About the Cover.
We are very honored to have the work of one of today's hottest illustrators grace our cover. We felt that with all that is being written in the trades and elsewhere about late 20th-century advertising being "self-aware," "self-conscious," even "self-parodic" the cover should reflect this. We realized that not everyone feels this way about contemporary advertising, but we are rightly reflecting a current and ongoing dialogue. Yes, advertising is a serious business, and students are training for a very important career. We personally think that advertising is one of the top five stories of the 20th century. But beginning around the time of the creative revolution, waxing and waning, and emerging full-blown in the 1990s, there has been a commercial self-consciousness in advertising. While we love advertising, we also want people to understand that we are aware of its shortcomings, and that same awareness exists within the industry itself. But art is for you to interpret, so do it.

About the Artist.
Lou Beach has been a freelance graphic designer for over 20 years. He has done work for a variety of publications, including *BusinessWeek, The New York Times, Wired,* and *Harper's.* As a founding partner and the creative director at ION, he worked with musicians David Bowie and Brian Eno, creating interactive CD-ROMs. He has also taught editorial illustration at The Art Center in Pasadena and at Otis Parsons in Los Angeles. Born in 1947 to Polish parents, he emigrated to the United States in 1951. After his third year of college in Buffalo, he decided to drop out, and he traveled to California, where he began his career as an artist making collages and studying Surrealist art. Over the years, he has traveled extensively and taken on a variety of jobs, such as truck driver and janitor, to support his career as an artist. He currently lives in Los Angeles with his wife and two children.

To Mildred Lucille Chambers O'Guinn
(1914–1998)
　　Thomas Clayton O'Guinn

To Dad
He was my hero
　　Chris Allen

In memory of my father, Joseph, who taught
me the three most important things in life
. . . how to throw a sinking fastball
. . . how to power shift
. . . and how to write
Thanks, Dad
　　Rich Semenik

Second Edition

ADVERTISING

Thomas C. O'Guinn
Professor of Advertising and Business Administration
Research Professor, Institute of Communications Research
University of Illinois, Urbana-Champaign

Chris T. Allen
Arthur Beerman Professor of Marketing
University of Cincinnati

Richard J. Semenik
Professor of Marketing
David Eccles School of Business
University of Utah-Salt Lake City

South-Western College Publishing
an International Thomson Publishing company I(T)P®

Cincinnati • Albany • Boston • Detroit • Johannesburg • London • Madrid • Melbourne • Mexico City
New York • Pacific Grove • San Francisco • Scottsdale • Singapore • Tokyo • Toronto

Publisher: Dave Shaut
Acquisitions Editor: Steve Scoble
Developmental Editor: Judith O'Neill
Marketing Manager: Sarah J. Woelfel
Production Editor: Sandra Gangelhoff
Media and Technology Editor: Kevin von Gillern
Media Production Editor: Robin K. Browning
Manufacturing Coordinator: Dana Began Schwartz
Internal and Cover Design: Craig LaGesse Ramsdell
Cover Illustration: copyright Lou Beach
Photo Researcher: Cary Benbow
Production House: Lachina Publishing Services
Printer: R.R. Donnelley & Sons Company, Roanoake Manufacturing Division

Printed in the United States of America
 2 3 4 5 6 7 8 9 10

International Thomson Publishing Europe
Berkshire House
168-173 High Holborn
London, WC1V7AA, United Kingdom

International Thomson Editores
Seneca, 53
Colonia Polanco
11560 Mèxico D.F. Mèxico

Nelson ITP, Australia
102 Dodds Street
South Melbourne
Victoria 3205 Australia

International Thomson Publishing Asia
60 Alberta Street #15-01
Albert Complex
Singapore 189969

Nelson Canada
1120 Birchmount Road
Scarborough, Ontario
Canada M1K 5G4

International Thomson Publishing Japan
Hirakawa-cho Kyowa Building, 3F
2-2-1 Hirakawa-cho, Chiyoda-ku
Tokyo 102, Japan

International Thomson Publishing Southern Africa
Building 18, Constantia Square
138 Sixteenth Road, P.O. Box 2459
Halfway House, 1685 South Africa

Library of Congress Cataloging-in-Publication Data

O'Guinn, Thomas C.
    Advertising / Thomas C. O'Guinn, Chris T. Allen, Richard J.
Semenik. — 2nd ed.
        p.   cm.
    Includes bibliographical references and indexes.
    ISBN 0-324-00661-6 (hardcover)
    1. Advertising.   2. Advertising media planning.   I. Allen, Chris
T.   II. Semenik, Richard J.   III. Title.
HF5821.034 1999   99-23028
659.1—dc21   CIP

This book is printed on acid-free paper.

BRIEF CONTENTS

v

CONTENTS

**PART THREE
Preparing the Message   302**

PREFACE

No doubt about it. Advertising has mystique. When we introduced the first edition of *Advertising,* we summed up our attitudes about our subject in this way:

Advertising is a lot of things. It's democratic pop culture, capitalist tool, oppressor, liberator, art, and theater, all rolled into one. It's free speech, it's creative flow, it's information, and it helps businesses get things sold. Above all, it's fun.

Like other aspects of business, though, good advertising is the result of hard work and careful planning. Don't let anyone snow you. Creating good advertising is an enormous challenge. This book was written by three people with lots of experience in both academic and professional settings. We worked hard to deliver a book that is both engaging and academically solid. We really got into this project. Yes, it was a lot of work, but it was also a labor of love. More than anything else, we want students who read our book to learn an awful lot about advertising—and have a good time doing it!

The second edition of *Advertising* emphasizes these same beliefs—in spades. Much has happened since we released the first edition that has strengthened our resolve in these beliefs about advertising. First, we learned from our adopters (over 300 of you) and from our students that the book's (sometimes brutal) honesty about the process of advertising was welcomed and applauded. We love this thing called advertising, but we also know that it is not always wonderful: It has its downside, and it can be totally frustrating to work with. On the other hand, it can still be a whole lot of fun.

Second, advertising continues to be buffeted by the turbulent world of ad industry evolution, new media expansion, and global competition. We were compelled to re-release this book just to keep current. In this edition, you will find the most current and extensive references to support our discussions of every aspect of advertising and lots and lots of detail.

Third, as much as we respected our academic and practitioner colleagues the first time around, we respect them even more now. Research for *Advertising²* turned up phenomenal talent in this industry, and we share our findings and surprises with you.

Once again, this book copies no one, yet pays homage to many. It will seem familiar and comfortable to you in many ways, and different and confrontational in others. More than anything, this book struggles to be honest, thoughtful, and imaginative. It acknowledges the complexity of human communication and consumer behavior while retaining a point of view. It tells you what the cutting-edge thinking is on various topics and what we're fairly certain about in the way of good advertising practices, but it also quickly admits that, on certain issues, no one really has a clue about a definitive, or "right way," to do it.

In terms of content and features, this book is loaded, simultaneously attuned to the vanguard and mindful of accepted wisdom. We pay particular attention to integrated marketing communications and to new media options such as advertising on the World Wide Web. We have guarded against immediate outdating by underlying our discussions of new media with principles and perspectives that will endure well after specific examples are obsolete. We have also tried our best to make life easier for the overworked instructor by offering a wide variety of ancillary materials, all written and coordinated by the authors, that will assist in teaching from the book and in fully engaging students on this fascinating topic.

Students will like this book. Some, we dare say, will even love it. It's current, and it has an edge. We spent considerable time reviewing student and instructor likes and dislikes with existing advertising textbooks in addition to examining their reactions to our own book. With this feedback, we devote pages and pictures, ideas and intelligence to creating a place for student and teacher to meet.

From Chapter I to Chapter 20. *Advertising* and its support package were written for use in all advertising classes taught anywhere in the university: in business and journalism schools as well as in mass communication and advertising departments. We recognize that many other fine textbooks are available for use in the introductory advertising class. Here are four good reasons why you'll want to get with it and take a close look at *Advertising*².

Compelling Fundamentals. We fully expect our book to continue to set the standard for coverage of new media topics. It is loaded with features and insights and commonsense perspectives about the new media. We were at the right place at the right time to build these issues into the first edition of *Advertising*. Now we have built on that competitive advantage and have incorporated new media coverage in *every* chapter.

That said, the real strength of this book is in its treatment of the fundamentals of advertising. One cannot appreciate the role of the new media—today or in the next millennium—without a solid understanding of the fundamentals. If you doubt our commitment to the fundamentals, take a good look at Chapters 2 through 9. Here we present compelling coverage of the key issues involved in preparing a sound advertising plan. Chapter 2 begins this process by providing students with a perspective on the structure of the advertising industry and the economic roots of the process. In Chapters 3 and 4, students will gain further insights by studying the evolution of modern-day advertising along its the social, ethical, and regulatory aspects. Chapter 5 provides a comprehensive treatment of how analysis of consumer behavior serves as the basis for sound advertising plans, and Chapter 6 establishes advertising's key role in executing coherent marketing strategies with respect to market segmentation, targeting, and positioning. The role of marketing and advertising research in laying the foundation for the plan is considered in Chapter 7, and the essentials of ad planning are consolidated and spelled out in Chapter 8.

Notice that we don't wait until the end of the book to bring international considerations into students' thinking. Global topics are integrated in every chapter throughout the text, because today's students must possess a global view. We incorporate our international chapter into the heart of the book—Chapter 9. Chapter 9 builds on the discussions in Chapter 8 and gives students a full view of the global advertising planning process. Chapters 10 to 20 cover the full array of issues that must be attended to in executing an advertising plan, from message development to media planning and evaluation.

So, *yes,* we have the new media covered; but, *no,* our new media coverage does not come at the expense of full coverage of the fundamentals of advertising.

Balanced New Media Coverage. If you have been waiting for an advertising text that will allow you to explore the possibilities of the new media, your wait is over. Where other books now in their fourth or fifth editions struggle to come to terms with the new media that now animate our industry, our book has new media at its foundation, providing coverage of advertising on the Internet and the World Wide Web at a depth and breadth not attempted elsewhere. Every chapter contains a boxed insert headed *New Media,* which furnishes contemporary examples of how the new media are affecting various aspects of advertising practice. And every chapter contains *Web Sightings,* application activities designed to bring chapter ads into real time, and the concept of new media to life. Every chapter ends with *Using the Internet* exercises that can be pursued via the Internet to help students learn about advertising, generally, and the Internet, specifically. In-depth consideration of new media vehicles is provided in Part Four of the book, "Placing the Message." Chapter 17 is all about advertising and marketing on the Internet and reviews many technical considerations for working in this new medium. Chapter 17 is the first of its kind among basic advertising texts. As we have already suggested, we fully expect that our book—a text with it all—to set the standard for coverage of new media topics.

Integrated IMC Coverage. Isn't it odd the way some authors treat integrated marketing communications (IMC) as if it were something disconnected from advertising? They seem to suggest that the two are naturally incompatible and in conflict. It's as though we might want to do one (mass media advertising) or the other (IMC), but certainly not both. We reject this mind-set about advertising and IMC as disabling.

To create effective advertising in the next millennium, students must appreciate the full range of communication tools available to them. We make this point as our concluding premise in Chapter 1, and return to it over and over again throughout the book. Part Four picks up on this general theme and presents a comprehensive treatment of the tools available to carry one's message to the consumer. While we give thorough consideration to traditional media, we also provide in-depth coverage of event sponsorship (Chapter 16), the wide array of possibilities in the area of sales promotion (Chapter 18), and the supportive role for PR and corporate advertising (Chapter 20). Is the direct marketing chapter in your old advertising book up to the standard of ours (Chapter 19)? Just wondering.

Throughout Part Four we provide continual reminders of the coordination challenges to be managed if advertising and promotions are to speak to the customer *in a single voice.* But the IMC coverage doesn't stop there—not by a long shot. Another unique feature of *Advertising* is the end-of-part case study, "From Principles to Practice: A Comprehensive IMC Case," which we developed in conjunction with Cincinnati Bell and its agency, Northlich Stolley LaWarre. This ongoing case takes students inside a company and an agency to learn how IMC is planned and executed. The result illustrates the full array of considerations involved in implementing integrated marketing communications. As you will see, Cincinnati Bell provided us with all the planning, strategy, and implementation information for its IMC campaign to introduce Cincinnati Bell Wireless services. We track the evolution of this campaign from its inception through its multimedia execution. This unique and comprehensive case vividly illustrates what it means to speak to the customer with multiple tools, but *in a single voice.* In addition, a video has been produced to highlight the coordination and creative aspects of this highly successful IMC effort.

Two additional features highlight our recognition of IMC. First, every chapter has an IMC box that relays an important IMC event or practice. Second, as a complement to our text, *IMC: An Integrated Marketing Communications Exercise* by Bernard Jakacki, is also available to take students through the creation and management of an IMC program.

Student Engagement and Learning. You will find that this book provides a sophisticated examination of advertising fundamentals in lively, concise language. We don't beat around the bush, and we're not shy about challenging a few conventions. In addition, the book features an attractive internal design and hundreds of illustrations. Reading this book will be an engaging experience for new students of advertising.

We sincerely want this to be a learning experience as well. The markers of our commitment to student learning are easily identified throughout the book. Every chapter begins with a statement of the learning objectives for that chapter. (For a quick appreciation of the coverage provided by this book, take a pass through it and read the learning objectives on the first page of each chapter.) Chapters are organized to deliver content that is responsive to each learning objective, and the chapter summaries are written to reflect what the chapter has offered with respect to each learning objective.

We also believe that students must be challenged to go beyond their reading to think about the issues raised in the book. Thus, you will note that the Questions for Review and Critical Thinking at the end of each chapter demand thoughtful analysis rather than mere regurgitation, and the Experiential Exercises will help students put their learning to use in ways that will help them take more away from the course than just textbook learning. Complete use of this text and its ancillary materials will yield a dramatic and engaging learning experience for students of all ages who are studying advertising for the first time.

If you think about these four reasons, and give our book a serious look, we believe you will be excited by the possibilities of using it in your classes.

A Closer Look at Some Second Edition Features.

How the Text Is Organized. *Advertising* is divided into four major parts:

- the process of advertising (Part One)
- the planning of advertising (Part Two)
- preparing the advertising message (Part Three)
- placing the advertising message (Part Four)

If you stare at this list long enough, it actually turns into the 4Ps of advertising. This sequence of presentation is meant to replicate the way clients and their agencies work through the advertising process. Throughout the book, we have tried to give students both the client's and the agency's perspective on advertising practices. Two outstanding supplementary videos, created and filmed exclusively for *Advertising,* give students additional insights into the client's and the agency's view of advertising. These two videos are discussed in detail on pages xiii–xiv.

Now, let us call your attention to some important chapter highlights:

Part One: The Process: Advertising in Business and Society.

Chapter 1: Advertising as a Process. Chapter 1 quickly sets the stage for what's to come. Departing from decades-old communication models, the chapter presents a different model of advertising, which highlights the advertiser's sensitivity to target audiences' expectations and motivations. With this opening perspective, we recognize renewed industry emphasis on the account planning process. Students learn that advertising is both a communications process and a business process, and they're shown why this is so. The book's seamless IMC coverage begins right here, with students introduced to the terminology and concept of coordinating and integrating promotional efforts to achieve advertising synergy and to speak to consumers *in a single voice*. It's a great beginning.

Chapter 2: The Structure of the Advertising Industry: Advertisers, Advertising Agencies, and Support Organizations. In this chapter, students read about six trends that are transforming the advertising industry today and the seismic changes the industry is experiencing in the 1990s. Students will see who the participants in the ad industry are today and the role each plays in the formulation and execution of ad campaigns. They will also learn how agencies are compensated for their services, including the trend toward fee-based compensation.

Chapter 3: The Evolution of Advertising. This chapter puts advertising in a historical context for students and provides numerous ads from the "good old days" to emphasize the historical concepts presented. But before the history lesson begins, students are given the straight scoop about advertising as a product of fundamental economic and social conditions—capitalism, the industrial revolution, manufacturers' pursuit of power, and modern mass communication—without which there would be no advertising process. Students then study the history of advertising through ten eras, seeing how advertising has changed and evolved, and how it is forged out of its social setting. Students will read about the Preindustrialization Era (pre-1800); the Era of Industrialization (1800 to 1875); the P. T. Barnum Era (1875 to 1918); the 1920s (1918 to 1929); the Depression (1929 to 1941); WWII and the Fifties (1941 to 1960); Peace, Love, and the Creative Revolution (1960 to 1972); the 1970s (1973 to 1980); the Republican Era (1980 to 1992); and the Second Nineties (1993 to present).

This chapter is rich with some of the most interesting ads representing advertising as a faithful documentation of social life in America. Definitely an entertaining and provocative chapter, it also gives students a necessary and important perspective on advertising before launching into advertising planning concepts and issues.

Chapter 4: Social, Ethical, and Regulatory Aspects of Advertising. Advertising is dynamic and controversial. In this chapter, students will examine a variety of issues concerning advertising's effects on societal well-being. Is advertising intrusive, manipulative, and deceptive? Does it waste resources, promote materialism, and perpetuate stereotypes? Or does it inform, give exposure to important issues, and raise the standard of living? After debating the social merits of advertising, students will explore the ethical considerations that underlie the development of campaigns and learn about the regulatory agencies that set guidelines for advertisers. Lastly, students are introduced to the concept of self-regulation and why advertisers must practice it.

Part Two: The Planning: Analyzing the Advertising Environment.

Chapter 5: Advertising and Consumer Behavior. This chapter on consumer behavior begins Part Two of the text. It describes consumer behavior, explaining it from two different perspectives. The first portrays consumers as systematic decision makers who seek to maximize the benefits they derive from their purchases. The second portrays consumers as active interpreters of advertising whose membership in various cultures, subcultures, societies, and communities significantly affects their interpretations and responses to advertising. Students, shown the validity of both perspectives, learn that, like all human behavior, the behavior of consumers is complex, multifaceted, and often symbolic. Understanding buyer behavior is a tremendous challenge to advertisers, who should not settle for easy answers if they want good relationships with their customers.

Chapter 6: Market Segmentation, Positioning, and the Value Proposition. This chapter begins with the compelling story of how Gillette used segmentation, position, and targeting to grow into a global consumer products powerhouse. Students are introduced to the sequence of activities often referred to as STP marketing—**s**egmenting, **t**argeting, and **p**ositioning—and to how advertising is both affected by and affects these basic marketing strategies. The remainder of the chapter is devoted to detailed analysis of how organizations develop market segmentation, positioning, and product differentiation strategies. The critical and difficult role of ad campaigns in successfully executing these strategies is emphasized over and over. Numerous examples of real-world campaigns that contrast different segmentation and positioning strategies keep the narrative fresh and fast moving. The chapter concludes by demonstrating that effective STP marketing strategies result in creating a perception of value in the marketplace.

Chapter 7: Advertising Research. This meaty and substantive chapter begins with the story of the Goodyear Aquatred tire, one of the most successful new tire introductions of all time, thanks to extensive and rigorous ad testing before and during the tire's release. This chapter covers the methods used in developmental research, the procedures used for pretesting messages prior to the launch of a campaign, the methods used to track the effectiveness of ads during and after a launch, and the many sources of secondary data that can aid the ad-planning effort. This chapter also provides coverage of the agency's new emphasis on account planning as a distinct part of the planning process. An accompanying Advertising Education Foundation video on research and advertising brings these concepts to life. If students don't understand the importance of advertising research and testing after reading this chapter, well, then . . . they didn't read the chapter.

Chapter 8: The Advertising Plan. This chapter begins by recounting the sequence of events and strategies behind the launch of Apple's new, colorful iMac computer. Through this opening vignette, students see the importance of constructing a sound ad plan before launching any campaign. But in addition, this introductory campaign for the iMac is an extraordinary example of IMC at work. After reading this chapter, students will be familiar with the basic components of an ad plan. They will understand two fundamental approaches for setting advertising objectives—the budgeting process, and the role of the ad agency in formulating an advertising plan. By the end of the chapter, students will understand the significance of the opening commentary in this chapter: ". . . you don't go out and spend $100 million promoting a new product that is vital to the success of a firm without giving the entire endeavor considerable forethought. Such an endeavor calls for a plan."

Chapter 9: Advertising Planning: An International Perspective. We begin this chapter with some of the many blunders in international advertising that make for some good belly laughs. But aside from the compelling content of this chapter, one of its most noteworthy features is the placement. While many books bury their international chapter at the end, we chose to place this chapter in the heart of the book, where it belongs, as part of the overall advertising planning effort. We think you'll find the chapter impressive in the number of international ads that are included and impressive in the way the fast-moving discussion unfolds: from a discussion of cultural barriers and overcoming them to an examination of the creative, media, and regulatory challenges that international advertising presents. The chapter ends with an insightful discussion of the differences between globalized and localized campaigns.

Part Three: Preparing the Message.

Chapter 10: Creativity and Advertising. Of the many features that we believe sets this book apart from all others, the addition of this new chapter is key. This chapter takes on the seemingly awkward task of "talking" about creativity. For all you creatives out there, you know this is a nearly impossible task. "If I could describe it, I wouldn't have to do it" is an all-too-familiar lament. But what we have tried to do for students in this chapter is completely different from all other texts. Rather than just describing the creative *process* (we do that in Chapters 11 and 12), we have tried to discuss the essence of what creativity is. First, we portray the challenges of the creative effort by describing the conflicts that arise between the poets and the killers (we'll let you go to the chapter to see who these combatants are). Next, we highlight the commentary and achievements of creative geniuses—both within the advertising industry and completely removed from it. The result is a thought-provoking and enriching treatment like no other that students will find.

Chapter 11: Message Development: Strategies and Methods. Building on Chapter 10, this chapter explores the role of creativity in message strategy from a refreshingly honest perspective—no one knows exactly how advertising creativity works. Ten message strategy objectives are presented along with the creative methods used to accomplish the objectives, including humor ads, slice-of-life ads, anxiety ads, sexual-appeal ads, slogan ads, and repetition ads. This chapter makes excellent use of visuals to dramatize the concepts presented.

Chapter 12: Copywriting. This chapter flows logically from the chapter on message development. In this chapter students learn about the copywriting process and the importance of good, hard-hitting copy in the development of print, radio, and television advertising. Guidelines for writing headlines, subheads, and body copy for print ads are given, as are guidelines for writing radio and television ad copy. The chapter closes with a discussion of the most common mistakes copywriters make and a discussion of the copy-approval process. And, of course, this chapter considers the issues surrounding the copywriting process in the highly constrained creative environment of the Internet.

Chapter 13: Art Direction and Production. The adopters of the first edition of *Advertising* told us that two chapters on art direction and production was overkill. We heeded your plea. Chapter 13 now combines discussion of print and broadcast media. Here, students learn about the strategic and creative impact of illustration, design, and layout, and the production steps required to get to the final ad. Numerous engaging full-color ads are included that illustrate important design, illustration, and layout concepts.

We also introduce students to what is often thought of as the most glamorous side of advertising: television advertising. Students learn about the role of the creative team and the many agency and production company participants involved in the direction and production processes. Students are given six creative guidelines for television ads, with examples of each. Radio is not treated as a second-class citizen in this chapter but is given full treatment, including six guidelines for the production of creative and effective radio ads. This chapter is comprehensive and informative without getting bogged down in production details.

Part Four: Placing the Message.

Chapter 14: Media Planning, Objectives, and Strategy. In this chapter, which begins Part Four, students see that a well-planned and creatively prepared campaign needs to be placed in media (and not just any media!) to reach a target audience and to stimulate demand. This chapter drives home the point that advertising placed in media that do not reach the target audience—whether new media or traditional media—will be much like the proverbial tree that falls in the forest with no one around: Does it make a sound? Students will read about the major media options available to advertisers today, the media-planning process, computer modeling in media planning, and the challenges that complicate the media-planning process.

Chapter 15: Media Evaluation: Print, Television, and Radio. The opening vignette for Chapter 15 highlights the battle going on for the favors of TV viewers. Cable television has slowly but surely made major inroads into the market share of broadcast television. This chapter focuses on evaluating media as important means for advertisers to reach audiences. The chapter details the advantages and disadvantages of newspapers, magazines, radio, and television as media classes and describes the buying and audience measurement techniques for each.

Chapter 16: Support Media, P-O-P Advertising, and Event Sponsorship. The story of Procter & Gamble's innovative poster campaign to promote Noxzema is exceptional—don't miss it. With P&G's posters as introduction, this chapter makes students aware of the vast number of support media options available to advertisers: event sponsorship, signage, outdoor billboards, transit advertising, aerial advertising, point-of-purchase displays, directories, and specialty items. If students do not already appreciate the challenge of integrating marketing communications before they get to this chapter, they certainly will afterward!

Chapter 17: Advertising on the Internet. The first edition of *Advertising* was the first introductory advertising book to devote an entire chapter to advertising on the Internet, and this revision continues to set the standard for Internet coverage. Today's employers expect college advertising students to know about the Internet and the creative and selling opportunities it presents to advertisers as part of their IMC strategy. This chapter presents a complete overview of advertising on the Internet and provides numerous Net activities to give students hands-on experience visiting and analyzing advertisers' Web sites. The chapter describes who's using the Internet today and the ways they are using it, identifies the advertising and marketing opportunities presented by the Internet, discusses fundamental requirements for establishing sites on the World Wide Web, and lays out the challenges inherent in measuring the cost effectiveness of the Internet versus other advertising media. This chapter doesn't assume that all students are already Internet gurus, but it won't insult those who are.

Chapter 18: Sales Promotion. Sales promotion is a multibillion-dollar business in the United States and is emerging as a global force as well. This chapter explains the rationale for different types of sales promotions. It differentiates between consumer and trade sales promotions and highlights the risks and coordination issues associated with sales promotions—a consideration overlooked by other texts. All of the following are discussed: coupons, price-off deals, premiums, contests, sweepstakes, sampling, trial offers, brand (formerly product) placements, refunds, rebates, frequency programs, point-of-purchase displays, incentives, allowances, trade shows, and cooperative advertising.

Chapter 19: Direct Marketing. This chapter opens with an example of direct marketing from the mayor of Beverly Hills promoting the virtues of her fair city and then moves quickly on to L. L. Bean and the well-known L. L. Bean mail-order catalog. Students quickly learn about Bean's emphasis on building an extensive mailing list, which serves as a great segue to database marketing. Students will learn why direct marketing continues to grow in popularity, what media are used by direct marketers to deliver their messages, and how direct marketing creates special challenges for achieving integrated marketing communications.

Chapter 20: Public Relations and Corporate Advertising. This chapter begins with the story of Microsoft's ongoing problems with the Justice Department and how the press coverage of the case represents a public relations disaster for the firm. It illustrates the point that while some public relations crises are beyond the control of the organization, some are of the company's own doing. This dynamic and engaging chapter explains the role of public relations as part of an organization's overall IMC strategy and details the objectives and tools of public relations in a way that attracts and holds student interest. The chapter differentiates between proactive and reactive public relations and the strategies associated with each. The chapter goes on to discuss the various forms of corporate advertising and the way each can be used as a means for building the reputation of an organization in the eyes of key constituents.

Inside Every Chapter.
Inside every chapter of *Advertising* you will find features that make this new book eminently teachable and academically solid, while at the same time fun to read. As we said earlier, this text was written and the examples were chosen to facilitate an effective meeting place for student and teacher. Who said learning has to be drudgery? It doesn't have to be and it shouldn't.

Dynamic Graphics and over 500 Ads and Exhibits. Ask any student and almost any instructor what an advertising book must include, and you will get as a top response—lots of ads. As you will see by quickly paging through *Advertising,* this is a book full of ads. Over 400 ads are used to illustrate important points made in the chapters. Each ad is referenced in the text narrative, tying the visual to the concept being discussed.

As you can see, the book's clean, classic, graphic layout invites you to read it; it dares you to put it down without reading just one more caption or peeking at just the next chapter.

Opening Vignettes. Every chapter in *Advertising* includes a classic or current real-world advertising story to draw students into the chapter and to stimulate classroom discussions. Each vignette illustrates important concepts that will be discussed in the chapter. For example, in Chapter 1, "Advertising as a Process," students are introduced to the world of advertising with the interesting story of how Mercedes-Benz abandoned its tried and true "engineering-based" ad appeals for rubber duckies and singing coyotes. In Chapter 2, "The Structure of the Advertising Industry," students read how Leo Burnett was whipsawed by changes in the industry and lost nearly $400 million in creative work—only to win back over $700 million in new business over the next 18 months. The chapters throughout the book continue with these types of lively introductions, ensuring that students get off to a good start with every chapter.

In-Chapter Boxes. Every chapter in *Advertising* contains boxed material that highlights interesting, unusual, or just plain entertaining information as it relates to the chapter. The boxes are not diversions unrelated to the text; rather, they provide information that can be fully integrated into classroom lectures. The boxes are for teaching, learning, and reinforcing chapter content. Three types of boxes are included in the text: New Media, Global Issues, and IMC. Let's take a look at each.

New Media. There is no greater challenge in the ad industry today than coping with the number and diversity of new media options available. This is especially true with respect to the Internet, and much of the coverage in the New Media boxes focuses on issues related to advertising and the Internet. Following is a sampling of the issues discussed in the New Media boxes:

- *The Internet Is Big—But Not As Big As Seinfeld*, Chapter 1
- *No Push in the Push—Yet*, Chapter 3
- *Truth Is, Gen X Is Still out There, If You Know Where and How to Look*, Chapter 6
- *Reaching Generations Y and Z*, Chapter 8
- *News Flash: World Wide Web NOT Worldwide*, Chapter 9
- *Writing Cybercopy—Don't Abandon All the Old Rules*, Chapter 12
- *Digizines: Don't Look for One While You Wait for the Dentist*, Chapter 15
- *Turning Green at the Cybermall*, Chapter 20

Global Issues. The Global Issues boxes provide an insightful real-world look at the numerous challenges advertisers face internationally. Many issues are discussed in these timely boxes, including the development of more standardized advertising across cultures with satellite-based television programming, how U.S.-based media companies such as MTV and Disney/ABC are pursuing the vast potential in global media, obstacles to advertising in emerging markets, and cross-cultural global research. The following is a sampling of the Global Issues boxes you'll find in *Advertising:*

- *Motorola's Global Campaign Takes Flight*, Chapter 1
- *East Meets West for PR Lessons*, Chapter 3
- *Value Segmentation Reaches Global Proportions*, Chapter 6
- *So Who Was It That Invented Salsa?*, Chapter 9
- *America's Newest Contribution to World Culture: Infomercials Go Global*, Chapter 11
- *You Know That KISS Thing—It Works for Global Ads, Too*, Chapter 12
- *Cosmo: To Russia with Love*, Chapter 15
- *Polaroid Sheds New Light on the Spice Girls*, Chapter 18

IMC. As we said earlier, we are committed to students' awareness of IMC activities in the industry and the role advertising plays in the process. The IMC boxes in each chapter highlight interesting and important IMC programs or issues. Here are some of the titles of IMC boxes in the text:

- *Taking It in the Shorts*, Chapter 1
- *Not Snake Oil—But Still Pretty Slick (For the Most Part)*, Chapter 3
- *Stalking the Holy Grail: Research Companies Join Forces to Track Synergies Promised by IMC*, Chapter 7
- *Daewoo Woos You*, Chapter 8
- *If Microsoft Is Doing It, It Must Be Right*, Chapter 12
- *Major Marketer Saving on Coupons*, Chapter 18
- *Event Sponsorship Acid Test*, Chapter 20

Web Sightings. In keeping with the new media distinctiveness of this book, you will find all new "Web Sightings" in each chapter. You can spot these Web Sightings by looking for the Web Sighting binoculars found above selected exhibits in each chapter. Students are asked to go to the Web site addresses provided to explore the advertiser's home page, bringing the ad in the book online and into real time. Questions are provided to prompt students to explore, explain, describe, compare, contrast, summarize, rethink, or analyze the content or features of the advertiser's home page. You can think of these Web Sightings as in-chapter experiential exercises and real-time cases. You can assign these Web Sightings as individual or group activities. They are also excellent discussion starters. A note: Most Web sites are listed with the prefix *http://*. While this is the technical address, most Web browsers don't require the user to type out this prefix, so it has been dropped from the URLs in this book.

Concise Chapter Summaries. Each chapter ends with a summary that distills the main points of the chapter. Chapter summaries are organized around the learning objectives so that students can use them as a quick check on their achievement of learning goals.

Key Terms with Page Citations. Each chapter ends with an alphabetical listing of the key terms found in the chapter along with page citations for easy reference. Key terms also appear in boldface in the text. Students can prepare for exams by scanning these lists to be sure they can define or explain each term.

Questions for Review and Critical Thinking. These end-of-chapter questions, written by the authors, are designed to challenge students' thinking and to go beyond the "read, memorize, and regurgitate" learning process. The Questions for Review and Critical Thinking sections require students to think analytically and to interpret data and information provided for them in the text. Detailed responses to these questions are provided in the Instructor's Manual.

Below is a sampling of the types of critical-thinking questions found in *Advertising:*

- If a firm developed a new line of athletic shoes, priced them competitively, and distributed them in appropriate retail shops, would there be any need for advertising? Is advertising really needed for a good product that is priced right?
- The 1950s were marked by great suspicion about advertisers and their potential persuasive powers. Do you see any lingering effects of this era of paranoia in attitudes about advertising today?
- Some contend that self-regulation is the best way to ensure fair and truthful advertising practices. Why would it be in the best interest of the advertising community to aggressively pursue self-regulation?
- Identify several factors or forces that make consumers around the world more similar to one another. Conversely, what factors or forces create diversity among consumers in different countries?
- Explain the two basic strategies for developing corporate home pages, exemplified in this chapter by Saturn and Absolut.
- Visit some of the corporate home pages described in this chapter, or think about corporate home pages you have visited previously. Of those you have encountered, which would you single out as being most effective in giving the visitor a reason to come back? What conclusions would you draw regarding the best ways to motivate repeat visits to a Web site?
- Everyone has an opinion on what makes advertisements effective or ineffective. How does this fundamental aspect of human nature complicate a copywriter's life when it comes to winning approval for his or her ad copy?

Experiential Exercises. At the end of each chapter, Experiential Exercises require students to apply the material they have just read by researching topics, writing short papers, preparing brief presentations, or interacting with professionals from the advertising industry. They require students to get out of the classroom to seek information not provided in the text. A number of these exercises are especially designed for teamwork, and many are classroom tested. Additional Experiential Exercises can be found in the Instructor's Manual.

Using the Internet. This unique set of Internet exercises is designed to get students on the Internet to examine the nature of the advertising that is there, to analyze the effectiveness of what they find, and to apply the Internet to fundamental advertising concepts presented in the text. Because the focus of these exercises is hands-on in nature, students will spend time accessing home pages using the Web site addresses provided and evaluating what they find. Application questions are provided for each exercise for students to answer after their Web site excursions. The application questions require students to apply the concepts taught in each chapter, making these surfing-the-Net exercises worthwhile and focused, not just browsing time. Additional Internet exercises can be found in the Instructor's Manual—for real diehard cyberhounds! Suggested answers to all of the Internet exercises can be found in the Instructor's Manual. Additionally, *Advertising*'s appendix provides the Web address of nearly every major advertiser that appears in the text.

Learning Objectives and a Built-In Integrated Learning System.

The text and test bank are organized around the learning objectives that appear at the beginning of each chapter, to provide you and your students with an easy-to-use, integrated learning system. A numbered icon like the one shown here ◀▶ identifies each chapter objective and appears next to its related material throughout the chapter. This integrated learning system can provide you with a structure for creating lesson plans as well as tests. A correlation table at the beginning of every chapter in the test bank enables you to create tests that fully cover every learning objective or that emphasize the objectives you feel are most important.

The integrated system also gives structure to students as they prepare for tests. The icons identify all the material in the text that fulfill each objective. Students can easily check their grasp of each objective by reading the text sections and reviewing the corresponding summary sections. They can return to appropriate text sections for further review if they have difficulty with end-of-chapter questions.

End-of-Part IMC Campaign: Cincinnati Bell^{SM} Wireless.

No introductory text would be complete without giving special attention to integrated marketing communications. At the end of each of the four parts of *Advertising* is a completely new ongoing case study of Cincinnati Bell and its Cincinnati Bell Wireless IMC campaign. These sections will help students better understand IMC by examining the topic in two ways. First, each section begins by discussing the basics of IMC and methods for creating effective integrated marketing communications. Second, each section applies the basic principles of IMC to the campaign developed for Cincinnati Bell Wireless. As students will discover, Cincinnati Bell used a wide range of communications tools to support its goal of introducing its brand to the fiercely competitive wireless market. As mentioned earlier, a video of this campaign has been produced to support the text discussion. Of course, these IMC sections are fully and colorfully illustrated. And, as with a lot of the features that distinguish this book, we were in the right place at the right time. The Cincinnati Bell Wireless campaign was the most successful wireless campaign in the nation.

A Full Array of Teaching/Learning Supplementary Materials.

Instructor's Manual. The author-written Instructor's Manual that accompanies *Advertising* provides comprehensive lecture outlines for each of the text's 20 chapters. These outlines average 10 to 12 pages per chapter and offer a complete and structured approach for presenting class lectures. The outlines also include marginal notations suggesting where the supplementary videos, PowerPoint slides, and color transparencies can be used to demonstrate points made in the text. A full set of PowerPoint transparency masters are included in the manual. In addition, the manual includes suggested answers for all exercises found in the text: Web Sightings, Questions for Review and Critical Thinking, and Using the Internet exercises. Finally, the manual contains additional Experiential and Using the Internet exercises, with suggested answers, for instructors seeking variety.

PowerPoint Slides. All images prepared as transparency masters in the Instructor's Manual are also available on PowerPoint software, versions 4.0 and 7.0. All you need is Windows to run the PowerPoint viewer, and an LCD panel for classroom display. The PowerPoint images can also be downloaded from our Web site at oguinn.swcollege.com.

Comprehensive Test Bank. This comprehensive test bank is organized around the text's learning objectives. At the beginning of each test bank chapter is a correlation table that classifies each question according to type, complexity, and learning objective covered.

Using this table, you can create exams with the appropriate mix of question types and level of difficulty for your class. You can choose to prepare tests that cover all learning objectives or emphasize those you feel are most important.

For each text chapter the test bank provides true/false, multiple choice, scenario application, and essay questions. There are a total of 2,000 questions. All questions have been carefully reviewed for clarity and accuracy. Questions are identified by topic and show the rationales and text pages where the rationales appear.

Testing Software. All items from the printed test bank are available on disk (either Windows or Macintosh format) through Thomson Learning Testing Tools™, a fully integrated suite of test creation, delivery, and course management tools. Thomson Learning Tools is provided free of charge to instructors at educational institutions that adopt *Advertising* by O'Guinn, Allen, and Semenik.

Color Transparency Package. Also available to instructors is a high-quality selection of full-color overhead transparencies. These transparencies include 25 ads and exhibits taken from the text as well as 75 additional ads not used in the text. Suggestions for incorporating these ads into lectures are included in the lecture outlines in the Instructor's Manual.

Award-Winning Video Package—Nobody Else Has the Clios! The following comprehensive and exciting video programs—including the Clio awards—represent the best package going and are available to supplement *Advertising.* These programs are designed to bring to life, in a fresh, cutting-edge, and energetic way, the advertising principles presented in the text.

From Principles to Practice: The Cincinnati Bell Wireless IMC Campaign. Produced exclusively to accompany the on-going IMC case that closes each major section of the text, this video features interviews with managers at Cincinnati Bell regarding their plans and expectations for the IMC campaign. From the agency side, creative directors and account supervisors at Northlich Stolley LaWarre tell their story of how this dynamic campaign was created.

Clio Awards 1998 Show Reel. This show reel (40-plus minutes long) contains the best of television advertising in 1998. No other advertising text on the market today includes the Clio awards as part of its supplementary package. We pursued the Clio ads not just because of their entertainment value but to expose students to the creative work of the best and brightest advertising minds. Today and for the past 40 years, Clio has heralded great accomplishments in advertising. The purpose of the Clios is to honor and inspire advertising excellence worldwide. You will find incorporating the Clio ads into your classroom lectures not only entertaining and inspiring, but an effective way to illustrate concepts presented in the text chapters.

The Advertising Education Foundation, Inc. (AEF). The 27-minute video entitled "Good-Bye Guesswork: How Research Guides Today's Advertisers" is a documentary that probes the dynamics of advertising research, strategic thinking, and concept testing from the viewpoint of three major advertisers and their ad agencies in three 9-minute segments: Campbell Soup Company with FCB/Leber Katz Partners, Maidenform with Ogilvy & Mather, and AT&T with McCann-Erickson Worldwide.

BusinessLink Video Series. A selection of videos, ranging in length from 10 to 15 minutes, are available at no cost to instructors who adopt *Advertising*. Produced exclusively for South-Western College Publishing by LEARNet, (a team of experienced advertising and marketing professors and video producers who specialize in instructional media) our BusinessLink videos add a visual dimension to course content. Videos cover a range of topics including integrated marketing communications, advertising strategy, client-based advertising, and market segmentation, and they feature a wide range of businesses such as Andersen Consulting, Ben & Jerry's, Burton Snowboards, Red Roof Inn, and World Gym, to name a few. Critical-thinking questions segment the video presentations, making it easy to stop the tapes to discuss pertinent issues. Descriptions of the videos and other information to help you integrate videos into your classroom lectures are provided in the Instructor's Manual, but we'll mention just two here:

Advertising Agency Relationships: W. B. Doner and Red Roof Inns. Red Roof Inns had been using the slogan "Sleep Cheap" when it hired the W. B. Doner agency to develop a new integrated marketing communications strategy to emphasize value instead of low price.

Client-Based Advertising: Andersen Consulting. In 1989 Andersen Consulting (AC) had two advertising challenges: to define its image in the marketplace and to establish a distinctive position. AC conducted marketing research and then initiated a very innovative corporate image advertising campaign that achieved impressive results.

★ ★ ★

This entire award-winning video package was designed to show students how advertising works in the real world, from the perspective of both the ad agency and the client, and to demonstrate for students some of the most current and creative examples of advertising worldwide. It's a dynamic, attention-getting, and engaging package you'll enjoy using in your classes.

Advertising Display Collection on CD-ROM. Open up the *Advertising Display Collection* CD-ROM and get an eyeful. It's a very desirable collection of over 300 ads from all the best agencies and advertisers. With files for on-screen display and printing to paper, the *Advertising Display Collection* gives you a remarkable library of images to enhance classroom presentations as well as remarkable control in deciding where and how to use them.

oguinn.swcollege.com. Go online at oguinn.swcollege.com for additional resources, ideas, content, and lots and lots of links to great Web sites.

IMC: An Integrated Marketing Communications Exercise.

This comprehensive supplementary package puts students in the role of client services manager at a major, full-service integrated marketing communications agency. The client, the Republic of Uruguay, wants the agency to create and manage a total marketing program for a new resort in Uruguay called Punta del Este. This approximately 100-page, semester-long project workbook includes step-by-step directions for students to follow. Cost tables are supplied, as are how-to worksheets on creative and media planning assignments. In addition to the traditional IMC mix, this exercise also takes students into the world of interactive media, because any successful presentation in the real world today will have to include a proposal integrating the Internet and other interactive media.

To begin the exercise, students are briefed on all aspects of the new resort: facts and details about Punta del Este, competition, research data, and the lore surrounding the resort. After the briefing, students are guided through the development of a four-part campaign recommendation for their client. They will create (1) a generalized communications statement complete with objectives and a strategy for segmentation, targeting, and product positioning; (2) a copy platform with their recommendations for TV and magazine ads; (3) a media plan, including interactive media; and (4) a promotion plan for travel industry intermediaries and travel consumers.

The correlating Instructor's Manual contains numerous suggestions and guidelines for the smooth implementation of this exercise into your course. It also offers suggestions for condensing the material, if you prefer a shorter exercise or one that focuses exclusively on advertising without the IMC topics.

This outstanding supplement was written by Bernard C. Jakacki of Ramapo College. In addition to writing this exercise, Professor Jakacki has tested it for four years with many college students and with advertising agency trainees. The response from users has been spectacular in terms of both its comprehensive content and the fun they have promoting Punta del Este. This tested and proven package is truly real-world in both orientation and design. [ISBN 0-538-87794-4]

Ad Campaign Planner.

Developed by Shay Sayre of California State University, Fullerton, this workbook presents complete yet concise instructions for developing an advertising campaign for one of two accounts. Using a series of specially designed worksheets, students are guided through the process of building a campaign step by step. Students organize an agency, profile a target market, conduct primary and secondary research, analyze the competition, develop an industry overview, evaluate the product/service, and prepare media plans, creative strategies, and promotions. Then, drawing on their worksheets, they construct an end-of-term written proposal and/or presentation. A sample campaign is included. [ISBN 0-538-87894-0]

Thomas C. O'Guinn
Chris T. Allen
Richard J. Semenik

ACKNOWLEDGMENTS

The most pleasant task in writing a textbook is the expression of gratitude to people and institutions that have helped the authors. We appreciate the support and encouragement we received from many individuals, including:

- Everyone at Cincinnati Bell and Northlich Stolley LaWarre who gave us tremendous help and support in creating the IMC case and its accompanying video. We especially want to thank CBW President and CEO Jack Cassidy and CBW Director of Marketing Mike Vanderwoude, as well as the following people at NSL: Mark Serrianne, president and CEO; Don Perkins, senior vice president and executive creative director; Mandy Reverman, account supervisor; Scott Aaron, account supervisor; Susan Cheney, direct marketing account supervisor; Mike Swainey, account manager; and Jay Pioch, assistant account manager.
- Mary Pommert, Custom Editorial Productions, for her diligent efforts in coordinating the development of the CBW/NSL video case.
- David Moore, vice president/executive producer at Leo Burnett, who gave us invaluable insights on the broadcast production process and helped us secure key materials for the text.
- Ann Schlosser, Owen Graduate School of Business, Vanderbilt University, for her help with our new media chapter.
- Kent Lancaster, University of Florida, for his assistance with our media chapter.
- Kimberly Paul, University of Texas at Austin and Intensity Designs, Austin, Texas, for her help with the creative chapters.
- Bernard C. Jakacki, Ramapo College, for providing a truly excellent IMC supplement. The timing of his work was serendipitous, and we're glad to have it as part of the *Advertising* package.
- Shay Sayre, California State University, Fullerton, for creating an ad campaign planner of exceptional quality.
- Nick Bean, b+b communicatioins, for taking on the challenge of preparing the PowerPoint slides, which serve as a truly useful lecture aid.

- Ross Stapleton-Gray, of TeleDiplomacy, Inc., and Georgetown University, for his fine efforts in preparing the Using the Internet exercises and the Web Sightings.
- John Weiss, Colorado State University, for his outstanding work in preparing an exceptional Test Bank. Thanks also to John H. Murphy II, University of Texas at Austin, for contributing to the upgrade.
- James Davis, University of Utah, for securing artwork and permission to use exhibits.
- Natasha I. Tolstikova, University of Illinois Urbana Champaign, for coordinating this massive project and providing important quality control.
- Matt Smith of Arnold, Finnegan & Martin for providing us with the Watermark ad and sketches in Chapter 13.
- Andrew Jaffe, Executive Director, Marella Oviedo, Director of Special Events, and the entire staff of the Clio Awards, a special acknowledgement is owed for providing us with the best advertising awards reel in the industry (www.clioawards.com).
- **Peter Sheldon,** University of Illinois: Chief Exhibitionist (yes, he made us say this). Peter is the creative heart and soul of this book. He picked most of the ads for this book, provided substantive editorial material and comments, and told us when we were out to lunch. Everybody says this, but in Peter's case it is really true: Without him, we couldn't have done it. He made the book a reality. His vision, talent, and wonderful humor was our daily blessing. Thanks, Peter.
- Mildred O'Guinn, who actually read every single word of the first edition and found the only misspelled word, one missed by countless computers, editors, authors, proofers, and so on: "Restritions," in Exhibit 9.16 on page 252. Very good job. Thanks.

We would also like to thank the many people at South-Western Publishing who made this project take shape and helped guide its development from start to finish: Dave Shaut, Craig LaGesse Ramsdell, Sarah Woelfel, Cary Benbow, Kevin von Gillern, Sandy Gangelhoff, and Dan Schwartz. We express gratitude, also, to our publisher's professional and committed sales force for the critically important customer feedback that we received all along the way.

We would also like to thank Steve Scoble, acquisitions editor, for his hard work, dedication, suggestions, and support throughout the project. A special thanks goes to Judy O'Neill, our developmental editor at South-Western, and Lachina Publishing Services, Inc., who skillfully and professionally guided the production of this book under the tightest of production deadlines. We would also like to thank Dreis Van Landuyt, who made the second edition possible by making the first edition such a success.

We are particularly indebted to our reviewers—past and present—and the following individuals whose thoughtful comments, suggestions, and specific feedback shaped the content of *Advertising*. Our thanks go to:

Priscilla LaBarbera
New York University

Lynne Boles
Procter & Gamble

Anne Cunningham
University of Tennessee

Robert Dwyer
University of Cincinnati

Jon Freiden
Florida State University

Cynthia Frisby
University of Missouri–Columbia

Corliss L. Green
Georgia State University

Scott Hamula
Keuka College

Wayne Hilinski
Penn State University

Karen James
Louisiana State University–Shreveport

Donald Jugenheimer
Southern Illinois University

James Kellaris
University of Cincinnati

Patricia Kennedy
University of Nebraska–Lincoln

Robert Kent
University of Delaware

William LaFief
Frostburg State University

Tina M. Lowrey
Rider University

Nancy Mitchell
University of Nebraska–Lincoln

Darrel Muehling
Washington State University

John Purcell
Castleton State College

Joe Regruth
Procter & Gamble

Debra Scammon
University of Utah

Kim Sheehan
University of Oregon

Alan Shields
Suffolk County Community College

Jan Slater
Syracuse University

Patricia Stout
University of Texas-Austin

Lynn Walters
Texas A & M

Brian Wansink
University of Illinois

Marc Weinberger
University of Massachusetts–Amherst

Gary B. Wilcox
University of Texas-Austin

Kurt Wildermuth
University of Missouri–Columbia

Christine Wright-Isak
Young & Rubicam

Molly Ziske
Michigan State University

PART ONE

PART ONE

THE PROCESS:

ADVERTISING

IN BUSINESS

AND SOCIETY

This first part of the book, "The Process: Advertising in Business and Society," sets the tone for our study of advertising. The chapters in this part of the book emphasize that advertising is much more than a wonderfully creative interpretation of important corporate marketing strategies. While it very much serves that purpose, advertising is a fundamental business and societal process that has evolved over time with culture, technology, and industry traditions.

To appreciate the true nature of advertising, we must first understand advertising as the complex, dynamic business and social process it is. Part One examines the first of the 4Ps of advertising: the *process* of developing and using advertising as a marketing and communications tool. In this first part of the text, the roots of the advertising process are revealed. Advertising is defined as both a business *and* a communications process, and the structure of the industry through which modern-day advertising exists is described. The evolution of advertising is traced from fairly modest beginnings through periods of growth and maturation. The complex and controversial social, ethical, and regulatory aspects of advertising conclude this opening part of the text.

Advertising as a Process

Chapter 1, "Advertising as a Process," defines advertising and positions it within a firm's overall marketing and communications programs. This chapter also analyzes advertising as a basic communications tool and as a marketing communications *process*. We introduce the concept of integrated marketing communications (IMC), which provides a new perspective on the way in which a full range of communications options is exercised to compete effectively, develop customer loyalty, and generate profits.

The Structure of the Advertising Industry

Chapter 2, "The Structure of the Advertising Industry," shows that effective advertising requires the participation of a variety of organizations, not just the advertiser. Advertising agencies, research firms, special production facilitators, media companies, Web site developers, and Internet portals are just some of the organizations that form the structure of the industry. Each plays a different role, and billions of dollars are spent every year for the services of various participants. This chapter also highlights that the structure of the industry is in flux. New media options and advertisers' interest in integrated marketing communications are forcing change in the industry. This chapter looks at the basic structure of the industry and at how that structure is changing.

The Evolution of Advertising

Chapter 3, "The Evolution of Advertising," sets the process of advertising into both an historical and contemporary context. Advertising has evolved and proliferated because of fundamental influences related to free enterprise, economic development, and tradition. Advertising as a business process and a reflection of social values has experienced many evolutionary periods of change as technology, business management practices, and social values have changed.

Social, Ethical, and Regulatory Aspects of Advertising

Chapter 4, "Social, Ethical, and Regulatory Aspects of Advertising," examines the broad societal aspects of the advertising process. From a social standpoint, we must understand that advertising has positive effects on the standard of living, addresses lifestyle needs, supports the mass media, and is a contemporary art form. Critics argue, though, that advertising wastes resources, promotes materialism, is offensive, and perpetuates stereotypes. The ethical issues in advertising focus on truth in advertising, advertising to children, and the advertising of controversial products.

Love

CHAP TER

**After reading and thinking about
this chapter, you will be able to
do the following:**

◀▶ Know what advertising is and what it
can do.

◀▶ Discuss a basic model of advertising
communication.

◀▶ Describe the different ways of classifying
audiences for advertising.

◀▶ Explain the key roles of advertising as a
business process.

◀▶ Recognize the effects of advertising in a
national economy.

The name Mercedes-Benz brings to mind rich images: fine engineering, quality crafts-manship, first-class service, prestige, rubber duckies, and singing coyotes. Rubber duck-ies and singing coyotes? Yes, rubber duckies and singing coyotes. When you see rubber duckies and singing coyotes in Mercedes ads, you know there is something new going on. There is, in fact, something of a revolution taking place at Mercedes-Benz, and the company's new attitude is being fueled, in part, by its energetic CEO, Jürgen Schrempp. This new attitude is manifesting itself both in the vehicles the company is producing and in the advertising being created for those vehicles. In its vehicle lineup, the vener-able and traditionally staid automaker recently displayed a wider variety of cars and new concepts at the Frankfurt auto show. Included were its first 4×4 sport-utility vehicle, a redesigned and lower priced E-Class sedan, and concept cars ranging from a two-passenger vehicle that "leans" into turns like a motorcycle to a high-mileage, low-pollution, full-size sedan that runs on liquid methanol.[1]

To match the innovativeness of its new vehicles, Mercedes-Benz has invested in new and exciting advertising. In one television ad, a stylish young couple (a nod to its traditional image) is taking a leisurely drive through a surrealistic world of mountains, streams, and sunsets in a Mercedes SL convertible. Partway through the drive, the cou-ple is serenaded by singing coyotes, and, later in the drive, a trio of fish salutes the trav-elers with a synchronized dive out of and back into a roadside pond (see Exhibit 1.1). This is not your typical Mercedes ad, and that seems to be just the point: to make clear that the Mercedes SL is not your typical Mercedes either. Other elements of this inte-grated campaign reflect innovation, but in a more subtle and understated manner. The print ads in Exhibits 1.2 and 1.3 are good examples. Each projects a basic and deep-felt human feeling—love—and ties this feeling to the Mercedes brand name with a subtle inclusion of the brand logo in the ad. Other versions of ads in this campaign highlight service and fun. The company hopes that together, these ads paint just the right mosaic for the new Mercedes.

Mercedes-Benz is a great example of an organi-zation that has taken dramatic steps in redesigning its products and then has taken equally dramatic steps in its advertising to reflect the change. Organizations like Mercedes have a good understanding of how to get the most out their advertising efforts. The com-bination of new, stylishly designed vehicles; strategic pricing; traditional service; and attention-getting advertising has pushed Mercedes sales to 700,000 units in 1997, up from 515,000 units in 1993.[2] But most people have significant misperceptions about the process of advertising and what it's supposed to do, what it can do, and what it can't do.

The general public's attitude toward advertising is ambivalent—most people like some of the ads they see or hear, but they may also say that they don't like advertising in general. Many think advertising deceives others, but rarely themselves. Most think it's a semi-glamorous profession, but one in which peo-ple are either morally bankrupt con artists or patho-logical liars. At worst, advertising is seen as hype, unfair capitalistic manipulation, banal commercial noise, mind control, postmodern voodoo, or out-right deception. Some believe it is the clearest

EXHIBIT 1.1

From a tradition of quality and coveted good taste comes a new genera-tion of style that rather self-consciously questions what makes a Mercedes memorable. www.mercedes-benz.com

1.   Alex Taylor III, "Revolution at Daimler-Benz," *Fortune,* November 10, 1997, 144–152.
2.   Ibid., 146.

EXHIBITS 1.2 AND 1.3

Mercedes-Benz has made a radical departure from its traditional advertising with this new campaign featuring only the brand logo.

marker of the decline of civilization and the undoing of meaning in the lives of ordinary people. Some of these descriptions of advertising reflect suspicions, biases, and superstitions that have long surrounded the industry. Yet some of these descriptions are, on occasion, regrettably true and precise.

At best, the average person sees advertising as amusing, informative, helpful, and occasionally hip. Advertising often helps consumers see possibilities and meanings in the things they buy and in the services they use. It can connect goods and services to the culture and liberate meanings that lie below the surface. It can turn mere products into meaningful brands and important possessions. For example, the advertising of Doyle Dane Bernbach for Volkswagen (see Exhibit 1.4) helped turn an unlikely automobile into a mobile social statement. The ads for the launch of the New Beetle (Exhibit 1.5) trade upon these roots, but deliver new looks and new meanings. Decades of advertising by Coca-Cola (an example is shown in Exhibit 1.6) have helped turn this brand of soft drink into a nearly universally recognized cultural icon. Coke is much more than a sweet, fizzy drink: it has enormous cultural capital and meaning. There are, of course, many less-dramatic and less well-known examples of the way advertising helps attract attention to products, such as the PowerQuest ad in Exhibit 1.7.

The truth about advertising lies somewhere between the extremes. Sometimes advertising is hard-hitting and powerful; at other times, it is boring and ineffective. Advertising can be enormously creative and entertaining, and it can be simply annoying. One thing is for sure: advertising is anything but unimportant. Advertising plays a pivotal role in world commerce and in the way we experience and live our lives. It is part of our language and our culture. It reflects the way we think about things and the way we see ourselves. It is both a complex communication process and a dynamic business process. Advertising is an important topic for you to study.

EXHIBIT 1.4

Advertising helps shape a product's image in the minds of consumers. Volkswagen used this ad from the 1960s to get consumers to replace the image of cars as "lemons" with the image of thrifty, dependable VWs.

EXHIBIT 1.5

In 1998, Volkswagen launched its celebrated New Beetle model with a series of ads recalling the original Beetle and evoking imagery from its target audience's past (www.vw.com/). Compare VW's campaign for the New Beetle with that of Apple Computer's new iMac (www.apple .com/), the most successful new product in Apple's history.

What Is Advertising?

Advertising means different things to different people. It's a business, an art, an institution, and a cultural phenomenon. To the CEO of a multinational corporation, such as Jürgen Schrempp, advertising is an essential marketing tool that helps create brand awareness and loyalty and stimulates demand. To the art director in an advertising agency, advertising is the creative expression of a concept. To a media planner, advertising is the way a firm uses the mass media to communicate to current and potential customers. To scholars and museum curators, advertising is an important cultural artifact, text, and historical record. Advertising means something different to all these people. In fact, sometimes determining just what is and what is not advertising is a difficult task. Keeping that in mind, we offer this definition:

Advertising is a paid, mass-mediated attempt to persuade.

As direct and simple as this definition seems, it is loaded with distinctions. Advertising is *paid* communication by a company or organization that wants its information disseminated. In advertising language, the company or organization that pays for advertising is called the **client** or **sponsor**.

First, if communication is *not* paid for, it's not advertising. For example, a form of promotion called *publicity* is not advertising because it is not paid for. Let's say Bruce Willis appears on the *Late Show with David Letterman* to promote his newest movie. Is this advertising? No, because the producer or film studio did not pay the *Late Show with David Letterman* for airtime. In this example, the show gets an interesting and popular guest, the guest star gets exposure, and the film gets plugged. Everyone is happy, but no advertising took place. But when the film studio produces and runs ads for the newest

Decades of consistent, high-quality advertising have made Coca-Cola one of the most recognizable brand names in the world. www.cocacola.com/

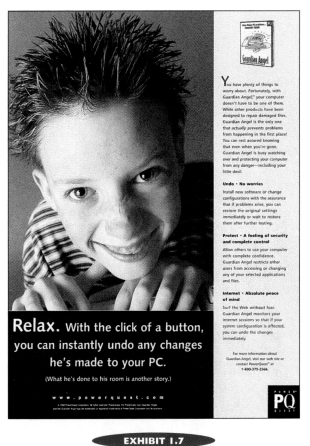

Advertising helps marketers attract attention to their brands and a brand's features. This ad for PowerQuest attracts attention with interesting photography. www.powerquest.com/

Bruce Willis movie on television and in newspapers across the country, this communication is paid for by the studio, and it most definitely is advertising.

For the same reason, public service announcements (PSAs) are not advertising either. True, they look like ads and sound like ads, but they aren't ads. They are not commercial in the way an ad is because they are not paid for like an ad. They are offered as information in the public (noncommercial) interest. When you hear a message on the radio that implores you to "Just Say No" to drugs, this sounds very much like an ad, but it is a PSA. Simply put, PSAs are excluded from the definition of advertising because they are unpaid communication.

Consider the two messages in Exhibits 1.8 and 1.9. These two messages have similar copy and offer similar advice. Exhibit 1.8 has persuasive intent, is paid-for communication, and appears in the mass-media. It is an advertisement. Exhibit 1.9 also has persuasive intent and appears in mass media outlets, but it is not advertising because it is not paid-for communication. PSAs are important and often strongly imitate their commercial cousins. For example, the Partnership for a Drug-Free America is taking on the "heroin chic" images of certain high-fashion advertising with a public service advertising campaign that takes the glamour out of heroin use.[3]

Second, advertising is *mass mediated*. This means it is delivered through a communication medium designed to reach more than one person, typically a large number—or mass—of people. Advertising is widely disseminated through familiar means—television, radio, newspapers, and magazines—and other media such as direct mail, billboards,

3.   Mercedes M. Cardona, "Drug Partnership Ads Tackle Heroin Use by Youth," *Advertising Age,* November 3, 1997, 8.

EXHIBITS 1.8 AND 1.9

The messages in Exhibits 1.8 and 1.9 communicate nearly identical information to the audience, but one is an advertisement and one is not. The message in Exhibit 1.8, sponsored by Trojan, is an advertisement because it is a paid-for communication. The message in Exhibit 1.9, sponsored by the U.K.'s Health Education Authority, has a persuasive intent similar to the Trojan ad, but it is not advertising—Exhibit 1.9 is a PSA. Why isn't the Health Education Authority PSA message an ad?
www.trojan.com/

"I didn't use one because I didn't have one with me."

GET REAL

If you don't have a parachute, don't jump, genius.

Helps reduce the risk

HOW FAR WILL YOU GO BEFORE YOU MENTION CONDOMS?

THIS FAR?

THIS FAR?

THIS FAR?

THIS FAR?

Today, no one can ignore the need to mention condoms. Have sex with someone without using one and not only could you risk an unwanted pregnancy, but you also risk contracting one of the many sexually transmitted diseases.

Like Herpes, Chlamydia, Gonorrhoea, and of course HIV, the virus which leads to AIDS.

So the question isn't if, but when you mention condoms. You could mention them at any moment leading up to sexual intercourse. In reality, it's not quite so easy.

Mention them too early and you might feel you look pushy or available. Leave it too late and you risk getting so carried away you might not mention them at all.

When is the easiest moment to say you want to use one? How about while you're still wearing your knickers? In this instance it would be picture three.

By now you've gone far enough to make it obvious that you both want to have sex. But not so far that you're in danger of getting emotionally and sexually carried away.

It's a perfect opportunity. So take it. Say you want to use a condom.

Say he hasn't got one? Well have one of your own at the ready just in case. It really doesn't matter whose you use.

And then you can go just as far as you like.

FOR MORE INFORMATION OR ADVICE ABOUT AIDS OR HIV, PHONE THE FREE NATIONAL AL   PINE ON 0800 567 123. IT'S OPEN 24 HOURS A DAY AND IS COMPLETELY CONFIDENTIAL.

the Internet, and videocassettes. The mass-mediated nature of advertising creates a communication environment where the message is not delivered in a face-to-face manner. This distinguishes advertising from personal selling as a form of communication.

Third, all advertising includes an *attempt to persuade*. To put it bluntly, ads are communication designed to get someone to do something. Even an advertisement with a stated objective of being purely informational still has persuasion at its core. The ad informs the consumer for some purpose, and that purpose is to get the consumer to like the brand and because of that liking to eventually buy the brand. In the absence of this persuasive intent, a communication might be news, but it would not be advertising.

At this point, we can say that for a communication to be classified as advertising, three essential criteria must be met:

1. The communication must be paid for.
2. The communication must be delivered to an audience via mass media.
3. The communication must be attempting persuasion.

It is important to note here that advertising can be persuasive communication not only about a product or service but also about an idea, a person, or an entire organization. When Colgate and Honda use advertising, this is product advertising and meets all three criteria. Likewise, when Dean Witter, Delta Air Lines, Terminix, or your dentist runs advertisements, it is service advertising and meets all three criteria.

But what about political advertising? Political ads "sell" candidates rather than commercial goods or services. Political advertisements may seem special because they are the only completely unregulated form of advertising; they are viewed as "political speech" and thus enjoy complete First Amendment protection. Still, political advertising meets our definition because it is paid-for communication, is mass mediated, and has a persuasive intent. Beyond the familiar political campaign advertising, political advertising is often undertaken in conjunction with lobbying efforts. Critics of President Clinton's health care plan used advertising to sway lawmakers and defeat a pending change in government health care coverage.[4] Political advertising can be for a candidate, as shown in Exhibit 1.10, or for a political organization, such as the National Rifle Association (NRA).

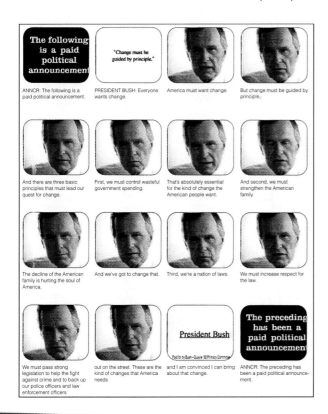

EXHIBIT 1.10

While this political message for George Bush during the 1992 presidential campaign is promoting a person and ideas, it meets the definitional test for advertising in general—it is paid-for communication, is placed in mass media, and has a persuasive intent. Check out www .democrats.org and www.rnc.org.

Although the Bush campaign ad does not ask anyone to buy anything (in terms of money), it is (1) paid for, (2) placed in a mass medium, and (3) an attempt to persuade members of the electorate to view George Bush and his agenda favorably. It represents another way advertising can persuade beyond the purchase of products and services. Many political candidates, environmental groups, human rights organizations, and political groups buy advertising and distribute it through mass media to persuade people to accept their way of thinking. They, too, are selling something.

Advertising, Advertisements, and Advertising Campaigns. Now that we have a working definition of advertising, we turn our attention to other important distinctions in advertising. An **advertisement** refers to a specific message that someone or some organization has placed to persuade an audience. An **advertising campaign** is a series of coordinated advertisements and other promotional efforts that communicate a reasonably cohesive and integrated theme. The theme may itself be made up of several claims or points but should advance an essentially singular theme. Successful advertising campaigns can be developed around a single advertisement placed in multiple media, or they can be made up of several different advertisements (more typical) with a similar look, feel, and message. The Lee Casuals ads in Exhibits 1.11 through 1.14

---

4. Ira Teinowitz, "Ad Campaigns Take Hold in Public-Policy Lobbying," *Advertising Age,* December 22, 1997, 14.

EXHIBITS 1.11 THROUGH 1.14

A well-conceived and well-executed advertising campaign offers consumers a series of messages with a similar look and feel. This series of ads for Lee Casuals is an excellent example of a campaign that communicates with similar images to create a unified look and feel. www.leecasuals.com/

represent an excellent use of similar look and feel to create an advertising campaign. Advertising campaigns can run for a few weeks or for many years. The advertising campaign is, in many ways, the most challenging aspect of advertising execution. It requires a keen sense of the complex environments within which an advertiser must communicate to different audiences and of how these messages interact with one another and an audience.

The vast majority of ads you see each day are part of broader campaigns. Furthermore, most individual ads would make little sense without the knowledge audience members have about ads for this particular product or for the product category in general. Ads are interpreted by consumers through their experiences with the product and with previous ads about the product. When you see a new Coca-Cola ad, you make sense of the ad through your history with Coca-Cola and its previous advertising. Even ads for a new brand or a new product are situated within audiences' broader knowledge of products, brands, and advertising. After years of viewing ads and buying brands, audiences bring a rich history and knowledge base to every communications encounter. These encounters between consumers and advertising underlie the discussion of our next topic.

Advertising as a Communication Process. Communication is a fundamental aspect of human existence, and advertising is communication. To understand advertising at all, you must understand something about communication in general and about mass communication in particular. At the outset, you must understand the basic aspects of how advertising works as a means of communication. To this end, let's consider a contemporary model of mass communication. We will apply this basic model of communication as a first step in understanding advertising.

A Model of Mass-Mediated Communication. As we said earlier, advertising is mass-mediated communication. It is communication that occurs, not face-to-face, but through a medium (such as radio, magazines, television, or a computer). While there are many valuable models of mass communication, a contemporary model of mass-mediated communication is presented in Exhibit 1.15. This model shows mass communication as a process of interacting individuals and institutions. It has two major components, each representing quasi-independent processes: production and reception.

Moving from left to right in the model, we first see the process of communication production, where the content of any mass communication is produced. An advertisement, like other forms of mass communication, is the product of institutions (such as networks, corporations, advertising agencies, and governments) interacting to produce content (what physically appears on a page as a print ad, or on a videotape as a television ad, or on a computer screen at a company's Web site). The creation of the advertisement is a complex interaction of the advertiser's message content; the advertiser's expectations

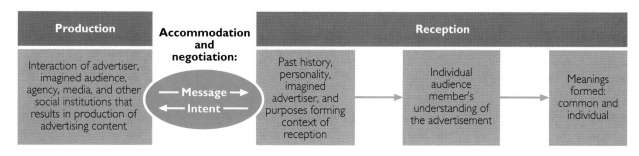

EXHIBIT 1.15

A model of mass-mediated communication.

regarding the target audience's desire for information (or their favorite strategies for avoiding it); the advertiser's assumptions about how the audience will interpret the words and images in an ad; and the conventions, rules, and regulations of the medium that transmits the message. Advertising is rarely (if ever) the product of an individual; rather, it is a collaborative (social) product.

Moving to the right, we see that accommodation and negotiation lie between the production and reception phases of the communication process. Accommodation and negotiation are processes of interpretation. Audience members have some ideas about how the advertiser wants them to interpret the ad. They also have their own needs, agendas, and preferred interpretations. They also know about the way other consumers think about this product and this message. Given all this, they arrive at an interpretation of the ad that makes sense, serves their needs, and is not usually wholly incompatible with the way the advertiser wanted consumers to see the ad. In other words, the receivers of the ad must *accommodate* these competing forces, meanings, and agendas and then *negotiate* a meaning, or an interpretation, of the ad. That's why we say that communication is inherently a *social* process: what a message means to any given consumer is a function, not of an isolated solitary thinker, but of an inherently social being responding to what he or she knows about the producers of the message, other receivers of it, and the social world in which the good or service and the message about it resides. Now, admittedly all this interpretation happens very, very fast and without much contemplation. Still, it happens. The level of conscious interpretation might be minimal (mere recognition) or it might be extensive (thoughtful, elaborate processing of an ad), but there is always interpretation. To even recognize an ad as an ad requires interpretation, albeit rapid and unnoticed interpretation. As members of a consumer culture, individuals have from a very early age been able to understand ads as ads and to perform very sophisticated interpretive acts. Humans are amazingly sophisticated, interpretive beings.

Within the reception process itself, individual members of the audience interpret an ad according to a set of factors governed largely by their salient social networks (their family, friends, and peers), their previous experience, and their motivations. Audience members bring with them their own rules of audience membership, that is, their own rules about how they will approach a message and interpret it. This is where the meaning of the ad is determined. The advertiser has significant input into the creation of *content,* but what the audience member makes of the ad (his or her interpretation) is the *meaning* the audience member gives it. It is critical to remember that content and meaning are not synonymous. For example, you and one of your friends can read the same book but interpret it very differently. The same is true of ads. A condom ad, for example, will most likely have different meanings depending on one's personal views toward sex. You and your grandmother may see things differently (or you may not). You create your own separate meanings based on your own social and cultural context and your own unique background and experiences. And both you and your grandmother will accommodate and negotiate the advertiser's message differently because of your different social situations and personal views toward sex. Regardless of what an advertiser intended the meaning to be, the actual meaning lies with the audience interpretation.

We say that the processes of production and reception are partially independent because, although the producers of a message can control the placement of an ad in a medium, they cannot control or even closely monitor the actual reception and interpretation of the ad. Audience members are exposed to advertising outside of the direct observation of the advertiser and are capable of interpreting advertising any way they want. (Of course, most audience interpretations are not completely "off the wall," either.) Likewise, audience members have little control over or input into the actual production of the message. Because of these aspects of communication, the model shows that both producers and receivers are thus "imagined," in the sense that the two don't have significant direct contact with one another but have a general sense of what the other is like.

(SFX: VARIOUS VOICES) WOMAN WHISPERS: It's 11:30

WOMAN: It's 11:30. WOMAN: It's 11:30

WOMAN: Diet Coke break. WOMAN: Diet Coke break.

WOMAN: Diet Coke break

(MUSIC) MAN SINGS: I don't want you

to be no slave.

I don't want you to work

all day.

But I want you to be true,

and I just wanna love to you, love to you.

WOMAN: See you tomorrow. WOMAN: 11:30.

WOMAN SINGS: Hm,hm. Love–(MUSIC OUT)

EXHIBIT 1.16

This ad is a good example of how the meaning of an ad can vary for different people. How would you interpret the meaning of this ad? Think of someone very different from you. What meaning might that person give this ad? www.cocacola.com/

The model in Exhibit 1.15 underscores the critical point that no ad contains a single meaning for all audience members. An ad for a pair of women's shoes means something different for women than it does for men. An ad that achieved widespread popularity is the ad for Diet Coke, shown in Exhibit 1.16, which may be interpreted differently by men and women. For example, does the ad suggest that men drink Diet Coke so they can be the object of intense daily admiration by a group of female office workers? Or does the ad suggest that Diet Coke is a part of a modern woman's lifestyle, granting her "permission" to freely admire attractive men in the same way women have been eyed by male construction workers (or executives) for years? The audience decides. Keep in mind that although individual audience members' interpretations will differ to some extent, they may be close enough to the advertiser's intent to make the ad effective. When members of an audience are similar in their background, social standing, and goals, they generally yield similar enough meaning from an ad for it to accomplish its goals.

The Audiences for Advertising. In the language of advertising, an **audience** is a group of individuals who receive and interpret messages sent from advertisers through mass media. In advertising, audiences are often targeted. A **target audience** is a particular group of consumers singled out for an advertisement or advertising campaign. Target audiences are *potential* audiences because advertisers can never be sure that the message will actually get through to them as intended. While advertisers can identify dozens of different target audiences, five broad audience categories are commonly described: household consumers, members of business organizations, members of a trade channel, professionals, and government officials and employees.

Audience Categories. Household consumers are the most conspicuous audience in that most mass media advertising is directed at them. Unilever, Miller Brewing, Saturn, The Gap, and Nationwide Insurance have products and services designed for the consumer market, and so their advertising targets household consumers. The most recent information indicates that there are 100 million households in the United States and approximately 270 million household consumers.[5] Total yearly retail spending by these households is about $3 trillion.[6] This huge audience is typically where the action is in advertising. Under the very broad heading of "consumer advertising," very fine audience distinctions are made by advertisers. Target audience definitions, such as men, 25 to 45, living in metropolitan areas, with incomes greater than $50,000 per year, are common.

Members of business organizations are the focus of advertising for firms that produce business and industrial goods and services, such as office equipment, production machinery, supplies, and software. While products and services targeted to this audience often require personal selling, advertising is used to create an awareness and a

5.   "1998 Survey of Buying Power," *Sales and Marketing Management* (1998), 10, 15, 19.
6.   Ibid, 19.

About 50 years cooler than an overhead projector.

The world's most popular data/video projectors.
Call for a free demo: 1-800-294-6400 or www.infocus.com/aa

It's the computer age. Why not present from one? With an In Focus® projector, you put your ideas up on a wall with brilliant color, graphics, and motion—letting you really take control of your audience. And you'll love our award-winning products like the new In Focus LP420 personal projector. It's just 6.8 pounds, incredibly bright, and at least 50 years cooler than an overhead.

InFocus®
Project yourself.

EXHIBIT 1.17

When members of business organizations use advertising to communicate, the ads often emphasize creating awareness of the company's brand. This ad for InFocus projectors is an example. www.infocus.com/

favorable attitude among potential buyers. Not-for-profit businesses such as universities, some research laboratories, philanthropic groups, and cultural organizations represent an important and separate business audience for advertising. Exhibit 1.17 is an example of an ad directed at members of business organizations.

Members of a trade channel include retailers, wholesalers, and distributors; they are an audience for producers of both household and business goods and services. Unless a producer can obtain adequate retail and wholesale distribution through a trade channel, the firm's products will not reach customers. Therefore, it is important to direct advertising at the trade level of the market. Various forms of advertising and promotion are instrumental in cultivating demand among members of a trade channel. Generally, the major promotional tool used to communicate with this group is personal selling. This is because this target audience represents a relatively small, easily identifiable group that can be reached with personal selling. When advertising is also directed at this audience, it can serve an extremely useful purpose, as we will see later in the section on advertising as a business process.

Professionals form a special target audience and are defined as doctors, lawyers, accountants, teachers, or any other professionals who have received special training or certification. This audience warrants separate classification because its members have specialized needs and interests. Advertising directed at professionals thus highlights products and services often uniquely designed to serve their more narrowly defined needs. In addition, the language and images used in advertising to this target audience rely on the esoteric terminology and unique circumstances that members of professions readily recognize. Advertising to professionals is predominantly carried out through trade publications. The ad for Prevacid in Exhibit 1.18 is an example of advertising directed to doctors.

Government officials and employees constitute an audience in themselves due to the large dollar volume of buying that federal, state, and local governments do. Government organizations such as schools and road maintenance operations buy huge amounts of various products. Producers of items such as furniture, construction materials, vehicles, fertilizers, computers, and business services all target this group with their advertising. Advertising to this audience group is dominated by direct mail advertising.

Audience Geography. Audiences can also be thought of in geographic terms. Because of cultural differences, very few ads can be effective for all consumers worldwide. However, so-called **global advertising** can be used for some brands. These are typically brands that are considered citizens of the world and whose manner of use does not vary tremendously by culture. Even though cultures vary significantly in their view of time and men's jewelry, Exhibits 1.19 and 1.20 show extremely similar executions of a Rolex ad. Firms that market brands, such as Singapore Airlines, IBM, Levi's, Sony, and Pirelli, attempt to develop and place advertisements with a common theme and presentation in all markets around the world where the firm's brands are sold. Global placement is possible only when a brand and the messages about that brand have a common

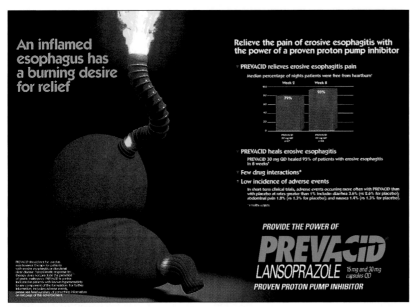

Professional audiences for advertising, such as doctors, lawyers, and engineers, have special needs and interests. This ad for Prevacid was run in a trade publication and offers medical doctors the kind of specialized information they desire about pharmaceutical products.

WEB : SIGHT : ING

No surprise—companies can tailor their advertising to target audiences and routinely do when the target is clear. The obvious audience difference here is language (German versus Italian), while other aspects—Rolex's appeal to an affluent elite who likely follow tennis, not NASCAR, and the Rolex brand imagery—remain the same. In Cyberspace, everywhere can be "local," and advertising on the Web seems more attuned to lifestyle than to geography, with English as the most common lingua franca. Although Rolex doesn't yet use the Web to advertise its products, a Web search at Yahoo! (www.yahoo .com) turns up a variety of retailers. Is the Web likely to be Rolex's best advertising channel anyway?

appeal across diverse cultures. Travelers in Asia seek the same benefits from an airline as travelers in the United States. Men in Europe want the same comfort from a razor when they shave as men in South America. Motorola had its agency, McCann-Erickson Worldwide, prepare global ads for its cell phones and pagers; their strategy is discussed in the Global Issues box on this page. There is, however, a very significant minority opinion that there is no such thing as global advertising, because communication can never be completely isolated from culture. Of course, the counterargument to this is that brands such as Coke, Sony, and IBM are part of a global consumer culture that recognizes no national borders. This argument is one of the longest running in the advertising profession.

International advertising occurs when firms prepare and place different advertising in different national markets. Each international market often requires unique or original advertising due to product adaptations or message appeals tailored specifically for that market. Unilever prepares different versions of ads for its laundry products for nearly every international market due to differences in the way consumers in different cultures approach the laundry task. Consumers in the United States use large and powerful washers and dryers and lots of hot water. Households in Brazil use very little hot water and hang clothes out to dry. Very few firms enjoy the luxury of having a brand with truly cross-cultural appeal and global recognition. Since this is true, most firms must pursue other-nation markets with international advertising rather than global advertising.

National advertising reaches all geographic areas of one nation. National advertising is the term typically used to describe the kind of advertising we see most often in the mass media in the domestic U.S. market.

Regional advertising is carried out by producers, wholesalers, distributors, and retailers that concentrate their efforts in a relatively large, but not national, geographic region. Best Buy, a regional consumer electronics and appliance chain, has distribution confined to a few states.

GLOBAL ISSUES

MOTOROLA'S GLOBAL CAMPAIGN TAKES FLIGHT

As successful and astute as Motorola has been in reinventing itself as a corporation, it did miss one major market trend—the rush by consumers to go digital with cell phone technology. As a result, Motorola's share of the U.S. market for cellular handset technology has dropped from 55 percent in 1995 to just 34.1 percent in 1998. The beneficiaries of Motorola's hesitancy are Nokia, whose 13.6 percent share increased to 24.4 percent, and Ericsson, whose share has rocketed from merely 2 percent to over 14 percent.

Motorola clearly needed a lift and a global ad campaign was conceived. Motorola challenged its advertising agency, McCann-Erickson Worldwide, to "find the friendliest means of telling consumers about the wealth of benefits Motorola technology brings." The challenge was to develop a global advertising campaign that would feature technology as the universal appeal across geographic and cultural boundaries. The campaign needed to be a corporate image campaign. The Motorola name was known in the market, but not preferred. Analysts at McCann-Erickson discovered that consumers weren't seeking out the brand; they thought it was "durable" but had no real affinity for who the company was or what the brand stood for. Bottom line: the brand lacked personality and a solid identity.

These conditions are classic prerequisites for a global image campaign that focuses on creating a relationship with a brand rather than relying on product feature appeals, as competitors often do. So a new campaign took flight—literally. Motorola launched a $100 million global campaign called "Wings," which features its batwinglike corporate logo. Television and print ads aim to beat back the challenge from Nokia and Ericsson and to change the corporate image from "sturdy" to "contemporary." The images in the campaign highlight a squadron of flight-related images: a nun pedaling a bike with a dove at her side; a woman in a chapel wearing giant feathered wings; a man tossing a paper airplane. In the background, Mick Jagger sings "You Can't Always Get What You Want." The voiceover intones, "They say flight is for the birds; Motorola says you are cleared for takeoff. . . . Motorola gives you wings. Wings set you free."

The unifying global theme, which is portable across geographic boundaries and cultures, is the message that Motorola technology has benefits for individuals—no matter where you are. As the text discussion points out, when a firm like Motorola can strike a universal chord, then a global ad campaign can become a reality.

Sources: Bradley Johnson and Mercedes M. Cardona, "Motorola Seeks Unifying Elements for Global Ads," *Advertising Age*, August 18, 1997, 8; Sally Goll Beaty, "Motorola's Image Campaign Set to Fly," *Wall Street Journal*, April 18, 1998, B14.

Because of the nature of the firm's market, it places advertising only in regions where it has stores.

Local advertising is essentially the same as regional advertising. **Local advertising** is directed at an audience in a single trading area, either a city or state. Exhibit 1.21 shows an example of this type of advertising.

Retail shopkeepers of all types rely on local media to reach customers. Under special circumstances, national advertisers will share advertising expenses in a market with local dealers to achieve specific advertising objectives. This sharing of advertising expenses between national advertisers and local merchants is called **cooperative advertising** (or **co-op advertising**). Exhibit 1.22 illustrates a co-op advertisement run by TUMI luggage and one of its retailers, Shapiro.

Advertising as a Business Process. ◁ For multinational organizations like IBM, as well as for small local retailers, advertising is a basic business tool that helps them communicate with current and potential customers. We need to understand advertising as a business process in two ways. First, we will consider the role advertising plays in the overall marketing program in firms. Second, we will take a broader look at the impact of advertising across economic systems.

The Role of Advertising in Marketing. To truly appreciate advertising as a business process, we have to understand the role advertising plays in a firm's marketing effort. Every organization must make marketing decisions. These decisions involve researching, developing, pricing, promoting, and distributing products and services for some target audience. The role of advertising in marketing relates to four important aspects of the marketing process: (1) designing a marketing mix; (2) achieving effective market segmentation, product differentiation, and positioning; (3) contributing to revenue and profit generation; and (4) enhancing customer satisfaction.

EXHIBIT 1.21

Daffy's is a clothing retailer with just one shop in New York City; it services a local geographic market. Retailers that serve a small geographic area use local advertising to reach their customers.

EVERY DAY OVER 1,000 COMPUTERS ARE BROKEN IN TRANSIT.

HAVE A SAFE TRIP.

INTRODUCING THE SAFECASE COMPUTER BRIEF

The revolutionary Safecase by TUMI cradles and suspends your computer, protecting it from damage while you travel.

Utilizing a patented suspension system including two sets of neoprene slings, the Safecase gives 4 times more protection against dropping than the average computer case.

TUMI Safecases are available in Ballistic nylon and full-grain Nappa leather.

FASHION PLACE
ZCMI CENTER
COTTONWOOD MALL
OGDEN CITY MALL
UNIVERSITY MALL
SOUTH TOWNE MALL
BOISE TOWNE SQUARE

TUMI

SHAPIRO
Luggage · Gifts · Leather
An Escape From The Ordinary Since 1917

EXHIBIT 1.22

National advertisers will often share advertising expenses with local retail merchants if the retailer features the advertiser's brand in local advertising. This sharing of expenses is called co-op advertising. Here a local retailer, Shapiro, is featuring TUMI brand luggage in this co-op ad.

Advertising's Role in Designing the Marketing Mix. A formal definition of marketing reveals that advertising (as a part of overall promotion) is one of the primary marketing tools available to any organization:

Marketing is the process of planning and executing the conception, pricing, promotion, and distribution of ideas, goods, and services to create exchanges that satisfy individual and organizational objectives.[7]

Marketing assumes a wide range of responsibilities related to the conception, pricing, promotion, and distribution of ideas, goods, or services. Many of you know that these four areas of responsibility and decision making in marketing are referred to as the **marketing mix.** The word *mix* is used to describe the blend of strategic emphasis on the product, its price, its promotion (including advertising), and its distribution when a brand is marketed to consumers. This blend, or mix, results in the overall marketing program for a brand. Advertising is important, but it is only one of the major areas of marketing responsibility *and* it is only one of many different promotional tools relied on in the marketing mix.

Generally speaking, the role of advertising in the marketing mix is to focus on the ability of the advertising effort to communicate to a target audience the value a product or service has to offer. Value consists of more than simply the product or service itself, though. Indeed, consumers look for value in the product or service, but they also demand such things as convenient location, credit terms, warranties and guarantees, and delivery. In addition, a wide range of emotional values such as security, belonging, affiliation, and prestige can also be pursued in the brand choice process. Because of consumers' search for such diverse values, marketers must determine which marketing mix ingredients to emphasize and how to blend the mix elements in just the right way to attract and satisfy customers. These mix ingredients play a significant role in determining the message content and placement of advertising.

Exhibit 1.23 lists the most common factors considered in each area of the marketing mix. You can see that product, price, promotion, and distribution really refer to a wide range of strategies that can be used to attract customers. The important point is that a firm's advertising effort must complement the overall marketing mix strategy being used by a firm.

Advertising's Role in Achieving Market Segmentation, Product Differentiation, and Positioning. For advertising to be effective, it must work to support the organization's general marketing strategies. Some of the most basic strategies for cultivating customers are market segmentation, product differentiation, and positioning. Advertising plays an important role in helping a firm execute these marketing strategies.

Market segmentation is the breaking down of a large, widely varied (*heterogeneous*) market into submarkets, or segments, that are more similar than dissimilar (*homogeneous*) in terms of what the consumer is looking for or is presumed to be looking for.

---

7.   The American Marketing Association definition, given here, is well accepted and appeared in *Marketing News,* March 1, 1985, 1.

Product	Promotion
Functional features	Amount and type of advertising
Aesthetic design	Number and qualifications of salespeople
Accompanying services	Extent and type of personal selling program
Instructions for use	Sales promotion—coupons, contests, sweepstakes
Warranty	Trade shows
Product differentiation	Public relations activities
Product positioning	Direct mail or telemarketing
	Event sponsorships
	Internet communications

Price	Distribution
Level:	Number of retail outlets
Top of the line	Location of retail outlets
Competitive, average prices	Types of retail outlets
Low-price policy	Catalog sales
Terms offered:	Other nonstore retail methods—Internet
Cash only	Number and type of wholesalers
Credit:	Inventories—extent and location
Extended	Services provided by distribution:
Restricted	Credit
Interest charges	Delivery
Lease/rental	Installation
	Training

Underlying the strategy of market segmentation are the facts that consumers differ in their wants and that the wants of one person can differ under various circumstances. The market for automobiles can be divided into submarkets for different types of automobiles based on the needs and desires of various groups of buyers. Identifying those groups, or segments, of the population who want and will buy large or small, luxury or economy, sport or sedan or minivan models is an important part of basic marketing strategy. Larger markets are, however, often broken up by more indirect criteria, such as age, marital status, gender, and income, since these data are widely collected and widely available and tend to be reasonably related to product and usage. Advertising's role in the market segmentation process is to develop messages that appeal to the wants and desires of different segments and then to transmit those messages via appropriate media. At present, advertisers are struggling with decisions concerning how much to invest in new media vehicles for reaching target segments. The difficulty of these decisions is highlighted in the New Media box on page 20.

Product differentiation is the process of creating a perceived difference, in the mind of the consumer, between an organization's brand and the competition's. Notice that this definition emphasizes that product differentiation is based on *consumer perception*. The perceived differences can be tangible differences, or they may be based on image or style factors. The critical issue is that consumers *perceive* a difference between brands. If consumers do not perceive a difference, then whether "real" differences exist or not does not matter. Product differentiation is one of the most critical of all marketing strategies. If a firm's brand is not perceived as distinctive and attractive by consumers, then consumers will have no reason to choose the brand over one from the competition or to pay higher prices for the "better" brand.

NEW MEDIA

THE INTERNET IS BIG—BUT NOT AS BIG AS *SEINFELD*

The Internet is posing some difficult problems for advertisers. Traditional media—television, radio, newspapers, magazines—have demonstrated their ability, over decades, to reach targeted audiences with persuasive and informative communications. But then along comes this new medium—the Internet—with all kinds of special potential. The headlines scream out every day about this potential: It's huge! It's hot! It's interactive! Grandmothers are online! Every school in America is getting wired!

But really, just how big is the Internet? Not that big—really. For all the hype and potential and conspicuousness, the Internet still reaches a much smaller audience than traditional media—and messages are a lot easier to ignore. For the record, here are some of the numbers. About 62 million people in the United States use the Internet. Of those 62 million, about 15 million are novices who first logged on in 1997. By age, the Internet reaches 11 percent of 12-to-17-year-olds, 38 percent of 18-to-34-year-olds, 36 percent of 35-to-49-year-olds, and only about 15 percent of those over 50. But these numbers lose more of their zip when you consider that the Internet reaches about 23 percent of households in the United States. Compare that with the fact that television reaches 98 percent of households and radio reaches 99.9 percent. Even cable television has a 67 percent penetration rate.

Want some more perspective? America Online brags that it now has 11 million subscribers. But during peak usage, AOL is serving only about 6,875,000 users at once. This is about half the homes that are tuned into *Nick Freno: Licensed Teacher* (a show that was cancelled for low ratings!) on the Warner Brothers television network. And bragging rights really fade when you consider that the final episode of *Seinfeld* was watched by about 80 million people!

One final point on the nonhugeness of the Internet is particularly interesting from an advertising perspective. Currently, advertisers have invested about $1.5 billion in Internet advertising, compared to the $73 billion invested in television, radio, newspapers, and magazines. In other words, the Internet represents only about 2 percent of traditional media from an advertising standpoint. Is the Internet exciting, dynamic, entertaining, informative, and important? Yes. Is it huge? No. Will it be huge? Maybe.

Advertising can help create a difference, in the mind of the consumer, between an organization's brand and its competitors' brands. The advertisement may emphasize performance features, or it may create a different image of the brand. The essential task for advertising is to develop a message that is distinctive and unmistakably linked to the organization's brand. The ads in Exhibits 1.24 and 1.25 are distinctive and pursue product differentiation with both function and image.

Positioning is the process of designing a brand so that it can occupy a distinct and valued place in the target consumer's mind relative to other brands and then communicating this distinctiveness through advertising. For example, Saab may want to "position" (in the consumer's mind) its new 9^3 somewhere between the new BMW 3 series and an Acura TL (see Exhibits 1.26 through 1.28). Notice that positioning, like product differentiation, is dependent on a perceived image. The importance of positioning can be understood by recognizing that consumers create a *perceptual space* in their minds for all the brands they might consider purchasing. A perceptual space is how one brand is seen on any number of dimensions—such as quality, taste, price, or social display value—in relation to those same dimensions in other brands.

The positioning decision really comprises two different decisions. A firm must decide on the **external position** for a brand—that is, the niche the brand will pursue relative to all the competitive brands on the market. Additionally, an **internal position** must be achieved with regard to the other similar brands a firm markets. For example, Procter & Gamble—with nearly a dozen laundry detergent brands on the market—has to be careful not to cannibalize, or steal market share from, one of its own brands. With the external-positioning decision, a firm must achieve a distinctive competitive position based on design features, pricing,

EXHIBITS 1.24 AND 1.25

An important role for advertising is to help a firm differentiate its brand from the competition with distinctive presentations. The Honda del Sol ad in Exhibit 1.24 draws attention to the car's removable roof as a basis for differentiation. The Wonderbra ad in Exhibit 1.25 also highlights this brand's superior design as a basis for differentiation. www.honda.com/

NEWTON WAS WRONG.

EXHIBIT 1.26

In this ad, which introduces its new 9³, Saab chooses not to take its tradition of safety for granted. And who doesn't think twice about driving through tunnels these days? www.saabusa.com

distribution, or promotion or advertising strategy. Some brands are positioned at the very top of their product category, like BMW's 740iL, priced around $65,500. Other brands seek a position at the low end of all market offerings, like the Chevrolet Metro, whose base price is $10,402.[8]

Effective internal positioning is accomplished by either developing vastly different products within a product line (Ben & Jerry's® ice cream, for example, offers plenty of distinctive flavors, as shown in Exhibit 1.29) or creating advertising messages that appeal to different consumer needs and desires. Procter & Gamble successfully avoids cannibalization in its laundry detergent line by internally positioning very similar brands using a combination of product design and effective advertising. While some of these brands assume different positions in the line due to substantive differences (a liquid versus a powder soap, for example), others with minor differences achieve distinctive positioning through advertising. One P&G brand is advertised as being effective on kids' dirty clothes, while another brand is portrayed as effective for preventing colors from running (see Exhibit 1.30). In this way, advertising helps create a distinctive position, both internally and externally, and minimizes cannibalization among similar brands.

8.   Pricing information at www.bmwusa.com/showroom/7series/by07/740iL.html and www.chevrolet.com/metro/index.htm. Accessed October 27, 1998.

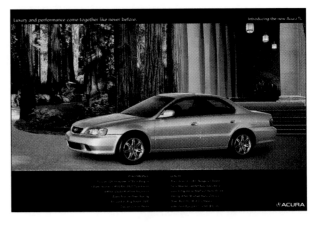

EXHIBITS 1.27 AND 1.28

Introducing new automobiles, both BMW and Acura neatly capture the be-safe/be-secure message seen in the Saab ad, but quickly move on to other perks of driving—the thrill and luxury of it, safety balanced by exhilaration. www.bmwusa.com *and* www.acura.com

EXHIBIT 1.29

Firms with multiple brands in a single product category have to internally position these brands to differentiate them from each other in the minds of consumers. Ben & Jerry's® achieves its product positioning by emphasizing the distinctly different flavors of each of its ice creams. www.benjerry.com/

EXHIBIT 1.30

When a firm has multiple brands in a product category, it must be careful to position these brands distinctively so as to avoid cannibalization of one brand's sales by another. Procter & Gamble successfully achieves both a competitive external position and a distinctive internal product line position for Cheer laundry detergent by advertising the brand as the leader in preventing colors from running. www.pg.com/

The methods and strategic options available to an organization with respect to market segmentation, product differentiation, and positioning will be fully discussed in Chapter 6. For now, recognize that advertising plays an important role in helping an organization put these essential market strategies into operation.

Advertising's Role in Contributing to Revenue and Profit Generation.

The fundamental purpose of marketing can be stated quite simply: to generate revenue. No other part of an organization has this primary purpose. In the words of highly regarded management consultant and scholar Peter Drucker, "Marketing and innovation produce results: all the rest are 'costs.'"[9] The results Drucker is referring to are revenues. The marketing process is designed to generate sales and therefore revenues for the firm.

The contribution to creating sales as part of the revenue-generating process is where advertising plays a significant role. As we have seen, advertising communicates persuasive information to audiences based on the values created in the marketing mix. This communication, which can highlight brand features, price, or availability through distribution, attracts customers. When a brand has the *right* features, the *right* price, the *right* distribution, and the *right* communication, sales will likely occur, and the firm generates revenue. In this way, advertising makes a direct contribution to the marketing goal of revenue generation. Notice that advertising *contributes* to the process of creating sales and revenue—it cannot be viewed as solely responsible for creating sales and revenue. Some organizations mistakenly see advertising as a panacea—the salvation for an ambiguous marketing mix strategy. Advertising alone cannot be held responsible for sales. Sales occur when a brand has a well-conceived and complete marketing mix—including good advertising.

The effect of advertising on profits is a bit more involved. This effect comes about when advertising can help give a firm greater flexibility in the price it charges for a product or service. Advertising can help create pricing flexibility by (1) contributing to economies of scale and (2) creating brand loyalty. When a firm creates large-scale demand for its product, the quantity of product produced is increased. As production reaches higher and higher levels, fixed costs (such as rent and equipment costs) are spread over a greater number of units produced. The result of this large-scale production is that the cost to produce each item is reduced. Lowering the cost of each item produced because of high-volume production is known as **economies of scale**.

When Colgate manufactures hundreds of thousands of tubes of its new Colgate Total toothpaste and ships them in large quantities to warehouses, the fixed costs of production and shipping per unit are greatly reduced. With lower fixed costs per unit, Colgate can realize greater profits on each tube of toothpaste sold. Advertising contributes to demand stimulation by communicating to the market about the features and availability of a brand. By contributing to demand stimulation, advertising contributes to the process of creating economies of scale, which ultimately translates into higher profits per unit.

Brand loyalty occurs when a consumer repeatedly buys the same brand. This loyalty can result from habit, brand images and brand names that are prominent in the consumer's memory, barely conscious associations with a brand's image, or some fairly deep meanings consumers have attached to the brands they buy. When consumers, through whatever set of these influences and meanings, are brand loyal, they are generally less sensitive to price increases for the brand. In economic terms, this is known as **inelasticity of demand**. When consumers are less price sensitive, firms have the flexibility to raise prices and increase profit margins. Advertising contributes directly to brand loyalty, and thus to inelasticity of demand, by persuading and reminding consumers of the satisfactions and values related to the brand.

Advertising's Role in Creating Customer Satisfaction.

How does advertising play a role in creating customer satisfaction? Once again, advertising can communicate how a brand addresses certain needs and desires and therefore plays an important role in attracting customers to brands they will find useful and satisfying. But advertising can go further. It can help link a brand's image and meaning to a consumer's social

---

9.   Peter F. Drucker, *People and Performance: The Best of Peter Drucker* (New York: Harper Collins, 1977), 90.

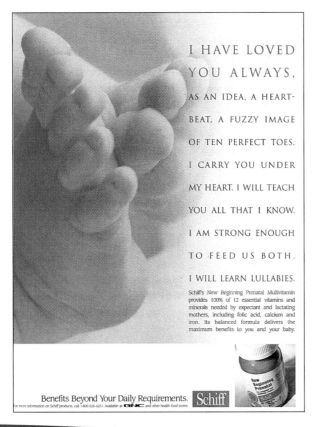

I HAVE LOVED YOU ALWAYS, AS AN IDEA, A HEART-BEAT, A FUZZY IMAGE OF TEN PERFECT TOES. I CARRY YOU UNDER MY HEART. I WILL TEACH YOU ALL THAT I KNOW. I AM STRONG ENOUGH TO FEED US BOTH. I WILL LEARN LULLABIES.

Schiff's New Beginning Prenatal Multivitamin provides 100% of 12 essential vitamins and minerals needed by expectant and lactating mothers, including folic acid, calcium and iron. Its balanced formula delivers the maximum benefits to you and your baby.

Benefits Beyond Your Daily Requirements. Schiff

For more information on Schiff products, call 1-800-526-6251. Available at GNC and other health food stores.

EXHIBIT 1.31

This message in this Schiff ad creates meaning for vitamins that goes beyond the daily nutrition role vitamins can play. What are the many meanings in this message offered to consumers?

environment and to the larger culture, and it can thus deliver a sense of personal connection for the consumer. Without advertising as a way to reveal the availability of brands and draw out these connections of broader meaning, a firm's ability to deliver customer satisfaction would be limited.

The Schiff ad for prenatal vitamins in Exhibit 1.31 is a clear example of how advertising can create deeper meaning and effect satisfaction. The message in this ad is not just about the health advantages of using a nutritional supplement during pregnancy. The message mines associations related to love and caring for an unborn or recently born child. Even the slogan for the brand, "Benefits Beyond Your Daily Requirements," plays on the sense that a vitamin is more than a vehicle for dosing up on folic acid. Other promotional tools, such as personal selling, sales promotions, public relations, and event sponsorship, simply cannot achieve such creative power or communicate all the potential meanings a brand can have to a consumer.

Types of Advertising. Advertisers develop and place advertisements for many reasons. Some of the most basic types of advertising are based on functional goals, that is, on what the advertiser is trying to accomplish. The functional goals for advertising include primary and selective demand stimulation, direct and delayed response advertising, and corporate advertising.

One potential function for advertising is primary demand stimulation, although this role is quite limited. In **primary demand stimulation**, an advertiser is seeking to create demand for a product category in general. In its pure form, the purpose of this type of advertising is to educate potential buyers about the fundamental values of a type of product rather than to emphasize the values of a specific brand within the product category. Both the National Fluid Milk Processor Promotion Board and the Florida Department of Citrus have tried to use primary demand stimulation advertising for their products, as shown in Exhibits 1.32 and 1.33.

Primary demand stimulation is challenging and costly, and research evidence suggests that it is only likely to have a perceivable impact for new products on the market—such as when the VCR was first developed and introduced to the market. With a product that is totally new to the market, consumers need to be convinced that the product category itself is available and valuable. When the VCR was first introduced in the United States, RCA, Panasonic, and Quasar (see Exhibit 1.34) ran primary demand stimulation advertising to explain to household consumers the value and convenience of taping television programs—something almost no one had ever done before at home. More recently, Thermoscan has been running advertisements in an attempt to stimulate primary demand for a thermometer that measures a baby's temperature in the ear rather than in the traditional location (see Exhibit 1.35). For organizations that have tried to stimulate primary demand in mature product categories, the results have been dismal. While the "mustache" campaign (see Exhibit 1.32 again), which tries to stimulate primary demand for milk, is very popular and gets widespread recognition, milk consumption has *declined* every year during the time of this

EXHIBIT 1.32

Advertising to stimulate primary demand is often tried by industry associations and advocacy groups, such as the National Fluid Milk Processor Promotion Board, rather than by specific manufacturers. On the Web, where communication is less regulated than in print, it may even be impossible to determine who is behind a message. Who is behind the Got Milk? site (www.gotmilk.org)? What is it selling? How does the message at Borden's Elsie the Cow site (www.elsiethecow.com) differ?

EXHIBIT 1.33

This ad promoting orange juice attempts to stimulate primary demand, or demand for a product category rather than demand for a particular brand. Decades of literature demonstrate no relationship between aggregate levels of advertising in an industry and overall demand in an industry. It appears that advertising is indeed suited only to selective (brand) demand stimulation.

campaign.[10] This is despite the fact that nearly $700 million has been invested in the campaign. Even if the attempts at primary demand have reduced the overall decline, it is still not a very impressive result. This should come as no surprise, though. Research has clearly indicated that attempts at primary demand in mature product categories have never been successful.[11]

While some corporations have tried primary demand stimulation, the true power of advertising is shown when it functions to stimulate demand for a particular company's brand. This is known as **selective demand stimulation**. The purpose of selective demand stimulation advertising is to point out a brand's unique benefits compared to the competition. For example, examine the Tropicana ad in Exhibit 1.36—it touts this brand's superiority (contrast this brand ad with the primary demand stimulation ad in Exhibit 1.33). Likewise, now that the VCR is past the stage of primary demand stimulation and is a mature product category, households accept the value of this product and

---

10. U.S. Bureau of the Census, *Statistical Abstract of the United States: 1995,* 115th ed., Washington, D.C., 1995; "Got Results?" *Marketing News,* March 2, 1998, 1.

11. For an excellent summary of decades of research on the topic, see Mark S. Abion and Paul W. Farris, *The Advertising Controversy: Evidence of the Economic Effects of Advertising* (Boston: Auburn House, 1981); J. C. Luik and M. S. Waterson, *Advertising and Markets* (Oxfordshire, UK: NTC Publications, 1996).

EXHIBIT 1.34

In the early days of the VCR, manufacturers stimulated primary demand for the product category with advertising that touted the basic value of the machine and the taping process itself.

each brand selectively appeals to different consumer needs. Current advertising for VCRs emphasizes brand features such as hi-fi sound, remote control, and voice recognition programming, as Exhibit 1.37 illustrates. This is selective demand stimulation.

Another important type of advertising involves functional goals related to the immediacy of consumer response. **Direct response advertising** is a type of advertising that asks the receiver of the message to act immediately. When an ad suggests that you "call this toll-free number" or "mail your $19.95 before midnight tonight," it is an example of direct response advertising. The ad in Exhibit 1.38 is a good example. Here, the company implores consumers to act quickly in order to obtain the Frank Sinatra collector's plate. That's direct response advertising.

While exceptions exist, direct response advertising is most often used for products that consumers are familiar with, that do not require inspection at the point of purchase, and that are relatively low-cost. The proliferation of toll-free numbers and the widespread use of credit cards have been a boon to direct response advertisers.

Delayed response advertising relies on imagery and message themes that emphasize the benefits and satisfying characteristics of a brand. Rather than trying to stimulate an immediate action from an audience, delayed response advertising attempts to develop recognition and approval of a brand over time. In general, delayed response advertising attempts to create brand awareness, reinforce the benefits of using a brand, develop a general liking for the brand, and create an image for a brand. When a consumer enters the purchase process, the information from delayed response advertising comes into play. Most advertisements we see on television and in magazines are of the delayed response type. Exhibit 1.39, an ad for hypo-allergenic detergent, provides an example of this common form of advertising.

Corporate advertising is not designed to promote a specific brand, but rather functions to establish a favorable attitude toward the company as a whole. Prominent users of corporate advertising are Phillips Petroleum, Xerox, and IBM. These firms have long-established corporate campaigns aimed at generating favorable public opinion

EXHIBIT 1.35

Advertising for ear thermometers is a recent attempt at primary demand stimulation, as this ad by Thermoscan demonstrates quite well. How is this attempt at primary demand stimulation different from the milk and orange juice attempts in Exhibits 1.32 and 1.33?

EXHIBIT 1.36

EXHIBIT 1.37

Selective demand stimulation advertising highlights a brand's superiority in providing satisfaction. In this ad, Tropicana touts its superiority as a brand of orange juice. Compare this ad to the primary demand ad in Exhibit 1.33.

With primary demand well established for the VCR product category, marketers now use selective demand stimulation to tout the distinctive features of their individual brands, as Toshiba is doing in this ad that features the V3 head cylinder. www.toshiba.com/

toward the corporation and its products. This type of advertising can also have an effect on the shareholders of a firm. When shareholders see good corporate advertising, it instills confidence and, ultimately, long-term commitment to the firm and its stock.

Another form of corporate advertising is carried out by members of a trade channel. Often, corporate advertising within a trade channel is referred to as *institutional advertising.* Retailers such as Nordstrom, County Seat, and Wal-Mart advertise to persuade consumers to shop at their stores. While these retailers may occasionally feature a particular manufacturer's brand in the advertising (County Seat often features Levi's, in fact), the main purpose of the advertising is to get the audience to shop at their store. Federated Department Stores, for example, invested $160 million in a campaign featuring the retailer's private label clothing lines—available only at Federated stores such as Charter Club and INC—which would encourage consumers to shop at Federated outlets.[12]

The Economic Effects of Advertising.

Our discussion of advertising as a business process has focused strictly on the use of advertising by individual business organizations. However, some aspects of advertising relate to broad effects across the entire economic system of a country and beyond.

---

12. Alice Z. Cuneo, "Federated Sets Big Private Label Push," *Advertising Age,* February 16, 1998, 8.

EXHIBIT 1.38

Direct response advertising asks consumers to take some immediate action. Direct response advertising is most often used with low-price products with which consumers have extensive experience.

EXHIBIT 1.39

Delayed response advertising attempts to reinforce the benefits of using a brand and create a general liking for the brand. This ad for "all" detergent is an example of delayed response advertising.

Advertising's Effect on Gross Domestic Product. Gross domestic product (GDP) is a measure of the total value of goods and services produced within an economic system. Earlier, we discussed advertising's role in the marketing mix. Recall that, as advertising contributes to marketing mix strategy, it can make a contribution to sales—along with the right product, the right price, and the right distribution. Because of this role, advertising is related to GDP in that it can contribute to levels of overall consumer demand when it plays a key role in introducing new products, such as VCRs, microcomputers, the Internet, or alternative energy sources. As demand for these new products grows, the resultant consumer spending fuels retail sales, housing starts, and corporate investment in finished goods and capital equipment. Consequently, GDP is affected by sales of products in new, innovative product categories.[13]

Advertising's Effect on Business Cycles. Advertising can have a stabilizing effect on downturns in business activity. There is evidence that many firms increase advertising during times of recession in an effort to spend their way out of a business downturn. Similarly, there is research to suggest that firms that maintain advertising during a recession perform better afterward, relative to firms that cut advertising spending.[14]

---

13. There are several historical treatments of how advertising is related to demand. See, for example, Neil H. Borden, *The Economic Effects of Advertising* (Chicago: Richard D. Irwin, 1942), 187–189; and John Kenneth Galbraith, *The New Industrial State* (Boston: Houghton Mifflin, 1967), 203–207.

14. See, for example, Marion L. Elmquist, "100 Leaders Parry Recession with Heavy Spending," *Advertising Age,* September 8, 1983, 1.

A Little Plastic Packaging
Can Help Prevent Bruising.

PLASTIC MAKES IT POSSIBLE™

EXHIBIT 1.40

Advertising affects the competitive environment in an economy. This ad by a plastics manufacturers council is fostering competition with manufacturers of other packaging materials.

Advertising's Effect on Competition. Advertising is alleged to stimulate competition and therefore motivate firms to strive for better products, better production methods, and other competitive advantages that ultimately benefit the economy as a whole. Additionally, when advertising serves as a way to enter new markets, competition across the economic system is fostered. For example, Exhibit 1.40 shows an ad in which plastics manufacturers present themselves as competitors to manufacturers of other packaging materials.

Advertising is not universally hailed as a stimulant to competition. Critics point out that the amount of advertising dollars needed to compete effectively in many industries is often prohibitive. As such, advertising can act as a barrier to entry into an industry—that is, a firm may have the capability to compete in an industry in every regard *except* that the advertising expenditures needed to compete are so great that the firm cannot afford to get into the business. In this way, advertising can actually serve to decrease the overall amount of competition in an economy.[15]

Advertising's Effect on Prices. One of the widely debated effects of advertising has to do with its effect on the prices consumers pay for products and services. Since advertising is a relatively costly process, then products and services would surely cost much less if firms did no advertising. Right? Wrong?

First, across all industries, advertising costs incurred by firms range from about 1 percent of sales in the automobile and retail industries to about 15 percent of sales in the personal care and luxury products businesses. Exhibit 1.41 shows the ratio of advertising to sales for various firms in selected industries. Notice that there is no consistent and predictable relationship between advertising spending and sales. Honda spent $578 million in advertising to generate about $21 billion in sales; Estée Lauder spent about as much as Honda but only generated about $2 billion in sales; and Wal-Mart only spent $290 million on advertising but generated over $112 billion in sales! Different products and different market conditions demand that firms spend different amounts of money on advertising. These same conditions make it difficult to identify a predictable relationship between advertising and sales.

It is true that the costs for advertising are built into the costs for products, which are ultimately passed on to consumers. But this effect on price must be judged against how much time and effort a consumer would have to spend in searching for a product or service without the benefit of advertising.

Second, the effect of economies of scale, discussed earlier, has a direct impact on prices. Recall that economies of scale serve to lower the cost of production by spreading fixed costs over a large number of units produced. This lower cost can be passed on to consumers in terms of lower prices, as firms search for competitive advantage with lower prices. Nowhere is this effect more dramatic than the price of personal computers. In the early 1980s, an Apple IIe computer that ran at about 1 MHz and had 64k of total memory cost over $3,000. Today, you can get a computer that is several hundred times faster with vastly increased memory and storage for far less. And, it is likely that

15. This argument was well articulated many years ago by Colston E. Warn, "Advertising: A Critic's View," *Journal of Marketing*, Vol. 26, No. 4 (October 1962), 12.

Advertising spending as a proportion of sales in selected industries, 1997 (dollars in millions).

Industry	Advertiser	U.S. Ad Spending	U.S. Sales	Advertising Spending as % of Sales
Apparel				**5.30**
	Levi Strauss	$ 244.6	$ 4,600.0	5.30
	Nike	501.7	5,055.0	9.10
Automobiles				**2.70**
	General Motors	3,087.4	127,128.0	2.42
	Ford	1,281.8	120,474.0	1.06
	Volkswagen	204.9	6,791.0	3.00
	Honda	578.1	21,190.7	2.72
Computers				**2.30**
	IBM	924.9	32,663.0	2.82
	Intel	630.5	11,053.0	5.69
	Microsoft	407.4	4,356.0	9.35
Food				**10.5**
	Nestlé SA	460.9	15,353.0	2.99
	Kellogg	558.2	3,961.8	14.08
	Campbell Soup	342.5	4,850.0	7.05
Personal care				**12.0**
	Procter & Gamble	2,743.2	18,460.0	14.8
	Gillette	578.4	3,682.8	15.6
	Estée Lauder	519.2	2,200.0	23.5
Retail				**3.30**
	JC Penney	906.2	30,546.0	2.96
	Circuit City Stores	450.2	8,870.8	5.07
	Wal-Mart	290.2	112,005.0	0.25

Sources: Industry averages were obtained from "1998 Advertising to Sales Ratios for the 200 Largest Ad Spending Industries," *Advertising Age*, June 29, 1998, 22. Advertising spending for individual firms was obtained from "100 Leading National Advertisers," *Advertising Age*, September 28, 1998, s47. Reprinted with permission from the June 29, 1998, and September 28, 1998, issues of *Advertising Age*, Crain Communications Inc., 1998.

companies like Gateway and Dell are spending more today on advertising than Apple did back in the 1980s. So the matter remains unresolved.

Advertising's Effect on Value. *Value* is the password for successful marketing in the new era. **Value** refers to a perception by consumers that a brand provides satisfaction beyond the cost incurred to acquire that brand. The value perspective of the modern consumer is based on wanting every purchase to be a "good deal." Value is added to the consumption experience by advertising. For example, many advertising professionals and academic researchers believe that the experience of eating at McDonald's or drinking a Coke is significantly enhanced by the expectations the advertising has created and reinforced within the consumer.

Advertising also affects a consumer's perception of value by contributing to the symbolic value and the social meaning of a brand. **Symbolic value** refers to what a product or service means to consumers in a nonliteral way. For example, branded clothing such as Guess? jeans or Doc Martens shoes has been said to symbolize self-concept for some consumers. Exhibits 1.42 and 1.43 show examples of ads seeking to

EXHIBITS 1.42 AND 1.43

Advertising contributes to the symbolic value that brands have for consumers. What is it about the ad for Levi's jeans in Exhibit 1.42 and the ad for Ray-Ban sunglasses in Exhibit 1.43 that contribute to the symbolic value of these brands? www.levi.com/menu *and* www.ray-ban.com/

create symbolic value for two well-known brands. In reality, all branded products rely to some extent on symbolic value; otherwise they would not be brands, but unmarked commodities.

Social meaning refers to what a product or service means in a societal context. For example, social class is marked by any number of products used and displayed to signify class membership, such as cars, beverages, and clothes. Exhibit 1.44 shows an ad for a service with clear social-class connections. Often, the product's connection to a social class addresses a need within consumers to move up in class.

Researchers from various disciplines have long argued that objects are never just objects. They take on meaning from culture, society, and from consumers.[16] It is important to remember that these meanings often become just as much a part of the product as some physical feature. Since advertising is an essential way in which the image of a brand is developed, it contributes directly to consumers' perception of the value of the brand. The more value consumers see in a brand, the more they are willing to pay to acquire the brand. If the image of a Gucci watch, a Lexus coupe, or a Four Seasons hotel is valued by consumers, then consumers will pay a premium to acquire that value. Waterford crystal and Gucci watches, shown in Exhibits 1.45 and 1.46, are examples of products that consumers pay premiums to own.

16. For a historical perspective, see Ernest Dichter, *Handbook of Consumer Motivations* (New York: McGraw-Hill, 1964), 6. For a contemporary view, see David Glenn Mic and Claus Buhl, "A Meaning-Based Model of Advertising Experiences," *Journal of Consumer Research,* vol. 19 (December 1992), 312–338.

EXHIBIT 1.44

Ads communicate social meaning to consumers, as a product or service carries meaning in a societal context beyond its use or purpose. This ad for United Airlines puts the company's service into such a context. www.ual.com/

EXHIBITS 1.45 AND 1.46

Waterford crystal and Gucci watches are two advertised products that consumers will pay premium prices to own. Both products have intrinsic value in that they epitomize the highest levels of quality craftsmanship. Such craftsmanship, in itself, may be enough to command premium prices in the marketplace.

Advertising and Integrated Marketing Communications. As we

discussed in the section on advertising's role in the marketing mix, it is important to recognize that advertising is only one of many promotional tools available. It is not always the main choice of companies because in many situations, another tool, such as personal selling, event sponsorship, or direct marketing, is better suited to the task at hand. Firms such as Levi Strauss & Co., featured in the IMC box on page 33, often employ a wide range of promotional tools to achieve desired communications results.

The concept of mixing various promotional tools has recently received widespread attention in the advertising industry and is referred to as integrated marketing communications.[17] **Integrated marketing communications (IMC)** is the process of using promotional tools in a unified way so that a synergistic communications effect is created. That is, firms review every form of communication in use, from the most elaborate full-production television ad to the letterhead on company stationery, for the impression each makes on consumers. Each form of communication is scrutinized during a given period to ensure that a singular, clear, compelling message is being communicated to the intended audience(s).

Although the basic ideas of IMC are not new,[18] the concept of coordinating and integrating promotional efforts to achieve a synergistic effect—that is, to ensure that the promotional effort is greater than the sum of its parts—has gained much greater sophistication and industry commitment in recent years.[19] Because of the growing emphasis on IMC in the advertising industry, IMC issues are raised in every chapter of this book in special boxes that highlight the strategy and coordination challenges of every aspect of advertising. In addition, four separate sections of this book are devoted

17. Don E. Schultz, Stanley Tannenbaum, and Robert Lauterborn, *Integrated Marketing Communications* (Lincolnwood, Ill.: NTC Books, 1993).

18. Marketing textbooks have been discussing "coordination of the promotional mix" for many years. As an example of a basic and traditional treatment of promotion that suggested coordination and integration of the promotional mix variables, see Roy T. Shaw, Richard J. Semenik, and Robert H. Williams, *Marketing: An Integrated-Analytical Approach,* 4th ed. (Cincinnati, Ohio: South-Western, 1981), 237–238.

19. Tom Duncan, "Integrated Marketing? It's Synergy," *Advertising Age,* March 8, 1993, 1.

TAKING IT IN THE SHORTS

For a brand that has been associated for decades with youthful rebellion, Levi's has an interesting problem: teenage indifference. While Levi's has successfully followed baby boomers into adulthood and middle age with jeans tailored to a changing body and new "casual" clothes like Dockers, the firm has lost its grip on teenagers. The firm completely missed the baggy rebellion of youth—including the droopy shorts.

The problem is not minimal. Levi's market share among kids is down from 33 percent to 26 percent. What is worse is the way kids talk about Levi's. Company executives were forced to endure video after video of focus group sessions in which teens talked about Levi Strauss as if it were a has-been—saying the jeans were uncool or only suited for their parents or older brothers and sisters. Meanwhile, competitors were attacking kids from the top and bottom— Tommy Hilfiger and Ralph Lauren on the top and JCPenney and Sears on the bottom. As one consultant put it, Levi Strauss was zagging while the world was zigging. But Levi Strauss does have a response. The company's SilverTab brand is very popular among more stylish young consumers. The brand has a median age of 18 for purchasers. It has a baggier fit and is on the right side of the fashion line.

So how does Levi's take advantage of this brand opportunity? By developing an exciting and effective integrated marketing communications program. Along with traditional magazine and television advertising—the mainstays of marketing clothes to teens—the firm has a wide array of new and different ways to reach teens. First, the company is sponsoring concerts by up-and-coming bands that play "Electronica" music. Next, characters on new, hot, teen-oriented shows such *Friends* and *Beverly Hills 90210* are outfitted in SilverTab jeans. Another piece of the communications puzzle is to make sure that Levi retailers maintain stylish presentation so that all aspects of the SilverTab communication are consistent and hip.

The use of various tools beyond major advertising is a way to reinforce the advertising themes and reach teens in different and interesting ways—classic integrated marketing communications. The trick will be to keep the company name viable among the Bob Dylan set.

Source: Linda Himelstein, "Levi's Is Hiking Up Its Pants," *Business Week*, December 1, 1997, 70, 75.

to integrated marketing communications. These sections conclude each of the four major parts of the book, parallel the emphasis of the text, and feature the complete story of the application of IMC concepts by Cincinnati Bell in its marketing of wireless phone services:

- *Cincinnati Bell:* The Process of Integrated Marketing Communications
- *Cincinnati Bell:* Planning Integrated Marketing Communications
- *Cincinnati Bell:* Preparing the Integrated Marketing Communications Message
- *Cincinnati Bell:* Placing and Coordinating Advertising and Supportive Communications

These special IMC sections are easy to find because each section begins with a distinctive color scheme that signals the beginning of an IMC section. These sections focus on the real-world IMC challenges faced by Cincinnati Bell during the planning, development, execution, and coordination of its integrated marketing communications. Cincinnati Bell and its advertising agency, Northlich Stolley LaWarre, have generously provided their advertising and other communication materials for use in this text. We believe that IMC is an important enough consideration in contemporary communications that its role alongside the advertising effort deserves comprehensive treatment. These sections serve as a real-world demonstration of all aspects of an integrated marketing communications effort.

SUMMARY

▶◀ Know what advertising is and what it can do.

Since advertising has become so pervasive, it would be reasonable to expect that you might have your own working definition for this critical term. But an informed perspective on advertising goes beyond what is obvious and can be seen on a daily basis. Advertising is distinctive and recog-

nizable as a form of communication by its three essential elements: its intent to persuade, its paid sponsorship, and its use of mass media. An advertisement is a specific message that an advertiser has placed to persuade or inform an audience. An advertising campaign is a series of ads with a common theme also placed to persuade or inform an audience over a specified period of time.

◉ Discuss a basic model of advertising communication.

Advertising cannot be effective unless some form of communication takes place between the advertiser and the audience. But advertising is about mass communication. There are many models that might be used to help explain how advertising works or does not work as a communication platform. The model introduced in this chapter features basic considerations such as the message-production process versus the message-reception process, and this model says that consumers create their own meanings when they interpret advertisements.

◉ Describe the different ways of classifying audiences for advertising.

While it is possible to provide a simple and clear definition of what advertising is, it is also true that advertising takes many forms and serves different purposes from one application to another. One way to appreciate the complexity and diversity of advertising is to classify it by audience category or by geographic focus. For example, advertising might be directed at households or government officials. Using another perspective, it can be global or local in its focus.

◉ Explain the key roles of advertising as a business process.

Many different types of organizations use advertising to achieve their business purposes. For major multinational corporations, such as Procter & Gamble, and for smaller more localized businesses, such as the San Diego Zoo, advertising is one part of a critical business process known as marketing. Advertising is one element of the marketing mix; the other key elements are the firm's products, their prices, and the distribution network. Advertising must work in conjunction with these other marketing mix elements if the organization's marketing objectives are to be achieved.

◉ Recognize the effects of advertising in a national economy.

In North America alone, billions of dollars are spent on advertising every year. Viewed in the aggregate, all of this advertising can have broad effects in an economy. These effects include the effect on gross domestic product through advertising's role in introducing new products, an effect on the upturns and downturns in business cycles, an effect on stimulating competition, and an effect on prices through economies of scale and elasticity of demand. Finally, advertising has an effect on the value of brands based on the symbolic value created by the images of advertising.

KEY TERMS

advertising (6)
client, or sponsor (6)
advertisement (9)
advertising campaign (9)
audience (13)
target audience (13)
household consumers (13)
members of business organizations (13)
members of a trade channel (14)
professionals (14)
government officials and employees (14)
global advertising (14)
international advertising (16)

national advertising (16)
regional advertising (16)
local advertising (17)
cooperative advertising (17)
marketing (18)
marketing mix (18)
market segmentation (18)
product differentiation (19)
positioning (20)
external position (20)
internal position (20)
economies of scale (23)
brand loyalty (23)

inelasticity of demand (23)
primary demand stimulation (24)
selective demand stimulation (25)
direct response advertising (26)
delayed response advertising (26)
corporate advertising (26)
gross domestic product (GDP) (28)
value (30)
symbolic value (30)
social meaning (31)
integrated marketing communications
    (IMC) (32)

QUESTIONS FOR REVIEW AND CRITICAL THINKING

1.   What does it mean when we say that advertising is intended to persuade? How do different ads persuade in different ways?

2.   Explain the differences between regional advertising, local advertising, and cooperative advertising. What would you look for in an ad to identify it as a cooperative ad?

3.   How do the goals of direct response versus delayed response advertising differ? How would you explain marketers' growing interest in direct response advertising?

4.   When can a firm use global advertising? How does global advertising differ from international advertising?

5.   Give an example of an advertising campaign that you know has been running for more than one year. Why do some advertising campaigns last for years, whereas others come and go in a matter of months?

6.   If a firm developed a new line of athletic shoes, priced them competitively, and distributed them in appropriate retail shops, would there be any need for advertising? Is advertising really needed for a good product that is priced right?

7.   Many companies now spend millions of dollars to sponsor and have their names associated with events such as stock-car races or rock concerts. Do these event sponsorships fit the definition for advertising given in this chapter?

8.   How does the process of market segmentation lead an organization to spend its advertising dollars more efficiently and more effectively?

9.   What does it mean to say that a brand has symbolic value? Is there any good reason to believe that consumers will actually pay higher prices for brands with the right symbolic value?

10.   What is the concept of integrated marketing communications? How are IMC and advertising related?

EXPERIENTIAL EXERCISES

1.   Find ads that fit the definition of primary demand, selective demand, direct response, and corporate advertising. What is the intended purpose of each type of advertising? Do the ads you selected achieve their objective? Explain why or why not.

2.   Find a magazine or newspaper ad that highlights the concept of "value" as it was explained near the end of the chapter. Avoid ads that explicitly say "value" or "value priced." Look for ads that tout a brand's features as the basis for value.

USING THE INTERNET

Pick a consumer product. Then go to Yahoo! (www .yahoo.com) and search for the product. Visit five sites that carry information about it. To search on Yahoo!, place a keyword in the empty box, then hit SEARCH. You may need to use different keywords to achieve the desired results. For each of the five sites, answer the following questions:

1.   Is the site promoting the product category or promoting a specific brand? What value does the site offer consumers?

2.   How helpful is the site for making a purchase decision in this product's category?

3.   Do you think this Web site is a reliable source of information? Why or why not?

4.   How effective is this site in communicating its message? If it has a persuasive message, how effective is it?

Visitors to a given Web site often come to it via a hierarchical site like Yahoo! or via a search engine by querying on keywords. But a lot of traffic can also be generated by referrals from other sites. The HotBot search engine permits queries on "links to" particular Web sites. Go to the HotBot site and choose the query option of "links to this URL." See how many and what sorts of sites link to sites you're familiar with; then try this query on:

www.yahoo.com

www.ibm.com

www.mtv.com

www.thex-files.com

1.   There are more than a half million links to the Yahoo! Web site, on pages across the Web. Why do you think this is?

2.   What reasons might lead a Web site developer to include a link to IBM's corporate Web site?

3.   One major problem with Web links is their brittleness: a link to a subpage on one of these sites could become broken if the site is reshuffled. What are the tradeoffs between links to specific pages, and general links to the top level of a Web site?

4.   How does *The X Files* television program site benefit from its community of fans?

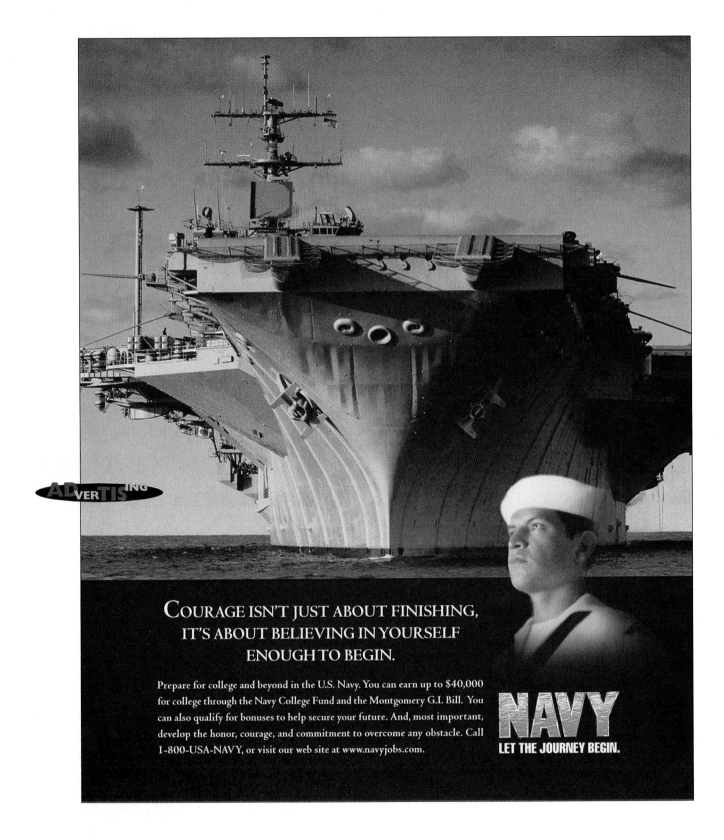

COURAGE ISN'T JUST ABOUT FINISHING,
IT'S ABOUT BELIEVING IN YOURSELF
ENOUGH TO BEGIN.

Prepare for college and beyond in the U.S. Navy. You can earn up to $40,000
for college through the Navy College Fund and the Montgomery G.I. Bill. You
can also qualify for bonuses to help secure your future. And, most important,
develop the honor, courage, and commitment to overcome any obstacle. Call
1-800-USA-NAVY, or visit our web site at www.navyjobs.com.

NAVY
LET THE JOURNEY BEGIN.

CHAP TER 2

After reading and thinking about this chapter, you will be able to do the following:

- Discuss six important trends transforming the advertising industry.

- Describe the size and scale of the advertising industry.

- Explain who the participants in the advertising industry are and the role each plays in the formulation and execution of advertising campaigns.

- Detail the diverse services that advertising agencies supply in the planning, preparation, and placement of advertising and explain how agencies are compensated for their services.

United Airlines, McDonald's, Miller Brewing, Kraft International, Reebok International—any advertising agency would be proud to list this group of advertisers in its client stable. But what about an advertising agency that *lost* the business of these prestigious advertisers over a 24-month period? That is exactly what happened to Leo Burnett Co., the largest advertising agency in the United States.

The exodus of such high-profile clients was devastating to employee morale. Leo Burnett was supposed to be the Rock of Gibraltar of advertising—conservative, confident, and very stable. Most of the account realignments were explained by clients' feeling that Burnett's processes were too tradition bound and bureaucratic, which ended up stifling creativity.[1] As Burnett's chairman and CEO, Richard B. Fizdale, put it: "It was all about how much more we can make, rather than how good our ads can be."[2] The Miller Lite account went to Fallon McElligott, where "ads by Dick" were created. United Airlines went to friendlier skies. McDonald's took a large part of its business a few blocks north to DDB Needham, where it came from back in the late 1970s. The Reebok business was lost because the client said it wanted to look "outside the mainstream to tap new ideas."[3] This was not supposed to happen at Burnett, but it did.

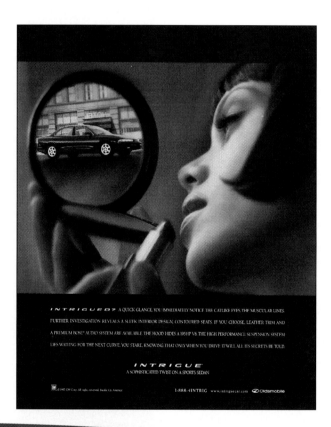

While this type of account jumping is becoming all too common, the really interesting part of the story is how Burnett responded. First, Leo Burnett quickly recouped revenue losses by adding $575 million in new media buying assignments from Procter & Gamble and (interestingly) Miller Brewing and by adding more than $713 million in other new business.[4] And the agency maintains a long and impressive list of clients, including Pillsbury, Procter & Gamble, Oldsmobile (see Exhibit 2.1), Motorola, Philip Morris, and others. But what was so hard to accept about the losses is that the agency's creative prowess—the soul of an agency and its most revered asset—was questioned.

The insularity of Burnett, the smugness that we know it all—that's changed.
—Mary Bishop, head of Procter & Gamble accounts[5]

Leo Burnett took the question of its creative abilities and responsiveness to client needs seriously and initiated massive changes at the agency. First, the agency split into seven "mini-agencies." Each mini-agency team is responsible for setting its own direction and for its own profit and loss statements. Each must also establish operating procedures and go after new business. The idea behind the mini-agency strategy is to make Burnett more nimble and to improve the creative environment. Three of the mini-agencies are centered on large company clients such as Allstate Corp., Eli Lilly & Co., and

EXHIBIT 2.1

Leo Burnett Co. has seen an exodus of important clients—United Airlines, McDonald's, and Miller Brewing. But the agency has recruited over $700 million in new business and continues to create outstanding ads for longstanding clients such as Oldsmobile. www.intriguecar.com/

1.   Mercedes M. Cardona, "Burnett Splitting Agency into Seven Mini-Shops," *Advertising Age,* November 17, 1997, 6.
2.   Johnson, Dirk, "Not So Jolly Now, a Giant Agency Retools," *New York Times,* March 22, 1998, Money and Banking, from http://archives.nytimes.com/archives/. Accessed September 2, 1998.
3.   Jeff Jensen and Chuck Ross, "Burnett USA Resigns $100 Mil Reebok Biz," *Advertising Age,* May 5, 1997, 68.
4.   Mercedes M. Cardona, "Burnett's Second Wind," *Advertising Age,* November 30, 1998, 1, 16–18.
5.   Johnson, "Not So Jolly Now, a Giant Agency Retools," op. cit.

Pillsbury. Of the other four agencies, two are centered on product types—retail and durables—and two handle combinations of unrelated clients. Each mini-agency has a complement of creative and managerial talent and several of the agencies will include representatives from Burnett's new media unit Starcom.[6] Burnett also added some "edge" by acquiring 49 percent of the hot British creative shop Bartle Bogle Hegarty; by employing Red Spider, a very hot British creative/management group (see Exhibit 2.2); and by establishing Vigilante, a New York "urban culture" unit,[7] presumably to offset some of what some consider to be Burnett's dated and sappy creative look. Still, Burnett's evolution and reorganization is likely to continue for some time as the agency tries to adapt to the dynamic, competitive, and creative environment of the advertising industry in the United States.[8]

An Industry in Transition.

The loss of clients, and ultimately the reorganization of a large and respected U.S. advertising agency such as Leo Burnett Co., signals the nature and magnitude of change that is occurring in the advertising industry. We will examine these changes in more detail shortly. But first we need to realize that the fundamental process of advertising, and the role it plays in organizations, has actually changed very little over the past 75 years. Certainly, the process has evolved with social and cultural trends, advances in technology, and evolving client desires. But the essence of the process—persuasive communication designed to stimulate demand and delivered to targeted audiences—has remained fairly constant.

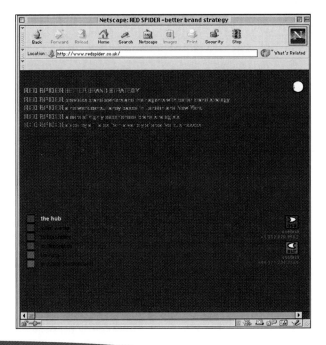

EXHIBIT 2.2

Leo Burnett hired Red Spider to bring something new and perhaps unexpected to its creative executions and client interactions. www .redspider.co.uk/

What *has* changed over the past 75 years or so and what Leo Burnett has reacted to is that the structure of the advertising industry is (again) in transition. As one analyst put it, "Just like manufacturing, the advertising industry is undergoing seismic change."[9] How has the industry changed, and how is it continuing to change? Well, interactive media options, advertising agency structure, client demands, compensation schemes, and creative techniques are just a few of the aspects of the industry undergoing significant and fundamental change.

The central issues in the Leo Burnett story highlight several aspects of change that have taken place in the structure of the advertising industry. First, advertisers like to believe that to maintain brand leadership in highly competitive markets characterized by impatient consumers, new and different creative executions are essential. Second, traditional factory-like advertising agencies are being replaced with a new, more adaptable and responsive type of agency. Many ad agencies formed by megamergers in the 1980s are dismantling their vertically integrated, multilayered management structures and re-engineering themselves into more nimble multiservice organizations that use dynamic management structures to prioritize creative thinking. Similarly, many advertisers are branching out from their traditional agencies and

6.   Cardona, "Burnett Splitting Agency into Seven Mini-Shops," op. cit.
7.   "Not So Jolly Now, a Giant Agency Retools," op. cit.
8.   "Reorganization Cuts 18 on Burnett Creative Staff," *Advertising Age,* June 1, 1998, 1.
9.   Patricia Sellers, "Do You Need Your Ad Agency?" *Fortune,* November 15, 1993, 148.

using smaller "boutique" agencies and consultants as a way to revitalize creative executions.[10] Third, the old commission method of paying for advertising (based on media spending) is giving way to fee-based systems. Now, only about 14 percent of advertisers still pay agencies the once-standard 15 percent commission (based on media billing). Burnett was one of the last of the big agencies to insist on 15 percent. Advertisers and agencies are working on various forms of "results-oriented" compensation schemes that move away from media expenditures as the basis for agency compensation.[11]

The reorganization at Leo Burnett illustrates just some of the important aspects of change in the advertising industry, but this story of one agency's struggles does not reveal the breadth of change taking place in the very structure of the industry. The structure of the advertising industry today is being altered by six important trends:

1. With the proliferation of cable television and direct marketing, and other alternative and new media, comes media fragmentation.
2. The tremendous proliferation of ads in an array of media, ranging from television ads to billboards to banner ads on the Internet, has resulted in so much clutter that the probability of any one advertisement breaking through and making a real difference continues to diminish.
3. New retail channels, including catalogs, TV shopping networks, online shopping, and price clubs are growing in influence.
4. A fragmentation of marketing budgets with companies has occurred, with a greater proportion of these budgets going to trade and consumer sales promotions.
5. Improved information systems are allowing retailers and distributors to exercise more control over many kinds of marketing decisions.
6. More and more advertisers are focusing their efforts on integrated marketing communications (IMC) programs. Advertisers now look to sales promotions, event sponsorships, new media options, and public relations as means to support and enhance the primary advertising effort. IMC is a global phenomenon, as the Global Issues box on page 44 highlights.

For years to come, these fundamental changes will affect the way advertisers think about communicating, the way advertising agencies serve their clients, and the way advertising is delivered to audiences. Large advertisers such as Procter & Gamble and Sprint are already demanding new and innovative programs to enhance the impact of their advertising. While the goal of persuasive communication remains intact, the changing structure used by the advertising industry to accomplish that goal is the central topic of this chapter.

The Scope of the Advertising Industry.   To fully understand the structure of the advertising industry, we need to appreciate the scope of advertising. By any measure, advertising is an enormous global business. Annual expenditures on advertising in the United States total about $200 billion, with nearly $425 billion being spent worldwide.[12] Advertising expenditures worldwide have been growing about 7 to 8 percent a year, with the United States, Great Britain, Asia, and Latin America leading the way.[13]

Another indicator of the scope of advertising is the investment made by individual firms. Exhibit 2.3 shows spending for 1996 and 1997 among the top 20 U.S. advertisers. Hundreds of millions of dollars—and in the case of the largest spenders, even billions of dollars—is truly a huge amount of money to spend annually on advertising.

10. Comments made by Martin Sorrell as represented in "Agencies Face New Battlegrounds: Sorrell," *Advertising Age,* April 13, 1998, 22.
11. Laura Petrecca, "Pay-for-Results Plans Can Boost Agencies: Execs," *Advertising Age,* September 8, 1997, 18, 20.
12. Zenith Media, *Advertising Expenditure Forecasts,* July 1998, 11.
13. Ibid. 1.

EXHIBIT 2.3

The top 20 leading advertisers in the United States.

Company	1997 U.S. Ad Dollars (in millions)	1996 U.S. Ad Dollars (in millions)	% Change
General Motors	$3,087.4	$2,376.4	29.9
Procter & Gamble Co.	2,743.2	2,581.2	6.3
Philip Morris Cos.	2,137.8	2,250.2	−5.0
Chrysler	1,532.4	1,422.6	7.7
Ford	1,282.8	1,197.1	7.1
Sears, Roebuck & Co.	1,262.0	1,216.5	3.7
Walt Disney Co.	1,249.7	1,263.5	−1.1
PepsiCo	1,244.7	1,235.2	0.8
Diageo	1,206.6	1,037.7	16.3
McDonalds Corp.	1,041.7	1,074.6	−3.1
Time Warner	1,013.2	1,037.7	−2.4
IBM	924.9	792.3	16.7
Johnson & Johnson	920.2	935.0	−1.6
Unilever	908.9	953.8	−4.7
JCPenney	906.2	815.5	11.1
Bristol-Meyers Squibb	885.2	742.0	19.3
Toyota Motor Corp.	851.9	782.8	8.82
Tricon Global Restaurants	851.2	879.9	−3.2
AT&T	781.1	1,070.1	−27.7
Sony	777.5	661.0	17.6

Source: "100 Leading National Advertisers," *Advertising Age,* September 28, 1998, S-4.

But we have to realize that the $3.0 billion spent by General Motors on advertising was just 2 percent of GM's sales. Similarly, Sears spent $1.2 billion, but this amount represented only about 3 percent of its sales. So, while the absolute dollars are large, the relative spending is much more modest. Overall, the 100 leading advertisers in the United States spent $58 billion on advertising in 1997, which was a healthy 8.6 percent increase over 1996. Still, there is no doubt that this rapidly increasing spending is related to increased clutter. Advertising may be quickly becoming its own worst enemy. Exhibit 2.4 shows the increase in advertising across the 20th century.

The Structure of the Advertising Industry. ◁▷ When we understand the structure of the advertising industry we know *who* does *what* in *what order* during the advertising process. The advertising industry is actually a collection of a wide range of talented people, all of whom have specialized expertise and perform necessary tasks in planning, preparing, and placing of advertising. Exhibit 2.5 shows the structure of the advertising industry by showing who the different participants are in the process.

Exhibit 2.5 demonstrates that *advertisers* (such as Kellogg's) can employ the services of *advertising agencies* (such as Leo Burnett) that may (or may not) contract for specialized services with various *external facilitators* (such as Simmons Market Research) in the

EXHIBIT 2.4

A graphical plot of the growth in advertising over this century.

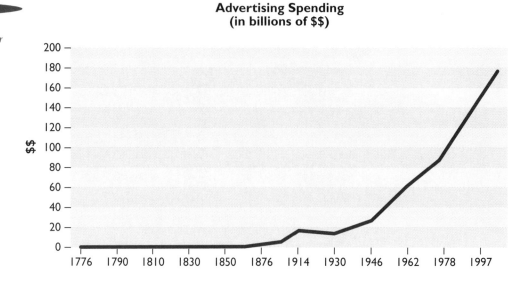

process, which results in advertising being transmitted with the help of various *media organizations* (such as the Nickelodeon cable network) to one or more *target audiences* (such as you).

Note the dashed line on the left side of Exhibit 2.5. This line indicates that advertisers do not always employ the services of advertising agencies. Nor do advertisers or agencies always seek the services of external facilitators. Some advertisers deal directly with media organizations for placement of their advertisements, sometimes receiving merely technical (rather than creative) assistance in the preparation of advertisements. This happens either when an advertiser has an internal advertising department that prepares all the materials for the advertising process, or when the media organizations (especially radio, television, and newspapers) provide technical assistance to advertisers in exchange for purchasing media time or space. The new interactive media formats also provide advertisers the opportunity to work directly with entertainment programming firms, such as Walt Disney and Sony, to provide integrated programming that features brand placements in the programming.

Each level in the structure of the advertising industry is complex. Let's take a look at each level, with particular emphasis on the nature and activities of advertising agencies. Advertising agencies provide the essential creative firepower to the advertising process and represent a critical link in the structure. As discussed earlier, advertising agencies are being transformed by competitive, cultural, and technological changes.

Advertisers.

A wide range of organizations—from your local pet store to multinational corporations—seek to benefit from the effects of advertising. The advertisers listed in Exhibit 2.3 each use advertising somewhat differently, depending on the type of product or service they sell or the position in the channel of distribution they occupy. The following categories describe the different types of advertisers and the role advertising plays for them.

Manufacturers and Service Firms.

Large national manufacturers of consumer products and services are the most prominent users of advertising, often spending hundreds of millions of dollars annually. Procter & Gamble, General Foods, MCI, and Merrill Lynch all have national or global markets for their products and services. The use of advertising by these firms is essential to creating awareness and preference for their brands. But advertising is not useful just to national or multinational firms; regional and local producers of household goods and services also rely heavily on advertising. For example, regional dairy companies sell milk, cheese, and other dairy products in regions usually comprising a few states. Several breweries and wineries also serve only regional

EXHIBIT 2.5

The structure of the advertising industry and the participants in the process.

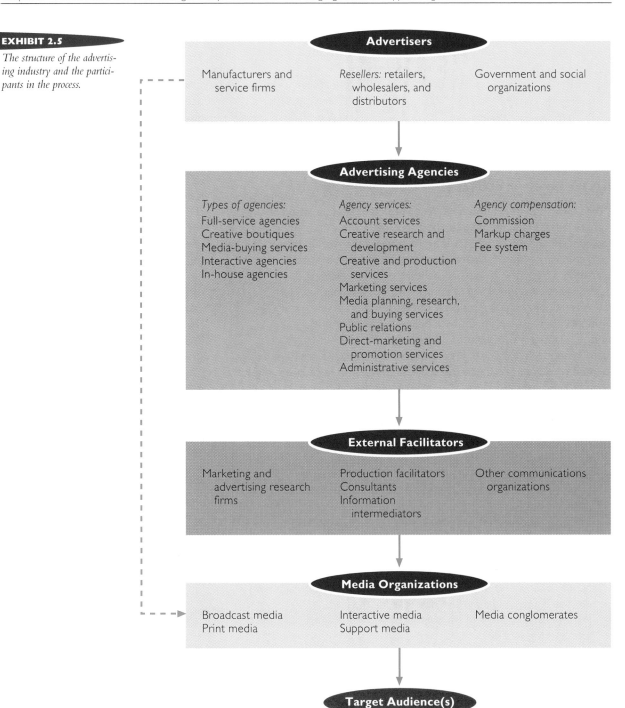

markets. Local producers of products are relatively rare, but local service organizations are common. Medical facilities, hair salons, restaurants, and art organizations are examples of local service providers that use advertising to create awareness and stimulate demand.

Firms that produce business goods and services also use advertising on a global, national, regional, and local basis. IBM and Xerox are examples of global companies that produce business goods and services. At the national and regional level, firms that supply agricultural and mining equipment and repair services are common advertisers, as are consulting and research firms. At the local level, firms that supply janitorial, linen, and bookkeeping services use advertising.

Resellers. The term *reseller* is simply a general description for all organizations in the marketing channel of distribution that buy products to resell to customers. As Exhibit 2.5 shows, resellers can be retailers, wholesalers, or distributors. These resellers deal with both household consumers and business buyers at all geographic levels.

Retailers that sell in national or global markets are the most visible reseller advertisers. Sears, The Limited, and McDonald's are examples of national and global retail companies that use various forms of advertising to communicate with customers. Regional retail chains, typically grocery chains such as Albertson's or department stores such as Dillard's, serve multistate markets and use media advertising appropriate for their customers. At the local level, small retail shops of all sorts rely on newspaper, radio, television, and billboard advertising to reach a relatively small geographic area.

Wholesalers and distributors, such as American Lock & Supply (which supplies contractors with door locks and hardware), are a completely different breed of reseller. Technically, these two groups deal with business customers only, since their position in the distribution channel dictates that they sell products either to producers (who buy goods to produce other goods) or to retailers (who resell goods to household consumers). Occasionally, an organization will call itself a wholesaler and sell to the public. Such an organization is actually operating as a retail outlet.

Wholesalers and distributors have little need for the mass-media outlets such as television and radio. Rather, they use trade publications, directory advertising such as the Yellow Pages, and direct mail as their main advertising media. Also, these firms tend to rely more heavily on personal selling and trade shows as promotional tools.

GLOBAL ISSUES

NESTLÉ TAKES IMC GLOBAL

While many U.S.-based firms are anxious to communicate with consumers in the seamless, multi-method style of IMC, few have embraced the concept and executed IMC as aggressively as the world's largest food company—Nestlé. The company president, Peter Brabeck-Letmathe, a 54-year-old Austrian, believes in communicating directly with consumers and in as many ways as possible.

Advertising remains a mainstay of Nestlé's overall promotional program, but Mr. Brabeck believes in building one-to-one relationships with customers in ways that advertising alone cannot. His attitude is fostered by what he believes are fragmented consumer and media markets and the growth in retailers' power relative to manufacturers (recall this discussion from Chapter 1). To cope with the fragmentation of advertising media, Nestlé has developed a variety of other communications/promotional alternatives to advertising:

- *Dialogue Clubs:* These clubs encourage consumers of Nestlé brands to communicate with the company and participate in new product development. Clubs are set up in Europe, North America, and the United Kingdom. Nestlé has a direct selling program through the clubs.
- *TV shopping networks:* Nestlé joined a TV shopping test and set up Easy Shop, a proprietary shopping program in two Swiss villages.
- *Internet:* Nestlé maintains a corporate Web site as well as individual sites for nearly every brand it markets.
- *Nestlé Loyalty Cards:* These swipe cards provide Nestlé buyers with discounts and build a massive database for the firm.
- *Joint Promotions:* The firm has partnered with an Italian airline and a food catalog retailer.

Ultimately, Mr. Brabeck wants "to know what my consumer is feeling, how he is changing, and what he is desiring." With that knowledge, the leader of Nestlé believes he can address those desires with "my products, my services, and my communications"—a sterling example of IMC at work.

Source: Suzanne Bidlake, "Nestlé CEO Strives for Dialogue That Individualizes Consumers," *Ad Age International,* January 1998, 33.

Government and Social Organizations. It may seem odd to include the government as an advertiser, but government bodies invest millions of dollars in advertising annually. In fact, in 1997 the U.S. government spent more than $620 million on advertising. The federal government's spending on advertising is concentrated in two areas: armed forces recruiting (as shown in Exhibit 2.6) and social issues. As an example, the U.S. government once used a television ad campaign with a budget of $55 mil-

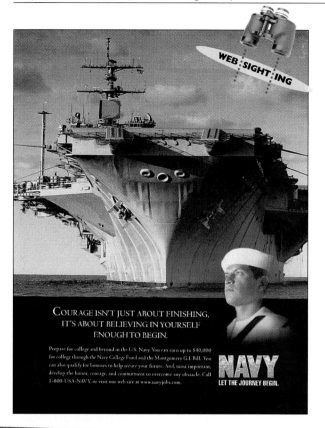

COURAGE ISN'T JUST ABOUT FINISHING,
IT'S ABOUT BELIEVING IN YOURSELF
ENOUGH TO BEGIN.

Prepare for college and beyond in the U.S. Navy. You can earn up to $40,000 for college through the Navy College Fund and the Montgomery G.I. Bill. You can also qualify for bonuses to help secure your future. And, most important, develop the honor, courage, and commitment to overcome any obstacle. Call 1-800-USA-NAVY, or visit our web site at www.navyjobs.com.

NAVY
LET THE JOURNEY BEGIN.

EXHIBIT 2.6

Today's Navy is not just a job, it's a journey, but, frankly, in a time of relative peace and with a wide range of opportunities in a booming private sector, it's a journey that fewer and fewer find intriguing. Uncle Sam wants you; you want something else. Check out the U.S. Navy's Web site at www.navy.mil and that of the Defense Department at www. pentagon.mil. Are these sites well integrated with the military's mass-media recruiting message?

lion for U.S. Army recruiting. The government purchased time on MTV and during NCAA basketball games to reach its target audience.[14] In addition, a large number of government publications are aimed at businesses to alert them to government programs or regulations.

State and local government agencies, especially health care and welfare organizations, attempt to shape behaviors (reduce child abuse, for example) or communicate with citizens who can use their services, such as potential Social Security and Medicare recipients. State governments also invest millions of dollars in promoting state lotteries and tourism. Advertising by social organizations at the national, state, and local level is common. The American Cancer Society and the United Way advertise their programs, seek donations, and attempt to shape behavior (deter drug use or encourage breast self-examination procedures, for example). National organizations such as these use both the mass media and direct mail.

Every state has its own unique statewide organizations, such as Citizens against Hunger, a state arts council, a tourism office, or a historical society. Social organizations in local communities represent a variety of special interests, from computer clubs to neighborhood child care organizations. The advertising used by social organizations has the same fundamental purposes as the advertising carried out by major multinational corporations: to stimulate demand and disseminate information. The ad by the Idaho Department of Commerce in Exhibit 2.7 promotes the state as an ideal area to locate businesses because of its lifestyle opportunities and favorable tax rates.

Few of the advertisers just discussed have the in-house expertise or resources to strategically plan and then prepare effective advertising. This is where advertising agencies play such an important role in the structure of the advertising industry.

Advertising Agencies. Most advertisers choose to enlist the services of an advertising agency in planning, preparing, and placing advertisements. The reason so many firms rely on advertising agencies is that agencies house a collection of professionals with very specialized talent, experience, and expertise. A formal definition of an advertising agency is as follows:

> *An **advertising agency** is an organization of professionals who provide creative and business services to clients related to planning, preparing, and placing advertisements.*

Advertising agencies can be global businesses. During the 1980s, several megamergers occurred, creating worldwide organizations to serve clients' advertising and marketing communications needs. Exhibit 2.8 shows the 1997 worldwide gross income of the 10 largest advertising agencies in the world. Note that the list is dominated by agencies with headquarters in New York City. The top 500 advertising agencies had worldwide income of more than $22 billion on gross billings of $174 billion in 1997.[15] This 11.3 percent increase shows the strength of investment in advertising globally.

14. Kevin Goldman, "Army Launches New TV Ad Campaign," *Wall Street Journal,* March 7, 1995, B10.
15. R. Craig Endicott, "Agency Report," *Advertising Age,* April 27, 1998, S1.

WEB SIGHT-ING

NOT ONLY IS LIFE LESS TAXING IN IDAHO... IT'S LITERALLY LESS TAXING.

You've probably heard about the great recreational opportunities, impressive natural beauty, and outstanding lifestyle Idahoans enjoy. But you might not know Idaho has the 13th lowest overall per capita tax burden in the country and the second lowest tax burden among western states. Our state tax revenues come from a balanced mix of personal income, corporate income, sales, and property taxes which generate stable funding for needed public services without unfairly burdening any sector. In fact, the Corporation for Enterprise Development ranked Idaho's tax and fiscal system as the second best in the nation. One positive result is that Idaho's per capita debt continues to be the lowest in the nation.

Companies in Idaho are finding our tax structure very business-friendly.

IDAHO *Works*

Idaho Department of Commerce • 700 West State Street • P.O. Box 83720 • Boise, Idaho 83720-0093
1-800-842-5858 • www.idoc.state.id.us

EXHIBIT 2.7

In The Grapes of Wrath, *California was the promised land for farmers driven from Oklahoma's Dust Bowl, promises passed by word of mouth and folk songs. Today, states, and even cities and countries, advertise their benefits and compete head-to-head for manufacturers, investors, and tourists, across a range of media. Take a trip to* www.idoc.state.id.us, *or* www.visitid.org, *or cross the border into Washington at* www.tourism.wa.gov. *Who is responsible for advertising on behalf of a state or a city? How do nations advertise themselves? Check out the U.S. Information Agency at* www.usia.gov.

The types of agency professionals who can help advertisers in the planning, preparation, and placement of advertising and other promotional activities include the following:

Account planners
Account supervisors
Art directors
Creative directors
Copywriters
Radio and television producers
Researchers
Artists
Technical staff—printing, film editing, and so forth
Marketing specialists
Media buyers
Public relations specialists
Sales promotion and event planners
Direct-marketing specialists
Web developers
Interactive media strategists

As this list suggests, an advertising agency can provide an advertiser with a host of services, from campaign planning through creative concepts to measuring advertising effectiveness. Several different types of agencies are available to the advertiser. An appreciation of the differences between types of agencies is important.

Full-Service Agencies. A **full-service agency** typically includes an array of advertising professionals to meet all the promotional needs of clients. Often, such an agency will also offer a global reach to the client. Young & Rubicam and McCann-Erickson Worldwide are examples of full-service agencies with global capabilities.

A full-service agency will attempt to have available not only the creative and technical personnel associated with advertising preparation, but also marketing and research personnel to help in the planning process. Additionally, various administrative services personnel are provided, which include everyone from high-level management (such as account supervisors) to clerical services. Account supervisors typically act as the liaison between the agency and the client. Administrative services can take care of such costly details as scheduling and billing.

Full-service agencies are not necessarily large organizations employing hundreds or even thousands of people. Small local shops can be full service with just a dozen employees. And big accounts can often go to smaller agencies. When American Honda Motor Co. put its Acura account up for review, it wanted "outstanding creative talent" no matter what size agency did the work. The account went to midsize agency Suissa Miller in Santa Monica, California.[16]

Creative Boutiques. A **creative boutique** typically emphasizes creative concept development, copywriting, and artistic services to its clients. An advertiser can employ this alternative for the strict purpose of infusing greater creativity into the message

16. Advertising Age Viewpoint editorial, "Why Midsize Shops Survive," *Advertising Age,* October 28, 1998, 26.

EXHIBIT 2.8

The world's top 10 advertising organizations in 1997.

Rank	Agency	Worldwide Gross Income ($ in U.S. millions)	% Change 1996–1997
1	Omnicom Group, New York	$4,154.3	10.8
2	WPP Group, London	3,646.6	6.3
3	Interpublic Group of Cos., New York	3,384.5	11.4
4	Dentsu Inc., Tokyo	1,997.6	3.0
5	Young & Rubicam, New York	1,497.9	10.4
6	True North Communications, Chicago	1,211.5	21.6
7	Grey Advertising, New York	1,143.0	11.2
8	Havas Advertising, Paris	1,033.1	6.0
9	Leo Burnett, Chicago	878.0	1.4
10	Hakuhodo, Tokyo	848.0	–5.5

Source: "Agency Report," *Advertising Age,* April 27, 1998, S-13. Reprinted with permission from the April 27, 1998, issue of *Advertising Age.* Copyright © Crain Communications Inc.

theme or individual advertisement. As one advertising expert put it, "If all clients want is ideas—lots of them, from which they can pick and mix to their hearts' delight—they won't want conventional, full-service agencies. They'll want fast, flashy fee-based idea factories."[17] Creative boutiques are these "idea factories." When an agency uses a boutique, then other aspects of advertising planning and placement are handled internally by the advertiser or contracted out to other external facilitators. Some large global agencies such as McCann-Erickson Worldwide are setting up "creative-only" project shops that mimic the services provided by creative boutiques.[18]

Media-Buying Services. While not technically an agency, a **media-buying service** is an independent organization that specializes in buying media time and space, particularly on radio and television, as a service to advertising agencies and advertisers. The task of buying media space has become more complex because of the proliferation of media options. An agency or advertiser will do the strategy planning for media placement and then turn to a media-buying service to do the actual buying of time and space. One additional advantage of using a media-buying service is that since it buys media in large quantities, it often acquires media time at a much lower cost than an agency or advertiser could. Also, media-buying services often have acquired time and space in "inventory" and offer last-minute placement to advertisers.

Interactive Agencies. The era of new media has created a new form of agency—the interactive agency. **Interactive agencies** help advertisers prepare communications for new media such as the Internet, interactive kiosks, CD-ROMs, and interactive television. Sometimes referred to as *cyberagencies,* these new ad agencies have specialized talent and expertise that many traditional full-service agencies do not have. Organizations such as Modem Media in Norwalk, Connecticut; Organic Online in San Francisco; and Network Publishing in Salt Lake City have created new media communications for some big-name companies: AT&T, Adolph Coors, Delta Air Lines, Saturn, and Kraft Foods.

Interactive agencies have technical personnel to help advertisers develop new media communications. They also keep other specialized talent to maintain computer file servers that not only manage the interactions with clients' communication, but also

17. "Agencies Face New Battlegrounds: Sorrell," op.cit.
18. Melanie Wells, "McCann Eyes Boutique," *Advertising Age,* June 27, 1994, 4.

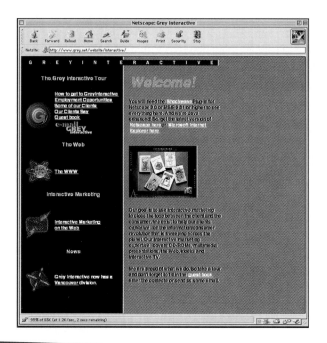

EXHIBIT 2.9

Cyberagency Grey Interactive Worldwide showcases its growing portfolio of new media executions at www.grey.net/website/interactive/ index.html

build databases for clients' future use—with both new and traditional media. At this point, many of the interactive agencies are dealing with clients' established full-service agencies. The creative history embodied in the general agency is valuable in preparing new media communications.

This is not to say that traditional full-service agencies are sitting idly by. Ogilvy & Mather, Grey Advertising, and Leo Burnett—some of the oldest agencies in the business—have developed special groups within their agencies to handle clients' new media needs. Grey Interactive Worldwide (formed within the main agency Grey Advertising; see Exhibit 2.9) was formed in 1992 and now creates interactive advertising materials for global clients such as Microsoft, KLM Royal Dutch Airlines, and British Telecom.[19] Chrysler, Toshiba, IBM, and American Express are examples of U.S. firms relying on their full-service agencies for their new media materials. It will be interesting to see if the new cyberagencies move to provide broader services or remain specialized.

In-House Agencies. An **in-house agency** is often referred to as the advertising department of a firm. This option has the advantage of greater coordination and control in all phases of the advertising process. The advertiser's own personnel have control over and knowledge of marketing activities, such as product development and distribution tactics. Another advantage is that the firm can essentially keep all the profits from commissions an external agency would have earned. As the senior VP for advertising and corporate communications at NEC explained about the firm's prospects for moving much of its $40 million Packard Bell account in-house, "We're certainly looking at taking some of the work in-house because it's more efficient."[20]

While the advantages of doing advertising work in-house are attractive, there are severe limitations. First, there may be a lack of objectivity, thereby constraining the execution of all phases of the advertising process. Second, it is highly unlikely that an in-house agency could ever match the breadth and depth of expertise available in an external agency. Third, you're not as likely to talk back or argue with the client, for their own good, because you are the client.

Advertising agencies represent an important link in the structure of the industry. At this point, we will consider the broad range of services agencies can provide to advertisers.

Agency Services. ◁ The types of services provided by an agency vary with the types of agencies just discussed. In a full-service agency, a wide range of creative, marketing, media, and administrative services are often provided to serve a client's complete advertising needs. A typical organizational structure for a full-service agency is shown in Exhibit 2.10. Exhibit 2.11 is an ad from Leo Burnett, the largest U.S. full-service agency. While not every full-service agency offers every service, the types of services that can be found in full-service agencies are discussed in the following sections.

19. Debra Aho Williamson, "Grey Interactive Finally Shines in Light of P&G Deal," *Advertising Age,* November 11, 1996, 42.
20. Bradley Johnson, "NEC May Move $40 Mil In-House," *Advertising Age,* April, 6, 1998, 48.

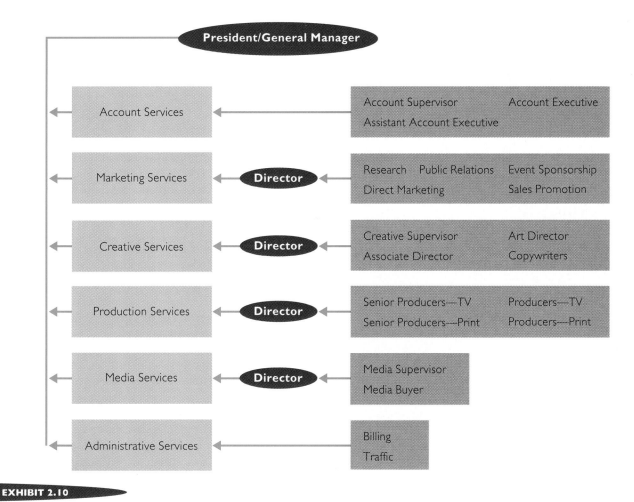

EXHIBIT 2.10

Typical organizational structure of a full-service advertising agency.

Account Services. Account services managers, who have titles such as account executive, account supervisor, or account manager, work with the client to determine how the client's product or service can benefit most from advertising. Account services entail identifying the benefits a product or service provides, its potential target audiences, and the best competitive positioning, and then developing a complete advertising plan. In some cases, account services in an agency can provide basic marketing and consumer behavior research. Some agencies have analysts doing research on basic consumer behavior and consumer values, product concept testing, and campaign evaluation.

Account services managers also work with the client in translating cultural and consumer values into advertising messages through the creative services in the agency. Finally, they work with media services to develop an effective media strategy for the best placement of advertisements to reach targeted audiences. One of the primary tasks in account services is to keep the various agency teams—creative, production, media—on schedule and within budget. In many agencies, account services are referred to as account management activities.

Marketing Services. Marketing services in an agency commonly include four areas: (1) research, (2) sales promotion and event sponsorship, (3) direct marketing, and (4) public relations. Research conducted by an agency for a client usually consists of the agency locating studies (conducted by commercial research organizations) that have bearing on a client's market or advertising objectives. The research group will help the client interpret the research and communicate these interpretations to the creative and

EXHIBIT 2.11

This ad created by full-service agency Leo Burnett demonstrates the staying power of a successful ad theme. Because Burnett has a full range of marketing support services to maintain and update Pillsbury's Doughboy, it can provide its creative and production people with information they need to adapt this well-known theme to changing consumer tastes.
www.pillsbury.com/

media people. Another type of research may actually be conducted by the agency. As mentioned in the account services discussion, some agencies can assemble consumers from the target audience to evaluate different versions of proposed advertising and determine whether messages are being communicated effectively. The ad agency BBDO has several proprietary research methods it employs for clients.

The sales promotion and event sponsorship marketing services that an agency may provide include the development of contests, sweepstakes, premiums, or special offers and in-store merchandising materials for a client. Many firms are adding event-marketing specialists in this area. These marketing experts help clients identify whether and how to sponsor events, such as major golf tournaments, auto races, or local community events such as parades and marathons.

Some agencies have developed in-house direct-marketing departments to serve clients' needs for direct mail and telemarketing efforts. This department plans and integrates direct-marketing activities with a firm's primary advertising effort. Direct mail pieces or phone campaigns can target audience members for special advertising messages or sales promotion efforts.

In this era of integrated marketing communications, agencies are finding that more clients demand assistance with integrating all forms of communication with the advertising effort. Some full-service agencies are adding public relations to their list of available marketing services. These firms are attempting to achieve as much control as possible over a client's marketing communications to ensure truly integrated marketing communications. We touched on IMC in Chapter 1, and we will continue to examine the issue throughout the text, with special emphasis in Part 4.

Creative and Production Services. Creative services personnel come up with the concepts that express the value of a company's brand in interesting and memorable ways. In simple terms, the creative group develops the advertising message. The creative group in an agency will typically include a creative director, art director, illustrators, and copywriters.

Production services includes producers (and sometimes directors) who take creative ideas and turn them into radio, television, and print advertisements. Producers are the ones who scout locations, hire directors, find the right actors and actresses, contract with production and postproduction houses, and generally manage and oversee the production of the finished advertisement. Creative and production services personnel in an agency bring to life the value that clients have to offer the market and express that value by producing polished advertising messages.

Some agencies also have producers for specialized support media efforts. Billboards, posters, transit advertising, and specialty advertising materials (giveaway items with the firm's logo, for example) are examples of support media.

Media-Planning and -Buying Services. Media-planning and -buying services handle the placement task in the advertising effort. The central challenge is to determine how a client's message can most effectively and efficiently reach the target audience. Media planners and buyers examine an enormous number of options to put together an effective media plan within the client's budget. But media planning and buying is much more than simply buying ad space. A wide range of media strategies can be implemented to enhance the impact of the message. Agencies are helping clients sort through the blizzard of new media options such as CD-ROM, videocassettes, interactive media, and the Internet. Quite a few agencies, such as Chiat/Day and Fallon McElligott, have already set up their own sites on the Internet in response to client demands that the Internet media option be made available to them.[21] The three positions typically found in the media area are media planner, media buyer, and media researcher. This is where the client's money is spent; it's very important.

Administrative Services. Like other businesses, advertising agencies have to manage their business affairs. Agencies have personnel departments, accounting and billing departments, and sales staffs that go out and sell the agency to clients. Most important to clients is the traffic department, which has the responsibility of monitoring projects to be sure that deadlines are met. Traffic managers make sure the creative group and media services are coordinated so that deadlines for getting ads into media are met. The job requires tremendous organizational skills and is critical to delivering the other services to clients.

Agency Compensation, Promotion, and Redesign.

Agency Compensation Plans. The way agencies get paid is somewhat different from the way other professional organizations are compensated. While accountants, doctors, lawyers, and consultants often work on a fee basis, advertising agencies often base compensation on a commission or markup system. We will examine the four most prevalent agency compensation methods: commissions, markup charges, fee systems, and newer pay-for-results plans.

Commissions. One method of agency compensation is the **commission system**, which is based on the amount of money the advertiser spends on media. Under this method, 15 percent of the total amount billed by the media organization is retained by the advertising agency as compensation for all costs in creating advertising for the client. The only variation is that the rate typically changes to $16\frac{2}{3}$ percent for outdoor media. Exhibit 2.12 provides a simple example of how an agency is compensated for an advertising campaign that costs $1 million for media time.

Over the past ten years, the wisdom of the commission system has been questioned by both advertisers and agencies themselves. As the chairman of a large full-service agency put it, "It's incenting us to do the wrong thing, to recommend network TV and national magazines and radio when other forms of communication like direct marketing or public relations might do the job better."[22]

EXHIBIT 2.12

Calculation of agency compensation using a traditional commission-based compensation system.

Agency bills client **$1,000,000** for television airtime

−

Agency pays television media **$ 850,000** for television airtime

=

Agency earns **$ 150,000** **15% commission**

21. Kevin Goldman, "Ad Agencies Slowly Set Up Shop at New Addresses on the Internet," *Wall Street Journal,* December 29, 1994, B5.
22. Sellers, "Do You Need Your Ad Agency?" 151–152.

Exhibit 2.13 shows that about 59 percent of all advertisers compensate their advertising agencies using a commission system. But, only about 14 percent of advertisers responding to a recent survey still use the traditional 15 percent commission, however. More advertisers use other percentage levels of commission—often negotiated levels—as the basis for agency compensation. Unilever, the Dutch consumer products company with extensive U.S. revenues, has some agencies on rates as low as 10.75 percent, depending on the agreement negotiated.[23]

Markup Charges. Another method of agency compensation is to add a percentage **markup charge** to a variety of services the agency purchases from outside suppliers. In many cases, an agency will turn to outside contractors for art, illustration, photography, printing, research, and production. The agency then, in agreement with the client, adds a markup charge to these services. The reason markup charges became prevalent in the industry is that many service providers do not give the agency a commission, as do the media. There is thus no way, other than by adding a markup percentage, for the agency to receive compensation for managing the work of outside contractors. A typical markup on outside services is 17.65 to 20 percent.

Fee Systems. A **fee system** is much like that used by consultants or attorneys, whereby the advertiser and the agency agree on an hourly rate for different services provided. The hourly rate can be based on average salaries within departments or on some agreed-upon hourly rate across all services. Recently, GM, the largest U.S. advertiser, agreed to a fee system in which compensation will be based on agency work and its thinking.[24]

Another version of the fee system is a fixed fee set for a project between the client and the agency. It is imperative that the agency and the advertiser agree on precisely what services will be provided, by what departments in the agency, over what specified period of time. In addition, the parties must agree on which supplies, materials, travel costs, and other expenses will be compensated beyond the fixed fee. Fixed-fee systems have the potential for causing serious rifts in the client-agency relationship because out-of-scope work can easily spiral out of control when so many variables are at play.

Pay-for-Results Compensation Plans. Recently, many advertisers and agencies alike have been working on compensation programs that base the agency's fee on the achievement of agreed-upon results.[25] Historically, agencies have not agreed to be evaluated on "results" because "results" have often been narrowly defined as sales. The key effect on an advertiser's sales result is based on factors outside the agency's control such

EXHIBIT 2.13

Agency compensation programs: 1992 versus 1995.

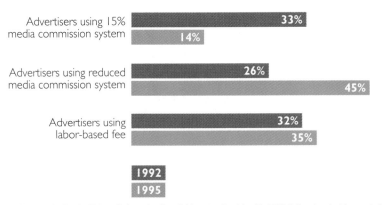

Advertisers using 15% media commission system — 33% (1992), 14% (1995)

Advertisers using reduced media commission system — 26% (1992), 45% (1995)

Advertisers using labor-based fee — 32% (1992), 35% (1995)

1992
1995

Source: Iris Cohen Selinger "Big Profits, Risks, with Incentive Fees," *Advertising Age,* May 15, 1995, 3. Reprinted with permission from the May 15, 1995, issue of *Advertising Age.* Copyright © Crain Communications Inc.

23. Pat Sloan and Laura Petrecca, "Unilever Panel to Propose Hike in Fees for Agencies," *Advertising Age,* November 3, 1997, 2.
24. Jean Halliday, "GM to Scrap Agency Commissions," *Advertising Age,* November 16, 1998, 1, 57.
25. Petrecca, "Pay-for-Results Plans Can Boost Agencies: Execs," *Advertising Age,* September 8, 1997, 18, 20.

as product features, pricing strategy, and distribution programs (that is, the overall marketing mix, not just advertising). These newer **pay-for-results compensation plans** tie advertising agency compensation to a pre-agreed-upon achievement of specified objectives. An agency may agree to be compensated based on achievement of sales levels, but more often (and more appropriately) communications objectives such as awareness, brand identification, or brand feature knowledge among target audiences will serve as the results criteria.

Agency Self-Promotion. To receive any form of compensation, an agency must win and keep clients. Winning clients is an expensive and risky undertaking. In the organizational structure of an agency, it is the account management people who, as liaisons with clients, are primarily responsible for ensuring that current clients are satisfied and new clients are cultivated. Recall that in the new Leo Burnett mini-agency structure, each agency team is now responsible for cultivating new business.

The typical method for agency self-promotion is for an agency to compete for an account when the account "comes up for review." This means that an advertiser has decided that a brand needs a new advertising approach and has put out the call for new ideas. When this occurs, an agency may decide (or may be invited) to take the risk and expense of competing for the account. In 1995, the Deutsch agency spent 95 days and deployed 50 of its 175 employees to the task of competing for the Volkswagen account. The final pitch alone cost a whopping $360,000—and the account was awarded to a competitor.[26]

In recent years, a record number of accounts have come up for review. While all that available business has made the industry exciting, there is a major frustration and cost for agencies. Aside from the expense of competing for new business, many advertisers are making "split decisions" in their reassignments. A split decision means that two or more agencies are assigned the work of developing advertising materials. When United Airlines decided to replace Leo Burnett, it split the assignment between Fallon McElligott in Minneapolis and Young & Rubicam in New York.[27] Similarly, AT&T uses four agencies and McDonald's uses three. Advertisers explain that they feel they can create a competitive environment and enhance the creativity of their advertising materials.

Aside from the expensive and cutthroat competition of account reassignments, another way agencies can compete for new business is to use the main tool of their trade—advertising! Exhibits 2.14 and 2.15 show how two agencies have promoted themselves, practicing what they preach.

Agency Redesign. As highlighted at the opening of the chapter, advertising agencies are reconsidering their role in the contemporary advertising environment. Major advertisers are now questioning the traditional role of mass media as the primary delivery mechanism for advertising. Some agencies are more fully integrating the research function. All of this has led many agencies to redesign themselves.

Much redesign is being done to serve all of an advertiser's marketing communications needs, and it is turning agencies into integrated marketing communications organizations. While few agencies are willing to change their designation from "advertising agency" to "IMC agency," more agencies are adding public relations, sales promotion, direct-marketing, and event-marketing departments. As more corporate dollars are being spent on these other forms of promotion, agencies are trying to keep that spending rather than letting it go to specialists in these areas. But the desire to redesign an agency to accommodate IMC desires of clients must be considered carefully, as the IMC box on page 55 highlights. While clients might *say* they want to pursue integrated marketing communications, the expense and complication of such a commitment often results in second thoughts and delays in implementation. As is said, the devil is in the details.

26. "VW Picks Arnold, Fortuna, Lawner," *Wall Street Journal,* March 28, 1995, B7.
27. Mark Gleason and Laura Petrecca, "Split Decisions Grow as Advertisers Seek Edge," *Advertising Age,* November 11, 1996, 1, 20, 22.

EXHIBIT 2.14

Self-promotion is an important advertising goal for any agency. By showcasing its creative prowess in this ad, J. Walter Thompson seeks both new clients and leverage in setting its compensation system.
www.jwtworld.com/

EXHIBIT 2.15

Go to the Arian, Lowe & Travis site on the Web at www.altadv.com. *What sort of image of the company does its Web site convey? How well does the Internet serve advertising agencies, in allowing them to display their capabilities? What if your agency specialized in television advertising? How could you best employ a Web site? TBWA/Chiat/Day (*www.chiatday*) has pioneered successful advertising campaigns for major brands, such as Apple Computer and Nike. How does Chiat/Day use its Web site to illustrate style, present work, and past achievements?*

Frank Costantini, Creative Director, e.p.t, JWT New York

LOOK WHO'S *expecting* ANOTHER EFFIE

An Effie for e.p.t.* One of 16 this year. One of over 100 in the last 10 years.

Effies won in the last 10 years.

WEB SIGHTING

AFTER SEEING OUR WORK THE BURNETT CREATIVE REVIEW BOARD DUBBED IT "PROVOCATIVE, OUTRAGEOUS, AND NASTY." WE MUST BE DOING SOMETHING RIGHT.

SEE FOR YOURSELF. CALL DARYL TRAVIS FOR A COPY OF OUR AGENCY'S LATEST REEL.

ARIAN, LOWE & TRAVIS

833 WEST CHICAGO AVENUE CHICAGO ILLINOIS 60622 (312) 243-3500

Another issue in agency redesign is preparing to serve clients' needs in applying interactive media to the process of communicating with customers. What can agencies do to retain an important role in this emerging media communication process? One firm that is keeping its agency involved by relying on both traditional advertising and the new interactive information superhighway is Sassaby Cosmetics. Sassaby's strategy for the introduction of a line of teen cosmetics called "jane" included a $3 million magazine advertising campaign supported by a 24-hour chat service on the Prodigy online information service. The Sassaby Cosmetics online chat group, dubbed "jane's brain," gave teenage girls a forum to talk to each other and to Sassaby about a range of topics, including, but not limited to, cosmetics and fashion.[28] Exhibit 2.16 is an example of another interactive Web site. This one is for O'Neill products— surfboards, snowboards, and other outdoor recreation products.

Precisely how agencies will reinvent themselves to better address client needs and adapt to new media options remains to be seen. Many agencies have already made significant organizational commitments. Ogilvy & Mather Direct has an extensive full-time staff in its Interactive Marketing Group working on interactive advertising disks with Forbes, kiosk-based systems with Kraft, and interactive television with AT&T. Saatchi & Saatchi has created Interactive Plus within its agency, and the group is doing extensive research on the future of interactive television and CD-ROM applications. Other agencies are setting up interactive task forces to determine how they will adapt to the new media options.[29] These actions signal changes to the structure of advertising agencies as well as to the evolving structure of the industry.

Both advertisers and their agencies are being cautious about commitments to new media options, however. The reason is that even though new media—particularly the Internet—are conspicuous and

I WANT MY IMC—SORT OF

As much lip service as advertisers give to pursuing the "one voice" and "seamless communication" that a well-designed IMC program can provide, there seems to be one major roadblock to implementation: the advertisers themselves! This is the opinion of one industry expert who has studied the IMC process for many years.

John McLaughlin, a marketing consultant, believes that major IMC efforts actually started with major advertising agencies about 25 years ago, when agencies began designing their organizations to provide all sorts of communications capabilities to their clients in addition to traditional advertising, as a way to ensure keeping all of their clients' business. These agencies added sales promotion, public relations, and direct mail departments, but the vast majority of clients didn't respond. The reasons:

- Clients didn't see a clear-cut cost advantage in dealing exclusively with a primary agency rather than several suppliers.
- Clients didn't have confidence in the ability of advertising agencies to deliver specialized services.
- Clients had strategic concerns about putting all their eggs in one creative/executional basket. If a client decided to replace an agency, a house of cards would come tumbling down around the firm's entire communication/promotional program.

Because of these concerns, advertisers not only hesitated to use their agencies' newly developed multiple capabilities but also delayed implementing IMC altogether. The task of developing multiple relationships with multiple agencies proved to be dysfunctional and expensive— but the original concerns about dealing with a sole agency remained. Creative constipation set in.

In the meantime, since agencies were not realizing widespread new business from newly formed divisions, many of them were disbanded or sold off. While some agencies still maintain broad-based staffs from multiple communications needs of clients, others choose to partner with outside agencies.

So, if IMC has not spread as quickly as everyone thinks it should have, Mr. McLaughlin says simply, "Blame it on the clients."

Source: John P. McLaughlin, "Why Is IMC Taking So Long? Blame It on the Clients," *Marketing News*, September 15, 1997, 27.

28. Pat Sloan, "A Sassy Approach to Cosmetics," *Advertising Age,* May 23, 1994, 17.
29. Melanie Wells, Jeff Jansen, Gary Levine, et al., "Desperately Seeking the Interactive Superhighway," *Advertising Age,* special section on interactive media and marketing, August 22, 1994, 14–15.

EXHIBIT 2.16

As agencies redesign themselves to provide more services, many are helping clients take advantage of the interactivity offered by the Internet. This Web site for O'Neill sport products provides both product information and event schedules to attract Web users. www.oneill.com/

entertaining, the full role of these new media in persuasive communication and, indeed, commerce remains unknown. By the beginning of 1998, only 7 million households had made any sort of purchase online. Another caution comes from the fact that although 23 percent of households are online, only about half of them have ever used the Internet to research a purchase.[30] Certainly, advertisers and agencies are preparing for the future of electronic communication, but at present the amount of persuasive communication reaching target audiences in new media pales in comparison to the $200 billion invested in sending persuasive communication through traditional media.

External Facilitators.

External Facilitators. While advertising agencies offer clients many services and are adding more, advertisers often need to rely on specialized external facilitators in planning, preparing, and placing advertisements. **External facilitators** are organizations or individuals that provide specialized services to advertisers and agencies. The most important of these external facilitators are discussed in the following sections.

Marketing and Advertising Research Firms.

Marketing and Advertising Research Firms. Many firms rely on outside assistance during the planning phase of advertising. Research firms such as Burke International and Simmons can perform original research for advertisers using focus groups, surveys, or experiments to assist in understanding the potential market or consumer perceptions of a product or services. Other research firms, such as SRI International, routinely collect data (from grocery store scanners, for example) and have these data available for a fee.

Advertisers and their agencies also seek measures of advertising effectiveness. After an advertisement has been running for some reasonable amount of time, firms such as Starch INRA Hooper will run recognition tests on print advertisements. Other firms such as Burke offer day-after recall tests of broadcast advertisements. Some firms specialize in message testing to determine whether consumers find advertising messages appealing and understandable. The exact nature and full range of research that can be conducted are covered in Chapter 7.

Consultants.

Consultants. A variety of consultants specialize in areas related to the advertising process. Advertisers can seek out marketing consultants for assistance in the planning stage. Creative and communications consultants provide insight on issues related to message strategy and message themes. Media experts can help an advertiser determine the proper media mix and efficient media placement. Two new types of consultants have emerged in recent years. One is a database consultant, who works with both advertisers and advertising agencies. Organizations such as Shepard Associates help firms identify and then manage databases that allow for the development of integrated marketing communications programs. Diverse databases from research sources dis-

30. Jared Sandberg, "On-Line Shopping Shows Signs of Life, But Still No Mass Appeal, Survey Says," *Wall Street Journal,* March 12, 1998.

cussed earlier can be merged or cross-referenced in developing effective communications programs. The other new type of consultant specializes in Web site development and management. These consultants typically have the creative skills to develop Web sites and corporate home pages and the technical skills to advise advertisers on managing the technical aspects of the user interface.

Production Facilitators. External production facilitators offer essential services both during and after the production process. Production is the area where advertisers and their agencies rely most heavily on external facilitators. All forms of media advertising require special expertise that even the largest full-service agency, much less an advertiser, may not retain on staff. In broadcast production, directors, production managers, songwriters, camera operators, audio and lighting technicians, and performers are all essential to preparing a professional, high-quality radio or television ad. Production houses can provide the physical facilities, including sets, stages, equipment, and crews, needed for broadcast production. Similarly, in preparing print advertising, graphic artists, photographers, models, directors, and producers may be hired from outside the advertising agency or firm to provide the specialized skills and facilities needed in preparing advertisements.

Once an advertisement has gone through the production process, further expertise is needed before the ad is placed in a medium. Postproduction processes in broadcast advertising include film developing and transferring, editing, special effects, sound mixing, and color matching. In print advertising, film developing and photo enhancement are typically carried out by external organizations.

The specific activities performed by external facilitators and the techniques employed by the personnel in these firms will be covered in greater detail at various points in the text. For now, it is sufficient to recognize the role these firms play in the advertising industry.

Information Intermediators. This form of external facilitator has emerged as a result of new technology and the desire on the part of advertisers to target audiences more precisely. An **information intermediator** collects customer purchase transaction histories, aggregates them across many firms that have sold merchandise to these customers, and then sells the customer names and addresses back to the firms that originally sold to these customers. Firms such as American Express, AT&T, and regional telephone companies are uniquely situated in the information management process to accumulate and organize such data, and they will likely emerge as information intermediators. These firms will gather and organize information on consumer transaction histories across a variety of different firms selling goods and services. Once this information is organized by an intermediator, it allows an advertiser to merge information about important target segments—what they buy, when they buy, and how they buy. With this information, both message themes and media placement can be more effectively and efficiently developed.

Other Communications Organizations. A complete discussion of the structure of the advertising industry must recognize that other types of communications organizations, beyond advertising agencies, play an important role in fulfilling the communications needs of advertisers. In an era when the concept of integrated marketing communications is receiving more and more attention, it is necessary to consider other organizations that provide advertisers with alternative opportunities to communicate with their target audiences. These other communications organizations act much like other external facilitators and provide advertisers with services that an advertising agency may not offer. The three communications organizations most often relied on are public relations firms, direct-marketing firms, and sales promotion specialists.

RADIOTVNET?

As the introduction to this chapter highlights, advertising is an industry in transition. There is little doubt that new media and new media interfaces are major contributors to this transition—and that such change presents many opportunities. One such opportunity is the broadcast of radio and television programming over the Internet. The firm leading this interface of media is broadcast.com (formerly AudioNet), which offers a wide range of radio, television, and proprietary broadcasts through its Internet site. By late 1998, broadcast.com offered the following media interfaces to Web users:

- Live continuous broadcasts of over 350 radio stations and networks
- Broadcasts of 17 television stations and cable networks
- Play-by-play game broadcasts and other programming of over 350 college and professional sports teams
- Live and on-demand corporate and special events
- Live music, including concerts and club performances
- On-demand music from the CD Jukebox, with over 2,100 full-length CDs
- Over 360 full-length audio books

With these capabilities, broadcast.com has broadcast of some the largest sporting events in Internet history, such as Super Bowls XXX, XXXI, and XXXII and the Stanley Cup playoffs. In entertainment, the Web site carried backstage interviews from the 1998 Academy Awards Webcast and concerts with such stars as Travis Tritt. And the company is also proud to claim to have broadcast the first live corporate stockholders' meeting on the Internet.

What is so different about this site as a medium is that it truly blurs media lines. On broadcast.com, a Web user can listen to a station while using the computer for other tasks—and the audio follows the user from site to site. Of course, video broadcast is its own Web attraction. The future of this sort of new medium, according to broadcast.com founder Mark Cuban, is that it allows online broadcast to reach a hard-to-reach demographic: white-collar workers at their desks. But the real future for this sort of hybrid medium and companies like broadcast.com is the extent to which advertisers see this as an effective way to transmit persuasive and informative messages. While standard messages are embedded in the transmission, will such messages be received with the same favorability (or lack of favorability) as they would have through the original medium? And does banner ad sponsorship work any better in this context than at standard Web sites?

These issues will ultimately be answered by Web users' response to Web broadcasting. For now, aggregators and broadcasters of streaming media programming on the Web offer one more choice to the fragmented media environment.

Sources: Michael Wilke, "AudioNet Rebroadcasts Live Radio, tv Signals to Sites," *Advertising Age*, June 2, 1997; www.broadcast.com/. Accessed September 30, 1998.

Public relations was identified in Chapter 1 as one of the components of a firm's promotional mix. **Public relations firms** handle the needs of organizations regarding relationships with the local community, competitors, industry associations, and government organizations. The tools of public relations include press releases, feature stories, lobbying, spokespersons, and company newsletters. Some public relations firms can conduct research to develop and test the impact of public relations efforts. The goal of public relations efforts is to communicate information about a firm, its products, and its employees so as to achieve public awareness, understanding, and goodwill.

Direct-marketing firms handle another of the promotional mix variables listed in Chapter 1. **Direct-marketing firms** maintain large databases of mailing lists as one of their services. Several of these firms can also design direct-marketing campaigns either through the mail or by telemarketing. Finally, **sales promotion specialists** design and then operate contests, sweepstakes, special displays, or coupon campaigns for advertisers. Since sales promotion is a specialized form of communication, experts in this area plan and then execute such promotions.

Media Organizations.

Someday, we will all work for the Mouse.
—Anonymous

The next level in the industry structure, shown in Exhibit 2.17, comprises the media available to advertisers. The media available for placing advertising, such as broadcast and print media, are well known to most of us simply because we're exposed to them daily. Exhibit 2.17, however, organizes this information into five specific categories.

EXHIBIT 2.17

Advertisers have an array of media organizations available to them. Notice that the choices range from traditional print and broadcast media to new media and diverse support media such as posters, directories, and event sponsorships.

Broadcast

Television
Major network
Independent station
Cable

Radio
Network
Local

Print

Magazines
By geographic coverage
By content

Direct Mail
Brochures
Catalogs
Videos

Newspapers
National
Statewide
Local

Specialty
Handbills
Programs

Interactive Media

Online Computer Services

Home-Shopping Broadcasts

**Interactive Broadcast
Entertainment Programming**

Kiosks

CD-ROM

Internet

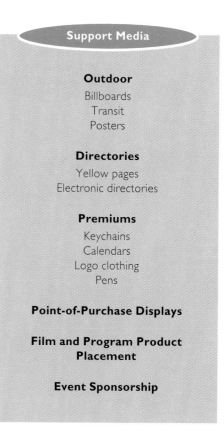

Support Media

Outdoor
Billboards
Transit
Posters

Directories
Yellow pages
Electronic directories

Premiums
Keychains
Calendars
Logo clothing
Pens

Point-of-Purchase Displays

**Film and Program Product
Placement**

Event Sponsorship

Media Conglomerates

Multiple Media Combinations
Time Warner
Viacom
TCI
Turner Broadcasting
Comcast
AT&T

Advertisers and their agencies turn to organizations that own and manage these media categories. Major television networks such as NBC or Fox, as well as national magazines such as *U.S. News & World Report* or *People,* provide advertisers with time and space—at considerable expense—for their messages. Other media options are more useful for reaching narrowly defined target audiences. Specialty programming on cable television, tightly focused direct mail pieces, and a well-designed outdoor campaign may be better ways to reach a specific audience. Note the inclusion of "Media Conglomerates" in this list. This category is included because organizations such as Time Warner and Viacom own and operate companies in broadcast, print, and interactive media. Most recently, Disney has vastly expanded its media presence with the purchase of the ABC television network and partial ownership in multiple Web sites, including ESPN SportsZone, NBA.com, NFL.com, and ABCnews.com.[31] These media organizations may soon control, coordinate, and integrate a variety of separate media options to the benefit (and no doubt expense) of advertisers.

Take particular notice of the interactive media and support media categories. Some very dramatically different media opportunities have arisen, particularly with the Internet—opportunities that, in fact, blur the media lines, as the New Media box on page 58 discusses. In the last 10 years, advertisers have invested more and more money in the nontraditional media options listed in these categories—although the traditional media of radio, television, magazines, and newspapers still command about 90 percent of advertisers' dollars. The obvious importance of the various media is that each provides a different form of access to an audience. Each of the media options listed in Exhibit 2.17 has its own unique advantages for transmitting information and reaching a particular audience. Strategic use of media options is critical to an effective and efficient advertising process and has become more important in recent years as firms craft complex and elaborate integrated marketing communications programs. The strategic opportunities and challenges of each medium are discussed in great detail in Part Four of this text.

---

31. Chuck Ross, "Disney Eyes Stake in Excite as Part of Bold Web Strategy," *Advertising Age,* June 1, 1998, 1, 52.

SUMMARY

◀▶ Discuss six important trends transforming the advertising industry.

The 1990s have proven to be a period of dramatic change for the advertising industry. Many factors have propelled this change. Cable television has increased its reach, and the growing popularity of direct-marketing programs and home shopping has diluted the impact of advertising delivered via mass media. Internet aggregators of radio and TV broadcasts and streaming video offer new hybrid media options for advertisers to consider. In addition to the growth and diversity of media, marketers have altered their budget allocations, with more funding going to sales promotion and event sponsorship, and less money allocated for conventional advertising. These changes have contributed to the emphasis on integrated marketing communications.

◀▶ Describe the size and scale of the advertising industry.

Advertising is an immense globalized business. Counting the many forms of advertising, annual global expenditures on advertising have reached nearly $450 billion. In the United States, companies such as Procter & Gamble, Philip Morris, and General Motors allocate billions of dollars to advertising their various brands every year. The advertising agencies that help companies like these develop advertising campaigns employ tens of thousands of people worldwide.

◀▶ Explain who the participants in the advertising industry are and the role each plays in the formulation and execution of advertising campaigns.

Many different types of organizations make up the advertising industry. To truly appreciate what advertising is all about, one must have a good handle on *who* does *what* and in *what order* in the creation and delivery of an advertising campaign. The process begins with an organization that has a message it wishes to communicate to a target audience. This is the advertiser. Next, advertising agencies are typically hired to launch a campaign, but other external facilitators are often brought in to perform specialized functions, such as identifying a sporting event for the advertiser to sponsor or helping the advertiser set up a Web page on the Internet. Since most campaigns use some type of mass media, advertisers and their agencies must also work with companies that have advertising time or space to sell.

◀▶ Detail the diverse services that advertising agencies supply in the planning, preparation, and placement of advertising and explain how agencies are compensated for their services.

Advertising agencies come in many varieties and offer diverse services to clients with respect to planning, preparing, and placing advertising. These services include market research and marketing planning, the actual creation and production of ad materials, the buying of media time or space for placement of the ads, and traffic management—keeping production on schedule. Some advertising agencies appeal to clients by offering a full array of services under one roof; others—such as creative boutiques—develop a particular expertise and win clients with their specialized skills. The four most prevalent ways to compensate an agency for services rendered are commissions, markups, fee systems, and the new pay-for-results programs.

KEY TERMS

advertising agency (45)
full-service agency (46)
creative boutique (46)
media-buying service (47)
interactive agencies (47)
in-house agency (48)
commission system (51)
markup charge (52)

fee system (52)
pay-for-results compensation plans (53)
external facilitators (56)
information intermediator (57)
public relations firms (58)
direct-marketing firms (58)
sales promotion specialists (58)

QUESTIONS FOR REVIEW AND CRITICAL THINKING

1.   Explain the problems Leo Burnett had with losing clients. Also explain how this largest of all U.S. ad agencies responded to the challenge of losing some clients.

2.   As cable-TV channels continue to proliferate and the TV-viewing audience becomes ever more fragmented, how would you expect the advertising industry to be affected?

3.   The U.S. Army spends millions of dollars each year trying to recruit young men and women into the armed services. Given the definition of advertising offered in Chapter 1, would it be correct to conclude that the U.S. Army is spending millions on advertising?

4.   Huge advertisers such as Procter & Gamble spend billions of dollars on advertising every year, yet they still rely on advertising agencies to prepare most of their advertising. Why doesn't a big company like this just do all its own advertising in-house?

5.   As marketers become more enamored with the idea of integrated marketing communications, why would it make sense for an advertising agency to develop a reputation as a full-service provider?

6.   Explain the viewpoint that a commission-based compensation system may actually give ad agencies an incentive to do the wrong things for their clients.

7.   What is it that makes ad production the area where advertisers and their agencies are most likely to call on external facilitators for expertise and assistance?

8.   Give an example of how the skills of a public relations firm might be employed to reinforce the message that a sponsor is trying to communicate through conventional ads.

EXPERIENTIAL EXERCISES

1.   During a two-day period, observe and list all of the media you come in contact with that carry advertising messages. Which media are most suitable for local advertisers? Which medium do you think is most effective in reaching you? Which do you think is least effective? If you were planning to open a pizza restaurant, which media choices do you think would be best for advertising? Explain your reasoning.

2.   Make an appointment with an account executive at an advertising agency in your city. Ask this person what he or she believes are the biggest challenges facing the advertising industry from his or her perspective. How does this person's perspective match the issues raised at the beginning of this chapter?

USING THE INTERNET

Visit the following five sites:

Dalbey & Denight: http://www.dalbey-denight.com

Modem Media; Poppe Tyson: www.poppe.com

DD&B Needham Interactive Communications: www.ddbniac.com

J. Walter Thompson: www.jwtworld.com

Trilium Interactive: www.trilium.com

For each of the sites, answer these questions:

1.   Is this a full-service advertising agency or a boutique that specializes in Internet advertising services?

2.   What specific services does the firm offer? What is its client base?

3.   Based on the Web site, what is the creative style of each firm?

4.   If you were a company selling mountain bikes, which firm would you choose? Justify your choice based on your answers to the preceding questions.

As with any other business, a part of an advertising firm's Web strategy is to use its presence to attract customers (clients).

1.   How do you think the agencies in the previous exercise attract "eyeballs" to their Web sites?

2.   Are the agencies listed in all the places they should be (e.g., in the correct categories on the Yahoo! site)? Use one or more search engines to search for one of the agencies by name.

3.   What sort of pages does your query find? How often do they represent authoritative content from the agency or from its clients (e.g., press releases) and how often do they represent "mainstream" news? What other sources did you encounter?

4.   Use the "links to this URL" query (described in Chapter 1's Using the Internet) to find links to one of these agencies' sites. Do advertisers often, seldom, or never mention their agency on their own Web sites?

—and he wonders why
she said "NO!"

 Could he have read her thoughts he would not have lost her. A picture of neatness herself, she detested slovenliness. And not once, but many times, she had noticed his ungartered socks crumpling down around his shoe tops. To have to apologize to her friends for a husband's careless habits was too much to ask. So she had to say "NO"—and in spite of his pleading couldn't tell him WHY.

No SOX Appeal Without

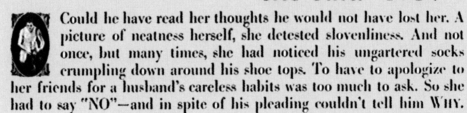

SINGLE GRIP

PARIS
GARTERS
NO METAL CAN TOUCH YOU
25c to 82
Dress Well and Succeed

DOUBLE GRIP

© 1928—A. STEIN & COMPANY—MAKERS—CHICAGO, NEW YORK, LOS ANGELES, TORONTO

CHAPTER 3

**After reading and thinking about
this chapter, you will be able to
do the following:**

◀▶ Explain why advertising is a natural feature
of capitalistic economic systems.

◀▶ Describe manufacturers' dependence
on advertising and branding in achieving
balanced relationships with retailers.

◀▶ Discuss 10 important eras in the evolution
of advertising in the United States, and
relate important changes in advertising
practice to more fundamental changes in
society and culture.

◀▶ Identify forces that may make the next
decade a period of dramatic change for
the advertising industry.

EXHIBIT 3.1

While this ad for Lux laundry powder may seem curious to us today, it reflected the anxiety of the 1930s, during the Great Depression. Just as today's advertising reflects the values of contemporary society, this ad emphasized some very real concerns of the time—the economic well-being and status of women.

The 1935 Lux advertisement shown in Exhibit 3.1 is undoubtedly curious to contemporary audiences. It is, however, typical of its time and very likely made perfect sense to its original audience. In the 1930s, in the middle of the Great Depression, anxiety about losing one's husband to divorce—and thus one's economic well-being—was not unfounded. Targeted to a new generation of stay-at-home housewives anxious about their exclusion from the modern world of their husbands, during a period when losing one's source of income could mean abject poverty or worse, in a society where daily bathing was still very rare but where self-doubt about personal hygiene was on the rise, such an ad may have pushed just the right buttons. If Lux can "remove perspiration odor from underthings," it might save more than colors and fabrics. It might save marriages. If Bob's romantic indifference continues, Sally may soon be back home with Mom or on the street. But with Lux on the scene, Bob goes home for dinner.

While some ads today use the same general technique to sell deodorants, soaps, and feminine hygiene products, this ad is certainly not read the same way today as it was in 1935. Ads are part of their times. Today, Sally would likely have a job and be far less economically vulnerable and socially isolated—not to mention that Sally and Bob would both be bathing more. So we see the 1930s in this ad in the same way that students of the future will view ads of our time: as interesting, revealing, but still distorted reflections of daily life in the late 20th century. Even in the 1930s consumers knew ads were ads; they knew that ads exaggerate, they knew that ads try to sell things, and they knew that ads don't exactly mirror everyday life. But, ads may look enough like life to work, sometimes.

This chapter is about the evolution of advertising. Over the decades, advertisers have tried many different strategies and approaches, and you can learn a lot from their successes and failures. You will also know when a given advertising technique is really something new or just hype. (As the New Media box on page 68 explains, Internet users, usually impatient for the next big thing, may have already cast their votes against push technology.) Besides being interesting, this history is very practical.

Fundamental Influences. ◀▶ In many discussions of the evolution of advertising, the process is often portrayed as having its origins in ancient times, with even primitive peoples practicing some form of advertising. Frankly, this is unlikely. Whatever those ancients were doing, they weren't advertising. Remember, advertising exists only as mass-mediated communication. As far as we know, there was no *Mesopotamia Messenger* or "Rome: Live at Five." So, while cavemen and cavewomen certainly were communicating with one another with persuasive intent, and perhaps even in a commercial context, they were not using advertising. Advertising is a product of modern times and mass media.

Before offering a brief social history of American advertising, we will first discuss some of the major factors that gave rise to it. Advertising, as we have defined it, came into being as a result of at least four major developments:

1. The rise of capitalism
2. The Industrial Revolution
3. Manufacturers' pursuit of power in the channel of distribution
4. The rise of modern mass media

The Rise of Capitalism. For advertising to become prominent in a society, the society must rely on aspects of capitalism in its economic system. The tenets of capitalism warrant that organizations compete for resources, called *capital,* in a free market environment. Part of the competition for resources involves stimulating demand for the organization's goods or services. When an individual organization successfully stimulates demand, it attracts capital to the organization in the form of money (or other goods) as payment. One of the tools used to stimulate demand is advertising.

The Industrial Revolution. The **Industrial Revolution** produced a need for advertising. Beginning about 1750 in England, the revolution spread to the United States and progressed slowly until the early 1800s, when the War of 1812 boosted domestic production. The emergence of the principle of interchangeable parts and the perfection of the sewing machine, both in 1850, coupled with the Civil War a decade later, laid the foundation for widespread industrialization. The Industrial Revolution took American society away from household self-sufficiency as a method of fulfilling material needs to marketplace dependency as a way of life. The Industrial Revolution was a basic force behind the rapid increase in a mass-produced supply of goods that required stimulation of demand, something that advertising can be very good at. By providing a need for advertising, the Industrial Revolution was a basic influence in its emergence.

As part of the broad Industrial Revolution, there were other equally revolutionary developments. First, there was a revolution in transportation, most dramatically symbolized by the east-west connection of the United States in 1869 by the railroad. This connection represented the beginnings of the distribution network needed to move the mass quantities of goods for which advertising would help stimulate demand. In the 1840s, the **principle of limited liability**, which restricts an investor's risk in a business venture to only his or her shares in a corporation rather than all personal assets, gained acceptance and resulted in the accumulation of large amounts of capital to finance the Industrial Revolution. Finally, rapid population growth and urbanization began taking place in the 1800s. From 1830 to 1860, the population of the United States increased nearly threefold, from 12.8 million to 31.4 million. During the same period, the number of cities with more than 20,000 inhabitants grew to 43. Historically, there is a strong relationship between per capita outlays for advertising and an increase in the size of cities.[1] Overall, the growth and concentration of population provided the marketplaces essential to the widespread use of advertising. As the potential grew for goods to be produced, delivered, and introduced to large numbers of people residing in concentrated areas, the stage was set for advertising to emerge and flourish.

1. Julian Simon, *Issues in the Economics of Advertising* (Urbana, Ill.: University of Illinois Press, 1970), 41–51.

Manufacturers' Pursuit of Power in the Channel of Distribution.

Another fundamental influence on the emergence and growth of advertising relates to manufacturers' pursuit of power in the channel of distribution. If a manufacturer can stimulate sizable demand for a brand, then that manufacturer can develop power in the distribution channel and essentially force wholesalers and retailers to sell that particular brand. Demand stimulation among consumers causes them to insist on the item at the retail or wholesale level; retailers and wholesalers have virtually no choice but to comply with consumers' desires and carry the desired item. Thus, the manufacturer has power in the channel of distribution and not only can force other participants in the channel to stock the brand, but also is in a position to command a higher price for the item. The marketing of Intel's Pentium chip is an excellent example of how one manufacturer, Intel, has developed considerable power in the computer distribution channel, establishing its product, the Pentium chip, as a premium brand.

A factor that turned out to be critical to manufacturers' pursuit of power was the strategy of **branding** products. Manufacturers had to develop brand names so that consumers could focus their attention on a clearly identified item. Manufacturers began branding previously unmarked commodities, such as work clothes and package goods, by the late 1800s, with Levi's (1873), Maxwell House (1873), Budweiser (1876), Ivory (1879), and Coca-Cola (1876) being among the first branded goods to show up on shopkeepers' shelves. Once a product had a brand mark and name that consumers could identify, the process of demand stimulation could take place. Of course, the essential tool in stimulating demand for a brand is advertising. Even today, when Procter & Gamble and Philip Morris spend many billions of dollars each year to stimulate demand for such popular brands as Crest, Charmin, Velveeta, and Miller Lite, wholesalers and retailers carry these brands because advertising has stimulated demand and brought consumers into the retail store looking for and asking for the brands.

Manufacturers' pursuit of power in the distribution channel is a standard facet of capitalistic economic

NO PUSH IN THE PUSH—YET

In advertising, the scope, direction, and importance of the Internet is the newest frontier—and the newest challenge. While the Internet itself is a broad fascination, advertisers need to understand strategic use of technology. One strategic application of Internet technology, "push," is defined as information delivered to Web users via their PCS over personal broadcast services or by e-mail. This information can include news, weather, stock reports, sports news, or a variety of other information specified by the user. This sort of communication option is exciting for advertisers because it theoretically allows the maximum in targeted communications—delivering a specific message to an identifiable target consumer.

Despite the clear advantage of targeting a communication to an individual, though, push has gotten a lukewarm response from both users and advertisers. One media analyst put it this way: "Push as a phenomenon hasn't gotten the amount of traction many expected it to get." Why not? The best guess is the poor response from Web users. Only 29.1 percent of Web users said they would be interested in using a push service, while a whopping 67.8 percent said they would not use one. Advertisers were just as uninterested. When surveyed about their intention to use the Web as a way to develop brand recognition, only 28 percent of advertisers said they would use a push service as a branding tool, while 96 percent said they would use a Web site and 88 percent said they would use banner ads.

The problem with push, according to some analysts, is that the system does not really lead to a direct interaction with the customer, any more than a newspaper delivered to your doorstep can be posited as a direct interaction. It is one step removed compared with a Web site, a banner ad, or even site sponsorship. But not every analyst has given up on push, however. Some believe that Web users are in an evolutionary stage and that broad consumer use of push systems is two to three years away. Such an assessment may be right on. Both Microsoft and Netscape have developed browsers that can push content to PCs. Microsoft's browser allows users to select from more than 700 channel partners that can deliver Web content to a PC's hard drive for offline viewing. Netscape's Netcaster service has formal agreements with content providers for about 150 channels of push content.

Sources: Kate Maddox, "Don't Push It, Say Users and Web Marketers," *Advertising Age*, November 10, 1997, S1; Bradley Johnson, "Netscape, Microsoft Continue Their Battle with Push Services," *Advertising Age*, November 10, 1997, S2.

systems. Generally, the economic system also needs to be advanced enough to feature a national market and a sufficient communication and distribution infrastructure through which power in the channel is pursued. It is just this sort of pursuit of power by manufacturers that is argued to have caused the widespread use of advertising in the United States.[2]

The Rise of Modern Mass Media.

Advertising is also tied to the rise of mass communication. With the invention of the telegraph in 1844, a communication revolution was set in motion. The telegraph not only allowed the young nation to benefit from the inherent efficiencies of rapid communication, but also did a great deal to engender a sense of national, or at least regional, community. People began to know and care about things going on thousands of miles away. Also, during this period, many new magazines designed for larger and less socially privileged audiences made magazines both a viable mass advertising medium and a democratizing influence on American society.[3] Through advertising in these mass-circulation magazines, national brands could be projected into national consciousness. National magazines made national advertising possible; national advertising made national brands possible. Without the rise of mass media, there would be no advertising.

It is critical to realize that for the most part, mass media in the United States is supported by advertising. Television networks, radio stations, newspapers, and magazines produce shows, articles, films, and programs, not for the ultimate goal of entertaining or informing, but to make a healthy profit from the sale of advertising. Media vehicles sell audiences.

Advertising in Practice.

So far, our discussion of the evolution of advertising has identified the fundamental social and economic influences that fostered its rise. Now we'll turn our focus to the evolution of advertising in practice. Several periods in this evolution can be identified to give us various perspectives on the process of advertising.

The Preindustrialization Era (pre–1800).

In the 17th century, printed advertisements appeared in newsbooks (the precursor to the newspaper).[4] The messages were informational in nature and appeared on the last pages of the tabloid. In America, the first newspaper advertisement is said to have appeared in 1704 in the *Boston News Letter*. Two notices were printed under the heading "Advertising" and offered rewards for the return of merchandise stolen from an apparel shop and a wharf.[5]

Advertising grew in popularity during the 18th century both in Britain and the American colonies. The *Pennsylvania Gazette* printed advertisements and was the first newspaper to separate ads with lines of white space.[6] As far as we know, it was also the first newspaper to use illustrations in advertisements. But advertising changed little over the next 70 years. While the early 1800s saw the advent of the penny newspaper, which resulted in widespread distribution of the news medium, advertisements in penny newspapers were dominated by simple announcements by skilled laborers. As one

2. Vincent P. Norris, "Advertising History—According to the Textbooks," *Journal of Advertising*, vol. 9, no. 3 (1980), 3–12.
3. Christopher P. Wilson, "The Rhetoric of Consumption: Mass-Market Magazines and the Demise of the Gentle Reader, 1880–1920," in *The Culture of Consumption: Critical Essays in American History, 1880–1980*, ed. Richard Wightman Fox and T. J. Jackson Lears (New York: Pantheon, 1983), 39–65.
4. Frank Presbrey, *The History and Development of Advertising* (Garden City, N.Y.: Doubleday, Doran & Company, 1929), 7.
5. Ibid., 11.
6. Ibid., 40.

historian notes, "Advertising was closer to the classified notices in newspapers than to product promotions in our media today."[7] Advertising was about to change dramatically, however.

The Era of Industrialization (1800 to 1875).

In practice, users of advertising in the mid- to late 1800s were trying to cultivate markets for growing production in the context of a dramatically increasing population. A middle class, spawned by the economic windfall of regular wages from factory jobs, was beginning to emerge. This newly developing populace with economic means was concentrated geographically in cities more than ever before.

By 1850, circulation of the **dailies,** as newspapers were then called, was estimated at 1 million copies per day. The first advertising agent—thought to be Volney Palmer, who opened shop in Philadelphia—basically worked for the newspapers by soliciting orders for advertising and collecting payment from advertisers.[8] This new opportunity to reach consumers was embraced readily by merchants, and at least one newspaper doubled its advertising volume from 1849 to 1850.[9]

With the expansion of newspaper circulation fostered by the railroads, a new era of opportunity emerged for the advertising process. Advertising was not universally hailed as an honorable practice, however. Without any formal regulation of advertising, the process was considered an embarrassment by many segments of society, including some parts of the business community. At one point, firms even risked their credit ratings if they used advertising—banks considered the practice a sign of financial weakness. This image wasn't helped much by advertising for patent medicines, which were the first products heavily advertised on a national scale. These advertisements promised a cure for everything from rheumatism and arthritis to "consumption" and respiratory affliction, as Exhibit 3.2 shows.

EXHIBIT 3.2

The expansion of newspaper circulation fostered more widespread use of advertising. Unfortunately, some of this new advertising did not contribute positively to the image of the practice. Ads like this one for a patent medicine carried outrageous claims, such as "Keep the blood pure."

The P. T. Barnum Era (1875 to 1918).

The only one who could ever reach me was the son of a preacher man.
—John Hurley and Ronnie Wilkins, "Son of a Preacher Man"; most notably performed by Dusty Springfield[10]

Shortly after the Civil War in the United States, modern advertising began. This is advertising that we would begin to recognize as advertising. While advertising existed during the era of industrialization, it wasn't until America was well on its way to being an urban, industrialized nation that advertising became a vital and integral part of the social landscape. From about 1875 to 1918, advertising ushered in what has come to be known as **consumer culture**, or a way of life centered on consumption. True, consumer culture was advancing prior to this period, but during this age it really took hold, and the rise of modern advertising had a lot to do with it. Advertising became a full-fledged industry in this period. It was the time of advertising legends: Albert

7. James P. Wood, *The Story of Advertising* (New York: Ronald Press, 1958), 45–46.
8. Daniel Pope, *The Making of Modern Advertising and Its Creators* (New York: William Morrow, 1984), 14.
9. Cited in Stephen Fox, *The Mirror Makers: A History of American Advertising and Its Creators* (New York: William Morrow and Company, 1984), 14.
10. Atlantic Recording Group.

Lasker, head of Lord and Thomas in Chicago, possibly the most influential agency of its day; Francis W. Ayer, founder of N. W. Ayer; John E. Powers, the most important copywriter of the period; Earnest Elmo Calkins, champion of advertising design; Claude Hopkins, influential in promoting ads as "dramatic salesmanship"; and John E. Kennedy, creator of "reason why" advertising.[11] These were the founders, the visionaries, and the artists who played principal roles in the establishment of the advertising business. One interesting sidebar is that several of the founders of this industry had fathers with the exact same occupation: minister. This very modern and controversial industry was founded in no small part by the sons of preachers. Interesting.

By 1900, total sales of patent medicines had reached $75 million—providing an early demonstration of the power of advertising.[12] This demonstration sent advertising in a new direction and set the stage for its modern form. During this period, the first advertising agencies were founded and the practice of branding products became the norm. Advertising was motivated by the need to sell the vastly increased supply of goods brought on by mass production and by the demands of an increasingly urban population seeking social identity through (among other things) branded products. In earlier times, when shoppers went to the general store and bought soap sliced from a large locally produced cake, advertising had little or no place. But with advertising's ability to create enormous differences between near-identical soaps, advertising suddenly held a very prominent place in early consumer culture. Advertising made unmarked commodities into social symbols and identity markers.

The advertising of this period was, until 1906, completely unregulated. In that year, Congress passed the **Pure Food and Drug Act**, which required manufacturers to list the active ingredients of their products on their labels. Still, its effect on advertising was minimal; advertisers could continue to say just about anything—and usually did. Many advertisements took on the style of a sales pitch for snake oil. The tone and spirit of advertising owed more to P. T. Barnum—"There's a sucker born every minute"—than to any other influence. The ads were bold, carnivalesque, garish, and often full of dense copy that hurled fairly incredible claims at prototype "modern" consumers. Ads from this era are shown in Exhibits 3.3 and 3.4.

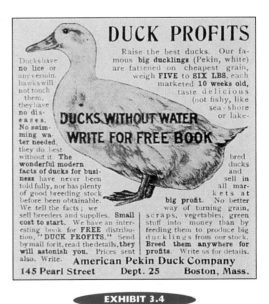

EXHIBIT 3.3

During the late 1800s and early 1900s, advertising began to make claims aimed at the "modern" consumer. Here, the 1900 Washer Company promises relief from all the drudgery of wash day.

EXHIBIT 3.4

Ads from the P. T. Barnum era were often densely packed with fantastic promises. This 1902 Saturday Evening Post advertisement featured many reasons why potential customers should get into the duck-raising business.

11. Fox, *The Mirror Makers,* op. cit.
12. Presbrey, *The History and Development of Advertising,* 16.

Several things are notable about these ads: lots of copy (words); the prominence of the product itself and the corresponding lack of surrounding social space, or context in which the product was to be used; small size; little color; few photographs; and plenty of hyperbole. Over this period there was variation, and some evolution, but this style was fairly consistent up until World War I.

Consider also the social context of these ads. It was a period of rapid urbanization, massive immigration, labor unrest, and significant concerns about the abuses of capitalism. Some of capitalism's excesses and abuses, in the form of deceptive and misleading advertising, were the targets of early reformers. It was also the age of suffrage, the progressive movement, motion pictures, and mass culture. The world changed rapidly in this period, and it was no doubt disruptive and unsettling to many—but advertising was there to offer solutions to the stresses of modern life, no matter how real, imagined, or suggested.

The 1920s (1918 to 1929). In many ways, the Roaring Twenties really began a couple of years early. After World War I, advertising found respectability, fame, and glamour. It was the most modern of all professions; it was, short of being a movie actor or actress, the most fashionable. According to popular perception, it was where the young, smart, and sophisticated worked and played. During the 1920s, it was also a place where institutional freedom rang. The prewar movement to reform and regulate advertising was completely dissipated by the distractions of the war and advertising's role in the war effort. During World War I, the advertising industry learned a valuable lesson: donating time and personnel to the common good is not only good civics but smart business.

The 1920s were prosperous times. Most Americans enjoyed a previously unequaled standard of living. It was an age of considerable hedonism; the pleasure principle was practiced and appreciated, openly and often. The Victorian Age was over, and a great social experiment in the joys of consumption was underway. Victorian sexual repression and modesty gave way to a more open sexuality and a love affair with modernity. Advertising was made for this burgeoning sensuality; advertising gave people permission to enjoy. Ads of the era exhorted consumers to have a good time and instructed them how to do it. Consumption was not only respectable, but expected. Being a consumer became synonymous with being a citizen.

During this post–World War I economic boom, advertising instructed consumers how to be thoroughly modern and how to avoid the pitfalls of this new age. It was during this era that consumers learned of halitosis from Listerine advertising and about body odor from Lifebuoy advertising (see Exhibit 3.5, a Lifebuoy ad from 1926). Not too surprisingly, there just happened to be a product with a cure for just about every social anxiety and personal failing one could imagine, many of which had supposedly been brought on as side effects of modernity. This was perfect for the growth and entrenchment of

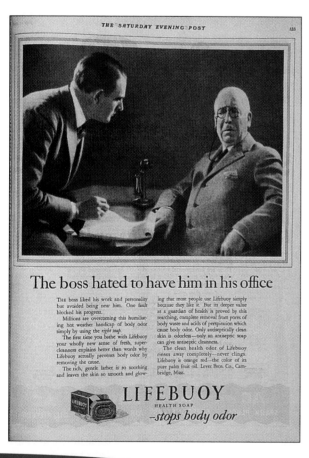

EXHIBIT 3.5

Many ads from the 1920s promised to relieve just about any social anxiety imaginable. Here, Lifebuoy offered a solution for people concerned that body odor could be standing in the way of career advancement.

advertising as an institution: Modern times bring on many wonderful new things, but the new way of life has side effects that, in turn, have to be fixed by even more modern goods and services. Thus, a seemingly endless chain was created: Needs lead to products, new needs are created by new products, newer products solve newer needs, and on and on. This chain of needs is essential to a capitalist economy, which must continue to expand in order to survive. It also makes a necessity of advertising.

Other ads from the 1920s emphasized other modernity themes, such as the division between public work space, the male domain of the office (see Exhibit 3.6), and the private, "feminine" space of the home (see Exhibit 3.7). Thus, two separate consumption domains were created, with women placed in charge of the latter, more economically important one. Advertisers soon figured out that women were responsible for as much as 80 percent of household purchases. While 1920s men were out in the "jungle" of the work world, women made most purchase decisions. So, from this time forward, advertising's primary target became women.

EXHIBIT 3.6

This 1920s-era Gulf advertisement focuses on technological progress and the male prerogative in promoting its advancement. With the wonders of technology now found in every living room, selling gasoline aims more at individual gratification than at social uplift: appeals to convenience, cost-consciousness, and environmental friendliness are all in evidence. www.gulfoil.com is Gulf's "friendly, neighborhood" presence in Cyberspace. Compare Gulf's site with those of other gasoline providers, like Mobil (www.mobil.com) and Amoco (www.amoco.com), that use their Web sites to talk about their sponsorship of autoracing and to help customers find their service stations.

EXHIBIT 3.7

Ads from the 1920s often emphasized modernity themes, like the division between public and private workspace. This Fels-Naptha ad shows the private, "feminine" space of the home.

Another very important aspect of 1920s advertising, and beyond, was the role that science and technology began to play. Science and technology were in many ways the new religions of the modern era. The modern way was the scientific way. So, one saw ads appealing to the popularity of science in virtually all product categories of advertising during this period. Ads even stressed the latest scientific offerings for child rearing and "domestic science," as Exhibits 3.8 and 3.9 demonstrate.

The style of 1920s ads was much more visual than in the past. Twenties ads showed slices of life, or carefully constructed "snapshots" of social life with the product. In these ads, the relative position, background, and dress of the people using or needing the advertised product was carefully crafted. These visual lessons were generally about how to fit in with the "smart" crowd, how to be urbane and modern by using the newest conveniences, and how not to fall victim to the perils and pressure of the new fast-paced modern world. The social context of product use became critical, as one can see in Exhibits 3.10 and 3.11.

Advertising during the 1920s chronicled the state of technology and styles for clothing, furniture, and social functions. Advertising specified social relationships between people and products by depicting the social settings and circumstances into which products fit. Some of the best illustrators, artists, and writers in the world worked on advertisements during this period, and some of the ads from this period are now being collected and sold as art. The 1922 Standard plumbing fixtures ad, shown in Exhibit 3.12, is an example of an ad now prized as a work of art. Also note the attention to the social setting into which plumbing fixtures were to fit. Is the ad really about plumbing?

In terms of pure art direction, the ads in Exhibits 3.13 through 3.15 are examples of the beauty of the period's look.

EXHIBITS 3.8 AND 3.9

The cultural theme of modernity in the 1920s emphasized science and technology. These ads for General Foods (Exhibit 3.8) and Pet Milk (Exhibit 3.9) tout the "domestic science" these brands brought to the home.

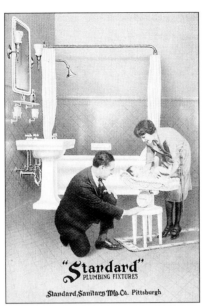

EXHIBITS 3.10 AND 3.11

As the Kodak (Exhibit 3.10) and Standard Sanitary (Exhibit 3.11) ads illustrate, ads from the 1920s often showed carefully constructed "snapshots" of social life with the products.

EXHIBIT 3.12

In an effort to make their advertising depict the technology and style of the era, advertisers in the 1920s enlisted the services of some of the best illustrators and artists of the time. So fine were the illustrations that many of them, like this Standard plumbing fixtures ad from 1922, are now prized by some as works of art.

EXHIBITS 3.13, 3.14, AND 3.15

These 1920s ads are more examples of the beautiful and stylish art direction of the period.

The very tough times of the Great Depression, depicted in this 1936 photo by Walker Evans, gave Americans reason to distrust big business and its tool, advertising.

The Depression (1929 to 1941).

By 1932 a quarter of American workers were unemployed. But matters were worse than this suggests, for three quarters of those who had jobs were working part-time—either working short hours, or faced with chronic and repeated layoffs. . . . Perhaps half the working population at one time or another knew what it was like to lose a job. Millions actually went hungry, not once but again and again. Millions knew what it was like to eat bread and water for supper, sometimes for days at a stretch. A million people were drifting around the country begging, among them thousands of children, including numbers of girls disguised as boys. People lived in shanty towns on the fields at edges of cities, their foods sometimes weeds plucked from the roadside.[13]

If you weren't there, you have no idea how bad it was. We don't, but our parents and grandparents did. It was brutal, crushing, and mean. It killed people; it broke lives. Those who lived through it and kept their dignity are to be deeply admired. It forever changed the way Americans thought about a great many things: their government, business, money, and, not coincidentally, advertising.

Just as sure as advertising was glamorous in the 1920s, it was villainous in the 1930s. It was part of big business, and big business, big greed, and big lust had gotten America into the great economic depression beginning in 1929—or so the story goes. The public now saw advertising as something bad, something that had seduced them into the excesses for which they were being punished.

Advertisers responded to this feeling by adopting a tough, no-nonsense advertising style. The stylish and highly aesthetic ads of the 1920s gave way to harsher and more cluttered ads. As one historian said, "The new hard-boiled advertising mystique

13. James Lincoln Collier, *The Rise of Selfishness in America* (New York: Oxford University Press, 1991), 162.

brought a proliferation of 'ugly,' attention-grabbing, picture-dominated copy in the style of the tabloid newspaper."[14] Clients wanted their money's worth, and agencies responded by cramming every bit of copy and image they could into their ads. This type of advertising persisted, quite likely making the relationship between the public and the institution of advertising even worse. The themes in advertisements traded on the anxieties of the day: losing one's job meant being a bad provider, spouse, or parent, unable to give the family what it needed (as seen in Exhibits 3.17 and 3.18). The cartoon-strip style also became very popular during this period. Exhibit 3.19 offers a typical 1930s-style ad.

Another notable event during these years was the emergence of radio as a significant advertising medium. During the 1930s, the number of radio stations rose to 814, and the number of radio sets in use more than quadrupled to 51 million. Radio was in its heyday as a news and entertainment medium, and it would remain so until the 1950s when television emerged. An important aspect of radio was its ability to create a new sense of community in which people thousands of miles apart listened to and became involved with their favorite radio soap opera, so termed in reference to the soap sponsors of these shows.

The J. Walter Thompson advertising agency was the dominant agency of the period. Stanley and Helen Resor and James Webb Young brought this agency to a leadership position through intelligent management, vision, and great advertising. Helen Resor was the first prominent woman advertising executive and was instrumental in J. Walter Thompson's success. Still, the most famous ad person of the era was a very interesting man named Bruce Barton. He was not only the leader of BBDO, but also a best-selling author, most notably of a 1924 book called *The Man Nobody Knows*.[15]

EXHIBITS 3.17 AND 3.18

The themes in advertising during the 1930s traded on the anxieties of the day, as these ads for Paris Garters (Exhibit 3.17) and the Association of American Soap and Glycerine Producers, Inc. (Exhibit 3.18) illustrate.

EXHIBIT 3.19

Another notable feature of 1930s advertising was the increasing use of the cartoon-strip style. The cartoon strip, like this one for Dr. West's toothpaste, could tell a fairly complex story of devastating social failure and then offer a wondrous solution with the advertiser's brand. This ad also shows how agencies were responding to advertisers' demands for copy-heavy ads.

14. Ibid., 303–304.
15. Bruce Barton, *The Man Nobody Knows* (New York: Bobbs-Merrill, 1924).

The book was about Jesus and portrayed him as the archetypal ad man. This blending of Christian and capitalist principles was enormously attractive to a people struggling to reconcile traditional religious thought, which preached against excess, and the new religion of consumption, which preached just the opposite.

Advertising, like the rest of the country, suffered dark days during this period. Agencies cut salaries and forced staff to work four-day weeks without being paid for the mandatory extra day off. Clients demanded frequent review of work, and agencies were compelled to provide more and more free services to keep accounts. Advertising would emerge from this depression, just as the economy itself did, during World War II. However, it would never again reach its predepression status. It became the subject of a well-organized and angry consumerism movement. Congress passed real reform in this period. In 1938 the Wheeler-Lea Amendments to the Federal Trade Commission Act deemed "deceptive acts of commerce" to be against the law; this was interpreted to include advertising. Between 1938 and 1940, the FTC issued 18 injunctions against advertisers, including "forcing Fleischmann's Yeast to stop claiming that it cured crooked teeth, bad skin, constipation and halitosis."[16] These agencies soon used these new powers against a few large national advertisers, including Fleischmann's Yeast (consumers were being advised to eat yeast cakes for better health and vitality) and Lifebuoy and Lux soaps.

EXHIBIT 3.20

Advertisers often used America's involvement in World War II as a way to link their products with patriotism. This link provided advertising with a much-needed image boost after the dark period of the late 1930s.
www.cocacola.com/

WWII and the Fifties (1941 to 1960).

Almost one-half of all women married while they were still teenagers. Two out of three white women in college dropped out before they graduated. In 1955, 41 percent of women "thought the ideal number of children was four."[17]

Many people mark the end of the depression with the start of America's involvement in World War II in December 1941. During the war, advertising often made direct reference to the war effort, as the ad in Exhibit 3.20 shows, linking the product with patriotism and helping to rehabilitate the tarnished image of advertising. During the war, advertisers sold war bonds and encouraged conservation. In addition, they encouraged women to join the workforce, as seen in the so-called Rosie the Riveter ads. The ad in Exhibit 3.21 for the Penn Railroad is a good example. During the war years, many women joined the workforce; of course, many left it after the war ended in 1945.

Following World War II, the economy continued to improve, and the consumption spree was on again. This time, however, public sentiment toward advertising was fundamentally different from what it had been in the 1920s. During the 1950s, when there was great concern about the rise of communism, the issue of "mind control" became an American paranoia, and many people suspected that advertising was involved. The country was filled with suspicion related to McCarthyism, the bomb,

16. Fox, *The Mirror Makers,* 168.
17. Brienes, W., *Young, White and Miserable.*

Meet **MRS.** Casey Jones

PENNSYLVANIA RAILROAD
Serving the Nation

EXHIBIT 3.21

During the war, advertisers encouraged women to join the workforce, as this ad for Penn Railroad illustrates.

repressed sexual thoughts, and aliens from outer space. Otherwise normal people were building bomb shelters in their backyards (see Exhibit 3.22) and wondering whether their neighbors were communists.

In this environment of fear, stories began circulating in the 1950s that advertising agencies were doing motivation research and using the psychological sell, which served only to fuel an underlying suspicion of advertising. It was also during this period that Americans began to fear they were being seduced by **subliminal advertising** (subconscious advertising) to buy all sorts of things they didn't really want or need. There had to be a reason that homes and garages were filling up with so much stuff; it must be all that powerful advertising—or so the story went. In fact, a best-selling 1957 book, *The Hidden Persuaders,* offered the answer: slick advertising worked on the subconscious.[18] Suspicions about slick advertising still persist. (See the IMC box on page 81.)

The most incredible story of the period involved a man named James Vicary. In 1957 he convinced the advertising world, and in fact the vast majority of the U.S. population, that he had successfully demonstrated a technique to get consumers to do exactly what advertisers wanted. He claimed to have placed subliminal messages in motion picture film, brought in audiences, and recorded the results. He claimed that the embedded messages of "Eat Popcorn" and

EXHIBIT 3.22

During the 1950s, with McCarthyism—and advertising—contributing to American paranoia, frightened people were building bomb shelters in their backyards.

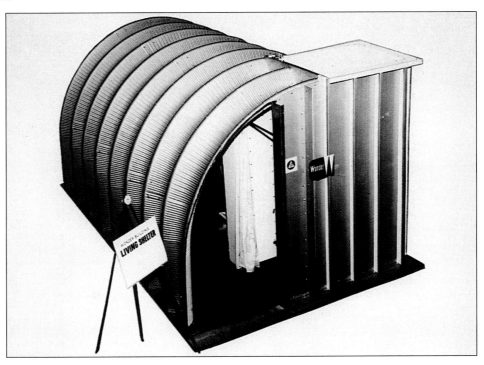

18. Vance Packard, *The Hidden Persuaders* (New York: D. McKay Co., 1957).

"Drink Coca-Cola" had increased sales of popcorn by 57.5 percent and Coca-Cola by 18.1 percent. He held press conferences and took retainer fees from advertising agencies. Later, he skipped town, just ahead of reporters who had figured out that none of this had ever happened. He completely disappeared, leaving no bank accounts and no forwarding address. He left town with about $4.5 million ($22.5 million in today's dollars) in advertising agency and client money.[19]

Wherever you are, Jim, you have to know that you pulled off the greatest scam in advertising history. The big problem is that a lot of people, including regulators and members of Congress, still believe in the hype you were selling and that advertisers can actually do such things. That's the real crime.

The 1950s were also about sex, youth culture, rock and roll, and television. In terms of sex, volumes could be written about the very odd and paradoxical fifties. On one hand, this was the time of neo-Freudian pop psychology and *Beach Blanket Bingo,* with sexual innuendo everywhere; at the same time, very conservative pronouncements about sexual mores were giving young Americans very contradictory messages. What's more, they would be advertised to with a singular focus and force never seen before, becoming, as a result, the first "kid" and then "teen" markets. Because of their sheer numbers, they would ultimately constitute an unstoppable youth culture—one that everyone else had to deal with and try to please—the baby boomers. They would, over their parents' objections, buy rock-and-roll records in numbers large enough to revolutionize the music industry. Now they buy golf clubs, cell phones, and mutual funds.

And then there was TV (Exhibit 3.23). Nothing like it had happened before. Its rise from pre–World War II science experiment to 90 percent penetration in U.S. house-

EXHIBIT 3.23

At first, advertisers didn't know what to do with television, the pre–World War II science experiment that reached 90 percent of U.S. households by 1960.

19. Stuart Rogers, "How a Publicity Blitz Created the Myth of Subliminal Advertising," *Public Relations Quarterly,* Winter 1992–1993, 12–17.

holds occurred during this period. At first, advertisers didn't know what to do with it, and did two- and three-minute commercials, typically demonstrations. Of course, they soon began to learn its look and language.

This era also saw growth in the U.S. economy and in household incomes. The suburbs emerged, and along with them there was an explosion of consumption. Technological change was relentless, and it fascinated the nation. The television, the telephone, and the automatic washer and dryer became common to the American lifestyle. Advertisements of this era were characterized by scenes of modern life, social promises, and a reliance on science and technology.

Into all of this, 1950s advertising projected a confused, often harsh, at other times sappy presence. It is rarely remembered as advertising's golden age. Two of the most significant advertising personalities of the period were Rosser Reeves of the Ted Bates agency, who is best remembered for his ultra-hard-sell style, and consultant Ernest Dichter, best remembered for his motivational research, which focused on the subconscious and symbolic elements of consumer desire. Exhibits 3.24 through 3.27 are representative of the advertising from this contradictory and jumbled period in American advertising.

These ads show what were becoming (or already were) mythic nuclear families, well behaved children, our "buddy" the atom, the last days of unquestioned faith in science, and rigid gender roles. In a few short years, the atom would no longer be our friend; we would question science; youth would rebel; and women and African-Americans would demand inclusion and fairness.

NOT SNAKE OIL—BUT STILL PRETTY SLICK (FOR THE MOST PART)

Marketers and advertisers long ago gave up the snake-oil—"it cures all"—claims of eras past. But modern technology enables advertisers to use multiple media to integrate their marketing communications in a way that is, well, pretty slick.

Let's say your grandmother suffers from arthritis and really needs to take medication to relieve her pain, but all the prescription arthritis pain medications upset her stomach. Magically, a coupon for $1.00 off Zantac antacid shows up in her mailbox. The reason? Glaxo Wellcome PLC, the makers of Zantac, know that various forms of prescription arthritis medication lead to nausea in a high percentage of cases. It just so happens that Granny is in a Glaxo Wellcome database of arthritis medication users and—voilà—the coupon gets sent out for Zantac.

Until recently, pharmaceutical marketers did not know, and could not know, who their prescription customers were. Doctors and pharmacists were sworn to keep the names of patients confidential. But recent changes in advertising regulations have relaxed restrictions. Now, about 300 new database marketing programs are available that track drug use. With this information, direct mail campaigns, magazine placement of ads, and even certain television media placements can be made with greater efficiency in reaching target customers.

Acquiring names and other vital information about target customers is not a matter of doctors and pharmacists violating confidentiality, though. In many cases, drug companies get the names of people who suffer from such sensitive conditions as depression and impotence from an unlikely source—the patients themselves. Many people give out their names and addresses when they call 800 numbers, subscribe to magazines, or fill out pharmacy questionnaires. For example, *Reader's Digest* sent a survey to 15 million of its subscribers asking them about their health problems. Over 3 million subscribers responded, and now *Reader's Digest* can target mailings to people with high cholesterol, to smokers, and to arthritis suffers. Many patients are outraged at the invasion of privacy, even though they gave out their names freely.

For the time being, firms such as Glaxo Wellcome are trying to understand the best way to use database information to the benefit of both the firm and the patient without violating the patient's sense of privacy and confidentiality.

Sources: William M. Bulkeley, "Prescriptions, Toll-Free Numbers Yield a Gold Mine for Marketers," *Wall Street Journal,* April 17, 1998, B1; Sally Beatty, "Reader's Digest Targets Patients by Their Ailments, *Wall Street Journal,* April 17, 1998, B1.

Advertising during the 1950s offered consumers contradictory messages. On one hand, technological change and economic progress created the widespread enthusiasm reflected in the Ford, IBM, and Atlas Tires ads in Exhibits 3.24, 3.25, and 3.27. On the other hand, consumer suspicions about slick advertising that worked on the subconscious led some advertisers to use hard-sell messages, like the one in the Serta ad shown in Exhibit 3.26 (lower left). www.ibm.com/ *and* www2.ford.com/

The new era of advertising in the 1960s was characterized by the creative revolution, during which the creative side of the advertising process rose to new prominence. The ads in Exhibits 3.28 and 3.29 reflect the advertising of the day—clean, minimalist, and sparse, with simple copy. These ads were developed by two advertising agencies closely associated with the creative revolution of the sixties: Leo Burnett in Chicago and Ogilvy & Mather in New York. www.kelloggs.com/

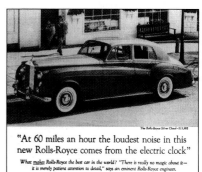

Through innovative advertising, Volkswagen has, over the years, been able to continually refuel its original message that its cars aren't expensive luxuries but as much a household staple as broccoli and ground round (and, at $1.02 a pound, cheaper than either!). Volkswagen's light, and fun, presence on the Web (www.vw.com/) is similar to that of Saturn (www.saturn.com), also being promoted as a company marching to the beat of a drummer different from that of its staid parent, General Motors (www.gm.com).

Peace, Love, and the Creative Revolution (1960 to 1972).

You say you want a revolution,
well, you know,
we all want to change the world.
—John Lennon and Paul McCartney, "Revolution"[20]

Advertising in the United States during the 1960s was slow to respond to the massive social revolution going on all around it. While the nation was struggling with civil rights, the Vietnam War, and the sexual revolution, advertising was often still portraying women and minorities in subservient roles. Based on the ads of the day, one would conclude that only white people bought and used products, and that women had few aspirations beyond service in the kitchen and the bedroom.

The only thing really revolutionary about 1960s advertising was the **creative revolution**. This revolution was characterized by the "creatives" (art directors and copywriters) having a bigger say in the management of their agencies. The emphasis in advertising turned "from ancillary services to the creative product; from science and research to art, inspiration, and intuition."[21] The look of advertising during this period was clean, minimalist, and sparse, with simple copy and a sense of self-effacing humor. The creative revolution, and the look it produced, is most often associated with three famous advertising agencies: Leo Burnett in Chicago; Ogilvy & Mather in New York; and Doyle Dane Bernbach in New York. They were led in this revolution by agency heads Leo Burnett, David Ogilvy, and Bill Bernbach. The Kellogg's Special K® cereal, Rolls-Royce, and Volkswagen ads pictured in Exhibits 3.28, 3.29, and 3.30 are 1960s ads prepared by these three famous agencies, respectively.

20. John Lennon and Paul McCartney, "Revolution," Northern Songs, 1968.
21. Fox, *The Mirror Makers*, 218.

EXHIBITS 3.31 AND 3.32

Not all the advertising in the 1960s was characterized by the spirit of the creative revolution. The ads in Exhibits 3.31 and 3.32 rely on more traditional styles and values. www.pepsiworld.com/ *and* www.goodyear.com/

Of course, it would be wrong to characterize the entire period as a creative revolution. Many ads in the 1960s still reflected traditional values and relied on relatively uncreative executions. Typical of many of the more traditional ads during the era are the Pepsi and Goodyear ads in Exhibits 3.31 and 3.32.

A final point that needs to be made about the era from 1960 to 1972 is that this was a period when advertising became generally aware of its own role in consumer culture—that is, advertising was an icon of a culture fascinated with consumption. While advertising played a role in encouraging consumption, it had become a symbol of consumption itself. While the creative revolution did not last long, advertising would always be different as a result. After the 1960s it would never again be quite as naive about its own place in society; it has since become much more self-conscious.

The 1970s (1973 to 1980).

Mr. Blutarski, fat, drunk, and stupid is no way to go through life.
—Dean Vernon Wormer (John Vernon) in *National Lampoon's Animal House,* 1978

Dean Wormer's admonition to John Belushi's character in *Animal House* captured essential aspects of the 1970s, a time of excess and self-induced numbness. This was the age of polyester, disco, and driving 55. The re-election of Richard Nixon in 1972 marked the real start of the 1970s. America had just suffered through its first lost war, four student protesters had been shot and killed by the National Guard at Kent State University in the spring of 1970, Mideast nations appeared to be dictating the energy policy of the United States, and we were, as President Jimmy Carter said late in this period, in a national malaise. In this environment, advertising again retreated into the tried-and-true but hackneyed styles of decades before. The creative revolution of the 1960s gave way to a slowing economy and a return to the hard sell. This period also

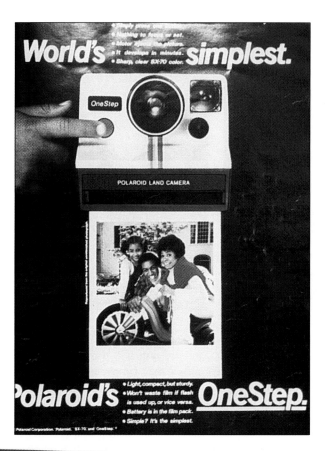

While a bad economy and a national malaise caused a retreat to the tried-and-true styles of decades before, a bright spot of 1970s advertising was the portrayal of people of color. This Polaroid ad is from 1978. www .polaroid.com/

marked the beginning of the second wave of the American feminist movement. In the 1970s, advertisers actually started to present women in "new" roles and to include people of color, as the 1978 Polaroid OneStep ad in Exhibit 3.33 shows.

The seventies was also the end of the sixties, and the end of whatever revolution one wished to speak of. This period became known as the era of self-help and selfishness. "Me" became the biggest word in the 1970s. What a great environment for advertising. All of society was telling people that it was not only OK to be selfish, but it was the right thing to do. Selfishness was said to be natural and good. A refrain similar to "Hey babe, I can't be good to you, if I'm not good to me," became a seventies mantra. Of course, being good to one's self often meant buying stuff.

Somewhat surprisingly, the seventies also resulted in added regulation and the protection of special audiences. Advertising encountered a new round of challenges on several fronts. First, there was growing concern over what effect $200 million a year in advertising had on children. A group of women in Boston formed **Action for Children's Television (ACT)**, which lobbied the government to limit the amount and content of advertising directed at children. Established regulatory bodies, in particular the **Federal Trade Commission (FTC)** and the industry's **National Advertising Review Board**, demanded higher standards of honesty and disclosure from the advertising industry. Several firms were subject to legislative mandates and fines because their advertising was judged to be misleading. Most notable among these firms were Warner-Lambert (for advertising that Listerine mouthwash could cure and prevent colds), Campbell's (for putting marbles in the bottom of a soup bowl to bolster its look), and Anacin (for advertising that its aspirin could help relieve tension). While advertising during this period featured more African-Americans and women, the effort to adequately represent and serve these consumers was minimal; advertising agency hiring and promotion practices with respect to minorities were formally challenged in the courts.

The most positive aspect of this period was not the result of efforts on the part of advertisers or their agencies, but rather the contribution of technology to the process of advertising. The 1970s signaled a period of growth in communications technology. Consumers began to surround themselves with devices related to communication. The development of the VCR, cable television, and the laserdisc player all occurred during the 1970s. Cable TV claimed 20 million subscribers by the end of the decade. Similarly, cable programming grew in quality, with viewing options such as ESPN, CNN, TBS, and Nickelodeon. As cable subscribers and their viewing options grew, advertisers learned how to reach more specific audiences through the diversity of programming on cable systems.

The process of advertising was being restricted by both consumer and formal regulatory challenges, yet technological advances posed unprecedented opportunities. It was the beginning of the merger mania that swept the industry throughout the end of the decade and into the next, a movement that saw most of the major agencies merge with one another and with non-U.S. agencies as well. This period in the evolution of advertising presented enormous challenges.

EXHIBITS 3.34 AND 3.35

One of the significant differences between advertising prepared in the 1960s and in the 1970s is that ads began focusing on the product itself, rather than on creative techniques. The Alpo ad in Exhibit 3.34 and the Spirit ad in Exhibit 3.35 represent this product-focused feature of 1970s advertising, which reflects the fact that management had taken control of agency activities during this era. www2.chryslercorp.com/

In all of this, the look of advertising was about as interesting as it was in the 1950s. Often, advertisements focused on the product itself, rather than on creative technique, as illustrated in the product-focused Alpo and Spirit ads in Exhibits 3.34 and 3.35. During this period, management took control and dominated agency activities. Alas, the MBA age was upon us. A very famous 1970s and 1980s CEO of a very large New York advertising agency, himself an ex-copywriter, was fond of saying that the worst thing that ever happened to advertising was the MBA. In agencies used to creative control, the idea of "bottom-liners" struck deep at the soul. Of course, all that money they made in the 1980s made them feel much better about the whole thing.

The Republican Era (1980 to 1992).

Greed is good.
—Gordon Gekko (Michael Douglas) in *Wall Street,* 1987.

"In 1980, the average American had twice as much real income as his parents had had at the end of WWII."[22] The political, social, business, and advertising landscape changed again around 1980 with the election of Ronald Reagan. The country made a sharp right, and conservative politics was the order of the day. There was, of course, some backlash and many countercurrents, but the conservatives were in the mainstream.

Many ads from the Republican era are particularly social-class and values conscious. They openly promote consumption, but in an understated and conservative way. The Royal Viking Line ad in Exhibit 3.36 is a good example of understated, class-conscious advertising. The quintessential 1980s ad may be the 1984 television ad for President Ronald Reagan's reelection campaign called "Morning in America." The storyboard for this ad is shown in Exhibit 3.37. This ad is soft in texture, but it gives an impression of firm reaffirmation of family and country. Other advertisers quickly followed with ads that looked similar to "Morning in America."

At the same time, several new, high-technology trends were emerging in the industry, which led to more-creative, bold, and provocative advertising. Television advertising of this period was influenced by the rapid-cut editing style of MTV, and some advertising near the end of the period played to at least someone's idea of Generation X, as the Pepsi ad in Exhibit 3.38 illustrates.

22. Collier, *The Rise of Selfishness in America,* 230.

Advertising from the Republican era openly promoted consumption, but in an understated way. This ad for the Royal Viking Line exemplifies this (sort of) subtle emphasis on consumption.

An ad that embodied the tone and style of 1980s advertising was Ronald Reagan's 1984 re-election campaign ad "Morning in America." The ad is soft in texture but firm in its affirmation of the conservative values of family and country.

This was also the age of the **infomercial**, a long advertisement that looks like a talk show or a half-hour product demonstration. If you watch late-night cable television, you've probably seen some guy lighting his car on fire as part of a demonstration for car wax. These very long ads initially aired in late-night television time slots, when audiences were small in number and airtime was relatively inexpensive. Infomercials have since spread to other off-peak time slots, including those with somewhat larger audiences, and they have gained respect along the way. The Psychic Friends Network, Soloflex, and Cher's hair-care line are all examples of products and services recently promoted on infomercials.

The Second Nineties (1993–present).

Modern advertising has entered its second century, and it's much more self-conscious than ever before. Winks and nods to the media-savvy audience are common. It is fast, and it is everywhere. It's being challenged by the World Wide Web and other new media, reshaped, and reinvented, but it's still advertising. (See Exhibits 3.39 and 3.40.)

In May 1994, Edwin L. Artzt, then chairman and CEO of Procter & Gamble, the $40-billion-a-year marketer of consumer packaged goods, dropped a bomb on the advertising industry. During an address to participants at the American Association of Advertising Agencies (4As) annual conference, he warned that agencies must confront a "new media" future that won't be driven by traditional advertising. While at that time P&G was spending about $1 billion a year on television advertising, Artzt told the 4As audience, "From where we stand today, we can't be sure that ad-supported TV programming will have a future in the world being created—a world of video-on-demand, pay-per-view, and subscription TV. These are designed to carry no advertising

EXHIBIT 3.38

While the success of the Republican era in using advertising to create political images led to many imitations, the Pepsi ad here marked a counter-current of rebellion that appealed to the younger markets. Is there evidence that this cultivated, youth-oriented image for Pepsi still drives the company's advertising? When you visit the Pepsi home page at www.pepsiworld.com/, *see if you can draw direct comparisons to the past campaign illustrated in this exhibit. Also compare this campaign to competitor Coca-Cola's at* www.cocacola.com/.

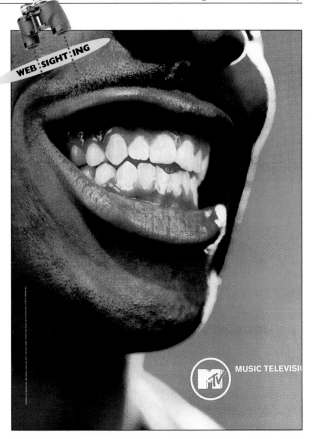

EXHIBIT 3.39

*While most MTV consumers likely don't routinely salivate, some no doubt do (and many more may wish they were having enough fun to do so). Contrast MTV On Line's (*www.mtv.com*) overt appeals to consumers who expect to be entertained as they seek information with the Academy of Ancient Music's more tranquil view of the appreciation of fine sound and discography (*www.aam.co.uk*).*

at all."[23] Then, just when the industry had almost recovered from Artzt's blast, William T. Esrey, chairman and CEO of Sprint, fired another volley almost exactly a year later at the same annual conference. Esrey's point was somewhat different but equally challenging to the industry. He said that clients are "going to hold ad agencies more closely accountable for results than ever before. That's not just because we're going to be more demanding in getting value for our advertising dollars. It's also because we know the technology is there to measure advertising impact more precisely than you have done in the past."[24] Esrey's point: Interactive media will allow direct measurement of ad exposure and impact, quickly revealing those that perform well, and those that do not.

Four years down the road, in August 1998, Procter & Gamble hosted an Internet "summit," due to "what is widely perceived as the poky pace of efforts to eliminate the difficulties confronted by marketers using on-line media to pitch products."[25] Some of these problems are technological in nature: incompatible technical standards, limited bandwidth, and not least, disappointing measurement of audience, exposure, and subsequent behavior. Advertisers such as P&G want to know what they are getting and what it costs when they place an Internet ad. Does anyone notice these ads, or do people click

23. This quote and information from this section can be found in Steve Yahn, "Advertising's Grave New World," *Advertising Age,* May 16, 1994, 53.
24. Kevin Godman, "Sprint Chief Lectures Agencies on Future," *Wall Street Journal,* April 28, 1995, B6.
25. Stuart Elliot, "The Media Business: Advertising; Procter and Gamble Calls Internet Marketing Executives to Cincinnati for a Summit Meeting." *New York Times,* Business and Financial Section, New York Times on the Web.

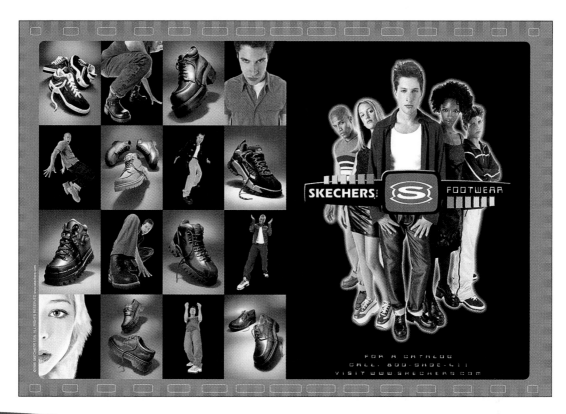

EXHIBIT 3.40

Advertising of the 1990s, represented in this Skechers Footwear ad, competes for the attentions of an increasingly media-savvy audience.

right past them? What would "exposure" in this environment mean? How do you use this medium to build brand relationships? At the end of this summit, P&G reaffirmed its commitment to the Internet.

Clearly, the future is hard to predict. While the pace of Internet advertising growth may be disappointing to P&G, it is impressive to others. It's still very early, and when a company such as P&G, which spends about $3 billion a year on advertising, is committed to something, one has to take it seriously. With 1998 online sales estimated at $6 billion,[26] it is clear that shopping and *buying* over the Internet is growing rapidly. However, the role of *advertising* itself in this medium is far from determined. We believe that, like in so many other similar situations, the initial tendency will be to rely on old forms until Internet advertising finds its own form; only then will it truly thrive.

Internet advertising has also brought the issues of audience measurement and definition into sharp focus. It has changed the way some consumers search for information, and it has become an entertainment medium for others. The problems that Procter & Gamble is dealing with may be as much a matter of how consumers behave as they are technological barriers. Chapter 17 deals with this topic in detail.

The Interactive Media Revolution. As you might imagine, the perspectives offered by the heads of Procter & Gamble and Sprint sent shock waves through the advertising industry. The technological changes that will occur during the last few years of the 20th century and the early years of the 21st century may create an era of great upheaval for advertising. Or, they may not.

At the crux of the turmoil is the new technology generally referred to as **interactive media**. With interactive media, consumers can call up games, entertainment,

26. Lorrie Grant, "On-line Shopping Soars," *USA Today,* December 15, 1998, 3B.

shopping opportunities, and educational programs on a subscription or pay-per-view basis. The belief is that consumers want the wide range of choices, the convenience, and the control such programming provides. To reach consumers through this new technology, big firms such as Procter & Gamble will most likely form joint ventures with major entertainment companies and participate in all phases of **integrated programming**. Using this approach, advertisers control the content of new media—such as CD-ROMs, interactive television, and online information services—to better control the destiny of their advertising.[27] The system would work something like this: A firm such as P&G finances media expenses; entertainment companies such as Sony provide production funding; cable TV operators such as Time Warner and TCI provide the airtime; and all parties promote the programming together and create a media event. In such a system, interactive technology can be used to actually engage consumers in commercials. For example, if a viewer wants to know what nail polish will match the lipstick she just saw in a commercial, she can interact with the programming and get an immediate answer. Thus, target audiences do not have to be broadly defined by age or geographic groups—individual households can be targeted through direct interaction with the audience member. Of course, there are those who believe that, at least in the case of television, consumers *do not* want to be interactive but passive. When they watch TV, they just want to watch TV and be left alone. The "audience" involvement of computers and the passivity of TV viewing may prove incompatible. We'll have to wait and see.

Reinventing the Advertising Process. The glaring omission in this new world of programming is traditional advertising as we know it today. This is a world where half-hour prime-time programming with 10 to 12 minutes of commercial interruption does not exist. How can advertising as a process survive in such a world? One answer lies in reinventing the process to fit the new ways of reaching audience members.

But we shouldn't jump to the conclusion that the very nature of advertising as a process will change. Advertising will still be a paid, mass-mediated attempt to persuade. As a business process, advertising will still be one of the primary marketing mix tools that contribute to revenues and profits by stimulating demand and nurturing brand loyalty. It is also safe to argue that consumers will still be highly involved in some product decisions and not so involved in others, so that some messages will be particularly relevant and others will be completely irrelevant to forming and maintaining attitudes about brands.

If advertising retains its character as both a business and a communication process, then how must the process be reinvented? The most dramatic change will be in the way advertising is prepared and delivered to the target audience. The likely scenario for the integrated, interactive advertisement of the future goes something like this: Prospective car buyers, from the comfort of their home, consider a variety of cars on their television screen. They change the model, position, color, and options on the vehicle with a click of a mouse. Then, having constructed one or more appealing versions of the desired vehicle, another click of the mouse sets an appointment for a test drive with a nearby dealer. The dealer brings the requested car to prospective buyers. If a buyer is ready to take action, the dealer representative can go online with a laptop computer to check inventory and leasing programs and then signal the dealership to prepare the necessary paperwork.[28]

Of course, like all predictions, this one is probably wrong, but not completely wrong. Several firms are experimenting with early hybrid versions of interactive advertising and promotion:

- Broadcast.com can now deliver 345 radio stations and networks, 17 television and cable stations, play-by-play sports, live music events, 360 full-length audio-books, and the like.

27. Scott Donaton and Pat Sloan, "Control New Media," *Advertising Age,* March 13, 1995, 1.
28. Jonathan Berry and Kathy Rebello, "What Is an Ad in the Interactive Future?" *Business Week,* May 2, 1994, 103.

- Shopper Vision, a Georgia home-grocery-shopping service, and Shoppers Express, a Maryland grocery-ordering and delivery service, are merging to form Shopper-VisionExpress and will develop interactive applications for television and online services.
- Intel has announced agreements with Prodigy, America Online, and others for test delivery of multimedia online services via cable.
- CUC International provides catalog-shopping services on CompuServe, and America Online is adding video to its text-based service.
- U.S. West is working with Nordstrom and J. C. Penney to develop interactive home-shopping services in the firm's new Interactive Video Services division.
- Turner Broadcasting System has introduced Turner Interactive, a line of interactive CD-ROMs.
- Procter & Gamble has agreed to participate in the Time Warner full-service network test in Orlando, Florida. This test is a prototype of cable interactive systems of the future.

The present era is certainly full of change and challenge for advertising, advertisers, and advertising agencies. But there is enormous opportunity as well, both in the United States and in foreign markets. One research study estimates that by the year 2003, the total dollar volume of interactive TV transactions will be $7.2 billion and that advertisers will have a clear role in bringing about consumer use of the technology.[29] Consumers will still need descriptive and persuasive information; how that information is developed and delivered will be the fascination of advertisers and their agencies for the coming years.

The Value of an Evolutionary Perspective.

To understand advertising in an evolutionary perspective is to appreciate the reasons for advertising's use in a modern industrialized society. Advertising was spawned by a market-driven system and grew through self-interest in capitalistic, free enterprise market economies. Efficient methods of production made advertising essential as a demand stimulation tool. Urbanization, transportation expansion, and communications advancements all facilitated the use and growth of advertising. The result is that advertising has become firmly entrenched as a business function, with deeply rooted economic and cultural foundations. This evolutionary perspective allows us to understand the more basic aspects of the role and impact of advertising. An interesting correlate to any discussion of the evolution of advertising is the evolution of marketing communications in emerging markets such as China. As the Global Issues box on page 92 shows, market fundamentals in China are very fundamental indeed.

Corporate leaders such as Artzt from Procter & Gamble and Esrey from Sprint have issued a challenge to traditional advertising methods and media. New technologies and the interactive media options they present are an important issue. But this should not be interpreted as the death of advertising, as some have argued.[30] In fact, paraphrasing Mark Twain, the death of advertising has been greatly exaggerated. Just when people were starting to describe advertising's sorrowful death at the hands of new media, we witnessed a surge in demand for traditional mass media space that set off a bidding war and the prospect of rationing time slots during the 1995–96 prime-time network television season![31] A record $10 billion in advance media time was purchased, and advertisers were scrambling for airtime. Now, in 1999, even though network television audiences appear to be shrinking, and virtually all broadcasters have

29. Scott Donaton, "Bates USA Survey Is Bullish on Interactive," *Advertising Age,* July 11, 1994, 26.
30. Roland Rust and Richard W. Oliver, "The Death of Advertising," *Journal of Advertising,* vol. 23, no. 4 (December 1994), 71–77.
31. Joe Mandese, "Sizzling TV Ad Sales May Spark Rationing," *Advertising Age,* May 15, 1995, 1.

purchased Internet services, they seem less worried about the survival of the medium or traditional advertising than they were a short time ago. The death of advertising at the hands of interactive media does, indeed, seem to have been greatly exaggerated. Echoing and extending the recent sentiments of one Wall Street analyst: we have to look back at failure after failure in the interactive media realm, and wonder if consumers really want to be that engaged, that much of the time. We'll see. Passivity has its fans. Just because we can be more interactive doesn't mean we will choose to be.

GLOBAL ISSUES

EAST MEETS WEST FOR PR LESSONS

Historically, public relations has been the sole province of Western economies committed to capitalism and free enterprise. Eastern cultures, especially those with control economies, had little use for the manipulative ways of public relations. Well, that's all changing now that several former control economies are adopting Western-like economic systems.

One such culture with an economy in transition is China. Just as communications structure and style have evolved in the United States over several decades, so too is the nature of communication evolving in China. Up to this point, public relations in China has been the equivalent of an exercise in government protocol. But, despite the non-Western nature of many public relations practices, public relations itself has been described as "as varied and sprawling as the largest and most populated country in the world." For example, the China Global Public Relations Company, which is part of the Xinhua News Agency, which in turn is owned and run by the state, employs nearly 100 PR practitioners. The main challenges for China Global are to try to represent a broad range of clients, many using different dialects, and to sort out the many and varied government regulations. China Global also has many impressive Western clients, including General Motors, Lockheed, Jaguar, Chrysler, and IBM.

Public relations in China is not restricted to Chinese firms, however. Large U.S. communications firms, such as Ogilvy & Mather, have offices in China. The director of Ogilvy & Mather feels that there is one big difference between the practice of public relations in the United States and in China: China is a market of fundamentals. Before an agency can get too creative or technical, the most rudimentary elements of client relations with constituents must be considered. At this point there is no reason for specialization in the PR task.

China has been a fascination of U.S. marketers and advertisers ever since it began to adopt Western marketing and advertising practices. Because of the sheer number of potential consumers, no U.S. firm is willing to ignore the Chinese market. But, as we have learned here, the process is one of focusing on the basics—a good lesson to learn for all forms of the communication process.

The 1990s have also brought changes to the concept of power in the distribution channel, which was discussed earlier as a fundamental influence on advertising. Power retailers—such as Wal-Mart, The Gap, Toys "R" Us, and Home Depot—are struggling to wrestle power away from manufacturers. The retailers' power in the channel is being exercised in two ways. First, mass merchandise discounters such as Wal-Mart and Home Depot are using **value pricing**—pricing that emphasizes quality and low price—to attract customers. Manufacturers must comply with the power of these retailers in the channel, and they are having a more difficult time getting consumers to demand their products when the retailer suddenly has a power base. Second, the emergence and popularity of retailers' **private label brands**—brands that carry the retailer name—have also affected manufacturers' use of advertising. Private label brands have emerged as formidable competition for national brands. The appeal of private labels is their lower price. Because of this, manufacturers have had to rely more on direct mail campaigns and sales promotions such as coupons and premiums to attract attention back to national brands.

Source: David Ritchey, "Mastering the Fundamentals: PR in China," *TACTICS*, September 1997, 16.

SUMMARY

Explain why advertising is a natural feature of capitalistic economic systems.

Although some might contend that the practice of advertising began thousands of years ago, it is more meaningful to connect advertising as we know it today with the emergence of capitalistic economic systems. In such systems, business organizations must compete for survival in a free market setting. In this setting, it is natural that a firm would embrace a tool that assists it in persuading potential customers to choose its products over those offered by others. Of course, advertising is such a tool. The explosion in production capacity that marked the Industrial Revolution gave demand stimulation tools added importance.

Describe manufacturers' dependence on advertising and branding in achieving balanced relationships with retailers.

Advertising and branding play a key role in the ongoing power struggle between manufacturers and their retailers. U.S. manufacturers began branding their products in the late 1800s. Advertising could thus be used to build awareness of and desire for the various offerings of a particular manufacturer. Retailers have power in the marketplace deriving from the fact that they are closer to the customer. When manufacturers can use advertising to build customer loyalty to their brands, they take part of that power back. Of course, in a capitalistic system, power and profitability go hand in hand.

Discuss 10 important eras in the evolution of advertising in the United States, and relate important changes in advertising practice to more fundamental changes in society and culture.

Social and economic trends, along with technological developments, are major determinants of the way advertising is practiced in any society. Before the Industrial Revolution, advertising's presence in the United States was barely noticeable. With an explosion in economic growth around the turn of the century, modern advertising was born: The P. T. Barnum era and the 1920s established advertising as a major force in the U.S. economic system. With the Great Depression and World War II, cynicism and paranoia regarding advertising began to grow. This concern led to refinements in practice and more careful regulation of advertising in the 1960s and 1970s. Consumption was once again in vogue during the Republican era of the 1980s. The new communication technologies that have emerged in the present era may effect significant changes in future practice.

Identify forces that may make the next decade a period of dramatic change for the advertising industry.

Integrated and *interactive* have become the advertising buzzwords of the nineties. These words represent notable developments that may reshape advertising practice. Integrated marketing communications may grow in importance as advertisers work with more-varied media options to reach markets that are becoming even more fragmented. A variety of advertisers are now experimenting with interactive media to learn how to make effective use of this new tool. Advertising in the next decade will continue to be a vibrant and challenging profession.

KEY TERMS

Industrial Revolution (67)
principle of limited liability (67)
branding (68)
dailies (70)
consumer culture (70)
Pure Food and Drug Act (71)
subliminal advertising (79)
creative revolution (83)

Action for Children's Television (ACT) (85)
Federal Trade Commission (FTC) (85)
National Advertising Review Board (85)
infomercial (87)
interactive media (89)
integrated programming (90)
value pricing (92)
private label brands (92)

QUESTIONS FOR REVIEW AND CRITICAL THINKING

1.   As formerly communist countries make the conversion to free market economies, advertising typically becomes more visible and important. Why would this be the case?

2.   Explain why there is a strong relationship between increasing urbanization and per capita spending.

3.   Why are manufacturers such as Nabisco and First Brands losing power in their channels of distribution? To whom, exactly, are they losing this power?

4.   Describe the various factors that produced an explosion of advertising activity in the P. T. Barnum era.

5.   The 1950s were marked by great suspicion about advertisers and their potential persuasive powers. Do you see any lingering effects of this era of paranoia in attitudes about advertising today?

6.   There were many important developments in the seventies that set the stage for advertising in the Reagan era. Which of these developments are likely to have the most enduring effects on advertising practice in the future?

7.   Ed Artzt, then chairman and CEO of Procter & Gamble, made a speech in May 1994 that rattled the cages of many advertising professionals. What did Artzt have to say that got people in the ad business so excited?

8.   Review the technological developments that have had the greatest impact on the advertising business. What new technologies are emerging that promise more profound changes for advertisers in the next decade?

EXPERIENTIAL EXERCISES

1.   As discussed in the chapter, one of the more popular forms of advertising today is the infomercial. Watch two infomercials. Describe the products advertised and what action the advertiser wants you to take. Do you think the infomercials are persuasive and believable? Why or why not? Call one of the two 800 numbers you saw advertised and ask a few pertinent questions about the product or request additional information. Describe the nature of your conversation and the outcome. Note: You *do not* have to buy anything to complete this exercise.

2.   Many contemporary magazines began publishing during the eras described in this chapter. Go to your library and find a copy of *Time* magazine (or any other general interest magazine) from the 1950s, '60s, '70s, '80s, and a current issue. Compare the ads in each decade to the other decades' ads. How are they different? Are there any similarities?

USING THE INTERNET

The Internet is an emerging communication medium that offers businesses fresh opportunities for satisfying customer needs. The following businesses each take advantage of the unique characteristics of the Internet to offer added value in competitive environments:

Southwest: www.iflyswa.com

FedEx: www.fedex.com

General Electric: www.ge.com

Holiday Inn: www.holiday-inn.com

Ticketmaster: www.ticketmaster.com

For each site, answer these questions:

1. What new service does the site offer to customers?

2. What is the value added by the Web site, as compared to traditional media?

3. How does the site strengthen the company's image? Increase profitability? Facilitate sales?

4. How does the site build stronger relationships between buyers and sellers?

K-Tel, like Ron Popeil's Ronco, is one of the legends of late-night television advertising, selling record albums "not available in any store," such as compilations of 1970s disco hits. K-Tel's stock had hovered on the NASDAQ exchange somewhere between $2 and $5 per share since the company's listing in 1993 . . . until early 1998 when K-Tel announced plans to debut on the Web, at which point the stock spiked to nearly $40 per share (and subsequently dropped, nearly as precipitously, to a far less feverish $6 or so). Visit the K-Tel Web site and check K-Tel's stock history on the Yahoo! stock quotes site:

www.ktel.com

quote.yahoo.com (stock symbol KTEL)

1. Why do you think Internet-related stocks are often so volatile?

2. How does K-Tel's brand image compare with that of a company such as CDNow, which has only had a "Cyber-space" presence as a comprehensive source for music CDs, and which doesn't (yet) make use of television advertising?

Andy Warhol
Three Coke Bottles, 1962
Synthetic polymer paint and silkscreen ink on canvas, 20 × 16 in.

CHAP TER 4

After reading and thinking about this chapter, you will be able to do the following:

- Assess the benefits and problems of advertising in a capitalistic society and debate a variety of issues concerning advertising's effects on society's well-being.

- Explain how ethical considerations affect the development of advertising campaigns.

- Discuss the role of government agencies in the regulation of advertising.

- Explain the meaning and importance of self-regulation for an advertising practitioner.

The social, ethical, and regulatory aspects of advertising are as dynamic and controversial as any of the strategic or creative elements of the process. What is socially responsible or irresponsible, ethically debatable, politically correct, or legal? The answers are constantly changing. As a society changes, so too do its perspectives. Like anything else with social roots and implications, advertising will be affected by these changes.

The social, ethical, and regulatory aspects of advertising provide some of its most memorable and defining moments. Consider these episodes in the history of advertising:

- In the late 1800s, patent medicine advertising dominated the media. Elixirs and medical devices promised cures for everything from paralysis to spinal irritation and malaria.
- Warner-Lambert began running advertising in 1921 that claimed Listerine mouthwash could prevent colds and sore throats. In 1975, the advertising was judged to be deceptive, and the firm was required to spend $10 million on "corrective advertising" to undo the misimpressions created by the claims.
- In 1990, an ad for Volvo automobiles showed a monster truck with oversized tires rolling over the roofs of a row of cars, crushing all of them except a Volvo. Volvo, which had developed a reputation for building safe and durable cars, had rigged the demonstration; the Volvo's roof had been reinforced, while the other cars' roof supports had been weakened.[1]
- In 1994, General Nutrition agreed to stop making unsubstantiated claims for more than 40 products, including Sleepers Diet, which the company claimed would help users lose weight while they slept. The company also agreed to pay a $2.4 million civil penalty.[2]
- In 1998, a coalition of organizations including the American Academy of Pediatrics and the American Public Health Association called on Anheuser-Busch to discontinue its popular advertising campaign featuring frogs, lizards, and other amphibians. Likening them to the infamous Joe Camel, critics claimed that these animated characters represented a purposeful effort to capture the interest and attention of children. Adding fuel to critics' concerns, a study by the ad agency Campbell Mithun Esty documented that more children ages 6 to 17 recognized the Budweiser lizards than recognized Barbie. Officials at Anheuser-Busch disputed the claim that their likable lizards were contributing to the problem of underage drinking.[3]

Advertising history includes all sorts of social, ethical, and legal lapses on the part of advertisers. However, advertising has also had its triumphs, moral as well as financial. Whether justified or not, criticisms of advertising can be naive and simplistic, often failing to consider the complex social and legal environment in which contemporary advertising operates. Sometimes they are right on.

The Social Aspects of Advertising. The social aspects of advertising are often volatile. For those who feel that advertising is intrusive and manipulative, it is usually the social aspects that provide the most fuel for heated debate.

We can consider the social aspects of advertising in several broad areas. On the positive side, we will consider advertising's effect on consumers' standard of living, its support of the mass media, and the role it plays in providing exposure to issues. Advertisers such as as Anheuser-Busch devote millions of dollars to promoting responsible drinking with advertisements like the one shown in Exhibit 4.1. As described in the IMC box on page 100, Anheuser-Busch has also launched a unique Web site at www.beeresponsible.com/ as part of an IMC campaign designed to combat drunk driving, underage drinking, and binge drinking. In addition, government organizations

1.   Steven W. Colford and Raymond Serafin, "Scali Pays for Volvo Ad: FTC," *Advertising Age,* August 26, 1991, 4.
2.   Jeanne Saddler, "General Nutrition to Pay FTC Penalty of $2.4 Million over False Advertising," *Wall Street Journal,* April 29, 1994, B10.
3.   Rekha Balu, "Anheuser-Busch Amphibian Ads Called Cold-Blooded by Doctors," *Wall Street Journal* April 10, 1998, B10.

EXHIBIT 4.1

This ad represents time and money spent by Anheuser-Busch to project a positive social message, yet the ad doesn't explicitly attempt to sell its products. Why is this choice important in a social-responsibility ad? www.budweiser.com/

EXHIBIT 4.2

Many types of organizations use advertising to get their message out. In this case the message is very serious. www.youthhiv.org/apait/

use advertising for many purposes, including the education of consumers about social programs, as illustrated in Exhibit 4.2.

On the negative side, we will examine a variety of social criticisms of advertising, ranging from the charge that advertising wastes resources and promotes materialism to the argument that advertising perpetuates stereotypes.

Our approach will be to offer pros and cons on several issues that critics and advertisers commonly argue about. Be forewarned—these are matters of opinion, with no clear right and wrong answers. You will have to draw your own conclusions.

Advertising Educates Consumers. Does advertising provide valuable information to consumers, or does it seek only to confuse or entice them? Here's what the experts on both sides have to say.

Pro: Advertising Informs. Supporters of advertising argue that advertising educates consumers, equipping them with the information they need to make informed purchase decisions. By regularly assessing information and advertising claims, consumers become more educated regarding the features, benefits, functions, and value of products. Further, consumers can become more aware of their own tendencies toward being persuaded and relying on certain types of product information. The argument has been offered that advertising is "clearly an immensely powerful instrument for the elimination of ignorance."[4] According to this argument, better-educated consumers enhance their lifestyles and economic power through astute marketplace decision making.

4.   George J. Stigler, "The Economics of Information," *Journal of Political Economy* (June 1961), 213–220.

A related argument is that advertising *reduces search time*—that is, the amount of time an individual must spend to search for desired products and services is reduced because of advertising. The large amount of readily available information allows consumers to easily assess the potential value of a particular product or service in the marketplace, without spending time and effort to evaluate the product in a retail setting. The information contained in an advertisement "reduces drastically the cost of search."[5]

TACKLING ALCOHOL ABUSE THROUGH INTEGRATED MARKETING COMMUNICATIONS

Why would the world's largest brewer and beer distributor also be a worldwide leader in the fight against alcohol abuse? Since 1982, when Anheuser-Busch launched its "Know When to Say When" ad campaign, it has spent over $200 million on advertising to promote responsible drinking among adults who choose to drink. In November of 1997 Anheuser-Busch celebrated the 15-year anniversary of its campaign by launching the Web site www.beeresponsible.com/ to continue the fight against alcohol abuse "one person at a time." Over this time period, distributors of Anheuser-Busch's brands, such as Budweiser and Bud Light, have also made substantial contributions to the campaign. In 1996 alone, Anheuser-Busch's distributors placed more than 26,000 advertisements in local newspapers, on billboards, and on radio and television, reminding consumers to drink responsibly. Distributors also worked at the grassroots level to train 18,000 bartenders, waiters, and waitresses on responsible serving techniques to help discourage drunk driving, and they provided nearly 25,000 free cab rides to bar and restaurant patrons. All this effort has produced some positive results. For example, the number of high school seniors who reported having five or more drinks in a row dropped 23 percent from 1982 to 1997, and according to the U.S. Department of Transportation, the number of people killed in teenage drunk-driving crashes declined from 3,597 in 1982 to 1,309 in 1996. While there is much more work to do in controlling alcohol abuse, the IMC campaign orchestrated by Anheuser-Busch appears to be having a desirable effect. As to the motives behind this effort, we choose to believe that the company just wants to do the right thing.

Source: www.beeresponsible.com/. Accessed July 2, 1998.

Con: Advertising Is Superficial.
Critics argue that advertising does not provide good product information at all. The basic criticism of advertising here is that it frequently carries little, if any, actual product information. What it does carry is said to be hollow ad-speak. Ads are rhetorical; there is no pure "information." All information in an ad is biased, limited, and inherently deceptive.

Critics claim that ads should contain information on functional features and performance results. Advertisers argue in response that, in many instances, consumers are interested in more than a physical, tangible material good with performance features and purely functional value. The functional features of a product may be secondary in importance to consumers in both the information search and the choice process. Advertising's critics often dismiss or ignore the totality of product benefits, including the hedonic (pleasure-seeking) aspects. The relevant information for the buyer relates to the criteria being used to judge the satisfaction potential of the product, and that satisfaction is quite often nonutilitarian. On the other hand, advertising apologists don't really understand how limited this "information" is. As evidence, they note how often the truth about products only comes about due to regulatory or legal action on this point. In truth, advertisers don't have the best record.

Advertising Improves the Standard of Living. Whether advertising raises or lowers the general standard of living is hotly debated. Opinions vary widely on this issue and go right to the heart of whether advertising is a good use or a waste of energy and resources.

5. Ibid., 220.

Pro: Advertising Lowers the Cost of Products. First, supporters argue that due to the economies of scale produced by advertising, consumers actually realize less-expensive products. As broad-based demand stimulation results in lower production and administrative costs per unit, lower prices are passed on to consumers. Second, a greater variety of choice in products and services stems from the increased probability of success firms realize from being able to introduce new products with the assistance of advertising. Third, the pressures of competition and the desire to have fresh, marketable products stimulate firms to produce improved products. Fourth, the speed and reach of the advertising process aids in the diffusion of innovations. This means that new discoveries can be communicated to a large percentage of the marketplace very quickly. Innovations succeed when advertising communicates their benefits to the customer.

All four of these factors can contribute positively to the standard of living and quality of life in a society. Advertising may be instrumental in bringing about these effects because it serves an important role in demand stimulation and keeping customers informed.

Con: Advertising Wastes Resources and Only Raises the Standard of Living for Some. One of the traditional criticisms of advertising is that it represents an inefficient, wasteful process that channels monetary and human resources in a society to the "shuffling of existing total demand," rather than to the expansion of total demand.[6] Advertising thus brings about economic stagnation and a lower standard of living. Critics say that a society is no better off with advertising because it does not stimulate demand—it only shifts demand from one brand to another. Similarly, critics argue that brand differences are trivial and the proliferation of brands does not offer a greater variety of choice, but rather a meaningless waste of resources, with confusion and frustration for the consumer.

Further, they argue that advertising is a tool of capitalism that just helps make the gap between rich and poor widen.

Advertising Affects Happiness and General Well-Being.
Critics and supporters of advertising differ significantly in their views about how advertising affects consumers' happiness and general well-being. As you will see, this is a complex issue with multiple pros and cons.

Con: Advertising Creates Needs. A common cry among critics is that advertising creates needs and makes people buy things they don't really need or even want. The argument is that consumers are relatively easy to seduce into wanting the next shiny bauble offered by marketers. For example, a quick examination of any issue of the magazine *Seventeen* reveals a medium intent on teaching the young women of the world to covet slim bodies and a glamorous complexion. Cosmetics giant Estée Lauder Cos. spends nearly 30 cents from every dollar of sales to promote its brands as the ultimate solution for those in search of the ideal complexion.[7]

Pro: Advertising Addresses a Variety of Needs. A good place to start in discussing whether advertising can create needs is to consider the nature of needs. Abraham Maslow, a pioneer in the study of human motivation, conceived that human behavior progresses through the following hierarchy of need states:

- *Physiological needs.* Biological needs that require the satisfaction of hunger, thirst, and basic bodily functions.
- *Safety needs.* The need to provide shelter and protection for the body and to maintain a comfortable existence.

6.   Richard Caves, *American Industry: Structure, Conduct, Performance* (Englewood Cliffs, N.J.: Prentice-Hall, 1964), 102.
7.   Nina Munk, "Why Women Find Lauder Mesmerizing," *Fortune,* May 25, 1998, 96–106.

- *Love and belonging needs.* The need for affiliation and affection. A person will strive for both the giving and receiving of love.
- *Esteem needs.* The need for recognition, status, and prestige. In addition to the respect of others, there is a need and desire for self-respect.
- *Self-actualization needs.* This is the highest of all the need states and is achieved by only a small percentage of people, according to Maslow. The individual strives for maximum fulfillment of individual capabilities.

It must be clearly understood that Maslow was describing basic human needs and motivations, not consumer needs and motivations. But, in the context of an affluent society, individuals will turn to goods and services to satisfy needs. Many products are said to directly address the requirements of one or more of these need states. Food and health care products, for example, such as those in Exhibits 4.3 and 4.4, relate to physiological needs. Home security systems and smoke detectors help address safety needs. Many personal care products, such as the skin care system shown in Exhibit 4.5, promote feelings of self-esteem, confidence, glamour, and romance.

In the pursuit of esteem, many consumers buy products they perceive to have status and prestige; expensive jewelry, clothing, automobiles, and homes are examples. Though it may be difficult to buy self-actualization, educational pursuits and high-intensity leisure activities can certainly foster the feelings of pride and accomplishment that contribute to self-actualization. Supporters maintain that advertising may be directed at many different forms of need fulfillment, but it is of little use in creating new needs.

EXHIBIT 4.3

Consumers always want products that taste good. Many advertisements appeal to this basic desire.

EXHIBIT 4.4

Many Johnson & Johnson products attempt to satisfy physiological needs. Does this ad provide motivation, need satisfaction, or both? www.jnj.com/.

EXHIBIT 4.5

"All you need is Guinot." In what sense might a person need Guinot?
www.lotions.com/guinot.html

Con: Advertising Promotes Materialism. It is also claimed that individuals' wants and aspirations may be distorted by advertising. The long-standing argument is that in societies characterized by heavy advertising, there is a tendency for conformity and status-seeking behavior, both of which are considered materialistic and superficial.[8] Material goods are placed ahead of spiritual and intellectual pursuits. Advertising, which portrays products as symbols of status, success, and happiness, contributes to the materialism and superficiality in a society. It creates wants and aspirations that are artificial and self-centered. This results in an overemphasis on the production of private goods, to the detriment of public goods (such as highways, parks, schools, and infrastructure).[9]

It is also thought by some that long-term exposure to advertising will destroy your soul and blind you to what really matters in life.

Pro: Advertising Reflects Society's Priorities. Although advertising is undeniably in the business of promoting the good life, defenders of advertising argue that it did not create the American emphasis on materialism. For example, in the United States, major holidays such as Christmas (gifts), Thanksgiving (food), and Easter (candy and clothing) have become festivals of consumption. This is the American way. Stephen Fox concludes his treatise on the history of American advertising as follows:

One may build a compelling case that American culture is—beyond redemption—money-mad, hedonistic, superficial, rushing heedlessly down a railroad track called Progress. Tocqueville and other observers of the young republic described America in these terms in the early 1800s, decades before the development of national advertising. To blame advertising now for these most basic tendencies in American history is to miss the point. . . . The people who have created modern advertising are not hidden persuaders pushing our buttons in the service of some malevolent purpose. They are just producing an especially visible manifestation, good and bad, of the American way of life.[10]

While we clearly live in the age of consumption, goods and possessions have been used by all cultures to mark special events, to play significant roles in rituals, and to serve as vessels of special meaning, long before there was modern advertising. Still, have we taken it too far? Is excess what we do best in consumer cultures?

Advertising: Demeaning and Deceitful, or Liberating and Artful? Without a doubt, advertisers are always on the lookout for creative and novel ways to grab and hold the attention of their audience. Additionally, many times an advertiser has a particular profile of the target customer in mind when an ad is being created. Both of these fundamental propositions about how ads get developed can spark controversy.

8.   Vance Packard, *The Status Seekers* (New York: David McKay, 1959).
9.   See, for example, George Katona, *The Mass Consumption Society* (New York: McGraw-Hill, 1964), 54–61; and John Kenneth Galbraith, *The Affluent Society* (Boston: Houghton Mifflin, 1958).
10. Stephen Fox, *The Mirror Makers: A History of American Advertising and Its Creators* (New York: William Morrow, 1984), 330.

EXHIBIT 4.6

What is the advertiser claiming in this ad? How about—a Versace gown is the ultimate in chic. viabazaar.com/versace/versace-home.html

Con: Advertising Perpetuates Stereotypes.

Advertisers often portray their target customer in advertisements, with the hope that individuals will relate to the ad and attend to its message. Critics charge that this practice yields a very negative effect—it perpetuates stereotypes. The portrayal of women, the elderly, and ethnic minorities is of particular concern. It is argued that women are still predominantly cast as homemakers, or as objects of desire (see Exhibit 4.6), despite the fact that women now hold top management positions and deftly head households. The elderly are often shown as helpless or ill, even though many active seniors enjoy a rich lifestyle. Critics contend that advertisers' propensity to feature African-American or Latin athletes in ads is simply a more contemporary form of stereotyping.

Pro: Advertisers Are Showing Much More Sensitivity.

Much of this sort of stereotyping is becoming part of the past. Advertisements from prior generations do show a vivid stereotyping problem. The ad in Exhibit 4.7 illustrates the gender stereotype that a good woman is one who can keep her man happy with her cooking abilities. Today, FedEx's advertising features an African-American woman prevailing over a group of white male executives in an important business deal. Advertisers are realizing that a diverse world requires diversity in the social reality that ads represent and help construct. However, many remain dissatisfied with the pace of change; the Body Shop ad in Exhibit 4.8, promoting something other than the body of a supermodel as a valid point of reference for women, is still the exception, not the rule.

Con: Advertising Is Often Offensive.

A pervasive and long-standing criticism of advertising is that it is often offensive and the appeals are typically in poor taste. Moreover, some would say that the trend in American advertising is to be rude, crude, and sometimes lewd, as advertisers struggle to grab the attention of consumers who have learned to tune out the avalanche of advertising messages they are confronted with each day.[11] Of course, taste is just that, a personal and inherently subjective evaluation. What is offensive to one person is merely satiric to another. What should we call an ad prepared for the International Advertising Festival in Cannes, designed to show the durability of Kadu surfer shorts? The ad showed Kadu shorts emerging from the stomach of a gutted shark.[12] (By the way, the agency that conceived this ad is now defunct.) A television ad depicting Adolf Hitler as a reformed spokesperson for a brand of potato chips, complete with the Nazi swastika morphing into the brand's logo, caused a predictable outcry in Thailand. Leo Burnett, the agency that prepared this ad for the Thai market, quickly withdrew it after protests from the Israeli embassy in Bangkok, and maintained the ad "was never intended to cause ill feelings."[13]

But not all advertising deemed offensive has to be as extreme as these examples. Many times, advertisers get caught in a firestorm of controversy because certain, and

11. Stuart Elliott, "A New Pitch for U.S. Ads: Lewd, Crude and Rude," *Herald International Tribune,* June 20, 1998, 1, 4.
12. "Objection, Your Honor," *The Advertising Age,* December 19, 1994, 19.
13. Pichayaporn Utumporn, "Ad with Hitler Causes a Furor in Thailand," *Wall Street Journal,* June 5, 1998, B8.

WEB SIGHTING

EXHIBIT 4.7

Advertisers today realize the diverse reality of consumers' lives. This Dove ad is a beautiful example of advertisers' efforts to represent that diversity. www.dovespa.com/

One day you realize that being soft is actually a sign of strength.

Dove® moisturizes your skin better than any soap in the world. Its unique one-quarter moisturizing lotion actually absorbs into your skin to help restore your natural softness. No wonder women everywhere have trusted Dove for over forty years to bring out their beautiful best. **Dove**

For the beauty that's already there.
www.DoveSpa.com

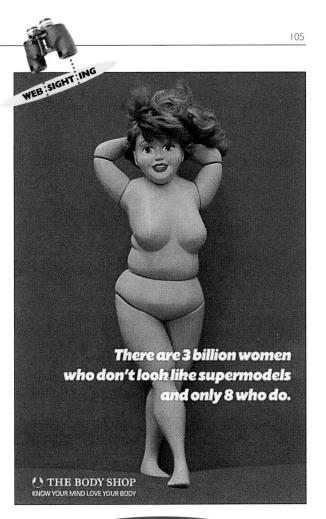

There are 3 billion women who don't look like supermodels and only 8 who do.

THE BODY SHOP
KNOW YOUR MIND LOVE YOUR BODY

EXHIBIT 4.8

The Body Shop (www.bodyshop.com/) is bucking trends by protesting the "super model" imagery often used in product advertising. While men's magazine sites, like Playboy *(www.playboy.com), triumphantly display airbrushed perfection and countless companies adorn everything from automobiles to breakfast cereal with the svelte and the athletic, the Web is (currently) a rather low-fidelity medium for transmitting glossy photographs. Sex may sell, but simple, bold, and clever graphics may be as useful for "eye candy" as anything ever exhibited by Versace Couture.*

sometimes relatively small, segments of the population are offended. The AIDS prevention campaign run by the Centers for Disease Control (CDC) has been criticized for being too explicit. A spokesperson for the Family Research Council said about the ads, "They're very offensive—I thought I was watching *NYPD Blue.*" A highly popular ad seen as controversial by some was the "People Taking Diet Coke Break" ad. In this television spot, a group of female office workers is shown eyeing a construction worker as he takes off his T-shirt and enjoys a Diet Coke. Coca-Cola was criticized for using reverse sexism in this ad.[14] While Coca-Cola and the CDC may have ventured into delicate areas, consider these advertisers, who were caught completely by surprise in finding that their ads were deemed offensive:

- In a public service spot developed by Aetna Life & Casualty insurance for measles vaccine, a wicked witch with green skin and a wart resulted in a challenge to the firm's ad from a witches' rights group.
- A Nynex spot was criticized by animal-rights activists because it showed a rabbit colored with blue dye.

14. Kevin Goldman, "From Witches to Anorexics, Critical Eyes Scrutinize Ads for Political Correctness," *Wall Street Journal,* May 19, 1994, B1, B10.

EXHIBIT 4.9

Oddly, frank talk about real-life issues is not all that common in advertising. Do you know anyone who would be put off by such frankness?
www.tampax.com/

- A commercial for Black Flag bug spray had to be altered after a war veterans' group objected to the playing of taps over dead bugs.

It should be emphasized that most consumers probably did not find these ads particularly offensive.[15] Perhaps it is the spirit of political correctness that causes such scrutiny, or maybe it is that consumers are so overwhelmed with ads that they have simply lost their tolerance. Or maybe some people just have too much time on their hands. And sometimes they correctly point to insensitivity on the part of advertisers. Whatever the explanation, marketers today are well advised to take care in broadly considering the tastefulness of their ads. Expect the unexpected. An unpretentious ad like that in Exhibit 4.9, featuring frank copy about mundane aspects of menstruation, could be expected to breach some consumers' sensibilities. However, the marketer in this case is willing to take the risk in the hopes that the frank approach will ring true with the target customer.

Pro: Advertising Is a Source of Fulfillment and Liberation. On the other end of the spectrum, some argue that the consumption that advertising glorifies is actually quite good for members of society. Most people sincerely appreciate modern conveniences that liberate us from the more foul facets of the natural, such as body odor, close contact with dirty diapers, and washing clothes by hand. Furthermore, this view holds that consumption is more likely to set one free than the slavish worship of an unpleasant, uncomfortable, and likely odoriferous, but natural, condition. Some observers remind us that when the Berlin Wall came down, those in the East did not immediately run to libraries and churches—they ran to department stores and shops. Before the modern consumer age, the consumption of many goods was restricted by social class. Modern advertising has helped bring us a democracy of goods. These observers argue that there is a liberating quality to advertising and consumption that should be appreciated and encouraged. Of course, liberation is viewed differently depending on where you stand.

Con: Advertisers Deceive via Subliminal Stimulation. There is much controversy, and almost a complete lack of understanding, regarding the issue of subliminal (below the threshold of consciousness) communication and advertising. Since there is much confusion surrounding the issue of subliminal advertising, perhaps this is the most appropriate point to provide some clarification: No one ever sold anything by putting images of breasts in ice cubes or the word *sex* in the background of an ad. Furthermore, no one at an advertising agency, except the very bored or the very eager to retire, has time to sit around dreaming up such things. We realize it makes for a great story, but hiding pictures in other pictures doesn't work to get anyone to buy anything. Although it is true that there is some evidence for some types of unconscious ad processing, these are effects generally related to repetition and ease of recall from memory, not the Svengali-

15. Ibid.

EXHIBIT 4.10

Artist Andy Warhol demonstrated that the most accessible art was advertising.

type hocus-pocus that has become advertising mythology. If the rumors are true that advertisers are actually using subliminal messages in their ads (and they aren't), the conclusion should be that they're wasting their money.[16]

Pro: Advertising Is Art. Finally, there are those who argue that one of the best aspects of advertising is its artistic nature. The pop art movement of the late 1950s and 1960s, particularly in London and New York, was characterized by a fascination with commercial culture. Some of this art critiqued consumer culture and simultaneously celebrated it. Above all, Andy Warhol (see Exhibit 4.10), himself a commercial illustrator, demonstrated that art was for the people and that the most accessible art was advertising. Art was not restricted to museum walls; it was on Campbell's soup cans, Lifesaver rolls, and Brillo pads. Advertising is anti-elitist, democratic art. As Warhol said about America, democracy, and Coke,

What's great about this country is that America started the tradition where the richest consumers buy essentially the same things as the poorest. You can be watching TV and see Coca-Cola, and you can know that the President drinks Coke, Liz Taylor drinks Coke, and just think, you can drink Coke, too. A Coke is a Coke and no amount of money can get you a better Coke than the one the bum on the corner is drinking. All the Cokes are the same and all the Cokes are good. Liz Taylor knows it, the President knows it, the bum knows it, and you know it.[17]

Advertising Has a Powerful Effect on the Mass Media.
One final issue that advertisers and their critics debate is the matter of advertising's influence on the mass media. Here again, we find a very wide range of viewpoints.

Pro: Advertising Fosters a Diverse and Affordable Mass Media.
Advertising fans argue that advertising is the best thing that ever happened to an informed democracy. Magazines, newspapers, and television and radio stations are supported by advertising expenditures. In 1997, advertising expenditures in the United States reached nearly $188 billion, with worldwide advertising expenditures estimated to be around $450 billion.[18] Much of this spending went to support television, radio, magazines, and newspapers. With this sort of monetary support of the media, citizens have access to a variety of information and entertainment sources at low cost. Network television and radio broadcasts would not be free commodities, and newspapers would likely cost two to four times more, in the absence of advertising support. Further, the demands of various segments of the population for specialized television and radio programming or special-interest magazines could not be economically served without the support of advertisers.

16. Timothy E. Moore, "Subliminal Advertising: What You See Is What You Get," *Journal of Marketing,* vol. 46 (Spring 1982), 38–47.
17. Andy Warhol, *The Philosophy of Andy Warhol: From A to B and Back Again* (New York: Harcourt Brace Jovanovich, 1975), 101.
18. *Advertising Age,* September 28, 1998, S50.

Jim Morrison 1943-1971   Janis Joplin 1943-1970

In advertising, they say one of the surest ways to get your message across is to put celebrities in your ad.

John Belushi 1949-1982   River Phoenix 1970-1993

Partnership for a Drug-Free America®

EXHIBIT 4.11

This ad both appeals to our fascination with celebrity and shocks the viewer with the realization that drug use can be fatal. At www .drugfreeamerica.org/, the Partnership for a Drug-free America hones its message that drug use is anything but glamorous. The Internet is rife with both authorized and (far more likely) unauthorized images of celebrities. This uncontrolled use of celebrity pics may dilute a message more compelling on TV or in magazines. Visit www.geocities.com/ Hollywood/Studio/2487/, a Web site dedicated to dead comedians, including John Belushi.

Others argue that advertising provides invaluable exposure to issues. When noncommercial users of advertising rely on the advertising process, members of society receive information on important social and political issues. Political candidates and proponents of political causes (for example, tax reform or environmental regulation) use advertising to inform voters. Similarly, various philanthropic organizations, such as the United Way and Special Olympics, use advertising to inform people of organization activities and to generate donations. At the local level, community fund-raisers for various artistic or community service organizations can benefit from advertising's ability to provide information efficiently to large numbers of people.

A dramatic example of the noncommercial use of advertising was the multimedia campaign launched in 1998 by the U.S. government, working in conjunction with the Partnership for a Drug-Free America.[19] At the campaign's launch in July of 1998, President Clinton pledged to outspend major advertisers such as Nike and Sprint to remind the American public of the ruinous power of drugs like heroin. Estimates at that time indicated that spending on the campaign over five years could approach $1 billion. A stockpile of nearly 400 ads was available for use in this comprehensive campaign. Some, like the one shown in Exhibit 4.11, involved the use of celebrities.

Con: Advertising Affects Programming.

Critics argue that advertisers who place ads in media have an unhealthy effect on shaping the content of information contained in the media. For example, if a magazine that reviews and evaluates stereo equipment tests the equipment of one of its large advertisers, the contention is that the publication will hesitate to criticize the advertiser's equipment.

Another charge leveled at advertisers is that they purchase airtime only on programs that draw large audiences. Critics argue that these mass market programs lower the quality of television because cultural and educational programs, which draw smaller and more selective markets, are dropped in favor of mass market programs. Additionally, television programmers have a difficult time attracting advertisers to shows that may be valuable, yet controversial. Programs that deal with abortion, sexual abuse, or AIDS may have trouble drawing advertisers who fear the consequences of any association with controversial issues.

The Ethical Aspects of Advertising.
Many of the ethical aspects of advertising border on and interact with both the social and legal considerations of the advertising process. **Ethics** are moral standards and principles against which behavior is judged. Honesty, integrity, fairness, and sensitivity are all included in a broad defini-

---

19. B. G. Gregg, "Tax Funds Bankroll New Anti-Drug Ads," *Cincinnati Enquirer,* July 10, 1998, A1, A17.

tion of ethical behavior. Much of what is judged as ethical or unethical comes down to personal judgment. We will discuss the ethical aspects of advertising in three areas: truth in advertising, advertising to children, and advertising controversial products.

Truth in Advertising. While truth in advertising is a key legal issue, it has ethical dimensions as well. The most fundamental ethical issue has to do with **deception**—making false or misleading statements in an advertisement. The difficulty regarding this issue, of course, is in determining just what is deceptive. A manufacturer who claims a laundry product can remove grass stains is exposed to legal sanctions if the product cannot perform the task. Another manufacturer who claims to have "The Best Laundry Detergent in the World," however, is perfectly within its rights to employ superlatives. Just what constitutes "The Best" is a purely subjective determination; it cannot be proved or disproved. The use of absolute superlatives such as "Number One" or "Best in the World" is sometimes called **puffery** and is considered completely legal. The courts have long held that superlatives are understood by consumers as simply the standard language of advertising and are interpreted by consumers as such.

It is likewise impossible to legislate against emotional appeals such as those made about the beauty or prestige-enhancing qualities of a product, because these claims are unquantifiable. Since these types of appeals are legal, the ethics of such appeals fall into a gray area. Beauty and prestige, it is argued, are in the eye of the beholder, and such appeals are neither illegal nor unethical. Although there are some narrowly defined legal parameters for truth in advertising (as we will discuss shortly), the ethical issues are not as clear-cut.

Advertising to Children. The desire to restrict advertising aimed at children is based on three concerns. First, it is believed that advertising promotes superficiality and values founded in material goods and consumption—as we discussed earlier in the broader context of society as a whole. Second, children are considered inexperienced consumers and easy prey for the sophisticated persuasions of advertisers. Third, advertising influences children's demands for everything from toys to snack foods. These demands create an environment of child-parent conflict. Parents find themselves having to say no over and over again to children whose desires are piqued by effective advertising.

There is also concern that many programs aimed at children constitute program-length commercials. Many critics argue that programs featuring commercial products, especially products aimed at children, are simply long advertisements. In 1990, critics pointed out that 70 programs were based on commercial products such as He-Man, the Smurfs, and the Muppets.[20] More recent examples include elaborate, hour-long television productions such as "Treasure Island: The Adventure Begins." Critics claim that a program such as this, which features a young boy's vacation at the Las Vegas resort Treasure Island, blurs the boundary between programming and advertising. The program was produced by the Mirage Resorts (owners of Treasure Island), and the one-hour time slot was purchased from a major network, as advertising time, for an estimated $1.7 million.[21] While the program looks like an adventure show, critics argue it merely promotes the theme park and casino to kids, without ever revealing its sponsor. There have been several attempts by special-interest groups to strictly regulate this type of programming aimed at children, but, to date, the Federal Communications Commission permits such programming to continue.

20. Patrick J. Sheridan, "FCC Sets Children's Ad Limits," *1990 Information Access Company,* vol. 119, no. 20 (1990), 33.
21. Laura Bird, "NBC Special Is One Long Prime-Time Ad," *Wall Street Journal,* January 21, 1994, B1, B4.

Advertising Controversial Products.
Some people question the wisdom of allowing the advertising of controversial goods and services, such as tobacco, alcoholic beverages, gambling and lotteries, and firearms. Most frequently criticized are the advertising of cigarettes and alcoholic beverages. Critics charge these firms with targeting children with their advertising and with making dangerous and addictive products appealing.[22] While advertising for these products is already restricted, there are serious efforts to impose even stricter constraints, such as banning pictures and imagery in outdoor cigarette advertising or banning the advertising of these products altogether. Cigarette smoking is said to kill as many as 300,000 people a year.

Critics have also called into question the targeting of ethnic and minority groups with products and advertising, such as with malt liquor ads. Similarly, the tobacco and alcohol industries have been the target of boycotts over their sponsorship of professional sporting events. These industries answer the critics with the counterclaim that the advertising is aimed at smokers and drinkers of legal age.[23]

Gambling and state-run lotteries represent another controversial product area with respect to advertising. What is the purpose of this advertising? Is it meant to inform gamblers and lottery players of the choices available? This would be selective demand stimulation. Or is such advertising designed to stimulate demand for engaging in wagering behavior? This would be primary demand stimulation. What of compulsive gamblers? What is the state's obligation to protect "vulnerable" citizens by restricting the placement or content of lottery advertising? When these vulnerable audiences are discussed, questions as to what is the basis for this vulnerability can become complex and emotionally charged. Those on one side of the issue argue that special audiences are among the "information poor," while those on the other side find such claims demeaning, patronizing, and paternalistic.

It is also critical to recognize that the courts have given limited First Amendment protection to advertising. As long as these products and services are legal and what is said about them is true, commercial free-speech advocates argue that there should be no further restrictions. One of the dangers civil libertarians point to is the so-called slippery slope, or the scenario that once government is given one opportunity to restrict the advertising of one legal product, this action will begin the slow but inevitable slide down a slippery slope to unwanted and broadly applied government censorship. The issues involved are a long way from being resolved and play themselves out virtually every day in the news.

While we can group the ethical issues of advertising into some reasonable categories, it is not as easy to make definitive statements about the status of ethics in advertising. Ethics will always be a matter of personal values and personal interpretation. Advertising's role in public policy will always be controversial.

The Regulatory Aspects of Advertising.
The term *regulation* immediately brings to mind government scrutiny and control of the advertising process. There are, indeed, various government bodies that regulate advertising. But consumers themselves and several different industry organizations exert as much regulatory power over advertising as government agencies. Three primary groups—consumers, industry organizations, and government bodies—regulate advertising in the truest sense: Together they shape and restrict the process. The government relies on legal restrictions, while consumers and industry groups use less-formal controls. Like the other topics in this chapter, regulation of advertising can be controversial, and opinions about what does and doesn't need to be regulated can be highly variable. Moreover, the topic of regulation could easily be an entire course of study in its own right, so here we present just an overview of major issues and major players.

---

22. Kathleen Deveny, "Joe Camel Ads Reach Children, Research Finds," *Wall Street Journal,* December 11, 1991, B1, B6.
23. Kevin Goldman, "Coors Ads Try Not to Attract Teen-Agers," *Wall Street Journal,* November 10, 1992, B10.

First we will consider the areas of regulation pursued most ardently, whether it be by the government, consumers, or industry groups. Then we will examine the nature of the regulation exerted by these groups.

Areas of Advertising Regulation.
There are three basic areas of advertising regulation: the content of advertisements, competitive issues, and advertising to children. Each area is a focal point for regulation. Probably the majority of complaints against advertisers and their advertising efforts has to do with the content of advertising. In general, critics and those who desire greater regulation of the advertising process feel that advertising does not provide enough information for consumers to make informed decisions. There are two main issues related to regulation of content: deception and unfairness.

Deception and Unfairness.
Agreement is widespread that deception in advertising is unacceptable. The problem, of course, is that it is as difficult to determine what is deceptive from a regulatory standpoint as from an ethical standpoint. The Federal Trade Commission's (FTC's) policy statement on deception is the authoritative source when it comes to defining deceptive advertising. It specifies the following three elements as essential in declaring an ad deceptive:[24]

1. There must be a representation, omission, or practice that is likely to mislead the consumer.
2. This representation, omission, or practice must be judged from the perspective of a consumer acting reasonably in the circumstance.
3. The representation, omission, or practice must be a "material" one. The basic question is whether the act or the practice is likely to affect the consumer's conduct or decision with regard to the product or service. If so, the practice is material, and consumer injury is likely because consumers are likely to have chosen differently if not for the deception.

If this definition of deception sounds like carefully worded legal jargon, that's because it is. It is also a definition that can lead to diverse interpretations when it is actually applied to advertisements in real life. Fortunately, as represented in Exhibit 4.12, the FTC now provides highly practical advice for anticipating what can make an ad deceptive (go to www.ftc.gov/bcp/guides/guides.htm under the section "Frequently Asked Advertising Questions"). One critical point about the FTC's approach to deception is that both implied claims and information that is missing from an ad can be bases for deeming an ad deceptive. Obviously, the FTC expects any explicit claim made in an ad to be truthful, but they also are on the lookout for ads that deceive through allusion and innuendo, or ads that deceive by not telling the whole story.

Many instances of deceptive advertising and packaging have resulted in formal government programs designed to regulate such practices. But as we discussed earlier, there can be complications in

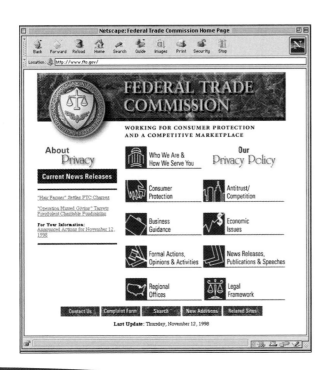

EXHIBIT 4.12

No government agency does more to regulate advertising than the Federal Trade Commission. Its Web site provides a wealth of current information about regulatory practices and standards. Check it out to get the latest news on the FTC's efforts to monitor the new frontier of advertising: Internet. www.ftc.gov/

---

24. For additional discussion of the FTC's definition of deception, see Gary T. Ford and John E. Calfee, "Recent Developments in FTC Policy on Deception," *Journal of Marketing,* vol. 50 (July 1986), 82–103.

regulating puffery. Conventional wisdom has argued that consumers don't actually believe extreme claims and realize that advertisers are just trying to attract attention. There are those, however, who disagree with this view of puffery and feel that it actually represents "soft-core" deception, because some consumers believe these exaggerated claims.[25]

While the FTC and the courts have been reasonably specific about what constitutes deception, the definition of unfairness in advertising has been left relatively vague until recently. In 1994, Congress ended a long-running dispute in the courts and in the advertising industry by approving legislation that defines **unfair advertising** as "acts or practices that cause or are likely to cause substantial injury to consumers, which is not reasonably avoidable by consumers themselves, and not outweighed by the countervailing benefits to consumers or competition."[26] This definition obligates the FTC to assess both the benefits and costs of advertising, and rules out reckless acts on the part of consumers, before a judgment can be rendered that an advertiser has been unfair.

Competitive Issues. Because the large dollar amounts spent on advertising may foster inequities that literally can destroy competition, several advertising practices relating to competition can result in regulation. Among them are cooperative advertising, comparison advertising, and using monopoly power.

Vertical cooperative advertising is an advertising technique whereby a manufacturer and dealer (either a wholesaler or retailer) share the expense of advertising. This technique is commonly used in regional or local markets where a manufacturer wants a brand to benefit from a special promotion run by local dealers. There is nothing illegal, per se, about the technique, and it is used regularly. The competitive threat inherent in the process, however, is that dealers (especially since the advent of department store chains) can be given bogus cooperative advertising allowances. These allowances require no effort or expenditure on the part of the dealer and thus represent hidden price concessions. As such, they are a form of unfair competition and are deemed illegal. If an advertising allowance is granted to a dealer, that dealer must demonstrate that the funds are applied specifically to advertising.

The potential exists for firms to engage in unfair competition if they use comparison ads inappropriately. **Comparison advertisements** are those in which an advertiser makes a comparison between the firm's brand and competitors' brands. The comparison may or may not explicitly identify the competition. Again, comparison ads are completely legal and are used frequently by all sorts of organizations. However, if the advertisement is carried out in such a way that the comparison is not a fair one, then there is an unjust competitive effect. The American Association of Advertising Agencies (4As) has issued a set of guidelines, shown in Exhibit 4.13, regarding the use of comparison ads. Further, the Federal Trade Commission may require a firm using comparison to substantiate claims made in an advertisement.

Finally, some firms are so powerful in their use of advertising that **monopoly power** by virtue of the advertising can become a problem. This issue normally arises in the context of mergers and acquisitions. As an example, the U.S. Supreme Court blocked the acquisition of Clorox by Procter & Gamble because the advertising power of the two firms combined would (in the opinion of the Court) make it nearly impossible for another firm to compete.

Advertising Aimed at Children. Critics argue that continually bombarding children with persuasive stimuli can alter their motivation and behavior. While government organizations such as the FTC have been active in trying to regulate advertising directed

25. Ivan Preston, *The Great American Blow Up* (Madison, Wis.: University of Wisconsin Press, 1975), 4.
26. Christy Fisher, "How Congress Broke Unfair Ad Impasse," *Advertising Age,* August 22, 1994, 34. For additional discussion of the FTC's definition of unfairness, see Ivan Preston, "Unfairness Developments in FTC Advertising Cases," *Journal of Public Policy and Marketing,* vol. 14, no. 2 (1995), 318–321.

EXHIBIT 4.13

American Association of Advertising Agencies guidelines for comparison advertising. www.aaaa.org/

The Board of Directors of the American Association of Advertising Agencies recognizes that when used truthfully and fairly, comparative advertising provides the consumer with needed and useful information. However, extreme caution should be exercised. The use of comparative advertising, by its very nature, can distort facts and, by implication, convey to the consumer information that misrepresents the truth. Therefore, the Board believes that comparative advertising should follow certain guidelines:

1. The intent and connotation of the ad should be to inform and never to discredit or unfairly attack competitors.
2. When a competitive product is named, it should be one that exists in the marketplace as significant competition.
3. The competition should be fairly and properly identified, but never in a manner or tone of voice that degrades the competitive product or service.
4. The advertising should compare related or similar properties or ingredients of the product, dimension to dimension, feature to feature.
5. The identification should be for honest comparison purposes and not simply to upgrade by association.
6. If a competitive test is conducted, it should be done by an objective testing source, preferably an independent one, so that there will be no doubt as to the veracity of the test.
7. In all cases, the test should be supportive of all claims made in the advertising based on the test.
8. The advertising should never use partial results or stress insignificant differences to cause the consumer to draw an improper conclusion.
9. The property being compared should be significant in terms of value or usefulness of the product to the consumer.
10. Comparatives delivered through the use of testimonials should not imply that the testimonial is more than one individual's thought unless that individual represents a sample of the majority viewpoint.

Source: American Association of Advertising Agencies

at children, industry and consumer groups have been more successful in securing restrictions. The consumer group known as Action for Children's Television was actively involved in getting Congress to approve the Children's Television Act (1990). This act limits the amount of commercial airtime during children's programs to 10½ minutes on weekdays and 12 minutes on weekends. The Council of Better Business Bureaus established a Children's Advertising Review Unit and has issued a set of guidelines for advertising directed at children. These guidelines emphasize that advertisers should be sensitive to the level of knowledge and sophistication of children as decision makers. The guidelines also urge advertisers to make a constructive contribution to the social development of children by emphasizing positive social standards in advertising, such as friendship, kindness, honesty, and generosity. Similarly, the major television networks have set their own guidelines for advertising aimed at children. The guidelines restrict the use of celebrities, prohibit exhortive language (such as "Go ask Dad"), and restrict the use of animation to one-third of the total time of the commercial.

Regulatory Agents. Earlier in this chapter it was noted that consumer and industry groups as well as government agencies all participate in the regulation of advertising. We will now discuss examples of each of these agents along with the kinds of influence they exert. Given the multiple participants, this turns out to be a highly complex activity that we can only overview in this discussion. Additionally, our discussion focuses on regulatory activities in the United States, but as suggested in the Global Issues box on page 114, advertising regulation can vary dramatically from country to country. Chapter 9 will provide additional insights on advertising regulation around the world, but we must emphasize that becoming an expert on the complex and dynamic topic of global ad regulation would literally require a lifetime of study.

GLOBAL ISSUES

SINO SNAKE OIL—ADVERTISING ETHICS NOW ENFORCED IN MAINLAND CHINA

The Chinese economic boom of recent years has been accompanied by a rapid growth of advertising in that country. In the last decade alone, ad spending has multiplied nearly 100 times over, with literally thousands of advertising agencies sprouting up in just the past few years. With the state-owned media companies under increasing pressure to remain profitable, however, the government stations have been loath to police advertising content and turn away vital ad dollars. Numerous misleading, inflated, or false product claims have ensued, with toothpaste that cures cancer, soap that wipes ten years off a woman's face, and a single-pill cure for hepatitis, among others. To curb abuse of the ill-defined regulations, Chinese officials passed their first comprehensive advertising law late in 1994. The enforcement has been both swift and sure; following a screening of nearly 1,500 television commercials in January 1995, the Chinese State Administration for Industry and Commerce found that 90 of the ads were in violation of the new law and blocked them from airing. The Chinese advertising community has taken notice. "Before they were just regulations," says Dennis Wong, managing director of Leo Burnett's Chinese operations. "Now they're laws."

Source: "Chinese Officials Attempt to Ban False Ad Claims," *Wall Street Journal*, February 28, 1995, B1. Printed by permission of the *Wall Street Journal*. © 1998 Dow Jones & Company, Inc. All Rights Reserved Worldwide.

Government Regulation. Governments have a powerful tool available for regulating advertising: the threat of legal action. In the United States, several different government agencies have been given the power and responsibility to regulate the advertising process. Exhibit 4.14 identifies the six agencies that have legal mandates concerning advertising, and their areas of regulatory responsibility.

Several other agencies have minor powers in the regulation of advertising, such as the Civil Aeronautics Board (advertising by air carriers), the Patent Office (trademark infringement), and the Library of Congress (copyright protection). The agencies listed in Exhibit 4.14 are the most directly involved in advertising regulation. Most active among these agencies is the Federal Trade Commission, which has the most power and is most directly involved in controlling the advertising process. The FTC has been granted legal power through legislative mandates and also has developed programs for regulating advertising.

The FTC's Legislative Mandates. The Federal Trade Commission was created by the FTC Act in 1914. The original purpose of the agency was to prohibit unfair methods of competition. In 1916, the FTC concluded that false advertising was one way in which a firm could take unfair advantage of another, and advertising was established as a primary concern of the agency.

It was not until 1938 that the effects of deceptive advertising on consumers became a key issue for the FTC. Until the passage of the Wheeler-Lea Amendment (1938), the commission was primarily concerned with the direct effect of advertising on competition. The amendment broadened the FTC's powers to include regulation of advertising that was misleading to the public (regardless of the effect on competition). Through this amendment, the agency could apply a cease-and-desist order, which required a firm to stop its deceptive practices. It also granted the agency specific jurisdiction over drug, medical device, cosmetic, and food advertising.

Several other acts provide the FTC with legal powers over advertising. The Robinson-Patman Act (1936) prohibits firms from providing phantom cooperative-advertising allowances as a way to court important dealers. The Wool Products Labeling Act (1939), the Fur Products Labeling Act (1951), and the Textile Fiber Products Identification Act (1958) provided the commission with regulatory power over labeling and advertising for specific products. Consumer protection legislation, which seeks to increase the ability of consumers to make more-informed product comparisons, includes the Fair Packaging and Labeling Act (1966), the Truth in Lending Act (1969), and the Fair Credit Report-

EXHIBIT 4.14

Primary government agencies regulating advertising.

Government Agency	Areas of Advertising Regulation
Federal Trade Commission (FTC)	Most widely empowered agency in government. Controls unfair methods of competition, regulates deceptive advertising, and has various programs for controlling the advertising process.
Federal Communications Commission (FCC)	Prohibits obscenity, fraud, and lotteries on radio and television. Ultimate power lies in the ability to deny or revoke broadcast licenses.
Food and Drug Administration (FDA)	Regulates the advertising of food, drug, cosmetic, and medical products. Can require special labeling for hazardous products such as household cleaners. Prohibits false labeling and packaging.
Securities and Exchange Commission (SEC)	Regulates the advertising of securities and the disclosure of information in annual reports.
U.S. Postal Service	Responsible for regulating direct mail advertising and prohibiting lotteries, fraud, and misrepresentation. It can also regulate and impose fines for materials deemed to be obscene.
Bureau of Alcohol, Tobacco, and Firearms	Most direct influence has been on regulation of advertising for alcoholic beverages. This agency was responsible for putting warning labels on alcoholic beverage advertising and banning active athletes as celebrities in beer ads. It has the power to determine what constitutes misleading advertising in these product areas.

ing Act (1970). The FTC Improvement Act (1975) expanded the authority of the commission by giving it the power to issue trade regulation rules.

Recent legislation has expanded the FTC's role in monitoring and regulating product labeling and advertising. For example, the 1990 Nutrition Labeling and Education Act (NLEA) requires uniformity in the nutrition labeling of food products and establishes strict rules for claims about the nutritional attributes of food products. The standard "Nutrition Facts" label required by the NLEA now appears on everything from breakfast cereals to barbecue sauce. The NLEA is a unique piece of legislation from the standpoint that two government agencies—the FTC and the FDA—play key roles in its enforcement.

The law also provides the FTC and other agencies with various means of recourse when advertising practices are judged to be deceptive or misleading. The spirit of all these acts relates to the maintenance of an equitable competitive environment and the protection of consumers from misleading information. It is interesting to note, however, that direct involvement of the FTC in advertising practices more often comes about from its regulatory programs and remedies than from the application of legal mandates.

The FTC's Regulatory Programs and Remedies. The application of legislation has evolved as the FTC exercises its powers and expands its role as a regulatory agency. This evolution of the FTC has spawned several regulatory programs and remedies to help enforce legislative mandates in specific situations.

The **advertising substantiation program** of the FTC was initiated in 1971 with the intention of ensuring that advertisers make available to consumers supporting evidence for claims made. The program was strengthened in 1972 when the commission forwarded the notion of "reasonable basis" for the substantiation of advertising. This extension suggests not only that advertisers should substantiate their claims, but also that the substantiation should provide a reasonable basis for believing the claims are true.[27] Simply put, before a company runs an ad, it must have documented evidence that supports the claim it wants to make in that ad. The kind of evidence required depends on the kind of claim being made. For example, health and safety claims will require competent and reliable scientific evidence that has been examined and validated by experts in the field (go to www.ftc.gov/ for additional guidance).

The consent order and the cease-and-desist order are the most basic remedies used by the FTC in dealing with deceptive or unfair advertising. In a **consent order**, an advertiser accused of running deceptive or unfair advertising agrees to stop running the advertisements in question, without admitting guilt. For advertisers who do not comply voluntarily, the FTC can issue a **cease-and-desist order**, which generally requires that the advertising in question be stopped within 30 days so a hearing can be held to determine whether the advertising is deceptive or unfair. For products that have a direct effect on consumers' health or safety (for example, foods), the FTC can issue an immediate cease-and-desist order.

Affirmative disclosure is another remedy available to the FTC. An advertisement that fails to disclose important material facts about a product can be deemed deceptive, and the FTC may require **affirmative disclosure**, whereby the important material absent from prior ads must be included in subsequent advertisements. The absence of important material information may cause consumers to make false assumptions about products in comparison to the competition. Such was the case with Geritol; the FTC ordered the makers of the product to disclose that "iron-poor blood" was not the universal cause of tiredness.

The most extreme remedy for advertising determined to be misleading is **corrective advertising**.[28] In cases where evidence suggests that consumers have developed incorrect beliefs about a brand based on deceptive or unfair advertising, the firm may be required to run corrective ads in an attempt to dispel those faulty beliefs. The commission has specified not only the message content for corrective ads, but also the budgetary allocation, the duration of transmission, and the placement of the advertising. The goal of corrective advertising is to rectify erroneous beliefs created by deceptive advertising, but it hasn't always worked as intended.

Another area of FTC regulation and remedy involves **celebrity endorsements**. The FTC has specific rules for advertisements that use an expert or celebrity as a spokesperson for a product. In the case of experts (those whose experience or training allows a superior judgment of products), the endorser's actual qualifications must justify his or her status as an expert. In the case of celebrities (such as Michael Jordan as a spokesperson for McDonald's), FTC guidelines indicate that the celebrity must be an actual user of the product, or the ad is considered deceptive.

These regulatory programs and remedies provide the FTC a great deal of control over the advertising process. Numerous ads have been interpreted as questionable under the guidelines of these programs, and advertisements have been altered. It is likely also that advertisers and their agencies, who are keenly aware of the ramifications of violating FTC precepts, have developed ads with these constraints in mind.

Yet it is certainly fair to conclude that advertising regulation is a dynamic endeavor that will challenge regulators far into the future. Of course, the most notable new challenge that regulators around the world must learn to cope with is advertising on the

27. For a discussion of the FTC advertising substantiation program and its extension to require reasonable basis, see Debra L. Scammon and Richard J. Semenik, "The FTC's 'Reasonable Basis' for Substantiation of Advertising: Expanded Standards and Implications," *Journal of Advertising,* vol. 12, no. 1 (1983), 4–11.

28. A history of the corrective-advertising concept and several of its applications are provided by Debra L. Scammon and Richard J. Semenik, "Corrective Advertising: Evolution of the Legal Theory and Application of the Remedy," *Journal of Advertising,* vol. 11, no. 1 (1982), 10–20.

Internet. For instance, while U.S. government agencies such as the FTC and FDA intend to extend their jurisdiction to the Internet, they clearly have a tiger by the tail. As just one example of current shortcomings, the New Media box on this page makes the point that the health care advice and products promoted on the Internet often resemble the snake-oil claims of the 1800s. Until a regulatory agency steps up to the challenge of the Internet, it will be up to the consumer to separate the quacks from the qualified.

MORE QUACKS THAN DUCKS UNLIMITED

Hit the World Wide Web for products and advice about medical problems and you can find some truly amazing promises. For instance, at **www.cleansingtime.com/,** a special-formula product was advertised with the claim that it "has had almost a 100% success ratio in completely removing all forms of skin cancers (including melanoma)." (And you thought you needed sunscreen!) Dr. John Renner, an expert on Web-based medical sites, has catalogued over 6,000 of them, and estimates that 1,200 to 1,500 offer useless or dangerous information. He contends that "there is no online FDA, no Internet medical board, and any doctor whose license has been revoked can operate his own Web site." People at the FDA don't exactly agree. Donald Pohl, a public health official with the FDA, recognizes that the quacks are out there, but acknowledges that "[w]e just don't have the resources or money to stop these people." So the government knows that the bad guys are out there; they just don't have the time or money to do anything about it. Feel better?

Source: "The Snake-Oil Side Step: The Feds Won't Touch the Real Villains," *YAHOO! Internet Life,* April 1998, 50.

Industry Self-Regulation.

Advertisers have come far in terms of their self-control and restraint. Some of this improvement is due to tougher government regulation, and some to industry self-regulation. **Self-regulation** is the industry's attempt to police itself. Supporters say it is a shining example of how unnecessary government intervention is, while critics point to it as a joke, an elaborate shell game. According to the critics, meaningful self-regulation occurs only when the threat of government action is imminent. How you see this controversy is largely dependent on your own personal experience and level of cynicism.

Several industry and trade associations and public service organizations have voluntarily established guidelines for advertising within their industries. The reasoning is that self-regulation is good for the advertising community as a whole and promotes the credibility, and therefore the effectiveness, of advertising itself. Exhibit 4.15 lists some organizations that have taken on the task of regulating and monitoring advertising, and the year when each established a code by which to judge the acceptability of advertising.

The purpose of self-regulation by these organizations is to evaluate the content and quality of advertisements specific to their industries. The effectiveness of such organizations depends on the cooperation of members and the policing mechanisms used. Each organization exerts an influence on the nature of advertising in its industry. Some are particularly noteworthy in their activities and warrant further discussion.

The National Advertising Review Board. One important self-regulation organization is the Council of Better Business Bureaus' National Advertising Review Board (NARB). The NARB is the operations arm of the National Advertising Division (NAD) of the Council of Better Business Bureaus. Complaints received from consumers, competitors, or local branches of the Better Business Bureau are forwarded to the NAD. Most such complaints come from competitors. After a full review of the complaint, the issue may be forwarded to the NARB and evaluated by a panel. The complete procedure for dealing with complaints is detailed in Exhibit 4.16.

The NAD maintains a permanent professional staff that works to resolve complaints with the advertiser and its agency before the issue gets to the NARB. If no resolution is achieved, the complaint is appealed to the NARB, which appoints a panel made up of

Organization	Code Established
Advertising Associations	
American Advertising Federation	1965
American Association of Advertising Agencies	1924
Association of National Advertisers	1972
Business/Professional Advertising Association	1975
Special Industry Groups	
Council of Better Business Bureaus	1912
Household furniture	1978
Automobiles and trucks	1978
Carpet and rugs	1978
Home improvement	1975
Charitable solicitations	1974
Children's Advertising Review Unit	1974
National Advertising Division/National Advertising Review Board	1971
Media Associations	
American Business Press	1910
Direct Mail Marketing Association	1960
Direct Selling Association	1970
National Association of Broadcasters	
Radio	1937
Television	1952
Outdoor Advertising Association of America	1950
Selected Trade Associations	
American Wine Association	1949
Wine Institute	1949
Distilled Spirits Association	1934
United States Brewers Association	1955
Pharmaceutical Manufacturers Association	1958
Proprietary Association	1934
Bank Marketing Association	1976
Motion Picture Association of America	1930
National Swimming Pool Institute	1970
Toy Manufacturers Association	1962

three advertiser representatives, one agency representative, and one public representative. This panel then holds hearings regarding the advertising in question. The advertiser is allowed to present the firm's case. If no agreement can be reached by the panel either to dismiss the case or to persuade the advertiser to change the advertising, then the NARB initiates two actions. First, the NARB publicly identifies the advertiser, the complaint

EXHIBIT 4.16

Flow diagram of the NAD and NARB regulatory process.

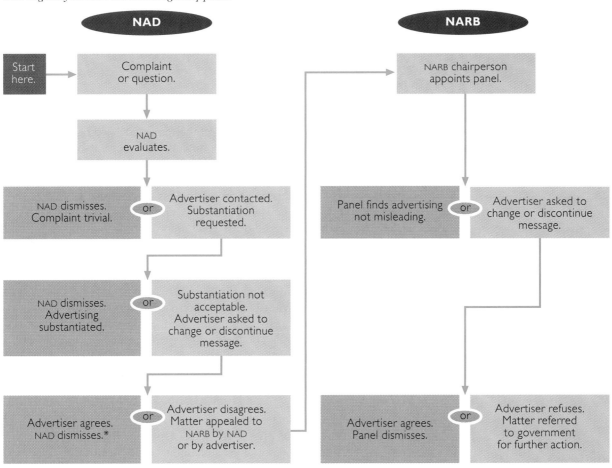

*If the complaint originated outside the system, the outside complainant can appeal at this point to the NARB chairperson for a panel adjudication. Granting of such an appeal is at the chairperson's discretion.

against the advertiser, and the panel's findings. Second, the case is forwarded to an appropriate government regulatory agency (usually the Federal Trade Commission).

The NAD and the NARB are not empowered to impose penalties on advertisers, but the threat of going before the board acts as a deterrent to deceptive and questionable advertising practices. Further, the regulatory process of the NAD and the NARB is probably less costly and time consuming for all parties involved than if every complaint were handled by a government agency.

State and Local Better Business Bureaus. Aside from the national Better Business Bureau (BBB), there are more than 140 separate local bureaus. Each local organization is supported by membership dues paid by area businesses. The three divisions of a local BBB—merchandise, financial, and solicitations—investigate the advertising and selling practices of firms in their areas. A local BBB has the power to forward a complaint to the NAD for evaluation.

Beyond its regulatory activities, the Better Business Bureau tries to avert problems associated with advertising by counseling new businesses and providing information to advertisers and agencies regarding legislation, potential problem areas, and industry standards.

Advertising Agencies and Associations. It makes sense that advertising agencies and their industry associations would engage in self-regulation. An individual agency is legally responsible for the advertising it produces and is subject to reprisal for deceptive claims. The agency is in a difficult position in that it must monitor not only the activities of its own people, but also the information that clients provide to the agency. Should a client direct an agency to use a product appeal that turns out to be untruthful, the agency is still responsible.

The American Association of Advertising Agencies (4As) has no legal or binding power over its agency members, but it can apply pressure when its board feels industry standards are not being upheld. The 4As also publishes guidelines for its members regarding various aspects of advertising messages. One of the most widely recognized industry standards is the 4As' Creative Code. The code outlines the responsibilities and social impact advertising can have and promotes high ethical standards of honesty and decency.

Media Organizations. Individual media organizations evaluate the advertising they receive for broadcast and publication. The National Association of Broadcasters (NAB) has a policing arm known as the Code Authority, which implements and interprets separate radio and television codes. These codes deal with truth, fairness, and good taste in broadcast advertising. Newspapers have historically been rigorous in their screening of advertising. Many newspapers have internal departments to screen and censor ads believed to be in violation of the newspaper's advertising standards. While the magazine industry does not have a formal code, many individual publications have very high standards.

Direct mail may have a poor image among many consumers, but its industry association, the Direct Marketing Association (DMA), is active in promoting ethical behavior and standards among its members. It has published guidelines for ethical business practices. In 1971, the association established the Direct Mail Preference Service, which enables consumers who wish to have their names removed from most direct mail lists.

A review of all aspects of industry self-regulation suggests not only that a variety of programs and organizations are designed to monitor advertising, but also that many of these programs are effective. Those whose livelihoods depend on advertising are just as interested as consumers and legislators in maintaining high standards. If advertising deteriorates into an unethical and untrustworthy business activity, the economic vitality of many organizations will be compromised. Self-regulation can help prevent such a circumstance and is in the best interest of all the organizations discussed here.

Consumers as Regulatory Agents. Consumers themselves are motivated to act as regulatory agents based on a variety of interests, including product safety, reasonable choice, and the right to information. Advertising tends to be a focus of consumer regulatory activities because of its conspicuousness. Consumerism and consumer organizations have provided the primary vehicles for consumer regulatory efforts.

Consumerism, the actions of individual consumers or groups of consumers designed to exert power in the marketplace, is by no means a recent phenomenon. The earliest consumerism efforts can be traced to 17th-century England. In the United States, there have been recurring consumer movements throughout the 20th century. *Adbusters* magazine is a recent one.

In general, these movements have focused on the same issue: Consumers want a greater voice in the whole process of product development, distribution, and information dissemination. Consumers commonly try to create pressures on firms by withholding patronage through boycotts. Some boycotts have been effective. Firms as powerful as Procter & Gamble, Kimberly-Clark, and General Mills all have responded to threats of boycotts by pulling advertising from programs consumers found offensive.[29]

29. Alix M. Freedman, "Never Have So Few Scared So Many Television Sponsors," *Wall Street Journal,* March 20, 1989, B4.

Consumer Organizations. The other major consumer effort to bring about regulation is through established consumer organizations. The following are the most prominent consumer organizations and their prime activities:

- *Consumer Federation of America (CFA).* This organization, founded in 1968, now includes over 200 national, state, and local consumer groups and labor unions as affiliate members. The goals of the CFA are to encourage the creation of consumer organizations, provide services to consumer groups, and act as a clearinghouse for information exchange between consumer groups.
- *Consumers Union.* This nonprofit consumer organization is best known for its publication of *Consumer Reports.* Established in 1936, Consumers Union has as its stated purpose "to provide consumers with information and advice on goods, services, health, and personal finance; and to initiate and cooperate with individual and group efforts to maintain and enhance the quality of life for consumers."[30] This organization supports itself through the sale of publications and accepts no funding, including advertising revenues, from any commercial organization.
- *Action for Children's Television (ACT).* ACT has been active in conjunction with the national Parent Teacher Association in initiating boycotts against the products of advertisers who sponsor programs that are violent in nature. On its own, ACT has lobbied government bodies to enact legislation restricting the use of premiums in advertising to children and the use of popular cartoon characters in promoting products.

These three consumer organizations are the most active and potent of the consumer groups, but there are literally hundreds of such groups organized by geographic location or product category. Consumers have proven that with an organized effort, corporations can and will change their practices. In one of the most publicized events in recent times, consumers applied pressure to Coca-Cola and, in part, were responsible for forcing the firm to re-market the original formula of Coca-Cola (as Coca-Cola Classic). If consumers are able to exert such a powerful and nearly immediate influence on a firm like Coca-Cola, one wonders what other changes they could effect in the market.

SUMMARY

◀▶ Assess the benefits and problems of advertising in a capitalistic society and debate a variety of issues concerning advertising's effects on society's well-being.

Advertisers have always been followed by proponents and critics. Proponents of advertising argue that it offers benefits for individual consumers and society at large. At the societal level, proponents claim, advertising helps promote a higher standard of living by allowing marketers to reap the rewards of product improvements and innovation. Advertising also "pays for" mass media in many countries, and provides consumers with a constant flow of information not only about products and services, but also about political and social issues.

Over the years critics have leveled many charges at advertising and advertising practitioners. Advertising expenditures in the multi-billions are condemned as waste-

ful, offensive, and a source of frustration for many in society who see the lavish lifestyle portrayed in advertising, knowing they will never be able to afford such a lifestyle. Critics also contend that advertisements rarely furnish useful information but instead perpetuate superficial stereotypes of many cultural subgroups. For many years, some critics have been concerned that advertisers are controlling us against our will with subliminal advertising messages.

◀▶ Explain how ethical considerations affect the development of advertising campaigns.

Ethical considerations are a concern when creating advertising, especially when that advertising will be targeted to children or will involve controversial products such as firearms, gambling, alcohol, or cigarettes. While ethical standards are a matter for personal reflection, it certainly

30. This statement of purpose can be found inside the cover of any issue of Consumer Reports.

is the case that unethical people can create unethical advertising. But there are also many safeguards against such behavior, including the corporate and personal integrity of advertisers.

◀▶ Discuss the role of government agencies in the regulation of advertising.

Governments typically are involved in the regulation of advertising. It is important to recognize that advertising regulations can vary dramatically from one country to the next. In the United States, the Federal Trade Commission (FTC) has been especially active in trying to deter deception and unfairness in advertising. The FTC was established in 1914, and since then a variety of legislation has been passed to clarify the powers of the FTC. The FTC has also developed regulatory remedies that have expanded its

involvement in advertising regulation, such as the advertising substantiation program.

◀▶ Explain the meaning and importance of self-regulation for an advertising practitioner.

Some of the most important controls on advertising are voluntary; that is, they are a matter of self-regulation by advertising and marketing professionals. For example, the American Association of Advertising Agencies has issued guidelines for promoting fairness and accuracy when using comparative advertisements. Many other organizations, such as the Better Business Bureau, the National Association of Broadcasters, and Action for Children's Television, participate in the process to help ensure fairness and assess consumer complaints about advertising.

KEY TERMS

ethics (108)
deception (109)
puffery (109)
unfair advertising (112)
vertical cooperative advertising (112)
comparison advertisements (112)
monopoly power (112)
advertising substantiation program (115)

consent order (116)
cease-and-desist order (116)
affirmative disclosure (116)
corrective advertising (116)
celebrity endorsements (116)
self-regulation (117)
consumerism (120)

QUESTIONS FOR REVIEW AND CRITICAL THINKING

1. Advertising has been a focal point of criticism for many decades. In your opinion, what are some of the key factors that make advertising controversial?

2. Proponents claim that because of mass media advertising, American consumers enjoy lower prices on a variety of products and services than would be the case if there were no mass media advertising. How could this be possible?

3. You have probably been exposed to hundreds of thousands of advertisements in your lifetime. In what ways does exposure to advertising make you a better or worse consumer?

4. Use Maslow's well-known hierarchy of needs to address critics' concerns that too much of advertising is directed at creating demand for products that are irrelevant to people's true needs.

5. What does it mean to suggest that an advertisement projects a stereotype? How might this problem of stereotyping be related to the process of market segmentation?

6. One type of advertising that attracts the attention of regulators, critics, and consumer advocates is advertising directed at children. Why is it the focal point of so much attention?

7. What is comparison advertising, and why does this form of advertising need a special set of guidelines to prevent unfair competition?

8. Explain why a marketer might be tempted to misuse cooperative-advertising allowances to favor some kinds of retailers over others. What piece of legislation empowered the FTC to stop these bogus allowances?

9.   The Nutrition Labeling and Education Act of 1990 is unique for a number of reasons. How has this act affected the day-to-day eating habits of many U.S. consumers? What makes this a special piece of legislation from an enforcement standpoint?

10. Some contend that self-regulation is the best way to ensure fair and truthful advertising practices. Why would it be in the best interests of the advertising community to aggressively pursue self-regulation?

EXPERIENTIAL EXERCISES

1.   In this chapter you read about the social aspects of advertising. Imagine you are speaking with an individual who is totally unfamiliar with life in the United States. To inform your companion about life here, find five magazine ads that reflect societal characteristics of Americans. Describe for your companion how each ad reflects American society and values.

2.   Critics of advertising fear the effect of advertising on adolescents. Did advertising make you do things you did not want to do when you were a teenager?

USING THE INTERNET

Visit the following four sites and consider the social and ethical issues each raises about advertising:

Global Casino: www.gamblenet.com

Stoli: www.stoli.com

Playboy: www.playboy.com

Frederick's of Hollywood: www.fredericks.com

1.   What issues would consumer advocate groups raise for this site? What personally concerns you about this site? Justify your arguments with information from the site.

2.   Many children surf the Net. Does that affect your previous evaluation of the site?

3.   What steps have these companies taken to regulate themselves?

4.   What regulations would you suggest for Internet advertising in light of these issues?

Now, visit the FTC site at www.ftc.gov and read the latest FTC news.

5.   Are there any pending regulations affecting advertising on the Internet?

Protection of children has been used as the basis for a number of legislative and regulatory proposals regarding the Internet. In addition to the problem of children's exposure to inappropriate content, children might also be targeted by marketers, in order to collect information that a more savvy, informed adult might regard as private. The Center for Media Education is one of the non-profit groups concerned with children's exposure to advertising in the new media. TRUSTe is a non-profit consortium that has established "trust marks" to indicate how a Web site handles information collected on site visitors; it has a Children's Privacy Seal Program to address the special concerns of young children's privacy, e.g., regarding parental consent. Visit these two sites:

Center for Media Education: www.cme.org

TRUSTe: www.truste.org

1.   How does the Internet compare with traditional media in terms of segregating audiences, e.g., to limit children's exposure to advertising?

2.   If you were a Web site manager, how might you try to filter your audience, whether to bar children (or, for that matter, bar adults) or to separate audiences by age group?

3.   Why might children require additional privacy protections?

FROM PRINCIPLES to Practice:

A COMPREHENSIVE IMC CASE

PART I
Client: Cincinnati Bell Inc.
Agency: Northlich Stolley LaWarre (NSL)
IMC Campaign: Cincinnati Bell Wireless (CBW)

Background and Participants.
In Chapter 1, we introduced the concept of integrated marketing communications (IMC). The rise in prominence of IMC makes it essential that this evolving perspective on marketing communication be understood in relation to mass media advertising. On the client side, sophisticated marketers such as Starbucks, Citibank, and Ford Motor Company are integrating IMC tools such as direct marketing, event sponsorship, sales promotions, and public relations, with or without mass media advertising, to build their brands.[1] On the agency side, a recent search for "integrated marketing communication agencies" on Lexis-Nexis and the Internet turned up over 200 agencies that were described as IMC service providers. Article after article in the trade press maintains that IMC has once and for all moved beyond the stage of a fad or buzzword to a lasting philosophical shift in the way marketers communicate with their customers.[2]

The IMC sections at the end of each part of this text will help you better understand integrated marketing communications by examining the topic in two ways. First, each section will discuss IMC relative to each part of the text to provide more concepts and principles for understanding this important approach. Second, we will bring these concepts to life through an in-depth and ongoing IMC case example. This example will feature the working relationship between a marketer and an ad agency in pursuit of the launch of a new wireless phone service. The client and agency who will be featured are Cincinnati Bell Inc. and Northlich Stolley LaWarre. You will learn a great deal about these two companies over the course of our four-part IMC case. More important, by closely examining the work of Northlich Stolley LaWarre in the launch of Cincinnati Bell Wireless, we can gain a concrete appreciation for the challenges and benefits of sophisticated IMC campaigns.

What Is IMC?
There are many good working definitions of IMC, including the following three:

> [A] concept of marketing communications planning that recognizes the added value of a comprehensive plan that evaluates the strategic role of a variety of communications disciplines—for example, general advertising, direct response, sales promotion, and public relations—and combines these disciplines to provide clarity, consistency and maximum communications impact.[3]

1. For discussions of how these and other marketers are using multiple communications options in an integrated way, see Robert Frank, "Pepsi Bets a Blue Can Will Spur Sales Abroad," *Wall Street Journal,* April 2, 1996, B8; Laura Petrecca, "Ikea Homes in on Office," *Advertising Age,* August 10, 1998, 16; and Betsy Spethmann, "Is Advertising Dead?" *PROMO Magazine,* September 1998, 32–36, 159–162.

2. For example, see Jim Osterman, "This Changes Everything," *Adweek,* May 15, 1995, 44–45; Kate Fitzgerald, "Beyond Advertising," *Advertising Age,* August 3, 1998, 1, 14.

3. This definition by the American Association of Advertising Agencies appeared in Don E. Schultz, "Integrated Marketing Communications: Maybe Definition Is in the Point of View," *Marketing News,* January 18, 1993, 17.

What is integrated marketing communications? It's a new way of looking at the whole, where once we only saw parts such as advertising, public relations, sales promotion, purchasing, employee communications, and so forth. It's realigning communications to look at it the way the customer sees it—as a flow of information from indistinguishable sources.[4]

IMC is the strategic coordination of multiple communication voices. Its aim is to optimize the impact of persuasive communication on both the consumer and nonconsumer (e.g., retailers, sales personnel, opinion leaders) audiences by coordinating such elements of the marketing mix as advertising, public relations, promotions, direct marketing, and package design.[5]

Notice that each of these definitions is compatible with the one we offered in Chapter 1: *IMC is the process of using various promotional tools in a unified way so that a synergistic communications effect is created.*

Factors Contributing to IMC's Rising Prominence.

Why has IMC become so popular over the past decade? Several significant and pervasive changes in the communications environment have contributed to the growing prominence of IMC:[6]

- *Fragmentation of media.* Media options available to marketers have proliferated at an astounding rate. Broadcast media now offer "narrow-casting" so specific that advertisers can reach consumers at precise locations, such as airports and supermarket checkout counters. The print media have proliferated dramatically as well. At one point, there were 197 different sports magazines on the market in the United States! The proliferation and fragmentation of media have resulted in less reliance on mass media and more emphasis on other promotional options, such as direct mail and event sponsorship.
- *Better audience assessment.* More sophisticated research methods have made it possible to more accurately identify and target specific market segments such as Asian Americans, teenagers, Hispanics, and dual-income households with no kids (DINKs). This leads the marketer away from mass media to promotional tools that reach only the segment that has been targeted.
- *Consumer empowerment.* Consumers today are more powerful and sophisticated than their predecessors. Fostering this greater power are more single-person households, smaller families, higher education levels, and more experienced consumers. Empowered consumers are more skeptical of commercial messages and demand information tailored to their needs.
- *Increased advertising clutter.* Not only are consumers becoming more sophisticated, they are becoming more jaded as well. The proliferation of advertising stimuli has diluted the effectiveness of any single message. There is no end in sight to this "message" proliferation.
- *Database technology.* The ability of firms to generate, collate, and manage databases has created diverse communications opportunities beyond mass media. These databases can be used to create customer and noncustomer profiles. With this information, highly targeted direct response and telemarketing programs can be implemented.
- *Channel power.* In some product and market categories, there has been a shift in power away from big manufacturers toward big retailers. The new "power retailers," such as WalMart, The Gap, Toys "R" Us, and Home Depot, are able to demand promotional fees and allowances from manufacturers, which diverts funds away from advertising and into special events or other promotions.

4. Don E. Schultz, Stanley I. Tannenbaum, and Robert F. Lauterborn, *Integrated Marketing Communications* (Lincolnwood, Ill.: NTC Business Books, 1993), xvii.
5. Esther Thorson and Jeri Moore, *Integrated Communication: Synergy of Persuasive Voices* (Mahwah, N.J.: Erlbaum, 1996), 1.
6. See additional discussion in Thorson and Moore, *Integrated Communication,* Chapter 1.

- *Accountability.* In an attempt to achieve greater accountability for promotional spending, firms have reallocated marketing resources from advertising to more short-term and more easily measurable methods, such as direct marketing and sales promotion.

All these factors have contributed to an increase in the diversity and complexity of the communications tools used by firms to inform and persuade target audiences. Mass media advertising still plays an important role in the communications programs of most firms, whether they are IMC oriented or not. But the opportunity to use other communication tools makes coordination and integration much more challenging than in the past. Both clients and advertising agencies, however, see the payoff as great:

Integrated marketing communications is emerging as one of the most valuable "magic bullets" a firm can use to gain competitive advantage.

—James C. Reilly, IBM

Integrated marketing communications identifies the dynamics of today's marketplace and teaches us how easy it is to prosper under the new rules of communication.

—Richard Fizdale, Leo Burnett[7]

Sounds Great . . . So What's So Hard about IMC?
Exhibit IMC 1.1 presents a hierarchy of participants that helps to illustrate the challenges that marketers will encounter when attempting to surround current or prospective customers with a "wall" of integrated marketing communications. Notice that the marketer typically brings to the process a marketing plan, goals and objectives, and perhaps a database that will identify current and prospective customers. These databases are developed from customer contacts or are purchased from specialty research firms. The marketer's advertising agency will help research the market, suggest creative strategies, and produce IMC materials. In addition, agencies can assist in placing materials in outlets that range from conventional mass media to event sponsorship to Internet advertising. The exhibit also shows the number of specialized marketing communication organizations that may need to be hired in conjunction with or in place of the firm's ad agency to execute the IMC campaign. Back in Chapter 2 we referred to such specialists as external facilitators. This is where the process starts to get messy.

The fact is that most ad agencies simply do not have all the internal expertise necessary to develop and manage every marketing communication tool. First and foremost, the ad agency is the expert in the development and placement of mass media advertising. This is especially the case for large advertising agencies. Mega-agencies such as those listed in Exhibit 2.8 became mega-agencies because of their prowess in mass media advertising. Because they have a lot invested in their mass media expertise, the large ad agency is routinely criticized for the tendency to push mass media as the best communication solution for any client.[8]

Hence, when marketers want other communication options, they often must turn to external facilitators to get the expertise they are looking for. For example, companies such as Avon and Ford's Lincoln Mercury division retain Wunderman Cato Johnson–Chicago just to help them with event management, and Pepsi and Philip Morris retain Cyrk-Simon Worldwide to design and run their Pepsi Stuff and Marlboro Miles branded-merchandise reward programs.[9] As reflected by the dashed line in Exhibit IMC 1.1, in many instances marketing organizations must literally bypass their traditional advertising agency to get the expertise they require for building their brands.

---

7. These quotes are taken from Schultz, Tannenbaum, and Lauterborn, *Integrated Marketing Communicaiton,* pages ix, xi, xii.
8. For example, see Osterman, "This Changes Everything"; Spethmann, "Is Advertising Dead?"
9. Spethmann, "Is Advertising Dead?"

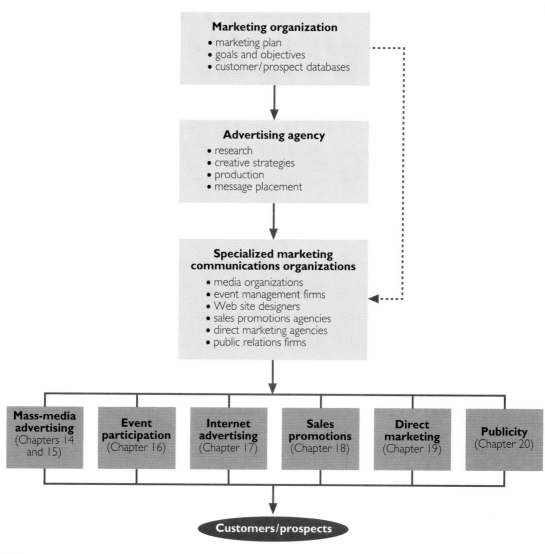

Marketing organization
- marketing plan
- goals and objectives
- customer/prospect databases

Advertising agency
- research
- creative strategies
- production
- message placement

Specialized marketing communications organizations
- media organizations
- event management firms
- Web site designers
- sales promotions agencies
- direct marketing agencies
- public relations firms

| Mass-media advertising (Chapters 14 and 15) | Event participation (Chapter 16) | Internet advertising (Chapter 17) | Sales promotions (Chapter 18) | Direct marketing (Chapter 19) | Publicity (Chapter 20) |

Customers/prospects

EXHIBIT IMC 1.1

The integrated marketing communications hierarchy.

Coordination and integration of a marketing communications program becomes much more complex as various external facilitators are brought into the picture. These diverse specialists often will view one another as competitors for the client's marketing dollars, and will most likely champion their particular specialty, be it event sponsorship, sales promotions, the Internet, direct marketing, or whatever. This is just human nature in a free enterprise system. But instead of ending up with coordination and integration, we now have a situation characterized by conflict and disintegration. Of course, conflict and disintegration are *not* what the marketer wants for his or her brand.

Advertising agencies of all sizes are well aware of these challenges, and as we noted in Chapter 2, many are attempting to redesign themselves to add more internal expertise that can foster the goals of IMC. Sometimes this redesign comes in the form of new cross-functional work units launched within the traditional agency under nifty names such as J. Walter Thompson USA's 35-person, Total Solutions Group; or DDB Needham Worldwide's 140-person, Beyond DDB.[10] Other times, expertise is added when big companies buy out smaller specialist firms to supplement their range of services.[11]

10. Fitzgerald, "Beyond Advertising."
11. Spethmann, "Is Advertising Dead?"

As you can see, this whole business of IMC is about bringing together the right combination of expertise to serve a particular client's marketing needs. This is always a complex undertaking with no easy answers.

The IMC process as it is depicted in Exhibit IMC 1.1 shows the participants and the tools of IMC. At the end of Part Two of the text, the "Planning an IMC Campaign" section will look at the strategic planning that goes into the development of an IMC program. And each of the chapters in Part Four will examine different tools to help you understand the options available for executing IMC campaigns. Specifically, Chapters 14 and 15 will emphasize traditional mass media tools, Chapter 16 will consider support media and event sponsorship, Chapter 17 looks at opportunities spawned by the Internet, Chapter 18 reviews the array of possibilities in sales promotion, Chapter 19 provides a comprehensive look at direct marketing, and Chapter 20 completes the set by discussing the public relations function. So if Exhibit IMC 1.1 is not completely clear to you at this point, fear not. There's more to come on all this! But enough about what's to come. Now let's meet the participants in our comprehensive IMC case.

An Agency in Pursuit of Integrated Marketing Communication . . .

Northlich Stolley LaWarre www.northlich.com/. Northlich Stolley LaWarre (NSL), based in Cincinnati, Ohio, was founded in 1949 but saved its most dramatic growth spurt for the decade of the nineties. In 1996 NSL's billings exceeded $100 million for the first time, and for 1998, *Adweek* magazine ranked NSL in the top 50 among Midwest ad agencies, with a net revenue of $15.9 million. NSL has served a diverse client base, including ChoiceCare/Humana Managed Healthcare, Fidelity Institutional Retirement Services, Procter & Gamble—Attends, Metamucil, Millstone Brands, Roto-Rooter Plumbing Services, and StarKist Seafood Products, to name a few. Samples of NSL's work on its own behalf and for some of its clients are shown in Exhibit IMC 1.2. NSL became the agency of record for Cincinnati Bell Inc. two years before the launch of Cincinnati Bell Wireless.

NSL executives attribute their success as a full-service communications agency to two defining principles:

> We carefully define and then exceed client expectations in all that we do.
> We strive to objectively measure the business results of everything we do.

Other elements of the NSL model for success include the following:

- Relentless pursuit of audience insights that leads to distinctive and preemptive value propositions for clients' brands.
- Targeted programs that divide and conquer with each constituency.
- Provocative advertising that disrupts the category and causes a chain reaction.
- Compelling demos that deliver memorable visualization benefits.
- Integrated communications that drive home the essence of a brand's value proposition in every vehicle.

While the folks at NSL usually refer to their company as an advertising agency, it is probably more accurate to think of NSL as an IMC agency. IMC at NSL means using whatever marketing tools are appropriate for the marketing problem at hand. That could mean that direct marketing must be used in conjunction with image-oriented advertising, or that PR alone is the best way to proceed. To truly leverage the power of

When I go out for coffee,
I have to take my passport.

Calzones $3.89
CHEESE AND 1 ITEM

LaRosa's 347-1111

EXHIBIT IMC 1.2

NSL advertising samples.

Here's how to make sure they
won't forget their lunch.

Classic Tuna Sandwich

The best thing between
breakfast and dinner.

Nutty Tuna Salad Pitas

a brand name and motivate consumers, it takes an intimate understanding of how to orchestrate different media and messages. The overriding goal is always to build the strength of the client's brand.

NSL employs on the order of 150 people full time. The NSL leadership team featured in Exhibit IMC 1.3 gives an indication of the range of expertise that NSL can marshall to serve clients' communication needs. This starts with an extensive client-service capability that includes strategic marketing planning, product positioning, and market research expertise. NSL also provides a full line of creative and production services for development of media advertising, collateral, packaging, point-of-purchase, direct-marketing, and other IMC materials. The direct-marketing department will assist clients with program design, strategy development, program oversight, measurement, and effectiveness evaluation. NSL offers complete media planning, buying, and postbuy evaluation, and has additional expertise in interactive marketing with specific capabilities in Web site design and construction. The public relations group at NSL also has full-service capabilities including media and community relations, consumer promotion activities, employee relations and crisis management. The combination of NSL's philosophy, its manageable size, its co-location of diverse capabilities, a team-oriented work environment, and its excellent range and depth of expertise puts NSL in an excellent position to fulfill its promise of integrated marketing communication.

In 1998, after 23 years with the agency, Mark Serrianne was named NSL's president and CEO. He is clearly an advocate for IMC. As executive vice president in 1987, Serrianne began the redesign of NSL from a conventional, mass-media-oriented ad agency to a full-service marketing communications firm. One conclusion should be obvious: The transformation from conventional to integrated is not something that happens overnight. In his view, NSL has created an internal culture that embraces and rewards integration. Simple aspects of the daily work environment at NSL feed into the drive for integration. For example, no one at NSL, including the CEO, has a private office. In Serrianne's view, the open-office policy "has created more energy . . . culturally sends a good message to everyone . . . and breaks down barriers between departments." At the same time, NSL's office complex is filled with numerous breakout rooms of various sizes that allow teams of employees to retreat and focus on clients' problems from a cross-departmental perspective. "Clients are

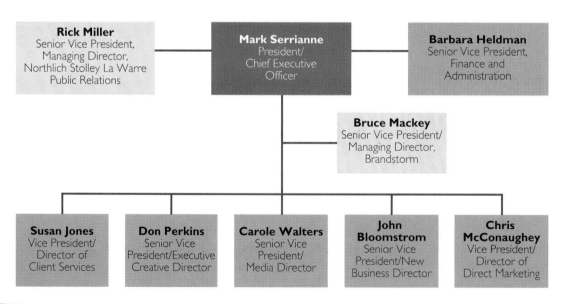

EXHIBIT IMC 1.3

The NSL leadership team.

convinced to buy integrated services," says Serrianne, "once you have some pretty good case histories and they have experience with our multidisciplinary teams."[12] We will see those multidisciplinary teams at work in the case history of the launch of Cincinnati Bell Wireless.

A Client in Pursuit of Integrated Marketing Communication . . .

Cincinnati Bell Inc. www.cincinnatibell.com/. The other key player in our ongoing IMC case history is Cincinnati Bell Inc., a diversified and innovative communications company that employed about 30,000 people in 1997. Cincinnati Bell Inc. is a multifaceted enterprise made up of subsidiary companies that compete in three major business domains. In the domain of information systems, Cincinnati Bell Information Systems Inc. (CBIS) supplies and administers customer-care and billing solutions for the communications and cable TV industries. In the domain of teleservices, MATRIXX Marketing Inc. provides a complete line of telemarketing solutions to a wide array of corporate customers. CBIS and MATRIXX are each market leaders in their business domains as measured by revenue, profit performance, and innovation.

Cincinnati Bell's third business domain is communication services. Its various units, such as Cincinnati Bell Telephone Company (CBT), Cincinnati Bell Long Distance, and Cincinnati Bell Supply Company, furnish local and long distance phone service, Yellow Pages and directory service, and telecommunications equipment in the Greater Cincinnati metropolitan market. Quoting from one of Cincinnati Bell's annual reports, "The Company's strategy is to be a leader in helping communication companies and marketing-intensive businesses worldwide compete more effectively through advanced billing, customer information, and teleservice solutions, while enhancing its position as the premier provider of communication services in Greater Cincinnati." Here we'd expect you to conclude that Cincinnati Bell is a lot more than just a sleepy little telephone service provider nestled on the banks of the Ohio River.

Indeed, in the communication services domain, CBT is explicitly dedicated to a strategy of being more than just "the phone company." CBT strives to offer products and services to assist its household customers in exploring their world and managing their lives, and to help small businesses in the dynamic new age of communication technologies. Products and services introduced by CBT that typify this commitment to rapid diffusion of new technologies include the CBT Feature Phone, PhoneGear, Fuse Internet access service, and direct broadcast satellite television from CBTV. Advertising for some of these products and services is shown in Exhibit IMC 1.4. The common theme represented by the Cincinnati Bell brand name is the commitment to superior service, quality, innovation, and value. These types of connections to the Cincinnati Bell brand name would of course become an asset when CBT decided that it was time to launch a new wireless phone service in the Greater Cincinnati metropolitan market.

In the fourth quarter of 1997, Cincinnati Bell Inc. signed a landmark agreement with AT&T Wireless Services that marked the birth of Cincinnati Bell Wireless (www.cbwireless.com). Previously, they hired away John F. (Jack) Cassidy from Cantel Cellular Services in Canada to become the new president of CBW. The stage was set for a tumultuous six-month period in which NSL and CBW would prepare to launch advanced personal communication services: voice, paging, and E-mail messaging, with other features and associated products. The strategy formulation that occurred in the period from November 1997 through the spring of 1998 will be described in the next installment of this IMC case history, at the end of Part Two.

---

12. Sue Fulton, "Local to National: One Agency's Strategy," *Ad Business Report*, June 1998, 1.

EXHIBIT IMC 1.4

CBT sample ads prior to its launch of wireless phone service: billboard, print, and direct mail.

IMC EXERCISES

1. Refer to the four definitions of integrated marketing communications (IMC) on pages 124 and 125, then write a definition of IMC in your own words. Explain why the integration of marketing communications tools is such a bold departure from traditional mass-media advertising.

2. It has been said that the biggest challenge of IMC is to speak to the customer via multiple communications tools in *a single voice*. What does *a single voice* mean, and what's so hard about achieving *a single voice* in an IMC campaign?

3. Examine the Northlich Stolley LaWarre (NSL) organizational structure, Exhibit IMC 1.3. How do you think this structure would compare to the structure of a more traditional advertising agency? How does the structure of NSL lend itself to the execution of the Cincinnati Bell Wireless IMC campaign?

4. Why would a regional company like Cincinnati Bell, Inc. seek out an advertising agency with IMC capabilities to launch its new wireless phone service? Why might Cincinnati Bell not want to rely on mass-media advertising alone to sell its new service? (Hint: Refer to the discussion of the factors contributing to IMC's rise: fragmentation of media, better audience assessment, consumer empowerment, increased advertising clutter, database technology, channel power, and accountability.)

PART TWO

THE PLANNING:
ANALYZING THE
ADVERTISING
ENVIRONMENT

Successful advertising campaigns rely on a clear understanding of how and why consumers make their purchase decisions. Successful campaigns are also usually rooted in sound marketing strategies and careful research about a brand's market environment. This understanding of the market, sound marketing strategy, and research are brought together in a formal advertising plan. Part Two, "The Planning: Analyzing the Advertising Environment," discusses several important bases for the development of an advertising plan and concludes with a look at ad planning for international markets.

Part Two of the text focuses on the second of the 4Ps of advertising—*planning*—and reveals the care and detail needed to effectively plan an advertising campaign. This planning stage provides advertisers with the information and insights needed to take on the creative challenges of the next stage of advertising, the preparation.

Advertising and Consumer Behavior Chapter 5, "Advertising and Consumer Behavior," begins with an assessment of the way consumers make product and brand choices. These decisions depend on consumers' involvement and prior experiences with the product in question. This chapter also addresses consumer behavior and advertising from both psychological and sociological points of view. It concludes with a discussion of how external factors, such as culture and reference groups, affect the way individuals make decisions.

Market Segmentation, Positioning, and the Value Proposition Chapter 6, "Market Segmentation, Positioning, and the Value Proposition," details how these three fundamental planning efforts are developed by an organization. With a combination of audience and competitive information, products and services are developed that have features and images that are both valued by target customers and are different from those of the competition. Finally, the way advertising contributes to communicating value to consumers is explained and modeled.

Advertising Research Chapter 7, "Advertising Research," discusses the types of research conducted by advertisers and the role information plays in planning an advertising effort. Advertisers do research before messages are prepared, during the preparation process, and after messages are running in the market. Without effective research, advertising planning is greatly compromised. The new aspects of the account planning process are also covered int this chapter.

The Advertising Plan Chapter 8, "The Advertising Plan," explains how formal advertising plans are developed. The inputs to the advertising plan are laid out in detail, and the process of setting advertising objectives—both communications and sales objectives—is described. The methods for setting an advertising budget are presented, including the widely adopted and preferred objective-and-task approach.

Advertising Planning: An International Perspective Chapter 9, "Advertising Planning: An International Perspective," introduces issues related to planning advertising targeted to international audiences. Global forces are creating markets that are more affluent, more accessible, and more predictable. In the midst of these trends toward international trade, marketers are redefining the nature and scope of the markets for their goods and services while adjusting to the creative, media, and regulatory challenges of competing across national boundaries.

CHAPTER 5

After reading and thinking about this chapter, you will be able to do the following:

◄► Describe the four basic stages of consumer decision making.

◄► Explain how consumers adapt their decision-making processes as a function of involvement and experience.

◄► Discuss how advertising may influence consumer behavior through its effects on various psychological states.

◄► Discuss the interaction of culture and advertising.

◄► Discuss the role of sociological factors in consumer behavior and advertising response.

The Japanese marketplace is one of the toughest competitive arenas in the world. Japanese consumers are among the most affluent and educated in the world. Giant U.S. corporations such as Procter & Gamble often struggle in this challenging environment. Up until 1995, P&G—maker of dishwashing products such as Dawn, Joy, Ivory, and Cascade—did not sell any dish soap in Japan.[1] Soaps are P&G's core business; P&G aspires to market all its brands around the world; and P&G is one of the most sophisticated companies in the world when it comes to executing multimillion-dollar advertising campaigns. But how to get started in Japan?

P&G used a tried-and-true formula. They sent their managers into the field to talk to consumers and study Japanese dishwashing rituals. They watched the Japanese wash their dishes, videotaped them washing dishes, and talked to them before, during, and after dishwashing. As a result of this careful observation, P&G researchers discovered one critical habit: Japanese homemakers, one after another, squirted out more liquid than was called for, more than was needed, and more than was effective. P&G managers interpreted this as a clear sign of consumers' frustrations with existing products. Implicitly, these consumers wanted a more powerful cleaning liquid, and were trying to get it by simply using more of their current brand. But it wasn't working.

P&G's chemical engineers in Kobe, Japan, went to work on a new, highly concentrated soap formula just for the frustrated Japanese consumer. The marketing pitch would be simple and to the point: A little bit of Joy cleans better, yet is easier on the hands. Encouraged by positive results in test marketing, P&G prepared for a nationwide launch in Japan.

For its advertising campaign P&G settled on a documentary-style TV ad in which a famous Japanese comedian named Junji Takada dropped in on unsuspecting homemakers (see Exhibit 5.1), with his camera crew in tow, to test Joy on the household's dirty dishes. Television ads featured a shot of a grease slick in a sink full of dirty dishes. One squirt of Joy and the grease disappeared. With this simple visual demonstration the ad communicated to consumers that the new Joy was more potent than their old brand. It wasn't long before Joy began racking up impressive market share gains throughout Japan.

Of course, P&G's Japanese competitors were quick to notice the success of Joy. The Kao Corporation (think of Kao as the P&G of Japan) conducted research to better understand Joy's success. Kao's research showed that more than 70 percent of Joy's users began using it because the TV ads persuaded them that this new brand offered superior performance. Now that's effective advertising! Kao's management admitted: "We had

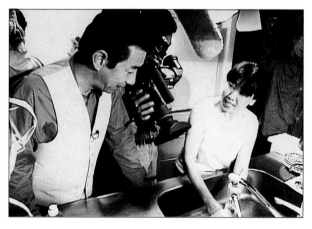

EXHIBIT 5.1

P&G used a documentary-style advertising campaign for its launch of Joy in Japan: on the road in search of greasy dishes. The interviewer is comedian Junji Takada. His celebrity status and sense of humor were important elements in creating likable and persuasive TV commercials. www.pg.com/

1.   Norihiko Shirouzu, "P&G's Joy Makes an Unlikely Splash in Japan," *Wall Street Journal,* December 10, 1997, B1.

mistakenly assumed Japanese didn't care much about grease-fighting power in dish soaps. The reality was that people were eating more meat and fried food and were frustrated about grease stains on their plastic dishes and storage containers."[2] Kao's lack of understanding of what was important to the customer led to a predictable outcome: Joy became Japan's best-selling dishwashing soap.

Many things must go right for a new brand to enter a crowded marketplace and achieve market leadership, as Joy did in Japan. The product's performance, its packaging, its pricing, and the advertising campaign must work synergistically to achieve this level of success. But success can commonly be traced back to understanding consumers, creating products that address their needs, and executing ad campaigns that persuade consumers that only one brand has just what they're looking for. As with Joy in Japan, insights about the behavior of consumers are crucial to advertising professionals. Before advertisers initiate campaigns for any product or service, they need a thorough understanding of what's important to the customer. This understanding greatly increases the advertiser's chance of effecting purchase behavior.

Chapters 1 through 4 provided important background and perspectives about the business of advertising. With this background in place, we are now ready to begin consideration of how one would actually go about planning for an advertising campaign. Where to begin? How does one get started? As you saw in the preceding success story about marketing dishwashing liquids in Japan, a great place to start is with unique insights about your consumers.

Consumer behavior is defined as the entire broad spectrum of things that affect, derive from, or form the context of human consumption. Like all human behavior, the behavior of consumers is complicated, rich, and varied. However, advertisers must make it their job to understand consumers if they want to experience sustained success in creating effective advertising. Sometimes this understanding comes in the form of comprehensive research efforts; other times in the form of years of experience and implicit theories; other times in the form of blind, dumb luck (rarely attributed as such). However this understanding comes about, it is a key factor for advertising success.

This chapter summarizes the concepts and frameworks we believe are most helpful in trying to understand consumer behavior. We will describe consumer behavior and attempt to explain it, in its incredible diversity, from two different perspectives. The first portrays consumers as reasonably systematic decision makers who seek to maximize the benefits they derive from their purchases. The second views consumers as active interpreters (meaning makers) of advertising, whose membership in various cultures, societies, and communities significantly affects their interpretation and response to advertising. These two perspectives are different ways of looking at the exact same people and the exact same behaviors. Though different in essential assumptions, both of these perspectives offer something valuable to the task of actually getting the work of advertising done.

The point is that no one perspective can adequately explain consumer behavior. Consumers are psychological, social, cultural, historical, and economical at the same time. For example, suppose a sociologist and a psychologist both saw someone buying a car. The psychologist might explain this behavior in terms of attitudes, decision criteria, and the like, while the sociologist would probably explain it in terms of the buyer's social environment and circumstances (that is, income, housing conditions, social class, the social value or "cultural capital" the brand afforded, and so on). Both explanations may be valid, but each is incomplete. The bottom line is that all consumer behavior is complex and multifaceted. Why you or any other consumer buys a movie ticket rather than a lottery ticket, or Pepsi rather than Coke, or Duracell rather than Eveready, is a function of psychological, economic, sociological, anthropological, historical, textual, and other forces. No single explanation is sufficient. With this in mind, we offer two basic perspectives on consumer behavior.

2.   Ibid.

Perspective One: The Consumer as Decision Maker. ◀▶ One way

to view consumer behavior is as a logical, sequential process culminating with the individual's reaping a set of benefits from a product or service that satisfies that person's perceived needs. In this basic view, we can think of individuals as purposeful decision makers who take matters one step at a time. All consumption episodes might then be conceived as a sequence of four basic stages:

1. Need recognition
2. Information search and alternative evaluation
3. Purchase
4. Postpurchase use and evaluation

The Consumer Decision-Making Process. A brief discussion of what typically happens at each

stage will give us a foundation for understanding consumers, and it can also illuminate opportunities for developing powerful advertising.

Need Recognition. The consumption process begins when people perceive a need. A **need state** arises when one's desired state of affairs differs from one's actual state of affairs. Need states are accompanied by a mental discomfort or anxiety that motivates action; the severity of this discomfort can be widely variable depending on the genesis of the need. For example, the need state that arises when one runs out of toothpaste would involve very mild discomfort for most people, whereas the need state that accompanies the breakdown of one's automobile on a dark and deserted highway in Minnesota in mid-February can approach true desperation.

One way advertising works is to point to and thereby activate needs that will motivate consumers to buy a product or service. For instance, nearly every fall, advertisers from product categories as diverse as autos, snowblowers, and footwear roll out predictions for another severe winter and encourage consumers to prepare themselves before it's too late. Such an appeal is very productive when the previous winter was especially severe and the advertiser does a good job of capturing the sights and sounds of last year's terrible storms.

Following an especially severe winter in the Northeast, Jeep dealers in New York State warned, "Last year's winter produced 17 winter storms. . . . This year, the *Old Farmer's Almanac* is predicting another winter with above-average snowfall." As a result of this campaign, Jeep dealers in the New York region sold every vehicle they could get their hands on.[3] Consumers in New York obviously responded to the advertiser's effort to activate a need state.

Many factors can influence the need states of consumers. For instance, as discussed in Chapter 4, Maslow's hierarchy of needs suggests that a consumer's level of affluence can have a dramatic impact on the types of needs he or she might perceive as relevant. The less fortunate are concerned with fundamental needs, such as food and shelter; more-affluent consumers may fret over which new piece of Williams-Sonoma kitchen gadgetry or other accouterment to place in their uptown condo. The former's needs are predominantly for physiological survival and basic comfort, while the latter's may have more to do with seeking to validate personal accomplishments and derive status and recognition through consumption. While income clearly matters in this regard, it would be a mistake to believe that the poor have no aesthetic concerns, or that the rich are always oblivious to the need for basic essentials. The central point is that a variety of needs can be fulfilled through consumption, and it is reasonable to suggest that consumers are looking to satisfy needs when they buy products or services.

Products and services should provide benefits that fulfill consumers' needs; hence, one of the advertiser's primary jobs is to make the connection between the two for the consumer. Benefits come in many forms. Some are more functional—that is, they

---

3.   Fara Warner, "Relishing and Embellishing Forecasts for Frigid Winter," *Wall Street Journal*, December 1, 1994, B1.

derive from the more objective performance characteristics of a product or service. Convenience, reliability, nutrition, durability, and economy are descriptors that refer to **functional benefits**.

Consumers may also choose products that provide **emotional benefits**; these are not typically found in some tangible feature or objective characteristic of a product. Emotional benefits are more subjective and may be perceived differently from one consumer to the next. Products and services help consumers feel pride, avoid guilt, relieve fear, and experience intense pleasure. These are powerful consumption motives that advertisers often try to activate. Can you find the emotional benefits promised in Exhibit 5.2?

Any advertiser must develop a keen appreciation for the kinds of benefits that consumers might derive from its product and brand. Even in the same product category, the benefits promised may be quite disparate. As shown in Exhibit 5.3, the makers of the Geo Metro portray their vehicle as the epitome of functional transportation. The

EXHIBIT 5.2

All parents want to be good to their child. This ad promises both functional benefits and emotional rewards for diligent parents.
www.jnj.com/

EXHIBIT 5.3

Functional benefits rule in this ad. Of course, the "tiny, little price tag" of the Geo Metro is a good place to start when promoting functionality.
www.chevrolet.com
/metro/index.htm

EXHIBIT 5.4

While the Dodge Neon and Geo Metro both target youthful, first-time car buyers, the Neon's promise has a different twist. Is the Neon promising just functional benefits? www.4adodge.com/neon/

Dodge Neon offers inexpensive transportation along with hipness and cuteness, per Exhibit 5.4. The makers of the Acura Integra GS-R sports coupe appeal to the emotional rewards of ownership with ads like that in Exhibit 5.5.

The ads for these three cars demonstrate the diversity of needs perceived by consumers, along with benefits offered by advertisers. If consumers do not know about or forget the benefits that a particular brand is supposed to provide, the maker's advertising effort is likely at fault.

Information Search and Alternative Evaluation. Given that a consumer has recognized a need, it is often not obvious what would be the best way to satisfy that need. For example, if you have a fear of being trapped in a blizzard in upstate New York, a condo on Miami Beach may be a much better solution than a Jeep or new snow tires. Need recognition simply sets in motion a process that may involve an extensive information search and careful evaluation of alternatives prior to purchase. Of course, during this search and evaluation, there are numerous opportunities for the advertiser to influence the final decision.

Once a need has been recognized, information for the decision is acquired through an internal or external search. The consumer's first option for information is to draw on personal experience and prior knowledge. This **internal search** for information may be all that is required. When a consumer has considerable prior experience with the products in question, attitudes about the alternatives may be well established and determine choice, as is suggested in the ad for Campbell's soup shown in Exhibit 5.6.

This ad makes no concession to functional benefits. Driving is about emotional rewards. But which emotional rewards? www.acura.com/

For a cultural icon such as Campbell's soup, an advertiser can assume that consumers have some prior knowledge. Here the advertiser seeks to enhance that knowledge to lead people to use more canned soup. www.campbellsoups.com/

An internal search can also tap into information that has accumulated in one's memory as a result of repeated advertising exposures. Affecting people's beliefs about a brand before their actual use of it, or merely establishing the existence of the brand in the consumer's consciousness, is a critical function of advertising. As noted in Chapter 1, the purpose of delayed response advertising is to generate recognition of and a favorable predisposition toward a brand so that when consumers enter into search mode, that brand will be one they immediately consider as a possible solution to their needs. If the consumer has not used a brand previously and has no recollection that it even exists, then that brand probably will not be the brand of choice.

It is certainly plausible that an internal search will not turn up enough information to yield a decision. The consumer then proceeds with an external search. An **external search** involves visiting retail stores to examine the alternatives, seeking input from friends and relatives about their experiences with the products in question, or perusing professional product evaluations furnished in various publications such as *Consumer Reports* or *Car and Driver*. In addition, when consumers are in an active information-gathering mode, they may be receptive to detailed, informative advertisements delivered through any of the print media, or they may be motivated to post a product inquiry on a corporate Web site.

During an internal or external search, consumers are not merely gathering information for its own sake. They have some need that is propelling the process, and their goal is to make a decision that yields benefits. The consumer searches and is simultaneously forming attitudes about possible alternatives. This is the alternative-evaluation component of the decision process, and it is another key phase for the advertiser to target.

Alternative evaluation will be structured by the consumer's consideration set and evaluative criteria. The **consideration set** is the subset of brands from a particular product category that becomes the focal point of the consumer's evaluation. Most product categories contain too many brands for all to be considered, so the consumer finds some way to focus the search and evaluation. For example, for autos, consumers may consider only cars priced less than $10,000, or only cars that have antilock brakes, or only foreign-made cars, or only cars sold at dealerships within a five-mile radius of their work or home. A critical function of advertising is to make consumers aware of the brand and keep them aware, so that the brand has a chance to be part of the consideration set. Virtually all ads try to do this.

As the search-and-evaluation process proceeds, consumers form evaluations based on the characteristics or attributes that brands in their consideration set have in common. These product attributes or performance characteristics are referred to as **evaluative criteria**. Evaluative criteria differ from one product category to the next and can include many factors, such as price, texture, warranty terms, color, scent, or fat content. As Exhibit 5.7 suggests, one traditional evaluative criterion for judging airlines has been on-time arrivals.

It is critical for advertisers to have as complete an understanding as possible of the evaluative criteria that consumers use to make their buying decisions. They must also know how consumers rate their brand in comparison with others from the consideration set. Understanding consumers' evaluative criteria furnishes a powerful starting point for any advertising campaign and will be examined in more depth later in the chapter.

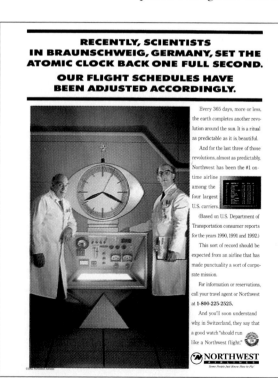

EXHIBIT 5.7

Advertisers must know the relevant evaluative criteria for their products. For an airline, on-time arrival is certainly an important matter.
www.nwa.com/

Purchase. At this third stage, purchase occurs. The consumer has made a decision, and a sale is made. Great, right? Well, to a point. As nice as it is to make a sale, things are far from over at the point of sale. In fact, it would be a big mistake to view purchase as the culmination of the decision-making process. No matter what the product category, the consumer is likely to buy from it again in the future. So, what happens after the sale is very important to advertisers.

Postpurchase Use and Evaluation. The goal for marketers and advertisers must not be simply to generate a sale; it must be to create satisfied and, ultimately, loyal customers. The data to support this position are quite astounding. Research shows that about 65 percent of the average company's business comes from its present, satisfied customers, and that 91 percent of dissatisfied customers will never buy again from the company that disappointed them.[4] Thus, consumers' evaluations of products in use become a major determinant of which brands will be in the consideration set the next time around.

Customer satisfaction derives from a favorable postpurchase experience. It may develop after a single use, but more likely it will require sustained use. Advertising can play an important role in inducing customer satisfaction by creating appropriate expectations for a brand's performance, or by helping the consumer who has already bought the advertised brand to feel good about doing so.

Advertising plays an important role in alleviating the cognitive dissonance that can occur after a purchase. **Cognitive dissonance** is the anxiety or regret that lingers after a difficult decision. Often, rejected alternatives have attractive features that lead people to second-guess their own decisions. If the goal is to generate satisfied customers, this dissonance must be resolved in a way that leads consumers to conclude that they did make the right decision after all. Purchasing high-cost items or choosing from categories that include many desirable and comparable brands can yield high levels of cognitive dissonance.

When dissonance is expected, it makes good sense for the advertiser to reassure buyers with detailed information about its brands. Postpurchase reinforcement programs might involve direct mail or other types of personalized contacts with the customer. This postpurchase period represents a great opportunity for the advertiser to have the undivided attention of the consumer and to provide information and advice about product use that will increase customer satisfaction.[5] It can also help marketers in getting consumers to think about their new purchase in the way advertisers want them to. For an example, see the ad for Isuzu shown in Exhibit 5.8.

Four Modes of Consumer Decision Making.

As you may be thinking about now, consumers aren't always deliberate and systematic; sometimes they are hasty, impulsive, or even irrational. The search time that people put into their purchases can vary dramatically for different types of products. Would you give the purchase of a toothbrush the same amount of effort as the purchase of a new stereo system? Probably not, unless you've been chastised by your dentist recently. Why is that T-shirt you bought at a concert more important to you than the brand of orange juice you had for breakfast this morning? Does buying a Valentine's gift from Victoria's Secret create different feelings than buying a newspaper for your father? When you view a TV ad for car batteries, do you carefully memorize the information being presented so that it will be there to draw on the next time you're evaluating the brands in your consideration set?

Some purchase decisions are just more engaging than others. In the following sections we will elaborate on the view of consumer as decision maker by explaining four decision-making modes that help advertisers appreciate the richness and complexity of consumer behavior. These four modes are determined by a consumer's involvement and prior experiences with the product or service in question.

---

4.   Terry G. Vavra, *Aftermarketing: How to Keep Customers for Life through Relationship Marketing* (Homewood, Ill.: Business One Irwin, 1992), 13.
5.   Ibid.

This ad offers lots of reassurance to those who buy an Isuzu Trooper. This vehicle not only will prove to be a great cargo hauler, but also will make purchasers the envy of their friends and family. www .isuzu.com/home.htm

The emotional appeal in this Casio ad is just one of many involvement devices. The play on water resistance also increases involvement as the reader perceives the double meaning. Describe how these devices work. How does Casio use involvement devices at its Web site, www.casio-usa.com/, *to encourage visitors to further explore its products on the site? Describe the involvement devices used by competitor Timex at its home page,* www.timex.com/.

Sources of Involvement. To accommodate the complexity of consumption decisions, those who study consumer behavior typically talk about the involvement level of any particular decision. **Involvement** is the degree of perceived relevance and personal importance accompanying the choice of a certain product or service within a particular context.[6] Many factors contribute to an individual's level of involvement with any given decision. People can develop interests and avocations in many different areas, such as cooking, photography, pet ownership, or exercise and fitness. Such ongoing personal interests can enhance involvement levels in a variety of product categories. Also, any time a great deal of risk is associated with a purchase—perhaps as a result of the high price of the item, or because the consumer will have to live with the decision for a long period of time— one should also expect elevated involvement.

Consumers can also derive important symbolic meaning from products and brands. Ownership or use of some products can help people reinforce some aspect of their self-image or make a statement to other people who are important to them. If a purchase carries great symbolic and real consequences—such as choosing the right gift for someone on Valentine's Day—it will be highly involving.

Some purchases can also tap into deep emotional concerns or motives. For example, many marketers, from Wal-Mart to Marathon Oil, have solicited consumers with an appeal to their patriotism. The ad for Casio watches (a Japanese product) in Exhibit 5.9 demonstrates that a product doesn't have to be American to wrap itself in the Stars and Stripes. For some individuals, this can be a powerful appeal that strikes an emotional chord. Here, the appeal to emotion influences the consumer's involvement with the decision.

Involvement levels vary not only among product categories for any given individual, but also among individuals for any given product category. For example, some pet owners will feed their pets only the expensive canned products that look and smell like people food. IAMS, whose ad is featured in Exhibit 5.10, understands this and made a special premium dog food for consumers who think of their pets as humans. Many other pet owners, however, are perfectly happy with 50-pound economy sizes.

Now we will use the ideas of involvement and prior experience to help conceive four different types of consumer decision making. These four modes are shown in Exhibit 5.11. Any specific consumption decision is based on a high or low level of prior experience with the product or service in question, and a high or low level of involvement. This yields the four modes of decision making: (1) extended problem solving; (2) limited problem solving; (3) habit or variety seeking; and (4) brand loyalty. Each is described in the following sections.

Extended Problem Solving. When consumers are inexperienced in a particular consumption setting yet find the setting highly involving, they are likely to engage in **extended problem solving**. In this mode, consumers go through a deliberate decision-making process that begins with explicit need recognition, proceeds with careful internal and external search, continues through alternative evaluation and purchase, and ends with a lengthy postpurchase evaluation.

Examples of extended problem solving come with decisions such as choosing a home or a diamond ring, as shown in Exhibit 5.12. These products are expensive, are publicly evaluated, and can carry a considerable amount of risk in terms of making an uneducated decision. Selecting one's first new automobile or choosing a college are two other consumption settings that may require extended problem solving. Extended problem solving is the exception, not the rule.

Limited Problem Solving. In this decision-making mode, experience and involvement are both low. **Limited problem solving** is a more common mode of decision making. In this mode, a consumer is less systematic in his or her decision making. The consumer has a new problem to solve, but it is not a problem that is interesting or engaging, so the information search is limited to simply trying the first brand encountered. For example, let's say a young couple have just brought home a new baby, and suddenly

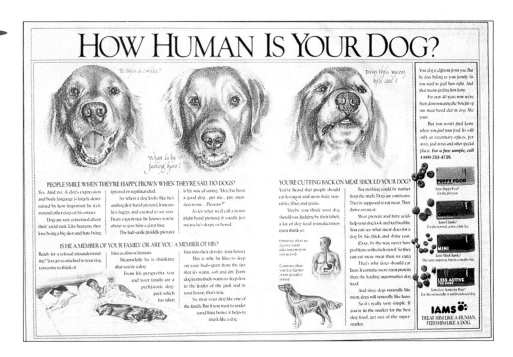

	High Involvement	Low Involvement
Low Experience	Extended problem solving	Limited problem solving
High Experience	Brand loyalty	Habit or variety seeking

they perceive a very real need for disposable diapers. At the hospital they received complimentary trial packs of several products, including Pampers disposables. They try the Pampers, find them an acceptable solution to their messy new problem, and take the discount coupon that came with the sample to their local grocery, where they buy several packages. In the limited problem-solving mode, we often see consumers simply seeking adequate solutions to mundane problems. It is also a mode in which just trying a brand or two may be the most efficient way of collecting information about one's options. Of course, smart marketers realize that trial offers can be a preferred means of collecting information, and they facilitate trial of their brands through free samples, inexpensive "trial sizes," or discount coupons.

Habit or Variety Seeking. Habit and variety seeking occur in settings where a decision is uninvolving and a consumer repurchases from the category over and over again. In terms of sheer numbers, habitual purchases are probably the most common decision-making mode. Consumers find a brand of laundry detergent that suits their needs, they run out of the product, and they buy it again. The cycle repeats itself dozens of times per year in an almost mindless fashion. Getting in the habit of buying just one brand can be a way to simplify life and minimize the time invested in "nuisance" purchases. When a consumer perceives little difference among the various competitive brands, it is easier to buy the same brand repeatedly. A lot of consumption decisions are boring but necessary. Habits help us minimize the inconvenience.

In some product categories where a buying habit would be expected, an interesting phenomenon called variety seeking may be observed instead. Remember, **habit** refers to buying a single brand repeatedly as a solution to a simple consumption problem. This can be very tedious, and some consumers fight the boredom through variety seeking. **Variety seeking** refers to the tendency of consumers to switch their selection among various brands in a given category in a seemingly random pattern. This is not to say that a consumer will buy just any brand; he or she probably has two to five brands that all provide similar levels of satisfaction to a particular consumption problem. However, from one purchase occasion to the next, the individual will switch brands from within this set, just for the sake of variety.

Variety seeking is most likely to occur in frequently purchased categories where sensory experience, such as taste or smell, accompanies product use.

*High involvement and low experience typically yield extended problem
solving. Buying an engagement ring is a perfect example of this scenario.
This ad offers lots of advice for the extended problem solver.*
www.adiamondisforever.com/

EXHIBIT 5.13

Dave Thomas of Wendy's combines the reliability of an easily recognizable celebrity with an appeal to variety-seeking behavior. How does this pairing encourage consumers to seek variety? How does Wendy's Web site, www.wendys.com/, encourage consumers to seek variety? How does rival McDonald's offer variety at its site, www.mcdonalds.com/?

Satiation will occur after repeated use and may leave the consumer looking for a fresh sensory experience. Product categories such as soft drinks and alcoholic beverages, snack foods, breakfast cereals, and fast food are prone to variety seeking, as you can see in the Wendy's ad in Exhibit 5.13.

Brand Loyalty. The final decision-making mode is typified by high involvement and rich prior experience. In this mode, **brand loyalty** becomes a major consideration in the purchase decision. Consumers demonstrate brand loyalty when they repeatedly purchase a single brand as their choice to fulfill a specific need. In one sense, brand-loyal purchasers may look as if they have developed a simple buying habit; however, it is important to distinguish brand loyalty from simple habit. Brand loyalty is based on highly favorable attitudes toward the brand and a conscious commitment to find this brand each time the consumer purchases from this category. Conversely, habits are merely consumption simplifiers that are not based on deeply held convictions. Habits can be disrupted through a skillful combination of advertising and sales promotions. Spending advertising dollars to persuade truly brand-loyal consumers to try an alternative can be a great waste of resources.

Brands such as Sony, Gerber, Levi's, Harley-Davidson, FedEx, and the Grateful Dead have inspired loyal consumers. Brand loyalty is something that any marketer aspires to have, but in a world filled with more-savvy consumers and endless product proliferation, it is becoming harder and harder to attain. Brand loyalty may emerge because the consumer perceives that one brand simply outperforms all others in providing some critical functional benefit. For example, the harried business executive may have grown loyal to FedEx's overnight delivery service as a result of repeated satisfactory experiences with FedEx—and as a result of FedEx's advertising that has repeatedly posed the question, Why fool around with anyone else?

Perhaps even more important, brand loyalty can be due to the emotional benefits that accompany certain brands. One of the strongest indicators for brand loyalty has to be the tendency on the part of some loyal consumers to tattoo their bodies with the insignia of their favorite brand. While statistics are not kept on this sort of thing, it would be reasonable to speculate that the worldwide leader in brand-name tattoos is Harley-Davidson. What accounts for Harley's fervent following? Is Harley's brand loyalty simply a function of performing better than its many competitors? Or does a Harley rider derive some deep emotional benefit from taking that big bike out on the open road and leaving civilization far behind? To understand loyalty for a brand such as Harley, one must turn to the emotional benefits, such as feelings of pride, kinship, and nostalgia that attend "the ride." Owning a Harley—perhaps complete with tattoo—makes a person feel different and special. Harley ads are designed to reaffirm the deep emotional appeal of this product.

Strong emotional benefits might be expected from consumption decisions that we classify as highly involving, and they are major determinants of brand loyalty. Indeed, with so many brands in the marketplace, it is becoming harder and harder to create loyalty for one's brand through functional benefits alone. To break free of this brand-parity problem and provide consumers with enduring reasons to become or stay loyal, advertisers are investing more and more effort in communicating the emotional benefits that might be derived from brands in categories as diverse as soup (Campbell's—"Good for the Soul") to cellular service (AirTouch—"Empowerment . . . Boundless . . . It can change your life").

In addition, as suggested by the New Media box on this page, more and more companies are exploring ways to use interactive media to create a dialogue with customers. The hope is that this dialogue may help foster brand loyalty. Amazon.com is frequently portrayed as one of the pioneers in using the World Wide Web as a loyalty-building medium.

Key Psychological Processes.

To complete our consideration of the consumer as a thoughtful decision maker, one key issue remains. We need to examine the explicit psychological consequences of advertising. What does advertising leave in the minds of consumers that ultimately may influence their behavior? For those of you who have previously taken psychology courses, many of the topics in this section will sound familiar.

As we noted earlier in the chapter, a good deal of advertising is designed to ensure recognition and create favorable predispositions toward a brand so that as consumers search for solutions to their problems, they will think of the brand immediately. The goal of any delayed-response ad is to effect some psychological state that will subsequently influence a purchase.

Two ideas borrowed from social psychology are usually the center of attention when discussing the psychological aspects of advertising. First is attitude. **Attitude** is defined as an overall evaluation of any object, person, or issue that varies along a continuum, such as favorable to unfavorable or positive to negative. Attitudes are learned, and if they are based on substantial experience with the object or issue in question, they can be held with great conviction. Attitudes make our lives easier because they simplify decision making; that is, when faced with a choice among several alternatives, we do not need to process new information or analyze the merits of the alternatives. We merely select the alternative we think is the most favorable. We all possess attitudes on thousands of topics, ranging from a religious sect to

NEW MEDIA

CYBERSPACE FOR RENT: BRAND BUILDERS LOOK TO THE INTERNET

The premise of interactive media seems ideally suited for brand development. After all, *interactive* by definition ensures a two-way communication between buyer and seller; communication builds relationships, and relationships translate into brand loyalty. Right? Well, the rules of online selling are far from established, but the medium may prove to be the most powerful tool ever in creating long-term relationships with brand-conscious consumers. Cyberbrand companies such as Amazon.com are working intently to lead the way.

Amazon.com uses a business model built entirely around the interactivity of the Web. Through a service referred to as BookMatcher, Amazon.com asks new customers to express their opinions about ten well-known books. From this exchange, customers' preferences are gauged and new titles are recommended. When a repeat customer visits the site, he or she is welcomed with a personalized greeting and offered a set of recommended titles based on previous purchases. Once customers' favorite authors are identified, the site also alerts them to any new titles by those authors each time they log on to browse Amazon.com's extensive cyber-bookshelves. Amazon.com's conscientious effort to build a loyal customer base through personalized interactivity appears to be on track: At the time of this writing repeat customers accounted for 60 percent of all orders placed. One of these repeaters summarized the appeal this way: "Amazon.com knows the books I like and is the first to tell me when these books come out. What could be a more powerful selling tool than that?"

Sources: "Working the Web," *Marketing Tools* (June 1997): 39–45; "Secrets of the New Brand Builders," *Fortune*, June 22, 1998, 170.

underage drinking. Marketers and advertisers, however, are most interested in one particular class of attitudes—brand attitudes.

Brand attitudes are summary evaluations that reflect preferences for various products and services. The next time you are waiting in a checkout line at the grocery,

Consumer 1	Consumer 2
Cadillacs are clumsy to drive	Cadillacs are sturdy and safe
Cadillacs are expensive	Cadillacs are a good investment
Cadillacs are gas guzzlers	Cadillacs are simple to maintain
Cadillacs are large	Cadillacs are good for long trips
Cadillacs are for senior citizens	Cadillacs are a symbol of one's success

take a good look at the items in your cart. Those items are a direct reflection of your brand attitudes.

But what is the basis for these summary evaluations? Where do brand attitudes come from? Here we need a second idea from social psychology. To understand *why* people hold certain attitudes, we need to assess their specific beliefs. **Beliefs** represent the knowledge and feelings a person has accumulated about an object or issue. They can be logical and factual in nature, or biased and self-serving. A person might believe that Cadillacs are large, garlic consumption promotes weight loss, and pet owners are lonely people. For that person, all these beliefs are valid and can serve as a basis for attitudes toward Cadillacs, garlic, and pets.

If we know a person's beliefs, it is usually possible to infer attitude. Consider the two consumers' beliefs about Cadillacs summarized in Exhibit 5.14. From their beliefs, we might suspect that one of these consumers is a Cadillac owner, while the other will need a dramatic change in beliefs to ever make Cadillac part of his or her consideration set. It follows that the brand attitudes of the two individuals are at opposite ends of the favorableness continuum.

People have many beliefs about various features and attributes of products and brands. Some beliefs are more important than others in determining a person's final evaluation of a brand. Typically, a small number of beliefs—on the order of five to nine—underlie brand attitudes.[7] These beliefs are the critical determinants of an attitude and are referred to as **salient beliefs**.

Clearly, we would expect the number of salient beliefs to vary between product categories. The loyal Harley owner who proudly displays a tattoo will have many more salient beliefs about his bike than he has about his brand of shaving cream. Also, salient beliefs can be modified, replaced, or extinguished. Exhibit 5.15 is a two-page ad from a Sears campaign designed to modify the salient beliefs of its target audience.

Since belief shaping and reinforcement can be one of the principal goals of advertising, it should come as no surprise that advertisers make belief assessment a focal point in their attempts to understand consumer behavior.

Multi-Attribute Attitude Models (MAAMs). **Multi-attribute attitude models (MAAMs)** provide a framework and set of procedures for collecting information from consumers to assess their salient beliefs and attitudes about competitive brands. Chapter 7 will furnish more detail on the topic of data collection procedures, so our purpose here is to highlight the basic components of a MAAMs analysis and illustrate how such an analysis can benefit the advertiser.

Any MAAMs analysis will feature four fundamental components:

- *Evaluative criteria* are the attributes or performance characteristics that consumers use in comparing competitive brands. In pursuing a MAAMs analysis, an advertiser must identify all evaluative criteria relevant to its product category.

7.   Icek Ajzen and Martin Fishbein, *Understanding Attitudes and Predicting Social Behavior* (Englewood Cliffs, N.J.: Prentice-Hall, 1980), 63.

- *Importance weights* reflect the priority that a particular evaluative criterion receives in the consumer's decision-making process. Importance weights can vary dramatically from one consumer to the next; for instance, some people will merely want good taste from their bowl of cereal, while others will be more concerned about fat and fiber content.

- The *consideration set* is that group of brands that represents the real focal point for the consumer's decision. For example, the potential buyer of a luxury sedan might be focusing on Acuras, BMWs, and Saabs. These and comparable brands would be featured in a MAAMs analysis. Cadillac could have a model, like its Seville, that aspired to be part of this consideration set, leading General Motors to conduct a MAAMs analysis featuring the Seville and its foreign competitors. Conversely, it would be silly for GM to include the Geo Metro in a MAAMs analysis with this set of imports.

- *Beliefs* represent the knowledge and feelings that a consumer has about various brands. In a MAAMs analysis, beliefs about each brand's performance on all relevant evaluative criteria are assessed. Beliefs can be matters of fact—Raisin Nut Bran has five grams of fat per serving, same as the six-inch Subway Club—or highly subjective—the Acura Integra sports coupe is the sleekest, sexiest car on the road. It is common for beliefs to vary widely among consumers.

In conducting a MAAMs analysis, we must specify the relevant evaluative criteria for our category, as well as our direct competitors. We then go to consumers and let them tell us what's important and how our brand fares against the competition on the various evaluative criteria. The information generated from this research will give us a

EXHIBIT 5.15

Belief change is a common goal in advertising. With its "Softer Side" campaign, Sears attempted to change beliefs about its stores as a source for women's fashions. www.sears.com/

better appreciation for the salient beliefs that underlie brand attitudes, and it may suggest important opportunities for changing our marketing or advertising to yield more favorable brand attitudes.

Three basic attitude-change strategies can be developed from the MAAMs framework. First, a MAAMs analysis may reveal that consumers do not have an accurate perception of the relative performance of our brand on an important evaluative criterion. For example, consumers may perceive that Crest is far and away the best brand of toothpaste for fighting cavities, when in fact all brands with a fluoride additive perform equally well on cavity prevention. Correcting this misperception could become our focal point if we compete with Crest.

Second, a MAAMs analysis could uncover that our brand is perceived as the best performer on an evaluative criterion that most consumers do not view as very important. The task for advertising in this instance would be to persuade consumers that what our brand offers (say, more baking soda than any other toothpaste) is more important than they had thought previously.

Third, the MAAMs framework may lead to the conclusion that the only way to improve attitudes toward our brand would be through the introduction of a new attribute to be featured in our advertising. For example, the advertisement in Exhibit 5.16 makes the case that a platinum sensor in the thermostat is something you should be looking for the next time you purchase an oven. Interested? Check it out at www.thermador.com/.

When marketers use the MAAMs approach, good things can result in terms of more-favorable brand attitudes and improved market share. When marketers carefully isolate key evaluative criteria, bring products to the marketplace that perform well on the focal criteria, and develop ads that effectively shape salient beliefs about the brand, the results can be dramatic—as we saw in the case of Joy in Japan. If you want another excellent example, turn to Chapter 7 and read how Goodyear used this approach to shape salient beliefs about its Aquatred tires.

Information Processing and Perceptual Defense. At this point you may have the impression that creating effective advertising is really a straightforward exercise. We carefully analyze consumers' beliefs and attitudes, construct ads to address any problems that might be identified, and choose various media to get the word out to our target customers. Yes, it would be very easy if consumers would just pay close attention and believe everything we tell them, and if our competition would kindly stop all of its advertising so that ours would be the only message that consumers had to worry about. Of course, these things aren't going to happen.

Why would we expect to encounter resistance from consumers as we attempt to influence their beliefs and attitudes about our brand? One way to think about this problem is to portray the consumer as an information processor who must advance through a series of stages before our message can have its intended effect. If we are skillful in selecting

WEB SIGHTING

EXHIBIT 5.16

Thermador (www.thermador.com/) wants you to get inside their product (not literally, of course), but to add to your evaluative criteria a new factor you've not thought about before. Intel (www.intel.com/) has raised this to a high art: Its "Intel Inside" campaign for the Pentium microprocessor is an integrated marketing communications masterpiece—how many other chips do you know by name, and what other products would you recall by a simple, short audio "stinger"?

appropriate media to reach our target, then the consumer must (1) pay attention to the message, (2) comprehend it correctly, (3) accept the message exactly as we intended, and (4) retain the message until it is needed for a purchase decision. Unfortunately, problems can and do occur at any or all of these four stages, completely negating the effect of our advertising campaign.

There are two major obstacles that we must overcome if our message is to have its intended effect. The first—the **cognitive consistency** impetus—stems from the individual consumer. Remember, a person develops and holds beliefs and attitudes for a reason: They help him or her make efficient decisions that yield pleasing outcomes. When a consumer is satisfied with these outcomes, there is really no reason to alter the belief system that generated them. New information that challenges existing beliefs can be ignored or disparaged to prevent modification of the present cognitive system. The consumer's desire to maintain cognitive consistency can be a major roadblock for an advertiser that wants to change beliefs and attitudes.

The second obstacle—**advertising clutter**—derives from the context in which ads are processed. Even if a person wanted to, it would be impossible to process and integrate every advertising message that he or she is exposed to each day. Pick up today's newspaper and start reviewing every ad you come across. Will you have time today to read them all? The clutter problem is further magnified by competitive brands making very similar performance claims. Now, was it Advil, Anacin, Aleve, Avia, Motrin, Nuprin, or Tylenol Gelcaps that promised you 12 hours of relief from your headache? (Can you select the brand from this list that isn't a headache remedy?) The simple fact is that each of us is exposed to hundreds of ads each day, and no one has the time or inclination to sort through them all.

Consumers thus employ perceptual defenses to simplify and control their own ad processing. It is important here to see that the consumer is in control, and the advertiser must find some way to engage the consumer if an ad is to have any impact. Of course, the best way to engage consumers is to offer them information about a product or service that will address an active need state. Simply stated, it is difficult to get people to process a message about your headache remedy when they don't have a headache. **Selective attention** is certainly the advertiser's greatest challenge and produces tremendous waste of advertising dollars. Most ads are simply ignored by consumers. They turn the page, change the station, mute the sound, head for the refrigerator, or just daydream or doze off—rather than process the ad.

Advertisers employ a variety of tactics to break through the clutter. Popular music, celebrity spokespersons, sexy models, rapid scene changes, and anything that is novel are devices for combating selective attention. Remember, as we discussed in Chapter 4, advertisers constantly walk that fine line between novel and obnoxious in their never-ending battle for the attention of the consumer. They really don't want to insult you or anyone else; they just want to be noticed. Of course, they often step over the annoyance line.

The battle for consumers' attention poses another dilemma for advertisers. Without attention, there is no chance that an advertiser's message will have its desired impact; however, the provocative, attention-attracting devices used to engage consumers often become the focal point of consumers' ad processing. They remember seeing an ad featuring 27 Elvis Presley impersonators, but they can't recall what brand was being advertised or what claims were being made about the brand. If advertisers must entertain consumers to win their attention, they must also be careful that the brand and message don't get lost in the shuffle.

Let's assume that an ad gets attention and the consumer comprehends its claims correctly. Will acceptance follow and create the enduring change in brand attitude that is desired, or will there be further resistance? If the message is asking the consumer to alter beliefs about the brand, expect more resistance. When the consumer is involved and attentive and comprehends a claim that challenges current beliefs, the cognitive consistency impetus kicks in, and cognitive responses can be expected. **Cognitive responses**

EXHIBIT 5.17

Cities can also engage in persuasive communications. Does this ad present an image of Detroit that is compatible with your prior beliefs? www.detroit.com/

EXHIBIT 5.18

Singapore's Tourism Board uses this ad to educate readers about its broad cultural diversity, and to tickle their curiosity (www.newasia -singapore.com/). Is Singapore an Asian city? Yes, but with influences from many cultures. The ad invites the reader to break out of a conceptual box, just as the Florida orange growers did with their "Orange juice: It's not just for breakfast anymore" campaign.

are the thoughts that occur to individuals at that exact moment in time when their beliefs and attitudes are being challenged by some form of persuasive communication. When these thoughts are negative in any way, the advertiser's goals are not served.[8]

Messages designed to reinforce existing beliefs, or shape beliefs for a new brand that the consumer was unaware of previously, are more likely to win uncritical acceptance. Compare the ads in Exhibit 5.17 and 5.18. In this example, think of the cities Detroit and Singapore as two brands competing for a tourist's attention (and ultimately, dollars). Each of these ads tries to affect beliefs and attitudes about its focal city. The cognitive consistency impetus that manifests in cognitive responses will work against the city that is more well known, especially when the ad challenges existing beliefs. Which ad do you find more challenging to your beliefs?

Shaping Attitudes via a Peripheral Route. For low-involvement products, such as batteries or tortilla chips, cognitive responses to advertising claims are not expected.[9] In such situations, attitude formation will often follow a more peripheral route, and peripheral cues become the focal point for judging the ad's impact. **Peripheral cues** refer to features of the ad other than the actual arguments about the brand's

---

8.   For an expanded discussion of these issues, see Richard E. Petty, John T. Cacioppo, Alan J. Strathman, and Joseph R. Priester, "To Think or Not to Think: Exploring Two Routes to Persuasion," in *Persuasion: Psychological Insights and Perspectives,* ed. Sharon Shavitt and Timothy C. Brock (Boston: Allyn and Bacon, 1994), 113–147.
9.   Ibid.

performance. They include an attractive or comical spokesperson, novel imagery, humorous incidents, or a catchy jingle. Any feature of the ad that prompts a pleasant emotional response could be thought of as a peripheral cue.

In the peripheral route the consumer can still learn from an advertisement, but the learning is passive and typically must be achieved by frequent association of the peripheral cue (for example, the Eveready Energizer Bunny) with the brand in question. It has even been suggested that classical conditioning principles might be employed by advertisers to facilitate and accelerate this associative learning process.[10] As consumers learn to associate pleasant feelings and attractive images with a brand, their attitude toward the brand should become more positive.

What do LeAnn Rimes, Jerry Seinfeld, Junji Takada, the Pillsbury Doughboy, Shaq, the Budweiser amphibians, and the song "Instant Karma" by John Lennon have in common? They and many others like them have been used as peripheral cues in advertising campaigns. When all brands in a category offer similar benefits, the most fruitful avenue for advertising strategy is likely to be the peripheral route, where the advertiser merely tries to maintain positive or pleasant associations with the brand by constantly presenting it with appealing peripheral cues. This strategy can be especially important for mature brands in low-involvement categories where the challenge is to keep the customer from getting bored,[11] but it is expensive because any gains made along the peripheral route are short-lived. Expensive TV air time, lots of repetition, and a never-ending search for the freshest, most popular peripheral cues demand huge advertising budgets. When you think of the peripheral route, think of the advertising campaigns for high-profile, mature brands such as Coke, Pepsi, Miller Lite, McDonald's, and Doritos. They entertain in an effort to keep you interested.

Perspective Two: The Consumer as Social Being.
The view of the consumer as decision maker is a popular one. It is not, however, without its limitations or its critics. Certainly, it tells only part of the story. It gives us information concerning consumer psychology, or what goes on in the mind of consumers. But in its effort to isolate psychological mechanisms, this approach often takes consumer behavior out of its natural social context, making consumers appear oddly utilitarian and overly rational. Critics in industry and academia alike believe that much of attitude advertising research (most popular in the industry in the 1950s and then again in the 1970s and early 1980s) has significantly less to do with the advertising of real products in the real world than with advancing attitude theory. Some go so far to say that whatever these psychologists are testing are not ads at all but have been reduced to experimental "stimulus material." Ads really exist only in the social world and natural environment. When removed from that environment they are no longer ads in any meaningful sense.

The rise of the "new image" advertising of the 1980's, in London and on the U.S. West Coast, was to some degree a reaction against narrowly defining the consumer as a rational decision maker. It was about image, position, and feelings. West Coast agencies began adopting what they called "British research," which was really just qualitative research as has been practiced by anthropologists, sociologists, and others for well over a century. The only thing really "British" about it at all is that some very hot London agencies had been doing research this way all along. (Actually, many had been, but these agencies used it as a point of differentiation.) This industry trend also resonated with a similar move in universities toward more interpretive, qualitative, and humanistic approaches. People began to see consumers as more than information

---

10. For additional discussion of this issue, see Frances K. McSweeney and Calvin Bierley, "Recent Developments in Classical Conditioning," *Journal of Consumer Research,* vol. 11 (September 1984): 619–631.

11. The rationale for cultivating brand interest for mature brands is discussed more fully in Karen A. Machleit, Chris T. Allen, and Thomas J. Madden, "The Mature Brand and Brand Interest: An Alternative Consequence of Ad-Evoked Affect," *Journal of Marketing,* vol. 57 (October 1993): 72–82.

EXHIBIT 5.19

Consuming at Crispy Corn.

processors and ads as more than attempts at attitude manipulation. Consumers do process information, but they also do a whole lot more. Furthermore, "information" itself is a rich and complex socioculturally bound textual product, interpreted in very sophisticated ways by very human beings.

So this section presents a second perspective on consumer behavior, a perspective concerned with social and cultural processes. It draws on basic ideas from anthropology, sociology, and communications, and it should be considered another part of the larger story of how advertising works. But, remember, this is just another perspective. We are still talking about the same consumers discussed in the preceding section; we are just viewing their behavior from a different vantage point. When it comes to the complexities of consumer behavior, we really can't have too many perspectives.

We are going to divide our discussion of this perspective in two: (1) one concerned with the context of reception, or the sociocultural environment in which consumers consume, and (2) one in which the ad itself is viewed as a socio-cultural text. This division also reflects the way that consumer behavior research is typically practiced in the advertising industry: In one domain it is concerned with how and why consumers consume (or don't consume) an advertised brand; in another, it focuses on studying (and evaluating) the advertisement itself (copy research).

Advertising in a Sociocultural Consumption Context. Consumers consume in a sociocultural context. Some major components of this context are discussed here.

Culture. Culture is what a people do, or "the total life ways of a people, the social legacy the individual acquires from his (her) group."[12] It is the way we eat, groom ourselves, celebrate, and mark our space and position. It is the way things are done. Cultures are often thought of as large and national, but in reality cultures are usually smaller, but

---

12. Gordon Marshall, ed., *The Concise Oxford Dictionary of Sociology* (New York: Oxford University Press, 1994), 104–105.

not necessarily geographic, such as urban hipster culture, teen tech-nerd culture, Junior League culture, and so on. It's usually easier to see and note culture when it's more distant and unfamiliar. For most people, this is when they travel to another place. For example, if you've traveled beyond your own country, you have no doubt noticed that people in other cultures do things differently. If you were to point this out to one of the locals, say to a Parisian, and say something like, "Boy, you guys sure do things funny over here in France," you would no doubt be struck (perhaps literally) with the locals' belief that it is not they, but you, who behave oddly. This is a manifestation of culture and points out that members of a culture find the ways they do things to be perfectly natural. Culture is thus said to be invisible to those who are immersed in it. Everyone around us behaves in a similar fashion, so we do not think about the existence of some large and powerful force acting on us all. But it's there; this constant background force is culture. Make no mistake, culture is real, and it affects every aspect of human behavior, including consumer behavior and response to advertising. Culture surrounds the creation, transmission, reception, and interpretation of ads.

CONSUMERS' PERCEPTIONS ARE AN ADVERTISER'S REALITY: TAKE THE FORMER SOVIET UNION, PLEASE

While advertising in traditional Eastern Bloc countries such as Poland is thriving under new market reforms, ad acceptance in the former heart of communism has been slow in coming. The reasons are varied. Many consumers there equate advertising in general with Cold War–era state-sponsored propaganda. Others feel that if a product has to be advertised, then it must not be very good. In fact, Russian consumers and their ex-Soviet neighbors are the most skeptical worldwide. In a global survey of some 40,000 individuals dispersed among 40 different countries, Roper Starch Worldwide found that only 9 percent of former Soviet Union residents believe that advertising actually contains useful information, compared with a global average of 38 percent.

Other interesting beliefs can be found throughout post-Soviet Central Asia. While sometimes they involve serious misperceptions (at least as we see things), consumers' beliefs are nonetheless an advertiser's reality. Barbie dolls are perceived as American and that's a good thing, but those that are shipped in from Hong Kong and stamped "Made in Hong Kong" are considered fakes. In Uzbekistan, smokers try to interpret the bar codes on Marlboro cigarettes to learn where that pack was made. If they perceive it to be American made, they will pay a premium price for it. But for food products, many old-fashioned consumers prefer Russian brands: U.S. brands carry much shorter sell-by dates that those from Russia, so people figure the Russian brands will last forever—they must be better. And poor Pepsi continues to struggle throughout Central Asia because it carries the stigma of having been the preferred cola of the stodgy old Soviet Union. There's still plenty of red in Central Asia, but a big part of that now is the ubiquitous red-and-white logo of Coca-Cola. Coke reigns supreme as the region's best known brand.

Sources: "Ex-Soviet States Lead World in Ad Cynicism," *Advertising Age,* June 5, 1995, 3; "Plying Ex-Soviet Asia with Pepsi, Barbie, and Barf," *Wall Street Journal,* May 6, 1998, B1.

When advertisers consider just why consumers consume certain goods or services, or why they consume them in a certain way, they are considering culture itself. Culture informs consumers' views about food, the body, gifts, possessions, a sense of self versus others, mating, courtship, death, religion, family, jobs, art, holidays, leisure, satisfaction, work . . . just about everything. For example, if you are Ocean Spray, you want to understand how the cultural ritual of Thanksgiving works so that you can sell more cranberries. What is Thanksgiving? Why do we value it? Why do we have the particular rituals we perform on that day? Or who makes up the rules of gift giving? If you are Tiffany, Barnes & Noble, or Hallmark, you have a very good reason to understand why people do things a certain way (for example, buy things for one holiday but not for another). The list is endless. When you're in the advertising business, you're in the culture business.

Values. Values are the defining expressions of culture. They express in words and deeds what is important to a culture. For example, some cultures value individual freedom, while others value duty to the society at large. Some value propriety and restrained behavior, while others value open expression. Values are cultural bedrock.

Cultural values, attitudes, and consumer behavior. Some believe that advertising can directly affect consumer behavior and, over time, cultural values as well.

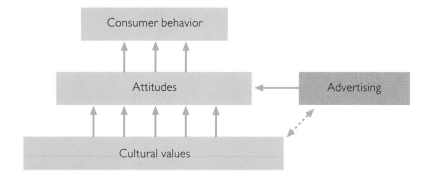

Values are enduring. They cannot be changed quickly or easily. They are thus different from attitudes, which advertisers believe can be changed through a single advertising campaign or even a single ad. Think of cultural values as the very strong and rigid foundation on which much more mutable attitudes rest. Exhibit 5.20 illustrates this relationship. Values are the foundation of this structure. Attitudes are, in turn, influenced by values, as well as by many other sources. Advertising has to be consistent with, but cannot easily or quickly change, values. It is thus senseless for an advertiser to speak of using advertising to change values in any substantive way. Advertising influences values in the same way a persistent drip of water wears down a granite slab—very slowly and through cumulative impact, over years and years. It is also the case that cultural values change advertising.

Everybody deserves a chance to express his or her individuality, right?
www.drmartens.com/

Typically, advertisers try to either associate their product with a cultural value or criticize a competitor for being out of step with one. For example, in America, to say that a product "merely hides or masks odors" would be damning criticism indeed, because it suggests that anyone who would use such a product doesn't really value cleanliness and thus isn't like the rest of us.

Advertisements must be consistent with the values of a people. If they are not, they will likely be rejected. Many argue that the best (most effective) ads are those that best express and affirm core cultural values. For example, one core American value is said to be individualism, or the predisposition to value the individual over the group. This value has been part of American culture for a very long time. Some hold that advertisements that celebrate or affirm this value (all else being equal, which it rarely is) are more likely to succeed than ones that denigrate or ignore it. Exhibit 5.21 shows an ad that leans heavily on this value.

Cultural capital describes the value that cultures place on certain consumption practices. For example, a certain consumption practice, say in-line skating, has a certain capital or social value (like money) for some segment of the population. If you own in-line skates (a certain amount of cultural capital) and can actually use them (more cultural capital), and look good while using them (even more capital), then this activity is like cultural currency or money in the bank. A Porsche has a certain cultural capital among some groups, as wearing khakis, drinking Bud, ordering the right Pinot Noir, knowing how to hail a cab, flying first class, or knowing the latest alternative band. This capital may be situated within a hipster culture, or a 40-something wine snob culture, or redneck culture. These are all cultures, and certain consumer practices are favored or valued more in each. Advertisers need to figure out which ones are valued more, and why, and how to make their product sought after because it has higher cultural capital. This is what "taste" is all about. These ads try to emphasize the cultural capital (and good taste) to be found in the product (Exhibits 5.22 and 5.23).

EXHIBITS 5.22 AND 5.23

What types of cultural capital do these products exhibit?

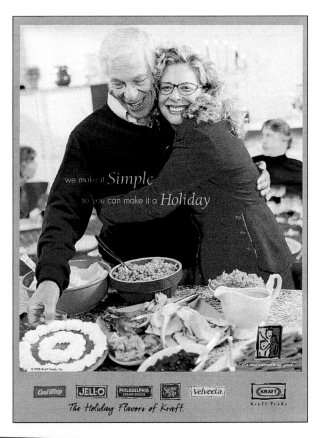

we make it *Simple*

so you can make it a *Holiday*

| CoolWhip | JELL-O | PHILADELPHIA CREAM CHEESE | Stove Top | Velveeta | | KRAFT |

The Holiday Flavors of Kraft

EXHIBIT 5.24

This ad promotes Kraft products as an integral part of family traditions.
www.kraftfoods.com/

Rituals. Rituals are "often-repeated formalized behaviors involving symbols."[13] Cultures participate in rituals. Cultures affirm, express, and maintain their values through rituals. Rituals are core elements of culture. They are a way in which individuals are made part of the culture, and a method by which the culture constantly renews and perpetuates itself. For example, ritual-laden holidays such as Thanksgiving, Christmas, and the Fourth of July help perpetuate aspects of American culture through their repeated re-enactment. Because they include consumption (for example, feasts and gift giving), they help intertwine national culture and consumption practices (see Exhibit 5.24). For example, Jell-O may have attained the prominence of a national food because of its regular usage as part of the Thanksgiving dinner ritual.[14] In the American South, it is common to eat black-eyed peas on New Year's Day to ensure good luck. In one sense it is "just done," but in another it is just done because it is a ritual embedded in a culture. If you are a canned-goods manufacturer, understanding this particular ritual is not a trivial concern at all.

But rituals don't have to be the biggest events of the year. There are also everyday rituals, such as the way we eat, clean ourselves, and groom. Think about all the habitual things you do from the time you get up in the morning until you crawl into bed at night. These things are done in a certain way; they are not random. Members of a common culture tend to do them one way, and members of other cultures do them other ways. Again, if you've ever visited another country, you have no doubt noticed significant differences. An American dining in Paris might be surprised to have sorbet to begin the meal and a salad to end it.

Daily rituals seem inconsequential because they are habitual and routine. If, however, someone tried to get you to significantly alter the way you do these things, he or she would quickly learn just how important and resistant to change these rituals are.

If a product or service cannot be incorporated into an already-existing ritual, it is very difficult and expensive for advertisers to effect a change. If, on the other hand, an advertiser can successfully incorporate the consumption of its good or service into an existing ritual, then success is much more likely.

Society. While culture is essentially what a people do, **society** is "a group of people who share a common culture, occupy a particular territorial area, and feel themselves to constitute a unified and a distinct entity."[15] Examples are American society, Southern society, and Eastern society. Within a society, many social forces and social institutions operate. Consumer behavior and advertising depend on the actions of these social institutions, agents, and forces. Social factors such as class, reference groups, gender, race, family, and community all have a significant impact on consumer behavior and the way consumers respond to advertising.

13. Ibid., 452.
14. Melanie Wallendorf and Eric J. Arnould, "We Gather Together: Consumption Rituals of Thanksgiving Day," *Journal of Consumer Research,* vol. 18, no. 1 (June 1991): 13–31.
15. Marshall, *Concise Oxford Dictionary of Sociology,* 498.

Social Class. Social class refers to a person's relative standing in a social hierarchy resulting from systematic inequalities in the social system. (These systematic inequalities are also known as social stratification.) Social class is a type of social stratification. Wealth, power, prestige, and status are not distributed equally within any society. People are rich or poor, are powerful or powerless, possess low status or high status, and so on. Race and gender are likewise unequally distributed within classes of power, income, and status. Thus a cross-section, or slice, of American society would reveal many different levels (or strata) of the population along these different dimensions.

Social class has historically been a fairly slippery concept. For example, some individuals possess higher social class than their income indicates, and vice versa. Successful plumbers often have higher incomes than college professors, but their occupation is (perhaps) less prestigious. Education also has something to do with social class, but a person with a little college experience and a lot of inherited wealth will probably rank higher than an insurance agent with an MBA. Thus income, education, and occupation are three important variables for indicating social class, but are still individually, or even collectively, inadequate at capturing its full meaning. Clearly, "complex combinations of social rewards and social opportunities compose social class."[16] Others have argued that the emergence of the New Class, a class of technologically skilled and highly educated individuals with great access to information and information technology, will change the way we define social class: "Knowledge of, and access to, information may begin to challenge property as a determinant of social class."[17]

Here, we use the term *social class* in a very inclusive sense. To us, social class includes not only economic criteria (such as income and property), but prestige, status, mobility, and a felt sense of similarity or communal belonging. Members of a social class tend to live in a similar way, have similar views and philosophies, and, most critically, tend to consume in similar ways. Markers of social class include what one wears, where one lives, and how one talks. In a consumer society, consumption marks or indicates social class in a myriad of ways. In fact, some believe that social class is the single biggest predictor of consumer behavior and consumer response to advertising. Despite the contributions to advertising practice by psychologists, in real-world advertising agencies, social class and its correlates dwarf everything else in terms of their use in actual advertising planning.

One reason for this is the power of social class in determining consumption tastes and preferences, including media habits, and thus exposure to various advertising media vehicles—for example, *RV Life* versus *Wine Spectator*. We think of tennis more than bowling as belonging to the upper classes, chess more than checkers, and Brie more than Velveeta. Ordering wine instead of beer has social significance, as does wearing Tommy Hilfiger rather than Lee jeans, or driving a Volvo rather than a Chevy. Social class and consumption are undeniably intertwined; they go hand in hand. In fact, cultural theorist Pierre Bourdieu argues that social class is such a powerful socializing factor that it "structures the whole experience of subjects," particularly when it comes to consumption.[18]

Consider some examples. Think about the purchases of equivalently priced cars, say a Saab and a Cadillac. The Saab is owned by a young architect, the Cadillac by the owner of a small construction company. These two consumers don't frequent the same restaurants, drink in the same bars, or eat the same kinds of foods. They don't belong to the same social class, and it is evident in their consumption. Think about the contents of the living rooms of those in various social classes. The differences are not due to money only, or the lack of it. Clearly, there is another dynamic at work here. Social-

16. James R. Kluegel and Eliot R. Smith, *Beliefs about Inequality: Americans' View of What Is and What Ought to Be* (New York: Aldine de Gruyter, 1986).
17. Alvin W. Gouldner, "The Future of Intellectuals and the Rise of the New Class," in *Social Stratification in Sociological Perspective: Class, Race and Gender,* ed. David B. Grusky (San Francisco: Westview Press, 1994), 711–729.
18. Pierre Bourdieu, "Distinction: A Social Critique of the Judgement of Taste," in *Social Stratification in Sociological Perspective: Class, Race and Gender,* ed. David B. Grusky (San Francisco: Westview Press, 1994), 404–429.

class-related consumption preferences reflect class-related value differences and different ways of seeing the world and the role of things in it; they reflect taste.

Class also becomes apparent when a person moves from one class into another. Consider the following example: Bob and Jill move into a more expensive neighborhood. Both grew up in lower-middle-class surroundings and moved into high-paying jobs after graduate school. They have now moved into a fairly upscale neighborhood, composed mostly of "older money." On one of the first warm Sundays, Bob goes out to his driveway and begins to do something he has done all his life: change the oil in his car. One of Bob's neighbors comes over and chats, and ever so subtly suggests to Bob that people in this neighborhood have "someone else" do "that sort of thing." Bob gets the message: It's not cool to change your oil in your own driveway. This is not how the new neighbors behave. It doesn't matter whether you like to do it or not; it is simply not done. To Bob, paying someone else to do this simple job seems wasteful and uppity. He's a bit offended, and a little embarrassed. But, over time, he decides that it's better to go along with the other people in the neighborhood. Over time, Bob begins to see the error of his ways and changes his attitudes and his behavior.

This is an example of the effect of social class on consumer behavior. Bob will no longer be a good target for Fram, Purolator, AutoZone, or any other product or service used to change oil at home. On the other hand, Bob is now a perfect candidate for quick oil change businesses such as Jiffy Lube. Consider the ads in Exhibits 5.25 and 5.26 in terms of social-class considerations. Which social classes do you believe are being targeted by these ads?

EXHIBITS 5.25 AND 5.26

These ads speak to two different social classes. www.chivas.com/ *and* www.millerlite.com/

Family. The consumer behavior of families is also of great interest to advertisers. Advertisers want not only to discern the needs of different kinds of families, but also to discover how decisions are made within families. The first is possible; the latter is much more difficult. For a while, consumer researchers tried to determine who in the traditional nuclear family (that is, Mom, Dad, and the kids) made various purchasing decisions. This was largely an exercise in futility. Due to errors in reporting and conflicting perceptions between husbands and wives, it became clear that the family purchasing process is anything but clear. While some types of purchases are handled by one family member, many decisions are actually diffuse nondecisions, arrived at through what consumer researcher C. W. Park aptly calls a "muddling through" process.[19] These "decisions" just get made, and no one is really sure who made them, or even when. For an advertiser to influence such a diffuse and vague process is indeed a challenge. The consumer behavior of the family is a complex and often subtle type of social negotiation. One person handles this, one takes care of that. Sometimes specific purchases fall along gender lines, but sometimes they don't.[20] While they may not be the buyer in many instances, children can play important roles as initiators, influencers, and users in many categories, such as cereals, clothing, vacation destinations, fast-food restaurants, and even computers. Still, some advertisers capitalize on the flexibility of this social system by suggesting in their ads who should take charge of a given consumption task, and then arming that person with the appearance of expertise so that whoever wants the job can take it and defend his or her purchases.

We also know that families have a lasting influence on the consumer preferences of family members. One of the best predictors of the brands adults use is the ones their parents used. This is true for cars, toothpaste, household cleansers, and many more products. Say you go off to college. You eventually have to do laundry, so you go to the store, and you buy Tide. Why Tide? Well, you're not sure, but you saw it around your house when you lived with your parents, and things seemed to have worked out okay for them, so you buy it for yourself. The habit sticks, and you keep buying it. This is called an **intergenerational effect**.

Advertisers often focus on the major or gross differences in types of families, because different families have different needs, buy different things, and are reached by different media. Family roles often change when both parents (or a single parent) are employed outside the home. For instance, a teenage son or daughter may be given the role of initiator and buyer, while the parent or parents serve merely as influences. Furthermore, we should remember that Ward, June, Wally, and the Beaver (Exhibit 5.27) are not (if they ever were) the norm (see Exhibit 5.28). There are a lot of single parents and second and third marriages. *Family* is a very open concept. In addition to the "traditional" nuclear family and the single-parent household, there is the extended family (nuclear family plus grandparents, cousins, and others) and the so-called alternative family (single and never-married mothers and gay and lesbian households with and without children, for example).

EXHIBIT 5.27

Who are the Cleavers?

19. C. Whan Park, "Joint Decisions in Home Purchasing: A Muddling-Through Process," *Journal of Consumer Research,* vol. 9 (September 1982): 151–162.

20. For an excellent article on this topic, see Craig J. Thompson, William B. Locander, and Howard R. Pollio, "The Lived Meaning of Free Choice: An Existential-Phenomenological Description of Everyday Consumer Experiences of Contemporary Married Women," *Journal of Consumer Research,* vol. 17 (December 1990): 346–361.

| Characteristics | All house-holds | Family households | | | | Nonfamily households | | |
| | | Total | Other families | | | Total | Female house-holder | Male house-holder |
			Married couple	Female house-holder	Male house-holder			
All households	102,528	70,880	54,317	12,652	3,911	31,648	17,516	14,133
Race and Hispanic origin								
White	86,106	59,511	48,066	8,308	3,137	26,596	14,871	11,725
White not Hispanic	77,936	52,871	43,423	6,826	2,622	25,065	14,164	10,901
Black	12,474	8,408	3,921	3,926	562	4,066	2,190	1,876
Hispanic[1]	8,590	6,961	4,804	1,612	545	1,630	754	875
Size of household								
1 person	26,327	NA	NA	NA	NA	26,327	15,317	11,010
2 people	32,965	28,722	21,833	5,290	1,598	4,243	1,850	2,393
3 people	17,331	16,640	11,595	3,858	1,187	691	232	459
4 people	15,358	15,090	12,427	2,008	654	268	76	192
5 people	7,048	6,972	5,743	924	306	76	17	59
6 people	2,232	2,195	1,807	293	95	37	21	15
7 or more people	1,267	1,260	911	278	70	7	3	4
Average size	2.62	3.24	3.26	3.18	3.22	1.24	1.17	1.33
Percent with own children								
under 18	33.9	49.0	46.5	60.8	46.0	NA	NA	NA

[1]People of Hispanic origin may be of any race.
U.S. Census Bureau, Current Population Survey. Available online at www.census.gov/population/socdemo/hh-fam/98ppla.txt. Internet release date: December 1, 1998.

EXHIBIT 5.28

American households by type and selected characteristics, 1998. Numbers are in thousands, except averages and percentages.

Beyond the basic configuration, advertisers are often interested in knowing things such as the age of the youngest child, the size of the family, and the family income. The age of the youngest child living at home tells an advertiser where the family is in terms of its needs and obligations (that is, toys, investment instruments for college savings, clothing, and vacations). When the youngest child leaves home, the consumption patterns of a family radically change. Advertisers love to track the age of the youngest child living at home and use it as a planning criterion.

Reference Groups. Obviously, other people and their priorities can have a dramatic impact on our consumption priorities, as suggested by the MasterCard ad in Exhibit 5.29. A **reference group** is any configuration of other people that a particular individual uses as a point of reference in making his or her own consumption decisions.

Reference groups can be small and intimate (you and the people sharing your neighborhood) or large and distant (you and all other people taking an advertising course). Reference groups can also vary in their degree of formal structure. They can exist as part of some larger organization—such as any business or employer—with formal rules for who must be part of the group and what is expected of the group in terms of each day's performance. Or they may be informal in their composition and agenda, such as a group of casual friends who all live in the same apartment complex.

Another way of categorizing reference groups involves the distinction between membership groups and aspirational groups.[21] **Membership groups** are those that we

21. For additional explanation of this distinction, see Michael R. Solomon, *Consumer Behavior* (Upper Saddle River, NJ: Prentice-Hall, 1996), 342–344.

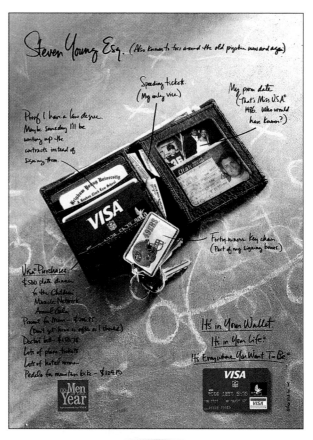

EXHIBIT 5.29

Aspirations play a large part in the message of this MasterCard ad.
www.mastercard.com/

EXHIBIT 5.30

This celebrity endorsement lets consumers hold something in common with a famous quarterback: owning a Visa card. www.visa.com/

interact with in person on some regular basis; we have personal contact with the group and its other members. **Aspirational groups** are made up of people we admire or use as role models, but it is likely we will never interact with the members of this group in any meaningful way. However, because we aspire to be like the members of this group, they can set standards for our own behavior. Professional athletes, movie stars, rock-and-roll bands, and successful business executives become role models whether they like it or not. Of course, advertisers are keenly aware of the potential influence of aspirational groups, and they commonly employ celebrities, from Grant Hill to Hanson, as endorsers for their products. (See also Exhibit 5.30.) After all, who wouldn't want to be, to paraphrase another ad, like Michael Jordan?

Reference groups affect our consumption in a variety of ways. At the simplest level, they can furnish information that helps us evaluate products and brands, and if we will actually consume a particular product (for example, tonight's dinner) with the group, the group's preferences may become hard to distinguish from our own. Additionally, reference groups play an important role in legitimizing the symbolic value of some forms of consumption—that is, individuals choose some brands because they perceive that using these products will enhance their image with a reference group, signal to others the particular reference group they belong to, or serve as a gift to another member of the group to let that person know how special he or she is. In this way products and brands end up offering consumers important **self-expressive benefits**. And where do products and brands get their symbolic meaning that makes them valuable as props for communicating with others? How did Cadillac become a symbol of status and Nike become a symbol of devotion to performance? Such symbolism is shaped and reaffirmed by years of consistent advertising, as long as the status conferred is consistent with the other coexisting social forces. Even great advertising will not succeed against the tide. And remember, much of what a brand means is determined by consumers, not just handed down by marketers.

Race and Ethnicity. Race and ethnicity provide other ways to think about important social groups. Answering the question of how race figures into consumer behavior is difficult. Our discomfort stems from having, on the one hand, the desire to say, "Race doesn't matter, we're all the same," and on the other hand not wanting (or not being able) to deny the significance of race in terms of reaching ethnic cultures and influencing a wide variety of behaviors, including consumer behavior. Obviously, a person's pigmentation, in and of itself, has almost nothing to do with preferences for one type of product over another. But because race has mattered in culture, it does matter in consumer behavior. To the extent that race is part of culture, it matters. Race clearly affects cultural and social phenomena. The United States is becoming an increasingly diverse culture (Exhibit 5.31). But how do we (and should we) deal with this reality?

There probably isn't an area in consumer behavior where research is more inadequate. We simply know next to nothing about the role of race in consumer behavior. This is probably because everyone is terrified to discuss it, and because most of the findings we do have are suspect. What is attributed to race is often due to another factor that is itself associated with race. For example, consumer behavior textbooks commonly say something to the effect that African-Americans and Hispanics are more brand loyal than their Anglo counterparts. Data on the frequency of brand switching is offered, and lo and behold, it does appear that white people switch brands more often. But why? Some ethnic minorities live in areas where there are fewer retail choices. When we statistically remove the effect of income disparities between white people and people of color, we see that the brand-switching effect often disappears. This suggests that brand loyalty is not a function of race, but of disposable income and shopping options.

Still, race does inform one's social identity to varying degrees. One is not blind to one's own ethnicity. African-Americans, Hispanics, and other ethnic groups have culturally related consumption preferences. It is not enough, however, for advertisers to say one group is different from another group. If they really want a good, long-term relationship with their customers, they must acquire, through good consumer research, a deeper understanding of who their customers are and how this identity is informed by culture, felt ethnicity, and race. In short, advertisers must ask why groups of consumers are different, and not settle for an easy answer. It wasn't until the

EXHIBIT 5.31

Ethnic diversity in America: projected U.S. population by race in millions (and percentage of total population by race).

Year	White	Black	Hispanic	Asian	American Indian
1996	194.4 (73.3%)	32.0 (12.1%)	27.8 (10.5%)	9.1 (3.4%)	2.0 (0.7%)
2000	197.1 (71.8%)	33.6 (12.2%)	31.4 (11.4%)	10.6 (3.9%)	2.1 (0.7%)
2010	202.4 (68.0%)	37.5 (12.6%)	41.1 (13.8%)	14.4 (4.8%)	2.3 (0.8%)
2020	207.4 (64.3%)	41.5 (12.9%)	52.7 (16.3%)	18.6 (5.7%)	2.6 (0.8%)
2030	210.0 (60.5%)	45.4 (13.1%)	65.6 (18.9%)	23.0 (6.6%)	2.9 (0.8%)
2040	209.6 (56.7%)	49.4 (13.3%)	80.2 (21.7%)	27.6 (7.5%)	3.2 (0.9%)
2050	207.9 (52.8%)	53.6 (13.6%)	96.5 (24.5%)	32.4 (8.2%)	3.5 (0.9%)

Source: U.S. Census Bureau.

mid- to late 1980s that most American corporations made a concerted effort to court the African-American consumer, or even to recognize their existence.[22] Efforts to serve the Hispanic consumer have been intermittent and inconsistent. This, coupled with a very sad historical corporate record is simply shameful. Sample ads directed at diverse audiences are shown in Exhibits 5.32 and 5.33.

Gender. **Gender** is the social expression of sexual biology, sexual choice, or both. Obviously, gender matters in consumption. But are men and women really that different in any meaningful way in their consumption behavior, beyond the obvious? Again, to the extent that gender informs a "culture of gender," the answer is yes. As long as men and women are the products of differential socialization, then they will continue to be different in some significant ways. There is, however, no definitive list of gender differences in consumption, because the expression of gender, just like anything else social, depends on the situation and the social circumstances. In the 1920s, advertisers openly referred to women as less logical, more emotional, the cultural stewards of beauty.[23] (Some say that the same soft, irrational, emotional feminine persona is still

EXHIBITS 5.32 AND 5.33

These two ads target Asian and Hispanic consumers.

22. Jannette L. Dates, "Advertising," in *Split Image: African Americans in the Mass Media,* ed. Jannette L. Dates and William Barlow (Washington, D.C.: Howard University Press, 1990), 421–454.

23. Roland Marchand, *Advertising: The American Dream* (Berkeley, Calif.: University of California Press, 1984).25. Laura Koss-Feder, "Out and About: Firms Introduce Gay-Specific Ads for Mainstream Products, Services," *Marketing News,* May 25, 1998, 1, 20.

invoked in 1990s advertising.) Advertising helps construct a social reality, with gender a predominant feature. Not only is it a matter of conscience and social responsibility to be aware of this construction, but it is good business as well. Advertisers must keep in mind, though, that it's hard to do business with people you patronize, insult, or ignore.

Obviously, gender's impact on consumer behavior is not limited to heterosexual men and women. Gay men and lesbian women are large and significant markets. Of late, these markets have been targeted by corporate titans such as IBM, United Airlines, and Citibank.[24] Again, these are markets that desire to be acknowledged and served, but not stereotyped and patronized. Exhibits 5.34 and 5.35 are ads targeted at lesbian and gay audiences.

In the late 1970s, advertisers discovered working women. In the 1980s, marketers discovered African-American consumers, about the same time they discovered Hispanic consumers. Later they discovered Asian-Americans, and just lately they discovered gays and lesbians. Of course, these people weren't missing. They were there all along. These "discoveries" of forgotten and marginalized social groups create some interesting problems for advertisers. Members of these groups, quite reasonably, want to be served just

EXHIBIT 5.34

Some advertisers are beginning to recognize the advantages of marketing to gay and lesbian consumers. Here, American Express recognizes the special financial challenges faced by lesbian couples.
www.americanexpress.com/

EXHIBIT 5.35

Here, André attempts to represent and appeal to gay consumers.

24. Laura Koss-Feder, "Out and About: Firms Introduce Gay-Specific Ads for Mainstream Products, Services," *Marketing News,* May 25, 1998, 1, 20.

like any other consumers. To serve these markets, consider what Wally Snyder of the American Advertising Federation said:

Advertising that addresses the realities of America's multicultural population must be created by qualified professionals who understand the nuances of the disparate cultures. Otherwise, agencies and marketers run the risk of losing or, worse, alienating millions of consumers eager to buy their products or services. Building a business that "looks like" the nation's increasingly multicultural population is no longer simply a moral choice, it is a business imperative.[25]

COMING TOGETHER . . . OVER SATURN

It sounded like a goofy idea: Invite every Saturn owner (about 600,000) to a "homecoming" at the Spring Hill, Tennessee, plant where their cars were "born." After all, who in their right mind would plan their vacation around a remote manufacturing facility? About 44,000 Saturn owners, that's who. Owners came from as far away as Alaska and Taipei; one couple ended up getting married by a United Auto Workers chaplain, with the Saturn president there to give away the bride. Another 100,000 Saturn owners participated in related, dealer-sponsored programs all over the United States. Add in the national publicity provided from the news media and ensuing Saturn ads depicting the event, and the idea isn't so goofy anymore. It's a masterful integrated marketing communications campaign that has helped build allegiance to the Saturn brand that is the envy of the automotive industry.

The genius of the Spring Hill Homecoming (and subsequent ads, such as Exhibit 5.36) is that Saturn's primary marketing strategy revolves around strong customer relations and service. The four-day event at the Tennessee plant rewarded customers for their purchase behavior and provided reassurance for new-car shoppers seeking the trust and relationships that allay service-related fears and the general mystery of new-car buying. Saturn's innovative approach is also integral to the overall strategy of its parent company, General Motors: The overwhelming majority of Saturn sales come from previous import owners, and not at the expense of other GM divisions. Actually, Saturn's retention programs just may be the greatest tangible benefit to arise from GM's earth-shaking $5 billion initial investment in the Saturn project.

Sources: "Savvy Companies Hold Customers," *Sales & Marketing Management*, December 1994, 15; Kevin L. Keller, *Strategic Brand Management* (Upper Saddle River, NJ: Prentice-Hall: 1998), 244–245; for an in-depth analysis of Saturn's brand building programs, see David Aaker, *Building Strong Brands* (New York: Free Press, 1996), Chapter 2.

Attention and representation without stereotyping from a medium and a genre that is known for stereotyping might be a lot to expect, but it's not that much.

Community. **Community** is a powerful and traditional sociological variable, considered by some to be the fundamental concept in sociology. It is defined as a "wide-ranging relationship of solidarity over a rather undefined area of life and interests."[26] Its meaning extends well beyond the idea of a specific geographic place. Communities can be imagined or even virtual.[27]

Advertisers are becoming increasingly aware of its power. It is important in at least two major ways. First, it is where consumption is grounded, where consumption literally lives. Products have social meanings, and community is the quintessential social domain, so consumption is inseparable from the notion of where we live. Communities may be the fundamental reference group, and they exhibit a great deal of power. A community may be your neighborhood, or it may be people like you with whom you feel a kinship, such as members of social clubs, other consumers who collect the same things you do, or people who have the same interests you do. In a consumer society, goods and services figure prominently in the symbolic fabric of communities. Communities may exist through a common text (such as an ad) or a product.

Second, the extent to which brands can derive power is determined in part by *brand community*. **Brand communities** are groups of consumers who feel a com-

25. Wally Snyder, "Advertising's Ethical and Economic Imperative," *American Advertising* (Fall 1992), 28.
26. Marshall, *Concise Oxford Dictionary of Sociology*, 72–73.
27. Benedict Anderson, *Imagined Community* (London: Verso, 1983).

GM's Saturn division has been a leader in promoting a sense of community among its owners. In this ad, that sense of community is cultivated through photographs from the Spring Hill Homecoming. Savvy Saturn marketers used the homecoming as a feature in advertising campaigns to show that the bond between Saturn owners and their cars is something special.
www.saturncars.com/index.html

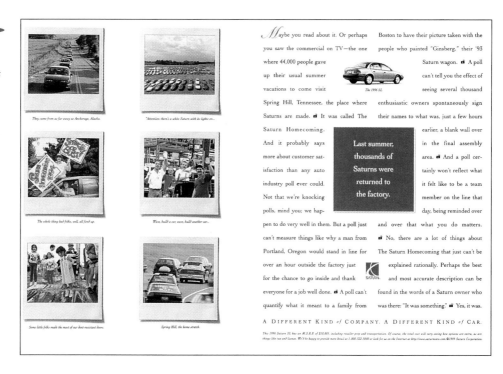

Kurt's strat is hardly just wood and wire.

monality and a shared purpose grounded or attached to a consumer good or service.[28] When owners of Doc Martens, Saabs, Mountain Dews, or Saturns experience a sense of connectedness by virtue of their common ownership or usage, a brand community exists. When two perfect strangers stand in a parking lot and act like old friends simply because they both own Saturns, a type of community is revealed. Indeed, Saturn's Spring Hill Homecoming, described in the IMC box on page 170, is considered a great marketing success story in the area of cultivating brand community. Exhibit 5.36 reinforces the communal appeal of Saturn.

Object Meaning. The things we buy, the things we consume, have meaning. All consumed objects (in fact, all material things) have sociocultural meaning. They are not just things. Look around you: the things in your home, the things in your room, the things in your car, your car itself, all things material, derive their meaning from society and culture. A Fender Stratocaster is not just a piece of wood with some wires and strings. It is also not just a fine musical instrument. It is an electric guitar. It is a Fender. It is the kind of guitar that Stevie Ray Vaughan, Eric Clapton, Kurt Cobain, Jimi Hendrix, and other famous guitarists have played (Exhibit 5.37). It is social history. What others think about it makes it

28.   Albert Muniz Jr. and Thomas O'Guinn, *Brand Community* (Berkeley, CA: unpublished manuscript).

something other than wood and wire. People give it meaning. A tuxedo is not just a coat and pants combo. It is worn on certain social occasions. Paper plates (not even Chinette) are not just plates made of paper. If you serve your guests a fine meal on them, they will notice. A Tag Heuer watch is not just a time piece; neither is a Timex or a 20-dollar Casio. They all mean something, and this meaning is derived socially. Advertisers try to influence this process. Sometimes they succeed; other times they don't. A lot of good research lately has demonstrated these observations. Some researchers have looked at more "ordinary" or "everyday" social meaning; others have delved into deeper meanings: the meanings of our most prized possessions, the things we could hardly stand to lose, something our parents or grandparents gave us, something that reminds us of someone dear, or something that would really be hard to explain just why it means so much. Just remember, all material things have meaning, as do activities. Smart advertisers must hope to understand relevant and widely shared social meaning in order to get consumers to appreciate their brand.

EXHIBIT 5.38

The consumer's cultural background often contributes to his or her inter-pretation of a text. Can you identify the cultural references in this ad?

Advertising as Social Text. Advertising is a sociocultural object. It is created, in a very real way, by society and culture. Individuals and groups of advertising professionals may actually physically craft ads, but the sociocultural environment "creates" them.

Advertising is also a text. It is "read" and interpreted by consumers. You can think of it as being like other texts, books, movies, posters, paintings, and so on. In order to "get" ads, you have to know something of the cultural code, or they would make no sense. In order to really understand a movie, to really get it, you have to know something about the culture that created it. Sometimes when you see a foreign film (even in your native tongue), you just don't quite get all the jokes and references, because you are not really good at reading the text. You don't possess the cultural knowledge necessary to really effectively "read" the text. So, ads are, just like these other forms, sociocultural texts. (See Exhibit 5.38.)

Ads Transmit Sociocultural Meaning. The link between culture and advertising is key. Anthropologist Grant McCracken has offered the model in Exhibit 5.39 to explain how advertising (along with other cultural agents) functions in the transmission of meaning. To understand advertising as a mechanism of meaning transfer is to understand a great deal about advertising. In fact, one could legitimately say that advertisers are really in the meaning-transfer business.

Think about McCracken's model as you examine the ad for Johnston and Murphy in Exhibit 5.40. The product—in this case, shoes—exists "out there" in the culturally constituted world, but it needs advertising to link it to certain social representations, certain slices of life. The advertiser

EXHIBIT 5.39

The movement of meaning.

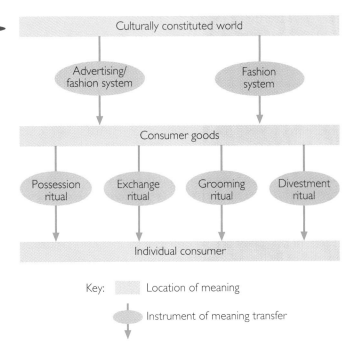

EXHIBIT 5.40

A Johnston & Murphy shoe is not just any shoe. One goal of this advertisement is to create a special meaning for this brand of men's shoes. www.johnstonmurphy.com/

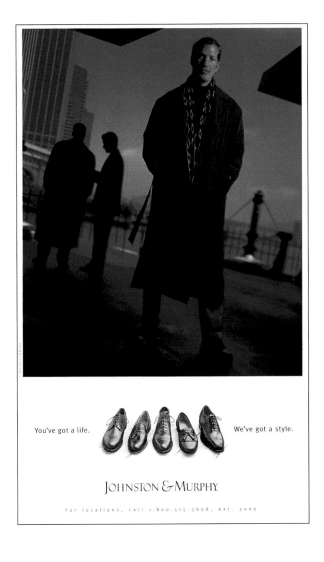

places the advertised product and the slice of social life in an ad to get the two to rub off on each other, to intermingle, to become part of the same social reality. In other words, the product is given social meaning by being placed within an ad that represents some social reality. This slice of life, of course, is the type of social setting in which potential customers might find, or desire to find, themselves. According to McCracken's model, meaning has moved from the world to the product (shoes) by virtue of its sharing space within the social frame of the advertisement. When a consumer purchases or otherwise incorporates that good or service into his or her own life, the meaning is transferred to the individual consumer. Meaning is thus moved from the world to the product (via advertising) to the individual. When the individual uses the product, that person conveys to others the meaning he or she and the advertisement have now given it. Their use incorporates various rituals that facilitate the movement of meaning from good to consumer.

Remember, the meaning of an ad does not exist inviolate and immutable within its borders. In fact, it doesn't exist there at all. Meaning is constructed in the minds of consumers, not delivered by advertisements. What an ad means is determined through a subtle but powerful process of meaning construction by consumers. What something means depends on who the consumer is, the strategy or motivation with which he or she receives the ad, and the ad itself. Consider texts in general: For some African-Americans, reading *Huckleberry Finn* is a very different experience than it is for white suburban middle-class kids. In fact, if the experience is so entirely different, then so is the text for these two groups. In other words, there is no single text. Since what a text means is really up to the reader, then we must acknowledge that who the reader is, in terms of major sociological factors, matters as well.[29]

Textual meaning is created through the interaction of sociological, cultural, and individual factors. So it is for ads. Ads are no less texts than is *Huckleberry Finn*. Consumers determine what ads mean, and since they are socially situated within significant groups, their interpretations will be affected by those group memberships.[30] Ads are created by organizations (social entities) through social processes, all affected by social actions. They are then interpreted according to social conventions and have their meanings determined through social interpretive processes.

Think about how different individuals might interpret the ads shown in Exhibits 5.41 and 5.42. Of course, the different meanings will not be random. While there will be variations, the meanings will have a certain commonality about them, because members of the same culture tend to bring similar cultural baggage to the interpretive event (reading the ad) and thus render similar interpretations. When advertisers include social and cultural factors in their analysis of consumer behavior, they dramatically enhance their chances of anticipating the meaning consumers will draw from advertisements.

Ads also become part of consumers' everyday language and conversation.[31] Characters, lines, and references all become part of conversations, thoughts, and—coming full circle—the culture. Children, co-workers, family members, and talk show hosts all pick up things from ads, and then replay them, adapt them, and recirculate them just like things from movies, books, and other texts. Ads, in may ways, don't exist just within the sociocultural context; they are the sociocultural context of our time.

29. Stanley Fish, *Is There a Text in This Class?* (Cambridge, Mass.: Harvard University Press, 1980).
30. Linda M. Scott, "The Bridge from Text to Mind: Adapting Reader Response Theory for Consumer Research," *Journal of Consumer Research,* vol. 21 (December 1994): 461–486; David Glenn Mick and Claus Buhl, "A Meaning-Based Model of Advertising Experiences," *Journal of Consumer Research,* vol. 19 (December 1992): 312–338.
31. Richard Eliot and Mark Ritson, unpublished manuscript.

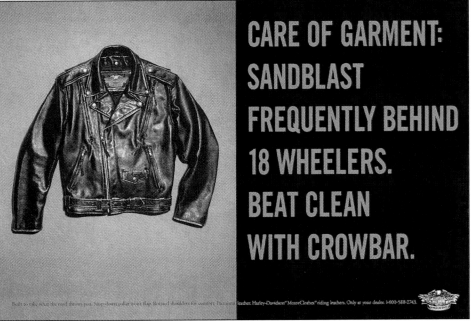

EXHIBITS 5.41 AND 5.42

How might different people interpret these ads, based on their differing social and cultural backgrounds? www.joeboxer.com/ *and* www.harley-davidson.com/

SUMMARY

◀▶ Describe the four basic stages of consumer decision making.

Advertisers need a keen understanding of their consumers as a basis for developing effective advertising. This understanding begins with a view of consumers as systematic decision makers who follow a predictable process in making their choices among products and brands. The process begins when consumers perceive a need, and it proceeds with a search for information that will help in making an informed choice. The search-and-evaluation stage is followed by purchase. Postpurchase use and evaluation then become critical as the stage in which customer satisfaction is ultimately determined.

Explain how consumers adapt their decision-making processes as a function of involvement and experience.

Some purchases are more important to people than others, and this fact adds complexity to any analysis of consumer behavior. To accommodate this complexity, advertisers often think about the level of involvement that attends any given purchase. Involvement and prior experience with a product or service category can lead to four diverse modes of consumer decision making. These modes are extended problem solving, limited problem solving, habit or variety seeking, and brand loyalty.

Discuss how advertising may influence consumer behavior through its effects on various psychological states.

Advertisements are developed to influence the way people think about products and brands. More specifically, advertising is designed to affect consumers' beliefs and brand attitudes. Advertisers use multi-attribute attitude models to help them ascertain the beliefs and attitudes of target consumers. However, consumers have perceptual defenses that allow them to ignore or distort most of the commercial messages to which they are exposed. When consumers are not motivated to thoughtfully process an advertiser's message, it may be in that advertiser's best interest to feature

one or more peripheral cues as part of the message.

Discuss the interaction of culture and advertising.

Advertisements are cultural products, and culture provides the context in which an ad will be interpreted. Advertisers who overlook the influence of culture are bound to struggle in their attempt to communicate with the target audience. Two key concepts in managing the impact of culture are values and rituals. Values are enduring beliefs that provide a foundation for more-transitory psychological states, such as brand attitudes. Rituals are patterns of behavior shared by individuals from a common culture. Violating cultural values and rituals is a sure way to squander advertising dollars.

Discuss the role of sociological factors in consumer behavior and advertising response.

Consumer behavior is an activity that each of us undertakes before a broad audience of other consumers. Advertising helps the transfer of meaning. Reference groups of various types have a dramatic influence on the consumption behavior of their individual members. Reference groups can be either groups we merely aspire to be part of, or groups, such as our families, that count us as members.

KEY TERMS

consumer behavior (139)
need state (140)
functional benefits (141)
emotional benefits (141)
internal search (142)
external search (144)
consideration set (144)
evaluative criteria (144)
customer satisfaction (145)
cognitive dissonance (145)
involvement (146)
extended problem solving (147)
limited problem solving (147)
habit (148)

variety seeking (148)
brand loyalty (149)
attitude (150)
brand attitudes (150)
beliefs (151)
salient beliefs (151)
multi-attribute attitude models
    (MAAMs) (151)
cognitive consistency (154)
advertising clutter (154)
selective attention (154)
cognitive responses (154)
peripheral cues (155)
culture (157)

values (158)
rituals (161)
society (161)
social class (162)
intergenerational effect (164)
reference group (165)
membership groups (165)
aspirational groups (166)
self-expressive benefits (166)
gender (168)
community (170)
brand communities (170)

QUESTIONS FOR REVIEW AND CRITICAL THINKING

1. When consumers have a well-defined consideration set and a list of evaluative criteria for assessing the brands in that set, they in effect possess a matrix of information about that category. Drawing on your experiences as a consumer, set up and fill in such a matrix for the category of fast-food restaurants.

2. Is cognitive dissonance a good thing or a bad thing from an advertiser's point of view? Explain how and why advertisers should try to take advantage of the cognitive dissonance their consumers may experience.

3. Most people quickly relate to the notion that some purchasing decisions are more involving than others. What kinds of products or services do you consider highly involving? What makes these products more involving from your point of view?

4. Explain the difference between brand-loyal and habitual purchasing. When a brand-loyal customer arrives at a store and finds her favorite brand is out of stock, what would you expect to happen next?

5. Describe three attitude-change strategies that could be suggested by the results of a study of consumer behavior using multi-attribute attitude models. Provide examples of different advertising campaigns that have employed each of these strategies.

6. Watch an hour of prime-time television and for each commercial you see, make a note of the tactic the advertiser employed to capture and hold the audience's attention. How can the use of attention-attracting tactics backfire on an advertiser?

7. What does it mean to say that culture is invisible? Explain how this invisible force serves to restrict and control the activities of advertisers.

8. Give three examples of highly visible cultural rituals practiced annually in the United States. For each ritual you identify, assess the importance of buying and consuming for effective practice of the ritual.

9. Are you a believer in the intergenerational effect? Make a list of the brands in your cupboards, refrigerator, and medicine cabinet. Which of these brands would you also expect to find in your parents' cupboards, refrigerator, and medicine cabinet?

10. "In today's modern, highly educated society, there is simply no reason to separate men and women into different target segments. Gender just should not be an issue in the development of marketing and advertising strategies." Comment.

EXPERIENTIAL EXERCISES

1. In this chapter, you learned about MAAMs. Divide into teams. Go to the toothpaste, toothbrush, cereal, or shampoo section of a grocery store. How many different brands are displayed? Develop a list of attributes for the product category your team chose. Are there any attributes associated with new products? What are they, and what brands have them? Which attributes are especially important to team members when buying a brand in this product category? Which attributes do team members find irrelevant? Discuss with the class the beliefs and attitudes various team members have toward the brands.

2. Watch people watch advertising, in a real situation. Take notes while observing. Record the conversation topics, the responses to the ads, the background noise, and all the other stuff going on. Then write a paragraph or two explaining what happens when people watch ads on TV. How could an advertiser use what you've learned to make a better ad?

USING THE INTERNET

Consumers often follow a predictable decision-making process when purchasing products. Web sites can be configured to influence a specific stage or several stages of the decision-making process. Visit the following sites:

Edmund's Automobile Buyer's Guides: www.edmund.com/

Izusu: www.izusu.com/

1. What stage or stages of the consumer decision-making process does each site address?

2. How do the sites differ in addressing the process of buying a car?

3. How do the sites differ in addressing functional and emotional benefits?

Now, compare the Amazon.com Books and Reebok sites:

Amazon.com Books: www.amazon.com/

Reebok: www.reebok.com/

4. What stage or stages of the consumer decision-making process does each site address?

5. How do the sites differ in developing brand loyalty?

6. How do the sites differ in producing customer satisfaction?

Both Amazon.com and Barnes & Noble use associates to help generate traffic and to lead customers in for specific book purchases. Read about each service's associates program on its Web site.

Amazon.com: www.amazon.com/

Barnes & Noble: www.barnesandnoble.com/

You can use the "links to this URL" query on HotBot (www.hotbot.com/) to find some of the sites with links to these booksellers.

A site that documents other companies' Web-based commissions is at www.markwelch.com/bannerad/baf_commission.htm.

1. How do Amazon.com and Barnes & Noble use their networks of associates to broaden their reach?

2. How might affiliate networks help to advertise in societal context?

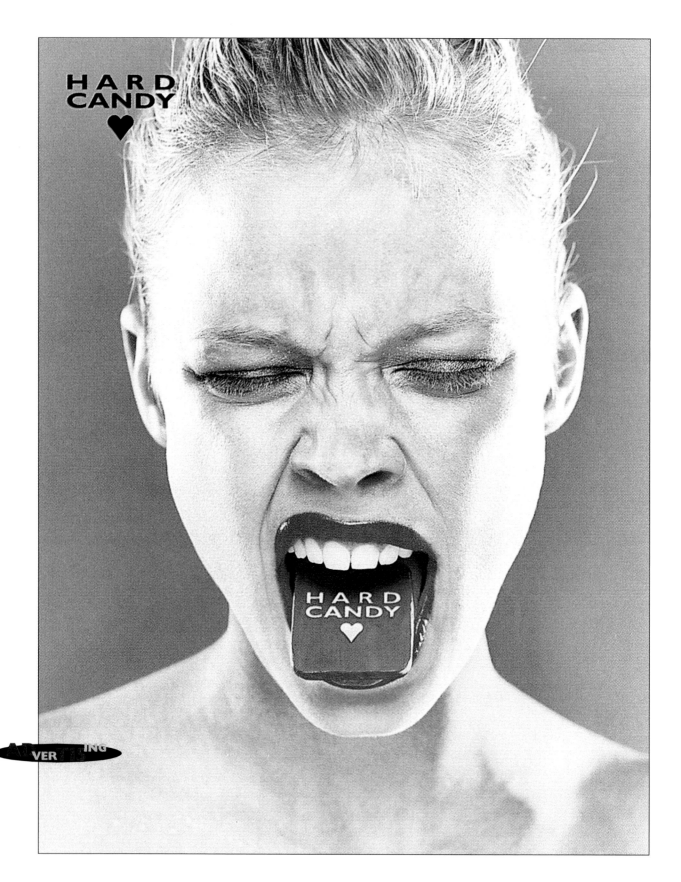

CHAPTER 6

**After reading and thinking about
this chapter, you will be able to
do the following:**

◀▶ Explain the process known as STP marketing.

◀▶ Describe different bases that marketers use
to identify target segments.

◀▶ Discuss the criteria used for choosing a
target segment.

◀▶ Identify the essential elements of an effective
positioning strategy.

◀▶ Review the necessary ingredients for creating a brand's value proposition.

It would be fair to say that executives at The Gillette Company in Boston, Massachusetts, have become prisoners of their own success. King C. Gillette invented the safety razor in 1903, and since that time male grooming habits and the "wet shave" have been the company's obsession. Few companies can demonstrate the growth rates and global success that Gillette Co. achieved in the 20th century. By the end of the century Gillette was able to claim that roughly two-thirds of all wet shaves around the world involved one of its razors, and that the company's profit growth was averaging nearly 15 percent annually.[1] Its advertising slogan—"Gillette: The Best a Man Can Get"— and products like its SensorExcel and MACH3 shaving systems were ubiquitous. Thus, the challenge for Gillette executives was how to maintain their company's success at growing sales and profits around the world. They could keep introducing more expensive (and more profitable) shaving systems like the MACH3, and try to reach every last wet-shaving male on the face of the planet, but at some point they literally would run out of new faces.

Many companies large and small share Gillette's problem: How do you keep growing when there are always natural limits to growth? Or, how do you keep growing in the face of effective competitors who also want to grow just as much as you do? Companies anticipate and address this problem through a process we will refer to as STP marketing. It is a critical process from an advertising standpoint because it leads to decisions about to whom we need to advertise, and the value proposition we will want to present to them.

To find sources for new growth, Gillette would need to identify new markets— someone other than wet-shaving males—to target with its new products and advertising campaigns. To make a long story short, Gillette decided to target wet-shaving females. The quintessential male-focused company would finally devote some of its considerable resources to address the unique shaving needs of women. And not just men's razors with pink handles (like the Daisy disposable razor, a failed Gillette product in the mid-1970s), but a complete line of products developed by women for women. When the strategy was announced, one competitor quipped, "What's your headline—Gillette discovers women?"[2]

In effect, Gillette had discovered women as a focal point for its considerable marketing and advertising efforts. But not all women; more specifically, Gillette would emphasize women in the 15-to-24-year-old range—a new target segment for Gillette. The thinking was that winning over youthful, wet-shaving females would create customers for life. Additionally, Gillette had the global marketplace in mind when it launched its "Gillette for Women: Are You Ready?" campaign. While women around the world are less likely to remove body hair than their counterparts in the United States (for example, Gillette estimates that 84 percent remove body hair in the United States versus 18 percent in Germany), younger women worldwide are most receptive to the idea. Gillette set out to tap the growth potential represented by the target segment of 15-to-24-year-old females around the world.

The program Gillette launched for these young women was multifaceted. It started with the Sensor shaving system for women, created by a female industrial designer, that featured a flat, wafer-shaped handle to give women better control while shaving. Other products followed, such as a high-end disposable razor named Agility and a line of shaving creams and after-shave products marketed under the brand name Satin Care. More money was allocated for global ad campaigns featuring ads such as those shown in Exhibits 6.1 and 6.2. This advertising, with the theme "Gillette for Women: Are You Ready?," was based on market research that showed most women perceive shaving as a nuisance or chore. Hence, they treat razors as a commodity item and are satisfied with inexpensive disposables. Gillette's advertising was designed to make this routine groom-

---

1.   Mark Maremont, "Gillette Finally Reveals Its Vision of the Future, and It Has 3 Blades," *Wall Street Journal,* April 14, 1998, A1, A10.
2.   Mark Maremont, "Gillette's New Strategy Is to Sharpen Pitch to Women," *Wall Street Journal,* May 11, 1998, B1, B16.

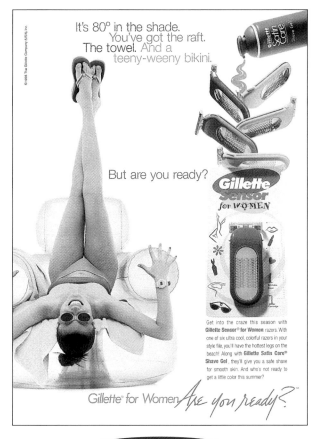

EXHIBIT 6.1

This was one of the first ads featured in Gillette's aggressive marketing program to young women. As suggested by the ad, most of each year's ad budget was concentrated on the peak season—summertime. www.gillette.com/

EXHIBIT 6.2

Gillette marketing executives were intent on elevating the role of shaving from the practical realm to the emotional realm. Would you agree that emotional benefits are promised by this ad? www.gillette.com/

ing chore more important and more glamorous, and, in the words of Gillette's VP of female shaving, "elevate the role of shaving beyond the practical to a more emotional realm."[3] In this "emotional realm," Gillette's hopes were that more women would be willing to pay a bit extra for products like Sensor and Satin Care.

By targeting wet-shaving young women, Gillette executives found a way to keep the company's sales and profits growing. Annual growth rates for women's products hovered around 20 percent, outperforming the men's division. Gillette followed sales gains with increases in its advertising budgets in an effort to reach its goal of $1 billion in revenues from women's products worldwide by the year 2001.[4] No matter how you cut it, that's a whole lot of wet shaves.

STP Marketing and the Evolution of Marketing Strategies.
The Gillette example illustrates the process that marketers use to decide whom to advertise to and what to say in that advertising. Gillette executives started with the diverse market of all women, and they broke the market down by age segments. They then selected 15-to-24-year-old females as their **target segment**. The target segment is the subgroup (of the larger market) chosen as the focal point for the marketing program and advertising campaign.

3. Ibid.
4. Ibid.

While markets are segmented, products are positioned. To pursue the target segment, a firm organizes its marketing and advertising efforts around a coherent positioning strategy. **Positioning** is the act of designing and representing one's product or service so that it will occupy a distinct and valued place in the consumer's mind. **Positioning strategy** involves the selection of key themes or concepts that the organization will feature when communicating this distinctiveness to the target segment. In Gillette's case, its executives first designed a line of products for the youthful female wet-shaver. They then came up with the positioning theme "Gillette for Women: Are You Ready?" to clearly distinguish this new line from their traditional male-oriented shaving systems. Finally, through skillful advertising, they communicated distinctive functional and emotional benefits to the target segment.

Notice the specific sequence, illustrated in Exhibit 6.3, that was played out in the Gillette example: the marketing strategy evolved as a result of segmenting, targeting, and positioning. This sequence of activities is often referred to as **STP marketing**, and it represents a sound basis for generating effective advertising.[5] While there are no formulas or models that guarantee success, the STP approach is strongly recommended for markets characterized by diversity in consumers' needs and preferences. In markets with any significant degree of diversity, it is impossible to design one product that would appeal to everyone, or one advertising campaign that would communicate with everyone. Organizations that lose sight of this simple premise often run into trouble.

Indeed, in most product categories one finds that different consumers are looking for different things, and the only way for a company to take advantage of the sales potential represented by different customer segments is to develop and market a different brand for each segment. No company has done this better than cosmetics juggernaut Estée Lauder. Lauder has over a dozen cosmetic brands, each developed for a different target segment of women.[6] For example, there is the original Estée Lauder brand, for women with conservative values and upscale tastes. Then there is Clinique, a nononsense brand that represents functional grooming for Middle America. Bobbi Brown Essentials are for the working mom who skillfully manages a career and her family and manages to look good in the process. M.A.C. is a brand for those who want to make a

EXHIBIT 6.3

Laying the foundation for effective advertising campaigns through STP marketing.

Segmenting

Breaking down diverse markets into manageable segments
Gillette's market: analyzed via demographic segmentation

Targeting

Choosing specific segments as the focal point for marketing efforts
Gillette's target segment: females, 15–24, worldwide

Positioning

Aligning the marketing mix to yield distinctive appeal for the target segment
Gillette's positioning: a new product line designed by women for women;
advertising theme—"Gillette for Women: Are You Ready?"

5.　For a more extensive discussion of STP marketing, see Philip Kotler, *Marketing Management* (Englewood Cliffs, N.J.: Prentice-Hall, 1994), Chapters 11 and 12.
6.　Nina Munk, "Why Women Find Lauder Mesmerizing," *Fortune,* May 25, 1998, 96–106.

bolder statement: its spokespersons have been RuPaul, a 6-foot 7-inch drag queen, and k.d. lang, the talented lesbian vocalist. Prescriptives is marketed to a hip, urban, multiethnic target segment, and Origins, with its earthy packaging and natural ingredients, is for consumers who are concerned about the environment. These are just some of the cosmetics brands offered by Estée Lauder to appeal to diverse target segments.

We offer the Estée Lauder example to make two key points before we move on. First, the Gillette example may have made things seem too simple: STP marketing is a lot more complicated than just deciding to target women or men. Gender alone is rarely specific enough to serve as a complete identifier of a target segment. Second, the cosmetics example shows that many factors beyond just age and gender can come into play when trying to identify valid target segments. For these diverse cosmetics brands we see that considerations such as attitudes, lifestyles, and basic values all may play a role in identifying and describing customer segments.

To illustrate these two points, examine the three ads in Exhibits 6.4, 6.5, and 6.6. All three of these ads ran in the magazine *Seventeen,* so it is safe to surmise that in all cases the advertiser was trying to reach adolescent females. But as you compare these exhibits, it should be pretty obvious that the advertisers were really trying to reach out to very different segments of adolescent females. To put it bluntly, it is hard to imagine a marine captain wearing either Clinique lipstick in Red Kiss or Hard Candy lip gloss. These ads were designed to appeal to different target segments, even though the people in these segments would seem the same if we only considered their age and gender.

EXHIBIT 6.4

The U.S. Armed Forces, including the Marines, are very aggressive and sophisticated advertisers. Here the Marines direct a message to basically the same target segment (from an age and gender standpoint) that was the focal point in Gillette's "Are You Ready?" campaign. www.usmc.mil/

EXHIBIT 6.5

The Clinique brand is positioned as elegant but sensible. Its Superlast Cream Lipstick doesn't even leave a smudge!

EXHIBIT 6.6

*Hard Candy comes by its hip style, perhaps in large part, because of its uninhibitedly energetic founding by Gen X twentysomething Dineh Mohajer, who was unhappy with the choices traditional cosmetics firms offered her (*www .hardcandy.com/*) and her market demographic. There must be something in that California air. Internet technology company Cisco co-founder Sandy Lerner created Urban Decay (*www.urbandecay.com*)—another alternative for the fashion-mad—out of a similar dissatisfaction with the offerings of companies like Lancôme (*www.lancome.com*).*

Beyond STP Marketing. If an organization uses STP marketing as its framework for strategy development, at some point it will find the right strategy, develop the right advertising, make a lot of money, and live happily ever after. Right? As you might expect, it's not quite that simple. Even when STP marketing yields profitable outcomes, one must presume that success will not last indefinitely. Indeed, an important feature of marketing and advertising—a feature that can make these professions both terribly interesting and terribly frustrating—is their dynamic nature. To paraphrase a popular saying, shifts happen—consumer preferences shift. Competitors improve their marketing strategies, or technology changes and makes a popular product obsolete. Successful marketing strategies need to be modified or may even need to be reinvented as shifts occur in the organization's competitive environment.

To maintain the vitality and profitability of its products or services, an organization has two options. The first entails reassessment of the segmentation strategy. This may come through a more detailed examination of the current target segment to develop new and better ways of meeting its needs, or it may be necessary to adopt new targets and position new products to them, as was the case with "Gillette for Women."

The second option is to pursue a product differentiation strategy. As defined in Chapter 1, product differentiation focuses the firm's efforts on emphasizing or even creating differences for its brands to distinguish them from the offerings of established competitors. Advertising plays a critical role as part of the product differentiation strategy because often the consumer will have to be convinced that the intended difference is meaningful. Product differentiation strategies try to make a brand appear different from competing brands, but it is consumers' perceptions of the difference that will determine the success of the strategy.

For example, when Church & Dwight Company introduced its Arm & Hammer Dental Care baking soda toothpaste, major toothpaste marketers such as Procter & Gamble and Colgate-Palmolive were not impressed. The product had a distinctive difference from traditional brands like Crest and Colgate, but would consumers find this difference meaningful? The answer turned out to be yes—the slightly salty taste and gritty texture of the Arm & Hammer brand proved popular with consumers; in no time, sales of baking soda toothpastes approached $300 million annually.[7]

The basic message is that marketing strategies and the advertising that supports them are never really final. Successes realized through proper application of STP marketing can be short-lived in highly competitive markets where any successful innovation is almost sure to be copied by competitors. Thus, the value creation process for marketers and advertisers is continuous; STP marketing must be pursued over and over again and may be supplemented with product differentiation strategies.

Virtually every organization must compete for the attention and business of some customer groups while de-emphasizing or ignoring others. In this chapter we will examine in detail the way organizations decide whom to target and whom to ignore in laying the foundation for their marketing programs and advertising campaigns. The critical role of advertising campaigns in executing these strategies is also highlighted.

Identifying Target Segments.   The first step in STP marketing involves breaking down large, diverse markets into more manageable submarkets or customer segments. This activity is known as **market segmentation**. It can be accomplished in many ways, but keep in mind that advertisers need to identify a segment with common characteristics that will lead the members of that segment to respond distinctively to a mar-

7.   Kathleen Deveny, "Anatomy of a Fad: How Clear Products Were Hot and Then Suddenly Were Not," *Wall Street Journal,* March 15, 1994, B1.

keting program. Additionally, for a segment to be really useful, advertisers must be able to reach that segment with information about the product. Typically this means that advertisers must be able to identify some media the segment uses that will allow them to get an advertising message to the segment. For example, teenage males can be reached efficiently through media such as MTV; selected rap, contemporary rock-and-roll, or alternative radio stations; and the Internet. As described in the New Media box on this page, one of the particularly appealing aspects of the Internet for advertisers is the way it allows them to reach valued target segments.

In this section we will review several ways that consumer markets are commonly segmented. Markets can be segmented on the basis of usage patterns and commitment levels, demographic and geographic information, psychographics and lifestyles, or benefits sought. Many times, segmentation schemes evolve in such a way that multiple variables are used to identify and describe the target segment. Such an outcome is desirable because more knowledge about the target will usually translate into better marketing and advertising programs.

NEW MEDIA

TRUTH IS, GEN X IS STILL OUT THERE, IF YOU KNOW WHERE AND HOW TO LOOK

The twentysomething consumer, referred to loosely as Generation X, remains a high priority in the segmentation strategies of many companies. One simple fact helps explain why: Their projected aggregate income by the year 2001 will be in the neighborhood of $1.8 trillion. Of course, like any other age cohort, there is too much diversity within this group to treat them as a single entity. There are, at the very least, four submarkets of Gen X'ers to consider—college and graduate students, up-and-coming professionals, and married couples with and without children. To reach the Gen X segment, you really must know who it is you're targeting within that segment. Then you can pick an advertising medium that will help you get your message to them.

Increasingly, the medium that marketers rely on is the Internet. Again, a simple fact helps explain why. The twentysomething cohort spends an average of 9.3 hours a week surfing the Net, compared to an average of 8.4 hours a week for the population in general, and 6.3 hours for people over age 50. Volkswagen of America is often cited as an example of a company that has been successful in communicating with Gen X'ers, and its Web site is a critical part of that dialogue. But it's not enough just to build a Web site and then expect Gen X to show up. The Web site works only as part of an integrated campaign where traditional broadcast advertising does its part by generating some curiosity and getting the consumer to use the Web. Easier said than done, because Gen X'ers have been raised on sophisticated advertising campaigns and can be very cynical about advertisers' motives. One Volkswagen executive offered this advice: "You want the ads to look like you're not trying too hard (and show) the product in a way that connects closely to the audience." Or, using terminology that you will get to later in this chapter, with Generation X, the best bet for your TV commercial may be an edgy dose of user-oriented positioning. They'll learn the benefits of your brand on their own when they visit your very hip Website.

Source: "Want to Catch Gen X? Try Looking on the Web," *Marketing News*, June 8, 1998, 20.

Usage Patterns and Commitment Levels.
One of the most common ways to segment markets is by consumers' usage patterns or commitment levels. With respect to usage patterns, it is important to recognize that for most products and services, some users will purchase much more frequently than others. It is common to find that **heavy users** in a category account for the majority of a product's sales and thus become the preferred or primary target segment. For example, Campbell Soup Company has discovered what it refers to as its extra-enthusiastic core users: folks who buy nearly 320 cans of soup per year.[8] That's enough soup to serve Campbell's at least six days a week every week. To maintain this level of devotion to the product, standard marketing thought holds that it is in Campbell's best interest to know these heavy users in great detail and make them a focal point of the company's marketing strategy.

While being the standard wisdom, the heavy-user focus has some

8.   Rebecca Piirto, *Beyond Mind Games: The Marketing Power of Psychographics* (Ithaca, N.Y.: American Demographics Books, 1991), 230.

potential downsides. For one, devoted users may need no encouragement at all to keep consuming. In addition, a heavy-user focus takes attention and resources away from those who do need encouragement to purchase the marketer's brand. Perhaps most important, various heavy users may be significantly different in terms of their motivations to consume, their approach to the product, or their image of the product.

Another segmentation option combines prior usage patterns with commitment levels to identify four fundamental segment types—brand-loyal customers, switchers (or variety seekers), nonusers, and emergent consumers.[9] Each segment represents a unique opportunity for the advertiser. **Nonusers** offer the lowest level of opportunity relative to the other three groups. **Brand-loyal users** are a tremendous asset if they are the advertiser's customers, but they are difficult to convert if they are loyal to a competitor.

Switchers, or **variety seekers**, often buy what is on sale or choose brands that offer discount coupons or other price incentives. Whether they are pursued through price incentives, high-profile advertising campaigns, or both, switchers turn out to be an expensive segment to try to win. Much can be spent in getting their business merely to have it disappear just as quickly as it was won.

Emergent consumers, however, offer the organization an important business opportunity. In most product categories, there is a gradual but constant influx of first-time buyers. The reasons for this influx vary by product category and include purchase triggers such as puberty, college graduation, marriage, birth of a child, divorce, job promotions, and retirement. Immigration can also be a source of numerous new customers for many product categories. Generation X has attracted the attention of marketers and advertisers because it is a large group of emergent adult consumers. But inevitably, Generation X will lose its emergent status and be replaced by a new generation, which some marketers are now already courting (you guessed it)—Generation Y.[10]

Emergent consumers are motivated by many different factors, but they share one important characteristic: Their brand preferences are still under development. Targeting emergents with messages that fit their age or social circumstances may produce modest effects in the short run, but it eventually may yield a brand loyalty that pays handsome rewards for the discerning organization. Of course, this was part of Gillette's rationale in targeting youthful females. As another example, credit card marketers actively recruit college students who have limited financial resources in the short term, but excellent potential as long-term customers. Exhibit 6.7 shows an American Express ad run in a college catalog that was designed to tap this potential.

Demographic Segmentation. **Demographic segmentation** is widely used in selecting target segments and includes basic descriptors such as age, gender, race, marital status, income, education, and occupation. Demographic information has special value in market segmentation because if an advertiser knows the demographic characteristics of the target segment, choosing media to efficiently reach that segment is much easier.

Demographic information has two specific applications. First, demographics are commonly used to describe or profile segments that have been identified with some other variable. If an organization had first segmented its market in terms of product usage rates, the next step would be to describe or profile its heavy users in terms of demographic characteristics such as age or income. In fact, one of the most common approaches for identifying target segments is to combine information about usage patterns with demographics.

9. Further discussion of this four-way scheme is provided by David W. Stewart, "Advertising in Slow-Growth Economies," *American Demographics* (September 1994), 40–46.
10. Joseph Pereira, "Board-Riding Youths Take Sneaker Maker on a Fast Ride Uphill," *Wall Street Journal,* April 16, 1998, A1, A8.

EXHIBIT 6.7

Emergent consumers represent an important source of long-term opportunity for many organizations. Have you ever thought of yourself as an emergent consumer? www.americanexpress.com/

Mobil Oil Corporation used such an approach in segmenting the market for gasoline buyers and identified five basic segments: Road Warriors, True Blues, Generation F3, Homebodies, and Price Shoppers.[11] Extensive research on more than 2,000 motorists revealed considerable insight about these five segments. At the one extreme, Road Warriors spend at least $1,200 per year at gas stations; they buy premium gasoline and snacks and beverages and sometimes opt for a car wash. Road Warriors are generally more affluent, middle-aged males who drive 25,000 to 50,000 miles per year. (Note how Mobil combined information about usage patterns with demographics to provide a detailed picture of the segment.) In contrast, Price Shoppers spend no more than $700 annually at gas stations, are generally less affluent, rarely buy premium, and show no loyalty to particular brands or stations. In terms of relative segment sizes, there are about 25 percent more Price Shoppers on the highways than Road Warriors. If you were the marketing vice president at Mobil Oil Corporation, which of these two segments would you target? Think about it for a few pages—we'll get back to you.

Second, demographic categories are frequently used as the starting point in market segmentation. This was the case in the Gillette example, where teenage females turned out to be the segment of interest. Additionally, film makers such as Konica USA, Kodak, and Fuji have attempted to tap diverse demographic segments with products such as high-speed "baby film" for new parents, complete photo-hobby kits for preteens, and hassle-free cardboard cameras for older people who want last-minute photos of the grandchildren.[12]

11.   Allanna Sullivan, "Mobil Bets Drivers Pick Cappuccino over Low Prices," *Wall Street Journal,* January 30, 1995, B1.

12.   Joan E. Rigdon, "Photography Companies Focus on Niches," *Wall Street Journal,* March 12, 1993, B1.

One demographic group that will receive increasing attention from advertisers in the years to come is the "woopies," or well-off older people. In the United States, consumers over 50 have more discretionary income than all other age segments combined. By the year 2025, the number of people over 50 will grow by 80 percent to become a third of the U.S. population. This growth in the woopie segment will be even more dramatic in other countries, such as Japan and the nations of Western Europe.[13] Still, like any other age segment, older consumers are a diverse group, and the temptation to stereotype must be resisted. Some marketers advocate partitioning older consumers into groups aged 50–64, 65–74, 75–84, and 85 or older, as a means of reflecting important differences in needs. Still, more thorough knowledge of this population is clearly needed.

Geographic Segmentation. Geographic segmentation needs little explanation other than to emphasize how useful geography is in segmenting markets. Geographic segmentation may be conducted within a country by region (for example, the Pacific Northwest versus New England), by state or province, by city, or even by neighborhood. Climate and topographical features yield dramatic differences in consumption by region for products such as snow tires and surfboards, but geography can also correlate with other differences that are not so obvious. Eating and food preparation habits, entertainment preferences, recreational activities, and other aspects of lifestyle have been shown to vary along geographic lines. Exhibits 6.8 and 6.9 show U.S. consumption patterns for Twinkies and for Obsession versus Old Spice. As you can see, where one lives does seem to affect preferences.

In recent years, skillful marketers have merged information on where people live with the U.S. Census Bureau's demographic data to produce a form of market segmentation known as **geodemographic segmentation.** Geodemographic segmentation identifies neighborhoods (that is, zip codes) around the country that share common demographic characteristics. One such system, known as PRIZM (potential rating index by zip marketing), identifies 62 market segments that encompass all the zip codes

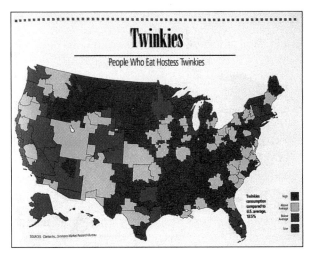

Source: Michael Weiss, *Latitudes and Attitudes* (Boston: Little, Brown, 1994), 17. Reprinted with permission of Simmons Market Research Bureau, Inc.

EXHIBIT 6.8

People who eat Hostess Twinkies.

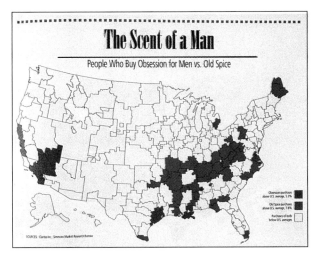

Source: Michael Weiss, *Latitudes and Attitudes* (Boston: Little, Brown, 1994), 45. Reprinted with permission of Simmons Market Research Bureau, Inc.

EXHIBIT 6.9

People who buy Obsession for Men versus Old Spice.

13. "The Rich Autumn of a Consumer's Life," *The Economist,* September 5, 1992, 67–68.

in the United States.[14] Each of these segments indicates similar lifestyle characteristics and can be found throughout the country.

For example, the American Dreams segment is found in many metropolitan neighborhoods and comprises upwardly mobile ethnic minorities, many of whom were foreign-born. This segment's product preferences are different from those of people belonging to the Rural Industria segment, who are young families with one or both parents working at low-wage jobs in small-town America. Systems such as PRIZM are very popular because of the depth of segment description they provide, along with their ability to precisely identify where the segment can be found.

Given PRIZM's success, it was logical to expect the same methods and technology to be applied on an international scale, and Experian, based in Nottingham, England, and Orange, California, is doing just that.[15] Experian has developed a geodemographic segmentation system for 18 countries (accounting for about 800 million consumers), including most of Western Europe, Australia and New Zealand, Japan, South Africa, and the United States. Such a system can prove very powerful for marketers with global aspirations, because it can tell them whether the segment they are pursuing in one country also exists in others. When a common customer segment exists in many countries (for example, middle-income, urban office workers), one marketing and advertising campaign can sometimes be used to appeal to them across national borders. Expect these systems to grow in popularity as the tools and technology spread around the world.

Psychographics and Lifestyle Segmentation.

Psychographics is a term that advertisers created in the mid-1960s to refer to a form of research that emphasizes the understanding of consumers' activities, interests, and opinions (AIOs).[16] Many advertising agencies were using demographic variables for segmentation purposes, but they wanted insights into consumers' motivations, which demographic variables did not provide. Psychographics were created as a tool to supplement the use of demographic data. Because a focus on consumers' activities, interests, and opinions often produces insights into differences in the lifestyles of various segments, this approach usually results in a **lifestyle segmentation**. Knowing details about the lifestyle of a target segment can be valuable for creating advertising messages that ring true to the consumer.

Lifestyle, or psychographic, segmentation can be customized with a focus on the issues germane to a single product category, or it may be pursued so that the resulting segments have general applicability to many different product or service categories. An example of the former is research conducted for Pillsbury to segment the eating habits of American households.[17] This "What's Cookin'" study involved consumer interviews with more than 3,000 people and identified five segments of the population, based on their shared eating styles:

- *Chase & Grabbits,* at 26 percent of the population, are heavy users of all forms of fast food. These are people who can make a meal out of microwave popcorn; as long as the popcorn keeps hunger at bay and is convenient, this segment is happy with its meal.
- *Functional Feeders,* at 18 percent of the population, are a bit older than the Chase & Grabbits but no less convenience oriented. Since they are more likely to have families, their preferences for convenient foods involve frozen products that are quickly prepared at home. They constantly seek faster ways to prepare the traditional foods they grew up with.

---

14. Christina Del Valle, "They Know Where You Live—and How You Buy," *Business Week,* February 7, 1994, 89.
15. Susan Mitchell, "Parallel Universes," *Marketing Tools,* November/December 1997, 14–17.
16. Piirto, *Beyond Mind Games,* 21–23.
17. Ibid., 222–23.

- *Down-Home Stokers,* at 21 percent of the population, involve blue-collar households with modest incomes. They are very loyal to their regional diets, such as meat and potatoes in the Midwest versus clam chowder in New England. Fried chicken, biscuits and gravy, and bacon and eggs make this segment the champion of cholesterol.
- *Careful Cooks,* at 20 percent of the population, are more prevalent on the West Coast. They have replaced most of the red meat in their diet with pastas, fish, skinless chicken, and mounds of fresh fruit and vegetables. They believe they are knowledgeable about nutritional issues and are willing to experiment with foods that offer healthful options.
- *Happy Cookers* are the remaining 15 percent of the population but are a shrinking segment. These cooks are family oriented and take substantial satisfaction from preparing a complete homemade meal for the family. Young mothers in this segment are aware of nutritional issues but will bend the rules with homemade meat dishes, casseroles, pies, cakes, and cookies.

Even these abbreviated descriptions of Pillsbury's five psychographic segments should make it clear that very different marketing and advertising programs are called for to appeal to each group. Exhibits 6.10 and 6.11 show ads from Pillsbury. Which segments are these ads targeting?

As noted, lifestyle segmentation studies can also be pursued with no particular product category as a focus, and the resulting segments could prove useful for many different marketers. A notable example of this approach is the VALS (for values and lifestyles) system developed by SRI International and marketed by SRI Consulting of Menlo Park, California.[18] The VALS framework was first introduced in 1978 with nine potential segments, but in recent years it has been revised as VALS 2 with eight market segments.

EXHIBIT 6.10

Which lifestyle segment is Pillsbury targeting with this ad? It looks like a toss-up between Chase & Grabbits and Functional Feeders.
info.pillsbury.com/

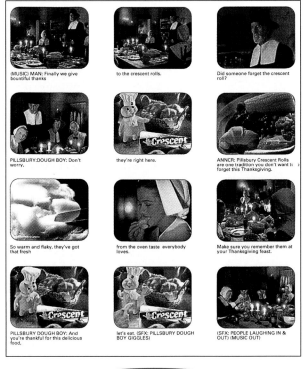

EXHIBIT 6.11

The convenience-oriented Functional Feeders seem the natural target for this novel ad. That Pillsbury Doughboy sure gets around!
info.pillsbury.com/

18. Ibid.; see Chapters 3, 5, and 8 for an extensive discussion of the VALS system.

EXHIBIT 6.12

The eight VALS 2 segments.
www.sri.com

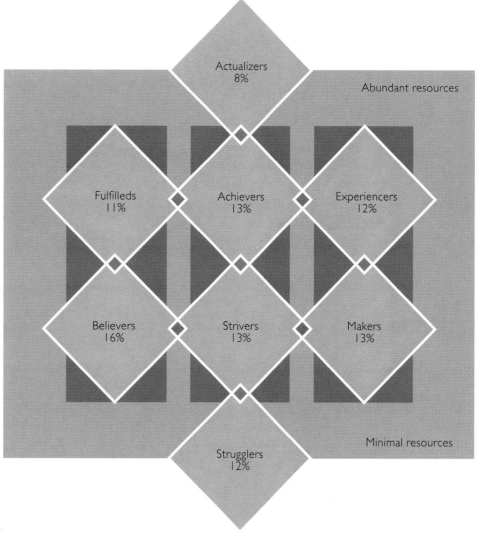

Source: SRI Consulting. VALS/Simmons, 1996.

As shown in Exhibit 6.12, these segments are organized in terms of resources (which includes more than age, income, and education) and personal orientation. For instance, the Experiencer is relatively affluent and action oriented. This enthusiastic and risk-taking group has yet to establish predictable behavioral patterns. Its members look to sports, recreation, exercise, and social activities as outlets for their abundant energy. SRI Consulting sells detailed information and marketing recommendations about the eight segments to a variety of marketing organizations. An example of a segmentation system akin to the VALS approach, but on a global scale, is reviewed in the Global Issues box on page 194.

Benefit Segmentation. Another segmentation approach developed by advertising researchers and used extensively over the past 30 years is **benefit segmentation**. In benefit segmentation, target segments are delineated by the various benefit packages that different consumers want from the same product category. For instance, different people want different benefits from their automobiles. Some consumers just want economical and reliable transportation; others want speed and excitement; and still others want luxury, comfort, and prestige. One product could not possibly serve such diverse benefit segments. Exhibits 6.13, 6.14, and 6.15 show three car ads that appeal to three different benefit segments.

EXHIBIT 6.13

Benefit segmentation really comes to life in the automobile market. For example, the Mitsubishi Spyder presents a distinctive set of benefits for one group of car buyers. www.mitsucars.com/

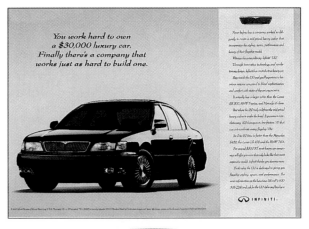

EXHIBIT 6.14

Here we see Infiniti execute the conventional approach in automotive advertising: Make the car the star of the show, and describe features and benefits. www.infinitimotors.com/

EXHIBIT 6.15

For years, Volvo has employed a benefit segmentation strategy by emphasizing safety features in its ads. How does this segment differ from the benefits targeted in the Infiniti and Mitsubishi ads? www.volvo.com/

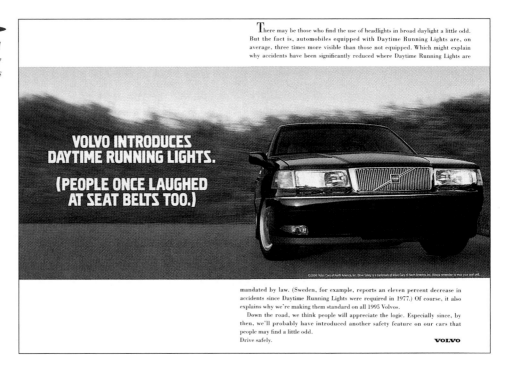

This notion of attempting to understand consumers' priorities and assess how different brands might perform based on criteria deemed important by various segments should have a familiar ring. If not, turn back to Chapter 5 and revisit our discussion of multi-attribute attitude models (MAAMS). The importance weights collected from individual consumers in MAAMS research often provide the raw material needed for identifying benefit segments.

Segmenting Business-to-Business Markets. Thus far, our discussion of segmentation options has focused on ways to segment **consumer markets**. Consumer markets are the markets for products and services purchased by individuals or households to satisfy

EXHIBIT 6.16

In business, it is common practice to employ outside expertise to solve specific problems, such as those created by diverse tax regulations around the world. In this ad, the accounting firm of Arthur Andersen highlights its credentials for doing just that. www.arthurandersen.com/

their specific needs. Consumer marketing is often compared and contrasted with business-to-business marketing. **Business markets** are the institutional buyers who purchase items to be used in other products and services or to be resold to other businesses or households. Although advertising is much more prevalent in consumer markets, products and services such as fax machines, cellular phones, and tax accounting (see Exhibit 6.16) are commonly promoted to business customers. Hence, segmentation strategies are also valuable for business-to-business marketers.

Business markets can be segmented using several of the options already discussed.[19] For example, business customers differ in their usage rates and geographic locations, so these variables may be productive bases for segmenting business markets. Additionally, one of the most common approaches uses the Standard Industrial Classification (SIC) codes prepared by the U.S. Census Bureau. SIC information is helpful for identifying categories of businesses and then pinpointing the precise locations of these organizations.

Some of the more sophisticated segmentation methods used by firms that market to individual consumers do not translate well to business markets.[20] For instance, rarely would there be a place for psychographic or lifestyle segmentation in the business-to-business setting. In business markets, advertisers fall back on simpler strategies that are easier to work with from the perspective of the sales force. Segmentation by a potential customer's stage in the purchase process is one such strategy. It turns out that first-time prospects, novices, and sophisticates want very different packages of benefits from their vendors, and thus they should be targeted separately in advertising and sales programs.

Prioritizing Target Segments.

Whether it is done through usage patterns or demographic characteristics or geographic location or benefit packages or any combination of options, segmenting markets typically yields a mix of segments that vary in their attractiveness to the advertiser. In pursuing STP marketing, the advertiser must get beyond this potentially confusing mixture of segments to a selected subset that will become the target for its marketing and advertising programs. Recall the example of Mobil Oil Corporation and the segments of gasoline buyers it identified via usage patterns and demographic descriptors. What criteria should Mobil use to help decide between Road Warriors and Price Shoppers as possible targets?

19. Kotler, *Marketing Management,* 278.
20. Thomas S. Robertson and Howard Barich, "A Successful Approach to Segmenting Industrial Markets," *Planning Forum* (November/December 1992), 5–11.

Perhaps the most fundamental criteria in segment selection revolve around what the members of the segment want versus the organization's ability to provide it. Every organization has distinctive strengths and weaknesses that must be acknowledged when choosing its target segment. The organization may be particularly strong in some aspect of manufacturing, like Gillette, which has particular expertise in mass production of intricate plastic and metal products. Or perhaps its strength lies in well-trained and loyal service personnel, like those at FedEx, who can effectively implement new service programs initiated for customers, such as next-day delivery "absolutely, positively by 10:30 A.M." To serve a target segment, an organization may have to commit substantial resources to acquire or develop the capabilities to provide what that segment wants. If the price tag for these new capabilities is too high, the organization must find another segment.

VALUE SEGMENTATION REACHES GLOBAL PROPORTIONS

As discussed in Chapter 5, consumers' core values are important to understand because they represent a permanent and stable influence on behavior. By appealing to people's basic values, it is possible to influence their purchase behavior. On the other hand, challenge consumers' basic values, and you're history. This is a particularly important issue as advertisers seek to extend their reach around the globe. The values that you take for granted in cultures you are familiar with need not apply on the other side of the world.

One way to address this challenging issue of values around the world is through market segmentation. Here the goal would be to identify value segments that span national borders. In 1997, Roper Starch Worldwide Inc. conducted research as a basis for worldwide value segmentation. They surveyed 1,000 people in their homes in 35 countries, and as part of the research had respondents rate the importance of 56 different values in their personal lives. From this survey, six global value segments were identified that spanned all 35 countries, but to varying degrees in each. Here are some highlights about each segment:

- *Strivers*—This is the largest of the six segments. They place more emphasis on material and professional goals than others. One of three people in developing Asia are Strivers, and just one in four in Russia.
- *Devouts*—This segment represents 22 percent of all adults. Tradition and duty are the priorities in these people's lives. Devouts are prevalent in the Middle East and in African countries, and are least common in developed Asia and Western Europe.
- *Altruists*—This group—18 percent of adults—has a keen interest in social and societal welfare issues. With a median age of 44, this is a more mature group. More Altruists live in Latin America and Russia than in any other countries.
- *Intimates*—Constituting 15 percent of the population from the countries sampled, these individuals value close personal relationships and family above all else. One in four Europeans and Americans fall into this segment, compared to just 7 percent of the population in developing Asia.
- *Fun Seekers*—This is the youngest group on average and has a male/female ratio of 54 to 46. Large numbers of Fun Seekers can be found in developing Asia; the segment as a whole represents about 12 percent of the population worldwide.
- *Creatives*—This is the smallest segment, estimated to be about 10 percent of the population worldwide. Their passions involve education, knowledge, and technology. Creatives are especially prevalent in Latin America and Western Europe.

Another major consideration in segment selection entails the size and growth potential of the segment. Segment size is a function of the number of people, households, or institutions in the segment, plus their willingness to spend in the product category. When assessing size, advertisers must keep in mind that the number of people in a segment of heavy users may be relatively small, but the extraordinary usage rates of these consumers can more than make up for their small numbers. In addition, it is not enough to simply assess a segment's size as of today. Segments are dynamic, and it is common to find marketers most interested in devoting resources to segments projected for dramatic growth. As we have already seen, the purchasing power and growth projections for people age 50 and older have made this a segment that many companies are targeting.

So does bigger always mean better when choosing target segments? The answer is a function of the third major criterion for segment selection. In choosing a target segment, an advertiser must also look at the **competitive field**—companies that

Source: "Global Segments from 'Strivers' to 'Creatives,'" *Marketing News*, July 20, 1998, 11.

compete for the segment's business—and then decide whether it has a particular expertise, or perhaps just a bigger budget, that would allow it to serve the segment more effectively.

When an advertiser factors in the competitive field, it often turns out that smaller is better when selecting target segments. Almost by definition, large segments are usually established segments that many companies have identified and targeted previously. Trying to enter the competitive field in a mature segment isn't easy because established competitors can be expected to respond aggressively with advertising campaigns or price promotions in an effort to repel any newcomer.

Alternatively, large segments may simply be poorly defined segments; that is, a large segment may need to be broken down into smaller categories before a company can understand consumers' needs well enough to serve them effectively. Again, the segment of older consumers—age 50 and older—is huge, but in most instances it would simply be too big to be valuable as a target. Too much diversity exists in the needs and preferences of this age group, so further segmentation based on other demographic variables, or perhaps via psychographics, is called for before an appropriate target can be located.

The smaller-is-better principle has become so popular in choosing target segments that it is now referred to as niche marketing. A **market niche** is a relatively small group of consumers who have a unique set of needs and who typically are willing to pay a premium price to the firm that specializes in meeting those needs.[21] The small size of a market niche often means it would not be profitable for more than one organization to serve it. Thus, when a firm identifies and develops products for market niches, the threat of competitors developing imitative products to attack the niche is reduced. Exhibit 6.17 is an example of an ad directed toward a very small niche, those who prefer imported Russian tubes for their high-end tube stereo amplifiers.

Niche marketing will continue to grow in popularity as the mass media splinter into a more and more complex and narrowly defined array of specialized vehicles. Specialized programming—such as the Health & Fitness Channel, the Cooking Channel, or the 24-hour Golf Channel—attracts small and very distinctive groups of consumers, providing advertisers with an efficient way to communicate with market niches.[22]

But now let's return to the question faced by Mobil Oil Corporation. Whom should it target—Road Warriors or Price Shoppers? Hopefully you will see this as a straightforward decision. Road Warriors are a more attractive segment in terms of both segment size and growth potential. Although there are more Price Shoppers in terms of sheer numbers, Road Warriors spend more at the gas station, making them the larger segment from the standpoint of revenue generation. Road Warriors are much more prone to buy those little extras, such as a sandwich and a car wash, that could be extremely profitable sources of new business. Mobil also came to the

EXHIBIT 6.17

Niche marketers are usually able to charge a premium price for their distinctive products. If you decide to go with Svetlana the next time you are buying amplifier tubes, expect to pay a little extra.
www.svetlana.com/

---

21. Kotler, *Marketing Management,* 267.
22. Patricia Sellers, "The Best Way to Reach Your Buyers," *Fortune,* Autumn/Winter 1993, 14–17.

conclusion that too many of its competitors were already targeting Price Shoppers. Mobil thus selected Road Warriors as its target segment and developed a positioning strategy it referred to as "Friendly Serve." Gas prices went up at Mobil stations, but Mobil also committed new resources to improving all aspects of the gas-purchasing experience.[23] Cleaner restrooms and better lighting alone yielded sales gains between 2 percent and 5 percent. Next, more attendants were hired to run between the pump and the snack bar to get Road Warriors in and out quickly—complete with their sandwich and beverage. Early results indicated that helpful attendants boosted station sales by another 15 to 20 percent. The Mobil case is a good example of how the application of STP marketing can rejuvenate sales, even in a mundane product category such as gasoline.

Formulating the Positioning Strategy.

Now that we have discussed the ways markets are segmented and the criteria used for selecting specific target segments, we turn our attention to positioning strategy. If a firm has been careful in segmenting the market and selecting its targets, then a positioning strategy—such as Mobil's "Friendly Serve" or Gillette's "The Best a Man Can Get"—should occur naturally. In addition, as an aspect of positioning strategy, we will begin to entertain ideas about how a firm can best communicate to the target segment what it has to offer. This is where advertising plays its vital role. A positioning strategy will include particular ideas or themes that must be communicated effectively if the marketing program is to be successful.

Essentials for Effective Positioning Strategies.

Any sound positioning strategy includes several essential elements. Effective positioning strategies are based on meaningful commitments of organizational resources to produce substantive value for the target segment. They also are consistent internally and over time, and they feature simple and distinctive themes. Each of these essential elements is described and illustrated in this section.

Let's begin with the issue of substance. For a positioning strategy to be effective and remain effective over time, the organization must be committed to creating substantive value for the customer. Take the example of Mobil Oil Corporation and its target segment, the Road Warriors. Road Warriors are willing to pay a little more for gas if it comes with extras such as prompt service or fresh coffee. So Mobil must create an ad campaign that depicts its employees as the brightest, friendliest, most helpful people you'd ever want to meet. The company asks its ad agency to come up with a catchy jingle that will remind people about the great services they can expect at a Mobil station. It spends millions of dollars running these ads over and over and wins the enduring loyalty of the Road Warriors. Right? Well, maybe, and maybe not. Certainly, a new ad campaign will have to be created to make Road Warriors aware of what the company has to offer, but it all falls apart if they drive in with great expectations and the company's people do not live up to them.

Effective positioning begins with substance. In the case of Mobil's "Friendly Serve" strategy, this means keeping restrooms attractive and clean, adding better lighting to all areas of the station, and upgrading the quality of the snacks and beverages available in each station's convenience store. It also means hiring more attendants, outfitting them in blue pants, blue shirts, ties, and black Reeboks, and then training and motivating them to anticipate and fulfill the needs of the harried Road Warrior.[24] Effecting meaningful change in service levels at its 8,000 stations nationwide is an expensive and time-consuming process for Mobil, but without some substantive change, there can be no hope of retaining the Road Warrior's lucrative business.

---

23. Chad Rubel, "Quality Makes a Comeback," *Marketing News,* September 23, 1996, 10.
24. Ibid.

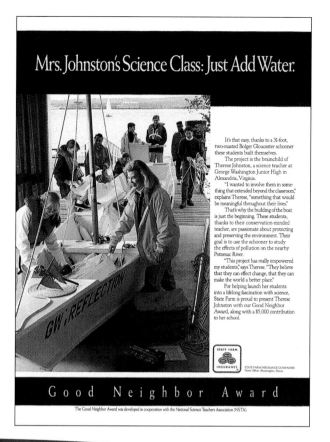

Mrs. Johnston's Science Class: Just Add Water.

It's that easy, thanks to a 31-foot, two-masted Bolger Gloucester schooner these students built themselves.

The project is the brainchild of Therese Johnston, a science teacher at George Washington Junior High in Alexandria, Virginia.

"I wanted to involve them in something that extended beyond the classroom," explains Therese, "something that would be meaningful throughout their lives."

That's why the building of the boat is just the beginning. These students, thanks to their conservation-minded teacher, are passionate about protecting and preserving the environment. Their goal is to use the schooner to study the effects of pollution on the nearby Potomac River.

"This project has really empowered my students," says Therese. "They believe that they can effect change, that they can make the world a better place."

For helping launch her students into a lifelong fascination with science, State Farm is proud to present Therese Johnston with our Good Neighbor Award, along with a $5,000 contribution to her school.

STATE FARM INSURANCE COMPANIES
Home Offices: Bloomington, Illinois

Good Neighbor Award

The Good Neighbor Award was developed in cooperation with the National Science Teachers Association (NSTA).

EXHIBIT 6.18

Consistency is a definite virtue in choosing and executing a positioning strategy. State Farm's "Good Neighbor" theme has been a hallmark of its advertising for many years. www.statefarm.com/

A positioning strategy also must be consistent internally and consistent over time. Regarding internal consistency, everything must work in combination to reinforce a distinct perception in the consumer's eyes about what a brand stands for. If we have chosen to position our airline as the one that will be known for on-time reliability, then we certainly would invest in things like extensive preventive maintenance and state-of-the-art baggage-handling facilities. There would be no need for exclusive airport lounges as part of this strategy, nor would any special emphasis need to be placed on in-flight food and beverage services. If our target segment wants reliable transportation, then this and only this should be the obsession in running our airline. This particular obsession has made Southwest Airlines a very formidable competitor, even against much larger airlines, as it has expanded it routes to different regions of the United States.[25]

A strategy also needs consistency over time. As we saw in Chapter 5, consumers have perceptual defenses that allow them to screen or ignore most of the ad messages they are exposed to. Breaking through the clutter and establishing what a brand stands for is a tremendous challenge for any advertiser, but it is a challenge made easier by consistent positioning. If year in and year out an advertiser communicates the same basic themes to the target segment, then the message may get through and shape the way consumers perceive the brand. An example of a consistent approach is the long-running "Good Neighbor" ads of State Farm Insurance. While the specific copy changes, the thematic core of the campaign does not change. Exhibit 6.18 shows a contemporary ad from this long-running campaign.

Finally, there is the matter of simplicity and distinctiveness. Simplicity and distinctiveness are essential to the advertising task. No matter how much substance has been built into a product, it will fail in the marketplace if the consumer doesn't perceive what the product can do. Keep in mind, in a world of harried consumers who can be expected to interrupt, ignore, or completely forget most of the ads they are exposed to, complicated, imitative messages simply have no chance of getting through. The basic premise of a positioning strategy must be simple and distinctive if it is to be communicated effectively to the target segment.

The value of simplicity and distinctiveness in positioning strategy is nicely illustrated by the success of GM's Pontiac division in the mid-1980s. This was a period when Japanese automakers were taking market share from their U.S. counterparts, and no American car company was being hit harder than General Motors. Pontiac, however, grew its market share in this period with a positioning strategy that involved a return to Pontiac's heritage from the 1960s as a performance car.[26] Pontiac's positioning strategy, which was communicated with a relentless barrage of advertisements like that shown in Exhibit 6.19, was "We Build Excitement."

25. Scott McCartney, "Southwest Airlines Lands Plenty of Florida Passengers," *Wall Street Journal,* November 11, 1997, B4.

26. Paul Ingrassia, "Pontiac Revives 'Sporty' Image, Setting a Marketing Example for Other GM Units," *Wall Street Journal,* August 15, 1986, 13.

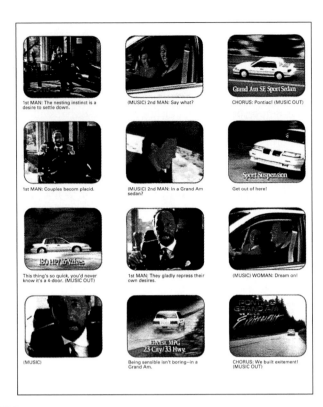

EXHIBIT 6.19

"We Build Excitement" is a perfect example of a single-benefit positioning theme. Pontiac has used this theme, with recent adaptations ("We Are Driving Excitement"), for more than a decade. www.pontiac.com/index.html

This was certainly a distinctive claim relative to GM's other stodgy divisions of that era, and its beauty was its simplicity. Pontiac's Grand Am featured distinctive styling and mechanics that furnished the substance to support the advertising claim, and it became a best-seller for Pontiac. Indeed, in this Pontiac positioning strategy we see substance, consistency, simplicity, and distinctiveness—all the essential elements for an effective positioning strategy.

Fundamental Positioning Themes.

Positioning themes that are simple and distinctive help an organization make internal decisions that yield substantive value for customers, and they assist in the development of focused ad campaigns to break through the clutter of competitors' advertising. Thus, choosing a viable positioning theme is one of the most important decisions faced by marketers and advertisers. In many ways, the *raison d'être* for STP marketing is to generate viable positioning themes.

Positioning themes take many forms, and like any other aspect of marketing and advertising, they can benefit from creative breakthroughs. Yet while novelty and creativity are valued in developing positioning themes, there are basic principles that should be considered when selecting a theme. Whenever possible, it is helpful if the organization can settle on a single premise—such as "Good Neighbor" or "We Build Excitement" or "Friendly Serve" or "Gillette for Women: Are You Ready?"—to reflect its positioning strategy.[27] In addition, three fundamental options should always be considered in selecting a positioning theme. These options are benefit positioning, user positioning, and competitive positioning.[28]

"We Build Excitement" and "Friendly Serve" are examples of **benefit positioning**. Notice in these premises that a distinctive customer benefit is featured. This single-benefit focus is the first option that should be considered when formulating a positioning strategy. As we saw in Chapter 5, consumers purchase products to derive functional, emotional, or self-expressive benefits, so an emphasis on the primary benefit they can expect to receive from a brand is fundamental. While it might seem that more compelling positioning themes would result from promising consumers a wide array of benefits, keep in mind that multiple-benefit strategies are hard to implement. Not only will they send mixed signals within an organization about what a brand stands for, but they will also place a great burden on advertising. Exhibit 6.20 shows an ad that executes a functional benefit positioning: Here the benefit is simply the capacity to create.

Functional benefits are the place to start in selecting a positioning theme, but in many mature product categories, the functional benefits provided by the various brands in the competitive field are essentially the same. In these instances the organization may turn to emotion in an effort to distinguish its brand. Emotional benefit positioning may involve a promise of exhilaration, like Pontiac's "We Build Excitement," or

27. A more elaborate case for the importance of a single, consistent positioning premise is provided in Al Ries and Jack Trout, *Positioning: The Battle for Your Mind* (New York: Warner Books, 1982).

28. Other basic options are discussed in David A. Aaker and J. Gary Shansby, "Positioning Your Product," *Business Horizons,* May/June 1982, 56–62.

In this no-nonsense ad we see the storage capacity of a Zip disk being highlighted. What specific features of this ad are designed to reinforce the message that a Zip disk enhances your capacity?
www.iomega.com/

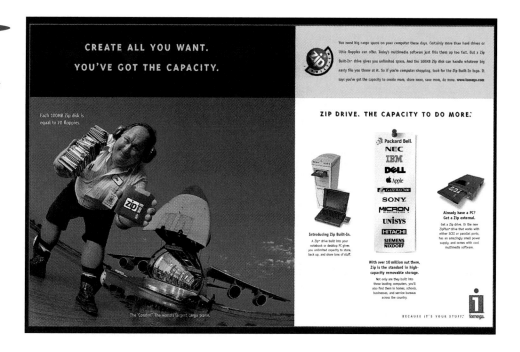

may feature a way to avoid negative feelings—such as embarrassment in social settings from bad breath, dandruff, or perspiration odor. Another sometimes controversial way to add emotion to one's positioning is by linking a brand with important causes that provoke intense feelings. Avon Products' CEO, James E. Preston, insisted that tie-ins with high-profile social issues can cut through the clutter of rivals' marketing messages.[29] His company supported breast cancer research in the United States and child nourishment programs in China. Likewise, Sears helped raise money for the homeless, Star-Kist has promoted dolphin-safe fishing practices, and Coors Brewing has funded public literacy programs—all as ways of offering a distinctive emotional benefit to their customers. Exhibit 6.21 demonstrates this type of emotional appeal in an ad for Virginia Power.

Self-expressive benefits can also be the bases for effective positioning strategies. With this approach, the purpose of an advertising campaign is to create distinctive images or personalities for brands, and then invite consumers into brand communities.[30] These brand images or personalities can be of value to individuals as they use the brands to make statements about themselves to other people. For example, feelings of status, pride, and prestige might be derived from the imagery associated with brands such as BMW, Rolex, and Ralph Lauren. Brand imagery can also be valued in gift-giving contexts. A woman who gives a man Obsession by Calvin Klein is probably expressing something different than the woman who gives Old Spice. Advertisers help brands have meaning and self-expressive benefits to distinguish them beyond their functional forms. In the Saab advertising shown in Exhibit 6.22, brand image is an invitation to reject superficiality and adopt an anti-image image. Show the world that you are independent and intelligent and not susceptible to the fads and fancies of automobile advertising: Find your own road . . . drive a Saab.

Besides benefit positioning, another fundamental option is **user positioning**. Instead of featuring a benefit or attribute of the brand, this option takes a specific profile of the target user as the focal point of the positioning strategy. For example, Rykä is positioned as the aquatic aerobic shoe for women only. This very focused positioning strategy is apparent in the ad in Exhibit 6.23.

29. Geoffrey Smith and Ron Stodghill, "Are Good Causes Good Marketing?" *Business Week,* March 21, 1994, 64–65.
30. Albert Muniz, Jr. and Thomas C. O'Guinn, "Brand Community," *Advances in Consumer Research,* vol. 23 (1994), 216.

Help Families In Need Add Some Extra Insulation To Their Homes This Winter.

This winter, your old sweaters can do a lot more than sit in the top of your closet, take up space in the attic, or clutter up your chest of drawers.

Your sweaters can help families all over Richmond who will be struggling to keep warm during the cold winter months ahead.

For those in our area who are facing difficult times—families in crisis, people with limited resources, children, the elderly, the disabled—winter is especially difficult.

Too often, many rely on high-risk heating sources such as space heaters, ovens, and even open fires to keep warm. Sometimes with tragic results.

But your sweaters can go a long way in helping people in need stay warm and safe.

Virginia Power, in partnership with WWBT-TV12 and United Way Services, has set aside one day in September when you can make a difference. It's called the Sweater Recycling Project, and it's easy

to participate. Just bring your usable sweaters to any of the 22 area Ukrop's Super Markets on Saturday, September 28, between 9 a.m. and 4 p.m.

We need sweaters in all sizes for adults and children. So please, look through all your closets and bring whatever you can spare.

Volunteers from Virginia Power will be on hand to accept your sweaters and deliver them to the Richmond Area Association for Retarded Citizens.

From there, they'll be given to United Way affiliated agencies, other health and human service organizations, churches, synagogues, social service departments, and to schools for distribution to people in need throughout the area.

So start gathering **VIRGINIA POWER** The More You Know, The Better.

your sweaters now. Then take them to your nearest Ukrop's on Saturday, September 28. It's something we can all feel a little warmer about this winter.

EXHIBIT 6.21

Virginia Power uses this ad to underscore that it's a local power company, inviting its neighbors to think of it more as a concerned citizen than a faceless utility. Locally- or regionally-oriented service providers can pitch themselves as cozier companions than the alternatives, as Southwest Airlines does (www.iflyswa.com) by letting Texas know it's special. By contrast, companies with a more virtual offering might abandon any appeal to physical community. Could you guess that America Online (www.aol.com) is headquartered in the Washington DC suburbs? Does anyone need to know? But AOL does paint itself as more family-oriented than other Internet providers and does so all without reference to place.

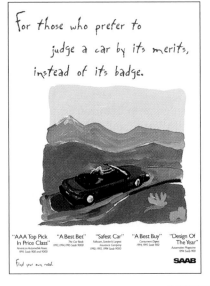

EXHIBIT 6.22

Saab advertising often emphasizes quality and performance, but there is symbolism here as well. Think of Saab imagery as anti-image imagery. www.saabusa.com/

EXHIBIT 6.23

The Aqueous 9H2O from Rykä is made for the female aqua fitness enthusiast. This is a nice example of user positioning. www.ryka.com/

User-oriented positioning themes are common when demographic and psycho-graphic variables have been combined to reveal a target segment's distinctive lifestyle. The task then becomes the positioning of products or services to fit that particular lifestyle. Exhibits 6.24 and 6.25 show ads for the Norwegian and Carnival cruise lines; the former clearly sets itself apart as a young person's romantic experience (that is, no kids), while the latter reaches out to a broader range of consumers, including families with children.

The third option for a positioning theme is **competitive positioning**. This option is sometimes useful in well-established product categories with a crowded com-petitive field. Here, the goal is to use an explicit reference to an existing competitor to help define precisely what your brand can do. Many times this approach is used by smaller brands to carve out a position relative to the market share leader in their cate-gory. For instance, in the analgesics category, many competitors have used market leader Tylenol as an explicit point of reference in their positioning strategies. Excedrin, for one, has attempted to position itself as the best option to treat a simple headache, granting that Tylenol might be the better choice to treat the various symptoms of a cold or the flu. As shown in Exhibit 6.26, Excedrin's strategy must have been effective, because Tylenol came back with a very pointed reply.

Now that you've seen the three fundamental options for creating a positioning strat-egy, we need to make matters a bit more messy. There is nothing that would prevent a

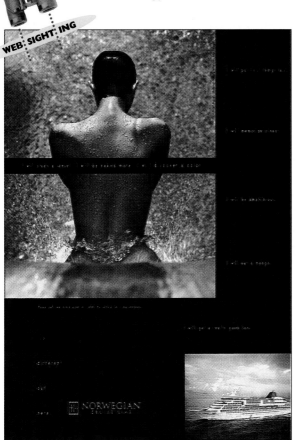

EXHIBIT 6.24

Norwegian Cruise Line's (www.ncl.com/) ad distinguishes it from other carriers by appealing to fun-loving adults. By contrast, Carnival (www.carnival.com/) wants to attract everyone and Olivia Cruises and Resorts (www.olivia.com/) precisely (and solely) targets gay women. While cruise lines can identify and zero in on diverse segments among the established market of regular cruise-goers, they've also got lots of room to grow: statistics are that only a scant few percent of Americans have ever taken a cruise.

EXHIBIT 6.25

Contrast the tone of this ad with that in Exhibit 6.24. See any differ-ences? www.carnival.com/

WEB SIGHT ING

EXHIBIT 6.26

In mature saturated markets where the performance features of brands don't change much over time, it is common to see competitors making claims back and forth in an effort to steal market share from one another. Powerhouse brands such as Tylenol usually don't initiate these exchanges, because they have the most to lose. This ad is a reply from the makers of Tylenol, responding to a campaign of a smaller competitor. www.tylenol.com/

person from combining these various options to create a hybrid involving two or more of them working together. The combination of benefit and user, and benefit and competitive, are quite common in creating positioning strategies. For example, the two Gillette ads you examined at the beginning of the chapter are hybrids involving the benefit/user combination. And if you look carefully at the ad in Exhibit 6.20, you'll see that it has a small element of competitive positioning to enhance its primary emphasis on benefit positioning. Do keep in mind that we're looking for a strategy that reflects substance, consistency, simplicity, and distinctiveness. But the last thing we'd want to do is give you guidelines that would shackle your creativity. So don't be shy about looking for creative combinations.

Repositioning. STP marketing is far from a precise science, so marketers do not always get it right the first time.[31] Furthermore, markets are dynamic. Things change. Even when marketers do get it right, competitors can react, or consumers' preferences may shift for any number of reasons, and what once was a viable positioning strategy must be altered if the brand is to survive. One of the best ways to revive an ailing brand or to fix the lackluster performance of a new market entry is to redeploy the STP process to arrive at a revised positioning strategy. This type of effort is commonly referred to as **repositioning**.

While repositioning efforts are a fact of life for marketers and advertisers, they present a tremendous challenge. When brands that have been around for some time are forced to reposition, perceptions of the brand that have evolved over the years must be changed through advertising. This problem is common for brands that become popular with one generation but fade from the scene as that generation ages and emergent consumers come to view the brand as passé. Cadillac and Lincoln both had this problem in the late 1990s as their key target segment continued to age, while younger consumers looked to Acura, BMW, Lexus, and Infiniti for prestige and sophistication in an automobile.[32]

Faced with fierce competition and plummeting market share, Nabisco set out to reposition its "new and improved" line of SnackWell's cookies and crackers in the summer of 1998.[33] In fact, this was the second attempt to reposition the failing Snack-Well's line in less than a year, a sure sign that the brand had lost its luster. And rather than feature the good taste or the low-fat content of its snacks, Nabisco attempted emotional benefit positioning. Their target segment was baby-boomer women with a high sense of self-worth. Their research had revealed that for this segment, "wellness" is not about looking good in a bathing suit, but about celebrating competencies and accomplishments. To "feed into" this celebration of self, one commercial opined: "At SnackWell's, we like to think that snacking shouldn't be just about feeding yourself, but, in some small way, about feeding your self-esteem."[34] The message here may be

---

31. Michael Gershman, *Getting It Right the Second Time* (Reading, Mass.: Addison-Wesley, 1990).
32. Robert L. Simison and Rebecca Blumenstein, "Cadillac and Lincoln Try to Regain Their Cachet," *Wall Street Journal,* July 3, 1997, B1, B8.
33. Vanessa O'Connell, "Nabisco Ads Push Cookies for Self-Esteem," *Wall Street Journal,* July 10, 1998, B5.
34. Ibid.

that failing brands in cluttered product categories can get pretty desperate for something compelling to say to the customer.

A highly successful repositioning executed in the 1990s was that of Mountain Dew, which was taken from relative obscurity to the official brand of Generation X. Exhibit 6.27 shows the storyboard for one television ad from Mountain Dew's popular "Thrill" campaign. Repositioning may also be pursued by prosperous brands in an effort to renew and amplify that prosperity. This type of repositioning is more of a fine-tuning rather that a fundamental overhaul and is exemplified by the Gateway (forget the 2000!) campaign described in the IMC box on page 204.

Capturing Your Strategy in a Value Proposition.

In this chapter we have presented several important concepts for understanding how marketers develop strategies for their brands that then have major implications for the advertising campaigns that are executed to build those brands. One needs to think about and research customer segments and target markets along with the competitive field to make decisions about various kinds of positioning themes that might be appropriate in guiding the creation of an ad campaign. Yes, as noted up front, it can get complicated. Furthermore, as time passes, and as new people from both the client and agency side are brought in to work on the brand team, it can be easy to lose sight of what the brand used to stand for in the eyes of the target segment. Of course, if the people who create the marketing and advertising programs for a brand get confused about the brand's desired identity, then the consumer is bound to get confused as well. This is a recipe for disaster. Thus, we need a way to capture and keep a record of what our brand is supposed to stand for in the eyes of the target segment. While there are many ways to literally capture one's strategy on paper, we recommend doing just that by articulating the brand's value proposition. If we are crystal clear in our own minds on what value we believe our brand offers to consumers, and everyone on the brand team shares that clarity, the foundation is in place for creating effective advertising.

At this point you should find the following definition of a **value proposition** as a natural extension of concepts that are already familiar; it simply consolidates the emphasis on customer benefits that has been featured in this and the previous chapter:

A brand's value proposition is a statement of the functional, emotional, and self-expressive benefits delivered by the brand that provide value to customers in the target segment. A balanced value proposition is the basis for brand choice and customer loyalty, and is critical to the ongoing success of a firm.[35]

Exhibit 6.28 emphasizes the point in our definition that we must have a balanced value proposition to be successful in the marketplace. On the one hand, if the set of benefits provided by the brand does not justify its price relative to competitive brands, then we've obviously got a problem. On the other hand, if our price is too low relative to the benefits the brand offers, then we are essentially giving away profits. Balance is optimal.

(MUSIC)

(SFX: MAN SCREAMS IN & OUT)

MEL TORME SINGS: You get no kick being thrown from a plane.

(SFX: MAN SCREAMS IN & OUT)

(SFX: ROCKET ZOOMS IN & OUT)
A thousand foot fall doesn't thrill them at all.

So tell me why should it be true,

that they get a kick

out of Dew.

Dew, Dew, Dew, Dew, Dew, Dew, Dew, Dew.

(MUSIC)

(MUSIC)

MAN: Alright, Mel! (MUSIC OUT)

EXHIBIT 6.27

Mel Torme accepts the "Do the Dew" challenge. Who would have thunk it—Mel Torme as a spokesperson to Generation X.

35. This definition is adapted from David Aaker, *Building Strong Brands* (New York: Free Press, 1996), Chapter 3.

Benefits?
- functional
- emotional
- self-expressive   • relative price

EXHIBIT 6.28

Don't let your value proposition get out of balance!

FOR GATEWAY: IMC, YES; 2000 AND COWS, NO

When Gateway pursued its repositioning campaign in 1998, it did so from a position of strength rather than as an act of desperation. This is the way you'd want it to be, if you had a choice. The new campaign had a very substantial IMC thrust in that one of Gateway's explicit goals was to create more synergy between its broadcast advertising and its 2,500 telemarketers. The broadcast ads were newly created to provoke interest and encourage people to call 1-800-GATEWAY. The telemarketing force was ready and waiting and was encouraged to begin the conversation with the question: What would you like your Gateway to do for you? Gateway was seeking a less technical dialogue with consumers and a better understanding of their true computing needs. Of course, the point of better understanding is to sell more Gateway computers.

Regarding the revised positioning strategy, Gateway's desire was to stress competency and currency without sacrificing its reputation as approachable and trustworthy. Perhaps it was in the name of competency that they decided to send the cows to the barn. It is a fair question: Do cows and state-of-the-art computer competency go hand in hand? Gateway marketing exec's decided not. Regarding the old Gateway 2000 logo, how can 2000 still appear current with the new millennium upon us? And who wants a name that could even vaguely be associated with the infamous Year 2000 computer paranoia? As it turns out, not Gateway.

Source: "Gateway 2000 Plans Shorter Name, Longer Client Talks, and No Cows," *Wall Street Journal*, April 24, 1998, B7.

Here are the extensive value propositions for two global brands that are likely familiar to you.[36]

McDonald's Value Proposition

Functional benefits: Good-tasting hamburgers, fries, and drinks served fast; extras such as playgrounds, prizes, premiums, and games.

Emotional benefits: Kids—fun via excitement at birthday parties; relationship with Ronald McDonald and other characters; a feeling of special family times. Adults—warmth via time spent enjoying a meal with the kids; admiration of McDonald's social involvement such as McDonald's Charities and Ronald McDonald Houses.

Nike's Value Proposition

Functional benefits: High-technology shoe that will improve performance and provide comfort.

Emotional benefits: The exhilaration of athletic performance excellence, feeling engaged, active, and healthy; exhilaration from admiring professional and college athletes as they perform wearing "your brand"—When they win, you win a little bit too.

Self-expressive benefits: Using the brand endorsed by high-profile athletes lets one's peers know your desire to compete and excel.

Notice from these two statements that over time many different aspects can be built into the value proposition for a brand. Brands like Nike may offer benefits in all three benefit categories, McDonald's from two of the three. Benefit complexity of this type is extremely valuable when the various benefits reinforce one another. In these examples, this cross-benefit reinforcement is especially strong for Nike, with all levels working together to deliver the desired state of performance excellence. The job of advertising is to carry the message to the target segment about the value that is offered by the brand. However, for brands with complex value propositions such as McDonald's and Nike, no single ad could be expected to reflect all aspects of the brand's

---

36. These examples are adapted from David Aaker, *Building Strong Brands* (New York: Free Press, 1996), Chapter 3.

value. However, if any given ad is not communicating some selected aspects of the brand's purported value, then we have to ask, why run that ad?

So from now on, everytime you see an ad, ask yourself, what kind of value or benefits is that ad promising the target customer? What is the value proposition behind this ad? We very definitely want you to carry forward this ability to select target segments and isolate value propositions as we zero in on the task of planning and implementing an advertising campaign.

SUMMARY

◀▶ Explain the process known as STP marketing.

The term *STP marketing* refers to the process of segmenting, targeting, and positioning. Marketers pursue this set of activities in formulating marketing strategies for their brands. STP marketing also provides a strong foundation for the development of advertising campaigns. While no single approach can guarantee success in marketing and advertising, STP marketing should always be considered when consumers in a category have heterogeneous wants and needs.

◀▶ Describe different bases that marketers use to identify target segments.

In market segmentation, the goal is to break down a heterogeneous market into more manageable subgroups or segments. Many different bases can be used for this purpose. Markets can be segmented on the basis of usage patterns and commitment levels, demographics, geography, psychographics, lifestyles, benefits sought, SIC codes, or stage in the decision process. Different bases are typically applied for segmenting consumer versus business-to-business markets.

◀▶ Discuss the criteria used for choosing a target segment.

In pursuing STP marketing, an organization must get beyond the stage of segment identification and settle on one or more segments as a target for its marketing and advertising efforts. Several criteria are useful in establishing the organization's target segment. First, the organization must decide whether it has the proper skills to serve the segment in question. The size of the segment and its

growth potential must also be taken into consideration. Another key criterion involves the intensity of the competition the firm is likely to face in the segment. Often, small segments known as market niches can be quite attractive because they will not be hotly contested by numerous competitors.

◀▶ Identify the essential elements of an effective positioning strategy.

The P in STP marketing refers to the positioning strategy that must be developed as a guide for all marketing and advertising activities that will be undertaken in pursuit of the target segment. As exemplified by Pontiac's "We Build Excitement" campaign, effective positioning strategies are rooted in the substantive benefits offered by the brand. They are also consistent internally and over time, and they feature simple and distinctive themes. Benefit positioning, user positioning, and competitive positioning are options that should be considered when formulating a positioning strategy.

◀▶ Review the necessary ingredients for creating a brand's value proposition.

Many complex considerations underlie marketing and advertising strategies, so some device is called for to summarize the essence of one's strategy. We advance the idea of the value proposition as a useful device for this purpose. A value proposition is a statement of the various benefits (functional, emotional, and self-expressive) offered by a brand that create value for the customer. These benefits as a set justify the price of the product or service. Clarity in expression of the value proposition is critical for development of advertising that sells.

KEY TERMS

target segment (181)
positioning (182)
positioning strategy (182)
STP marketing (182)
market segmentation (184)
heavy users (185)
nonusers (186)
brand-loyal users (186)
switchers, or variety seekers (186)
emergent consumers (186)
demographic segmentation (186)
geodemographic segmentation (188)

psychographics (189)
lifestyle segmentation (189)
benefit segmentation (191)
consumer markets (192)
business markets (193)
competitive field (194)
market niche (195)
benefit positioning (198)
user positioning (199)
competitive positioning (201)
repositioning (202)
value proposition (203)

QUESTIONS FOR REVIEW AND CRITICAL THINKING

1.   While STP marketing often produces successful outcomes, there is no guarantee that these successes will last. What factors can erode the successes produced by STP marketing, forcing a firm to reformulate its marketing strategy?

2.   Why does the persuasion required with a product differentiation strategy present more of a challenge than the persuasion required with a market segmentation strategy?

3.   Explain the appeal of emergent consumers as a target segment. Identify a current ad campaign targeting an emergent-consumer segment.

4.   It is often said that psychographics were invented to overcome the weaknesses of demographic information for describing target segments. What unique information can psychographics provide that would be of special value to advertisers?

5.   What criteria did Mobil Oil Corporation weigh most heavily in its selection of Road Warriors as a target segment? What do you think will be the biggest source of frustration for Mobil in trying to make this strategy work?

6.   Explain why smaller can be better when selecting segments to target in marketing strategies.

7.   What essential elements of a positioning strategy can help overcome the consumer's natural tendency to ignore, distort, or forget most of the advertisements he or she is exposed to?

8.   Identify examples of current advertising campaigns featuring benefit positioning, user positioning, and competitive positioning.

9.   Carefully examine the Gillette ads displayed in Exhibits 6.1 and 6.2. What positioning theme (benefit, user, or competitive) is the basis for these ads? If you say benefit positioning, what form of benefit promise (functional, emotional, or self-expressive) is being made in these ads? Write a statement of the value proposition that you believe is reflected by these two ads.

10. Look around your room or apartment and find a product that you consider one of your favorite brands. Consider what it is about this brand that makes it a personal favorite for you. Is it functional, emotional, self-expressive, or some combination of these different types of benefits that you particularly value about this brand?

EXPERIENTIAL EXERCISES

1. General Motors is attempting to reposition the image of Oldsmobile in the minds of consumers. Ask three adults to discuss with you their current impression of, beliefs about, and attitude toward Oldsmobile. Would they purchase an Oldsmobile today? Why or why not? Briefly describe what each adult said and indicate the extent to which you think the brand needs to be repositioned.

Develop two rough ads for Oldsmobile using competitive, benefit, or user positioning.

2. Pick three magazines you think are targeted to different segments. Pick two ads from each magazine that support your contention.

USING THE INTERNET

The soft drink market has become increasingly competitive, with several companies seeking to capture market share and sustain consistent growth. What was once referred to as the cola wars has now expanded to the Internet and includes more companies than Coca-Cola and Pepsi. Visit each of these sites supported by soft drink companies:

Pepsi: www.pepsi.com

Snapple: www.snapple.com

Jolt: www.joltcola.com

Gatorade: www.gatorade.com

1. Describe each brand's target segment in terms of demographics, psychographics, and lifestyles.

2. Compare the four sites and describe their positioning strategies. How does each site create a specific position?

3. How does the positioning reflected in each Web site match with the target segment?

4. How effective is each site at differentiating its brand from its competitors'?

The same products can be advertised to different market segments through different media outlets, with differing appeals (e.g., emphasizing a car's safety rating in a family-oriented publication and its power and agility in a magazine targeting single men). Many companies using the Internet, however, have a single Web page for a given product and, most likely, a single corporate Web site.

Some companies have been energetic in securing Internet domain names beyond the one secured and registered for their corporate Web site. Procter & Gamble, for instance, has registered domain names for many of its brands and for many generic words associated with its products or with conditions that might recommend them (e.g., www.diarrhea.com).

Visit these following sites:

www.pg.com

www.vidalsassoon.com

www.diarrhea.com

1. How does the Internet pose a challenge to segmenting markets?

2. How might a company ensure that its messages best match its audiences on the Web?

GENTLEMEN, START YOUR FOLLICLES.

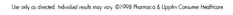

THE NEW ROGAINE.
45% MORE HAIR
THAN WITH ANYTHING YOU COULD BUY BEFORE.

And to get you started right, there's the Rogaine Starter Kit. You get more than just Rogaine Extra Strength for Men. You get the "Getting Started" video with Coach Mike Holmgren, and Progaine® Shampoo to care for thinning hair.

Use only as directed. Individual results may vary. ©1998 Pharmacia & Upjohn Consumer Healthcare

www.rogaine.com

CHAP
TER 7

**After reading and thinking about
this chapter, you will be able to
do the following:**

◁▷ Explain the purposes served by and
methods used in developmental advertising research.

◁▷ Discuss the various procedures used
for pretesting advertising messages prior
to a complete launch of an advertising
campaign.

◁▷ Discuss the various methods used to track
the effectiveness of ad executions during
and after the launch of a full-blown advertising campaign.

◁▷ Identify the many sources of secondary
data that can aid the ad-planning effort.

The Goodyear Aquatred tire was one of the most successful new tire introductions of all time. Goodyear's ability to compete successfully against foreign competitors, particularly Michelin and Yokohama, was greatly enhanced by the Aquatred. It also contributed significantly to record levels of profits for Goodyear. Managers at Goodyear attributed much of the initial success of the Aquatred to the introductory advertising campaign. This campaign featured "The Bucket"—a television commercial that showed how many buckets of water an Aquatred tire could disperse every mile.

Strategists at Goodyear believe "The Bucket" advertising was so successful because the ad went through extensive and rigorous testing before and during the product's release. While the product was being developed, marketing strategists at Goodyear determined that a unique tread design with outstanding performance features would provide the basis for a compelling positioning strategy. Then, before the tire was ready for market introduction, Goodyear and its advertising agency, J. Walter Thompson–Detroit, started researching several alternative television messages. First, the agency tested two different basic message formats. One was a testimonial by a user (called "Richard on Aquatreds"); the other was an ad that featured the tire's traction on wet, snowy roads (called "Skiing"). Based on this preliminary research, Goodyear and its agency concluded that a product performance ad emphasizing functional benefit positioning would be the best format for the introductory Aquatred campaign.

The agency moved forward based on the research and developed "The Bucket" as an ad that specifically featured both the performance and demonstration dimensions. "Skiing" and "The Bucket" were aired during the four-week introductory period for Aquatred. Exhibit 7.1 shows the **storyboard** (the shot-by-shot sequence agencies use to depict the scenes from a television ad) for "The Bucket."

Once the product was introduced, Goodyear tracked the effectiveness of "The Bucket" and "Skiing" using a persuasion rating system. These results were compared to the sales of the Aquatred in various market areas. The firm discovered that both ads were having a significant and positive impact on sales; that "The Bucket" campaign was the most powerful; and that both ads became less effective after a four-week period. Goodyear also realized that the ads were contributing to a level of consumer demand beyond the firm's production capacity, so the advertising was actually scaled back to balance demand with supply.

Goodyear and its advertising agency used several different types of research to plan the introductory advertising campaign for the Aquatred tire. First, marketing research performed by Goodyear determined what product features and performance characteristics would provide the basis for a distinctive positioning strategy. Next, advertising research determined that a product demonstration ad, rather than a testimonial, would be more effective. Finally, when the two demonstration ads began running during the tire's introduction, persuasion and sales measures were tracked to assess these ads' relative effectiveness.[1]

EXHIBIT 7.1

Goodyear and its ad agency determined that a demonstration ad would be most effective in launching the new Aquatred tire.
www.goodyear.com/

---

1. Information on Goodyear's development of Aquatred advertising is adapted from Ronald P. Conlin, "Goodyear Advertising Research: Past, Present, and Future," *Journal of Advertising Research,* Research Currents (May/June 1994), RC-7–RC-10.

The Role of Research.

The experience of Goodyear highlights the role of research. Managerial experience in a product category and a history of marketing to a particular target segment are extremely valuable but often insufficient to fully meet the challenges of advertising planning.

By drawing on research, an advertiser can better understand what will be useful in an advertisement. This is not to say that research information makes decisions for advertisers. It's more that research increases the probability of making a good decision or, conversely, reduces the probability of making a bad one (assuming the research is well conceived and executed). Still, no matter how comprehensive the research may be, decision making still relies on decision makers' interpretations, and ultimately on their judgment.

Several issues must be addressed regarding marketing and advertising research. First, what is the difference between marketing and advertising research? **Marketing research** is defined as the systematic gathering, recording, and interpretation of information related to all marketing mix variables. **Advertising research** is a specialized form of marketing research that focuses on the planning, preparation, and placement of advertising. In a practical sense, advertising research is any research conducted by an advertising agency. While some agencies have all but gotten out of the research business, others are scrambling to take on any research jobs that will bring in a little extra revenue (those that bill on a fee basis) or allow them to hang on to an important client. Creative-driven agencies tend to value research less than others.

Research comes into the advertising process at several points. It is often used to assist a marketer in determining which segment of the market to target. Research also plays a role in helping the creatives understand the audience members to whom their ads will speak, and which buttons to push. It is also used to make go/no-go decisions, to determine when to pull an ad that is worn out, and to evaluate the performance of an ad agency. Unfortunately, it is also commonly misused.

As you can see, advertising research is used to judge advertising, but who judges advertising research, and how? First of all, not enough people, in our opinion, question and judge research. Research is not magic or truth, and it should never be confused with such. Issues of reliability, validity, trustworthiness, and meaningfulness should be seriously considered when research is used to make important decisions. **Reliability** means that the method generates generally consistent findings over time. **Validity** means that the information generated is relevant to the research questions being investigated. In other words, the research investigates what it seeks to investigate. **Trustworthiness** is a term usually applied to qualitative data, and it means exactly what it implies: Can one, knowing how the data were collected, trust them, and to what extent? Most difficult of all is the notion of **meaningfulness**. Just what does a piece of research really mean (if anything)? It is important for advertising professionals to take a moment (or several) and consider the limitations inherent in their data and in their interpretations. Too few take the time.

Account Planning versus Advertising Research.

Jon Steel, Director of Account Planning and Vice Chairman of Goodby, Silverstein and Partners (their clients are Anheuser-Busch, California—"Got Milk?"—Milk Producers, Nike, Porsche, and Hewlett-Packard, among others), has called account planning "the biggest thing to hit American advertising since Doyle Dane Bernbach's Volkswagen campaign."[2] That may be stretching it a bit (it is), but account planning is a big story in the industry. What is it? Well, good question.

Account planning is defined in contrast to traditional advertising research. It differs mostly in three ways. First, in terms of organization, agencies that use this system typically assign an "account planner" to work as co-equal with the account

---

2.   Jon Steel, *Truth, Lies & Advertising: The Art of Account Planning* (New York: John Wiley & Sons, 1998), jacket.

executive on a given client's business. Rather than depending on a separate research department's occasional involvement, the agency assigns the planner to a single client (just like an advertising executive) to stay with the projects on a continuous basis. (Even though, in this organizational scheme, there is typically an account planning department.) In the more traditional system, the research department would get involved from time to time as needed, and members of the research department would work on several different clients' advertising. (There are several derivations on this theme.)

Another difference is that this organizational structure puts research in a different, and more prominent, role. In this system, researchers (or "planners") seem to be more actively involved throughout the entire advertising process and seem to have a bigger impact on it as well. (Of course, some of the difference is more agency self-promotion than reality.) Agencies that practice "account planning" tend to do more developmental, and less evaluative, research. Third, "planning agencies" tend to do more qualitative and naturalistic research than their more traditional counterparts. But these differences, too, seem fairly exaggerated. Even though Jay Chiat called planning "the best new business tool ever invented,"[3] Jon Steel puts it closer to the less hyperbolic truth:

In my view, planning, when used properly, is the best old *business tool ever invented. Because if the agency has a true planning philosophy, it is interested in only one thing, and that is getting the advertising right for its existing clients. Its planners are being smart about their strategic research; they have good working relationships with other departments, especially the creative department; and most important, when they take rough advertising concepts and show them to target consumers, they are not only honest in their appraisal, but they are listened to. Not always necessarily agreed with, but at least their point of view is seriously considered. Under such circumstances, it is more likely that the advertising will be effective, and that advertising will then become a powerful tool with which to attract new clients.[4]*

Developmental Advertising Research.   ◖◗ Developmental advertising research is used to generate advertising opportunities and messages. It helps the creatives and the account team figure out things such as the target audience's street language and profile. It provides critical information used by creatives in actually producing ads. It is conducted early in the process so there is still an opportunity to influence the way the ads come out. Developmental advertising research is broadly defined and serves many purposes. Because of this, many consider it the most valuable kind of advertising research. Several of the purposes served by developmental research are reviewed in the following sections.

Idea Generation.   Sometimes an ad agency is called on to invent new, yet meaningful, ways of presenting an advertised good or service to a target audience. The outcome might take the form of a repositioning strategy for the advertiser. For example, after many years of representing its parks as the ultimate family destination, Disney and its ad agencies have now positioned its theme parks as adult vacation alternatives for couples whose children have grown and gone off on their own.

Where does an advertiser get ideas for new and meaningful ways to portray a brand? Direct contact with the customer can be an excellent place to start. Qualitative research involving observation of customers, brainstorming sessions with customers, and extended interviews with customers can be great devices for fostering fresh thinking about a brand. (Disney probably got its idea for repositioning by simply observing how many older couples were visiting its parks without children in tow!) Direct contact with and

3.   Ibid, 42.
4.   Ibid, 43.

aggressive listening to the customer can fuel the creative process at the heart of any great advertising campaign. It can also be a great way to anticipate and shape marketplace trends, as seen in the Global Issues box on this page.

GLOBAL ISSUES

JAPAN'S MARKETING BELLWETHER? THE TEENAGE GIRL

For many marketers in Japan, aggressive listening to the customer begins and ends with adolescent females. It seems that high school girls in Japan have an unusual ability to predict consumer product successes, and, when targeted with special promotions, are also able to create favorable hype for products that can turn those products into family favorites. For example, Coca-Cola used focus groups of teenage girls to help fine-tune the marketing program for its fermented-milk drink Lactia. The girls suggested a light and smooth consistency for the product, and a short, stubby bottle with a pink label. Coke followed this advice and then handed out 30,000 of the stubby bottles to high school girls, to help generate favorable word-of-mouth during the brand's launch. Lactia is now one of Japan's most popular beverages.

What could account for this special status of young women as a focal point in market research? Japanese marketing executives say that the girls are simply much more open and honest than their modest and tradition-bound elders. Additionally, these young women are very value-conscious consumers, and thus have good insights when inexpensive products are the focal point of the research. And, they often have a substantial say in their mothers' selections of food items for the entire family. When Meiji Milk Products of Japan introduced its breath-cleansing Chinese tea under the brand name Oolong Socha, it did so with the advice of teenage girls. It soon became a family favorite. Yasuo Odo, a Meiji Milk brand manager, commented: "We were flabbergasted. We didn't think high school girls were that close with their parents these days."

And what about teenage boys? One market research consultant in Tokyo put it this way: "Most Japanese high school boys have trouble articulating. They're no help for our purposes."

Source: Norihiko Shirouzu, "Japan's High-School Girls Excel in Art of Setting Trends," *Wall Street Journal,* April 24, 1998, B1.

Environmental Analysis.

Environmental analysis generates information on the uncontrollable variables in the broad business environment. **Environmental analysis** tries to assess the potential influence of social and cultural trends, economics, and politics on the consumer and the social environment into which the advertising will be projected. Such analysis provides useful information for advertising planning in terms of both the opportunities to communicate effectively with audiences and the barriers to implementation. Exhibit 7.2 shows the type of information gathered during environmental analysis. All of these data help situate (put in context) the advertising message.

Audience Definition.

Market segmentation is one of the first and most important marketing decisions a firm must make. As discussed in the last chapter, the goal of market segmentation is to identify target audiences that represent the best match between the firm's market offering and consumers' needs and desires. Basic data about audience sizes along with their demographic profiles are absolutely critical in this process. As suggested by the New Media box on page 216, this is every bit as important to the Internet advertiser as it is to those working in more conventional media.

Furthermore, new market opportunities are commonly discovered when you get to know your audience. As an example, the national hardware trade association discovered that 49.6 percent of the purchases of tools needed for simple emergency repairs— plungers, ladders, fire extinguishers, pipe decloggers—were made by women.[5] Once a target segment or segments have been identified, advertising planning can proceed with a determination of the message that will be most meaningful to the consumers in the segment. In addition, information about the best potential segments allows for the efficient media placement of advertisements. The finding on women's purchases of

5.   Jeffery D. Zbar, "Hardware Builds Awareness among Women," *Advertising Age,* July 11, 1994, 18.

EXHIBIT 7.2

Environmental analysis.

Environment	Information Gathered
Demographic	Demographics are population characteristics. Among the important dimensions of the demographic environment are population density, age distribution, geographic population distribution, household size and composition, and population ethnicity. The demographic environment is of critical importance to advertisers because population characteristics affect demand for various goods and services. Further, accurate information on the demographic environment allows marketers to make inferences regarding behavior, thus providing a basis for predicting future consumption patterns.
Social and cultural	One of the most important and yet most difficult external environmental factors to gauge is the social and cultural environment. The social and cultural environment is related to the broad-based values evident in a society. In recent history, changes in such social and cultural values have spawned multibillion-dollar industries in the United States. The value placed on health and fitness has given rise to the health food industry and the spa and fitness center industry, as well as a huge boost to the outdoor recreation industry. Social and cultural trends may evolve slowly but have an enormous effect on goods and services (and advertising) prevalent in a society. Among the significant social and cultural trends over the past 30 years that have shaped demand in the United States are the changing family structure, the importance of time and convenience, the emphasis on health and fitness, the changing gender roles, a concern for the natural environment, and attitudes toward wealth and status seeking.
Economic	Several economic factors affect the ability of firms to successfully market and advertise goods and services. Fundamental features of the economy, such as gross domestic product, interest rates, and inflation, influence the ability (and desire) of both household and business consumers to spend. Some industries are more sensitive to economic conditions than others. Traditionally, the automobile industry (and other durable goods industries), tourism, and housing suffer the most if economic conditions sour. Conversely, basic consumer packaged goods, pharmaceuticals, and some business goods categories suffer little from a general slowdown in the economy. Of the enormous number of economic statistics available, some of the more popular for firms to monitor are household income and spending patterns, the consumer price index, and consumer confidence.
Political/regulatory	The effects of the political and regulatory environment come from both government and nongovernment sources. Numerous restrictions have been imposed on marketing and advertising practices by both federal and state governments. The federal agencies that have the most direct and obvious effect on marketing and advertising practices are the Federal Trade Commission (FTC), the Food and Drug Administration (FDA), and the Federal Communications Commission (FCC). Recall that consumers, industry associations, and the media all have informal regulatory powers over a firm's marketing and advertising practices. Consumers can boycott products or form special-interest groups. Industry trade associations and media organizations have codes of behavior they generally follow.
Technological	Technological change doesn't affect just the products or services a firm can market. Technology affects the values and behavior of a society. With regard to advertising specifically, if the information superhighway makes it feasible to communicate with individual consumers in an interactive media format, the nature of advertising will change dramatically. Similarly, if technology promotes telecommuting, then consumption of and demand for automobiles, gasoline, fast food, clothing, and a variety of other work-related products will be changed. A long-term and visionary perspective on technology and its impact is essential.
Competitive	The activities of competitors have an obvious effect on both marketing and advertising planning. Firms must monitor competitors to respond to competitive maneuvers. What is less obvious, though, is the threat from indirect competition. This is the threat of competition from new alternatives. For example, there is the threat to the airline industry from teleconferencing. The primary decision with regard to the competitive environment for advertising planning is the extent to which a direct response to competition will be undertaken or whether more basic, noncompetition-based strategies will be pursued.

Builders Square targets a new segment for hardware: women.
www.builderssquare.com/

hardware led Builders Square, the home improvement retailer, to run ads targeting the women's market in *Home, House Beautiful,* and *Better Homes & Gardens,* as the ad in Exhibit 7.3 shows.[6]

Audience Profiling. Perhaps the most important service provided by developmental advertising research is the profiling of target audiences for the creatives. Creatives need to know as much as they can about the people to whom their ads will speak. This research is done in many ways. One of the most popular is through lifestyle research. Lifestyle research, also known as AIO (activities, interests, and opinions) research, uses survey data from consumers who have answered questions about themselves. From the answers to a wide variety of such questions, advertisers are able to get a pretty good profile of those consumers they are most interested in talking to. Since the data also contain other product usage questions, advertisers are able to account for a consumption lifestyle as well. These profiles present the creative staff with a finer-grained picture of the target audience and their needs, wants, and motivations. Of course, the answers to these questions are only as valuable as the questions are valid. In-depth interviews with individual consumers provide an excellent source of information to supplement the findings from AIO research.

Methods and Procedures Used in Developmental Research. One of the key methods for developmental research purposes is the **focus group**. A focus group is a brainstorming session with target customers to come up with new insights about the brand—"Six people sitting around a table eating pizza and discussing your product category with market researchers watching through a one-way mirror is the essence of focus groups."[7] This method brings together from 6 to 12 consumers with a professional moderator to guide the discussion. These consumers are first asked some general questions; then, as the session progresses, the questioning becomes more focused and moves to detailed issues about the brand in question. Clients tend to like focus groups because they can understand them and observe the data being collected.

While focus groups provide an opportunity for in-depth discussion with consumers, they are not without limitations. Even multiple focus groups represent a very small sample of the target audience, and advertisers must remember that generalization is not the goal. The real goal is to get or test a new idea and gain depth of information. Greater depth of information allows for a greater understanding of the context of actual usage and its subtleties.

It also takes great skill to lead a focus group effectively. Without a well-trained and experienced moderator, some individuals will completely dominate, or at least annoy, the others. Focus group members feel empowered and privileged; they have been made experts by their selection, and they will sometimes give the moderator all sorts of strange answers that may be more a function of trying to impress other group members than anything having to do with the product in question.

6.   Ibid.
7.   Jeffery A. Trachtenberg, "Listening the Old-Fashioned Way," *Forbes,* October 5, 1987, 202, 204.

Projective techniques are designed to allow consumers to project thoughts and feelings (conscious or unconscious) in an indirect and unobtrusive way onto a theoretically neutral stimulus. (Seeing zoo animals in clouds, or faces in ice cubes, is an example of projection.) Projective techniques share a history with Freudian psychology and depend on notions of unconscious or even repressed thoughts. Projective techniques often consist of offering consumers fragments of pictures or words and asking them to complete the fragment. The most common projective techniques are association tests, sentence or picture completion, dialogue balloons, and story construction. While there is little doubt that people can, and do, project, the trustworthiness, validity, and usefulness of these techniques are often suspect.

Association tests ask consumers to express their feelings or thoughts after hearing a brand name or seeing a logo. In **sentence and picture completion**, a researcher presents consumers with part of a picture or a sentence with words deleted and then asks that the stimulus be completed. The picture or sentence relates to one or several brands of products in the category of interest. For example, a sentence completion task might be: *Most American-made cars are* _____. The basic idea is to elicit honest thoughts and feelings. Of course, consumers usually have some idea of what the researcher is looking for. Still, one can get some reasonably good data from this method.

Dialogue balloons offer consumers the chance to fill in the dialogue of cartoonlike stories, much like those in the comics in the Sunday paper. The story usually has to do with a product use situation. **Story construction** asks consumers to tell a story about people depicted in a scene or picture. Respondents might be asked to tell a story about the personality of the people in the scene, what they are doing, what they were doing just before this scene, what type of car they drive, and what

FAR FROM AN EXACT SCIENCE: INTERNET AUDIENCE TRACKING

Media Metrix (MM) of New York and RelevantKnowledge (RK) of Atlanta are two key players in the new business of Internet audience tracking. Both have gained notoriety as a result of their monthly top 25 most-visited site rankings, and each also offers other more detailed reports about Internet audiences. For example, they can provide details about your site's penetration among all online households; how long surfers stay at your site per day; and gender, age, and other demographic statistics about Web surfers. Although there are notable differences in how one goes about getting these data for Internet versus television or radio audiences, one thing is very much the same: A lot of people complain about the results.

One complainer—Rich LeFurgy, senior VP of Internet advertising at ESPN/ABC News—says to just have a look at their monthly top 25 listings. It is common to find that as many as a third of the 25 sites appearing in the two companies' lists don't overlap—an odd outcome, to be sure, when both companies claim to be ranking the same thing. LeFurgy also contends that both companies badly underestimate actual site visitations. In one count of ESPN page views, MM's estimate was 41 million and RK's was 94 million, but ESPN's internal logs showed 168 million. Obviously, Internet audience tracking is not an exact science.

On the other hand, executives at MM and RK are quick to defend their methods from critics such as Rich LeFurgy, and are quick to make claims about the superiority of their own methods versus the competitor's. MM says its data is more accurate than RK's because it draws on a much larger sample (30,000 versus 11,000) in conducting its surveys. MM president Mary Anne Packo claims: "The key difference is that our focus is on measuring the whole digital media space—not only Web sites but the online services and the non-Web services such as Pointcast." RK management counters that their method of sampling Internet users is superior, making raw sample size irrelevant. Clearly, both organizations are still learning how to cope with challenges posed by the new media. But then, who isn't?

Source: Russell Shaw, "Online Ratings Are a Growing Business, with Firms Including RelevantKnowledge and Media Metrix," *Electronic Media*, March 2, 1998, 17.

type of house they live in. Again, the idea is to use a less direct method to less obtrusively bring to the surface some often-unconscious mapping of the brand and its associations.

One specific method that has enjoyed growing popularity in developmental applications is the Zaltman Metaphor Elicitation Technique (ZMET).[8] This technique draws out people's buried thoughts and feelings about products and brands by encouraging participants to think in terms of metaphors. A metaphor simply involves defining one thing in terms of another. ZMET draws metaphors from consumers by asking them to spend time thinking about how they would visually represent their experiences with a particular product or service. Participants are asked to make a collection of photographs and pictures from magazines that reflect their experience. For example, in research conducted for DuPont, which supplies raw material for many pantyhose marketers, one person's picture of spilled ice cream reflected her deep disappointment when she spots a run in her hose. In-depth interviews with several dozen of these metaphor-collecting consumers can often reveal new insights about consumers' consumption motives, which then may be useful in the creation of products and ad campaigns to appeal to those motives.

Many times advertisers also need feedback about new ideas before they spend a lot of money to turn the idea into a new marketing or advertising initiative. A **concept test** seeks feedback designed to screen the quality of a new idea, using consumers as the final judge and jury. Concept testing may be used to screen new ideas for specific advertisements or to assess new product concepts. How the product fits current needs and how much consumers are willing to pay for the new product are questions a concept test attempts to answer. For example, would consumers trust a yogurt product coming from the makers of Jell-O? Exhibit 7.4 makes one think so. Concept tests of many kinds are commonly included as part of the agenda of focus groups to get quick feedback on new product or advertising ideas. Concept testing is also executed via survey research when more generalizable feedback is desired.

EXHIBIT 7.4

Yogurt seems a natural fit with the other products for which Jell-O is best known. www.kraftfoods.com/

The Experiences of the Consumer.

Consumers live real lives, and their behavior as consumers is intertwined throughout these real lives. More and more, researchers are attempting to capture more of the experiences of consumers.[9] Advertising researchers can situate their messages far better if they understand the lives of their target audience. Various types of qualitative research attempt to do this. This general type of research uses prolonged observation and in-depth study of individuals or small groups of consumers, typically in their own social environment. This work is usually accomplished through field work, or going to where the consumer lives and consumes. The advertising industry has long appreciated the value of qualitative data and is currently moving to even more strongly embrace extended types of field work.

8.   For three different viewpoints on ZMET, compare Kevin Lane Keller, *Strategic Brand Management* (Upper Saddle River, N.J.: Prentice-Hall, 1998), 317–320; Ronald B. Lieber, "Storytelling: A New Way to Get Close to Your Customer," *Fortune,* February 3, 1997, 102–108; and Gerald Zaltman, "Rethinking Market Research: Putting People Back In," *Journal of Marketing Research,* vol. 34 (November 1997), 424–437.
9.   Craig J. Thompson, William B. Locander, and Howard Pollio, "Putting Consumer Experience Back into Consumer Research: The Philosophy and Method of Existential Phenomenology," *Journal of Consumer Research,* vol. 16 (June 1989), 133–147.

Fundamental Issues in Message Evaluation.

At the heart of any successful advertising campaign is a message that engages a consumer and gives him or her a reason to believe in the brand. It should thus come as no surprise that much of the research conducted by ad agencies and their clients deals with message testing. Message-testing research comes in two basic types: One occurs before an ad is placed (a pretest); the other occurs after an ad is placed (a posttest). There is no one right way to test a message, and as a result one can find conflicting advice about how to execute this research function. This diversity of opinion stems from multiple and sometimes competing testing criteria or outright confusion about what an ad must do to be considered effective.

Motives and Expectations.

Message testing can be a function of logic and adaptive decision making, or it may be driven by custom and history. In the best case, reliable, valid, trustworthy, and meaningful tests are appropriately applied. In the worst case, tests in which few still believe continue to thrive because they represent "the way we have always done things." More typically, however, industry practice falls somewhere in between. The pressure of history and the felt need for normative data (which allows comparisons with the past) partially obscure questions of appropriateness and validity. This makes for an environment in which the best test is not always done, and the right questions are not always asked.

This brings us to motives and expectations. Just what is it that advertising people want out of their message tests? The answer, of course, depends on who you ask. Generally speaking, the account team wants some assurance that the commercial or ad does essentially what it's supposed to do. Many times, the team simply wants whatever the client wants. The client typically wants to see some numbers, generally meaning **normative test scores**; in other words, the client wants to see how well a particular ad scored against average commercials of its type that were tested previously. The creatives who produced the ad often believe there is no such thing as the average commercial, and they are quite sure that if there are average commercials, theirs are not among them. Besides benefiting the sales of the advertised product or service, the creatives wouldn't mind another striking ad on their reel or in their book. Message-testing tools also generate a type of report card, and some people, particularly on the creative side of advertising, resent getting report cards from people in suits. (Who wouldn't?) Creatives also argue that these numbers are often misleading and misapplied. Often they're right.

Whenever people begin looking at the numbers, there is a danger that trivial differences can be made monumental. Other times, the required measure is simply inappropriate. Still other times, creatives wishing to keep their jobs simply give the client what he or she wants, as suggested in Exhibit 7.5. If simple recall is what the client wants, then increasing the frequency of brand mentions might be the answer. It may not make for a better commercial, but it may make for a better score and, presumably, a happy client in the short run.

Despite the politics involved, message-testing research is probably a good idea most of the time. Properly conducted, such research can yield important data that management can then use to determine the suitability of an ad. It's far better to shelve an expensive commercial than run (or continue to run) something that will produce little good and may even do harm.

Dimensions for Message Assessment.

There are many standards against which ads are judged. Of course, picking the right criteria is not always an easy task, but it is the essence of effective message evaluation. An ad like that in Exhibit 7.6 could be judged along many dimensions and with several criteria. However, we will discuss four basic dimensions on which a message could be evaluated: whether or not the ad imparts knowledge about the brand, shapes attitudes and preferences, attaches feeling and emotion, or legitimizes the brand as one that is right for its target audience.

EXHIBIT 7.5

Creative pumps up DAR numbers.

Bob, a creative at a large agency, has learned from experience how to deal with lower-than-average day-after recall (DAR) scores. As he explains it, there are two basic strategies: (1) Do things that you know will pump up the DAR. For example, if you want high DARs, never simply super (superimpose) the brand name or tag at the end of the ad. Always voice it over as well, whether it fits or not. You can also work in a couple of additional mentions in dialogue; they may stand out like a sore thumb and make consumers think, "Man, is that a stupid commercial," because people don't talk that way. But it will raise your DARs. (2) Tell them (the account executive or brand manager and other suits) that this is not the kind of product situation that demands high DARs. In fact, high DARs would actually hurt them in the long run due to quick wearout and annoyance. Tell them, "You're too sophisticated for that ham-handed kind of treatment. It would never work with our customers." You can use the second strategy only occasionally, but it usually works. It's amazing.

WEB SIGHTING

EXHIBIT 7.6

Rogaine almost certainly tested its message heavily before settling on such a macho, racing-evocative theme. Pharmacia & Upjohn use its Rogaine Web site (www.rogaine.com/) to further communicate with customers (e.g., with online discussion groups). While one suspects that the average Rogaine user might find more interesting places to "hang out" online, the sort of feedback Pharmacia & Upjohn might get from encouraging customers to talk amongst themselves could be valuable, and, with the Web as the forum, far less expensive to gather than convening conventional focus groups on a continual basis.

Impart Knowledge. It is commonly assumed that advertising generates thoughts, some of which are at some point retrieved to then influence purchase. Some ads are judged effective if they leave this cognitive residue, or knowledge about the brand. This knowledge may take many different forms. It could be a jingle, a tag line, the recognition of a product symbol, or merely brand-name recognition. Generally, tests of recall and recognition are featured when knowledge generation is the advertiser's primary concern.

Shape Attitudes. Attitudes can tell us a lot about where a brand stands in the consumer's eyes. Attitudes can be influenced both by what people know and by what people feel about a brand. In this sense, attitude or preference is a summary evaluation that ties together the influence of many different factors. Advertisers thus may view attitude shaping or attitude change as a key dimension for assessing advertising effectiveness. Message-testing research is frequently structured around the types of attitude measures discussed in Chapter 5.

Attach Feelings and Emotions. Advertisers have always had a special interest in feelings and emotions. Ever since the "atmospheric" ads of the 1920s, there has been the belief that feelings may be more important than thoughts as a reaction to certain ads. While this philosophy waxes and wanes, there has been a renewed interest in developing better measures of the feelings and emotions generated by advertising.[10] This has included better paper-and-pencil measures as well as dial-turning devices with which those watching an ad turn a dial in

10. Stuart J. Agres, Julie A. Edell, and Tony M. Dubitsky, eds., *Emotion in Advertising* (Westport, Conn.: Quorum Books, 1990). See especially Chapters 7 and 8.

either a positive or negative direction to indicate their emotional response to the ad. Participants' responses are tracked by computer and can be aggregated and superimposed over the ad during playback to allow account executives and brand managers to see the pattern of affective reactions generated by the ad.

Legitimize the Brand. A **resonance test** is one in which the goal is to determine to what extent the message resonates or rings true with target-audience members.[11] This method fits well with consumer-experience research. The question becomes, Does this ad match consumers' own experiences? Does it produce an affinity reaction? Do consumers who view it say, "Yeah, that's right; I feel just like that"? Do consumers read the ad and make it their own?[12] In the view of some, this is the direction in which message evaluation research needs to move. The assessment dimension here reflects the effectiveness of advertising for legitimizing a brand with its target audience.

Pretest Message Research.
Because so much time, effort, and expense are involved in the development of advertising messages, most organizations pretest their message to gauge consumer reaction *before* advertisements are placed. A variety of tools may be used in pretesting.

Communications Tests.
A **communications test** simply seeks to see whether a message is communicating something close to what is desired. Communications tests are usually done in a group setting, with data coming from a combination of pencil-and-paper questionnaires and group discussion. They are done with one major thought in mind: to prevent a major disaster, to prevent communicating something the creators of the ad are too close to see but that is entirely obvious to those consumers first seeing the ad. This could be an unintended double entendre or an unseen sexual allusion. It could be an unexpected interpretation of the visual imagery in an ad as that ad is moved from country to country around the world. Remember, if the consumer sees unintended things, it doesn't matter whether they're intended or not—to the consumer, they're there. However, advertisers should balance this against the fact that communications test members feel privileged and special, and thus they may try too hard to see things. This is another instance where well-trained and experienced researchers must be counted on to draw a proper conclusion from the testing.

Magazine Dummies.
Dummy advertising vehicles are mock-ups of magazines that contain editorial content and advertisements, as a real magazine would. Inserted in the dummy vehicle is one or more test advertisements. Once again, consumers representing the target audience are asked to read through the magazine as they normally would. The test is usually administered in consumers' homes and therefore has some sense of realism. Once the reading is completed, the consumers are asked questions about the content of both the magazine and the advertisements. Questions relating to recall of the test ads and feelings toward the ad and the featured product are typically asked. This method is most valuable for comparing different message options.

11. David Glenn Mick and Claus Buhl, "A Meaning-Based Model of Advertising Experiences," *Journal of Consumer Research,* vol. 19 (December 1992), 317–338.
12. Linda Scott, "The Bridge from Text to Mind: Adapting Reader Response Theory for Consumer Research," *Journal of Consumer Research,* vol. 21 (December 1994), 461–486.

Theater Tests. Advertisements are also tested in small theaters, usually set up in or near shopping malls. Members of the theater audience have an electronic device through which they can express how much they like or dislike the advertisements shown. Simulated shopping trips can also be a part of this type of research. The problem with the **theater test** is that it is difficult to determine whether the respondent is really expressing feelings toward the ad or the product being advertised. Given the artificial and demanding conditions of the test, experienced researchers are again needed to interpret the results.

This form of message pretesting has become quite common in the United States, and as a result considerable data are available for judging the validity of this approach. John Philip Jones, a professor of communications at Syracuse University, has conducted analyses on these data and his conclusions are very supportive.[13] He contends that even if this form of message pre-testing yields some incorrect predictions about ads' potential effectiveness (as it surely will), an advertiser's success rate with this tool is bound to improve relative to that which would be realized without it.

Thought Listings. It is commonly assumed that advertising generates thoughts, or cognitions, during and following exposure. Message research that tries to identify specific thoughts that may be generated by an ad is referred to as **thought listing**, or cognitive response analysis.

Here the researcher is interested in the thoughts that a finished or near-finished ad generates in the mind of the consumer. Typically, cognitive responses are collected by having individuals watch the commercial in groups and, as soon as it is over, asking them to write down all the thoughts that were in their minds while watching the commercial. The hope is that this will capture what the potential audience members made of the ad and how they responded, or talked back, to it.

These verbatim responses can then be analyzed in a number of ways. Usually, simple percentages or box scores of word counts are used. The ratio of favorable to unfavorable thoughts may be the primary interest of the researcher. Alternatively, the number of times the person made a self-relevant connection—that is, "That would be good for me" or "That looks like something I'd like"—could be tallied and compared for different ad executions.

Attitude-Change Studies. The typical **attitude-change study** uses a before-and-after ad exposure design. People from the target market are recruited, and their pre-exposure attitudes toward the advertised brand as well as toward competitors' brands are taken. Then they are exposed to the test ad, along with some dummy ads. Following this exposure, their attitudes are measured again. The goal, of course, is to gauge the potential of specific ad versions for changing brand attitudes.

Attitude-change studies are often conducted in a theater test setting. These tests often use a constant-sum measurement scale. A subject is asked to divide a sum (for example, 100 points) among several (usually three) brands. For example, they would be asked to divide 100 points among three brands of deodorants in relation to how likely they are to purchase each. They do this before and after ad exposure. A change score is then computed. Sometimes this change score is adjusted by the potential change, so as not to unfairly penalize established brands.

13. John Philip Jones, "Advertising Pre-Testing: Will Europe Follow America's Lead?" *Commercial Communications,* June 1997, 21–26.

The reliability of these procedures is fairly high. Yet how meaningful are change scores? This is change premised on a single ad exposure (sometimes two) in an unnatural viewing environment. Many advertisers believe that commercials don't register their impact until after three or four exposures. Still, a significant swing in before and after scores with a single exposure suggests that something is going on, and that some of this effect might be expected when the ad reaches real consumers in the comfort of their homes.

To test attitude change in regard to print ads, test ads can be dropped off at the participants' homes in the form of magazines. The test ads have been tipped in, or inserted. Subjects are told that the researcher will return the next day for an interview. They are also told that as part of their compensation for participating, they are being entered in a drawing. At that point, they are asked to indicate their preferences on a wide range of potential prizes. The next day when the interviewer returns, he or she asks for these preferences a second time. This is the postexposure attitude measure.

There aren't many attitude-change studies in radio. This may be because most people view radio as a medium best used for building awareness and recall, and not for the higher-order goal of attitude change.

Physiological Measures. Several message pretests use physiological measurement devices. **Physiological measures** detect how consumers react to messages, based on physical responses. **Eye-tracking systems** have been developed to monitor eye movements across print ads. With one such system, respondents wear a goggle-like device that records (on a computer system) pupil dilations, eye movements, and length of view by sectors within a print advertisement. Another physiological measure is a **psychogalvanometer,** which measures galvanic skin response (GSR). GSR is a measure of minute changes in perspiration, which suggest arousal related to some stimulus—in this case, an advertisement.

Voice response analysis is another high-tech research procedure. The idea here is that inflections in the voice when discussing an ad indicate excitement and other physiological states. In a typical application, a subject is asked to respond to a series of ads. These responses are tape recorded and then computer analyzed. Deviations from a flat response are claimed to be meaningful. Other, less frequently used physiological measures record brain wave activity, heart rate, blood pressure, and muscle contraction.

All physiological measures suffer from the same drawbacks. While we may be able to detect a physiological response to an advertisement, there is no way to determine whether the response is to the ad or the product, or which part of the advertisement was responsible for the response. In some sense, even the positive-negative dimension is obscured. Without being able to correlate specific effects with other dimensions of an ad, physiological measures are of minimal benefit.

Since the earliest days of advertising, there has been a fascination with physiological measurement. Advertising's fascination with science is well documented, with early attempts at physiology being far more successful as a sales tool than as a way to actually gauge ad effectiveness. There is something provocative about scientists (sometimes even in white lab coats) wiring people up; it seems so precise and legitimate, as reflected in Exhibit 7.7. Unfortunately—or fortunately, depending on your perspective—these measures tell us little beyond the simple degree of arousal attributable to an ad. For most advertisers, this minimal benefit doesn't justify the expense and intrusion involved with physiological measurement.

Commercial Pretest Services. Pretest message research can often be conducted by an advertiser in conjunction with its advertising agency. However, several commercial pretesting services provide full-service pretesting for both television and print advertisements. Some of these service providers are described in Exhibit 7.8.

EXHIBIT 7.7

*The legitimatizing effect of
science on advertising testing.*

EXHIBIT 7.7

*The legitimatizing effect of
science on advertising testing.*

Experimentation in the Marketplace—Pilot Testing.
Before committing to the expense of
a major campaign, advertisers often take their message-testing programs into the field.
Pursuing message evaluation with experimentation in the marketplace is known as
pilot testing. This extended testing can be of the do-it-yourself variety, or it can be
accomplished via a commercial service provider. Several well-known service providers
are featured in Exhibit 7.9.

The fundamental options for pilot testing fall into one of three classes. **Split-cable
transmission** allows testing of two different versions of an advertisement through
direct transmission to two separate samples of similar households within a single, well-
defined market area. This method provides exposure in a natural setting for heightened
realism. Factors such as frequency of transmission and timing of transmission can be
carefully controlled. The advertisements are then compared on measures of exposure,
recall, and persuasion.

Split-run distribution uses the same technique as split-cable transmission, except
the print medium is used. Two different versions of the same advertisement are placed
in every other copy of a magazine. This method of pilot testing has the advantage of
using direct response as a test measure. Ads can be designed with a reply card that can
serve as a basis of evaluation. Coupons and toll-free numbers can also be used. The
realism of this method is a great advantage in the testing process. Expense is, of course,
a major drawback.

Finally, a **split-list experiment** tests the effectiveness of various aspects of direct
mail advertising pieces. Multiple versions of a direct mail piece are prepared and sent to
various segments of a mailing list. The version that pulls (produces sales) the best is
deemed superior. The advantage of all the pilot-testing methods is the natural and real
setting within which the test takes place. A major disadvantage is that competitive or
other environmental influences in the market cannot be controlled and may affect the
performance of one advertisement without ever being detected by the researcher. Such
effects provide an inaccurate comparison between test ads.

EXHIBIT 7.8

Commercial services for pretesting advertising messages.

Television Pretesting Services

Research Systems Corporation: ARS Persuasion System. This is the system Goodyear used to pretest its Aquatred advertisements. The ARS System employs 800 to 1,200 respondents in several market areas. These respondents view television ads embedded in television programs. Before and after viewing, respondents are asked to choose sets of products they would pick if they were chosen as a winner of a door prize. The persuasion measure is the number of respondents who choose the test product after exposure versus those who chose the product before exposure. Three days after exposure, a subsample is telephoned to measure recall and understanding of the test ad.

Gallup & Robinson InTeleTest. This test uses in-home viewing of a videotaped program with six test commercials and six normal commercials embedded. Testing is done in 10 different cities, with 150 male and female respondents. Respondents are told they are viewing a proposed new television program. The day after viewing the program, a researcher conducts a telephone interview and takes recall measures related to the advertising in the program. Later, respondents view a tape that contains only the test ads, and they then provide an evaluation of recognition, likability, and general reaction to each ad.

Video Storyboard Tests (VST). The VST is specifically designed to test rough versions of television ads. The ads are prepared from storyboards and music soundtracks by VST. One-on-one interviews are conducted after individual respondents are shown the storyboard ads on a television monitor. Respondents are asked questions relating to persuasion, liking, believability, and other features of the ad. VST can provide benchmark measures for other products in the category as a basis for rating the test ad.

Print Pretesting Services

Perception Research Services (PRS). PRS evaluates all types of print advertising using an eye-tracking camera that follows the respondent's eye movement around a print advertisement. Respondents that fit a target audience profile are allowed to view a print ad as long as they desire. The camera records the length of time for which and the sequence in which some ad elements are viewed, other elements are overlooked, and copy is read. A postsession interview identifies recall, likability of the ad, main idea perceptions, purchase interest, and product image.

ASI: Print Plus. ASI offers print ad pretesting through national magazines or its own dummy magazine vehicle, called *Reflections*. Testing is done in five markets in the United States. Test participants are told they are taking part in a public-opinion survey and are given a magazine to read in their home. A telephone interview is conducted the following day to determine recall and other dimensions of the test ad. Participants are asked to review four ads, after which a feature evaluation and product interest list is administered.

Video Storyboard Tests (VST). VST tests all forms of rough and fully finished print ads in its dummy vehicle magazine, called *Looking at Us*. Respondents are told they are examining a pilot issue of a new magazine. Individual interviews are conducted in shopping malls, where respondents rate ads on persuasion, product uniqueness, believability, competitive strength, likes and dislikes, and reactions to headlines.

Source: Adapted from descriptions in Jack Haskins and Alice Kendrick, *Successful Advertising Research Methods* (Chicago: NTC Business Books, 1993), 318–328.

EXHIBIT 7.9

Commercial services for pilot testing advertising messages.

Television Pilot Testing

Gallup & Robinson: In-View. This service provides on-air testing of both rough and finished advertisements. One market area in the East, Midwest, and West is selected, and randomly selected samples of 100 to 150 subjects are targeted for the test. The test ad is aired on an independent network station with a former prime-time program now in syndication. Subjects are called *before* the program is aired and invited to watch for the purpose of evaluating the program itself. Researchers obtain day-after recall measures and ask questions regarding idea communication and persuasion for the test ad.

ASI: Recall Plus and Persuasion Plus. Unlike the Gallup & Robinson test, ASI uses cable transmission to test ads on a recruited audience. A standard random sample is 200 respondents drawn from a minimum of two test cities. In Recall Plus, respondents are called the day of the test and invited to preview a new television program. The program includes four noncompeting test advertisements and one filler nontest ad. Day-after recall and effectiveness measures are then taken. The Persuasion Plus test uses the same methods as Recall Plus, with the addition of brand-choice measures. More extensive screening of participants is done in the recruiting stage with respect to brand usage and preference. Then, within two hours after viewing the test program, Persuasion Plus respondents are interviewed and, in the context of prize drawing, asked to choose the brands they would most like to have. A "Tru-Share" persuasion score is calculated on the pretest and posttest brand preferences.

Print Pilot Testing

Gallup & Robinson: Rapid Ad Measurement (RAM). Regular readers of *Time* and *People* magazines are recruited in five metropolitan areas to participate in studies. Gallup & Robinson then offers advertisers the chance to buy advertising space in test issues of these magazines, which are delivered to 150 participants' homes in each test area. A telephone interview is conducted the day after delivery, and, after magazine reading has been verified, respondents are asked if they recall ads for a list of brands and companies. Detailed measures are obtained for recall, idea communication, and persuasion of the text ad.

Source: Adapted from descriptions in Jack Haskins and Alice Kendrick, *Successful Advertising Research Methods* (Chicago: NTC Business Books, 1993), 334–337.

Posttest Message Tracking.

Posttest message tracking assesses the performance of advertisements during or after the launch of an advertising campaign. Common measures of an ad's performance are recall, recognition, awareness and attitude, and purchase behavior.

Recall Testing.

By far the most common method of advertising research is the recall test. The basic idea is that if the ad is to work, it has to be remembered. Following on this premise is the further assumption that the ads best remembered are the ones most likely to work. Thus the objective of these tests is to see just how much, if anything, the viewer of an ad remembers of the message. Recall is used in the testing of print, television, and radio advertising.

In television, the basic procedure is to recruit a group of individuals from the target market who will be watching a certain channel during a certain time on a test date. They are asked to participate ahead of time, and simply told to watch the show. A day after exposure, the testing company calls the individuals on the phone and determines, of those who actually saw the ad, how much they can recall. The procedure generally starts with questions such as, Do you remember seeing an ad for laundry detergent? If so, do you remember the brand? If the respondent remembers, she or he is asked to replay the commercial; if not, further aids or prompts are given. The interview is generally tape recorded and transcribed. The verbatim interview is coded into various categories representing levels of recall, typically reported as a percentage. Recall testing for radio ads follows procedures similar to those for television.

In a typical print recall test, a consumer is recruited from the target market, generally at a shopping mall. He or she is given a magazine to take home. Many times the magazine is an advance issue of a real publication; other times it is a fictitious magazine created only for testing purposes. The ads are tipped in, or inserted, into the vehicle. Some companies alter the mix of remaining ads; others do not. Some rotate the ads (put them in different spots in the magazine) so as not to get effects due to either editorial context or order. The participants are told that they should look at the magazine and that they will be telephoned the following day and asked some questions. During the telephone interview, **aided recall** is assessed. This involves a product-category cue, such as, Do you remember seeing any ads for personal computers? The percentage who respond affirmatively and provide some evidence of actually remembering the ad are scored as exhibiting aided recall. Other tests go into more detail by actually bringing the ad back to the respondent and asking about various components of the ad, such as the headline and body copy. Recall tests are more demanding for participants than are recognition tests, which are described next.

Some research indicates there is little relation between recall scores and sales effectiveness.[14] But doesn't it make sense that the best ads are the ads best remembered? This seemingly simple question has perplexed academics and practitioners for a long time.

Recognition Testing. Recognition tests ask magazine readers and television viewers whether they remember having seen particular advertisements and whether they can name the company sponsoring the ad. For print advertising, the actual advertisement is shown to respondents, and for television advertising, a script with accompanying photos is shown. For instance, a recognition test might ask, Do you remember seeing the ad in Exhibit 7.10? This is a much easier task than recall in that respondents are cued by the very stimulus they are supposed to remember, and they aren't asked to do anything more than say yes or no. Do you think any complications might arise in establishing recognition of the ads displayed in Exhibits 7.10 and 7.11?

Companies that do this kind of research follow some general procedures. Subscribers to a relevant magazine are contacted and asked if an interview can be set up in their home. The readers must have at least glanced at the issue to qualify. Then each tar-

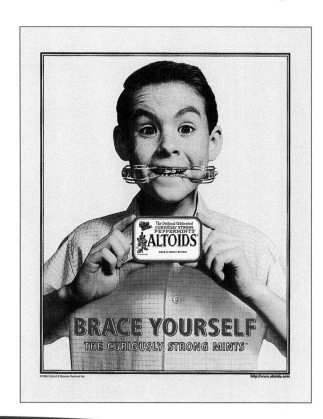

EXHIBIT 7.10

Recognition testing uses the ad itself to test whether consumers remember it and can associate it with its brand and message. This unusual, comically fanciful image would likely make this ad easy to recognize. But imagine this ad with the Altoids brand name blacked out. If consumers remember the ad, will they also remember the Altoids brand name? Novel imagery sometimes actually distracts readers, enticing them to overlook brand names. www.altoids.com/

14. Rajeev Batra, John G. Meyers, and David A. Aaker, *Advertising Management,* 5th ed. (Upper Saddle River, N.J.: Prentice-Hall, 1996), 469.

WEB SIGHT ING

EXHIBIT 7.11

MM = 2000. What's that? Although M&M Mars might singlehand-edly re-educate the American consumer on how to count in Roman numerals, that's clearly not the real intent of this ad. The happy accident of M&M's two-M name provides the opportunity to peg the company brand to a prominent event: the turn of the new millennium. Whether or not there's any official correlation between the candy and the millennial benchmark, consumers will doubtless consume thousands of M&M's as Y2K officially dawns. M&M's may have a disadvantage in Cyberspace, though, because Web addresses can't incorporate ampersands. Would you guess to find them at www.m-ms.com?

get ad is shown, and the readers are asked if they remember seeing the ad (if they *noted* it), if they read or saw enough of the ad to notice the brand name (if they *associated* it), and if they claim to have read at least 50 percent of the copy (if they *read most* of it). This testing is usually conducted just a few days after the current issue becomes available.

There is a longer history of recognition scores than of any other testing method. There are norma-tive data on many types of ads. The biggest problem with this test is that of a yea-saying bias. In other words, many people say they recognize an ad that in truth they haven't seen. After a few days, do you really think you could correctly remember which of the three ads in Exhibits 7.12, 7.13, and 7.14 you really saw, if you saw the ads under natural viewing conditions?

Recognition tests suffer from two other prob-lems. First, because direct interviewing is involved, the test is expensive. Second, because respondents are given visual aids, the risk of overestimation threatens the meaningfulness of the collected data.

Awareness and Attitude Tracking.

Tracking studies measure the change in an audi-ence's brand awareness and attitude before and after an advertising campaign. This common type of advertising research is almost always conducted as a survey. Members of the target market are surveyed on a fairly regular basis to detect any changes. Any change in awareness or attitude is usually attributed (rightly or wrongly) to the advertising effort. The problem with these types of tests is the inability to isolate the effect of advertising on awareness and attitude amid a myriad of other influences—media reports, observation, friends, competitive advertising, and so forth.

Behavior-Based Evaluation.
Advertisements in both print and broadcast media that offer the audi-ence the opportunity to place an inquiry or respond directly through a Web site, reply card, or toll-free phone number, produce **inquiry/direct response mea-sures**. An example is displayed in Exhibit 7.15. These measures are quite straightfor-ward in the sense that advertisements that generate a high number of inquiries or direct responses, compared to historical benchmarks, are deemed effective. Addi-tional analyses may compare the number of inquiries or responses to the number of sales generated. These measures are not relevant for all types of advertising. Ads designed to have long-term image-building or brand-identity effects should not be judged using such short-term response measures.

With the advent of universal product codes (UPCs) on product packages and the proliferation of cable television, research firms are now able to engage in single-source research to document the behavior of individuals in a respondent pool by tracking their behavior from the television set to the checkout counter. **Single-source tracking measures** provide information from individual households about brand purchases,

EXHIBITS 7.12, 7.13, AND 7.14

All of these ads, so strikingly similar, do little to (1) differentiate the product, (2) make it memorable for the consumer, or (3) promote the brand, though presumably GM and Ford had intended to do all three with these ads. (Remember Ricardo Montalban's touting the "rich, Corinthian leather" interior of a luxury car? Probably. But do you remember which car or have any idea what Corinthian leather is?) General Motors' Cadillac Division has tried to break out of the seemingly generic luxury car bin with its Catera model (www.catera.com), a "Caddy that zigs," with mixed results. Has Ford broken any new ground in its approach to advertising its luxury SUV, the Navigator (www.lincolnvehicles.com)?

EXHIBIT 7.15

The use of an 800 number or other behavior-based activity is an attractive feature of inquiry/direct response measures for evaluating advertising effectiveness. What are the key advantages to this kind of research? The E★Trade home page, www.etrade.com/index .html, demonstrates a key advantage of the Internet for advertising: its interactivity. Customers can respond easily and quickly, making a response more likely. Also, the interactivity goes both ways—the company can respond to the customer. How does this two-way interactivity benefit the company? See how competitor Charles Schwab www .schwab.com/, takes advantage of Internet interactivity.

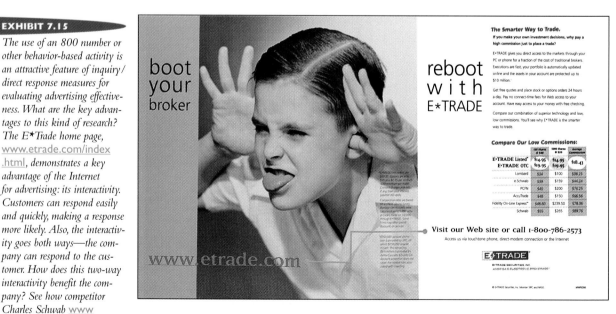

coupon use, and television advertising exposure by combining grocery store scanner data and devices attached to the households' televisions (called *peoplemeters*), which monitor viewing behavior. These sophisticated measures are used to gauge the impact of advertising and promotions on consumers' actual purchases. The main problem with these measures is that it is impossible to determine what aspects of advertising had positive effects on consumers. The IMC box on this page raises additional considerations about the complications that can be anticipated in evaluating the various elements in an integrated marketing communications campaign.

STALKING THE HOLY GRAIL: RESEARCH COMPANIES JOIN FORCES TO TRACK SYNERGIES PROMISED BY IMC

The underlying thesis of IMC is that all the communication tools at the advertiser's disposal can and should be used in combination to get the message across to the target segment. Direct marketing, sales promotion, event sponsorship, PR, and traditional broadcast advertising should be employed in an integrated program to reach the consumer. The hoped-for outcome is what Esther Thorson and Jeri Moore have referred to as "a synergy of persuasive voices." In combination, the various communication tools are supposed to produce an effect where the whole is greater than the sum of the individual parts. Sounds wonderful in theory, but how do we know that such synergies are actually being achieved in IMC campaigns? Can we measure the effects of all the individual parts and then also quantify the synergistic effect due to them working in combination? Simply stated, we don't know, and we aren't even close to being able to validate the hoped-for synergistic effect. As represented by advertising researchers Helen Katz and Jacques Lendrevie, this is truly the search for IMC's Holy Grail.

But you have to start somewhere, and two advertising research companies have merged their evaluative know-how to begin the search. A. C. Nielsen and IPSOS-ASI now offer a testing service they call "Market Drivers" to begin to sort out the joint effects of advertising and sales promotion. The fact that these former competitors joined forces to launch this service makes the point that the search for IMC's Holy Grail will require a new way of doing business. Market Drivers combines Nielsen's data on in-store sales with ASI's ad-testing capabilities to measure the joint effectiveness of advertising and sales promotion. The tool may be used in preparing a company's IMC plan or measuring the success of a program after it is launched. Expensive? Yes and no. The base price of $100,000 per project doesn't seem that bad if you think of it as a piece of the Holy Grail.

Sources: Helen Katz and Jacques Lendrevie, "In Search of the Holy Grail: First Steps in Measuring Total Exposures of an IMC Program," in Esther Thorson and Jeri Moore, eds., *Integrated Communication* (Mahwah, N.J.: Lawrence Erlbaum Associates, 1996), Chapter 14; James B. Arndorfer, "ACNielsen Market Drivers Will Gauge Promos' Punch," *Advertising Age*, February 23, 1998, 8.

Commercial Posttest Services. Exhibit 7.16 lists the most widely recognized commercial posttest message services. Overall, posttesting is appealing because of the strong desire to track the continuing effectiveness of advertising in a real-world setting. However, the problems of expense, delay of feedback, and inability to separate sources of effect are compromises that need to be understood and evaluated when using this form of message testing.

A Final Thought on Message Testing. None of these methods are perfect. There are challenges to reliability, validity, trustworthiness, and meaningfulness with all of them. Advertisers sometimes think that consumers watch new television commercials the way they watch new, eagerly awaited feature films, or that they listen to radio spots like they listen to a symphony, or read magazine ads like a Steinbeck novel. Work by James Lull and other naturalistic researchers and ethnographers demonstrates what we as Americans know: We watch TV while we work, talk, eat, and study; we use it as a night-light, background noise, and baby-sitter.[15] Likewise, we typically thumb through magazines very, very quickly. While these traditional methods of message testing have their strengths, more naturalistic methods are clearly recommended.

15. James Lull, "How Families Select Television Programs: A Mass Observational Study," *Journal of Broadcasting*, vol. 26, no. 4 (1982), 801–811.

EXHIBIT 7.16

Commercial services for posttesting advertising messages.

Gallup & Robinson: Magazine Impact Research Service (MIRS). This service from Gallup & Robinson tests advertisements that appear in selected issues of major consumer magazines, including *Time, Playboy, Sports Illustrated, Business Week, Bon Appetit, People,* and others. Male and female respondents who have read at least two of the last four issues of one or more of the test magazines (but not the current issues used for the testing) are recruited in 10 metropolitan areas. Test magazines are delivered to participants, who are interviewed by phone the next day. Fifteen brand and product categories are examined, with questions relating to recall, idea communication, and persuasion.

ASI: Print Plus. This service is similar to ASI's pretesting service, discussed earlier. Male and female samples are drawn in five test markets for posttesting general consumer magazines. Participants are told they are in a public-opinion survey of magazines. A distinct feature of the ASI test is that brand attitude is measured before exposure to the test ad, in the context of a prize drawing for a dollar amount of a product (and brand) chosen by the participant. After delivery of the test magazines and verification of reading, recall and feature communication are tested. Re-exposure to four test ads is carried out to measure interest in the product. A postexposure brand preference is taken in the prize-drawing context for each category of advertisement tested. Pretest and posttest preference measures provide a persuasion index.

Starch INRA Hooper: Message Report Service. Starch provides the most extensive posttesting service available. Testing is available for 700 issues of all forms of magazines, including professional and trade publications. More than 75,000 subjects are interviewed each year by Starch. Starch draws samples from 20 to 30 urban locations for each test. Interviewers turn the pages of a publication and ask subjects about each ad under study. Along with demographic data on subjects, Starch produces the following evaluations for each ad:

- *Noted readers*—the percentage who remember having previously seen the ad in the issue being studied.
- *Associated readers*—the percentage who remember seeing the ad and are able to associate it with a brand or advertiser.
- *Read-most readers*—the percentage who read at least half of the material in the ad.

Starch INRA Hooper: Impression Study. This Starch service is designed to posttest ads that appear in print, television, and outdoor media. The measures are more qualitative and designed to identify the communication effects of advertising. Personal interviews are conducted in which subjects are shown an ad and then asked to describe in their own words their reactions with respect to the ad's meaning, the outstanding features of the ad, and the impressions formed from both the visual and written aspects of the ad.

Information Resources (IRI): Panel Data. While IRI's national sample of homes that maintain a diary on their purchases and media habits is not strictly designed to give detailed posttest message information, the panel data can provide some insights. The data from the households can be used to correlate promotional efforts with sales, which gives an indirect measure of message effectiveness. Of course, lack of control makes such a measure tenuous at best.

Secondary Data.
Apart from the primary data collection methods just discussed, there is a wealth of available secondary data. Information obtained from existing sources is referred to as **secondary data**. Secondary data have the distinct advantages of being far less costly to obtain than primary data and more immediately available.

Secondary Data Sources.
Secondary data are abundant and should be considered before an advertiser initiates primary research. Four typical places to find secondary data are internal company sources, government sources, commercial sources, and professional publications.

Internal Company Sources. Some of the most valuable data are available within a firm itself and are, therefore, referred to as internal company sources of secondary data. Commonly available information within a company includes strategic marketing plans, old research reports, customer service records, warranty registration cards, letters from customers, customer complaints, and various sales figures (by region, by customer type, by product line). All provide a wealth of information relating to the proficiency of the company's advertising programs and, more generally, changing consumer tastes and preferences.

Government Sources. Various government organizations generate data on factors of interest to advertising planners; information on population and housing trends, transportation, consumer spending, and recreational activities in the United States is available through government documents. Exhibit 7.17 gives a listing and brief description of some relevant government sources of secondary data. Also go to www .lib.umich.edu/libhome/Documents.center/federal.html for 140 or so pages of great links to data from federal, state, and international goverment sources. You might also

EXHIBIT 7.17

Government sources of secondary data pertinent to advertising.

Government Data Source	Type of Information
Census of population	This counts the population of the nation. Information can be obtained for the nation as a whole or by state, city, county, or region. Different volumes identify the citizenry by age, gender, income, race, marital status, and other demographic features. Published every 10 years in years ending with 0.
Census of housing	Housing units are described based on size, number of inhabitants, type of fuel used, number and type of major appliances, and condition and value of structures. Major urban areas are broken down by city block. Published every 10 years in years ending with 0.
Census of service industries	Identifies service providers by category and geographic area and indicates sales, employment, and number of units. Taken in years ending in 2 and 7.
Census of transportation	Identifies usage of three major transportation modes: passenger car, truck, and bus. Some 24,000 households were surveyed in 1977, and information includes number of trips, number of people taking trips, duration, means of travel, and destination. Taken in years ending in 2 and 7.
Census of retail trade	Provides detailed information on retail activity, including number of retail outlets, total sales, and employment. Also published in years ending in 2 and 7. Statistics are available for relatively small geographic areas, such as counties and cities.
Survey of current business	This survey is published monthly by the Bureau of Economic Analysis of the Department of Commerce. It provides information on general business indicators, real estate activity, commodity prices, personal consumption expenditures, and income and employment by industry. There are 2,600 different series in the survey, most of which contain data on the past four years.

Population Projections 17

No. 17. Resident Population Projections, by Age and Sex: 1995 to 2050

[In thousands, except as indicated. As of July. See headnote, table 3]

YEAR	Total	Under 5 years	5 to 13 years	14 to 17 years	18 to 24 years	25 to 34 years	35 to 44 years	45 to 54 years	55 to 64 years	65 to 74 years	75 to 84 years	85 years and over
TOTAL												
Lowest series:												
1995	262,051	19,892	34,140	14,519	25,281	41,435	42,023	30,142	21,166	18,881	11,023	3,547
2000	270,259	18,034	35,869	15,564	25,306	37,286	44,565	35,813	23,370	18,217	12,132	4,101
2005	276,316	16,951	34,668	16,542	27,309	35,121	41,898	40,475	28,203	17,984	12,600	4,564
2010	281,180	16,653	32,100	16,425	29,005	35,934	37,703	42,833	33,422	19,933	12,115	5,055
2020	289,553	17,336	31,272	14,404	26,764	40,218	36,362	36,228	39,890	28,513	13,439	5,127
2025	292,092	17,036	31,916	14,356	25,447	39,427	38,788	34,137	37,395	32,090	16,309	5,191
2030	292,902	16,519	31,773	14,792	25,260	36,593	40,553	34,921	33,656	33,800	19,228	5,808
2040	290,351	16,202	30,299	14,537	26,092	35,429	36,957	38,921	32,508	28,486	22,691	8,229
2050	285,502	16,250	30,174	13,986	24,920	36,106	35,791	35,443	36,185	27,665	19,088	9,894
Middle series:												
1995	263,434	20,181	34,262	14,591	25,465	41,670	42,150	30,224	21,241	18,963	11,087	3,598
2000	276,241	19,431	36,547	15,811	25,911	38,237	45,123	36,170	23,690	18,551	12,438	4,333
2005	288,286	19,333	36,843	16,947	28,238	36,792	43,075	41,219	28,870	18,623	13,265	5,082
2010	300,431	20,017	36,213	17,388	30,220	38,179	39,659	44,099	34,552	20,978	13,157	5,969
2020	325,942	21,957	38,701	17,119	30,456	43,553	39,662	38,885	42,262	30,910	15,480	6,959
2025	338,338	22,372	40,455	17,897	30,585	44,299	42,590	37,534	40,455	35,361	19,274	7,515
2030	349,993	22,689	41,528	18,820	31,802	43,572	45,040	38,936	37,429	37,984	23,348	8,843
2040	371,505	23,978	43,069	19,747	34,510	46,127	45,134	44,224	37,701	33,968	29,206	13,840
2050	392,031	25,382	45,742	20,630	35,710	49,462	47,739	44,337	42,920	34,628	26,588	18,893
Highest series:												
1995	264,715	20,470	34,380	14,659	25,643	41,907	42,294	30,295	21,295	19,008	11,139	3,626
2000	281,957	20,938	37,206	16,045	26,498	39,198	45,797	36,501	23,910	18,733	12,649	4,483
2005	299,941	22,076	39,099	17,333	29,131	38,444	44,443	41,979	29,311	18,990	13,687	5,445
2010	319,536	24,108	40,756	18,331	31,383	40,358	41,772	45,470	35,322	21,586	13,805	6,644
2020	363,213	27,960	47,760	20,174	34,302	46,735	43,000	41,674	44,162	32,313	16,729	8,405
2025	386,595	29,602	51,206	22,094	36,274	49,102	46,380	41,010	43,047	37,396	21,058	9,427
2030	410,991	31,472	54,296	23,745	39,423	50,832	49,467	42,984	40,729	40,776	25,855	11,410
2040	463,579	36,246	61,516	26,653	44,998	58,392	53,705	49,454	42,279	38,127	33,472	18,736
2050	522,098	41,404	70,680	30,400	50,494	65,872	61,394	53,662	48,751	40,095	32,028	27,318
MALE (middle series)												
1995	128,685	10,344	17,556	7,503	12,958	20,835	20,911	14,777	10,101	8,420	4,274	1,005
2000	135,101	9,958	18,738	8,129	13,177	19,059	22,425	17,692	11,321	8,385	4,980	1,238
2005	141,121	9,908	18,895	8,716	14,360	18,301	21,372	20,193	13,842	8,559	5,463	1,512
2010	147,187	10,262	18,575	8,949	15,382	18,991	19,620	21,631	16,603	9,744	5,574	1,855
2020	159,897	11,263	19,866	8,816	15,513	21,703	19,601	18,389	20,414	14,561	6,837	2,399
2025	166,012	11,476	20,765	9,216	15,578	22,084	21,062	18,301	19,519	16,755	8,693	2,561
2030	171,690	11,635	21,312	9,691	16,197	21,721	22,294	18,988	18,008	18,081	10,643	3,122
2040	182,049	12,289	22,091	10,161	17,571	22,998	22,361	21,597	18,125	16,174	13,566	5,116
2050	192,098	13,008	23,460	10,614	18,181	24,675	23,681	21,690	20,696	16,552	12,446	7,094
FEMALE (middle series)												
1995	134,749	9,837	16,707	7,087	12,507	20,835	21,238	15,447	11,140	10,544	6,814	2,593
2000	141,140	9,473	17,811	7,681	12,734	19,178	22,697	18,477	12,369	10,166	7,458	3,095
2005	147,165	9,425	17,948	8,230	13,878	18,491	21,702	21,028	15,027	10,065	7,802	3,570
2010	153,245	9,756	17,637	8,438	14,839	19,188	20,038	22,468	17,949	11,235	7,583	4,114
2020	166,045	10,693	18,835	8,303	14,943	21,849	20,060	19,896	21,848	16,348	8,606	4,662
2025	172,326	10,896	19,689	8,680	15,007	22,216	21,528	19,232	20,936	18,606	10,581	4,954
2030	178,303	11,054	20,216	9,131	15,606	21,851	22,746	19,947	19,421	19,903	12,705	5,721
2040	189,456	11,689	20,978	9,585	16,939	23,129	22,773	22,647	19,576	17,794	15,640	8,724
2050	199,933	12,374	22,282	10,016	17,530	24,787	24,057	22,647	22,224	18,076	14,141	11,799
PERCENT DISTRIBUTION (middle series)												
1995	100.0	7.7	13.0	5.4	10.1	16.6	15.7	10.8	8.2	7.2	4.1	1.3
2000	100.0	7.0	13.2	5.7	9.4	13.8	16.3	13.1	8.6	6.7	4.5	1.6
2005	100.0	6.7	12.8	5.9	9.8	12.8	14.9	14.3	10.0	6.5	4.6	1.8
2010	100.0	6.7	12.1	5.8	10.1	12.7	13.2	14.7	11.5	7.0	4.4	2.0
2020	100.0	6.7	11.9	5.3	9.3	13.4	12.2	11.9	13.0	9.5	4.7	2.1
2025	100.0	6.6	12.0	5.3	9.0	13.1	12.6	11.1	12.0	10.5	5.7	2.2
2030	100.0	6.5	11.9	5.4	9.1	12.4	12.9	11.1	10.7	10.9	6.7	2.5
2040	100.0	6.5	11.6	5.3	9.3	12.4	12.1	11.9	10.1	9.1	7.9	3.7
2050	100.0	6.5	11.7	5.3	9.1	12.6	12.2	11.3	10.9	8.8	6.8	4.8

Source: U.S. Bureau of the Census, *Current Population Reports*, P25-1104.

EXHIBIT 7.18

A sample of secondary data available from the government, in this case the Statistical Abstract of the United States.

check out the International Social Survey Programme at www.zuma-mannheim.de/boege/issp. Another very cool site is the National Archives Online, www.nara.gov/.

The array of consumer data available from government sources is a particularly useful starting place in advertising planning for businesses of all sizes, as suggested by the data in Exhibit 7.18. Such publications are reasonably current, and many are available at public libraries. This means that even a small-business owner can access large amounts of information for advertising-planning purposes at little cost.

Commercial Sources. Since information has become such a critical resource in marketing and advertising decision making, commercial data services have emerged to provide data of various types. Firms specializing in this sort of information tend to concentrate their data-gathering efforts on household consumers. Exhibit 7.19 lists some of the more prominent commercial sources of marketing and advertising information.

Information from these sources is reasonably comprehensive and is normally gathered using reasonably sound methods. The cost of information from these sources is greater than information from government sources. Despite the greater expense, information from commercial sources still generally costs less than primary data generation.

Professional Publications. Another secondary data source is professional publications. Professional publications are periodicals in which marketing and advertising professionals report significant information related to industry trends or new research findings. Exhibit 7.20 provides a listing of publications that frequently contain secondary data for advertising planning, along with their Web addresses. It probably goes without saying for today's Web-savvy college student that the Internet can be an advertiser's best friend when looking for secondary data of almost any kind.

In marketing and advertising, there are several academic, trade, and general business publications carrying research studies and industry statistics that can contain valuable secondary data. It may be that precisely the information a firm needs has been reported in a recent publication. Failure to explore such publications before initiating primary data collection is a major oversight.

Limitations of Secondary Data. As convenient and cost-effective as secondary data can be, they are not perfect. There are several potential problems with secondary data, and these problems may make the information poorly suited for decision making:

- The information can be out of date.
- The data may be expressed in categories different from the information desired. For example, the variable of interest to a firm may be the total number of women between ages 18 and 25 in a certain geographic area. Published secondary data may provide statistics on women younger than 18 and from ages 19 to 29.

EXHIBIT 7.19

Examples of commercial sources of secondary data.

Commercial Information Source	Type of Information
Dun & Bradstreet Market Identifiers	DMI is a listing of 4.3 million businesses that is updated monthly. Information includes number of employees, relevant SIC codes that relate to the businesses' activities, location, and chief executive. Marketing and advertising managers can use the information to identify markets, build mailing lists, and specify media to reach an organization. www.dnb.com/
Nielsen Retail Index	Nielsen auditors collect product inventory turnover data from 1,600 grocery stores, 750 drugstores, and 150 mass merchandise outlets. Information is also gathered on retail prices, in-store displays, and local advertising. Data from the index are available by store type and geographic location. www.nielsenmedia.com/
National Purchase Diary Panel	With more than 13,000 families participating, NPD is the largest diary panel in the United States. Families record on preprinted sheets their monthly purchases in 50 product categories. Information recorded includes brand, amount purchased, price paid, use of coupons, store, specific version of the product (flavor, scent, etc.), and intended use.
Roper Starch Advertisement Readership	The Roper Starch service tracks readership of more than 70,000 advertisements appearing in 1,000 consumer and farm publications, newspapers, and business periodicals. More than 100,000 personal interviews are conducted each year to determine the readership of the ads. Starch uses a recognition approach, which rates each ad on the extent of readership it was able to stimulate. Data on headlines, copy, and other component parts of an ad are also recorded.
Nielsen Television Index	This is one of the most familiar commercial services, since the Nielsen ratings receive so much popular press. The index provides estimates of the size and characteristics of the audience for television programs. Data are gathered through an electronic device attached to participating households' television sets. The device records the times the TV is on and what channel is tuned in. Reports on viewership are published biweekly.
Consumer Mail Panel	This panel is operated by a firm called Market Facts. There are 45,000 active participants at any point in time. Samples are drawn in lots of 1,000. The overall panel is said to be representative of different geographic regions in the United States and Canada, then broken down by household income, urbanization, and age of the respondent. Data are provided on demographic and socioeconomic characteristics as well as type of dwelling and durable goods ownership.
Information Resources	One of the leading organizations in single-source research, where all phases of a consumer's media exposure and, ultimately, purchase behavior are tracked. This firm is also recognized for its research on the impact of grocery store promotional programs (PromotioScan) and coupon redemption.

Publication	Web Address
Advertising Age	www.adage.com/
Adweek	www.adweek.com/
Adweek Asia	www.asianad.com/
American Demographics	www.demographics.com/publications/AD/
Brandweek	www.brandweek.com/
Business Week	www.businessweek.com/
Creative	www.creativemag.com/
Fast Company	www.fastcompany.com
Forbes	www.forbes.com/
Fortune	www.fortune.com/
Guerrilla Marketing	www.gmarketing.com/
InfoWorld	www.infoworld.com/
KidScreen	www.kidscreen.com/
Progressive Grocer	www.progressivegrocer.com/
Promo	www.mediacentral.com/promo/
Sales and Marketing Management	www.salesandmarketing.com/
IEG Sponsorship Report	www.sponsorship.com/
Sports Marketing Quarterly	www.fitinfotech.com/smq/smqpage.html
Target Marketing	www.targetonline.com/
Wall Street Journal	www.wsj.com/

- The unit of measurement may be different from the unit needed for analysis. Secondary data sources may report income figures for individuals, families, households, or spending units. If the unit of measure is not the same as the one desired by the decision maker, then the data are severely limited.
- The source of the data may not be totally objective. For example, industry trade associations may generate and report data that make their industry look good.

Secondary data offer a low-cost and speedy method for gaining information, but they should be scrutinized for currency, the qualifications of the data collection organization, any special interests associated with the data generation effort, and, most importantly, relevance and meaning.

SUMMARY

Explain the purposes served by and methods used in developmental advertising research.

Advertising research can serve many purposes in the development of a campaign. There is no better way to generate fresh ideas for a campaign than to listen carefully to the customer. Environmental analysis is also valuable in the planning process to help determine opportunities for effective communication. Audience definition and profiling are fundamental to effective campaign planning and rely on advertising research. In the developmental phase, advertisers use diverse tools for gathering information. Survey research, focus groups, projective techniques, the ZMET, and concept testing are some of the common tools used for developmental purposes.

Discuss the various procedures used for pretesting advertising messages prior to a complete launch of an advertising campaign.

Another major type of advertising research is that devoted to message testing prior to the launch of a campaign. Communications tests, dummy advertising vehicles, and theater tests are basic tools used for message pretesting. The thought-listing technique and attitude-change studies are important approaches for pretesting the persuasiveness of a message. Commercial testing services may be used prior to launch of a full-blown campaign for both pretesting and pilot testing. Pilot testing is a form of marketplace experimentation that provides data about how messages may perform when they reach the consumer. Since there is no one right way to test a message, it is important for an advertiser to be aware of the various options and the virtues and limitations of each.

Discuss the various methods used to track the effectiveness of ad executions during and after the launch of a full-blown advertising campaign.

Advertisers commonly track the performance of their messages during and after the launch of an ad campaign. Recall and recognition testing are two traditional tools that allow an advertiser to assess whether a message has broken through the competitive clutter to register with the target audience. Brand awareness and attitude surveys are also commonly employed in tracking a campaign's impact. Behavior-based evaluation has a strong following and is made possible by direct response measures and single-source research. A number of commercial suppliers provide posttest evaluation services.

Identify the many sources of secondary data that can aid the ad-planning effort.

Before investing in new or primary research, an advertiser is well advised to examine the information available through secondary sources. Secondary data are inexpensive and immediately accessible. The ongoing evolution of the Internet and the World Wide Web will put more and more secondary data at the researcher's fingertips. Sources of secondary data include a firm's internal records, the government, commercial suppliers, and professional publications. Knowing the limitations of secondary data is a necessary prerequisite for informed use of this important tool.

KEY TERMS

storyboard (210)
marketing research (211)
advertising research (211)
reliability (211)
validity (211)
trustworthiness (211)
meaningfulness (211)
account planning (211)
environmental analysis (213)
focus group (215)
projective techniques (215)
association tests (216)
sentence and picture completion (216)
dialogue balloons (216)
story construction (216)
concept test (217)
normative test scores (218)
resonance test (220)

communications test (220)
dummy advertising vehicles (220)
theater test (221)
thought listing (221)
attitude-change study (221)
physiological measures (222)
eye-tracking systems (222)
psychogalvanometer (222)
pilot testing (223)
split-cable transmission (223)
split-run distribution (223)
split-list experiment (223)
posttest message tracking (225)
aided recall (226)
inquiry/direct response measures (227)
single-source tracking measures (227)
secondary data (230)

QUESTIONS FOR REVIEW AND CRITICAL THINKING

1.   What does it mean to profile the target audience? What is the value of audience profiling? Identify three different types of information commonly used in developing audience profiles.

2.   Focus groups turn out to be one of the advertising researcher's most versatile tools. Explain how focus groups are valuable in conducting concept tests, resonance tests, and communications tests. Describe the basic features of focus group research that could lead to inappropriate generalizations about the preferences of the target audience.

3.   ZMET is a technique that advertisers may use in place of focus groups. What aspects of ZMET and focus groups are similar? What particular features of ZMET could foster richer understanding of consumers' motives than is typically achieved with focus groups?

4.   Identify issues that could become sources of conflict between brand managers and advertising creatives in the message-pretesting process. What could go wrong if people in an ad agency take the position that what the client wants, the client gets?

5.   Explain the key distinction between pretesting and pilot testing. What is it about direct mail advertising that makes it so amenable to pilot testing? Do you think the ease of pilot testing has anything to do with the growing popularity of direct mail as an advertising option?

6.   Attitude-change research is another versatile tool for message testing. Identify the key differences that distinguish an attitude-change study being conducted for pretesting purposes from an attitude-change study being conducted for posttesting purposes.

7.   Normative test scores help the advertiser put test results for a new ad in proper context. Do you think it would be a good idea to compare scores for recognition versus recall tests as another way to "put things in context"? Explain your position.

8.   How would you explain the finding that ads that achieve high recall scores don't always turn out to be ads that do a good job in generating sales? Are there some features of ads that make them memorable but could also turn off consumers and dissuade them from buying the brand? Give an example from your experience.

9.   What is the meaning of the phrase *single-source research*? What is the connection between the UPCs one finds on nearly every product in the grocery store and this thing called single-source research?

10. Discuss in detail the limitations of secondary data. Given these limitations, how do you justify the statement in this chapter that the failure to explore secondary data sources before initiating primary data collection represents a serious oversight?

EXPERIENTIAL EXERCISES

1.   In this chapter you learned about advertising research methods that help managers avoid costly mistakes. Find an example of a print ad or describe a broadcast ad you feel is truly awful. Explain your objections. Now imagine that you have the opportunity to conduct advertising research before the ad actually runs. What type or types of research would you recommend that management conduct?

Explain your recommendations and how the research might have changed the ad you selected.

2.   Visit the *Advertising Age* Web site (www.adage.com) and the Centers for Disease Control and Prevention Web site (www.cdc.gov). How do these sites provide secondary data?

USING THE INTERNET

Visit *The X-Files* site (www.thex-files.com) and continue to the fan forum.

1.   How could the makers of *The X-Files* use the information exchanged in the fan forum to better understand their viewers?

2.   What other established research method or methods is this discussion forum similar to?

Visit Vanderbilt University's Project 2000 site (http://www2000.ogsm.vanderbilt.edu/) and read about research efforts to measure Internet usage and consumer behavior on the Web. Visit the CommerceNet site research area (www.commercenet.com/research/) to read their collection.

Identify and compare the different research methods used to study and describe Internet usage.

3.   Which methods were most appropriate? What are the shortcomings of each method?

4.   How does the use of multiple methods increase your confidence in the final results?

Visit the Hot Wired site (www.hotwired.com) and find the user registration form.

5.   As a potential registrant, are you comfortable with giving out this information?

6.   Pick out a few questions you think are important, and suggest their value to Hot Wired. As a marketer, what additional information would you request?

The Hollywood Stock Exchange (www.hsx.com) is a free auction simulation that lets visitors buy and sell "stocks" and "bonds" in movies, actors, and actresses, using play money. A part of its revenue model comes from selling banner advertising, to expose those playing the game to movie-related ads, but the Exchange also serves as a means to measure the "buzz" around movies (including before their commercial release). While the Internet is far from suited to movie-quality audio and video at present, one can imagine it as the future medium of field testing.

1.   How would you assess the validity of the Hollywood Stock Exchange as a predictor of a movie's potential?

2.   How susceptible might something like the Hollywood Stock Exchange be to manipulation (for example, to "pump" a movie stock's value as a marketing ploy)?

3.   What features might you consider adding to the site to increase its value to movie producers?

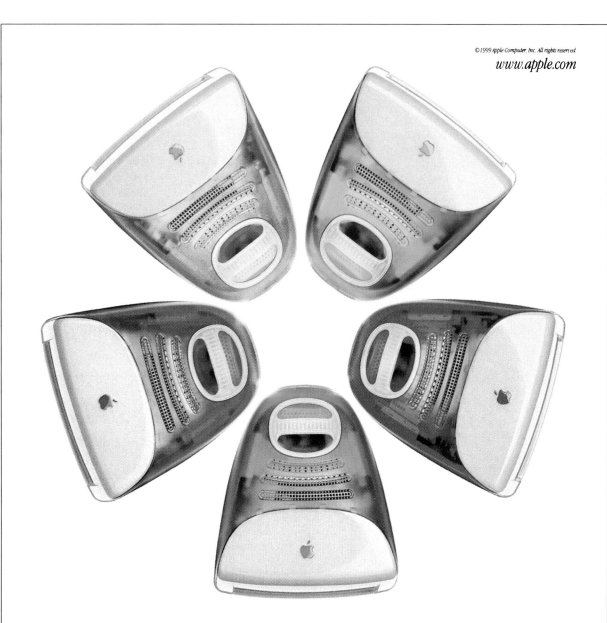

www.apple.com

Collect all five.

Think different.™

CHAPTER 8

**After reading and thinking about
this chapter, you will be able to
do the following:**

◀▶ Describe the basic components of an
advertising plan.

◀▶ Compare and contrast two fundamental approaches for setting advertising
objectives.

◀▶ Explain various methods for setting
advertising budgets.

◀▶ Discuss the role of the advertising agency
in formulating an advertising plan.

. . . Think Different.

This was the battle cry in all advertising for Apple Computer as the new millennium approached. But it seemed that no one was listening. The once high-flying computer manufacturer was floundering in a PC/Windows onslaught. In June 1998 Apple's U.S. retail market share had fallen to a mere 2 percent.[1] The company that had once rocked the computer business with its innovative Macintosh computer and its provocative "1984" TV commercial (see Exhibit 8.1) was approaching virtual extinction. Could Apple be saved?

Apple found itself in a real mess. And we want to emphasize that the severity of its problems went well beyond what one might be able to fix with a fresh advertising campaign and a catchy slogan like "Think Different." To rebound, Apple would need inspired leadership and, most important, a series of innovative new products to capture the imagination of consumers around the world. The leadership would have to come from its celebrated founder and on-again/off-again CEO—Steve Jobs. The new product designed to salvage the company was the iMac personal computer.

Put yourself in the shoes of Steve Jobs. The company that you helped create was adrift and you desperately needed a major new product success to turn things around. You have decided to stake the future of your company on a new product called iMac. A great new product with a creative and comprehensive IMC campaign are your best hope for reviving the company.

Only time will tell if the iMac is truly a great product. However, we are very impressed with the integrated marketing communications campaign that Jobs and his ad agency orchestrated in launching the iMac. As you will see, he held nothing back in his determined effort to save Apple.

One way to think of the iMac is as the first in a new generation of Internet appliances. It was a system designed first and foremost to get households hooked to the Net. As described by Steve Jobs, "iMac does for Internet computing what the original Macintosh did for personal computing. Macintosh let anyone use a computer and iMac lets anyone get on to the Internet quickly and easily." Regarding his IMC campaign, Jobs went on to say, "We're launching this campaign because we want the world to know that iMac is the computer for the tens of millions of consumers who want to get to the Internet easily, quickly, and affordably."[2] Jobs, of course, was not just grasping at straws: His market research at the time was telling him that one of consumers' primary motives for buying a personal computer was to hook up to the Internet.

While the iMac actually went on sale August 14, 1998, its launch campaign was initiated three months before at a surprise unveiling of the machine before an audience of media types in the same auditorium where Macintosh was introduced.[3] In other parallels with the 1984 launch of Macintosh, Jobs departed from his usual dress code by wearing a suit and keeping the iMac prototype behind a veil on stage until he was ready to spring it on his unsuspecting audience. Mr. Jobs stated at the time: "We figured we'd have a surprise and then let people feed on it before they could get it."[4] In the weeks leading up to August 14, Jobs's sneak preview had the desired effect of creating an iMac buzz across Web sites frequently visited by loyal Mac users.

Mr. Jobs and his public relations machine continued to strut their stuff in the hours leading up to the first public sale of the iMac at 12:01 A.M. on August 14. Working with loyal retailers, Apple's PR people created 20-foot-high inflatable iMac balloons to fly above retail stores at the Midnight Madness event on August 14, 1998. A Cupertino, California, retailer added giant searchlights and scheduled part of its midnight iMac delivery using four Volkswagen New Beetles on loan from a local dealer. Of course, TV

1.   Bradley Johnson, "Jobs Orchestrates Ad Blitz for Apple's New iMac PC," *Advertising Age,* August 10, 1998, 6.
2.   "Apple Launches Its Largest Marketing Campaign Ever for iMac," www.apple.com/pr/library/. Accessed August 13, 1998.
3.   Jim Carlton, "From Apple, a New Marketing Blitz," *Wall Street Journal,* August 14, 1998, B1.
4.   Ibid.

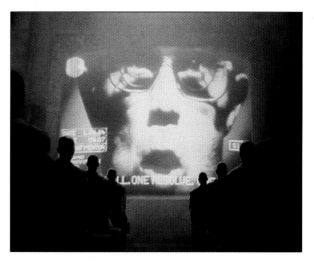

EXHIBIT 8.1

This 1984 ad, which launched the Macintosh, was enormously successful for Apple and is now a legend in the advertising industry. www.apple.com/

crews from every station in the Bay Area were there to cover the action and report it all to the world the next day. Summarizing the state of affairs at ground zero, one salesperson at a CompUSA Superstore in San Francisco said:"I don't think even Apple expected it to be this crazy; We're having trouble keeping iMacs on the shelves."[5]

And that was just for starters. As the new iMac was going on sale, Apple executives also announced the start of the largest IMC campaign in the history of the company, where paid media advertising costs were expected to run more than $100 million between August 15 and December 31, 1998. (Yes, it did appear that Mr. Jobs was betting the future of his company on the success of the iMac.) These are just some of the key elements of the campaign:[6]

Television advertising—National TV ads began August 16 on *The Wonderful World of Disney* and continued on programs such as *News Radio* and *The Drew Carey Show*, and on cable shows such as *South Park* and *Larry King Live*. TV ads were also placed in the top 10 metro markets—Boston; Chicago; Los Angeles; New York; San Francisco; Philadelphia; Washington D.C.; Seattle; Minneapolis; and Denver. TV ads began airing in Europe and Asia in September 1998.

Outdoor advertising—Billboards also went up in the top 10 metro markets. As shown in Exhibit 8.2, they featured a photo of the iMac and one of the following copy lines: "Chic. Not Geek"; "Sorry, no beige"; "Mental floss"; and "I think, therefore iMac." This last copy line was attributed to Mr. Magic—Steve Jobs.

Magazine advertising—An informative 12-page iMac insert was distributed through leading magazines such as *Time, People, Sports Illustrated,* and *Rolling Stone.* Over 15 million copies were put in consumers' hands in the first few weeks after launch. This more than doubled the amount of inserts ever distributed by Apple in any prior campaign. Four pages from this insert are displayed in Exhibit 8.3.

Radio advertising—A five-day countdown to the iMac launch was executed through a network of 20 nationwide radio companies. This promotions featured iMac giveaways each day of the week preceding Midnight Madness. Apple's was the most comprehensive radio campaign in the United States the week of August 10, 1998.

EXHIBIT 8.2

Apple's iMac launch used outdoor billboards like this one in the 10 top metro markets across the United States. What value proposition do you see being addressed by this billboard?

5.   "iMac Makes a Midnight Debut," www.macweek.com/. Accessed August 15, 1998.
6.   "Apple Launches its Largest Marketing Campaign Ever for iMac."

To everyone who thinks
computers are too
complicated, too costly
or too beige:

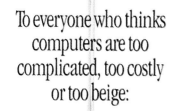

One decision. One box.
One price. $1,299.

The world's easiest-to-use computer is also
the world's easiest-to-buy.

iMac comes in one box, with everything you need, for one low price: $1,299.
And there are two simple ways to buy one.

You can visit your authorized Apple
reseller, who can provide personalized
advice and service. (Call 1-800-538-9696
for the nearest location.)

You can also visit us any time at the
Apple Store™ on the web at www.apple.com
or call us at 1-800-795-1000.

Think different.™

*U.S. estimated retail price. © 1998 Apple Computer, Inc. All rights reserved. Apple, the Apple logo, AppleWorks, Macintosh and PowerBook are registered trademarks and iMac, the Apple Store and Think different are trademarks of Apple Computer, Inc. Adobe is a trademark of Adobe Systems Inc. FileMaker is a registered trademark of FileMaker, Inc. PowerPC is a trademark of IBM Corp. Virtual PC is a trademark of Connectix Corp. SRS is a registered trademark of SRS Labs, Inc. Mention of non-Apple products is for informational purposes only and constitutes neither an endorsement nor a recommendation. 12/11/98.

Amazingly simple.

Live long enough and you begin to recognize a
pattern: Lots of parts = complicated. Few parts =
easy. iMac is the poster child for "easy."

The whole system, with its gorgeous hi-res
display and stereo speakers, comes in one ready-
to-go package. Instead of a thick installation
manual, all you need is this
installation paragraph:

Plug in the power cord.
Plug in the modem cord.
Attach the keyboard and
mouse. And that's it. You're off to the races.

Or the Louvre. Or the Library of Congress. Or
the CD store. Or the stadium. Or the concert hall.
Or Mars. Or—well, you get the idea.

When you combine the excitement of the
internet with the simplicity of iMac, there's no
limit to what you can do.

EXHIBIT 8.3

Apple (www.apple.com/) has consistently broken new ground in its product advertising. Former Chairman John Sculley, who came to Apple from PepsiCo, contrasted the company with his former margins-focused employer, as an agent of incessant innovation and radical change. Apple ads certainly seem to find endless ways to herald the new, the innovative, the unordinary better, perhaps, than any others. Prior to the iMac's release, Apple had already launched a "Think Different" campaign with images of famous iconoclasts but "Think Different" continues to play a role in Apple's marketing of the iMac. (One wonders, though, at the "too beige" jab: While most PCs can be painted with that brush, so too, could Apple's Macintosh product line!)

EXHIBIT 8.4

Of course, Apple's home page featured the iMac in November 1998. The interactivity of the Web makes it the perfect medium for anticipating and answering questions about the technical features of a product such as a new PC.

Cooperative advertising—Apple also joined forces with its local retailers in cooperative advertising efforts around the United States. For example, Apple worked with the New York dealer DataVisions Inc. to help sponsor iMac ads on movie screens in all 600 of Long Island's theaters. Other dealers participated in software and T-shirt giveaways, and CompUSA launched newspaper ads that for the first time promoted Apple products exclusively.

Web site features and promotions—Of course, everything you could ever want to know about the iMac and the iMac product launch was available for the world to peruse at www.apple.com. Exhibit 8.4 shows that Apple homepage as of November 1998.

Early reports suggested that the iMac IMC campaign was having the kind of effect that Steve Jobs wanted. Without a doubt it created renewed consumer interest in the Apple brand, and market research showed that iMac was winning over previous Windows users as well as households buying their first personal computer.[7] Both these developments would be crucial to the long-term success of the iMac. As the high-profile CEO of Apple, Mr. Jobs received a good deal of the praise for iMac's provocative ad campaign. However, he quickly demurred and assigned the credit to his advertising agency—TBWA Chiat/Day of Venice, California. Said Jobs: "Creating great advertising, like creating great products, is a team effort. I am lucky to work with the best talent in the industry."[8] Indeed, it would be impossible to launch a campaign of this scale without great teamwork between agency and client.

While we have merely scratched the surface in describing all that was involved in the campaign that launched the iMac, we hope this example gives you a taste for the complexity that can be involved in executing a comprehensive IMC effort. And you don't go out and spend $100 million promoting a new product that is vital to the success of a firm without giving the entire endeavor considerable forethought. Such an endeavor calls for a plan. As you will see in this chapter, Jobs, Apple, and Chiat/Day followed the process of building an advertising effort based on several key features of the advertising plan. An advertising plan is the culmination of the planning effort needed to create effective advertising.

The Advertising Plan and Its Marketing Context.   An ad plan

should be a direct extension of a firm's marketing plan. As suggested in the closing section of Chapter 6, one device that can be used to explicitly connect the marketing plan with the advertising plan is the statement of a brand's value proposition. A statement of what the brand is supposed to stand for in the eyes of the target segment derives from the firm's marketing strategy, and will guide all ad-planning activities. The advertising plan, including all integrated marketing communications, is a subset of the larger marketing plan. The IMC component must be built into the plan in a seamless and syner-

7.   Jim Carlton, "Apple Reports Tripling in Profit; Sales Jump Is First in Three Years," *Wall Street Journal,* January 14, 1999, B6.
8.   Bradley Johnson, "Jobs Orchestrates Ad Blitz for Apple's New iMac PC," *Advertising Age,* August 10, 1998, 6.

gistic way. Everything has to work together, whether the plan is for Apple or for a business with far fewer resources. And as Steve Jobs noted about his iMac campaign, there is no substitute for good teamwork between agency and client in the development of compelling marketing and advertising plans.

An **advertising plan** specifies the thinking and tasks needed to conceive and implement an effective advertising effort. We particularly like the iMac example because it illustrates the wide array of options that can be deployed in creating interest and communicating the value proposition for a brand. Jobs and his agency choreographed public relations activities, promotions and giveaways, cooperative advertising, broadcast advertising, billboard advertising, Web site development, and more, as part of the iMac launch. An advertising planner should review all the options before selecting an integrated set to communicate with the target audience. We wish to emphasize that advertising planners must think beyond traditional broadcast media when considering the best way to break through the clutter of the modern marketplace and get their message across to the focal customer.

Exhibit 8.5 shows the components of an advertising plan. It should be noted that there is a great deal of variation in advertising plans from advertiser to advertiser. Our discussion of the advertising plan will focus on the seven major sections shown in Exhibit 8.5: the introduction, situation analysis, objectives, budgeting, strategy, execution, and evaluation. Each of these advertising plan components is discussed in the following sections.

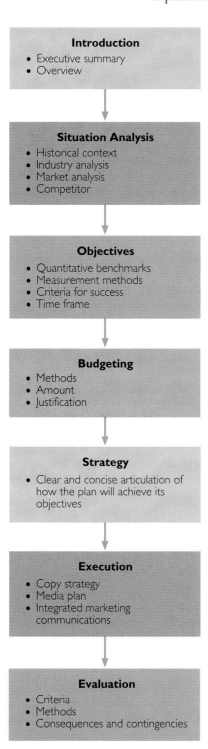

Introduction. The introduction of an advertising plan consists of an executive summary and an overview. An executive summary, typically two paragraphs to two pages in length, is offered to state the most important aspects of the plan. This is the take-away; that is, it is what the reader should remember from the plan. It is the essence of the plan.

As with many documents, an overview is also customary. An overview ranges in length from a paragraph to a few pages. It sets out what is to be covered, and it structures the context. All plans are different, and some require more of a setup than others. Don't underestimate the benefit of a good introduction. It's where you can make or lose a lot of points with your boss or client.

Situation Analysis. When someone asks you to explain a decision you've made, you may say something such as, "Well, here's the situation . . ." In what follows, you probably try to distill the situation down to the most important points and how they are connected in order to explain why you made the decision. An ad plan **situation analysis** is no different. It is where the client and agency lay out the most important factors that define the situation, and then explain the importance of each factor.

An infinite list of potential factors (for example, demographic, social and cultural, economic, political/regulatory) define a situation analysis. Some books offer long but incomplete lists. We prefer to play it straight with you: There is no complete list of situational factors. The idea is not to be exhaustive or encyclopedic when writing a plan, but to be smart in choosing the few important factors that really describe the situation, and then explain how the factors relate to the advertising task at hand. Market segmentation and consumer

EXHIBIT 8.5

The advertising plan.

EXHIBIT 8.6

What is the image this ad establishes for the American Express card? How is this image a response to the company's situation analysis? Link your answer to a discussion of market segmentation and product positioning. Who is reached by this ad and how does reaching this segment fit into the overall strategy for American Express? www.americanex press.com/

behavior research provide the organization with insights that can be used for a situation analysis, but ultimately you have to decide which of the many factors are really the most critical to address in your advertising. This is the essence of management.

Let's say you represent American Express. How would you define the firm's current advertising situation? What are the most critical factors? What image has prior advertising, like that in Exhibit 8.6, established for the card? Would you consider the changing view of prestige cards to be critical? What about the problem of hanging onto an exclusive image while trying to increase your customer base by having your cards accepted at discount stores, such as Kmart? Does the proliferation of gold and platinum cards by other banks rate as critical? Do the very low interest rates offered by bank cards seem critical to the situation? What about changing social attitudes regarding the responsible use of credit cards? What about the current high level of consumer debt?

Think about how credit card marketing is influenced by the economic conditions of the day and the cultural beliefs about the proper way to display status. In the early eighties, it was acceptable for advertisers to tout the self-indulgent side of plastic (for example, MasterCard's slogan "MasterCard, I'm bored"). Today, charge and credit card ads often point out just how prudent it is to use your card for the right reasons. Now, instead of just suggesting you use your plastic to hop off to the islands when you feel the first stirrings of a bout with boredom, credit card companies are far more likely to detail a few of the functional benefits of their cards, as reflected in Exhibit 8.7.

Basic demographic trends may be the single most important situational factor in advertising plans. Whether it's baby boomers or Generation X, Y, or Z, where the numbers are is usually where the sales are. As the population distribution varies with time, new markets are created and destroyed. The baby-boom generation of post–World War II disproportionately dictates consumer offerings and demand simply because of its size. As the boomers age, companies that offer the things needed by tens of millions of aging boomers will have to devise new appeals. Think of the consumers of this generation needing long-term health care, geriatric products, and things to amuse themselves in retirement. Will they have the disposable income necessary to have the bountiful lifestyle many of them have had during their working years? After all, they aren't the greatest savers. And what of the X'ers? Are the needs of the current twentysomethings fundamentally different from those of boomers? Is it conceivable, as shown in the Sony ad in Exhibit 8.8, that some products might even be able to bridge the generation gap? And, as discussed in the New Media box on page 249, the next great challenge for advertisers will be finding ways to reach a new generation of skeptics.

Historical Context. No situation is entirely new, but all situations are unique. Just how a firm arrived at the current situation is very important. Before trying to design Apple's iMac campaign, an agency should certainly know a lot about the history of all the principal players, the industry, the brand, the corporate culture, critical moments in the company's past, its big mistakes and big successes. All new decisions are situated in a firm's history, and an agency should be diligent in studying that history. For example, would an agency pitch new business to Green Giant without knowing something of the brand's history and the rationale behind the Green Giant? The history of the Green

A decade ago, credit card issuers would compete either on rates or on the solidity of their banks' good names. Today, cards are bundled with a variety of offers and spun to fit any of a number of lifestyles or interests. Visit Citibank's site (www.citibank.com/us/cards/) to see what it means when it says, "A card for every purchase": cards for cash back toward a new car, for frequent flyer miles, for points toward Sony products, or for monthly golf tips. Any wonder why American consumers have run up high personal debt? Too much going on to notice that credit card companies send bills as well!

Sony positions its version of the wireless phone as a high-tech answer to an age-old problem. Ring true to you? www.sony.com/

Giant dates back decades, as the ad in Exhibit 8.9 shows. The fact is that no matter what advertising decisions are made in the present, the past has a significant impact.

Apart from history's intrinsic value, sometimes the real business goal is to convince the client that the agency knows the client's business, its major concerns, and its corporate culture. A brief history of the company and brand are included to demonstrate the thoroughness of the agency's research, the depth of its knowledge, and the scope of its concern.

Industry Analysis. An **industry analysis** is just that; it focuses on developments and trends within an industry and on any other factors that may make a difference in how an advertiser proceeds with an advertising plan. An industry analysis should enumerate and discuss the most important aspects of a given industry, or the supply side of the supply-demand equation. For example, if you were designing advertising for Blockbuster Video, you might be concerned that movie rentals have been significantly lower industrywide. Are consumers watching fewer movies? No. In this particular industry, film distributors are discovering that they can make more money by selling films directly to the public at deeply discounted prices. Also, satellite distribution of movies is cutting directly into sales of video rental chains. There is also the problem of changing home technologies. What if the new DVD completely wipes out the inferior videocassette?

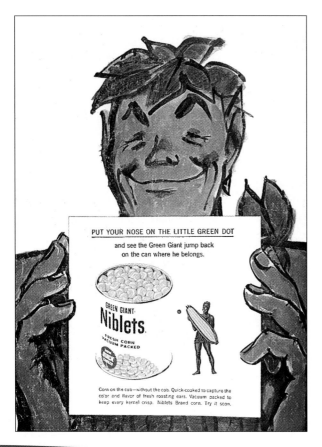

EXHIBIT 8.9

Knowing a brand's history can guide the development of future campaigns. www.greengiant.com/

Certainly these issues have an impact on the long-term future of companies like Blockbuster, but even in the short term they have meaning. If you're Blockbuster, you want someone to come up with some advertising that slows or reduces this trend. You want your agency to figure out what is unique about going to a video store. Maybe it means more integrated promotion efforts, such as tie-ins with fast-food restaurants and toy stores, appearances by celebrities, or a chance to win tickets to a sporting event. One thing is clear—you can't ignore the trends in an industry.

Market Analysis. A **market analysis** is the flip side of industry analysis; it is the demand side of the equation. In a market analysis, an advertiser examines the factors that drive and determine the market for the firm's product or service. First, the advertiser needs to decide just exactly what the market is for the product. Most often, the market for a given good or service is simply defined as current users. The idea here is that consumers figure out for themselves whether they want the product or not and thus define the market for themselves, and for the advertiser. This approach has some wisdom to it. It's simple, easy to defend, and very conservative. Few executives get fired for choosing this target market. However, it completely ignores those consumers who might otherwise be persuaded to use the product.

A market analysis commonly begins by stating just who the current users are, and (hopefully) why they are current users. Consumers' motivations for using one product or service but not another may very well provide the advertiser with the means toward a significant expansion of the entire market. If the entire pie grows, the firm's slice usually does as well. The advertiser's job in a market analysis is to find out the most important market factors and why they are so important. It is at this stage in the situation analysis that account planning can play an important role.

Competitor Analysis. Once the industry and market are studied and analyzed, attention is turned to **competitor analysis**. Here an advertiser determines just exactly who the competitors are, discussing their strengths, weaknesses, tendencies, and any threats they pose.

Suppose you are creating advertising for Fuji 35-mm film. Who are your competitors? Is Kodak, with its dominant market share, your only real competitor? Are Agfa and Konica worth worrying about? Would stealing share from these fairly minor players amount to much? What has Kodak done in the past when Fuji has made a move? What are Kodak's advantages? For one, it may have successfully equated memories with photographs and with trusting the archiving of these memories to Kodak film. Does Kodak have any weaknesses? Is it as technologically advanced as Fuji? Japanese technologies are often thought to be superior to American. Could Kodak be characterized as stodgy and old-fashioned? What of recent product innovations? What about financial resources? Can Kodak swat Fuji like a fly? Or does Fuji have deep pockets, too? What would happen if Fuji tripled its advertising and directly compared its product to Kodak's? All of these questions would be addressed for each competitor in a competitor analysis.

Identifying who the real competition is can make a big difference. For example, if you managed the National Cattlemen's Beef Association, you might expect that lamb, pork, and poultry producers would be your primary competitors. Right? Well, declin-

REACHING GENERATIONS Y AND Z

Today's teens (Generation Y) and preteens (Generation Z) are critical for short- and long-term marketing success. Several facts support this premise. Generations Y and Z have $27 billion of their own money to spend, and their disposable income is growing at a rate of 20 percent per year. Y and Z, with both parents working, or in single-parent families, are taking on more household responsibilities. Many times this includes doing the shopping for the family. Marketers know that brand familiarity established at a young age can turn into brand loyalty as that consumer ages: If you wait until they reach twenty-something, it may already be too late to start. And there is always the basic matter of market size. Generation Y is projected to top out at 35 million consumers by 2010, making them a larger cohort than the aging baby boomers.

Generations Y and Z represent a tremendous challenge for advertisers because, if anything, the generation gap just keeps getting bigger. Dr. James McNeal, a researcher at Texas A&M University, puts it bluntly: "Marketers' intuitions and youthful memories can't tell them how societal changes and technology have made young folks different from even a generation ago." Many factors contribute to this increasing distance between generations. Global communications have accelerated trends, as cable TV and the Internet bring ideas to young minds from around the world. Indeed, Generations Y and Z are the first to grow up with a complete array of technology tools, and take for granted beepers, cell phones, and laptop computers as everyday helpers. And kids today are very skeptical of traditional broadcast advertising, perhaps because they are bombarded with so many marketing messages. Researchers estimate that Generation Z is exposed to 3,000 to 5,000 messages a week, compared to about 1,000 per week for Generation X at a similar life stage.

Relying on the traditional broadcast media simply can't be enough with youthful and media-savvy consumers. But the future appears bright for the advertiser who has learned how to capitalize on the interactive properties of the World Wide Web, especially for engaging Generation Z. While most advertisers are still learning on this front, today's most popular Web sites with Generation Z—such as www.disney.com/ and www.nick.com/—provide some clues about what works. Principle #1: You have to give young consumers more than text and pretty pictures; they want to be involved and build something or solve something or win something. Principle #2: Kids want to connect and be recognized. Herein lies the beauty of the Web as a promotional tool: Its infinite capacity for interactivity lets inventive advertisers create games and contests that allow winners to be recognized and contestants to interact with one another. This is the power of the Web to engage your new consumer.

Source: David Vaczek, "Problem Children," *Promo Magazine,* July 1998, 37–46.

ing sales of veal in the past decade were ultimately attributed to ad campaigns by animal-rights groups depicting shoddy practices of some cattle producers. Consumers became concerned about the way veal calves were being raised, and it affected their eating habits, especially in restaurants. Finally, veal producers recognized their problem and, through their trade association, developed advertising to try to improve sales. However, they chose to avoid direct confrontation with animal-rights advocates. Instead, they reacted with a low-key print campaign targeted at chefs rather than consumers to remind them of veal's versatility as an entree. While the trade association's budget for veal advertising is just $1.1 million per year, the campaign has had a very positive impact on per capita consumption of veal in the United States.[9]

Objectives. Advertising objectives lay the framework for the subsequent tasks in an advertising plan and take many different forms. Objectives identify the goals of the advertiser in concrete terms. The advertiser, more often than not, has more than one objective for an ad campaign. An advertiser's objective may be: (1) to increase consumer awareness of and curiosity about its brand, (2) to change consumers' beliefs or attitudes about its product, (3) to influence the purchase intent of its customers, (4) to stimulate trial use of its product or service, (5) to convert one-time product users into repeat purchasers, (6) to switch consumers from a competing brand to its brand, or (7) to increase sales. (Each of these objectives is discussed briefly in the following paragraphs.) The advertiser may have more than one objective at the same time. For example, a swimwear company may state its advertising objectives as follows: to maintain the company's brand image as the market leader in adult female swimwear and to increase revenue in this product line by 15 percent.

9.   Daniel Rosenberg, "Veal Industry Focuses on Chefs in Countering Animal Rights Ads," *Wall Street Journal,* March 18, 1998, B3.

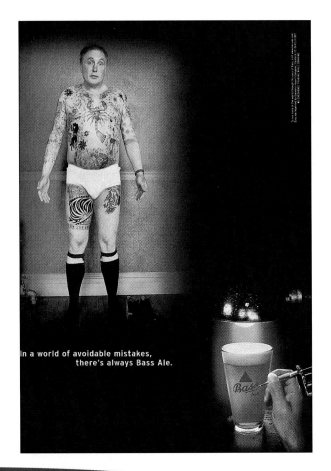

In a world of avoidable mistakes,
there's always Bass Ale.

EXHIBIT 8.10

Besides enhancing top-of-the-mind awareness, this ad appears designed to foster a more favorable attitude toward the brand, through its use of off-beat humor. www.bassale.com/

Creating or maintaining brand awareness and interest is a popular advertising objective. Brand awareness is an indicator of consumer knowledge about the existence of the brand and how easily that knowledge can be retrieved from memory. For example, an advertiser might ask a consumer to name five brands of fast food. **Top-of-the-mind awareness** is represented by the brand listed first. Ease of retrieval from memory is important because for many consumer goods or services, ease of retrieval is predictive of market share. An ad like that in Exhibit 8.10 is designed to promote top-of-the-mind awareness in a category where brand choice has been complicated by an incredible proliferation of alternatives.

Beliefs are knowing with some degree of certainty that certain things are true. For example, you may believe that FedEx is the most reliable next-day delivery service or that Saturn has a no-pressure sales environment. You may believe that gingivitis is the scourge of the Western world, and no one is safe from it. These are all important beliefs for marketers. In the case of Crest or any other toothpaste that promises to prevent gingivitis, the idea that this disease is prevalent is important when setting advertising objectives.

Creating or changing attitudes is another popular advertising objective. As we saw in Chapter 5, one way to go about changing people's attitudes is to give them new information designed to alter their beliefs. Alternatively, attitude change may be pursued by consistently associating one's brand with other likable objects or settings to effect a direct change in liking. Information-dense ads are designed to change attitudes by first altering beliefs, whereas entertaining ads are designed to influence attitudes through direct affect transfer. And even for an information-intensive service such as a mutual fund, there are times when the most prudent advertising goal is to build brand awareness and make your fund more likable by using entertaining or humorous advertising. In 1998 there were 8,900 different mutual funds being marketed to U.S. consumers.[10] In this sea of competitive clutter, if your advertising can't get you noticed and make your fund likable, you are destined to drown.

Purchase intent is another popular criterion in setting objectives. Purchase intent is determined by asking consumers whether they intend to buy a product or service in the near future. The appeal of influencing purchase intent is that intent is closer to actual behavior, and thus closer to the desired sale, than are attitudes. While this makes sense, it does presuppose that consumers can express their intentions with a reasonably high degree of reliability. Sometimes they can, sometimes they cannot. Purchase intent, however, is fairly reliable as an indicator of relative intention to buy, and it is, therefore, a worthwhile advertising objective.

Trial usage reflects actual behavior and is commonly used as an advertising objective. Many times, the best that we can ask of advertising is to encourage the consumer to try our brand once. At that point, the product or service must live up to the expectations created by our advertising. In the case of new products, stimulating trial usage is

---

10.   Vanessa O' Connell, "Alliance Capital Tries to Spice up Funds with Offbeat TV Spots," *Wall Street Journal,* March 25, 1998, B8.

critically important. In the marketing realm, the angels sing when the initial purchase rate of a new product or service is high.

The **repeat purchase**, or conversion, objective is aimed at the percentage of consumers who try a new product and then purchase it a second time. A second purchase is reason for great rejoicing. The odds of long-term product success go way up when this percentage is high.

Brand switching is the last of the advertising objectives mentioned here. In some brand categories, switching is commonplace, even the norm. In others it is rare. When setting a brand-switching advertising objective, the advertiser must neither expect too much, nor rejoice too much, over a temporary gain. Persuading consumers to switch brands can be a long and arduous task.

Communications versus Sales Objectives. 👀 Some analysts argue that as a single variable in a firm's overall marketing mix, it is not reasonable to set sales expectations for advertising when other variables in the mix might undermine the advertising effort or be responsible for sales in the first place.

In fact, some advertising analysts argue that communications objectives are the *only* legitimate objectives for advertising. This perspective has its underpinnings in the proposition that advertising is but one variable in the marketing mix and cannot be held solely responsible for sales. Rather, advertising should be held responsible for creating awareness of a brand, communicating information about product features or availability, or developing a favorable attitude that can lead to consumer preference for a brand. All of these outcomes are long term and based on communications impact. Central to a strict communications perspective is the belief that since it is impossible to judge sales impact directly from advertising, then sales objectives should not be part of advertising objectives. For a product such as the one being advertised in Exhibit 8.11, it is easy to appreciate the folly of a sales objective. This ad is obviously designed to get you to pick up the phone and call John Rosanvallon, or when you're in Paris, Jean-Claude Bouxin. John and Jean would like to sell you a jet.

There are some major benefits to maintaining a strict communications perspective in setting advertising objectives. First, by viewing advertising as primarily a communications effort, marketers can consider a broader range of advertising strategies. Second, they can gain a greater appreciation for the complexity of the overall communications process. Designing an integrated marketing communications program with sales as the sole objective neglects aspects of message design, media choice, public relations, or sales force deployment that can be effectively integrated across all phases of a firm's communication efforts. Using advertising messages to support the efforts of the sales force (as in Exhibit 8.11) is an example of coordinating the communications process and the IMC effort.

The desire of organizations to tie their advertising effort to sales is certainly understandable.

WEB SIGHT-ING

It helps to come from a powerful gene pool.

Engineered with passion

EXHIBIT 8.11

Dassault (www.dassault-aviation.com) is known for its weapons systems; but this ad is intended to remind readers that that expertise extends to consumer markets as well, with such products as the Falcon Jet (www.falconjet.com). Right. Exactly how many of us will tear this ad out of the magazine we find it in and make a note to call John or Jean-Claude? Even if no one is prompted by this ad to order a personal aircraft, much of the audience will process a message that contributes to a general (and favorable, the company hopes) impression of the Dassault brand.

After all, the average person assumes a fairly direct relationship between advertising and sales. With more and more emphasis on accountability in spending, firms are scrutinizing budgets and the performance of all aspects of the marketing program, including advertising. Despite all the compelling arguments to maintain a heavy emphasis on communications, firms still have a keen eye trained on sales.

While there is a natural tension between those who advocate sales objectives and those who push communications objectives, nothing precludes a marketer from using both categories of objectives when developing an advertising plan. Indeed, combining sales objectives such as market share and household penetration with communication objectives such as awareness and attitude change can be an excellent means of motivating and evaluating an advertising campaign.[11]

Characteristics of Workable Advertising Objectives. Objectives that enable a firm to make intelligent decisions about resource allocation must be stated in an advertising plan in terms specific to the organization. Articulating such well-stated objectives is easier when advertising planners do the following:

1. *Establish a quantitative benchmark.* Objectives for advertising are measurable only in the context of quantifiable variables. Advertising planners should begin with quantified measures of the current status of market share, awareness, attitude, or other factors that advertising is expected to influence. The measurement of effectiveness in quantitative terms requires a knowledge of the level of variables of interest *before* an advertising effort, and then afterward. For example, a statement of objectives in quantified terms might be "Increase the market share of heavy users of the product category using our brand from 22 to 25 percent." In this case, a quantifiable and measurable market share objective is specified.

2. *Specify measurement methods and criteria for success.* It is important that the factors being measured are directly related to the objectives being pursued. It is of little use to try to increase the awareness of a brand with advertising and then judge the effects based on changes in sales. If changes in sales are expected, then measure sales. If increased awareness is the goal, then change in consumer awareness is the only legitimate measure of success. This may seem obvious, but in a classic study of advertising objectives, it was found that claims of success for advertising were unrelated to the original statements of objective in 69 percent of the cases studied.[12] In this research, firms cited increases in sales as proof of success of advertising when the original objectives were related to factors such as awareness, conviction to a brand, or product use information. Yet another recent complication for measurement stems from vehicles such as the World Wide Web. The interactive media have presented a substantial challenge with respect to establishing success criteria.[13]

3. *Specify a time frame.* Objectives for advertising should include a statement of the period of time allowed for the desired results to occur. In some cases, as with direct response advertising, the time frame may be immediate or a 24-hour period. For communications-based objectives, the measurement of results may not be undertaken until the end of an entire multiweek campaign. The point is that the time period for accomplishment of an objective and the related measurement period must be stated in advance in the ad plan.

These criteria for setting objectives help ensure that the planning process is organized and well directed. By relying on quantitative benchmarks, an advertiser has guidelines for making future decisions. Linking measurement criteria to objectives provides a basis for the equitable evaluation of the success or failure of advertising.

11. John Philip Jones, "Advertising's Crisis of Confidence," *Marketing Management,* vol. 2, no. 1 (1993), 15–24.

12. Stewart Henderson Britt, "Are So-Called Successful Advertising Campaigns Really Successful?" *Journal of Advertising Research,* vol. 9 (1969), 5.

13. Sally Beatty, "P&G, Rivals and Agencies Begin Attempt to Set On-Line Standards," *Wall Street Journal,* August 24, 1998, B6.

Finally, the specification of a time frame for judging results keeps the planning process moving forward. As in all things, however, moderation is a good thing. A single-minded obsession with watching the numbers can be dangerous in that it minimizes or entirely misses the importance of qualitative and intuitive factors.

GLOBAL ISSUES

IBM COMBS THE GLOBE FOR E-BUSINESS

When is a computer not just a computer? Well, in IBM's way of thinking about things, that would be when a computer is an e-business tool. Faced with potent competitors such as Compaq, Hewlett-Packard, and Dell, IBM needed a way to reposition its laptops and PCs to accelerate its sales. Building on its own much-mimicked e-business concept, it was logical for IBM to pursue a repositioning of these products as e-business tools. The marketing strategy was to launch a revamped product line designed specifically to help companies get on the Internet and other networks to boost their business. A carefully orchestrated ad campaign could help consumers see IBM computers in this new light.

The e-business campaign was launched with extravagant eight-page inserts in various national newspapers. This was followed by giant IBM posters plastered on construction sites, in airports and in subway stations in major metropolitan markets, along with magazine and TV ads and the ever-present Web site promotion. To add a touch of style and grace to its campaign, IBM employed a photographer who previously specialized in glamour shots for Clinique cosmetics. These stylish black-and-white photos of products such as the IBM ThinkPad were a common element throughout the various media used in this repositioning campaign.

How much to spend on a campaign to promote e-business tools around the world? This year-long global campaign was funded at the $100 million level. Gee, $100 million here and $100 million there, and all of a sudden you're talking about some real money. IBM spends on the order of $750 million dollars each year on advertising.

Source: Raju Narisetti, "IBM Blitz to Introduce E-Business Tools," *Wall Street Journal*, April 15, 1998, B4.

Budgeting. One of the most agonizing tasks is budgeting the funds for an advertising effort. As described in the Global Issues box on this page, firms like IBM routinely spend hundreds of millions of dollars on advertising. Normally, the responsibility for the advertising budget lies with the firm itself. Within a firm, budget recommendations come up through the ranks, from a brand manager to a category manager and ultimately to the executive in charge of marketing. The sequence then reverses itself for the allocation and spending of funds. In a small firm, such as an independent retailer, the sequence just described may include only one individual who plays all the roles.

In some cases, a firm will rely on its advertising agency to make recommendations regarding the size of the advertising budget. When this is done, it is typically the account executive in charge of the brand who will analyze the firm's objectives and its creative and media needs and then make a recommendation to the company. The account supervisor's budget planning will likely include working closely with brand and product-group managers to determine an appropriate spending level.

To be as judicious and accountable as possible for spending money on advertising, advertisers rely on various methods for setting an advertising budget. To appreciate the benefits (and failings) of each of these methods, we will consider each of them separately.

Percentage of Sales. A **percentage-of-sales approach** to advertising budgeting calculates the advertising budget based on a percentage of the prior year's sales or the projected year's sales. This technique is easy to understand and operationalize. The budget decision makers merely specify that a particular percentage of either last year's sales or the current year's estimated sales will be allocated to the advertising process. It is common to spend between 2 and 12 percent of sales on advertising.

While simplicity is certainly an advantage in decision making, the percentage-of-sales approach is fraught with problems. First, when a firm's sales are decreasing, the advertising budget will automatically decline. Periods of decreasing sales may be precisely the time when a firm needs to increase spending on advertising; if a percentage-of-sales budgeting method is being used, this won't happen. Second, this budgeting method can easily result in overspending on advertising. Once funds have been earmarked, the tendency is to find ways to spend the budgeted amount. Third, the most serious drawback from a strategic standpoint is that the percentage-of-sales approach does not relate advertising dollars to advertising objectives. Basing spending on past or future sales is devoid of analytical evaluation and implicitly presumes a direct cause-and-effect relationship between advertising and sales. But here, sales cause advertising.

A variation on the percentage-of-sales approach that firms may use is the **Unit-of-sales approach** to budgeting, which simply allocates a specified dollar amount of advertising for each unit of a brand sold (or expected to be sold). This is merely a translation of the percentage-of-sales method into dollars per units sold. The unit-of-sales approach has the same advantages and disadvantages as the percentage-of-sales approach.

Share of Market/Share of Voice. With this method, employed by many firms, a firm monitors the amount spent by various significant competitors on advertising and allocates an amount equal to the amount of money spent by competitors or an amount proportional to (or slightly greater than) the firm's market share relative to the competition.[14] Exhibit 8.12 shows the relationship between share of market and share of voice for two fierce competitors: Coke and Pepsi.

With this method, an advertiser will achieve a **share of voice**, or an advertising presence in the market, equal to or greater than the competitors' share of advertising voice. This method is often used for advertising budget allocations in new-product introductions. Conventional wisdom suggests that some multiple, often 2.5 to 4 times the desired first-year market share, should be spent in terms of share-of-voice advertising expenditures. For example, if an advertiser wants a 2 percent first-year share, it would need to spend up to 8 percent of the total dollar amount spent in the industry (for an 8 percent share of voice). The logic is that a new product will need a significant share of voice to gain notice among a group of existing, well-established brands.[15] To achieve significant share of voice for its new toothpaste with baking soda and peroxide, Colgate-Palmolive spent $40 million in the first six months on advertising.[16] This sort of massive spending on a product launch can give a brand visibility in a crowded market but would be far out of line relative to competitors' spending.

EXHIBIT 8.12

Share of market versus share of voice, 1992 cola market. Figures are in millions of U.S. dollars.

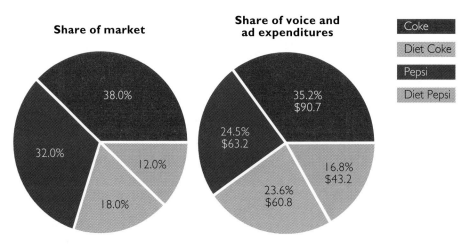

Source: Taken from *Market Share Reporter* (Detroit: Gale Research, 1994), 100. Share of voice/ad expenditures computed from January to December 1992 in LNA/Media Watch Multi-Media Service (New York: 1992), 186, 209, 392. Copyright © 1994, Gale Research, Inc. All rights reserved. Reproduced by permission.

14. The classic treatment of this method was first offered by James O. Peckham, "Can We Relate Advertising Dollars to Market-Share Objectives?" in Malcolm A. McGiven, ed., *How Much to Spend for Advertising* (New York: Association of National Advertisers, 1969), 24.
15. James C. Shroer, "Ad Spending: Growing Market Share," *Harvard Business Review* (January–February 1990), 44.
16. Pat Sloan, "Colgate Packs $40M behind New Toothpaste," *Advertising Age,* December 12, 1994, 36.

Although this technique is sound in the sense that it shows a heightened awareness of competitors' activities, there is some question as to whether it can or should be used. First, it may be difficult to gain access to precise information on competitors' spending. Second, there is no reason to believe that competitors are spending their money wisely or in a way even remotely related to what the decision-making firm wants to accomplish. Third, the flaw in logic in this method is the presumption that every advertising effort is of the same quality and will have the same effect from a creative execution standpoint. Nothing could be further from the truth. Multimillion-dollar advertising campaigns have been miserable failures, and limited-budget campaigns have been big successes.

Response Models. Using response models to aid the budgeting process is a fairly widespread practice among larger firms.[17] The belief is that greater objectivity can be maintained with such models. While this may or may not be the case, response models do provide useful information on what a given company's advertising response function looks like. An **advertising response function** is a mathematical relationship that associates dollars spent on advertising and sales generated. To the extent that past advertising predicts future sales, this method is valuable. Using marginal analysis, an advertiser would continue its spending on advertising as long as its marginal spending was exceeded by marginal sales. Marginal analysis answers the advertiser's question, "How much more will sales increase if we spend an additional dollar on advertising?" As the rate of return on advertising expenditures declines, the wisdom of additional spending is analyzed.

Theoretically, this method leads to a point where an optimal advertising expenditure results in an optimal sales level and, in turn, an optimal profit. The relationship between sales, profit, and advertising spending is shown in the marginal analysis graph in Exhibit 8.13. Data on sales levels, prior advertising expenditures, and consumer awareness are typical of the numerical input to such quantitative models.

Unfortunately, the advertising-to-sales relationship assumes simple causality, and we know that that assumption isn't true. Many other factors, in addition to advertising, affect sales directly. Still, some feel that the use of response models is a better budgeting method than guessing or applying the percentage-of-sales or other budgeting methods discussed so far.

Sales ($)

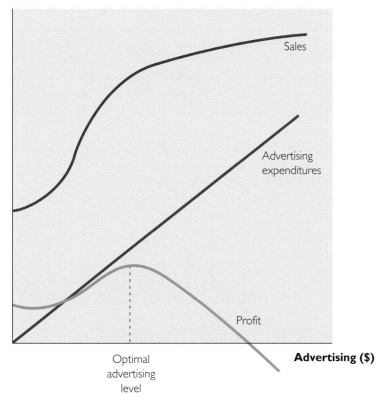

Optimal advertising level

Advertising ($)

Source: David A. Aaker, Rajeev Batra, and John G. Meyers, *Advertising Management,* 4th ed. (Englewood Cliffs, N.J.: Prentice-Hall, 1992), 469. Reprinted by permission of Prentice-Hall, Inc., Upper Saddle River, N.J.

EXHIBIT 8.13

Sales, profit, and advertising curves used in marginal analysis.

17. James E. Lynch and Graham J. Hooley, "Increasing Sophistication in Advertising Budget Setting," *Journal of Advertising Research* (February–March, 1990), 72.

Objective and Task. The methods for establishing an advertising budget just discussed all suffer from the same fundamental deficiency: a lack of specification of how expenditures are related to advertising goals. The only method of budget setting that focuses on the relationship between spending and advertising objectives is the **objective-and-task approach**. This method begins with the stated objectives for an advertising effort. Goals related to production costs, target audience reach, message effects, behavioral effects, media placement, duration of the effort, and the like are specified. The budget is formulated by identifying the specific tasks necessary to achieve different aspects of the objectives.

There is a lot to recommend this procedure for budgeting. A firm identifies any and all tasks it believes are related to achieving its objectives. Should the total dollar figure for the necessary tasks be beyond the firm's financial capability, then a reconciliation must take place. But even if a reconciliation and a subsequent reduction of the budget results, the firm has at least identified what *should* have been budgeted to pursue its advertising objectives.

The objective-and-task approach is the most logical and defensible method for calculating and then allocating an advertising budget. It is the only budgeting method that specifically relates advertising spending to the advertising objectives being pursued. It is widely used among major advertisers. For these reasons, we will consider the specific procedures for implementing the objective-and-task budgeting method.

Implementing the Objective-and-Task Budgeting Method. Proper implementation of the objective-and-task approach requires a data-based, systematic procedure. Since the approach ties spending levels to specific advertising goals, the process depends on proper execution of the objective-setting process described earlier. Once a firm and its agency are satisfied with the specificity and direction of stated objectives, a series of well-defined steps can be taken to implement the objective-and-task method. These steps are shown in Exhibit 8.14 and summarized in the following sections.

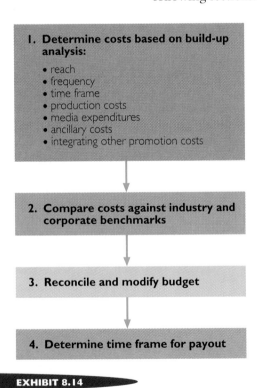

EXHIBIT 8.14

Steps in implementing the objective-and-task approach.

Determine costs based on build-up analysis. Having identified specific objectives, an advertiser can now begin determining what tasks are necessary for the accomplishment of those objectives. In using a **build-up analysis**—building up the expenditure levels for tasks—the following factors must be considered in terms of costs:

- *Reach:* The advertiser must identify the geographic and demographic exposure the advertising is to achieve.
- *Frequency:* The advertiser must determine the number of exposures required to accomplish desired objectives.
- *Time frame:* The advertiser must estimate when communications will occur and over what period of time.
- *Production costs:* The decision maker can rely on creative personnel and producers to estimate the costs associated with the planned execution of advertisements.
- *Media expenditures:* Given the preceding factors, the advertiser can now define the appropriate media, media mix, and frequency of insertions that will directly address objectives. Further, differences in geographic allocation, with special attention to regional or local media strategies, are considered at this point.
- *Ancillary costs:* There will be a variety of related costs not directly accounted for in the preceding factors. Prominent

among these are costs associated with advertising to the trade and specialized research unique to the campaign.

- *Integrating other promotional costs:* In this era of integrated marketing communications, an advertising budget must be considered in the context of spending on other promotional efforts. Some of these promotional expenditures will directly support mass media advertising. Others will have distinct objectives, but as we have seen from an IMC standpoint, the theme and any spending issues need to be coordinated across the various elements of the IMC campaign.

Compare costs against industry and corporate benchmarks. After compiling all the costs through a build-up analysis, an advertiser will want to make a quick reality check. This is accomplished by checking the percentage of sales that the estimated set of costs represents relative to industry standards for percentage of sales allocated to advertising. If most competitors are spending 4 to 6 percent of gross sales on advertising, how does the current budget compare to this percentage? Another recommended technique is to identify the share of industry advertising that the firm's budget represents. Another relevant reference point is to compare the current budget with prior budgets. If the total dollar amount is extraordinarily high or low compared to previous years, this variance should be justified based on the objectives being pursued. The use of percentage of sales on both an industry and internal corporate basis provides a reference point only. The percentage-of-sales figures are not used for decision making per se, but rather as a baseline comparison to judge whether the budgeted amount is so unusual as to need reevaluation.

Reconcile and modify the budget. It is always a fear that the proposed budget will not meet with approval. It may not be viewed as consistent with corporate policy related to advertising expense, or it may be considered beyond the financial capabilities of the organization. Modifications to a proposed budget are common. Having to make radical cuts in proposed spending is disruptive and potentially devastating. The objective-and-task approach is designed to identify what a firm will need to spend in order to achieve a desired advertising impact. To have the budget level compromised after such planning can result in a totally impotent advertising effort because necessary tasks cannot be funded.

Every precaution should be taken against having to radically modify a budget. Planners should be totally aware of corporate policy and financial circumstance *during* the objective-setting and subsequent task-planning phases. This will help reduce the extent of budget modification, should any be required.

Determine time frame for payout. It is important that budget decision makers recognize when the budget will be available for funding the tasks associated with the proposed effort. Travel expenses, production expenses, and media time and space are tied to specific calendar dates. For example, media time and space are often acquired and paid for far in advance of the completion of finished advertisements. Knowing when and how much money is needed will usually increase the odds of the plan being carried out smoothly.

If these procedures are followed for the objective-and-task approach, an advertiser will have a defendable and agreeable advertising budget with which to pursue advertising objectives. One point to be made, however, is that the budget should not be viewed as the final word in funding an advertising effort. The dynamic nature of the market and rapid developments in media require flexibility in budget execution. This can mean changes in expenditure levels, but it can also mean changes in payout allocation.

Like any other business activity, an advertiser must take on an advertising effort with clearly specified intentions for what is to be accomplished. Intentions and expectations for advertising are embodied in the process of setting objectives. Armed with information from market planning and an assessment of the type of advertising needed to support marketing plans, advertising objectives can be set. These objectives should be in place before steps are taken to determine a budget for the advertising effort, and before the creative work begins. Again, this is not always the order of things, even though it should be. These objectives will also affect the plans for media placement.

Strategy. Strategy represents the mechanism by which something is to be done. It is an expression of the means to an end. All of the other factors are supposed to result in a strategy. Strategy is what you do, given the situation and objectives. There are an infinite number of possible advertising strategies. For example, if you are trying to get more top-of-the-mind awareness for your brand of chewing gum, a simple strategy would be to employ a high-frequency, name-repetition campaign. Exhibit 8.15 presents an ad from Danskin's campaign designed to broaden the appeal of its products beyond dance accessories to the much larger fitness-wear market. Danskin's advertising strategy features unique "fitness" celebrities as implicit endorsers of the Danskin brand.

EXHIBIT 8.15

This ad provides an excellent example of repositioning. The slogan says it all: "DANSKIN—Not Just for Dancing." www.danskin.com/

More sophisticated goals call for more sophisticated strategies. You are limited only by your resources: financial, organizational, and creative. Ultimately, strategy formulation is a creative endeavor. It is best learned through the study of what others have done in similar situations and through a thorough analysis of the focal consumer.

To assist in strategy formulation, a growing number of ad agencies have created a position called the **account planner** (see Chapter 7). This person's job is to synthesize all relevant consumer research and draw inferences from it that will help define a coherent advertising strategy. As with so many things, experience counts in this crucial role.

DAEWOO WOOS YOU

As a counterpoint to some of the other campaign examples featured in this chapter, consider the case of Daewoo Motor America and the approach it took in launching a line of three new automobiles in the U.S. marketplace. We offer the Daewoo launch as an illustration that an IMC campaign does not have to mean using every possible advertising medium imaginable. Daewoo chose simplicity: a grassroots, promotion-laden effort aimed at college towns.

Shunning glitzy, stylish ads in the national broadcast media, Daewoo arrived on foot—that is, on the feet of 2,000 Daewoo Campus Advisors (DCAs) at about 400 college campuses throughout the United States. Daewoo recruited DCAs through campus newspapers and radio stations, and more than 3,000 applicants queued up. After training sessions over the summer, these student DCAs were expected to reach out to their classmates on behalf of Daewoo. DCAs put in 8 to 10 hours per week passing out brochures, giving presentations to groups and clubs, and promoting on-campus Ride-and-Drive events. They received commissions of about $400 on each referral and were given the opportunity to purchase a Daewoo at "significant" discounts. Perhaps you are now driving Daewoo's Leganza sedan, the Nubria compact, or the sporty Lanos. (If so, be a good sport and share with your classmates what it was that convinced you to go with Daewoo!)

But why the grassroots approach? For starters, Daewoo wanted to get noticed quickly by a market segment that would be pivotal to the company's long-term survival in the American market, and they didn't want to spend a lot of money doing it. Students promoting to fellow students, recent grads, faculty, and parents seemed like an efficient strategy. Additionally, Daewoo took the one-to-one approach with prospective customers to ensure that it would distinguish itself from other Korean automakers who had been plagued by poor-quality reputations throughout North America.

You have to admire Daewoo's willingness to try unconventional approaches. In Britain, where Daewoo Motors has been quite successful, they sell their cars in department stores and door-to-door. Many times, finding another way can turn out to be the best way.

Source: Al Urbanski, "The Old College Try," *Promo Magazine*, July 1998, 49, 50.

Execution. The actual "doing" is the execution of an ad plan. It is the making and placing of ads across all media. To quote a famous bit of advertising copy from a tire manufacturer, this is where "the rubber meets the road." There are two elements to the execution of an advertising plan: determining the copy strategy and devising a media plan.

Copy Strategy. A copy strategy consists of copy objectives and methods, or tactics. The objectives state what the advertiser intends to accomplish, while the methods describe how the objectives will be achieved. Part Three of this text will deal extensively with these executional issues.

Media Plan. The media plan specifies exactly where ads will be placed and what strategy is behind their placement. In a truly integrated marketing communications environment, this is much more complicated than it might first appear. Back when there were just three broadcast television networks, there were already more than a million different combinations of placements that could be made.

With the explosion of media and promotion options today, the permutations are almost infinite. Moreover, the IMC box on this page illustrates that in some instances, an ad campaign may involve no mass media advertising at all.

It is at this point—devising a media plan—where all the money is spent, and so much could be saved. This is where the profitability of many agencies is really determined. Media placement strategy can make a huge difference in profits or losses and is considered in great depth in Part Four of this text.

Integrated Marketing Communications. The IMC effort should be spelled out in the media plan. It should be seamless with the rest of the plan. Sometimes IMC is the dominant aspect of the marketing effort, as is the case with Rhino Records. One could argue that Rhino is the all-time undisputed champion of creative PR and sales promotion, both integral aspects of IMC.

Rhino Records began as a used-album record store in West Los Angeles. Records were displayed in fruit crates on sawhorses. Rhino management would do just about anything to gain loyal customers. For example, they offered customers a nickel if they would take home a copy of a Danny Bonaduce album and promise to actually listen to it.[18] They pressed records in the shapes of animals. Perhaps their greatest feat was recording and selling a kazoo-orchestra recording of Led Zeppelin's "Whole Lotta Love." It sold 15,000 copies. A well-known street person in Los Angeles, Wild Man Fischer, was asked to record "Go to Rhino Records." At first the recording was given out as a promotional bonus to customers, but then it found its way to the BBC and actually made the pop charts in the UK.[19] Rhino issued offerings such as *The World's Worst Records,* which actually came with a barf bag,[20] and a collection of seventies tunes called *Have a Nice Day.* Soon Rhino was a record label as well as a record store. In 1978 it produced an influential album of then-unsigned L.A. bands, called *Saturday Night Pogo,* and *Cover Me,* a collection of bands covering Bruce Springsteen. Today you can find Rhino on the World Wide Web and in ads in popular magazines.

Everything Rhino does has a synergy and integration to it. The lesson from Rhino should not be lost: Don't make IMC a static, me-too formula. When practiced creatively, IMC can be amazing, and amazingly successful.

Evaluation. Last but not least in an ad plan is the evaluation component. This is where an advertiser determines how the agency will be graded: what criteria will be applied and how long the agency will have to achieve the agreed-upon objectives. It's critically important for the advertiser and agency to understand the evaluation criteria up front. Of course, the advertiser has the power to change its agency any time it wishes, regardless of whether or not the criteria are being met. In short, advertising agencies are at the mercy of their clients, fair or unfair.

The Role of the Advertising Agency in Advertising Planning.
Now that we have covered key aspects of the advertising planning process, one other issue should be considered. Because many advertisers rely heavily on the expertise of an advertising agency, understanding the role an agency plays in the advertising planning process is important. What contribution to the planning effort can and should an advertiser expect from its agency?

The discussion of advertising planning to this point has emphasized that the advertiser is responsible for the marketing-planning inputs as a type of self-assessment that identifies the firm's basis for offering value to customers. This assessment should also clearly identify, in the external environment, the opportunities and challenges that can be addressed with advertising. A firm should bring to the planning effort a well-articulated statement of a brand's value proposition and the marketing mix strategies designed to gain and sustain competitive advantage. However, when client

18. Stephen Fried, "Loony Tunes: Rhino Records' Utterly Gonzo Sensibility Is Turning Out to Be Good Business," *GQ,* April 1992, 76.
19. "B-Rated Rock and Roll," *Newsweek,* October 7, 1985, 90.
20. Fried, "Loony Tunes."

and agency are working in harmony, the agency may take an active role in helping the client formulate the more general marketing plan. Indeed, when things are going right, it can be hard to say exactly where the client's work ended and the agency's work began. This is the essence of teamwork, and as Steve Jobs noted in the case of iMac: "Creating great advertising, like creating great products, is a team effort."

But the advertising agency's crucial role, as a partner in the advertising effort, is to translate the current market and marketing status of a firm and its advertising objectives into advertising strategy and, ultimately, finished advertisements. An agency can serve its clients best by taking charge of the preparation and placement stages. Here, message strategies and tactics for the advertising effort and for the efficient and effective placement of ads in media need to be hammered out. At this point, the firm (as a good client) should turn to its agency for the expertise and talent needed for planning and executing at the stage where creative execution brings marketing strategies to life. There are two basic models for the relationship between agencies and their clients: adversarial or partnering. The former is too common; the latter is certainly preferred.

SUMMARY

◀▶ Describe the basic components of an advertising plan.

An advertising plan is motivated by the marketing planning process and provides the direction that ensures proper implementation of an advertising campaign. An advertising plan incorporates decisions about the segments to be targeted, communications and/or sales objectives with respect to these segments, and salient message appeals. The plan should also specify the dollars budgeted for the campaign, the media that will be employed to deliver the messages, and the measures that will be relied on to assess the campaign's effectiveness.

◀▶ Compare and contrast two fundamental approaches for setting advertising objectives.

Setting appropriate objectives is a crucial step in developing any advertising plan. These objectives are typically stated in terms of communications or sales goals. Both types of goals have their proponents, and the appropriate types of objectives to emphasize will vary with the situation. Communications objectives feature goals such as building brand awareness or reinforcing consumers' beliefs about a brand's key benefits. Sales objectives are just that: They hold advertising directly responsible for increasing sales of a brand.

◀▶ Explain various methods for setting advertising budgets.

Perhaps the most challenging aspect of any advertising campaign is arriving at a proper budget allocation. Companies and their advertising agencies work with several different methods to arrive at an advertising budget. A percentage-of-sales approach is a simple but naive way to deal with this issue. In the share-of-voice approach, the activities of key competitors are factored into the budget-setting process. A variety of quantitative models may also be used for budget determination. The objective-and-task approach is difficult to implement, but with practice it is likely to yield the best value for a firm's advertising dollars.

◀▶ Discuss the role of the advertising agency in formulating an advertising plan.

An advertising plan will be a powerful tool when firms partner with their advertising agencies in its development. The firm can lead this process by doing its homework with respect to marketing strategy development and objective setting. The agency can then play a key role in managing the preparation and placement phases of ad campaign execution.

KEY TERMS

advertising plan (245)

situation analysis (245)

industry analysis (247)

market analysis (248)

competitor analysis (248)

top-of-the-mind awareness (250)

purchase intent (250)

trial usage (250)

repeat purchase (251)

brand switching (251)

percentage-of-sales approach (253)

unit-of-sales approach (254)

share of voice (254)

advertising response function (255)

objective-and-task approach (256)

build-up analysis (256)

account planner (259)

QUESTIONS FOR REVIEW AND CRITICAL THINKING

1.   Review the materials presented in this chapter (and anything else you may be able to find) about Apple's launch of the iMac. Based on the advertising utilized, what do you surmise must have been the value proposition for iMac at the time of its launch?

2.   Find an example of cooperative advertising in your local newspaper. Why would computer manufacturers such as Apple, IBM, or Compaq want to participate in cooperative advertising programs with their retailers?

3.   Explain the connection between marketing strategies and advertising plans. What is the role of target segments in making this connection?

4.   Describe five key elements in a situation analysis and provide an example of how each of these elements may ultimately influence the final form of an advertising campaign.

5.   How would it ever be possible to justify anything other than sales growth as a proper objective for an advertising campaign? Is it possible that advertising could be effective yet not yield growth in sales?

6.   What types of objectives would you expect to find in an ad plan that featured direct response advertising?

7.   Write an example of a workable advertising objective that would be appropriate for a product like Crest Tartar Control toothpaste.

8.   In what situations would share of voice be an important consideration in setting an advertising budget? What are the drawbacks of trying to incorporate share of voice in budgeting decisions?

9.   What is it about the objective-and-task method that makes it the preferred approach for the sophisticated advertiser? Describe how build-up analysis is used in implementing the objective-and-task method.

10. Briefly discuss the appropriate role to be played by advertising agencies and their clients in the formulation of marketing and advertising plans.

EXPERIENTIAL EXERCISES

1.   In this chapter you read about the role of industry analysis in marketing and advertising planning. Divide into teams and select one product category, such as soft drinks, fast foods, vitamin supplements, health foods, or athletic footwear. Identify the external variables that tend to influence that industry. Assign the variables to group members. Describe how each variable should be monitored by

industry advertisers. Find one newspaper or magazine article that examines a variable you have targeted, and discuss the significance of the article for your industry.

2.   Pick a product that you use regularly—your watch or even your favorite bookstore. Based on your personal knowledge, identify an advertising objective for this brand.

A successful advertising plan should include an integrated marketing communications strategy. The following companies have extensive advertising budgets allocated across multiple media vehicles. Explore the following sites and determine the creative style and type of information available at each site:

Budweiser: www.budweiser.com

Guess: www.guess.com

Jeep: www.jeepunpaved.com

NBA: www.nba.com

For each site, answer the following questions:

1.   From your experience with past and current promotions for the company or organization, how does the site fit with all these communications? Are there similarities? Differences? Does the site reinforce the promotions? Does it offer additional information?

2.   In what ways are the differences you have noticed between the site and other media due to the different characteristics of the Internet itself?

3.   Create a personal standard for advertising quality by listing several criteria that apply to different media. Compare the quality of the Web site with that of promotions in other media. In your judgment, did the company or organization allocate too much, too little, or just the right amount of resources on its Web site?

Franchised organizations seem to be faced with a special challenge on the Internet, as a function of its ability to grant a publishing voice to nearly anyone that wants one colliding with the need (or at least desire) to maintain corporate control over communications strategy.

Tupperware (www.tupperware.com) and Takeout Taxi (which had no corporate Web site as of late 1998) are two companies that rely on independent operators to represent the company in the field, and both have had problems reconciling the global and local aspects of advertising. Tupperware has a policy of discouraging its distributors from creating their own Web sites.

Search the Tupperware site to find its distributor locator service.

1.   How effective is this site in helping you find a Tupperware distributor near you?

2.   How might an individual Tupperware distributor use the Web to be more effective?

3.   What issues would Tupperware need to weigh in crafting their Web-based advertising policy?

Numerous Takeout Taxi franchises have their own Web pages, scattered around the Net (try a Yahoo! or HotBot search on "takeout taxi" to find some).

4.   How effective do you think these individual franchise Web pages are?

5.   Why do you think there's no central Takeout Taxi Web site?

6.   If you were designing one, how might you use it?

SkyPort

見たいだけ、見せてあげる。

見たい番組ばっかり、見ていたい。そんなわがままは、1チャンネル1ジャンルのCSにまかせなさい。6つのTV放送と5つの通信放送が見られるCSスカイポートなら、好きなジャンルを次から次へと楽しめます。CSチューナー内蔵テレビや、CSチューナー内蔵ビデオがあれば、あとはCSアンテナを設置するだけ。そろいもそろった11チャンネルが、あなたの好奇心を欲求不満にさせません。

スカイポートTV

スカイポート通信

CHAPTER 9

After reading and thinking about this chapter, you will be able to do the following:

◀▶ Explain the types of audience research that are useful for understanding cultural barriers that can interfere with effective communication.

◀▶ Identify three distinctive challenges that complicate the execution of advertising in international settings.

◀▶ Describe the three basic types of advertising agencies that can assist in the placement of advertising around the world.

◀▶ Discuss the advantages and disadvantages of globalized versus localized advertising campaigns.

International advertising blunders are a rich part of advertising lore. Cruise the Internet and you will find many examples:[1]

> The name Coca-Cola in China was first rendered as "Ke-kou-ke-la." Unfortunately, Coke did not discover until after thousands of signs had been printed that the phrase means "bite the wax tadpole" or "female horse stuffed with wax," depending on the dialect. Coke then researched 40,000 Chinese characters and found a close phonetic equivalent, "ko-kou-ko-le," which can be loosely translated as "Happiness in the mouth."

> In Taiwan, the translation of the Pepsi slogan "Come alive with the Pepsi Generation" came out as "Pepsi will bring your ancestors back from the dead."

> Scandinavian vacuum manufacturer Electrolux used the following in an American ad campaign: "Nothing sucks like an Electrolux."

> When Parker Pen marketed a ballpoint pen in Mexico, its ads were supposed to say, "It won't leak in your pocket and embarrass you." Instead the ads said that "It won't leak in your pocket and make you pregnant."

Humorous or not, such episodes remind us that communicating with consumers around the world is a special challenge.

International advertising is advertising that reaches across national and cultural boundaries. Unfortunately, a great deal of international advertising in the past was nothing more than translations of domestic advertising. Often, these translations were at best ineffective, at worst offensive. The day has passed, however—if there ever was such a day—when advertisers based in industrialized nations could simply "do a foreign translation" of their ads. Today, international advertisers must pay greater attention to local cultures. While this chapter is written by Americans, we have tried hard to write about advertising from an international perspective. We argue that the real issue is not nations, but cultures.

As we said in Chapter 5, culture is a set of values, rituals, and behaviors that define a way of life. Culture is typically invisible to those who are immersed within it. Communicating *across* cultures is not easy. It is, in fact, one of the most difficult of all communication tasks, largely because there is no such thing as culture-free communication. Advertising is a cultural product; it means nothing outside of culture. Culture surrounds advertising, informs it, gives it meaning. To transport an ad across cultural borders, one must respect, and hopefully understand, the power of culture.

This chapter augments and extends the advertising planning framework offered in Chapter 8. We add some necessary international planning tools along with a discussion of the special challenges found in advertising around the world.

Ads depend on effective communication, and effective communication depends on shared meaning. The degree of shared meaning is significantly affected by cultural membership. When an advertiser in culture A wants to communicate with consumers in culture B, it is culture B that will surround the created message, form its cultural context, and significantly affect how it will be interpreted.

Some products and brands may belong to a global consumer culture more than to any one national culture. Such brands travel well, as do their ads, because there is already common cultural ground on which to build effective advertising. The Libertel phone and McDonald's ads in Exhibits 9.1 and 9.2 provide examples of products and brands with wide, if not "global," appeal. Wireless phones have emerged as a global product seemingly overnight, providing functionality that is easy to appreciate through technological advances that many consumers around the world have come to take for granted. McDonald's, although clearly an American icon, has become a part of the global landscape, thus facilitating something of a global image. Such examples, how-

---

1. These examples are quoted directly from Robert Kirby, "Kirby: Advertising Translates Into Laughs," *Salt Lake Tribune,* www.sltrib.com/. Accessed February 24, 1998.

EXHIBIT 9.1

Can you translate this Dutch ad? The three-part headline reads: "I got my eyes from my mother. I got my sense of humor from my mother. And I got my mobile phone from my dad." www.libertel.com/

EXHIBIT 9.2

Piled high with pickle, onion, ketchup, and mustard, the McDonald's hamburger is the quintessential example of a global brand. It's "home" Web site is at www.mcdonalds.com; *McDonald's Brazilian Web presence is* www.mcdonalds.com.br. *Of course, what's underneath all those fixings might depend on cultural context: In India, where sacred cows are, indeed, sacred, that universally recognized burger might necessarily not be beef! As a vast multinational, McDonald's has also drawn its share of protests, including the McSpotlight Web site (*www.mcspotlight.org*).*

ever, are few and far between, and as "global" as they may be, they are still affected by the local culture as to their use and, ultimately, their meaning.

The Pepsi Challenge in Brazil: Confronting a Global Brand.

Consider this cross-cultural advertising challenge: Your major competitor has 88 percent of the market; you have 7 percent. The market has a history of loyalty to your competitor; you are considered an upstart. Although you have made recent market gains, your competitor claims that the gains are merely a result of its inability to keep up with demand. Welcome to the battle between Pepsi and Coke in Brazil. Coke is dominant in the $6 billion Brazilian soft drink market.

The stakes in the Brazilian cola market are indeed high. Brazil is not only a huge market—it ranks as the world's fourth largest in soft drink consumption—but also a young market. More than 30 percent of Brazil's population is between 10 and 24 years old—the prime cola-drinking ages. These youthful consumers, if captured now, may be brand loyal for a lifetime.

Pepsi faced an enormous challenge. Coca-Cola had carefully nurtured massive market share over decades—so much so that when a person in Brazil asked for *uma coca*, it didn't mean "a cola" to most Brazilians, it meant "a Coke." What's more, Coke was in no way complacent. It regularly launched $40 to $50 million advertising campaigns in Brazil to defend market share. What could Pepsi do, and why did Pepsi think that challenging Coke in the Brazilian market was even feasible?

Brazil is in the midst of a massive economic revolution that is changing the lives and lifestyles of most Brazilians. The Brazilian government's economic reform program—called the "plan *real*" after the new monetary unit, the *real,* on which it is based—brought inflation down from more than 1,000 percent a year into single digits. While stubborn currency problems have remained, the removal of this "inflation tax" gave Brazilians a new standard of living. To the extent that Pepsi's advertising appeal could be wrapped up in this social change, Pepsi had an opportunity to create common cultural ground between a brand known for youth and irreverence and a culture in the midst of dramatic change.

In 1995, Pepsi started a massive $500 million marketing and advertising offensive to gain the loyalty of the 145 million prime cola drinkers in Brazil. The campaign took an integrated marketing communications approach—advertising, sales promotions, support media, and public relations. The program was anchored by 20 television commercials produced by the Brazilian ad agency Almap BBDO in São Paulo. This $100 million TV campaign employed ads featuring young people touting the recent changes in Brazil. Each television ad ended with the same shot—a Brazilian teen holding up a can of Pepsi and speaking the tag line of the ad, "Now we have a choice."[2] Another part of the campaign was the print ad in Exhibit 9.3, which connected Brazil's cultural change with Pepsi.

Pepsi's challenge was formidable. Coca-Cola is one of the most highly respected marketing and advertising organizations in the world, with more than 70 percent of its annual sales coming from markets outside the United States.[3] Some argue that Coke is one of the few brands that is part of a global consumer culture. In the view of Coca-Cola strategists, there is enough homogeneity across cultures that the look and feel of

EXHIBIT 9.3

As an example of international advertising, how does this Pepsi ad take advantage of the particular cultural and economic conditions in Brazil? Does the use of an integrated marketing communications approach have special considerations when implemented in international markets? www.pepsi.com/

2.   Claudia Penteado, "Pepsi's Brazil Blitz," *Advertising Age,* January 16, 1995, 12.
3.   "In Japan, Coke Is Still It," *International Herald Tribune,* July 18, 1995, 15.

both the product and the advertising for Coke can be largely standardized, with some fairly minor adaptations. For example, as adaptations, Coca-Cola uses Coke Light as a brand name instead of Diet Coke in countries where the word *diet* is legally restricted for commercial use. Coke also uses a slightly sweeter formula for the syrup in Middle Eastern markets to accommodate local tastes. And in the biggest exception to its global rule, Coke aggressively markets a brand by the name of Thums Up in India, where its base Coca-Cola brand has never achieved the popularity typical in nearly every other country of the world.[4]

What is important, though, is that Coca-Cola has a global perspective whereby the entire world is viewed as a market, and the product and advertising planning proceed from that premise. Coca-Cola may be the ultimate global brand, with more loyalty around the world than any other. Just ask the folks at Pepsi.

Overcoming Cultural Barriers.

Global trade initiatives such as the General Agreement on Tariffs and Trade (GATT) and the North American Free Trade Agreement (NAFTA) are designed to facilitate trade and economic development across national borders. These initiatives signal the emergence of international markets that are larger, more accessible, and perhaps more homogeneous. A nice example of this emerging homogenization between two NAFTA trading partners is discussed in the Global Issues box on this page. In the midst of this trend toward more and more international trade, marketers are redefining the nature and scope of the markets for their goods and services, which, in turn, redefines the nature and scope of advertising and the advertising planning effort. This means that firms must be more sensitive to the social and economic differences of various international markets.

Exhibit 9.4 offers perspective on the kinds of companies that are most committed and successful in marketing and advertising around the world. All the firms listed in Exhibit 9.4 compete in either consumer products or the automotive markets. These are corporate titans such as P&G, Toyota, and Coke. Today, however, most companies consider their markets to extend beyond national boundaries and across cultures. Hence, advertisers must come to terms with how they are going to effectively overcome cultural barriers in trying to communicate with consumers around the world.

GLOBAL ISSUES

SO WHO WAS IT THAT INVENTED SALSA?

When it comes to fast food in Mexico, the taco remains supreme. They are sold on every street corner. Steak, pork, chicken, and fish tacos are always available, broiled or steamed, with corn or flour tortillas, piled high with chilies and salsa. Vendors set up for the breakfast crowd and usually stay in place till about midnight. But sales of the taco in Mexico have been slumping of late. Why? Because Mexican fast-food consumers can now also choose from pizza at Domino's and Pizza Hut, hamburgers at McDonald's and Jack in the Box, and cold sandwiches at their local Subway. Getting hungry yet?

In the United States, "Americanized" Mexican food continues to grow in popularity. "Tex-Mex" has become a food genre that is popular around the world. U.S. consumers chow down on chili dogs, nachos, Doritos, Tostitos, and salsa brands such as Victoria and Ortega, to get their taste of Old Mexico. The irony of course is that products such as these are largely invented in the United States to appeal to the U.S. consumer's idealized sense of what Mexican food must be like.

The ultimate staple of the native Mexican diet is salsa and fresh chilies. They are at the table for breakfast, lunch, and dinner. Here we clearly observe the homogenization effect on consumer preferences that evolves between close trading partners. Salsa brands made in the United States now fill the shelves of grocery stores in Mexico, side by side with Mexican brands. Now Mexican consumers can choose the salsa with a taste of Old USA to spice up their fish tacos at breakfast. Perhaps the next phase of this cultural fusion will be Mexican firms exporting ketchup, hamburgers, and soft drinks to the United States, and U.S. firms responding with tequila and corn tortillas exported to Mexico. Such is life in the new global economy.

Source: Ignacio Vazquez, "Mexicans Are Buying 'Made in USA' Food," *Marketing News*, August 31, 1998, 14.

---

4.   Nikhil Deogun, "For Coke in India, Thums Up Is the Real Thing," *Wall Street Journal,* April 29, 1998, B1.

EXHIBIT 9.4

Top 15 global marketers by ad spending outside the United States. Figures are in millions of U.S. dollars.

Rank	Advertiser (Parent Company)	Headquarters	Non-U.S. Ad Spending 1996	U.S. Ad Spending 1996
1	Procter & Gamble Co.	Cincinnati	$2,479.1	$2,622.7
2	Unilever	Rotterdam/London	2,355.3	948.5
3	Nestlé SA	Vevey, Switzerland	1,574.7	402.5
4	Toyota Motor Corp.	Toyota City, Japan	988.6	800.3
5	PSA Peugeot-Citroen SA	Paris	958.6	0.0
6	Volkswagen AG	Wolfsburg, Germany	933.2	171.8
7	Nissan Motor Co.	Tokyo	855.2	557.4
8	Coca-Cola Co.	Atlanta	832.2	612.3
9	Philip Morris Cos.	New York	813.0	2,278.9
10	General Motors Corp.	Detroit	773.1	2,373.4
11	Ford Motor Co.	Dearborn, Michigan	741.0	1,179.2
12	Mars Inc.	McLean, Virginia	731.2	557.6
13	Renault SA	Paris	664.1	0.0
14	Kao Corp.	Tokyo	628.4	22.6
15	Fiat SpA	Turin, Italy	606.3	1.4

Source: www.adage.com/, accessed August 31, 1998.

Barriers to Successful International Advertising. Adopting an international perspective is often difficult for marketers. The reason is that experiences gained over a career and a lifetime create a cultural "comfort zone"—that is, one's own cultural values, experiences, and knowledge serve as a subconscious guide for decision making and behavior. International advertisers are particularly beset with this problem.

Managers must overcome two related biases to be successful in international markets. **Ethnocentrism** is the tendency to view and value things from the perspective of one's own culture. A **self-reference criterion (SRC)** is the unconscious reference to one's own cultural values, experiences, and knowledge as a basis for decisions. These two closely related biases are primary obstacles to success when conducting marketing and advertising planning that demands a cross-cultural perspective.

A decision maker's SRC and ethnocentrism can inhibit his or her ability to sense important cultural distinctions between markets. This in turn can blind advertisers to their own culture's "fingerprints" on the ads they've created. Sometimes these are offensive or, at a minimum, markers of "outsider" influence. Outsiders aren't always welcome; other times, they just appear ignorant.

For example, AT&T's "Reach Out and Touch Someone" advertising campaign was viewed as much too sentimental for most European audiences. Similarly, AT&T's "Call USA" campaign, aimed at Americans doing business in Europe, was negatively perceived by many Europeans. The ad featured a harried American businessman whose language skills were so poor that he could barely ask for assistance in a busy French hotel to find a telephone. European businesspeople are typically fluent in two or three languages and have enough language competence to ask for a telephone. This ad, with its portrayal of Americans as culturally inept and helpless, created a negative association for AT&T among European businesspeople. Granted, the target market was Americans in foreign assignments, but the perspective of the ad was still decidedly ethnocentric and offensive to Europeans.

The only way you can have any hope at all of counteracting the negative influences that ethnocentrism and SRC have on international advertising decision making is to be constantly sensitive to their existence and to the virtual certainty of important differences between cultures that will somehow affect your best effort. Even with the best cross-cultural analysis, it is still likely that problems will present themselves. However, without it, it is a virtual certainty.

Cross-Cultural Audience Research. Analyzing audiences in international markets can be a humbling task. If firms have worldwide product distribution networks—as do Nestlé, Unilever, and Philip Morris—then international audience analysis will require dozens of separate analyses. There really is no way to avoid the task of specific audience analysis. This typically involves research in each different country, generally from a local research supplier. There are, however, good secondary resources that may provide broad-based information to advertisers about international markets. The U.S. Department of Commerce has an International Trade Administration (ITA) division that helps companies based in the United States develop foreign market opportunities for their products and services. The ITA publishes specialized reports that cover most of the major markets in the world and provide economic and regulatory information. The United Nations' *Statistical Yearbook* is another source of general economic and population data. The yearbook, published annually, provides information for more than 200 countries. This type of source provides some helpful information for the international advertiser. Unfortunately, it's rarely enough.

An international audience analysis will also involve evaluation of economic conditions; demographic characteristics; values; custom and ritual; and product use and preferences.

Country	GDP	Ad $ as % of GDP
United States	$8,476	1.34
Japan	4,260	0.87
Germany	2,216	0.88
France	1,449	0.64
United Kingdom	1,339	1.49
Italy	1,190	0.55
China	1,029	0.47
Canada	646	0.79
Brazil	563	1.66
India	449	0.39
Mexico	434	1.14
Argentina	345	0.80
South Africa	146	1.06
Hungary	48	1.57
Vietnam	25	0.36

Source: *Advertising Expenditures Forecast* (Zenith Media, July 1998).

EXHIBIT 9.5

National economies in 1998, ranked by GDP in billions of U.S. dollars.

Economic Conditions. One way to think about the economic conditions of a potential international audience is to break the world's markets into three broad classes of economic development: less-developed countries, newly industrialized countries, and highly industrialized countries. These categories provide a basic understanding of the economic capability of the average consumer in a market and thus help place consumption in the context of economic realities. Exhibit 9.5 shows a mix of countries in different stages of economic development as indicated by their gross domestic products (GDP) in 1998. This exhibit also details dollars spent on advertising as a percentage of GDP, by country.

Less-developed countries represent nearly 75 percent of the world's population. Some of these countries are plagued by drought and civil war, and their economies lack almost all the resources necessary for development: capital, infrastructure, political stability, and trained workers. Many of the products sold in these less-developed economies are typically not consumer products, but rather business products used for building infrastructure (such as heavy construction equipment) or agricultural equipment.

Newly industrialized countries have economies defined by change; they are places where traditional ways of life that have endured for centuries are changing and modern consumer cultures have emerged in a few short years. This creates a very particular set of problems for the outside advertiser trying to hit a moving target, or a culture in rapid flux.

Rapid economic growth in countries such as Singapore, Malaysia, and Taiwan has created a new middle class of consumers with radically different expectations than their counterparts of a mere decade ago. Asian consumers are relatively heavy users of media-based information. The latest global trends in fashion, music, and travel have shorter and shorter lag times in reaching this part of the world. Many U.S. firms already have a strong presence in these markets with both their products and their advertising, like the Tropicana brand shown in Exhibit 9.6.

The **highly industrialized countries** of the world are the countries with both a high GDP and a high per capita income. These countries have also invested heavily over many years in infrastructure—roads, hospitals, airports, power-generating plants, and educational institutions. Within this broad grouping, an audience assessment will focus on more-detailed analyses of the market, including the nature and extent of competition, marketing trade channels, lifestyle trends, and market potential. Firms pursuing opportunities in highly industrialized countries proceed with market analysis in much the same way it would be conducted in the United States. While the advertising in these countries will often vary based on unique cultural and lifestyle factors, consumers in these markets are accustomed to seeing a full range of creative appeals for

EXHIBIT 9.6

This ad for Tropicana exemplifies the rapid changes occurring in many Asian countries. Traditional values are giving way to a focus on consumption and consumer culture.

goods and services. Additionally, as exemplified by the IMC box on this page, we would expect to see active experimentation with the World Wide Web as a marketing tool in most highly industrialized countries.

CYBERPOINTS FOR SITE VISITS

Loyalty or frequency reward programs (for example, any of the major airlines' frequent-flyer programs) have long been a reliable tactic for direct marketers. Such programs create reward systems to promote a behavior that the marketer deems desirable. In Europe, this tactic has found its way to the World Wide Web. If a new British-based program fares well, consumers around the world may one day visit Web sites not because of interest or entertainment, but instead because it will enable them to "earn" free stuff.

Holders of the SMART card in Britain can earn points just by visiting the Web sites of participating U.K.–based businesses and clicking on a flashing "credits" icon. Points can then be redeemed for gifts and movie tickets. The rationale behind SMART's cyber-offering is to grow its base of cardholders and generate awareness and exposure for the various company sponsors. Of course, it is the hope of each sponsor that Web surfers who come to their home page merely to earn the free points will then fully explore the Web site to learn more about the products and services offered. Initial sponsors in this innovative program included Shell U.K., UCI Cinemas, and Victoria Wine liquor stores. SMART program managers in Britain claimed that theirs was the first program anywhere in the world that promoted Web site visits with the frequency reward tactic, and they predicted that one day these "virtual" points may emerge as a new form of global currency. That being the case, perhaps Europe will forgo the Euro and find its new common currency in cyberspace.

Source: Suzanne Bidlake, "Loyalty Card Links with Web," *Advertising Age International,* January 1998, 40.

Demographic Characteristics. Information on the demographic characteristics of nations is generally available. Both the U.S. Department of Commerce and the United Nations publish annual studies of population for hundreds of countries. Advertisers must be sensitive to the demographic similarities and differences in international markets. The demographics of a population, including size of population, age distribution, income distribution, education levels, occupations, literacy rates, and household size, can dramatically affect the type of advertising prepared for a market. Large-scale demographic trends are important to advertisers. For example, those thinking of entering international markets should keep in mind that roughly 20 percent of the world's population, generally residing in the highly industrialized countries, controls 75 percent of the world's wealth and accounts for 75 percent of all consumption.[5]

While much has been written about the graying of the U.S. population, other parts of the world do not follow this pattern. In the Middle East, Africa, and Latin America, roughly 40 percent of the population is currently under the age of 20.[6] Increases and decreases in the proportion of the population in specific age groups are closely related to the demand for particular products and services. As populations continue to increase in developing countries, new market opportunities emerge for products and services for young families and teens. Similarly, as advanced-age groups continue to increase in countries with stable population rates, the demand for consumer products and services such as health care, travel services, and retirement planning will also increase.

One of the most interesting demographic evolutions is taking place in Asian countries. By the year 2010, an additional 400 million people will be born in the Pacific Rim region. In addition, in the year 2000, 30 percent of the population will be in their thirties and forties and will have migrated from rural to urban areas. In just 30 years, South Korea's population has flip-flopped to 73 percent urban from 72 percent rural.[7]

5.   Clive Cook, "Catching Up," in *The World in 1994* (special issue) *The Economist,* Winter 1993, 15–16.
6.   Adapted from Richard Sookdeo, "The New Global Consumer," *Fortune,* Autumn/Winter 1993, 68–79.
7.   Ford S. Worthy, "A New Mass Market Emerges," *Fortune,* Fall 1991.

Advertising messages must accommodate the new experiences of the now urban and middle-age audiences. In addition, advertising strategies must place ads in media that efficiently reach these audiences.

Values. Cultural values are enduring beliefs about what is important to the members of a culture. They are the defining bedrock of a culture. They are an outgrowth of the culture's history and its collective experience. (Even though there are many cultures within any given nation, many believe that there are still enough shared values to constitute a meaningful "national culture," like "American culture.") For example, the value of individualism enjoys a long and prominent place in American history and is considered by many to be a core American value. Other cultures seem to value the group or collective more. Even though a "collectivist" country like Japan may be becoming more individualistic, there is still a Japanese tradition that favors the needs of the group over those of the individual. In Japan, organizational loyalty and social interdependence are values that promote a group mentality. Japanese consumers are thus thought to be more sensitive to appeals that feature stability, longevity, and reliability, and they find appeals using competitive comparisons to be confrontational and inappropriate.[8]

Some researchers believe this continuum from individualism to collectivism to be a stable and dependably observed cultural difference among the peoples of the world. Exhibits 9.7 and 9.8 show two ads that appear to reflect this difference. The Scotch ad in Exhibit 9.7 shows an appeal to individualism; it ran in the United States. The IBM ad shown in Exhibit 9.8 reflects a collectivist approach; it is from Japan. Scotch whiskey certainly has a social component in actual use, and computers are not typically considered group products by Americans. But IBM appears to have adapted its message accordingly for advertising in a "collectivist" culture.[9]

Custom and Ritual. Among other things, rituals perpetuate a culture's connections to its core values. They seem perfectly natural to members of a culture, and they can often be performed without much thought (in some cases, hardly any) regarding their deeper meaning. Many consumer behaviors involve rituals, such as grooming, gift giving, or preparing food. To do a good job in cross-cultural advertising, the rituals of other cultures must be not only appreciated, but also understood. This requires in-depth and extended research efforts. Quick marketing surveys rarely do anything in this context, except invite disaster. Ignorance compounded by arrogance has unfortunately been the norm in both industry and academic research in this context.

One of the most devastating mistakes an advertiser can make is to presume that consumers in one culture have the same rituals as those in another. Religion is an obvious expression of values in a culture. In countries adhering to the precepts of the Islamic religion, which includes most Arab countries, traditional religious beliefs restrict several products from being advertised at all, such as alcohol and pork. Other restrictions related to religious and cultural values include not allowing women to appear in advertising and restricting the manner in which children can be portrayed in advertisements.[10] Each market must be evaluated for the extent to which prevalent customs or values translate into product choice and other consumer behaviors.

Understanding values and rituals can represent a special challenge (or opportunity) when economic development in a country or region creates tensions between the old and the new. The classic example is the dilemma that advertisers face as more wives leave the home for outside employment, creating tensions in the home about who should do the housework. Most recently, this tension over traditional gender assignments in household chores has been particularly acute in Asia, and advertisers there

8.   Johny Johansson, "The Sense of Nonsense: Japanese TV Advertising," *Journal of Advertising* (March 1994), 17–26.
9.   S. Han and S. Shavitt, "Persuasion and Culture: Advertising Appeals in Individualistic and Collectivistic Societies," *Journal of Experimental Social Psychology,* vol. 30 (1994), 326–350.
10. Marian Katz, "No Women, No Alcohol: Learn Saudi Taboos before Placing Ads," *International Advertiser* (February 1986), 11; Barbara Sundberg Baidpt, *International Advertising Handbook* (Boston: Lexington Books, 1989), 220–221.

EXHIBIT 9.7

Individualism is a core value in U.S. culture and is reflected by the message of this Johnnie Walker ad. In contrast, the IBM ad in Exhibit 9.8 appeals to the collectivist nature of Asian culture.

EXHIBIT 9.8

How does the IBM ad shown here underscore the collectivist values important to Japanese consumers? Even if you don't read Japanese, what is it about the ad that communicates these values right away?
www.ibm.com/

have tried to respond by featuring husbands as homemakers. For example, an ad for vacuum cleaners made by Korea's LG Electronics showed a woman lying on the floor exercising and giving herself a facial with slices of cucumbers, while her husband cleaned around her. The ad received mixed reviews from women in Hong Kong and South Korea, with younger women approving but their mothers disapproving.[11] (Sound familiar?) The advertiser's dilemma in situations like these is how to make ads that reflect real changes in a culture, without alienating important segments of consumers by appearing to push the changes. Not an easy task!

Product Use and Preferences. Information about product use and preferences is available for many markets. The major markets of North America, Europe, and the Pacific Rim typically are relatively heavily researched. In recent years, A. C. Nielsen has developed an international database on consumer product use in 26 countries. Also, Roper Starch Worldwide has conducted "global" studies on product preferences, brand loyalty, and price sensitivity in 40 different countries. The Roper Starch study revealed that consumers in India were the most brand loyal (34 percent of those surveyed), and that German and Japanese consumers showed the greatest tendency for price sensitivity (over 40 percent of survey consumers in each market).[12]

11.   Louise Lee, "Depicting Men Doing Housework Can Be Risky for Marketers in Asia," *Wall Street Journal,* August 14, 1998, B6.
12.   Leah Rickard, "Ex-Soviet States Lead World in Ad Cynicism," *Advertising Age,* May 5, 1995, 3.

Studies by firms such as Nielsen and Roper Starch do not dispute that consumers around the world display vastly different product use characteristics and preferences. One area of great variation is personal-care products. There is no market in the world like the United States, where consumers are preoccupied with the use of personal-care products such as toothpaste, shampoo, deodorant, and mouthwash. Procter & Gamble, maker of brands such as Crest, Pert, Secret, and Scope, among others, learned the hard way in Russia with its Wash & Go shampoo. Wash & Go (comparable to Pert in the United States) was a shampoo and conditioner designed for the consumer who prefers the ease, convenience, and speed of one-step washing and conditioning. Russian consumers, accustomed to washing their hair with bar soap, didn't understand the concept of a hair conditioner, and didn't perceive a need to make shampooing any more convenient.

Other examples of unique and culture-specific product uses and preferences come from Brazil and France. In Brazil, many women still wash clothes by hand in metal tubs, using cold water. Because of this behavior, Unilever must specially formulate its Umo laundry powder and tout its effectiveness under these washing conditions.

In France, men use cosmetics much like those used by women in the United States. Advertising must, therefore, be specifically prepared for men and placed in media to reach them with specific male-oriented appeals. As another example, Exhibit 9.9 shows an ad directed toward French women—some of whom are relatively less accustomed (compared to women in the United States) to shaving their legs and underarms—for a razor designed for just such a purpose. The ad uses both pictures and text to promote the behavior. Perhaps no less ambitious is the attempt to sell canned paella to the culinary-proud French, illustrated in Exhibit 9.10.

The Challenges in Executing Advertising Worldwide. Cross-cultural audience research on basic economic, social, and cultural conditions is an essential starting point for planning international advertising. But even with excellent audience analysis, three formidable and unique challenges face the advertiser: the creative challenge, the media challenge, and the regulatory challenge.

The Creative Challenge. Written or spoken language is a basic barrier to cross-cultural communication. Ads written in German are typically difficult for those who speak only Arabic—this much is obvious. We've all heard stories of how some literal translation of an ad said something very different than what was intended. For example, when Sunbeam introduced the Mist-Stick mixer into the German market, the firm ran into a fairly severe language problem. The word *Mist* spelled and pronounced precisely the same way in German means "manure." The word *Stick* translates roughly as "wand." Sunbeam was attempting to introduce a "manure wand" for use in German food preparation.[13]

What is less obvious, however, is the role of **picturing** in cross-cultural communication. There is a widely held belief that pictures are less culturally bound than are words, and that pictures can speak to many cultures at once. International advertisers are increasingly using ads that feature few words and rely on pictures to communicate. This is, as you might expect, a bit more complicated than it sounds.

First, picturing *is* culturally bound. Different cultures use different conventions or rules to create representations (or pictures) of things. Pictures, just like words, must be "read" or interpreted, and the "rules of reading" pictures vary from culture to culture. People living in Western cultures assume that everyone knows what a certain picture means. This is not true and is another example of ethnocentrism. Photographic two-dimensional representations are not even recognizable as pictures to those who have

13. David Ricks, *Big Business Blunders: Mistakes in Multi-National Marketing* (Homewood, Ill.: Dow Jones–Irwin, 1983), 66.

EXHIBIT 9.9

It's been said that "all politics are local," but so too is personal hygiene. The United Kingdom's Wilkinson might encounter difficulties in selling its Lady Protector, specifically designed for shaving women's legs and underarms, in France, a country where that has generally not been less common. The company's Web site (www.wilkinson-sword.com) is admirably multilingual, though, appealing to British, French and Germans (alas, as hirsute as the French, traditionally). Might Wilkinson have done better to have "Americanized" a Web site as well?

EXHIBIT 9.10

Advertisers need to be sensitive to the product use and preferences prevalent in a market. A good example is Exhibit 9.10: Here, Garbit is offering canned paella to the French—an unlikely product preference for a culinary-proud audience.

not learned to interpret such representations. Symbolic representations that seem so absolute, common, and harmless in one culture can have varied, unusual, and even threatening meaning in another. A picture may be worth a thousand words, but those words may not mean something appropriate—or they may be entirely unintelligible or tasteless—to those in another culture. Think about the ads in Exhibits 9.11 to 9.14. Which of these ads seem culture bound? Which would seem to easily cross cultural borders? Why?

All of these ads depend on knowing the way to correctly interpret the ad, but some require more cultural knowledge than others. For example, if the audience doesn't know the story of the dish that ran away with the spoon, then the Oneida ad in Exhibit 9.13 is probably not as engaging as it otherwise might be. Do you have to know who Tiny Tim was to understand the ad for Kenwood? What does giving a rose mean in other cultures? Is a big bare belly going to reflect the same level of status in Germany, India, and Argentina?

A few human expressions, such as a smile, are widely accepted to mean a positive feeling. Such expressions and their representations, even though culturally connected, have widespread commonality. But cultureless picture meanings do not exist. A much larger contributor to cross-cultural commonalities are those representations that are a part of a far-flung culture of commerce and have thus taken on similar meanings in

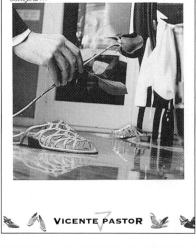

EXHIBITS 9.11 TO 9.14

Which of these ads seem most bound to their national cultures, based on the pictures used in the ads? Which feature pictures that are less culturally bound? www.kenwoodcorp .com/, www.oneida .com/, *and* www .airbus.com/

many different nations. With sports playing an ever-larger role in international commerce, the sports hero is often used to symbolize common meaning across cultural boundaries. What do you think? Is Michael Jordan Michael Jordan, no matter what he is selling, or where he is selling it?[14]

The Media Challenge.
Of all the challenges faced by advertisers in international markets, the media challenge may be the greatest. Exhibit 9.15 shows many of the traditional media options for reaching consumers around the world.

Media Availability and Coverage.
Some international markets simply have too few media options. In addition, even if diverse media are available in a particular international market, there may be severe restrictions on the type of advertising that can be done or the way in which advertising is organized in a certain medium.

Many countries have dozens of subcultures and language dialects within their borders, each with its own newspapers and radio stations. This complicates the problem of deciding which combination of newspapers or radio stations will achieve the desired coverage of the market. The presence of a particular medium in a country does not necessarily make it useful for advertisers if there are restrictions on accepting advertising. The most prominent example is the BBC networks in the United Kingdom, where advertising is still not accepted. While the UK does have commercial networks in both radio and television, the BBC stations are still widely popular. Or consider the situation with regard to television advertising in Germany and The Netherlands. On the German government-owned stations, television advertising is banned on Sundays and holidays and restricted to four five-minute blocks on other days. In The Netherlands, television advertising cannot constitute more than 5 percent of total programming time, and most time slots must be purchased nearly a year in advance. Similar circumstances exist in many markets around the world.

Newspapers are actually the most localized medium worldwide, and they require the greatest amount of local market knowledge to be correctly used as an advertising option. In Mexico, for example, advertising space is sold in the form of news columns, without any notice or indication that the "story" is a paid advertisement. This situation influences both the placement and layout of ads. Turkey has more than 350 daily national newspapers; The Netherlands has only three. Further, many newspapers (particularly regional papers) are positioned in the market based on a particular political philosophy. Advertisers must be aware of this, making certain that their brand's position with the target audience does not conflict with the politics of the medium.

The best news for advertisers from the standpoint of media availability and coverage is the emergence of several global television networks made possible by satellite technology. Viacom bills its combined MTV Networks (MTVN) as the largest TV network in the world, with a capability to reach over 300 million households worldwide.[15] MTVN not only can provide media access, but also offers expertise in developing special promotions to Generations X, Y, and Z around the world. MTVN has facilitated international campaigns for global brands such as Pepsi, Swatch, Sega, and BMX Bikes.[16] CNN, the worldwide news network, can be seen in 100 countries and specifically offers newly acquired access to the vast Indian market.[17]

Another development affecting Europe and Asia is direct broadcast by satellite (DBS). DBS transmissions are received by households through a small, low-cost receiving dish. STAR TV, which stands for Satellite Televisions Asian Region, currently sends BBC and U.S. programming to 17 million Asian households and hotels. Ultimately, STAR TV could reach 3 billion people, making it the most widely viewed medium in

14. Roger O. Crockett, "Yikes! Mike Takes a Hike," *Business Week,* January 25, 1999, 74–76.

15. "On-Air Opportunities," *Television Business International,* vol. 49 (January 1998), 1.

16. Ibid.

17. Todd Pruzan, "Global Media: Distribution Slows but Rates Climb," *Advertising Age International,* January 16, 1995, I–19; "India Will Allow CNN Broadcasts," July 12, 1995, 9.

EXHIBIT 9.15

Advertising Age International's *global media lineup.*

Media	Ownership	Circulation or Number of Households
PRINT		
Business Week	The McGraw-Hill Cos.	1.08 million
Computerworld/InfoWorld	IDG	1.9 million
The Economist	The Economist Group	684,416
Elle	Hachette Filipacchi	5.1 million
Elle Deco	Hachette Filipacchi	1.5 million
Financial Times	Pearson PLC	363,525
Forbes Global Business & Finance	Forbes	860,000**
Fortune	Time Warner	915,000
Harvard Business Review	Harvard Business School Publishing	220,000
International Herald Tribune	The New York Times/ The Washington Post Co.	222,930
National Geographic	National Geographic Society	8.8 million
Newsweek Worldwide	The Washington Post Co.	4.2 million
PC World	IDG	3.6 million
Reader's Digest	Reader's Digest Association	26 million
Scientific American	Yerlagsgruppe Hoitzbrinck	562,150
TIME	Time Warner	5.6 million
USA Today International	Gennett Co.	2.2 million† (Mon.–Thurs.) 2.6 million (Friday edition)
The Wall Street Journal	Dow Jones & Co.	4.3 million
TV		
Animal Planet	Discovery Communications/BBC	4.9 million*
BBC World	BBC Worldwide	60 million
Cartoon Network	Time Warner	125.5 million
CNBC	NBC/Dow Jones & Co. (only 100% NBC-owned in U.S.)	136 million**
CNN International	Time Warner	221 million
Discovery Networks International	Discovery Communications	144 million
ESPN	Walt Disney Co./Hearst Corp.	242 million
MTV Networks	Viacom	285 million
TNT	Time Warner	104.2 million

*Includes 45 million homes in the United States
**Excludes Latin America
†For international edition only

Source: *Advertising Age International*, February 8, 1999, 23.

EXHIBIT 9.16

Direct broadcast by satellite allows households to receive television transmissions via a small, low-cost receiving dish. This is an ad for Skyport TV promoting its satellite service in the Asian market.

the world.[18] An ad for one of STAR TV's partners in the Asian market is shown in Exhibit 9.16.

Additionally, global expansion of the Internet may one day offer advertisers economical access to huge new markets. But that day has yet to arrive. As described in the New Media box on page 284, it would be inappropriate to presume that the Internet is equally accessible or equally important to consumers in various parts of the world. (See Chapter 17.)

Media Costs and Pricing. Confounding the media challenge is the issue of media costs and pricing. As discussed earlier, some markets have literally hundreds of media options (recall the 350 Turkish newspapers). Whenever a different medium is chosen, separate payment and placement must be made. Additionally, in many markets, media prices are subject to negotiation—no matter what the official rate cards say. The time needed to negotiate these rates is a tremendous cost in and of itself.

Global coverage is an expensive proposition. For example, a four-color ad in *Reader's Digest* costs nearly half a million dollars.[19] Should the advertiser desire to achieve full impact in *Reader's Digest,* then the ad should be prepared in all 20 of the different languages for the international editions—again, generating substantial expense.

Exhibit 9.17 provides a nice summary of advertising expenditures in different media around the world, and documents that ad spending is on the rise just

EXHIBIT 9.17

Summary of world advertising expenditures. Figures are in millions of U.S. dollars.

Major Media*	1996	1997	1998	1999	2000
North America	105,569	112,583	118,904	124,898	131,167
Europe	72,923	78,606	83,421	87,700	92,165
Asia/Pacific	61,702	67,226	67,226	70,362	73,996
Latin America	21,051	24,214	26,741	29,614	33,127
Africa/M East	5,281	6,123	6,809	7,570	8,437
Sub Total	**266,525**	**288,751**	**303,100**	**320,143**	**338,891**
Direct Mail					
North America	31,990	33,621	35,303	37,107	38,888
Europe	29,786	31,395	32,996	34,613	36,274
Japan	2,711	2,860	2,969	3,082	3,165
Miscellaneous Media**					
USA	33,369	35,037	36,789	38,592	40,367
Japan	10,052	10,605	11,008	11,426	11,735
Total	**374,434**	**402,269**	**422,165**	**444,962**	**469,320**

*TV, Print, Radio, Cinema, and Outdoor
**Includes point-of-sale/sales promotion expenditure
Source: *Advertising Expenditures Forecast* (Zenith Media, July 1998).

18. Thomas McCarroll, "New Star over Asia," *Time,* August 9, 1993, 53.
19. Pruzan, *op. cit.*

about everywhere. Both ad rates and the demand for ad space are on the increase. In some markets, advertising time and space are in such short supply that, regardless of the published rate, a bidding system is used to escalate the prices. As you will see in Chapter 14, media costs represent the majority of costs in an advertising budget. With the seemingly chaotic buying practices in some international markets, media costs are indeed a great challenge in executing cost-effective advertising campaigns.

The Regulatory Challenge. The regulatory restrictions on international advertising are many and varied, reflecting diverse cultural values, market by market. The range and specificity of regulation can be aggravatingly complex. Tobacco and liquor advertising are restricted (typically banned from television) in many countries, although several lift their ban on liquor after 9 or 10 P.M. With respect to advertising to children, Austria, Canada, Germany, and the United States have specific regulations. Other products and topics monitored or restricted throughout the world are drugs (Austria, Switzerland, Germany, Greece, and The Netherlands), gambling (United Kingdom, Italy, and Portugal), and religion (Germany, United Kingdom, and The Netherlands).

This regulatory complexity, if anything, continues to grow. For instance, the European Union has proposed restrictions for the placement of advertising on teleshopping, pay-per-view, and movie-on-demand channels.[20] Generally, advertisers must be sensitive to the fact that advertising regulations can, depending on the international market, impose limitations on the following:

- The types of products that can be advertised
- The types of appeals that can be used
- The times during which ads for certain products can appear on television
- Advertising to children
- The use of foreign languages (and talent) in advertisements
- The use of national symbols, such as flags and government seals, in advertisements
- The taxes levied against advertising expenditures

In short, just about every aspect of advertising can be regulated, and every country has its own peculiarities with respect to ad regulation. More examples of the regulatory differences among nations are featured in Exhibit 9.18.

Advertising Agencies around the World.

An experienced and astute agency can help an advertiser deal with the creative, media, and regulatory challenges just discussed. In Brazil, using a local agency is essential to get the creative style and tone just right. In Australia, Australian nationals must be involved in certain parts of the production process. And in China, trying to work through the government and media bureaucracy is nearly impossible without the assistance of a local agency.

Advertisers in the United States have three basic alternatives in choosing an agency to help them prepare and place advertising in other countries: They can use a global agency, an international affiliate, or a local agency.

The Global Agency. The consolidation and mergers taking place in the advertising industry are creating more and more **global agencies**, or worldwide agencies. Most of these global advertising organizations continue to show healthy revenue growth, as advertisers attempt to extend their reach to consumers worldwide. As you might expect, New York, London, Tokyo, Chicago, and Paris have become the advertising capitals of the world.

The great advantage of a global agency is that it will know the advertiser's products and current advertising programs (presuming it handles the domestic adver-

20. Bruce Crumley, "EU Proposal May Limit TV Spots," *Advertising Age,* January 9, 1995, 12.

EXHIBIT 9.18

Sample advertising regulations around the world.

United Kingdom	No television advertising for cigarettes, politics, hypnotists, gambling, religion, or charities. The Independent Broadcasting Authority (IBA) carefully monitors television advertising for "appropriateness." Recently, the major independent television network, ITV, has decided to start running liquor ads. This reverses a long-standing policy.[1]
France	No television advertising for tobacco, alcohol, margarine, or diet products. Tourism outside the country cannot be promoted. Children may be used only in ads for children's products. Supermarket advertising is discouraged (though not illegal) for fear that traditional food shops will suffer.
Germany	There are several volumes of regulation published by the German Advertising Federation (ZAW). Advertising cannot instill fear or promote superstition or discrimination. Children may not be used to promote products. Product claims must be carefully documented. No television advertising for cigarettes, religion, charities, narcotics, or prescription drugs. No advertising of any kind for war-related toys. The German regulatory system can act swiftly and effectively. An advertising campaign (for the Italian clothing firm Benetton) that featured child laborers and an oil-soaked seabird was deemed morally offensive because it exploited "pity for commercial purposes." The ads were immediately banned from print publication.[2]
Italy	Italy is one of the few international markets in which comparative ads are allowed. Testimonial statements must be authenticated. No television advertising for cigarettes, gambling, jewels, furs, clinics, or hospitals.
Sweden	Regulatory constraints in Sweden are hard to pin down. First, the two government-controlled television stations and the three government-controlled radio stations do not accept advertising. The independent media are just starting to evolve within the country, and cable broadcasts are being sent from outside the country. The Swedes do not allow the use of young, attractive models in cigarette advertising.
Brazil	Price advertising is carefully regulated by the Brazilian government. Restrictions on television advertising include no advertising for alcohol, cigarettes, or cigars until after 9 P.M. Nudity in Brazilian ads is unregulated. The Brazilian government is committed to economic growth, and the new, more stable currency is causing tremendous change in the consumption culture. While there are good markets for many U.S. goods, Brazilians frown on ads made by U.S. agencies.
Australia	Restrictions on Australian advertising are fairly basic, with one major exception—the Australian government has mandated that 80 percent of all advertising running in Australia must be created by Australian companies. Deception is subject to regulation. Cigarettes are banned from television advertising.
Japan	For a country of strict rules and regulations, there is much flexibility in the interpretation of advertising regulation—with the exception of comparison and hard-sell advertising. As long as good taste prevails, nudity is permitted. There are no laws governing the use of a product by a spokesperson. The one area of high scrutiny is exaggeration of claims.
China	As we have seen recently with copyright infringement and intellectual property disputes, the regulatory system for commercial transactions in China is still in a state of infancy. The "regulation" of advertising has much more to do with understanding traditions and complying with standard business practice. For example, many media organizations will discriminate against advertisers who use an agency, in an attempt to circumvent agency commissions. Some have been known to refuse to execute a media plan submitted by an agency. Specific restrictions are placed on comparative ads and "slanderous propaganda."

1. Laurel Wentz, "UK TV to Accept Liquor Ads," *Advertising Age,* June 5, 1995, 8.
2. Brandon Mitchener, "German Court Rules against Benetton," *International Herald Tribune,* July 7, 1995, 13.

NEWS FLASH: WORLD WIDE WEB NOT WORLDWIDE

The race is on: AT&T has signed on a dozen of the 30 or so nations it needs to launch Africa One, a $2 billion underwater fiber-optic cable network that surrounds the African continent and connects constituent nations to one another and to the World Wide Web. Meanwhile, the 15-year-old Pan African News Agency has taken a wireless approach and plans to expand a skeleton satellite network that currently allows bureaus in 13 African nations to send and receive articles instantly. Someday soon, we may freely converse online with our African cousins and welcome them to the cyberfold. Or maybe not. In many regions of sub-Saharan Africa, some 90 percent of individuals have never placed a phone call, let alone connected to the Net via a modem. Even in Africa's most developed nation, South Africa, the stated priorities do not include networks and interactivity. President Nelson Mandela frequently lists the hierarchy of needs for his country, such as basic medical care, schooling, fresh water, and electricity, without mention of either computers or telephones.

By contrast, one might expect that a highly industrialized country such as Japan would be fully plugged into the World Wide Web. Yes and no. While to be sure, Web development in Japan is far beyond that of the African continent, it is nowhere near the stage taken for granted in the United States. The Internet only began to catch on in Japan in 1994, with the lifting of previous restrictions and regulations by the Japanese government. With a population of 126 million people in 1998, Japan had only 8.5 million Internet users. And only about half of these had browsers that could access the Web, with the other half being members of self-contained systems. Additionally, the Web continues to lack cultural diversity, and the overwhelming majority of Web sites are in English. Obviously, if you can't read English, the Web will be less useful to you. Moreover, local phone charges are very expensive in Japan, and up until recently the Japanese government did not permit yen-based credit card transactions on the Web. While the barriers to the Web's advancement in Japan are certainly less severe than those in Africa, there are barriers just the same.

So while the Web's influence continues to grow around the world, the fact that we call it "World Wide" is probably a nice example of U.S. ethnocentrism. We see the world as we see ourselves . . .

Sources: "Builders of Info-Highway Hope to Reshape Priorities in Africa," *Wall Street Journal,* June 9, 1995, B5; "Web's Heavy U.S. Accent Grates on Overseas Ears," *Wall Street Journal,* September 26, 1996, B4; "Report from Tokyo," *Marketing News,* May 25, 1998, 2.

tising duties). With this knowledge, the agency can either adapt domestic campaigns for international markets or launch entirely new campaigns. Another advantage is the geographic proximity of the advertiser to the agency headquarters, which can often facilitate planning and preparation of ads. The size of a global agency can be a benefit in terms of economies of scale and political leverage.

Their greatest disadvantage stems from their distance from the local culture. Exporting meaning is never easy. This is no small disadvantage to agencies that actually believe they can do this. Most, however, are not that naive or arrogant (some are), and they have procedures for acquiring local knowledge.

The International Affiliate.

Many agencies do not own and operate worldwide offices, but rather have established foreign-market **international affiliates** to handle clients' international advertising needs. Many times these agencies join a network of foreign agencies or take minority ownership positions in several foreign agencies. The benefit of this arrangement is that the advertiser typically has access to a large number of international agencies that can provide local market expertise. These international agencies are usually well established and managed by foreign nationals, which gives the advertiser a local presence in the international market, while avoiding any resistance to foreign ownership. This was the reasoning behind Coca-Cola's decision to give local creative responsibility for advertising its Coke Classic brand in Europe to the French agency Publicis SA.[21]

Although Coke Classic is a global brand, Coke felt that the French agency was better suited to adapt U.S. ad campaigns for European use.

The risk of these arrangements is that while an international affiliate will know the local market, it may be less knowledgeable about the advertiser's brands and competi-

21. Daniel Tilles, "Publicist Gets a Sip of Coke Account," *International Herald Tribune,* July 7, 1995, 13.

tive strategy. The threat is that the real value and relevance of the brand will not be incorporated into the foreign campaign.

The Local Agency. The final option is for an advertiser to choose a **local agency** in every foreign market where advertising will be carried out. Local agencies have the same advantages as the affiliate agencies just discussed: They will be knowledgeable about the culture and local market conditions. Such agencies tend to have well-established contacts for market information, production, and media buys. But the advertiser that chooses this option is open to administrative problems. There is less tendency for standardization of the creative effort; each agency in each market will feel compelled to provide a unique creative execution. This lack of standardization can be expensive, and potentially disastrous for brand imagery when the local agency seeks to make its own creative statement without a good working knowledge of a brand's heritage.[22] Finally, working with local agencies can create internal communication problems, which increases the risk of delays and errors in execution.

Globalized versus Localized Campaigns.

One additional issue must be resolved. This key issue involves the extent to which a campaign will be standardized versus localized across markets. In discussions of this issue, the question is often posed as, How much can the advertiser globalize the advertising? **Globalized campaigns** use the same message and creative execution across all (or most) international markets. Exhibits 9.19 and 9.20 show ads from Jack Daniel's globalized campaign. By contrast, **localized campaigns** involve preparing different messages and creative executions for each market a firm has entered.

The issue is more complex than simply a question of globalized versus localized advertising. Both the brand and its overall marketing strategy must be examined. The marketer must first consider the extent to which the brand can be standardized across markets, and then the extent to which the advertising can be globalized across markets. The degree to which advertising in international markets can use a common appeal, versus whether the ads prepared for each market must be customized, has been a widely debated issue.

Those who favor the globalized campaign assume that similarities as well as differences between markets should be taken into account. They argue that standardization of messages should occur whenever possible, adapting the message only when absolutely necessary. For example, Mars's U.S. advertisements for Pedigree dog food have used golden retrievers, while poodles were deemed more effective for the brand's positioning and image in Asia. Otherwise, the advertising campaigns were identical in terms of basic message appeal.[23]

Those who argue for the localized approach see each country or region as a unique communication context, and they claim that the only way to achieve advertising success is to develop separate campaigns for each market.

The two fundamental arguments for globalized campaigns are based on potential cost savings and creative advantages. Just as organizations seek to gain economies of scale in production, they also look for opportunities to streamline the communication process. Having one standard theme to communicate allows an advertiser to focus on a uniform brand or corporate image worldwide, develop plans more quickly, and make maximum use of good ideas. Thus, while Gillette sells hundreds of different products in more than 200 countries around the world, its corporate philosophy of globalization is

22. Leon E. Wynter, "Global Marketers Learn to Say No to Bad Ads," *Wall Street Journal,* April 1, 1998, B1.
23. Zachary Schiller and Rischar A. Melcher, "Marketing Globally, Thinking Locally," *International Business Week,* May 13, 1991, 23.

Clockwise from top left, that's Jack Daniel, Jess Motlow, Lem Tolley, Frank Bobo and Jess Gamble. (Jimmy's in the middle).

JACK DANIEL'S HEAD DISTILLER, Jimmy Bedford, has lots of folks looking over his shoulder.

Since 1866, we've had only six head distillers. (Every one a Tennessee boy, starting with Mr. Jack Daniel himself.) Like those before him, Jimmy's mindful of our traditions, such as the oldtime way we smooth our whiskey through 10 feet of hard maple charcoal. He knows Jack Daniel's drinkers will judge him with every sip. So he's not about to change a thing. The five gentlemen on his wall surely must be pleased about that.

SMOOTH SIPPIN'
TENNESSEE WHISKEY

Tennessee Whiskey • 40-43% alcohol by volume (80-86 proof) • Distilled and Bottled by
Jack Daniel Distillery, Lem Motlow, Proprietor, Route 1, Lynchburg (Pop 361), Tennessee 37352
Placed in the National Register of Historic Places by the United States Government.

飲酒は20歳を過ぎてから

洞穴に湧くこの水と樽を世話するリチャード・マギー。
それは、テネシーの自然が育んでくれた2つの驚異だ。
ジャック・ダニエル蒸溜所の谷間では、ピュアで鉄分を含まない水が、洞穴の泉から
何百万年もの間、湧き続けている。ウイスキーづくりに理想的なその水を
すくっているのが、マギー。洞穴の泉ほどではないが、誰よりも古くから、
誰よりも多く、樽をころがし、ウイスキーの世話を続けている名人だ。
まだ、味わっていない方は、ぜひ、ご一飲を。
テネシーの2つの驚異なしには生まれなかったジャック・ダニエルの
格別な滑らかさを、きっと確かめていただけるに違いない。

JACK DANIEL'S
TENNESSEE WHISKEY
テネシーウイスキー ジャック・ダニエル
容量750ml・4,600円 希望小売価格(消費税込み) 輸入・販売サントリー株式会社

EXHIBITS 9.19 AND 9.20

Globalized advertising campaigns maintain a highly similar look and feel across international markets. These Jack Daniel's ads from the United States and Japan demonstrate how a global brand can use a global campaign. Can you identify the common themes used in these two ads?
www.jackdaniels.com/

expressed in its "Gillette—the Best a Man Can Get" theme. This theme is attached to all ads for men's toiletry products, wherever they appear.[24]

In recent years, several aspects of the global marketplace have changed in such a way that the conditions for globalized campaigns are more favorable. Specifically, these conditions fostering the use of such campaigns are as follows:[25]

- *Global communications.* Worldwide cable and satellite networks have resulted in television becoming a truly global communications medium. MTV's 200 European advertisers almost all run English-language-only campaigns in the station's 28-nation broadcast area. These standardized messages will themselves serve to homogenize the viewers within these market areas.
- *The global teenager.* Global communications, global travel, and the demise of communism are argued to have created common norms and values among teenagers

24. Bill Saporito, "Where the Global Action Is," *Fortune,* Autumn/Winter 1993, 63; Mark Maremont, "Gillette Finally Reveals Its Vision of the Future, and It Has 3 Blades," *Wall Street Journal,* April 14, 1998, A1, A10.
25. This list is adapted from Henry Assael, *Consumer Behavior and Marketing Action,* 5th ed. (Cincinnati, Ohio: South-Western/International Thomson Publishing, 1995), 491–494.

around the world. One advertising agency videotaped the rooms of teenagers from 25 countries, and it was hard to tell whether the room belonged to an American, German, or Japanese teen. The rooms had soccer balls, Levi jeans, NBA jackets, and Sega video games.[26] In response to such similarity, Swatch has created a worldwide campaign aimed at teenagers that uses the same image in all international markets and merely changes the copy in print ads to adapt to language differences.

- *Universal demographic and lifestyle trends.* Demographic and lifestyle trends that emerged in the 1980s in the United States are manifesting themselves in markets around the world. More working women, more single-person households, increasing divorce rates, and fewer children per household are now widespread demographic phenomena that are affecting lifestyles. The rising number of working women in Japan caused Ford Motor Company to prepare ads specifically targeted to this audience.

- *The Americanization of consumption values.* Perhaps of greatest advantage to U.S. advertisers is the Americanization of consumption values around the world. American icons are gaining popularity worldwide, especially due to the exportation of pop culture fueled by the U.S. entertainment industry. This trend has become so pervasive that some countries are seeking ways to shield themselves from U.S. entertainment exports. A recent meeting of culture ministers from 19 nations, including Canada, Britain, Mexico and Sweden, discussed proposals for exempting cultural "products" from international free-trade pacts. The ultimate target of this discussion by these czars of local culture was undeniably "Made in the USA" entertainment products.[27]

All of these forces are creating an environment where a common message across national boundaries becomes more possible. To the extent that consumers in various countries hold the same interests and values, "standardized" images and themes can be effective in advertising.

Arguments against globalization tend to center on issues relating to local market requirements and cultural constraints within markets. The target audiences in different countries must understand and place the same level of importance on brand features or attributes for a globalized campaign to be effective. In many cases, different features are valued at different levels of intensity, making a common message inappropriate. Also, if a globalized campaign defies local customs, values, and regulations, or if it ignores the efforts of local competition, then it has little chance of being successful.

It is sometimes the case that local managers do not appreciate the value of globalized campaigns. Since they did not help create the campaign, they may drag their feet in implementing it. Without the support of local managers, no globalized campaign can ever achieve its potential.

Developing global brands through standardized campaigns can be successful only when advertisers can find similar needs, feelings, or emotions as a basis for communication across cultures. Creating culture-free ads is an impossibility, but the global marketer may be able to draw upon enough commonality to be effective.

Finally, global marketers need to distinguish between strategy and execution when using a global approach to advertising. The basic need identified may well be universal, but communication about the product or service that offers satisfaction of the need may be strongly influenced by cultural values in different markets and thus may work against globalization. Recall the example of AT&T's "Reach Out and Touch Someone" campaign. The campaign was highly successful in the United States in communicating the universal need to keep in touch with loved ones, but it was viewed by European audiences as too sentimental in style and execution. For another example, take a look at Exhibit 9.21. What do you think of this Italian ad for Yokohama tires? Would it play in Peoria?

---

26. Shawn Tully, "Teens: The Most Global Market of All," *Fortune,* May 16, 1994, 90.
27. Terry Teachout, "Cultural Protectionism," *Wall Street Journal,* July 10, 1998, W11.

EXHIBIT 9.21

Using standardized campaigns for global brands is difficult. This Italian Yokohama ad (www.yokohamatire.com) may suit Italian sensibilities, but how will it play in Peoria? Many American tire ads stress safety (e.g., the ad showing a baby securely nestled in a solid, sensible tire), and performance in adverse weather, not a torrid romance with the road. Might this be a consequence of differences in who buys tires? When both mom and dad drive (and take for service) their own cars, the whole of the family's considerations come into play.

SUMMARY

Explain the types of audience research that are useful for understanding cultural barriers that can interfere with effective communication.

All of us wear cultural blinders, and as a result we must overcome substantial barriers in trying to communicate with people from other countries. This is a major problem for international advertisers as they seek to promote their brands around the world. To overcome this problem and avoid errors in advertising planning, cross-cultural audience analysis is needed. Such analyses involve evaluation of economic conditions, demographic characteristics, customs, values, rituals, and product use and preferences in the target countries.

Identify three distinctive challenges that complicate the execution of advertising in international settings.

Worldwide advertisers face three distinctive challenges in executing their campaigns. The first of these is a creative challenge that derives from differences in experience and meaning among cultures. Even the pictures featured in an ad may be translated differently from one country to the next. Media availability, media coverage, and media costs vary dramatically around the world, adding a second complication to international advertising. Finally, the amount and nature of advertising regulation vary dramatically from country to country and may force a complete reformulation of an ad campaign.

Describe the three basic types of advertising agencies that can assist in the placement of advertising around the world.

Advertising agencies provide marketers with the expertise needed to develop and execute advertising campaigns in international markets. Marketers can choose to work with global agencies, local agencies in the targeted market, or an international affiliate of the agency they use in their home country. Each of these agency types brings different advantages and disadvantages on evaluative dimensions such as geographic proximity, economies of scale, political leverage, awareness of the client's strategy, and knowledge of the local culture.

Discuss the advantages and disadvantages of globalized versus localized advertising campaigns.

A final concern for international advertising entails the degree of customization an advertiser should attempt in campaigns designed to cross national boundaries. Globalized campaigns involve little customization among countries, whereas localized campaigns feature heavy customization for each market. Standardized messages bring tremendous cost savings and create a common brand image worldwide, but they may miss the mark with consumers in different nations. As consumers around the world become more similar, globalized campaigns are likely to become more prevalent. Teenagers in many countries share similar values and lifestyles and thus make a natural target for globalized campaigns.

KEY TERMS

international advertising (266)
ethnocentrism (270)
self-reference criterion (SRC) (270)
less-developed countries (271)
newly industrialized countries (272)
highly industrialized countries (272)

picturing (276)
global agencies (282)
international affiliates (284)
local agency (285)
globalized campaigns (285)
localized campaigns (285)

QUESTIONS FOR REVIEW AND CRITICAL THINKING

1. Coca-Cola is one of the world's best-known brands and most successful global marketers. Given this state of affairs, why would Pepsi challenge Coke's dominant position in Brazil? Is Pepsi using a globalized or localized campaign in Brazil?

2. In this chapter we discuss the challenges advertisers face in Asia when it comes to representing husbands and wives in ads for products such as laundry detergents and vacuum cleaners. Why is this a challenging issue in Asia today? Would you expect that advertisers face this same challenge in other parts of the world? Where?

3. If you were creating a media strategy for a global advertising campaign, what emphasis would you put on newspapers in executing your strategy? What factors complicate their value for achieving broad market coverage?

4. Explain the appeal of new media options such as direct broadcast by satellite and the World Wide Web for marketers who have created globalized advertising campaigns.

5. Compare and contrast the advantages of global versus local ad agencies for implementing international advertising.

6. Identify several factors or forces that make consumers around the world more similar to one another. Conversely, what factors or forces create diversity among consumers in different countries?

7. Teens and retired people are two market segments found worldwide. If these two segments of European consumers were each being targeted for new advertising campaigns, which one would be most responsive to a globalized ad campaign? Why?

EXPERIENTIAL EXERCISES

1. As discussed in the chapter, it is extremely important to understand cultural differences before developing advertising for foreign countries. For example, personal-care products seem to be a preoccupation of consumers in the United States. Write a report on how consumers in Russia, Brazil, and France appear to differ from their u.s. counterparts when it comes to the use of personal-care products. Explain how these differences will affect American advertisers developing ads for personal-care products in these countries. You may wish to talk with someone who

is familiar with advertising in these countries, or go to the university or local library and browse through consumer magazines published in these countries to see which products are being advertised and which are not.

2. Go to the Internet and search for information on emerging markets, like Hungary and Poland. Gather data off the Web on these markets that would be useful for international advertising planning.

USING THE INTERNET

A company's advertising efforts may be globalized or largely localized, and advertising agencies also operate on both global and local scales. Visit the sites for Gitam International (www.gitam.co.za) and Chiat/Day (www.chiatday.com/).

1.   Which agency appears to be more global? What aspects of each site give you this impression?

2.   If you owned a business that operates exclusively in South Africa and were seeking an advertising agency, which would you choose? What is it about the agency that has influenced your decision? How would your answers change if your South African-based business operated on a global scale?

    Visit the IBM site (www.ibm.com/).

3.   How is this site both globalized and localized?

4.   Are all messages communicated in English, or in other languages as well? What effect do you think the Web will have on English as the universal language?

Early online provider Prodigy was crushed in its original U.S. market by America Online and hundreds of other large and small Internet service providers. Prodigy arose, like the Phoenix, by diversifying into niche businesses, including targeting specific, underserved foreign markets, most notably, in the People's Republic of China (www .prodigychina.com).

1.   How does the Prodigy China Web site (a joint venture with Sino Telecom) handle the two languages?

2.   Is English this site's "first language"?

3.   What particular problems might one encounter in working with both a Latin alphabet, and a calligraphically-based language like Chinese?

FROM PRINCIPLES to Practice:

A COMPREHENSIVE IMC CASE

PART II
Planning Integrated Marketing Communications for the Launch of Cincinnati Bell Wireless

There is nothing new about planning promotional efforts around a mix of different promotional tools. Depending on a firm's objectives, different tools and different combinations of tools may be used. For example, TV advertising is relied on more heavily for establishing brand awareness; sales promotions are used to cause short-term spikes in demand; direct marketing is used to motivate action from a well-defined target audience; and public relations can help a firm manage media reports about its activities.

This range of promotional devices and their application under different conditions is common. But the planning of integrated marketing communications goes beyond merely using the right tool under the right conditions. Strategic planning for IMC is distinguished from the traditional use of multiple promotional tools by four important factors:[1]

- *An outside-in approach is used to plan communications.* Traditionally, communications have been planned from the inside out; that is, firms have historically begun the planning process by setting communications goals that fulfill brand and/or corporate information or differentiation objectives. In planning IMC, a firm starts with the customer or prospect and works backward, identifying what the customer deems important information. This outside-in approach helps ensure that the customer gets information when and how she or he wants it, rather than when and in what form the firm deems appropriate.
- *IMC planning requires comprehensive and detailed knowledge about customers and prospects.* IMC programs are more database driven than traditional promotional programs. This feature is exemplified by American Express. With its huge database of cardholders and travelers, AmEx has detailed information on tens of millions of people. So detailed, in fact, that it can send out special promotions in monthly bills to as few as 20 people.[2]
- *An IMC plan is built around brand contacts.* Brand contacts are all the ways in which customers or prospective customers come in contact with the organization: packaging, employee contacts, in-store displays, sales literature, and media exposure. Each contact must be evaluated for clarity and consistency with the overall IMC program.
- *Control of an IMC plan is highly centralized.* The effectiveness of an IMC program is greatly increased by appointing a single person or a team to control and evaluate all contacts with targeted customers.

---

1. See Don E. Schultz, "Maybe We Should Start All Over with an IMC Organization," *Advertising Age,* October 25, 1993, 8; and Don E. Schultz, Stanley Tannenbaum, Robert Lauterborn, *Integrated Marketing Communications* (Lincolnwood, IL: NTC Business Books, 1993).
2. Jonathan Berry, "Database Marketing," *Business Week,* September 5, 1994, 56.

A Model for Planning Integrated Marketing Communications.

There are many different models that one might use for direction in the process of planning an IMC campaign. To put the Cincinnati Bell Wireless campaign in a proper context, and to be consistent with our discussion of planning issues in the last five chapters, we will frame this discussion using the strategic planning triangle proposed by advertising researchers Esther Thorson and Jeri Moore.[3] As reflected in Exhibit IMC 2.1, the apexes of the planning triangle entail the segment(s) selected as targets for the IMC campaign, the brand's value proposition, and the array of persuasion tools that might be deployed to achieve campaign objectives.

In planning for an IMC campaign, a firm starts with the customer or prospect and works backward, identifying what the customer deems important information. Hence, we place identification and specification of the target segment as the paramount apex in the triangle. Building a consensus between the client and the agency about which customer segments will be targeted is essential to the campaign's effectiveness. Complex IMC campaigns may end up targeting multiple segments; when this is so, it is critical to analyze if and how different target segments will interact to support or disparage the campaign. As suggested in Chapter 6, compelling advertising begins with descriptions and insights about one's target segment(s) that are both personal and precise.

The second important apex in the planning triangle entails specification of the brand's value proposition. Per Chapter 6, a brand's value proposition is a statement of the functional, emotional, and self-expressive benefits delivered by the brand that provide value to customers in the target segment. In formulating the value proposition, one should consider both what a brand has stood for or communicated to consumers in the past, as well as what new types of value or additional benefits one wants to claim for the brand going forward. For mature and successful brands, reaffirming the existing value proposition may be the primary objective for any campaign. When launching a new brand, there is an opportunity to start from scratch in establishing the value proposition. For Cincinnati Bell Wireless (CBW), which was a combination of something old (Cincinnati Bell), and something new (Wireless), the challenge was to draw on the strengths of the old as a foundation for claims about the new.

The final apex of the planning triangle considers the various persuasion tools that may be deployed in executing the campaign. A complete description of the tools is yet to come. Chapters 14 and 15 will emphasize traditional mass media tools; Chapter 16 will consider support media, point-of-purchase advertising, and event sponsorship; Chapter 17 looks at the Internet advertising option; Chapter 18 reviews the array of possibilities in sales promotion; Chapter 19 provides a comprehensive look at direct marketing; and Chapter 20 completes the set by discussing the public relations function. The mix of tools used will depend on the objectives that are set for the IMC campaign in question. For example, building awareness of and excitement about a new brand such as CBW will be accomplished most effectively via mass media and event sponsorship, whereas bringing consumers into retail stores with an intent to purchase may require a sales promotion, delivered to the targeted customer via a direct mail

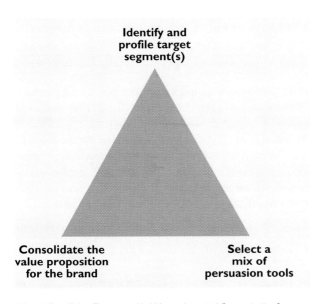

Identify and profile target segment(s)

Consolidate the value proposition for the brand

Select a mix of persuasion tools

Adapted from Esther Thorson and Jeri Moore, *Integrated Communication: Synergy of Persuasive Voices* (Mahwah, N.J.: Erlbaum, 1996).

EXHIBIT IMC 2.1

Thorson and Moore's IMC planning triangle.

3. Esther Thorson and Jeri Moore, *Integrated Communication: Synergy of Persuasive Voices* (Mahwah, N.J.: Erlbaum, 1996).

offer, with a telemarketing follow-up. As you will see, one of the most admirable aspects of the IMC campaign designed by Northlich Stolley LaWarre (NSL) for the CBW launch was its skillful use of multiple persuasion tools working in harmony to sell the product. That's right, we want to emphasize: *to sell the product*. Marketers such as Cincinnati Bell fund IMC campaigns to get results that affect their companies' revenues and profitability. The campaign that launched CBW did just that.

Assessing CBW's Situation Prior to Launch.
As described in Chapter 8, an effective campaign begins with a keen appreciation for the critical elements of one's situation. There is an infinite list of potential factors (for example, demographic, social and cultural, economic, political/regulatory) that may be considered in analyzing the situation. However, the idea is to be smart in choosing the few important factors that really describe the situation, and then explain how the factors relate to the task at hand. To appreciate the task that NSL faced in planning the campaign to launch CBW requires an appreciation for several key elements of the situation.

Historical Context.
Cincinnati Bell officially launched its wireless phone service on May 11, 1998. However, this particular launch was just one in a continuing series of new products and services involving the Cincinnati Bell brand name. Moreover, in 1998 Cincinnati Bell celebrated its 125-year anniversary in the Greater Cincinnati metropolitan market under the banner "Celebrating 125 Years of Innovation." Some important milestones in the history of the company are listed in Exhibit IMC 2.2. In addition, as illustrated by the sample ads in Exhibit IMC 2.3, a common theme across ads for its various products and services was the slogan "People you know you can rely on." Obviously, the launch of CBW should not be viewed as an isolated event, and the Cincinnati Bell brand name carried with it equities that provided a sound foundation for the launch of a wireless service. Certainly, it was a name widely known in the local market, and one that connoted superior service, quality, innovation, and value. These types of connections to the Cincinnati Bell brand would of course be tremendous assets in the launch of CBW.

Industry Analysis.
Telecommunications is a dynamic, technical, and complex business. Building a product and service network that would deliver good value to the wireless phone customer was the responsibility of Cincinnati Bell and its partners. Although it is beyond the scope of this discussion to explain the interworkings of the telecommunications business, some familiarity with key industry issues is essential for appreciating the business opportunity that CBW launched to capitalize on in May of 1998.

In the winter of 1998, the wireless phone marketplace in Cincinnati, and for that matter, nationwide, was on the brink of bedlam. As one writer put it at the time:

Well, the future of (wireless) is now. And while some of its promises are already being fulfilled, all of the new (and sometimes incompatible gear) and advanced services have had an unintended impact: It's wireless chaos out there.[4]

Executives at Cincinnati Bell realized that in a marketplace typified by chaos, the rewards would go to companies that offered consumers simple solutions and good value. Out of chaos often comes wonderful business opportunity.

Critical to understanding this opportunity is the distinction between analog cellular and digital PCS (for *personal communication services*) wireless phones. CBW would launch a new digital PCS offering to the Greater Cincinnati marketplace. Its primary competition at launch would be analog cellular providers. Analog cellular was the

---

4.   Chris O' Malley, "Sorting Out Cellphones," *Popular Science*, February 1998, 55.

INTEGRATED MARKETING COMMUNICATIONS

EXHIBIT IMC 2.2

Cincinnati Bell: Celebrating 125 years of innovation

A Corporate Timeline ...

1873—City & Suburban Telegraph Association (now Cincinnati Bell) founded

1876—Alexander Graham Bell invents the telephone

1877—First telephone installed in Cincinnati

1907—First Yellow Pages directory published

1975—911 emergency service activated

1984—First fiber optic cable installed

1990—Cincinnati Reds sweep Oakland in the World Series

1992—Cincinnati Bell pioneered the self-healing fiber optic network

1996—First telecommunication company to offer Internet access: Fuse

1997—1,000,000th access line installed

1997—Ranked one of the nation's top two providers of trouble-free local phone service

1998—First to offer Internet Call Manager

1998—Ranked highest independent telecommunications company for Web technology

1998—Cincinnati Bell: Celebrating 125 years of innovation

established technology that introduced most of us to the concept of a wireless phone. Across the United States, analog service providers all rely on the same transmission methods and thus can handle calls for each others' customers, for a heavy "roaming fee." Hence, you can make an analog cellular call almost anywhere in the United States. The common transmission standard for analog also meant that consumers could select from a wide variety of phone models, ranging from the low-cost Nokia 232 to the pricey ($800 to $1,200) but chic Motorola StarTAC 8600.[5]

Digital PCS was the new kid on the block, and offered some important advantages over analog. Digital PCS can be marketed at lower prices vis-à-vis analog because digital technology allows providers to expand capacity to handle calls much more easily than is the case for analog service. Also, because digital service always relies on a computer-mediated stream of ones and zeros, digital messages can be more easily encrypted, thus eliminating many forms of "cellular fraud" that plague analog systems. Digital technology also opens the door for add-on services such as E-mail and Internet access, and the sound quality for digital is superior to that of analog. Finally, the agreement that Cincinnati Bell Inc. signed with AT&T Wireless Services in the fourth quarter of 1997 made Cincinnati Bell Wireless part of a nationwide system that would allow CBW customers to use their phones in 400 cities across the United States. Opportunity was knocking, but only if CBW could get its value proposition in front of consumers before the competition.

Local Competition. In the winter of 1998 Cincinnati Bell worked closely with its agency NSL in an effort to capitalize on the competitive advantages in digital PCS. At the time, only one other PCS provider existed in the Cincinnati market under the brand name GTE Wireless. However, GTE Wireless had not been aggressive in convincing Cincinnatians of the benefits of digital PCS, and was further hampered by a very limited calling area. More established competition came from analog cellular providers, and two of these—Ameritech Cellular and AirTouch Cellular—had strong brand identity in the local market. As part of the planning process, CBW and NSL would have to resolve a

5.   Ibid.

INTEGRATED MARKETING COMMUNICATIONS

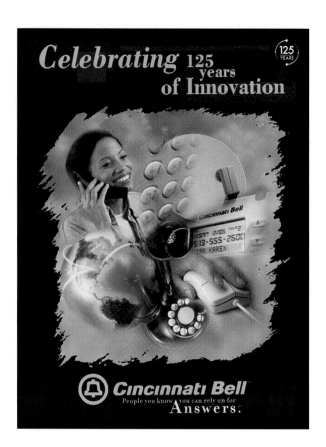

EXHIBIT IMC 2.3

Cincinnati Bell sample ads prior to the wireless launch.

fundamental dilemma created by the local competition. That is, should they concentrate the launch campaign on signing up first-time wireless phone users, or should they seek to steal customers away from the entrenched analog competition? The resolution of this dilemma would come through a thorough segmentation analysis.

Market Analysis. CBW was preparing to launch its service in the face of surging demand for both digital PCS and analog cellular. Nationwide, the market for these services had more than doubled from 1995 to 1998, to over 60 million subscribers.[6] Market growth rates approaching 30 percent annually had several companies scrambling to take advantage of this opportunity (for example, Sprint would introduce its PCS service to the Cincinnati market in November 1998), so CBW executives pressed for their launch as soon as was humanly possible. The Federal Communications Commission estimates the Cincinnati marketplace to be about 1.9 million people. Given a national penetration rate of 25 percent,[7] this translates into a potential market of 475,000 wireless phone subscribers in Greater Cincinnati. Who among these should be targeted in the CBW launch? How many of these could CBW hope to sign on to its service in the first 90 days after launch? These would be pivotal questions hotly debated by NSL and CBW personnel leading up to their May 11 blastoff.

Pinpointing the Target Segment for Launch.

NSL and CBW would draw on various forms of market research in preparing for the spring launch. Both quantitative and qualitative research tools uncovered important consumer insights that benefited the planning process. For example, survey research established that the number one motivation for sign-up among new users was concern for safety of a family member. Hence, if the decision was to target non-users, alleviating concerns about safety when a family member is traveling or away from home would have to be the primary appeal. Additionally, focus group research established that many consumers felt confused and overwhelmed by the growing number of wireless phone deals and options. Consumers don't like marketplace chaos, so the supplier that can make things simple would have almost instant appeal. Moreover, in a finding that had to warm the hearts of executives at Cincinnati Bell, consumers also rated corporate identity and credibility as becoming increasingly important in the decision about which wireless service to choose.

Synthesizing the various market research studies and developing a consensus between client and agency about who should be the primary launch target for the IMC campaign was achieved, as described in Chapter 6, via an in-depth segmentation analysis. The general framework that was developed to structure this analysis is summarized by the diagram in IMC Exhibit 2.4. As reflected in the diagram, usage considerations and demographic factors were combined to isolate a number of different market segments. Guided by this framework, an analysis was pursued that ultimately produced consensus about the primary launch target. In the discussion that follows, two specific segments will be profiled to provide an appreciation for the details that must be considered in planning for a major new product launch. As we noted earlier, compelling advertising begins with descriptions and insights about one's target segment(s) that are both personal and precise.

- *Mid-level executives—profile and motivations.* One market segment carefully assessed as the launch target was mid-level executives who were current users of another wireless service. This segment was primarily college-educated males who embraced technology and were early adopters of many advanced technologies, including the

6. Mike Boyer, "Wireless Wars," *Cincinnati Enquirer*, November 15, 1998, E1, E4.
7. Ibid.

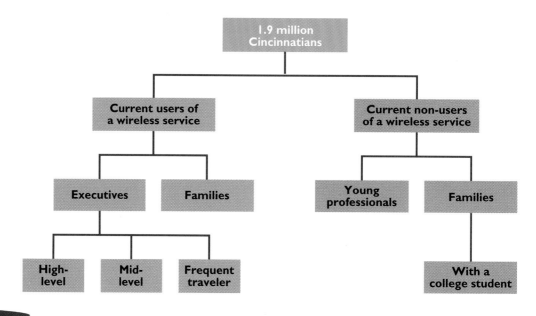

EXHIBIT IMC 2.4

The CBW/NSL segmentation framework: Spring 1998.

Internet. These individuals looked at their wireless phone as a productivity-enhancing device for their work, and were receptive to any features in a wireless phone, such as E-mail, voice mail, or text messaging, that could make them more productive. Most of these executives indicated that price was a key factor that would make them switch carriers, and many also acknowledged that they probably could find a better deal if they spent the time to comparison shop. Poor customer service, erratic sound quality, and restrictive calling zones were also concerns among those in this market segment.

- *Families with a child in college—profile and motivations.* Families with one or more children in college represented an important segment of non-users. Here, the purchase of the service would most likely be by the parent, whereas the primary user was projected to be the student. Both parents and students looked to a wireless phone as offering safety and security. Parents also wanted to be able to reach their student at a moment's notice and expressed a lack of confidence in roommates or other means of passing on important messages to their college student. However, parents expressed concerns about the phone being misused once it was out of their control; they wanted to realize the security and convenience of a wireless phone while controlling costs. Parents as primary purchasers did not represent early adopters of new technologies and thus were especially intimidated by various options regarding contracts, pricing, coverage zones, and add-on features. They just wanted an easy and safe way to get direct access to their son or daughter at college. Hence, for this market segment, a familiar brand name that parents already trusted would be a great asset in winning their new business.

The two market segments profiled above reflect the dilemma faced by CBW and NSL as they approached the launch date in May 1998. Should they attempt to steal savvy customers from established competitors such as Ameritech Cellular and Air-Touch Cellular, or appeal to the novice customer who had previously never used wireless? This is a tough choice because it can be hard to get savvy customers to switch when they already have a product or service that is filling their requirements, and it can be hard to get novice customers to take the plunge and sign on for something new, especially when that "something new" involves advanced technology such as PCS digital.

In either case, CBW would need a carefully orchestrated communications campaign to break through the clutter of the marketplace to convince the launch target that CBW did offer something special, just for them. And it should be clear that there is no way CBW could have it both ways. That is, the fast-track business executive and the concerned parent of a college student would require very different appeals and persuasion tools. CBW and NSL would have to choose one as the target segment for their launch, or risk coming to the marketplace with a diluted message that would leave all segments confused about CBW's value proposition. Value-proposition ambiguity would hand the opportunity of taking first-mover advantage in the Cincinnati PCS digital market to a competitor such as Sprint or GTE.

So, which would you choose—current users or non-users? Before you read on, stop and give this some thought. Reflecting on the example of Mobil Oil that was described back in Chapter 6 will help you make this call.

CBW and NSL selected mid- and high-level executives who currently were using another wireless service as the primary targets for the their launch of PCS digital in Cincinnati. The rationale for this launch target was much like the one Mobil Oil used in targeting Road Warriors. Recall that although Road Warriors were outnumbered by Price Shoppers, Road Warriors spend more at the gas station, making them the larger segment from the standpoint of revenue generation and profit potential. Likewise for MOPEs (managers, owners, professionals, and entrepreneurs) when it comes to use of a wireless phone: They make much heavier use of the wireless service in terms of minutes called per month, versus household users. And the way Cincinnati Bell makes money on a service like this is when customers are actually using the phone. Having a phone at home in the kitchen drawer that no one ever uses unless there is an unwanted emergency was not the usage scenario that excited the CBW/NSL team. Hence, MOPEs became the launch target.

Launch Strategy and the CBW Value Proposition.

The launch strategy was set: MOPEs using another wireless service would be targeted for conversion to PCS digital from Cincinnati Bell. The value proposition to be advanced through a diversified IMC campaign would feature the functional benefits of this new service. Various media and methods would be deployed to communicate a compelling value proposition around these benefit claims:

- *Simple pricing, better value.* No contracts to sign; subscribers choose a simple pricing plan, like 500 minutes for $49/month or 1,600 minutes for $99/month.
- *Member of the AT&T Wireless Network.* As a member of AT&T's nationwide network, CBW offered customers complete wireless access in over 400 cities at one "hometown rate."
- *Worry-free security.* Digital PCS allows secure business transactions that may be compromised over analog cellular.
- *The coolest phone on the planet.* CBW launched its service with the feature-laden Nokia 6160 wireless phone. It really is a cool phone: The kind you want people to see you using.

Cincinnati Bell had several important benefit claims to make for its service in comparison to the analog cellular competition. In addition, it had a tremendous advantage from the standpoint of the combined brand equities of its strategic partners, which surely contributed to the credibility of all its claims. Specifically, its claim of a nationwide network was instantly validated by its association with AT&T, and the quality of its phone gear per se was supported by brand-building ads (see Exhibit IMC 2.5) and high-visibility event sponsorship (for example, the Nokia Sugar Bowl) that made Nokia one of the best-known portable-phone brands at the time of launch. In combination, the Cincinnati Bell, AT&T, and Nokia brand names were an imposing triad that would establish instant credibility for Cincinnati Bell Wireless.

EXHIBIT IMC 2.5

Another asset in the CBW launch: The Nokia 6100 Series Digital Phone.

Another Nokia discovery:

Dead batteries are inconvenient.

That's why we make the Nokia 6100 Series digital phones with long battery life. Up to eight hours of talk time and 14 days of standby time. So whether you're talking with a client or playing one of the phone's built-in games, you'll have plenty of time. Once again, we got a jump on the competition.

NOKIA
CONNECTING PEOPLE

Objectives and Budget.

With all this opportunity staring them in the face, NSL was clearly challenged to produce dramatic results with the launch of CBW. Jack Cassidy, CBW's President, stated the initial objective for launch simply and forcefully: "Get me activations!" Although activating a customer does not necessarily create a satisfied or profitable customer, everything starts with an activation. And while the distinction between communication and sales objectives discussed in Chapter 8 was not lost on Mr. Cassidy, he clearly was just interested in the sale. Since it is the client that pays the bills, it is the client's prerogative to determine a campaign's objectives. NSL's work would be judged initially on the basis of the number of new customers who signed on for CBW's service. Mr. Cassidy and his associates at Cincinnati Bell specified as their goal for the calendar year 1998 16,868 new CBW customers. Given the estimate of 475,000 potential wireless customers in the Greater Cincinnati market, Mr. Cassidy was looking for an immediate market penetration in excess of 3.5 percent.

The initial thinking was that the first eight months of advertising for CBW would be supported by a $3 million budget. Starting in May 1998, all marketing communications would be directed at the Greater Cincinnati market, but about 90 days after launch the market space would be expanded to include the Dayton, Ohio, market, which would increase the scope of the overall market from 1.9 to 3.2 million people. This $3 million budget for May through December may not seem all that impressive on first glance, but if we project it to a year-long nationwide campaign we can immediately grasp the level of importance Cincinnati Bell was placing on this launch. Specifically, if such a campaign were to be executed for 12 months in the top 50 metro markets across the United States, the $3 million budget would translate into a $225 million program. Per Chapter 8, this would be a commitment on par with that made by Steve Jobs in launching his new iMac in the second half of 1998. Clearly, the folks at Cincinnati Bell were committed to making a "big-time" investment in their launch of CBW, and they were expecting "big-time" results. These expectations would create many sleepless nights for the NSL personnel working on CBW.

The Mix of Persuasion Tools.

Now, while the folks at NSL knew that their work would be evaluated initially on the basis of Mr. Cassidy's "Get me activations!," they first conceived their challenge in terms of more fundamental communication objectives. To get new customers, the IMC campaign would first have to create brand awareness, then generate interest in the brand, and finally bring people into retail outlets where they could buy their Nokia 6160 phone (at a special introductory price of $99) and activate their service. In Part IV of this case history, substantial details will be provided about the various elements of the campaign that were deployed to launch CBW. For example, television, radio, and outdoor ads were created to build brand awareness for CBW; print ads were used to provide information about specific features; event sponsorships were placed to create excitement and visibility for the new service; and a sophisticated direct marketing effort was launched in conjunction with sales promotion to motivate MOPEs to visit retail stores and close the deal. Indeed, nearly all the persuasion tools discussed in Chapters 14 through 20 were considered as part of this comprehensive IMC campaign. But would they really produce the kind of results that the client was looking for? Stay tuned . . .

IMC EXERCISES

1. Explain how the planning of integrated marketing communications (IMC) goes well beyond merely choosing the right promotional tool at the right time.
2. Refer to Exhibit 2-1, Thorson and Moore's IMC Planning Triangle. Who did Cincinnati Bell Wireless (CBW) identify as the primary market segments for its new wireless phone service? How did it profile each market segment? What was the value proposition CBW planned to communicate to its targeted market?
3. One of the ways Northlich Stolley LaWarre (NSL) and Cincinnati Bell Wireless (CBW) gather data is through focus group research. Develop a list of 10 questions you would use in a focus group of potential wireless phone users to identify their preferences and values related to wireless phone use. If you are a wireless phone user, think back to the reasons why you decided to subscribe. Recalling your own reasons for subscribing will assist you in drafting your questions.
4. In Chapter 5, we learned that products and services should provide benefits that fulfill consumers' needs. List three *functional* and three *emotional* benefits a consumer might derive from subscribing to a wireless phone service.

PART THREE

PREPARING THE MESSAGE

This part, "Preparing the Message," marks an important passage in our study of advertising. The topics to this point have raised the essential process and planning issues that make advertising what it is as a communication and business tool. Now we need to take the plunge into the actual *preparation* of advertising—the third of the 4Ps of advertising.

One of the most insightful observations on the creative process in advertising was made by Jim Nelson, a well-seasoned advertising executive: "Creativity is a misunderstood phenomenon. The key isn't simply brilliant insight from above, but hard work here below. For my money, you need two things: tough, analytical thinking and intuitive, creative imagination. Rubbing them together may cause friction, but it may also set fire to a real people-moving idea." (A. Jerome Jewler, *Creative Strategy in Advertising*, 3rd ed. (Belmont, Calif.: Wadsworth Publishing, 1989), 61.)

The valuable insight in this comment is that creativity and the creative process should not be totally separated from the analytical, strategic planning effort. Rather, when they are "rubbed" together, the result can be advertising that has impact and the power to move people. This section of the text explores aspects of the creation process and creativity as an important role in effective advertising.

Creativity and Advertising As a famous dancer once said, "If I could describe dancing, I wouldn't have to do it." Well, we feel the same way about creativity in advertising—it really is impossible to describe. But we do our best to give you insights into the creative process by giving examples of how the creative process is worked out in an advertising context—how the "creatives" work with the "strategists." Offering more than just examples of creative practice in advertising, we try to provide insights by offering the observations of seven creative geniuses of the 20th century. Creativity is the soul of advertising and this chapter tries to show the magic that is advertising.

Message Strategy Chapter 11, "Message Strategy: Objectives and Methods," begins by describing how creativity is often expressed as "the big idea." The big idea is a key message appeal that has the power to move people. You will also learn in this chapter that effective message development is a lot of work beyond creativity. A wide range of message objectives and strategies, which require astute insights from consumer and market analysis, can be used to develop messages. In the end, you will see that what ultimately communicates to a target audience is what that audience finds relevant and interesting.

Copywriting Chapter 12, "Copywriting," focuses on the enormous challenge of writing the descriptions that accompany print and broadcast advertising. This chapter explores the development of copy from the creative plan through dealing with the constraints and opportunities of the medium that will carry the message. This chapter also highlights guidelines for writing effective copy and common mistakes in copywriting. A full discussion of radio and television advertising formats, which provide the context for copy development, is also provided. At the end of this chapter is a discussion of a typical copy approval process used by advertisers and agencies.

Art Direction and Production In Chapter 13, "Art Direction and Production," you will first learn about creating effective print advertisements destined for magazines, newspapers, or direct-marketing promotions. The nature of the illustration, design, and layout components of print advertising are considered. Then, the exciting and complex process of creating broadcast advertising is discussed. This part of the chapter describes the people and techniques involved in creating television and radio ads. The emphasis in this chapter is on the creative team and how creative concepts are brought to life. The chapter follows a preproduction, production, and postproduction sequence. Also highlighted in this chapter are the large numbers of people outside the agency who facilitate the production effort.

CHAPTER 10

**After reading and thinking about
this chapter, you will be able to
do the following:**

◀▶ Describe the core characteristics of great
creative minds.

◀▶ Contrast the role of an advertising
agency's creative department with that of
its business managers/account executives
and explain the tensions between them.

◀▶ Identify the controls imposed on agency
creatives that can undermine an agency's
ability to create consistently superior work.

The creative mind plays with the objects it loves.

—C.G. Jung[1]

This is the kind of conference room that can be very scary. When you enter the room, the lights come on like magic. But they don't burst on in a blaze. They come up very, very slowly. A spooky kind of slowly. When the lights are full, the room is perfectly lit—no shadows, no glare. Then there are the floor-to-ceiling windows—tall enough so that Shaq would need a ladder to clean them. What's more, this corner conference room on the 50th floor gives you a 120-degree view of Manhattan (or L.A., or Dallas, or Chicago, or Seattle). All very intimidating.

But not as intimidating as the meetings that go on here. You see, this is sort of a modern-day Colosseum. It's not supposed to be that way in this era of "relationships" and "partnering." But like the lions and the Christians, this is where the poets meet the killers.[2] There is no real bloodshed, but there are battered egos and bloodied relationships.

The poets are the creatives from the ad agency—the art directors, copywriters, graphic artists, and account planners who are dedicated to making advertising exciting, aesthetic, compelling, and edgy. The poets are dedicated to conceiving advertising that makes clients nervous enough to rise out of their seats, pace the floor, and jingle the change in their pockets.[3]

The killers are the clients—or, more specifically, the marketing- and strategy-trained managers from the client who wield the anything-but-aesthetic bottom-line sword against the poets' creative prowess. It's not that the killers don't like the poets. It's not that they don't like advertising. It *is* that they like sales and want the poets to talk about sales. But the poets have a higher calling. Neither side means to wage a bloody battle, and the meetings never start with either side intending it to be that way. But these are tense times: new media, more old media, monster databases, astute audiences, shareholders clamoring for higher earnings per share.

No ad campaign in recent history has locked the poets against the killers in mortal battle like Nissan's "Mr. K" campaign (see Exhibit 10.1). Mr. K was the kindly guy who used to show up at the end of Nissan ads. The creative community loved the campaign, but the Nissan dealers were sitting on unmoved inventory. The result was the resignation of Nissan USA president Bob Thomas. The battle lines drawn around this campaign were so severe that ad agency types didn't even want to talk about it. One creative director said that talking about the Mr. K campaign with his clients "was kind of like the McCarthy hearings. You know, 'Are you now, or have you ever been, an admirer of Nissan's advertising?'"[4] The latest casualties of unmoved inventory were "Ads by Dick." These

Maybe traffic jams happen because cars like to be with other cars.

EXHIBIT 10.1

Nissan's "Mr. K" campaign pitted the poets against the killers.
www.nissan.com/

1.   Carl G. Jung, cited in Astrid Fitzgerald, *An Artist's Book of Inspiration: A Collection of Thoughts on Art, Artists, and Creativity* (New York: Lindisfarne, 1996), 58.
2.   Anthony Vagnoni, "Creative Differences," *Advertising Age,* November 17, 1997, 1, 28, 30.
3.   This description of clients' nervous reactions is credited to Mike Dunn, founder and principal of Dunn Communications, Salt Lake City, Utah.
4.   Vagnoni, "Creative Differences," 28.

were the offbeat Miller Lite ads, like the one featured in Exhibit 10.2, that featured rampaging beavers and furry animals living in armpits. The light-beer category grew 2.7 percent in 1998, while Miller Lite's volume grew only 2.4 percent—oops.[5]

But the debate doesn't center on offbeat, unusual ads. The debate is much more central to the entire advertising process. It centers on the creative role of advertising. One side says you must *sell* with advertising, and selling means giving consumers facts they can use to make decisions. The other side says you have to *build an emotional bond* between consumers and brands, and that process requires communicating much more than product attributes. Bob Kuperman, president and CEO of TBWA Chiat/Day North America, puts it quite simply: "Before you can be believed, you have to be liked."[6] The killers who favor selling—and believe that there are plenty of killer/rationalists on the agency side as well as the client side—point to the historic failures of emotional advertising: any Alka-Seltzer campaign, Joe Isuzu, Mr. K, and Ads by Dick. They say that such campaigns are creatively self-indulgent and grossly inefficient. Fortunately, the poets and killers are not always working at cross purposes, as shown in the IMC box on page 308.

While the killers call creative advertising inefficient, the poets are starting to lose their patience. In a speech to the European Association of Advertising Agencies, CEO of Saatchi & Saatchi Worldwide Kevin Roberts said, "[I]t seems like it's open season on attacking agencies nowadays, everyone's jumping on the bandwagon. Clients, management consultants, Silicon Valley hot shot technic nerds and even Rance Crain of *Ad Age*. Enough's enough! In the words of my New Zealand compatriot, Xena, Warrior Princess: 'Stop staring at me before I take your eyes out!!'"[7]

Creativity, Science, and Magic. We have to be honest with you—writing about creativity feels a little silly. Don't get us wrong—we love to sit around and talk about creative endeavors and creative people. In fact, we're pretty creative people ourselves, and we think we know creativity when we see it. But trying to nail creativity down to a set of principles, mental operations, or traits seems like a good deal of hubris to us, and

---

EXHIBIT 10.2

Miller Lite's "Ads by Dick" were popular among creatives, but left Miller with unmoved inventory.
www.millerlite.com/

("Naked/Texas": 60 Radio)

(SFX: MILLER TIME MUSIC)
ANNCR.: Not long ago we asked Dick, the Creative Superstar behind Miller Lite advertising, to come up with a Miller Time radio concept just for beer-loving Texans. Dick said, "OK." Dick said he liked radio ads because you could get away with more naughty stuff than in TV. We weren't sure what Dick meant by this, so we asked him to explain. Dick said, for example, that you can't show naked people in TV commercials. But by merely saying the words "naked people" in a radio commercial, you force listeners to picture naked people in their minds. Here is what Dick wants you to picture in your mind while listening to his commercial. Naked people. Naked people in Texas. Naked Texans going to the refrigerator and getting a Miller Lite. Wearing nothing . . . except cowboy boots . . . with spurs, drinking Miller Lite. Naked. This had been a very naughty Miller Time presentation for Texas by Dick. Thank you for your time.
SINGERS: Miller Time.
ANNCR.: Miller Brewing Company, Fort Worth, Texas.

Fallon McElligott (Minneapolis, MN), ad agency
Miller Lite, Client

---

5.   Sally Beatty, "Remeber Dick? He Was Miller's Attempt to Woo Cool Drinkers," *Wall Street Journal,* May 4, 1999, 1.
6.   Vagnoni, "Creative Differences," 1.
7.   Kevin Roberts, "Making Magic," keynote address to the European Advertising Agencies Association conference, Budapest, Hungary, October 16, 1998. Available online at www.saatchikevin.com/speeches/magic.html.

maybe a good measure of folly as well. It's a little like writing scientific analysis about some other forms of magic, such as love (see poet Patti Smith):

THE CLIENT AND THE AGENCY AGREE! REALLY!

When it comes to creative execution, the client and agency often part their oh-so-partnership ways—as we have seen. The "poet" creative types and the "killer" brand manager can have vastly different ideas on the best way to represent the brand.

But there is one point on which the poets and the killers often agree. When it comes to success in communication—including the creative execution—clear brand identity is a mutually shared aspiration. Evidence of sharing this goal was recently discovered in the automobile industry. When automotive brand managers and agency executives were asked how important a unified image was for their auto brand, a whopping 92 percent indicated it was either extremely important, very important, or important.

A good example of the unification of a brand image is the Dodge line of vehicles. When Dick Johnson was appointed chief creative officer of BBDO Worldwide, he put a complete stop to all "car-on-road" film footage for TV ads. "One more car going down one more wet road is not going to move any needles." Instead, he wanted an image and slogan for Dodge that told the story of the brand's redesign. This gave birth to the tagline "We're changing everything" for the launch of the 1992 Dodge Intrepid. The phrase acknowledged what consumers had already known—everything at Dodge needed to be changed.

The theme of change was unified across all Dodge vehicles. When the 1993 Dodge Ram pickup was introduced, Johnson abandoned the traditional truck advertising featuring the "work" shot of the owner hauling and the "leisure" shot of the owner at play. He also did away with traditional images for the Dodge Caravan minivan: no shots of mom hauling kids around.

The overall effect is a unified brand image that translates into brand identity in the minds of consumers. Whether the creative execution is wildly unusual or somewhat staid, creatives and brand managers can agree on one thing. If an advertising execution creates clear and appealing brand image—it's a good execution.

Source: Frank S. Washington, "Key to Strong Brand Image: Unified Marketing Strategy," *Advertising Age*, April 6, 1998, S-20.

Now I lay me down to sleep
Pray the Lord my soul to keep
Kiss to kiss, breath to breath
My soul surrenders astonished to death
Night of wonder promise to keep
Set our sails channel the deep
Capture the rapture, two hearts meet
Minds entwined in a single beat

—"Frederick," Patti Smith[8]

What does science have to say to that? Nothing; it can't compete. Art triumphs. One might just as well try to dissect the first few notes of a great song, any moment of a Michael Jordan highlight reel, great sex, or a thunderstorm rolling across the plains. It's a mystery, but you pretty much know when it's working for you. So it feels a little foolish even trying to be analytic and definitive about something so inherently artful, soulful, and human.

Still, with that said, we believe that any book on advertising really needs some attention to creativity, the thing that most people think about when they think about advertising. And, in reality, it is the thing that makes the advertising world go round. Without it, there is really no advertising. Creativity is advertising's soul. Yet most advertising textbooks say relatively little about it. They give you some technical information on typefaces and T-squares, but little about creativity itself. We want to talk a little about the magic and mystical art of advertising creativity. So, we will.

We will do this by speaking of creativity in general, creativity in the advertising world, and the creative-management interface/friction zone. It's an entertaining story, but it doesn't always support the myth of orderly business. It's way too messy, way too human; so avert your eyes if you must.

Creativity across Domains.

What lies behind us and what lies before us are tiny matters, compared to what lies within us.

—Ralph Waldo Emerson[9]

8.   Patti Smith, "Frederick," *Patti Smith Complete* (New York: Doubleday, 1998), 107.
9.   Ralph Waldo Emerson, cited in The Quotations Archive (www.aphids.com/quotes).

Nobody sees a flower—it is so small it takes time—we haven't time—and to see takes time, like to have a friend takes time.

—Georgia O'Keeffe [10]

Creativity, in its essence, is the same no matter what the domain. People who create, create, whether they write novels, take photographs, ponder the particle physics that drives the universe, craft poetry, write songs, play a musical instrument, dance, make films, design buildings, or paint. Or make ads. To some people, discussing advertising professionals alongside great writers or painters seems heresy. We disagree. We don't put much stock in the high art–low art distinction. Great ads can be truly great creative accomplishments.

Creativity is generally seen as a gift, a special way of seeing the world. It is. Throughout the ages, creative people have been seen as special, revered and reviled, admired and held in contempt, loved and hated. They have served as powerful political instruments (for good and evil), and they have been ostracized, imprisoned, and killed for their art. Creativity has been associated with various forms of madness:

Madness, provided it comes as the gift of heaven, is the channel by which we receive the greatest blessings. . . . [T]he men of old who gave their names saw no disgrace or reproach in madness; otherwise they would not have connected it with the name of the noblest of all arts, the art of discerning the future, and called by our ancestors, madness is a nobler thing than sober sense. . . . [M]adness comes from God, whereas sober sense is merely human.

—Socrates[11]

Creativity reflects early childhood experiences, social circumstances, and mental styles.

In one of the best books ever written on creativity, *Creating Minds,* Howard Gardner examines the lives and works of seven of the greatest creative minds of the 20th century: Sigmund Freud, Albert Einstein, Pablo Picasso (see Exhibit 10.3), Igor Stravinsky, T. S. Eliot, Martha Graham, and Mahatma Gandhi.[12] His work reveals fascinating similarities. We share his work and revelations about these seven extraordinarily creative people in order to better discuss the creative life and mind.

While all of these people have benefited tremendously from good public relations efforts, Gardner reveals quite a few things we didn't know about these seven. Some are not too surprising; others are not too flattering. All seven of these individuals, from physicist to modern dancer, were

self confident, alert, unconventional, hardworking, and committed obsessively to their work. Social life or hobbies are almost immaterial, representing at most a fringe on the creators' work time.[13]

EXHIBIT 10.3

Pablo Picasso, seen here in a self-portrait, was one of the greatest creative minds of the 20th century.

10. Georgia O'Keeffe, cited in Julia Cameron with Mark Bryan, *The Artist's Way: A Spiritual Path to Creativity.* New York: Putnam, 1995.

11. Socrates, cited in Plato, *Phaedrus and the Seventh and Eighth Letters,* Walter Hamilton, trans. (Middlesex, England: Penguin, 1970), 46–47, cited in Kay Redfield Jamison, *Touched with Fire: Manic-Depressive Illness and the Artistic Temperament* (New York: Free Press, 1993), 51.

12. Howard Gardner, *Creating Minds: An Anatomy of Creativity Seen through the Lives of Freud, Einstein, Picasso, Stravinsky, Eliot, Graham, and Gandhi* (New York: Basic Books, 1993).

13. Gardner, *Creating Minds,* 364.

Apparently, total commitment to one's craft is the rule. While this commitment sounds pretty positive, there is also a darker reflection of this trait:

[T]he self confidence merges with egotism, egocentrism, and narcissism: highly absorbed, not only wholly involved in his or her own projects, but likely to pursue them at costs of other individuals.[14]

Let's be clear: One should not stand between a great creator and his or her work. It's not safe; you'll have tracks down your back. Or maybe the creator will just ignore you to death. Not coincidentally, these great creative minds had troubled personal lives and simply did not have time for the more ordinary people (such as their families). According to Gardner, they were generally not very good to those around them. This was true even of Gandhi.[15]

All seven of these great creatives were also great self-promoters.[16] Widely recognized creative people are not typically shy about getting exposure for their work. They are shameless in their efforts to gain public attention, putting their work before the public eye. Apparently, fame in the creative realm rarely comes to the self-effacing and timid.

All seven of these great creators were, very significantly, childlike in a critical way. All of them had the ability to see things as a child does. Einstein spent much of his career revolutionizing physics by pursuing in no small way an idea he produced as a child: What would it be like to move along with a strand of pure light? His work was marked by his ability to conceive of things that were seemingly contradictory and highly conceptual. Likewise, Picasso commented that it ultimately was his ability to paint as a child (along with amazingly superior technical skills) that explained much of his greatness. At an exhibition of children's paintings he said, "When I was their age I could draw like Raphael, but it has taken me a whole lifetime to learn to draw like them."[17] Freud's obsession and interpretation of his childhood dreams had a significant role in what is arguably his greatest work, *The Interpretation of Dreams.*[18] T. S. Eliot's poetry demonstrated imaginative abilities that typically disappear past childhood. The same is true of Martha Graham's modern dance. Even Gandhi's particular form of social action was formulated with a very simple and childlike logic at its base. There is apparently something not yet ruined by adult socialization in childhood. These artists and creative thinkers never lost that ability. It is the ability to see the ordinary as extraordinary, to see the bogeyman in the shadows and really hear the monster under the bed, to not have their particular form of imagination beaten out of them by the process of "growing up." It is the ability to take flights of fancy with the most limited materials and in the most ordinary and mundane circumstances. This is a form of rule breaking. The creative person suspends or sees past the rules of everyday, ordinary perception. Those are the rules that bind most of us to ordinariness, that prevent us from being "creative."

Of course, the problem with this childlike thinking is that these individuals also behaved as children throughout most of their lives. Their social behavior was egocentric and selfish. They expected those around them to be willing sacrifices at the altar of their gift. Gardner put it this way: "[T]he carnage around a great creator is not a pretty sight, and this destructiveness occurs whether the individual is engaged in solitary pursuit or ostensibly working for the betterment of humankind."[19] These people often feel that the rules do not apply. They are intensely competitive, often seeing the world as a zero-sum game (if someone else wins something, they lose something). They can, however, be extraordinarily charming when it suits their ambitions. They could be

14. Ibid.
15. Ibid.
16. Ibid.
17. Pablo Picasso, cited in Gardner, *Creating Minds,* 145.
18. Gardner, *Creating Minds,* 145; Sigmund Freud, *The Interpretation of Dreams,* in A. A. Brill, ed., *The Basic Writings of Sigmund Freud* (New York: Modern Library, 1900/1938).
19. Gardner, *Creating Minds,* 369.

monsters at home, and darlings when performing. Of course, these seven may be extreme cases, but Gardner argues that they are not wholly unrepresentative of successful creative people in general. The expected tension that comes from being an emotional child in an adult's body and living in an adult social world provides a type of energy that actually motivates and invigorates creative people. The constant social turmoil feeds their energy, and helps them feel as marginal as they desire, and apparently they do desire marginality.[20]

Gardner says, "each creator was determinedly marginal and was willing to give up much to retain this marginality."[21] They found very different ways of achieving it, but all seven worked very hard at being at the margins of their fields, or marginal in intimate or family relationships, or marginal in society in general. This marginality seems to have been absolutely necessary to these people, and provided them with some requisite energy.

Another fascinating pattern emerges concerning the moments of greatest creativity:

At the time of greatest contribution these creators often moved from a period of life in which they were comfortable with many persons to a period of maximum isolation, at the moment of their major discovery, only to return to a larger, and perhaps more accepting, world in the later years of life. Second, at the time of their greatest isolation, these creators needed, and benefitted from, a special relation to one or more supportive individuals.[22]

Great creators seem to long to be left alone, particularly at or near the time of their greatest contribution, but have a very significant relationship with at least one significant other. This might be a colleague, a friend, a spouse, or a lover. There was among these great creators a need to turn inward during times of great creativity, driving away all but the significant others. The fate of these significant others was generally one of self-sacrifice and little reward.

Perhaps most important, these great creative minds were "productive every day."[23] Picasso averaged 300 drawings a year; Eliot wrote all the time; Stravinsky worked ten hours a day; Einstein would go days without sleep; Freud and Graham were workaholics of the first order; and Gandhi toiled every day of his life, his written works filling 90 volumes.[24] Being extremely creative is not part of a lazy lifestyle.

Emotional stability did not mark these creative lives either. All but Gandhi had a major mental breakdown at some point in their lives, and Gandhi suffered from at least two periods of severe depression (see Exhibit 10.4). Extreme creativity, just as the popular myth suggests, seems to come at some psychological price.

Creative people seem to exploit what Gardner calls *asynchrony*, or the state of being out of synch with one or more of the three critical domains. To explain this, we use the notion of the creative triangle offered by Csikszentmilhaly (Exhibit 10.5).[25] As you can see, there are three elements: other people (knowledgeable experts) in the creator's field, the individual, and the work (for example, painting, politics, dance, or physics). The creative person has to find not balance, but imbalance or asynchrony. Being out of synch with one or more of these forces (that is, being seen as marginal in their field, marginal in society, marginal in their relationships) causes an energy, a force that pushes the creative process. As a result, the creator creates, bringing things back into balance only momentarily, and then back to asynchrony.[26] It is argued that Picasso created enormous turmoil in his personal life in order to keep the creative process going. As

20. Ibid.
21. Ibid.
22. Ibid.
23. Ibid., 372.
24. Ibid.
25. M. Csikszentmilhaly, "Society, Culture, and Person: A Systems View of Creativity," in R. J. Sternberg, ed., *The Nature of Creativity* (New York: Cambridge University Press, 1988), 325–339.
26. Gardner, *Creating Minds*, 380–383.

EXHIBIT 10.4

*Gandhi once said,
"But for my faith in
God, I should have
been a raving maniac."*

EXHIBIT 10.5

*Csikszentmilhaly's
creative triangle.*

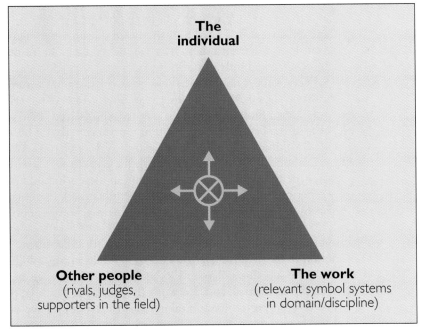

Adapted from Howard Gardner, *Creating Minds: An Anatomy of Creativity Seen through the Lives of Freud, Einstein, Picasso, Stravinsky,
Eliot, Graham, and Gandhi* (New York: Basic Books, 1993).

Gardner puts it, "creativity is the capacity to exploit, or profit from, an apparent misfit
or lack of smooth connection within the triangle of creativity. In the extent to which
they seek conditions of asynchrony, receiving a kind of thrill or flow from experience
from being "at the edge," creative standouts make Faustian bargains."[27]

So we see a picture of creatives that is both positive and negative, admirable, and a
bit frightening. Still, we are talking about seven extraordinary individuals. Perhaps these

27. Ibid.

traits are not seen in the average creative person, or maybe they are. Perhaps the demands of being part of a relatively structured and corporate creative environment such as an ad agency does not afford or allow such negative social behaviors to emerge or to be tolerated for long. But that really doesn't seem to be the case; these same traits seem to inhabit the realms of creatives in general, and advertising in particular.

Recognizing Creativity.
Of course, there are many theories as to why creative people are creative—why they can see things differently. Many artists have their own theories; some involve notions of suffering and being an outsider. Other creative people find such characteristics romanticized, self-serving, and excuses for undersocialized and overprivileged children.

Can One Become Creative?
This is a very big question. The popular answer in a democratic society would be to say, "Yes, sure; you too can be Picasso." Well, it's not quite that way. It really depends on what one means by "creativity." For starters, determining "creativity" is about as simple as nailing Jell-O to a wall. Is a person creative because he or she can produce a creative result? Or is a person creative because of the way he or she thinks? Further, who gets to determine what is creative and what is not? When an elephant paints holding a brush with its trunk, and the paintings sell for thousands of dollars, does it mean that the elephant is creative? Or is the next teen-throb band creative because they sell a gazillion albums? Clearly, public acceptance may not be the best measuring stick. Yet, is it inconsequential? Are only critics allowed to determine what is creative?

Critical acceptance certainly has its own set of shortcomings. While generally trained in some aesthetic form or fashion, critics are really granted questionable authority. Critics often have their own agenda and can be just as big morons as just about anyone else. They often seek to advance a particular view, politic, or sensibility. They are commonly biased against the popular, simply because it is popular. Ultimately, all critical standards and aesthetics are socially determined. So, who says what is right? Who says what is creative? More and more, there is a populist movement to challenge the privileged position of the critic, and to assert that we the audience are perfectly capable of rendering creative judgement. On the other hand, to the extent that critics are able to point to technical standards, can make important connections to other works, or in any other way better inform the "reader" of the ad, then their view should be considered, even valued.

Creativity in the Business World.
The difficulty of determining who is creative and who is not, or what is creative and what is not, in the artistic world is paralleled in the business world. Certainly, no matter how this ambiguous monster is defined, creativity is viewed in the business world as a positive trait for employees. It's been said that "creative individuals assume almost mythical status in the corporate world."[28] Everybody needs them, but no one is sure who or what they are.

Some people who study creativity in business believe that everybody is creative, albeit in different ways. For example, *adaptation/innovation theory* maintains that the way people think when facing creative tasks places them on a continuum between being an adaptor and being an innovator.[29] **Adaptors** tend to work within the existing paradigm, whereas innovators treat the paradigm as part of the problem. In other words, adaptors try to do things better. **Innovators** try to do things differently.[30] It can be

28. T. A. Matherly and R. E. Goldsmith, "The Two Faces of Creativity," *Business Horizons,* 1985, 8–11.
29. M. Kirton, "Adaptors and Innovators: A Description and Measure," *Journal of Applied Psychology,* vol. 61, no. 5 (1976), 622–629.
30. M. Kirton, "Adaptors and Innovators in Organizations," *Human Relations,* vol. 33, no. 4 (1980), 213–224.

NEW MEDIA

CREATIVITY ON THE INTERNET—THE MORE THINGS CHANGE, THE MORE THEY STAY THE SAME

While the Internet itself is a creative medium, that does not mean that everything that appears on the Net is creative. In fact, banner ads and corporate Web sites can be downright boring and eminently ignorable. And just because the Net is new and dynamic, that doesn't mean that all the rules of creative development of messages are abandoned.

First, youth, and especially teens, are very brand-conscious. Despite their new-media savvy and desire for interesting communications, they have not abandoned a brand orientation. Second, brands were established, in part, as a result of mass communications using the one-way circuitry of broadcast and print. If you said "Just do it" often enough, you could establish a brand identity in the marketplace.

The problem is that the two points above create a third point: In the interactive world of N-Gen customers, a brand may be harder to establish and may even evaporate. Here is the problem. In a networked information environment, receivers are not receiving information on the advertiser's terms—that is, a preset message on a repetitive schedule—but rather are sorting information on their terms. For example, grocery shoppers using the Peapod Web site can ask for all products in a certain category sorted by different choice criteria. Currently, the top two criteria for, say, peanut butter are price and fat content. This produces the "healthiest" peanut butter, according to the Net user's information criteria. Kraft didn't get a chance to have an impact on the decision with an image campaign.

What this potentially means from a creative standpoint is that good brands will correspond more closely to good products. Good brands will have to know the market better because kids are using "softbots," or "bots" software, to tirelessly search the Web for products that interest them. The key is that creatives will understand the choice criteria and develop creative responses once the bots locate the brand site. With this understanding, the challenge will be to create a brand "badge" that displays instantly apparent universal meaning. Without the drone of mass media repetition, creatives will have to score quickly with brand image and brand meaning.

The brand, then, is the catch-22 of N-Gen culture. N-Gen'ers identify and are loyal to brands, but they are building a culture that is antithetical to the mass communications important to brand establishment and identity. This contradiction is creating a shift from broadcast dictatorship to interactive democracy—but still depends, absolutely, on brand identity.

argued that adaptors and innovators are equally creative.[31] However, between and within organizations, one mode of creative problem solving may be more conducive to success than the other.[32]

This approach has a certain commonsense appeal. The CEO of an airline might reward and promote an employee who created a way to get customers through the ticket line faster using technology the airline was using in a different part of its operations. However, the same CEO might not respond as favorably to an employee who created a rising set of service expectations on the part of customers. The commonsense appeal has its limitations—especially if you were an employee at a bank in 1970 who figured out a way to keep customers out of the bank. You might have gotten laughed out of a job. Luckily, ten years later you could deposit your unemployment checks at the ATM around the corner. See the New Media box on this page for an example of how technology has changed one aspect of the creative approach to advertising.

Creativity is the ability to consider and hold together seemingly inconsistent elements and forces. This ability to step outside of the everyday logic, to free oneself of thinking in terms of "the way things are" or "the way things have to be" apparently allows creative people to put things together in a way that, once we see it, makes sense, is interesting, is creative. To see love and hate as the same entity, to see "round squares," or to imagine time bending like molten steel is to have this ability. It reveals its own logic, and then we say, "I see."

Source: Don Tapscott, "Net Culture Reshapes Brand Opportunities," *Advertising Age*, November 10, 1997, 34.

31. Ibid., Matherly and Goldsmith, "The Two Faces of Creativity."
32. Kirton, "Adaptors and Innovators in Organizations."

Advertising Agencies, the Creative Process, and the Product.

As an employee in an agency creative department, you will spend most of your time with your feet up on a desk working on an ad. Across the desk, also with his feet up, will be your partner—in my case, an art director. And he will want you to talk about movies.

In fact, if the truth be known, you will spend fully one-fourth of your career with your feet up talking about movies.

The ad is due in two days. The media space has been bought and paid for. The pressure's building. And your muse is sleeping off drunk behind a dumpster somewhere. Your pen lies useless. So you talk movies.

That's when the traffic person comes by. Traffic people stay on top of a job as it moves through the agency. Which means they also stay on top of you. They'll come by to remind you of the horrid things that happen to snail-assed creative people who don't come through with the goods on time.

So, you try to get your pen moving. And you begin to work. And working in this business, means staring at your partner's shoes.

That's what I've been doing from 9 to 5 for almost 20 years. Staring at the bottom of the disgusting tennis shoes on the feet of my partner, parked on the desk across from my disgusting tennis shoes. This is the sum and substance of life at an agency.

—Luke Sullivan[33]

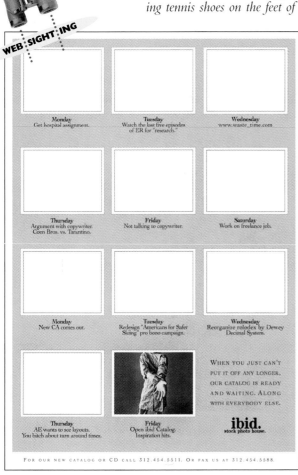

WEB SIGHTING

Companies like ibid (www.ibidphoto.com) cater to the creative: The ibid catalog offers images to jump-start the imagination.

Exhibit 10.6 is illustrative of many creative pursuits: lots of time trying to get an idea, or the right idea. You turn things over and over in your head, trying to see the light. You try to find that one way of seeing it that makes it all fall in place. Or, it just comes to you, real easy, just like that. Magic. Every creative pursuit involves this sort of thing. However, advertising, like all creative pursuits, is unique in some respects. Ad people come into an office and try to solve a problem, always under time pressure, given to them by some businessperson. Often this problem is poorly defined, and there are competing agenda. They work for people who seem not to be creative at all, and doing their best not to let them be creative. They are housed in the "creative department," which makes it seem as if it's some sort of warehouse where the executives keep all the creativity so they can find it when they need it, and so it won't get away. This implies that one can pick some up, like getting extra batteries at Wal-Mart.

Oil and Water.
Here are some thoughts on management and creativity by advertising greats:

The majority of businessmen are incapable of original thinking, because they are unable to escape from the tyranny of reason. Their imaginations are blocked.

—William Bernbach[34]

33. Luke Sullivan, "Staring at Your Partner's Shoes," in *Hey Whipple, Squeeze This: A Guide to Creating Great Ads* (New York: Wiley, 1998), 20–22.

34. William Bernbach, cited in Thomas Frank, *The Conquest of Cool: Business Culture, Consumer Culture, and the Rise of Hip Consumerism* (Chicago: University of Chicago Press, 1997).

If you're not a bad boy, if you're not a big pain in the ass, then you are in some mush in this business.

—George Lois[35]

So, you can see this topic rarely yields tepid, diplomatic comments. Advertising is produced through a social process. As a social process, however, it's marked by struggles for control and power that occur within departments, between departments, and between the agency and its clients on a daily basis. Exhibit 10.7 shows a T-shirt sent by an agency to invite its clients to an East Coast phenomenon called a "crab pickin'." Bushels of soft-shell crabs are smashed and picked clean using various sharp objects, then devoured. The shirt says quite a bit about life in an agency on a bad day.

Most research concerning the contentious environment in advertising agencies places the creative department in a central position within these conflicts. We know of no research that has explored conflict within or between departments in an advertising agency that doesn't place the creative department as a focus of the conflict. One explanation hinges on reactions to the uncertain nature of the product of the creative department. Because clients hold the power of final approval, members of the account service team see an advertisement as a product they must control before the client sees it.[36] This creates a great deal of tension between the creative department and the account service department. In addition, individuals in the account service department and in the creative department of an advertising agency do not always share the same ultimate goals for advertisements (sorry, Pollyana; it's true). Individuals in the creative department see an advertisement as a vehicle to communicate a personal creative ideology that will further their careers. (See Exhibit 10.8.) The account manager, serving as liaison between client and agency, sees the goal of the communication as achieving some predetermined objective in the marketplace.[37] Another source of conflict is attributed to differing perspectives due to differing background knowledge of the members of creative groups and the account service team. Account managers must be

EXHIBIT 10.7

A commentary on life in an advertising agency on a bad day.

35. George Lois, cited in Randall Rothenberg, *Where the Suckers Moon* (New York: Knopf, 1994), 135–172.
36. A. J. Kover and S. M. Goldberg, "The Games Copywriters Play: Conflict, Quasi-Control, a New Proposal," *Journal of Advertising Research,* vol. 25, no. 4 (1995), 52–62.
37. Elizabeth Hirschman, "The Effect of Verbal and Pictorial Advertising Stimuli on Aesthetic, Utilitarian and Familiarity Perceptions," *Journal of Advertising,* 1985, 27–34.

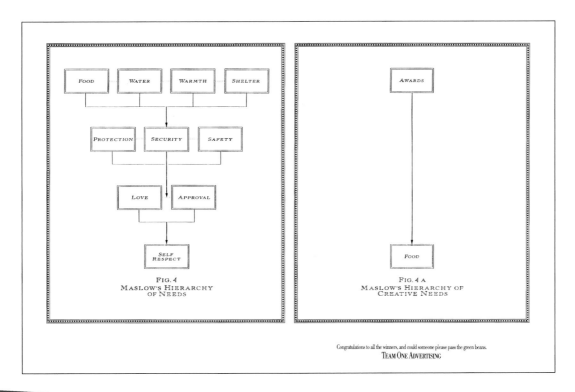

Congratulations to all the winners, and could someone please pass the green beans.
TEAM ONE ADVERTISING

EXHIBIT 10.8

Team One Advertising (www.teamoneadv.com) has an interesting spin on what motivates agency creatives; here, it parodies Maslow's hierarchy to make its point. Compare this print advertisement with the imagery, words, and ideas on display at Team One's Web site. Both are, in part, self-promotional and self-congratulatory. When an agency is both client and creator, how do the struggles for power and control of the creative product change?

generalists with broad knowledge, whereas creatives (copywriters and art directors) are specialists who must possess great expertise in a single area.[38]

Regardless of its role as a participant in conflict, the creative department is recognized as an essential part of an advertising agency's success. It is the primary consideration of potential clients when they select advertising agencies.[39] Creativity has been found to be crucial to a positive client/advertiser relationship. Interestingly, clients see creativity as an overall agency trait, whereas agency people place the responsibility for it firmly on the shoulders of the creative department.[40] However, there is evidence that, although the client may hold the entire agency responsible for the creative output, they may still unknowingly place the creative department in a position of primary responsibility. An interview with 20 of the largest advertising clients in the United States found that failing to produce effective advertisements was the single unforgivable shortcoming an agency could have.[41]

However, many clients don't recognize their role in killing the very same effective ideas that they claim to be looking for (Exhibit 10.9). Anyone who has worked in the creative department of an advertising agency for any length of time has a full quiver of client stories—like the one about the client who wanted to produce a single 30-second spot for his ice cream novelty company. The creative team went to work and brought in a single spot that everyone agreed delivered the strategy perfectly, set up further possible spots in the same campaign, and in the words of the copywriter, was just damn

38. B. G. Vanden Berg, S. J. Smith, and J. W. Wickes, "Internal Agency Relationships: Account Service and Creative Personnel," *Journal of Advertising,* vol. 15, no. 2 (1986), 55–60.
39. D. West, "Restricted Creativity: Advertising Agency Work Practices in the U.S., Canada and the U.K." *Journal of Creative Behavior,* vol. 27, no. 3 (1993), 200–213.
40. P. C. Michell, "Accord and Discord in Agency-Client Perceptions of Creativity," *Journal of Advertising Research,* vol. 24, no. 5 (1984), 9–24.
41. M. Kingman, "A Profile of a Bad Advertising Agency," *Advertising Age,* November 23, 1981, 53–54.

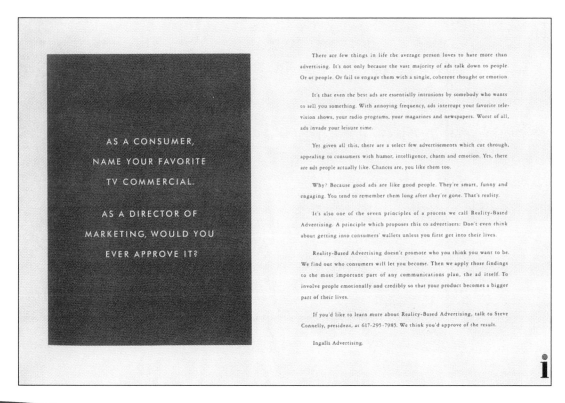

EXHIBIT 10.9

What clients like and what clients approve are often two very different things.

funny. It was the kind of commercial that you actually look forward to seeing on television. During the storyboard presentation, the client laughed in all the right places, and admitted the spot was on strategy. Then the client rejected the spot.

The client said the agency was trying to force him into a corner where he had to approve the spot, since they didn't show him any alternatives. The agency went back to work. Thirty-seven alternatives were presented over the next six months. Thirty-seven alternatives were killed. Finally, the client approved a spot, the first spot from half a year earlier. There was much rejoicing. One week later, he canceled the production, saying he wanted to put the money behind a national couponing effort instead. Then he took the account executive out to lunch and asked why none of the creatives liked him.

Or the potato chip client that told an agency that the next campaign they came up with needed to be the best work they had ever done. The new product the client was introducing was crucial to the overall success of the company. The agency put every team in the house to work on it for 16 hours a day, two weeks straight. The result? The client loved the work, saying it was indeed the best work he had ever seen. In fact, instead of the single product-introduction ad he had asked for, the client approved four ads. There was a client/agency group hug. One week later, the client fired the agency, asking why they hadn't ever presented this kind of work before.

Or the newspaper client that wanted to encourage people who didn't read the newspaper to read the newspaper. Only one mandate, though. The ads had to appear in the client's newspaper since the space was free.

It's easy and sometimes fun to blame clients for all of the anxieties and frustrations of the creatives. Especially if you work in a creative department. You can "diss" the clients all you want and, since they aren't in the office next to you, they can't hear you. But, despite the obvious stake that creative departments have in generating superior advertising, it should be mentioned that no creative ever put $200 million of his own money behind a campaign. Clients not only foot the bills, they also approach agencies with creative problems in the first place. Read the Global Issues box on this page and try imagining an agency's creative department not being piqued by the chance to have all the world as its stage just because the client may sulk a lot.

GLOBAL ISSUES

HOW IMPORTANT IS BRAND IDENTITY? IT MEANS THE WORLD TO COMPAQ

Compaq has hired an identity consultant to lead a global brand study so the world's number-one PC maker and its ad agency—Ammirati Puris Lintas—can prepare a global ad campaign. The consulting firm will scrutinize absolutely everything about Compaq's "brand architecture": packaging, product names, brochures, and advertising materials.

Compaq is not alone in the drive to identify and accentuate brand identity. A host of technology firms, including Gateway and Hewlett-Packard, have also embarked on identity campaigns. Part of the motivation is the very real threat that consumers will perceive homogeneity between tech brands. After all, it does seem as if one gigabyte is about like the next, and how different can MHz be anyway? But, beyond the threat, there is the massive global opportunity. *If* a compelling brand identity is agreed upon and *if* the advertising and supportive materials can be aligned for solidifying this identity, then a truly global brand can emerge.

This opportunity for global brand identity is the flip side of the original threat of perceived homogeneity. The flip side of consumers perceiving similarity among tech brands is that the tendency to see similarity is a cross-cultural phenomenon. This means that the ability to communicate on similar terms is high—a Brit, an American, and a Brazilian are likely to desire the same features in a tech product. If a compelling and universal brand image can be discovered, its potential for global acceptance is high.

Compaq's global campaign will cost as much $200 million to effectively establish. It may be rolled out on a global basis or on a regional basis depending on the creative elements and the need to customize versus standardize the images. But, in this case, brand identity really does mean the world to Compaq.

Source: Bradley Johnson, "Compaq Joins Tech Rush For Identity Consultants," *Advertising Age*, January 19, 1998, 47.

Indeed, you can't always blame the clients. Sometimes the conflicts and problems that preclude wonderful creative work occur within the walls of the advertising agency itself.

That agency can be a very complex social system. The way this system works can have a very real effect on creative output. In her work on influences on creativity, researcher Theresa Amabile lists different social-environmental factors that affect creativity.[42] This list includes such things as the work environment, education, family influences, and societal, political, and cultural influences.[43] Therefore, to understand creativity within an agency, you must consider personality variables, motivational variables, and the sociocultural environment.[44]

We are not suggesting that you should downplay the importance of the personal cognitive systems of the Einsteins, Gandhis, and Picassos of advertising. Instead, you should recognize that innate abilities and understandings are mediated by social influences and contextual influences such as the physical environment and task variables. In short, it's crucial to understand that external complexities affect the creative process in very real ways.

To say there can be a bit of conflict between the creative department and the other departments of an advertising agency is a bit like saying there can be a bit of conflict when Jerry Springer walks into a studio.

In advertising, the conflict often centers on the creative department and the account management department. It's no wonder that creatives feel as if their creative output is put under a microscope. The creative department is recognized as an essential part of an advertising agency's success. What does a potential client consider to be of

42. Amabile
43. Ibid.
44. Sternberg, 1996.

primary importance when choosing an advertising agency? Creativity. What is one of the crucial factors in a positive client/agency relationship? Again, creativity.[45] So why doesn't everybody pull together and love each other within an agency?

When a client is unhappy, they fire the agency. Billings and revenue drop. Budgets are cut. And pink slips drop. It's no wonder that conflict occurs. When someone is looking out for his or her job, it's tough not to get involved in struggles over control of the creative product. Account managers function as the conduit from agency to client and back. Every day when they walk in the door, their prime responsibility is to see that the client is purring and happy. Since clients hold the final power of approval over creative output, the members of the account team see an advertisement as a product they must control before the client sees it.[46] Members of the creative department resent the control. They feel as if their work is being judged by a group whose most creative input should be over what tie or scarf goes best with a pinstriped suit.

Members of the account management team perceive the creatives as experts in the written word or in visual expression. However, they believe that creatives don't understand advertising strategy or business dealings.

As with most things, the truth probably lies somewhere in the murky middle. Unfortunately, except at a few fortunate agencies (Exhibit 10.10), the chances for total recognition of each departments' talents are slim. As stated earlier, the backgrounds of the people in each department are just too different, the organizational structures too much of a problem.

EXHIBIT 10.10

How to identify a good advertising executive.

For some 25 years I was an advertising agency "AE," eventually rising through the crabgrass to become a founder, president, chairman and now chairman emeritus of Borders, Perrin and Norrander, Inc.

During all those years, I pondered the eternal question: Why do some advertising agencies consistently turn out a superior creative product while others merely perpetuate mediocrity? Is the answer simply to hire great writers and art directors? Well, certainly that has a lot to do with it, but I would suggest that there is another vital component in the equation for creative success.

Outstanding creative work in an ad agency requires a ferocious commitment from all staffers, but especially from the account service person. The job title is irrelevant—account executive, account manager, account supervisor—but the job function is critical, particularly when it comes to client approvals. Yes, I am speaking of the oft-maligned AE, the "suit" who so frequently is the bane of the Creative Department.

So how in the wide world does one identify this rare species, this unusual human being who is sensitive to the creative process and defends the agency recommendations with conviction and vigor? As you might expect, it is not easy. But there are some signals, some semihypothetical tests that can be used as diagnostic tools:

To begin with, look for unflappability, a splendid trait to possess in the heat of battle. In Australia last year I heard a chap tell about arriving home to "find a bit of a problem" under his bed. An eight-foot python had slithered in and coiled around the man's small dog. Hearing its cries, he yanked the snake out from under the mattress, pried it loose from the mutt, tossed it out the door and "dispatched it with a garden hoe." Was he particularly frightened or distressed? Not at all. "I've seen bigger snakes," he said, helping himself to another Foster's Lager. Now, that's the kind of disposition which wears well in account service land.

Source: Wes Perrin, "How to Identify a Good AE," *Communication Arts Advertising Annual 1988* (Palo Alto, CA: Coyne and Blanchard, Inc., 1988), 210.

45. D. C. West, "Cross-National Creative Personalities, Processes, and Agency Philosophies," *Journal of Advertising Research,* vol. 33, no. 5 (1993), 53–62.
46. Kover and Goldberg, "The Games Copywriters Play."

EXHIBIT 10.11

Companies like Working Computer (www.clientsandprofits.com) provide tools to help manage some of the most complex machinery imaginable: the human being. Why do you think the Clients & Profits ad highlights that the software runs on the Macintosh, given that so many of the computers in the world aren't Macs?

So how does an agency successfully address this tension? The ad in Exhibit 10.11 suggests that it can be done with the right computer software. In most instances, though, the truth may be that it can't. Beyond the philosophy may be a simple fact: Individuals in the account service departments and creative departments of advertising agencies do not always (even usually) share the same ultimate goals for advertisements. Sorry, but that's often the way it is.

For an account manager to rise in his or her career, he or she must excel in the care and feeding of clients. It's a job of negotiation, gentle prodding, and ambassadorship. For a creative to rise, the work must challenge. It must arrest attention. It must provoke. At times, it must shock. It must do all the things a wonderful piece of art must do. Yet, as we indicated earlier, this is all the stuff that makes for nervous clients. And that is an account executive's nightmare.

This nightmare situation for the account executives produces the kind of ads that win awards for the creatives. People who win awards are recognized by the award shows in the industry. Their work gets published in *The One Show* and *Communication Arts* and appears on the Clios. These people become in demand and they are wined and dined by rival agencies (Exhibit 10.12). And they become famous and, yes, rich by advertising standards. Are they happier, better people? Some are. Some aren't. Ask one sometime. In the most honest moments, do they think sales as much as *One Show*s and Addys? So the trick is, how do you get creatives to want to pursue cool ads that also sell? Let them win awards even though it may have nothing to do with boosting sales, or more simply, let them keep their job?

Art and Science. ◆▷ *There are a lot of great technicians in advertising. And unfortunately they talk the best game. They know all the rules. They can tell you that [pictures of] people in an ad will get you greater readership. They can tell you that body copy should be broken up for easier and more inviting reading. They can give you fact after fact after fact. They are the scientists of advertising. But there's one little rub. Advertising is fundamentally persuasion and persuasion happens to be not a science, but an art.*

—William Bernbach[47]

The difficulty of assessing the effectiveness of an advertisement has also created antagonism between the creative department and the research department.[48] (The ads in Exhibits 10.13 and 10.14 clearly were not copy-tested.) Vaughn states that the tumultuous social environment between creative departments and research departments represents the "historical conflict between art and science . . . these polarities have been argued philosophically as the conflict between Idealism and Materialism or

47. Ibid.
48. Kover and Goldberg, "The Games Copywriters Play."

WE'D LIKE TO TELL ALL OF TONIGHT'S AWARD HUNGRY, SMART ASS, HOLIER-THAN-THOU ADDY WINNERS EXACTLY WHERE THEY CAN GO.

FCB   (312) 440-5301

CATHY J. WALEJESKI
CREATIVE RECRUITER

FOOTE, CONE & BELDING
FCB CENTER, 101 EAST ERIE
CHICAGO, IL 60611-2897, FAX (312) 751-3501

EXHIBIT 10.12

Foote, Cone & Belding (www.fcbsf.com) is in the hunt for creatives, using a bit of sassy, pun-in-cheekiness to signal that resumes are wanted. What challenges do you think the Foote, Cone & Belding HR department faces in hiring and retaining the best and the brightest (beyond borrowing some of the company's creative time to produce clever recruitment ads)?

If you don't like this ad, we'll find out why.

For accurate and objective advertising research, call Kevin Menk at (612) 331-9222.

 Project Research, Inc.

1313 Fifth Street SE, Minneapolis, MN 55414

We could fill this page with interesting information about our research company, but research indicates you wouldn't read it.

Project Research, Inc.

1313 Fifth Street SE, Minneapolis, MN 55414
(612) 331-9222

EXHIBITS 10.13 AND 10.14

Research on an ad's effectiveness is an important, difficult, and unpopular task.

Rationalism and Empiricism."[49] In the world of advertising, people in research departments are put in the unenviable position of judging the creatives. So, once again, they are put in a position where "science" judges art. Creatives don't like this, particularly when it's usually pretty bad science, or not science at all. Of course, researchers are sometimes creative themselves, and they don't typically enjoy being an additional constraint on those in the creative department.

Why Does Advertising Need Creativity?

Who needs creativity? Consumers do. Clients do. Creativity allows the consumer to see the brand in new and desired ways. It can accomplish the increasingly elusive breakthrough. Most marketing is about establishing brand relationships—creating and maintaining brand image and position. It is the creative execution that really allows this to happen. Advertising makes brands and relationships, and creative makes advertising. It puts the brand in a social context. It makes things into brands. And, as suggested by Exhibit 10.15, "bad" creatives will surely destroy a client's brand.

With all this talk of competition, envy, madness, constraint, and frustration, we could have written a do-it-yourself marriage counseling book. The world of advertising, despite these problems, is as Jerry Della Femina said: "The most fun you can have with your pants on."[50] It's one of the few places left where really creative people can go to express themselves and make a living. And remember:

All literature is yet to be written. Poetry has scarce chanted its first song. The perpetual admonition of nature to us is "The world is new, untried. Do not believe the past. I give you the universe a virgin today."

—Ralph Waldo Emerson[51]

49. Vaughn, 1995.

50. Jerry Della Femina, *From those Wonderful Folks Who Gave You Pearl Harbor, Front-Line Dispatches from the Advertising War.* (New York: Simon and Schuster, 1970), 244.

51. Ralph Waldo Emerson, cited in Fitzgerald, *An Artist's Book of Inspiration,* 14.

EXHIBIT 10.15

Assuring poor creative.

One of the advantages of being a practitioner-turned-educator is the opportunity to interact with a large number of agencies. Much like Switzerland, an academic is viewed as a neutral in current affairs and not subject to the suspicions of a potential competitor.

The result of my neutral status has been the opportunity to watch different agencies produce both great and poor work. And, as a former associate creative director, I'd like to share the trends I've seen in the development of bad creative. The revelation: Bad work is more a matter of structure than talent. Here are 12 pieces of advice if you want to institutionalize bad creative work in your agency:

1. Treat your target audience like a statistic.

Substituting numbers for getting a feel for living, breathing people is a great way to make bad work inevitable. It allows you to use your gut instinct about "women 55 to 64" rather than the instinct that evolves from really understanding a group of folks. The beauty with staying on the statistical level is that you get to claim you did your homework when the creative turns out dreadful. After all, there were 47 pages of stats on the target.

2. Make your strategy a hodgepodge.

Good ads have one dominant message, just one. Most strategies that result in lousy work have lots more than one. They are political junkyards that defy a creative wunderkind to produce anything but mediocrity. So make everybody happy with the strategy and then tell your creatives to find a way to make it all work. You'll get bad work, for sure.

3. Have no philosophy.

William Bernbach believed in a certain kind of work. His people emulated his philosophy and produced a consistent kind of advertising that built a great agency. Now, to be controversial, I'll say the exact same thing about Rosser Reeves. Both men knew what they wanted, got it and prospered.

The agency leaders who do hard sell one day, then new wave the next, create only confusion. More important, the work does not flow from a consistent vision of advertising and a code of behavior to achieve that advertising. Instead, there is the wild embrace of the latest fashion or the currently faddish bromide making the rounds at conventions. So beware of those who have a philosophy and really are true to it. They are historically at odds with lousy work.

4. Analyze your creative as you do a research report.

The cold, analytical mind does a wonderful job destroying uncomfortable, unexpected work. Demand that every detail be present in every piece of creative and say it is a matter of thoroughness. The creative work that survives your ice storm will be timid and compromised and will make no one proud.

5. Make the creative process professional.

"Creative types collect a paycheck every two weeks. They'd better produce and do it now. This is, after all, a business." The corporate performance approach is a highly recommended way of developing drab print and TV. Treating the unashamedly artistic process of making ads as if it were an offshoot of the local oil filter assembly plant promises to destroy risk-taking and morale. Your work will become every bit as distinctive as a gray suit. More important, it will be on schedule. And both are fine qualities in business and we are a business, aren't we?

6. Say one thing and do another.

Every bad agency says all the right things about risk-taking, loving great creative, and admiring strong creative people. It is mandatory to talk a good game and then do all the things that destroy great work. This will help keep spirits low and turnover high in the creative who is actually talented. And then you'll feel better when they leave after a few months because you really do like strong creative people—if they just weren't so damn defensive.

7. Give your client a candy store.

To prove how hard you work, insist on showing numerous half-thought-out ideas to your client. The approved campaign will have lots of problems nobody thought about and that will make the final work a mess.

Campaigns with strong ideas are rare birds, and they need a great deal of thinking to make sure they're right. So insist on numerous campaigns and guarantee yourself a series of sparrows rather than a pair of eagles.

8. Mix and match your campaigns.

Bring three campaigns to your client, and then mix them up. Take a little bit of one and stick it on another. Even better, do it internally. It's like mixing blue, red, and green. All are fine colors, but red lacks the coolness of blue. Can't we add a little? The result of the mix will be a thick muddy clump. Just like so many commercials currently on the air.

9. Fix it in production.

Now that your procedure has created a half-baked campaign that is being mixed up with another, tell the creative to make it work by excellent production values. Then you can fire the incompetent hack when the jingle with 11 sales points is dull.

10. Blame the creative for bad creative.

After all, you told them what they should do. ("Make it totally unexpected, but use the company president and the old jingle.") The fault lies in the fact that you just can't find good talent anymore. Never mind that some creative departments have low turnover and pay smaller salaries than you do.

11. Let your people imitate.

"Chiat/Day won awards and sales for the Apple *1984* commercial, so let's do something like that for our stereo store account." This approach works wonders because your imitation appears lacking the original surprise that came from a totally expected piece of work. You can even avoid the controversy that surrounded Chiat/Day when half the industry said the ad was rotten. Your imitation can blend right in with all the other imitations and, even better, will have no strategic rationale for your bizarre execution.

12. Believe posttesting when you get a good score.

That way you can be slaughtered by your client when your sensitive, different commercial gets a score 20 points below norm. The nice things you said about posttesting when you got an excellent score with your "singing mop" commercial cannot be taken back. If you want to do good work, clients must somehow be made to use research as a tool. If you want to do bad creative, go ahead, and believe that posttesting rewards excellent work.

Naturally, a lot of bad creative results from egomania laziness, incompetence, and client intractability—but a lot less than most believe. I have found that bad work usually comes from structures that make talented people ineffective and that demand hard work, human dedication, and tremendous financial investment to produce work that can be topped by your average high school senior.

John Sweeney, a former associate creative director at Foote, Cone & Belding, Chicago, teaches advertising at the University of North Carolina–Chapel Hill.

SUMMARY

◀▷ Describe the core characteristics of great creative minds.

A look at the shared sensibilities of great creative minds provides a constructive starting point for assessing the role of creativity in the production of great advertising. What Picasso had in common with Gandhi, Freud, Eliot, Stravinsky, Graham, and Einstein—including a strikingly exuberant self-confidence, (childlike) alertness, unconventionality, and an obsessive commitment to the work—both charms and alarms us. Self-confidence, at some point, becomes crass self-promotion; an unconstrained childlike ability to see the world as forever new devolves, somewhere along the line, into childish self-indulgence. Without creativity, there can be no advertising. How we recognize and define creativity in advertising rests on our understanding of the achievements of acknowledged creative geniuses from the worlds of art, literature, music, science, and politics.

◀▷ Contrast the role of an advertising agency's creative department with that of its business managers/account executives and explain the tensions between them.

What it takes to get the right idea (a lot of hard work), and the ease with which a client or agency manager may dismiss that idea, underlies the contentiousness between an agency's creative staff and its managers and clients—between the poets and the killers. Creatives provoke. Managers control. Ads that win awards for creative excellence don't necessarily fulfill a client's business imperatives. All organizations deal with the competing agendas of one department versus another, but, in advertising agencies, this competition plays out at an amplified level.

◀▷ Identify the controls imposed on agency creatives that can undermine an agency's ability to create consistently superior work.

Creative superiority—that most-coveted of all agency attributes—can be undone if too many checks are put on creative impulses. Mediocrity has the opportunity to take hold of an agency's creative executions if target audiences are defined by numbers alone or if your message strategy becomes too much of a hodgepodge because someone thinks an ad can communicate more than one dominant theme. Other sure routes to producing lackluster advertising include not having a consistent philosophy, overanalyzing the work, "professionalizing" the creative process, and saying one thing but doing another. Going overboard to keep clients happy also can sour an agency's creative output. Presenting lots of ideas to a client just to prove how hard you've worked is a mistake, as is mixing elements from diverse campaign in hopes of coming up with one really great campaign. It shouldn't be assumed that half-baked ideas can be improved with excellent production value. Other don'ts include blaming the creative for a bad execution (when the account executive and client directed its creation), imitating the highly successful work of another agency, and believing that posttesting scores always reward creative excellence.

KEY TERMS

adaptors (313)

innovators (313)

QUESTIONS FOR REVIEW AND CRITICAL THINKING

1. Over the years, creativity has been associated with various forms of madness and mental instability. In your opinion, what is it about creative people that prompts this kind of characterization?

2. Think about a favorite artist, musician, or writer. What is unique about the way he or she represents the world? What fascinates you about the vision he or she creates?

3. A lot of credence is given in this chapter to the idea that tension (of various sorts) fuels creative pursuits. Explain the connection between creativity and tension in terms of Csikszentmilhaly's creative triangle.

4. What role should critics play in determining what is creative and what is not?

5. Which side of this debate do you have more affinity for: Are people creative because they can produce creative results or are they creative because of the way they think? Explain.

6. What forces inside an advertising agency can potentially compromise its creative work? Is compromise always to be avoided? Imagine that you are an agency creative. Define *compromise*. Now imagine that you are an account executive. How does your definition of *compromise* change?

7. Choose an ad from the book that represents exemplary creativity to you. Explain your choice.

8. Examine Exhibit 10.15. Using this exhibit as your guide, generate a list of ten principles to facilitate creativity in an advertising agency.

EXPERIENTIAL EXERCISES

1. Explain why you are a creative person in *exactly* 100 words. You *do not* have the option of claiming you are not creative.

2. Describe what the advertising process will be like in the year 2025. Include a description of media and the way an agency works.

USING THE INTERNET

Any new Internet venture encounters a serious challenge long before the first customer walks in the virtual door: What will it be named? Increasingly, the naming question becomes "what's *left*?", with millions of possibilities already gobbled up by other businesses and by domain name speculators.

Visit Network Solutions (www.networksolutions.com), which was awarded a contract by the National Science Foundation (NSF) to serve as the registrar for the COM, NET, and ORG top-level domains.

Visit also the U.S. Patent and Trademark Office, which has put its database of registered trademarks on the Web at www.uspto.gov.

Yahoo! (www.yahoo.com) lists a variety of companies in the business of domain name brokering.

The Internet Corporation for Assign Names and Numbers (ICANN) (www.icann.org) is a new, nonprofit organization created to provide a governing body for domain name issues.

1. How important is an Internet domain name to a business?

2. Your company has finally gotten around to creating a Web site for your flagship product, which you've manufactured for twenty years, only to find that some college kid owns the most appropriate domain name and wants $100,000 for it. What are your options?

3. Given that the Internet is, by all accounts, in its infancy, and useful domain names are already scarce, what alternatives might be considered?

One approach to deciding where to put the sidewalks on a new college campus is to not put in any in the first year, and to watch where the paths develop in the grass. One can learn a lot just by observing how people collectively traverse a space, including Cyberspace. Alexa (http://www.alexa.com) hopes to let users navigate the World Wide Web based on others' behavior, developing recommendations on the basis of observed similarities (many people who visit Site A also visit Site B), the joint presence of links on a single page (if A links to B, C, and D, they all might have similar content), and so on.

Alexa can be used as a powerful research tool— try using it to find sites and pages relevant to your own research.

1. How reflective are Alexa's associations of the Web surfing population as a whole?

2. How accurate do you think Alexa's measures of site size, traffic, freshness, and so on, are?

3. How might Alexa's databases be open to manipulation by the unscrupulous marketer?

Since Alexa's databases are compiled in large part through data collected from Alexa users, they will be biased toward the preference and interests of Alexa users—most likely won't be Net "newbies," but more experienced and technically-savvy users.

ALTOIDS
THE CURIOUSLY STRONG MINTS™

http://www.altoids.com

CHAPTER

After reading and thinking about this chapter, you will be able to do the following:

◖▶ Identify ten objectives of message strategy.

◖▶ Identify methods for executing each message strategy objective.

There are those who say it was brilliant and inspired. Others argue it was a capricious and expensive exercise in grandstanding. In January 1984, during the third quarter of the Super Bowl, Apple Computer introduced the Macintosh with a 60-second spot. The ad, known as "1984" (turn back to Exhibit 8.1), climaxed with a young athletic woman hurling a mallet through a huge projection screen in a monochromatic vision of a hypercorporate and ugly future.[1] On the big screen was an Orwellian Big Brother instructing the masses. As the ad closed, with the near soulless masses obediently chanting the corporate-state mantra in the background, the following simple statement appeared on the television screens of millions of viewers: "On January 24th, Apple Computer will introduce Macintosh. And you'll see why 1984 won't be like 1984."

What made this advertisement particularly newsworthy is that it cost $400,000 to produce (very expensive for its day) and another $500,000 to broadcast, yet it was broadcast only *once*. It was a creative superevent. The three major networks covered the event on the evening news, and the ad went on to become *Advertising Age*'s Commercial of the Decade for the 1980s. But why? It wasn't just its high cost and single play. It wasn't just its very stylish, but disturbing look (directed by Ridley Scott [*Bladerunner*]). It wasn't just about an ad that told us that we could be the person we wanted to be, rather than the one we had to be. It was more that the ad captured and articulated something important lying just below the surface of mid-1980s American culture. It was about us versus them, threatened individuals versus faceless corporations. It was about the defiant rejection of sterile corporate life and the celebration of individuality through, of all things, a computer. Archrival IBM was implicitly cast as the oppressive Big Blue (that is, Big Brother) and Apple as the good anti-corporate corporation. The ad captured the moment and, most critically, served up a consumer product as popular ideology. Apple became the hip, the young, the cool, the democratic, the populist, the anti-establishment computer. It was the computer of the non-sellout, or at least of those who wished to think of themselves that way.

As we've said before, you can rarely go wrong by emphasizing individuality in the United States. Likewise, if you can link your product to a strong social movement, so much the better, as long as the trend lasts. If you can also serve a large and under-served market segment (for example, cyber-insecure consumers unwilling to deal with DOS, ready to use a mouse, and generally anti-button-down corporate), even better. Steve Hayden, the "1984" copywriter, described the ad this way: "We thought of it as an ideology, a value set. It was a way of letting the whole world access the power of computing and letting them talk to one another. The democratization of technology—the computer for the rest of us."[2]

With "1984," Apple and advertising agency Chiat/Day wanted to focus attention on a new product and completely distinguish Apple and the Macintosh from Big Blue, IBM. Macintosh was going to offer computing power to the people. This declaration of computing independence was made on the most-watched broadcast of the year. Forty-six percent of all U.S. households were tuned to the 1984 Super Bowl. With the Macintosh, Apple offered an alternative and very hip cyber-ethos for those who felt alienated or intimidated by the IBM world. The "1984" ad offered a clear choice, a clear instruction: Buy a Mac, keep your soul. And it worked. Macintosh and Apple grew and prospered. For quite a while, "the rest of us" was a pretty big group.

Of course, there is another lesson here: Nothing lasts forever, not even a great creative idea. Things change. Advertising has to evolve along with the situation, or the brand may suffer. As great as this ad was (and it was) and as much success as the Mac and Apple had, things didn't stay so good. Some believe that the seeds of Apple's own near demise may have been the result of hanging on to this idea of "the rest of us" just a little too long. Apple effectively cultivated an us-versus-them ethic, which worked well to help establish a brand position and even a sense of brand community, but Apple failed to keep the Apple tent inclusive and big. The rest-of-us ethos became something of a problem.

1. The term "ugly future" was first used in this context by Connie Johnson, University of Illinois, in the late 1970s.
2. This quote appears in Bradley Johnson, "10 Years after 1984: The Commercial and the Product That Changed Advertising," *Advertising Age,* January 10, 1994, 12.

Jump back to the present. Today, Apple's future is uncertain and, some believe, threatened by a failure to recognize and adapt to changes in the marketplace. Because Apple refused to license its operating system until 1995 (and then changed its mind again), Macs became a relatively expensive alternative. Coupled to a premium price, the "rest of us" came to be regarded by some as evidence of Apple's snooty and elitist attitude. The "rest of us" seemed to think they were better (more hip, cooler, more arty, more *au courant*, and so on) than us—not necessarily a desirable product attribute if a company hopes to sell a lot of computers. Once the skid hit software availability, Apple came perilously close to extinction.

Now, with the return of co-founder Steve Jobs, Apple has once again teamed up with TBWA Chiat/Day to launch the iMac (Exhibit 11.1), and it seems that things could turn around yet again. With the return of Jobs, the company made a profit of around $309 million after a loss of $1 billion in the previous Jobs-less year. And over 278,000 people took iMacs home with them in the first six weeks on the market.[3] Is Apple back tapping into the soul of American culture? We'll have to wait and see. But it's unlikely that Apple will conquer the American consciousness the way it did in 1984. Back then, Apple's advertising was unquestionably superior. No one can ever take that away. It was truly creative, and it advanced Apple's strategy. Apple and Chiat/Day deserve a great deal of credit.

Message Strategy.

An advertising strategy is a summary statement of all essential and defining planning, preparation, and placement decisions. One major component of an advertising strategy is the **message strategy**. The message strategy consists of objectives and methods. It defines the goals of the advertiser and how those goals will be achieved. This chapter offers ten message strategy objectives and discusses and illustrates the methods often used to satisfy them. This is not an exhaustive list, but it covers many of the most common and important message strategy objectives. Exhibit 11.2 summarizes the ten message strategy objectives presented here.

Objective: Promote Brand Recall.

Since the very beginning, a major goal of advertisers has been to get consumers to remember the brand's name. This is typically referred to as the brand recall objective. Of course, advertisers not only want consumers to remember their name, but also want that name to be the first name consumers remember.

EXHIBIT 11.1

The launch of the iMac.
www.apple.com/

3.   David Kirkpatrick, "The Second Coming of Apple," *Fortune*, November 9, 1998, 86–92.

EXHIBIT 11.2

Message strategy objectives and methods.

Objective: What the Advertiser Hopes to Achieve	Method: How the Advertiser Plans to Achieve the Objective
Promote brand recall: To get consumers to recall its brand name(s) first; that is, before any of the competitors' brand names	Repetition ads Slogan and jingle ads
Link a key attribute to the brand name: To get consumers to associate a key attribute with a brand name and vice versa	Unique selling proposition (USP) ads
Instill brand preference: To get consumers to like or prefer its brand above all others	Feel-good ads Humor ads Sexual-appeal ads
Scare the consumer into action: To get consumers to buy a product or service by instilling fear	Fear-appeal ads
Change behavior by inducing anxiety: To get consumers to make a purchase decision by playing to their anxieties; often, the anxieties are social in nature	Anxiety ads
Transform consumption experiences: To create a feeling, image, or mood about a brand that is activated when the consumer uses the product or service	Transformational ads
Situate the brand socially: To give the brand meaning by placing it in a desirable social context	Slice-of-life ads Light fantasy ads
Define the brand image: To create an image for a brand by relying predominantly on visuals rather than discourse	Image ads
Persuade the consumer: To convince consumers to buy a product or service through high-engagement discourse	Reason-why ads Hard-sell ads Comparison ads Information-only ads Testimonial ads Demonstration ads Advertorial Infomercials
Invoke a direct response: To get consumers to take immediate buying action, typically by providing a toll-free number	Call or click now ads

Advertisers want their brand name to be "top of mind" or at least in the *evoked set*, a small list of brand names (typically less than five) that come to mind when a product or service category (for example, airlines, soft drinks, photographic film) is recalled. In the case of parity (few major differences between brands) products (for example, laundry soaps) and other "low-involvement" goods and services, the first brand remembered is often the most likely to be purchased. First-remembered brands are often the most popular brands. Consumers may infer popularity, desirability, and even superiority from the ease with which they recall brands. So, how do advertisers promote easy recall? There are several methods.

Method: Repetition. 👀 As simple as it sounds, repetition is a tried-and-true way of gaining easier retrieval from memory. This is done not only through buying a lot of ads (although that certainly helps), but also by repeating the brand name within the ad copy itself. The idea is that things said more often will be remembered more easily than

TALKING DOG: Kibbles 'n Bits,

Kibbles 'n Bits, I'm gonna get me

some Kibbles 'n Bits.

(SFX-DOG PANTS) Kibbles 'n Bits,

Kibbles 'n Bits.

I'm gonna get me some Kibbles 'n Bits.

ANNCR: Ken-L Ration introduces Kibbles 'n Bits, a brand new idea.

It's two new dog foods in one.

Kibbles, a new crunchy meaty-tasting dry. And bits, a new chewy burger-style food.

You'll crunch it, chomp it, absolutely devour it.

Kibbles 'n Bits, two great new dog foods in one.

TALKING DOG: Kibbles 'n Bits, Kibbles 'n Bits, I'm gonna get me more Kibbles 'n Bits. (BARKS)

EXHIBIT 11.3

Repeating the brand name in an ad can help establish the name in receivers' memory. This ad for Kibbles 'n Bits may have established a record for brand name repetition in a 30-second ad. www.kibbles-n-bits.com/

things said less frequently. When the consumer stands in front of the laundry detergent aisle, you can't expect deliberate and extensive consideration of product attributes: Just the recall of a name, a previous judgment, or (most often) habit drives the purchase decision. Getting into the consumer's evoked set gets you closer to preference and, ultimately, to brand loyalty. This type of advertising tries to keep existing users as much as it tries to get new ones, usually more so. The example from Kibbles 'n Bits, shown in Exhibit 11.3, may have set the record for brand mentions in one ad.

Method: Slogans and Jingles. Slogans are linguistic devices that link a brand name to something memorable, due to the slogan's simplicity, meter, rhyme, or some other factor. (For an example of how Panasonic has reinvigorated its 30-year-old slogan "Just Slightly Ahead of Our Time," see the IMC box on page 335.) Jingles do the same thing, just set to music. Examples are numerous: "Bud-Weis-Er"; "You Deserve a Break Today"; "Tide's In, Dirt's Out"; "The Best Part of Waking Up Is Folgers in Your Cup"; "You're in Good Hands with Allstate"; "Like a Good Neighbor, State Farm Is There"; "We Love to Fly and It Shows"; "Two, Two, Two Mints in One"; "Get Met, It Pays"; and "It Keeps on Going and Going and Going." No doubt you've heard a few of these before. Slogans and jingles allow for rehearsal and often rely on things that can enhance retrieval, such as metaphors and similes.

Objective: Link a Key Attribute to the Brand Name. Sometimes advertisers want consumers to remember a single attribute along with the brand name. If done well, ads employing this strategy objective achieve an echo effect: The attribute helps in the recall of the brand name, and the brand name is linked to one key attribute. This type of advertising is most closely identified with the "Rosser Reeves" **unique selling proposition (USP)** style.

Method: USP. While one does not have to adopt a Reeves style (that is, hard sell, "tests," and a bit annoying), the idea of emphasizing one and only one brand attribute is a very good idea. Ads that try to link several attributes to a brand while working to establish recall often fail. Good examples of successful ads of this sort are "All-Temp-a-Cheer" and the USP offered in Exhibit 11.4—an extremely strong example of this approach. See also the Global Issues box on page 337 for a global application of this approach.

Objective: Instill Brand Preference. The brand-preference objective is fairly universal. Advertisers want consumers to like (and better yet, prefer) their brand. Liking gets you closer to preference than does not-liking. So, liking the brand is good. Liking is different from awareness or top-of-mind recall. Liking is measured in attitudes and is expressed as a feeling. There are many approaches to getting the consumer to like one's brand. Let's look at some of the general approaches; most specific executions are finer distinctions within these more general ones.

Method: Feel-Good Ads. These ads are supposed to work through affective association. They are supposed to link the good feeling elicited by the ad with the brand: You like the ad, you like the brand. While the actual theory and mechanics of this seemingly simple reflex are more complex than you might think (and more controversial), the basic idea is that by creating ads with positive feelings, advertisers will lead consumers to associate those positive feelings with the advertised brand, leading to a higher probability of purchase. As Steve Sweitzer of the Hal Riney and Partners advertising agency said:

[C]onsumers want to do business with companies they LIKE. If they LIKE us, they just may give us a try at the store. What a concept. Sometimes just being liked is a strategy.[4]

The evidence on how well this method works is mixed and equivocal. It may be that positive feelings are transferred to the brand, or it could be that they actually interfere with remembering the message or the brand name. Liking the ad doesn't necessarily mean liking the brand. But message strategy development is a game of probability, and liking may, more times than not, lead to a higher probability of purchase. There are certainly practitioners who continue to believe in the method's intuitive appeal.

The exact mechanisms by which this liking linkage occurs are debated or unknown. We believe that ultimately what creates a good feeling is the product of interpretation on the part of the audience member. This interpretation may be informed by fairly simple associations or by more complex and elaborated thoughts. The interpretive processes of humans are, however, very sophisticated. Humans can make sense of and otherwise "get" complex advertising texts loaded with symbols, innuendo, jokes, and so on, in a split second. While we don't understand why some feel-good ads work and others do not, we do know that paying greater attention to the social context of likely target consumers, and the manner in which consumers "read" ads, is critical. Some pos-

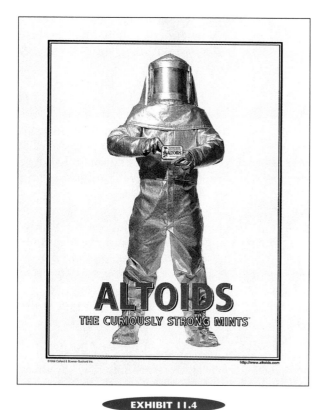

EXHIBIT 11.4

The "Rosser Reeves" unique selling proposition style in action. www.altoids.com/

EXHIBIT 11.5

Chevy's feel-good "Like a Rock" truck ads create positive associations for working-class Americans. www.chevrolet.com/

4. The One Club e-mail discussion, July 27, 1997, as published in *One: A Magazine for Members of the One Club for Art and Copy,* vol. 1, no. 2 (Fall 1997), 18.

itive attitudes toward the ad don't seem to result in positive attitudes toward the brand because they are not "read" for that purpose, or the interpretive context works against liking the brand. You may love ads for Miller Lite, but be a Budweiser drinker. You may think, "Nice ads—wish they made a good beer." Or, you might love the new iMac ads, but don't ever, ever, ever want to be an Apple snob. Still, other feel-good advertising campaigns work. For example, the long-running and apparently successful Chevrolet truck television campaign "Like a Rock," shown in Exhibit 11.5, features the music of Bob Seger and scenes of hardworking, patriotic Americans and their families. It seems to work for a lot of consumers. The good feeling it produces may be the result of widely shared patriotic associations and the celebration of working-class Americans evoked by the advertising.

PANASONIC TAKES THE INTEGRATION PLUNGE

Panasonic has long been criticized as a company that was more focused on selling products than on building a long-term brand franchise. That is all changing now as the firm has committed to an integrated marketing makeover that will bring the same look and feel to advertising, packaging, and promotions.

Panasonic decided that particularly for the holiday buying season—when 60 percent of all consumer electronics are traditionally sold—it would use the same creative approach to promote products across all brand categories. Spending across all media increased about 30 percent over prior years with double-digit increases to persist over several years. The firm decided that TV and print would command the largest portion of the ad budget for consumer electronics and home appliances.

During its first effort in the new era of integration, a six-week spot TV campaign was launched in nine key markets, including New York, Chicago, and Los Angeles. Even though the media buy was regional, it appeared to be national because of promotional tie-ins with ABC's *Monday Night Football* and *The Wonderful World of Disney* along with onscreen billboards. The 30-second spots for three different product categories—camcorder, digital video disc player, and combination TV/computer monitor—all shared the same creative look, with black-and-white images, color footage, and computer animation. The print part of the integrated campaign focused on travel magazines and trade books borrowing images from the broadcast versions.

As a link to the past, Panasonic will keep the "Just Slightly Ahead of Our Time" tagline. In true "one-voice" fashion, that slogan has been with the firm since 1969 and will carry through this new era of integration.

Source: Bradley Johnson, "Panasonic's $15 Million Ad Blitz to Build Brand," *Advertising Age*, November 10, 1997, 4.

Delta Air Lines could show how often its planes depart and arrive on schedule. Instead, it shows the happy reunion of family members and successful business meetings, which create a much richer message, a wider field of shared meanings. The emotions become the product attribute and are linked to the brand—or does the text simply resonate with common lived experience? Hopefully, the consumer makes the desired linkage. Consider Kodak's highly successful print and television campaign that highlighted the "Memories of Our Lives" with powerful scenes: a son coming home from the military just in time for Christmas dinner, and a father's reception dance with his newly married daughter. Here, Kodak makes it clear that it is in the memory business, and Kodak memories are good memories. Good feelings are a desirable product attribute. Back in the mid 1980s every advertiser around was scrambling to understand consumer emotions. Agencies were promising results because of their superior understanding of human emotion. Like most trends, it ran its course, and now these types of ads, while still popular, are far less common. In Exhibit 11.6, Entenmann's attempts to evoke nostalgic feelings of a simpler time through the use of Norman Rockwell paintings.

Method: Humor Ads. The goal of a humor ad is pretty much the same as that of other feel-good ads, but humor is a bit of a different animal altogether. The goal of humor in advertising is to create in the receiver a pleasant and memorable association with the product. Recent advertising campaigns as diverse as those for Miller Lite beer ("Can Your Beer Do This?"), Magnavox consumer electronics (the disappearing remote control), and Little Caesar's ("Pizza-Pizza") have all successfully used humor as the primary message theme. But research suggests that the positive impact of humor is not as strong as the intuitive appeal of the approach. Quite simply, humorous versions of advertisements often do not prove to be more persuasive than nonhumorous versions of the same ad—or research is simply inadequate to detect the difference.

How many times have you been talking to friends about your favorite ads, and you say something like, "Remember the one where the guy knocks over the drink, and then says. . . ." Everybody laughs, and then maybe someone says something like, "I can't remember who it's for, but what a great ad." Wrong; this is not a great ad. You remember the gag, but not the brand. Not good. How come with some other funny ads you can recall the brand? The difference may be that ads in which the payoff for the humor is an integral part of the message strategy better ensure the memory link between humor and brand. If the ad is merely funny and doesn't link the joke (or the punch line) to the brand name, then the advertiser may have bought some very expensive laughs. Hint: Clients rarely consider this funny.

An example of an explicitly linked payoff is the Bud Light "Give Me a Light" campaign of the early 1980s. "Miller Lite" was quickly becoming the generic term for light beer. To do something about this, Bud Light came up with the series of "Give Me a Light" ads to remind light beer drinkers that they had to be a little more specific in what they were ordering. The ads showed customers ordering "a light" and getting spotlights, landing lights, searchlights, and other types of lights. The customer would then say, "No, a Bud Light." The ads were not only funny, but also made the point perfectly: Say "Bud Light," not just "a light," when ordering a beer. In addition, the message allowed thousands of customers and would-be comedians in bars and restaurants to repeat the line in person, which amounted to a lot of free advertising. The campaign by then Needham, Harper and Steers–Chicago (now DDB Needham) was a huge success. (See Exhibit 11.7.)

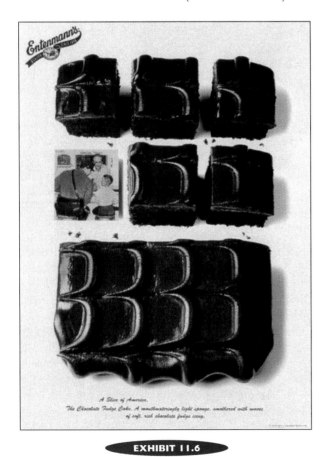

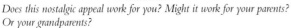

EXHIBIT 11.6

Does this nostalgic appeal work for you? Might it work for your parents? Or your grandparents?

EXHIBIT 11.7

These popular Bud Light ads were successful because they were humorous and created a link between the humor and the brand.
www.budweiser.com/

Miller Brewing is an advertiser that has both reaped the benefits of humor in its recent ad campaigns and suffered from its risks. The original "Less Filling—Tastes Great" campaigns that pitted famous retired athletes against one another rose to great prominence in the late 1970s and through nearly the entire decade of the 1980s. Sports fans could hardly wait for the next installment of the campaign. But the campaign, while highly successful overall, ultimately ran into the problem of wearout. The brand began to lose market share and is still struggling to regain past glories.

In light of research findings, there are several cautions associated with the use of humor as a message tactic:

- Humorous messages may adversely affect comprehension.
- Humorous messages can wear out as quickly as after three exposures, leaving no one laughing, especially the advertiser.[5]
- Humorous messages may attract attention but may not increase the effectiveness or persuasive impact of the advertisement.

HERE'S THE KEY TO GLOBAL SUCCESS: TWIST, LICK, AND DUNK

Long a secret vice of U.S. consumers, the wicked pleasure of dunking an Oreo cookie in milk will soon be shared by people all over the world. New global campaigns in Argentina, Taiwan, and South Africa will offer consumers translated versions of long-running U.S. "Moments" ads where children teach family members how to eat an Oreo cookie "properly."

Like many multinational product marketers, Nabisco is venturing abroad with a single ad agency network (FCB Worldwide) with a brand that is showing slow growth in the United States but burgeoning growth in foreign markets. Last year Oreo sales grew 37 percent outside the United States, despite a preference for biscuits in Europe and less-sweet treats, such as dried fruits, in Asia. The push outside the United States has been a huge success. From a base of 30 countries in 1993, the Oreo brand cookie is now in more than 100 countries.

The new Oreo ads replace individual country ads. One clever "adaptation" was Oreo's U.K. launch, where an unaltered 1998 American TV spot for Oreos was run with "British English" subtitles: "It's an Oreo" was translated into "a strangely black yet oddly delicious biscuit," and "All right. Let's have it" was translated into "I am interested in your offer."

While Nabisco feels it has several brands with global potential, the firm chose to focus on Oreo. The president of Nabisco International put it this way: Oreo has "unique characteristics: twist, lick and dunk is ownable only for Oreo."

Source: K. C. Swanson, "Oreo's Global Twist and Dunk," *Advertising Age*, September 14, 1998, 1.

Method: Sex Appeal. Because they are directed toward humans, ads tend to focus on sex from time to time. Not a big surprise.[6] But does sex sell? In a literal sense, the answer is no, because nothing, not even sex, *makes* someone buy something. However, sexual appeals are attention getting and occasionally arousing, which may affect how consumers feel about a product. Some believe in a type of classical conditioning involving sex in ads. Evidence for this effect is scant, but it is not without its proponents. Like all other interpretation of ads by humans, context is extremely important in sexual-appeal messages. Knowing just what constitutes sex appeal is not easy. Is it showing skin? How much skin? What's the difference between the celebration of a beautiful body and its objectification? Motive? Politics?

Can you use sex to help create a brand image? Sure you can. Calvin Klein and many other advertisers have used sexual imagery successfully to mold brand image. But these are for products such as clothes and perfumes, which emphasize how one looks, feels, and smells. Does the same appeal work as well for cars, telephones, computer peripherals, or file cabinets? How about breakfast cereals? In general, no. But because humans are complex and messy creatures, we cannot say that sex-appeal ads never work in such categories. Sometimes they do. In 1993, the print ads rated most successful in *Starch Tested*

5.   This claim is made by Video Storyboards Tests, based on its extensive research of humor ads, and cited in Kevin Goldman, "Ever Hear the One about the Funny Ad?" *Wall Street Journal,* November 2, 1993, B11.
6.   The political left often complains about exploitation, objectification, and the oppressive patriarchy found in advertising. The right, on the other hand, sees sexual ads as evidence of moral decay and the excesses of secular humanism. While some of these charges are regrettably true, to both the right and left the sin is really often nothing more than that it's advertising, low culture and commercial at that. If the images were from the 17th century and hung in a museum, they would be okay, but because they are popular culture and commercial, they must approach pornography. Go figure.

EXHIBITS 11.8 AND 11.9

A popular advertising method is to use sexual-appeal messages. This Iron Bed ad and the Scandinavian public service announcement for cancer prevention use light sexual content in an attempt to attract attention and affect receivers' feelings. Ads that use muted sex appeal often test very high on recall. What about their effect on brand preference?

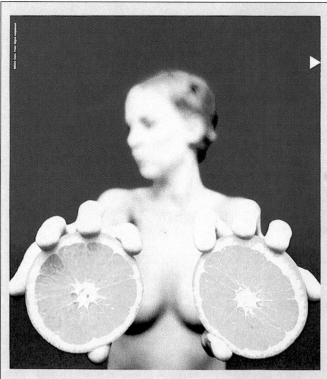

FRUKT OG GRØNNSAKER REDUSERER RISIKOEN FOR Å FÅ BRYSTKREFT

EXHIBITS 11.10 AND 11.11

Does sex sell?

GENTLEMEN,
START YOUR IGNITION

Lighter by JOHN HARDY

Copy were ads using muted sexual appeal.[7] The ads shown in Exhibits 11.8 and 11.9 use a sexual-appeal message to one degree or another. How effective do you think these ads are in fulfilling the objective of instilling brand preference?

Just as the jury is out on whether sex can sell products, it's also unclear as to whether sex can sell textbooks. In case it does work, we've included a few extra exhibits for you to consider and analyze. What do you think of the ads in Exhibits 11.10 and 11.11?

Objective: Scare the Consumer into Action. Sometimes the idea is simply to scare the consumer. Again, this not a difficult concept. You've probably heard of fear; perhaps you've even experienced it yourself. Sometimes advertisers adopt the scare-the-consumer-into-action objective. Fear is an extraordinarily powerful emotion and may be used to get consumers to take some very important action. However, it must be used strategically and judiciously to work well, or even work at all.

Method: Fear-Appeal Ads. A fear appeal highlights the risk of harm or other negative consequences of not using the advertised brand or taking some recommended action. The intuitive belief about fear as a message tactic is that fear will motivate the receiver to buy a product that will reduce or eliminate the portrayed threat. For example, Radio Shack spent $6 million to run a series of ads showing

At last,
tights you can
take off
with the
lights on.

Aristoc Sensuous.

7.   Leah Richard, "Basic Approach in Ads Looks Simply Superior," *Advertising Age,* October 10, 1994, 30.

a dimly lit unprotected house, including a peacefully sleeping child, as a way to raise concerns about the safety of the receiver's valuables, as well as his or her family. The campaign used the theme "If security is the question, we've got the answer." The ad closed with the Radio Shack logo and the National Crime Prevention Council slogan, "United against Crime."[8] Similarly, the ad in Exhibit 11.12 for Body Alarm cuts right to the chase: It capitalizes on fears of not being able to cry for help during a bodily attack.

The contemporary social environment has provided advertisers with an ideal context for using fear appeals. In an era of drive-by shootings, carjackings, and gang violence, Americans fear for their personal safety. Manufacturers of security products such as alarm and lighting security systems play on this fearful environment[9] (see Exhibit 11.13). Other advertisers have recently tried fear as an appeal. One such advertiser, the Asthma Zero Mortality Coalition, urges people who have asthma to seek professional help and uses a fear appeal in its ad copy: "When those painful, strained breaths start coming, keep in mind that any one of them could easily be your last." The creator of the ad states, "Sometimes you have to scare people to save their lives."[10]

Unfortunately, research does not offer such an absolute conclusion on the effectiveness of fear as a message tactic. Fear as a tactic in advertising has generated controversy. Social psychologists and marketing researchers have disagreed on the effective-

EXHIBIT 11.12

How does this ad for the Body Alarm embody the scare-the-consumer-into-action-objective? Does this ad have ethical implications? How so?

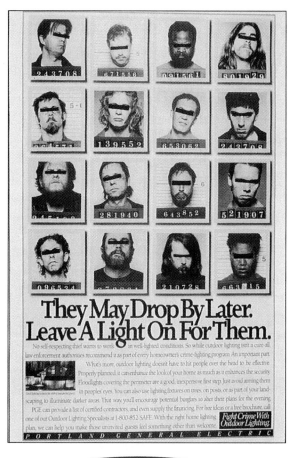

EXHIBIT 11.13

Not all scare-the-consumer ads are based on the possibility of bodily harm; this ad plays on one's fear of being burglarized.
carmen.artsci.washington.edu/propaganda/fear.htm.

8.   Jeffery D. Zbar, "Fear!" *Advertising Age,* November 14, 1994, 18.
9.   Ibid.
10. Emily DeNitto, "Healthcare Ads Employ Scare Tactics," *Advertising Age,* November 7, 1994, 12.

ness of a fear-based appeal. Traditional research wisdom indicates that intense fear appeals actually short-circuit persuasion and result in a negative attitude toward the advertised brand.[11] It seems that receivers get so anxious about the fear-inducing message that they focus on the fear and not on overcoming it. Other researchers argue that the tactic is beneficial to the advertiser.[12] More recent research on fear appeals suggests that the effectiveness of this method is difficult to evaluate. Still, it stands to reason that too much fear may occupy so much cognitive work space that the types of inferences needed to take action may never occur. It may also come down to how explicitly the suggestions for avoiding the harm are made. Using fear messages without offering a way out seems more likely to fail than does inducing moderate levels of fear coupled with suggesting an actionable behavior promised to reduce or eliminate the danger.

Objective: Change Behavior by Inducing Anxiety.

Like fear, anxiety is not pleasant. In fact, it's pretty awful. Most people try to avoid feeling anxious. They try to minimize, moderate, and alleviate anxiety. Often people will buy or consume things to help them in their continuing struggle with anxiety. They might watch television, smoke, exercise, eat, or take medication. They might also buy mouthwash, deodorant, condoms, a safer car, or even a retirement account, and advertisers know this. Advertisers pursue a change-behavior-by-inducing-anxiety objective by playing on consumer anxieties.

Method: Anxiety Ads.

There are many things to be anxious about. Advertisers realize this and use many settings to demonstrate why you should be anxious and what you can do to alleviate the anxiety. Social, medical, and personal-care products frequently use anxiety ads. The message conveyed in anxiety ads is that (1) there is a clear and present danger, and (2) the way to avoid this danger is to buy the advertised brand. When Head and Shoulders dandruff shampoo is advertised with the theme "You never get a second chance to make a first impression" (Exhibit 11.14), the audience realizes the power of Head & Shoulders in saving them the embarrassment of having dandruff.

Other anxiety ads tout the likelihood of being stricken by gingivitis, athlete's foot, calcium deficiency, body odor, and on and on. The idea is that these anxiety-producing conditions are out there, and they may affect you unless you take the appropriate action. The danger is often negative social judgment. Procter & Gamble has long relied on such presentations for its household and personal-care brands. In fact, Procter & Gamble has used this approach so consistently over the years that in some circles the anxiety tactic is referred to as the P&G approach. One of the more memorable P&G social anxiety ads is the scene where husband and wife are busily cleaning the spots off the water glasses before dinner guests arrive because they didn't use P&G's Cascade dishwashing product, which, of course, would have prevented the glasses from spotting. Most personal-care products have used this type of appeal. In Exhibit 11.15 Scope suggests that your breath might stand in the way of everlasting love. Feel a touch of anxiety? How's your breath?

EXHIBIT 11.14

Ads such as this one for Head & Shoulders dandruff shampoo play on consumers' fear of social embarrassment. www.pg.com/

11. Irving L. Janis and Seymour Feshbach, "Effects of Fear Arousing Communication," *Journal of Abnormal Social Psychology* 48 (1953), 78–92.
12. Michael Ray and William Wilkie, "Fear: The Potential of an Appeal Neglected by Marketing," *Journal of Marketing*, vol. 34, no. 1 (January 1970), 54–62.

Objective: Transform Consumption Experiences. You know how sometimes it's hard to explain to someone else just exactly why a certain experience was so special, why it felt so good? It wasn't just this thing, or that thing; it was that the entire experience was somehow better than the sum of the individual facets. Sometimes, that feeling is at least partly due to your expectations of what something will be like, your positive memories of previous experiences, or both. Sometimes advertisers try to provide that very anticipation and/or familiarity, bundled up in a positive memory of an advertisement, to be activated during the consumption experience itself. It is thus said to have transformed the consumption experience.

Method: Transformational Ads. The idea behind transformational advertising is that it can actually make the consumption experience better. For example, after years of advertising by McDonald's, the experience of eating at McDonald's is actually transformed or made better by virtue of what you know and feel about McDonald's each time you walk in. Transformational advertising messages attempt to create a brand feeling, image, and mood that is activated when the consumer uses the product or service. Transformational ads that are acutely effective are said to connect the experience of the advertisement so closely with the brand that consumers cannot help but think of the advertisement (or in a more general sense, be informed by the memory of many ads), when they think of the brand. Exhibit 11.16 is as much about the fun feelings connected with McDonald's as it is about the taste of the food.

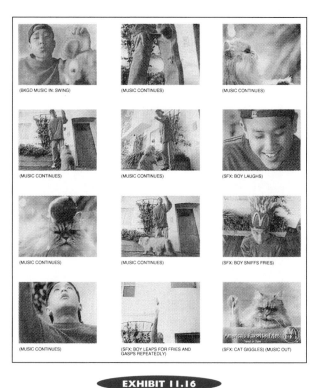

EXHIBIT 11.15

Another example of a social anxiety ad. www.scope-mouthwash.com/

EXHIBIT 11.16

What kinds of images and moods does this transformational ad from McDonald's evoke? www.mcdonalds.com/

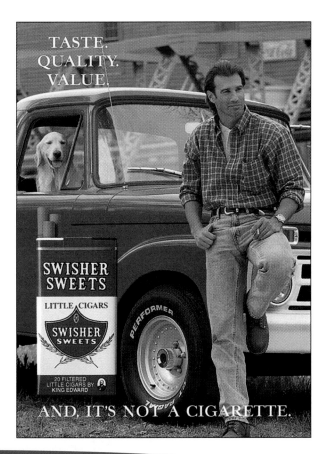

TASTE.
QUALITY.
VALUE.

SWISHER
SWEETS

LITTLE CIGARS

SWISHER
SWEETS

20 FILTERED
LITTLE CIGARS BY
KING EDWARD

AND, IT'S NOT A CIGARETTE.

EXHIBITS 11.17 AND 11.18

Slice-of-life ads depict an idealized user in a typical setting, with the user benefiting from a brand. Receivers are then supposed to identify with the user or scene, and the brand acquires social meaning for receivers.
www.prudential.com/

Objective: Situate the Brand Socially.

Maybe you haven't given it much thought, but if you're ever going to understand advertising, you have to get this: Objects have social meanings. While it applies to all cultures, this simple truth is at the very center of consumer cultures. In consumer cultures such as ours, billions of dollars are spent in efforts to achieve specific social meanings for advertised brands. Advertisers have long known that by placing their product in the right social setting, their brand takes on some of the characteristics of its surroundings. These social settings are created in advertising. In advertising, a product is placed into a custom-created social setting perfect for the brand, a setting in which the brand excels. Hopefully, this becomes the way in which the consumer remembers the brand, as fitting into this manufactured social reality. Advertisers often set a situate-the-brand-socially objective by creating an ad that places a brand in a socially desirable context.

Method: Slice-of-Life Ads. By placing a brand in a social context, it gains social meaning by association. Slice-of-life advertisements depict a usage situation gaining benefits and satisfaction from using the brand. Often these ads are visual and depict a social setting; the social context surrounding the brand rubs off and gives the brand social meaning (Exhibit 11.17). Other times, they do it with words (Exhibit 11.18). Receivers may, of course, reject or significantly alter that meaning.

Live well.
"I always tell newlyweds that if you're willing to go halfway, it's not enough. You have to go beyond. The basic idea in a happy marriage is the basic idea in life. The decision to be happy."

Make a plan.
"We always had a five-year plan. I think life is like an ocean, and the waves go up and down and no wave stays up forever."

Be your own rock.
Prudential offers life insurance, investments, real estate and health care that can help you manage your life. And live well.

ThePrudential

http://www.prudential.com

Method: Light Fantasy. Some ads use a form of light fantasy. These ads allow receivers to pretend a little and think about themselves in the position of the rich, the famous, or the accomplished. For example, the average guy wearing a particular athletic shoe can feel like an NBA all-star. The advertisement in Exhibit 11.19 appeals to the fantasies of just about anyone who has ever played the lottery. Chances are you are not going to win, but it sure is fun to think about the possibilities while you wait to hear someone else's number drawn.

Objective: Define the Brand Image.

Madonna has an image; Michael Jordan has an image; so do Saab and Pepsi. Just like people, brands have images. Images are the most apparent and most prominently associated characteristics of a brand. They are the thing consumers most remember or associate with a brand. Advertisers are in the business of creating, adjusting, and maintaining images—in other words, they often engage in the define-the-brand-image objective.

Method: Image Ads. Image advertising means different things to different people. To some, it means the absence of hard product information. To others, it refers to advertising that is almost exclusively visual. This is an oversimplification, but it is true that most image advertising tends toward the visual. In both cases, it means an attempt to link certain attributes to the brand, rather than to engage the consumer in any kind of discourse. Sometimes these linkages are quite explicit, such as using a tiger to indicate the strength of a brand. Other times, the linkages are implicit and subtle, such as the colors and tones associated with a brand. Check out the ads in Exhibits 11.20 and 11.21.

Objective: Persuade the Consumer.

Advertising that attempts to persuade is high-engagement advertising. Its goal is to convince the consumer, through a form of commercial discourse, that a brand is superior. The persuasion objective requires a significantly high level of cognitive engagement with the audience. The receiver has to think about what

EXHIBIT 11.19

By taking a light fantasy approach, it would seem that the New York Lottery (www.nylottery.org) wants to keep all of us dreaming. But because a considerable chunk of the monies taken in by lotteries are applied to local investment (e.g., schools or municipal general funds), they've become a very contentious issue on the Internet, where non-lottery states and municipalities are concerned at the ease with which taxpayers can send their fantasies—and their dollars—to far-away places. The Multi-State Lottery Association (www.powerball.com) is using the Web to let you share in the fantasies of others, reading about what happened to past winners. It's been said that lotteries are "a tax on people who are bad at math." Do you think the Web is a good medium to sell customers on playing the lottery?

Image advertising from Mercedes-Benz.

Nouveau Mercedes SL

SKYY Vodka (www.skyyvodka.com) evokes an ideal; at its Web site, an unfolding cinematic fantasy allows you to suspend time and indulge in the glamour of a bygone era. Long before Russia slipped behind the Iron Curtain and despite the economic chaos and environmental degradation it suffers in the Cold War's aftermath today, "Russia" was, and perhaps always will be, pristine snow, wild nature, and fine alcoholic beverages to the American consumer.

the advertiser is saying. The receiver must engage in a form of mental argument with the commercial. For example, an ad says, "In a Mercedes, you wouldn't get stuck behind a Lexus on the road. . . . Why would you get stuck behind one at your dealer?" You might read that and say to yourself, "Hey, what's wrong with Lexus? I think Lexus is great. Forget this." Or you might say, "Yeah, if I could afford a Mercedes, I'd buy a really great car." Or maybe you would say to yourself, "Hey, that's right. . . . You know, maybe I should consider a Mercedes next time. They're probably not much more than a Lexus." The point is that in a persuasion ad, there is an assumed dialogue between the ad and the receiver.

Method: Reason-Why. In a reason–why ad, the advertiser reasons with the potential consumer. The ad points out to the receiver that there are reasons why this brand will be satisfying and beneficial. Advertisers are usually relentless in their attempt to reason with consumers when using this method. They begin with some claim, like "Seven great reasons to buy Brand X," and then proceed to list all seven, finishing with the conclusion (implicit or explicit) that only a moron would, after such compelling evidence, do anything other than purchase Brand X. Other times, such as in Exhibit 11.22, the reason or reasons why to use a product can be presented deftly, memorably, and rationally. The biggest task to this method is making sure that the reason why makes sense and that consumers care. Consumer research is important before this appeal is attempted.

EXHIBIT 11.22

What are the advantages of using the advertiser's product? Reason-why ads use a rational appeal.

Method: Hard-Sell. Hard-sell ads are characteristically high pressure and urgent. Phrases such as "act now," "limited time offer," "your last chance to save," and "one-time-only sale" are representative of this method. The idea is to create a sense of urgency so consumers will act impulsively. Of course, many consumers have learned how to decode and otherwise discount these messages, decreasing their effectiveness and persuasive ability.

Method: Comparison Ads. Comparison advertisements are ads in which a brand's ability to satisfy consumers is demonstrated by comparing its features to those of competitive brands. Comparisons can be an effective and efficient means of communicating a large amount of information in a clear and interesting way, or they can be extremely confusing. Comparison as a technique has traditionally been used by marketers of convenience goods, such as pain relievers, laundry detergents, and household cleaners. More recently, advertisers in a wide range of product categories have tried comparison as their main message method. AT&T and MCI have had a long-running feud over whose rates are lower for household consumers, which may have completely confused everyone. Even luxury car makers BMW and Lexus have recently targeted each other with comparative claims.[13] In one ad, BMW attacks the sluggish performance of Lexus with the message, "According to recent test results, Lexus' greatest achievement in acceleration is its price." Not to be left out, the Acura dealers of Southern California entered the luxury car advertising skirmish by stating, "We could use a lesser leather in our automobiles, but then we'd be no better than Rolls-Royce."

Using comparison in an advertisement can be direct and name competitors' brands, or it can be indirect and refer only to the "leading brand" or "Brand X." In Exhibit 11.23, the "other brands" may not be named, but readers have a pretty good idea if their credit card company is one of the bad guys. The following are conclusions about the use of comparison as a message tactic:

- Direct comparison by a low-share brand to a high-share brand increases the attention on the part of receivers and increases the purchase intention of the low-share brand.
- Direct comparison by a high-share brand to a low-share brand does not attract additional attention and increases awareness of the low-share brand.
- Noncomparative claims by high-share brands are more effective than either direct or indirect comparison at enhancing purchase intention.
- Indirect comparison by moderate-share brands to either high- or low-share brands is more effective than direct comparison at enhancing the purchase intention of moderate-share brands.
- Direct comparison is more effective if members of the target audience have not demonstrated clear brand preference in their product choices.
- Direct comparison is more effective if the television medium is employed to make the comparison.[14]

13. Jim Henry, "Comparative Ads Speed Ahead for Luxury Imports," *Advertising Age,* September 12, 1994, 10.
14. Conclusions in this list are drawn from William R. Swinyard, "The Interaction between Comparative Advertising and Copy Claim Variation," *Journal of Marketing Research* 18 (May 1981), 175–186; Cornelia Pechmann and David Stewart, "The Effects of Comparative Advertising on Attention, Memory, and Purchase Intentions," *Journal of Consumer Research* (September 1990), 180–191; and Sanjay Petruvu and Kenneth R. Lord, "Comparative and Noncomparative Advertising: Attitudinal Effects under Cognitive and Affective Involvement Conditions," *Journal of Advertising* (June 1994), 77–90.

AFTER 30 DAYS, MOST CHARGE CARD COMPANIES GIVE YOU A WARNING.

WE GIVE YOU ANOTHER 30 DAYS.

There must be a catch, right? Actually, no. We understand that sometimes a three-day business trip turns into three weeks and, by necessity, you could use some extra time to pay your bill. That's why we always give you the convenience of an extra billing period to pay when you need it, interest-free. Another difference is having a real person answer your calls and help you, 24 hours a day. We also give you an award winning rewards program that allows you to earn miles that can be redeemed on every major U.S. airline. And, of course, the Diners Club Card is welcomed by airlines, hotels, car rental companies and millions of other places you go. Call us at 1 800 2 DINERS. We'll answer all of your questions, no extra charge.

Diners Club International

3887 12345s 7890

BREAKING THE PLASTIC MOLD.™

CITIBANK O®

EXHIBIT 11.23

Comparison ads compare the advertiser's brand to one or more competitors. Here, Diners Club is indirectly comparing the convenience of its credit card service to those of other charge card companies. www.dinersclub.com/

There is also evidence that comparison advertising is not appropriate and will not be effective when one or more of the following are true:

- The fundamental brand appeal is emotional rather than logical.
- The brand is a new product in the product category.
- The product category is characterized by insignificant functional differences between brands, thus making comparisons trivial.
- The competition has powerful counterclaims that can be made in retaliation to the original comparison.
- The brand has distinctive features that can differentiate it from the competition in the absence of comparison.[15]

There are some risks to the advertiser with the use of the comparison tactic. The firm sponsoring a comparative ad is sometimes perceived as less trustworthy, and comparative ads are sometimes evaluated as more offensive and less interesting than non-comparative ads.

Method: Information-Only Ads. First, there is really no such thing. All ads exist to sell a good or service, sooner or later. An "information-only" ad presents facts about a product or service. Of course, these facts are not randomly selected but are chosen for persuasive reasons, which means there is no such thing as a purely information-only ad. A brand with distinctive features can use the information-only message tactic to great advantage. These ads often use a visual to help the audience identify the product features being highlighted. For example, BMW gives you all kinds of information about its new 7-series in Exhibit 11.24. Read

EXHIBIT 11.24

An "information-only" ad from BMW. www.bmwusa.com/

What we don't change   THE NEW 7-SERIES 🔵

15. In general, comparative advertisements are not more effective than noncomparative ads when the intention is to affect brand attitude. For a current review of literature on conditions related to the effectiveness of comparative advertising, see Cornelia Pechmann and David Stewart, "The Psychology of Comparative Advertising," in *Attention, Attitude and Affect in Response to Advertising,* E. M. Clark, T. C. Brock, and D. W. Steward, eds. (Hillsdale, N.J.: Erlbaum, 1994), 79–96.

the New Media box on this page—will the information-wariness of modern consumers have an impact on these kinds of ads?

Method: Testimonial Ads. A frequently used message tactic is to have a spokesperson who champions the brand in an advertisement, rather than simply providing information. When an advocacy position is taken by a spokesperson in an advertisement, this is known as a **testimonial**. The value of the testimonial lies in the authoritative presentation of a brand's attributes and benefits by the spokesperson. There are three basic versions of the testimonial message tactic.

CONSUMERS FIGHT BACK—MORE INFORMATION MEANS LESS ATTENTION

The ever-expanding media landscape has given advertisers more ways to reach consumers. More is better, right? Wrong. What at first would seem to be nothing but pure advantage and opportunity for advertisers has a significant and disturbing flaw. With so much information coming their way, consumers are now fighting information load in the only way they know how—paying less attention.

A new survey by Iconocast (www.iconocast.com/), a leading Internet newsletter, found that 17 percent of respondents reported that they were scanning articles as a way to handle information overload. One of the main culprits, of course, in the information onslaught is the Internet. With an added staple of some estimated 35 new media—discussion lists, e-mail, newsletters, and Web sites being major additions—marketers are trying to understand the impact that so much information is having on consumers. The survey found that consumers are paying less attention to media as a way to survive the information tidal wave. For example, respondents indicated that they were decreasing their use of traditional media, with 17 percent using TV less, 13 percent cutting back on consumer magazines, and 13 percent cutting back on computer magazines. Some respondents offered that they were coping with the information overload by "drinking more latte" or taking St. John's Wort as an antidepressant.

In all seriousness though, Iconocast editor Michael Tchong indicates that "Earlier studies have shown that the info deluge is causing a lot of stress, even depression, among some users. This survey suggests that the many hundreds of thousands of works the media pour out each day are largely for naught as more readers hunker down to uncover 'just the facts, ma'am.' I believe that publishers will have to start paying careful attention to counter information obsolescence."

It is interesting to note that this Internet newsletter does not cite the Internet as a source of information overload—perhaps *the* source of the most stress and feelings of being overwhelmed. Nor did the survey indicate the extent to which consumers were cutting back on their use of the Web.

Source: Iconocast company press release, September 10, 1998. Available online at www.iconocast.com/.

The most conspicuous version is the *celebrity testimonial*. Sports stars such as Michael Jordan (McDonald's) and Arnold Palmer (Pennzoil, Cadillac) are favorites of advertisers. Actresses such as Candice Bergen (Sprint) and supermodels such as Cindy Crawford (Pepsi) are also widely used. The belief is that a celebrity testimonial will increase an ad's ability to attract attention and produce a desire in receivers to emulate or imitate the celebrities they admire.

Whether this is really true or not, the fact remains that a list of top commercials is dominated by ads that feature celebrities.[16] Of course, there is the ever-present risk that a celebrity will fall from grace, as several have in recent years, and potentially damage the reputation of the brand for which he or she was once the champion.

Expert spokespersons for a brand are viewed by the target audience as having expert product knowledge. The GM Parts Service Division created an expert in Mr. Goodwrench, who was presented as a knowledgeable source of information. A spokesperson portrayed as a doctor, lawyer, scientist, gardener, or any other expert relevant to a brand is intended to increase the credibility of the message being transmitted. There are also real experts. Advertising for The Club, a steering-wheel locking device that deters auto theft, uses police officers from several U.S. cities to demonstrate the effectiveness of the product. Some experts can also be celebrities. This is the case when Michael Jordan gives a testimonial for Nike basketball shoes.

---

16.   Kevin Goldman, "Year's Top Commercials Propelled by Star Power," *Wall Street Journal,* March 16, 1994, B1.

EXHIBIT 11.25

Demonstrating a brand's performance helps receivers appreciate the satisfaction the brand has to offer. Here, Hallmark demonstrates its ability to provide just the right words. www.hallmark.com/

There is also the *average-user testimonial*. Here, the spokesperson is not a celebrity or portrayed as an expert but rather as an average user speaking for the brand. The philosophy is that the target market can relate to this person. Solid theoretical support for this testimonial approach comes from reference group theory. An interpretation of reference group theory in this context suggests that consumers may rely on opinions or testimonials from people they consider similar to themselves, rather than on objective product information. Simply put, the consumer's logic in this situation is "That person is similar to me and likes that brand; therefore, I will also like that brand." In theory, this sort of logic frees the receiver from having to scrutinize detailed product information by simply substituting the reference group information. Of course, in practice, the execution of this strategy is nowhere near that easy. Consumers are very sophisticated at detecting this attempt at persuasion.

Method: Demonstration. How close an electric razor shaves, how green a fertilizer makes a lawn, or how easy an exercise machine is to use are all product features that can be demonstrated by using a method known simply as the demonstration ad. "Seeing is believing" is the motto of this school of advertising. When it's done well, the results are striking. There are a thousand ways to say that Hallmark greeting cards can find the right five words when you can't. Instead, in Exhibit 11.25, Hallmark decided to demonstrate it.

Method: Advertorial. An **advertorial** is a special advertising section designed to look like the print publication in which it appears. Advertorials are so named because they have the look of the editorial content of a magazine or newspaper but really represent a long and involved advertisement for a firm and its product or service. The *Wall Street Journal, Redbook,* and *New York Magazine* have all carried advertorials. *Sports Illustrated* has inserted advertorials for the Kentucky Derby and the Indianapolis 500. The potential effectiveness of this technique lies with the increased credibility that comes from the look and length of the advertisement. These features have, however, raised controversy. Some critics believe that most readers aren't even aware they're reading an advertisement because of the similarity in appearance to the publication.[17]

Method: Infomercials. With the **infomercial**, an advertiser buys from 5 to 60 minutes of television time and runs a documentary/information/entertainment program that is really an extended advertisement. An infomercial is the television equivalent of an advertorial. Real estate investment programs, weight-loss and fitness products, motivational programs, and cookware have dominated the infomercial format. A 30-minute infomercial can cost from $50,000 to $1.2 million to put on the air. The program usually has a host who provides information about a product and typically brings on guests to give testimonials about how successful they have been using the

17. Cynthia Crossen, "Proliferation of 'Advertorials' Blurs Distinction between News and Ads," *Wall Street Journal,* April 21, 1988, 33.

featured product. Most infomercials run on cable stations, although networks have sold early-morning and late-night time as well. Recently, big firms have used infomercials. Philips Electronics has had great success with a 30-minute adventure-like infomercial for its compact disc interactive (CD-I) player. Philips spent nearly $20 million to produce and buy prime-time media for the infomercial but contends the infomercial has much more impact than the print advertising it replaced.[18] Apple Computer also ran a 30-minute infomercial as part of the advertising campaign to introduce its new lower-priced Macintosh, the Performa. The ad was targeted to families looking to buy their first computer and was a huge success. The infomercial generated four times as many telephone inquiries as Apple anticipated.[19]

Not all advertisers have had such good success with infomercials. After spending nearly half a million dollars to produce and air a 30-minute infomercial promoting a Broadway show, the producers pulled the ad after three weeks. The toll-free number to order tickets drew an average of only 14 calls each time the ad ran.[20] However, infomercials can have tremendous sales impact. Many leading infomercials rely on celebrity spokespeople as part of the program.

WEB SIGHTING

EXHIBIT 11.26

FannieMae (www.openthedoor.org) wants to walk you right in the door—if not right into your new house, at least into the Fannie Mae foyer. An 800 number is a powerful mechanism for invoking a direct response, as is, increasingly, a Web address. Given the stakes—a home purchase is the single largest commitment of money most households ever make—home buyers receive a lot of attention on the Web. Banks and other lenders take care to highlight home mortgage offerings and provide prospects with tools from cost-of-living comparisons to mortgage payment calculators (www.crestarmortgage.com). How might one use the Web to both capture and keep the attention of a prospective homebuyer?

Objective: Invoke a Direct Response.

A direct response advertising appeal implores the receiver to act immediately. It's a blend of hard selling and impulse buying. Price appeals associated with special sales or the convenience of ordering from the comfort of one's home form the basis of the direct response objective. Local retailers and national direct merchants such as L. L. Bean and J. Crew are the most frequent users of this message strategy. In some cases, organizations use more feature-laden appeals in their direct response advertising, as does the FannieMae Foundation in its informational guides on the home-buying process (see Exhibit 11.26). The main characteristic of such ads, however, is encouraging the audience to respond immediately by calling a toll-free number.

Method: Call or Click Now. Direct response ads have become more prevalent in recent years for several reasons. First, many direct response messages feature a price-oriented appeal. In today's era of value-oriented, price-conscious consumers, direct response messages provide an ideal opportunity for offering consumers a discount via a mail-in coupon or special television offer that is a price-based appeal. Second, firms have developed sophisticated databases that allow them to specifically target well-defined customer groups. Such databases can be tailored to geographic areas, demographic characteristics of audiences, or past product

18. Kevin Goldman, "Philips Infomercial Does Its Thing in Popular TV Watching Hours," *Wall Street Journal,* September 23, 1993, B6.

19. Kevin Goldman, "Apple Plans Infomercial Aimed at Families," *Wall Street Journal,* January 4, 1994, B3; Jacqueline M. Graves, "The Fortune 500 Opt for Infomercials," *Fortune,* March 6, 1995, 20.

20. Kevin Goldman, "Broadway Hopeful Flops with Debut of Infomercial," *Wall Street Journal,* April 29, 1994, B3.

use as ways to target different audiences. The firm can then send a specific and different message to each target audience. Third, advertisers are demanding more evidence that the dollars they spend on advertising are having an impact. Ad agencies have found that direct response messages offer the most tangible evidence of advertising impact, and they are using the technique as a means of accountability.

★ ★ ★ ★ ★ ★ ★

Message development is where the advertising battle is usually won or lost. It's where real creativity exists. It's where the agency has to be smart and figure out just how to turn the wishes of the client into effective advertising. It is where the creatives have to get into the minds of consumers, realizing that the advertisement will be received by different people in different ways. Great messages are developed by people who can put themselves into the minds of their audience members and anticipate their response, leading to the desired outcomes. They create social texts that resonate with the lived experience of their consumers.

SUMMARY

◀▷ Identify ten objectives of message strategy.

Advertisers can choose from a wide array of message strategy objectives as well as methods for implementing these objectives. Three fundamental message objectives are brand recall, key brand attribute, and brand preference. The advertiser may also seek to activate negative emotional states such as fear or anxiety as the means to motivate brand purchase. Transformational advertising seeks to influence the nature of the consumption experience. A message may also feature the brand in an important social context to heighten the brand's appeal. Enhancing brand imagery is another common message objective and can be contrasted with designing messages to produce immediate action. Finally, many advertising messages are designed with the primary intent of persuading the customer. A wealth of approaches are used to effect persuasion, including comparison ads, testimonials, and infomercials.

◀▷ Identify methods for executing each message strategy objective.

Advertisers employ any number of methods to achieve their objectives. To get consumers to recall a brand name, repetition, slogan, and jingle ads are often produced. Sometimes the objective is only to link a key attribute to a brand. For this, many turn to USP ads. Feel-good ads, humorous ads, and sexual-appeal ads can raise a consumer's preferences for one brand over another. Fear-appeal ads, judiciously used, can motivate purchases, as can ads that play on other anxieties. Transformational ads attempt to enrich the consumption experience. With slice-of-life ads and light fantasy ads the goal is to situate a brand in a desirable social context. Ads that primarily use visuals define brand image. If the goal is to persuade a consumer to buy, comparison ads, testimonials, and demonstration ads all do the trick. Finally, call- or click-now ads aim to invoke direct response.

KEY TERMS

message strategy (331)
unique selling proposition (USP) (333)
comparison advertisements (346)

testimonial (348)
advertorial (349)
infomercial (349)

QUESTIONS FOR REVIEW AND CRITICAL THINKING

1.   Review the chapter opener about the success of Apple's "1984" commercial. What was the idea at the heart of this ad that helped make the Macintosh a success? A decade later, Apple's big idea has worn out. What went wrong?

2.   Once again, reflect on the "1984" commercial. As this chapter suggested, consumers are active interpreters of ads, and one of the virtues of the "1984" ad was that it invited the audience to become involved and make an interpretation. Thinking about the "1984" ad, what sorts of interpretations could a consumer make that would benefit the brand? Conversely, what sorts of interpretations might a person make, after a single exposure to this ad, that would be detrimental to Macintosh?

3.   Explain the difference between brand recall and brand preference as message objectives. Which of these objectives do you think would be harder to achieve, and why?

4.   Procter and Gamble has had considerable success with the message strategy involving anxiety arousal. How does P&G's success with this strategy refute the general premise that the best way to appeal to American consumers is to appeal to their pursuit of personal freedom and individuality?

5.   Discuss the merits of unique selling proposition (USP) ads. Is it possible to have a USP that is not the "big idea" for an ad campaign?

6.   Review the dos and don'ts of comparison advertising and then think about each of the brand pairs listed here. Comment on whether you think comparison ads would be a good choice for the product category in question, and if so, which brand in the pair would be in the most appropriate position to use comparisons: Ford versus Chevy trucks; Coors Light versus Bud Light beer; Nuprin versus Tylenol pain reliever; Brut versus Obsession cologne; Wendy's versus McDonald's hamburgers.

7.   How can advertisers use some message "strategy" in Web ads? Are there ways to overcome the creativity constraints?

EXPERIENTIAL EXERCISES

1.   Describe one of your favorite feel-good ads, print or broadcast. Are you a loyal purchaser of the brand being promoted? If so, what is it about the ad that leads you to purchase the product? If not, what feel-good ads promote brands you are loyal to? What is your conclusion about the effectiveness of feel-good ads?

2.   Find two ads from each of the following two product categories: automobiles and credit cards. Compare the appeal used by two advertisers. What are the similarities? What are the differences?

USING THE INTERNET

Advertisers use a variety of message strategies and methods for accomplishing their strategic goals. Visit the following sites:

Clinique: www.clinique.com

Ragu: www.eat.com

Sprint: www.sprint.com/college/

For each site, answer the following questions:

1.   Is there a big idea behind the site?

2.   What is the fundamental message objective?

3.   How have the site designers used creativity to achieve this objective?

4.   How is the site designed relative to the message issues raised in the New Media box on page 348?

Amazon.com uses reader reviews—a form of average user testimonial—to give consumers a better feeling for the books they sell. This can be a double-edged sword, unless Amazon.com exercises editorial control to massage or discard frivolous or offensive reviews. Still, Amazon.com's approach is quite different from traditional brick and mortar stores, who would only spend expensive print advertising space to tout authors and reflect only a positive experience in finding a good read on their shelves.

Visit Amazon.com (www.amazon.com) and look at some of the reader reviews; try adding your own review of a book you like (or perhaps, of one you don't!).

1.   How might you, as an author, feel about Amazon.com's permitting negative reviews?

2.   Is advertising any particular book a secondary consideration behind developing the site as an informative, user-engaging environment?

3.   As traditional stores do, does Amazon.com highlight particular authors (presumably for a premium)?

IF OTHER RADIO STATIONS ARE MIDDLE OF THE ROAD, WE'RE LYING DRUNK IN A DITCH.

XfM 104.9

LONDON'S ONLY ALTERNATIVE

CHAPTER 12

**After reading and thinking about
this chapter, you will be able to do
the following:**

- Explain the need for a creative plan in the copywriting process.

- Detail the components of print copy, along with important guidelines for writing effective print copy.

- Describe various formatting alternatives for radio ads and articulate guidelines for writing effective radio copy.

- Describe various formatting alternatives for television ads and articulate guidelines for writing effective television copy.

We live in an age when just about everything carries a warning label of some sort. Objects in rearview mirrors may be closer than they appear. Hair dryers should not be used in the shower. Using a lawn mower to trim the hedge may result in injury.

In this spirit, the authors of this book urge you to read the warning label in Exhibit 12.1. Yet, unlike the examples given earlier, the truth expressed here may not be quite so obvious, the danger not so clear. You know how some people just have to divide up the world into neat little parcels and categories. These are the same people who neatly place copywriters in one box on the organizational chart, and art directors in another. But in practice, it's not that simple. It's far too simplistic to state that copywriters are responsible for the verbal elements in an ad and art directors are responsible for the visual elements. In fact, copywriters and art directors function as partners and are referred to as the **creative team** in agencies. The creative team is responsible for coming up with the **creative concept** and for guiding its execution. The creative concept, which can be thought of as the unique creative thought behind a campaign, is then turned into individual advertisements. During this process, copywriters often suggest the idea for magnificent, arresting visuals. Likewise, art directors often come up with killer headlines.

As you can see in Exhibits 12.2 and 12.3, some ads have no headlines at all; some have no visuals. Still, in most cases, both a copywriter and an art director are equally involved in creating an ad. This doesn't mean that copywriting and art directing are one and the same. This chapter and the next will show that the talent and knowledge needed to excel in one area differ in many ways from those needed to excel in the other. Still, one must recognize that not all copywriting is done by copywriters and not all art directing is done by art directors.

Understanding copywriting is as much about the people who write copy as it is about the product studies, audience research, and other information that copywriters draw upon to create effective copy. Copywriting is, in fact, mostly about the fairly magical relationship between creator and creation, between writer and text, writer and brand. It is more about art than science. Copywriting is writing, and writing is a form of crafted magic. Magic cannot be taught. If (and it's a big if) you have a gift to begin with, then you can learn technique. But technique alone is not enough. Gifts are gifts—they come from somewhere else. Writing long paragraphs won't make you William Faulkner any more than writing self-effacing copy will make you Bill Bernbach. Likewise, trying to treat a discussion of copywriting like a step-by-step discussion of how to change the oil in your car is sadly silly and thoroughly useless. Still, there are things—some of them principles, some of them hints and tips—that can be learned from the creators of some of the greatest advertising of all time. Furthermore, even if you don't plan to be a copywriter, knowing something about the craft is essential to any working understanding of advertising. Knowing something about the craft is also essential to selling good ideas in global markets, as shown in the Global Issues box on page 358.

EXHIBIT 12.1

While copywriters are primarily responsible for writing the verbal descriptions in ads and art directors are primarily responsible for the visuals, they act as partners and often come up with great ideas outside their primary responsibility.

WARNING: The Difference Between Copywriters And Art Directors May Not Be As Great As You Think.

While most effective ads use multiple copy components—headline, subhead, body copy, visual—some ads excel by focusing on a single component. The Richmond Technical Center ad in Exhibit 12.2 succeeds without the use of an illustration. Similarly, the ad for Clamato in Exhibit 12.3 uses no copy or headline, but the illustration communicates brilliantly. www.clamato.com/

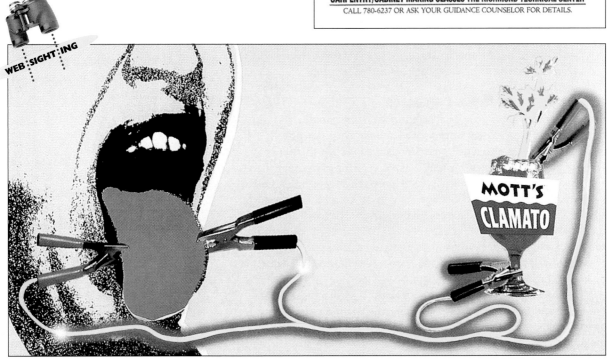

Lesson one:
How to avoid getting a nickname like Lefty, Stumpy or Knuckles.

CARPENTRY/CABINET MAKING CLASSES THE RICHMOND TECHNICAL CENTER
CALL 780-6237 OR ASK YOUR GUIDANCE COUNSELOR FOR DETAILS.

WEB SIGHTING

*Mott markets Clamato (*www.clamato.com*) with a certain in-your-face zeal, which this ad conveys entirely with illustration. Although the ad doesn't use words, one of Mott's current, sassy slogans for Clamato "boasts" that the product is "99.9% clam free." (Clamato, which once had a much higher clam content, now uses only a trace of clam broth for zest.) Is the brand forever doomed to be perceived as too "clammy"? Mott's irreverent take on clams—its raison d'être—makes for an interesting contrast with Smucker's treatment of its century-old family name: "With a name like Smucker's, it has to be good" (*www.smucker.com*).*

Let's begin with some fairly general thoughts on copywriting from some of the most influential people in the history of advertising:

If you think you have a better mousetrap, or shirt, or whatever, you've got to tell people, and I don't think that has to be done with trickery, or insults, or by talking down to people. . . . The smartest advertising is the advertising that communicates the best and respects consumers' intelligence. It's advertising that lets them bring something to the communication process, as opposed to some of the more validly criticized work in our profession which tries to grind the benefits of a soap or a cake mix into a poor housewife's head by repeating it 37 times in 30 seconds.[1]

—Lee Clow, creator of the Apple Macintosh "1984" advertisement

1.   Jennifer Pendleton, "Bringing New Clow-T to Ads, Chiat's Unlikely Creative," *Advertising Age,* February 7, 1985, 1.

As I have observed it, great advertising writing either in print or television is disarmingly simple. It has the common touch without being or sounding patronizing. If you are writing about baloney, don't try to make it sound like Cornish hen, because that is the worst kind of baloney. Just make it darned good baloney.[2]

—Leo Burnett, founder of the Leo Burnett agency, Chicago

YOU KNOW THAT KISS THING—IT WORKS FOR GLOBAL ADS, TOO

Years ago, some management guru said, "Keep It Simple, Stupid," giving birth to the KISS rule in American management philosophy. Well, it turns out that KISS has a place in global advertising as well.

Over the last decade, advertisers have been getting better and better at creating advertising campaigns that succeed on a global level. The International Advertising Festival at Cannes demonstrates that fact annually. More and more of the winning campaigns are global campaigns, not just domestic market campaigns. They work as well in Boston as they do in Brussels. What is also a demonstrated fact annually is that these winning campaigns are actually quite simple in terms of message theme and visual structure. Certainly, particular product categories lend themselves more readily to a global stage than do others. Lifestyle products such as soft drinks, jeans, sneakers, and candy translate well across cultures. Nike, Pepsi, and Levi's speak to the world and each has been the subject of memorable, award-winning campaigns. But what makes these brands so well suited to a global audience—even beyond the natural fit of lifestyle product categories?

The campaigns that work best on a global scale are those where the brand and its imagery are inextricably one and the same. Innovative product demonstrations or images where the pictures tell the story are the foundation of effective global advertising. Advertising that succeeds in the global arena draws on four constants: Simplicity, Clarity, Humor, and Clever demonstration. SCHC doesn't exactly spell KISS, but the reason that global ads that highlight these qualities can bridge the complexities and distinctiveness of one culture to another is simple. Granted, what is funny to a Brit may be lost on a Brazilian, but the key is to find not the culturally bound humor in a demonstration, but the culturally shared humor. When it comes to copy, simplicity and clarity rule. Aside from their inherent value, their ability to communicate across cultures is, well, clear. In short, actually *trying* to bridge cultures may be just the thing that complicates the situation. Reducing a brand and its message to the simplest and most common human values has a great chance of succeeding.

Source: Jay Schulberg, "Successful Global Ads Need Simplicity, Clarity," *Advertising Age*, June 30, 1997, 17.

Why should anyone look at your ad? The reader doesn't buy his magazine or tune his radio and TV to see and hear what you have to say. . . . What is the use of saying all the right things in the world if nobody is going to read them? And, believe me, nobody is going to read them if they are not said with freshness, originality and imagination.[3]

—William Bernbach, cofounder of one of the most influential agencies during the 1960s, Doyle Dane Bernbach

Never write an advertisement which you wouldn't want your family to read. Good products can be sold by honest advertising. If you don't think the product is good, you have no business to be advertising it. If you tell lies, or weasel, you do your client a disservice, you increase your load of guilt, and you fan the flames of public resentment against the whole business of advertising.[4]

—David Ogilvy's ninth of eleven commandments of advertising

Finally, the following observation on the power of a good advertisement, brilliant in its simplicity, is offered by one of the modern-day geniuses of advertising:

Imagination is one of the last remaining legal means to gain an unfair advantage over your competition.[5]

—Tim McElligott, cofounder of a highly creative and successful Minneapolis advertising agency

Good copywriters must always bring spirit and imagination to adver-

2.   Leo Burnett, "Keep Listening to That Wee, Small Voice," in *Communications of an Advertising Man* (Chicago: Leo Burnett, 1961), 160.

3.   Cited in Martin Mayer, *Madison Avenue, U.S.A.* (New York: Pocket Books, 1954), 66.

4.   David Ogilvy, *Confessions of an Advertising Man* (New York: Atheneum, 1964), 102.

5.   Tim McElligott is credited with making this statement in several public speeches during the 1980s.

When you're only No.2, you try harder. Or else.

Little fish have to keep moving all of the time. The big ones never stop picking on them.

Avis knows all about the problems of little fish.

We're only No.2 in rent a cars. We'd be swallowed up if we didn't try harder.

Avis can't afford to relax.

There's no rest for us.

We're always emptying ashtrays. Making sure gas tanks are full before we rent our cars. Seeing that the batteries are full of life. Checking our windshield wipers.

And the cars we rent out can't be anything less than spanking new Plymouths.

And since we're not the big fish, you won't feel like a sardine when you come to our counter.

We're not jammed with customers.

EXHIBIT 12.4

One of the great names in advertising is William Bernbach, and the memorable and highly effective "We Try Harder" campaign for Avis Rent a Car was produced by his agency, Doyle Dane Bernbach.
www.avis.com/

Hathaway and the Duke's stud groom

EXHIBIT 12.5

David Ogilvy, to many a guru in advertising, created the Hathaway Shirt Man (complete with an eye patch) as a way to attract attention and create an image for the Hathaway brand many years ago.

tising. Lee Clow, Leo Burnett, William Bernbach, and David Ogilvy have created some of the most memorable advertising in history: the "We're Number 2, We Try Harder" Avis campaign (William Bernbach); the Hathaway Shirt Man ads (David Ogilvy); the Jolly Green Giant ads (Leo Burnett); and the "1984" Apple Macintosh ad (Lee Clow). See Exhibits 12.4 and 12.5 for samples of their work. When these advertising legends speak of creating good ads that respect the consumer's intelligence and rely on imagination, they assume good copywriting.

Copywriting and the Creative Plan.

Writing well, rule #1: Write well.

—Luke Sullivan, copywriter and author

Copywriting is the process of expressing the value and benefits a brand has to offer, via written or verbal descriptions. Copywriting requires far more than the ability to string product descriptions together in coherent sentences. One apt description of copywriting is that it is a never-ending search for ideas combined with a never-ending search for new and different ways to express those ideas.

Effective copywriters are well-informed, astute advertising decision makers with creative talent. Copywriters are able to comprehend and then incorporate the complexities of marketing strategies, consumer behavior, and advertising strategies into a brief yet powerful communication. They must do so in such a way that the copy does not interfere with but rather enhances the visual aspects of the message.

Imagine you're a copywriter at Saatchi & Saatchi/London. Your client? The British Army. You've read a stack of books on military training. You've sat in on endless meetings. You've waded through volumes of material on people's perceptions and misperceptions of members of the military. Now your job is simple: Take all the charts, numbers, and strategies and turn them into a simple, emotionally moving, intellectually involving campaign such as the one in Exhibits 12.6 through 12.8.

An astute advertiser will go to great lengths to provide copywriters with as much information as possible about the objectives for a particular advertising effort. The responsibility for keeping copywriters informed lies with the client's marketing managers in conjunction with account executives and creative directors in the ad agency. They must communicate the foundations and intricacies of the firm's marketing strategies to the copywriters. Without this information, copywriters are left without guidance and direction, and they must rely on intuition about what sorts of information are relevant and meaningful to a target audience. Sometimes that works; most of the time, it does not.

A **creative plan** is a guideline used during the copywriting process to specify the message elements that must be coordinated during the preparation of copy. These elements include main product claims, creative devices, media that will be used, and special creative needs a product or service might have. One of the main challenges faced by a copywriter is to make creative sense out of the maze of information that comes from the message development process. Part of the challenge is creating excitement around what can otherwise be dull product features. For example, the challenge for the copywriter responsible for the ad in Exhibit 12.9 was to express the expected feature of reliability in a sport-utility vehicle in an unexpected fashion.

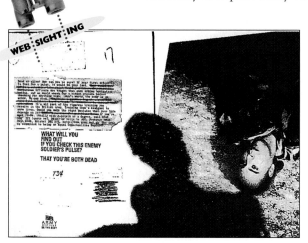

EXHIBITS 12.6, 12.7, AND 12.8

Each of these ads catches the reader's attention by proposing heady, responsibility-laden dilemmas to an audience whose most vexing career question might otherwise be "Do you want fries with that?" (Or chips, as they say across the pond.) Visit www.army.mod.uk/army/ and contrast these spots with the message conveyed in the U.S. Army's recruiting ad, as shown in Exhibit 12.12, which focuses on individual (and monetary) enrichment.

EXHIBIT 12.9

Reliability in an SUV is expected; expressing it in just these eleven words is not.

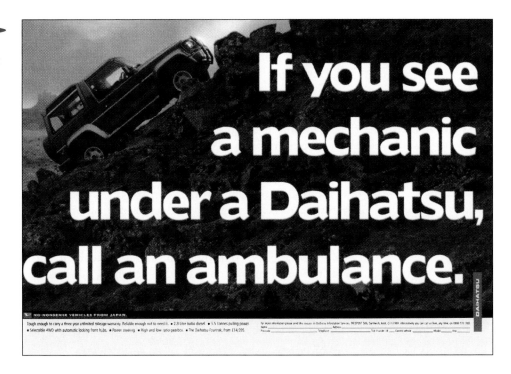

Another aspect of the challenge is bringing together various creative tools (such as illustration, color, sound, and action) and the copy. Copy must also be coordinated with the media that will be used. All of these factors are coordinated through the use of a creative plan. Some of the elements considered in devising a creative plan are the following:

- the single-most important thought you want a member of the target market to take away from the advertisement
- the product features to be emphasized
- the benefits a user receives from these features
- the media chosen for transmitting the information and the length of time the advertisement will run
- the suggested mood or tone for the ad
- the ways in which mood and atmosphere will be achieved in the ad
- the production budget for the ad[6]

These considerations can be modified or disregarded entirely during the process of creating an ad. For example, sometimes a brilliant creative execution demands that television, rather than print, be the media vehicle of choice. Occasionally, a particular creative thought may suggest a completely different mood or tone than the one listed in the creative plan. A creative plan is best thought of as a starting point, not an endpoint, for the creative team. Like anything else in advertising, the plan should evolve and grow as new insights are gained. Once the creative plan is devised, the creative team can get on with the task of creating the actual advertisement.

Copywriting for Print Advertising.
In preparing copy for a print ad, the first step in the copy development process is deciding how to use (or not use) the three separate components of print copy: the headline, the subhead, and the body copy. Be aware that the full range of components applies most directly to print ads that appear in

---

6.   The last two points in this list were adapted from A. Jerome Jewler, *Creative Strategy in Advertising,* 3rd ed. (Belmont, Calif.: Wadsworth Publishing Company, 1989), 196.

magazines, newspapers, or direct mail pieces. These guidelines also apply to other "print" media such as billboards, transit advertising, and specialty advertising, but all media are in effect different animals. More detail on these "support" media is presented in Chapter 16.

The Headline.

The **headline** in an advertisement is the leading sentence or sentences, usually at the top or bottom of the ad, that attracts attention, communicates a key selling point, or achieves brand identification. Many headlines fail to attract attention, and the ad itself then becomes another bit of clutter in consumers' lives. Lifeless headlines do not compel the reader to examine other parts of the ad. Simply stated, a headline can either motivate a reader to move on to the rest of an ad or lose the reader for good.

Purposes of a Headline. In preparing a headline, a copywriter begins by considering the variety of purposes a headline can have in terms of gaining attention or actually convincing the consumer. In general, a headline can be written to pursue the following purposes:

- *Give news about the brand.* A headline can proclaim a newsworthy event focused on the brand. "Champion Wins Mt. Everest Run" and "25 of 40 Major Titles Won with Titleist" are examples of headlines that communicate newsworthy events about Champion spark plugs and Titleist golf balls. The Red Dog ad in Exhibit 12.10 uses this approach quite cleverly.
- *Emphasize a brand claim.* A primary and perhaps differentiating feature of the brand is a likely candidate for the headline theme. "30% More Mileage on Firestone Tires" highlights durability.
- *Give advice to the reader.* A headline can give the reader a recommendation that (usually) is followed by results provided in the body copy. "Increase Your Reading Skills" and "Save up to 90% on Commissions" both implore the reader to take the

EXHIBIT 12.10

Does this headline attract attention or arouse interest in the audience to read the copy? Is this an effective way to give news about the brand? www.reddog.com/

EXHIBIT 12.11

Giving readers advice in a headline can attract attention and stimulate interest in the body copy. MCI's 1-800-COLLECT uses just such an approach in this Mother's Day ad. www.mci.com/

EXHIBIT 12.12

This ad uses its headline to succinctly select a prospect. www.army.mil/

advice of the ad. The headline in Exhibit 12.11 advises readers to call Mom this Mother's Day.

- *Select prospects.* Headlines can attract the attention of the intended audience. "Good News for Arthritis Sufferers" and "Attention June Graduates" are examples of headlines designed to achieve prospect selection. The headline in the recruiting ad shown in Exhibit 12.12 is designed to attract the attention of college students.

- *Stimulate the reader's curiosity.* Posing a riddle with a headline can serve to attract attention and stimulate readership. Curiosity can be stimulated with a clever play on words or a contradiction. Take, for example, the headline "With MCI, Gerber's Baby Talk Never Sounded Better." The body copy goes on to explain that Gerber Products (a maker of baby products) uses the high technology of MCI for its communication needs. Does the headline in the ad shown in Exhibit 12.13 get your attention? It was written for that purpose.

- *Set a tone or establish an emotion.* Language can be used to establish a mood that the advertiser wants associated with its product. Teva sports sandals has an ad with the headline "When you die, they put you in a nice suit and shiny shoes. As if death didn't suck enough already." Even though there is no direct reference to the product being advertised, the reader has learned quite a bit about the company doing the advertising and the types of people expected to buy the product. The headline in the ad shown in Exhibit 12.14 accomplishes the same objective.

- *Identify the brand.* This is the most straightforward of all headline purposes. The brand name or label is used as the headline, either alone or in conjunction with a word or two. The goal is to simply identify the brand and reinforce brand-name recognition. Advertising for Brut men's fragrance products often uses merely the brand name as the headline.

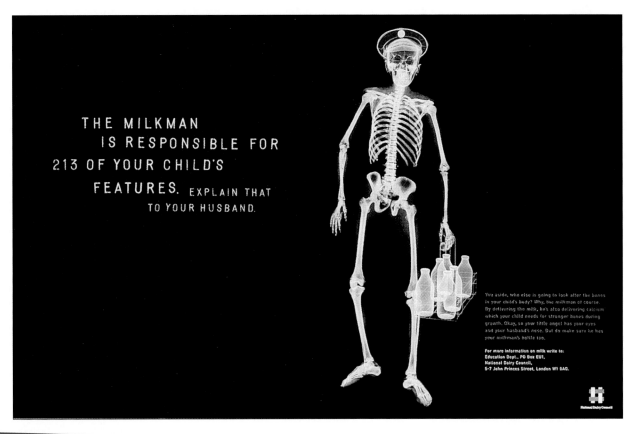

EXHIBIT 12.13

A headline that creates curiosity motivates readers to continue reading, perhaps after a slight disconcerting pause. www.milk.co.uk/

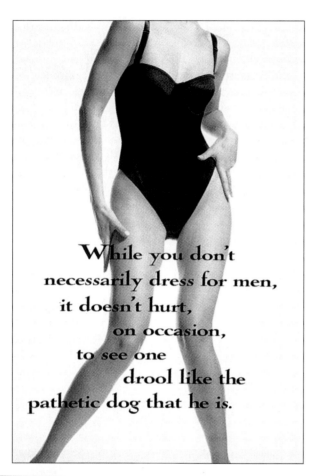

While you don't necessarily dress for men, it doesn't hurt, on occasion, to see one drool like the pathetic dog that he is.

EXHIBIT 12.14

Headlines can set a tone and establish a mood that the advertiser desires for a brand. This ad for Bodyslimmers women's apparel does just that.

Guidelines for Writing Headlines. Once a copywriter has firmly established the purpose a headline will serve in an advertisement, several guidelines can be followed in preparing the headline. The following are basic guidelines for writing a good headline for print advertisements:

- Make the headline a major persuasive component of the ad. Five times as many people read the headline as the body copy of an ad. If this is your only opportunity to communicate, what should you say? The headline "New Power. New Comfort. New Technology. New Yorker" in a Chrysler ad communicates major improvements in the product quickly and clearly.
- Appeal to the reader's self-interest with a basic promise of benefits coming from the brand. For example, "The Temperature Never Drops Below Zerex" promises engine protection in freezing weather from Zerex antifreeze.
- Inject the maximum information in the headline without making it cumbersome or wordy.
- Limit headlines to about five to eight words.[7] Research indicates that recall drops off significantly for sentences longer than eight words.
- Include the brand name in the headline.
- Entice the reader to read the body copy.
- Entice the reader to examine the visual in the ad. An intriguing headline can lead the reader to carefully examine the visual components of the ad.
- Never change the typeface in a headline. Changing the form and style of the print can increase the complexity of visual impression and negatively affect the readership.
- Never use a headline whose persuasive impact depends on reading the body copy.
- Use simple, common, familiar words. Recognition and comprehension are aided by words that are easy to understand and recognize.

This set of guidelines is meant only as a starting point. A headline may violate one or even all of these basic premises and still be effective. And it is unrealistic to try to fulfill the requirements of each guideline in every headline. This list simply offers general safeguards to be considered. Test the list for yourself using the ads in Exhibits 12.15 through 12.17. Which, if any, of these ten guidelines do these ads comply with? And which ones do they torch? Which of these guidelines would you say are most important for creating effective headlines?

7.   Based in part on Jewler, *Creative Strategy in Advertising,* 232–233; Albert C. Book, Norman D. Cary, and Stanley I. Tannenbaum, *The Radio and Television Commercial* (Lincolnwood, Ill.: NTC Business Books, 1984), 22–26.

There are ten general guidelines for writing headlines. How do you rate the headlines in these ads relative to the guidelines?

EXHIBIT 12.17

A powerful message in a scant dozen words: The headline paints the issue as one of civil liberty and conjures a familiar menace. Morbid (quite literally) curiosity might lead you to read the body copy, but the message has been delivered as smoothly as an intravenous feed. The Hemlock Society USA's Web site (www2.privatel.com/hemlock/) presumes you're already sympathetic to the cause and is far more pedestrian than its print advertising.

A truly great piece of advice:

Certain headlines are currently checked out. You may use them when they are returned. Lines like "Contrary to popular belief . . . " or "Something is wrong when . . . " These are dead. Elvis is dead. John Lennon is dead. Deal with it. Remember, anything that you even think *you've seen, forget about it. The stuff you've never seen? You'll know when you see it, too. It raises the hair on the back of your neck.*[8]

—Luke Sullivan

Originality is good.

The Subhead.   A **subhead** consists of a few words or a short sentence and usually appears above or below the headline. It includes important brand information not included in the headline. The subhead in the ad for Clorox in Exhibit 12.18 is an excellent example of how a subhead is used to convey important brand information not communicated in the headline. A subhead serves basically the same purpose as a headline—to communicate key selling points or brand information quickly. A subhead is normally in print larger than the body copy, but smaller than the headline. In many cases, the subhead is more lengthy than the headline and can be used to communicate more complex selling points. The subhead should reinforce the headline and, again, entice the reader to proceed to the body copy.

Subheads can serve another important purpose: stimulating a more complete reading of the entire ad. If the headline attracts attention, the subhead can stimulate movement through the physical space of the ad, including the visual. A good rule of thumb is the longer the body copy, the more appropriate the use of subheads. Most creative directors try to keep the use of subheads to the barest minimum, however. They feel that if an ad's visual and headline can't communicate the benefit of a product quickly and clearly, the ad isn't very good.

The Body Copy.   More good advice:

I don't think people read body copy. I think we've entered a frenzied era of coffee-guzzling, fax-sending channel surfers who honk the microsecond the light turns green and have the attention span of a flashcube. If the first five words of the body copy aren't: "may we send you $700.00," word 6 isn't read. Just my opinion, mind you.[9]

It's our opinion too.

Body copy is the textual component of an advertisement and tells a more complete story of a brand. Effective body copy is written in a fashion that takes advantage of and reinforces the headline and subhead, is compatible with and gains strength from the visual, and is interesting to the reader. Whether or not body copy is interesting is a function of how accurately the copywriter and other decision makers have assessed various components of message development, and how good the copywriter is. The most elaborate body copy will probably be ineffective if it is "off strategy." It will not matter if it's very clever, but has little to do in advancing the strategy.

8.   Luke Sullivan, *Hey Whipple, Squeeze This: A Guide to Creating Great Ads* (New York: Wiley), 78.
9.   Ibid, 85.

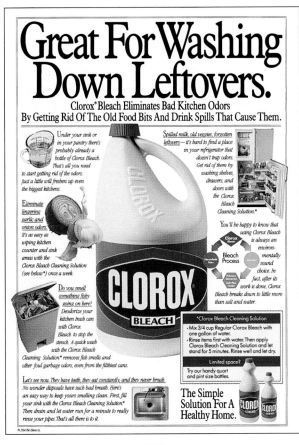

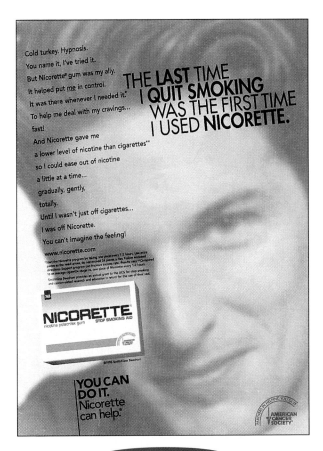

EXHIBIT 12.18

Subheads include important brand information not included in the head-line. Where is the subhead in this Clorox ad? What does the subhead accomplish that the headline does not? www.clorox.com/

EXHIBIT 12.19

In this testimonial ad from Nicorette, a spokesperson tells his story directly to the reader. www.nicorette.com/

There are several standard techniques for preparing body copy. The **straight-line copy** approach explains in straightforward terms why a reader will benefit from use of a brand. This technique is used many times in conjunction with a benefits message strategy. Body copy that uses **dialogue** delivers the selling points of a message to the audience through a character or characters in the ad. The Nicorette ad shown in Exhibit 12.19 is an example of the testimonial technique. A **testimonial** uses dialogue as if the spokesperson is having a one-sided conversation with the reader through the body copy. Dialogue can also depict two people in the ad having a conversation, a technique often used in slice-of-life messages.

Narrative as a method for preparing body copy simply displays a series of statements about a brand. A person may or may not be portrayed as delivering the copy. It is difficult to make this technique lively for the reader, so the threat of writing a dull ad using this technique is ever present. **Direct response copy** is, in many ways, the least complex of copy techniques. In writing direct response copy, the copywriter is trying to highlight the urgency of acting immediately. Hence, the range of possibilities for direct response copy is more limited. In addition, many direct response advertisements rely on sales promotion devices, such as coupons, contests, and rebates, as a means of stimulating action. Giving deadlines to the reader is also a common approach in direct response advertising.

These techniques for copywriting establish a general set of styles that can be used as the format for body copy. Again, be aware that any message objective can be employed within any particular copy technique. There are a vast number of compatible combinations.

Guidelines for Writing Body Copy. Regardless of the specific technique used to develop body copy, the probability of writing effective body copy can be increased if certain guidelines are followed. However, guidelines are meant to be just that—guidelines. Copywriters have created excellent ads that violate one or more of these recommendations. Generally, however, body copy for print ads has a better chance of being effective if these guidelines are followed:

- *Use the present tense whenever possible.* Casting brand claims in the past or future reduces their credibility and timeliness. Speaking to the target audience about things that have happened or will happen sounds like hollow promises.
- *Use singular nouns and verbs.* An ad is normally read by only one person at a time, and that person is evaluating only one brand. Using plural nouns and verbs simply reduces the focus on the item or brand attribute being touted and makes the ad less personal.
- *Use active verbs.* The passive form of a verb does little to stimulate excitement or interest. The use of the active verb in Pontiac's "We Build Excitement" slogan suggests something is happening, and it's happening *now.*
- *Use familiar words and phrases.* Relying on familiar words and phrases to communicate in an interesting and unique way poses a formidable challenge for a copywriter. Familiar words can seem common and ordinary. The challenge is to creatively stylize what is familiar and comfortable to the reader so that interest and excitement result.
- *Vary the length of sentences and paragraphs.* Using sentences and paragraphs of varying lengths not only serves to increase interest but also has a visual impact that can make an ad more inviting and readable.
- *Involve the reader.* Talking *at* the receiver or creating a condescending mood with copy results in a short-circuited communication. Copy that impresses the reader as having been written specifically for him or her reduces the chances of the ad being perceived as a generalized, mass communication.
- *Provide support for the unbelievable.* A brand may have features or functions that the reader finds hard to believe. Where such claims are critical to the brand's positioning in the market and value to the consumer, it is necessary to document (through test results or testimonials) that the brand actually lives up to the claims made. Without proper support of claims, the brand will lose its credibility and therefore its relevance to the consumer.
- *Avoid clichés and superlatives.* Clichés are rarely effective or attention getting. The average consumer assumes that a brand touted through the use of clichés is old-fashioned and stale. Even though the foundation for puffery as a message method is the use of superlatives (*best, superior, unbeatable*), it is wise to avoid their use. These terms are worn out and can signal to the consumer that the brand has little new or different to offer.[10]

Copywriting for Cyberspace.

While some take the position that writing is writing, we see enough evidence that the rapidly evolving medium of cyberspace has its own style, its own feel, and its own writing. Part of this is due to its history. Cybercopy evolved

---

10. The last three points in this list were adapted from Kenneth Roman and Jan Maas, *The New How to Advertise* (New York: St. Martin's Press, 1992), 18–19.

WRITING CYBERCOPY: DON'T ABANDON ALL THE OLD RULES

Writing effective copy for print and broadcast media is difficult enough, but what kind of copy does the average Net surfer find appealing? No one really knows, but we do know a few things about early users of the Internet and World Wide Web. First, users of the Internet are there first and foremost because it is an information environment. It is hard to imagine someone getting up in the morning, turning on the computer, and seeking out ads. Quite to the contrary, the beauty of the Internet in the minds of many has been its freedom from advertising.

Second, when Internet users visit a site, that visit may last only a few seconds. *HotWired* magazine says that on a good day, it can have 600,000 "hits," or visits, some lasting only a few seconds—just long enough for the visitor to quickly scan what is available and then, if not intrigued, move on to another site. The chance to communicate online thus may be even more fleeting than the opportunity offered by radio or television. Third, advertisers have to accept that cyberspace may soon become just as cluttered with competing ads as the traditional media. Some experts predict that annual online advertising will rise to $7.1 billion globally by 2002.

In the end, the rules for writing effective copy in cyberspace may not be all that different from the general rules for copywriting. Once a browser is attracted to a site for the information it offers, she or he will, oh by the way, bump into ads. The new opportunity is to make these ads and their copy interactive according to an individual consumer's interest. If an IBM advertisement can lead a consumer through a series of alternative click-and-proceed paths, then customization of ads is the new copywriting opportunity offered by the interactive environment.

Sources: "Cerfin' the Net," *Sales and Marketing Management*, March 1995, 18-23; Julie Chao, "Tallies of Web-Site Browsers Often Deceive," *Wall Street Journal*, June 21, 1995, B1; Bruce Judson, "Luring Advertisers' Prospects to Web," *Advertising Age*, August 7, 1995, 16. Steven Oberbeck, "Continued Growth in Internet Ads, Users Forecast," *Salt Lake Tribune*, March 21, 1999. www.sltrib.com/999/mar/03211999/business/91988.htm. Accessed March 22, 1999.

from a very techno-speak community, with a twentysomething, Gen-X-meets-techno-nerd kind of voice. Cybercopy's style has been influenced by this history. The medium itself, its structure and its active nature, suggests a type of writing closer to print than to television copy, but not really traditional print copy either. This is a medium where audience has a significantly different meaning than in traditional one-way (noninteractive) media. Audience members often come more directly to cyberads than the average print audience. In other cases, cyberads pop up as one moves from Web page to Web page. Sometimes they are downright roadblocks, but most often they are just annoyances and, thus, are pretty much like ads in other traditional media. But even in most of those cases, the cyberaudience is not as passive as television or radio audiences. All of this suggests something new. There seems to be more incentive to read cybercopy than traditional print advertising. In the beginning, there was little enough ad clutter in cyberspace, making it fairly east to break through. (With increased Internet advertising, this has changed.) Further, much cybercopy is direct response, thus dictating copy style. At this point we believe that the basic principles of good print advertising discussed earlier in the chapter (and reconsidered in the New Media box on this page) generally apply, but a type of copy that assumes an active and engaged audience is preferred. Still, remember that odds are that they are not there for your ads, and they have mouses in their hands. Consider the cyberads in Exhibits 12.20 through 12.23. What do these different forms suggest to you about cyberwriting?

Copywriting for Broadcast Advertising.

Relative to the print media, radio and television present totally different challenges for a copywriter. It is obvious that the audio and audiovisual capabilities of radio and television provide different opportunities for a copywriter. The use of sound effects and voices on radio and the ability to combine copy with color and motion on television provide vast and exciting creative possibilities.

Compared to the print media, however, the broadcast media have inherent limitations for a copywriter. In the print media, a copywriter can write longer and more involved copy to better communicate complex brand features. For consumer shopping goods such as automobiles or home satellite systems, a brand's basis for competitive

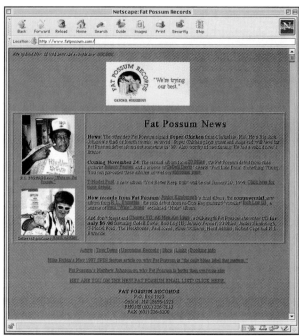

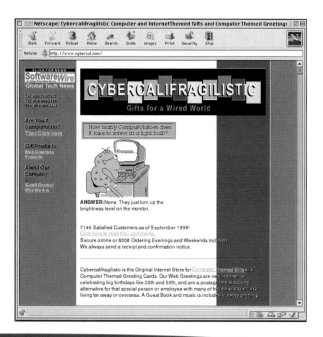

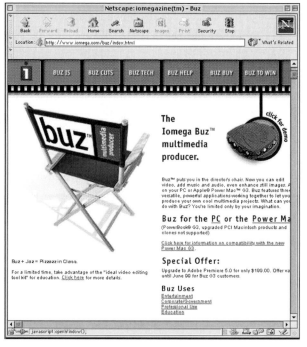

EXHIBITS 12.20, 12.21, 12.22, AND 12.23

Cybercopy represents a new type of ad writing—closer to print than to television copy, but not really traditional print copy either. What do these four cyberads suggest to you about cyberwriting?

differentiation and positioning may lie with complex, unique functional features. In this case, the print media provide a copywriter the time and space to communicate these details, complete with illustrations. In addition, the printed page allows a reader to dwell on the copy and process the information at a personalized, comfortable rate.

These advantages do not exist in the broadcast media. Radio and television offer a fleeting exposure. In addition, introducing sound effects and visual stimuli can distract the listener or viewer from the copy of the advertisement. Despite the additional creative opportunities radio and television offer, the essential challenge of copywriting remains.

Writing Copy for Radio.

Your spot just interrupted your listener's music. It's like interrupting people having sex. If you're going to lean in the bedroom door to say something, make it good: "Hey your car's on fire."[11]

Some writers consider radio the ultimate forum for copywriting creativity. While the radio is restricted to an audio-only presentation, a copywriter is free from some of the harsher realities of visual presentations. Yet it has been said that radio *is* visual. The copywriter must (it is almost inevitable) create images in the minds of listeners. The creative potential of radio rests in its ability to stimulate a theater of the mind, which allows a copywriter to create images and moods for an audience that transcend those created in any other medium.

Despite these creative opportunities, the drawbacks of this medium should never be underestimated. Few radio listeners ever actively listen to radio programming, much less the commercial interruptions. (Talk radio is an obvious exception.) Radio may be viewed by some as the theater of the mind, but others have labeled it audio wallpaper—wallpaper in the sense that radio is used as filler or unobtrusive accompaniment to reading, driving, household chores, or homework. If it was absent, the average person would miss it, but the average person would be hard-pressed to recall the radio ads aired during dinner last evening.

The most reasonable view of copywriting for radio is to temper both the enthusiasm of the theater-of-the-mind perspective and the pessimism of the audio-wallpaper view. (Of course, "reasonable" creative solutions often are destined to be mind-numbingly dull.) A radio copywriter should recognize the unique character of radio and exploit the opportunities it offers. First, radio adds the dimension of sound to the copywriting task, and sound (other than voices) can become a primary tool in creating copy. Second, radio can conjure images in the mind of the receiver that extend beyond the starkness of the brand "information" actually being provided. Radio copywriting should, therefore, strive to stimulate each receiver's imagination.

Writing copy for radio should begin in the same way writing copy for print begins. The copywriter must review components of the creative plan so as to take advantage of and follow through on the marketing and advertising strategies specified and integral to the brand's market potential. Beyond that fundamental task, there are particular formats for radio ads and guidelines for copy preparation the writer can rely on for direction.

Radio Advertising Formats.

There are four basic formats for radio advertisements, and these formats provide the structure within which copy is prepared: the music format, the dialogue format, the announcement format, and the celebrity announcer format. Each of these formats is discussed here.

Music. Since radio provides audio opportunities, music is often used in radio ads. One use of music is to write a song or jingle in an attempt to communicate in an attention-getting and memorable fashion. Songs and jingles are generally written specifically to accommodate unique brand copy. On occasion, an existing tune can be used, and the copy is fit to its meter and rhythm. This is especially true if the music is being used to capture the attention of a particular target segment. Tunes popular with certain target segments can be licensed for use by advertisers. Advertisements using popular tunes by Garbage and Barry Manilow would presumably attract two very different audiences. Singing and music can do much to attract the listener's attention and enhance recall.

11. Sullivan, *Hey Whipple, Squeeze This: A Guide to Creating Great Ads,* 131.

Singing can also create a mood and image with which the product is associated. Modern scores can create a contemporary mood, while sultry music and lyrics create a totally different mood.

But what of jingles? While some love them—and let's face it, they have survived for over a hundred years in advertising—there are some hazards in the use of singing or jingles. Few copywriters are trained lyricists or composers. The threat is ever present that a musical score or a jingle will strike receivers as amateurish and silly. To avoid this, expert songwriters are often used. Further, ensuring that the copy information dominates the musical accompaniment takes great skill. The musical impact can easily overwhelm the persuasion and selling purposes of an ad. Still, just try to get a really good jingle out of your head. You may go to your grave with it on your mind.

Another use of music in radio commercials is to open the ad with a musical score and/or have music playing in the background while the copy is being read. The role of music here is generally to attract attention. This application of music, as well as music used in a song or jingle, is subject to an ongoing debate. If a radio ad is scheduled for airing on music-format stations, should the music in the ad be the same type of music the station is noted for playing, or should it be different? One argument says that if the station format is rock, for example, then the ad should use rock music to appeal to the listener's taste. The opposite argument states that using the same type of music simply buries the ad in the regular programming and reduces its impact. There is no good evidence to suggest that music similar to or different from station programming is superior.

Dialogue. The dialogue technique, described in the section on print copywriting, is commonly used in radio. There are difficulties in making narrative copy work in the short periods of time afforded by the radio medium (typically 15 to 60 seconds). The threat is that dialogue will result in a dull drone of two or more people having a conversation. (You hear enough of that, right?) To reduce the threat of boredom, many dialogues are written with humor, like the one in Exhibit 12.24. Of course, some believe that humor is overused in radio.

Announcement. Radio copy delivered by an announcer is similar to narrative copy in print advertising. The announcer reads important product information as it has been prepared by the copywriter. Announcement is the prevalent technique for live radio spots delivered by disc jockeys or news commentators. The live setting leaves little opportunity for much else. If the ad is prerecorded, sound effects or music may be added to enhance the transmission.

Celebrity Announcer. Having a famous person or persons deliver the copy is alleged to increase the attention paid to a radio ad. Most radio ads that use celebrities do not fall into the testimonial category. The celebrity is not expressing his or her satisfaction with the product, but merely acting as an announcer. Some celebrities (such as James Earl Jones) have distinctive voice qualities or are expert at the emphatic delivery of copy. It is argued that these qualities, as well as listener recognition of the celebrity, increase attention to the ad.

Guidelines for Writing Radio Copy.
The unique opportunities and challenges of the radio medium warrant a set of guidelines for the copywriter to increase the probability of effective communication. The following are a few suggestions for writing effective radio copy:

- *Use common, familiar language.* The use of words and language easily understood and recognized by the receiver is even more important in radio than in print copy preparation.

EXHIBIT 12.24

Dialogue ads prepared for radio often use humor as a way to attract and hold attention. Here is the script for a dialogue ad prepared for Toyota.
www.toyota.com/

ENGINEER:	Um, before we start, the advertising guys have had to take out a few things for legal reasons.
ANNCR:	Well, read them out and I'll cross them off the script.
ENGINEER:	Okay, delete line one where it says that the hot Toyota Corolla SX is faster than an F18 fighter.
ANNCR:	Yeah, I wondered about that.
ENGINEER:	Then the next bit, where it says this Hot Hatch is so hot it comes with a free date with Kim Basinger.
ANNCR:	Shame, big selling point I thought.
ENGINEER:	And they had a few problems with promising that the Corolla Hot Hatch can seat a whole football team in comfort.
ANNCR:	Right.
ENGINEER:	Then that whole section from "By Royal Command" to "You'll get an infectious disease if you don't buy one."
ANNCR:	Including, um, "Guaranteed to increase your IQ by twenty points?"
ENGINEER:	Just a sec', I'll check.
CLIENT:	No, lose it.
ANNCR:	It's lost.
ENGINEER:	Right, what does that leave us with?
ANNCR:	The 100kW Toyota Corolla SX. This Hot Hatch is really hot ...
ENGINEER:	Nothing else.
ANNCR:	Just the usual music at the end.
(MUSIC:	OH WHAT A FEELING, COROLLA)

- *Use short words and sentences.* The probability of communicating verbally increases if short, easily processed words and sentences are used. Long, involved, elaborate verbal descriptions make it difficult for the listener to follow the copy.
- *Stimulate the imagination.* Copy that can conjure up concrete and stimulating images in the receiver's mind can have a powerful impact on recall.
- *Repeat the name of the product.* Since the impression made by a radio ad is fleeting, it may be necessary to repeat the brand name several times before it will register. The same is true for location if the ad is being used to promote a retail organization.
- *Stress the main selling point or points.* The premise of the advertising should revolve around the information that needs to be presented. If selling points are mentioned only in passing, there is little reason to believe they'll be remembered.
- *Use sound and music with care.* By all means, a copywriter should take advantage of all the audio capabilities afforded by the radio medium, including the use of sound effects and music. While these devices can contribute greatly to attracting and holding the listener's attention, care must be taken to ensure that the devices do not overwhelm the copy and therefore the persuasive impact of the commercial.
- *Tailor the copy to the time, place, and specific audience.* Take advantage of any unique aspect of the advertising context. If the ad is specified for a particular geographic region, use colloquialisms unique to that region as a way to tailor the message. The same is true with time-of-day factors or unique aspects of the audience.[12]

The Radio Production Process.
Radio commercial production highlights the role of the copywriter. There is no art director involved in the process. Further, the writer is relatively free to plan nearly any radio production he or she chooses because of the significantly reduced costs of radio execution compared to television. In radio, there are far fewer

12. Book, Cary, and Tannenbaum, *The Radio and Television Commercial,* op. cit.

expert participants than in television. This more streamlined form of production does not mean, however, that the process is more casual. Successful fulfillment of the objectives of an advertisement still requires the careful planning and execution of the production process.

Exhibit 12.25 lists the stages and timetable of a fairly complex radio production: a fully produced commercial. Again, this is a realistic and reasonable timetable once script and budget approval have been secured. The production process for radio is quite similar to the production process for television. Once the copy strategy and methods for the commercial are approved, the process begins with soliciting bids from production houses. The producer reviews bids and submits the best bid for advertiser approval. When the best bid (not always the lowest-priced bid) is identified, the agency submits an estimate to the advertiser for approval. The bid estimate includes both the production house bid and the agency's estimates of its own costs associated with production. When the agency and the advertiser agree, then the producer can award the job to a production house.

After awarding the job to a production house, the next step is to cast the ad. A radio ad may simply have an announcer, in which case the casting job is relatively simple. If the dialogue technique is used, two or more actors and actresses may be needed. Additionally, musical scores often accompany radio ads, and either the music has to be recorded, which includes a search for musicians and possibly singers, or prerecorded music has to be obtained for use by permission. Securing permission for existing music, especially if it is currently popular, can be costly. Much music is in the public domain, that is, it is no longer rigidly protected by copyright laws and is available for far less cost. Closely following the casting is the planning of special elements for the ad, which can include sound effects or special effects, such as time compression or stretching, to create distinct sounds.

Final preparation and production entails scheduling a sound studio and arranging for the actors and actresses to record their pieces in the ad. If an announcer is used in addition to acting talent, the announcer may or may not record with the full cast; her or his lines can be incorporated into the tape at some later time. Music is generally recorded separately and simply added to the commercial during the sound-mixing stage.

It is during the actual production of the ad that the copywriter's efforts become a reality. As in television production, the copywriter will have drawn on the copy platform plans approved in the message development stage to write copy for the radio spot. The script used in the production of a radio advertisement serves the same purpose that the storyboard does in television production. Exhibit 12.26 is a typical radio script.

EXHIBIT 12.25

The timetable of a fully produced radio commercial, once script and budget approval have been secured.

Activity	Time
Solicit bids from production houses/other suppliers	I week
Review bids, award job, submit production estimate to advertiser	I week
Select a cast (announcer, singers, musicians)	I week
Plan special elements (e.g., sound effects); make final preparations; produce tape	I week
Edit tape	Less than I week
Review production (advertiser)	I week
Mix sound	Less than I week
Duplicate tape; ship to stations	I week
Total	6 to 7 weeks

CLIENT: *King's Daughters' Medical Center*
PROJECT: *Family Care Radio (REV 3)*
JOB #: *4600–195*
DATE: *November 9, 1995*
JYG

Doctors :60 Radio

(MUSIC UP AND THROUGHOUT)

ANNCR: No wonder people hate to change doctors.

Your doctor has seen you at your absolute worst—when your eyes are all watery, your skin has turned that kind of sick, greenish color and your breath's so bad, you don't want to be in the same room with yourself. Worse yet, your doctor has seen you in one of those gown things that just doesn't cover you up as well as you'd like.

When you have a physician who knows you that well, the last thing you want is the new one who doesn't know you at all.

Well, King's Daughters' had that in mind when we opened our Family Care Centers in Grayson, Catlettsburg and South Shore. The doctor you see at your Family Care Center is also on staff at our medical center.

So, if you or anyone in your family ever needs hospital care, the same doctor who treats them here can treat them there. Not a doctor they don't know.

King's Daughters' wants to provide you more than a convenient, well-equipped facility. We want to make sure you have someone you can feel comfortable feeling bad around.

The Family Care Centers of King's Daughters' Medical Center. The right care. Right here.

Note that the copywriter must indicate the use of sound effects (SFX) on a separate line to specify the timing of these devices. Further, each player in the advertisement is listed by role, including the announcer (ANNCR), who may or may not be needed, depending on the commercial.

One important element of writing radio copy not yet discussed is the number of words of copy to use given the length of the radio ad. As a general rule, word count relative to airtime is as follows:

10 seconds	20 to 25 words
20 seconds	40 to 45 words
30 seconds	60 to 65 words
60 seconds	120 to 125 words
90 seconds	185 to 190 words[13]

The inclusion of musical introductions, special effects, or local tag lines (specific information for local markets) reduces the amount of copy in the advertisement. Special sound effects interspersed with copy also shorten copy length. The general rules for number of words relative to ad time change depending on the form and structure of the commercial.

After production, the tape goes through editing to create the best version of the production. Then, after advertiser approval, a sound mix is completed in which all

13. Sandra E. Moriarty, *Creative Advertising: Theory and Practice,* 2nd ed. (Englewood Cliffs, N.J.: Prentice-Hall, 1991), 293.

music, special sound effects, and announcer copy are mixed together. The mixing process achieves proper timing between all audio elements in the ad and ensures that all sounds are at the desired levels. After mixing, the tape is duplicated and sent to radio stations for airing.

Expenses for a radio ad should be in the $30,000 to $50,000 range, although big-name talent can push that cost way up.

The most loosely structured production option essentially requires no production at all. It is called a fact sheet. A **fact sheet radio ad** is merely a listing of important selling points that a radio announcer can use to ad-lib a radio spot. This method works best with radio personalities who draw an audience because of their lively, entertaining monologues. The fact sheet provides a loose structure so the announcer can work in the ad during these informal monologues. The risk, of course, is that the ad will get lost in the chatter and the selling points will not be convincingly delivered. On the positive side, radio personalities many times go beyond the scheduled 30 or 60 seconds allotted for the ad.

Another loosely structured technique is the live script. The **live script radio ad** involves having an on-air radio personality, such as a DJ or talk-show host, read the detailed script of an advertisement. Normally there are no sound effects, since such effects would require special production. The live script ensures that all the selling points are included when the commercial is delivered by the announcer. These scripts are not rehearsed, however, and the emphasis, tone, and tempo in the delivery may not be ideal. The advantage of a live script is that it allows an advertiser to submit a relatively structured commercial for airing in a very short period of time. Most stations can work in a live script commercial in a matter of hours after it is received. Exhibit 12.27 shows that a live script is, indeed, read right over the air.

EXHIBIT 12.27

A live script radio ad has an on-air personality read a detailed script over the air. Normally, there are no sound effects or music to accompany the ad—just the announcer's voice.

Writing Copy for Television.

Great print can make you famous. Great TV can make you rich.

—Anonymous[14]

Rule #1 in producing a great TV commercial. First, you must write one.

—Luke Sullivan

The ability to create a mood or demonstrate a brand in use gives television wonderful capabilities; it also affords you the ability to really screw up in magnificent fashion for a very large and expensive audience (no pressure here!). Obviously, copy for television must be highly sensitive to the ad's visual aspects. It is a visual medium; you should try to not let the words get in the way.

The opportunities inherent to television as an advertising medium represent challenges for the copywriter as well. Certainly, the inherent capabilities of television can do much to bring a copywriter's words to life. But the action qualities of television can create problems. First, the copywriter must remember that words do not stand alone. Visuals, special effects, and sound techniques may ultimately convey a message far better than the cleverest turn of phrase. Second, television commercials represent a difficult timing challenge for the copywriter. It is necessary for the copy to be precisely coordinated with the video. If the video portion were one continuous illustration, the task would be difficult enough. Contemporary television ads, however, tend to be heavily edited (that is, lots of cuts), and the copywriting task can be a nightmare. The copywriter not only has to fulfill all the responsibilities of proper information inclusion (based on creative platform and strategy decisions), but also has to carefully fit all the information within, between, and around the visual display taking place. To make sure this coordination is precise, the copywriter, producer, and director assigned to a television advertisement work together closely to make sure the copy supports and enhances the video element. The road map for this coordination effort is known as a storyboard. A **storyboard** is a important shot-by-important-shot sketch depicting in sequence the visual scenes and copy that will be used in a television advertisement. The procedures for coordinating audio and visual elements through the use of storyboards will be presented in Chapter 13, when television production is discussed.

Television Advertising Formats.

Because of the broad creative capability of the television medium, there are several alternative formats for a television ad: demonstration, problem and solution, music and song, spokesperson, dialogue, vignette, and narrative. Each is discussed here. Again, this is not an exhaustive list, but rather a sampling of popular forms.

Demonstration. Due to television's abilities to demonstrate a brand in action, demonstration is an obvious format for a television ad. Do it if you can. Brands whose benefits result from some tangible function can effectively use this format. Copy that accompanies this sort of ad embellishes the visual demonstration. The copy in a demonstration is usually straight-line copy, but drama can easily be introduced into this format, such as with the Radio Shack home security system that scares off a burglar or the Fiat braking system that saves a motorist from an accident. Demonstration with

---

14. Cited in Sullivan, *Hey Whipple, Squeeze This: A Guide to Creating Great Ads,* 103.

sight and sound lets viewers appreciate the full range of features a brand has to offer. The commercial in Exhibit 12.28 was created at an agency in Sao Paulo, Brazil, but the clarity of the demonstration is convincing in just about any culture.

Problem and Solution. In this format, a brand is introduced as the savior in a difficult situation. This format often takes shape as a slice-of-life message, in which a consumer solves a problem with the advertised brand. Dishwashing liquids, drain openers, and numerous other household products are commonly promoted with this technique. A variation on the basic format is to promote a brand on the basis of problem prevention. A variety of auto maintenance items and even insurance products have used this approach.

Music and Song. Many television commercials use music and singing as a creative technique. The various beverage industries (soft drinks, beer, and wine) frequently use this format to create the desired mood for their brands. Additionally, the growth of image advertising has resulted in many ads that show a product in action accompanied by music and only visual overlays of the copy. This format for television advertising tends to restrict the amount of copy and presents the same difficulties for copywriting as the use of music and song in radio copywriting. Did you wonder if Burger King would ever run out of pop songs to use to peddle fast food? A logo, a few captions, a product shot, and songs ranging from "Tempted" to "So Hot" to the theme from *Welcome Back Kotter* have been used to great success for the franchise.

EXHIBIT 12.28

Demonstration with sight and sound lets viewers appreciate the full range of features a brand has to offer; this commercial created by an ad agency in Brazil is a good example.

(**SFX:** MOTORCYCLE SOUNDS)
SUPER: Honda C-100 Dream. Up to 700 Km per
                     liter or 30 seconds with a single drop.
SUPER: C-100 Dream, Start It, Ride It, And Love It.
SUPER: Honda. The World's Best Emotion.

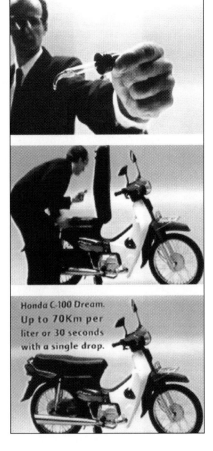

Spokesperson. The delivery of a message by a spokesperson can place a heavy emphasis on the copy. The copy is given precedence over the visual and is supported by the visual, rather than vice versa. Expert, average-person, and celebrity testimonials fall into this formatting alternative. An example of the effective use of an expert spokesperson is Tiger Woods for Titleist.

Dialogue. As in a radio commercial, a television ad may feature a dialogue between two or more people. Dialogue-format ads pressure a copywriter to compose dialogue that is believable and keeps the ad moving forward. Most slice-of-life ads in which a husband and wife or friends are depicted using a brand employ a dialogue format.

Vignette. A vignette format uses a sequence of related advertisements as a device to maintain viewer interest. Vignettes also give the advertising a recognizable look, which can help achieve awareness and recognition. The Taster's Choice couple featured in a series of advertisements in the United States and Great Britain is an example of the vignette format.

Narrative. A narrative is similar to a vignette but is not part of a series of related ads. Narrative is a distinct format in that it tells a story, like a vignette, but the mood of the ad is highly personal, emotional, and involving. A narrative ad often focuses on story-telling and only indirectly touches on the benefits of the brand. Many of the "heart-sell" ads by McDonald's, Kodak, and Hallmark use the narrative technique to great effect. (See Exhibit 12.29.)

EXHIBIT 12.29

A narrative ad often focuses on storytelling and only indirectly touches on the benefits of the brand.

SUPER:	Your parents, your children, yourself.
SIGOURNEY WEAVER:	You owe it to your parents, for they brought you into this world.
SUPER:	Who do you love the least?
WEAVER:	You owe it to your children, for you did the same for them. But the day may arrive when both debts come due. When you may have no choice but to borrow from your own retirement to educate a child or care for a parent. Into whose eyes can you look and say you just can't help?
SUPER:	Insurance for the unexpected.
WEAVER:	For in both, you will surely see your own.
SUPER:	Investments for the opportunities.
SUPER:	John Hancock (Olympic rings) world-wide sponsor.

Guidelines for Writing Television Copy.
Writing copy for television advertising has its own set of unique opportunities and challenges. The following are some general guidelines:

- *Use the video.* Allow the video portion of the commercial to enhance and embellish the audio portion. Given the strength and power of the visual presentation in television advertising, take advantage of its impact with copy.
- *Support the video.* Make sure that the copy doesn't simply hitchhike on the video. If all the copy does is verbally describe what the audience is watching, an opportunity to either communicate additional information or strengthen the video communication has been lost.
- *Coordinate the audio with the video.* In addition to strategically using the video, it is essential that the audio and video do not tell entirely different stories.
- *Sell the product as well as entertain the audience.* Television ads can sometimes be more entertaining than television programming. A temptation for the copywriter and art director is to get caught up in the excitement of a good video presentation and forget that the main purpose is to deliver persuasive communication.
- *Be flexible.* Due to media-scheduling strategies, commercials are produced to run as 15-, 20-, 30-, or 60-second spots. The copywriter may need to ensure that the audio portion of an ad is complete and comprehensive within varying time lengths.
- *Use copy judiciously.* If an ad is too wordy, it can create information overload and interfere with the visual impact. Ensure that every word is a working word and contributes to the impact of the message.
- *Reflect the brand personality and image.* All aspects of an ad, copy and visuals, should be consistent with the personality and image the advertiser wants to build or maintain for the brand.
- *Build campaigns.* When copy for a particular advertisement is being written, evaluate its potential as a sustainable idea. Can the basic appeal in the advertisement be developed into multiple versions that form a campaign?[15]

Slogans.
Copywriters are often asked to come up with a good slogan or tag line for a product or service. A **slogan** is a short phrase in part used to help establish an image, identity, or position for a brand or an organization, but mostly used to increase memorability. A slogan is established by repeating the phrase in a firm's advertising and other public communication as well as through salespeople and event promotions. Slogans are often used as a headline or subhead in print advertisements, or as the tag line at the conclusion of radio and television advertisements. Slogans typically appear directly below the brand or company name, as in all Lee jeans advertising: "The Brand That Fits." Some of the more memorable and enduring ad slogans are listed in Exhibit 12.30.

A good slogan can serve several positive purposes for a brand or a firm. First, a slogan can be an integral part of a brand's image and personality. BMW's slogan, "The Ultimate Driving Machine," does much to establish and maintain the personality and image of the brand. Second, if a slogan is carefully and consistently developed over time, it can act as a shorthand identification for the brand and provide information on important brand benefits. The long-standing slogan for Allstate Insurance, "You're in Good Hands with Allstate," communicates the benefits of dealing with a well-established insurance firm. A good slogan also provides continuity across different media and between advertising campaigns. Nike's "Just Do It" slogan has given the firm an underlying theme for a wide range of campaigns and other promotions throughout the 1990s. In this sense, a slogan is a useful tool in helping to bring about thematic integrated marketing communications for a firm. Microsoft's slogan—"Where do you want to go today?"—is all about freedom, but the company approach to integrated communications is more sophisticated than just brandishing its slogan with a vengeance. See the IMC box on page 382.

---

15.   The last three points in this list were adapted from Roman and Maas, *The New How to Advertise.*

Brand/Company	Slogan
Allstate Insurance	You're in Good Hands with Allstate.
American Express	Don't Leave Home Without It.
American Stock Exchange	The Smarter Place to Be.
AT&T (consumer)	Reach Out and Touch Someone.
AT&T (business)	AT&T. Your True Choice.
Beef Industry Council	Real Food for Real People.
BMW	The Ultimate Driving Machine.
Budweiser	This Bud's for You.
Chevrolet trucks	Like a Rock.
Cotton Industry	The Fabric of Our Lives.
DeBeers	Diamonds Are Forever.
Delta Airlines	You'll Love the Way We Fly.
Ford	Have You Driven a Ford Lately?
Gemini Consulting	Worldwide Leader in Business Transformation.
Goodyear	The Best Tires in the World Have Goodyear Written All over Them.
Lincoln	What a Luxury Car Should Be.
Microsoft (online)	Where Do You Want to Go Today?
Northwestern Mutual	The Quiet Company.
Panasonic	Just Slightly Ahead of Our Time.
Prudential Insurance	Get a Piece of the Rock.
Saturn	A Different Kind of Company. A Different Kind of Car.
Sharp	From Sharp Minds Come Sharp Products.
Smith Barney	We Make Money the Old-Fashioned Way. We Earn It.
Toshiba	In Touch with Tomorrow.
Toyota	Everyday.
Visa	It's Everywhere You Want to Be.

Common Mistakes in Copywriting.

The preceding discussions have shown that print, radio, and television advertising present the copywriter with unique challenges and opportunities. Copy in each arena must be compatible with the various types of ads run in each medium and the particular capabilities and liabilities of each medium and format. Beyond the guidelines for effective copy in each area, some common mistakes made in copywriting can and should be avoided:

- *Vagueness.* Avoid generalizations and words that are imprecise in meaning. To say that a car is stylish is not nearly as meaningful as saying it has sleek, aerodynamic lines.
- *Wordiness.* Being economical with descriptions is paramount. Copy has to fit in a limited time frame (or space), and receivers bore easily. When boredom sets in, effective communication often ceases.
- *Triteness.* Using clichés and worn-out superlatives was mentioned as a threat to print copywriting. The same threat (to a lesser degree, due to audio and audiovisual

capabilities) exists in radio and television advertising. Trite copy creates a boring, outdated image for a brand or firm.

- *Creativity for creativity's sake.* Some copywriters get carried away with a clever idea. It's essential that the copy in an ad remain true to its primary responsibility: communicating the selling message. However, copy that is extraordinarily funny or poses an intriguing riddle yet fails to register the main selling theme will simply produce another amusing advertising failure.

The Copy Approval Process.

"The client has some issues and concerns about your ads." This is how account executives announce the death of your labors: "issues and concerns." To understand the portent of this phrase, picture the men lying on the floor of that Chicago garage on St. Valentine's Day. Al Capone had issues and concerns with these men.

I've had account executives beat around the bush for 15 minutes before they could tell me the bad news. "Well, we had a good meeting."

Yes, you say, "but are the ads dead?"

"We learned a lot?"

"But are they dead?"

"Wellll, . . . They're really not dead. They are just in a new and better place."

—Luke Sullivan[16]

IF MICROSOFT IS DOING IT, IT MUST BE RIGHT

Microsoft has a reputation for doing things right and succeeding. After all, with sales approaching $20 billion and profit margin hovering around 30 percent, it's hard to argue with its decision making.

So when Microsoft takes one of its veteran executives, Jon Reingold, and creates a new position called VP–Corporate Marketing, with the expressed purpose of helping the company "speak with a more consistent voice," it's probably worth paying attention to. When a company says it wants to "speak with a more consistent voice," this is classic integrated marketing communications rising to the forefront.

In Microsoft's case, the issue of wanting an IMC approach to communications has a unique twist. According to an internal corporate memo on the matter, Reingold will not only guide Microsoft's brand ad campaigns, but will also be in charge of coordinating public relations and public affairs units. These are the divisions in the firm that deal with Washington, D.C., influencers. Given the firm's highly publicized legal problems with the Department of Justice, including the public affairs division in corporate marketing initiatives makes sense at this point in the firm's history.

But beyond the unique wrinkles, the main challenge will be to ensure that all forms of buyers, from information technology corporate buyers to desktop users, understand Microsoft and its products. Mr. Reingold puts it this way: "I am sure we could do a better job letting folk know what Microsoft really stands for. We have a great story to tell. Being consistent across our communications certainly helps us to be more effective doing that."

In order to help the process along, Microsoft will rely on Wieden & Kennedy in Portland, Oregon, as its lead agency and will spend about $300 million on measured media. Anderson & Lembke in San Francisco will handle online development.

Source: Bradley Johnson, "Microsoft Aims 3 Ad Drives at Small Business Users," *Advertising Age*, February 16, 1998, 43.

The final step in copywriting is getting the copy approved. For many copywriters, this is the most dreaded part of their existence. During the approval process, the proposed copy is likely to pass through the hands of a wide range of client and agency people, many of whom are ill prepared to judge the quality of the copy. The challenge at this stage is to keep the creative potency of the copy intact. As David Ogilvy suggests in his commandments for advertising, "Committees can criticize advertisements, but they can't write them."[17]

The copy approval process usually begins within the creative department of an advertising agency. A copywriter submits draft copy to either the senior writer or the creative director,

16. Sullivan, *Hey Whipple, Squeeze This: A Guide to Creating Great Ads,* 182.
17. Ogilvy, *Confessions of an Advertising Man,* 101.

Agency

Account Planning

↓

Copywriter

↓

Senior Writer
Creative Director

↓

Account Management Team
Legal Department

Client

↓

Product Manager
Brand Manager
Marketing Staff

↓

Senior Executives

EXHIBIT 12.31

The copy approval process.

or both. From there, the redrafted copy is forwarded to the account management team within the agency. The main concern at this level is to evaluate the copy on legal grounds. After the account management team has made recommendations, a meeting is likely held to present the copy, along with proposed visuals, to the client's product manager, brand manager, and marketing staff. Inevitably, the client representatives feel compelled to make recommendations for altering the copy. In some cases, these recommendations realign the copy in accordance with important marketing strategy objectives. In other cases, the recommendations are amateurish and problematic. From the copywriter's point of view, they are rarely welcome, although the copywriter usually has to act like they are.

Depending on the assignment, the client, and the traditions of the agency, the creative team may also rely on various forms of copy research. Typically, copy research is either developmental or evaluative. **Developmental copy research** can actually help copywriters at the early stages of copy development by providing audience interpretations and reactions to the proposed copy. **Evaluative copy research** is used to judge copy after it's been produced. Here, the audience expresses its approval or disapproval of the copy used in an ad. Copywriters are not fond of these evaluative report cards. In our view, they are completely justified in their suspicion; for many reasons, state-of-the-art evalutive copy research just isn't very good. Most of the time, it's awful, maybe even a crime. Just because someone calls it science doesn't mean a thing.

Finally, copy should always be submitted for final approval to the advertiser's senior executives. Many times, these executives have little interest in evaluating advertising plans, and they leave this responsibility to middle managers. In some firms, however, top executives get very involved in the approval process. The various levels of approval for copy are summarized in Exhibit 12.31 and parodied in Exhibit 12.32. For the advertiser, it is best to recognize that copywriters, like other creative talent in an agency, should be allowed to exercise their creative expertise with guidance but not overbearing interference. Copywriters seek to provide energy and originality to an often dry marketing strategy. To override their creative effort violates their reason for being.

EXHIBIT 12.32

Advertisers should allow copy-editors to exercise their creative expertise with guidance but not overbearing interference, as this Dilbert *cartoon humorously illustrates.*

Source: *Dilbert* reprinted by permission of United Features Syndicate, Inc.

SUMMARY

◄1► Explain the need for a creative plan in the copywriting process.

Effective ad copy must be based on a variety of individual inputs and information sources. Making sense out of these diverse inputs and building from them creatively is a copywriter's primary challenge. A creative plan is used as a device to assist the copywriter in dealing with this challenge. Key elements in the creative plan include product features and benefits that must be communicated to the audience, the mood or tone appropriate for the audience, and the intended media for the ad.

◄2► Detail the components of print copy, along with important guidelines for writing effective print copy.

The three unique components of print copy are the headline, subhead, and body copy. Headlines need to motivate additional processing of the ad. Good headlines communicate information about the brand or make a promise about the benefits the consumer can expect from the brand. If the brand name is not featured in the headline, then that headline must entice the reader to examine the body copy or visual material. Subheads can also be valuable in helping lead the reader to and through the body copy. In the body copy, the brand's complete story can be told. Effective body copy must be crafted carefully to engage the reader, furnish supportive evidence for claims made about the brand, and avoid clichés and exaggeration that the consumer will dismiss as hype.

◄3► Describe various formatting alternatives for radio ads and articulate guidelines for writing effective radio copy.

Four basic formats can be used to create radio copy. These are the music format, the dialogue format, the announcement format, and the celebrity announcer format. Guidelines for writing effective radio copy start with using simple sentence construction and language familiar to the intended audience. When the copy stimulates the listener's imagination, the advertiser can expect improved results as long as the brand name and the primary selling points don't get lost. When using music or humor to attract and hold the listener's attention, the copywriter must take care not to shortchange key selling points for the sake of simple entertainment.

◄4► Describe various formatting alternatives for television ads and articulate guidelines for writing effective television copy.

Several formats can be considered in preparing television ad copy. These are demonstration, problem and solution, music and song, spokesperson, dialogue, vignette, and narrative. To achieve effective copy in the television medium, it is essential to coordinate the copy with the visual presentation, seeking a synergistic effect between audio and video. Entertaining to attract attention should again not be emphasized to the point that the brand name or selling points of the ad get lost. Developing copy consistent with the heritage and image of the brand is also essential. Finally, copy that can be adapted to various time lengths and modified to sustain audience interest over the life of a campaign is most desirable.

KEY TERMS

creative team (356)
creative concept (356)
copywriting (359)
creative plan (360)
headline (362)
subhead (366)
straight-line copy (367)
dialogue (367)
testimonial (367)

narrative (367)
direct response copy (367)
fact sheet radio ad (376)
live script radio ad (376)
storyboard (377)
slogan (380)
developmental copy research (383)
evaluative copy research (383)

QUESTIONS FOR REVIEW AND CRITICAL THINKING

1. Explain the applications for copy research in the copywriting process. What other forms of consumer or market research might be particularly helpful in developing effective ad copy?

2. Pull ten print ads from your favorite magazine. Using the classifications offered in this chapter, what would you surmise was the copywriter's intended purpose for each of the headlines in your ten print ads?

3. How does audience influence the style of writing exhibited in cyberads? How do you characterize the writing at www.iomega.com/ shown in Exhibit 12.23?

4. Discuss the advantages and disadvantages of music as a tool for constructing effective radio ads.

5. Listen with care to the radio ads in 30 minutes of programming on your favorite radio station. Then do the same for 30 minutes of programming on a parent's or grandparent's favorite station. Identify ads that did the best job of using terms and jargon familiar to the target audience of each station. What differences in mood or tone did you detect among ads on the two stations?

6. Compare and contrast the dialogue and narrative formats for television ads. What common requirement must be met to construct convincing TV ads using these two formats?

7. Entertainment is both the blessing and the curse of a copywriter. Is it conceivable that ads that merely entertain could actually prove valuable in stimulating sales? If so, how so?

8. Describe the four common categories of mistakes that copywriters must avoid. From your personal experience with all types of ads, are there other common mistakes that you believe copywriters are prone to make on a regular basis?

9. Everyone has his or her own opinion on what makes advertisements effective or ineffective. How does this fundamental aspect of human nature complicate a copywriter's life when it comes to winning approval for his or her ad copy?

EXPERIENTIAL EXERCISES

1. Divide into groups. Your team assignment is to study and improve upon local car dealer television advertising. Watch two or three television commercials by local car dealers. Discuss what you found good or bad about the ads. Seize upon the worst commercial and develop a list of suggestions to improve it. Apply your thoughts to the generation of a storyboard for a much-improved commercial.

2. Find two print ads that do not use a subhead. Craft three subheads for each ad and defend the role each plays in improving the ads.

USING THE INTERNET

There are several major elements used when producing advertising copy. Visit the following sites:

Leggs: www.leggs.com

Valvoline: www.valvoline.com

Pontiac: www.pontiac.com

1. What is the creative concept behind each site?

2. Which of the headlines is the most appealing? What features are most effective in a headline for a Web page?

3. Do you think that the body copy for each site supports the headline? What aspects of the body copy do you think are most effective? Least effective?

4. Which site exhibits the most unity between headline, subhead, and body copy? How does this unity support the creative concept?

CNET's news.com site (www.news.com) is a typical Web news collection site, running original content and citing stories from a great many sources on the Web.

1. How does news.com's style of delivering news resemble or differ from that of sites delivering advertising?

2. How well do CNET's headlines do at conveying the sense of what information is available to the reader who'll take the time to click through?

3. How does the use of subheads in links to current articles enhance their impact?

AT A TIME LIKE THIS, THERE ARE SEVERAL
THINGS YOU MIGHT FIND USEFUL.

Dive knife.

Depth gauge.

Shark repellent.

Oxygen.

COMPUWARE.
What do you need most?

For application development, testing and management, four out of five of the world's
largest corporations rely on Compuware. People and software for business applications.

©1998 Compuware Corporation   800.521.9353   www.compuware.com

CHAPTER 13

After reading and thinking about this chapter, you will be able to do the following:

◀▶ Identify the basic purposes, components, and formats of print ad illustrations.

◀▶ Describe the principles and components that help ensure the effective design of print ads.

◀▶ Detail the stages that art directors follow in developing the layout of a print ad.

◀▶ Discuss the activities and decisions involved in the final production of print ads.

◀▶ Identify the various players who must function as a team to produce television ads.

◀▶ Discuss the specific stages and costs involved in producing television ads.

◀▶ Describe the major formatting options for television ad production.

A hundred years ago advertisers largely relied on words to persuade consumers. They argued with consumers, attempted to reason with them, cajoled them . . . and occasionally lied to them. Then somewhere in the early 20th century, particularly noticeable after about 1910, advertisers began a move away from words and toward pictures. This trend would extend throughout the 20th century, and into the 21st. Advertising has become more and more visual. There are several reasons for this. Among them are (1) improved technologies, which facilitate better and more affordable illustration; (2) the inherent advantage of pictures to quickly demonstrate goods and services; (3) the ability to build brand "images" through visuals; (4) the legalistic advantage of pictures over words in that the truth or falsity of a picture is virtually impossible to determine; (5) the fact that pictures, although just as cultural as words, permit a certain type of portability that words do not; and (6) the fact that pictures allow advertisers to place brands in desired social contexts, thus transferring important social meaning to them.

Not coincidentally, the role of the art director has grown more and more important relative to the copywriter. This is a visual age, and like it or not, the primacy of the word has been challenged by pictures in contemporary advertising. Copywriting is obviously still vital to advertising, but there's a new sheriff in town, and she is an art director. We can learn from the experience of advertising practice. So, let's show and tell.

Illustration, Design, and Layout.

We begin with a discussion of three primary visual elements of a print ad: illustration, design, and layout. We then identify aspects of each that should be specified, or at least considered, as a print ad is being prepared. An advertiser must appreciate the technical aspects of coordinating the visual elements in an ad with the mechanics of the layout and ultimately with the procedures for print production. A discussion of illustration, design, and layout brings to the fore the role of art direction in print advertising.

Initially, the art director and copywriter decide on the content of an illustration. Then the art director, often in conjunction with a graphic designer, takes this raw idea for the visual and develops it further. Art directors, with their specialized skills and training, coordinate the design and illustration components of a print ad. The creative director oversees the entire process. Most often, the copywriter is still very much in the loop.

Illustration.

Illustration, in the context of print advertising, is the actual drawing, painting, photography, or computer-generated art that forms the picture in an advertisement.

Illustration Purposes. There are several specific, strategic purposes for illustration, which can greatly increase the chances of effective communication. The basic purposes of an illustration are the following:

- to attract the attention of the target audience
- to make the brand heroic
- to communicate product features or benefits
- to create a mood, feeling, or image
- to stimulate reading of the body copy
- to create the desired social context for the brand

Attract the Attention of the Target Audience. One of the primary roles of an illustration is to attract and hold attention. With all the advertising clutter out there today, this is no easy task. In some advertising situations (for example, the very early stages of a new product launch, very "low involvement" repeat purchase items), just being noticed by consumers *may* almost be enough. In most cases, however, just being noticed is a necessary, but not sufficient, goal. An illustration is made to communicate with a particular target audience and, generally, must support other components of the ad to achieve the intended communication impact. So, what do you think of the ads in Exhibits 13.1 and 13.2? Impact?

Make the Brand Heroic. One traditional role of art direction is to make the brand heroic. Very often this is done by the manner in which the brand is presented via illustration. Visual techniques such as backlighting, low-angle shots, and dramatic use of color can communicate heroic proportions and qualities. (See Exhibit 13.3.) David Ogilvy suggests that if you don't have a particular story to tell in the ad, then make the package the subject of the illustration.[1]

Communicate Product Features or Benefits. Perhaps the most straightforward illustration is one that simply displays brand features, benefits, or both. Even though a print ad is static, the product can be shown in use through an "action" scene or even through a series of illustrations. The benefits of product use can be demonstrated with before-and-after shots or by demonstrating the result of having used the product. (See Exhibit 13.4.)

Create a Mood, Feeling, or Image. Brand image is projected through illustration. The myriad of ways this is done is beyond enumeration, but the illustration, interacting with the packaging, associated brand imagery (for example, the brand logo), and evoked feelings, all contribute. The "mood" of an ad can help this along. Pursuing these purposes with a print ad depends on the technical execution of the illustration. The lighting, color, tone, and texture of the illustration can have a huge impact. The photograph used as the illustration in the print ad for Mass Mutual in Exhibit 13.5 captures a feeling of tenderness and security with its tone and texture.

Stimulate Reading of the Body Copy. Just as a headline can stimulate examination of the illustration, the illustration can stimulate reading of the body copy. Since body copy generally carries the essential selling

EXHIBITS 13.1 AND 13.2

Would anyone be bored by these images?

EXHIBIT 13.3

Visual techniques can make a brand heroic.

1.   David Ogilvy, *Ogilvy on Advertising* (New York: Vintage Books, 1985), 77.

NEC communicates product features and benefits through a series of product-in-action photographs. www.nec.com/

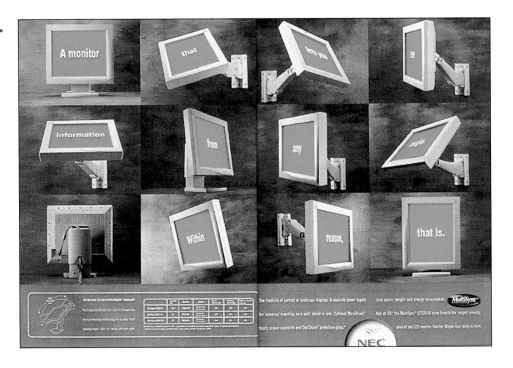

message, any tactic that encourages reading is useful. (See Exhibit 13.6.) Illustrations can create curiosity and interest in readers. To satisfy that curiosity, readers may proceed to the body copy for clarification. (This is not easy; body copy often looks boring and tedious, because it often is.) Normally, an illustration and headline need to be fully coordinated and play off each other for this level of interest to occur. One caution is to avoid making the illustration too clever a stimulus for motivating copy reading. Putting cleverness ahead of clarity in choosing an illustration can confuse the receiver and cause the body copy to be ignored. As one expert puts it, such ads win awards but can camouflage the benefit offered by the product.[2] Gillette's reliance on print advertising to launch its Mach3 razor worldwide underscores the importance of choosing illustrations that spur on the reading of body copy, as noted in the Global Issues box on page 392.

Create the Desired Social Context for the Brand. As described earlier, advertisers need to associate or situate their brand within a type of social setting, thereby linking it with certain "types" of people and certain lifestyles. Establishing desired social contexts is probably the most important function of modern art direction. Look at the ad in Exhibit 13.7 and then think about what it would mean if the product were divorced from the social context. (See Exhibit 13.8.) See what we mean. Context can be (and usually is) everything.

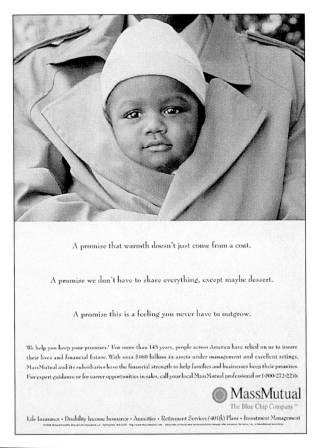

How does the illustration of an infant in this ad help create a mood or feeling? Are children appropriate subjects for an insurer's ads?
www.massmutual.com/

2.   Tony Antin, *Great Print Advertising* (New York: Wiley, 1993), 38.

EXHIBIT 13.6

Bicycles and information systems auditing . . . do they have much in common? The illustration in this KPMG ad (www.kpmg.com) should resonate with nearly anyone who lives or works in a city. The copy constructs the analogy: a bike frame was secured, with a fine lock, but that wasn't quite enough security, in the end, was it? The image invites readers to imagine all of the ways their information systems might be at risk; little additional copy is required.

EXHIBITS 13.7 AND 13.8

3Com's Palm Computing platform with and without social context. www.3com.com/

Illustration Components. Various factors contribute to the overall visual presentation and impact of an illustration. Size, color, and medium affect viewers. Individual decisions regarding size, color, and medium are a matter of artistic discretion and creative execution. There is some evidence of the differing effects of various decisions made in each of these areas. But remember, the interpretation and meaning of any visual representation cannot be explained completely by a series of rules or prescriptive how-tos. Thankfully, it's not that simple.

Size. Does doubling the size of an illustration double the probability that the illustration will achieve its intended purpose? The answer is probably no. There is no question that greater size in an illustration may allow an ad to compete more successfully for the reader's attention, especially in a cluttered media environment. Generally speaking, illustrations with a focal point immediately recognizable by the reader are more likely to be noticed and comprehended. Conversely, illustrations that arouse curiosity or incorporate action score high in attracting attention but have been found to score low in inducing the reading of the total ad.[3]

Color. While not every execution of print advertising allows for the use of color (because of either expense or the medium being employed), color is a creative tool with important potential. Some products (such as furniture, floor coverings, or expensive clothing) may depend on color to accurately communicate a principal value. Color can also be used to emphasize a product feature or attract the reader's attention to a particular part of an ad. But remember, color has no fixed meaning, so no hard

3.   Daniel Starch, *Measuring Advertising Readership and Results* (New York: McGraw-Hill, 1966), 83.

rules can be offered. Color is cultural, situational, and contextual. Saying that red always means this or blue always means that is a popular but unfounded myth. It's simply not true.

GLOBAL ISSUES

ONE OF THE BEST GOES GLOBAL WITH PRINT

One of the undisputed leaders in global marketing is Gillette. For the past decade this U.S. firm has earned over 50 percent of its revenue outside the United States. When Gillette began planning the global ad blitz for the critically important Mach3 shaver, a good portion of the media strategy specified print as a vehicle for reaching consumers in key global markets.

Overall, Gillette plans to spend about $200 million in advertising over the first year in launching the new razor worldwide. The company is relying on its experience and great success with the introductions of the Sensor in 1989 and the SensorExcel razors in 1994. The Mach3 media mix includes TV, radio, print, outdoor, and Internet ads. All versions of the campaign will capitalize on the high-tech theme of the product. All advertising will also retain the highly successful and now anthemlike slogan "The Best a Man Can Get."

The role of the print version of the campaign is carefully conceived with the overall effort. The print ads will explain the product in greater detail than ads in other media vehicles. The key message issue is that the new product has a patented DLC (Diamond-Like Carbon) coating, and three carefully engineered blades, the blades have precise positioning, and the razor has a unique forward-pivoting action.

It is clear that the role for the print campaign takes advantage of the inherent capabilities of the print medium. In print, the receiver can be provided with greater amounts of information and the detail can be fully explained. This is something that Gillette cannot accomplish with 30-second television spots, radio spots, or billboard ads. In addition, the ability to selectively target particular users is much greater with the print media across many global markets.

A key to the campaign will be to induce trial use. An analyst believes that "if people try Mach3, you'll have 99% conversion."

Source: Sharon T. Klahr, "Gillette Puts $300 Million Behind Its Mach3 Shaver," *Advertising Age,* April 20, 1998, 6.

Medium. The choice of **medium** for an illustration is the decision regarding the use of drawing, photography, or computer graphics.[4] Drawing represents a wide range of creative presentations, from cartoons to pen-and-ink drawings to elaborate watercolor and oil paintings. Photos have an element of believability as representations of reality (even though they can be just as manipulated as any other form of representation.) Further, photos can often be prepared more quickly and at much less expense than other forms of art. Photographers all over the world specialize in different types of photography: landscape, seascape, portrait, food, and architecture, for example. The American Society of Magazine Photographers is a clearinghouse for nearly 5,000 photographers whose work is available as off-the-shelf images.[5] Photographs can be cropped to any size or shape, retouched, color corrected, and doctored in a number of ways to create the desired effect.

With advancing technology, artists have discovered the application of computer graphics to advertising illustrations. Computer graphics specialists can create and manipulate images. With respect to illustrations for print advertising, the key development has been the ability to digitize images. Digitizing is a computer process of breaking an image (illustration) into a grid of small squares. Each square is assigned a computer code for identification.

With a digitized image, computer graphics specialists can break down an illustration and reassemble it or import other components into the original image. Age can be added or taken away from a model's face, or the Eiffel Tower can magically appear on Madison Avenue. The creative possibilities are endless with computer graphics. Exhibit 13.9 is an example of an ad with multiple images imported through computer graphics. Some art directors are very fond of these software solutions. Adobe Photoshop is

4.   This section is adapted from Sandra E. Moriarty, *Creative Advertising: Theory and Practice,* 2nd ed. (Englewood Cliffs, N.J.: Prentice-Hall, 1991), 139–141.
5.   G. Robert Cox and Edward J. McGee, *The Ad Game: Playing to Win* (Englewood Cliffs, N.J.: Prentice-Hall, 1990), 44.

Given the nature of Hewlett-Packard's products, do you think that the composite image chosen for this ad—obviously computer generated and enhanced—is a good choice? www.hp.com/

the industry leader in imaging software. Visitors to Adobe's home page at www.adobe.com/ can download a free program that allows them to try their hand at manipulating photo images (Exhibit 13.10).

The size, color, and media decisions regarding an illustration are difficult ones. It is likely that strategic and budgetary considerations will heavily influence choices in these areas. Once again, an advertiser should not constrain the creative process more than is absolutely necessary, and even then you should probably back off a bit.

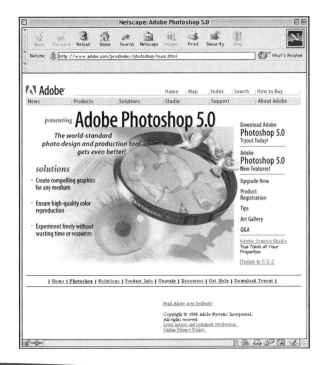

Adobe Photoshop—the industry leader in imaging software. www.adobe.com/

Illustration Formats. The just-discussed components represent a series of decisions that must be made in conceiving an illustration. Another important decision is how the product or brand will appear as part of the illustration. **Illustration format** refers to the choices the advertiser has for displaying its product. There are product shots of all sorts: some emphasize the social context and meaning of the product or service; others are more abstract (see Exhibit 13.11). Obviously, the illustration format must be consistent with the copy strategy set for the ad. The creative department and the marketing planners must communicate with one another so that the illustration format selected helps pursue the specific objectives set for the total ad campaign.

The Strategic and Creative Impact of Illustration. Defining effectiveness is a matter of first considering the basic illustration purposes, components, and formats we've just discussed. Next, these factors need to be evaluated in the context of marketing strategy, consumer behavior, and

As I See It, #41 in a series
Charles Sheaffe
'The One That Got Away'
Polaroid Transfer Photography

THE BOLD LOOK
OF **KOHLER**.

How do you capture a spirit? Look to an Artist Editions lavatory, tile and accessories. The Pheasant™ lavatory is inspired by 19th century illustrations. To revisit and reawaken the mastery of a time gone by. Don't let this one get away. See the Yellow Pages for a KOHLER® Registered Showroom, call 1-800-4-KOHLER, ext. XX to order product literature, or visit www.kohlerco.com.
©1998 by Kohler Co.

EXHIBIT 13.11

The somewhat surreal illustration format used in this ad helps involve the audience in the ad's copy. Would other formats work as well?
www.kohlerco.com/

campaign planning. At this point there is a lot of negotiation, discussion and explaining. If everything works out, the ad(s) go forward.

Design. ◐▷ **Design** is "the structure itself and the plan behind that structure" for the aesthetic and stylistic aspects of a print advertisement.[6] Design represents the effort on the part of creatives to physically arrange all the components of a printed advertisement in such a way that order and beauty are achieved—order in the sense that the illustration, headline, body copy, and special features of the ad are easy to read; beauty in the sense that the ad is visually pleasing to a reader.

Certainly, not every advertiser has an appreciation for the elements that constitute effective design, nor will every advertiser be fortunate enough to have highly skilled designers as part of the team creating a print ad. As you will see in the following discussions, however, there are aspects of design that directly relate to the potential for a print ad to communicate effectively based on its artistic form. As such, design factors are highly relevant to creating effective print advertising. The New Media box on page 395 makes clear that this is a lesson yet to be learned by many advertisers on the World Wide Web.

Principles of Design. Principles of design govern how a print advertisement should be prepared. The word *should* is carefully chosen in this context. It is used because, just as language has rules of grammar and syntax, visual presentation has rules of design. The **principles of design** relate to each element within an advertisement *and* to the arrangement of and relationship between elements as a whole.[7] Principles of design suggest the following:

- A design should be in balance.
- The proportion within an advertisement should be pleasing to the viewer.
- The components within an advertisement should have an ordered and directional pattern.
- There should be a unifying force within the ad.
- One element of the ad should be emphasized above all others.

We will consider each of these principles of design and how they relate to the development of an effective print advertisement. Of course, as surely as there are rules, there are occasions when the rules need to be broken. An experienced designer knows the rules and follows them, but is also prepared to break the rules to achieve a desired outcome. But first, you learn the rules.

6.   This discussion is based on Roy Paul Nelson, *The Design of Advertising,* 5th ed. (Dubuque, Iowa: Wm. C. Brown, 1985), 126.
7.   Ibid., 129-136.

Balance. Balance in an ad is an orderliness and compatibility of presentation. Balance can be either formal or informal. **Formal balance** emphasizes symmetrical presentation—components on one side of an imaginary vertical line through the ad are repeated in approximate size and shape on the other side of the imaginary line. Formal balance creates a mood of seriousness and directness and offers the viewer an orderly, easy-to-follow visual presentation (see Exhibit 13.12).

WEB ADS FLUNK DESIGN TEST

In its short history, the Internet's World Wide Web has attracted thousands of companies. Marketers of goods and services, from Acura to Zima, all want to take advantage of snazzy graphics and color photos to parade their wares before millions of computer users.

How good are the home pages, corporate Web sites, and advertising created by these new cyberspace advertisers? Not so good. The judgment is that many of them serve up the online equivalent of junk mail. In the words of an executive vice president at MCI Communications, "It's hideous."

The problem seems to be that too little design creativity, the hallmark of outstanding print advertising, is finding its way to Web sites. The typical home page is filled with turgid company profiles, hokey product pitches, and bland marketing material. One Web user wrote in an Internet posting, "Too many Web pages are designed like drive-by billboards that are about as interesting and informative as rocks in the road."

The explanation for firms flunking the Web design test so badly seems to be a combination of lack of experience, premature posting on the Web, and limited funds to create a more aesthetically pleasing site. Some marketers, in their urgency to set up a Web storefront, have simply dumped online whatever text-based marketing materials are on hand. Other firms simply scan in their print ads or photos from annual reports and let those materials form the visual foundation for the site. A spokesperson for Boeing said of his firm's online effort, "We aren't inventing anything new." In terms of Boeing's future efforts to spiff up its site, he said, "That takes some resources. The times are such that that's not in the cards."

In the view of one expert, the lack of attention to design could ultimately undermine a firm's success on the Web. Bob O'Keefe, a professor at Rensselaer Polytechnic Institute who tracks business use of the Internet, believes that if a firm's site lacks style and sophistication, Internet users "may subconsciously dismiss [the firm] and never have anything to do with [it] down the road."

Of course, not every corporate Web site gets a failing grade. For those Web organizations that are totally depending on attracting users and keeping them, such as broadcast.com, the Web site can be visually appealing, easy to use, and best yet, very fast. But other (non-Web) organizations such as the Gap (www.gap.com/) can produce very appealing sites. At the Gap Web site, you can tour a virtual store and fill your "shopping bag" on-line. But you can also check out new bands and download a cut from a new CD.

Source: Bart Ziegler, "In Cyberspace the Web Delivers Junk Mail," *Wall Street Journal*, June 13, 1995, B1.

Informal balance emphasizes asymmetry—the optical weighing of nonsimilar sizes and shapes. Exhibit 13.13 shows an advertisement using a range of type sizes, visuals, and colors to create a powerful visual effect that achieves informal balance. Informal balance in an ad should not be interpreted as imbalance. Rather, components of different sizes, shapes, and colors are arranged in a more complex relationship providing asymmetrical balance to an ad. Informal balance is more difficult to manage in that the placement of unusual shapes and sizes must be precisely coordinated.

Proportion. Proportion has to do with the size and tonal relationships between different elements in an advertisement. Whenever two elements are placed in proximity, proportion results. In a printed advertisement, proportional considerations include the relationship of the width of an ad to its depth; the width of each element to the depth of each element; the size of one element relative to the size of every other element; the space between two elements and the relationship of that space to a third element; and the amount of light area as opposed to the amount of dark area. Ideally, factors of proportion vary so as to avoid monotony in an ad. Further, the designer should pursue pleasing proportions, which means the viewer will not detect mathematical relationships between elements. In general, unequal dimensions and distances make for the most lively designs in advertising (Exhibit 13.14).

Order. Order in an advertisement is also referred to as sequence or, in terms of its effects on the reader "gaze motion." The designer's goal is to establish a relationship among elements that leads the reader through the ad in some controlled fashion. A designer can create a logical path of visual components to control eye movement. The eye has a "natural" tendency to move from left to right, from up to down, from large elements to small elements, from light to dark, and from color to noncolor. Exhibit 13.15 is an example of ads that induce the reader's eye to move from the upper left to the lower right based on the elements of order. Order also includes inducing the reader to jump from one space in the ad to another, creating a sense of action. The essential contribution of this design component is to establish a visual format that results in a focus or several focuses.

Proportion, when expertly controlled, can result in an inspired display of the oversized versus the undersized. www.bmwusa.com/

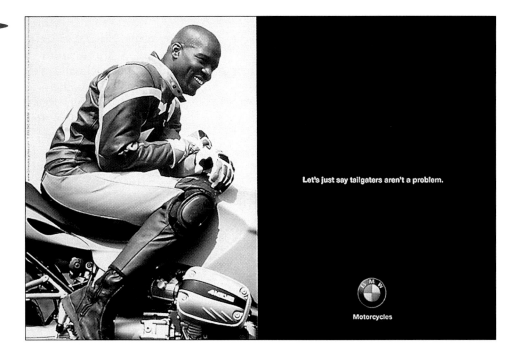

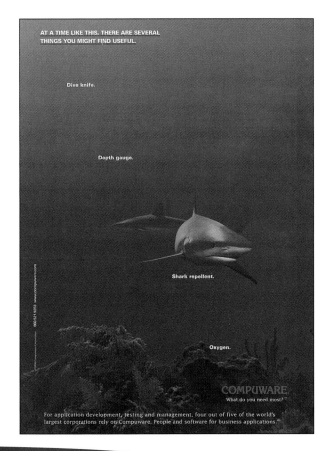

The order of elements in this ad for Compuware controls the reader's eye, moving it from left to right and from top to bottom.

Unity. Ensuring that the elements of an advertisement are tied together and appear to be related is the purpose of unity. Considered the most important of the design principles, unity results in harmony among the diverse components of print advertising: headline, subhead, body copy, and illustration. Several design techniques contribute to unity. The **border** surrounding an ad keeps the ad elements from spilling over into other ads or into the printed matter next to the ad. **White space** at the outside edges creates an informal border effect. The indiscriminate use of white space within an ad can separate elements and give an impression of disorder. The proper use of white space can be dramatic and powerful and draw the receiver's attention to the most critical elements of an ad. Exhibit 13.16 shows a classic example of the effective use of white space. Exhibit 13.17 shows that it wasn't just the look of the Beetle that made a comeback decades later: the effective use of white space came along for the ride, too.

The final construct of unity is the axis. In every advertisement, an axis will naturally emerge. The **axis** is a line, real or imagined, that runs through an ad and from which the elements in the advertisement flare out. A single ad may have one, two, or even three axes running vertically and horizontally. An axis can be created by blocks of copy, by the placement of illustrations, or by the items within an illustration, such as the position and direction of a model's arm or leg. Elements in an ad may violate the axes, but when two or more elements use a common axis as a starting point, unity is enhanced.

Think small.

Our little car isn't so much of a novelty any more.
A couple of dozen college kids don't try to squeeze inside it.
The guy at the gas station doesn't ask where the gas goes.
Nobody even stares at our shape.
In fact, some people who drive our little

flivver don't even think 32 miles to the gallon is going any great guns.
Or using five pints of oil instead of five quarts.
Or never needing anti-freeze.
Or racking up 40,000 miles on a set of tires.
That's because once you get used to

some of our economies, you don't even think about them any more.
Except when you squeeze into a small parking spot. Or renew your small insurance. Or pay a small repair bill.
Or trade in your old VW for a new one.
Think it over.

EXHIBITS 13.16 AND 13.17

The effective use of white space—past and present—to highlight the critical aspect of the ad: the product. www.vw.com/

A design can be more forceful in creating unity by using either a three-point layout or a parallel layout. A **three-point layout structure** establishes three elements in the ad as dominant forces. The uneven number of prominent elements is critical to creating a gaze motion in the viewer. (See Exhibit 13.18.) **Parallel layout structure** employs art on the right-hand side of the page and repeats the art on the left-hand side. This is an obvious and highly structured technique to achieve unity (see Exhibit 13.19).

Emphasis. At some point in the decision making process, someone needs to decide which major component—the headline, subhead, body copy, or illustration—will be emphasized. The key to good design relative to emphasis is that one item is the primary but not the only focus in an ad. If one element is emphasized to the total exclusion of the others, then a poor design has been achieved, and ultimately a poor communication will result.

Balance, proportion, order, unity, and emphasis are the basic principles of design. As you can see, the designer's objectives go beyond the strategic and message-development elements associated with an advertisement. Design principles relate to the aesthetic impression an ad produces. Once a designer has been informed of the components that will comprise the headline, subhead, body copy, and illustration to be included in the ad, then advertising and marketing decision makers *must* allow the designer to arrange those components according to the principles of creative design.

The engine's in the front, but its heart's in the same place.

Drivers wanted. VW

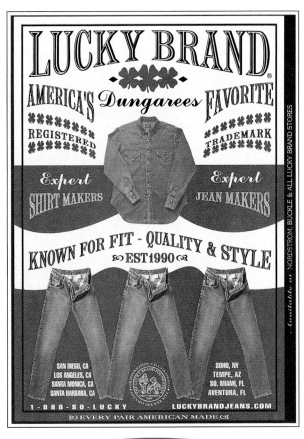

EXHIBIT 13.18

A three-point layout structure, brought to you by Hot Sails Maui.
www.hotsailsmaui.com/

EXHIBIT 13.19

Parallel layout structure at work. www.luckybrandfootwear.com/

Layout.

In contrast to design, which emphasizes the structural concept behind a print ad, layout is the mechanical aspect of design—the physical manifestation of design concepts. A **layout** is a drawing or digital rendering of a proposed print advertisement, showing where all the elements in the ad are positioned. An art director uses a layout to work through various alternatives for visual presentation and sequentially develop the print ad to its final stages. It is part and parcel of the design process and inextricably linked to the development of an effective design. While some art directors still work with traditional tools—layout tissue, T-square, triangle, and markers—many work in computerized layout programs, such as QuarkXpress.

An art director typically proceeds through various stages in the construction of a final design for an ad. The following are the different stages of layout development, in order of detail and completeness, that an art director typically uses.

Thumbnails. Thumbnails are the first drafts of an advertising layout. The art director will produce several thumbnail sketches to work out the general presentation of the ad. While the creative team refines the creative concept, thumbnails represent placement of elements—headline, images, body copy, and tag line. Headlines are often represented with zigzag lines and body copy with straight, parallel lines. An example of a thumbnail is shown in Exhibit 13.20. Typically, thumbnails are drawn at one quarter the size of the finished ad.

Rough Layout. The next step in the layout process is the **rough layout**. Unlike a thumbnail sketch, a rough layout is done in the actual size of the proposed ad and is usually created with a computer layout program, such as QuarkXpress. This allows the art director to experiment with different headline fonts and easily manipulate the placement and size of images to be used in the ad. A rough layout is often used by the advertising agency for preliminary presentation to the client. Exhibit 13.21 features a rough layout.

Comprehensive. The comprehensive layout, or **comp**, is a polished version of an ad. Now, for the most part, computer generated, it is a representation of what the final ad will look like. At this stage, the final headline font is used, the images to be used—photographs or illustrations—are digitized and placed in the ad, and the actual body copy is often included on the ad. Comps are generally printed in full color, if the final ad is to be in color, on a high quality printer. Comps that are produced in this way make it very easy for the client to imagine (and approve) what the ad will look like when it is published.

Mechanicals. After the client has approved the comprehensive layouts, the production art department creates the final version of an ad, the **mechanical**, that will be sent to the printer. Working with the art director, the production artist refines the ad by adjusting the headline spacing (kerning), making any copy changes the client has requested, and placing high-quality digitized (scanned or digitally created) versions of images (illustrations or photographs) to be used. The production artist uses a variety of computer programs such as Adobe Photoshop and Adobe Illustrator to create the ad. A layout program is used to assemble all of the elements of the ad—images and type. Although there are many programs available to perform these tasks, QuarkXpress is the standard for the advertising industry, along with the Macintosh computer platform.

The client will make one last approval of the mechanical before it is sent to the printer. Changes that a client requests, prior to the ad being sent to the printer, are still easily and quickly made. A digital file is then sent either electronically or by mail to the printer. (Prior to the use of computers to generate mechanicals, a small copy change could result in hours of work on the part of the production artists and a large bill to the client.)

EXHIBIT 13.20

A thumbnail showing the transition from idea to advertisement.

EXHIBIT 13.21

A rough layout.

EXHIBIT 13.22

A comp layout.

The stages of layout development discussed here provide the artistic blueprint for a print advertisement (see Exhibit 13.23). At this point, the practical matters of choosing the look and style of a print ad can be considered. We now turn our attention to the matter of print production.

Production in Print Advertising.

The production process in print advertising represents the technical and mechanical activities that transform a creative concept and rough layout into a finished print advertisement. While the process is fundamentally technical, some aspects of print production directly relate to the strategic and design goals of the print ad. Different type styles can contribute to the design quality, readability, and mood in an advertisement. Our purpose in this section, however, is to provide a basic familiarity with production details. It is our goal to outline the sequence of activities and proper time frame related to print production and the various options available for print preparation.

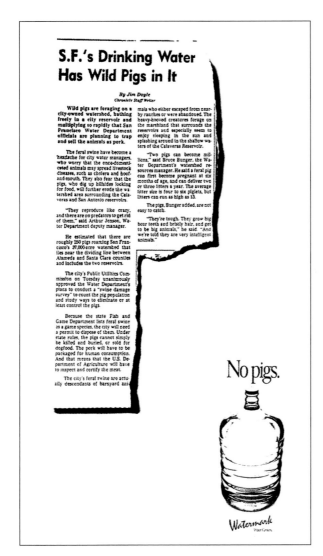

The finished ad.

The Print Production Schedule.

The advertiser is only partly in control of the timing of the print advertisement. While plans can be made to coordinate the appearance of the ad with overall marketing strategies, it must be recognized that the print media will have specifications regarding how far in advance and in what form an ad must be received to appear in print. The deadline for receipt of an ad is referred to as the **closing date**. Closing dates for newspapers can be one or two days before publication. For magazines, the closing date may be months ahead of publication. Exhibit 13.24 describes the sequence of events and the amount of time between stages for a typical magazine ad production schedule.

As you can see from this typical schedule, from the time design work begins until the ad appears in magazine publication, 13 to 21 weeks' time can be involved. For newspaper advertising, the time is typically much shorter, perhaps 1 to 2 weeks (maybe days), but this still represents a fairly long planning and execution period. Advertisers must be aware that such advance planning is necessary to accommodate the basic nature of print production.

Print Production Processes.

Seven major processes can be used in print production.[8] Depending on the medium (newspaper, magazine, direct mail, or specialty advertising), the length of the print run (quantity), the type of paper being used, and the quality desired in reproduction, one of the following processes is used: letterpress, offset lithography, gravure, flexography, electronic, laser, and inkjet

---

8.   This discussion is based in part on Michael H. Bruno, ed., *Pocket Pal: A Graphic Arts Production Handbook,* 13th ed. (New York: International Paper, 1983), 24–31.

EXHIBIT 13.24

*Preparation and production
schedule for a magazine
advertisement.*

Stage	Time
Creative work begins	Copy platform approved
Creative work completed and approved	2 weeks
Artwork ordered (photography or art)	1 day
Artwork completed	2 weeks
Working layout ordered	1 day
Working layout including art complete	1 week
Finished materials to printer (engraver)	5 days
First proof from printer	2 weeks
Final proof from printer	5 days
Printer (engraver) to plate preparation	5 days
Plates shipped to publication	5 days
Publication date of issue	4 to 12 weeks
Total time	13 to 21 weeks

printing. Advances in technology have made computer print production an ideal alternative under certain conditions.

Letterpress draws its name from the way it "presses" type onto a page. Typesetters hand placed, or set, each letter for a printed page in a tray, separating lines of text with bars of lead. These trays would then be inked and "pressed" onto the paper to transfer the ink type or image, similar to how we might currently use a rubber stamp. Today, handset type is a thing of the past, and individual metal type has been replaced with metal or rubber plates that are typeset from a computer program. The most common use for the letterpress today is finishing activities, such as embossing and scoring.

Offset lithography is by far the most common printing method. This process prints from a flat, chemically treated surface—a plate—wrapped around a cylinder that attracts ink to the areas to be printed and repels ink from other areas; the basic idea is oil and water don't mix. The inked image is then transferred to a rubber blanket on a roller and from this roller the impression is carried to paper. Depending on the length of the run (quantity of pieces needed) either a sheet-fed or web press would be used.

Gravure method of printing also prints from a plate. However, unlike the offset plate, the gravure plate is engraved. This method of printing is most commonly used for very large runs, such as the Sunday newspaper supplements, to maintain a high quality of printing clarity.

Flexography is similar to offset lithography because it also uses a rubber blanket to transfer images. It differs from offset in that this process uses water-based ink instead of oil-based ink, and printing can be done on any surface. Because of this versatility of printing surface, flexography is most commonly used in packaging.

Electronic, laser, and inkjet are also known as plateless printing. The widespread use of computer technology has made printing very small runs, as few as one piece, in full color or black and white, with very sharp image quality on a variety of different papers, very easy. The advertising industry often uses software connected to a color photocopier to generate color comps for clients. The colors may not be exactly as they would be if a printer had produced the piece, but for comping purposes this method is both timely and inexpensive. Laser and inkjet printing are also plateless printing processes that are directly connected to a computer to transfer information. However, unlike the large color comping machines, laser and inkjet printers are affordable for home use. On a larger scale, both *Time* and *Fortune* use inkjet printers to address magazines to their subscribers.

Computer Print Production. Integrating the printing production process with the computer has changed the printing business considerably. First, by having digital files, printers no longer need to photograph pasted-up versions of ads. Film can be generated directly from digital files and, in turn, printing plates are made from the film. Second, the proofing process—double checking that the colors to be printed are correct—can be generated well before the print job is on the press. Iris prints, polar proofs, and watermark prints are all extremely high-quality proofing methods. Though these proofing methods are expensive, they are only a small fraction of the cost to reprint a piece. Last, with the increasing use of electronic file transfer, files can be sent quickly to printers.

As stated earlier, choice of the proper printing process depends on the requirements of the advertisement with regard to the medium being used, the quantity being printed, the type of paper being printed on, and the level of quality needed. With respect to magazines, the production process is mandated by the publisher of a particular vehicle within the medium. Print production processes are independent publishing decisions.

Typography in Print Production.

The issues associated with typography have to do with the typeface chosen for headlines, subheads, and body copy, as well as the various size components of the type (height, width, and running length). Designers agonize over the type to use in a print ad because decisions about type affect both the readability and the mood of the overall visual impression. For our purposes, some knowledge of the basic considerations of typography is useful for an appreciation of the choices that must be made.

Categories of Type. Typefaces have distinct personalities, and each can communicate a different mood and image. A **type font** is a basic set of typeface letters. For those of us who do word processing on computers, the choice of type font is a common decision. In choosing type for an advertisement, however, the art director has thousands of choices based on typeface alone.

There are six basic typeface groups: blackletter, roman, script, serif, sans serif, and miscellaneous. The families are divided by characteristics that reflect the personality and tone of the font. **Blackletter**, also called gothic, is characterized by the ornate design of the letters. This style is patterned after hand-drawn letters in monasteries where illuminated manuscripts were created. You can see blackletter fonts used today in very formal documents, such as college diplomas. **Roman** is the most common group of fonts used for body copy because of its legibility. This family is characterized by the use of thick and thin strokes in the creation of the letter forms. **Script** is easy to distinguish by the linkage of the letters in the way that cursive handwriting is connected. Script is often found on wedding invitations and documents that are intended to look elegant or of high quality. **Serif** refers to the strokes or "feet" at the ends of the letter forms. Notice the serifs that are present in these letters as you read. Their presence helps move your eye across the page, allowing you to read for a long time without losing your place or tiring your eyes. **Sans serif** fonts, as the name suggests, do not have serifs, hence the use of the French word "sans," meaning without. Sans serif fonts are typically used for headlines and not for body copy. **Miscellaneous** includes typefaces that do not fit easily into the other categories. Novelty display, garage, and deconstructed fonts all fall into this group. These fonts were designed specifically to draw attention to themselves and not necessarily for their legibility. The following example displays serif and sans serif type:

This line is set in serif type.

This line is set in sans serif type.

Type Measurement. There are two elements of type size. **Point** refers to the size of type in height. In the printing industry, type sizes run from 6 to 120 points. Now, with computer layout programs such as QuarkXpress, the range is much larger, between 2

EXHIBIT 13.25

A range of type point sizes.

This is 8 point type

This is 12 point type

This is 18 point type

This is 36 point type

This is 60 point type

and 720 points. Exhibit 13.25 shows a range of type sizes for comparison purposes. **Picas** measure the width of lines. A pica is 12 points wide, and each pica measures about one-sixth of an inch. Layout programs make it very easy for the art director to fit copy into a designated space on an ad by reducing or enlarging a font with a few strokes on the keyboard.

Readability. It is critical in choosing type to consider readability. Type should facilitate the communication process. The following are some traditional recommendations when deciding what type to use (however, remember that these are only guidelines and should not necessarily be followed in every instance):

- Use capitals and lowercase, NOT ALL CAPITALS.
- Arrange letters from left to right, not up and down.
- Run lines of type horizontally, not vertically.
- Use even spacing between letters and words.

Different typefaces and styles also affect the mood conveyed by an ad. Depending on the choices made, typefaces can connote grace, power, beauty, modernness, simplicity, or any number of other qualities.

Art Direction and Production in Cyberspace.

Cyberspace is its own space. It is its own medium, too. It's not television or radio, but, at this point, it's closer to print than to anything else. It's an active medium rather than a passive one (people generally come to it rather than the other way around). While the basic principles of art direction (design and concept) apply, the medium is fundamentally different in the way its audience comes to it, navigates it, and responds to it. This is one of the real challenges of electronic advertising.

In most respects, cyberproduction does not differ significantly from print, radio, or television production, but it does differ from these traditional media in how aspects of production are combined with programming language, such as HTML, and with each other. Advances in streaming audio and digital video keep art direction and production in cyberspace a moving target. Still, at this point, most Internet advertising is, essentially, print advertising. Most is either produced in traditional ways and then digitized and combined with text or created entirely with computer design packages. Exhibits 13.26 through 13.29 are pretty representative of what's out there.

All media have to find their own way, their own voice. This is not just an aesthetic matter. It's figuring out what works, which has something to do with design. How the

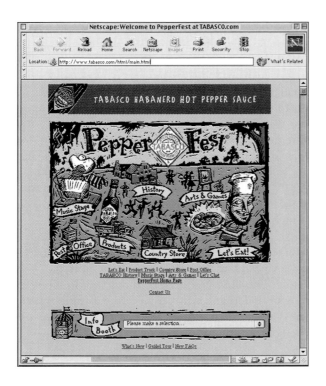

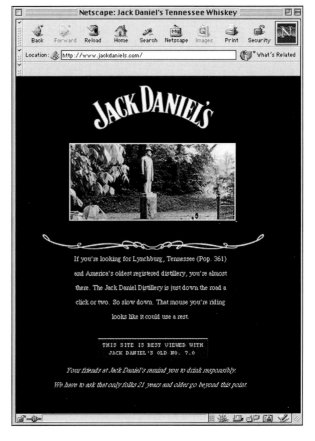

EXHIBITS 13.26 THROUGH 13.29

Art direction and production in cyberspace—four examples of what's out there.

information is laid out matters. If you go back and look at the first few years of television advertising, you have to say that they really didn't fully understand the medium or the ways audiences would use this new technology. The ads went on forever and seemed to be written for radio. In fact, many of the early TV writers were radio writers. They tried to make television radio.

This same phenomenon seems to be happening with Web sites. They look more like print ads than something truly Web-ish. Yet, unlike print ads, Web sites have the ability to change almost immediately. If a client wants to change a copy point, for example, it can happen many times in one afternoon. And Web consumers demand change. Though frequent changes may seem time consuming and expensive, they ensure return visits from audiences. Many clients, however, are slow to integrate the Web into their overall communication strategy. Thus, many sites appear to be neglected, distant relatives to their high-profile cousins, TV and print.

There is also a rapidly growing clutter problem. Web pages are often very busy, with lots of information crammed into small spaces. Advertisers, while not yet knowing what this medium can do, are convinced that they must be in it. In short, the Web is not print *or* television: It is electronic and fluid, and must be thought of in this way. In terms of design, this means trying to understand why people come to various sites, what they are looking for, what they expect to encounter, what they expect in return for their very valuable click. The design has to be an expression of this.

Art Direction and Production in Television Advertising.

There have been few (if any) things that have more changed the face of advertising (or contemporary culture) than television. Like other media, television first struggled to find its best form, but soon did. In many ways, television was simply made for advertising. It is everywhere, serving as background to much of daily life. If you are in a room and a television is on, you will find yourself watching it. Want to kill a good party? Turn on a television. Did you ever try to talk to someone sitting across from you when your back is to the television? You just about have to offer money and/or sex to get their attention. In the Oscar-winning film *Network,* a television anchorman believes that God has chosen him as a modern-day prophet. When he asks God, "Why me?" God replies, "Because you're on television, dummy." Everybody watches TV, no matter what they tell you.

Television is about moving visuals. Sometimes, it's just about leaving impressions, or setting moods, or getting you to notice; sometimes it tells stories. Many believe that the very best television ads work just as well with the sound turned off, that the best television tells its story visually. Of course, this is what film critics have said about master film directors, such as John Ford (Exhibit 13.30) and Alfred Hitchcock (Exhibit 13.31), both of whom learned their craft in silent films.

Still, it must be said that an awful lot of TV spots are very reliant on copy. In fact, entire genres of television ads rely heavily on repetitive brand mentions, or dialogue-dependent narratives. Of late, rapid cuts and sparse dialogue seem to be the way of the TV creatives, but this phase will probably change before the next full moon. Advertising is, in so many respects, fashion.

Art Direction in Television Advertising.

The primary creative directive for TV is the same as for other media: effective communication. Television presents some unique challenges, however. Due to its complexity, television production involves a lot of people. These people have different but often overlapping expertise, responsibility, and authority. This makes for a myriad of complications and calls for tremendous organizational skills. At some point, individuals who actually shoot the film or the tape are brought in to execute the copywriter's and art director's concepts. At this point, the creative process becomes intensely collaborative: The film director applies his or her craft and is respon-

EXHIBITS 13.30 AND 13.31

Two of the very best filmmakers—and storytellers—ever: John Ford and Alfred Hitchcock.

sible for the actual production. The creative team (i.e., art director and copywriter) rarely relinquishes control of the project, even though the film director may prefer exactly that. But who really has creative authorship is typically unclear. Getting the various players to perform their particular specialty at just the right time, while avoiding conflict with other team members, is an ongoing challenge in TV ad production.

The Creative Team in Television Advertising. The vast and ever-increasing capability of the broadcast media introduces new challenges and complexities to the production process. One aspect of these complexities is that aside from the creative directors, copywriters, and art directors who assume the burden of responsibility in the production of print advertising, we now encounter a host of new and irreplaceable creative and technical participants. The proper and effective production of broadcast advertising depends on a team of highly capable creative people: agency personnel, production experts, editorial specialists, and music companies. An advertiser and its agency must consider and evaluate the role of each of these participants. Descriptions of the roles played by the participants in television advertising are provided in Exhibit 13.32.

Creative Guidelines for Television Advertising. Just as for print advertising, there are general creative principles for television advertising.[9] These principles are not foolproof or definitive, but they certainly represent good advice. Again, truly great creative work has no doubt violated some or all of these conventions; as described in the IMC box on

---

9. These guidelines were adapted from A. Jerome Jewler, *Creative Strategy in Advertising,* 3rd ed. (Belmont, Calif.: Wadsworth, 1989), 210-211; Nelson, *The Design of Advertising,* 296.

EXHIBIT 13.32

The creative team for television advertising production.

Agency Participants

Creative director (CD). The creative director manages the creative process in an agency for several different clients. Creative directors typically come from the art or copywriting side of the business. The main role of the CD is to oversee the creative product of an agency across all clients.

Art director (AD). The art director and the copywriter work together to develop the concept for a commercial. The AD either oversees the production of the television storyboard or actually constructs the storyboards. In addition, the AD works with the director of the commercial to develop the overall look of the spot.

Copywriter. The copywriter is responsible for the words and phrases used in an ad. In television and radio advertising, these words and phrases appear as a script from which the director, creative director, and art director work during the production process. Together with the AD, the copywriter also makes recommendations on choice of director, casting, and editing facility.

Account executive (AE). The account executive acts as a liaison between the creative team and the client. The AE has the responsibility for coordinating scheduling, budgeting, and the various approvals needed during the production process. The AE can be quite valuable in helping the advertiser understand the various aspects of the production process. Account executives rarely have direct input into either the creative or technical execution of an ad.

Executive producer. The executive producer in an agency is in charge of many line producers, who manage the production at the production site. Executive producers help manage the production bid process. They also assign the appropriate producers to particular production jobs.

Producer. The producer supervises and coordinates all the activities related to a broadcast production. Producers screen director reels, send out production bid forms, review bids, and recommend the production house to be used. The producer also participates in choosing locations, sets, and talent. Normally, the producer will be on the set throughout the production and in the editing room during postproduction, representing agency and client interests.

Production Company Participants

Director. The director is in charge of the filming or taping of a broadcast advertising production. From a creative standpoint, the director is the visionary who brings the copy strategy to life on film or tape. The director also manages the actors, actresses, musicians, and announcers used in an ad to ensure that their performances contribute to the creative strategy being pursued. Finally, the director manages and coordinates the activities of technical staff. Camera operators, sound and lighting technicians, and special effects experts get their assignments from the director.

Producer. The production company also has a producer present, who manages the production at the site. This producer is in charge of the production crew and sets up each shoot. The position of cameras and readiness of production personnel are the responsibility of this producer.

Production manager. The production manager is on the set of a shoot, providing all the ancillary services needed to ensure a successful production. These range from making sure that food service is available on the set to providing dressing rooms and fax, phone, and photocopy services. The production manager typically has a production assistant (PA) to help take care of details.

Camera department. Another critical part of the production team is the camera department. This group includes the director of photography, camera operator, and assistant camera operator. This group ensures that the lighting, angles, and movement are carried out according to the plan and the director's specification.

Art department. The art department that accompanies the production company includes the art director and other personnel responsible for creating the set. This group designs the set, builds background or stunt structures, and provides props.

Editors. Editors enter the production process at the postproduction stage. It is their job, with direction from the art director, creative director, producer, or director, to create the finished advertisement. Editors typically work for independent postproduction houses and use highly specialized equipment to cut and join frames of film or audiotape together to create the finished version of a television or radio advertisement. Editors also synchronize the audio track with visual images in television advertisements and perform the transfer and duplication processes to prepare a commercial for shipping to the media.

page 412, recent research suggests that television creatives have something yet to learn from print executions.

- *Use an attention-getting and relevant opening.* The first few seconds of a television commercial are crucial. A receiver can make a split-second assessment of the relevance and interest a message holds. An ad can either turn a receiver off or grab his or her attention for the balance of the commercial with the opening. Remember, remote controls are rarely too far away. This truism should not be ignored. Channel surfing is a very real phenomenon. It is getting so incredibly easy to avoid commercials that you, as an advertiser, must have a good hook to suck viewers in. Ads just don't get much time to develop. Of course, there is the belief that "slower" ads (ads that take time to develop) don't wear out as quickly as the quick hit-and-run-ads. So, if you have a huge (almost inexhaustible) supply of money, an ad that "builds" might be best. If you don't, go for the quick hook. In Exhibit 13.33, IBM juxtaposed imagery and product in a very attention-getting way.

- *Emphasize the visual.* The video capability of television should be highlighted in every production effort. To some degree, this emphasis is dependent on the creative concept, but the visual should carry the selling message even if the audio portion is ignored by the receiver. In Exhibit 13.34, Coke tells its story with a minimum of words. Exhibit 13.35 shows one of the most famous political ads of all time, an ad that helped cement Lyndon Johnson's win over Barry Goldwater in 1964 by painting Goldwater as a near madman who might get us into a nuclear war.

- *Coordinate the audio with the visual.* The images and copy of a television commercial must reinforce each other rather than pursue separate objectives. Such divergence between the audio and visual portions of an ad only serves to confuse and distract the viewer. In Exhibit 13.36, Portland General Electric uses both words and visuals to convince viewers of the dangers of downed power lines.

- *Persuade as well as entertain.* It is tempting to produce a beautifully creative television advertisement rather than a beautifully effective television advertisement. The vast potential of film lures the creative urge in all the production participants. Creating an entertaining commercial is an inherently praiseworthy goal *except* when the entertainment value of the commercial completely overwhelms its persuasive impact. In Exhibit 13.37, Hewlett-Packard sells its photo-quality printers with a humorous yet persuasive demonstration of their reproductive powers.

EXHIBIT 13.33

IBM (www.ibm.com) employs a little attention-grabbing dissonance: nuns bantering about operating systems. What's next? Monks with modems? Although the ad is certainly memorable, it might also remind you that buying software may well mire you in tech jargon. Apple's iMac ads (www.imac.com) take on technical intractibility directly (why should a nun have to know what flavor operating system she's running?), disparaging other personal computers as too unruly. 3Com's message in Exhibit 13.7 (www .3com.com), also, is less focused on technology per se, than on why it really matters.

(IN FRENCH WITH ENGLISH SUBTITLES)

NUN 1:   I'm trying to get that new operating system, Chicago, but they keep pushing back the release date.

NUN 2:   That new OS/2 Warp from IBM looks pretty hot.

NUN 1:   OS/2 Warp?

NUN 2:   I just read about it in *Wired.* You get true multitasking, easy access to the internet.

NUN 1:   I'm dying to surf the 'net.

(SFX: PAGER BEEPING)

NUN 1:   Whoops. My beeper.

SUPER: SOLUTIONS FOR A SMALL PLANET.

Good television creative work emphasizes the visual component of an ad. This Coca-Cola ad needs only three words of copy to deliver its message.
www.cocacola.com/

(MUSIC: '30s ROMANTIC)
SUPER: ALWAYS FEELS RIGHT.

A classic political advertisement from the Johnson for President campaign (1964).

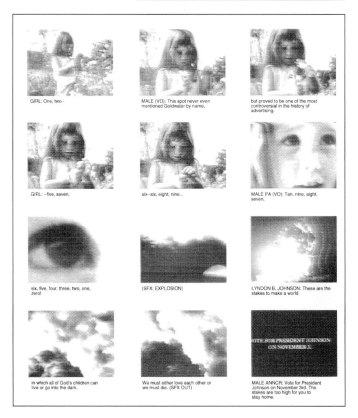

(MUSIC: MOODY, WIND INSTRUMENTS)
ANNCR: The frightening thing about downed power
         lines is that it's impossible to tell if they're dan-
         gerous or not. Just like it's hard to tell a harm-
         less bull snake from a deadly cottonmouth.
         Now, would you pick one up . . . hoping it's the
         harmless snake? If you see a downed power
         line, don't touch it. Call PGE. We'll handle it.
SUPER: PORTLAND GENERAL ELECTRIC.

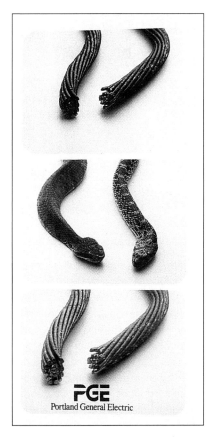

(SFX: QUIET TICKING OF CLOCK)
(SFX: WRESTLING ON TV)
GRANDPA: Ohhhhhh!
(SFX: THUD)
BABY: Wahhhhhhhhhhh!
GRANDPA: Don't worry, honey. Mom and Dad will be
            right back.
GRANDPA: Pretty baby!
BABY: Wahhhhhhhhhhh!
(SFX: SUDDEN QUIET)
(SFX: CLOCK TICKING)
ANNCR: HP photo-quality printers. Good enough to
            fool almost anyone.
SUPER: BUILT BY ENGINEERS. USED BY NORMAL
            PEOPLE.

EXHIBITS 13.36 AND 13.37

*The audio and visual components of an ad must work together to effectively communicate.
These ads from Portland General Electric and Hewlett-Packard have well-coordinated audio
and video components.*

- *Show the product.* Unless a commercial is using intrigue and mystery surrounding the product, the product should be highlighted in the ad. Close-ups and shots of the brand in action help receivers recall the brand and its appearance.

The Production Process in Television Advertising.

The television production process can best be understood by identifying the activities that take place before, during, and after the actual production of an ad. These stages are referred to as preproduction, production, and postproduction. (Hope we're not getting too technical.) By breaking the process down into this sequence, we can appreciate both the technical and the strategic aspects of each stage.

Preproduction.

The **preproduction** stage is that part of the television production process in which the advertiser and the advertising agency (or in-house agency staff) carefully work out the precise details of how the creative planning behind an ad can best be brought to life with the opportunities offered by television. Exhibit 13.38 shows the sequence of six events in the preproduction stage.

Storyboard and Script Approval. As Exhibit 13.38 shows, the preproduction stage begins with storyboard and script approval. A **storyboard** is a shot-by-shot sketch depicting, in sequence, the visual scenes and copy that will be used in an advertisement. A **script** is the written version of an ad; it specifies the coordination of the copy elements with the video scenes. The script is used by the producer and director to set the location and content of scenes, by the casting department to choose actors and actresses, and by the producer in budgeting and scheduling the shoot. Exhibit 13.39 is part of a storyboard from the Miller Lite "Can Your Beer Do This?" campaign, and Exhibit 13.40 shows the related script. This particular spot was entitled "Ski Jump" and involved rigging a dummy to a recliner and launching the chair and the dummy from a 60-meter ski jump.

EVEN $44 BILLION DOESN'T IMPRESS CONSUMERS

Despite the fact that advertisers spend $44 billion for time on the major television networks and cable TV advertising, a new study shows that consumers consider print ads more entertaining and less offensive than television commercials. The study, conducted by Video Storyboard Tests in New York, showed that more consumers considered print ads "artistic" and "enjoyable."

The 2,000 consumers surveyed blasted TV ads compared to their print counterparts: 34 percent of respondents thought print ads were artistic, compared with 15 percent for television ads; 35 percent thought print ads were enjoyable, compared to 13 percent for television; and, most surprising, 33 percent of consumers felt print ads were entertaining, compared to only 18 percent for TV ads. Much of the artistic impact and positive reaction to print ads comes from the illustrations used. The illustration is primary in creating the mood for a print ad, which ultimately affects consumers' feelings about and image of a brand.

While the study's sponsors were somewhat surprised by the survey results, some industry executives felt that print ads were finally getting the credit they deserve. Richard Kirshenbaum, chair and chief creative officer of Kirshenbaum, Bond & Partners, a New York advertising and public relations firm, is one such believer. In fact, Kirshenbaum says that when he looks to hire a new person for a creative position in his agency, "I always look at the print book first because I think it is harder to come up with a great idea on a single piece of paper."

But as impressed as consumers say they are by the aesthetics and style of print ads, television executives (as you might expect) dismiss the findings. One network official said, "Nothing will replace the reach and magnitude of an elaborately produced television spot. TV ads get talked about. Print ads don't." This executive must have missed the Benetton and Absolut print campaigns.

Source: Kevin Goldman, "Consumers Like Print Ads Better Than Those on TV, Study Says," *Wall Street Journal*, June 6, 1995, B13; Robert J. Coen, McCann Erikson WorldGroup, "Industry Advertising Expenditure Data," June 1998, at the McCann-Erickson Web site, www.mccann.com/. Accessed November 20, 1998.

The art director and copywriter are significantly involved at this stage of production. It is important that the producer has discussed the storyboard and script with the creative team and fully understands the creative concept and objectives for the advertisement before production begins. Since it is the producer's responsibility to solicit

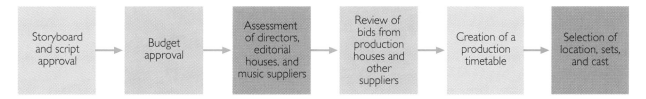

EXHIBIT 13.38

Sequence of events in the preproduction stage of television advertising.

bids for the project from production houses, the producer must be able to fully explain to bidders the requirements of the job so that cost estimates are as accurate as possible.

Budget Approval. Once there is agreement on the scope and intent of the production as depicted in the storyboard and script, the advertiser must give budget approval. The producer needs to work carefully with the creative team and the advertiser to estimate the approximate cost of the shoot, including production staging, location costs, actors, technical requirements, staffing, and a multitude of other considerations. It is essential that these discussions be as detailed and comprehensive as possible, because it is from this budget discussion that the producer will evaluate candidates for the directing role and solicit bids from production houses to handle the job.

EXHIBIT 13.39

How does this storyboard for a Miller Lite Beer ad save the advertiser time and money during the television production process? www.millerlite.com/

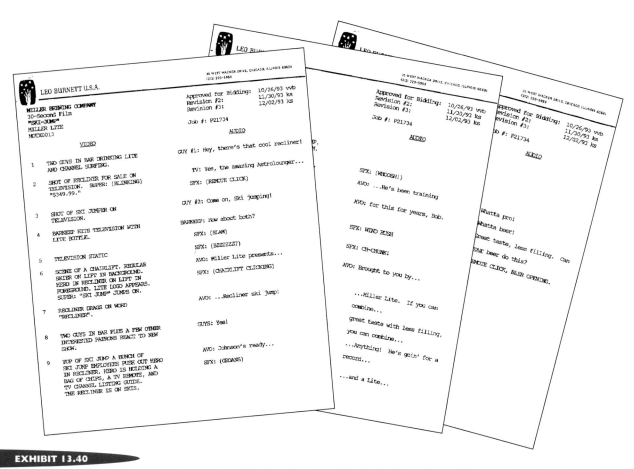

EXHIBIT 13.40

This is the script for the Miller Lite "Can Your Beer Do This?" ad shown in Exhibit 13.40. The producer and director use the script to set locations and the content of scenes and for budgeting and scheduling. The script is also used to choose actors and actresses.

Assessment of Directors, Editorial Houses, Music Suppliers. A producer has dozens (if not hundreds) of directors, postproduction editorial houses, and music suppliers from which to choose. An assessment of those well suited to the task must take place early in the preproduction process. Directors of television commercials, like directors of feature films, develop specializations and reputations. Some directors are known for their work with action or special effects. Others are more highly skilled in working with children, animals, outdoor settings, or shots of beverages flowing into a glass ("pour shots").

The director of an advertisement is responsible for interpreting the storyboard and script and managing the talent to bring the creative concept to life. A director specifies the precise nature of a scene, how it is lit and how it is filmed. In this way, the director acts as the eye of the camera. Choosing the proper director is crucial to the execution of a commercial. Aside from the fact that a good director commands a fee anywhere from $8,000 to $25,000 per day, the director can have a tremendous effect on the quality and impact of the presentation. An excellent creative concept can be undermined by poor direction. The agency creative team should be intimately involved in the choice of directors. Among the now-famous feature film directors who have made television commercials are Ridley Scott (Apple), John Frankenheimer (AT&T), Woody Allen (Campari), Spike Lee (Levi's, Nike, the Gap, Barney's), and Federico Fellini (Coop Italia). (See Exhibits 13.41 and 13.42.)

Similarly, editorial houses (and their editors) and music suppliers (and musicians) have particular expertise and reputations. The producer, the director, and the agency creative team actively review the work of the editorial suppliers and music houses that are particularly well suited to the production. In most cases, geographic proximity to the agency facilities is important; as members of the agency team try to maintain a tight

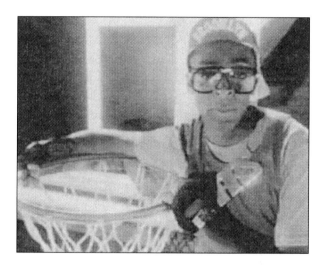

EXHIBITS 13.41 AND 13.42

Examples of famous feature film directors who have made television commercials are Ridley Scott, director of Apple's "1984" campaign and the 1982 movie Blade Runner, *and Spike Lee, who directed 1989's* Do the Right Thing *as well as the "Morris Blackman" Nike ads.* www.apple.com/ *and* www.nike.com/

schedule, editorial and music services that are nearby facilitate the timely completion of an ad. Because of this need, editorial and music suppliers have tended to cluster near agencies in Chicago, New York, and Los Angeles.

Review of Bids from Production Houses and Other Suppliers. Production houses and other suppliers, such as lighting specialists, represent a collection of specialized talent and also provide needed equipment for ad preparation. The expertise in production houses relates to the technical aspects of filming a commercial. Producers, production managers, sound and art specialists, camera operators, and others are part of a production house team. The agency sends a bid package to several production houses. The package contains all the details of the commercial to be produced and includes a description of the production requirements and a timetable for the production. An accurate timetable is essential because many production personnel work on an hourly or daily compensation rate.

To give you some idea of the cost of the technical personnel and equipment available from production houses, Exhibit 13.43 lists some key production house personnel

EXHIBIT 13.43

Sample costs for production personnel and equipment.

Personnel	Cost
Director	$8,000–25,000/day
Director of photography	3,000/day
Producer	800/day
Production assistant	200/day
Camera operator	600/day
Unit manager	450/day

Equipment	
Production van (including camera, lighting kit, microphones, monitoring equipment)	$2,500–4,000/day
Camera	750–1,000/day
Grip truck with lighting equipment and driver	400–500/day
Telescript with operator	600–700/day
Online editing with editor and assistant editor	250–400/hour

who would participate in shooting a commercial, and the typical daily rates (for a ten-hour day) for such personnel and related equipment. Also listed are the rental costs of various pieces of equipment. These costs vary from market to market, but it is obvious why production expenses can run into the hundreds of thousands of dollars. The costs listed in the exhibit represent only the daily rates for production time or postproduction work. In addition to these costs are overtime costs, travel, and lodging (if an overnight stay is necessary).

Most agencies send out a bid package on a form developed by the agency. An example of such a bid form is provided in Exhibit 13.44. By using a standardized form, an agency can make direct comparisons between production house bids. A similar form can be used to solicit bids from other suppliers providing editorial or music services. The producer reviews each of the bids and revises them if necessary. From the production house bids *and* the agency's estimate of its own costs associated with production (travel, expenses, editorial services, music, on-camera talent, and agency markups), a production cost estimate is prepared for advertiser review and approval. Once the advertiser has approved the estimate, one of the production houses is awarded the job. The lowest production bid is not always the one chosen. Aside from cost, there are creative and technical considerations. A hot director costs more than last year's model. The agency's evaluation of the reliability of a production house also enters into the decision.

Creation of a Production Timetable. In conjunction with the stages of preproduction just discussed, the producer will be working on a **production timetable**. This timetable projects a realistic schedule

			TALENT COUNT		
NAME / LENGTH	TYPE	OC	EXT	VO	
1					
2					
3.					
4.					

CLIENT:
PRODUCT:
DATE:
A. E.:
ACCT. SUP.:
WRITER:
A. D.:
C. D.:

	ESTIMATE	ACTUAL
PRODUCTION CO.		
EDITING		
MUSIC		
TALENT		
ARTWORK/CC PACKAGES		
RECORDING STUDIO		
VIDEOTAPE TRANSFERS		
ANIMATION		
CASTING		
SUB TOTAL NET		
% A. C.		
TRAVEL		
SHIPPING		
TOTAL GROSS COST		

NOTES:

EXHIBIT 13.44

Advertising agencies use a bid form to make comparisons between production house bids and provide the client with an estimate of production costs.

for all the preproduction, production, and postproduction activities. To stay on budget and complete the production in time to ship the final advertisement to television stations for airing, an accurate and realistic timetable is essential. A timetable must allow a reasonable amount of time to complete all production tasks in a quality manner. Exhibit 13.45 is a timetable for a national 30-second spot, using location shooting.

Realize that a reasonable timetable is rarely achieved. Advertisers often request (or demand) that an agency provide a finished spot (or even several spots) in times as short as four or five weeks. Because of competitive pressures or corporate urgency for change, production timetables are compromised. Advertisers have to accept the reality that violating a reasonable timetable can dramatically increase costs and puts undue pressure on the creative process—no matter what the reason for the urgency. In fact, a creative director at one agency often told clients that they could pick any two selections from the following list for their television commercials: good, fast, and reasonably priced.[10]

Selection of Location, Sets, and Cast. Once a bid has been approved and accepted, both the production house and the agency production team begin to search for appropriate, affordable locations if the commercial is to be shot outside a studio setting. Studio production warrants the design and construction of the sets to be used.

A delicate stage in preproduction is casting. While not every ad uses actors and actresses, when an ad calls for individuals to perform roles, casting is crucial. Every individual appearing in an ad is, in a very real sense, a representative of the advertiser. This is another reason why the agency creative team stays involved. Actors and actresses help set the mood and tone for an ad and affect the image of the brand. The successful execution of various message strategies is dependent on proper casting. For instance, a slice-of-life message requires actors and actresses with whom the target audience can readily identify. Testimonial message tactics require a search for particular types of people, either celebrities or common folks, who will attract attention and be credible to the audience. The point to remember is that successfully casting a television commercial depends on much more than simply picking people with good acting abilities. Individuals must be matched to the personality of the brand, the nature of the audience, and the scene depicted in the ad. A young male actor who makes a perfect husband in a laundry detergent ad may be totally inappropriate as a rugged outdoorsman in a chain-saw commercial.

EXHIBIT 13.45

Example of a reasonable timetable for shooting a 30-second television advertisement.

Activity	Time
Assess directors/editorial houses/music suppliers	1 week
Solicit bids from production houses/other suppliers	1 week
Review bids, award jobs to suppliers, submit production estimate to advertiser	1 week
Begin preproduction (location, sets, casting)	1 to 2 weeks
Final preparation and shooting	1 to 2 weeks
Edit film	1 week
Agency/advertiser review of rough-cut film	1 week
Postproduction (final editing, voice mix, record music, special effects, etc.) and transfer of film to video; ship to media	2 weeks
Transfer film to videotape; ship to stations	1 week
Total	10 to 12 weeks

10. Peter Sheldon, former creative director and current doctoral student, University of Illinois.

Production. The **production stage** of the process, or the **shoot**, is where the storyboard and script come to life and are filmed. The actual production of the spot may also include some final preparations before the shoot begins. The most common final preparation activities are lighting checks and rehearsals. An entire day may be devoted to *prelight,* which involves setting up lighting or identifying times for the best natural lighting to ensure that the shooting day runs smoothly. Similarly, the director may want to work with the on-camera talent along with the camera operators to practice the positioning and movement planned for the ad. This work, known as *blocking,* can save a lot of time on a shoot day, when many more costly personnel are on the set.

Lighting, blocking, and other special factors are typically specified by the director in the script. Exhibit 13.46 is a list of common directorial specifications that show up in a script and are used by a director to manage the audio and visual components of a commercial shoot.

EXHIBIT 13.46

Instructions commonly appearing in television commercial scripts.

Script Specification	Meaning
CU	Close-up.
ECU	Extreme close-up.
MS	Medium shot.
LS	Long shot.
Zoom	Movement in or out on subject with camera fixed.
Dolly	Movement in or out on subject moving the camera (generally slower than a zoom).
Pan	Camera scanning right or left from stationary position.
Truck	Camera *moving* right or left, creating a different visual angle.
Tilt	Camera panning vertically.
Cut	Abrupt movement from one scene to another.
Dissolve	Smoother transition from one scene to another, compared to a cut.
Wipe	Horizontal or vertical removal of one image to replace it with a new image (inserted vertically or horizontally).
Split screen	Two or more independent video sources occupying the screen.
Skip frame	Replacement of one image with another through pulsating (frame insertion of) the second image into the first. Used for dramatic transitions.
Key insert, matte, chromakey	Insertion of one image onto another background. Often used to impose product over the scene taking place in the commercial.
Super title	Lettering superimposed over visual. Often used to emphasize a major selling point or to display disclaimers/product warnings.
SFX	Sound effects.
VO	Introducing a voice over the visual.
ANN	Announcer entering the commercial.
Music under	Music playing in the background.
Music down and out	Music fading out of commercial.
Music up and out	Music volume ascending and abruptly ending.

Shoot days are the culmination of an enormous amount of effort beginning all the way back at the development of the copy platform. They are the execution of all the well-laid plans by the advertiser and agency personnel. The set on a shoot day is a world all its own. For the uninformed, it can appear to be little more than high-energy chaos, or a lot of nothing going on between camera setups. For the professionals involved, however, a shoot has its own tempo and direction, including a whole lot of nothing going on.

Production activities during a shoot require the highest level of professionalism and expertise. A successful shoot depends on the effective management of a large number of diverse individuals—creative performers, highly trained technicians, and skilled laborers. Logistical and technical problems always arise, not to mention the ever-present threat of a random event (a thunderstorm or intrusive noise) that disrupts filming and tries everyone's patience. There is a degree of tension and spontaneity on the set that is a necessary part of the creative process but must be kept at a manageable level. Much of the tension stems from trying to execute the various tasks of production correctly and at the proper time.

Another dimension to this tension, however, has to do with expense. As pointed out earlier, most directors, technicians, and talent are paid on a daily rate plus overtime after ten hours. Daily shooting expenses, including director's fees, can run $80,000 to $120,000 for just an average production, so the agency and advertiser, understandably, want the shoot to run as smoothly and quickly as possible.

There is the real problem of not rushing creativity, however, and advertisers often have to learn to accept the pace of production. For example, a well-known director made a Honda commercial in South Florida, where he shot film for only one hour per day—a half-hour in the morning and a half-hour at twilight. His explanation? "From experience you learn that cars look flat and unattractive in direct light, so you have to catch the shot when the angle [of the sun] is just right."[11] Despite the fact that the cameras were rolling only an hour a day, the $9,000-per-hour cost for the production crew was charged all day for each day of shooting. Advertisers have to accept, on occasion, that the television advertising production process is not like an assembly line production process. Sweating the details to achieve just the right look can provoke controversy—and often does.

The Cost of Television Production. Coordinating and taking advantage of the skills offered by creative talent is a big challenge for advertisers. The average 30-second television commercial prepared by a national advertiser can run up production charges from $100,000 to $500,000 and even more if special effects or celebrities are used in the spot.[12] The cost of making a television commercial increased nearly 400 percent between 1979 and 1993.[13] Part of that increase is attributed to the escalating cost of creative talent, such as directors and editors. Other aspects of the cost have to do with more and better equipment being used at all stages of the production process, and longer shooting schedules to ensure advertiser satisfaction.

Exhibit 13.47 shows the average production costs for national 30-second television ads of various types and in various industries. Notice that the average expense for a 30-second spot tends to be higher for commercials in highly competitive consumer markets, such as beer, soft drinks, autos, and banking, where image campaigns (which require high-quality production) are commonly used. Conversely, average production costs tend to be lower for advertisements in which functional features or shots of the product often dominate the spot, as with household cleansers and office equipment.

---

11. Jeffrey A. Trachtenberg, "Where the Money Goes," *Forbes*, September 21, 1987, 180.
12. Joe Mandese, "Study Shows Cost of TV Spots," *Advertising Age*, August 1, 1994, 32.
13. Information for the average cost of a 30-second ad in 1979 was taken from Ronald Alsop, "Advertisers Bristle as Charges Balloon for Splashy TV Spots," *Wall Street Journal*, June 20, 1985, 29. Information for the average cost of a 30-second ad in 1993 was taken from Peter Caranicas, "4A's Survey Shows Double-Digit Hike in Spot Production Costs," *Shoot*, July 15, 1994, 1, 40–42.

Average production costs for national 30-second television spots.

Product Category	Average Cost for 30-Second Spot
Banking/financial/insurance	$535,000
Beer/wine	516,000
Corporate image	397,000
Soft drinks/snacks	332,000
Autos/trucks/motorcycles	323,000
Apparel/clothing	289,000
Beauty/fashion/cosmetics	257,000
Furniture/appliances	226,000
Consumer services/national retail stores	189,000
Drugs/toiletries	157,000
Gifts/toys/hobbies/recreation	154,000
Household products	145,000
Office equipment/computers	97,000
Type of Commercial	
Special effects	$254,000
Interview/testimonial (avg. person and celebrity)	249,000
Multistory/vignettes	246,000
Animation	210,000
Large-scale product performance (e.g., auto)	208,000
Song/dance	187,000
Monologue	172,000
Tabletop/food	111,000
Specific Length	
15 seconds	$100,000
30 seconds	257,000
45 seconds	271,000
60 seconds	589,000

Source: Data from American Association of Advertising Agencies (4As) survey of 1,864 national spots produced in 1993, cited in Peter Caranicas, "4A's Survey Shows Double-Digit Hike in Spot Production Costs," *Shoot,* July 15, 1994, 40.

The high and rising cost of television production has created some tensions between advertisers and their ad agencies. Most agencies and production companies respond by saying that advertisers are demanding to stand out from the clutter, and to do so requires complex concepts and high-priced talent.[14] Conversely, when an advertiser is not so image conscious, ways can be found to stand out without spending huge dollar amounts.

The important issue in the preparation of all television advertising, regardless of cost, is that the production process has direct and significant effects on the communication impact of a finished advertisement. A well-conceived copy strategy can fall flat if

14. Caranicas, "4A's Survey Shows Double-Digit Hike in Spot Product Costs," 42.

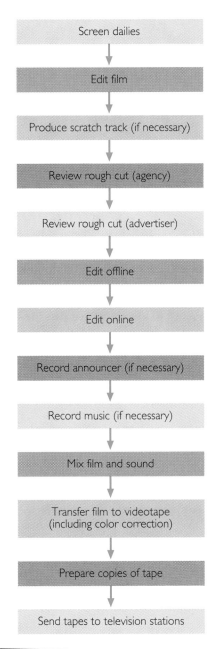

Screen dailies

↓

Edit film

↓

Produce scratch track (if necessary)

↓

Review rough cut (agency)

↓

Review rough cut (advertiser)

↓

Edit offline

↓

Edit online

↓

Record announcer (if necessary)

↓

Record music (if necessary)

↓

Mix film and sound

↓

Transfer film to videotape
(including color correction)

↓

Prepare copies of tape

↓

Send tapes to television stations

EXHIBIT 13.48

*Sequence of events in television commercial
postproduction.*

the execution at the point of production is poor. As one advertiser put it, "We don't want to be penny wise and pound foolish. If we're spending $10 million to buy TV time, we shouldn't threaten creative integrity just to cut production cost to $140,000 from $150,000."[15] One rule of thumb is to ask for ten percent of the planned media buy for production. They may not give it to you, but it's nice if you can get it, unless they are planing a very small media buy.

Postproduction. Once filming is completed, several postproduction activities are required before the commercial is ready for airing. At this point, a host of additional professional talent enters the process. Film editors, audio technicians, voice-over specialists, and musicians may be contracted. Exhibit 13.48 shows the sequence of events in the postproduction phase.

The first step in postproduction is review of the **dailies**—scenes shot during the previous day's production. Such screening may result in reshooting certain segments of the ad. Once dailies are acceptable to the agency, the editing process begins. **Editing** involves piecing together various scenes or shots of scenes, called *takes,* to bring about the desired visual effect. Most editing involves making decisions about takes shot at different angles, or subtle differences in the performance of the talent. If music is to be included, it will be prepared at this point using a **scratch track**, which is a rough approximation of the musical score using only a piano and vocalists.

A rough cut of the commercial is then prepared by loading the video dailies into an *Avid computer* to digitize and time-code the tape. The **rough cut** is an assembly of the best scenes from the shoot edited together using the quick and precise access afforded by digital technology. Using the offline Avid computer on the digitized rough cut, various technical aspects of the look of a commercial can be refined—color alterations and background images, for example. The final editing of the advertisement—which includes repositioning of elements, correcting final color, and adding fades, titles, blowups, dissolves, final audio, and special effects—is done with online equipment in online rooms equipped for final editing. **Online editing** involves transferring the finalized rough cut onto one-inch videotape, which is of on-air quality suitable for media transmission.

The personnel and equipment required for postproduction tasks are costly. Film editors charge about $150 to $200 per hour, and an editing assistant is about $50 per hour. An offline computer costs about $100 per hour. When online editing begins, the cost goes up, with online rooms running about $700 per hour. The reason for the dramatic difference in cost between offline editing and online editing is that offline edits are done on a single machine to produce a rough, working version of an ad. The online room typically includes many specialized machines for all the final effects desired in the ad. Additionally, a mixing room for voice and music costs about $400 per day.

In all, it is easy to see why filmed television commercials are so costly. Scores of people with specialized skills and a large number of separate tasks are included in the process. The procedures also reflect the complexity of the process. Aside from the mechanics of production, a constant vigil must be kept over the creative concept of the advertisement. Despite the complexities, the advertising industry continues to turn out high-quality television commercials on a timely basis.

---

15. Alsop, "Advertisers Bristle as Charges Balloon for Splashy TV Spots," op. cit.

Production Options in Television Advertising.   Several production options are available to an advertiser in preparing a television commercial. Eighty percent of all television commercials prepared by national advertisers use film as the medium for production. The previous discussion of production procedures, in fact, described the production process for a filmed advertisement. **Film** (typically 35 mm) is the most versatile medium and produces the highest-quality visual impression. It is, however, the most expensive medium for production and is also the most time-consuming.

A less-expensive option is **videotape**. Videotape is not as popular among directors or advertisers for a variety of reasons. Tape has far fewer lines of resolution, and some say videotape results in a flatter image than film. Its visual impressions are more stark and have less depth and less color intensity. While this can sometimes add to the realism of a commercial, it can also detract from the appearance of the product and the people in the ad. The obvious advantages of videotape—its lower costs, no need to process before viewing, and its flexibility—make it very appealing. New **digital video (DV)** formats may challenge film, however. These advantages have prompted production houses (especially television station–based production facilities) to use videotape as the medium of choice in filming infomercials.[16] Infomercials can actually benefit from the starkness and realism of the videotape format.

There is always the choice of live television commercial production. **Live production** can result in realism and the capturing of spontaneous reactions and events that couldn't possibly be re-created in a rehearsed scene. It is clear, however, that the loss of control in live settings threatens the carefully worked-out objectives for a commercial. On occasion, local retailers (such as auto dealers) use live commercials to execute direct response message strategies. Such a technique can capture the urgency of an appeal.

Two techniques that do not neatly fit the production process described earlier are animation and stills. **Animation** (and the variation known as Claymation) is the use of drawn figures and scenes (such as cartoons) to produce a commercial. Keebler cookie and California Raisin commercials use characters created by animators and Claymation artists. Animated characters, such as Tony the Tiger, are frequently incorporated into filmed commercials for added emphasis. A newer form of animation uses computer-generated images. Several firms, such as TRW, have developed commercials totally through the use of computers. The graphics capabilities of giant-capacity computers make futuristic, eye-catching animation ads an attractive alternative. And the "ads" show up on time.

Still production is a technique whereby a series of photographs or slides is filmed and edited so that the resulting ad appears to have movement and action. Through the use of pans, zooms, and dissolves with the camera, still photographs can be used to produce an interesting yet low-cost finished advertisement.

The production option chosen should always be justified on both a creative and a cost basis. The dominance of filmed commercials is explainable by the level of quality of the finished ad and the versatility afforded by the technique. A local retailer or social service organization may not need or may not be able to afford the quality of film. In cases where quality is less significant or costs are primary, other production techniques are available.

16. Kevin Goldman, "CBS to Push Videotaping of Infomercials," *Wall Street Journal,* November 15, 1994, B6.

SUMMARY

◆▶ Identify the basic purposes, components, and formats of print ad illustrations.

With few exceptions, illustrations are critical to the effectiveness of print ads. Specifically, illustrations can serve to attract attention, make the brand heroic, communicate product features or benefits, create a mood and enhance brand image, stimulate reading of the body copy, or create the desired social context for the brand. The overall impact of an illustration is determined in part by its most basic components: size, use of color, and the medium used to create the illustration. Another critical aspect of the illustration's effectiveness has to do with the format chosen for the product in the illustration. Obviously, a print ad cannot work if the consumer doesn't easily identify the product or service being advertised.

◆▶ Describe the principles and components that help ensure the effective design of print ads.

In print ad design, all the verbal and visual components of an ad are arranged for maximum impact and appeal. Several principles can be followed as a basis for a compelling design. These principles feature issues such as balance, proportion, order, unity, and emphasis. The first component of an effective design is focus—drawing the reader's attention to specific areas of the ad. The second component is movement and direction—directing the reader's eye movement through the ad. The third component is clarity and simplicity—avoiding a complex and chaotic look that will deter most consumers.

◆▶ Detail the stages that art directors follow in developing the layout of a print ad.

The layout is the physical manifestation of all this design planning. An art director uses various forms of layouts to bring a print ad to life. There are several predictable stages in the evolution of a layout. The art director starts with a hand-drawn thumbnail, proceeds to the digitized rough layout (or semicomp), and continues with a tight comp that represents the look of the final ad. With each stage, the layout becomes more concrete, and more like the final form of the advertisement. The last stage, the mechanical, is the form the ad takes as it goes to final production.

◆▶ Discuss the activities and decisions involved in the final production of print ads.

Timing is critical to advertising effectiveness: Advertisers must have a keen understanding of production cycles to have an ad in the consumer's hands at just the right time.

In addition, there are many possible means for actually printing an ad. These range from the letterpress to screen printing to computer print production. As with many aspects of modern life, the computer has had a dramatic impact on print ad preparation and production. Before a print ad can reach its audience, a host of small but important decisions need to be made about the type styles and sizes that will best serve the campaign's purposes.

◆▶ Identify the various players who must function as a team to produce television ads.

The complexity of ad production for television is unrivaled and thus demands the inputs of a variety of functional specialists. From the ad agency come familiar players such as the art director, copywriter, and account executive. Then there are a host of individuals who have special skills in various aspects of production for this medium. These include directors, producers, production managers, and camera crews. Editors will also be needed to bring all the raw material together into a finished commercial. Organizational and team-management skills are essential to make all these people and pieces work together.

◆▶ Discuss the specific stages and costs involved in producing television ads.

The intricate process of TV ad production can be broken into three major stages: preproduction, production, and postproduction. In the preproduction stage, scripts and storyboards are prepared, budgets are set, production houses are engaged, and a timetable is formulated. Production includes all those activities involved in the actual filming of the ad. The shoot is a high-stress activity that usually carries a high price tag. The raw materials from the shoot are mixed and refined in the postproduction stage. Today's editors work almost exclusively with computers to create the final product—a finished television ad. If all this sounds expensive, it is!

◆▶ Describe the major formatting options for television ad production.

Film is the preferred option for most TV ads because of the high-quality visual impression it provides. Videotape suffers on the quality issue, and live television is not practical in most cases. Animation is probably the second most popular formatting option. With continuing improvements in computer graphics, computer-generated images may one day become a preferred source of material for TV ad production. Still production can be an economical means to bring a message to television.

KEY TERMS

illustration (388)
medium (392)
illustration format (393)
design (394)
principles of design (394)
balance (395)
formal balance (395)
informal balance (395)
border (397)
white space (397)
axis (397)
three-point layout structure (398)
parallel layout structure (398)
layout (399)
thumbnails (399)
rough layout (399)
comp (400)
mechanical (400)
closing date (401)
letterpress (402)
offset lithography (402)
gravure (402)
flexography (402)
electronic, laser, and inkjet printing (402)
type font (403)

blackletter (403)
roman (403)
script (403)
serif (403)
sans serif (403)
miscellaneous (403)
point (403)
picas (404)
preproduction (412)
storyboard (412)
script (412)
production timetable (416)
production stage, or shoot (418)
dailies (421)
editing (421)
scratch track (421)
rough cut (421)
online editing (421)
film (422)
videotape (422)
digital video (DV) (422)
live production (422)
animation (422)
still production (422)

QUESTIONS FOR REVIEW AND CRITICAL THINKING

1.   Is there anyone out there who would rather watch black-and-white television than color? If not, why would any advertiser choose to run a black-and-white print ad in a medium that supports color? Can you think of a situation where a black-and-white ad might be more effective than a color ad?

2.   *Effective* turns out to be a very elusive concept in any discussion of advertising's effects. In what ways might an illustration in a print ad prove to be effective from the point of view of a marketer?

3.   This chapter reviewed five basic principles for print ad design: balance, proportion, order, unity, and emphasis. Give an example of how each of these principles might be employed to enhance the selling message of a print ad.

4.   Creativity in advertising is often a matter of breaking with conventions. Peruse an issue of your favorite maga-

zine or newspaper to find examples of ads that violate the five basic principles mentioned in the previous question.

5.   Why is it appropriate to think of print as a static medium? Given print's static nature, explain how movement and direction can be relevant concepts to the layout of a print ad.

6.   For an art director who has reached the mechanicals stage of the ad layout process, explain the appeal of computer-aided design versus the old-fashioned paste-up approach.

7.   Explain the role of the production company in the evolution of a television commercial. As part of this explanation, be certain you have identified each of the unique skills and specialties that people in the production company bring to the ad development process.

8. Compare and contrast the creative guidelines for TV offered in this chapter with those offered for magazine ads in the previous chapter. Based on this analysis, what conclusions would you offer about the keys to effective communication in these two media?

9. Identify the six steps involved in the preproduction of a television ad and describe the issues that an art director must attend to at each step if his or her goals for the ad are to be achieved.

10. Without a doubt, a television ad shoot is one of the most exciting and pressure-packed activities that any advertising professional can take part in. List the various factors or issues that contribute to the tension and excitement that surrounds an ad shoot.

11. Review the formatting options that an art director can choose from when conceiving a television ad. Discuss the advantages of each option and describe the situation for which each is best suited.

EXPERIENTIAL EXERCISES

1. Find an ad that uses an effective illustration and explain what makes it effective. Find two other ads, one that uses formal balance, and one that uses informal balance. Do you find these ads equally appealing? Why or why not? Finally, find an ad that seems to lack any good visuals, and explain whether is it good or bad advertising, and why. What conclusions can you draw about the use of illustrations in print ads?

2. Over the past decade the success of MTV has inspired a unique style of television ad. Watch an hour of programming on MTV, and list the ads shown in that hour. How would you describe the MTV style commercial? How large a role does the video editor play in creating this style of commercial?

USING THE INTERNET

When designing an advertisement, both the verbal and visual components of the ad are arranged to maximize impact and appeal. Visit the Internet Link Exchange site (www.linkexchange.com) and view the results of the most recent banner ad contest. Choose the three ads that you like the most.

For each ad, explain how the ad uses the principles of design to achieve its impact on the viewer:

1. Which is more dominant, the illustration or the copy?

2. What element receives the most emphasis?

3. Does the ad use formal or informal balance?

4. How would you characterize the typeface?

5. Does the ad make effective use of white space?

6. Which of these banner ads is most effective at influencing you to click on it? What aspects of ad design are the most appealing?

Many Web-based advertisers provide alternatives to site visitors, recognizing the range of means of access (e.g., where low-speed modems may make a heavy graphics site slow to a crawl), and the likelihood that some visitors will be technologically (or even sensorily) limited.

Select some of the sites you regularly use, and check their suitability for use by the visually-handicapped with the "Bobby" service: www.cast.org/bobby/

1. How well do these sites rate with Bobby?

2. How much care has been put into making the sites accessible to all viewers (or listeners, perhaps)?

Unlike other media, where content is published or broadcast with no immediate means to assess its impact, the Web is a truly interactive medium: as visitors click through a site, they provide feedback on what they find worth reading, or seeing, or listening to.

3. How might you determine how well a Web site was meeting the needs of visitors with special needs?

FROM PRINCIPLES to Practice:
A COMPREHENSIVE IMC CASE

PART III
Preparing the IMC Campaign to Launch
Cincinnati Bell Wireless

In Parts I and II of our comprehensive IMC case, we introduced you to a client and an ad agency who together, in the spring of 1998, were preparing for the launch of a new digital phone service in the Greater Cincinnati market.

Now it is time to take an inside look at the process of actually preparing the elements of an integrated marketing communications campaign. This stressful, stop-and-go process must be managed in such a way that the tension and stress do not stifle the creativity that is always required for breakthrough advertising. Many different types of expertise must be folded into the process to take advantage of multiple communication tools, and countless details must be attended to if the various tools are to work together to produce the synergy that is the reason for pursuing an IMC campaign in the first place. Collaboration between agency and client is key to ensure that the approval process proceeds in a timely fashion, but with all the planning and forethought there still needs to be an element of spontaneity that allows both client and agency to capitalize on the last-minute big ideas that always infiltrate the process just when you think you have everything decided.

Tension, stress, creativity, deadlines, collaboration, synergy, conflict, misunderstandings, expertise, complexity, details, details, details . . . these are all things that characterize the process of preparing to launch an IMC campaign. How is it possible for people to survive and work through the array of challenges that characterize campaign preparation? How is it possible, in the people-intensive business of advertising design and production, for order ever to emerge from the chaos?

Making Beautiful Music Together: Coordination, Collaboration, and Creativity.
Metaphors help us understand, so let's use a metaphor to appreciate the challenge of executing sophisticated IMC campaigns. Executing an IMC campaign is very much like the performance of a symphony orchestra. To produce glorious music, many individuals must make their unique contributions to the performance, but it only sounds right if the maestro brings it all together at the critical moment. The next time you attend the performance of a symphony orchestra, get there early so that you can hear each individual musician warming up his or her instrument. Reflect on the many years of dedicated practice that this individual put in to master his or her instrument. Reflect on the many hours of practice that this individual put in to learn his or her specific part for tonight's performance. As you sit there listening to the warmup, notice how the random collection of sounds becomes increasingly painful to the ears. With each musician doing his or her own thing, the sound is a collection of hoots and clangs that grows louder as the performance approaches. Mercifully, the maestro finally steps to the podium to quell the cacophony. All is quiet for a moment. The musicians focus on their sheet music for reassurance,

even though by now they could play their individual parts in their sleep. Finally, the maestro calls the orchestra into action. As a group, as a collective, as a team, with each person executing a specific assignment as defined by the composer, under the direction of the maestro, they make beautiful music together.

So it goes in the world of advertising. Preparing and executing breakthrough IMC campaigns is a people-intensive business. Many different kinds of expertise will be needed to pull it off, and this means many different people must be enlisted to play a variety of roles. But there must be some order imposed on the collection of players. Frequently, a maestro will need to step in to give the various players a common theme or direction for their work. Beyond this need for leadership, the effort must also be guided by a strategy if this collective is to produce beautiful music together. Of course, the goal for this kind of music is a persuasive harmony that makes the cash register sing!

As the advertising profession has become increasingly driven by the premise of integrated marketing communication, there has been a growing recognition of the importance of a professional approach to teamwork as the engine for getting things done. Professors Larry Weisberg and Brett Robbs of the University of Colorado state the case this way:

Advertising always has been a team sport. But the advent of integrated marketing communications has made effective teamwork more important than ever. It also has made it more difficult to achieve, because IMC requires competing functional areas—e.g., advertising, promotions, and public relations—to work together as one. . . . To ready students for the workplace, it isn't enough to just give them a strong understanding of IMC. We also need to equip them with the team skills that enable them to practice IMC effectively.[1]

Without a doubt, the coordination and collaboration required for IMC execution require sophisticated teamwork. Moreover, the creative essence of the campaign can be aided and elevated by a thoughtful, team approach. Teams possess a potential for synergy that allows them to rise above the talents of their individual members on many kinds of tasks.[2] (Yes, the whole can be greater than the sum of the individual parts.)

Our Cincinnati Bell Wireless example is replete with stories of successful teamwork. We will share some of those stories subsequently; however, we'd first like to make the point that successful teamwork can't be left to chance. It must be planned for and facilitated if it is to occur with regularity. In the remainder of this section we will introduce several concepts and insights about teams that are offered to encourage you to take teamwork more seriously. We will review research concerning what it is that makes teams effective, along with basic principles for effective teamwork. Then we will turn to our Cincinnati Bell Wireless example to bring the concepts to life.

What We Know about Teams. We fully expect that every college student, by the time they read this textbook, will have taken a class where part of their grade was determined by teamwork. Get used to it. More and more instructors in all sorts of classes are incorporating teamwork as part of their courses because they know that interpersonal skills are highly valued in the real world of work. In fact, there is an impressive body of evidence from research on management practices which indicates that teams have become essential to the effectiveness of modern organizations. In their book, *The Wisdom of Teams*, management consultants Jon Katzenbach and Douglas Smith review many valuable insights about the importance of teams in today's world of work. Here we summarize several of their key conclusions.[3]

1. Larry Weisberg and Brett Robbs, "Team Conflict: Teaching IMC Students to Handle It," *Marketing News*, August 3, 1998, 10–11.
2. Arthur B. VanGundy, *Managing Group Creativity* (New York: American Management Association, 1984).
3. Jon R. Katzenbach and Douglas K. Smith, *The Wisdom of Teams: Creating the High-Performance Organization* (Boston: Harvard Business School Press, 1993).

Teams Rule! There can be little doubt that teams have become the primary means for getting things done in a growing number and variety of organizations. The growing number of performance challenges faced by most businesses—as a result of factors such as more demanding customers, technological changes, government regulation, and intensifying competition—demand speed and quality in work products that are simply beyond the scope of what an individual can hope to offer. In many instances, teams are the only valid option for getting things done. This is certainly the case for executing integrated marketing communications campaigns.

It's All about Performance. Research shows that teams are effective in organizations where senior management makes it perfectly clear that teams will be held accountable for performance. Teams are expected to produce results that satisfy the client and yield financial gains for the organization. As we will see in subsequent examples, this performance motive as the basis for teams is a perfect fit in an IMC services provider such as NSL.

Synergy through Teams. Modern organizations require many kinds of expertise to get the work done. The only reliable way to mix people with different expertise to generate solutions where the whole is greater than the sum of the parts is through team discipline. Research shows that blending expertise from diverse disciplines often produces the most innovative solutions to many different types of business problems.[4] The "blending" must be done through teams.

The Demise of Individualism? Rugged individualism is the American Way. Always look out for number one! But are we suggesting that a growing reliance on teams in the workplace must mean a devaluation of the individual and a greater emphasis on conforming to what the group thinks? Not at all. Left unchecked, of course, an "always look out for number one" mentality can destroy teams. But teams are not incompatible with individual excellence. To the contrary, effective teams find ways to let each individual bring his or her unique contributions to the forefront as the basis for their effectiveness. When an individual does not have his or her own contribution to make, then one can question that person's value to the team. Or, as NSL's CEO Mark Serrianne is fond of saying, "If you and I both think alike, then one of us is unnecessary."

Teams Promote Personal Growth. Finally, an added benefit of teamwork is that it promotes learning for each individual team member. In a team, people learn about their own work styles and observe the work styles of others. This learning makes them more effective team players in their next assignment.

Leadership in Teams. A critical element in the equation for successful teams is leadership. Leadership in teams is a special form of leadership; it is not a matter of the most senior person in the team giving orders and expecting others to follow. Leadership in teams is not derived from the power and authority granted by one's standing in an organization. It is not a function of some mysterious accident at birth that grants some of us the ability to lead, while others must be content to follow. All of us can learn to be effective team leaders: It is a skill worth learning.

Leaders do many things for their teams to help them succeed.[5] Teams ultimately must reach a goal to justify their standing, and here is where the leader's job starts. The leader's first job is to help the team build consensus about the goals they hope to achieve and the approach they will take to reach those goals. Without a clear sense of

4.   Dorothy Leonard and Susaan Straus, "Putting Your Company's Whole Brain to Work," *Harvard Business Review*, July/August 1997, 111–121.
5.   Katzenbach and Smith, *The Wisdom of Teams,* Chapter 7.

purpose, the team is doomed. Once goals and purpose are agreed upon, then the leader plays a role in ensuring that the work of the team is consistent with the strategy or plan. This is a particularly important role in the context of creating IMC campaigns because there must always be a screen or filter applied to ensure that each element is supporting the overriding communication goal.

Leaders may also specify roles for various individuals and set and reaffirm ground rules that facilitate open communication in the team. Additionally, team leaders may serve as the point of contact for the team with others in the organization or a client outside the organization.

Finally, team leaders must help do the real work of the team. Here the team leader must be careful to contribute ideas without dominating the team. There are also two key items team leaders should never do: *They should not blame or allow specific individuals to fail, and they should never excuse away shortfalls in team performance.*[6] Mutual accountability must always be emphasized over individual performance.

Teams as the Engine for Coordination, Collaboration, and Creativity in the Launch of Cincinnati Bell Wireless.

A multimillion-dollar product launch such as that of Cincinnati Bell Wireless will require the coordination and collaboration of hundreds of individuals. These individuals will include employees from Bell and Northlich plus a variety of outside vendors, each contributing their own particular expertise, to make the launch a success. Without skillful teamwork involving dozens of discrete teams working at various levels and on various tasks, there could be no hope of executing an integrated campaign.

That team effort has many manifestations, but it must begin with a partnership between agency and client. When Mark Serrianne of NSL was asked what one needs to be successful in executing an IMC campaign, the first thing he said was, "You have to have a great client—a client that wants a partnership role." In the launch of Cincinnati Bell Wireless, we see client and agency working as partners to execute a successful launch. Cincinnati Bell brought to the table exactly those things that any good client must provide: technical expertise in their product category, financial resources, keen insights about competitive strategy, and a deep appreciation for the critical role of retailer support. From the agency side, NSL brought a tireless commitment to understanding the consumer as a basis for effective communication, and a depth of expertise and experience in the design, preparation, and placement of a broad array of communication tools. Each looked to the other to do their job; in particular, we see in this example a client that trusted its agency to do the job of preparing and placing a full-scale IMC campaign. That trust is critical because it frees the agency to do its most crucial task: creating breakthrough communications that will disrupt the category and drive business results.

The NSL Account Team.

As expressed by Mark Serrianne, the NSL philosophy on teamwork is embodied by the account team. This team of experts from the various disciplines within the agency is charged with bringing a campaign into being for its focal client. Every account team must have a leader, or account supervisor, who becomes the critical communication liaison to the client, and who seeks to facilitate and coordinate a dialogue among the disciplines represented on the team. But, consistent with our earlier discussion about team leadership, the NSL account supervisor is definitely not identified as the highest-ranking person on the team, whose job it is to give orders, sit back, and let other people do all the work. The account supervisor is a working member of the team who also is responsible for encouraging and coordinating the efforts of other team members.

6. Katzenbach and Smith, *The Wisdom of Teams,* 144.

Half the battle in making teams work is getting the right people on the team in the first place. This begins with the account supervisor. The NSL account team for the CBW launch was lead by Mandy Reverman. Mandy was basically hired by NSL from Campbell-Ewald, Advertising–Detroit, to direct the CBW launch. Over a seven-year period with Campbell-Ewald, Mandy had gained considerable experience in account management and team leadership through her work for Chevrolet and Toyota auto dealerships. Automotive retailer groups are a demanding clientele who expect to see a direct effect on sales from the advertising they sponsor in specific metro markets. As it turns out, these were the same kinds of expectations that CBW had for its advertising in the Greater Cincinnati metro market in the spring of 1998. Mandy thus had the right background to oversee the CBW account team.

Mandy views the role of team leader as the hub of a wheel, with various spokes that reach out to diverse disciplinary expertise. The hub connects the spokes and ensures that all of them work in tandem to make the wheel roll smoothly. Using Mandy's wheel metaphor, her spokes are represented by team members from direct marketing, public relations, broadcast media, graphic design, creative, and accounting. To illustrate the multilayered nature of the team approach to IMC, each team member can also be thought of as a hub in his or her very own wheel. For example, the direct marketing member on the account team was team leader for her own set of specialists charged with preparing direct marketing materials for the CBW launch. Through this type of multilevel "hub-and-spokes" design, the coordination and collaboration essential for effective IMC campaigns can be achieved.

Teams Moderate Tension in the Copy Approval Process.

As discussed in Chapter 12, in the deadline-driven and pressure-packed activity of campaign preparation, one predictable source of tension between agency and client is the copy approval process. This was certainly evident in the CBW launch, not only because of the time pressures that accompanied this launch, but also because of the unique partnership between Cincinnati Bell and AT&T that was forged in the creation of CBW. While the AT&T network was critical to the credibility of the CBW service, the partnership with AT&T also gave executives from that organization a say in the copy approval process. This turned out to be one of the most frustrating aspects of the launch for the NSL creative team, because AT&T's executives were far removed from the actual process of ad development. According to one NSL insider, this is the painstaking part of the process: "It is hard to keep people motivated to work the details when what appear to be insignificant changes are requested by a distant third party."

So how do you keep people motivated when these last-minute requests to shift scenes and sentences are made on work that you thought was finished? First of all, the communication that is facilitated through teamwork is essential to working through the copy approval process. Delays caused by miscommunication are certain to heighten tensions and create dysfunctional outcomes. Moreover, the mutual accountability that goes with effective teams must also come into play. The copywriters or art directors that have to respond with last-minute changes must accept their roles as team players, and move forward on the changes for the sake of the team.

Teams Liberate Decision Making.

When the right combination of expertise is assembled on a team, what appears to be casual or spur-of-the-moment decision making can turn out to be more creative decision making. The value of divergent, spontaneous input as a basis for decisions is beautifully illustrated by the team-oriented approach that NSL and CBW employed during the shoot of their television commercials. Key members of the "shoot team" included the account supervisor from NSL, Mandy Reverman, and her steadfast partner from the client side, Mike Vanderwoude, marketing director at CBW. They joined the production manager, art director, and copywriter to create a working team that didn't just bring their storyboards to life in the shoot. Through a lively give-

and-take on the site, they created engaging video that was on strategy and delivered a message that wireless customers in Cincinnati were just ready and waiting to hear.

Exhibit IMC 3.1 is an example of one of the storyboards that this working team started with at a shoot. This ad, titled "Classroom," is seeded with the core strategy that drove much of the advertising for the launch. The message of the ad was that Cincinnati Bell Wireless is a superior solution because it is both simpler and more economical than cellular. You don't need to know advanced calculus to figure out the benefits of Cincinnati Bell Wireless. But the final ad that evolved from this board shows many departures from its rather languid script. This is because, during the shoot, the working team fed off one another's ideas to continue to develop and refine the ad's expression of "simple terms" and "it's just a better deal" than cellular. Individual scenes were shot over and over again, testing various deliveries of new executions that the working team was creating on the spur of the moment. This liberated the team, the talent, and the director to produce a final product that delivers on the simplification message in a most compelling way.

More About Teams and Creativity. As the preceding example reflects, creativity in the preparation of an IMC campaign can be fostered by the trust and open communication that are hallmarks of effective teams. But it is also true that the creativity required for breakthrough campaigns will evolve as personal work products generated by individuals laboring on their own. Both personal and team creativity are critical in the preparation of IMC campaigns. The daunting task of facilitating both usually falls in the lap of an agency's creative director.

EXHIBIT IMC 3.1

Cincinnati Bell Wireless storyboard: "Classroom."

The position of creative director in any ad agency is very special because, much like the maestro of the symphony orchestra, the creative director must encourage personal excellence, but at the same time demand team accountability. Don Perkins, senior VP and executive creative director at NSL, sees his job as channeling the creative energies of the dozens of individuals in his group. Don acknowledges that creativity has an intensely personal element; in his view, original creation is motivated by the desire to satisfy one's own ego or sense of self. But despite the intimate character he ascribes to creativity, Don clearly appreciates the need for team unity. Many of the principles he relies on for channeling the creativity of his group could in fact be portrayed as key tenets for team leadership. In orchestrating NSL's creative teams, Don relies on the following principles:

• Take great care in assigning individuals to a team in the first place. Be sensitive to their existing work loads, and the proper mix of expertise required to do the job for the client.
• Get to know the work style of each individual. Listen carefully. Since creativity can be an intensely personal matter, one has to know when it is best to leave people alone, versus when one needs to support them in working through the inevitable rejection.
• Make teams responsible to the client. Individuals and teams are empowered when they have sole responsibility for performance outcomes.
• Beware of adversarial relationships between individuals and between teams. They can quickly lead to mistrust that destroys camaraderie and synergy.
• In situations where the same set of individuals will work on multiple teams over time, rotate team assignments to foster fresh thinking.

To Ensure the Uniform Look, Turn to Teams. While we're probably starting to sound like a broken record on this team thing, let's take just one more example. Exhibits IMC 3.2, 3.3, and 3.4 show a direct mail piece, point-of-purchase brochures, and a billboard facing that were created by three different NSL designers for the CBW launch. These and dozens of other elements of the launch campaign were created to have a uniform look that supported the integrated premise of the campaign. But how does one get this uni-

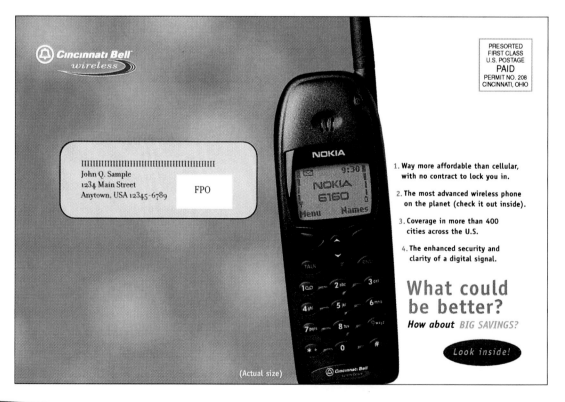

EXHIBIT IMC 3.2

CBW launch: direct mail piece.

form look when in fact these dozens of different items will inevitably be the work products of dozens of different individuals? Sure. You guessed it. If you want a uniform look, you must rely on teamwork.

The materials in the three exhibits feature several common design elements, including colors, line art, fonts, background, and of course, the CBW logo. These elements were selected through an internal competition that Don Perkins and his design director orchestrated in the NSL design department. From this competition, a design standard was chosen, and the graphic artist who created that design became the leader of an ad hoc design team. That artist thereafter coordinated the efforts of different designers as they prepared various materials for the campaign, and served the critical role that leaders often fulfill as filters to ensure collaboration, which in this specific case emerged as the "uniform look." Here we see once again that the fundamentals of effective teams—communication, trust, complementary expertise, and leadership—produce the desired performance outcome. There's simply no alternative. Teams rule!

EXHIBIT IMC 3.3

CBW launch: P-O-P brochures.

EXHIBIT IMC 3.4

CBW launch: billboard facing.

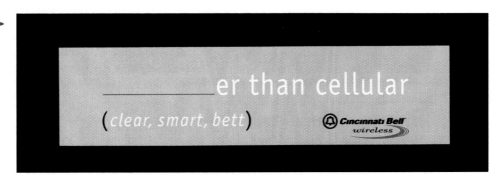

IMC EXERCISES

1. In the case you read that "advertising always has been a team sport, but the advent of IMC has made effective teamwork more important than ever. It also has made it more difficult to achieve." Explain how the growing emphasis on IMC makes effective teamwork more difficult to achieve.
2. What insight(s) about teams does Mark Serrianne, CEO of Northlich Stolley LaWarre, provide when he states, "if you and I both think alike, then one of us is unnecessary"?
3. In the launch of Cincinnati Bell Wireless, we see client and agency working together as a partnership to execute a product launch. What did each "bring to the table" to create the partnership? In your opinion, who plays the greater role in creating a successful partnership: the client or the agency?
4. The creative director in an advertising agency has the daunting task of channeling the creative energies of dozens of individuals, while demanding team accountability. If the expression of creativity is personal and highly individualized, how can teamwork possibly foster creativity? What might a creative director do to "allow creativity to happen" in a team environment? Explain how the saying "The whole is greater than the sum of its parts" fits into a discussion of creativity and teamwork.

PART FOUR

PLACING THE MESSAGE: MEDIA AND SUPPORTIVE COMMUNICATIONS

Once again we pass into a new and totally different area of advertising, "Placing the Message: Media and Supportive Communications." We are now at the point where reaching the target audience is the key issue. The challenge of message preparation gives way to the last of the 4Ps of advertising: *placement* of the message.

Beyond the formidable challenge of effectively choosing media to reach the target audience, contemporary advertisers are demanding even more from the placement decision: synergy and integration. Throughout the first three parts of the text, the issue of integrated marketing communications was raised whenever the opportunity existed to create coordinated communications. Indeed, the Cincinnati Bell sections at the end of each part are included to highlight the IMC issue. But nowhere is IMC more critical than at the media placement and supportive communications stage. Here, audiences may be exposed to the advertiser's messages through a wide range of different media and promotional efforts—each with a unique quality and tone for communication. The advertiser is challenged to ensure that if diverse communications options are chosen for placing the message, there is still a "one-voice" quality to the over-all communication program.

Media Planning, Objectives, and Strategy

Maintaining integration is indeed a challenge in the contemporary media environment. Chapter 14, "Media Planning, Objectives, and Strategy," begins with an overview of major media options. The media-planning process is explored next, including a discussion of media objectives, strategies, choices, and scheduling issues. Next, the complexity of the current media environment is discussed. Finally, media choice is considered in the context of integrated marketing communications. This chapter is enhanced with media strategy exercises and access to media data.

Media Evaluation: Print, Television, and Radio

Chapter 15, "Media Evaluation: Print, Television, and Radio," offers an analysis of the major media options available to advertisers. The chapter follows a sequence in which the advantages and disadvantages of each medium are discussed, followed by considerations of cots, buying procedures, and audience measurement techniques.

Support Media, P-O-P Advertising, and Event Sponsorship

Chapter 16, "Support Media, P-O-P Advertising, and Event Sponsorship," reflects the extraordinary range of options available to today's advertiser, from billboards and transit advertising to event sponsorship, point-of-purchase (p-o-p) advertising, and the most elaborate online services. The chapter focuses on P-O-P advertising and event sponsorship because of the dramatic growth and impact of these activities. The examples in this chapter highlight how creative advertisers and their agencies can be in finding unique and interesting ways to reach target markets.

Advertising on the Internet

The newest and perhaps greatest challenge for advertisers has recently presented itself—the Internet. Chapter 17, "Advertising on the Internet," describes this new and formidable technology available to advertisers. This chapter is truly a key to the text and to understanding the new advertising environment. Basic terminology and procedures are described. A multitude of Web sites are offered for exploration.

Sales Promotion

Chapter 18, "Sales Promotion," describes the ways that event sponsorships, contests, sweepstakes, and price incentives attract the attention of customers. The impact of many sales promotion techniques is much easier to measure than the impact of advertising, thus prompting some marketers to shift spending from advertising to promotion, and thus making promotion an important contemporary topic. Highlighted in this chapter are the fundamental differences between the purpose of advertising and the purpose of sales promotion.

Direct Marketing

Consumers' desire for greater convenience and marketers' never-ending search for competitive advantage has spawned tremendous growth in direct marketing. Chapter 19, "Direct Marketing," considers this area, which is a combination of both marketing and promotion. With direct marketing, advertisers communicate to a target audience, but they also seek an immediate response and a way to distribute the brand.

Public Relations and Corporate Advertising

Chapter 20, "Public Relations and Corporate Advertising," concludes the discussion of media and supportive communications. Public relations offers opportunities for positive communication but also provides damage control when negative events affect an organization. Corporate advertising is image-, cause-, or advocacy-focused and can serve a useful role in supporting an advertiser's broader brand advertising programs.

COURT TV CAPTURES WOMEN 18-49.

(MUST BE THE MEN IN UNIFORM)

WOMEN 18-49 / VPVH M-F / 8-11PM	
COURT TV	**458**
LIFETIME	429
FX	424
E!	391
HGTV	318
FOOD	308
USA	275
DISCOVERY	250

They're America's most wanted audience.
And COURT TV has them locked up.

Since unveiling our new prime time lineup January 1, COURT TV is attracting a higher concentration of Women 18-49 than the networks you may be buying.

So if you want to capture these women, COURT TV holds the key. Check out the evidence on the left, then call Gig Barton at (212) 692-7859.

COURT TV®
www.courttv.com

CHAP TER 14

**After reading and thinking about
this chapter, you will be able to:**

◖◗ Describe the major media options
available to advertisers.

◖◗ Detail the important components of
the media-planning process.

◖◗ Explain the applications of computer
modeling in media planning.

◖◗ Discuss five additional challenges that
complicate the media-planning process.

Ed Artzt, then the chairman and CEO of Procter & Gamble, sent shock waves through the advertising industry in 1994 when he boldly proclaimed that "from where we stand today, we can't be sure that ad-supported TV programming will have a future in a world of video-on-demand, pay-per-view, and subscription TV. These are designed to carry no advertising at all."[1] Artzt followed that blast with another, just weeks before he stepped down as head of P&G in 1995. This time his point was that advertisers need to control the content of new media—such as CD-ROMs, interactive television, and online information services—to better control the placement of their advertising. Specifically, he said that "content is king, and for advertisers, content is programming. We have to develop it. We have to share in its ownership, and we have to market it through whatever channels the new technologies deem most effective and most efficient for reaching consumers."[2] Exhibit 14.1 shows one form of the new media—a World Wide Web site—that Artzt is alluding to. In 1998 P&G, with its new president and chief executive, Durk Jager, in place, hosted an Internet advertising summit meeting, again demonstrating its new media commitment and leadership.

But while big advertisers such as P&G respect the power and potential of new media, they also recognize the vast presence of traditional media. Artzt's position on television, for example, is that "broadcast television is still the best way to achieve the reach and frequency advertisers need to build consumers' loyalty to our products and services." Rich Wilson, P&G Worldwide vice president of media, concurs. "For packaged goods marketers, . . . advertising will continue to be the prime way we communicate our products' benefits; while we do some limited sponsorship, it is generally as a supplement to traditional media."[3]

Driven by digital TV, the explosion of channel choices, audience fragmentation, and advertising free channels, other large and influential advertisers such as General Motors, Disney, Pepsi, Kellogg, and Heineken are pursuing opportunities for sponsorship, advertiser-funded programming, and innovative media. Philip Guarascio, vice president and general manager of marketing and advertising for General Motors, has also taken the position that advertisers need to be involved in developing the content of programming for traditional and new media. To further its programming efforts, GM has entered into an agreement with Time Warner to develop proprietary new media applications that will run on new media platforms, from CD-ROM to two-way television. Finally, Disney's $19 billion acquisition of the ABC television network gives the entertainment conglomerate a broad foundation for controlling both traditional media and new media options being developed with ABC.[4] (See Exhibit 14.2). Whatever traditional divide there was between advertiser and programmer seems to be getting smaller all the time.

An Overview of the Major Media.

To this point, we have studied advertising as a process that includes the planning and preparation of creative advertising materials. Placing the message is the next step. A well-planned and creatively prepared campaign needs to be placed in media to reach the target audience and stimulate demand for a brand. Have the activities of firms such as P&G and General Motors changed the very nature of media placement decisions? The answer, simply, is no, not yet.

What these firms see are new opportunities to shape the media environment to their advantage. For now the basic process of choosing channels through which a

1.   Steve Yahn, "Advertising's Grave New World," *Advertising Age,* May 16, 1994, 1, 53.
2.   Scott Donaton and Pat Sloan, "Control New Media," *Advertising Age,* March 13, 1995, 1.
3.   Donaton and Sloan, "Control New Media," 8; Alasdair Reid, "P&G Will Make Use of Any New Medium That Proves Effective," *ASAP,* September 18, 1998, 28.
4.   Amanda Lutchford, "Can TV Ads Survive Digital?" *ASAP,* October 16, 1997, 12; Joe Mandese, "Is It Magic Kingdom or an Evil Empire?" *Advertising Age,* August 7, 1995.

EXHIBIT 14.1

Advertisers are struggling with the choice between investing in traditional media and gaining control of new media options—such as the World Wide Web. Some advertisers believe that controlling information in new media is the wave of the future. This Web site devoted to inline skating features product information and links to mail-order companies. www.bauer.com/skating.html

EXHIBIT 14.2

Disney's acquisition of the ABC television network has broadened Disney's media options. www.disney.com/

message can be sent is fundamentally the same: How can an advertisement or campaign be placed in media to reach a target audience effectively and efficiently? Recall that Artzt expressed P&G's desire for media control in almost precisely these words.

No matter how new the media are, how great a marketing plan is, and how insightful or visionary advertising strategists are, poor message placement will undermine even the best-laid plans. Advertising placed in media that do not reach the target audience— whether via new media or traditional media—will be much like the proverbial tree that falls in the forest with no one around: Does it make a sound? From an advertising standpoint, it doesn't matter. Advertising placed in media that do not reach target audiences will not achieve the communications or sales impact an advertiser desires. For example, if an ad for Victoria's Secret or for an Ultimate Fighting Championship pay-per-view event were placed on a family cable network like PaxNet (see Exhibit 14.3), it would be unlikely to affect the thoughts and actions of the audience in a positive way.

To gain perspective on media placement, we need to understand the opportunities for communicating with audiences and, as the opening discussion highlighted, the challenges of new media options. From both a global and domestic standpoint, the media industry is large and complex. From the mergers and acquisitions of large U.S. media firms such as Disney/ABC, Warner Communications, and AT&T/TCI, to the global communications

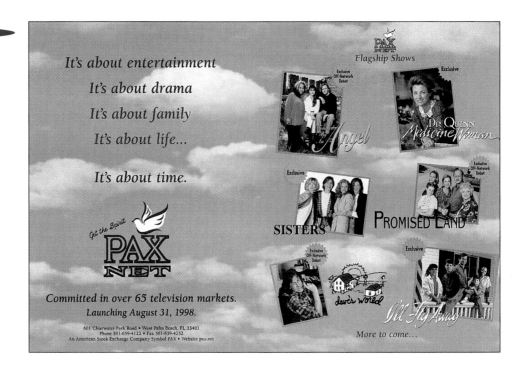

possibilities of the Intelsat satellite project (undertaken by Motorola) and the World Wide Web, media options seem to be in a perpetual state of accelerating turmoil.

To begin to appreciate the nature of media placement challenges and opportunities, let's consider the largest media organizations in the world. From the 2.9 million daily readers of the *Wall Street Journal* around the world to the estimated 250 million viewers of MTV, global reach with highly accessible media is becoming a reality. Many of these global media organizations have large audiences outside of North America. BBC World-wide TV, based in London, has more than 7.2 million viewers throughout Asia, and NBC has 65 million viewers in Europe. Likewise, as shown in Exhibit 14.4, *Time* magazine is actively expanding into new markets overseas.

Another way to gain a perspective on the nature of message placement options is to examine the media environment in the United States. Exhibits 14.5 and 14.6 provide interesting information in this regard. In Exhibit 14.5, total media expenditures by media category are listed. Notice that less than half of media expenditures in the United States are made in what are referred to as measured media. The **measured media**—television, radio, newspapers, magazines, the Internet, and outdoor media—are listed in detail in Exhibit 14.5. But notice that spending on these measured media, nearly $78 billion, represents only about 45 percent of all U.S. expenditures for 1997. **Unmeasured media**, which include direct mail, promotion, co-op, couponing, catalogs, special events, and other ways to reach business, farm, and household consumers, are estimated at nearly 22 percent higher than the measured media total.

The other noteworthy aspect of Exhibit 14.5 is the tremendous increase in expenditures in Internet advertising. This signals that some advertisers are accepting this medium to enhance their total advertising effort. (See Chapter 17 for more on this.) Indeed, wouldn't you expect an online-based business to advertise on the Internet? For an example of how suretrade.com—an online brokerage firm—apportions its advertising dollars on- and offline, see the IMC box on page 449.

Exhibit 14.6 reveals a different dimension of the media placement environment in the United States. Marketers in some product categories spend more on media and rely more on certain types of media than others. Notice that this media-spending list is headed by automobile marketers and then retailers, who each invested more than

$10.5 billion in measured media in 1997. Not surprisingly, retailers relied most on local newspapers ($5.4 billion), as did the auto advertisers ($4.2 billion).

Another aspect of media placement revealed in Exhibit 14.6 is that those advertisers with the broadest consumer product lines, such as food, cosmetics, and beverages, spend the most money placing their advertisements on network television—the medium with the broadest consumer market coverage. Direct response companies, on the other hand, invest most heavily in consumer magazines, which reach the most well-defined target audiences.

The Media-Planning Process.

This wealth of media options demands incredible attention to detail in the media-planning process. Some basic terminology is essential to understanding this effort. A **media plan** specifies the media in which advertising messages will be placed to reach the desired target audience. A **media class** is a broad category of media, such as television, radio, or newspapers. A **media vehicle** is a particular option for placement within a media class. For example, *Newsweek* is a media vehicle within the magazine media class.

A media plan includes objectives, strategies, media choices, and a media schedule for placing a message. Exhibit 14.7 shows the specific components of a media plan. Recall from Chapter 8 that the advertising plan, developed during the planning stage of the advertising effort, is the driving force behind a media plan. Market and advertising research determines that certain media options hold the highest potential. Thus, in reality, the media-planning process takes place simultaneously with the overall development of the advertising plan.

Notice in Exhibit 14.7 that media planners set media objectives, identify strategies, make media choices, and finally set a media schedule, including the media-buying process. We will discuss each component of the media-planning process.

WEB SIGHTING

EXHIBIT 14.4

American magazines like Time *have long pulled in news from all over the world and, increasingly, are pushing their content into the hands of non-U.S. readers, in their own languages. In a globalized market for information* Time (www.time.com) *shares a shelf next to the* Economist (www.economist.com). *Will a Portuguese edition of* Time *gain it more space and more readership? The Web is a boon to multi-language publishers, who can reach readers from the "everywhere" that is cyberspace without having to worry about geography. In the physical world of print, though, what considerations might a publisher weigh in launching a new edition?*

Media Objectives.

Media objectives set specific goals for a media placement: Reach the target audience, determine the geographic scope of placement, and identify the message weight, or the total mass of advertising delivered against a target audience.

The first and most important media objective is that the media chosen *reach the target audience* (Exhibits 14.8 and 14.9). Recall that the definition of a target audience can be demographic, geographic, or based on lifestyle or attitude dimensions. Unfortunately, media planners are often put in the awkward and unenviable position of trying to target a media effort based on weak secondary data from media organizations.

EXHIBIT 14.5

Advertising spending by media category in the United States, 1996–1997 (figures are in millions of dollars).

Media	1997	1996	% change	Media as % of total 1997	Media as % of total 1996
Magazines	$12,701.1	$11,213.8	13.3	6.8	6.4
Sunday magazines	1,016.6	942.4	7.9	0.5	0.7
Local newspapers	15,777.5	13,928.9	13.3	8.4	7.9
National newspapers	1,650.0	1,437.0	14.8	0.9	0.8
Outdoor	1,462.7	1,107.5	32.1	0.8	0.6
Network TV	15,225.1	14,739.6	3.3	8.1	8.4
Spot TV	14,534.6	14,017.7	3.7	7.8	8.0
Syndicated TV	2,515.0	2,326.1	8.1	1.3	1.3
Cable TV networks	5,781.9	4,728.4	22.3	3.1	2.7
Network radio	865.6	805.9	7.4	0.5	0.5
National spot radio	1,684.2	1,463.9	15.1	0.9	0.8
Internet	544.8	220.5	147.1	0.3	0.1
Yellow Pages	10,849.0	10,849.0	0	5.8	6.2
Total measured media	84,608.2	77,780.5	8.8	45.1	44.4
Estimated unmeasured media	102,920.8	97,449.5	5.6	54.9	55.6
Grand total	187,529.0	175,230.0	7.0	100.0	100.0

Source: "100 Leading National Advertisers," *Advertising Age*, September 28, 1998, S50. Reprinted with permission from the September 28, 1998, issue of *Advertising Age*. Copyright © Crain Communications Inc. 1998.

EXHIBIT 14.6

Media expenditures in the United States by selected product categories, 1997 (figures are in millions of dollars).

Product Category	1997 Total Ad Spending	Leading Medium	
Automotive	$13,325.5	Local newspapers	$4,236.3
Retail	10,664.5	Local newspapers	5,464.2
Toiletries and cosmetics	3,640.5	Network television	1,467.1
Food	3,361.6	Network television	1,034.9
Direct response companies	1,887.4	Consumer magazines	1,094.5
Beer, wine, and liquor	1,089.2	Network television	436.0
Soaps, cleansers, polishes	710.5	Network television	274.5
Sporting goods	409.9	Consumer magazines	190.3
Pets and pet food	360.1	Network television	127.8
Household furnishings	329.1	Consumer magazines	197.1

Source: "100 Leading National Advertisers," *Advertising Age*, September 28, 1998, S50. Reprinted with permission from the September 28, 1998, issue of *Advertising Age*. Copyright © Crain Communications Inc. 1998.

The Media Plan

1. Media objectives
   a. Reach the target audience
   b. Geographic scope of media placement
   c. Message weight

2. Media strategies
   a. Reach and frequency
   b. Continuity: continuous, flighting, pulsing
   c. Audience duplication
   d. Length or size of advertisements

3. Media choices
   a. Media mix: concentrated, assorted
   b. Media efficiency: cost per thousand (CPM),
      cost per thousand—target market (CPM—TM),
      cost per rating point (CPRP)
   c. Competitive media assessment

4. Media scheduling and buying

EXHIBIT 14.7

The media-planning process.

If advertisers are willing to spend extra money, however, there are media research organizations that provide detailed information on the media habits and purchase behaviors of target audiences; this information can greatly increase the precision with which media choices are made. The two most prominent providers of demographic information correlated with product usage data are Mediamark Research (MRI) and Simmons Market Research Bureau (SMRB). An example of the type of information supplied is shown in Exhibit 14.10, where market statistics for four brands of men's aftershave and cologne are compared: Eternity for Men, Jovan Musk, Lagerfeld, and Obsession for Men. The most-revealing data are contained in columns C and D. Column C shows each brand's strength relative to a demographic variable, such as age or income. Column D provides an index indicating that particular segments of the population are heavier users of a particular brand. Specifically, the number expresses each brand's share of volume as a percentage of its share of users. An index number above 100 shows particular strength for a brand. The strength of Eternity for Men as well as Obsession for Men is apparent in both the 18–24 and the 25–34 age cohorts.

Recently, even more sophisticated data have become available. Research services such as A. C. Nielsen's Home★Scan and Information Resources' BehaviorScan are referred to as **single-source tracking services**, which offer information not just on demographics but also on brands, purchase size, purchase frequency, prices paid, and media exposure. BehaviorScan is the most comprehensive, in that exposure to particular television programs, magazines, and newspapers can be measured by the service. With demographic, behavioral, and media-exposure correlates provided by research services like these, advertising and media planners can address issues such as the following:

- How many members of the target audience have tried the advertiser's brand, and how many are brand loyal?
- What appears to affect brand sales more—increased amounts of advertising, or changes in advertising copy?
- What other products do buyers of the advertiser's brand purchase regularly?
- What television programs, magazines, and newspapers reach the largest number of the advertiser's audience?[5]

Another critical element in setting advertising objectives is determining the *geographic* scope of media placement. In some ways, this is a relatively easy objective to set. Media planners merely need to identify media that cover the same geographic area as the advertiser's distribution system. Obviously, spending money on the placement of ads in media that cover geographic areas where the advertiser's brand is not distributed is

---

5.   Donaton and Sloan, "Control New Media."

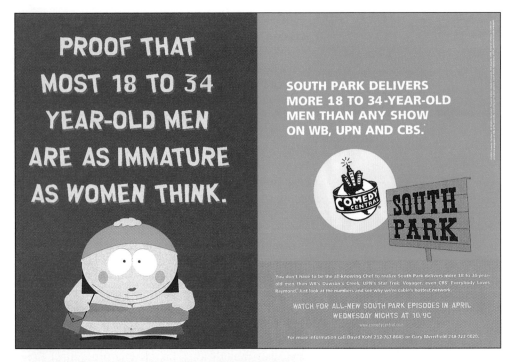

EXHIBITS 14.8 AND 14.9

Who are the target audiences for these ads? www.comedycentral.com/ *and* www.courttv.com/

16   AFTERSHAVE LOTION & COLOGNE FOR MEN

BASE: MEN	TOTAL U.S. '000	ETERNITY FOR MEN A '000	B % DOWN	C % ACROSS	D INDEX	JOVAN MUSK A '000	B % DOWN	C % ACROSS	D INDEX	LAGERFELD A '000	B % DOWN	C % ACROSS	D INDEX	OBSESSION FOR MEN A '000	B % DOWN	C % ACROSS	D INDEX
All Men	92674	2466	100.0	2.7	100	3194	100.0	3.4	100	1269	100.0	1.4	100	3925	100.0	4.2	100
Men	92674	2466	100.0	2.7	100	3194	100.0	3.4	100	1269	100.0	1.4	100	3925	100.0	4.2	100
Women	-	-			-	-			-	-			-	-			-
Household Heads	77421	1936	78.5	2.5	94	2567	80.4	3.3	96	1172	92.4	1.5	111	2856	72.7	3.7	87
Homemakers	31541	967	39.2	3.1	115	1158	36.3	3.7	107	451	35.5	1.4	104	1443	36.8	4.6	108
Graduated College	21727	583	23.7	2.7	101	503	15.8	2.3	67	348	27.4	1.6	117	901	23.0	4.1	98
Attended College	23842	814	33.0	3.4	128	933	29.2	3.9	113	*270	21.3	1.1	83	1283	32.7	5.4	127
Graduated High School	29730	688	27.9	2.3	87	1043	32.7	3.5	102	*460	36.3	1.5	113	1266	32.2	4.3	101
Did not Graduate High School	17374	*380	15.4	2.2	82	*715	22.4	4.1	119	*191	15.0	1.1	80	*475	12.1	2.7	65
18-24	12276	754	30.6	6.1	231	*391	12.2	3.2	92	*7	0.5	0.1	4	747	19.0	6.1	144
25-34	20924	775	31.4	3.7	139	705	22.1	3.4	98	*234	18.5	1.1	82	1440	36.7	6.9	162
35-44	21237	586	23.8	2.8	104	1031	32.3	4.9	141	*311	24.5	1.5	107	838	21.3	3.9	93
45-54	14964	*202	8.2	1.4	51	*510	16.0	3.4	99	*305	24.0	2.0	149	481	12.3	3.2	76
55-64	10104	*112	4.6	1.1	42	*215	6.7	2.1	62	*214	16.9	2.1	155	*245	6.2	2.4	57
65 or over	13168	*37	1.5	0.3	10	*342	10.7	2.6	75	*198	15.6	1.5	110	*175	4.4	1.3	31
18-34	33200	1529	62.0	4.6	173	1096	34.3	3.3	96	*241	19.0	0.7	53	2187	55.7	6.6	156
18-49	62950	2228	90.4	3.5	133	2460	77.0	3.9	113	683	53.9	1.1	79	3315	84.5	5.3	124
25-54	57125	1563	63.4	2.7	103	2246	70.3	3.9	114	850	67.0	1.5	109	2758	70.3	4.8	114
Employed Full Time	62271	1955	79.3	3.1	118	2141	67.0	3.4	100	977	77.0	1.6	115	2981	76.0	4.8	113
Part-time	5250	*227	9.2	4.3	163	*141	4.4	2.7	78	*10	0.8	0.2	14	*300	7.7	5.7	135
Sole Wage Earner	21027	554	22.5	2.6	99	794	24.9	3.8	110	332	26.2	1.6	115	894	22.8	4.3	100
Not Employed	25153	*284	11.5	1.1	42	912	28.6	3.6	105	*281	22.2	1.1	82	643	16.4	2.6	60
Professional	9010	*232	9.4	2.6	97	*168	5.3	1.9	54	*143	11.3	1.6	116	504	12.8	5.6	132
Executive/Admin./Managerial	10114	*259	10.5	2.6	96	*305	9.6	3.0	88	*185	14.6	1.8	134	353	9.0	3.5	82
Clerical/Sales/Technical	13212	436	17.7	3.3	124	*420	13.2	3.2	92	*231	18.2	1.7	128	741	18.9	5.6	132
Precision/Crafts/Repair	12162	624	25.3	5.1	193	*317	9.9	2.6	76	*168	13.2	1.4	101	511	13.0	4.2	99
Other Employed	23022	631	25.6	2.7	103	1071	33.5	4.7	135	*261	20.6	1.1	83	1173	29.9	5.1	120
H/D Income $75,000 or More	17969	481	19.5	2.7	101	*320	10.0	1.8	52	413	32.5	2.3	168	912	23.2	5.1	120
$60,000 - 74,999	10346	*368	14.9	3.6	134	*309	9.7	3.0	87	*142	11.2	1.4	100	495	12.6	4.8	113
$50,000 - 59,999	9175	*250	10.2	2.7	103	*424	13.3	4.6	134	*153	12.1	1.7	122	*371	9.4	4.0	95
$40,000 - 49,999	11384	*308	12.5	2.7	102	*387	12.1	3.4	99	*134	10.6	1.2	86	580	14.8	5.1	120
$30,000 - 39,999	12981	*360	14.6	2.8	104	542	17.0	4.2	121	*126	10.0	1.0	71	*416	10.6	3.2	76
$20,000 - 29,999	13422	*266	10.8	2.0	75	*528	16.5	3.9	114	*164	12.9	1.2	89	*475	12.1	3.5	84
$10,000 - 19,999	11867	*401	16.3	3.4	127	*394	12.3	3.3	96	*67	5.3	0.6	41	*481	12.3	4.1	96
Less than $10,000	5528	*31	1.3	0.6	21	*291	9.1	5.3	153	*69	5.4	1.2	91	*194	4.9	3.5	83

Source: Mediamark Research Inc., Mediamark Research Men's, Women's Personal Care Products Report (Mediamark Research Inc., Spring 1997), 16. Reprinted with permission.

EXHIBIT 14.10

Commercial research firms can provide advertisers with an evaluation of a brand's relative strength within demographic segments. Exhibit 14.10 is a typical data table from Mediamark Research showing how various men's aftershave and cologne brands perform in different demographic segments.
www.mediamark.com/

wasteful. As shown in Exhibit 14.11, the targeting of specific geographic markets has the additional benefit of allowing advertisers to cater messages directly to the people in those geographic areas.

When factors such as brand performance or competitors' activities are taken into account, media objectives for geographic scope become more complicated. For example, the strength of microbreweries in the northeastern and northwestern United States has forced major national brewers such as Miller Brewing and Anheuser-Busch not only to develop specialty beers, such as Red Wolf, but also to alter their geographic media objectives to provide different coverage based on the competitive intensity of these markets. In markets where microbreweries are particularly strong, Miller and A-B buy extra media time or run special promotions to combat the competition.

Some analysts suggest that when certain geographic markets demonstrate unusually high purchasing tendencies by product category or by brand, then geo-targeting should be the basis for the media placement decision. **Geo-targeting** is the placement of ads in geographic regions where higher purchase tendencies for a brand are evident. For example, in one geographic area the average consumer purchases of Prego spaghetti sauce were 36 percent greater than the average consumer purchases nationwide. With this kind of information, media buys can be geo-targeted to reinforce high-volume users.[6]

6.   This section and the example are drawn from Erwin Ephron, "The Organizing Principle of Media," *Inside Media,* November 2, 1992.

IT'S HARD TO SELL
"POP"
TO PEOPLE WHO DRINK
"SODA."

Every savvy marketer knows that, although they both have identical ingredients, pop and soda are completely different things depending on what part of the country you're in. On local television stations, you can speak to customers in the language they identify with. Local television also allows you to concentrate your message in the areas where you sell the most product. For a better way to connect your brand to local communities, call the Television Bureau of Advertising toll-free at 1-877-486-2528 or see our site at www.tvb.org **LOCAL TV** A better connection

EXHIBIT 14.11

Targeting local markets. www.tvb.org/

The final media objective is *message weight,* the total mass of advertising delivered. **Message weight** is the gross number of advertising messages or exposure opportunities delivered by the vehicles in a schedule. An important issue in message weight is that the measurement includes duplication of exposure; that is, an individual may be counted more than one time in a message weight calculation. Unduplicated audience measurement, known as *reach,* is discussed in the next section, dealing with media strategies. Media planners are interested in the message weight of a media plan because it provides a simple indication of the size of the advertising effort being placed against a specific market.

Message weight is typically expressed in terms of gross impressions. **Gross impressions** represent the sum of exposures to the entire media placement in a media plan. Planners often distinguish between two types of exposure. *Potential ad impressions* or *opportunities* to be exposed to ads are the most common meanings and refer to exposures by the media vehicle carrying advertisements (for example, a program or publication). *Message impressions,* on the other hand, refers to exposures to the ads themselves. Information on ad exposure probabilities can be obtained from a number of companies, including Nielsen, Simmons, Roper-Starch, Gallup & Robinson, Harvey Research, and Readex. This information can pertain to particular advertisements, campaigns, media vehicles, product categories, ad characteristics, and target groups.

For example, consider a media plan that, in a one-week period, placed ads on three television programs and in two national newspapers. The sum of the exposures to the media placement might be as follows:

		Gross Impressions	
		Media Vehicle	**Advertisement**
Television:	Program A audience	16,250,000	5,037,500
	Program B audience	4,500,000	1,395,000
	Program C audience	7,350,000	2,278,500
Sum of TV exposures		28,100,000	8,711,000
Newspapers:	Newspaper 1	1,900,000	376,200
	Newspaper 2	450,000	89,100
Sum of newspaper exposures		2,350,000	465,300
Total gross impressions		30,450,000	9,176,300

Of course, this does not mean that 30,450,000 separate people were exposed to the programs and newspapers or that 9,176,300 separate people were exposed to the advertisements. Some people who watched TV program A also saw program B and read newspaper 1, as well as all other possible combinations. This is called **between-vehicle duplication**. It is also possible that someone who saw the ad in newspaper 1 on Monday saw it again in newspaper 1 on Tuesday. This is **within-vehicle duplication**. That's why we say that the total gross impressions number contains audience duplication. Data available from services such as SMRB report both types of duplication so that they may be removed from the gross impressions to produce the unduplicated estimate of audience, called *reach.* (You should know, however, that the math involved in such calculations is fairly complex.) The concept of reach is discussed in the next section.

The message weight objective provides only a broad perspective for a media planner. What does it mean that a media plan for a week produced more than 30 million gross impressions? It means only that a fairly large number of people were potentially exposed to the advertiser's message. This does not mean that message weight is unimportant, however; it provides a general point of reference. When Toyota Motors introduced the Avalon in the U.S. market, the $40 million introductory ad campaign featured 30-second television spots, newspaper and magazine print ads (see Exhibit 14.12 for an example), and direct mail pieces. The highlight of the campaign was a nine-spot placement on a heavily watched Thursday evening TV show, costing more than $2 million. The message weight of this campaign in a single week was enormous—just the type of objective Toyota's media planners wanted for the brand introduction.[7]

Media Strategies.

Media objectives provide the foundation for media selection. The true power of a media plan, though, is in the media strategy. This strategy is expressed in decisions made with respect to a media vehicle's reach and frequency, the continuity of media placement, the audience duplication, and the length and size of advertisements. Good media strategy decisions help ensure that messages placed in chosen media have as much impact as possible.

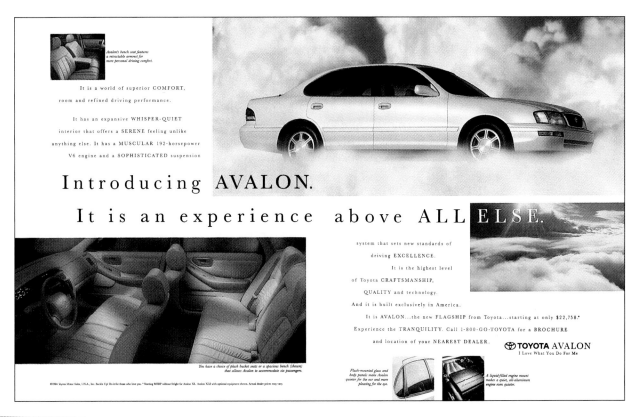

EXHIBIT 14.12

What is the importance of message weight for the introduction of a new product such as the Avalon? Is it important that the advertiser be able to distinguish between gross impressions and audience reach in this type of campaign? At the Web site for Toyota at www.toyota.com/, options include virtual showrooms, feedback forms, and an owners-only link that may help the company measure advertising impact and reach. Compare the Toyota site to Nissan's at www.nissan.com/. What is a striking difference between these two sites? Which site uses the new media most effectively? Why?

7.   Bradley Johnson, "Toyota's New Avalon Thinks Big, American," *Advertising Age,* November 14, 1994, 46.

EXHIBIT 14.13

Reach is an important measure of a media vehicle's effectiveness.

Reach and Frequency. Reach refers to the number of people or households in a target audience that will be exposed to a media vehicle or schedule at least one time during a given period of time (see Exhibit 14.13). It is often expressed as a percentage. If an advertisement placed on the hit network television program *ER* is watched at least once by 30 percent of the advertiser's target audience, then the reach is said to be 30 percent. Media vehicles with broad reach are ideal for consumer convenience goods, such as toothpaste and cold remedies. These are products with fairly simple features, and they are frequently purchased by a broad cross-section of the market. Broadcast television, cable television, and national magazines have the largest and broadest reach of any of the media, due to their national and even global coverage. For example, as explained in the Global Issues box on page 450, placing ads on cable TV is an excellent method to achieve broad reach across Latin America.

Frequency is the average number of times an individual or household within a target audience is exposed to a media vehicle in a given period of time (typically a week or a month). For example, say an advertiser places an ad on a weekly television show with a 20 rating (20 percent of households) four weeks in a row. The show has an (unduplicated) reach of 43 (percent) over the four-week period. So, frequency is then equal to $(20 \times 4)/43$, or 1.9. This means that an audience member had the opportunity to see the ad an average of 1.9 times.

An important measure for media planners related to both reach and frequency is **gross rating points (GRP)**. GRP is the product of reach times frequency ($GRP = r \times f$). When media planners calculate the GRP for a media plan, they multiply the rating (reach) of each vehicle in a plan times the number of times an ad will be inserted in the media vehicle and sum these figures across all vehicles in the plan. Exhibit 14.14 shows the GRP for a combined magazine and television schedule.

EXHIBIT 14.14

Gross rating points (GRP) for a media plan.

Media Class/Vehicle	Rating (reach)	Number of Ad Insertions (frequency)	GRP
Television			
ER	25	4	100
Law & Order	20	4	80
Good Morning America	12	4	48
Days of Our Lives	7	2	14
Magazines			
People	22	2	44
Travel & Leisure	11	2	22
U.S. News & World Report	9	6	54
Total			362

The GRP number is used as a relative measure of the intensity of one media plan versus another. Whether a media plan is appropriate or not is ultimately based on the judgment of the media planner.

TAKING NO CHANCES—ADS THAT GO OFF- AND ONLINE

Suretrade.com (www.suretrade.com/) is the new online brokerage service from Quick & Reilly—a flat-fee brokerage service for trading stocks, bonds, mutual funds, and other securities. When the brokerage introduced this online trading version of its service, it took no chance in trying to communicate with potential customers. Quick & Reilly invested heavily in both offline and online advertising.

Offline, the firm used cable TV and print advertising designed to draw potential customers to the site. The online advertising offered more details about how Suretrade.com worked and allowed visitors to click through the service itself. Like many companies that are adding Web activities to their integrated marketing communications mix, Quick & Reilly used separate agencies for the online versus the offline ad development. CKS/SiteSpecific in New York created the online ads, while Wieden & Kennedy handled the traditional media ads.

One of the interesting aspects of this particular integration of new electronic and traditional media is that Quick & Reilly is not just splitting messages, they are pretty much splitting their $30 million annual budget between the two options. A consultant to Suretrade.com revealed that "[W]e're essentially pretty close to splitting the advertising budget for the fourth quarter about 50/50 between online and offline."

In true IMC style, both the online and offline campaigns focus on the same message objective—creating awareness for the Suretrade.com brand name. During the Weiden & Kennedy TV commericals, the Internet address name stayed on the screen for the full 30 seconds while a variety of scenes rotated through the background. The account executive explained that "[W]e feel we can convey a lot of information by focusing on the logo." The online campaign appeared on about 50 sites.

The president of the online agency described the IMC synergy of the two campaigns this way: "You see the commercial and then you go online and you see a sponsorship and then when you go to the Suretrade.com site, you're ready to sign up. You get the best of online with the best of offline."

Source: Beth Snyder, "Off-, Online Ads Provide One-Two Punch for Broker," *Advertising Age*, November 17, 1997, 32.

Advertisers often struggle with the dilemma of increasing reach at the expense of frequency, or vice versa. At the core in this struggle are the concepts of effective frequency and effective reach. **Effective frequency** is the number of times a target audience needs to be exposed to a message before the objectives of the advertiser are met—either communications objectives or sales impact. Many factors affect the level of effective frequency. New brands and brands laden with features may demand high frequency. Simple messages for well-known products may require less-frequent exposure for consumers to be affected. While most analysts agree that one exposure will typically not be enough, there is debate about how many exposures are enough. A common industry practice is to place effective frequency at three exposures, but analysts argue that as few as two or as many as nine exposures are needed to achieve effective frequency.[8]

Effective reach is the number or percentage of consumers in the target audience that are exposed to an ad some minimum number of times. The minimum–number estimate for effective reach is based on a determination of effective frequency. If effective reach is set at four exposures, then a media schedule must be devised that achieves at least four exposures over a specified time period within the target audience.

Continuity. The second important strategic decision in the media plan is about continuity. **Continuity** is the pattern of placement of advertisements in a media schedule. There are three strategic scheduling alternatives: continuous, flighting, and pulsing. **Continuous scheduling** is a pattern of placing ads at a steady rate over a period of time. Running one ad each day for four weeks during the soap opera *General Hospital* would be a continuous pattern. Similarly, an ad that appeared in every issue of *Redbook* magazine for a year would also be

8.   For a complete discussion of the evolution of the concepts of effective reach and effective frequency, see Jack Z. Sissors and Lincoln Bumba, *Advertising Media Planning,* 5th ed. (Lincolnwood, Ill.: NTC Business Books, 1996), 115–147.

continuous. **Flighting** is another media-scheduling strategy. Flighting is achieved by scheduling heavy advertising for a period of time, usually two weeks, then stopping advertising altogether for a period, only to come back with another heavy schedule.

GLOBAL ISSUES

REACHING THE LATIN AMERICAN CONSUMER: ADVERTISERS PLUG IN TO CABLE

With a potential audience of 470 million consumers, advertisers are keeping a keen eye on Latin America, including Mexico, Argentina, Venezuela, Chile, and Brazil. The traditional and emerging professional elite that occupies top professional and executive positions represents 14 percent of the population. In addition, the professional and skilled middle class represents 33 percent of the population. The size and growing professionalism of the population is just a foundation for advertisers' interest.

What makes Latin America an exciting prospect for U.S. advertisers is the ability to reach this huge potential audience with increased precision and efficiency. Latin America is increasingly the target of pan-regional advertising. Pan-regional ads are created for the entire Latin American market rather than for a single country. Satellite and cable television systems are reaching upscale consumers and raising the prospect of extended, multicountry reach for international advertisers. The unifying factor making pan-regional campaigns more effective and cost-efficient is that while fewer than 16 percent of Latin American homes have cable or satellite access, these consumers control more than 50 percent of the region's disposable income.

Typical of the marketers who have adopted a pan-regional approach to reach their target markets are MasterCard International and FedEx. MasterCard uses images of ocean sunsets and urban energy to create a Latin American campaign around its tag line "One currency." The vice president of marketing for MasterCard says, "For us, it's pretty easy because it's international utility that we are selling." FedEx has advertised in Latin America since 1984 but broke its first pan-regional campaign in 1994. With the niche programming offered by cable, FedEx can hit specific demographic groups with ESPN and the Discovery Channel.

With the reach provided by cable and the growth of the upper and middle class, pan-regional campaigns by firms such as MasterCard, FedEx, Coca-Cola, and Shell Oil have boosted advertising spending by 9 percent annually in the region, to nearly $20 billion. Overall, the future looks bright for reaching and selling to Latin American consumers.

Sources: Jeffery D. Zbar, "Latin America," *Advertising Age International*, March 11, 1996, 119; Jeffery D. Zbar, "Advertisers Drop Markets for Latin Buy," *Advertising Age International*, March 11, 1996, 120.

Flighting is often used to support special seasonal merchandising efforts or new product introductions, or as a response to competitors' activities. The financial advantages of flighting are that discounts might be gained by concentrating media buys in larger blocks. Communication effectiveness may be enhanced because a heavy schedule can achieve the repeat exposures necessary to achieve consumer awareness. For example, the ad in Exhibit 14.15 was run heavily in December issues of magazines, to take advantage of seasonal dessert consumption patterns.

Finally, **pulsing** is a media-scheduling strategy that combines elements from continuous and flighting techniques. Advertisements are scheduled continuously in media over a period of time, but with periods of much heavier scheduling (the flight). Pulsing is most appropriate for products that are sold fairly regularly all year long but have, like clothing, certain seasonal requirements.

Length or Size of Advertisements. Beyond whom to reach, how often to reach them, and in what pattern, media planners must make strategic decisions regarding the length of an ad in electronic media or the size of an ad in print media. Certainly, the advertiser, creative director, art director, and copywriter have made determinations in this regard as well. Television advertisements (excluding infomercials) can range from 10 seconds to 60 seconds, and sometimes even two minutes, in length. Is a 60-second television commercial always six times more effective than a 10-second spot? Of course, the answer is no. Is a full-page newspaper ad always more effective than a two-inch, one-column ad? Again, not necessarily. Advertisers use full-page newspaper ads when a product claim warrants it. This was the case with Quaker Oats when the FDA determined that oatmeal had beneficial dietary effects, as shown in Exhibit 14.16.

WEB SIGHTING

Why is this man smiling?

OLD FASHIONED QUAKER OATS 100% NATURAL

**FDA Proposes
First Food-Specific Health Claim:**

Diets high in oatmeal and low in saturated fat and
cholesterol may reduce the risk of heart disease.

The Food and Drug Administration has tentatively determined that there is enough scientific evidence to support the claim that a diet high in oatmeal and low in saturated fat and cholesterol may reduce the risk of heart disease. Through April 3, 1996, the FDA will be accepting comments from all interested parties before finalizing its decision. Choosing a diet that is low in saturated fat and cholesterol and includes plenty of fruits, grains and vegetables may help lower your risk of heart disease. Other heart healthy steps to take include watching your weight and exercising regularly. And, of course, if you have elevated cholesterol levels, consult your physician.

EXHIBIT 14.15

An example of a print ad that was flighted during December—a month in which whipped-cream dessert toppings figure prominently.
www.reddi-wip.com/

EXHIBIT 14.16

When the Food and Drug Administration announced that oatmeal might have several beneficial health effects, Quaker Oats took the opportunity to run full-page newspaper ads in USA Today. The Web gives companies the opportunity to tell "the rest of the story" in tremendous detail, letting the consumer wander in whatever direction is of interest; Quaker Oats' Web site (www.quakeroats.com) does everything from honoring African-American women as community leaders (remember, this is the company that used Aunt Jemima to market its syrup—best to show a '90s face!) to explain the opportunities it provides small business suppliers. Do you think most purchasers of Quaker Oats products visit the site? Compare Claritin, a pharmaceutical brand (www.claritin.com). Early in its marketing campaign, Claritin used rather sparse print ads that neither made medicinal claims, nor had to be cluttered with legal disclaimers, but they did note Claritin's Web address.

The decision about the length or size of an advertisement depends on the creative requirements for the ad, the media budget, and the competitive environment within which the ad is running. From a creative standpoint, ads attempting to develop an image for a brand may need to be longer in broadcast media or larger in print media to offer more creative opportunities. On the other hand, a simple, straightforward message announcing a sale may be quite short or small, but it may need heavy repetition. From the standpoint of the media budget, shorter and smaller ads are, with few exceptions, much less expensive. If a media plan includes some level of repetition to accomplish its objectives, the lower-cost option may be mandatory. From a competitive perspective, matching a competitor's presence with messages of similar size or length may be essential to maintain the share of mind in a target audience. Once again, the size and length decisions are a matter of judgment between the creative team and the media planner, tempered by the availability of funds for media placement.

Media Choices. The next stage of the media-planning process focuses on media selection. Exhibit 14.17 gives general ratings for the major media. The advertiser and the agency team determine which media class is appropriate for the current effort, based on criteria similar to those listed in Exhibit 14.17. These criteria give a general orientation to major media and the inherent capabilities of each media class.

Media choice addresses three distinct issues: media mix, media efficiency, and competitive media assessment.

Media Mix. In making specific media choices for placing advertisements, media planners have to decide what sort of media mix to use. The **media mix** is the blend of different media that will be used to effectively reach the target audience. There are two options for a media planner with respect to the media mix: a concentrated media mix or an assorted media mix.[9] A **concentrated media mix** focuses all the media placement dollars in one medium. The rationale behind this option is that it allows an advertiser to have great impact on a specific audience segment. A highly concentrated media mix can give a brand an aura of mass acceptance, especially within an audience

EXHIBIT 14.17

Evaluation of traditional major media options.

| Characteristics | Medium | | | | | | | | |
	Broadcast TV	Cable TV	Radio	News-paper	Maga-zines	Direct Mail	Outdoor	Transit	Directory
Reach									
Local	M	M	H	H	L	H	H	H	M
National	H	H	L	L	H	M	L	L	M
Frequency	H	H	H	M	L	L	M	M	L
Selectivity									
Audience	M	H	H	L	H	H	L	L	L
Geographic	L	M	H	H	M	H	H	H	H
Audience reactions									
Involvement	L	M	L	M	H	M	L	L	H
Acceptance	M	M	M	H	M	L	M	M	H
Audience data	M	L	L	M	H	H	L	L	M
Clutter	H	H	H	M	M	M	M	L	H
Creative flexibility	H	H	H	L	M	M	L	L	L
Cost factors									
Per contact	L	L	L	M	M	H	L	L	M
Absolute cost	H	H	M	M	H	H	M	M	M

H = High, M = Moderate, L = Low

9.   Arnold M. Barban, Steven M. Cristol, and Frank J. Kopec, *Essentials of Media Planning: A Marketing Viewpoint,* 3rd ed. (Lincolnwood, Ill.: NTC Business Books, 1993), 76–80.

with restricted media exposure.[10] The range of benefits possible from a concentrated media mix are as follows:

- It may allow the advertiser to be dominant in one medium relative to the competition.
- Brand familiarity might be heightened, especially within target audiences that have a narrow range of media exposure.
- Concentrating media buys in high-visibility media, such as prime-time television or large advertising sections in premium magazines, can create enthusiasm and loyalty in a trade channel. Distributors and retailers may give a brand with heavily concentrated media exposure preferential treatment in inventory or shelf display.
- A concentration of media dollars may result in significant volume discounts from media organizations.

An **assorted media mix** employs multiple media alternatives to reach target audiences. The assorted mix can be advantageous to an advertiser because it facilitates communication with multiple market segments. By using a mix of media, an advertiser can place different messages for different target audiences in different media. In general, the advantages of an assorted media mix are as follows:

- An advertiser can reach different target audiences with messages tailored to each target's unique interests in the product category or brand.
- Different messages in different media reaching a single target may enhance the learning effect.
- Assorted media placement will increase the reach of a message, compared to concentrating placement in one medium.
- The probability of reaching audiences exposed to diverse media is greater with an assorted media mix.

One caution should be offered with the assorted media mix approach. Since different media placements require different creative and production efforts, the cost of preparing advertisements can increase dramatically. Preparing both print and broadcast versions of an ad may draw funds away from media expenditures. Using funds for multiple preparations likely will come at the expense of other important goals, such as gross impressions or GRP.

Media Efficiency. Each medium under consideration in a media plan must be scrutinized for the efficiency with which it performs. In other words, which media deliver the largest target audiences at the lowest cost? A common measure of media efficiency is cost per thousand. **Cost per thousand (CPM)** is the dollar cost of reaching 1,000 (the M in CPM comes from the roman numeral for 1,000) members of an audience using a particular medium. The CPM calculation can be used to compare the relative efficiency of two media choices within a media class (magazine versus magazine) or between media classes (magazine versus radio). The basic measure of CPM is fairly straightforward; the dollar cost for placement of an ad in a medium is divided by the total audience and multiplied by 1,000. Let's calculate the CPM for a full-page black-and-white ad in the Friday edition of *USA Today:*

$$\text{CPM} = \frac{\text{cost of media buy}}{\text{total audience}} \times 1{,}000$$

$$\text{CPM for } USA\ Today = \frac{\$72{,}000}{5{,}206{,}000} \times 1{,}000 = \$13.83$$

10. Leo Bogart, *Strategy in Advertising,* 2nd ed. (Lincolnwood, Ill.: NTC Business Books, 1984), 147.

These calculations show that *USA Today* has a CPM of $13.83 for a full-page black-and-white ad. But this calculation shows the cost of reaching the entire readership of *USA Today*. If the target audience is restricted to male college graduates in professional occupations, then the **cost per thousand–target market (CPM–TM)** calculation might be much higher for a general publication such as *USA Today* than for a more specialized publication such as *Fortune* magazine:

$$\text{CPM-TM for } \textit{USA Today} \quad = \quad \frac{\$72,000}{840,000} \times 1,000 = \$85.71$$

$$\text{CPM-TM for } \textit{Fortune} \quad = \quad \frac{\$54,800}{940,000} \times 1,000 = \$58.30$$

You can see that the relative efficiency of *Fortune* is much greater than that of *USA Today* when the target audience is specified more carefully and a CPM–TM calculation is made. An advertisement for business services appearing in *Fortune* will have a better CPM–TM than the same ad appearing in *USA Today*.

Information about ad cost, gross impressions, and target audience size is usually available from the medium itself. Detailed audience information to make a cost per thousand–target market analysis also is available from media research organizations, such as Simmons Market Research Bureau (for magazines) or A. C. Nielsen (for television). Cost information also can be obtained from Standard Rate and Data Service (SRDS) and Bacon's Media Directories, for example.

Like CPM, a **cost per rating point (CPRP)** calculation provides a relative efficiency comparison between media options. In this calculation, the cost of a media vehicle, such as a spot television program, is divided by the program's rating. (A rating point is equivalent to 1 percent of the target audience—for example, television households in the designated rating area tuned to a specific program.) Like the CPM calculation, the CPRP calculation gives a dollar figure, which can be used for comparing TV program efficiency. The calculation for CPRP is as follows, using television as an example.

$$\text{CPRP} \quad = \quad \frac{\text{dollar cost of ad placement on a program}}{\text{program rating}}$$

For example, an advertiser on WLTV (Univision 23) in the Miami–Ft. Lauderdale market may wish to compare household CPRP figures for 30-second announcements in various dayparts on the station. The calculations for early news and prime time programs are as follows.

$$\text{CPRP for WLTV early news} \quad = \quad \frac{\$2,205}{9} = \$245$$

$$\text{CPRP for WLTV prime time} \quad = \quad \frac{\$5,100}{10} = \$510$$

Clearly an early news daypart program delivers households more efficiently at $245 CPRP, less than half that of prime time, with approximately 90 percent of the typical prime-time rating.

It is important to remember that these efficiency assessments are based solely on costs and coverage. They say nothing about the quality of the advertising and thus should not be viewed as indicators of advertising effectiveness. When media efficiency measures such as CPM and CPM–TM are combined with an assessment of media objectives and media strategies, they can be quite useful. Taken alone and out of the broader campaign-planning context, such efficiency measures may lead to ineffective media buying.

Competitive Media Assessment. While media planners normally do not base an overall media plan on how much competitors are spending or where competitors are placing their ads, a competitive media assessment can provide a useful perspective. A competitive media assessment is particularly important for product categories in which all the competitors are focused on a narrowly defined target audience. This condition exists in several product categories in which heavy-user segments dominate consumption: snack foods, soft drinks, beer and wine, and chewing gum are examples. Brands of luxury cars and financial services also compete for common-buyer segments.

When a target audience is narrow and attracts the attention of several major competitors, an advertiser must assess its competitors' spending and the relative share of voice its brand is getting. **Share of voice** is a calculation of any one advertiser's brand expenditures relative to the overall spending in a category:

$$\text{share of voice} = \frac{\text{one brand's advertising expenditures in a medium}}{\text{total product category advertising expenditures in a medium}}$$

This calculation can be done for all advertising by a brand in relation to all advertising in a product category, or it can be done to determine a brand's share of product category spending on a particular advertising medium, such as network television or magazines. For example, athletic-footwear marketers spend approximately $310 million per year in measured advertising media. Nike and Reebok are the two top brands, with approximately $160 million and $55 million respectively in annual expenditures in measured advertising media. The share-of-voice calculations for both brands follow.

$$\text{Share of voice, Nike} = \frac{\$160 \text{ million}}{\$310 \text{ million}} \times 100 = 51.6\%$$

$$\text{Share of voice, Reebok} = \frac{\$55 \text{ million}}{\$310 \text{ million}} \times 100 = 17.7\%$$

Together, both brands dominate the product category advertising with a nearly 70 percent combined share of voice. Yet Nike's share of voice is nearly three times that of Reebok.

Research data, such as that provided by Competitive Media Reporting, can provide an assessment of share of voice in up to ten media categories. A detailed report shows how much a brand was advertised in a particular media category versus the combined media category total for all other brands in the same product category. Knowing what competitors are spending in a medium and how dominant they might be allows an advertiser to strategically schedule within a medium. Some strategists believe that scheduling in and around a competitor's schedule can create a bigger presence for a small advertiser.[11]

Consider how Leo Burnett scheduled advertising for Miller Lite on Super Bowl Sunday in 1994. Since the Super Bowl delivers such a high proportion of the beer-drinking target audience, strategists at Burnett were faced with the prospect of a very dense competitive environment—and a very expensive one, at $1 million for a 30-second spot. Anheuser-Busch had already scheduled its "Bud Bowl" spots during the Super Bowl. So, instead of going head-to-head with Anheuser-Busch in a cluttered, million-dollar-per-spot environment, Miller bought heavily during the pregame show. In this way, the brand achieved good exposure in the target segment without extraordinary expense in a cluttered environment.

As with the media efficiency measures discussed in the previous section, a competitive media assessment is normally not the only foundation for media planning. A competitive media assessment contains valuable information; however, media objectives and media strategies should be the driving forces behind media planning.

---

11. Andrea Rothman, "Timing Techniques Can Make Small Ad Budgets Seem Bigger," *Wall Street Journal,* February 3, 1989, B4; also see Robert J. Kent and Chris T. Allen, "Competitive Interference Effects in Consumer Memory for Advertising: The Role of Brand Familiarity," *Journal of Marketing* (July 1994): 97–105.

Media Scheduling and Buying. Media scheduling and buying are activities that take place throughout the planning effort. Media scheduling focuses on several issues related to timing and impact.[12] All aspects of timing, reach, frequency, and competitive media assessment are evaluated during the scheduling phase. In addition, the total media schedule is evaluated with respect to CPM or gross impressions to gauge the impact the entire schedule delivers in each time frame. Seasonal buying tendencies in the target segment also have a major impact on scheduling. Scheduling media more heavily when consumers show buying tendencies is referred to as **heavy-up scheduling**.[13]

One of the most important aspects of the media-scheduling phase involves creating a visual representation of the media schedule. Exhibit 14.18 shows a media schedule flowchart that includes both print and electronic media placement. With this visual representation of the schedule, the advertiser has tangible documentation of the overall media plan.

Once an overall media plan and schedule are in place, the focus must turn to media buying. **Media buying** entails securing the electronic media time and print media space specified in the schedule. An important part of the media-buying process is the agency of record. The **agency of record** is the advertising agency chosen by the advertiser to purchase time and space. The agency of record coordinates media discounts and negotiates all contracts for time and space. Any other agencies involved in the advertising effort submit insertion orders for time and space within those contracts.

Rather than using an agency of record, some advertisers use a **media-buying service**, which is an independent organization that specializes in buying large blocks of

EXHIBIT 14.18

A media flowchart gives an advertiser a visual representation of the overall media plan.

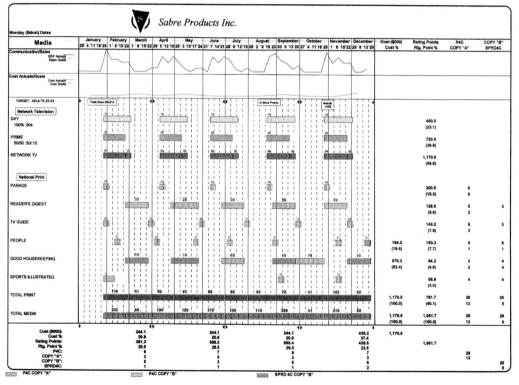

Source: Telmar Information Services Corp., FlowMaster for Windows™, New York, 1999. Reprinted with permission.

12. John J. Burnett, *Promotion Management* (Boston: Houghton Mifflin, 1993), 520–521.
13. Sissors and Bumba, *Advertising Media Planning,* 309–310.

media time and space and reselling it to advertisers (see Exhibit 14.19). Some agencies have developed their own media-buying units to control both the planning and the buying process.[14] Regardless of the structure used to make the buys, media buyers evaluate the audience reach, CPM, and timing of each buy. The organization responsible for the buy also monitors the ads and estimates the actual audience reach delivered. If the expected audience is not delivered, then media organizations have to **make good** by repeating ad placements or offering a refund or price reduction on future ads. For example, making good to advertisers because of shortfalls in delivering 1998 Winter Olympics prime-time cost CBS an estimated 400 additional 30-second spots.[15]

Computer Media-Planning Models. ❖ The explosion of available data on markets
and consumers has motivated media planners to rely heavily on electronic databases, computers, and software to assist with the various parts of the media-planning effort.

Nearly all of the major syndicated research services offer electronic data to their subscribers, including advertisers, agencies, and media organizations. These databases contain information helpful in identifying target markets and audiences, estimating or projecting media vehicle audiences and costs, and analyzing competitive advertising activity, among many others. Companies that offer data electronically, such as Nielsen, Arbitron, MRI, SMRB, Scarborough, and the Audit Bureau of Circulations, also typically provide software designed to analyze their own data. Such software often produces summary reports, tabulations, ranking, reach-frequency analysis, optimization, simulation, scheduling, buying, flowcharts, and a variety of graphical presentations.

Advertisers that use a mix of media in their advertising campaigns often subscribe to a variety of electronic data services representing the media they use or consider using. However, the various syndicated services do not provide standardized data, reports, and analyses that are necessarily comparable across media categories. Also, individual syndicated service reports and analyses may not offer the content and depth that some users prefer. Nor do they typically analyze media categories that they do not measure. Consequently, media software houses such as Interactive Market Systems (IMS) and Telmar Information Services Corp. (Telmar) offer hundreds of specialized and standardized software products that help advertisers, agencies, and media organizations worldwide develop and evaluate markets, audiences, and multi-media plans. Exhibit 14.20 shows typical screens from one such computer program. The first screen is reach and cost data for spot TV ads, and the second screen is the combined reach and cost data for spot TV and newspaper ads.

Computerization and modeling can never substitute for planning and judgment by media strategists. Computer modeling does, however, allow for the assessment of a wide range of possibilities before making costly media buys.

EXHIBIT 14.19

An example of a media-buying service.

14. Joe Mandese, "Ayer Adjusts to Complex Media Buys," *Advertising Age,* December 12, 1994, 6.
15. "CBS Faces Olympics Make-Goods." Available online at www.adage.com/, February 19, 1998.

```
------------------------------------------------------
ADplus(TM) RESULTS:  SPOT TV (30S)

Walt Disney World        Frequency (f) Distributions
Off-Season Promotion     -------------------------------
Monthly                      Vehicle          Message
                          -------------    -------------
Target:    973,900         f   % f   % f+    % f   % f+
Jacksonville DMA Adults   ---  ----- -----   ----- -----
                           0   5.1   ---     9.1   ---
Message/vehicle = 32.0%    1   2.0   94.9    7.5   90.9
                           2   2.2   92.9    8.1   83.4
                           3   2.3   90.7    8.1   75.2
                           4   2.4   88.3    7.8   67.1
                           5   2.4   85.9    7.2   59.3
                           6   2.5   83.5    6.6   52.1
                           7   2.5   81.0    6.0   45.5
                           8   2.5   78.5    5.3   39.5
                           9   2.5   76.0    4.7   34.2
                          10+  73.5  73.5   29.5   29.5
                          20+  49.8  49.8    6.1    6.1

Summary Evaluation
------------------
Reach 1+ (%)                     94.9%           90.9%
Reach 1+ (000s)                  923.9           885.3

Reach 3+ (%)                     90.7%           75.2%
Reach 3+ (000s)                  882.9           732.8

Gross rating points (GRPs)     2,340.0           748.8
Average frequency (f)             24.7             8.2
Gross impressions (000s)      22,789.3         7,292.6
Cost-per-thousand (CPM)            6.10           19.06
Cost-per-rating point (CPP)         59             186
```

Vehicle List	Rating	Ad Cost	CPM-MSG	Ads	Total Cost	Mix %
WJKS-ABC-AM	6.00	234	12.51	30	7,020	5.1
WJXT-CBS-AM	6.00	234	12.51	30	7,020	5.1
WTLV-NBC-AM	6.00	234	12.51	30	7,020	5.1
WJKS-ABC-DAY	5.00	230	14.76	60	13,800	9.9
WJXT-CBS-DAY	5.00	230	14.76	60	13,800	9.9
WTLV-NBC-DAY	5.00	230	14.76	60	13,800	9.9
WJKS-ABC-PRIM	10.00	850	27.27	30	25,500	18.4
WJXT-CBS-PRIM	10.00	850	27.27	30	25,500	18.4
WTLV-NBC-PRIM	10.00	850	27.27	30	25,500	18.4
		Totals:	19.06	360	138,960	100.0

```
------------------------------------------------------
ADplus(TM) RESULTS:  DAILY NEWSPAPERS (1/2 PAGE), SPOT TV (30S)

Walt Disney World        Frequency (f) Distributions
Off-Season Promotion     -------------------------------
Monthly                      Vehicle          Message
                          -------------    -------------
Target:    973,900         f   % f   % f+    % f   % f+
Jacksonville DMA Adults   ---  ----- -----   ----- -----
                           0   1.2   ---     4.0   ---
Message/vehicle = 28.1%    1   0.8   98.8    4.9   96.0
                           2   0.9   98.0    5.9   91.1
                           3   0.9   97.2    6.5   85.2
                           4   1.0   96.2    6.7   78.7
                           5   1.1   95.2    6.8   72.0
                           6   1.1   94.2    6.6   65.2
                           7   1.2   93.0    6.3   58.6
                           8   1.3   91.8    5.9   52.4
                           9   1.3   90.6    5.5   46.5
                          10+  89.3  89.3   41.0   41.0
                          20+  73.3  73.3    9.6    9.6

Summary Evaluation
------------------
Reach 1+ (%)                     98.8%           96.0%
Reach 1+ (000s)                  962.6           934.6

Reach 3+ (%)                     97.2%           85.2%
Reach 3+ (000s)                  946.5           829.7

Gross rating points (GRPs)     3,372.0           948.0
Average frequency (f)             34.1             9.9
Gross impressions (000s)      32,839.9         9,232.3
Cost-per-thousand (CPM)           10.96           38.99
Cost-per-rating point (CPP)        107             380
```

Vehicle List	Rating	Ad Cost	CPM-MSG	Ads	Total Cost	Mix %
1 DAILY NEWSPAPERS		Totals:	114.00	80	221,040	61.4
Times-Union	42.00	8,284	104.93	20	165,680	46.0
Record	4.00	866	115.18	20	17,320	4.8
News	3.20	926	153.95	20	18,520	5.1
Reporter	2.40	976	216.35	20	19,520	5.4
2 SPOT TV (30S)		Totals:	19.00	360	138,960	38.6
WJKS-ABC-AM	6.00	234	12.51	30	7,020	2.0
WJXT-CBS-AM	6.00	234	12.51	30	7,020	2.0
WTLV-NBC-AM	6.00	234	12.51	30	7,020	2.0
WJKS-ABC-DAY	5.00	230	14.76	60	13,800	3.8
WJXT-CBS-DAY	5.00	230	14.76	60	13,800	3.8
WTLV-NBC-DAY	5.00	230	14.76	60	13,800	3.8
WJKS-ABC-PRIM	10.00	850	27.27	30	25,500	7.1
WJXT-CBS-PRIM	10.00	850	27.27	30	25,500	7.1
WTLV-NBC-PRIM	10.00	850	27.27	30	25,500	7.1
		Totals:	38.99	440	360,000	100.0

Source: Kent M. Lancaster, ADplus with FlowMaster™: For Multi-Media Advertising Planning, Windows™ edition. New York: Telmar Information Services Corp. and Media Research Institute, Inc., 1999. Reprinted with permission.

EXHIBIT 14.20

The explosion of data about markets and consumers has caused advertisers to rely more on computerized media-planning tools.

Other Ongoing Challenges in the Media Environment.

Several additional challenges add to the complexity of media planning. To explain these additional complications, we will review five dynamic aspects of the media environment: the proliferation of media options; insufficient and inaccurate information; escalating media costs; interactive media; and the complications of media choice in the new era of integrated marketing communications.

The Proliferation of Media Options.

One of the most daunting challenges for media placement is simply keeping track of the media options available. There are two areas where media proliferation is occurring. First, there has been an expansion of traditional media, both globally and in the United States. Where there were once just three broadcast television networks, there are now five or six. Cable television is also expanding rapidly, and the new smaller satellite dishes now offer consumers an even greater range of pro-

Before Your Customers Get On The Plane, We'll Take Them Around The World

With CNN Airport Network, you can offer waiting air travellers live, breaking news, plus up-to-the-minute reports on business, sports, weather and entertainment — updated around the clock.

It's a unique way to serve your customers while they wait for their flight.

And it's easy, because we do all the work — from installing state-of-the-art satellite equipment and televisions, to providing quality programming from CNN, the world's news leader.

So get on board — because this is one round-the-world flight you and your travellers simply shouldn't miss.

CNN Airport Network

FOR MORE INFORMATION CALL: DEBORAH LUNN COOPER/404.827.4454 (USA)

PARTICIPATING AIRPORTS

Atlanta-Hartsfield International Airport	Houston Intercontinental Airport	Raleigh-Durham International Airport
Boston-Logan International Airport	John F. Kennedy International Airport	Salt Lake City International Airport
Cincinnati/Northern Kentucky	LaGuardia Airport	San Francisco International Airport
International Airport	Memphis International Airport	Sarasota-Bradenton Airport
Chicago O'Hare International Airport	Miami International Airport	Seattle-Tacoma International Airport
Dallas/Fort Worth International Airport	Minneapolis/St. Paul International Airport	Southwest Florida International Airport
Detroit Metro Wayne County Airport	Nashville International Airport	Springfield-Branson Regional Airport
	Newark International Airport	Washington Dulles International Airport
	Orlando International Airport	Washington National Airport

EXHIBIT 14.21

How does the proliferation of media options such as CNN's Airport Network affect strategic decisions about media scheduling and media buying? Can you think of other products or services that might benefit from an increased focus on place-based media? At the CNN Web site, www.cnn.com/, the news is more interactive, because CNN lets you choose the headlines and stories you want to learn about. How do you think this will affect advertisers? Will ads be scheduled by individual story themes or by categories of news? To see how another news organization is using new media options, visit ABC News online at www.realaudio.com/contentp/abc.html to sample audio files. Does the use of Internet audio have implications for media-scheduling and media-buying decisions?

gramming. New magazines are being launched at a rate of more than one per day.[16] Advertisers can reach older consumers with *Modern Maturity*, preschoolers with *Sesame Street Magazine,* and everyone in between with numerous other magazines.

Second, new media are being developed to reach consumers in more and different ways. Retailers mail videotapes to consumers in carefully designated geographic areas to entice a trip to their retail store. Interactive video kiosks in Minneapolis grocery stores dispense Minnesota Twins baseball tickets and advertise team merchandise.[17] Turner Broadcasting has developed the CNN Airport Network, one of many new place-based media that reach consumers when they're not at home. The Airport Network transmits advertising along with news and entertainment programming to airport terminal gates around the United States. Advertisers who market travel-related services, such as American Express and AT&T, find this new media vehicle an ideal option. Exhibit 14.21 illustrates this new place-based network.

Interactive video kiosks, CD-ROM ads, online information services, movie theater ads (see Exhibit 14.22)—little is left untouched by the long arm of advertising placement. Many of the players in new media are big names in traditional media as well. The trade association Magazine Publishers of America estimates that more than 200 magazines are already involved with new media distribution platforms. This includes some of the biggest names in magazine publishing, such as *Newsweek* and *Time.*[18] *Newsweek* has attracted advertisers such as Honda, Chrysler, and Fidelity Investments now that the magazine has an interactive version on the Prodigy online service. There are many new players in the new media environment as well. *Launch* is a CD-ROM music magazine that contains reviews of albums with three 30-second song clips from each album, full-motion video interviews with popular bands, and three-minute movie reviews. *Launch* signed big advertisers such as Reebok International, Janus Mutual Funds, and Sony Electronics to an inaugural issue at $12,000 apiece. Overall, new media advertising is still low priced because the new media, at this point, lack the broad reach of traditional media. The typical CD-ROM magazine has a total audience of 150,000, versus five to ten times that for a traditional magazine. Of course, the creative flexibility of interactive sound and motion available on the CD-ROM format far exceeds the capabilities of print magazines.

Finally, the evolution of what used to be called direct mail into a new form of direct marketing, which will be discussed in detail in Chapter 19, has also created new opportunities for advertisers. The evolution began with the airlines and their in-flight magazines, and now firms of all types have started to publish newsletters, news magazines, and catalogs targeted at their current customers. As a way to increase efficiency in

16. Laura Loro, "Heavy Hitters Gamble on Launches," *Advertising Age,* October 19, 1992, S-13–S-14.
17. Debra Aho, "Kiosks: The Good, the Bad & Ugly," *Advertising Age,* January 17, 1994, 13.
18. Keith J. Kelly, "Publishers Pine for Cyber-Profits," *Advertising Age,* March 13, 1995, S-22.

shhhhh...we're watching a commercial

SCREENVISION
CINEMA NETWORK
IT'S MORE THAN TV. IT'S THE MOVIES.
1-800-ADFILMS

EXHIBIT 14.22

Movie-theater ads are yet another "new" media option.
www.screenvis.com/

reaching target audiences, advertisers have essentially created their own in-house media options. For example, TIAA-CREF, the largest pension fund in the world, publishes a quarterly news magazine called *The Participant*. Similarly, Physicians Mutual Insurance has a quarterly publication called *Between Friends,* which is mailed to insureds and passes along safety information, household tips, comments from customers, and a short memo from the president of the firm. These created media are efficient in that current and past customers are reached. The probability that the receiver will pay attention to the message is greater because there is some affinity for the firm sending the message.

Insufficient and Inaccurate Information. Placing ads in media that reach the intended target audience and few nontarget audience members is a tremendous challenge. The truth is that much of the information advertisers must use to make media choices is either insufficient for identifying how to reach a target audience or simply inaccurate. All the information used to identify who is using what medium at what time and in what numbers is generated as secondary data by large commercial media research organizations. Secondary data are frequently out-of-date or do not provide the category of measurement the marketer or advertiser is interested in.

Many of the problems related to media information are unique to the measurement situation; others are simply a matter of lack of availability. For example, no service provides audience measures for both AM and FM listening for *every* market in the United States. Another frustrating problem for advertisers is the accuracy of the measurement of television audience size. A nagging concern exists about the way television audiences have been measured. All television audience measurement services provide information on either individuals or homes tuned in to programs. These measures have been used as surrogates for actual exposure for many years. But, as we all know from personal experience, the fact that a household is tuned in to a program (as measured by a device attached to the television set) does not mean that exposure to the ad or attention to the ad has been achieved.

Nielsen, which holds a virtual monopoly on national television ratings in the United States, has been under pressure to improve the accuracy of its ratings.[19] Indeed, several firms, including General Electric (the parent of NBC), Disney/ABC, and CBS, have paid for a statistical analysis to examine ways of improving the ratings process. Some television stations have even dropped out of the

---

19. See Joe Mandese, "Rivals' Ratings Don't Match Up," *Advertising Age,* February 24, 1992, 50.

Nielsen rating program, claiming that the measurement periods, known as sweep periods, create an artificial measurement context.[20] (See Exhibit 14.23.) Nielsen has also come under fire for the accuracy of its methods in markets outside the United States. In Japan, Nielsen has been criticized for the way it breaks down the audiences for Japanese television broadcast programs.[21] Problems with media-audience measurement are among the reasons why so much pretesting of messages is done. Pretesting provides a "controlled" (albeit artifical) measure of effectiveness. In an environment where measuring the actual audience is so imprecise, advertisers are opting for pretesting rather than posttesting. In reality, both are problematic.

Finally, media organizations often provide information to advertisers in ways that are only marginally useful. While it is possible to get detailed information on the age, gender, and geographic location of target audiences, these characteristics may not be relevant to audience identification. Not all brands show clear tendencies among consumer groups based on Simmons or MRI data. Rather, consumer behavior is much more often influenced by peer groups, lifestyles, attitudes, and beliefs—which don't show up on commercial research reports. If we base our target marketing on these behavioral and experiential factors, then we would logically want to choose our media in the same way. But such information is often not available from media organizations, nor is it likely to be forthcoming (due to the cost of gathering these data). In fairness, some media kits from magazines targeted to upper-income consumers (such as *Smithsonian Magazine*) provide fairly detailed information on past purchase behaviors and some leisure activities. This information is the exception rather than the rule, however, and even then a lot is being assumed.

Escalating Media Costs.   While advertisers have always complained about media costs, the situation may be reaching a critical point. The cost of newspaper and magazine ads can reach into the hundreds of thousands of dollars for a single page. In 1998, the average cost

EXHIBIT 14.23

Advertisers debate whether television ratings are an accurate measure of audience.

20. "TV Station Drops Nielsen," *Marketing News,* March 11, 1996, 1.
21. Jennifer Cody, "Broadcasters Pan Nielsen Japan's Ratings," *Wall Street Journal,* November 9, 1994, B8.

for a 30-second spot during the Super Bowl was $1.3 million and in 1999 it escalated to $1.6 million. Spots during prime-time network television programs cost $80,000 to $500,000 for 30 seconds.

A REALLY STICKY SITUATION

You've read about all sorts of new media—electronic kiosks, virtual billboards, electronic newsletters, even rocket ships. But for something really new in media, you have to go to the 3M company in Minneapolis. You know, the people who brought you the little yellow sticky Post-it notes? Well, now there are Post-it Software Notes for Internet designers.

This is the way an electronic Post-it note works. The software program allows developers and online marketers to "stick" a digital Post-it note onto their Web sites to grab visitors' attention. Because visitors to the site can "drag" the note off the Web to their own computer desktops, it's an ingenious way for developers to keep their site and message in front of the receiver both off- and online. Once the Post-it is on the user's desktop, the note serves as a hot link back to the site. With a double click, the note launches the user's Web browser and sends him or her back to the marketer's site for another visit.

Another version of the program is designed for professional users. Developers can incorporate animation and sound into an electronic Post-it note. Using an .AVI file, a designer can animate the company logo, key a message to activate, or launch more complicated applications. The software will also allow a designer to create "play" and "stop" buttons that put control of the animation or sound in the hands of the visitor. This sort of capability will encourage more interaction between the visitor and the Post-it note.

The final capability is of value to both the marketer and the professional designer. The Post-it software can also generate notes specific to each individual site visitor. This is an ideal way to customize a message, which overcomes the major drawback of mass media–distributed messages. It is also a way to create an online receipt function for a site. This works especially well for marketers because with this function, a visitor can order a product directly from the Post-it message link rather than transferring to the home page.

Overall, the Post-it has tremendous potential for making it easier for marketers and visitors to link to each other. And because it seems so much more like communication and cyber-linkage, consumers may find it a very comfortable environment. If you want to check out the program and a pretty Web-savvy site, go to www.3m.com/webnotes/.

Source: 3M Company press release, August 26, 1998, Web delivered over Yahoo!

These sorts of price increases, as well as the high absolute dollar amount for media placement, have made advertisers scrutinize their media costs. Some advertisers are questioning the wisdom of massive expenditures on media with broad reach, such as network television. For the time being, big advertisers are still investing more in all forms of traditional mass media, but that might be changing with the growth of interactive media and the greater attention being paid to integrated marketing communications.[22]

Interactive Media. Aside from the escalating cost of traditional mass media options, the media environment has gotten considerably more challenging as interactive media have been refined. **Interactive media** reach beyond television and include kiosks in shopping malls or student unions, as you can read in the New Media box on this page. Also included are interactive telephones, interactive CDs, online services, the Internet, and online versions of magazines. Even such traditional, upscale outlets as Christie's auction house have started using home pages on the World Wide Web to publicize upcoming events (see Exhibit 14.24). The confounding factor for media placement decisions is that if consumers truly do begin to spend time with interactive media, they will have less time to spend with traditional media such as television and newspapers. This will force advertisers to choose whether to participate in (or develop their own) interactive media. (Chapter 17 deals exclusively with the Internet, including the audience measurement problems.)

In the beginning, a few shopping networks, such as QVC, and a few retailers, such as Macy's and Nordstrom, found interactive technology well suited to serving their customers with greater ease and conve-

22. Robert J. Coen, "Look for Bid Up of Desirable Media," *Advertising Age,* November 7, 1994, S-20–S-22.

nience. But interactive media are growing beyond a few retail-shopping experiments. U.S. West has announced ambitious plans to invest several billion dollars to build multimedia networks in 20 cities in the United States through 1999.[23] Although no one knows for sure whether consumers will use interactive television for home shopping, education, games, movie rental, or other entertainment programming, the chairman and CEO of U.S. West, Richard D. McCormick, says firmly, "We want consumers to have access to any piece of information in the multimedia sense, anytime they want it."[24] Big players such as Time Warner, Bell Atlantic, Tele-Communications, and Cablevision Systems see similar potential in interactive media, because they are all developing their own interactive options for advertisers.

Media Choice and Integrated Marketing Communications.
A final complicating factor in the media environment is that more firms are adopting an integrated marketing communications (IMC) perspective, which relies on a broader mix of communication tools. IMC is the process of creating a comprehensive communication plan using a broad range of promotional options in a unified way. Promotional

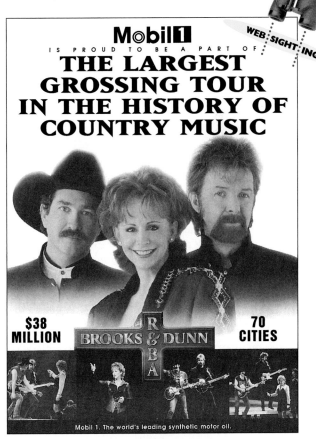

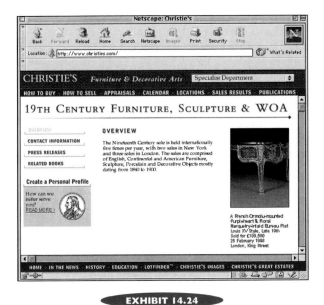

EXHIBIT 14.24

Online and interactive media have become popular even among upscale, traditional organizations. www.christies.com/

EXHIBIT 14.25

Mobil, like many major corporations, uses arts sponsorship for broader exposure. Mobil runs the gamut from PBS's Masterpiece Theater, to Country & Western, and, of course, sponsors a racing team. Mobil's Web site (www.mobil.com) is much more focused on its products, probably because its brand is so strongly tied to gasoline and other petroleum products—would you go looking for operatic tidbits at a gas station? Mobil and Exxon (www.exxon.com) announced plans to merge in 1998. What might the future implications for the Mobil brand be? www.pbs.org

23. Leslie Cauley, "U.S. West Prepares to Make a Big Splash in Multimedia," *Wall Street Journal,* January 10, 1994, B4.
24. Ibid.

options such as event sponsorship (Exhibit 14.25), direct marketing, sales promotion, and public relations are drawing many firms away from traditional mass media advertising. But these new approaches still require coordination with the advertising that remains. Some of the more significant implications for media planning to achieve IMC are as follows:

- The reliance on mass media will be reduced as more highly targeted media are integrated into media plans. Database marketing programs and more sophisticated single-source data research will produce more tightly focused efforts through direct marketing and interactive media options.
- More precise media impact data, not just media exposure data, will be needed to compare media alternatives. Advertisers will be looking for proof that consumers exposed to a particular medium are buyers, not just prospects.
- Media planners will need to know much more about a broader range of communication tools: event sponsorship, interactive media, direct marketing, and public relations. They will need to know more about the impact and capabilities of these other forms of promotion to fully integrate communications.
- Central control will be necessary for synergistic, seamless communication. At this point, it is unclear who will provide this central control—the advertiser, the advertising agency, the copywriter, or the media planner. There is some reason to believe that, because of the need for integration and coordination, media planners will emerge as more critically important to the communications process than they have ever been in the past.[25]

SUMMARY

Describe the major media options available to advertisers.

No advertising campaign can achieve its objectives without skillful use of one or several media vehicles. Poor media selection will in the end undermine any advertising campaign. Media planners today are faced with a wide variety of options for message placement. These options may be generally categorized as either measured or unmeasured media. Measured media include familiar alternatives such as television, radio, magazines, and newspapers. Unmeasured media are more varied and include direct mail, store catalogs, and event sponsorship.

Detail the important components of the media-planning process.

A media plan specifies the media vehicles that will be used to deliver the advertiser's message. Developing a media plan entails setting objectives such as effective reach and frequency and determining strategies to achieve those objectives. Media planners use several quantitative indicators, such as CPM and CPRP, to help them judge the efficiency of prospective media choices. The media-planning process culminates in the scheduling and purchase of a mix of media vehicles expected to deliver the advertiser's message to specific target audiences at precisely the right time to affect their consumption decisions.

Explain the applications of computer modeling in media planning.

As is true in so many aspects of modern life, the computer has become an essential tool for the media planner. The detailed information available and the myriad of choices that must be made in working up a media schedule lend themselves to computer modeling. Modeling allows a planner to economically gauge the potential impact of alternative plans before making a media buy. Computer models can also be used to rate media vehicles in terms of their efficiency in reaching a target segment. These models are important decision-support tools in media planning.

Discuss five additional challenges that complicate the media-planning process.

Several additional factors complicate media planning. Simply keeping track of all the options is a challenge, given that new options are constantly being invented. Inadequate information and rising media costs are additional hurdles. The emergence of interactive media presents advertisers with new, untested vehicles. This incredible array of choices creates many dilemmas for the media planner who seeks to achieve integrated marketing communications.

25. Adapted from Sissors and Bumba, *Advertising Media Planning*, 6–7, 51–60.

KEY TERMS

measured media (440)
unmeasured media (440)
media plan (441)
media class (441)
media vehicle (441)
media objectives (441)
single-source tracking services (443)
geo-targeting (445)
message weight (446)
gross impressions (446)
between-vehicle duplication (446)
within-vehicle duplication (446)
reach (448)
frequency (448)
gross rating points (GRP) (448)
effective frequency (449)
effective reach (449)

continuity (449)
continuous scheduling (449)
flighting (450)
pulsing (450)
media mix (452)
concentrated media mix (452)
assorted media mix (453)
cost per thousand (CPM) (453)
cost per thousand–target market (CPM–TM) (454)
cost per rating point (CPRP) (454)
share of voice (455)
heavy-up scheduling (456)
media buying (456)
agency of record (456)
media-buying service (456)
make good (457)
interactive media (462)

QUESTIONS FOR REVIEW AND CRITICAL THINKING

1. Why have Ed Artzt and other senior business leaders been so outspoken in recent years about the need to influence content and programming in the mass media? What are Artzt and others seeking for their companies?

2. Media plans should of course take a proactive stance with respect to customers. Explain how geo-targeting and heavy-up scheduling can be used in making a media plan more proactive with respect to customers.

3. Carefully watch one hour of television and record the time length of each advertisement. Using your perceptions about the most and least persuasive ads during this hour of television, develop a hypothesis about the value of long versus short advertising messages. When should an advertiser use long instead of short ads, to accomplish what goals?

4. Review the mathematics of the CPM and CPRP calculations, and explain how these two indicators can be used to assess the efficiency and effectiveness of a media schedule.

5. Assume that you are advising a regional snack-food manufacturer whose brands have a low share of voice.

Which pattern of continuity would you recommend for such an advertiser? Would you place your ads in television programming that is also sponsored by Pringles and Doritos? Why or why not?

6. Media strategy models allow planners to compare the impact of different media plans, using criteria such as reach, frequency, and gross impressions. What other kinds of criteria should a planner take into account before deciding on a final plan?

7. You have probably visited Web sites on the Internet for many different products and brands. How would you rate the World Wide Web as a medium for delivering commercial messages? Use the evaluative dimensions listed in Exhibit 14.10 as a guide for your assessment of the Web.

8. Discuss the issues raised in this chapter that represent challenges for those who champion integrated marketing communications. Why would central control be required for achieving IMC? If media planners wish to play the role of central controller, what must they do to qualify for the role?

EXPERIENTIAL EXERCISES

1.   Divide into teams. For one day have each member of the team record all the ways that marketers send messages about their goods or services. Discuss which messages, if any, you found yourselves taking in, and what it was about those messages that made them effective. Think about a message that got through to you primarily because of repetition. What is your attitude and purchasing behavior toward such advertisers? Present your findings to the class.

2.   Look at the schedule for NBC network television and TNT cable television for an entire day. (Don't watch all the shows; just look in the listing guide!)

How does the programming seem to be different? Are there times during the day when the programming is similar?

USING THE INTERNET

Choose a company that currently has a Web site, and assume you are the Internet media planner for this company.

1.   What other Web sites would you suggest placing banner ads on?

2.   What combination of high-traffic or narrowly focused sites does your media plan consist of? What is it about your company that makes it pay off to use a high-traffic site?

3.   Explain how these placements will reach people in your company's target market.

4.   What is the scheduling plan for each site you place banner ads on?

The Internet is an interesting (and perhaps challenging) new medium for companies that have successfully mined unique niches. SkyMall (www.skymall.com) is the company that puts that catalog in the pocket of the seat in front of you on your business flight to the coast. The analysis was obvious: a well-heeled business traveler, trapped in his or her seat for hours, imagining all of the things they'd rather be doing. Why not shop for monogrammed golf balls, inspirational tapes, or facial tanners?

1.   It's easy to reach customers if their only alternative reading starts "In the event of nausea, open bag and . . .," but what might drive traffic to SkyMall's Web site?

2.   How might SkyMall use its diverse publication media to support each other?

3.   Is the SkyMall Web site likely to be as effective as its in-flight catalogs?

The Complete Men's Magazine

Men'sJournal

If You Aren't Going All
The Way, Why Go At All?

–Joe Namath

"Shape of Your Life," Men's Journal Volume 7, Number 2, March 1998

CHAPTER 15

**After reading and thinking about
this chapter, you will be able to do
the following:**

◀▶ Detail the pros and cons of newspapers
as a media class, identify newspaper types,
and describe buying and audience measurement for newspapers.

◀▶ Detail the pros and cons of magazines as
a media class, identify magazine types, and
describe buying and audience measurement for magazines.

◀▶ Detail the pros and cons of television as
a media class, identify television types, and
describe buying and audience measurement for television.

④ Detail the pros and cons of radio as a
media class, identify radio types, and
describe buying and audience measurement for radio.

Do you like watching MTV? How about FX or Nickelodeon? Do you occasionally tune in to SportsCenter on ESPN to catch up on the day's sporting news? What about TNN and its country music programming? Congratulations—you are a member of the "least desirable segment of the population."[1] At least you are far as the marketing people at CBS—a major *broadcast* rather than cable network—are concerned. CBS offered this opinion in a direct mail marketing promotion to advertisers in the hope of gaining back revenue lost to cable over the last ten years.

The battle for your TV viewership and everyone else's in the United States is starting to heat up. Currently, advertisers spend about $10 to $12 billion with cable networks for advertising time. While the four major broadcast networks—ABC, CBS, Fox, and NBC—still command more dollars at about $14 to $15 billion per year, cable's revenues are growing at more than twice the rate of the networks'.[2] And that, claims Joe Ostrow, president of the Cabletelevision Advertising Bureau, has the networks "running scared."[3] Cable advocates claim that the networks are denying a major trend in television viewership, which shows that people are moving to cable and away from network. During the 1997–1998 television season, for example, the average prime-time rating for basic cable channels climbed to an average of 21.8, up from 19.4 the previous season. During the same time period, the average network rating fell from 37.2 to 35.7.

It is clear that the networks still command the largest audiences and will for some time to come. In fact, they are quick to point out this total "reach" advantage to potential advertisers. But the gap in reach is starting to close (see Exhibit 15.1), and cable broadcasters point out that they still have the distinct advantage of offering more narrowly defined programming, which attracts a more well-defined audience—a tremendous advantage in the eyes of many advertisers. And for the time being, the broad reach of broadcast programming comes with a tremendous cost premium. Hugely successful primetime network programs such as *ER* command over $500,000 for a 30-second spot. In contrast, advertisements on the most successful cable programs cost only a fraction of that: Advertising on ESPN regular season NFL football is about $105,000, and Comedy Central's *South Park* gets only about $50,000.[4]

Over the next several years, the battle between the networks and cable will continue to escalate. No doubt, there will be more ventures by the networks into cable—currently NBC owns and operates CNBC, and Disney, which owns ABC, also owns ESPN and the Disney cable channel. But the broadcast networks want to maintain leadership because of

WEB SIGHTING

70 MILLION*

Cable subscribers depend on The Weather Channel.

They all have to live with the weather. And they all get The Weather Channel.

Boy, do they get it. Viewers rank TWC as their 4th most valuable cable network.** That's made TWC the 3rd most powerful TV brand out there.*** Ahead of the likes of NBC, CBS, and ABC.

In other words, people watch, and they care—a lot. And isn't that what you're looking for?

THE WEATHER CHANNEL

weather.com

* Source: Nielsen People Meter Included Sample, April 1998.
** Both Research, 1997.
*** The Myers Report, Nov. 10, 1997.

EXHIBIT 15.1

Cable networks have proliferated and grown, reducing the former "big three" American broadcast networks' share of the market by appealing to narrow interest segments. Although it's unlikely that all but a few of The Weather Channel's 70 million viewers leave the dial tuned to TWC day in and day out (www.weather.com), consumers who can pick and choose their programming á la carte are less likely to be riveted to a single bit-of-everything network either. Will major networks like ABC (www.abc.com), CBS (www.cbs.com), NBC (www.nbc.com), and Fox (www.fox.com) be "pecked to death by ducks" as specialty cable channels optimize for slices of their viewership? Or will they develop special themes (e.g., Fox's upstart, irreverent-kid-on-the-block theme) to retain audiences?

1.   Kyle Pope and Leslie Cauley, "In Battle for TV Ads, Cable Is Now the Enemy," *Wall Street Journal,* May 6, 1998, B1, B6.
2.   Kathy Haley, "As Cable Audiences Grow, Revenues Follow," *Advertising Age,* June 8, 1998, A3.
3.   Pope and Cauley, "In Battle for TV Ads, Cable Is Now the Enemy," op. cit.
4.   Joe Mandese, "Cable TV," *Advertising Age,* April 13, 1998, S-1, S-4.

the premium price they can command for advertising time slots. It will be an interesting competition to watch—especially for those of us in the "least desirable segment of the population."

The Importance and Process of Media Evaluation.

The competition between broadcast and cable networks offers some insight into the importance of the media evaluation process. Media decisions made by advertisers ultimately determine which media companies earn the billions of dollars of revenue for print, television, and radio advertising slots. This chapter focuses on the challenge advertisers face in evaluating these media as important means for reaching their audiences. As the discussion of media planning in the previous chapter emphasized, even great advertising will not achieve communications and sales objectives if the media placement misses the target audience.

Our evaluation of print, television, and radio media will concentrate on several key aspects of using these major media options. With respect to the print media— newspapers and magazines—we will first consider the advantages and disadvantages of the media themselves. Both newspapers and magazines have inherent capabilities and limitations that advertisers must take into consideration in building a media plan. Next, we will look at the types of newspapers and magazines that advertisers have to choose from. Finally, we will identify buying procedures and audience measurement techniques.

Discussion of television and radio media follows. First, the types of television and radio options are described. Next, the advantages and disadvantages of television and radio are examined. Finally, the buying procedures and audience measurement techniques are identified.

Print, television, and radio media represent the major alternatives available to advertisers for reaching audiences. While much has been said—and more will be said in the following chapters—about increased spending on new media and integrated marketing communications, about 35 percent of all advertising dollars spent in the United States still goes to traditional print radio and television media.[5] In addition, the vast majority of creative effort—and money—is expended on print and broadcast advertising campaigns. Despite the many intriguing opportunities that new media options offer, print and broadcast media will likely form the foundation of most advertising campaigns for years to come. The discussions in this chapter will demonstrate why these media represent such rich communication alternatives for advertisers.

Print Media Evaluation.

You might think that the print media are lifeless and lack impact compared to the broadcast media options. Think again. Consider the problems that faced Absolut vodka. In 1980, Absolut was on the verge of extinction. The Swedish brand was selling only 12,000 cases a year in the United States—not enough to even register a single percentage point of market share. The name Absolut was seen as gimmicky; bartenders thought the bottle was ugly and hard to pour from; and to top things off, consumers gave no credibility at all to a vodka produced in Sweden, which they knew as the land of boxy-looking cars and hot tubs.

The TBWA advertising agency in New York set about the task of overcoming these liabilities with print advertising alone because spirits ads were banned from broadcast at the time. The agency took on the challenge of developing magazine and newspaper ads that would build awareness, communicate quality, achieve credibility, and avoid Swedish clichés etched in the minds of American consumers. The firm came up with one of the most famous and successful print campaigns of all time. The concept was to feature the strange-shaped Absolut bottle as the hero of each ad, in which the only copy was a two-word line always beginning with *Absolut* and ending with a "quality"

5.   R. Craig Endicott, "Top 100 Mega Brands," *Advertising Age,* July 13, 1998, S-2.

word such as *perfection* or *clarity*. The two-word description evolved from the original quality concept to a variety of clever combinations. "Absolut Centerfold" appeared in *Playboy* and featured an Absolut bottle with all the printing removed, and "Absolut Wonderland" was a Christmas-season ad with the bottle in a snow globe like the ones that feature snowy Christmas scenes.

In the end, the Absolut campaign was not only a creative masterpiece, but also a resounding market success. Absolut had become the leading imported vodka in the United States. The vodka with no credibility and the ugly bottle had become sophisticated and fashionable with a well-conceived and well-placed print campaign.[6]

The great success of Absolut vodka demonstrates that not every brand needs a multimedia, new media, interactive, database-managed advertising effort to achieve outstanding communications and sales impact. The marketing and advertising strategists for Absolut used one media class—print—and one media vehicle—magazines—to bring the brand from near oblivion to market leadership. The reason print media alone was able to accomplish this task relates to some of the inherent capabilities of print, which we will identify shortly. We will discuss the full range of issues in print advertising, beginning with newspapers and then turning our attention to magazines.

Newspapers as an Advertising Medium.

Newspaper is the medium that is most accessible to the widest range of advertisers. Advertisers big and small—even you and I when we want to sell that old bike or snowboard—can use newspaper advertising. In fact, investment in newspaper advertising reached $41.6 billion in 1997—second only to television in attracting advertising dollars.[7] Exhibits 15.2 and 15.3 show the top ten advertisers in national and local newspapers. Notice three features of the spending data in these exhibits. First, the list of national newspaper advertisers includes many business products and services. Several national newspapers reach primarily business audiences. Second, notice that the list of local newspaper advertisers is dominated by retailers. Newspapers are, of course, ideally suited to reaching a narrow geographic area—precisely the type of

EXHIBIT 15.2

Top ten national newspaper advertisers. Figures are in millions of U.S. dollars.

Rank	Advertiser	National Newspaper Ad Spending		
		1997	1996	% Change
1	IBM Corp.	$32.0	$21.9	46.2
2	Compaq Computer Corp.	28.4	17.2	65.4
3	General Motors	26.2	29.1	−10.1
4	Ford Motor Co.	25.9	21.1	22.33
5	Charles Schwab	25.2	20.2	25.03
6	BMW	21.9	7.8	181.7
7	Hewlett-Packard	21.7	7.5	189.8
8	FMR Corp.	19.5	27.2	−28.3
9	Dow Jones & Co.	17.4	27.4	−36.5
10	Merrill Lynch & Co.	17.0	15.1	12.5

Source: *Advertising Age*, September 28, 1998, s32. Reprinted with permission from the September 28, 1998, issue of *Advertising Age*. Copyright © Crain Communications Inc. 1998.

6.   Information about the Absolut vodka campaign was adapted from information in Nicholas Ind, "Absolut Vodka in the U.S.," in *Great Advertising Campaigns* (Lincolnwood, Ill.: NTC Business Books, 1993), 15–32.
7.   Robert J. Coen, "Ad Revenue Growth Hits 7% in 1997 to Surpass Forecasts," *Advertising Age,* May 18, 1998, 50.

EXHIBIT 15.3

Top ten local newspaper advertisers. Figures are in millions of U.S. dollars.

Rank	Advertiser	Local Newspaper Ad Spending		
		1997	1996	% Change
1	Federated Department Stores	$446.9	339.5	31.6
2	May Department Stores Co.	358.8	312.9	14.7
3	Circuit City Stores	293.0	250.3	17.1
4	Sears, Roebuck & Co.	227.1	196.1	15.8
5	Dillards	215.8	164.7	31.0
6	Dayton Hudson Corp.	189.4	158.8	19.3
7	J. C. Penney Co.	159.1	114.6	38.9
8	Time Warner	134.5	124.0	8.5
9	Kmart	109.4	70.0	56.3
10	Walt Disney Co.	109.3	112.6	–2.9

Source: *Advertising Age*, September 28, 1998, s30. Reprinted with permission from the September 28, 1998, issue of *Advertising Age*. Copyright © Crain Communications Inc. 1998.

audience retailers want to reach. Finally, look at how much more money is spent by the top ten local advertisers than by the national advertisers. This is because the national advertisers use newspaper advertising as part of a multimedia plan, while local advertisers, even though they are national companies, often rely on newspapers as the primary medium for reaching their well-defined geographic target audiences.

There are some sad truths about the current status of newspapers as a medium. Since the early 1980s, newspapers across the United States have been suffering circulation declines, and the trend has continued into the mid-1990s.[8] What may be worse is that the percentage of adults reading daily newspapers is also declining. About 61 percent of adults in the United States read a daily newspaper, compared with about 78 percent in 1970.[9] Much of the decline in both circulation and readership comes from the fact that both morning and evening newspapers have been losing patronage to television news programs. While shows such as *Good Morning America* and *Dateline* cannot provide the breadth of coverage that newspapers can, they still offer news, and they offer it in a lively multisensory format.

Declining newspaper readership and circulation is not a problem in other parts of the world. In Japan, the average household subscribes to several newspapers. In England, newspaper readership has remained strong over many decades. And in several European markets, there is high newspaper circulation among households and businesses.

Advantages of Newspapers. Newspapers may have lost some of their impact and luster over the past two decades, but they do reach more than 50 percent of U.S. households, representing more than 132 million adults. And, as mentioned earlier, newspapers are still an excellent medium for retailers targeting local geographic markets. But broad reach isn't the only attractive feature of newspapers as a medium. Newspapers offer other advantages to advertisers:

- *Geographic selectivity.* Daily newspapers in cities and towns across the United States offer advertisers the opportunity to reach a well-defined geographic target audience. Some newspapers are beginning to run zoned editions, which target even

8.   Keith J. Kelly, "Newspapers See Decline Continue," *Advertising Age,* November 14, 1994, 41.
9.   *Facts about Newspapers 1995* (Reston, Va.: Newspaper Association of America, 1995), 4.

more narrow geographic areas within a metropolitan market. Zoned editions are typically used by merchants doing business in the local area; national marketers such as Kellogg and Colgate can use the paper carrier to deliver free samples to these zoned areas.

- *Timeliness.* The newspaper is one of the most timely of the major media. Because of the short time needed for producing a typical newspaper ad and the regularity of daily publication, the newspaper allows advertisers to reach audiences in a timely way. This doesn't mean on just a daily basis. Newspaper ads can take advantage of special events or a unique occurrence in a community—like the Infiniti ad in Exhibit 15.4, which ties into the popular Chicago Auto Show.

- *Creative opportunities.* While the newspaper page does not offer the breadth of creative options available in the broadcast media, there are things advertisers can do in a newspaper that represent important creative opportunities. Since the newspaper page offers a large and relatively inexpensive format, advertisers can provide a lot of information to the target audience at relatively low cost. This is important for products or services with extensive or complex features that may need lengthy and detailed copy. The Tire America ad in Exhibit 15.5 needs just such a large format to provide detail about tire sizes and prices.

EXHIBIT 15.4

One of the advantages of the newspaper as a medium is its timeliness. Ads can be timed with special events, like this ad for Infiniti timed to run with the Chicago Auto Show. www.infinitimotors.com/

EXHIBIT 15.5

The newspaper medium offers a large format for advertisers. This is important when an advertiser needs space to provide the target audience with extensive information, as Tire America has done with this ad featuring tire sizes and prices.

- *Credibility.* Newspapers still benefit from the perception that "if it's in the paper it must be the truth." This, combined with the community image of most newspapers, creates a favorable environment for an advertisement.
- *Audience interest.* Newspaper readers are interested in the information they are reading. While overall readership may be down in the United States, those readers that remain are loyal and interested. Many readers buy the newspaper specifically to see what's on sale at stores in the local area, making this an ideal environment for local merchants.
- *Cost.* In terms of both production and space, newspapers offer a low-cost alternative to advertisers. The cost per contact may be higher than with the television and radio options, but the absolute cost for placing a black-and-white ad is still within reach of even a small advertising budget.

Disadvantages of Newspapers. Newspapers offer advertisers many good opportunities. Like every other media option, however, newspapers have some significant disadvantages.

- *Limited segmentation.* While newspapers can achieve good geographic selectivity, the ability to target a specific audience ends there. Newspaper circulation simply cuts across too broad an economic, social, and demographic audience to allow the isolation of specific targets. The placement of ads within certain sections can achieve minimal targeting by gender, but even this effort is somewhat fruitless. Some newspapers are developing special sections to enhance their segmentation capabilities. Many papers are offering kids' news sections targeted at 9-to-13-year-olds.[10] An example is shown in Exhibit 15.6. In addition, more and more newspapers are being published to serve specific ethnic groups, which is another form of segmentation.
- *Creative constraints.* The opportunities for creative executions in newspapers are certainly outweighed by the creative constraints. First, newspapers have poor reproduction quality. Led by *USA Today,* most newspapers now print some of their pages in color. But even the color reproduction does not enhance the look of most products. For advertisers whose product images depend on accurate, high-quality reproduction (color or not), newspapers simply have severe limitations compared to other media options. Second, newspapers are a unidimensional medium—no sound, no action. For products that demand a broad creative execution, this medium is not the best choice.

EXHIBIT 15.6

Many newspapers are trying to increase their target selectivity by developing special sections for advertisers, as in this kids' section.

10. Scott Hume and Ira Teinowitz, "KidNews Gets 'A' from Young Set," *Advertising Age,* October 5, 1992, S-6.

- *Cluttered environment.* The average newspaper is filled with headlines, subheads, photos, and announcements—not to mention news stories. This presents a terribly cluttered environment for an advertisement. To make things worse, most advertisers in a product category try to use the same sections to target audiences. For example, all the home equity loan and financial services ads are in the business section, and all the women's clothing ads are in the local section.

- *Short life.* In most U.S. households, newspapers are read quickly and then discarded (or, hopefully, stacked in the recycling pile). The only way advertisers can overcome this limitation is to buy several insertions in each daily issue, buy space several times during the week, or both. In this way, even if a reader doesn't spend much time with the newspaper, at least multiple exposures are a possibility.

The newspaper has creative limitations, but what the average newspaper does, it does well. If an advertiser wants to reach a local audience with a simple black-and-white ad in a timely manner, then the newspaper is the superior choice.

Types of Newspapers. All newspapers enjoy the same advantages and suffer from the same limitations to one degree or another. But there are different types of newspapers from which advertisers can choose. Newspapers are categorized by target audience, geographic coverage, and frequency of publication.

- *Target audience.* Newspapers can be classified by the target audience they reach. The five primary types of newspapers serving different target audiences are general population newspapers, business newspapers, ethnic newspapers, gay and lesbian newspapers, and the alternative press. **General-population newspapers** serve local communities and report news of interest to the local population. Newspapers such as the *Kansas City Star,* the *Dayton Daily News,* and the *Columbus Dispatch* are examples. **Business newspapers** such as the *Wall Street Journal, Investor's Business Daily* (United States), and the *Financial Times* (United Kingdom) serve a specialized business audience. **Ethnic newspapers** that target specific ethnic groups are growing in popularity. Most of these newspapers are published weekly. The *New York Amsterdam News* and the *Michigan Chronicle* are two of the more than 200 newspapers in the United States that serve African-American communities. The Hispanic community in the United States has more than 300 newspapers. One of the most prominent is *El Diario de las Americas* in Miami. **Gay and lesbian newspapers** exist in most major (and many smaller) markets. Readership typically extends considerably beyond gay and lesbian readers. So-called **alternative press newspapers**, such as the *L.A. Weekly* (www.laweekly.com/), the *Austin Chronicle* (www.auschron.com/current/), and the *Octopus* of Champaign-Urbana, Illinois (www.cuoctopus.com), are very viable vehicles for reaching typically young and entertainment-oriented audiences.

- *Geographic coverage.* As noted earlier, the vast majority of newspapers are distributed in a relatively small geographic area—either a large metropolitan area or a state. Newspapers such as the *Tulsa World* and the *Atlanta Journal,* with circulations of 170,000 and 140,000 respectively, serve a local geographic area. The other type of newspaper in the United States is a national newspaper. *USA Today* was, from its inception, designed to be distributed nationally, and it currently has a circulation of 1.4 million. The *New York Times,* the *Los Angeles Times,* and the *Christian Science Monitor,* each with a circulation of about 1 million, have evolved into national newspapers.

- *Frequency of publication.* The majority of newspapers in the United States are called *dailies* because they are published each day of the week, including Sunday. There are a smaller number of *weeklies,* and these tend to serve smaller towns or rural communities. Finally, another alternative for advertisers is the Sunday supplement, which is published only on Sunday and is usually delivered along with the Sunday edition of a local newspaper. The most widely distributed Sunday supplements—*Parade* magazine and *USA Weekend*—are illustrated in Exhibit 15.7.

Sunday supplements such as
Parade *magazine and* USA
Weekend *offer advertisers
another alternative for placing
newspaper ads.*

Categories of Newspaper Advertising. Just as there are categories of news-papers, there are categories of newspaper advertising: display advertising, inserts, and classified advertising.

- *Display advertising.* Advertisers of goods and services rely most on display advertising. **Display advertising** in newspapers includes the standard components of a print ad—headline, body copy, and often an illustration—to set it off from the news content of the paper. An important form of display advertising is co-op advertising sponsored by manufacturers. In **co-op advertising**, a manufacturer pays part of the media bill when a local merchant features the manufacturer's brand in advertising. Co-op advertising can be done on a national scale as well. (See Exhibit 15.8.) Intel invests more than $200 million annually in co-op advertising with PC manufacturers who feature the "Intel Inside" logo in their ads.[11]
- *Inserts.* There are two types of insert advertisements. Inserts do not appear on the printed newspaper page but rather are folded into the newspaper before distribution. An advertiser can use a **preprinted insert**, which is an advertisement delivered to the newspaper fully printed and ready for insertion into the newspaper. The second type of insert ad is a **free-standing insert (FSI)**, which contains cents-off coupons for a variety of products and is typically delivered with Sunday newspapers. The Pizza Hut ad in Exhibit 15.9 is part of a free-standing insert.
- *Classified advertising.* **Classified advertising** is newspaper advertising that appears as all-copy messages under categories such as sporting

Retailers who feature a particular brand can receive co-op advertising money for media placement. www.ebel.com/

11. Bradley Johnson, "Intel Co-op Boost Is Boon for TV, Radio," *Advertising Age,* April 3, 1995, 3.

EXHIBIT 15.9

This example of a free-standing insert (FSI) from Pizza Hut shows how an ad can be delivered via a newspaper distribution system without having to become part of the paper itself. What are the production and attention-getting advantages that this insert provides?
www.pizzahut.com/

goods, employment, and automobiles. Many classified ads are taken out by individuals, but real estate firms, automobile dealers, and construction firms also buy classified advertising.

Costs and Buying Procedures for Newspaper Advertising.
When an advertiser wishes to place advertising in a newspaper, the first step is to obtain a rate card from the newspaper. A **rate card** contains information on costs, closing times (when ads have to be submitted), specifications for submitting an ad, and special pages or features available in the newspaper. The rate card also summarizes the circulation for the designated market area and any circulation outside the designated area.

The cost of a newspaper ad depends on how large the advertisement is, whether it is black-and-white or color, how large the total audience is, and whether the newspaper has local or national coverage. Advertising space is sold in newspapers by the **column inch**, which is a unit of space one inch deep by one column wide. Each column is $2\frac{1}{16}$ inches wide. Most newspapers have adopted the **standard advertising unit (SAU)** system for selling ad space, which defines unit sizes for advertisements. There are 57 defined SAU sizes for advertisements in the system, so that advertisers can prepare ads to fit one of the sizes. Many newspapers offer a volume discount to advertisers who buy more than one ad in an issue or buy multiple ads over some time period.

When an advertiser buys space on a **run-of-paper (ROP)** basis, which is also referred to as a run-of-press basis, the ad may appear anywhere, on any page in the paper. A higher rate is charged for **preferred position**, in which the ad is placed in a specific section of the paper. **Full position** places an ad near the top of a page or in the middle of editorial material. Exhibit 15.10 shows how a full-position ad looks in a newspaper.

Measuring Newspaper Audiences.
There are several different dimensions to measuring newspaper audiences. The reach of a newspaper is reported as the newspaper's circulation. **Circulation** is the number of newspapers distributed each day (for daily newspapers) or each week (for weekly publications). **Paid circulation** reports the number of copies sold through subscriptions and newsstand distribution. **Controlled circulation** refers to the number of copies of the newspaper that are given away free. The Audit Bureau of Circulations (ABC) is an independent organization that verifies the actual circulation of newspapers.

Rates for newspaper advertising are not based solely on circulation numbers, however. The Newspaper Association of America estimates that 2.28 people read each copy of a daily newspaper distributed in the United States. **Readership** of a newspaper is a measure of the circulation multiplied by the number of readers of a copy. This number, of course, is much higher than the circulation number and provides a total audience figure on which advertisers base advertising rates. To give you some idea of costs, a full-page four-color ad in *USA Today* costs about $100,000, and a full-page black-and-white ad in the *Wall Street Journal* costs about $175,000. A full-page ad in your local newspaper is, of course, considerably less—probably around $10,000 to $15,000. Remember, though, that few advertisers, national or local, purchase an entire page.

EXHIBIT 15.10

Print paper layout is important: Hence, the scramble of print journalists to see their stories positioned not only on the front page but also "above the fold" (i.e., readable when the paper is folded in a newsstand display (the priciest of all newspaper real estate). This full-position ad for Leath Furniture, surrounded by editorial content that attracts a reader's attention, may garner more eyeballs than one buried in an advertising-only insert, and advertisers pay higher rates for such placement for this reason. For all of its purported advantages over newsprint, is the Internet as effective in giving advertisers a similiar grip on readers' attention? Why have some companies developed blocking software to let Web readers screen out banner advertising? See Internet Mute's interMute Web site at www.intermute.com.

The Future of Newspapers. At the outset of this chapter, we talked about the fact that newspaper circulation has been in a long, sustained downward trend, and that readership is following the same pattern. To survive as a viable advertising medium, newspapers will have to evolve with the demands of both audiences and advertisers, who provide them with the majority of their revenue. One research study indicates that to compete in the future as a viable advertising medium, newspapers will have to do the following:

- Continue to provide in-depth coverage of issues that focus on the local community.
- Increase coverage of national and international news.
- Provide follow-up reports of news stories.
- Maintain and expand their role as the best local source for consumers to find specific information on advertised product features, availability, and prices.
- Provide the option of shopping through an online newspaper computer service.[12]

12. Ronald Redfern, "What Readers Want from Newspapers," *Advertising Age,* January 23, 1995, 25.

Magazines as an Advertising Medium.

The marketing director for Schwinn Cycling & Fitness wanted to resurrect the company's bicycle division. Schwinn had been pummeled by worthy competitors such as Trek and Specialized over the past decade, and he felt certain one of the underlying problems was that the image of the brand was outdated. To begin solving this image problem, the marketing director first instructed the firm's advertising agency to develop a $10 million magazine campaign. One of Schwinn's ads from this campaign is shown in Exhibit 15.11. The ads were placed in specialty biking magazines and were aimed at mountain-biking and race-biking enthusiasts. Schwinn integrated the magazine campaign with a broad promotional strategy that included event sponsorship and interactive mall kiosks. While Schwinn is still a distant third in the U.S. bike market, sales climbed 18.4 percent during the restructured advertising and promotional period.

Schwinn's emphasis on magazine advertising—much like Absolut's— was part of an effort to upgrade the brand image and turned out to be an excellent strategic decision. Magazines, more than any other media option, provide advertisers with a choice of highly selective alternatives that offer a wide variety of formats and contexts. The top ten magazines in the United States, based on revenue, are listed in Exhibit 15.12. This list suggests the diversity of magazines as a media class. Exhibit 15.13 shows the top ten advertisers in magazines.

Like newspapers, magazines have advantages and disadvantages, come in different types, offer various ad costs and buying procedures, and measure their audiences in specific ways. We will consider these issues now.

Advantages of Magazines. Magazines have many advantages relative to newspapers. These advantages make them more than just an ideal print medium—many analysts conclude that magazines are, in many ways, superior to even broadcast media alternatives.

EXHIBIT 15.11

Schwinn Cycling & Fitness relied on magazine ads like this one to upgrade its brand image and regain lost market share from Trek and Specialized.
www.schwinn.com/

EXHIBIT 15.12

Top ten magazines by gross revenue, 1997. Figures are in millions of U.S. dollars.

Magazine	Total Revenue	Ad Revenue	Paid Circulation
TV Guide	$1,122,219	$408,844	13,103,187
People	1,006,893	588,504	3,608,111
Sports Illustrated	820,696	548,617	3,223,810
Time	805,923	533,198	4,155,806
Reader's Digest	567,891	212,322	15,038,708
Newsweek	561,212	408,510	3,177,407
Better Homes & Gardens	518,776	377,451	7,605,187
Parade	517,239	517,239	36,791,000
PC Magazine	398,193	333,513	1,176,351
Business Week	379,822	329,675	901,891

Source: *Advertising Age*, June 15, 1998, S-6. Reprinted with permission from the June 15, 1998, issue of *Advertising Age*. Copyright © Crain Communications Inc. 1998.

EXHIBIT 15.13

Top ten magazine advertisers. Figures are in millions of U.S. dollars.

Rank	Advertiser	Magazine Ad Spending 1997	Magazine Ad Spending 1996	% Change
1	General Motors Corp.	$588.4	$456.4	28.9
2	Procter & Gamble Co.	363.4	272.7	32.3
3	Philip Morris Cos.	345.4	338.6	2.0
4	Chrysler Corp.	327.9	269.2	21.8
5	Ford Motor Co.	284.8	280.5	1.6
6	Time Warner	180.1	157.3	14.5
7	Toyota Motor Corp.	149.1	126.1	18.3
8	Johnson & Johnson	140.8	154.0	−8.6
9	Unilever	131.1	125.3	4.6
10	L'oreal	104.3	91.2	14.3

Source: *Advertising Age*, September 28, 1998, s26. Reprinted with permission from the September 28, 1998, issue of *Advertising Age*. Copyright © Crain Communications Inc. 1998.

- *Audience selectivity.* The overwhelming advantage of magazines relative to other media—print or broadcast—is the ability of magazines to attract, and therefore target, a highly selective audience. This selectivity can be based on demographics (*Woman's Day*), lifestyle (*Muscle & Fitness*), or special interests (*Mountain Biking*), as shown in Exhibit 15.14. The audience segment can be narrowly defined, as is the one that reads *Modern Bride,* or it may cut across a variety of interests, as does the one for *Newsweek.* Magazines also offer geographic selectivity on a regional basis, as does *Southern Living* or city magazines, such as *Atlanta,* which highlight happenings in major metropolitan areas. Also, large national publications have multiple editions for advertisers to choose from. *Better Homes & Gardens* has 85 different specific market editions, and *Time* offers advertisers a different edition for each of the 50 states. Recently, publishers of leading women's magazines have discovered that global expansion is facilitated by the ability of newspapers to be tightly targeted. The Global Issues box on page 484 highlights the global capability of magazines.

- *Audience interest.* Perhaps more than any other medium, magazines attract an audience because of content. While television programming can attract audiences through interest as well, magazines have the additional advantage of voluntary exposure to the advertising. Golfers are interested in golf equipment like that shown in Exhibit 15.15 and advertised in *Golf Digest,* while auto enthusiasts find the accessory equipment in *Car and Driver* appealing.

- *Creative opportunities.* Magazines offer a wide range of creative opportunities. Because of the ability to vary the size of an ad, use color, use white space, and play off the special interests of the audience, magazines represent a favorable creative environment. Also, because the paper quality of most magazines is quite high, color reproduction can be outstanding—another creative opportunity. In an attempt to expand the creative environment even further, some advertisers have tried various other creative techniques: pop-up ads, scratch-and-sniff ads, ads with perfume scent strips, and even ads with small computer chips that have flashing lights and play music. The Clarins ad in Exhibit 15.16 shows how an advertiser can take advantage of the creative opportunities offered by magazines.

EXHIBIT 15.14

One distinct advantage of magazines over most other media options is the ability to attract and target a highly selective audience. Magazines such as Mountain Biking *attract an audience based on special interests and activities.*

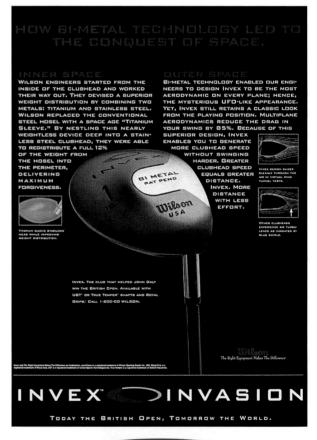

EXHIBIT 15.15

Magazines can attract readers with specialized content, and in so doing, they attract advertisers. This ad by Wilson appeared in Golf Digest. www.wilsonsports.com/

EXHIBIT 15.16

Magazines offer unique creative opportunities to advertisers. Perfume marketers such as Clarins include scent strips in their magazine ads for consumers to sample.

- *Long life.* Many magazines are saved issue-to-issue by their subscribers. This means that, unlike newspapers, a magazine can be reexamined over a week or a month. Some magazines are saved for long periods for future reference, such as *Architectural Digest, National Geographic,* and *Travel & Leisure.* In addition to multiple subscriber exposure, this long life increases the chance of pass-along readership as people visit the subscriber's home (or professional offices) and look at magazines.

Many magazines are realizing solid revenue and readership gains. Publications such as *Time, Fortune,* and *Good Housekeeping* have realized revenue gains over 10 percent. Overall, major magazines tracked by the Publishers' Information Bureau showed a gain of 3.9 percent in ad pages and a very strong 11.8 percent in growth overall revenue in 1997.[13]

Disadvantages of Magazines. The disadvantages of magazines as a media choice have to do with their being too selective in their reach and with the recent proliferation of magazines.

- *Limited reach and frequency.* The tremendous advantage of selectivity discussed in the previous section actually creates a limitation for magazines. The more narrowly defined the interest group, the less overall reach a magazine will have. Since most magazines are published monthly or perhaps every two weeks, there is little chance for an advertiser to achieve frequent exposure using a single magazine. To overcome this limitation, advertisers often use several magazines targeted at the same audience. For example, many readers of *Better Homes & Gardens* may also be readers of *Architectural Digest.* By placing ads in both publications, an advertiser can increase both reach and frequency within a targeted audience.
- *Clutter.* Magazines are not quite as cluttered as newspapers, but they still represent a fairly difficult context for message delivery. The average magazine is about half editorial and entertainment content and half advertising material, but some highly specialized magazines contain as much as 80 percent advertising.[14] And this advertising, given the narrowly defined audiences, tends to be for brands in direct competition with each other. In addition to this clutter, there is another sort of clutter that has recently begun to plague magazines. As soon as a new market segment is recognized, there is a flood of "me-too" magazines. This may be good in terms of coverage, but it may devalue individual ads and the vehicles in which they appear. As an example, by mid-1995 there were 30 magazines aimed at Generation X, the highly sought-after segment of young adults. With names like *Blaster* and *Subnation,* these Gen X publications have circulations from less than 1,000 to about 350,000.[15]
- *Long lead times.* Advertisers are required to submit their ads as much as 90 days in advance of the date of publication. If the submission date is missed, there can be as much as a full month's delay in placing the next ad. And once an ad is submitted, it cannot be changed during that 90-day period, even if some significant event alters the communications environment.

13. R. Craig Endicott, "Ad Age 300," *Advertising Age,* June 15, 1998, S-1.
14. Thomas R. King, "Bride's Magazine Takes Cake in Ad Clutter," *Wall Street Journal,* January 4, 1990, B8.
15. Todd Pruzan, "Advertisers Wary of Generation X Titles," *Advertising Age,* October 24, 1994, S-22.

- *Cost.* While the cost per contact in magazines is not nearly as high as in some media (direct mail in particular), it is more expensive than most newspaper space, and many times the cost per contact in the broadcast media. The absolute cost for a single insertion can be prohibitive. For magazines with large circulation, such as *Modern Maturity* and *Good Housekeeping,* the cost for a one-time four-color ad runs from $100,000 to about $250,000.

GLOBAL ISSUES

COSMO: TO RUSSIA WITH LOVE

Publishers of major women's magazines in the United States are racing to enter new countries and appeal to new readers as a means of expanding revenue. From the harsh winter clime of Russia to the sultry heat of Southeast Asia, *Cosmopolitan, Elle,* and *Marie Claire* race for the devotion of a young, global audience.

Traditionally, magazines have been very culture bound. Only the most widely circulated news or general-interest magazines could find a global market. But the publishers of these leading women's magazines are trying to make the culture adaptation necessary to attract readers—and then advertisers—to global versions. *Cosmo Girl,* for example, is being published in 33 international editions, with a goal of about 40 international editions. *Elle* is prepared to offer 29 editions and *Marie Claire,* a French fashion and lifestyle magazine, is planning distribution in 26 markets.

How is the race for global readers going? Not so well—yet. *Cosmopolitan* is in the lead with 4 million copies distributed outside the United States; *Elle* claims 3.5 million copies and *Marie Claire* about 2.5 million copies. The problem, however, is not so much readers as the ability to attract global ad packages. Part of the problem is that if the magazine is not fine-tuned to the tastes of the region, advertisers are less inclined to see a long-term potential. To help the fine-tuning process, publishers are finding local partners who help them include localized or regionalized editorial content. Local publishing partners also understand publishing and distribution infrastructure, which will translate directly into profits.

So, while going global for magazines has great potential in attracting selective target markets on a worldwide basis, it requires careful customization of the publication. Whether a large number of publishers will take on the challenge of multiple national editions remains to be seen.

Source: Claire Wilson and Rebecca A. Fannin, "Magazine Marathon," *Ad Age International,* May 1997, i16–i16.

Types of Magazines. The magazine medium is highly fragmented, with more than 12,000 magazine titles published annually in the United States and literally hundreds of titles introduced every year. A useful classification scheme for magazines is to categorize them by major target audience: consumer, business, and farm publications.

- *Consumer publications.* Magazines that appeal to consumer interests run the gamut from international news to sports, education, age-group information, and hobbies. These include magazines written specifically for men (*Men's Journal*—see Exhibit 15.17), women (*Woman's Day*), and ethnic groups (*Ebony*). Many new consumer magazines appeal to the lifestyle changes of the 1980s and 1990s: *New Woman, Men's Health.* Advertisers invested over $13 billion in advertising in consumer magazines in 1997.[16] The top five magazines in this category are listed in Exhibit 15.18.
- *Business publications.* Business magazines come in many different forms. Each major industry has a trade publication, such as *InfoWorld* in the computer industry, that highlights events and issues in that industry. Professional publications are written for doctors, lawyers, accountants, and other professional groups. *American Family Physician* publishes articles for family practitioners and carries advertising from many pharmaceutical manufacturers. General-interest business magazines such as *Fortune* and *Forbes* cut across all trades, industries, and professions. The leading business magazine categories are listed in Exhibit 15.19.
- *Farm publications.* The three major farm publications in the United States and their approximate paid circulations are *Farm Journal* (197,000), *Successful Farming* (476,000), and *Progressive Farmer* (286,000). These magazines provide technical information

16. R. Craig Endicott, "Ad Age 300," S-2.

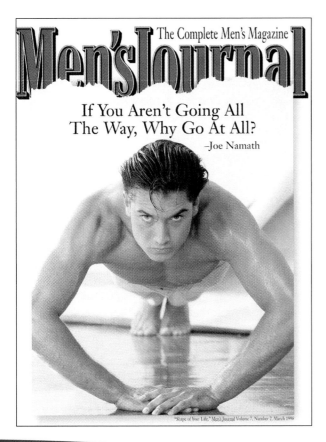

The Complete Men's Magazine

Men's Journal

If You Aren't Going All The Way, Why Go At All?

–Joe Namath

"Shape of Your Life," Men's Journal Volume 7, Number 2, March 1998

EXHIBIT 15.17

In the consumer magazine category, publishers try to appeal to target audience's special interest. Men's Journal *deals with contemporary issues facing men in health, fitness, and career challenges.*

about farming techniques as well as business management articles to improve farmers' profitability. In addition to national publications, regional farm magazines and publications focus on specific aspects of the industry.

In this new media environment, it is important to recognize that many consumer and business publications are now available in digital format over the Internet. Magazines that are available electronically have been dubbed "digizines." The evolution of the digizine is highlighted in the New Media box on page 488. Over 250 magazines now offer their titles in a digital version. There are several advantages of the digizine format for both the publisher and the subscriber. First, a publisher is often able to tap a different segment—the Internet-savvy user—with an electronic format. Second, the publisher also may realize lower costs in publishing a digizine in that there are no paper costs and distribution costs are greatly reduced. Finally, some advertisers may find the digital version a better environment for advertising than the more cluttered printed version.

From the subscriber's standpoint, the digizine is easily accessible through the subscriber's PC, movement through the magazine is facilitated by standard keyword search conventions, and, for the environmentally conscious, no recycling is needed. Finally, for subscribers to magazines that deal with computer or Internet content, the digizine is the ideal and preferred format. Ziff-Davis Publishing discovered that consumers with acute interest in the Internet were far more likely to subscribe to a digital version, of the company's *Yahoo! Internet Life* than the traditional print version, with 75 to 80 percent of new subscribers coming from Internet-based subscriptions.[17]

Costs and Buying Procedures for Magazine Advertising. The cost for magazine space varies dramatically. As with newspapers, the size of an ad, its position in a publication, its creative execution (black-and-white or color or any special techniques),

EXHIBIT 15.18

Top five consumer magazine categories, ranked by revenue, 1997. Figures are in millions of U.S. dollars.

Magazine Category	Total Revenue	Ad Revenue	Paid Circulation	Top Magazine in Classification
Newsweeklies	$5,049.0	$2,946.2	32,901,287	*TV Guide*
Women's	3,733.0	2,256.4	59,293,304	*Good Housekeeping*
General editorial	3,212.6	1,749.8	111,676,278	*Reader's Digest*
Home service and home	1,842.3	1,185.4	29,437,101	*Better Homes & Gardens*
Business and finance	1,708.7	1,307.3	10,687,306	*Business Week*

Source: *Advertising Age,* June 15, 1998, S-28. Reprinted with permission from the June 15, 1998, issue of *Advertising Age.* Copyright © Crain Communications Inc. 1998.

17. Ann Marie Kerwin, "'Internet Life' Taps Yahoo! Site for Subscribers," *Advertising Age,* June 15, 1998, 60.

Top five business magazine categories, ranked by revenue, 1997. Figures are in millions of U.S. dollars.

Magazine Category	Total Revenue	Ad Revenue	Paid Circulation	Top Magazine in Classification
Computers/internet	$2,653.9	$2,339.5	8,348,069	*PC Magazine*
Electronic engineering	257.1	257.1	0	*Electronic Engineering Times*
Travel, retail	182.0	180.7	50,309	*Travel Agent*
Medical and surgical	159.3	124.0	723,651	*New England Journal of Medicine*
Business	145.9	91.4	646,551	*Barron's*

Source: *Advertising Age*, June 15, 1998, S-28. Reprinted with permission from the June 15, 1998, issue of *Advertising Age*. Copyright © Crain Communications Inc. 1998.

and its placement in a regular or special edition of the magazine all affect costs. The main cost, of course, is based on the magazine's circulation. A full-page four-color ad in *Reader's Digest* costs $150,000; a full-page four-color ad in *People* costs about $106,000; a full-page ad in *Skiing* costs about $25,000; and a full-page ad in *Surreal,* a Gen X magazine with a paid circulation of 3,000, is only $500.

Each magazine has a rate card that shows the cost for full-page, half-page, two-column, one-column, and half-column ads. A rate card also shows the cost for black-and-white, two-color, and four-color ads. Rate cards for magazines, as with newspapers, have been the standard pricing method for many years. In recent years, however, more and more publishers have been willing to negotiate rates and give deep discounts for volume purchases—discounts as large as 20 to 30 percent off the published card rate.[18] The rate card in Exhibit 15.20 shows the kind of discount advertisers can get for volume purchases.

In addition to standard rates, there is an extra charge for a **bleed page**. On a bleed page, the background color of an ad runs to the edge of the page, replacing the standard white border. **Gatefold ads**, or ads that fold out of a magazine to display an extra-wide advertisement, also carry an extra charge. Gatefolds are often used by advertisers on the inside cover of upscale magazines. An example is the ad for dishes and flatware in Exhibit 15.21.

Advertisers can earn large-volume discounts when they buy multiple insertions. Notice that when advertisers buy space in Marketing News, *a trade publication, the cost for eight insertions of a ½-page horizontal ad is about 12.5 percent less per insertion.*

Marketing News General Advertising Rates

	1x	4x	8x	14x	20x	26x	40x
Full Page	$2615	$2355	$2290	$2220	$2155	$2090	$1960
Full Spread	$4925	$4430	$4310	$4185	$4065	$3940	$3695
Pony Page	$2125	$1910	$1860	$1805	$1755	$1700	$1595
Pony Spread	$4050	$3645	$3545	$3440	$3340	$3240	$3040
4/7 Page (vert.)	$1950	$1755	$1705	$1655	$1610	$1560	$1460
1/2 Page (horiz.)	$1750	$1575	$1530	$1485	$1445	$1400	$1310
3/7 Page	$1570	$1415	$1375	$1335	$1295	$1255	$1175
2/5 Page	$1465	$1320	$1280	$1245	$1210	$1170	$1100
2/7 Page	$1090	$980	$955	$925	$900	$870	$815
1/4 Page	$985	$885	$860	$835	$815	$790	$740
1/5 Page	$775	$695	$680	$660	$640	$620	$580
1/7 Page	$545	$490	$475	$465	$450	$435	$410
1/10 Page	$415	$375	$365	$355	$345	$335	$310
1/14 Page	$305	$275	$265	$260	$250	$245	$230
Ads smaller than 5 col. in.	$90/col. in.	$80	$78	$76	$74	$72	$68

18. Lisa I. Fried, "New Rules Liven Up the Rate-Card Game," *Advertising Age,* October 24, 1994, S-8.

Gatefold ads display extra-wide advertisements, like this one for Lenox dishes.

When buying space in a magazine, advertisers must decide among several placement options. A run-of-press advertisement can appear anywhere in the magazine, at the discretion of the publisher. The advertiser may pay for several preferred positions, however. **First cover page** is the front cover of a magazine; **second cover page** is the inside front cover; **third cover page** is the inside back cover; and **fourth cover page** is the back cover. When advertisers prepare **double-page spreads**—advertisements that bridge two facing pages—it is important that no headlines or body copy run through the gutter, which is the fold between the magazine pages.

Buying procedures for magazine advertising demand that an advertiser follow several guidelines and honor several key dates. A **space contract** establishes a rate for all advertising placed in a publication by an advertiser over a specified period. A **space order**, also referred to as an *insertion order*, is a commitment by an advertiser to advertising space in a particular issue. It is accompanied by production specifications for the ad or ads that will appear in the issue. The dates that an advertiser must be aware of are as follows:

- **Closing date:** The date when production-ready advertising materials must be delivered to a publisher for an ad to make an issue.
- **On-sale date:** The date on which a magazine is issued to subscribers and for newsstand distribution. Most magazines put issues on sale far in advance of the cover date.
- **Cover date:** The date of publication appearing on a magazine.

Measuring Magazine Audiences. Most magazines base their published advertising rates on **guaranteed circulation**, which is a stated minimum number of copies of a particular issue that will be delivered to readers. This number guarantees for advertisers that they are achieving a certain minimum reach with an ad placement. In addition, publishers estimate **pass-along readership**, which is an additional number of people, other than the original readers, who may see a publication. Advertisers can verify circulation through the Audit Bureau of Circulations, which reports total and state-by-state circulation for magazines, as well as subscriber versus newsstand circulation. When an advertiser wants to go beyond basic circulation numbers, the syndicated magazine

DIGIZINES: DON'T LOOK FOR ONE WHILE YOU WAIT FOR THE DENTIST

Blender. @NZone. Abound. Launch. Sound like names for the latest, hippest magazines? They are. But don't look for one the next time you go to the dentist. These new magazines can be found only in cyberspace. In fact, they are so hip, they're not even called magazines—they've been dubbed *digizines*. These four digizines, along with dozens of others, are published only online or on CD-ROM. Several publishers with good ideas for new magazines are skipping the cost, risk, and clutter of the newsstand and going straight to cyberspace.

While content and advertising look a bit like that in a traditional magazine, a digizine is not confined by traditional print media rules. Michael Rogers, executive producer of broadband products for the *Washington Post,* says, "There are no preconceptions on the part of the audience. They're not going to expect things to be in the electronic magazine that are in the print magazine and then be disappointed." The opportunities and capabilities of cyberspace make the digizine a truly new medium.

The rush to electronic magazine publishing was more like a crawl in 1993. A few big-name publications with lots of brand awareness and loyal readers were put online first by America Online. Publications such as *Time* and *Car and Driver* offered a low-risk way for consumers to venture into cyberspace. But the lukewarm response to such trusted publications opened the door to a swarm of newcomers. In addition to *Blender, Trouble & Attitude,* and *Launch*—aimed primarily at Gen X'ers—humor, music, business, and men's magazines are being published or planned for online or CD-ROM distribution. Their ranks include titles such as *Urban Desires, Word, Melvin, Nautilus,* and *eGG* (*electronic Gourmet Guide*).

Attracting advertisers will, of course, be a key to the success of digizines. Most online publications charge by the megabyte, although some seem to be dreaming up space charges just to see where the cost limits for advertisers might be. Rates range from $500 per megabyte for an audio trade digizine called *Control,* to $2,500 per meg for *Launch,* which guarantees advertisers a circulation of 150,000 discs priced at $8.95 and distributed through music and software retailers. *Launch* has been the most successful digizine at attracting mainline advertisers. The first issue included ads by Reebok, Dewar's Scotch, Cadbury, Schweppes, Warner Brothers, and Levi Strauss. *Launch* uses a cityscape internal design throughout the disc that allows readers to access ads in interesting and entertaining ways. For example, the Dewar's ads can be accessed by clicking on billboards in the city. The reader can enter a movie theater to view a trailer for Warner Brothers' *Batman Forever.*

The brightest future for digizines may actually lie with the pioneers such as *Launch.* As one digizine publisher put it, "We don't look anything like a print magazine. A print magazine couldn't do what we're doing. You have to find something compelling for the consumer. *Newsweek Interactive* is just not compelling."

Source: Scott Donaton, "Not Your Father's Magazine," *Advertising Age,* April 10, 1995, 18, 20.

research services such as Simmons Market Research Bureau and Mediamark Research can provide additional information. Through personal interviews and respondent-kept diaries, these services provide advertisers with information on reader demographics, media use, and product usage.

The Future of Magazines.
Magazines have had a roller-coaster history over the past 10 to 15 years. Currently, revenues and ad pages are up, and advertisers are finding the advantages of magazines well suited to their current needs. Two factors are likely to be major influences on magazines as an advertising medium in the future. First, magazines will, like other media options, have to determine how to adapt to new media options. More than 250 magazines now offer online versions with computer services such as America Online, Compu-Serve, and Prodigy. As discussed earlier, these electronic versions have several advantages to both the publisher and the subscriber, but it remains to be seen whether advertisers believe there are advantages. To date, these digizines have attracted minimal ad spending. Some analysts feel that for online advertising to be successful, it must be unintrusive. Such ads will have to be interactive, educational, or entertaining.[19] Until online magazine publication proves viable, advertisers are likely to stay with traditional formats.

The second factor affecting the future of magazines is a robust environment for mergers and acquisitions. Recent years have seen dozens of merger and acquisition deals each year in the magazine industry. Buyers are looking for two benefits in acquiring publications: economies of scale in traditional print publication and new media outlets. In the last few years, the pursuit of these advantages has resulted in over $2 billion a year in mergers and acquisitions.[20]

19. Scott Donaton, "New Creative Tools Give Online Titles Hope for Bolstering Ad Revenues," *Advertising Age,* October 24, 1994, S-18.

20. Ann Marie Kerwin, "Execs Predict '98 Mergers Aplenty for Magazines," *Advertising Age,* June 15, 1998, S-30.

Television and Radio Media Evaluation. When you say the word *advertising,* the average person thinks of television and radio advertising. It's easy to understand why. Television advertising can be advertising at its very best. With the benefit of sight and sound, color and music, action and special effects, television advertising can be the most powerful advertising of all. It has some other advantages as well. In many parts of the world, particularly in the United States, television is the medium most widely used by consumers for entertainment and information. Radio advertising also has key advantages. The ability to reach consumers in multiple locations and the creative power of radio rank as important communications opportunities.

Advertisers readily appreciate the power of television and radio advertising and invest billions of dollars a year in these media. This section of the chapter will describe the nature of the television and radio media. First, we will look at the options available to advertisers. Next, as with the print media, we'll consider the inherent advantages and disadvantages of these media. Finally, each evaluation concludes with a discussion of buying procedures and techniques for audience measurement.

Television as an Advertising Medium. 🔊 To many, television is the medium that defines what advertising is. With its multisensory stimulation, television offers the chance for advertising to be all that it can be. Television presents two extraordinary opportunities to advertisers. First, the diversity of communication possibilities allows for outstanding creative expression of a brand's value. Dramatic color, sweeping action, and spectacular sound effects can cast a brand in an exciting and unique light. Second, once this expressive presentation of a brand is prepared, it can be disseminated to millions of consumers, often at a fraction of a penny per contact.

These opportunities have not been lost on advertisers. In the United States in 1997, advertisers invested more than $44.5 billion in television advertising for media time alone—this does not include the many billions of dollars spent on production costs. And advertisers are finding television more and more to their liking. The $44.5 billion was a full 10.5 percent increase over the prior year's spending.[21] To fully appreciate all that television means to advertisers, we need to understand much more about this complex medium.

Television Categories. Without careful evaluation, the natural tendency is to classify television as a single type of broadcast medium. When we turn on the television, we simply decide what program we find interesting and then settle in for some entertainment. The reality is that over the past 15 to 20 years, several distinct versions of television have evolved, from which consumers can choose for entertainment and advertisers can choose for reaching those consumers. There are four different alternatives: network, cable, syndicated, and local television. Exhibit 15.22 shows the spending in these television categories for 1996 and 1997. Notice that while all the options showed solid growth in advertising receipts, the fastest growth was in cable television.

EXHIBIT 15.22

Spending by advertisers in the four television categories. Figures are in millions of U.S. dollars.

	Total Measured Advertising Spending		
	1997	**1996**	**% Change**
Spot TV	$14,534.6	$14,017.7	3.7
Network TV	15,225.1	14,739.6	3.3
Cable TV	5,781.9	4,728.4	22.3
Syndicated TV	2,515.0	2,326.1	8.1

Source: R. Craig Endicott, "The Top 100 Mega Brands," *Advertising Age,* July 13, 1998, S-2. Reprinted with permission from the July 13, 1998, issue of *Advertising Age.* Copyright © Crain Communications.

21. Coen, "Ad Revenue Growth Hits 7% in 1997 to Surpass Forecasts," 50.

Let's examine the nature of each of these four options for television advertising.

- *Network television.* **Network television** broadcasts programming over airwaves to affiliate stations across the United States under a contract agreement. Advertisers can buy time within these programs to reach audiences in hundreds of markets. There are currently four major broadcast television networks in the United States: Disney/American Broadcasting Company (ABC), the Columbia Broadcasting System (CBS), the Fox network (Fox), and the National Broadcasting Company (NBC). Two additional competitors in network television have only recently begun to broadcast. WB, a new network financed by Time Warner, started with 50 affiliate stations and four programs on Wednesday nights. The network estimates it will reach about 80 percent of U.S. households. The other new network is United Paramount Network (UPN), which began broadcasting in January of 1995 with only five shows over two nights of programming. Exhibit 15.23 displays the top ten network television advertisers.

- *Cable television.* From its modest beginnings as community antenna television (CATV) in the 1940s, cable television has grown into a worldwide communications force. **Cable television** transmits a wide range of programming to subscribers through wires rather than over airwaves. In the United States, more than 70 million households (75 percent of all U.S. households) are wired for cable reception and receive on average more than 30 channels of sports, entertainment, news, music video, and home-shopping programming. Cable's power as an advertising option has grown enormously over the past decade, as the chapter opening scenario highlighted. During the 1997–1998 season, cable's share of prime-time ratings in the United States rose to 21.8 percent of the viewing audience and cable's share of the total-day audience reached 33.4 percent, compared with the major networks' 39.1 percent.[22]

Aside from more programming on cable, which distinguishes this category of television from the networks, another aspect is the willingness of cable networks to invest in original programming. With the success of programs such as USA Network's *La Femme Nikita* and *Pacific Blue,* cable networks are investing record dollar amounts in new programs to continue to attract well-defined audiences.[23]

EXHIBIT 15.23

Top ten network TV advertisers. Figures are in millions of U.S. dollars.

Rank	Advertiser	Network TV Ad Spending		
		1997	**1996**	**% Change**
1	General Motors Corp.	$819.3	$613.9	33.5
2	Procter & Gamble Co.	662.2	600.5	10.3
3	Johnson & Johnson	473.7	506.9	–6.5
4	Philip Morris Cos.	464.3	396.5	17.1
5	Ford Motor Co.	341.9	331.2	3.2
6	Diageo	324.8	288.7	12.5
7	Chrysler Corp.	301.4	288.6	4.5
8	McDonald's	295.5	372.0	–20.6
9	Walt Disney Co.	263.9	267.2	–1.2
10	Tricon Global Restaurants	258.2	284.9	–9.4

Source: *Advertising Age,* September 28, 1998, s38. Reprinted with permission from the September 28, 1998, issue of *Advertising Age.* Copyright © Crain Communications Inc. 1998.

22. Haley, "As Cable Audiences Grow, Revenues Follow," A3.
23. Andrew Bowser, "Networks Increase Original Programming," *Advertising Age,* June 8, 1998, A4.

EXHIBIT 15.24

Cable television's global reach.

Cable Network	Reach (millions of homes)	Programming
BBC World	40	News, Entertainment
MTV	294.3	Music television
CNN International	162.6	News/information
TNT/Cartoon Network	115.8	Entertainment
ESPN	217.8	Sports
Discovery Channel	101.2	Education/entertainment
CNBC	149.2	Business news/information
USA Network	47.7	Entertainment

Source: "Global Media," *Ad Age International,* February 1997, i4. Reprinted with permission from the February 1997 issue of *Ad Age International.* Copyright © Crain Communications Inc. 1997.

The other feature of cable that is not to be underestimated is the global potential of cable networks. Exhibit 15.24 shows the global reach of the largest cable networks. Cable now reaches literally billions of viewers worldwide, making it a truly global medium for multinational firms to reach their audiences.

- *Syndicated television.* Television syndication is either original programming or programming that first appeared on network television. It is then rebroadcast on either network or cable stations. Syndicated programs provide advertisers with proven programming that typically attracts a well-defined, if not enormous, audience. There are several types of television syndication. **Off-network syndication** refers to programs that were previously run in network prime time. Some of the most popular off-network syndicated shows are *Home Improvement* and *Seinfeld.* **First-run syndication** refers to programs developed specifically for sale to individual stations. The most famous first-run syndication show is *Star Trek: The Next Generation.* **Barter syndication** takes both off-network and first-run syndication shows and offers them free or at a reduced rate to local television stations, with some national advertising presold within the programs. Local stations can then sell the remainder of the time to generate revenues. This option allows national advertisers to participate in the national syndication market conveniently. Some of the most widely recognized barter syndication shows are *Jeopardy* and *Wheel of Fortune.*
- *Local television.* **Local television** is the programming other than the network broadcast that independent stations and network affiliates offer local audiences. Completely independent stations broadcast old movies, sitcoms, or children's programming. Network affiliates get about 90 hours of programming a week from the major networks, but they are free to broadcast other programming beyond that provided by the network. News, movies, syndicated programs, and community interest programs typically round out the local television fare.

As you can see, while all television may look the same to the average consumer, advertisers actually have four distinct options to consider. Regardless of which type of television transmission advertisers choose, television offers distinct advantages to advertisers as a way to communicate with target audiences.

Advantages of Television. Throughout the book, we have referred to the unique capability of television as an advertising medium. There must be some very good reasons why advertisers such as AT&T, General Motors, and Procter & Gamble invest hundreds of millions of dollars annually in television advertising. The specific advantages of this medium are as follows:

- *Creative opportunities.* The overriding advantage of television compared to other media is, of course, the ability to send a message using both sight and sound. With recent advances in transmission and reception equipment, households now have brilliantly clear visuals and stereo-enhanced audio to further increase the impact of television advertising. In addition, special effects perfected for films such as *The Mask* are now making their way into advertising prepared for television.

- *Coverage, reach, and repetition.* Television, in one form or another, reaches more than 98 percent of all households in the United States—an estimated 260 million people. These households represent every demographic, economic, and ethnic segment in the United States, which allows advertisers to achieve broad coverage. We have also seen that the cable television option provides reach to hundreds of millions of households throughout the world. Further, no other medium allows an advertiser to repeat a message as frequently as television.

- *Cost per contact.* For advertisers that sell to broadly defined mass markets, television offers a cost-effective way to reach millions of members of a target audience. The average prime-time television program reaches 11 million households, and top-rated shows can reach more than 20 million households. This brings an advertiser's cost-per-contact figure down to an amount unmatched by any other media option.

- *Audience selectivity.* Television programmers are doing a better job of developing shows that attract well-defined target audiences. **Narrowcasting** is the development and delivery of specialized programming to well-defined audiences. Cable television is far and away the most selective television option. Cable provides not only well-defined programming, but also entire networks—such as MTV and ESPN—built around the concept of attracting selective audiences. The Fox network has also carefully developed its narrowcasting capabilities. Exhibit 15.25 shows the various programming efforts undertaken by Fox to reach youth audiences.

Disadvantages of Television. Television has great capabilities as an advertising medium, but it is not without limitations. Some of these limitations are serious enough to significantly detract from the power of television advertising.

- *Fleeting message.* One problem with the sight and sound of a television advertisement is that it is gone in an instant. The fleeting nature of a television message, as opposed to a print ad (which a receiver can contemplate), makes message impact difficult. Some advertisers invest huge amounts of money in the production of television ads to overcome this disadvantage.

- *High absolute cost.* While the cost per contact of television advertising is the best of all media, the absolute cost may be the worst. The average cost of airtime for a single 30-second television spot during prime time is just over $100,000. The average cost of producing a 30-second television spot is around $200,000. These costs make television advertising prohibitively expensive for many advertisers. Of course, large, national consumer products companies—for which television advertising is best suited anyway—find the absolute cost acceptable for the coverage, reach, and repetition advantages discussed earlier.

WEB SIGHTING

EXHIBIT 15.25

Part of the major networks' answer to the challenge of new media is to join 'em, even as they fight off others' new offerings. The availability of new outlets, both on cable and on the Internet, means opportunities to distill specialty content for narrower audiences (perhaps from content the network already owns and airs in less volume on its main channel). The ability to command higher advertising fees when an audience can be selected, through narrowcasting, to more exactly match an advertiser's offerings is one of television's advantages as an advertising medium. Compare Fox Kids (www.foxkids.com) and the Cartoon Network (www.cartoon network.com), both of which are targeting the same demographic.

- *Poor geographic selectivity.* While programming can be developed to attract specific audiences, program transmission cannot target geographic areas nearly as well. For a national advertiser that wants to target a city market, the reach of a television broadcast is too broad. Similarly, for a local retailer that wants to use television for reaching local segments, the television transmission is likely to reach a several-hundred-mile radius—which will increase the advertiser's cost with little likelihood of drawing patrons.

- *Poor audience attitude and attentiveness.* Since the inception of television advertising, consumers have bemoaned the intrusive nature of the commercials. Just when a movie is reaching its thrilling conclusion—on come the ads. The involuntary and frequent intrusion of advertisements on television has made television advertising the most distrusted form of advertising among consumers.

Along with—and perhaps as a result of—this generally bad attitude toward television advertising, consumers have developed ways of avoiding exposure. Making a trip to the refrigerator or conversing with fellow viewers are the preferred low-tech ways to avoid exposure. On the high-tech side, **channel grazing**, or using a remote control to monitor programming on other channels while an advertisement is being broadcast, is the favorite way to avoid commercials. When programs have been videotaped for later viewing, zapping and zipping are common avoidance techniques. **Zapping** is the process of eliminating ads altogether from videotaped programs. **Zipping** is the process of fast-forwarding through advertisements contained in videotaped programs.

New technology has created yet another potential method for avoiding advertising—and this development has advertisers greatly concerned. The problems centers on the so-called "V-chip." The **V-chip** is a device that can block television programming based on the newly developed program rating system. It was developed as a way for parents to block programming that they do not want their children to see. While that was the original and intended use for the V-chip, the technology can be easily adapted to block advertisements as well. Two manufacturers, RCA and Panasonic, say they want to build television sets with this sort of technology. Advertisers and broadcasters, of course, are challenging the rights of these manufacturers to build such sets. The consequences of sets with V-chips that block ads could be devastating to advertising revenues.

- *Clutter.* All the advantages of television as an advertising medium have created one significant disadvantage: clutter. The major television networks run about 13 minutes of advertising during each hour of prime-time programming, and cable broadcasts carry about 17 minutes of advertising per hour.[24] Aside from the sheer number of intrusive minutes of advertising, these minutes are jammed with messages. In 1980, 96 percent of all television ads were 30 seconds in length. In 1992, only 63 percent of all ads were 30 seconds long, and 32 percent were the newer 15-second ads.[25] This has significantly increased the number of messages audiences are exposed to, and it has caused a much more cluttered environment for communication and persuasion.

- *Buying Procedures for Television Advertising.* Discussions in Chapters 13 and 14 as well as in this chapter have identified the costs associated with television advertising from both a production and a space standpoint. Here we will concentrate on the issue of buying time on television. Advertisers buy time for television advertising through sponsorship, participation, and spot advertising.

- *Sponsorship.* In a **sponsorship** arrangement, an advertiser agrees to pay for the production of a television program and for most (and often all) of the advertising that appears in the program. Sponsorship is not nearly as popular today as it was in the early days of network television. Contemporary sponsorship agreements have attracted big-name companies such as AT&T and IBM, who often sponsor sporting events, and Hallmark, known for its sponsorship of dramatic series.

---

24. Kevin Goldman, "TV Promotional Clutter Irks Ad Industry," *Wall Street Journal,* February 11, 1994, B6.
25. Wayne Walley, "Popularity of :15s Falls," *Advertising Age,* January 14, 1994, 41.

- *Participation.* The vast majority of advertising time is purchased on a participation basis. **Participation** means that several different advertisers buy commercial time during a specific television program. No single advertiser has a responsibility for the production of the program or a commitment to the program beyond the time contracted for.

- *Spot advertising.* **Spot advertising** refers to all television advertising time purchased from and aired through local television stations. Spot advertising provides national advertisers the opportunity to either adjust advertising messages for different markets or intensify their media schedules in particularly competitive markets. Spot advertising is the primary manner in which local advertisers, such as car dealers, furniture stores, and restaurants, reach their target audiences with television.

A final issue with respect to buying television advertising has to do with the time periods and programs during which the advertising will run. Once an advertiser has determined that sponsorship, participation, or spot advertising (or, more likely, some combination of the last two) meets its needs, the time periods and specific programs must be chosen. Exhibit 15.26 shows the way in which television programming times are broken into **dayparts**, which represent segments of time during a television broadcast day.

The dayparts are important to advertisers because the size and type of audience varies by daypart. Morning audiences tend to be predominantly made up of women and children. The daytime daypart is dominated by women. Prime time has the largest and most diverse audiences. Once dayparts have been evaluated, specific programs within dayparts are chosen. As we have discussed, programs are developed and targeted to specific audiences, and advertisers match their ad buying to the program audience profiles. Let's turn our attention to these television audience issues.

Measuring Television Audiences. Television audience measurements identify the size and composition of audiences for different television programming. Advertisers choose where to buy time in television broadcasts based on these factors. These measures also set the cost for television time. The larger the audience or the more attractive the composition, the more costly the time will be.

The only source for *both* network and local audience information is A. C. Nielsen. Arbitron is another source for network measurement, but it abandoned local measurement in 1993.

The following are brief summaries of the information used to measure television audiences.

- *Television households.* **Television households** is an estimate of the number of households that are in a market and own a television. Since more than 98 percent of all households in the United States own a television, the number of total households and the number of television households are virtually the same, about 95.9 million. Markets around the world do not have the same level of television penetration.

EXHIBIT 15.26

Television broadcast dayparts (in Eastern time zone segments).

Morning	7:00 A.M. to 9:00 A.M., Monday through Friday
Daytime	9:00 A.M. to 4:30 P.M., Monday through Friday
Early fringe	4:30 P.M. to 7:30 P.M., Monday through Friday
Prime-time access	7:30 P.M. to 8:00 P.M., Sunday through Saturday
Prime time	8:00 P.M. to 11:00 P.M., Monday through Saturday 7:00 P.M. to 11:00 P.M., Sunday
Late news	11:00 P.M. to 11:30 P.M., Monday through Friday
Late fringe	11:30 P.M. to 1:00 A.M., Monday through Friday

- *Households using television.* **Households using television (HUT),** also referred to as *sets in use,* is a measure of the number of households tuned to a television program during a particular time period.
- *Program rating.* A **program rating** is the percentage of television households that are in a market and are tuned to a specific program during a specific time period. Expressed as a formula, program rating is

$$\text{program rating} = \frac{\text{TV households tuned to a program}}{\text{total TV households in the market}}$$

A **ratings point** indicates that 1 percent of all the television households in an area were tuned to the program measured. If an episode of *The X-Files* is watched by 19.5 million households, then the program rating would be calculated as follows:

$$\text{X-Files rating} = \frac{19,500,000}{95,900,000} = 20 \text{ rating}$$

The program rating is the best-known measure of television audience, and it is the basis for the rates television stations charge for advertising on different programs. Recall that it is also the way advertisers develop their media plans from the standpoint of calculating reach and frequency estimates, such as gross rating points.

- *Share of audience.* **Share of audience** provides a measure of the proportion of households that are using television during a specific time period and are tuned to a particular program. If 65 million households are using their televisions during the *X-Files* time slot, the share of audience measure is:

$$\text{X-Files share} = \frac{\text{TV households tuned to a program}}{\text{total TV households using TV}} = \frac{19,500,000}{65,000,000} = 30 \text{ share}$$

The Future of Television. The future of television is exciting for several reasons. First, the emerging interactive era will undoubtedly affect television as an advertising medium. Prospects include viewer participation in mystery programs and game shows in which household viewers play right along with studio contestants. While this interactivity is intriguing, there are varying opinions about how popular it might be. Early experiments with interactivity have been met with a less than enthusiastic response from consumers.[26]

Another major change that will affect the future of television is emerging transmission technology. **Direct broadcast by satellite (DBS)** is a program delivery system whereby television (and radio) programs are sent directly from a satellite to homes equipped with small receiving dishes. This transmission offers the prospect of hundreds of different channels. While advertisers will still be able to insert advertising in programs, the role of networks and cable stations in the advertising process will change dramatically. Recently, DBS technology has added a new capability. Rather than transmitting directly to homes, a Japanese company has developed a system to deliver programming to automobiles. The Global Issues box on page 496 tells the story of this satellite transmission system.

Finally, **high-definition television (HDTV)** promises to offer consumers picture and audio clarity that is a vast improvement over current technology. While HDTV equipment will certainly have the capability to reproduce images and sound with extraordinary quality, the uncertainties of visual and audio transmission may compromise the ability of the new HDTV sets to do so.

While it is hard to predict what the future will hold, one thing seems sure—television will continue to grow as an entertainment and information medium for households. The

---

26. William M. Buckeley and John R. Wilke, "Can the Exalted Vision Become a Reality? Early Attempts Show Viewers May Be Leery," *Wall Street Journal,* October 14, 1993, B1.

convenience, low cost, and diversity of programming make television an ideal medium for consumers. Additionally, television's expansion around the world will generate access to huge new markets. Television, despite its limitations, will continue to be an important part of the integrated communications mix of many advertisers.

Radio as an Advertising Medium.

Radio may seem the least glamorous and most inconspicuous of the major media. This perception does not jibe with reality. Radio plays an integral role in the media plans of some of the most astute advertisers. Because of the unique features of radio, advertisers invested $13.4 billion in the medium in 1997.[27] There are good reasons why advertisers of all sorts turn to radio as a means to reach their target audiences. Let's turn our attention to the different radio options available to advertisers.

COUCH POTATOES TAKE TO THE ROAD IN JAPAN

A Japanese company with the backing of such industrial giants as Toyota Motors, Toshiba, and Fujitsu has developed a satellite broadcasting service that will allow moving vehicles to receive TV signals, digital sound, and electronic data. Nihon Mobile Broadcasting Corporation (NMBC) claims it will be able to transmit 30 TV channels by the year 2000. A more advanced system can accommodate 80 channels.

The company will use satellite technology developed by its partner, Toshiba, which allows the use of a very compact antenna (about the size of a pen) that can pick up signals even in vehicles moving at high speeds. Weather does not seem to affect the reception. Most automakers in Japan offer an optional LCD monitor for use with navigational systems. These monitors can already receive land-based TV broadcasts, but only when the car is not moving. The adaptation to the new NMBC system is believed to be quite plausible.

The company plans to hold subscription rates low, at about $6.00 to $7.00 per month, with the intention of building an audience base quickly. Initial projects peg sales at 2 million subscribers by the year 2003 and 10 million by 2010.

Of course, none of this considers the potential restrictions on use of the device while the car is moving. And you thought you had problems with drivers using their cell phones.

Source: Jon Herskovitz, "TV to Go: Japan's Cars Are Next Satellite Target," *Advertising Age International*, June 8, 1998, 11.

Radio Categories.

Radio offers an advertiser several options for reaching target audiences. The basic split of national and local radio broadcasts presents an obvious, geographic choice. More specifically, though, advertisers can choose among the following categories, each with specific characteristics: networks, syndication, and AM versus FM.

- *Networks.* **Radio networks** operate much like television networks in that they deliver programming via satellite to affiliate stations across the United States. Network radio programming concentrates on news, sports, business reports, and short features. Some of the more successful radio networks that draw large audiences are ABC, CNN, and AP News Network.

- *Syndication.* **Radio syndication** provides complete programs to stations on a contract basis. Large syndicators offer stations complete 24-hour-a-day programming packages that totally relieve a station of any programming effort. Aside from full-day programming, they also supply individual programs, such as talk shows. Large syndication organizations such as Westwood One and Satellite Music Network place advertising within programming, making syndication a good outlet for advertisers.

- *AM versus FM.* AM radio stations send signals that use amplitude modulation (AM) and operate on the AM radio dial at signal designations 540 to 1600. AM was the foundation of radio until the 1970s. Today, AM radio broadcasts, even the new stereo AM transmissions, cannot match the sound quality of FM. Thus, most AM

27. Coen, "Ad Revenue Growth Hits 7% in 1997 to Surpass Forecasts," op. cit.

stations focus on local community broadcasting or news and talk formats that do not require high-quality audio. Talk radio has, in many ways, been the salvation of AM radio. Radio is, of course, now available via the Web. (For example, check out the very cool *Roe and Garry Show* on www.wlsam.com, 3 to 7 P.M. central, Monday through Friday.) Since 1990, the number of stations that have devoted the bulk of their programming to the talk format has nearly tripled from 405 stations to 1130.[28] FM radio stations transmit using frequency modulation (FM). FM radio transmission is of a much higher quality. Because of this, FM radio has attracted the wide range of music formats that most listeners prefer.

Types of Radio Advertising. Advertisers have three basic choices in radio advertising: local spot radio advertising, network radio advertising, or national spot radio advertising. Spot radio advertising attracts 80 percent of all radio advertising dollars in a year—about $10.5 billion. In **local spot radio advertising**, an advertiser places advertisements directly with individual stations rather than with a network or syndicate. Spot radio dominates the three classes of radio advertising because there are more than 9,000 individual radio stations in the United States, giving advertisers a wide range of choices. And spot radio reaches well-defined geographic audiences, making it the ideal choice for local retailers.

Network radio advertising is advertising placed within national network programs. Since there are few network radio programs being broadcast, only about $600 million a year is invested by advertisers in this format.

The last option, **national spot radio advertising**, offers an advertiser the opportunity to place advertising in nationally syndicated radio programming. The leading national spot radio advertisers are listed in Exhibit 15.27. An advertiser can reach millions of listeners by contracting with Westwood One for *Casey Kasem's Top 40 Countdown,* which is carried by thousands of stations across the United States. National spot radio advertising accounted for about $2.4 billion in radio revenues in 1997.[29]

Advantages of Radio. While radio may not be the most glamorous or sophisticated of the major media options, it has some distinct advantages over newspapers, magazines, and television.

EXHIBIT 15.27

Top ten national spot radio advertisers. Figures are in millions of U.S. dollars.

| Rank | Advertiser | National Spot Radio Ad Spending | | |
		1997	1996	% Change
1	MCI WorldCom	$52.9	$ 8.6	515.7
2	Viacom	29.8	20.0	48.9
3	Bell Atlantic Corp.	25.9	17.7	46.1
4	SBC Communications	25.4	20.4	24.5
5	CompUSA	24.8	21.6	14.6
6	US West	24.7	18.2	35.8
7	News Corp.	24.3	30.9	−21.4
8	General Motors	21.5	24.3	−11.6
9	GTE Corp.	18.8	8.5	120.7
10	Montgomery Ward & Co.	17.8	14.4	23.8

Source: *Advertising Age,* September 28, 1998, s45. Reprinted with permission from the September 28, 1998, issue of *Advertising Age.* Copyright © Crain Communications Inc. 1998.

28. Kelly Shermach, "Talk Radio Attracts Ads As Well As Listeners," *Marketing News,* January 30, 1995, 8.
29. Coen, "Ad Revenue Growth Hits 7% in 1997 to Surpass Forecasts," op. cit.

- *Cost.* From both a cost-per-contact and absolute-cost basis, radio is often the most cost-effective medium available to an advertiser. A full minute of network radio time can cost between $5,000 and $10,000—an amazing bargain compared to the other media we've discussed. In addition, production costs for preparing radio ads are quite low; an ad often costs nothing to prepare if the spot is read live during a local broadcast.

- *Reach and frequency.* Radio has the widest exposure of any medium. It reaches consumers in their homes, cars, offices, and backyards, and even while they exercise. The wireless and portable features of radio provide an opportunity to reach consumers that exceeds all other media. The low cost of radio time gives advertisers the opportunity to frequently repeat messages affordably.

- *Target audience selectivity.* Radio can selectively target audiences on a geographic, demographic, and psychographic basis. The narrow transmission of local radio stations gives advertisers the best opportunity to reach narrowly defined geographic audiences. For a local merchant with one store, this is an ideal opportunity. Radio programming formats and different dayparts also allow target audience selectivity. CBS Radio recently converted 4 of 13 stations to a rock-and-roll oldies format to target 35-to-49-year-olds—in other words, the baby boomers.[30] Hard rock, new age, easy listening, country, classical, and talk radio formats all attract different audiences. Radio dayparts, shown in Exhibit 15.28, also attract different audiences. Morning and afternoon/evening drive times attract a male audience. Daytime attracts predominantly women; nighttime, teens.

- *Flexibility and timeliness.* Radio is the most flexible medium because of very short closing periods for submitting an ad. This means an advertiser can wait until close to an air date before submitting an ad. With this flexibility, advertisers can take advantage of special events or unique competitive opportunities in a timely fashion.

- *Creative opportunities.* While radio may be unidimensional in sensory stimulation, it can still have powerful creative impact. Recall that radio has been described as the theater of the mind. Ads such as the folksy tales of Tom Bodett for Motel 6 or the eccentric humor of Stan Freberg are memorable and can have tremendous impact on the attitude toward a brand. In addition, the musical formats that attract audiences to radio stations can also attract attention to radio ads. Audiences that favor certain music may be more prone to an ad that uses recognizable, popular songs.[31]

General Motors felt that the creative opportunities in radio were good enough to make radio an important part of the integrated marketing communications effort for the Cadillac Seville. The Cadillac division of GM launched an IMC campaign for the Seville that included cable TV, outdoor ads, transit ads, and radio. The IMC box on page 499 tells the entire story of this campaign.

Disadvantages of Radio. As good as radio can be, it also suffers from some severe limitations as an advertising medium. Advertising strategists must recognize these disadvantages when deciding what role radio can play in an integrated marketing communications program.

EXHIBIT 15.28

Radio dayparts.

Morning drive time	6:00 A.M. to 10:00 A.M.
Daytime	10:00 A.M. to 3:00 P.M.
Afternoon/evening drive time	3:00 P.M. to 7:00 P.M.
Nighttime	7:00 P.M. to 12:00 A.M.
Late night	12:00 A.M. to 6:00 A.M.

30. Kevin Goldman, "CBS Radio Retunes to Music of the '70s," *Wall Street Journal,* December 30, 1993, B5.
31. Kevin Goldman, "Hot Songs Are Wooing Younger Ears," *Wall Street Journal,* January 2, 1993, B1.

- *Poor audience attentiveness.* Just because radio reaches audiences almost everywhere doesn't mean that anyone is paying attention. Remember that radio has also been described as audio wallpaper. It provides a comfortable background distraction while a consumer does something else—hardly an ideal level of attentiveness for advertising communication. When a consumer is listening and traveling in a car, he or she often switches stations when an ad comes on and divides his or her attention between the radio and the road.

- *Creative limitations.* While the theater of the mind may be a wonderful creative opportunity, taking advantage of that opportunity can be difficult, indeed. The audio-only nature of radio communication is a tremendous creative compromise. An advertiser whose product depends on demonstration or visual impact is at a loss when it comes to radio. And like its television counterpart, a radio message creates a fleeting impression that is often gone in an instant.

- *Fragmented audiences.* The large number of stations that try to attract the same audience in a market has created tremendous fragmentation. Think about your own local radio market. There are probably four or five different stations that play the kind of music you like. Or, consider that in the past few years, more than 1,000 radio stations in the United States have adopted the talk radio format. This fragmentation means that the percentage of listeners tuned to any one station is likely very small.

- *Chaotic buying procedures.* For an advertiser who wants to include radio as part of a national advertising program, the buying process can be sheer chaos. Since national networks and syndicated broadcasts do not reach every geographic market, an advertiser has to buy time in individual markets on a station-by-station basis. This could involve dozens of different negotiations and individual contracts.

Buying Procedures for Radio Advertising. While buying procedures to achieve national coverage may be chaotic, this does not mean they are completely without structure. Although the actual buying may be time-consuming and expensive if many stations are involved, the structure is actually quite straightforward. Advertising time can be purchased from networks, syndications, or local radio stations. Recall that among these options, advertisers invest most heavily in local placement. About 80 percent of annual radio advertising is placed locally. About 15 percent is allocated to national spot placement, and only 5 percent is invested in network broadcasts.

The other factor in buying radio time relates to the time period of purchase. Refer again to Exhibit 15.28. This shows the five basic daypart segments from which an

---

RADIO PLAYS KEY ROLE IN IMC CAMPAIGN FOR CADILLAC SEVILLE

The Cadillac division of General Motors is trying to convince luxury car buyers that the redesigned Cadillac Seville can compete with the German luxury cars Mercedes and BMW. Cadillac launched an integrated marketing communications campaign that included cable TV, outdoor billboards, transit ads, and radio commercials. The ads were targeted to 35-to-64-year-old males with household incomes of at least $100,000. The entire campaign was supported by $44 million in spending on measured media.

One of the key decisions in the IMC campaign was the commitment by the ad agency, D'Arcy Masius Benton & Bowles, to use radio ads as a prominent component. The Cadillac radio ads aired on the most popular radio stations in the company's 15 geographic target markets. As part of the radio campaign, disc jockeys at the stations did live broadcasts with the Seville on display. "We generated over 20,000 leads from those live remotes," said Ed Berger, the Seville brand manager. "They are people who don't currently own a Cadillac Seville, but said they were interested in more information."

Managers at Cadillac are pleased with the results of the campaign. The combined media effort, including radio, has helped push sales 23.9 percent ahead of the year before.

Source: Frank S. Washington, "Cadillac Push for Seville Helps Boost Sales 23.9%," *Advertising Age*, June 15, 1998, 75.

advertiser can choose. The time period decision is based primarily on a demographic description of the advertiser's target audience. Recall that drive-time dayparts attract a mostly male audience, while daytime is primarily female, and nighttime is mostly teen. This information, combined with programming formats, guides an advertiser in a buying decision.

As with magazine buying, radio advertising time is purchased from rate cards issued by individual stations. Run-of-station ads—ads that the station chooses when to run—cost less than ads scheduled during a specific daypart. The price can also increase if an advertiser wants the ad read live on the air by a popular local radio personality hosting a show during a daypart.

The actual process of buying radio time is relatively simple. A media planner identifies the stations and the dayparts that will reach the target audience. Then the rates and daypart availabilities are checked to be sure they match the media-planning objectives. At this point, agreements are made regarding the number of spots to run in specified time frames.

Measuring Radio Audiences. There are two primary sources of information on radio audiences. Arbitron ratings cover 260 local radio markets. The ratings are developed through the use of diaries maintained by listeners who record when they listened to the radio and to what station they were tuned. The *Arbitron Ratings/Radio* book gives audience estimates by time period and selected demographic characteristics. Several specific measures are compiled from the Arbitron diaries:

- **Average quarter-hour persons:** The average number of listeners tuned to a station during a specified 15-minute segment of a daypart.
- **Average quarter-hour share:** The percentage of the total radio audience that was listening to a radio station during a specified quarter-hour daypart.
- **Average quarter-hour rating:** The audience during a quarter-hour daypart expressed as a percentage of the population of the measurement area. This provides an estimate of the popularity of each station in an area.
- **Cume:** The cumulative audience, which is the total number of different people who listen to a station for at least five minutes in a quarter-hour period within a specified daypart. Cume is the best estimate of the reach of a station.
- RADAR (Radio's All Dimension Audience Research) is the other major measure of radio audiences. Sponsored by the major radio networks, RADAR collects audience data twice a year based on interviews with radio listeners. Designated listeners are called daily for a one-week period and asked about their listening behavior. Estimates include measures of the overall audience for different network stations and audience estimates by market area. The results of the studies are reported in an annual publication, *Radio Usage and Network Radio Audiences.* Media planners can refer to published measures such as Arbitron and RADAR to identify which stations will reach target audiences at what times across various markets.

SUMMARY

◀▶ Detail the advantages and disadvantages of newspapers as a media class, identify different types of newspapers, and describe buying and audience measurement for newspapers.

Newspaper types cluster into three categories: target audience, geographic coverage, and frequency of publication. As a media class, newspapers provide an excellent means for reaching local audiences with informative advertising messages. Precise timing of message delivery can be achieved at modest expenditure levels. But for products that demand creative and colorful executions, this medium simply cannot deliver. Newspaper costs are typically transmitted via rate cards and are primarily a function of a paper's readership levels.

◀▶ Detail the advantages and disadvantages of magazines as a media class, identify different types of magazines, and describe buying and audience measurement for magazines.

Three important magazine types are consumer, business, and farm publications. Because of their specific editorial content, magazines can be effective in attracting distinctive groups of readers with common interests. Thus, magazines can be superb tools for reaching specific market segments. Also, magazines facilitate a wide range of creative executions. Of course, the selectivity advantage turns into a disadvantage for advertisers trying to achieve high reach levels. Costs of magazine ad space can vary dramatically because of the wide array of circulation levels achieved by different types of magazines.

◀▶ Detail the advantages and disadvantages of television as a media class, identify different types of television, and describe buying and audience measurement for television.

The four basic forms of television are network, cable, syndicated, and local television. Television's principal advantage is obvious: Because it allows for almost limitless possibilities in creative execution, it can be an extraordinary tool for affecting consumers' perceptions of a brand. Also, it can be an efficient device for reaching huge audiences; however, the absolute costs for reaching these audiences can be staggering. Lack of audience interest and involvement certainly limit the effectiveness of commercials in this medium. The three ways that advertisers can buy time are through sponsorship, participation, and spot advertising. As with any medium, advertising rates will vary as a function of the size and composition of the audience that is watching.

◀▶ Detail the advantages and disadvantages of radio as a media class, identify different types of radio, and describe buying and audience measurement for radio.

Advertisers can choose from three basic types of radio advertising: local spot, network radio, or national spot advertising. Radio can be a cost-effective medium, and because of the wide diversity in radio programming, it can be an excellent tool for reaching well-defined audiences. Poor listener attentiveness is problematic with radio, and the audio-only format places obvious constraints on creative execution. Radio ad rates are driven by considerations such as the average number of listeners tuned to a station at specific times throughout the day.

KEY TERMS

general-population newspapers (476)
business newspapers (476)
ethnic newspapers (476)
gay and lesbian newspapers (476)
alternative press newspapers (476)
display advertising (477)
co-op advertising (477)
preprinted insert (477)
free-standing insert (FSI) (477)
classified advertising (477)
rate card (478)
column inch (478)
standard advertising unit (SAU) (478)
run-of-paper (ROP) or run-of-press (478)
preferred position (478)
full position (478)
circulation (478)
paid circulation (478)
controlled circulation (478)
readership (478)
bleed page (486)
gatefold ads (486)
first cover page (487)
second cover page (487)
third cover page (487)
fourth cover page (487)
double-page spreads (487)
space contract (487)
space order (487)
closing date (487)
on-sale date (487)
cover date (487)
guaranteed circulation (487)

pass-along readership (487)
network television (490)
cable television (490)
off-network syndication (491)
first-run syndication (491)
barter syndication (491)
local television (491)
narrowcasting (492)
channel grazing (493)
zapping (493)
zipping (493)
V-chip (493)
sponsorship (493)
participation (494)
spot advertising (494)
dayparts (494)
television households (494)
households using television (HUT) (495)
program rating (495)
ratings point (495)
share of audience (495)
direct broadcast by satellite (DBS) (495)
high-definition television (HDTV) (495)
radio networks (496)
radio syndication (496)
local spot radio advertising (497)
network radio advertising (497)
national spot radio advertising (497)
average quarter-hour persons (500)
average quarter-hour share (500)
average quarter-hour rating (500)
cume (500)

QUESTIONS FOR REVIEW AND CRITICAL THINKING

1. Magazines certainly proved to be the right media class for selling Absolut vodka. Why are magazines a natural choice for vodka advertisements? What has Absolut done with its advertising to take full advantage of this medium?

2. What advantages do publishers perceive of "digizines" versus a traditional, printed version of a magazine?

3. Reach and frequency can be perceived as conflicting goals in media planning. Evaluate each of the four major media classes discussed in this chapter in terms of how well they would serve reach-versus-frequency objectives.

4. Peruse several recent editions of your town's newspaper and select three examples of co-op advertising. What objectives do you believe the manufacturers and retailers are attempting to achieve in each of the three ads you've selected?

5. Place your local newspaper and an issue of your favorite magazine side by side and carefully review the content of each. From the standpoint of a prospective advertiser, which of the two publications has a more dramatic problem with clutter? Identify tactics being used by advertisers in each publication to break through the clutter and get their brands noticed.

6. The costs involved in preparing and placing ads in television programming such as the Super Bowl broadcast can be simply incredible. How is it that advertisers such as Pepsi or Nissan can justify the incredible costs that come with this media vehicle?

7. Think about the television viewing behavior you've observed in your household. Of the four means for avoiding TV ad exposure discussed in this chapter, which have you observed in your household? What other avoidance tactics do your friends and family use?

8.   The choice between print and broadcast media is often portrayed as a choice between high- and low-involvement media. What makes one medium inherently more involving than another? How will the characteristics of an ad's message affect the decision to employ an involving versus an uninvolving medium?

9.   For an advertiser that seeks to achieve nationwide reach, can radio be a good buy? What frustrations are likely to be encountered in using radio for this purpose?

EXPERIENTIAL EXERCISES

1.   Buy a weekday copy of your local daily newspaper. About what portion of the newspaper is devoted to advertising? What types of local advertisers are dominant? About how many national advertisers appear in the issue? Are there any two-color or four-color ads? Finally, describe the extent to which preprints or inserts are included in the paper.

2.   Next time you go to a bookstore, check out the magazine rack. How many magazines can you find that appeal to special interests? How many magazines are targeted to men versus women?

3.   Make an appointment at a local television or radio station. Ask to have an interview with the media sales people. Ask them how they try to sell advertising time and space to local advertisers. How is the local time and space allocated relative to the national "feed"?

USING THE INTERNET

The impact of ads placed in print media can depend on the editorial content and style of the publication within which the ad is placed. Visit the following newspaper and magazine sites and find one banner ad on each:

Boston Globe: www.boston.com

New York Times: www.nytimes.com

Pathfinder: www.pathfinder.com

U.S. News & World Report: www.usnews.com

Elle: www.ellemag.com

1.   Evaluate the fit between the advertiser and the Web publication. Does the style of the publication match the corporate image of the advertiser?

2.   Give a general description for the type of people that would visit each publication's site. What type of people would be interested in what is being advertised? How similar are your descriptions?

3.   Which banner ad had the most impact? How does the effectiveness of a banner ad depend on how long it takes the banner ad to appear on your screen and where the banner ad is positioned on the page?

Newspaper classified ads face a strong challenge from new media, and particularly from the Internet. Their text-only format make them ideal for searching in electronic (soft-copy) form, which recommends that they be transitioned to the Net. But as that transition from print to the Net happens, is there any limit to who can replicate the idea? Numerous competitors to the papers have constructed classified ad Web sites, with services vying with local newspapers leading the pack.

Visit the following sites, each of which hosts electronic classified ads in some fashion:

Microsoft Sidewalk: www.sidewalk.com

Apartments.com: www.apartments.com

Classified Warehouse: www.classifiedwarehouse.com

Match.com: www.match.com

1.   Which of the sites seems to be of greater or lesser threat to the print papers' reign in classified advertising?

2.   How does each make use of features of the Internet not available to ads in print?

Read about how the newspaper industry is assessing the future of classifieds at the Newspaper Association of America's Web site: www.naa.org

3.   What percentage of newspapers' revenues are derived from classified ads?

4.   How large is the industry, and what are the trends?

Look as good as the woman your date is hitting on.

Next time Noxzema.

CHAPTER 16

After reading and thinking about this chapter, you will be able to do the following:

◀▶ Describe the role of support media in a comprehensive media plan.

◀▶ Explain the appeal of P-O-P advertising as an element of an IMC program.

◀▶ Justify the growing popularity of event sponsorship as another supportive component of a media plan.

◀▶ Discuss the challenges presented by the ever-increasing variety of media for achieving integrated marketing communications.

David Dorfman, co-owner of Insite Advertising, sells media space. But not just any media space. David and his partner Marc Miller sell access to the ad space in 250 restrooms of trendy bars, restaurants, and nightclubs throughout New York City. Marketers such as RJR Nabisco, the Joe Boxer Corporation, and Procter & Gamble have bought into Mr. Dorfman's program. He comments: "What we sell to advertisers is a captive audience with a prime demographic of 21 to 35 years old. And it's gender specific! So you can get either men or women and eliminate the waste."[1]

Marketers of the Noxzema brand decided that women's restrooms throughout Manhattan was a place they wanted to be. The thinking was that Noxzema had been around forever, and it was time for a facelift. Noxzema needed something fresh, edgy, unexpected, and new. It needed to be part of a medium that would help it move up the hip scale and that would challenge women to think, "Whoa, what brand has the nerve to do and say that?" It needed to be in the restroom.

So working with the company's ad agency, Leo Burnett, Noxzema brand managers created a series of small advertising signs like those shown in Exhibit 16.1, featuring in-your-face humor such as "It's not the lighting" and "Did someone miss her beauty sleep?", with the common tagline "Next time Noxzema." Oh yeah, one more detail. These signs were hung in frames on the walls across from the mirrors in about 115 trendy restaurants and clubs in chic Manhattan neighborhoods. The signs were meant to be read in the mirror exactly at that point in time when a woman might be thinking about her face and appearance before returning to the crowded dance floor. Perhaps, then, this is an example of being at the right place at the right time to deliver an

EXHIBIT 16.1

These are two of the ad posters created for Noxzema's assault on women's restrooms in Manhattan. All the posters were meant to be read in the mirror. Hold this exhibit up to a mirror, and you too may see the light. www.pg.com/

1.   Stuart Elliott, "P&G Takes a Most Unusual Tack with Its New, In-Your-Face Ads," *New York Times*, June 3, 1998.

in-your-face, "HEY, LOOK AT ME" message, for a brand that had become a little too familiar, and a little too boring. In addition, quirky campaigns like this one often attract the attention of business writers in conventional media and lead to valuable, free exposure for the brand. Indeed, many of the details of this example are drawn from an article about it that appeared in a business column from the *New York Times*. Not bad coverage for bathroom advertising!

As you no doubt have already recognized, perhaps in a restroom near you, advertisers are always on the lookout for new venues to advance their messages. And this can lead them to unconventional places. The Noxzema example reflects the growing interest among marketers in finding unusual media vehicles meant to reach niche markets, particularly in urban locations, where new market trends often originate. Other such niche media include trucks that drive endlessly through city streets as mobile billboards; ads beamed onto the sides of office buildings; racks of postcard ads, which are again placed in trendy restaurants and nightspots; ads printed on coffee cups with coordinated signage attached to coffee carts; and even small signs attached to the backs of messenger bikes that patrol the canyons of downtown, corporate America.

The Noxzema example is also a nice prelude to this chapter because it illustrates several of the chapter's basic themes. It makes the point that advertisers are constantly on the lookout for new, cost-effective ways to break through the clutter of competitors' advertisements to register their appeals with carefully targeted consumers. Of course, as soon as a new vehicle begins to deliver results, many will make it part of their media plans, and the clutter problem returns. Additionally, these new forms of media can be wonderful outlets for experimentation and creative expression. As one Leo Burnett executive said about the Noxzema campaign, "Risk these days is living in the middle of the road where most of the cars can pass over you. Instead, you take an attitude, you take a point of view, which is cool."[2] Many of the media options discussed in this chapter present low-cost means for trying something different—and maybe trying something cool.

Although print and broadcast media continue to draw the lion's share of advertising expenditures, many other options exist for communicating with consumers. This chapter will examine a set of options commonly referred to as support media. Traditional support media such as signs and billboards have been around for many years, but are enjoying renewed interest from advertisers. Additionally, alternatives such as point-of-purchase advertising and event sponsorship continue to produce impressive results and thus are receiving more and more funding from many marketers. In a world possessed with integrated marketing communication, effective deployment of a broad array of support media has become a critical component of media planning.

Traditional Support Media. ◖▶ This section will feature traditional support media: outdoor signage and billboard advertising, transit and aerial advertising, specialty advertising, and directory advertising. **Support media** are used to reinforce or extend a message being delivered via some other media vehicle; hence the name *support media*. They can be especially productive when used to deliver a message near the time or place where consumers are actually contemplating product selections. Since these media can be tailored for local markets, they can have value to any organization that wants to reach consumers in a particular venue, neighborhood, or metropolitan area.

Outdoor Signage and Billboard Advertising. Billboards, posters, and outdoor signs are perhaps the oldest advertising form.[3] Posters first appeared in North America when they were used during the Revolutionary War to keep the civilian population informed about

2. Ibid.
3. Ann Cooper, "All Aboards," *Adweek*, May 9, 1994, 3–10.

the war's status. In the 1800s they became a promotional tool, with circuses and politicians being among the first to adopt this new medium. With the onset of World War I, the U.S. government turned to posters and billboards to call for recruits, encourage the purchase of war bonds, and cultivate patriotism. Exhibits 16.2 and 16.3 show some of these early uses of outdoor advertising. By the 1920s outdoor advertising also enjoyed widespread commercial applications and, until the invention of television, was the medium of choice when an advertiser wanted to communicate with visual imagery.

While the rise of television stifled the growth of outdoor advertising, the federal highway system that was laid across the nation in the sixties pumped new life into billboards. The 40-foot-high burgers and pop bottles were inevitable, but throughout the seventies and eighties billboards became an outlet for creative expression in advertising. One exceptional example of using the medium to its fullest was a Nike campaign run in the mid-eighties featuring high-profile athletes, such as Olympian Carl Lewis, performing their special artistry.[4] Today, the creative challenge posed by outdoor advertising is as it has always been—to grab attention and communicate with minimal verbiage and striking imagery, as do the billboards in Exhibits 16.4 and 16.5.

In excess of $2.0 billion was spent to deliver advertisers' messages on the 400,000 billboards across the United States in 1999.[5] Outdoor advertising offers several distinct

EXHIBIT 16.2

Advertising in the United States began with posters and billboards. Circuses were the early pioneers in this medium. ringling.com/

EXHIBIT 16.3

Public service announcements also got their start in posters and billboards. Here we see an appeal to patriotism featuring the potent combination of the Boy Scouts and the U.S. government. www.publicdebt.treas.gov/sav/sav.htm

4. Ibid.
5. Ronald Grover, "Billboards Aren't Boring Anymore," *Business Week*, September 21, 1998, 88, 89.

EXHIBIT 16.4

Minimal verbiage is one key to success with billboard advertising. This example easily satisfies the minimal-verbiage rule. www.horst-salons.com/

EXHIBIT 16.5

As with all media, creativity is a must in making effective use of billboards. Soaring above the clutter to grab the attention of passing motorists is the goal of this execution.

advantages.[6] This medium provides an excellent means to achieve wide exposure of a message in specific local markets. Size is, of course, a powerful attraction of this medium, and when combined with special lighting and moving features, billboards can be captivating. Billboards created for Dayton Hudson in Minneapolis have even wafted a mint scent throughout the city as part of a candy promotion for Valentine's Day.[7] Billboards also offer around-the-clock exposure for an advertiser's message and are well suited to showing off a brand's distinctive packaging or logo.

Billboards are especially effective when they reach viewers with a message that speaks to a need or desire that is immediately relevant. For example, British Airways runs a single billboard in Manhattan along the freeway to JFK and LaGuardia airports, featuring a spectacular shot of its Concorde jet at takeoff.[8] The board simply reads "London Bridge" and provides a constant reminder that British Airways should be in one's consideration set when traveling to Europe from New York City. This strategic reinforcement of a brand's presence and relevance represents the best that outdoor advertising has to offer. Another example of putting one's message in the right place at the right time to enhance its appeal is illustrated by Exhibit 16.6.

Billboards have obvious drawbacks. Long and complex messages simply make no sense on billboards; some experts suggest that billboard copy should be limited to no more than six words.[9] Also, the impact of billboards can vary dramatically depending on their location, and assessing locations is tedious and time-consuming. To assess locations, companies typically must send individuals to the site to see if the location is desirable.[10] This activity, known in the industry as **riding the boards**, can be a major investment of time and money. Moreover, the Institute of Outdoor Advertising rates billboards as expensive in comparison to several other media alternatives.[11] Considering that billboards are constrained to short messages, are often in the background, and are certainly not the primary focus of anyone's attention, their costs may be prohibitive for many advertisers.

EXHIBIT 16.6

This sign uses the perfect slogan for a sports venue. Has there ever been a referee who didn't need glasses?

6.   Jack Z. Sissors and Lincoln Bumba, *Advertising Media Planning* (Lincolnwood, Ill.: NTC Business Books, 1993).
7.   Grover, "Billboards Aren't Boring Anymore," op. cit.
8.   Cooper, "All Aboards," op. cit.
9.   *Yellow Pages and the Media Mix* (Troy, Mich.: Yellow Pages Publishers Association, 1990).
10. Kevin Goldman, "Spending on Billboards Is Rising; Video Tool Makes Buying Easier," *Wall Street Journal,* June 27, 1994, B6.
11. Sissors and Bumba, *Advertising Media Planning*.

Despite the costs, and the criticism by environmentalists that billboards represent a form of visual pollution, spending on outdoor advertising has been increasing at an increasing rate, and because of important technological advances, the future looks secure for billboards.[12] The first of these advances combines the videotaping of billboard sites and their surroundings with software from International Outdoor Systems of London.[13] This tool reduces the amount of time and money that executives must spend riding the boards, and it helps them design boards to fit in with the surroundings at a particular location. The software package not only allows advertisers to view billboard sites via videotape, but also allows them to insert mock-ups of different billboard executions into the specific location pictured on their computer screen. This design tool and time-saving system should make outdoor advertising a more attractive option for many advertisers.

Perhaps even more important to the future of billboard advertising is the development of computer-aided production technology for board facings.[14] Until a few years ago, billboard creation and painting was a labor-intensive process that could take a crew of workers several days to complete, and quality control from board to board was always problematic. Now, thanks to computer graphics, the biggest players are designing their boards digitally. One consequence of computer-aided design is that the time needed to get a campaign up and running on multiple boards has been reduced from months to days. Additionally, board facings can be produced in unlimited quantities with total quality control. The advent of computer-directed painting brings magazine-quality reproduction to billboards in any market. And digital design has set the stage for a major infusion of creativity in billboard advertising. If the designer can think it, he or she now can execute it on a billboard. The rapid deployment, quality control, and creative expression that now are possible in executing billboards and outdoor signage have attracted a whole new group of big-name advertisers—such as Disney, Sony, Microsoft, America Online, and Amazon.com—to the great outdoors.[15]

Transit and Aerial Advertising.

Transit advertising is a close cousin to billboard advertising, and in many instances it is used in tandem with billboards. The phrase **out-of-home media** is commonly used to refer to the combination of transit and billboard advertising, but as illustrated in Exhibits 16.7, 16.8, and 16.9, out-of-home ads appear in many venues, including on backs of buildings, at construction sites, and in sports stadiums. Transit ads may appear as signage on terminal and station platforms, or actually envelop mass transit vehicles, as exemplified in Exhibit 16.10. Some cash-strapped cities and towns even allow transit advertising on police cars, school buses, and garbage trucks.[16]

Transit advertising can be valuable when an advertiser wishes to target adults who live and work in major metropolitan areas.[17] The medium reaches people as they travel to and from work, and because it taps into daily routines repeated week after week, transit advertising offers an excellent means for repetitive message exposure. In large metro areas such as New York—with its 200 miles of subways and 3 million subway riders—transit ads can reach large numbers of individuals in a cost-efficient manner.

When working with this medium, an advertiser may find it most appropriate to buy space on just those trains or bus lines that consistently haul people from the demographic segment being targeted. This type of demographic matching of vehicle with target is always preferred as a means of deriving more value from limited ad budgets. Transit advertising can be appealing to local merchants because their

12. Grover, "Billboards Aren't Boring Anymore," op. cit.
13. Goldman, "Spending on Billboards Is Rising," op. cit.
14. Cyndee Miller, "Outdoor Gets a Makeover," *Marketing News,* April 10, 1995, 26.
15. Grover, "Billboards Aren't Boring Anymore," op. cit.
16. Douglas A. Blackmon, "New Ad Vehicles: Police Car, School Bus, Garbage Truck," *Wall Street Journal,* February 20, 1996, B1.
17. Sissors and Bumba, *Advertising Media Planning.*

EXHIBIT 16.7

This wonderful old building has a big, flat backside facing a major interstate freeway. No wonder then that the Gap wants to keep it in jeans.
www.gap.com/

EXHIBIT 16.8

Here an array of poster ads is displayed across the plywood wall marking the boundary of a construction site. They are inviting riders on the Converse Tram shown in Exhibit 16.10 to plug into the Holland Festival.
www.hollandfestival.nl

message may reach a passenger as he or she is traveling to a store to shop. For some consumers, transit ads are the last medium they are exposed to before making their final product selection.

Transit advertising works best for building or maintaining brand awareness; as with outdoor billboards, lengthy or complex messages simply cannot be worked into this medium. Also, transit ads can easily go unnoticed in the hustle and bustle of daily life. People traveling to and from work via a mass transit system are certainly one of the hardest audiences to engage with an advertising message. They can be bored, exhausted, absorbed by their thoughts about the day, or occupied by some other medium. Given the static nature of a transit poster, breaking through to a harried commuter can be a tremendous challenge.

WEB SIGHTING

EXHIBIT 16.9

As this Fenway Park score-board shows, signage and advertiser slogans are standard fare at the ballpark. None of these scoreboard ads sport Web addresses, although Cracker-jack (www.crackerjack .com) and these advertised brands all have homes on the Web. Does it matter? Which of the advertised brands might you need more information on? Is selection of a cream-versus jam-filled doughnut predicated on nutritional research, or is Dunkin' Donuts (www.dunkin donuts.com) just hoping you'll pick up a dozen on the way home from the park? Why do you think each advertiser chose to pick this particular place to advertise?

EXHIBIT 16.10

The story is the same all over the world. Mass transit has become an advertising vehicle too. www.converse.com/

When an advertiser can't break through on the ground or under the ground, it may have to look skyward. **Aerial advertising** can involve airplanes pulling signs or banners, skywriting, or those majestic blimps. For several decades, Goodyear had blimps all to itself; however, in the nineties, new blimp vendors came to the market with smaller, less-expensive blimps that made this medium surge in popularity with other advertisers.[18] Virgin Lightships now flies a fleet of small blimps that measure 70,000 cubic feet in size and can be rented for advertising purposes for around $200,000 per month. Not to be outdone, Airship International flies full-size blimps, about 235,000 cubic feet in

18. Fara Warner, "More Companies Turn to Skies as Medium to Promote Products," *Wall Street Journal,* January 5, 1995, B6.

size, which it promotes as offering 200 percent more usable ad space than the competition's mini-blimps.

Sanyo, Fuji Photo, MetLife, and Anheuser-Busch have clearly bought into the appeal of an airborne brand presence. The Family Channel has also been a frequent user of Virgin Lightships' mini-blimps over sporting events such as the Daytona 500 NASCAR race. A recall study done after one such event showed that 70 percent of target consumers remembered the Family Channel as a result of the blimp flyovers.[19] Blimps carrying television cameras at sporting events also provide game coverage that can result in the blimp's sponsor getting several on-air mentions. This brand-name exposure comes at a small fraction of the cost of similar exposure through television advertising.

Perhaps the best indication that blimp advertising does produce results is the growing blimp traffic over major sporting events. When a medium proves itself, more and more marketers will want it in their media plans. Of course, the irony is that as a medium becomes more attractive and hence cluttered, its original appeal begins to be diluted. We see this occurring with aerial advertising. With more and more blimps showing up at sporting events, networks can be choosy about which one gets the coveted on-air mention. Besides carrying an overhead camera for them, networks now demand that blimp sponsors purchase advertising time during the event if they want an on-air mention. Additionally, the sportscaster's casual banter about the beautiful overhead shots from so-and-so's wonderful blimp have now been replaced by scripted commentary that is written out in advance as part of the advertising contract.[20] As we've noted before, this cycle of uniqueness and effectiveness, followed by clutter and dilution of effectiveness, is one that repeats itself over and over again in the challenging world of advertising.

Specialty Advertising. No one can say for sure, but it is believed that modern-day specialty advertising came into being around 1840. An insurance salesperson in Auburn, New York, wanted local businesses to post information about his insurance offerings. When the owners declined to help, he bought calendars, attached the information he had wanted to post, and presented the wall calendars as gifts. The local business owners were pleased with the gift, hung the calendars in their stores, and the rest, as they say, is history. Lest you think that items such as calendars and kitchen magnets are too trivial to be worth serious consideration, *PROMO Magazine*'s estimate of expenditures on such items in 1997 was nearly $12 billion, up 25 percent from the previous year.[21]

The insurance salesperson's wall calendar illustrates the essence of all modern specialty advertising. **Specialty-advertising items** have three defining elements: (1) they contain the sponsor's logo and perhaps a related promotional message; (2) this logo and message appear on a useful or decorative item; and (3) the item is given freely, as a gift from the sponsor. This third element distinguishes specialty-advertising items from those referred to as premiums.[22] **Premiums** are items that carry the logo of a sponsor and are offered "free" or at a reduced charge to motivate the purchase of a related product or service. For example, the next time you receive a "free" souvenir movie cup with the purchase of a super-size Coke at McDonald's, you're taking home a premium.

Literally thousands of different items have been used for specialty-advertising purposes, but the majority of these fall into five broad categories: wearables, writing instruments, desk or office accessories, calendars, and glassware or ceramics.[23] T-shirts, bumper stickers, coffee mugs, matchbooks, ashtrays, cups and glasses, buttons, decals, clocks, pens

19. Ibid.

20. Bill Richards, "Bright Idea Has Business Looking Up for Ad Blimps," *Wall Street Journal*, October 14, 1997, B1.

21. "Targeting Drives Growth," in *PROMO's 6th Annual SourceBook '99* (Stamford, Conn.: *PROMO Magazine*, 1999), 16.

22. Dan S. Bagley, *Understanding Specialty Advertising* (Irving, Tex.: Specialty Advertising Association International, 1990).

23. Ibid.

Wherever you go, there we are.

Where do the leading Fortune 500 companies go for the best in sports promotional baseballs, footballs and basketballs?

FOTOBALL® USA, INC.
The industry leader in quality promotional baseballs, footballs, basketballs, hockey pucks, soccer balls and our exclusive Fototire™, the miniature replica Goodyear Eagle racing tire.

IMC/FOTOBALL®
INSYNQ MARKETING CONCEPTS
3738 RUFFIN ROAD • SAN DIEGO, CA • 92123
619-467-9900 • 1-800-325-3686 • Fax 619-467-9947
www.fotoball.com
Circle No. 065 on Reader Service Card

EXHIBIT 16.11

Specialty-advertising items come in all shapes and sizes. Let INSYNQ Marketing concepts (that's right, IMC) of San Diego, California, be your one-stop shopping headquarters for the ever-popular sports ball. www.fotoball.com/

and pencils, mouse pads, balloons, litter bags, coin holders, note pads, rulers, and yardsticks are all examples of specialty-advertising items. But if sports balls are your thing, you're probably going to want to call Fotoball USA. See their ad in Exhibit 16.11.

Using specialty-advertising items to carry a brand name has several appealing aspects.[24] First, they can be made available on a selective basis. Whether they are sent by mail, distributed only in a local trading area, or passed out by salespeople to target customers, the dispensing of these items can be carefully monitored. This ensures cost effectiveness and literally puts a message into the hands of prospective customers. Second, unlike other media options, specialty-advertising items can hang around for long periods of time. For example, a Friskies wall calendar will reinforce the virtues of Friskies cat food day in and day out for at least a year. Third, specialty advertising can help build goodwill. Young or old, people like to receive gifts. When executed with good taste, specialty-advertising programs can generate the goodwill that is an important asset for any brand.

Specialty advertising shares the space limitation problems of many other support media. Coffee mugs, coin holders, and the like provide little space for detailing the virtues of a brand; relative to the vast array of information that people are exposed to on a daily basis, what can be said on the back of a matchbook is easily overlooked. In addition, the mind-boggling variety of items to choose from for specialty advertising makes selection complex and time-consuming. (See for yourself at www.promomart.com/.) This decision must be made carefully, because associating a brand name with items that some might see as junk or trinkets always has the potential of backfiring by cheapening the brand's image.

Directory Advertising. The last time you reached for a phone directory to appraise the local options for Chinese or Mexican food, you probably didn't think about it as a traditional support medium. However, yellow pages advertising plays an important role in the media mix for many types of organizations, as is evidenced by the $11.5 billion that was spent in this medium in 1997.[25] The top 15 Yellow Pages advertisers for 1997, according to the Yellow Pages Publishers Association, are listed in Exhibit 16.12. A wealth of current facts and figures about this media option are available at www.yppa.org/.

A phone directory can play a unique and important role in consumers' decision-making processes. While most support media keep a brand name or key product information in front of a consumer, yellow pages advertising helps people follow through on their decision to buy. By providing the information that consumers need to actually find a particular product or service, the Yellow Pages can serve as the final link in a

24. Rebecca Piirto Heath, "An Engraved Invitation," *Marketing Tools*, November/December 1997, 36–42.
25. *Yellow Pages: Facts & Media Guide 1998* (Troy, Mich.: Yellow Pages Publishers Association, 1998) 7.

The top 15 yellow pages advertisers. Figures are in millions of U.S. dollars.

1997	Advertiser	Yellow Pages Advertising		
		1997	1996	% Change
1	General Motors Corp.	$28.0	$28.0	0.0
2	U-Haul	27.3	25.8	5.8
3	Sears, Roebuck & Co.	25.6	23.0	11.3
4	Midas International	17.8	18.0	−1.1
5	Ford Motor Co.	16.6	17.3	−4.0
6	ServiceMaster Co.	16.0	15.0	6.7
7	Ryder Truck	15.0	15.0	0.0
8	Chrysler Corp.	14.0	13.8	1.4
9	Allstate Insurance Group	13.5	12.5	8.0
10	Volunteer Hospitals of America	13.5	13.5	0.0
11	AT&T Corp.	13.0	12.0	8.3
12	Roto-Rooter	12.0	11.0	9.1
13	Meineke	10.8	10.7	0.9
14	State Farm Mutual Auto Insurance Co.	10.5	10.0	5.0
15	Budget Rent A Car	10.5	9.5	10.5

Source: Yellow Pages Publishers Association.

buying decision. Because of their availability and consumers' familiarity with this advertising tool, yellow pages directories provide an excellent means to supplement awareness-building and interest-generating campaigns that an advertiser might be pursuing through other media.

On the downside, the proliferation and fragmentation of phone directories can make this a difficult medium to work in.[26] Many metropolitan areas are covered by multiple directories, some of which are specialty directories designed to serve specific neighborhoods, ethnic groups, or interest groups. Selecting the right set of directories to get full coverage of large sections of the country can be a daunting task. Additionally, working in this medium requires long lead times, and over the course of a year information in a yellow pages ad can easily become dated. There is also limited flexibility for creative execution in the traditional paper format.

Because of emerging technologies, the phone directory of the future may evolve into a form that allows advertisers considerably more room for creative execution. Regional Bell companies like Bell Atlantic and Nynex are developing interactive directory options that could one day contribute to a paperless society.[27] The system would allow consumers with personal computers to search for Chinese restaurants in Boston and retrieve current menu information online, along with photographs of the dining room and service staff. Bell Atlantic is also working with CD technology to deliver directory listings on television sets. The CD-based system can offer full-motion video and stereo sound, along with an interactive capability that could allow a customer to create a personalized map from home to the restaurant or retailer selected.

Additionally, many Web sites such as www.bigyellow.com/ and www.superpages. com/ now provide online access to yellow page–style databases that allow for individualized searches at one's desktop. Exhibit 16.13 features the home page for BigYellow. Other high-profile Web players such as Yahoo! and Microsoft Network

26. *Yellow Pages and the Media Mix.*
27. Leslie Cauley, "Nynex and Prodigy Team Up on Yellow Pages That Will Provide On-Line Listings and Ads," *Wall Street Journal,* December 10, 1993, B1.

WEB SIGHTING

EXHIBIT 16.13

Certain categories of Web sites naturally attract sponsorship. Others, like BigYellow (www.bigyellow.com/) and Switchboard.com (www. switchboard.com), also attract directories. Why might an ad for FTD Florists (www.ftd.com) be appropriate for BigYellow?

(national.sidewalk.msn.com/) have also developed online directories as components of their service offerings for Web surfers. While the emergence of these Internet options cannot be a good thing for traditional yellow pages publishers, the threat they pose can be alleviated through the development of new business models. What that new model should be remains unclear, but most agree that simply dumping the traditional A to Z printed Yellow Pages onto the Internet is not the answer.[28] The key question is, when will marketers decide that they are better served by having their product or service described via an online directory rather than a paper directory? That day hasn't come yet, but if and when it does, the demand for yellow paper is going to go way down.

When Support Media Are More Than Support Media. There are going to be times when the capabilities and economies of support media lead them to be featured in one's media plan. Obviously, in such instances, it would be a misnomer to label them as merely supportive. Out-of-home media used creatively and targeted in major metropolitan markets are especially compelling in this regard. A couple of examples should make this point clear.

There will be times when the particular advantages of transit advertising fit a marketer's communication objectives so perfectly that this medium will not be used merely as a support medium, but instead, as the primary means for reaching customers. Donna Karan's DKNY line of clothing, accessories, and cosmetics has relied heavily on transit advertising to reach its target audience in Manhattan.[29] For starters, the firm bought out the ten-car subway train that runs under Lexington Avenue on Manhattan's East Side and filled it with sophisticated image ads for DKNY. Not coincidentally, this particular subway train runs under the Bloomingdale's store on 59th Street, where DKNY had a supershop featuring all the products in its extensive line. DKNY ads have also appeared on the shuttles from Times Square to Grand Central Terminal, and at subway stations in the city. For DKNY, extensive advertising on and under the streets of New York City reflects its general strategy of using unconventional locations to create awareness and distinctive imagery for the DKNY product line.

Altoids, "the curiously strong mints" made in England since 1780, used a similar strategy to invigorate its brand in 12 major U.S. cities. Turns out that Altoids' target segment of young, socially active adults living in urban neighborhoods are very hard to reach with conventional broadcast or print advertising. Perhaps they are just too busy being socially active. Whatever, using geodemographic segmentation systems like those described in Chapter 6, it is not hard to identify their neighborhoods. So Altoids and its ad agency Leo Burnett set out to plaster those neighborhoods with quirky advertising signage on telephone kiosks, bus shelters, and the backs of buses. Once again, quirky rules! In each of the 12 targeted metro areas, sales of Altoids increased by over 50 percent.[30] Now that's invigorating.

28. *Yellow Pages: Facts & Media Guide 1998,* 4, 5.
29. Fara Warner, "DKNY Takes Upscale Ads Underground," *Wall Street Journal,* October 6, 1994, B5.
30. Brad Edmondson, "The Drive/Buy Equation," *Marketing Tools,* May 1998, 28–31.

Point-of-Purchase (P-O-P) Advertising.   From 1981 to 1997, marketers'

annual expenditures on point-of-purchase (P-O-P) advertising rose from $5.1 to $13.1 billion per year.[31] Why this dramatic growth? First, consider that P-O-P is the only medium that places advertising, products, and a consumer together in the same place at the same time. Then, think about these results. Research conducted by the Point-of-Purchase Advertising Institute (www.popai.com/) indicates that 70 percent of all product selections involve some final deliberation by consumers at the point of purchase. (Data cited in POPAI U.S. Consumer Buying Habits Study, 1995, pp.17–18. Conducted by POPAI in conjunction with Meyers Research Center.) Additionally, a joint study sponsored by Kmart and Procter & Gamble found that P-O-P advertising boosted the sales of coffee, paper towels, and toothpaste by 567 percent, 773 percent, and 119 percent, respectively.[32] With results like these, it is plain to see why P-O-P advertising is one of the fastest-growing categories in today's marketplace.

P-O-P advertising refers to materials used in the retail setting to attract shoppers' attention to one's product, convey primary product benefits, or highlight pricing information. It can take many forms. In-store displays, banners, shelf signs, wall units, and floor stands are traditional and economical means of drawing attention to a brand in a retail setting. As will be discussed in Chapter 18, P-O-P displays may also feature price-off deals or other consumer sales promotions. A corrugated cardboard dump bin and an attached header card featuring the brand logo or related product information can be produced for pennies per unit. When filled with a product and placed as a freestanding display at retail, sales gains usually follow.

A dump bin with tower display for Nabisco's Barnum's Animals crackers is shown in Exhibit 16.14. This 76-inch-tall cardboard tower spent 14 weeks in design before being mass-produced and rolled out across the country. The gorilla towers, along with their tiger and elephant predecessors, are the cornerstone of the advertising strategy for Barnum's.[33] While other Nabisco brands such as Oreo's, Chips Ahoy, and Nilla Wafers are supported by more comprehensive advertising programs, they too benefit from P-O-P displays like that in Exhibit 16.15.

Effective deployment of P-O-P advertising requires careful coordination with the marketer's sales force. Gillette found this out in 1996 when it realized it was wasting money on lots of P-O-P materials and displays that retailers simply ignored.[34] Gillette sales reps visit about 20,000 stores per month, and are in a position to know what retailers will and will not use. Gillette's marketing executives finally woke up to this fact when their sales reps told them, for example, that 50 percent of the shelf signs being shipped to retailers from three separate suppliers were going directly to retailers' garbage bins. Reps helped redesign new display cards that mega-retailers such as Wal-Mart approved for their stores and immediately put into use. Now any time Gillette launches a new P-O-P program, it tracks its success through the eyes and ears of 20 of its sales reps who have been designated as monitors for the new program. Having a sales force that can work with retailers to develop and deliver effective P-O-P programs is yet another critical element for achieving integrated marketing communication.

Technological developments will have a major impact on the appeal of P-O-P advertising in the future. Interactive electronic displays remain expensive relative to traditional low-tech options, such as the Tylenol floor stand in Exhibit 16.16. But as their costs come down, high-tech displays are likely to see broader application. Warner-Lambert has shown good results from on-shelf computers placed in 600 Canadian drugstores.[35] At $250 per unit, these computers help consumers sort through the maze

31. Data cited in Lisa Z. Eccles, "P-O-P Scores with Marketers," *Advertising Age,* September 26, 1994, P1–P4; Leah Haran, "Point of Purchase: Marketers Getting with the Program," *Advertising Age,* October 23, 1995, 33; and "The 1998 Annual Report of the Promotion Industry," in *PROMO's 6th Annual SourceBook '99* (Stamford, Conn.: PROMO Magazine, 1999), 10, 11.

32. Eccles, "P-O-P Scores with Marketers," P1–P4; Haran, "Point of Purchase: Marketers Getting with the Program," 33.

33. Yumiko Ono, "'Wobblers' and 'Sidekicks' Clutter Stores, Irk Retailers," *Wall Street Journal,* September 8, 1998, B1.

34. Nicole Crawford, "Keeping P-O-P Sharp," *PROMO Magazine,* January 1998, 52, 53.

35. Lisa Z. Eccles, "Technology Gives P-O-P a New Look," *Advertising Age,* September 26, 1994, P6.

EXHIBIT 16.14

While this is an elaborate dump bin, it is a dump bin nonetheless. For a brand such as Barnum's Animals, dump bin design and deployment will be a primary element in the advertising plan. www.nabisco.com/

EXHIBIT 16.15

Surprise! Surprise! Nabisco knows that packaged cookies are often an impulse purchase. If you've got milk, you've got to have some cookies. This P-O-P display is tailored to capitalize on the cookie-buying impulse. www.nabisco.com/

EXHIBIT 16.16

The crowded competitive field for OTC pharmaceuticals makes standing out from the crowd absolutely essential. This "Tylenol Store" was created especially for one of Tylenol's biggest retailing clients—Wal-Mart. www.tylenol.com/

of over-the-counter cough, cold, and allergy remedies, leading them to select from Warner-Lambert brands such as Actifed and Benadryl. In the United States, interactive kiosks provide a similar function in 2,900 pharmacies across the country, generating 33 million customer contacts per year.[36] Advances in the materials used to construct traditional displays, such as new powder coatings that can give a cardboard display the look of chrome, zinc, or brass plating, will also keep the dollars flowing to P-O-P advertising. Additional possibilities are featured in the New Media box on page 521.

Event Sponsorship.

Marketers large and small have realized that the effectiveness of traditional broadcast media continues to erode as media become more fragmented and consumers become more distracted. No one knows this better than the one of the world's biggest advertisers—General Motors. GM spends more than $2 billion annually in traditional media such as TV, radio, and magazines.[37] But as indicated by Exhibit 16.17, growing

36. Kelly Shermach, "New CD Products Show Times Are A-Changin'," *Marketing News,* March 27, 1995, 11.
37. Fara Warner, "Under Pressure, GM Takes Its Sales Show on the Road," *Wall Street Journal*, November 4, 1998, B1.

EXHIBIT 16.17

Money well spent? www.gm.com/

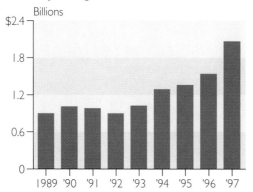

GM Is Spending More on Ads ...

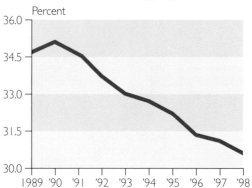

But Its Market Share Is Slipping

Sources: Competitive Media Reporting, General Motors.

expenditures in these media were not producing the desired impact on market share. As one GM executive put it, "You have to find other ways to touch customers than hammering them with network television."[38]

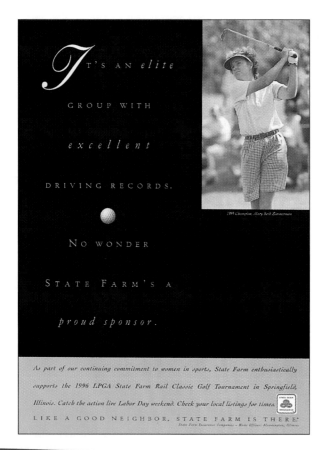

It's an *elite* GROUP WITH *excellent* DRIVING RECORDS. No WONDER STATE FARM'S A *proud sponsor.*

As part of our continuing commitment to women in sports, State Farm enthusiastically supports the 1996 LPGA State Farm Rail Classic Golf Tournament in Springfield, Illinois. Catch the action live Labor Day weekend. Check your local listings for times.
LIKE A GOOD NEIGHBOR, STATE FARM IS THERE.
State Farm Insurance Companies • Home Offices: Bloomington, Illinois

EXHIBIT 16.18

Sports sponsorship continues to grow in popularity as an advertising tool. Here, State Farm uses a clever play on words to validate its association with the LPGA. www.statefarm.com/

GM has experimented with a number of ways to "get closer" to its prospective customers. Most entail sponsoring events that get consumers in direct contact with its vehicles, or sponsoring events that associate the GM name with causes or activities that are of interest to its target customers. For example, GM has sponsored a traveling slave-ship exhibition, a scholarship program for the Future Farmers of America, and Seventh Avenue's week of fashion shows in New York City. GM has also launched a movie theater on wheels that travels to state fairs, fishing contests, and auto races to show its 15-minute "movie" about the Silverado pickup truck. Like many marketers large and small, GM is shifting more of its advertising budget into event sponsorship.[39]

Event sponsorship has some similarities with the other advertising and promotional options discussed thus far in this chapter. Event sponsorship often is used to support or supplement other ongoing advertising efforts. Thus, while it is not quite accurate to think of event sponsorship as a support *medium*, there will be times when it plays a supportive role in the media plan akin to that of out-of-home or specialty advertising. Additionally, event sponsorship can provide a base for wonderful synergies with other tactical options such as sales promotions and public relations. Some of these synergies will be made apparent in this chapter, and are then elaborated on in Chapters 18 and 20. As always, the IMC challenge is to get multiple tactical alternatives working together to break through the clutter of the marketplace and register the message with the target customer.

38. Ibid.
39. Ibid.

Who Else Uses Event Sponsorship?

Event sponsorship is a special and increasingly popular way to reach consumers. **Event sponsorship** involves a marketer providing financial support to help fund an event, such as a rock concert or golf tournament (see Exhibit 16.18). In return, that marketer acquires the rights to display a brand name, logo, or advertising message on-site at the event. If the event is covered on TV, the marketer's brand and logo may also receive exposure with the television audience. In 1997 marketers' expenditures for event sponsorship approached $6 billion, with about two-thirds of this total coming from sports sponsorship.[40]

P-O-P GOES I-N-T-E-R-A-C-T-I-V-E

Traditionally, point-of-purchase displays have offered customers an easy-to-spot, attractive product display, featured a two-for-one offer, or perhaps even dispensed a money-saving coupon. Well, P-O-P has leaped into the future with high-tech displays that not only make shopping more interesting for consumers, but also can generate valuable data for advertisers.

Everbrite of Greenfield, Wisconsin, has introduced a line of interactive P-O-P units that provide a variety of services to both consumers and marketers. One unit prints coupons, product use recommendations, and prescription drug information. The real power of this type of unit lies in the fact that the display is linked to information sources by telephone lines. This means an advertiser can change or update the unit's output daily to provide unique and timely information to consumers.

Another high-tech P-O-P unit can link as many as 30 microcomputers. A host PC supplies the entire network with a database containing product information and graphic displays. When a customer interacts with the computer (which looks like a video display unit), the printer is programmed to print a coupon for the specific product in which the consumer is interested.

These new P-O-P units can also be used to gather information *from* consumers. A Toyota dealership in San Diego ran a direct mail game. To find out if they won a prize, consumers had to visit the dealership and swipe the bar code of their game piece on a bar-code reader P-O-P display. The display also asked consumers, now identified by name and zip code location, their impressions of various Toyota products and programs. These data then are fed into the dealership's database for future direct mail campaigns.

P-O-P displays are no longer the lifeless pyramid of products stacked at the end of an aisle. They can interact with consumers and gather data for advertisers to produce better-integrated promotional programs. Audio chips, motion displays, and high-intensity lighting are also being employed to bring P-O-P displays to life. But the primary goal for P-O-P advertising never changes: that is, to make your brand stand out in a crowd.

Sources: Kelly Shermach, "Great Strides Made in P-O-P Technology," *Marketing News,* January 2, 1995; "P-O-P Gains, But Girds for Tobacco Withdrawal," in *PROMO's 6th Annual SourceBook '99* (Stamford, Conn.: *PROMO Magazine,* 1999), 14, 15.

Event sponsorship can take many forms. The events can be international in scope, like the Olympics, or they may have a local flavor, like a chili cook-off in Amarillo, Texas. The events may have existed on their own, with marketers offering funding after the fact, or marketers may literally create an event they can sponsor, in hopes of engaging a segment of their customers. Events provide a captive audience, may receive live coverage by radio and television, and often are reported in the print media. Hence, event sponsorship can both yield face-to-face contact with real consumers and receive simultaneous and follow-up publicity in the mass media.

The list of companies participating in event sponsorships seems to grow with each passing year. Sprint, Atlantic Records, Citibank, and a host of other companies have sponsored tours and special appearances for recording artists such as Brandy, Jewel, Elton John, and the Rolling Stones. Sprint reportedly paid $6 million to the Stones to fund their "Bridges to Babylon" tour, and as suggested by the ad in Exhibit 16.19, were grateful for the opportunity to be associated with "the World's Greatest Rock 'n' Roll Band." To capitalize on the growing popularity of women's NCAA college basketball, State Farm Insurance launched the Hall of Fame Tip-Off Classic.[41] If you have ever hit the beaches for spring break, you already know that companies such as Coca-Cola, MCI, and Sega will be there to greet

40. "Sponsorships Grow without the Olympics," in *PROMO's 6th Annual SourceBook '99* (Stamford, Conn.: *PROMO Magazine,* 1999), 20, 23.
41. Patrick M. Reilly, "Rich Marketing Alliances Keep Music Stars Glowing," *Wall Street Journal,* January 22, 1998, B1; Joan O'C. Hamilton, "The Hoopla over Women's Hoops," *Business Week,* April 10, 1995, 46.

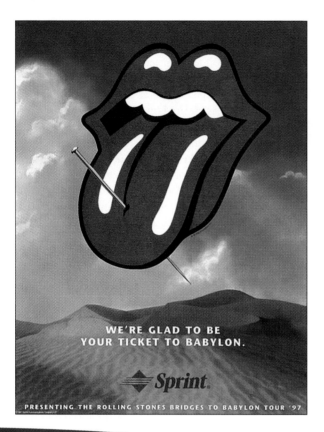

EXHIBIT 16.19

Over the years, the one-time bad boys of rock and roll have been courted by all manner of corporate sponsors. Cries of "Sellout!" were directed at the Stones for the $6 million deal they signed with Sprint (www .sprint.com/). But, the Rolling Stones (est. 1962) could legitimately argue that they (not Sprint) are the bigger brand name, and that only the truly naive believe that people who actually make the music are less deserving of the rewards than the big corporations. www.stones.com/

you. Research conducted by Intercollegiate Communications, Inc. has even established that 65 percent of college students on break not only accept corporate events on the beach, they expect and look forward to them.[42] With the growing interest in stock-car racing and an expanded NASCAR circuit that includes races all over the United States, major brands such as Canon, Tide, Gillette, Winston, McDonald's, and Kodak are scrambling for the privilege to spend $4 million a year to sponsor their very own race car.[43] Andersen Consulting has dabbled in golf and auto racing funding, and was also a proud sponsor of the "Van Gogh Masterpieces" art exhibit at the National Gallery of Art in Washington, D.C.[44] There can be no doubt that more marketers of all types will pursue event sponsorship in the future, and as indicated by the Global Issues box on page 523, this is by no means a uniquely North American development.

The Appeal of Event Sponsorship. In the early days of event sponsorship, it often wasn't clear what an organization was receiving in return for its sponsor's fee. Even today, many critics contend that sponsorship, especially of sporting events, can be ego-driven and thus a waste of money.[45] Company presidents are human, and they like to associate with sports stars and celebrities. This is fine, but when sponsorship of a golf tournament, for example, is motivated mainly by a CEO's desire to play in the same foursome as Jack Nicklaus or Tiger Woods, the company is really just throwing away advertising dollars.

One of the things fueling the growing interest in event sponsorship is that many companies are now finding ways to make a case for the effectiveness of their sponsorship dollars. Boston-based John Hancock Mutual Life Insurance has been a pioneer in developing detailed estimates of the advertising equivalencies of its sponsorships.[46] John Hancock began sponsoring a college football bowl game in 1986 and soon after had a means to judge the value of its sponsor's fee. Hancock employees scoured magazine and newspaper articles about their bowl game to determine name exposure in print media. Next they'd factor in the exact number of times that the John Hancock name was mentioned during television broadcast of the game, along with the name exposure in pregame promos. In 1991, Hancock executives estimated that they received the equivalent of $5.1 million in advertising exposure for their $1.6 million sponsorship fee. One John Hancock executive called this result "an extraordinarily efficient media buy."[47] However, as the television audience for the John Hancock bowl dwindled in subsequent years, Hancock's estimates of the bowl's value also plunged. Subsequently,

42. Dan Hanover, "School's Out!" *PROMO Magazine*, February 1998, 42–46.
43. Chris Roush, "Red Necks, White Socks, and Blue-Chip Sponsors," *Business Week,* August 15, 1994, 74; Alex Taylor III, "Can NASCAR Run in Bigger Circles?" *Fortune,* February 5, 1996, 38.
44. "Andersen Revamps Logo, Readies $100 Million," *Brandweek,* June 22, 1998, 1.
45. William M. Bulkeley, "Sponsoring Sports Gains in Popularity; John Hancock Learns How to Play to Win," *Wall Street Journal,* June 24, 1994, B1.
46. Michael J. McCarthy, "Keeping Careful Score on Sports Tie-Ins," *Wall Street Journal,* April 24, 1991, B1.
47. Ibid.

Hancock moved its sports sponsorship dollars into other events, such as the Winter Olympics from Lillehammer, Norway, and the U.S. Gymnastics Championships.

Other research is also providing hard evidence for the value of sponsorship. Studies conducted with various types of sports fans by Performance Research of Newport, Rhode Island, indicate that fan loyalty can be converted to sales. Among stock-car racing fans, 70 percent say they frequently buy the products they see promoted at the racetrack. For baseball, tennis, and golf, these commitment levels run at 58 percent, 52 percent, and 47 percent, respectively.[48] These findings suggest that racing fans in particular have specific product preferences that advertisers can identify and appeal to, and explain why marketers are flocking to the racetrack to get their brand names on the hood of a stock car or on the cap of a stock-car driver.

So how is it conceivable that a company such as Procter & Gamble could justify sponsorship of the Tide Car, shown in Exhibit 16.20? Well, first of all, lots of women are NASCAR fans and lots of women buy Tide. Additionally, P&G's own research jibes with that mentioned in the previous paragraph: NASCAR fans really are loyal to the brands that sponsor cars and have absolutely no problem with marketers plastering their logos all over their cars and their drivers. This translates into incredible visibility and exposure for the Tide brand during a race and in subsequent race coverage. Indeed, when it comes to TV exposure, NASCAR's average per-event TV ratings are second only to NFL football,[49] and without a doubt, brands are truly the stars of the show during any NASCAR event. When asked directly how they value the nationally telecast images of driver Ricky Rudd in his Tide jumpsuit standing in the winner's circle next to his screaming orange Tide Car, a tight-

GLOBAL ISSUES

EVENT SPONSORSHIP HITS CHINA

Marketers around the world want to be associated with culturally appropriate events. These events provide exposure and networking opportunities that foster global expansion. And with China being one of the largest developing economies in the world, it is a hot spot for event sponsorship. Thus, when the decision was made to perform Puccini's classic opera *Turandot* in the Forbidden City, international marketers were ready with their checkbooks to help underwrite the lavish $15 million production.

Of course, the location is perfect: Giacomo Puccini set his opera in Beijing's Forbidden City. The opera was conducted by Zubin Mehta, directed by Zhang Yimou, and performed outdoors by a cast of 1,000. The extravagant production was expected to draw 20,000 spectators, even with the equally extravagant ticket prices ranging from $150 to $1,500. Sponsors covet the association with affluent, cosmopolitan people that an event like this attracts. Banks and accounting firms were at the head of the line for sponsorship rights, and were joined by companies such as Time Inc., Ericsson Telecommunications, and Tricon Global Restaurants. To be a sponsor, any international firm needed to first establish a joint-venture relationship with a Chinese company, as required by the Chinese government.

So what is there to eat at the opera? Fortunately, Tricon's Pizza Hut and KFC were part of the event, selling their fast food on site. Chicken wings, Puccini, and the Forbidden City: It just doesn't get any better than that!

Source: Kate Fitzgerald, "China's International Culture Club," *Advertising Age,* August 3, 1998, 22, 23.

lipped P&G spokesperson would only say: "We have had the Tide race car as part of the Tide marketing program for many years, so obviously, we think it's a good way to reach consumers."[50] Obviously.

Event sponsorship can furnish a unique opportunity to foster brand loyalty at other kinds of events as well. When marketers connect their brand with the potent emotional experiences often found at rock concerts, in sport stadiums, or on Fort Lauderdale beaches in mid-March, positive feelings may be attached to that brand. As part

48. Roush, "Red Necks, White Socks, and Blue-Chip Sponsors," 74.
49. Sam Walker, "NASCAR Gets Coup as Anheuser Is Set to Raise Sponsorship Role," *Wall Street Journal,* November 13, 1998, B6.
50. Jeff Harrington, "P&G Bubbling over Tide Car's NASCAR Win," *Cincinnati Enquirer,* August 10, 1997, 11.

of its spring break promotion, Coca-Cola sponsors dance contests on the beach, where it hands out thousands of cups of Coke and hundreds of Coca-Cola T-shirts each day. The goal is to build brand loyalty with those 18-to-24-year-old students who've come to the beach for fun and sun. As assessed by one of Coke's senior brand managers, "This is one of the best tools in our portfolio."[51] Likewise, the brand may serve as a lasting reminder that links an individual to a special experience. Additionally, since various types of events attract well-defined target audiences, marketers can and should choose to sponsor just those events that help them reach a desired target.

For instance, a "who's who" of the European brewing industry lines up to sponsor professional soccer teams such as Britain's Chelsea football club. Brewers such as Bass PLC and Carlsberg AS want to reach beer-drinking soccer fans in hopes that the fans will become as loyal to their beers as they are to their favorite soccer team. This union of beer sponsors, soccer clubs, and emotional, unruly fans has created a backlash in countries such as France, which has banned club sponsorship by alcohol companies. Other brewers have tried to avoid the rowdy image of European soccer. Heineken, based in The Netherlands, has a multiyear deal with the International Tennis Federation both because its managers want the international exposure and because they believe that perceptions of tennis as a more civilized sport better match the refined imagery they try to convey to the "sophisticated" beer drinker.[52] However, in 1998 Heineken relented at least temporarily as it ran a number of local promotions in conjunction with Holland's entry in the World Cup Soccer Championships. Given the incredible fan support generated for a World Cup team, Heineken simply could not pass on this loyalty-building opportunity. Hup Holland!

Seeking a Synergy around Event Sponsorship. As we have seen, one way to justify event sponsorship is to calculate the number of viewers who will be exposed to a brand either at the event or through media coverage of the event, and then assess whether the sponsorship provides a cost-effective way of reaching the target segment. This approach assesses sponsorship benefits in direct comparison with traditional advertising media. Some experts now maintain, however, that the benefits of sponsorship can be fundamentally different from anything that traditional media might provide. These additional benefits can take many forms.

51.   Bruce Horovitz, "Students Get Commercial Crash Course," *USA Today*, March 22, 1995, B1–B2.
52.   Tara Parker-Pope, "Brewers' Soccer Sponsorships Draw Fire," *Wall Street Journal,* February 27, 1995, B1.

Events can be leveraged as ways to entertain important clients, recruit new customers, motivate the firm's salespeople, and generally enhance employee morale. Events provide unique opportunities for face-to-face contact with key customers. Marketers commonly use this point of contact to distribute specialty-advertising items so that attendees will have a branded memento to remind them of the rock concert or soccer match. Marketers may also use this opportunity to sell premiums such as T-shirts and hats, administer consumer surveys as part of their marketing research efforts, or distribute product samples. As you will see in Chapter 20, a firm's event participation may also be the basis for public relations activities that then generate additional media coverage. When it comes to additional media coverage, advertisers are truly relentless: As shown in the IMC box on this page, some are even experimenting with virtual reality as yet another way to get more mileage out of their event sponsorship.

SPORTS SPONSORS LOOK TO VIRTUAL REALITY

One of the primary motives of any company sponsoring a sporting event is to get exposure for its brand name as part of the televised coverage. The IMC mantra has us always seeking synergies, and event sponsorship dollars clearly go further when your brand name ends up on center court. Watch any sporting event from almost any country in the world, and you will see brand-name signage cleverly placed so that TV cameras always have something to sell.

But now, the limits of physical space need no longer be a constraint. New technology that might be thought of as virtual advertising offers to revolutionize sports sponsorship. Virtual advertising had its first major test at the Toshiba Tennis Classic, where Toshiba utilized technology from the Israeli company SciDel to literally place its logo on center court. While this "virtual logo" was not visible to the live audience at the match, it was prominent in the televised image. The unsuspecting TV viewer simply would not know that this branded logo was not actually painted on the tennis court.

Are there other venues where the virtual billboard might be of interest to sports sponsors? Of course! One especially lucrative possibility is soccer—one of the most watched sports worldwide. Soccer is a prime candidate because it is hard to use traditional TV ads with soccer, where the nonstop action of the sport provides for few commercial breaks. Additionally, virtual ad signage can be easily customized for local viewers. So viewers of a World Cup match between Italy and Brazil could have customized logos/signage appear on the TV screen, virtually, country by country. Is this a dream come true for advertisers, or what?

Source: Brian C. Fenton, "Truth in Advertising," *Popular Mechanics,* January 1997, 37.

John Hancock Mutual Life has shown remarkable creativity in maximizing the benefits it derived from the $24 million it spent for its five-year sponsorship of the Olympic Games.[53] Of course, association with a high-profile event such as the Summer Games in Atlanta yields broad exposure for the John Hancock name, but Hancock has also been skillful in taking advantage of its sponsor status with local programs. For instance, in conjunction with the Winter Games, Hancock sponsored hockey clinics featuring Olympians from the 1980 gold-medal-winning team. Children and their parents turned out in droves. While the clinics were designed for children, the parents who brought them became immediate prospects for Hancock sales representatives. It is this sort of synergy between sponsorship and local selling efforts that organizations often fail to strive for in maximizing the benefits of their sponsorship expenditures.

The Coordination Challenge.

When we add various support media to the many options that exist in print and broadcast media, we have an incredible assortment of choices for delivering messages to a target audience. And it doesn't stop there. As you have seen, marketers and advertisers are constantly searching for new, cost-effective

53. Bulkeley, "Sponsoring Sports Gains in Popularity."

ways to break through the clutter and reach consumers. Important developments in information technologies will only accelerate this search for new options as the traditional mass media undergo profound changes.

In concluding this chapter, a critical point about the media explosion needs to be reinforced. Advertisers have a vast and ever-expanding array of options for delivering messages to their potential customers. From cable TV to national newspapers, from virtual billboards to home pages on the World Wide Web, the variety of options is staggering. The keys to success for any advertising campaign are choosing the right set of options to engage a target segment and then coordinating the placement of messages to ensure coherent and timely communication. Achieving this coordination is easier said than done.

Many factors work against coordination. As advertising has become more complex, organizations often become reliant on functional specialists. For example, an organization might have separate managers for advertising, event sponsorship, and direct marketing. Specialists, by definition, focus on their specialty and can lose sight of what others in the organization are doing.[54] Specialists also want their own budgets and typically argue for more funding for their particular area. Internal competition for budget dollars often yields rivalries and animosities that work against coordination.

Coordination is also complicated by the fact that few ad agencies have all the internal skills necessary to fulfill clients' demands for integrated marketing communications.[55] The interactive media discussed in Chapter 17 have been a special challenge for traditional ad agencies in recent years. Thus, to develop its Zima Website, Coors Brewing employed Modem Media, an interactive-only ad agency based in Norwalk, Connecticut.[56] Coors's traditional advertising agency, Foote, Cone & Belding, was not involved in this Internet project. But with each additional external organization employed to help deliver messages to customers, coordination problems become more complicated.[57]

Remember from the discussion of IMC in previous chapters that the objective underlying this coordination is to achieve a synergistic effect. Individual media can work in isolation, but advertisers get more from their advertising dollars if various media and promotional tools build on one another and work together. Even marketing giants such as Gillette are challenged by the need for coordination. In fact, large size and global scale probably just make things harder. As we saw back in Chapter 6, Gillette is determined to dominate the wet-shaving business for men and women around the world. This will involve the launch of new products such as its Agility disposable shavers for women with multimillion-dollar advertising campaigns and loyalty-building promotional activities on Florida's beaches, and perhaps even a bumper sticker on Gillette's NASCAR entry. But it also requires effective deployment of Gillette's salesforce to negotiate and schedule P-O-P displays for Agility so that the brand stands out from the crowd in the retail setting, inviting shoppers to act on the interest that was created for the brand by mass media advertising. Making all these components work together and speak to the consumer with a "single voice" is at the heart of integrated marketing communication.

The coordination challenge does not end here. Chapters that follow will add more levels of complexity to this challenge. Topics to come include Internet advertising, sales promotion, direct marketing, and public relations. These activities entail additional contacts with a target audience that should reinforce the messages being delivered through broadcast, print, and support media. Integrating these efforts to speak with one voice represents a marketer's best and maybe only hope for breaking through the clutter of competitive advertising to engage with a target segment in today's crowded marketplace.

54.   Don E. Schultz, Stanley I. Tannenbaum, and Robert F. Lauterborn, *Integrated Marketing Communications* (Lincolnwood, Ill.: NTC Business Books, 1993).

55.   Don E. Schultz, "Why Ad Agencies Are Having So Much Trouble with IMC," *Marketing News,* April 26, 1993, 12; Kate Fitzgerald, "Beyond Advertising," *Advertising Age,* August 3, 1998, 1, 14.

56.   Joan E. Rigdon, "Hip Advertisers Bypass Madison Avenue When They Need Cutting-Edge Web Sites," *Wall Street Journal,* February 28, 1996, B1. For an in-depth description of the Zima Internet launch, see Cathy Taylor, "Z Factor," *Adweek,* February 6, 1995, 14–16.

57.   Don E. Schultz, "New Media, Old Problem: Keeping Marcom Integrated," *Marketing News,* March 29, 1999, 11, 12.

SUMMARY

◐▷ Describe the role of support media in a comprehensive media plan.

The traditional support media include out-of-home media along with specialty and directory advertising. Billboards and transit advertising are excellent means for carrying simple messages into specific metropolitan markets. Aerial advertising is becoming more prevalent and can be a great way to break through the clutter. Specialty-advertising items and premiums are useful for getting and keeping a brand name in front of a customer. Finally, directory advertising can be a sound investment because it helps a committed customer locate an advertiser's product.

◐▷ Explain the appeal of P-O-P advertising as an element of an IMC program.

Expenditures on P-O-P advertising continue to grow at a rapid pace. The reason is simple: P-O-P can be an excellent sales generator when integrated with an overall advertising campaign. P-O-P displays may call attention to one's brand, remind consumers of key benefits provided by one's brand, or offer price-off deals as a final incentive to purchase. Retailers' cooperation is key in making P-O-P programs work; getting their cooperation requires diligent efforts from the marketer's sales force in the field.

◐▷ Justify the growing popularity of event sponsorship as another supportive component of a media plan.

The list of companies sponsoring events grows with each passing year, and the events include a wide variety of activities. Of these various activities, sports attract the most sponsorship dollars. Sponsorship can help in building brand familiarity; it can promote brand loyalty by connecting a brand with powerful emotional experiences; and in most instances it allows a marketer to reach a well-defined target audience. Events can also facilitate face-to-face contacts with key customers and present opportunities to distribute product samples, sell premiums, and conduct consumer surveys.

◐▷ Discuss the challenges presented by the ever-increasing variety of media for achieving integrated marketing communications.

The tremendous variety of media options we have seen thus far represents a monumental challenge for an advertiser who wishes to speak to a customer with a single voice. Achieving this single voice is critical for breaking through the clutter of the modern advertising environment. However, the functional specialists required for working in the various media have their own biases and subgoals that can get in the way of IMC. We will return to this issue in subsequent chapters as we explore other options available to marketers in their quest to persuade customers.

KEY TERMS

support media (507)
riding the boards (510)
transit advertising (511)
out-of-home media (511)
aerial advertising (513)

specialty-advertising items (514)
premiums (514)
P-O-P advertising (518)
event sponsorship (521)

QUESTIONS FOR REVIEW AND CRITICAL THINKING

1.   Explain the important advancements in technology that are likely to contribute to the appeal of billboards as an advertising medium.

2.   Critique the out-of-home media as tools for achieving reach-versus-frequency objectives in a media plan.

3.   Explain the unique role for directory advertising in a media plan. Given what you see happening on the Internet, what kind of future do you predict for traditional yellow pages advertising?

4.   When would it be appropriate to conclude that tools such as transit or P-O-P advertising are serving more than just a supportive role in one's media plan? Give an example of each of these tools being used as the principal element in the advertising plan, either from your own experience or from examples that were offered in this chapter.

5.   During your next visit to the grocery store, identify three examples of P-O-P advertising. How well were each of these displays integrated with other aspects of a more comprehensive advertising campaign? What would you surmise are the key factors in creating effective P-O-P displays?

6.   Present statistics to document the claim that the television viewing audience is becoming fragmented. What are the causes of this fragmentation? Develop an argument that links this fragmentation to the growing popularity of event sponsorship.

7.   Event sponsorship can be valuable for building brand loyalty. Search through your closets, drawers, or cupboards and find a premium or memento that you acquired at a sponsored event. Does this memento bring back fond memories? Would you consider yourself loyal to the brand that sponsored this event? If not, why not?

8.   Explain why new media contribute to the need for functional specialists in ad preparation. What problems do these and other functional specialists create for the achievement of integrated marketing communications?

EXPERIENTIAL EXERCISES

1.   In this chapter you learned about traditional support media. When you are driving down a busy street, what types of commercial messages do you see? Which ones do you think are most effective, and why? How could an advertiser conduct formal, systematic research to determine whether its outdoor advertising messages are effective? What other traditional support media alternatives are available in your town? The next time you go to a movie, record the ways in which an advertiser could get a message to you. How much influence does support media advertising have on your purchasing decisions?

2.   Look through your local newspaper for entertainment or tourist events that are taking place in town this weekend. First, record how many of them have corporate sponsorships. Next, evaluate whether the event itself is consistent with the product category of the sponsor. If you disagree with some of the "match-ups," think of a sponsor that would be more appropriate for the event than the current sponsor.

USING THE INTERNET

Choose three Web addresses you either remember from or can find in traditional advertising media. Visit these three sites.

For each site, answer the following questions:

1.   In what way is the Web address placed within the advertisement? How do the characteristics of the Web address within the advertisement make it more memorable and encourage you to actually visit the site?

2.   Does the Web site communicate the same message or messages that the traditional media advertisement is attempting to communicate? Does the content of the site tend to reinforce or detract from the image of the product advertised?

3.   How effectively does the site use new media marketing tools such as interactivity and visual imagery?

Compare your experience on the Web with the density of advertising in a "real world" event setting, for example, in a sports arena or at an exhibition. From the Nike "swoosh" on the players' jerseys, to the blimps above, advertising seems ubiquitous. But as much as the Web has become rife with banner ads, it's still a relatively narrow window on a desktop otherwise controlled by the user. In their attempts to get in front of consumers, some sites have "piggy-backed" on others' content in ways that might be considered innovative or, depending on your stake, annoying.

The news-oriented Web site TotalNEWS was accused of bad practices and threatened with law suits when it used "framing" to place its own ads next to other services' Web content. Visit TotalNEWS (www.totalnews.com) and note the forms of advertising they currently host, and how they represent other news sites' content.

1.   How does TotalNEWS capture consumers, while still according the sites whose content it's "borrowing" their own access to the consumer?

A celebrated (or, more accurately, infamous) Web site is Whitehouse.com, which uses its similarity to Whitehouse.gov (the Web site for the President of the United States, a reasonably famous guy, to be sure!) and Web surfers' carelessness and the fact that most Web sites end in ".com" to grab traffic. Unlike the White House site, Whitehouse.com is a porn-oriented site.

Visit both the White House (www.whitehouse.gov) and Whitehouse.com (www.whitehouse.com) Web sites (or skip the latter, and take our word for it . . . it's a porn-oriented Web site!).

2.   How ethical is Whitehouse.com's approach to generating traffic? Is it legal? Is it wise?

Some Web sites are based on domain names that are typographical errors for other, popular sites, e.g., www.atlavista.com (as opposed to the popular altavista.com search engine site). Try creating some typo-domains of your own, and see if someone has put up a site at that (erroneous) destination.

3.   How do you think the site creators are using such sites?

your fly is open

$3.95 flat rate shipping

An outlet store in your home
(no assembly required)

40 million locations
in the U.S. alone

Your personal catalog
Pick your sizes and favorite designers

24 hours
a day

Much better
than a print
catalog

Trends, tips
and fashion
advice

shirts
jackets
pantsandshorts
outerwear
andmuchmore

**More top
designers**
than the
Hamptons

savings of 25% to 75%

Money Back guarantee

Best search system
since Lassie

Superior security

Cha-ching!

They say you can attract more flies with honey than vinegar.
Personally, we recommend savings and selection. Bluefly.com is your
own personal outlet store where you can shop for name brand and top designer clothing
from the comfort of your own home or the convenience of your office.
Bluefly is now open. And this fly never closes.

bluefly.comsm **it's wear to go**sm

Bluefly.com is brought to you by Pivot Rules, Inc., a NASDAQ SmallCap Company: PVTR, PVTRW. 'Pivot Rules 1998

CHAPTER 17

**After reading and thinking about
this chapter, you will be able to do
the following:**

- Describe who uses the Internet and the
  ways they are using it.

- Identify the advertising and marketing
  opportunities presented by the Internet.

- Discuss fundamental requirements for
  establishing viable sites on the World
  Wide Web.

- Explain the challenges inherent in measuring the cost-effectiveness of the Internet
  versus other advertising media.

- Describe how the Internet is changing the
  way consumers shop and buy.

Moses went walking with the staff of wood. Yeah, yeah, yeah, yeah.
Newton got beaned by the apple good. Yeah, yeah, yeah, yeah.
Egypt was troubled by the horrible asp. Yeah, yeah, yeah, yeah.
Mister Charles Darwin had the gall to ask. Yeah, yeah, yeah, yeah.
Hey Andy did you hear about this one? Tell me, are you locked in the punch?
Hey Andy are you goofing on Elvis? Hey, baby. Are you having fun?
If you believed they put a man on the moon, man on the moon.
If you believe there's nothing up my sleeve, then nothing is cool.

—"Man on the Moon," R.E.M./Athens Ltd.

Technology changes everything. When it is communications technology, it can change something very fundamental. So it is with the latest communications revolution. The connected consumer is connected to other consumers in real time, and with connection comes community, empowerment, even liberation. The Internet can be emancipatory, but is something else lost? Has technology again changed human consciousness the way the telegraph did? The way television did? Are more solitary individuals sitting at computers really connected in any meaningful way? Is this revolution? Well, "revolutions" are more common than they used to be. Still, what does seem truly revolutionary about the Internet is the ability to alter the basic nature of communication within the commercial channel. This much seems fairly clear. It may or may not change the way we think about ourselves, society, or God, but it will probably change the way we think about the stuff we buy, and how we look for it and talk about it. Hey baby. Are you having fun?

An Overview of Cyberspace.

The **Internet** is a global collection of computer networks linking both public and private computer systems. It was originally designed by the U.S. military to be a decentralized, highly redundant, and thus reliable communications system in the event of a national emergency. Even if some of the military's computers crashed, the Internet would continue to perform. Today the Internet comprises a combination of computers from government, educational, military, and commercial sources. In the past few years the number of computers connected to the Internet has approximately doubled every year, from 2 million in 1994 to 5 million in 1995 to about 10 million in 1996. In mid-1998, there were estimated to be around 90 million people connected to the Internet in the United States and Canada,[1] and 155 million people worldwide (www.euromktg.com/). Of course, don't let the imputed precision fool you; these are only estimates. At this point, no one knows exactly how many people use the Internet. The numbers vary depending on who is counting, how the counting is done, and the definition of an Internet user. In fact, this counting problem turns out to be a huge problem for the Internet as an advertising medium. If you can't count exposures to ads in any kind of reliable and meaningful way, many advertisers simply aren't interested in paying the Internet's relatively expensive rates.

The Basic Parts.

There are four main components of the Internet: electronic mail, IRC, Usenet, and the World Wide Web. **Electronic mail** (E-mail) allows people to send messages to one another. In 1998, there were close to 800 billion E-mails sent from within the United States, which may explain the proliferation of services, technologies, and devices that support electronic messaging and the advertising associated with them—an example of which is seen in Exhibit 17.2. **Internet Relay Chat (IRC)** makes it possible for people to "talk" electronically in real time with each other, despite their geographical separation. For people with common interests, **Usenet** provides a forum for sharing knowledge in a public "cyberspace" that is separate from their E-mail program. Finally,

---

1.   *Business Week,* "The Click Here Economy," June 22, 1998, 122–172.

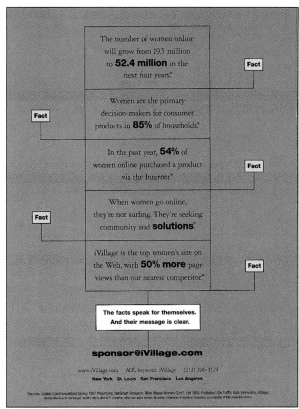

The Internet is changing the way people live, work, and shop. Marketers and advertisers will continue to be challenged well into the next century by this new, interactive medium.
www.ivillage.com/

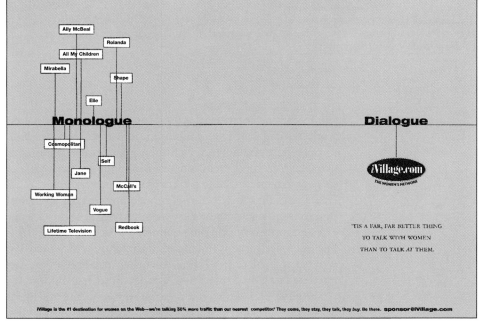

with the **World Wide Web (WWW)**, people can access an immense database of information in a graphical environment through the use of programs called Web browsers (such as Netscape and Internet Explorer). Most Web sites are listed with the prefix *http://,* which stands for *hypertext transfer protocol,* or rules of interaction between the Web browser and the Web server that are used to deal with hypertext. Because most Web browsers assume the file will be in hypertext, they don't require users to type out the prefix.

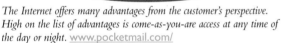

The Internet offers many advantages from the customer's perspective. High on the list of advantages is come-as-you-are access at any time of the day or night. www.pocketmail.com/

EXHIBIT 17.3

AT&T's WorldNet Service provides one Internet access option. www.att.net/wns/maxim

To use the Internet, the user's personal computer must be connected to the network in some way. The most common way to access the Internet is by using a modem to call a host computer, which then provides the client computer access to the Internet. The four most common access options are through a commercial online service, such as America Online; a corporate gateway, such as AT&T's WorldNet Service (Exhibit 17.3); a local Internet service provider; or an educational institution. In addition to using one of these networks, a personal computer needs software to communicate and move around while online, such as a Web browser and/or E-mail application. For example, if one is interested in the graphic-oriented World Wide Web, then software such as Netscape Navigator or Microsoft Internet Explorer is needed. If one is interested only in E-mail, then a program such as Eudora would suffice.

Exhibit 17.4 shows Internet usage around the world. As you can see, the United States, Canada, and Western Europe account for most of the "worldwide" Web traffic. Internet users are, at present, disproportionately affluent white American males. The United Kingdom, Western Europe, and parts of Southeast Asia are growing in both absolute and relative terms, as shown in the Global Issues box on page 537. In the United States, internet demographics are changing daily, and the trend favors a somewhat more representative slice of the population. Like many communication technologies, the Internet started rather upscale, but is now broadening. Just how far it will broaden remains to be seen.

EXHIBIT 17.4

Internet usage around the world.

Country	Population in Millions	Computers per 1,000 People	Internet Users per 1,000 People	Year 2000 Projected Estimate of Users per 1,000 People	Percentage of the World's Internet Users
Argentina	35.10	43.1	2.64	26.12	.09
Australia	18.8	366	178	412.9	3.35
Brazil	164.5	24.4	5.23	30.66	.86
Canada	29.04	363.7	148.9	386.9	4.33
China	1,228	5.08	.15	2.98	.18
Finland	5.1	354	244.5	448.8	1.25
France	58.64	233.6	20.03	211.7	1.17
Germany	81.67	231.4	49.76	278.2	4.07
Iceland	.27	356.3	227.3	423.3	.061
India	965	2.88	.15	1.55	.15
Israel	5.27	219.3	49.53	247.7	.26
Japan	126.3	227.7	63.06	172	7.97
Mexico	97.5	40.6	3.2	19.9	.31
Norway	4.36	362.6	231.1	431.2	1.01
Russia	150.5	31.3	4.02	33.23	.60
Singapore	2.95	315.5	141.2	370	.42
South Africa	47.5	31.4	12.4	37.43	.59
Ukraine	51.89	18.5	1.46	25.29	.076
United Kingdom	58.55	282.5	99.53	288	5.83
United States	268.8	450.2	203.4	478.4	54.7

Source: Internet Industry Almanac (Computer Industry Almanac Inc., 1998).

Internet Media. Internet advertising tactics differ in the degree to which the advertisement is "pushed" onto the consumer or requested ("pulled") by the consumer. Internet advertising that uses a push strategy is akin to traditional advertising tactics: The marketer delivers the communication to the consumer at the marketer's choosing, retaining control over when, where, and how the advertising message is delivered. Advertising delivered via E-mail and Usenet typically involves push strategies, and, as will be discussed, if done improperly, can lead to considerable backlash. With pull tactics, consumers have control over advertising exposure. That is, consumers seek information at their own convenience. This strategy is most common on the World Wide Web.

Advertising through Electronic Mail and Newsgroups. E-mail is an Internet function that allows users to communicate much as they do using standard mail. Some marketers have used this function of the Internet to communicate with potential consumers. A variety of companies collect E-mail addresses and profiles that allow advertisers to direct E-mail to a specific group. The DM Group (www.dm1.com/) maintains a list of E-mail groups and has reportedly collected hundreds of thousands of E-mail addresses. However, widespread E-mail advertising has not yet materialized due to significant consumer resistance to marketers' direct mailings to personal E-mail addresses. As techniques and guidelines are better established for direct E-mail advertising, it may become more accepted in the future. Many believe it's only a matter of time, because, historically, advertisers have rarely worried about being too intrusive.

People who wish to discuss specific topics through the Internet often join electronic mailing lists, or **listservs**. Thousands of mailing lists are available on an incredible variety of topics. We show the top 25 listservs, by number of subscribers, in Exhibit 17.5. A message sent to the list's E-mail address is then re-sent to everybody on the mailing list. A niche for commercial services that collect and sell listservs certainly exists and is already attracting attention. Still, advertisers need to be cautious here, since it is currently considered in very bad taste to openly sell products via listservs, particu-

EXHIBIT 17.5

The top 25 public listserv groups (by number of subscribers).

Listserv Address	Description	Number of Subscribers
hotdeals@mail.180096hotel.com	Hotel reservations network/best fares discount travel newsletter	501,800
course_list@prenhall.com	Listserv plus master list	272,519
eol-dispatch@dispatch.cnet.com	E!Mail electronic newsletter	242,246
eol-inbox@dispatch.cnet.com	E!Mail electronic newsletter	231,140
bezerknews@pangaea.berksys.com	Berkeley Systems Bezerk News	229,876
dilbert_news@listserv.unitedmedia.com	Dogbert's new ruling class	210,777
ignpresspass@listserv.imagine-inc.com	The IGN presspass list	183,683
javascripts-l@listserv.earthweb.com	javascripts.com info	171,055
dietcity-aol@peach.ease.lsoft.com	The resource for diet and nutrition info on AOL	164,621
value-mail@lists.emaildirect.com	Value-Mail	136,713
dietcity@peach.ease.lsoft.com	The resource for diet and nutrition info on the Web	126,551
brain@ml.software.ne.jp	Bunka Hoso Brain	110,603
alloymaillist@listserv.alloyonline.com	Alloy E-mags (html version)	110,131
wonnews@pangaea.berksys.com	The World Opponent Network (WON.net) newsletter	97,683
subscribers-javascripts-com@listserv.earthweb.com	javascripts.com info	96,313
developer-com@listserv.earthweb.com	The developer.com announcement list	96,181
msn-uk-news@announce.microsoft.com	MSN Update	94,795
symposium-webcast@listserv.gartner.com	Gartner's Symposium Webcast	94,538
burpeenews@dispatch.garden.org	A gardening newsletter from Burpee and the National Gardening Association	94,368
microsoft_security@announce.microsoft.com	Microsoft product security notification service	89,671
computerworld_daily@listserv.computerworld.com	No definition	88,958
emerge@stockplayer.com	Stockplayers	85,106
click-it@pegasus.thisco.com	Click-it! Weekends from TravelWeb, Inc.	85,037
selfhelp@peach.ease.lsoft.com	The resource for diet and nutrition info on the Web	84,990
bvdailynote@mailserv.digitalcity.com	Black Voices daily note list	72,928

Source: L-Soft International. Available online at www.lsoft.com/scripts/wl.exe?xs=10000. Accessed March 28, 1999.

larly when there is no apparent connection between the mailing list's theme and the advertised product. Product information shared through these mailing lists can be likened to traditional word-of-mouth communications and is, at the moment, still in the hands of users. Again, it's likely that the temptation to defy the current taboo will be too strong for advertisers to resist much longer.

AFFLUENT EUROPEANS ARE GOING ONLINE

The most affluent Europeans say they are watching more pan-European TV but fewer of them claim to be reading international newspapers and magazines, apparently because of a large increase in the number of wealthy Europeans who are spending more time on the Internet. The annual European Media and Marketing Survey showed that most large, established pan-European television channels managed to maintain their share of viewership and post single-digit growth in actual viewership. Smaller channels racked up double-digit growth and added large blocks of viewers. For example, Eurosport remained the most-watched channel, reaching 12.7 million viewers in an average week. But the Discovery Channel and CNBC added over 500,000 and 300,000 viewers, respectively, with CNBC's viewership growing an astounding 90 percent during 1997.

The most intriguing finding in the survey, though, is what appears to be a migration from traditional print media to Internet use among wealthy Europeans. Among daily titles such as *The Financial Times, International Herald Tribune,* and *USA Today,* average readership fell by double-digit percentages. Among weekly titles, only *Newsweek* recorded a slight increase. This is in contrast to the solid gains registered in Internet usage. Internet usage among survey respondents increased dramatically to 31 percent in 1997 from 21 percent in 1996. Among heavy Internet users (defined as daily users), the usage rate doubled to 12 percent. Heavy users are found significantly more often in the United Kingdom and Ireland, Nordic countries, and the Netherlands.

There may be a silver lining in these data, however. First, those respondents who were avid readers were also heavy users of the Internet. Second, few of the European publications have established a significant Web presence. These two factors taken together mean that there may be a solid future for online versions of traditional print publications.

Source: Bill Britt, "EMS Finds More Affluent Europeans Going Online," *Advertising Age International,* August 17, 1998, 9.

Usenet is a collection of discussion groups in cyberspace. People can read messages pertaining to a given topic, post new messages, and answer messages. For advertisers, this is an important source of consumers who care about certain topics. For example, the Usenet group alt.beer is an excellent place for a new microbrewery to promote its product. Advertisers can also use Usenet as a source of unobtrusive research, getting the latest opinions on their products and services. Television shows such as *The X-Files* often monitor Usenet groups, such as alt.tv.x-files, to find out what people think about the show. Usenet is also used as a publicity vehicle for goods and services. Usenet represents a relatively self-segmented word-of-mouth channel.

Uninvited commercial messages sent to listservs, Usenet groups, or some other compilation of E-mail addresses is a notorious practice known as **spam**. For example, more than 6 million people were once spammed at a cost of only $425. In retaliation, such organizations as the Coalition Against Unsolicited Commercial Email (www.cauce.org/) have compiled resources for fighting spam as well as a blacklist of advertisers who have used spam. For an ambitious and gutsy advertiser, such a tactic could prove an enormously cost-effective advertising buy, or it could provoke a great deal of hate mail, resentment, or even more dire consequences, including a loss of business reputation.[2] Again, the point is for advertisers to make sure they are at least wanted guests, and not despised intruders into what often amount to virtual communities.[3]

The **World Wide Web (WWW)** is a universal database of information available to most Internet users, and its graphical environment makes navigation simple and exciting. Of all the options available for Internet advertisers, the WWW holds the greatest

2.   S. Garfinkel, "Spam King! Your Source for Spams Netwide!" *Wired,* February 1996, 84.
3.   For a discussion of spamming versus targeted E-mail pitches, see Dana Garber, "Spam Has Choicer Cuts," CNN Interactive (August 10, 1998). cnn.com/TECH/computing/9808/10/tastyspam.idg/. Accessed March 28, 1999.

potential. It allows for detailed and full-color graphics, audio transmission, delivery of in-depth messages, 24-hour availability, and two-way information exchanges between the advertiser and customer. For some people, spending time on the Web is replacing time spent viewing other media, such as print, radio, and television. There is one great difference between the Web and other cyberadvertising vehicles: It is the consumer who actively searches for the advertiser's home page. Of course, Web advertisers are attempting to make their pages much easier to find and, in reality, harder to avoid.

Surfing the World Wide Web. By using software such as Netscape, consumers can simply input the addresses of Web sites they wish to visit and directly access the information available there. However, the Web is a library with no card catalog. There is no central authority that lists all possible sites accessible via the Internet. This condition leads to *surfing*— gliding from home page to home page. Users can seek and find different sites in a variety of ways: through search engines, through direct links with other sites, and by word of mouth. Some functions previously allowed only to librarians are now granted to Internet users.

To use a **search engine**, a user types in a few keywords and the search engine then finds all sites that correlate with the keywords. Search engines all have the same basic user interface but differ in how they perform the search and in the amount of the WWW accessed. There are four distinct styles of search engines: hierarchical, collection, concept, and robot. There are also the special cases of Web community sites and mega–search engines.

Hierarchical Search Engines. Yahoo! is an example of a search engine built on a hierarchical, subject-oriented guide. (See Exhibit 17.6.) All sites have to fit into a certain category. For example, Stolichnaya vodka is indexed as Business and Economy/ Companies/Drinks/Alcoholic/Vodka. Users are thus able to find and select a category as well as all the relevant Yahoo! sites. Going to Business and Economy/Companies/ Sports/Snowboarding/Board Manufacturers, for instance, gives a list of nearly 60 companies that sell snowboards on the Web. We show some of them in Exhibit 17.7.

By checking these sites, a person could find a snowboard company and buy a snowboard over the Web. Although hierarchical sites like Yahoo! are great for doing general searches, they do have some significant limitations. For example, Yahoo!'s database of Web sites contains only submissions; that is, Yahoo! does not actually perform a search of the Web for sites but only contains sites that users tell it about. Because of this, Yahoo! omits a significant portion of the vast information available on the Web.

Collection Search Engines. This second type of search engine is exemplified by AltaVista, shown in Exhibit 17.8. AltaVista uses a *spider*, which is an automated program that crawls around the Web and collects information. As of mid-1999, the collection of Web pages indexed by AltaVista stood at 1.2 million. With AltaVista, a person can perform a text search on all of these sites, resulting in access to literally tens of billions of words. For example, the search for the phrase *vampire books*, shown in Exhibit 17.9, finds 581 Web pages that contain this exact phrase.

Because of the sheer quantity of Web pages, AltaVista ranks the best matches first. The relatively large amount of information available on AltaVista mandates that users know what they are really interested in; otherwise, they will be flooded with information.

Concept Search Engines. Excite is a concept search engine. Here, a concept rather than a word or phrase is the basis for the search. Using the vampire example, the top sites with the concept *vampire books* are shown in Exhibit 17.10. To narrow the search, simply clicking on one of the sites found in the original search with the Excite icon enables another search based on the selected link. The percentage key gives the user an idea of how close a particular site is to his or her concepts. This is a very efficient way

EXHIBIT 17.6

Search engines are familiar to any accomplished Web user. Among the most familiar of these engines is Yahoo! www.yahoo.com/

EXHIBIT 17.7

Yahoo! is hierarchical by design. This search result for snowboard manufacturers provides a nice illustration of the hierarchical format of Yahoo! www.yahoo.com/

EXHIBIT 17.8

AltaVista is another popular Web search engine. By design, it provides access to more of the Web's content than does Yahoo! www.altavista.digital.com/

EXHIBIT 17.9

This result from AltaVista illustrates the vast content available on the World Wide Web. This search turned up 30,000 Web pages containing the terms vampire and books. www.altavista.digital.com/

EXHIBIT 17.10

Excite represents yet another option for searching the WWW. Excite executes a concept search that allows the user to converge quickly on a concept of particular interest. www.excite.com/

EXHIBIT 17.11

A natural-language search engine such as Ask Jeeves lets users search on topics using normal English syntax. www.ask.com/

of searching, producing relatively focused results compared to AltaVista and with the added ability of using the results of a search to further modify the search. The downside is that concept search engines such as Excite lack the comprehensiveness of collection search engines. Ask Jeeves (Exhibit 17.11) allows users to conduct searches using natural-language questions such as, "Who was the fourteenth president of the United States?" (Answer: Franklin Pierce, 1853-1857.)

Robot Search Engines. The newest technique employs robots ("bots") to do the "legwork" for the consumer by roaming the Internet in search of information fitting certain user-specified criteria. For example, there are shopping robots that specialize in finding the best deals for your music needs (www.BargainFinder.com/), insurance needs (www.insuremarket.com/), or traveling needs (www.travelocity.com/) (Exhibit 17.12). Web retailers concerned that such robots will result in an electronic marketplace governed entirely by price rather than brand loyalty have designed their sites to either refuse the robot admission to the site or to confuse the robot.[4]

Other Ways to Find Sites. Many people have created their own Web pages, which list their favorite sites. This is a fabulous way of finding new and interesting sites—as well as feeding a person's narcissism. For example, here is our Web address: oguinn.swcollege.com/. Since this page is maintained, updated, and checked regularly, it is a good resource for someone interested in advertising. Although most people find Web pages from Internet resources (over 80 percent of respondents in one survey find Web pages from search engines or other Web pages), sites can also be discovered through traditional word-of-mouth communica-

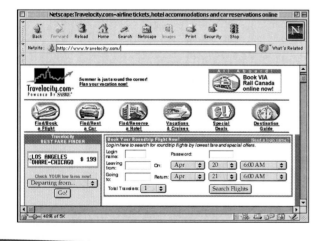

EXHIBIT 17.12

The Travelocity site is an example of a shopping robot.
www.travelocity.com/

tions. Internet enthusiasts tend to share their experiences on the Web through discussions in coffeehouses, reading and writing articles, Usenet, and other non-Web venues. In fact, over two-thirds of respondents participating in the 1998 survey reported learning of Web pages from friends or from printed media. Moreover, a recent survey reveals that including the company's URL in print advertisements is becoming an increasingly common practice, especially in business and computer magazines[5] (Exhibit 17.13). There are also Web community sites such as www.the globe.com/, and mega–search engines—those that combine several search engines at once (www.dogpile.com/).

Portals. Some search engines, such as Yahoo! and Lycos, are focusing their attention on becoming *portals*, or starting points, for Internet exploring. America Online is an example of a Web portal. In addition to providing its own content, AOL serves as a convenient and well-organized entrance to the Web. From AOL (Exhibit 17.14), a Web surfer can jump to many locations highlighted by AOL, particularly commercial sites that pay AOL to be featured in this way. Portals are more interested in channeling surfers to particular sites, especially commercial ones.

When considering search engines, remember their limitations: "Let's make it clear. None of the searchers—none of them—index everything on the web. No search engine can claim to have a perfect record of everything out there."[6]

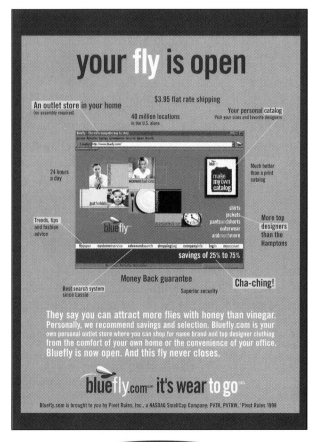

EXHIBIT 17.13

It's getting harder to find print ads that don't include the URL of the company's Web site. www.bluefly.com/

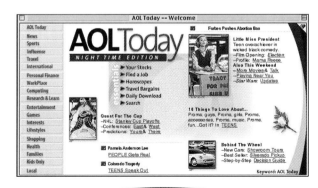

EXHIBIT 17.14

America Online is one of many Web portals that provide a convenient entrance to the Internet. www.aol.com/

5.   Ann E. Schlosser and Alaina Kanfer, "Current Advertising on the Internet: The Benefits and Usage of Mixed-Media Advertising Strategies," in D. Schumann and E. Thorson, eds., *Advertising and the World Wide Web* (Mahwah, NJ: Lawrence Erlbaum Associates, 1999), 41-60.
6.   Josh Bernoff, a senior analyst at Forrester Research, quoted in K. Hafner and J. Tanaka, "This Web's for You," *Newsweek,* April 1, 1996, 75.

Advertising and Marketing on the Internet. In 1995, $54.7 million

was spent advertising on the Internet. Spending in 1996 was around $300 million. In 1997 it jumped to just around $1 billion, and in 1998 it was somewhere around $2 billion. So, in terms of total dollars, Internet advertising is growing at a very nice clip. This is not, however, the whole story. At the same time, the cost of advertising on the Internet is actually falling; it dropped about 6 percent in 1998. So as demand for cyberadvertising goes up, apparently so does supply. Furthermore, don't let the big numbers impress you too much. Internet advertising still represents only about 1 percent of all United States advertising; when one counts all promotion dollars it's less than half of 1 percent. In other words, as one researcher said, "For AT&T, the Web budget is a rounding error."[7] For perspective, billboard (outdoor) advertising, perhaps advertising's least glamorized medium, grew at a rate of almost 9 percent in 1997, and accounted for almost twice as much advertising as the Internet. Despite all the hype, many large advertisers such as Best Buy have stayed out of cyberadvertising entirely. Still, Internet advertising growth is substantial, and its significance goes well beyond the raw numbers. What makes it significant is its prominent and central role in a true communications revolution. So while no one is sure how blue the sky is, there is no shortage of self-interested promotion and hype intermingled with truly significant changes in communication. Separating them is no easy task. For example, Shabang .net isn't the only online shopping service that indulges in a little revolutionary zeal from time to time, but hype done well certainly has its admirers (Exhibit 17.15).

On a cost-per-thousand (CPM) basis, Web ads are pricey. Exhibit 17.16 compares Web advertising costs with other traditional sources. Proponents of the Internet counter by saying that the real attraction of the Internet is not found in raw numbers and CPMs, but in terms of highly desirable, highly segmentable, and highly motivated audiences (Exhibits 17.17 and 17.18). They argue that the Internet is great for niche marketing—that is, for reaching only those consumers most likely to buy what the advertiser is selling. Well, this is partially true.

EXHIBIT 17.15

Shabang!, an online shopping service, takes advantage of the hype surrounding the "communications revolution" of the Internet.
www.shabang.net/

EXHIBIT 17.16

Comparing advertising costs on the Internet versus traditional media.

Type	Cost	Total Exposures	Cost per Thousand
TV: 30-second, network news	$ 85,000	12,000,000	$ 5.42
Magazine: full-color, national weekly+	$185,000	8,100,000	$43.55
Newspaper: full-page, midsize city	$ 81,000	514,000	$60.31
World Wide Web: online magazine, one-month placement	$ 15,000	200,000	$75.00

Source: Forrester Research, from *Newsweek*, April 1996, 76. Reprinted with permission of Forrester Research, Inc.

7.   Ibid.

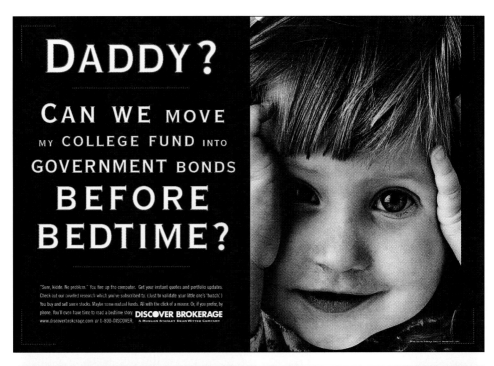

Visitors to certain types of sites are likely to be highly motivated to purchase what the company is selling—and to be prime targets for niche marketers.
www.discoverbrokerage.com/

The current Internet audience is relatively affluent, so the Internet audience does have the means to buy. In the cases where there is an active search for product or service information on the Internet, there is also a predisposed and motivated audience. This makes the Internet something fairly special among advertising-supported vehicles. On the other hand, there are enormous audience measurement problems; we don't really know who sees or notices Internet advertising with much certainty. So, advertisers don't know exactly what they are buying. This bothers them. Further, there is some evidence that audience tolerance for Web advertising is actually declining. One recent study finds that "over time, [consumers are] even less tolerant of it than they have been" (which

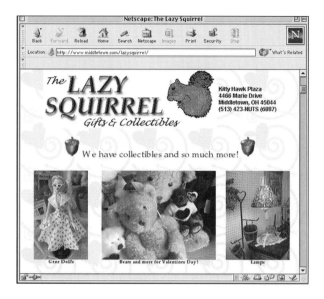

EXHIBIT 17.19

How affordable is Web advertising for local retailers?
www.middletown.com/lazysquirrel/

wasn't all that tolerant in the first place outside of the early "techno-geek" audience). The number of Web users who say they actively avoid the ads is up, and the number who say they notice ads is down. This is consistent with the experience of advertising history in general: As advertising becomes more common, fewer ads are noticed, fewer are accepted, and fewer make any impact at all. Each ad thus becomes less powerful as they become more common, familiar, and annoying. Advertising has always had a way of being a victim of its own success. It's interesting that some advertising historians note that advertising has declined in power since the 1920s, when there was relatively little of it, and mass advertising was relatively new. What's more, Internet advertising comes into an already crowded and highly cluttered media and information environment.

While most large ad agencies have been busy buying Internet ad agencies, the manner in which they have been absorbed, integrated, and used by the agency behemoths is less than impressive. Most of the big agencies want Internet units of their own, but aren't sure what to do with them once they get them. Interestingly, advertising agencies actually express a degree of pessimism concerning the effectiveness of advertising on the Internet, due to the many questions that exist concerning measurement and efficiency. They're also not sure how *they* will make more money on the Internet. (Funny how that works.) Still, a large majority of agencies include interactive advertising as a valuable part of the media mix of the future. To be a player, you've got to have a Web advertising effort; after all, this is the advertising business. For a big national advertiser, the cost of entry is relatively affordable, but for the smaller this is less and less the case. While local advertisers can get on the WWW, who will notice becomes the real question. (Take a look at the Web offering of a Middletown, Ohio, retailer of gifts and collectibles, The Lazy Squirrel, in Exhibit 17.19, and ask yourself that who–will–notice question again.) It all depends.

Regardless of the lack of effective measurement and evaluation of reach, the narrow audience composition, and the unknown impact of Web advertising, companies seem to be afraid of being left behind. Apparently, there is some prestige attached to advertising on the WWW, or at least a feeling of inadequacy to not be there. In addition, most advertisers want to have a well-established Web image in the future, so getting involved now makes sense, even if the best strategy for doing so is unclear. In response, many agencies have established their own home pages, are making strong efforts at gaining expertise with the Web, and are even establishing separate departments to handle interactive media. Agencies have emerged that handle only Internet advertising (Exhibit 17.20), and most agency reviews now include a presentation of Internet credentials. See Exhibit 17.21 for some agency Internet sites.

Who Advertises on the Internet? The pie graphs in Exhibit 17.22 demonstrate that advertising on the Web, compared to television and magazines, for example, is incredibly concentrated among a very few, very inside advertisers. This will have to change if the WWW is to really challenge traditional media.

Types of Web Advertising. There are several ways for advertisers to post advertising messages on the Web. The most basic route is by establishing a corporate home page. These pages

EXHIBIT 17.20

Some top interactive agencies.

Agency	Headquarters
AGENCY.COM	New York
iXL	Atlanta, GA
Modem Media.Poppe Tyson	Westport, CT
Grey New Technologies	New York
THINK New Ideas	New York
CKS Group	Cupertino, CA
c2o Interactive Architects	Dallas, TX
Organic Online	San Francisco
Strategic Interactive Group	Boston
USWeb	Santa Clara, CA

EXHIBIT 17.21

Examples of sites developed by ad agencies.

uts.cc.utexas.edu/~ccho/adworld.html	www.abracadabra.com/
www.am.com/	www.chiatday.com/factory/
www.advbl.com/	www.uswebcks.com/
www.adwork.co.id/	www.collemcvoy.com/
www.apltd.com/	www.ca.dk/
www.arnoldnet.com/	www.execpc.com/~adaid/core.html
www.aubreyco.com/aubrey/	www.cjrw.com/
www.austinknight.com/	www.chcmultimedia.com/
www.bch.com/	www.dbaadv.com/
www.twintowers.com/baratti	www.dgastl.com/
www.bates-dorland.co.uk/intro2.html	www.dnaadv.com/
ireland.iol.ie/resource/bates/index.html	www.dsw.com/
www.webcom.com/~bear/	www.dillonweb.com/
www.cre8ive.com/	www.netvertising.com/
www.blkbx.com/inthebox.html	www.emamulti.com/
www.blitzmedia.com/	www.ejl.com/
www.bluemarble.com/logo.html	www.fallon.com/
www.brouillard.com/	www.cybertising.com/
www.browncommunications.com/	www.fnl.com.au/
www.carwax.com/index2.htm	www.french-rogers.com/

clearly identify the company and the brand that supports the site. The style of sites ranges from those explicitly focused on the presentation of specific product benefits, to those based on special interests or lifestyle topics (which indirectly push the product), to those that actually let the consumer purchase the product.

The other way for marketers to advertise on the Web is through ads on entertainment, media, or corporate sites. Besides the actual ad purchased on a media company's

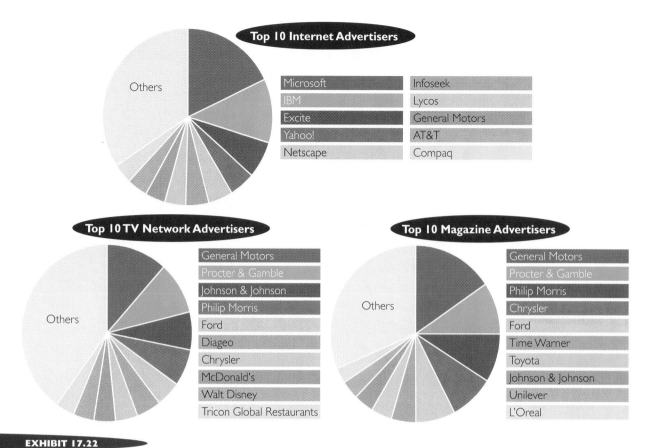

Top 10 Internet Advertisers

Others

Microsoft	Infoseek
IBM	Lycos
Excite	General Motors
Yahoo!	AT&T
Netscape	Compaq

Top 10 TV Network Advertisers

Others

General Motors
Procter & Gamble
Johnson & Johnson
Philip Morris
Ford
Diageo
Chrysler
McDonald's
Walt Disney
Tricon Global Restaurants

Top 10 Magazine Advertisers

Others

General Motors
Procter & Gamble
Philip Morris
Chrysler
Ford
Time Warner
Toyota
Johnson & Johnson
Unilever
L'Oreal

EXHIBIT 17.22

Prominence of cyber-insider advertising on the Internet.

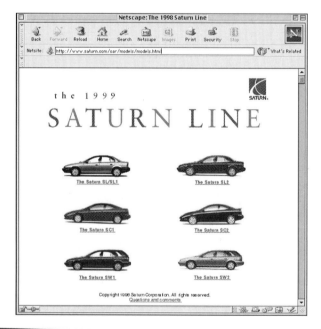

EXHIBIT 17.23

Saturn's corporate home page provides the surfer with a vast array of information about the Saturn line. It also takes advantage of the Web's interactive capability by encouraging questions and comments from those who visit the site. www.saturncars.com/index.html

Web site, the advertiser can also get a link to its own home page. So, if a consumer is browsing on Yahoo! and sees a Toyota banner ad, he or she can click on the ad and be taken straight to Toyota's home page.

Corporate Home Pages. The Saturn site shown in Exhibit 17.23 is an example of a **corporate home page**. The Saturn site allows people to find out about the line of Saturn cars, pricing, specifications, and the closest dealers. This product-oriented site also allows consumers to request brochures, communicate their comments and questions to the Saturn corporation, and find a dealer when they are ready to make a purchase. Absolut Vodka has an extremely interactive, truly innovative site in which surfers can create music mixes that are enhanced with flashing, moving images. Once a visitor creates his or her mix, it can be E-mailed off to fellow Internet users. This site, shown in Exhibit 17.24, was developed by Red Sky Interactive, a San Francisco agency that specializes in interactive communications.

A corporate site that falls toward the lifestyle end of the spectrum is the Crayola FamilyPlay site displayed in Exhibit 17.25. Rather than focusing on its

EXHIBIT 17.24

The Absolut site is less about product information than sites like Saturn's, and more about entertainment. Providing an entertaining encounter is one of the ways that advertisers can promote repeat visits and favorable word of mouth for their sites. www.absolutvodka.com/

EXHIBIT 17.25

The Crayola site is lifestyle based, providing activities and information for kids and their parents. www.crayola.com/

rather famous product, the company decided to focus on the needs of the parents and children that use Crayola crayons. Visitors can do such things as read bedtime stories, search for local child care providers, discover hints on getting kids to help with housework, and browse movie reviews for family-oriented flicks. And, of course, there is a link to a page where kids can create art with computerized Crayolas. Although the Crayola site provides a starting point to browsing the Net (the site even provides a child-safe Web browser), the company name is displayed and the content of the site helps to build a positive image for Crayola.

Banner Ads. **Banner ads** are paid placements on other sites that contain editorial material. An additional feature of banner ads is that consumers not only see the ad but also can make a quick trip to the advertiser's home page by clicking on the ad. Thus, the challenge of creating and placing banner ads is not only to catch people's attention but also to entice them to visit the advertiser's home page and stay for a while. Many high-traffic Web sites that provide information content have started to rely on advertisers to support their services. Sites such as Yahoo! and HotWired often have banner advertisements. Exhibit 17.26 shows an example of a banner ad on the *National Enquirer* Web site.

A hightraffic site offers a relatively high level of exposure to an advertising message. Much like placing advertisements within traditional print media such as newspapers and magazines, advertisers can

The use of banner ads shows some of the potential for leveraging advertising formats on the Web. Visit the National Enquirer *site and click on a banner ad. How effective are banner ads for a Web site? Or for the advertiser sponsoring them?* www.nationalenquirer.com

purchase space on sites providing a diversity of editorial content, such as the *New York Times, Chicago Tribune, Los Angeles Times, Wall Street Journal, USA Today, Newsweek, U.S. News & World Report, Car and Driver, Atlantic Monthly,* TimeWarner Communications, and ESPN.

A more targeted option is to place banner ads on sites that attract specific market niches. For example, a banner ad for running shoes would be placed on a site that offers information related to running. This option is emerging as a way for advertisers to focus more tightly on their target audiences. Currently, advertisers consider WWW users to be a focused segment of their own. However, as the Web continues to blossom, marketers will begin to realize that, even across the entire Web, there are sites that draw specific subgroups of Web users. These niche users have particular interests that may represent important opportunities for the right advertiser.

A pricing evaluation service for banner ads is offered by Interactive Traffic. The I-Traffic Index computes a site's advertising value based on traffic, placement and size of ads, ad rates, and evaluations of the site's quality.[8] Forrester Research assesses the costs of banner ads on a variety of sites and what advertisers get for their money, as shown in Exhibit 17.27. Complicating the matter now is the fact that consumer resistance to banner ads is increasing. First, most online consumers do not click on Web banner ads. For example, one survey found that only 1 percent of surfers click on banner ads.[9] Second, many consumers resent banner ads, which they see as intrusive and annoying; banner ads increase Web

Advertising costs on the Web.

Site	Rate	Deliverables
ESPN SportsZone	$100,000/quarter; $300,000/year	Estimated 542,000 users/week; 20.5 million hits/week; exclusive and rotating placement
HotWired	$13,000–$15,000/month	Minimum 100,000 banner views guaranteed; weekly traffic reports; discounts for *Wired* advertisers
Netscape	$30,000/month	Estimated 1 million impressions; estimated CPM of $25–$30
Pathfinder	$30,000/quarter	Free position in Pathfinder marketplace; weekly tracking reports
Yahoo! search page	$20,000/1 million impressions	Estimated 2.9 million hits/month; 135 million search results (cumulative)

Source: Forrester Research and *Advertising Age,* January 8, 1996, 25. Reprinted with permission of Forrester Research, Inc.

8.   K. Cleland, "SRDS, I Join Interactive Frenzy," *Advertising Age,* October 16, 1995, 22.
9.   *The Economist,* September 26, 1998.

page load times due to their complex graphics and animation. Supporting this trend are fixes called *ad blockers*, which allow consumers to screen out banner ads. For example, one ad blocker program called *AdWipe* allows a surfer to load pages sans banner ads.[10] At the same time, the banner advertisement should be designed with downloading time in mind. In 1998, nearly two-thirds of netizens reported that one of the biggest problems with the Web is that banner ads take too long to download.[11]

Enhanced banner ads are another option. These are banner ads with the complete information already in the ad, as opposed to having to click for additional information. Or they may have audio or some other enhancement to make them something more than the standard banner. Enhanced banner ads, at least for the moment, perform better than their unenhanced relatives.

Pop-up ads: The idea is borrowed from TV. A surfer wants to go to a certain site but has to wade through an ad page first, just as a television viewer must watch a commercial before seeing a favorite show. It is often not merely a word from a sponsor, but invitations to link to another related site. A pop-up ad opens a separate window. The more times people click on these ads, the more money can be charged for the privilege of advertising.

Establishing a Site on the World Wide Web.

While setting up a Web site can be done fairly easily, setting up a commercially viable one is a lot harder and a lot more expensive. A Web site can be "boot-strapped" onto an existing site for very little money, allowing the new site to take advantage of the current site's hardware, software, and Internet connection. However, the actual designing of the Web site's pages will still need to be done, and if you get lucky and actually have people show up at your site and want to conduct business with you, then it gets expensive: Some authorities say about three-quarters of a million dollars for baseline technology. That's probably a little high, but realistically you'll need about half a million. Setting up an attractive site costs more because of the need for specialized designers to create the site and, most important, to constantly update the site. The basic hardware for a site can be a personal computer, and the software to run the site ranges from free to several thousand dollars, depending on the number of extras needed. A site anticipating considerable traffic will need to plan for higher-capacity connections—and hence, a bigger phone bill.[12]

Getting Surfers to Come Back.

For advertisers, getting those on the Internet (*netizens*, as they are commonly called) to come back to their site is a primary concern. A site with pages showing the product and its specifications may have no appeal beyond attracting a single visit. There may be little or no entertainment value to bring people back again and again. Surfing various business home pages reveals countless boring corporate Web pages. According to research, most Web sites include rich product descriptions, mimicking brochures.[13] Although such Web sites might satisfy the needs of netizens searching for specific product information, they are unlikely to attract and capture the interest of people simply browsing the Web. For browsers, the advertiser should incorporate involving, interactive features into the site, such as online games or videos.[14] One area in the Cartoon Network site, shown in Exhibit 17.28, allows kids to help direct the action in a special made-for-the-Web interactive cartoon entitled *Pink Donkey and the Fly*. Thus, it is important for advertisers to be sure to learn about their

10. *San Francisco Chronicle,* August 26, 1998.

11. GVU, 1998.

12. *Information Week,* December 7, 1998, G2–G3.

13. Schlosser and Kanfer, "Current Advertising on the Internet," 41–60.

14. Schlosser and Kanfer, "Culture Clash in Internet Marketing," in M.J. Shaw, R. Blanning, T. Strader, and A. Whinston, eds., *Handbook on Electronic Commerce* (New York: Springer-Verlag, 1999).

EXHIBIT 17.28

Interactive entertainment is a useful tool for Web advertisers such as the Cartoon Network. www.cartoonnetwork.com/

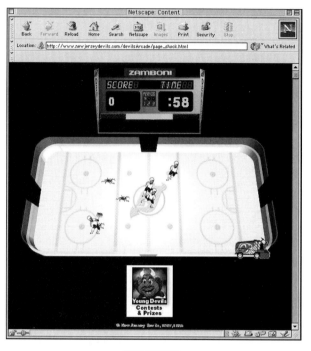

EXHIBIT 17.29

The New Jersey Devils site offers multiple reasons to return: team scores, interviews, merchandise, games, and more. www.newjerseydevils.com/

customers before setting up a site. Good consumer and communications research can be useful in this context.

A well developed site can keep customers coming back for more. A good example is the New Jersey Devils Web page (www.newjerseydevils.com/). Visitors can do more than just read how their favorite NHL team did the night before. They can read in-depth interviews with players, coaches, and even team trainers. Visitors compete for fan-of-the-month awards, while younger fans get a chance to be sportswriters. Tickets, schedules, and team merchandise are readily available. And, of course, no visit to the New Jersey Devils site is complete without a rousing game of Zamboni Master, where players race around the Devils' arena in a Zamboni, repairing damage inflicted by invasions of opposing teams (see Exhibit 17.29). These features give people multiple reasons to continue to visit the site. Such an approach to Web-presence design has been referred to as *rational branding* and stresses the need for a brand's Web site to provide some unique informational resource to justify visiting it. These features give people multiple reasons to continue to visit the site.

A popular content-oriented Web site is HotWired (Exhibit 17.30). The site is continually updated with information on a wide variety of topics, from arts and music to commentary on the Internet and politics. It is not focused on selling a product per se; instead, it is an entertainment site. Like a good corporate site, the HotWired site is continually changing to appeal to repeat users. Another site of this style is SportsLine USA, shown in Exhibit 17.31, which allows users to check out continually updated exclusive coverage, enter contests, and chat with sports superstars. If people stumble on these sites and like them, chances are they will be return visitors.

EXHIBITS 17.30 AND 17.31

Continual information updates also keep Web surfers coming back to sites such as HotWired and SportsLine USA. www.hotwired.com/ *and* www.sportsline.com/

One crucial Web site feature (regardless of whether consumers are searching for specific information or browsing the Web) is the presence of multiple navigational tools; the more navigational tools available, the more the visitor will like the site.[15] Navigational tools help guide the visitor around the site; examples include home and section icons, a search engine that is specific to the site, and a site index. Just as consumers need a cable guide to help them enjoy their cable services, so too do consumers need resources to help them realize and enjoy all the possibilities of the site. Remodeling a site is a costly investment: According to Forrester Research Inc., adding search and other personalization features to a site can cost $300,000 to $425,000. Many argue that such an investment is worthwhile, since the consequences of a poorly designed site include lost revenues and the erosion of brand image.[16]

Thus, the objective of having repeat customers depends on substance, ease of use, and entertainment value. Netizens are discriminating in that while nice pictures are interesting, sites that have considerable repeat users offer something more. This can be product information and ongoing technical support, or it can be general news about a product, original writing, or the latest or most comprehensive information about just about anything. At the same time, the company should ensure that the advertising information and graphics can be easily downloaded by their consumers. Above all, it has to satisfy the consumer's goal for visiting the site—pure and simple.

15. Schlosser and Kanfer, "Current Advertising on the Internet," 41-60.
16. Harvey, *Upside*, February 1999.

EXHIBIT 17.32

Keyword searches connect consumers seeking information with advertisers who have registered their sites with online search engines.
www.lycos.com/

Purchasing Keywords on Search Engines. Online search engines such as Yahoo! sell *keywords*. An advertiser can purchase a keyword such that its banner appears whenever users select that word for a search. For example, when a user searches for a keyword such as *inn* on the search engine Lycos, he or she will see an ad from a directory for bed-and-breakfast inns, as shown in Exhibit 17.32.

Keyword sponsorship on Lycos costs around five cents per impression ($50 CPM). Sponsorship on Yahoo! costs a bit more.[17] These search engines let advertisers pay a flat monthly fee or a per-impression fee (based on how many people see the ad). Thus, getting a popular word may result in a considerable number of impressions and a higher bill. The other factor is effectiveness. The Infoseek search engine claims buy rates from 2 to 36 percent, while other engines claim that keyword ads do not significantly differ from the banner ads in effectiveness. However, keyword ads are a great way to get a product in front of someone interested in that general category.

Promoting Web Sites. Building a Web site is only the first step; the next is promoting it. Several firms specialize in promoting Web sites, including WebStep (www.mmgco.com/webstep .html). The quickest and most effective route is to notify appropriate Usenet groups. The other key method is to register the site with search engines such as Yahoo! and AltaVista. With Yahoo!, because it is a hierarchical search engine, it is important to pick keywords that are commonly chosen, yet describe and differentiate that site. Other places to register are with the growing Yellow Pages on the Internet (for example, www.bigyellow.com/) and with appropriate listserv groups. It is also important to send out press releases to Internet news sites. E-mail as a form of direct mail is another method to promote the site. Conventional media can be effective as well; a well-placed address for a Web site in a printed publication can draw considerable business. Remember the Absolut site mentioned earlier in the chapter? Exhibit 17.33 shows one way the company recruited visitors to the site. And the cars.com print ad in Exhibit 17.34 shows the URL twice in large type, while the careful reader can find "cars.com" no fewer than 10 times.

If an advertiser wants to draw people to its Web site as one of the goals of a television commercial, the address should be visible on the screen long enough for viewers to capture and actually remember the site address. The necessary length of time can range from 3 to 5 seconds, depending on the length and memorability of the address. Whatever traditional advertising vehicle is used, it is important that the product advertised in traditional media is easily found at the promoted Web site.[18]

Integration with Other Media. Advertisers are starting to rethink their strategies for Web-based advertising. They have come to realize that Internet advertising cannot simply be a transfer of advertising from other media. For example, a television campaign that is designed to generate a mood or image for the product does not work well on the Internet, nor do magazine ads. Instead, the Internet has its own strengths and weaknesses, like all other media. For example, the Internet is great for providing detailed information that is beyond the scope of other media. Given this strength, the Internet can play a pivotal role in an IMC campaign: Media such as television and print ads can

17. J. Hodges, "Words Hold the Key to Web Ad Packages," *Advertising Age,* January 15, 1996.
18. Schlosser and Kanfer, "Current Advertising on the Internet," 41-60.

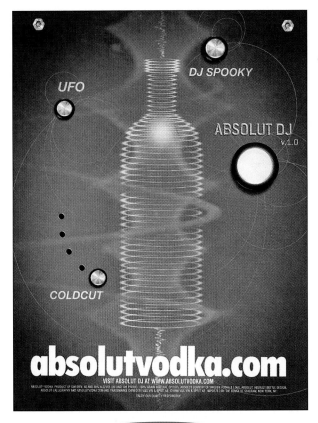

Many advertisers promote their Web sites through other media, such as print and TV ads. www.absolutvodka.com/

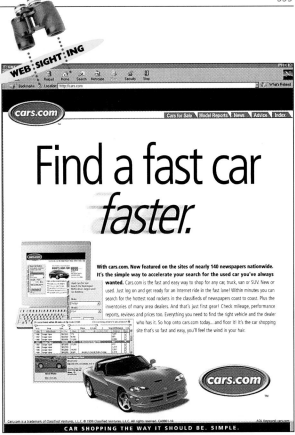

*If you can't beat 'em, join 'em. Cars.com (*www.cars.com*)—a site that pools together car-related classifieds from Gannett, Times Mirror, and others—is the newspapers' answer to the threat that Web-based "category killers" represent to their livelihood. It remains to be seen if Classified Ventures (*www.classifiedventures.com*) lasts much longer than New Century Network, a previous grand alliance of newspapers to develop Web-based solutions in answer to the new-media threats to print publishing. New Century Network was formed, then disbanded when the newspapers found themselves competing more than cooperating. How would a small, geographically local newspaper benefit from having Cars.com as a part of its Web site?*

be used to create a powerful image, while the Web site can provide detailed information on the product and help close the sale. See the IMC box on page 554 to find out how Times Mirror is blending different media and different sponsors to attract sports fans.

Saturn uses a similar multimedia strategy. It promotes its Web site with quirky image ads in TV and print, such as the one in which a college student orders a Saturn over the Internet and has it delivered, much the same way a pizza is delivered. The print and TV ads build an image for the brand and refer consumers to the corporate Web page. Once there, consumers can learn more about the product, put together a package that satisfies their particular needs, calculate lease rates and monthly payments, and get in contact with a Saturn dealer in their vicinity. As a result of Saturn's integrated campaign, traffic to the Saturn Web site tripled and Saturn now receives 80 percent of its sales leads from the Internet.[19]

19. *San Francisco Chronicle,* August 26, 1998.

Measurement and Security Issues.

The information a Web site typically gets when a user connects with a site is the IP address of the Internet site that is requesting the page, what page is requested, and the time of the request. This is the minimum amount of information available to a Web site. If a site requires registration, additional information (for example, E-mail address, zip code, gender, age, or household income) is requested directly from the user. Attempts at registration (and easy audience assessment) have been largely rejected by consumers, but plenty of service providers, such as I/PRO, are available to guide advertisers through Web measurement options (see Exhibit 17.35).

Several terms, such as *hits, pages, visits, users,* and *reach* are used in Web audience measurement. **Hits** represent the number of elements requested from a given page and consequently provide almost no indication of actual Web traffic. For instance, when a user requests a page with four graphical images, it counts as five hits. Thus by inflating the number of images, a site can quickly pull up its hit count. An example of this is *Penthouse*'s site. The *Penthouse* site gets 3 million hits a day, placing it among the top Web sites. However, this total of 3 million hits translates into only 80,000 people daily. Thus, hits do not translate into the number of people visiting a site. A *click-through* is a measure of the number of page elements (*hyperlinks*) that have actually been requested (that is, "clicked through" from the banner ad to the link). It is typically 1 to 2 percent of hits.

Pages (or page views) are defined as the pages (actually the number of html files) sent to the requesting site. However, if a down-

IT'S THE INTERNET, IT'S A MAGAZINE, IT'S A TV BROADCAST—NO, IT'S ALL THREE!

The Times Mirror Internet magazines group is putting together a cohesive network of sports sites that draw on three different forms of media to attract and hold visitors. The catalyst for the development of the network was Times Mirror Magazines' acquisition of the Interzine group of Web sites.

The key to the network is the crossing of multiple media from the traditional print and broadcast media into the world of cybercommunication. For example, a key "network" features the flagship "zine" Sporting News Online (www.sportingnews.com/), the online version of the popular sports magazine, which will provide MSNBC, the cable TV affiliate of NBC, with sports coverage. Under this arrangement, *Sporting News* will provide content to MSNBC, which will deliver the co-branded sports news to its viewers. Content will also be linked back to the Sporting News site. The deal includes promotion of both providers online, and MSNBC-TV mentions Sporting News Online during its content broadcasts.

Of course, the test of success comes when advertisers start signing up and make the partnership a lucrative arrangement. One advertiser that is expanding its relationship is Ford Motor Company, which in the past has sponsored Sporting News Online's college football and Best Sport Cities features. Ford announced that it will sponsor a special one-time football section that will appear both in the print version of *Sporting News* and the online version. Another advertiser, Dr. Pepper, has signed as the college football anchor sponsor, and IBM is planning to sponsor U.S. Open coverage.

This blending of media is novel and unusual at this point. But as media organizations see ways to integrate the Web into their traditional media distribution systems, advertisers will also have a better way to integrate the communications they send to target audiences.

Source: Beth Snyder, "Times Mirror Interzines Begins to Gel as Network," *Advertising Age,* August 31, 1998, 22.

loaded page occupies several screens, there is no indication that the requester examined the entire page. Also, it "doesn't tell you much about how many visitors it has: 100,000 page views in a week could be 10 people reading 10,000 pages, or 100,000 people reading one page, or any variation in between."[20] **Visits** are the number of occasions in which a user X interacted with site Y after time Z has elapsed. Usually Z is set to some standard time such as 30 minutes. If the user has not interacted with the site until after 30 minutes has passed, this would be counted as a new visit. **Users** (also known as *unique visitors*) are the number of different "people" visiting a site (a new user is determined from the user's registration with the site) during a specified period of time.

20. "Let's Get This Straight: Reach for the Hits" at www.salonmagazine.com/21st/rose/laag/02/05straight2.html.

EXHIBIT 17.35

I/PRO (www.ipro.com) was a fairly early arrival on the Internet scene, recognizing that, as the Web filled up with publishers and advertisers, it would see the same need for auditors and mediators as did the print world. While in some ways the Internet is far more open to scrutiny, since every keystroke of every user is captured somewhere (if not in several somewheres), it's still a fast and loose new medium, in need of professional rigor. Professional service companies, like I/PRO, clarify interactions of buyers and sellers. What risks does an advertiser assume by opting not to use a third-party auditor?

Besides the address, page, and time, a Web site can find out the referring link address. This allows a Web site to discover what links people are taking to the site. Thus, a site can analyze which links do in fact bring people to the site. This can be helpful in Internet advertising planning. The problem is that what is really counted are *similar unique IP numbers*. Many Internet service providers use a *dynamic IP number*, which is different every time a given user logs in through their service: so "you might show up as 30 different unique visitors to a site you visited daily for a month."[21]

Log analysis software is measurement software that not only provides information on hits, pages, visits, and users, but also lets a site track audience traffic within the site. A site could determine which pages are popular and expand on them. It is also possible to track the behavior of people as they go through the site, thus providing inferential information on what people find appealing and unappealing. An example of this software is MaxInfo's WebC, which allows advertisers to track what information is viewed, when it is viewed, how often it is viewed, and where users go within a site.[22] An advertiser can then modify the content and structure accordingly. It can also help advertisers understand how buyers make purchase decisions in general.[23] It still isn't possible, however, to know what people actually do with Web site information.

There are plenty of companies such as I/PRO, NetCount, and Interse offering measurement services for interactive media. And, as exemplified in the New Media box on page 556, plenty of advice is available on how to do research on the Net. Yet there is no industry standard for measuring the effectiveness of one interactive ad placement over another. There also is no standard for comparing Internet with traditional media placements. Moreover, demographic information on who is using the WWW is severely limited. Until these limitations are overcome, many advertisers will remain hesitant about spending substantial dollars for advertising on the World Wide Web.

The new deal in town is the Media Metrix reach index. Media Metrix and its competitors (for example, Net Ratings, owned by Nielsen) are invoking older technology to address the problem: sampling through a "Nielsen family" model. Sampling is used to draw a representative set of families. Tracking software is installed on the users' computers, and then data is collected and transmitted back to the companies. These data are projected to the universe of Internet users. The figure that has become the standard is the reach figure; here it represents the percentage of these users who visit a site in any one-month period. Of course, there are systematic biases built in, such as undercounting of workplace surfing. Some critics simply have a problem with applying the reach concept to this new medium at all:

As a measure of Web use, reach is weighted toward the superficial: It favors sprawling sites with vast collections of largely unrelated pages (like, for instance Geo-Cities) over well-focused sites that collect specific groups of users with shared interests. Say one site has 200,000 loyal users

21. Ibid.
22. Ibid.
23. Eric Johnson, Marketing Doctoral Consortium, Wharton Business School, August 1995.

USING THE NET TO RESEARCH AUDIENCES

A new medium for the new media is using cybercommunication for doing marketing and advertising research. This is particularly relevant with respect to the challenges facing advertisers in trying to understanding Internet users. Finding out who Net users are is a first step, and finding out what they value about the Internet is another important task. Crimson Communications of Menlo Park in California recently gained valuable insights for strategic decision making by gathering information from Internet users. The managing director of Crimson, Glenn Gow, offers these guidelines for gathering information about Internet audiences:

- *Target the right audience.* Gather names from people visiting your Web site. They already have an interest in your company or brand and will be more responsive. Crimson Communications realized a 45 percent response rate by tapping site visitors for information.
- *Pretest the survey.* As with any survey instrument, test the questionnaire first. A short online test is necessary, since this is the context within which the survey will be administered.
- *Personalize the survey.* Personalization, to the extent possible, will increase response rates.
- *Mix in open-ended questions.* Use check boxes and rating scales to make responding easy. But also mix in open-ended questions to allow respondents to express their thoughts. Such open-ended responses often yield valuable copy points or tagline opportunities.
- *Follow up.* The proliferation of E-mail has created E-mail limbo for many messages. Follow up the original request with reminder messages. One reminder is probably appropriate. Harassing a potential customer with multiple requests for a response will accomplish nothing.
- *Ask for permission, online, to contact respondents offline.* Include in the survey a request to telephone the respondent. Phone interviews can yield much richer information than structured surveys.
- *Be prepared for all types of responses.* Some people use these kinds of opportunities to vent their frustrations. Be prepared for some nasty messages, particularly since some users think it is poor "netiquette" to conduct research on the Internet.
- *Recognize biases.* Conducting research on the Internet has at least two inherent biases. First, you can contact only active users—but nonusers may hold the key to critical understanding. Second, as with any survey, there will be some self-selection biases in those who choose to respond.

Source: "Eight Tips for Conducting Research over the Net," *PROMO Magazine*, December 1995, 23.

who visit regularly; another has little regular traffic, but its wide variety of pages turn up in enough disparate search-engine results to attract brief visits during the course of a month from, say, 5 million visitors. The two sites may have identical page-view counts. The former site may actually have a more valuable franchise to sell to advertisers or to hand over to e-commerce partners—but the latter site wins the reach contest by a landslide.[24]

Technical Aspects of the Measurement Problem. When a computer is connected to the Internet, it has a unique IP address, such as 204.17.123.5. When a link to a Web site such as www.yahoo.com/ is clicked on, a computer converts this textual representation into a number that is the unique IP address for Yahoo!. This computer then requests from Yahoo! its home page, and in return it gives Yahoo! its unique IP address so Yahoo! knows the address of the requester. Thus the only information a computer at a site such as Yahoo! receives is an IP address, along with the material the user is actually requesting. Note that a textual IP address is not the same thing as an E-mail address. E-mail addresses are similar but follow a different protocol on the Internet.

A Web site log file contains the IP addresses of the computers requesting information. However, an IP address does not usually correspond to just one person. Many systems dynamically assign IP addresses to computers connected to the Internet. Therefore a person visiting a site in two different sessions may have a different IP address each time. For an advertiser, this means it is unclear exactly how many different people visited the site. Even if a requesting computer has a permanent static address, thus allowing a site to keep track of a specific computer, the site still doesn't know who is actually using the computer. The computer could be used by one graduate student in his or her apartment, or it could be in a computer lab where hundreds of different people have access to the same computer.

24. adage.com/interactive/articles/19961223/article1.html.

A Web site can track how many machines accessed the site, but this does not correspond to how many people actually visited the Web site. One estimate is that the number of visitors exceeds IP addresses by about 15 percent.[25] Thus it is currently difficult to know exactly who is visiting a site, and if the visitors are revisiting. The only obvious enhancement would be implementing unique IDs in Web browsers. This would identify a specific computer visiting the site. However, this has not been seen as feasible due to current privacy concerns. It also leaves the possibility of many different people using the same computer, such as would occur in a computer lab.

The Caching Complication. To conserve resources on the Web, there is a system known as **caching**. Caching is a kind of active memory. Once a page is downloaded, the cache on the computer saves that page so it can be immediately accessed. Commercial online services such as America Online cache heavily trafficked sites on their computers so users get quicker response times when they request that page. Suppose a person first goes to a Web site's home page. After clicking on a link to go somewhere else, the user decides to go back to the home page. Instead of asking the Web site again for that home page, the cache will have stored it in anticipation of the user wanting it again. This conserves Internet resources, commonly called **bandwidth**, because the user is not needlessly requesting the same material twice. However, this complicates matters in measuring activity at the site because once a person has cached a page, the Web site has no idea whether the user repeatedly and prolongedly visited the page, or whether the user immediately moved on.

Technological solutions can reduce the amount of caching, thus allowing sites better data on how often a page is viewed, but it comes with the cost of additional bandwidth for the site and a slower response time for the person viewing the site. Caching may result in fewer page requests to a Web site than have actually occurred. Moreover, if a person hits the reload button, a Web site will register more traffic than there actually is. While cache-busting technology (technology that allows sites to look inside users' computer caches to determine the true number of pages) does exist, its widespread use seems unlikely in the near future.

Payment. Internet advertisers pay for ads in several ways. Many pay in terms of **impressions**. It's supposed to mean the number of times a page with your ad on it is viewed; in reality these are roughly equivalent to hits, or opportunities to view. Often these are priced as flat fees—so many dollars for so many impressions. Others price with **pay-per-click**, which is in all reality the same as impressions. Others pay in **click-throughs**. A click-through "occurs when the visitor sees or reads the ad and clicks on it, taking them directly to the advertisers Web site. . . . The overall average for click throughs for all web advertising is around 2%."[26] Others will buy on cost per lead (documented business leads) or cost per actual sale (very rare). A *net rate* refers to the 15 percent discounted rate given to advertising agencies, although direct deals with portals and browsers are very common.

Security and Privacy. Any Web user can download text, images, and graphics from the World Wide Web. Although advertisers place trademark and copyright disclaimers on their online displays, advertisers on the Web have to be willing to accept the consequence that their trademarks and logos can be copied without authorization. Currently, there is no viable policing of this practice by users. Thus far, advertisers have taken legal action only against users who have taken proprietary materials and blatantly used them in a fashion that is detrimental to the brand or infringes on the exclusivity of the advertiser's own site. This may change.

---

25. J. Udell, "Damn Lies," *Byte*, February 1996, 137.
26. E. Weise, "P&G Changes Way Ads Paid For," *Cincinnati Enquirer*, April 29, 1996, A3.

With respect to consumer privacy, the Coalition for Advertising Supported Information & Entertainment (CASIE) has suggested five goals for advertisers, which we've reproduced in Exhibit 17.36. Striving for these goals will certainly contribute to the loyalty and confidence that consumers possess for a brand. Privacy is a legitimate concern for Internet users, and will likely be one for civil libertarians and regulators as well.

Currently, most Internet users are quite wary about providing personal information or registering with a site sponsor. Forcing people to register to gain access to a site may discourage potential visitors, but the information gained from this process can be valuable to an advertiser. Combining user profiles with records on each person's activities while browsing the site allows advertisers to determine what aspects of both the site and the product appeal to each type of consumer. Requesting people to register for access to additional information, as C-Net and HotWired do, is becoming increasingly common. Another way of obtaining visitor information is a cookie. A **cookie** is a coded identifier that is downloaded to the visitor's computer, where it resides, often undetected, but not really hidden. A cookie allows the Internet server both to keep track of a client or user throughout his or her visit to a site and also to collect a surprising amount of data on the user.[27] Cookie technology both offers a benefit for advertisers wishing to know their clients better and raises obvious privacy concerns for clients. The visitor is typically unaware of the downloaded cookie.

The Intel Pentium III has raised the privacy versus identification issue a few notches. The Pentium III, released in late February 1999, has a unique ID on the chip itself. The data the company collected when you bought and registered your machine

EXHIBIT 17.36

CASIE's goals for privacy for marketing on interactive media.

1. We believe it is important to educate consumers about how they can use interactive technology to save time and customize product and service information to meet their individual needs. By choosing to share pertinent data about themselves, consumers can be provided the product information most relevant to them and can help marketers service them more economically and effectively.

2. We believe any interactive electronic communication from a marketer ought to disclose the marketer's identity.

3. We believe that marketers need to respect provacy in the use of "personal information" about individual consumers collected via interactive technology. "Personal information" is data not otherwise available via public sources. In our view, personal information ought to be used by a marketer to determine how it can effectively respond to a consumer's needs.

4. We believe that if the marketer seeks personal information via interactive electronic communication, it ought to inform the consumer whether the information will be shared with others. We also believe that before a marketer shares such perosnal information with others, the consumer ought to be offered an option to request that personal information not be shared. Upon receiving such a request, the marketer ought to keep such personal information confidential and not share it.

5. We believe consumers ought to have the ability to obtain a summary of what personal information about them is on record with a marketer that has solicited them via interactive electronic communication. In addition, a consumer ought to be offered the opportunity to correct personal information, request that such information be removed from the marketer's database (unless the marketer needs to retain it for generally accepted and customary accounting and business purposes), or request that the marketer no longer solicit the customer.

Source: Coalition for Advertising Supported Information and Entertainment. Available online at www.casie.com/guidel/priv.html. Accessed March 28, 1999.

27. "Persistent Client State HTTP Cookies;" Hoffman and Novak, "Commercialization of the World Wide Web."

and software are then linked to the chip ID. This feature, when enabled, allows those to whom you link your computer to know exactly who you are. Under pressure from privacy advocacy groups, Intel has agreed to ship the machines with the chip ID feature turned off. However, just how easy it is to turn it back on, and who can do that, and how, is still unresolved at the time of this writing.

E-Commerce: Buying on the Web.

In our view, much of the truly revolutionary aspect of the Internet story is not so much about advertising per se, but how the Internet has changed the way consumers seek out and buy things. This has been the truly revolutionary aspect. It has allowed consumers unprecedented access to product information, as well as an efficient way to see how other consumers feel and think about various brands. It allows greater consumer-to-consumer contact, easier comparison shopping, and easier feedback from consumer to marketer.

Just remember:

Even by the most generous accounts, online retail sales remain only a tiny fraction of what's sold in physical stores or through mail order catalogs—even in the Web's most popular product categories. Online book sales will account for less than 5% of all US book sales last year . . . online music sales? Less than 2%. Even online travel sales—which will reach $1.8 billion this year, leading all consumer products (except IT products) sold online—won't even reach 1% of the $488 billion in total US travel spending. Web-based advertising revenue remains minuscule compared with broadcast and print—just 0.4% of agency bookings this year.[28]

Other Types of Cybermarketing.

Virtual Malls. Setting up a Web site and placing it inside a virtual mall is another strategy useful to Web marketers. A **virtual mall** is a gateway to a group of Internet storefronts that provide access to mall sites by simply clicking on a category of store, as shown in the Mall Internet site in Exhibit 17.37. The nature of virtual malls varies widely from mall to mall. Compared with Mall Internet, the Virtual Mall, shown in Exhibit 17.38, features a more local orientation from west Boston. The advantage of malls for an advertiser is the opportunity to attract browsers to its site, much like the way window shopping works in the physical world. Check out CyberShop: "The online mall allows virtual shoppers to browse by department or brand. Offerings range from gourmet food stuffs to housewares to women's accessories, and include constantly updated sale items. Found at: http://cybershop.com/."

Coupons. Companies such as Coupons Online (www.couponpages.com/) distribute coupons via the Internet and via the sites of other commercial online services. Coupons Online simply allows users to print coupons on their home printers and then take them to the store for redemption. The company charges clients anywhere from $3 to $15 per thousand coupons distributed. The average cost to manufacturers for coupons distributed via freestanding inserts is $7 per thousand. However, only a small portion of those coupons are even clipped (2 to 3 percent redemption rate), whereas with online coupons the manufacturer is paying only per thousand clipped, or in this case printed, by consumers.[29]

Event Marketing. The Web is also an avenue for ties to event and sports marketing. For instance, both the Super Bowl and the Oscars had Web sites in 1999. The site is

28. Udell, "Damn Lies," 137.
29. Wilke, "Catalina, Coupons Online in Tests," 15.

EXHIBIT 17.37

Often one finds old metaphors used in pioneering new industries. The first cars were "horseless carriages;" the first aggregations of businesses on the Net were dubbed "malls." Sites like Mall Internet (mall-internet .com) help to provide some familiar structure to the Web, which has been likened to a library books lying in heaps on the floor without a card catalog! Yahoo! (www.yahoo.com) probably lists all of the businesses one finds on Mall Internet. Does Yahoo!'s existence make the mall unnecessary? What features of a "meat space" (or traditional, bricks-and-mortar mall) might translate well into Cyberspace? What features would make as much sense as a buggywhip in a sport utility vehicle?

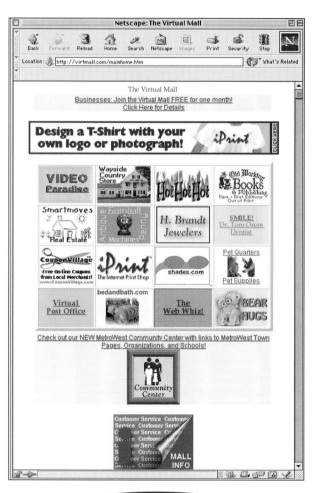

EXHIBIT 17.38

The ability to update message components is a real advantage of virtual malls. Visit the Virtual Mall (www.virtmall.com/) and contrast the presentation of information here with the kind you get from a standard search engine, such as Yahoo! (www.yahoo.com/) or Lycos (www.lycos.com/).

promoted during the program, and sponsors get their logos on the site, have links to their own home pages, and have an opportunity to provide editorial content for the event site.[30]

Sales Support. The Internet equivalent to response vehicles such as 800 numbers and postcards is E-mail. Home pages have the ability to provide an E-mail option for those who visit the site to respond to the advertiser and ask for further information. As with 800 numbers, an advertiser has to make sure that the E-mail account is adequately staffed to respond to queries in a timely manner.

---

30. Johnson, "Microsoft Developing Oscar's Web Site," 2.

Managing the E-Community.

The Internet, in addition to providing a new means for advertisers to communicate to consumers, also provides consumers a new and efficient way to communicate with one another. In fact, the social aspect of the Internet is one of the most important reasons for its success. Via Usenet newsgroups, IRC, and even Web pages, consumers have a new way to interact and form communities. Sometimes communities form online among users of a particular brand. These online brand communities behave much like a community in the traditional sense, such as a small town or ethnic neighborhood. They have their own cultures, rituals, and traditions. Members create detailed Web pages devoted to the brand. Members even feel a sense of duty or moral responsibility to other members of the community. For example, among many Volkswagen drivers, it is a common courtesy to pull over to help another VW broken down on the side of the road. Saab and Saturn drivers feel a similar sense of obligation to help others who use the same brand when they are in trouble.

In most respects, such communities are a good thing. One of the reasons members of these communities like to get together is to share their experiences in using the brand. They can share what they like about the brand and what it means to them, or suggest places to go to buy replacement parts or have the product serviced. However, advertisers need to be careful not to alienate members or turn them off of the brand. These consumers can also share their dislikes about recent changes in the brand and its advertising, rejecting them if severe enough. Since the Internet makes it easier for members of these communities to interact, brand communities are likely to proliferate in coming years. Consequently, dealing effectively with these communities will be one of the challenges facing advertisers. Some brands appear to embrace them. Saab, for example, devotes part of its Web site to the Saab brand community (see Exhibit 17.39).

EXHIBIT 17.39

The development and perpetuation of brand communities is perhaps one of the strongest advantages of advertising on the Internet.
www.saabusa.com/

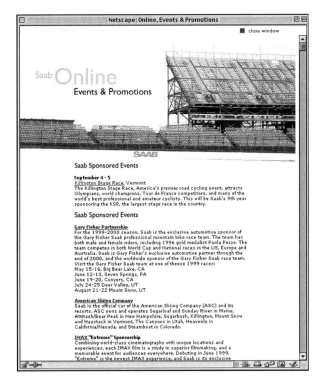

EXHIBIT 17.40

Computer-Mediated Environment/Brand Community Model.

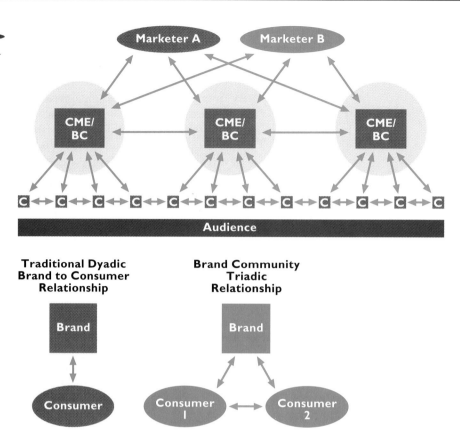

Of course, this creates new management issues as well. One of the most intriguing ideas for marketers has been how to access and utilize consumer word-of-mouth. The Internet has made the collection and management of this data much easier. Marketers can monitor Usenet discussions, develop proprietary search engines that scour the Web to find who is saying what about new products, and so on. A marketer can see what consumers are saying about its product or its competitors. Most important, the consumer link is greatly strengthened (see Exhibit 17.40).

SUMMARY

■❯ Describe who uses the Internet and the ways they are using it.

The Internet is a network of public and private computer systems. Millions of computers around the world are interconnected in this modern-day wonder. No one knows for sure how many people are using the Net, but everyone projects that the number of users will continue to grow. The characteristics of those who use the Internet make them an attractive audience for advertisers. To reach this audience, advertisers have four vehicles: E-mail, listservs, Usenet, and the World Wide Web. Of these, the World

Wide Web clearly holds the greatest potential for advertisers. The WWW is a remarkable information resource, and surfing the Web using one of several search engines allows one to tap the resource. Web surfing is also emerging as a form of personal entertainment and thus represents a threat to traditional print and broadcast media.

■❯ Identify the advertising and marketing opportunities presented by the Internet.

Facing uncertainty about what they might hope to gain, advertisers and marketers nevertheless have flocked to the

WWW. This interest by their clients has naturally forced ad agencies to develop expertise in Internet advertising. The two primary ways that advertisers establish themselves on the Web are by developing corporate home pages or placing banner ads. Other forms of marketing activity observed on the Web include virtual malls, online coupon distribution, support for event marketing, and sales support that promotes one-to-one contact between marketers and their customers.

Discuss fundamental requirements for establishing viable sites on the World Wide Web.

Establishing a presence on the Web is relatively inexpensive when compared to the costs involved in mass media advertising, but updating and servicing a site are critical to its value and demand a continuing investment of time and money. In establishing and maintaining a site, one of the key goals must be to build in sources of information and entertainment that will keep surfers coming back to the site. Plain product information and promotion are not going to yield repeat visits. Also, to make a site valuable, an advertiser has to get a surfer to the site in the first place. This is no small undertaking in the chaotic order of the WWW. Purchasing keywords that connect a site to appropriate points of departure on a search engine such as Yahoo!, or promoting the site via any number of other media, is necessary to get surfers to make an initial visit. Once there, they must find a reason to come back.

Explain the challenges inherent in measuring the cost-effectiveness of the Internet versus other advertising media.

To fulfill the Net's potential as an advertising medium, measurement tools must be developed that allow comparisons of the cost-effectiveness of the Internet versus traditional media. Better descriptive information on who is actually using the Net is also needed. Not surprisingly, current tracking mechanisms tally how often other computers have visited a particular Web site, but they cannot tell who the people were that operated the visiting computer. A memory technique known as caching adds further complications for tracking the frequency of visits to Web sites. Finally, privacy and anonymity have been characteristics highly valued by Internet users. If these are things that an audience values, getting detailed descriptions of such an audience will be a challenge.

Describe how the Internet is changing the way consumers shop and buy.

Although it is important to remember that online retail sales represent only a fraction of what is sold through other venues, the Internet is having an impact on shopping and buying behavior by facilitating access to product information, comparison shopping, community among brand users, and direct communication between consumer and advertiser.

KEY TERMS

Internet (532)
electronic mail (532)
Internet Relay Chat (IRC) (532)
Usenet (533)
World Wide Web (WWW) (533)
listservs (536)
spam (537)
search engine (538)
corporate home page (547)
banner ads (548)
hits (554)
pages (555)

visits (555)
users (555)
log analysis software (555)
caching (557)
bandwidth (557)
impressions (557)
pay-per-click (557)
click-throughs (557)
cookie (558)
virtual mall (559)

QUESTIONS FOR REVIEW AND CRITICAL THINKING

1. In the face of considerable uncertainty about audience size, audience composition, and cost-effectiveness, advertisers have nonetheless been flocking to the World Wide Web. What is it about the Web that advertisers have found so irresistible?

2. How can an understanding of search engines and how they operate benefit an organization initiating an ad campaign on the WWW?

3. Explain the two basic strategies for developing corporate home pages, exemplified in this chapter by Saturn and Absolut.

4. Niche marketing will certainly be facilitated by the WWW. What is it about the WWW that makes it such a powerful tool for niche marketing?

5. Visit some of the corporate home pages described in this chapter, or think about corporate home pages you have visited previously. Of those you have encountered, which would you single out as being most effective in giving the visitor a reason to come back? What conclusions would you draw regarding the best ways to motivate repeat visits to a Web site?

6. Why is an agreement between Ford and Sporting News Online such big news for advertisers with an interest in the WWW? Regarding the agreement between the two described in this chapter's IMC box, in what sense does it push integrated communications to a higher standard?

7. The Internet was obviously not conceived or designed to be an advertising medium. Thus, some of its characteristics have proven perplexing to advertisers. If advertising professionals had the chance to redesign the Internet, what single change would you expect they would want to make to enhance its value from an advertising perspective?

EXPERIENTIAL EXERCISES

1. Television commercials often end with a Web site address. After viewing a television ad, go to the Web site address given. Are the television and Web site messages coordinated? Is there a synergy between the two messages? Does the Web site refer to the television ad or to any print ads? Find a print ad for the same brand. Does the print ad include the Web site address? What does this exercise tell you about the coordination of advertising for the brand you selected? Find a print ad for the same brand. Does the print ad include the Web site address? What does this exercise tell you about the coordination of advertising for the brand you selected?

2. Find what you think are the five best Web ads and the five worst. Explain your choices.

USING THE INTERNET

Use the following search engines to find sites of interest to you:

Yahoo!: www.yahoo.com

Alta Vista: www.altavista.com

Excite: www.excite.com

Based on your experiences with the search engines, answer the following questions:

1. What are the unique advantages that each search engine offers?

2. What are the disadvantages of each search engine?

3. What type of search best takes advantage of each search engine's unique characteristics?

4. Which of the search engines do you prefer to use? Why?

Many major sites, be they search sites or pioneering electronic commerce sites like Amazon.com, are taking steps to establish themselves as "portals" (that is, the place at which users—and, more specifically, consumers, who can be both advertised and sold to—"enter" Cyberspace). Often this is done through strategic alliances and the aggregation of a number of disparate services on top of a single common infrastructure. The goal is to be able to provide anything and everything required at the portal site, so as not to let the customer wander off.

Visit the following sites, some of which are allied with each other:

HotBot: www.hotbot.com

Amazon.com: www.amazon.com

Lycos: www.lycos.com

Yahoo!: www.yahoo.com

CDNow: www.cdnow.com

1. What sorts of sites would have the best claim on the "portal" title?

2. How do the sites complement or support each other, to further the idea of a portal?

3. How are Web sites made "sticky," so that the customer doesn't wander off?

THE MOUNTAIN DEW SNOWBOARD FESTIVAL.
2 DAYS OF LETTING YOUR INNER CHILD RUN AMUCK.

Demo gear from 50 of the coolest companies to ever attack the slopes. Plus free lessons, tunes and plenty of Dew. So whip out to the mountains and show Jack Frost who runs the hill.

Dec. 13-14	Jan. 10-11	Jan. 24-25	Jan. 31-Feb. 1	Feb. 7-8
Ski Windham, NY	Winter Park, CO	Snowbird Ski Resort, UT	Heavenly Ski Resort, CA	Snow Valley, CA

do the dew

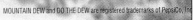

CHAPTER 18

After reading and thinking about this chapter, you will be able to do the following:

- Explain the popularity of and rationale for different forms of sales promotions.

- Describe the purposes and characteristics of sales promotions directed at consumers.

- Describe the purposes and characteristics of sales promotions directed at the trade.

- Discuss the risks and coordination issues associated with sales promotion.

WEB SIGHTING

THE EASIEST INTERNET ONLINE SERVICE JUST GOT EASIER!

ALL-NEW AOL 4.0!

100 Hours FREE!

all-new! America Online GOLD 4.0!

The all-new version of America Online is easier, faster and better than ever. It's a snap to install, comes with FREE 24-hour customer service, and connects you with lots of stuff you can't find anywhere else.

TO EXPERIENCE IT FIRSTHAND, CALL 1-800-4-ONLINE.

AMERICA Online

So easy to use, no wonder it's #1

Availability may be limited, especially during peak times
© 1998 America Online, Inc.

EXHIBIT 18.1

AOL, the Godzilla of giveaways.

The new titans of technology—AOL, Yahoo!, Network Associates—have discovered a new way to generate revenue fast: They give their products away. That's right, they give them away. These fast-growing, highly successful companies have discovered an alternative to advertising—sales promotion. More specifically, they have discovered the power of distributing free samples.

Of course, giving away free samples is not a new sales promotion technique. Toothpaste, shampoo, and snack food marketers have been giving out free samples for decades. But giving away intellectual property, such as software, *is* new and America Online is the Godzilla of giveaways (see Exhibit 18.1). AOL has blanketed the United States with diskettes and CD-ROMs offering consumers a free one-month trial of its Internet services. No distribution channel was left untapped in trying to reach consumers with the free diskettes: They were stashed in boxes of Rice Chex cereal, in United Airlines in-flight meals, and in packages of Omaha Steaks—not to mention inside the plastic sack along with your local Sunday paper that the neighborhood kid delivered.

This is not to say that software companies have abandoned advertising—hardly. In the past five years, advertising in the technology sector has increased from about $600 million to over $2 billion, making it one of the fastest growing advertising markets in the United States. But what makes sales promotion sampling so attractive is that it takes all the risk away from consumer trial. Consumers with computers, of course, can give AOL or Yahoo a try without investing a penny or making a long-term commitment to a piece of software. If they like what they see, they can sign up for a longer period of time.

The technology companies have embraced the concept and accepted the main liabilities of sampling—cost and time. But as the vice president of worldwide marketing for Sun Microsystems put it: "You know what URL stands for don't you? Ubiquity first, Revenues Later."[1]

These technology companies have discovered that sales promotion can be a valuable component of the overall promotional program—and that the potential impact of sales promotion is quite different from advertising. Because of the potential of various sales promotion techniques, corporations of all types have invested in sales promotion, making it an enterprise worth $80 billion dollars a year in the United States. Sales promotion is also emerging as a global force as firms try to introduce U.S. brands into distant markets. The "message" in a sales promotion features price reduction (or free sample), a prize, or some other incentive for consumers to try a brand or visit a retailer. Sales promotion has proven to be a popular complement to mass media advertising because it accomplishes things advertising cannot. Let's consider the full range of sales promotion techniques and how they are carried out by companies.

---

1.   Patricia Nakache, "Secrets of the New Brand Builders," *Fortune,* June 22, 1998, 167–170.

Basic Forms of Sales Promotion.

Mass media advertising suffers from having effects that are hard to measure in the short run. This is not the case with sales promotion. Sales promotion is a conspicuous activity undertaken to make things happen in a hurry. Used properly, sales promotion is capable of almost instant demand stimulation.

Formally defined, **sales promotion** is the use of incentive techniques that create a perception of greater brand value among consumers or distributors. The intent is to create a short-term increase in sales by motivating trial use or encouraging larger purchases or repeat purchases. **Consumer-market sales promotion** includes coupons, price-off deals, premiums, contests and sweepstakes, sampling and trial offers, brand (product) placements, rebates, frequency programs, and event sponsorship. All are ways of inducing household consumers to purchase a firm's brand rather than a competitor's brand. Notice that some incentives reduce price, offer a reward, or encourage a trip to the retailer. **Trade-market sales promotion** uses point-of-purchase displays, incentives, allowances, trade shows, or cooperative advertising as ways of motivating distributors, wholesalers, and retailers to stock and feature a firm's brand in their merchandising programs.

The Importance and Growth of Sales Promotion.

Sales promotion is designed to affect demand differently than does advertising. As we have learned throughout the text, most advertising is designed to have awareness-, image-, and preference-building effects for a brand over the long run. The role of sales promotion, on the other hand, is primarily to elicit an immediate purchase from a customer. Coupons, samples, rebates, sweepstakes, and similar techniques offer a consumer an immediate incentive, as exemplified in Exhibit 18.2, which shows Pepsi logo items as a form of premium available to consumers.

EXHIBIT 18.2

Some forms of sales promotion turn the consumer into a walking billboard for the brand. Do you have your Pepsi Stuff?
www.pepsi.com/

EXHIBIT 18.3

The purposes of sales promotion versus advertising.

Purpose of Sales Promotion	Purpose of Advertising
Stimulate short-term demand	Cultivate long-term demand
Encourage brand switching	Encourage brand loyalty
Induce trial use	Encourage repeat purchases
Promote price orientation	Promote image/feature orientation
Obtain immediate, often measurable results	Obtain long-term effects, often difficult to measure

Other sales promotions, such as brand placements (getting the company's brand placed in a movie or on a TV show) and frequency programs (for example, frequent-flyer programs), provide an affiliation value with a brand, which increases a consumer's ability and desire to identify with a particular brand. Sales promotions featuring price reductions, such as coupons, are effective in the convenience goods category, where frequent purchases, brand switching, and a perceived homogeneity among brands characterize consumer behavior.

Sales promotions are used across all consumer goods categories and in the trade market as well. When a firm determines that a more immediate response is called for—whether the target customer is a household, business buyer, distributor, or retailer—sales promotions are designed to provide the incentive. The goals for sales promotion versus advertising are compared in Exhibit 18.3. Notice the key differences in the goals for these different forms of promotion.

The Importance of Sales Promotion.

The importance of sales promotion in the United States should not be underestimated. Sales promotion may not seem as stylish and sophisticated as mass media advertising, but expenditures on this tool are impressive. In recent years, sales promotion expenditures have grown at an annual rate of about 10–12 percent, compared to a 7–9 percent rate for advertising.[2] By the late 1990s, the investment by marketers in sales promotions reached nearly $80 billion.[3] Add to that figure consumer savings by redeeming coupons and rebates and the figure exceeds $150 billion.[4]

It is important to realize that advertising agencies specializing in advertising planning, creative preparation, and media placement typically do not prepare sales promotion materials for clients. These activities are delegated either to a subsidiary of the main agency or to specialized sales promotion agencies. A list of the top ten sales promotion agencies is shown in Exhibit 18.4.

The development and management of an effective sales promotion program requires a major commitment by a firm. Procter & Gamble estimates that during any given year, 25 percent of sales force time and 30 percent of brand management time is spent on designing, implementing, and overseeing sales promotions.[5] The rise in the use of sales promotion and the enormous amount of money being spent on various programs makes it one of the most prominent forms of marketing activity. But again, it must be undertaken only under certain conditions and then carefully executed for specific reasons.

Growth in the Use of Sales Promotion.

Marketers have shifted the emphasis of their promotional spending over the past decade. Most of the shift has been away from mass media

2.   Russ Brown, "Sales Promotion," *Marketing and Media Decisions,* February 1990, 74.

3.   "1998 Annual Report of the Promotion Industry," *PROMO Magazine,* July 1998, S3–S37.

4.   Kenneth Wylie, "Marketing Services," special report, *Advertising Age,* July 11, 1994, S1–S10.

5.   Robert D. Buzzell, John A. Quelch, and Walter J. Salmon, "The Costly Bargain of Sales Promotion," *Harvard Business Review* (March/April 1990), 141–149.

Largest sales promotion agencies in the United States, ranked by revenue. Figures are in millions of U.S. dollars.

Rank	Agency	U.S. Sales Promotion Revenue, 1997	% Change 1996 to 1997
1	Carlson Marketing Group	$160.2	8.6
2	Alcone Marketing Group	115.5	5.0
3	Gage Marketing Group	85.0	–0.8
4	Frankel & Co.	77.7	23.7
5	YLP Inc.	51.0	22.9
6	HMG Worldwide	45.8	0.6
7	Cyrk Worldwide	42.8	27.9
8	Integer Group	33.0	28.7
9	GMR Marketing	31.9	26.6
10	Ryan Partnership	28.3	16.6

Source: "Marketing Service Shops Near $3 Billion in Revenue," *Advertising Age*, April 27, 1998, S-12. Reprinted with permission from the April 27, 1998 issue of *Advertising Age*. Copyright © Crain Communications Inc. 1998.

advertising and toward consumer and trade sales promotions. In 1981, the budget for promotions among packaged goods companies in the United States averaged 43 percent for advertising, 34 percent for trade promotions, and 23 percent for consumer promotions. Currently, the budget allocation stands at about 25 percent for advertising, 47 percent for trade promotions, and 28 percent for consumer promotions.[6] There are several reasons why some marketers have shifted their funds from mass media advertising to sales promotions:

Demand for Greater Accountability. In an era of cost cutting and downsizing, companies are demanding greater accountability across all functions, including marketing, advertising, and promotions. When activities are evaluated for their contribution to sales and profits, it is often difficult to draw specific conclusions regarding the effects of advertising. Conversely, the immediate effects of sales promotions are typically easier to document. Another plus for the accountability of sales promotion is that ACNielsen and IPSOs–ASI research firms have developed *Market Drivers,* a new research program that evaluates the effects of sales promotions.[7] The program combines Nielsen's store sales data with the IPSOs–ASI copy-testing measures to identify the effects of sales promotions versus ads in communicating to target segments. But this measurement is not cheap. The companies estimate that using the *Market Drivers* program runs about $100,000 per project.

Short-Term Orientation. Several factors have created a short-term orientation among managers. Pressures from stockholders to produce better quarter-by-quarter revenue and profit per share is one factor. A bottom-line mentality is another factor. Many organizations are developing marketing plans—with rewards and punishments for performance—based on short-term revenue generation.[8] This being the case, tactics that can have short-term effects are sought. Thus the increased popularity of sales promotion.

Consumer Response to Promotions. The precision shopper of the nineties is demanding greater value across all purchase situations, and the trend is "battering overpriced brands."[9] These precision shoppers search for extra value in every product

6.   *16th Annual Survey of Promotional Practices* (Stamford, Conn.: Donnelley Marketing, 1994), 6.
7.   James B. Arndorfer, "ACNielsen Market Drivers Will Gauge Promos' Punch," *Advertising Age,* February 23, 1998, 8.
8.   "What Happened to Advertising," *Business Week,* September 23, 1991, 66.
9.   Rahul Jacob, "Beyond Quality and Value," *Fortune,* Autumn/Winter 1993, 8–11.

purchase. Coupons, premiums, price-off deals, and other sales promotions increase the value of a brand in these shoppers' minds. This positive response goes beyond value-oriented consumers. For consumers who are not well informed about the average price in a product category, a brand featuring a coupon or price-off promotion is sensed to be a good deal and will likely be chosen over competitive brands.[10]

Proliferation of Brands. Each year, thousands of new brands are introduced into the consumer market. The drive by marketers to design products for specific market segments to satisfy ever more narrowly defined needs has caused a proliferation of brands that creates a mind-dulling maze for consumers. At any point in time, consumers can choose from approximately 64 spaghetti sauces, 103 snack chips, 54 laundry detergents, 91 cold remedies, and 69 disposable diaper varieties.[11] As you can see in Exhibit 18.5, gaining attention in this blizzard of brands is no easy task. Often marketers turn to sales promotions—product placements, contests, coupons, and premiums—to gain some recognition in a consumer's mind and stimulate a trial purchase.

Increased Power of Retailers. Retailers such as Home Depot, The Gap, Toys "R" Us, and the most powerful of all, Wal-Mart, now dominate in the United States. These powerful retailers have responded quickly and accurately to the new environment for retailing, where consumers are demanding more and better products and services at lower prices. Because of the lower-price component of the retailing environment, these retailers are demanding more deals from manufacturers. Many of the deals are delivered in terms of trade-oriented sales promotions: point-of-purchase displays, slotting fees (payment for shelf space), case allowances, and cooperative advertising allowances. In the end, manufacturers use more and more sales promotion devices to gain and maintain good relations with the new, powerful retailers—a critical link to the consumer.

Media Clutter. A nagging and traditional problem in the advertising process is clutter. Many advertisers target the same customers because their research has led them to the same conclusion about whom to target. The result is that advertising media are cluttered

Marketers commonly turn to sales promotion in an effort to stand out from the crowd at the point of purchase. This exhibit nicely illustrates what the marketer (and the consumer!) is faced with in the cluttered retail environment. Notice the point-of-purchase promotions attached to the shelves.

10. Leigh McAlister, "A Model of Consumer Behavior," *Marketing Communications,* April 1987, 26–28.
11. Gabriella Stern, "Multiple Varieties of Established Brands Muddle Consumers, Make Retailers Mad," *Wall Street Journal,* January 24, 1992, B1, B9.

with ads all seeking the attention of a common target. One way to break through the clutter is to feature a sales promotion. In print ads, the featured deal is often a coupon. In broadcast advertising, sweepstakes and premium offers can attract listeners' and viewers' attention. The combination of advertising and creative sales promotions can be a good way to break through the clutter, as suggested by the New Media box on page 574.

Sales Promotion Directed at Consumers.

It is clear that U.S. consumer-product firms have made a tremendous commitment to sales promotion in their overall marketing plans. During the 1970s, marketers allocated only about 30 percent of their budgets to sales promotion, with about 70 percent allocated to mass media advertising. Today, some estimate the percentages as just the opposite, with nearly 75 percent being spent on sales promotions.[12] Although the fundamental goal of sales promotion is to generate a sharp increase in short-term demand, some marketing strategists also believe that proper application of these techniques can make a long-term contribution.[13]

Objectives for Consumer-Market Sales Promotion.
To help ensure the proper application of sales promotion, specific strategic objectives should be set. The following basic objectives can be pursued with sales promotion in the consumer market:

EXHIBIT 18.6

Sales promotions are commonly used to encourage consumers to stock up. In this exhibit, multiple incentives are being offered to promote larger and repeat purchases. www.francoamerican.com/

- *Stimulate trial purchase.* When a firm wants to attract new users, sales promotion tools can reduce the consumer's risk of trying something new. A reduced price or offer of a rebate may stimulate trial purchase. When Keebler wanted to attract trial use in eight key Hispanic markets, it created the Keebler Kids Club, which featured giveaways and the *Keebler Kids Quiz Show,* which gave Spanish-speaking youngsters the chance to win college scholarships.[14]

- *Stimulate repeat purchases.* In-package coupons good for the next purchase, or the accumulation of points with repeated purchases, can keep consumers loyal to a particular brand. The most prominent frequency programs are found in the airline industry, where competitors such as Delta, American, and United try to retain their most lucrative customers by enrolling them in frequency programs. Frequent flyers can earn free travel, hotel stays, gifts, and numerous other perks through the programs. Recently, fast-food chains such as McDonald's have started frequency programs (the McExtra card) to keep customers coming back in the brand switching–prone fast-food industry.[15]

- *Stimulate larger purchases.* Price reductions or two-for-one sales can motivate consumers to stock up on a brand, thus allowing firms to reduce inventory or increase cash flow. Shampoo is often double-packaged to offer a value to consumers. Exhibit 18.6 is a sales promotion aimed at stimulating a larger purchase.

12. *15th Annual Survey of Promotional Practices* (Stamford, Conn.: Donnelley Marketing, 1993), 6.
13. B. Spethmann, "Money and Power," *Brandweek,* March 15, 1993, 21.
14. "Best in the World," *Promo,* November 1995, 39.
15. Louise Kramer, "McD's Eyes Rollout of Loyalty Card," *Advertising Age,* April 27, 1998, 3.

A SCREAMING DEAL—LITERALLY

While 13- and 14-year-olds have long puzzled their parents with strange adolescent behavior, in 1994 parents and teachers alike were particularly baffled when kids started screaming the word "Sega" in seemingly random fashion. The genesis of the Sega scream turned out to be a TV commercial tagline that caught on like wildfire with kids. But Sega wasn't satisfied to merely have kids all over the United States shrieking the brand name at the top of their lungs. Sega cleverly leveraged the phenomenon into a series of promotions and an Internet-based contest and turned the scream into a marketing mantra.

Among a series of integrated promotions that included events, product tie-ins, on-pack promotions, and multimedia efforts, Sega developed an online contest to let Sega screamers test their howl against the experts. Specifically, visitors to Sega's Web site could upload to Sega to compare their screaming against that of Tom Kalinske—the company president. Then, users could download his version to be played back on their home computer system.

Tom Abramson, vice president of marketing and promotions, is the architect of Sega's award-winning promotional programs. *Advertising Age* named Sega the 1994 Promotional Marketer of the Year. Abramson came to Sega after working with the Ice Capades, the Harlem Globetrotters, and Walt Disney World. Aside from the Sega Screaming Contest, he has conceived of such popular promotions as the Sega Worldwide Video Tournament (the finals of which took place at Alcatraz Prison) and special, limited flavors of Life Savers candy to promote Sega's new Sonic 3 game.

But for all the creativity and aggressiveness of Abramson's promotions, he puts a premium on coordinating the promotional activities at Sega with the company's advertising. In his view, "Advertising sets the stage for our attitude and gets us into the heads of our users. But we use promotions and events to get Sega into the hands of consumers every day, by reaching into their school notebooks, lunch boxes, Little League and football practices, and their weekend parties."

Source: Kate Fitzgerald, "Sega 'Screams' Its Way to the Top," *Advertising Age*, March 20, 1995, S-2.

- *Introduce a new brand.* Because sales promotion can attract attention and motivate trial purchase, it is commonly used for new brand introduction. When the makers of Curad bandages wanted to introduce their new kid-size bandage, 7.5 million sample packs were distributed in McDonald's Happy Meal sacks. The promotion was a huge success, with initial sales exceeding estimates by 30 percent.[16]
- *Combat or disrupt competitors' strategies.* Because sales promotions often motivate consumers to buy in larger quantities or try new brands, they can be used to disrupt competitors' marketing strategies. If a firm knows that one of its competitors is launching a new brand or initiating a new advertising campaign, a well-timed sales promotion offering deep discounts or extra quantity can disrupt the competitors' strategy. Add to the original discount an in-package coupon for future purchases, and a marketer can severely compromise competitors' efforts. *TV Guide* magazine used a sweepstakes promotion to combat competition. In an effort to address increasing competition from newspaper TV supplements and cable-guide magazines, *TV Guide* ran a Shopping Spree Sweepstakes in several regional markets. Winners won $200 shopping sprees in grocery stores—precisely the location where 65 percent of *TV Guide* sales are realized.[17]

- *Contribute to integrated marketing communications.* In conjunction with advertising, direct marketing, public relations, and other programs being carried out by a firm, sales promotion can add yet another type of communication to the mix. Sales promotions suggest an additional value, with price reductions, premiums, or the chance to win a prize. This is an additional and different message within the overall communications effort.

16. Glen Heitsmith, "Still Bullish on Promotion," *Promo*, July 1994, 40.
17. "*TV Guide* Tunes in Sweepstakes," *PROMO Magazine*, November 1995, 1, 50.

Consumer-Market Sales Promotion Techniques.

Several techniques are used to stimulate demand and attract attention in the consumer market. Some of these are coupons, price-off deals, premiums, contests and sweepstakes, samples and trial offers, product placement, rebates, frequency programs, and event sponsorship.

Coupons. A **coupon** entitles a buyer to a designated reduction in price for a product or service. Coupons are the oldest and most widely used form of sales promotion. The first use of a coupon is traced to around 1895, when the C. W. Post Company used a penny-off coupon as a way to get people to try its Grape-Nuts cereal. Annually, about 300 billion coupons are distributed to American consumers, with redemption rates ranging from 2 percent for gum purchases to nearly 45 percent for disposable diaper purchases. Exhibit 18.7 shows coupon redemption rates for several product categories. In 1997, consumers in the United States saved nearly $6.5 billion through coupon use.[18]

There are five advantages to the coupon as a sales promotion tool:

- The use of a coupon makes it possible to give a discount to a price-sensitive consumer while still selling the product at full price to other consumers. A price-sensitive customer takes the time to clip the coupon and carry it to the store; a regular consumer merely buys the product at full price.
- The coupon-redeeming customer is often a competitive-brand user, so the coupon can induce brand switching.
- A manufacturer can control the timing and distribution of coupons. This way a retailer is not implementing price discounts inappropriately.
- A coupon is an excellent method of stimulating repeat purchases. Once a consumer has been attracted to a brand, with or without a coupon, an in-package coupon can induce repeat purchase. The long-standing belief is that in-package coupons stimulate greater brand loyalty than media-distributed coupons. While an in-package coupon is designed to encourage repeat purchase and brand loyalty, retailers believe that coupons attached to the store shelf and distributed at the point of purchase are the most effective.[19]

EXHIBIT 18.7

Product categories with the highest percentage of purchases made with coupons.

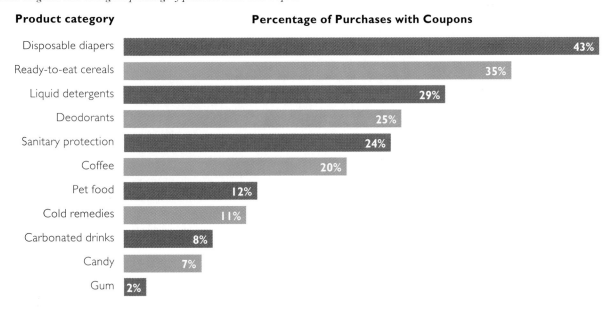

Product category	Percentage of Purchases with Coupons
Disposable diapers	43%
Ready-to-eat cereals	35%
Liquid detergents	29%
Deodorants	25%
Sanitary protection	24%
Coffee	20%
Pet food	12%
Cold remedies	11%
Carbonated drinks	8%
Candy	7%
Gum	2%

18. "1998 Annual Report of the Promotion Industry," S3.
19. Data displayed in *Advertising Age,* May 10, 1993, S-5.

- Coupons can get regular users to trade up within a brand array. For example, users of low-price disposable diapers may be willing to try a premium variety with a coupon.

The use of coupons is not without its problems. There are administrative burdens and risks with coupon use:

MAJOR MARKETER SAVING ON COUPONS

Procter & Gamble, considered by many the top marketing organization in the world, is testing a program of major cutbacks in coupon use. P&G has eliminated couponing for all its brands in the Buffalo, Rochester, and Syracuse markets and plowed the savings into value pricing and brand building. Early test results suggest that supermarkets in the area are reporting solid gains in the sales of P&G brands.

P&G's test is the latest step in a downward trend in coupon distribution and consumer redemption of coupons. In 1992, consumers redeemed 7.7 billion cents-off coupons at grocery and drug retail outlets. In 1995, that number had fallen to 5.8 billion (a 20 percent decline). By 1997, the number had fallen again to about 4.7 billion coupons, which represented an anemic 1.7 percent redemption rate. In addition, coupon distribution by marketers fell 6 percent in 1995, to 291.1 billion. There is no doubt that Procter & Gamble is leading the way in this decline. Within its $5 billion annual marketing and promotions budget, P&G has reduced national coupon expenditures by 50 percent since 1990.

The success of the P&G test has led other marketers, also disenchanted with the drawbacks of couponing, to consider a similar cutback. As the discussion in this chapter points out, while coupons can attract attention and have positive effects on short-term demand, the liabilities of couponing can be troublesome. A spokesperson has said that P&G's own studies show that coupons are an "inherently inefficient way to promote products." Further, retailers are tired of the time and expense of handling manufacturer coupons that don't address their local market needs or strategic agendas.

This move away from broad national couponing should not be interpreted as a death knell for coupons as a promotional tool, however. Couponing will always have a place in marketers' integrated marketing communications agenda. As a way to introduce a new brand or highlight a new feature of an old brand, coupons are necessary as a supportive element to major advertising campaigns across a wide range of conditions.

Sources: Pat Sloan, "P&G Tops Rivals in No-Coupon Push," *Advertising Age,* January 15, 1996, 3; Kate Fitzgerald, "P&G's Zero-Coupon Move Sparks Related Cutbacks by Competitors," *Advertising Age,* March 18, 1996; "1998 Annual Report of the Promotion Industry," *PROMO Magazine,* July 1998, S-5.

- While coupon price incentives and the timing of distribution can be controlled by a marketer, the timing of redemption cannot. Some consumers redeem coupons immediately; others hold them for months. Expiration dates printed on coupons help focus the redemption time but may compromise the impact of coupons.

- Coupons do attract competitors' users and some nonusers, but there is no way to prevent current users from redeeming coupons with their regular purchases. Heavy redemption by regular buyers merely reduces a firm's profitability. This has led some firms to consider eliminating coupons from their arsenal of marketing tools.[20] The IMC box on this page describes one company's approach to coordinating coupons with other components in its overall integrated marketing communications mix.

- Couponing entails careful administration. Coupon programs include much more than the cost of the face value of the coupon. There are costs for production and distribution and for retailer and manufacturer handling. In fact, the cost for handling, processing, and distribution of coupons is equal to about $2/3$ of the face value of the coupon.[21] Procter & Gamble has distributed as many as 773 million coupons for its Folgers coffee brand with administrative costs totaling more than $14 million.[22] Marketers need to track these costs against the amount of product sold with and without coupon redemption.

20. "P&G to Experiment with Ending Coupons," *Marketing News,* February 12, 1996, 11.
21. "1998 Annual Report of the Promotion Industry," S37.
22. "Coffee's On," *PROMO Magazine,* February 1996, 48–49.

- Fraud is a chronic and serious problem in the couponing process. The problem relates directly to misredemption practices. There are three types of misredemption that cost firms money: redemption of coupons by consumers who do not purchase the couponed brand; redemption of coupons by salesclerks and store managers without consumer purchases; illegal collection or copying of coupons by individuals who sell them to unethical store merchants, who in turn redeem the coupons without the accompanying consumer purchases.

Price-Off Deals. The price-off deal is another straightforward technique. A **price-off deal** offers a consumer cents or even dollars off merchandise at the point of purchase through specially marked packages. The typical price-off deal is a 10 to 25 percent price reduction. The reduction is taken from the manufacturer's profit margin rather than the retailer's. Manufacturers like the price-off technique because it is controllable. Plus, the price off, judged at the point of purchase, can effect a positive price comparison against competitors. Consumers like a price-off deal because it is straightforward and automatically increases the value of a known brand. Regular users tend to stock up on an item during a price-off deal. Retailers are less enthusiastic about this technique. Price-off promotions can create inventory and pricing problems for retailers. Also, most price-off deals are snapped up by regular customers, so the retailer doesn't benefit from new business.

Premiums. Premiums are items offered free, or at a reduced price, with the purchase of another item. Many firms offer a related product free, such as a free granola bar packed inside a box of granola cereal. Service firms, such as a car wash or dry cleaner, may use a two-for-one offer to persuade consumers to try the service.

There are two options available for the use of premiums. A **free premium** provides consumers with an item at no cost; the item is either included in the package of a purchased item or mailed to the consumer after proof of purchase is verified. The most frequently used free premium is an additional package of the original item or a free related item placed in the package. Some firms do offer unrelated free premiums, such as balls, toys, and trading cards. These types of premiums are particularly popular with cereal manufacturers.

A **self-liquidating premium** requires a consumer to pay most of the cost of the item received as a premium, as shown in Exhibit 18.8. Self-liquidating premiums are particularly effective with loyal customers. However, these types of premiums must be used cautiously. Unless the premium is related to a value-building strategy for a brand, it can, like other sales promotions, serve to focus consumer attention on the premium rather than on the benefits of the brand. Such an outcome could cause erosion of brand equity.

Contests and Sweepstakes. Contests and sweepstakes can draw attention to a brand like no other sales promotion technique. Technically, there are important differences between the two. A **contest** has consumers compete for prizes based on skill or ability. Winners in a contest are determined by a

EXHIBIT 18.8

Premiums take many shapes and sizes. What is it about this premium offer that makes it self-liquidating? www.jell-o.com/

panel of judges or based on which contestant comes closest to a predetermined crite-rion for winning, such as picking the total points scored in the Super Bowl. Contests tend to be somewhat expensive to administer because each entry must be judged against winning criteria.

A **sweepstakes** is a promotion in which winners are determined purely by chance. Consumers need only to enter their names in the sweepstakes as a criterion for winning. Sweepstakes often use official entry forms as a way for consumers to enter the sweepstakes. Publishers Clearing House has run a high-profile sweepstakes in the United States since 1967. Other popular types of sweepstakes use scratch-off cards. Instant-winner scratch-off cards tend to attract customers. Gasoline retailers, grocery stores, and fast-food chains commonly use scratch-off cards as a way of build-ing and maintaining store traffic. Sweepstakes can also be designed so that repeated trips to the retail outlet are necessary to gather a complete set of winning cards. Research indicates that for contests and sweepstakes to be effective, marketers must design them in such a way that consumers perceive value in the prizes and find play-ing the games intrinsically interesting.[23]

Contests and sweepstakes can span the globe. British Airways ran a contest with the theme "The World's Greatest Offer," in which it gave away thousands of free airline tickets to London and other European destinations. While the contest increased aware-ness of the airline, a spokesperson said there was definitely another benefit: "We're cre-ating a database with all these names. All those people who didn't win will be getting mail from us with information on other premium offers."[24]

Contests and sweepstakes often create excitement and generate interest for a brand, but the problems of administering these promotions are substantial. Primary among the problems are the regulations and restrictions on such promotions. Advertisers must be sure that the design and administration of a contest or sweepstakes complies with both federal and state laws. Each state may have slightly different regulations. The legal problems are complex enough that most firms hire agencies that specialize in contests and sweepstakes to administer the programs.

Another problem is that the game itself may become the consumer's primary focus, while the brand becomes secondary. The technique thus fails to build long-term con-sumer affinity for a brand. This problem is inherent to most forms of sales promotion, not just contests and sweepstakes.

The final problem with contests and sweepstakes relates to the IMC effort a firm may be attempting. It is hard to get any message across in the context of a game. The consumer's interest is focused on the game, rather than on any feature or value message included in the contest or sweepstakes communication. A related problem is that if a firm is trying to develop a quality or prestige image for a brand, contests and sweep-stakes may contradict this goal.

Sampling and Trial Offers. Getting consumers to simply try a brand can have a powerful effect on future decision making, as in the AOL sampling program described at the beginning of the chapter. **Sampling** is a technique designed to provide a consumer with a trial opportunity, as Exhibit 18.9 illustrates. Saying that sampling is a popular technique is an understatement. Estimates suggest that nearly 90 percent of consumer-product companies use sampling and invest approximately 15 percent of their total pro-motional budget in the technique.[25] A recent survey shows that consumers are very favorable toward sampling; 92 percent of consumers surveyed preferred a free sample to a coupon.[26] Sampling is particularly useful for new products, but should not be reserved for new products alone. It can be used successfully for established brands with weak

23. James C. Ward and Ronald Paul Hill, "Designing Effective Promotional Games: Opportunities and Problems," *Jour-nal of Advertising,* vol. 20, no. 3 (September 1991), 69–81.
24. Thomas R. King, "Marketers Bet Big with Contests to Trigger Consumer Spending," *Wall Street Journal,* April 4, 1991, B8.
25. "Sampling Continues to Be a Popular Choice," *Advertising Age,* May 16, 1993, 2.
26. Kate Fitzgerald, "Survey: Consumers Prefer Sampling over Coupons," *Advertising Age,* January 29, 1996, 9.

When A Cigar Can Make You
Forget Havana,
That's One-Upmannship

For Special Sample Offer, Call: 1-800-863-3456

The H. Upmann trademark is registered in the United States by a subsidiary of Consolidated Cigar Corporation and should not be confused with the identical trademark used by others in other countries. Consolidated's Dominican H. Upmann is available in the United States at fine tobacconists everywhere.

EXHIBIT 18.9

Sometimes, as Freud said, a cigar is just a cigar, though here it's also a promotional sample. Toll-free 800 numbers have made sampling nearly instantaneous and painless for consumers. With this ad, Consolidated Cigar shows that it is just a few button presses away from putting its H. Upmann brand into your hands. The World Wide Web takes 800 numbers a step further, making it possible for any company, anywhere, to capture requests for product samples at virtually no cost (and no delay). But commerce still balks at borders (some offers can't be made, depending on jurisdiction), and, in the case of tobacco, it may take a return phone call to verify that an adult is asking for this stogie. www.hupmann.com

market share in specific geographic areas. Kraft recently put its sampling program "on-tour" and handed out free samples of items from its existing product lines at Vince Gill concert sites.[27]

Five techniques are used in sampling. **In-store sampling** is popular for food products and cosmetics. This is a preferred technique for many marketers because the consumer is at the point of purchase and may be swayed by a direct encounter with the brand. Increasingly, in-store demonstrators are handing out coupons as well as samples. **Door-to-door sampling** is extremely expensive because of labor costs, but it can be effective if the marketer has information that locates the target segment in a well-defined geographic area. Some firms enlist the services of newspaper delivery people, who pack the sample with daily or Sunday newspapers as a way of reducing distribution costs. **Mail sampling** allows samples to be delivered through the postal service. Again, the value here is that certain zip-code markets can be targeted. A drawback is that the sample must be small to be economically feasible. Specialty-sampling firms, such as Alternative Postal Delivery, provide targeted geodemographic door-to-door distribution as an alternative to the postal service.

On-package sampling, a technique in which the sample item is attached to another product package, is useful for brands targeted to current customers. Attaching a small bottle of Ivory conditioner with a regular-sized container of Ivory shampoo is a logical sampling strategy. Finally, **mobile sampling** is carried out by logo-emblazoned vehicles that dispense samples, coupons, and premiums to consumers at malls, shopping centers, fairgrounds, and recreational areas. Marketers at Pennzoil are finding that intercepting prospects while they're at play or engaged in activities that complement product use is a good way to influence awareness, use, and preference.[28]

Of course, sampling has its critics. Unless the product has a clear value and benefit over the competition, simple trial of the product is unlikely to persuade a consumer to switch brands. This is especially true for convenience goods because consumers perceive a high degree of similarity among brands, even after trying them. The perception of benefit and superiority may have to be developed through advertising in combination with sampling. In addition, sampling is expensive. This is especially true in cases where a sufficient quantity of a product, such as shampoo or laundry detergent, must be given away for a consumer to truly appreciate a brand's values. Finally, sampling can be a very imprecise process. Despite the emergence of special agencies to handle sampling programs, a firm can never completely ensure that the product is reaching the targeted audience.

Trial offers have the same goal as sampling—to induce consumer trial use of a brand—but they are used for more expensive items. Exercise equipment, appliances, watches, hand tools, and consumer electronics are typical of items offered on a trial basis. Exhibit 18.10 shows an offer, aimed at sales managers, to try a $199 package of

27.   Kate Fitzgerald, "Samples Go on Tour," *Advertising Age,* May 5, 1997, 37.
28.   Jean Halliday, "Pennzoil Hits Road with Promotion for New Motor Oil," *Advertising Age,* June 15, 1998, 32.

EXHIBIT 18.10

For expensive products such as exercise equipment or computer software, sampling is impractical. The familiar alternative is the 30-day, risk-free trial offer. www.formulanet.com/

computer software free for a limited time. Trials are offered for as little as 1 day to as long as 90 days. The expense to the firm, of course, can be formidable. Segments chosen for this promotional device must have high sales potential.

Brand (Product) Placement. Brand placement (often erroneously referred to as product placement) is the sales promotion technique of getting a marketer's brand featured in movies and television shows. The use of a brand by actors and actresses or the mere association of a brand with a popular film or television show can create a positive image or, occasionally, a demonstrated sales impact for a brand. Marketers and advertisers used to think brand placements affected only consumers' perceptions of a brand, much like advertising. But recent brand placements have shown that the technique can have a sales impact like a traditional sales promotion. For example, consider these results:

- When British agent 007, James Bond, switched from his traditional Aston-Martin sports car to the new BMW Z3, a brand placement in the Bond film *Goldeneye,* along with a tightly coordinated dealer promotion program, resulted in 6000 pre-delivery orders for the Z3.
- Sales of Nike sneakers and apparel jumped after the release of the hit movie *Forrest Gump.* The film featured the star Tom Hanks getting a pair of Nike running shoes as a gift, which his character, Gump, believes is "the best gift anyone could get in the whole wide world." Later in the film, Gump wears a Nike T-shirt during a cross-country run.
- When Jennifer Gray danced in retro oxford sneakers in the film *Dirty Dancing,* the shoe's manufacturer, Keds, saw a huge increase in sales.
- One of the biggest beneficiaries of a product placement was Bausch and Lomb. Tom Cruise wore distinctive Bausch and Lomb Ray-Ban sunglasses in the film *Risky Business,* and the glasses were featured on the movie poster as well. Ray-Ban sales rocketed to all-time highs after the film's release.[29]

The newfound power of brand placement has been surprising, but the process is relatively simple. Once a movie studio or television production team approves a script and schedules production, placement specialists, either in-house or working for specialty agencies, go to work. They send the script to targeted companies in an effort to sell the placement opportunities. If a company agrees, then little more is involved than having the brand sent to the studio for inclusion in the film or program. Marketers such as BMW and Coke play a more formative role, but they are exceptions.

Brand placement, like any other communications effort, shows varying results. If the brand name is spoken aloud, such as Gene Hackman telling Tom Cruise to help himself to a Red Stripe beer during the film *The Firm,* the impact can be dramatic. Similarly, prominent use by a celebrity of a featured brand, such as Mel Gibson clearly drinking a Dr. Pepper or Dennis Quaid eating at McDonald's, can achieve 40 to 50 percent recognition within an audience. Less obvious placements, such as when Bond

---

29. Blair R. Fischer, "Making Your Product the Star Attraction," *PROMO Magazine,* July 1996, 58.

smashes a car into a Heineken beer truck—referred to as background placements—are considered by some a waste of money.[30]

Rebates. Rebates started in the mid-1970s when auto dealers feared price freezes would be imposed by the government as a means to curb inflation. Auto dealers discovered that a rebate on the purchase price of a car was a way around the impending freeze. The price freeze never materialized, but the rebate survived as a sales promotion technique. A **rebate** is a money-back offer requiring a *buyer* to mail in a form requesting the money back from the manufacturer, rather than the *retailer* (as in couponing). The rebate technique has been refined over the years and is now used by a wide variety of marketers. A recent survey of packaged goods companies revealed that 76 percent had used a money-back offer.[31] Rebates are particularly well suited to increasing the quantity purchased by consumers, so rebates are commonly tied to multiple purchases.

Another reason for the popularity of rebates is that few consumers take advantage of the rebate offer after buying a brand.[32] The best estimate of consumer redemption of rebate offers by the research firm Market Growth Resources is that only 5 to 10 percent of buyers ever bother to fill out and then mail in the rebate request.

EXHIBIT 18.11

The use of frequency programs can help build a sustained customer base. The reference to the frequency program in this Marriott ad closely ties the sales promotion to the advertising campaign. www.marriott.com

Frequency Programs. In recent years, one of the most popular sales promotion techniques among consumers has been frequency programs. **Frequency programs**, also referred to as *continuity programs,* offer consumers discounts or free product rewards for repeat purchase or patronage of the same brand or company. These programs were pioneered by airline companies. Frequent-flyer programs such as Delta Air Lines' SkyMiles, frequent-stay programs such as Marriott's Honored Guest Award program, and frequent-renter programs such as Hertz's #1 Club are examples of such loyalty-building activities. But frequency programs are not reserved for big national airline and auto-rental chains. Chart House Enterprises, a chain of 65 upscale restaurants, successfully launched a frequency program for diners, who earned points for every dollar spent. Frequent diners were issued "passports," which were stamped with each visit. Within two years, the program had more than 300,000 members.[33] Exhibit 18.11 features Marriott's frequency program.

Event Sponsorship. When a firm sponsors or co-sponsors an event, such as an auto race, charity marathon, or rock concert, the brand featured in the event immediately gains a credibility with the event audience. The audience attending (or participating) in an event already has a positive attitude and affinity for the context—they chose to attend or participate voluntarily. When this audience encounters a brand in this very favorable reception environment, the brand benefits from the already favorable audience attitude.

30. "Motion Pictures, Moving Brands," *PROMO Magazine,* January 1996, 44.

31. William M. Buckeley, "Rebates' Secret Appeal to Manufacturers: Few Consumers Actually Redeem Them," *Wall Street Journal,* February 10, 1998, B1.

32. Ibid.

33. Kerry J. Smith, "Building a Winning Frequency Program—The Hard Way," *PROMO Magazine,* December 1995, 36.

Exhibit 18.12 shows an ad announcing Mountain Dew's sponsorship of popular snowboarding events. Sponsorship has grown to be the fifth most popular form of promotion used by U.S. firms, with about $6 billion invested annually.[34] But do not conclude that sponsorships are good only in the United States. The Global Issues box on page 583 shows that firms have found this sales promotion technique effective as a global strategy as well.

Sales Promotion Directed at the Trade.

Sales promotions directed at members of the trade—wholesalers, distributors, and retailers—are designed to stimulate demand in the short term and help push the product through the distribution channel. Effective trade promotions can generate enthusiasm for a product and contribute positively to the loyalty distributors show for a brand. With the massive proliferation of new brands and brand extensions, manufacturers need to stimulate enthusiasm and loyalty among members of the trade.

WEB SIGHTING

THE MOUNTAIN DEW SNOWBOARD FESTIVAL.
2 DAYS OF LETTING YOUR INNER CHILD RUN AMUCK.
Demo gear from 50 of the coolest companies to ever attack the slopes. Plus free lessons, tunes and plenty of Dew. So whip out to the mountains and show Jack Frost who runs the hill.

| Dec. 13-14 Ski Windham, NY | Jan. 10-11 Winter Park, CO | Jan. 24-25 Snowbird Ski Resort, UT | Jan. 31-Feb. 1 Heavenly Ski Resort, CA | Feb. 7-8 Snow Valley, CA |

EXHIBIT 18.12

Event sponsorship exposes a company to an audience of its choice. Here, PepsiCo (www.pepsiworld.com) is promoting its Mountain Dew brand soft drink to a Generation X audience, pitching its product as the sort of radical beverage that goes with extreme sports. (One suspects that zero Gen Xers would recall an older Mountain Dew campaign image of a hillbilly moonshiner.) Many events are very strongly associated with certain industries and product categories (e.g., NASCAR goes with smokeless tobacco, and the more upscale Virginia Slims sponsors tennis). Coca Cola recently introduced Surge (www.surge.com) to compete head-to-head with Mountain Dew in the noncola market; no doubt the "Surge X-treme Expo!" will soon follow.

Objectives for Trade Promotions.

As in the consumer market, trade-market sales promotions should be undertaken with specific objectives in mind. Four primary objectives can be identified for these promotions:

- *Obtain initial distribution.* Because of the proliferation of brands in the consumer market, there is fierce competition for shelf space. Sales promotion incentives can help a firm gain initial distribution and shelf placement. Like consumers, members of the trade need a reason to choose one brand over another when it comes to allocating shelf space. A well-conceived promotion incentive may sway them.
- Bob's Candies, a small family-owned business in Albany, Georgia, is the largest candy cane manufacturer in the United States. But Bob's old-fashioned candy was having trouble keeping distributors. To reverse the trend, Bob's designed a new name, logo, and packaging for the candy canes. Then, each scheduled attendee at the All-Candy Expo trade show in Chicago was mailed three strategically timed postcards with the teaser question "Wanna Be Striped?" The mailing got a 25 percent response rate, and booth visitations at the trade show were a huge success.[35]
- *Increase order size.* One of the struggles in the channel of distribution is over the location of inventory. Manufacturers prefer that members of the trade maintain large inventories so the manufacturer can reduce inventory-carrying costs. Similarly, members of the trade would rather make frequent, small orders and carry little inventory. Sales promotion techniques can encourage wholesalers and retailers to order in large quantities, thus shifting the inventory burden to the channel.

34. "1998 Annual Report of the Sponsorship Industry," S5.
35. Lee Duffey, "Sweet Talk: Promotions Position Candy Company," *Marketing News,* March 30, 1998, 11.

• *Encourage cooperation with consumer-market sales promotions.* It does a manufacturer little good to initiate a sales promotion in the consumer market if there is little cooperation in the channel. Wholesalers may need to maintain larger inventories, and retailers may need to provide special displays or handling during consumer-market sales promotions. To achieve synergy, marketers often run trade promotions simultaneously with consumer promotions.

GLOBAL ISSUES

POLAROID SHEDS NEW LIGHT ON THE SPICE GIRLS

When Polaroid embarked on the worldwide introduction of one of its few on-camera products—a flat, disposable flashlight dubbed PolaPulse—the company invested $10 million in specially prepared 15-second television spots to run in 16 countries including the United States, United Kingdom, Germany, France, Australia, and Spain. Polaroid relied on the pan-European ad agency Bartle Bogle Hegarty in London to prepare the ads.

Such a creative preparation and placement strategy is not unusual. What is unusual is the rest of Polaroid's promotional program for the new product. Beyond the television spots, the PolaPulse will also get wide exposure through sales and giveaways at Spice Girls concerts around the world, where the flashlight will be sold as "Spice Lights." To help ease the new product into the world of events, the company also plans running on-screen spots in movie theaters both in the United States and abroad. This strategy is designed to ultimately encourage the sale of the lights in movie theaters as well.

The PolaPulse has a patented ultrathin battery with a shelf life of five years. This is one of the first forays by Polaroid outside the instant camera market using its existing technology. Because of the importance of the launch, the firm wanted to go beyond merely using television spots and branch out into not only event sponsorship of the Spice Girls tours, but also sales outside the norm at the events.

Source: Carol Krol, "Polaroid Takes to Events in Global Launch of Flashlight," *Advertising Age,* June 30, 1997, 8.

• *Increase store traffic.* Retailers can increase store traffic through special promotions or events. Door-prize drawings, parking-lot sales, or live radio broadcasts from the store are common sales promotion traffic builders. Burger King has become a leader in building traffic at its 6,500 outlets with special promotions tied to Disney movie debuts. Beginning in 1991 with a *Beauty and the Beast* tie-in promotion, Burger King has set records for generating store traffic with premium giveaways. The *Pocahontas* campaign distributed 55 million toys and glasses. Most recently, a promotion tie-in with Disney's huge success *Toy Story* resulted in 50 million toys, based on the film's characters, being given away in $1.99 Kid Meals.[36]

Trade-Market Sales Promotion Techniques.

When marketers devise incentives to encourage purchases by members of the trade, they are executing a **push strategy**; that is, sales promotions directed at the trade help push a product into the distribution channel until it ultimately reaches consumers. The sales promotion techniques used with the trade are point-of-purchase displays, incentives, allowances, trade shows, sales training programs, and cooperative advertising.

Point-of-Purchase Displays. Product displays and information sheets are useful in reaching the consumer at the point of purchase and often encourage retailers to support one's brand. P-O-P promotions can help win precious shelf space and exposure in a retail setting. From a retailer's perspective, a P-O-P display should be designed to draw attention to a brand, increase turnover, and possibly distribute coupons or sweepstakes entry forms. Exhibit 18.13 shows a typical P-O-P display. Advertisers invested $13 billion in P-O-P materials in 1997. This is more than was spent on either magazine or radio advertising.[37]

36. Editors' Special Report, "Having It Their Way," *PROMO Magazine,* December 1995, 79–80.
37. "1998 Annual Report of the Promotion Industry," S5.

EXHIBIT 18.13

As noted by Exhibit 18.5, the point of purchase is an important competitive battleground. Here we see an excellent illustration of one marketer's effort to take control of that battleground.
www.gillette.com/

Incentives. Incentives to members of the trade include a variety of tactics not unlike those used in the consumer market. Awards in the form of travel, gifts, or cash bonuses for reaching targeted sales levels can induce retailers and wholesalers to give a firm's brand added attention. The incentive does not have to be large or expensive to be effective. Weiser Lock offered its dealers a Swiss Army knife with every dozen cases of locks ordered. The program was a huge success. A follow-up promotion featuring a Swiss Army watch was an even bigger hit.

One risk with incentive programs for the trade is that salespeople can be so motivated to win an award that they may try to sell the brand to every customer, whether it fits that customer's needs or not. Also, a firm must carefully manage such programs to minimize ethical dilemmas. An incentive technique can look like a bribe unless it is carried out in a highly structured and open fashion.

Allowances. Various forms of allowances are offered to retailers and wholesalers with the purpose of increasing the attention given to a firm's brands. **Merchandise allowances**, in the form of free products packed with regular shipments, are payments to the trade for setting up and maintaining displays. The payments are typically far less than manufacturers would have to spend to maintain the displays themselves. Shelf space has become so highly demanded, especially in supermarkets, that manufacturers are making direct cash payments, known as **slotting fees**, to induce food chains to stock an item. The proliferation of new products has made shelf space such a precious commodity that these fees now run in the hundreds of thousands of dollars per product.

Trade Shows. Trade shows are events where several related products from many manufacturers are displayed and demonstrated to members of the trade. Company representatives are on hand to explain the products and perhaps make an important contact for the sales force. The use of trade shows must be carefully coordinated and can be an important part of trade-oriented promotional programs. Trade shows can be critically important to a small firm that cannot afford advertising and has a sales staff too small to reach all its potential customers. Through the trade-show route, salespeople can make far more contacts than would be possible with direct sales calls.

James Bond's
Choice

Seamaster Professional
Automatic chronometer.
Water-resistant to 300m/1000ft.
OMEGA — Swiss made since 1848.

007
Tomorrow Never Dies

Fine Jewelry & Jewel Gallery
LIBERTY HOUSE
Honolulu, HI

Ω
OMEGA

EXHIBIT 18.14

Here again we see an example of cooperation between a manufacturer and retailers. Here Omega is featuring not only the brand placement of the watch in a James Bond movie, but also the co-op advertising effort of a Hawaiian retailer. www.omega.ch/

Sales-Training Programs. An increasingly popular trade promotion is to provide training for retail store personnel. This method is used for consumer durables and specialty goods, such as personal computers, home theater systems, heating and cooling systems, security systems, and exercise equipment. The increased complexity of these products has made it important for manufacturers to ensure that the proper factual information and persuasive themes are reaching consumers at the point of purchase. For personnel at large retail stores, manufacturers can hold special classes that feature product information, demonstrations, and training about sales techniques.

Another popular method for getting sales-training information to retailers is the use of videotapes and brochures. Manufacturers can also send sales trainers into retail stores to work side by side with store personnel. This is a costly method, but it can be very effective because of the one-on-one attention it provides.

Cooperative Advertising. Cooperative advertising as a trade promotion technique is referred to as **vertical cooperative advertising**. (Such efforts are also called *vendor co-op programs*.) Manufacturers try to control the content of this co-op advertising in two ways. They may set strict specifications for the size and content of the ad and then ask for verification that such specifications have been met. Alternatively, manufacturers may send the template for an ad, into which retailers merely insert the names and locations of their stores. Just such an ad is featured in Exhibit 18.14. Notice that the James Bond and Omega watch components are national with the co-op sponsorship of the Hawaiian retailer highlighted in the lower right.

The Risks of Sales Promotion. Sales promotion can be used to pursue important sales objectives. As we have seen, there are a wide range of sales promotion options for both the consumer and trade markets. But there are also significant risks associated with sales promotion, and these risks must be carefully considered.

Creating a Price Orientation. Since most sales promotions rely on some sort of price incentive or giveaway, a firm runs the risk of having its brand perceived as cheap, with no real value or benefits beyond low price. Creating this perception in the market contradicts the concept of integrated marketing communication. If advertising messages highlight the value and benefit of a brand only to be contradicted by a price emphasis in sales promotions, then a confusing signal is being sent to the market.

Borrowing from Future Sales. Management must admit that sales promotions are typically short-term tactics designed to reduce inventories, increase cash flow, or show periodic boosts in market share. The downside is that a firm may simply be borrowing from future

sales. Consumers or trade buyers who would have purchased the brand anyway may be motivated to stock up at the lower price. This results in reduced sales during the next few time periods of measurement. This can play havoc with the measurement and evaluation of the effect of advertising campaigns or other image-building communications. If consumers are responding to sales promotions, it may be impossible to tease out the effects of advertising.

Alienating Customers. When a firm relies heavily on sweepstakes or frequency programs to build loyalty among customers, particularly their best customers, there is the risk of alienating these customers with any change in the program. Airlines suffered just such a fate when they tried to adjust the mileage levels needed for awards in their frequent-flyer programs. Ultimately, many of the airlines had to give concessions to their most frequent flyers as a conciliatory gesture.

Time and Expense. Sales promotions are both costly and time-consuming. The process is time-consuming for the marketer and the retailer in terms of handling promotional materials and protecting against fraud and waste in the process. As we have seen in recent years, funds allocated to sales promotions are taking dollars away from advertising. Advertising is a long-term, franchise-building process that should not be compromised for short-term gains.

Legal Considerations. With the increasing popularity of sales promotions, particularly contests and premiums, there has been an increase in legal scrutiny at both the federal and state levels. Legal experts recommend that before initiating promotions that use coupons, games, sweepstakes, and contests, a firm check into lottery laws, copyright laws, state and federal trademark laws, prize notification laws, right of privacy laws, tax laws, and FTC and FCC regulations.[38] The best advice for staying out of legal trouble with sales promotions is to carefully and clearly state the rules and conditions related to the program so that consumers are fully informed.

The Coordination Challenge—
IMC and Sales Promotion.
There is an allure to sales promotion that must be put into perspective. Sales promotions can make things happen—quickly. While managers often find the immediacy of sales promotion valuable, particularly in meeting quarterly sales goals, sales promotions are rarely a viable means of long-term success. But when used properly, sales promotions can be an important element in a well-conceived IMC campaign. Key to their proper use is coordinating the message emphasis and the placement of sales promotions with the advertising effort. When advertising and sales promotion are well coordinated, the impact of each is enhanced—a classic case of synergy.

Message Coordination. The typical sales promotion should either attract attention to a brand or offer consumers and the trade greater value: reduced price, more product, or the chance to win a prize or an award. In turn, this focused attention and extra value act as an incentive to choose the promoted brand over other brands. One of the coordination problems this presents is that advertising messages, designed to build long-term loyalty, may not seem totally consistent with the extra-value signal of the sales promotion.

38. Maxine S. Lans, "Legal Hurdles Big Part of Promotions Game," *Marketing News,* October 24, 1994, 15.

This is the classic problem that advertisers face in coordinating sales promotion with an advertising campaign. First, advertising messages tout brand features or emotional attractions. Then, the next contact a consumer may have with the brand is an insert in the Sunday paper offering a cents-off coupon. These mixed signals can be damaging for a brand.

Increasing the coordination between advertising and various sales promotion efforts requires only the most basic planning. First, when different agencies are involved in preparing sales promotion materials and advertising materials, those agencies need to be kept informed by the advertiser regarding the maintenance of a desired theme. Second, simple techniques can be used to carry a coordinated theme between promotional tools. The use of logos, slogans, visual imagery, or spokespersons can create a consistent presentation. As illustrated in Exhibit 18.15, even if advertising and sales promotion pursue different purposes, the look and feel of both efforts may be coordinated. The more the theme of a promotion can be tied directly to the advertising campaign, the more impact these messages will generally have on the consumer.

Media Coordination. Another key in coordination involves timing. Remember that the success of a sales promotion depends on the consumer believing that the chance to save money or receive more of a product represents enhanced value. If the consumer is not aware of a brand and its features and benefits, and does not perceive the brand as a worthy item, then there will be no basis for perceiving value—discounted or not. This means that appropriate advertising should precede price-oriented sales promotions for them to be effective. The right advertising can create an image for a brand that is appropriate for a promotional offer. Then, when consumers are presented with a sales promotion, the offer will impress the consumer as an opportunity to acquire superior value.

EXHIBIT 18.15

One simple principle for enhancing the impact of any sales promotion is to feature logos or visual imagery common in the brand's advertising. These examples from Progresso illustrate the common-look principle. www.pillsbury.com/main/brands/progresso.html

Conclusions from Recent Research.

The synergy theme prominent in the preceding discussion is not just a matter of speculation. Recent research using single-source data generated by A. C. Nielsen reaffirms many of the primary points of this chapter.[39] John Philip Jones has reported the major conclusions of this research:

- The short-term productivity of promotions working alone is much more dramatic than that of advertising. Promotions that involve price incentives on average yield a 1.8 percent increase in sales for each 1 percent price reduction. A 1 percent increase in advertising yields just a 0.2 percent sales increase on average.
- The average cost of a 1 percent reduction in price is always far greater than the cost of a 1 percent increase in advertising. Thus, more often than not, sales promotions featuring price incentives are actually unprofitable in the short term.
- It is rare that a sales promotion generates a long-term effect. Hence, there are no long-term revenues to offset the high cost of promotions in the short run. Successful advertising is much more likely to yield a profitable return over the long run, even though its impact on short-run sales may be modest.
- While both advertising and sales promotions may be expected to affect sales in the short run, the evidence suggests that the most powerful effects come from a combination of the two. The impact of advertising and promotions working together is dramatically greater than the sum of each sales stimulus working by itself.
- According to Jones, "The strong synergy that can be generated between advertising and promotions working together points very clearly to the need to integrate the planning and execution of both types of activity: the strategy of Integrated Marketing Communications."[40]

SUMMARY

Explain the popularity of and rationale for different forms of sales promotions.

Sales promotions use diverse incentives to motivate action on the part of consumers or distributors. They serve different purposes than does mass media advertising, and for some companies, sales promotions receive substantially more funding than does mass media advertising. The growing dependence on these promotions can be attributed to the heavy pressures placed on marketing managers to account for their spending and meet sales objectives in short time frames. Deal-prone shoppers, brand proliferation, the increasing power of large retailers, and media clutter have also contributed to the rising popularity of sales promotion.

Describe the purposes and characteristics of sales promotions directed at consumers.

Sales promotions directed at consumers can serve various goals. For example, they can be employed as means to

stimulate trial, repeat, or large-quantity purchases. They are especially important tools for introducing new brands or for reacting to a competitor's advances. Coupons, price-off deals, and premiums provide obvious incentives for purchase. Contests, sweepstakes, and product placements can be excellent devices for stimulating brand interest. A variety of sampling techniques are available to get a product into the hands of the target audience. Rebates and frequency programs provide rewards for repeat purchase.

Describe the purposes and characteristics of sales promotions directed at the trade.

Sales promotions directed at the trade can also serve multiple objectives. They are a necessity in obtaining initial distribution of a new brand. For established brands, they can be a means to increase distributors' order quantities or obtain retailers' cooperation in implementing a consumer-directed promotion. P-O-P displays can be an excellent tool for gaining preferred display space in a retail setting. Incentives and allowances can be offered to distributors to

39. John Philip Jones, *When Ads Work* (New York: Lexington Books, 1995).
40. Ibid., 56.

motivate support for a brand. Trade shows, sales training, and cooperative advertising programs are additional devices for effecting retailer support.

🔵 Discuss the risks and coordination issues associated with sales promotion.

There are important risks associated with heavy reliance on sales promotion. Offering constant deals for a brand is a good way to erode brand equity, and it may simply be borrowing sales from a future time period. Constant deals can also create a customer mindset that leads consumers to abandon a brand as soon as a deal is retracted. Sales promotions are expensive to administer and fraught with legal complications. Sales promotions yield their most positive results when carefully integrated with the overall advertising plan.

KEY TERMS

sales promotion (569)
consumer-market sales promotion (569)
trade-market sales promotion (569)
coupon (575)
price-off deal (577)
premiums (577)
free premium (577)
self-liquidating premium (577)
contest (577)
sweepstakes (578)
sampling (578)
in-store sampling (579)
door-to-door sampling (579)

mail sampling (579)
on-package sampling (579)
mobile sampling (579)
trial offers (579)
brand placement (580)
rebate (581)
frequency programs (581)
push strategy (583)
merchandise allowances (584)
slotting fees (584)
trade shows (585)
vertical cooperative advertising (586)

QUESTIONS FOR REVIEW AND CRITICAL THINKING

1. Compare and contrast sales promotion and mass media advertising as marketing tools. In what ways do the strengths of one make up for the limitations of the other? What specific characteristics of sales promotions account for the high levels of expenditures that have been allocated to them in recent years?

2. What is brand proliferation and why is it occurring? Why do consumer sales promotions become more commonplace in the face of rampant brand proliferation? Why do trade sales promotions become more frequent when there is excessive brand proliferation?

3. Pull all the preprinted and free-standing inserts from the most recent edition of your Sunday newspaper. From them find an example of each of these consumer-market sales promotions: coupon, free premium, self-liquidating premium, contest, sweepstakes, and trial offer.

4. In developing an advertising plan, synergy may be achieved through careful coordination of individual elements. Give an example of how mass media advertising might be used with on-package sampling to effect a positive synergy. Give an example of how event sponsorship might be used with mobile sampling to achieve a positive synergy.

5.   Consumers often rationalize their purchase of a new product with a statement such as, "I bought it because I had a 50-cent coupon and our grocery was doubling all manufacturers' coupons this week." What are the prospects that such a consumer will emerge as a loyal user of the product? What must happen if he or she is to become loyal?

6.   Early in the chapter, it was suggested that large retailers like Wal-Mart are assuming greater power in today's marketplace. What factors contribute to retailers' increasing power? Explain the connection between merchandise allowances and slotting fees and the growth in retailer power.

7.   In your opinion, are ethical dilemmas more likely to arise with sales promotions directed at the consumer or at the trade? What specific forms of consumer or trade promotions seem most likely to involve or create ethical dilemmas?

8.   Many marketers argue that consumer sales promotions do not work unless a great deal of time and money are first invested in advertising. What logic might you offer to support this contention? Why would advertising be required to make a sales promotion work?

EXPERIENTIAL EXERCISES

1.   Buy a Sunday newspaper. Make a list of the sales promotions offered by manufacturers, and attach a few examples. Make a second list of the sales promotions offered by retailers, and attach a few examples. Are there any other types of organizations that use sales promotion offers within the newspaper?

2.   Next time you go to a grocery store, record the number of sales promotion techniques you encounter. There should be at least three different sales promotions going on in any grocery store at any point in time.

USING THE INTERNET

Sales promotions attempt to motivate consumers to take action. Some Web sites encourage people to visit and use what the site has to offer through promotions. Visit the following sites:

www.couponpages.com

www.pch.com

www.shareware.com

For each site, answer the following questions:

1. What type of promotional tool is the site using?

2. Is the promotion easy to understand? What does it offer?

3. How much effort on your part does the promotion require?

4. What action does the promotion encourage?

5. Is the promotion effective?

The Internet's origins as a sort of "gift economy," where its builders freely shared basic software and academic sources of content were offered without thought of generating revenue, has had a strong influence on "what works" in Internet commerce. Numerous business models are based on distributing free software or services, deriving revenues in other ways. Some services, such as Tripod (www.tripod.com) and GeoCities (www.geocities.com), offer consumers free Web pages.

1. How do these services make use of advertising to generate revenue?

Qualcomm's Eudora (www.eudora.com) is one of the Internet's best known E-mail products.

2. How does Qualcomm structure its product and service offerings to produce (eventually) revenue from paying customers?

HotMail (www.hotmail.com) demonstrated the wisdom of giving away E-mail for free, when the start-up company was bought by Microsoft for an estimated several hundred million dollars.

3. What sort of people would find HotMail a useful service?

4. What products and services might be best to advertise to HotMail customers?

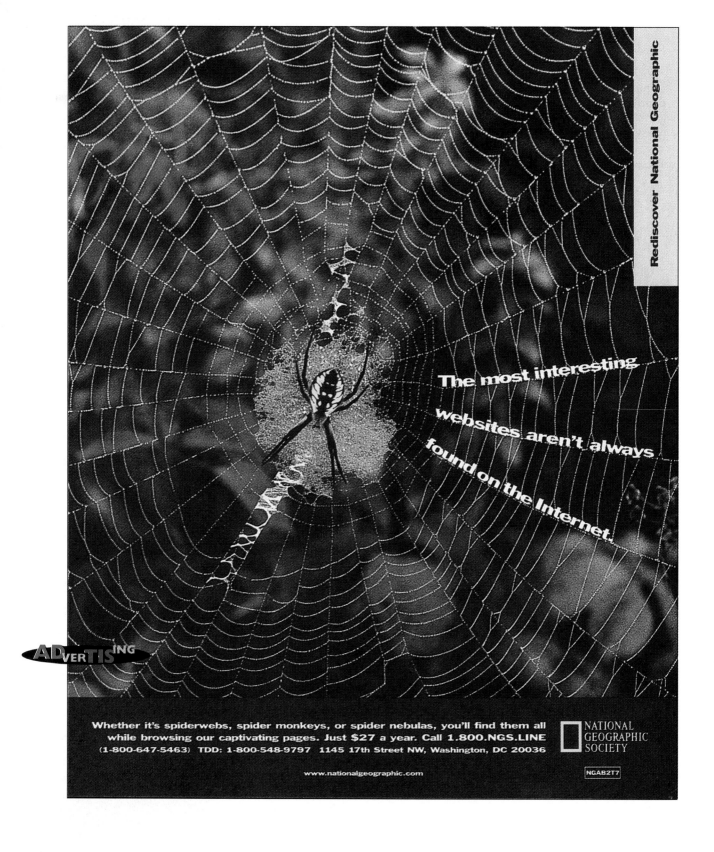

CHAPTER 19

After reading and thinking about this chapter, you will be able to do the following:

◀▶ Identify the three primary purposes served by and explain the growing popularity of direct marketing.

◀▶ Distinguish a mailing list from a marketing database and review the many applications of each.

◀▶ Describe the prominent media used by direct marketers in delivering their messages to the customer.

◀▶ Articulate the added challenge created by direct marketing for achieving integrated marketing communication.

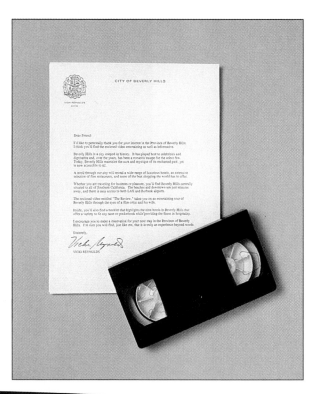

EXHIBIT 19.1

In direct marketing, it is common to seek a dialogue with the target customer. In this example, the mayor pursues that dialogue with a letter and video about her "Province of Beverly Hills."
www.ci.beverly-hills.ca.us/

Book clubs, cable TV, magazines, software, video-tapes, credit cards, life insurance, kitchen knives, and Tony Bennett CDs—ads for these and many other products and services fill the mailboxes of America with an endless stream of enticements and special offers. But did you get the letter from the mayor of Beverly Hills, promoting the virtues of her fair city for your next vacation? If you are part of the mayor's target segment, then you received her letter espousing the magic of Beverly Hills:

I think one of the most distinctive aspects of Beverly Hills is its atmosphere: the welcome comfort of a small community, combined with the dynamic energy of a big city. Beverly Hills plays host to the finest shopping and dining the world has to offer—all within walking distance from your hotel. And to top it off, the city is bathed in almost year-round sunshine.

The mayor closed with this promise about the magic of Beverly Hills: "I'm sure you will find that Beverly Hills is more than a city. It is a feeling."[1]

More than 12 million tourists visit Beverly Hills each year and spend about $60 million just in the city's elegant hotels.[2] Thus it is easy to understand that the mayor would have a marketing budget of about $1.5 million to get her message out to affluent travelers who might be considering Southern California as a vacation destination. Additionally, as is the case in many direct-marketing campaigns these days, the mayor's letter contains an offer that allows readers to quickly learn more about the product she is selling.[3] Her letter offers a free videotape titled *The Review,* which takes viewers on a leisurely tour around town as seen through the eyes of a film critic and his wife. This tape, of course, turns out to be the Beverly Hills highlight package—the posh shops on Rodeo Drive, gourmet restaurants, exclusive homes and gardens, and plush hotel accommodations. You know—the lifestyles of the rich and famous. Beauty, glamour, prestige, and security are the selling points that the mayor communicates with the videotape.

Do you remember receiving such a letter (see Exhibit 19.1) from the mayor of Beverly Hills? Probably not, we would guess, unless you have a very wealthy aunt, or one incredible part-time job. The mayor's direct mail campaign was precisely targeted. Her letter with its offer of the free video was mailed to just 100,000 households with incomes in excess of $100,000. This direct mail campaign was supplemented with ads in elite magazines such as *Condé Nast Traveler* and *The New Yorker.* The mayor's marketing plan appears sound, but you've got to wonder—did she sign all those letters herself?

The Evolution of Direct Marketing.
Like the mayor of Beverly Hills, marketers in all types of organizations large and small are allocating larger chunks of their budgets to direct-marketing activities. In this chapter we will examine the growing field of direct marketing and explain how it may be used to both complement and supplant other forms of advertising. Carefully coordinated advertising campaigns and

1.   Laura Loro, "Beverly Hills' Inviting Idea," *Advertising Age,* March 20, 1995, 24.
2.   Ibid.
3.   Junu Bryan Kim, "Marketing with Video," *Advertising Age,* May 22, 1995, S1.

direct-marketing programs produce the synergy that spells the difference between success and failure in the marketplace. Before we examine the evolution of direct marketing and look at the many reasons for its growing popularity, we need a better appreciation for what people mean when they use the phrase *direct marketing*. The "official" definition of direct marketing from the Direct Marketing Association (DMA) provides a starting point:

Direct marketing *is an interactive system of marketing which uses one or more advertising media to effect a measurable response and/or transaction at any location.*[4]

When examined piece by piece, this definition furnishes an excellent basis for understanding the scope of direct marketing.[5]

Direct marketing is interactive in that the marketer is attempting to develop an ongoing dialogue with the customer. Direct-marketing programs are commonly planned with the notion that one contact will lead to another and then another, so that the marketer's message can become more focused and refined with each interaction. In the Beverly Hills example, the mayor started the dialogue with her letter to 100,000 potential customers, who were offered a chance to respond by requesting the *Review* videotape. Those requesting the video would go on the mayor's hot-prospect list; hot prospects might be targeted for future mailings or even telephone contacts. The mayor might also turn over the hot-prospect list to local hotels or restaurants to let them furnish information requested by the customer.

The DMA's definition also notes that multiple media can be used in direct-marketing programs. This is an important point for two reasons. First, we do not want to equate direct mail and direct marketing. Any media can be used in executing direct-marketing programs, not just the mail. Second, as we have noted before, a combination of media is likely to be more effective than any one medium used by itself.

Another key aspect of direct-marketing programs is that they almost always are designed to produce some form of immediate, measurable response.[6] In the mayor's case, the immediate response to her letter could be measured by how many requests for the videotape were received. Direct-marketing programs may also be designed to produce an immediate sale. The customer might be asked to return an order form with $49.99 to get a copy of *Zelda 64* by Nintendo, or to call an 800 number with a credit card handy to get 22 timeless hits on a CD called *The Very Best of Tony Bennett*. Because of this emphasis on immediate response, direct marketers are always in a position to judge the effectiveness of a particular program. As we shall see, this ability to gauge the immediate impact of a program has great appeal to marketers.

The final phrase of the DMA's definition notes that a direct-marketing transaction can take place anywhere. The key idea here is that customers do not have to make a trip to a retail store for a direct-marketing program to work. Follow-ups can be made by mail, over the telephone, on the Internet, or via an express delivery service. It is probably apparent that pure direct marketers such as Amazon.com or CDnow.com pose a real threat to those who have made their living operating a traditional retail store.[7]

Direct Marketing—A Look Back.
From Johannes Gutenberg to Benjamin Franklin to Richard Sears, Alvah Roebuck, and Lillian Vernon, the evolution of direct marketing has involved some of the great pioneers in business. As Exhibit 19.2 shows, the practice of direct marketing today is shaped by the successes of many notable mail-order companies and catalog merchandisers.[8] Among these, none is more exemplary than L. L.

---

4.   Bob Stone, *Successful Direct Marketing Methods* (Lincolnwood, Ill.: NTC Business Books, 1994), 5.
5.   The discussion to follow builds on that of Stone, *Successful Direct Marketing Methods*, op. cit.
6.   Don E. Schultz and Paul Wang, "Real World Results," *Marketing Tools,* April/May 1994, 40–47.
7.   Patrick M. Reilly, "In the Age of the Web, a Book Chain Flounders," *Wall Street Journal*, February 22, 1999, B1, B4.
8.   See Edward Nash, "The Roots of Direct Marketing," *Direct Marketing Magazine,* February 1995, 38–40; Patricia Seremet, "The Queen of the Catalog: Lillian Vernon, Entrepreneur," *Marketing News,* June 8, 1998, 17.

EXHIBIT 19.2

Direct-marketing milestones.

c. 1450	Johannes Gutenberg invents movable type.
1667	The first gardening catalog is published by William Lucas, an English gardener.
1744	Benjamin Franklin publishes a catalog of books on science and industry and formulates the basic mail-order concept of customer satisfaction guaranteed.
1830s	A few mail-order companies began operating in New England, selling camping and fishing supplies.
1863	The introduction of penny postage facilitates direct mail.
1867	The invention of the typewriter gives a modern appearance to direct-mail materials.
1872	Montgomery Ward publishes his first "catalog," selling 163 items on a single sheet of paper. By 1884 his catalog grows to 240 pages, with thousands of items and a money-back guarantee.
1886	Richard Sears enters the mail-order business by selling gold watches and makes $5,000 in his first six months. He partners with Alvah Roebuck in 1887, and by 1893 they are marketing a wide range of merchandise in a 196-page catalog.
1912	L. L. Bean founds one of today's most admired mail-order companies on the strength of his Maine Hunting Shoe and a guarantee of total satisfaction for the life of the shoe.
1917	The Direct Mail Advertising Association is founded. In 1973 it becomes the Direct Mail/Direct Marketing Association.
1928	Third-class bulk mail becomes a reality, offering economies for the direct-mail industry.
1950	Credit cards first appear, led by the Diners' Club travel and entertainment card. American Express enters in 1958.
1951	Lillian Vernon places an ad for a monogrammed purse and belt and generates $16,000 in immediate business. She reinvests the money in what becomes the Lillian Vernon enterprise. Vernon recognizes early on that catalog shopping has great appeal to time-pressed consumers.
1953	Publishers Clearing House is founded and soon becomes a dominant force in magazine subscriptions.
1955	Columbia Record Club is established, and eventually becomes Columbia House—the music-marketing giant.
1967	The term *telemarketing* first appears in print, and AT&T introduces the first toll-free 800 service.
1983	The Direct Mail/Direct Marketing Association drops Direct Mail from its name to become the DMA, as a reflection of the multiple media being used by direct marketers.
1984	Apple introduces the Macintosh personal computer.
1992	The number of people who shop at home surpasses 100 million in the United States.
1998	The Direct Marketing Association, www.the-dma.org/, eager to adapt its members' bulk mailing techniques for the Internet, announces it will merge with the Association for Interactive Media, www.interactivehq.org/.

Sources: Adapted from the DMA's "Grassroots Advocacy Guide for Direct Marketers" (1993). Reprinted with permission of the Direct Marketing Association, Inc.; Rebecca Quick, "Direct Marketing Association to Merge with Association of Interactive Media," *Wall Street Journal,* October 12, 1998, B6.

Bean. Bean founded his company in 1912 on his integrity and $400. His first product was a unique hunting shoe made from a leather top and rubber bottom sewn together. Other outdoor clothing and equipment soon followed in the Bean catalog.

A look at the L. L. Bean catalog of 1917 (black and white, just 12 pages) reveals the fundamental strategy underlying Bean's success. It featured the Maine Hunting Shoe

Direct marketing pioneer L. L. Bean has always been a relationship builder. Bean's original 100% guarantee of satisfaction, now appearing in cyberspace, is at the heart of the company's relationship with its customers. www.llbean.com/

and other outdoor clothing with descriptive copy that was informative, factual, and low-key. On the front page was Bean's commitment to quality. It read: *"Maine Hunting Shoe—guarantee. We guarantee this pair of shoes to give perfect satisfaction in every way. If the rubber breaks or the tops grow hard, return them together with this guarantee tag and we will* replace them, free of charge. Signed, L. L. Bean."[9] Bean realized that long-term relationships with customers must be based on trust, and his guarantee policy was aimed at developing and sustaining that trust.

As an astute direct marketer, Bean also showed a keen appreciation for the importance of building a good mailing list. For many years he used his profits to promote his free catalog via advertisements in hunting and fishing magazines. Those replying to the ads received a rapid response and typically became Bean customers. Bean's obsession with building mailing lists is nicely captured by this quote from his friend, Maine native John Gould: "If you drop in just to shake his hand, you get home to find his catalog in your mailbox."[10]

By 1967 Bean sales approached $5 million, and by 1990 they had exploded to $600 million, as the product line was expanded to include more apparel and recreation equipment. Today, L. L. Bean is still a family-operated business that emphasizes the basic philosophies of its founder, which are carefully summarized at the company's Web site at www.llbean.com/. Quality products, understated advertising, and sophisticated customer-contact and distribution systems still drive the business. Additionally, L. L.'s 100 percent satisfaction guarantee can still be found in every Bean catalog, and it remains at the heart of the relationship between Bean and its customers. Bean's steadfast guarantee is shown in Exhibit 19.3 as it appears in cyberspace.

Direct Marketing Today. Direct marketing today is rooted in the legacy of mail-order giants and catalog merchandisers such as L. L. Bean, Lillian Vernon, Publishers Clearing House, and JCPenney. Today, however, direct marketing has broken free from its mail-order heritage to become a tool used by all types of organizations throughout the world. Although many types of businesses and not-for-profit organizations are making use of direct marketing, it is common to find that such direct-marketing programs are not carefully integrated with an organization's other advertising efforts. Integration should be the goal for advertising and direct marketing; impressive evidence supports the thesis that integrated programs are more effective than the sum of their parts.[11]

Because many different types of activities are now encompassed by the label *direct marketing*, it is important to remember the defining characteristics spelled out in the DMA definition given earlier. Direct marketing involves an attempt to interact or create a dialogue with the customer; multiple media are often employed in the process, and direct marketing is characterized by the fact that a measurable response is immediately available for assessing a program's impact. With these defining features in mind, we can see that direct-marketing programs are commonly used for three primary purposes.

9.   Allison Cosmedy, *A History of Direct Marketing* (New York: Direct Marketing Association, 1992), 6.
10.   Ibid.
11.   Ernan Roman, *Integrated Direct Marketing* (Lincolnwood, Ill.: NTC Business Books, 1995).

EXHIBIT 19.4

This Honda ad is simple and direct—visit us on the Web. Web addresses (or URLs, uniform resource locators) are rather blunt objects: a single front door to the whole of the organization and its offerings. Creating multiple points of entry, for example, www.honda.com/economy versus www.honda.com/luxury (does Honda make a luxury car?), might help to discriminate customers by their interest, but at the risk of a longer, less memorable address. Of course, once the customer has arrived on a Web site, various means exist to try to establish the interactive exchange that characterizes direct marketing—how might Honda design its "electronic foyer" to start that process?

As you might imagine, the most common use of direct marketing is as a tool to close a sale with a customer. This can be done as a stand-alone program, or it can be carefully coordinated with a firm's other advertising. Telecommunications companies such as AT&T, MCI, and Sprint make extensive use of the advertising/direct-marketing combination.[12] For example, MCI has spent heavily on TV advertising to promote its Friends & Family discount-calling program. This advertising is used to familiarize and justify the program for consumers and is followed up through both direct-mail and telemarketing campaigns to convert customers to the program. In response, AT&T has used TV advertising to mock the calling-circle concept at the heart of MCI's program, while promoting its own discount plan. AT&T also makes extensive use of direct-marketing follow-ups to close sales.

A second purpose for direct-marketing programs is to identify prospects for future contacts and, at the same time, provide in-depth information to selected customers. This of course was the purpose of the Beverly Hills program discussed at the beginning of the chapter, in which the mayor was looking to initiate a dialogue with prospective customers through the mail. Since dialogue and interactivity are at the heart of successful direct marketing programs, it will come as no surprise that direct marketers are eager to adapt their methods to the Internet,[13] and as described in the New Media box on page 600, many believe that this transition will be swift and far-reaching. Even a simple print ad like that in Exhibit 19.4 may be viewed as a marketer's attempt to induce an electronic dialogue with a prospective customer.

Direct-marketing programs are also initiated as a means to engage customers, seek their advice, furnish helpful information about using a product, reward customers for using a brand, or in general foster brand loyalty, as the direct mail promotion for Infiniti in Exhibit 19.5 illustrates. As another example, the manufacturer of Valvoline motor oil seeks to build loyalty for its brand by encouraging young car owners to join the Valvoline Performance Team.[14] To join the team, young drivers just fill out a questionnaire that enters them into the Valvoline database. Team members receive posters, special offers on racing-team apparel, news about racing events in which Valvoline has provided sponsorship, and promotional reminders at regular intervals that reinforce the virtues of Valvoline for the driver's next oil change.

If you're still not convinced that everyone is getting on the direct-marketing bandwagon, consider the example of Kraft General Foods. Using the names and addresses that consumers provide when redeeming coupon and rebate offers, Kraft amassed a database of more than 30 million users of its products.[15] Kraft constantly refines this massive file by sending surveys to those on the list. From these surveys, Kraft discerns

12. Kate Fitzgerald, "AT&T, MCI Ringing Up Bigger Cash Lures," *Advertising Age,* May 8, 1995, 6.
13. Rebecca Quick, "Direct Marketing Association to Merge with Association of Interactive Media," *Wall Street Journal,* October 12, 1998, B6.
14. Nash, "The Roots of Direct Marketing," op. cit.
15. Jonathan Berry, "Database Marketing," *Business Week,* September 5, 1994, 56–62.

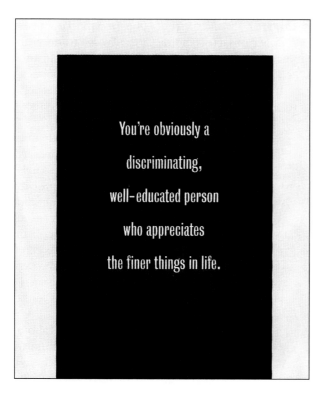

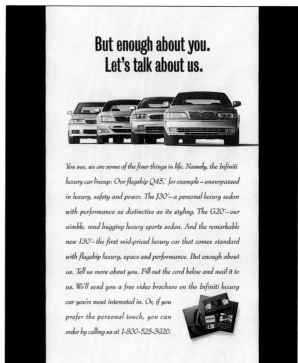

EXHIBIT 19.5

The distinguishing feature of a marketing database is direct input from the customer. This advertisement for Infiniti seeks to gather information and initiate a dialogue with the target customer. Do you see any parallels here vis-á-vis the approach used by the mayor of Beverly Hills?
www.infinitimotors.com/

the interests of different customers and responds with nutrition information, cooking tips, recipes, and coupons for specific brands that the person has used in the past or new brands that they are encouraged to try. (Here's your sample tip: Use Kraft Miracle Whip rather than butter or margarine the next time you make grilled cheese sandwiches, and don't forget the Velveeta!) Kraft's direct-marketing strategy is based on the premise that the more information consumers have about its various brands such as Miracle Whip and Velveeta, the more likely they are to remain loyal to those brands.

What's Driving the Growing Popularity of Direct Marketing?

The growth in popularity of direct marketing is due to a number of factors. Some of these have to do with changes in consumer lifestyles and technological developments that in effect create a climate more conducive to the practice of direct marketing. In addition, direct-marketing programs offer unique advantages vis-á-vis conventional mass media advertising, leading many organizations to shift more of their marketing budgets to direct-marketing activities.

From the consumer's standpoint, direct marketing's growing popularity might be summarized in a single word—*convenience*. Dramatic growth in the number of dual-income and single-person households has reduced the time people have to visit retail stores. Direct marketers provide consumers access to a growing range of products and services in their homes, thus saving many households' most precious resource—time.

More liberal attitudes about the use of credit and the accumulation of debt have also contributed to the growth of direct marketing. Credit cards are the primary means of payment in most direct-marketing transactions. The widespread availability of credit cards makes it ever more convenient to shop from the comfort of one's home.

Developments in telecommunications have also facilitated the direct-marketing transaction. After getting off to a slow start in the late sixties, toll-free 800 numbers have exploded in popularity to the point where one can hardly find a product or a catalog that does not include an 800 number for interacting with the manufacturer. And whether one is requesting that videotape about Beverly Hills, ordering a twill polo shirt from Eddie Bauer, or inquiring about an OzziRoo mountain bike like the one shown in Exhibit 19.6, the preferred mode of access for most consumers has been the 800 number.

Another technological development having a huge impact on the growth of direct marketing is the computer. Did you know that your parents' new Buick has more computer power than the Apollo spacecraft that took astronauts to the moon? The incredible diffusion of computer technology sweeping

NEW MEDIA

DIRECT MARKETERS EMBRACE THE INTERNET

All signs point to the World Wide Web as the direct marketer's ultimate tool. In the late 1990s online sales began to surge. In 1998 Dell Computer was generating $5 million dollars every day in Internet sales, and Amazon.com ended the year with sales in excess of $600 million. Total online sales for 1998 were estimated at $7.8 billion, and optimistic predictions about additional growth were rampant; for example, Forrester Research Inc. projected that online sales would grow to $108 billion by 2003.

But can you really make money on the Internet? This was one of the questions that researchers from Gruppo, Levey & Company posed to 60 direct marketers as the new millennium approached. A survey of executives from companies like Avon Products, L. L. Bean, Fidelity Investments, and Lenox Collections documented that traditional direct marketers were scrambling to upgrade their Internet presence, and only 2 percent of those surveyed saw no hope for turning a profit from Internet sales. Conversely, 39 percent said that their online sales had been profitable literally from the day they launched their Web sites, and most of the rest projected profits beginning in a matter of months.

The Internet is a natural evolution for direct marketers because it allows them to employ tools and tactics that have been practiced and perfected in other channels. For instance, 69 percent of the companies in the Gruppo survey said they established their initial presence online by simply putting up their complete catalogs. Additionally, direct marketing techniques such as targeting with customized offers, database marketing, and seasonal promotions are easily adapted to the Web.

What has been the direct marketers' biggest source of frustration? Survey respondents answered that not enough data are available currently about individual customers and their histories of online purchases. But perhaps this isn't such a bad thing. Sounding a hopeful note on the super-sensitive privacy issue, one of the survey's administrators said, "I think direct marketers are being careful because they're trying to balance privacy concerns with (their) need to gather information." Moreover, among the largest companies in the survey (annual sales of $100 million+), 75 percent said they had no intention of selling information about their Internet customers to other firms. Respecting the customer's privacy is good business, if you want a long-term (and profitable) relationship with that customer. Keep this premise in mind when you set out to make your fortune in cyberspace.

Sources: Carol Krol, "Primed for Online," *Advertising Age*, January 4, 1999, 20; Heather Green, "'Twas the Season for E-Splurging," *Business Week*, January 18, 1999, 40, 42.

EXHIBIT 19.6

Convenience for the customer is a major factor driving the popularity of direct marketing. A key contributor to that convenience is the omnipresent 800 number.

through all modern societies has been a tremendous boon to direct marketers. The computer now allows firms to track, keep records on, and interact with something like 5 million customers for what it cost to track a single customer in 1950.[16] Kraft General Foods obviously could not track and interact with 30 million of its customers without computer technology. As we will see in an upcoming discussion, the computer power now available for modest dollar amounts is fueling the growth of direct marketing's most potent tool—the marketing database.

And just as the computer has provided direct marketers with the tool they need to handle massive databases of customer prospects, it has also provided the convenience-oriented consumer with the tool he or she needs to comparison shop with the point and click of a mouse. What could be more convenient than logging on to the Internet and pulling up a shopping agent such as www.compare.com/ to check prices on everything from toaster ovens to snowboards? Many have projected that the Internet will become such a focal point for electronic commerce that traditional retailers must either re-invent themselves online, or face extinction.[17] If you haven't yet taken the plunge, check out a few of the sites listed in Exhibit 19.7, and draw your own conclusions about the future of online shopping.

Interactive television also promises to be an attractive vehicle for intensified direct marketing. Companies such as Time Warner, Spiegel, Sharper Image, The Nature Company, Warner Brothers Studio Store, Williams-Sonoma, and Chrysler are working together to develop the technical capabilities to deliver a wide array of interactive services

16.   Don Peppers and Martha Rogers, "The End of Mass Marketing," *Marketing Tools,* March/April 1995, 42–51.
17.   Gary Hamel and Jeff Sampler, "The E-Corporation," *Fortune,* December, 7, 1998, 80–92.

www.amazon.com/

www.apple.com/education/hed/students/

www.belgianexperts.com/

www.catalogcity.com/

www.cdnow.com/

www.collegedepot.com/

www.dell.com/client/edu/essentials.htm

www.efollett.com/

www.expedia.com/

www.fastweb.com/

www.gamedealer.com/

www.netmarket.com/

www.studentmkt.com/

www.travelcity.com/

www.varsitybooks.com/

EXHIBIT 19.7

Fifteen diverse shopping destinations on the Internet.

through consumers' TV sets.[18] The day is coming when marketers of all sorts will be able to carry on interactive dialogues with consumers in their homes via the television.

Direct-marketing programs also offer some unique advantages that make them appealing compared with what might be described as conventional mass marketing. A general manager of marketing communications with AT&T's consumer services unit put it this way: "We want to segment our market more; we want to learn more about individual customers; we want to really serve our customers by giving them very specific products and services. Direct marketing is probably the most effective way in which we can reach customers and establish a relationship with them."[19] As you might expect, AT&T is one of those organizations shifting more and more of its marketing dollars into direct-marketing programs.

The appeal of direct marketing is enhanced further by the persistent emphasis on producing measurable effects. For instance, in direct marketing, it is common to find calculations such as **cost per inquiry (CPI)** or **cost per order (CPO)** being featured in program evaluation.[20] These calculations simply divide the number of responses to a program by that program's cost. When calculated for each and every program an organization conducts over time, CPI and CPO data quickly help an organization appreciate what works and what doesn't work in its competitive arena.

This emphasis on producing and monitoring measurable effects is realized most completely through an approach called *database marketing*. Working with a database, direct marketers can target specific customers, track their actual purchase behavior over time, and experiment with different programs for affecting the purchasing patterns of these customers.[21] Obviously, those programs that produce the best outcomes become the candidates for increased funding in the future. Let's look into database marketing.

Database Marketing. ❧ If any ambiguity remains about what makes direct marketing different from marketing in general, that ambiguity can be erased by the database. The one characteristic of direct marketing that distinguishes it from marketing more generally is its emphasis on database development.[22] Knowing who the best customers are along with what and how often they buy is a direct marketer's secret weapon. This knowledge accumulates in the form of a marketing database.

Databases used as the centerpieces in direct-marketing campaigns take many forms and can contain many different layers of information about customers. At one extreme is the simple mailing list that contains nothing more than the names and addresses of possible customers; at the other extreme is the customized marketing database that augments names and addresses with various additional information about customers' characteristics, past purchases, and product preferences. Understanding this distinction between mailing lists and marketing databases is important in appreciating the scope of database marketing.

18.   Lindsey Kelly, "Interactive TV's Rough Road," *Advertising Age,* March 13, 1995, S12–S16.
19.   Gary Levin, "AT&T Exec: Customer Access Goal of Integration," *Advertising Age,* October 10, 1994, S1.
20.   Stone, *Successful Direct Marketing Methods,* 620.
21.   Schultz and Wang, "Real World Results," op. cit.
22.   Stone, *Successful Direct Marketing Methods,* Chapter 2.

Mailing Lists. A **mailing list** is simply a file of names and addresses that an organization might use for contacting prospective or prior customers. Mailing lists are plentiful, easy to access, and inexpensive.[23] For example, CD-ROM phone directories now available for less than $200 provide a cheap and easy way to generate mailing lists.[24] More-targeted mailing lists are available from a variety of suppliers. These suppliers offer lists such as the 107,521 active members of the Association of Catholic Senior Citizens; the 174,600 Kuppenheimer male-fashion buyers; the 825,000 subscribers to *Home* magazine; and the 189,000 buyers of products from the Smith & Hawken gardening catalog.[25]

Each time you subscribe to a magazine, order from a catalog, register your automobile, fill out a warranty card, redeem a rebate offer, apply for credit, join a professional society, or log in at a Web site, the information you provided about yourself goes on another mailing list. These lists are freely bought and sold through many means, including the Internet. Sites such as www.worldata.com/ and www.ira-ondemand.com/ allow one to buy names and addresses after sorting on demographic and zip-code information for about 15 cents per record. Visa, MasterCard, and American Express are gladly accepted.

Two broad categories of lists should be recognized: the internal, or house list, versus the external, or outside list. **Internal lists** are simply an organization's records of its customers, subscribers, donors, and inquirers. **External lists** are purchased from a list compiler or rented from a list broker. At the most basic level, internal and external lists facilitate the two fundamental activities of the direct marketer: Internal lists are the starting point for developing better relationships with current customers, whereas external lists help an organization cultivate new business.

List Enhancement. Name-and-address files, no matter what their source, are merely the starting point for database marketing. The next step in the evolution of a database is mailing-list enhancement. Typically this involves augmenting an internal list by combining it with other, externally supplied lists or databases. External lists can be appended or integrated with a house list.

One of the most straightforward list enhancements entails simply adding or appending more names and addresses to an internal list. Proprietary name-and-address files may be purchased from other companies that operate in noncompetitive businesses.[26] With today's computer capabilities, adding these additional households to an existing mailing list is simple. Many well-known companies such as Sharper Image, American Express, Bloomingdale's, and Hertz sell or rent their customer lists for this purpose.

A second type of list enhancement involves incorporating information from external databases into a house list. Here the number of names and addresses remains the same, but an organization ends up with a more complete description of who its customers are. Typically, this kind of enhancement includes any of four categories of information:

- *Demographic data*—the basic descriptors of individuals and households available from the Census Bureau.
- *Geodemographic data*—information that reveals the characteristics of the neighborhood in which a person resides.
- *Psychographic data*—data that allows for a more qualitative assessment of a customer's general lifestyle, interests, and opinions.
- *Behavioral data*—information about other products and services a customer has purchased; prior purchases can help reveal a customer's preferences.[27]

23. John Kremer, *The Complete Direct Marketing Sourcebook* (New York: John Wiley & Sons, 1992).
24. Ira Teinowitz, "Let Your Keyboard Do the Walking," *Advertising Age,* February 20, 1995, 22.
25. Kremer, *The Complete Direct Marketing Sourcebook.*
26. Terry G. Vavra, "The Database Marketing Imperative," *Marketing Management* 2, no. 1 (1993): 47–57.
27. Ibid.

List enhancements that entail merging existing records with new information rely on software that allows the database manager to match records based on some piece of information the two lists share. For example, matches might be achieved by sorting on zip codes and street addresses.

Many suppliers gather and maintain databases for the sole purpose of list enhancement. Infobase Premier is an enhancement file offered by Infobase Services and is particularly notable for its size and array of available information. Infobase Premier contains 170 different pieces of information about 200 million American consumers. Because of its massive size, this database has a high match rate (60 to 80 percent) when it is merged with clients' internal lists.[28] A more common match rate between internal and external lists is 45 to 60 percent. As with most things, list enhancement services are now available on the Web at sites such as www.imarketinc.com/. For its product named MarketPlace Pro, iMarket inc. promises match rates of 50 to 75 percent.

The Marketing Database. Mailing lists come in all shapes and sizes, and by enhancing internal lists they obviously can become rich sources of information about customers. But for a mailing list to qualify as a marketing database, one important additional type of information is required. Although a marketing database can be viewed as a natural extension of an internal mailing list, a **marketing database** also includes information collected directly from individual customers.[29] Developing a marketing database involves pursuing dialogues with customers and learning about their individual preferences and behavioral patterns. This can be potent information for hatching marketing programs that will hit the mark with consumers.

State-of-the-art direct marketing today has database development as its defining feature. According to one survey of marketing practitioners, 56 percent of retailers and manufacturers have database development under way, another 10 percent will soon begin development, and a whopping 85 percent believe that a marketing database will be a requirement to remain competitive after the year 2000.[30]

Aided by the dramatic escalation in processing power that comes from every new generation of computer chip, marketers see the chance to gather and manage more information about every individual who buys, or could buy, from them. Their goal might be portrayed as an attempt to cultivate a kind of cybernetic intimacy with the customer. A marketing database represents an organization's collective memory, which allows the organization to give customers the personalized attention that once was characteristic of the corner grocer in small-town America. For example, using its database of millions of cardmembers, American Express generates specific marketing programs almost person by person; some of the offers that AmEx sends out with its bill statements each month go to as few as 20 people.[31] This remarkable capability to sort through millions and speak to individuals is made possible by a marketing database. One of American Express's cardmember offers is shown in Exhibit 19.8.

While you might find this concept of cybernetic intimacy a bit far-fetched, it certainly is the case that a marketing database can have many valuable applications. Before we look at some of these applications, let's review the terminology introduced thus far. We now have seen that direct marketers use mailing lists, enhanced mailing lists, and/or marketing databases as the starting points for developing many of their programs. The crucial distinction between a mailing list and a marketing database is that the latter includes direct input from customers. Building a marketing database entails pursuing an ongoing dialogue with customers and continuous updating of records with new information. While mailing lists can be rich sources of information for program develop-

28. Ibid.
29. Herman Holtz, *Databased Marketing* (New York: John Wiley & Sons, 1992).
30. Berry, "Database Marketing," op. cit.
31. Ibid.

AMERICAN EXPRESS®

Presents

SONY MAXIMUM TELEVISION™

Once you've experienced it,
you'll never want to watch TV any other way.

Price
Guarantee
Plus

FOR CARDMEMBERS ONLY

Smart, Simple Price
Guarantee *Plus*...
• **Free** Shipping and Handling
• **Interest-Free**
  Monthly Payments
• **Free** 1,000 Bonus
  Membership Rewards℠ Points
• **Free** Return Pick Up

SONY.

EXHIBIT 19.8

The ability to tailor a specific program or campaign based on how a target market has behaved in the marketplace is a distinct advantage of a marketing database. In this exhibit, how do you think Sony and American Express select card members as good targets for this ad? At the American Express Web site, www.americanexpress.com/, you might visit the small-business exchange where the company shares information useful to small-business owners while gathering more information for its databases in return. To see how a competitor can build its databases by recording site visits, check out some of the services at the home page for Visa International at www.visa.com/.

ment, a marketing database has a dynamic quality that sets it apart. A marketing database can be an organization's living memory of who its customers are and what they want from the organization.

Marketing Database Applications.

Many different types of customer-communication programs are driven by marketing databases. One of the greatest benefits of a database is that it allows an organization to quantify how much business the organization is actually doing with its current best customers. A good way to isolate the best customers is with a recency, frequency, and monetary (RFM) analysis.[32] An **RFM analysis** asks how recently and how often a specific customer is buying from a company, and how much money he or she is spending per order and over time. With this transaction data, it is a simple matter to calculate the value of every customer to the organization and identify those customers that have given the organization the most business in the past. Past behavior is an excellent predictor of future behavior, so yesterday's best customers are likely to be any organization's primary source of future business.

RFM analysis allows an organization to spend marketing dollars to achieve maximum return on those dollars. Promotions targeted at best customers will typically pay off with handsome returns. For example, Claridge Hotel & Casino uses its frequent-gambler card—CompCard Gold—to monitor the gambling activities of its 350,000 active members.[33] Promotions such as free slot-machine tokens, monogrammed bathrobes, and door-to-door limo services are targeted to best customers. Such expenditures pay for themselves many times over because they are carefully targeted to people who spend freely when they choose to vacation at Claridge's resort hotels.

A marketing database can also be a powerful tool for organizations that seek to create a genuine relationship with their customers. The makers of Ben & Jerry's ice cream use their database for two things: to find out how customers react to potential new flavors and product ideas, and to involve their customers in social causes.[34] In one recent program, their goal was to find 100,000 people in their marketing database who would volunteer to work with Ben & Jerry's to support the Children's Defense Fund. Jerry Greenfield, cofounder of Ben & Jerry's, justifies the program as follows: "We are not some nameless conglomerate that only looks at how much money we make every year. I think the opportunity to use our business and particularly the power of our business as a force for progressive social change is exciting."[35] Of course, when customers feel genuine involvement with a brand like Ben & Jerry's, they also turn out to be very loyal customers.

32. Rob Jackson and Paul Wang, *Strategic Database Marketing* (Lincolnwood, Ill.: NTC Business Books, 1994).
33. Berry, "Database Marketing," op. cit.
34. Murray Raphel, "What's the Scoop on Ben & Jerry?" *Direct Marketing Magazine,* August 1994, 23–24.
35. Ibid.

EXHIBIT 19.9

Building relationships with existing customers is a key application of the marketing database. No company has placed more emphasis on this than Saturn. www.saturncars.com/index.html

Reinforcing and recognizing preferred customers can be another valuable application of the marketing database. This application may be nothing more than a simple follow-up letter that thanks customers for their business or reminds them of the positive features of the brand to reassure them that they made the right choice. As illustrated in Exhibit 19.9, GM's Saturn division uses its "branded" newsletter to continuously remind owners of the joys of driving a Saturn.

To recognize and reinforce the behaviors of preferred customers, marketers in many fields are experimenting with frequency-marketing programs that provide concrete rewards to frequent customers. **Frequency-marketing programs** have three basic elements: *a database,* which is the collective memory for the program; *a benefit structure,* which is designed to attract and retain customers; and *a communication strategy,* which emphasizes a regular dialogue with the organization's best customers.[36] As suggested by the Global Issues box on page 607, these loyalty-building programs can be found in all corners of the world.

Spectrum Foods, a San Francisco–based company with 15 upscale restaurants in California, has had considerable success with its frequency-marketing program known by diners as Table One.[37] Table One members earn points each time they dine. They can earn $25 award certificates, $250 shopping sprees at Nordstrom, or, for really frequent diners, trips to Italy and Mexico. Spectrum's program also includes free benefits such as valet parking, preferred reservations, and exclusive invitations to wine tastings and special dinners. Spectrum Foods has received a positive response to this program. Table One members dine at Spectrum's restaurants more often, spend more money each time they dine, and recommend the program to their friends—which has helped Spectrum grow its business at twice the industry average.

Another common application for the marketing database is cross-selling.[38] Since most organizations today have many different products or services they hope to sell, one of the best ways to build business is to identify customers who already purchase some of a firm's products and create marketing programs aimed at these customers but featuring other products. If they like our ice cream, perhaps we should also encourage them to try our frozen yogurt. If they have a checking account with us, can we interest them in a credit card? If customers dine in our restaurants on Fridays and Saturdays, with the proper incentives perhaps we can get them to dine with us midweek, when we really need the extra business. A marketing database can provide a myriad of opportunities for cross-selling.

A final application for the marketing database is a natural extension of cross-selling. Once an organization gets to know who its current customers are and what they like about various products, it is in a much stronger position to go out and seek new cus-

36. Richard Barlow, "Starting a Frequency Marketing Program," *Direct Marketing Magazine,* July 1994, 35.
37. Greg Gattuso, "Restaurants Discover Frequency Marketing," *Direct Marketing Magazine,* February 1995, 35–36.
38. Jackson and Wang, *Strategic Database Marketing.*

tomers. Knowledge about current customers is especially valuable when an organization is considering purchasing external mailing lists to append to its marketing database. If a firm knows the demographic characteristics of current customers—knows what they like about products, knows where they live, and has insights about their lifestyles and general interests—then the selection of external lists will be much more efficient. The basic premise here is simply to try to find prospects who share many of the same characteristics and interests with current customers. And what's the best vehicle for coming to know the current, best customers? Marketing-database development is that vehicle.

LOYALTY PROGRAMS KNOW NO BOUNDARIES

Loyalty programs such as frequent-flyer plans or credit card points are familiar by now to consumers around the world. But when an economy goes into recession, local marketers must fight ever harder to retain their customers. So what does your local video rental store offer as a reward for your repeat business? Discounts? Coupons? Store merchandise? Free popcorn or soda? Well how about a blood test?

To win the loyalty of its customers, KPS Video of Hong Kong launched its new Elite Card with the usual discounts on future rentals and store merchandise. But in a unique offer made in conjunction with Asian Medical Diagnostic Centers, the card also allowed renters to accumulate points that could be redeemed for blood counts, AIDS tests, cholesterol screenings, and other medical procedures. Was this an act of desperation by a local merchant in tough economic times, or savvy marketing based on keen insight about local market conditions? That's a hard call to make, but we should add that the program was launched in the same year that Hong Kong residents experienced widespread concern and near panic about the so-called bird flu epidemic. Turns out this was a banner year for blood testing in Hong Kong. Olivia Kan, marketing director for KPS Retail Stores, put it this way: "We found that because of the disease epidemic earlier this year in Hong Kong, people are more conscious about this kind of thing."

But will the free blood test have global appeal as an incentive for movie rentals? Well, while we would always defer to the judgment of local marketers such as Olivia Kan, our best advice on this one is, isn't free popcorn a whole lot more fun?

Source: Sarah Tilton, "Asia's 'Loyalty Card' Promotions Multiply in Crisis, and Get Stranger," *Wall Street Journal,* September 1, 1998, B2.

The Privacy Concern. One

very large dark cloud looms on the horizon for database marketers, and that cloud is consumers' concerns about invasion of privacy. It is easy for marketers to gather a wide variety of information about consumers, and this is making the general public nervous. In a recent Equifax/Harris poll, 65 percent of those surveyed said that protecting the privacy of consumer information has emerged as an issue that they are very concerned about.[39] Many Americans are uneasy about the way their personal information is being gathered and exchanged by businesses and the government without their knowledge, participation, or consent. Of course, the Internet only amplifies these concerns because the Web makes it a whole lot easier for all kinds of people and organizations to get access to personal information.

From time to time, state and federal lawmakers have proposed legislation to limit businesses' access to personal information, but not much has been accomplished. Direct marketers have been effective in blocking regulation by convincing lawmakers that they can police themselves. For example, the Direct Marketing Association has a toll-free hotline that consumers can call to have their names removed from mailing lists. However, it is not widely used by consumers. Privacy advocates contend that the hotline is primarily a public relations tool used by industry lobbyists to convince lawmakers that legislation is unnecessary.[40] One place you can go to learn more about how to protect the privacy of personal information is www.ftc.gov/privacy/protect.htm/.

Individual organizations can address their customers' concerns about privacy if they remember two fundamental premises of database marketing. First, a primary goal for

39. Susan Mitchell, "The Personal Is Political," *Marketing Tools,* January/February 1998, 14–19.
40. Mark Lewyn, "You Can Run, but It's Tough to Hide from Marketers," *Business Week,* September 5, 1994, 60–61.

developing a marketing database is to get to know customers in such a way that an organization can offer them products and services that better meet their needs. The whole point of a marketing database is to keep junk mail to a minimum by targeting only exciting and relevant programs to customers. If customers are offered something of value, they will welcome being in the database.

Second, developing a marketing database is about creating meaningful, long-term relationships with customers. If you want someone's trust and loyalty, would you collect personal information from them and then sell it to a third party behind their back? We hope not! When collecting information from customers, an organization must help them understand why it wants the information and how it will use it. If the organization is planning on selling this information to a third party, it must get customers' permission. If the organization pledges that the information will remain confidential, it must honor that pledge. Integrity is fundamental to all meaningful relationships, including those involving direct marketers and their customers. Recall that it was his integrity as much as anything else that enabled L. L. Bean to launch his successful career as a direct marketer.

Media Applications in Direct Marketing. 👁 While mailing lists and marketing databases are the focal point for originating most direct-marketing programs, information and arguments need to be communicated to customers in implementing these programs. As we saw in the definition of direct marketing offered earlier in this chapter, multiple media can be deployed in program implementation, and some form of immediate, measurable response is typically an overriding goal. The immediate response desired may be an actual order for services or merchandise, a request for more information, or the acceptance of a free trial offer. Because advertising conducted in direct-marketing campaigns is typified by this emphasis on immediate response, it is commonly referred to as **direct response advertising**.

As you probably suspect, **direct mail** and **telemarketing** are the direct marketer's prime media. However, all conventional media, such as magazines, radio, and television, can be used to deliver direct response advertising, and nowadays, don't forget to check that E-mail from Nike. In addition, a dramatic transformation of the television commercial—the infomercial—has become especially popular in direct marketing. Let's begin our examination of these media options by considering the advantages and disadvantages of the dominant devices—direct mail and telemarketing.

Direct Mail. Direct mail has some notable faults as an advertising medium, not the least of which is cost. It can cost 15 to 20 times more to reach a person with a direct mail piece than it would to reach that person with a television commercial or newspaper advertisement.[41] Additionally, in a society where people are constantly on the move, mailing lists are commonly plagued by bad addresses. Each bad address represents advertising dollars wasted. And direct mail delivery dates, especially for bulk, third-class mailings, can be unpredictable. When the timing of an advertising message is critical to its success, direct mail can be the wrong choice.

But as suggested by the ad from the U.S. Postal Service in Exhibit 19.10 (hardly an unbiased source), there will be times when direct mail is the right choice. Direct mail's advantages stem from the selectivity of the medium. When an advertiser begins with a database of prospects, direct mail can be the perfect vehicle for reaching those prospects with little waste. Also, direct mail is a flexible medium that allows message adaptations on literally a household-by-household basis.[42] For example, through surveys conducted with its 15 million U.S. subscribers, Reader's Digest has amassed a huge marketing database detailing the health problems of specific subscribers.[43] In the database are

41. Stone, *Successful Direct Marketing Methods*, 362.
42. Jack Z. Sissors and Lincoln Bumba, *Advertising Media Planning* (Lincolnwood, Ill.: NTC Business Books, 1994).
43. Sally Beatty, "Drug Companies Are Minding Your Business," *Wall Street Journal,* April 17, 1998, B1, B3.

771,000 arthritis sufferers, 679,000 people with high blood pressure, 206,000 with osteoporosis, 460,000 smokers, and so on. Using this information, Reader's Digest sends its subscribers disease-specific booklets containing advice on coping with their afflictions, wherein it sells advertising space to drug companies that have a tailored message that they want to communicate to those with a particular problem. This kind of precise targeting of tailored messages is the hallmark of direct marketing.

Direct mail as a medium also lends itself like no other to testing and experimentation. For example, with direct mail it is common to test two or more different appeal letters using a modest budget and a small sample of households.[44] The goal is to establish which version effects the largest response. When a winner is decided, that form of the letter is backed by big-budget dollars in launching the organization's primary campaign.

In addition, with direct mail, the choice of formats an organization can send to customers is virtually limitless. It can mail large, expensive brochures; videotapes; computer disks; or CDs. It can use pop-ups (Exhibit 19.11), foldouts, scratch-and-sniff strips, or just simple postcards. If a product can be described in a limited space with

EXHIBIT 19.10

This ad from the U.S. Postal Service reads like a textbook discussion of the advantages of using direct mail as part of an integrated marketing communications program. USPS is both the beneficiary, and the victim, of the arrival of information technology to the process of direct marketing—the boom in direct mail, and an explosion of new postal customers pumping postcards, letters, and packages into USPS's systems, came with the arrival of large databases and powerful computers to cross reference and filter them. On the other hand, a steady migration toward new media and, in particular, the Internet, is pushing customers to other providers; the Postal Service has no comparable monopoly on E-mail, and is only one of many carriers of the packages flowing from Web-based E-commerce purchases. How might the Postal Service imagine its future prospects in the Information Age? www.usps.gov/

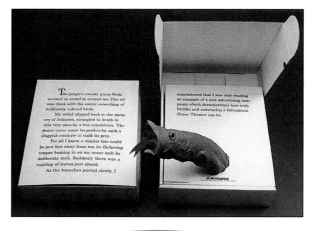

EXHIBIT 19.11

Direct mail is a versatile medium. Everything from a simple postcard to a pop-up snake can be delivered through the mail. www.mitsubishi.com/

44. Pamela Sebastian, "Charity Tries Two Letters to Melt Cold Hearts," *Wall Street Journal,* November 22, 1994, B1.

minimal graphics, there really is no need to get fancy with the direct mail piece. The double postcard (DPC) format has an established track record of outperforming more expensive and elaborate direct mail packages.[45] Moreover, if an organization follows U.S. Postal Service guidelines carefully in mailing DPCs, the pieces can go out as first-class mail for reasonable rates. Since the Postal Service supplies address corrections on all first-class mail, using DPCs usually turns out to be a winner on either CPI or CPO measures, and DPCs can be an effective tool for cleaning up the bad addresses in a mailing list!

Telemarketing. Telemarketing is probably the direct marketers' most potent tool. As with direct mail, contacts can be selectively targeted, the impact of programs is easy to track, and experimentation with different scripts and delivery formats is simple and practical. And because telemarketing involves real, live, person-to-person dialogue, no medium produces better response rates.[46] Telemarketing shares many of direct mail's limitations. Telemarketing is very expensive on a cost-per-contact basis, and just as names and addresses go bad as people move, so too do phone numbers. It is typical in telemarketing programs to find that 15 percent of the numbers called are inaccurate.[47] Further, telemarketing does not share direct mail's flexibility in terms of delivery options. When you reach people in their home or workplace, you have a limited amount of time to convey information and request some form of response.

If you have a telephone, you already know the biggest concern with telemarketing. It is a powerful yet highly intrusive medium that must be used with discretion. High-pressure telephone calls at inconvenient times can alienate customers. Telemarketing gives its best results over the long run if it is used to maintain constructive dialogues with existing customers and qualified prospects.[48]

For example, Kayla Cosmetics of Burbank, California, uses telemarketing to generate 93 percent of its sales from a marketing database of 19,000 customers.[49] Kayla's phone operators maintain ongoing dialogues with customers, and even though it may be months between contacts, each customer always works through the same personal operator when placing orders with Kayla. When that customer calls or is contacted by Kayla, her records, with purchase histories and personal details, appear immediately on the operator's computer screen. The first comment the customer hears from a Kayla operator is not "What item did you want to buy today?" but something like "What did you name your new baby?" Using technology and well-trained employees to add a personal touch to telemarketing efforts is a good way to get the most from this medium. Of course, such a personal response might make some people uncomfortable.

E-mail. Perhaps the most controversial tool deployed by direct marketers in recent years has been unsolicited or "bulk" E-mail. Commonly referred to as spam, this junk E-mail can get you in big trouble with consumers. In a worst-case scenario, careless use of the E-mail tool can earn one's company the label of a "spammer" across the Internet, and because of the community-oriented character of Internet communications, can then be a continuing source of negative publicity. Once a spammer, always a spammer . . . and your reputation is shot.

On the other hand, the awesome potential of this electronic tool will continue to attract the interest of direct marketers. Low cost, timely delivery, and easy availability of E-mail addresses are tremendous attractions. As shown in the IMC box on page 611, marketing giants such as Nike continue to experiment with targeted E-mail messaging

45. Michael Edmondson, "Postcards from the Edge," *Marketing Tools,* May 1995, 14.
46. Sissors and Bumba, *Advertising Media Planning.*
47. Ibid.
48. Stone, *Successful Direct Marketing Methods,* Chapter 14.
49. William Dunn, "Building a Database," *Marketing Tools,* July/August 1994, 52–59.

NIKE MARKETERS DECIDE TO DO E-MAIL

When it comes to using the tools of direct marketing, it would be fair to say that just about everybody has gotten into the game. Take for example Nike Inc. Renowned for its marketing muscle and high-profile TV ad campaigns featuring the royalty of professional sports, Nike decided to take a more integrated approach in launching *Engineered for Women Athletes*, a new line of women's-only products. The initial launch included 11 new shoes such as the Air Propensity, a walking shoe, as well as a bevy of basketball shoes endorsed by WNBA stars such as Lisa Leslie, Cynthia Cooper, and Sheryl Swoopes. Six months later Nike would add 11 more products to its women's-only repertoire, all of which had undergone specific design and engineering to make them anatomically correct for a woman's foot. With so much to explain and so many different products to talk about, Nike marketers decided to rely more heavily on the tools of direct marketing in an integrated launch campaign. As with any IMC campaign, the goal was to get the right message to just the right consumer.

Like any good direct marketer, Nike built its launch campaign around its customer database. Through its established relationships with numerous leagues and sports associations nationwide, its Internet site, and its in-box mail-in program that generates 180,000 response cards monthly, Nike has amassed a customer database of more than 6 million Nike users. About 2.4 million of these are women. Obviously, these 2.4 million previous Nike customers became a focal point in the launch of the *Engineered for Women Athletes* line. Of course, once you know who your customer is, where they live physically and electronically, and what they've purchased from you in the past, broadcast media such as television are not your best choice for delivering a targeted appeal about a specific new product. Targeted messages in this launch were delivered via postcards, product brochure mailings, and E-mail—more proof that direct marketing tools and tactics may have been conceived initially by the likes of L. L. Bean and Lillian Vernon, but now have been embraced by marketers in most companies large and small.

Source: Theresa Howard, "Nike Set to Run with Two New Product Lines: Postcards, E-Mail Will Help Shoemaker Target Women," *DM News*, July 20, 1998, 1, 58.

as part of their integrated marketing communication campaigns. There definitely is a school of thought that says some consumers are not averse to receiving targeted E-mail advertisements, and that as the Internet continues to evolve as an increasingly commercial medium, those companies that observe proper etiquette on the Net (dare we say Netiquette) will be rewarded through customer loyalty.[50]

Our advice is to stay away from the low-cost temptations of bulk E-mail. The quickest way to get flamed and damage your good name is to start sending out bulk E-mails to people who do not want to hear from you. Instead, through database development, ask your customers for permission to contact them via E-mail. Honor their requests. Don't abuse the privilege by selling their E-mail addresses to other companies, and when you do contact them, have something important to say. Take the high road. Build a relationship with the customer based on trust and respect for his or her privacy. Call us naive if you like, but we submit that integrity is a great foundation for building a successful business, off or on the Internet.

Direct Response Advertising in Other Media. Direct marketers have experimented with many other methods in trying to convey their appeals for a customer response. Using magazines, a popular device for executing a direct marketer's agenda is the bind-in insert card.[51] Thumb through a copy of any magazine and you will see how effective these light-cardboard inserts are in stopping the reader and calling attention to themselves. Insert cards not only promote their products but also offer the reader an easy way to order a pair of Optek sport sunglasses, request a free sample of Skoal smokeless tobacco, or select those ten free CDs that will make the reader a member of the BMG Music Club. The card in Exhibit 19.12 comes from *Wired* magazine, and is designed to facilitate contact through the mail. But for those that prefer something more immediate, Iridium also offers both the Web address and its toll-free number. Now that's covering all the bases!

50. Kenneth Leung, "Marketing with Electronic Mail without Spam," *Marketing News*, January 19, 1998, 11; Marshall M. Rosenthal, "Rethinking Spam," *Marketing Tools*, June 1997, 28–33.
51. Stone, *Successful Direct Marketing Methods*, 250–252.

KEEP ME IN TOUCH.

Please send me more information about Iridium Service.

Name   Mr. / Mrs. / Ms.
(Circle one)   First, Last

Company Name

Address Business/Home
(Circle one)

Town/City   State

Zip Code   Country
Telephone   Fax

E-mail Address

Please take a minute to answer these questions. Your answers will help us to better serve your needs.

Are you a cellular or satellite phone user? (Check all that apply.)   ☐ Cellular   ☐ Satellite   ☐ No, I am not.
What is the name of your cellular service provider?_____ Satellite service provider?_____
Do you subscribe to a paging service?   ☐ Yes   ☐ No
In the past year, how many times have you traveled internationally?_____ Domestically?_____
What type of business or industry are you employed in?_____
How would you acquire this service?   ☐ Purchase it and not be reimbursed.   ☐ Purchase it and be reimbursed.
☐ My employer would purchase and provide me with the service.   ☐ Not sure.

**THANK YOU. PLEASE MAIL THIS POSTAGE-PAID CARD.
YOU CAN ALSO VISIT OUR WEBSITE AT WWW.IRIDIUM.COM
OR CALL US AT 1-888-IRIDIUM.**

WIRED

EXHIBIT 19.12

This is a bind-in insert card for Iridium's satellite-based phone service. Note that Iridium requests several pieces of personal information for building its marketing database, and attempts to justify the request with the phrase: "Your answers will help us to better serve your needs." Is that enough assurance for you to submit personal information to Iridium? What do you think Iridium will do with the information it collects? Iridium is an excellent candidate for the use of direct marketing strategies, given its service: the average Joe isn't going to spend several dollars per minute for a satellite phone call. Placing ads in WIRED is a healthy step toward filtering the audience, though it may be that the average WIRED reader is less inclined to fill out a paper form (what a retro concept, dude . . . colored dye on dead trees!), and will whip out the cell phone for the 800 number, or surf over to Iridium's site (www.iridum.com/) on the Web. www.wired.com

When AT&T introduced the first 800 service in 1967, it simply could not have known how important this service would become to direct marketing. Newspaper ads from the *Wall Street Journal* provide toll-free numbers for requesting everything from package delivery (1-800-PICK-UPS) to notebook PC's (1-800-TOSHIBA). If you watch late-night TV, you may know the 800 number to call to order the Grammy-winning CD by Walter Ostanek and his polka band. IDS Financial Services, a division of American Express, featured its 800 number in radio ads as part of a two-step offer designed to generate prospects for its financial planning business. IDS operators took the caller's name, address, phone number, and age to input into a marketing database, and they offered to book the caller for a consultation. IDS found this radio-based campaign more than twice as profitable as the direct mail campaigns it had used previously.[52] Additionally, as exemplified by Exhibit 19.13, magazine ads are commonly used to provide an 800 number to initiate contact with customers. As these diverse examples indicate, toll-free numbers make it possible to use nearly any medium for direct response purposes.

Infomercials. The infomercial is a novel form of direct response advertising that merits special mention. An **infomercial** is fundamentally just a long television advertisement made possible by the lower cost of ad space on many cable and satellite channels. They range in length from 3 to 60 minutes, but the common length is 30 minutes. Although producing an infomercial is more like producing a television program than it is like producing

52. Nancy Coltun Webster, "Radio Tuning In to Direct Response," *Advertising Age,* October 10, 1994, S14–S15.

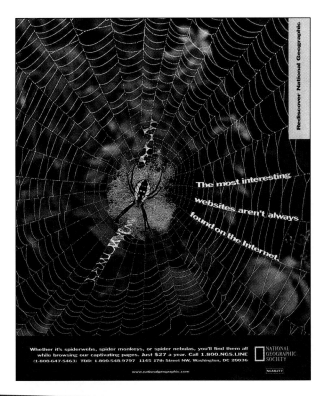

Rediscover National Geographic

The most interesting websites aren't always found on the Internet.

Whether it's spiderwebs, spider monkeys, or spider nebulas, you'll find them all while browsing our captivating pages. Just $27 a year. Call 1.800.NGS.LINE (1-800-647-5463) TDD: 1-800-548-9797 1145 17th Street NW, Washington, DC 20036

NATIONAL GEOGRAPHIC SOCIETY

www.nationalgeographic.com

NGA8277

EXHIBIT 19.13

Here again we see the direct marketer's favorite tool. Look for the World Wide Web to replace the 800 number as the direct marketer's favorite tool, say by 2003. www.nationalgeographic.com/

a 30-second commercial, infomercials are all about selling. There appear to be several keys to successful use of this unique vehicle.

A critical factor is testimonials from satisfied users. Celebrity testimonials can help catch a viewer as he or she is channel surfing by the program, but celebrities aren't necessary, and, of course, they add to the production costs. Whether testimonials are from celebrities or from folks just like us, one expert summarizes matters this way: "Testimonials are so important that without them your chances of producing a profitable infomercial diminish hugely."[53]

Another key point to remember about infomercials is that viewers are not likely to stay tuned for the full 30 minutes. An infomercial is a 30-minute direct response sales pitch, not a classic episode of *Seinfeld* or *The Simpsons.* The implication here is that the call to action should come not just at the end of the infomercial; most of the audience could be long gone by minute 28 into the show. A good rule of thumb in a 30-minute infomercial is to divide the program into 10-minute increments and close three times.[54] Each closing should feature the 800 number that allows the viewer to order the product or request more information. And an organization should not offer information to the customer unless it can deliver speedy follow-up; same-day response should be the goal in pursuing leads generated by an infomercial.

Many different types of products and services have been marketed using infomercials, and now via Internet extensions such as www.iqvc.com/. CD players, self-help videos, home exercise equipment, kitchen appliances, and hair restoration treatments have all had success with the infomercial. And while it is easy to associate the infomercial with things such as the Ronco *Showtime* Rotisserie & BBQ (yours for just four easy payments of $39.95!), many familiar brands have experimented with this medium. Brand marketers such as Quaker State, America Online, Primestar, Lexus, Magnavox, Hoover, KalKan, and Bissell have all used infomercials to help inform consumers about their offerings.[55]

While the infomercial has become a versatile tool, one final point needs to be made about making profitable use of this tool. If the primary goal in running infomercials is order solicitation, it is difficult to generate a profit for any item priced below $40 or $50.[56] The costs to produce and air an infomercial make it almost impossible to generate adequate cash flow from an item that can support a price of, say, only $19.95. If a firm is working with moderately priced items, the solution may be to bundle them together. If the product can justify a price of only $19.95, sell it in sets of three for $49.99, or, better yet, offer two for $49.99 with a third item free for those who call the 800 line immediately. Then, the firm must be prepared: 80 percent of all calls generated by infomercials occur within five minutes of the focal call to action.[57] If callers get a busy signal or are put on hold, many will have second thoughts, and will put their credit cards back in their wallets.

53. Herschell Gordon Lewis, "Information on Infomercials," *Direct Marketing Magazine,* March 1995, 30–32.
54. Ibid.
55. Kathy Haley, "Infomercials Score for Brand-Name Advertisers," *Advertising Age,* September 8, 1997, A1, A2.
56. Lewis, "Information on Infomercials," op. cit.
57. Paul Kerstetter, "When Consumers Actually Respond to Infomercial Airings," *Adweek Infomercial Sourcebook,* 1994, 12–15.

The Coordination Challenge Revisited.

As you have seen in the previous four chapters, the wide variety of media available to an advertiser poses a tremendous challenge with respect to coordination and integration. Organizations are looking to achieve the synergy that can come when various media options reach the consumer with a common and compelling message. However, to work in various media, functional specialists both inside and outside an organization need to be employed. It then becomes a very real problem to get the advertising manager, special events manager, sales promotion manager, and new-media manager to work in harmony. And now we must add to the list of functional specialists the direct-marketing manager.

The evolution and growing popularity of direct marketing raises the challenge of achieving integrated marketing communications to new heights. In particular, the development of a marketing database commonly leads to interdepartmental rivalries and can create major conflicts between a company and its advertising agency. The marketing database is a powerful source of information about the customer; those who do not have direct access to this information will be envious of those who do. Additionally, the growing use of direct-marketing campaigns must mean that someone else's budget is being cut. Typically, direct-marketing programs come at the expense of conventional advertising campaigns that might have been run on television, in magazines, or in other mass media.[58] Since direct marketing takes dollars from those activities that have been the staples of traditional ad agency business, it is easy to see why advertising agencies view direct marketing with some resentment.[59] Similarly, it is easy to see why large advertising agencies are interested in buying up smaller, fast-growing direct-marketing companies.[60] If you can't beat 'em, buy 'em!

There are no simple solutions for achieving integrated marketing communications, but one approach that many organizations are experimenting with is the establishment of a marketing-communications manager, or *marcom manager* for short.[61] A **marcom manager** plans an organization's overall communications program and oversees the various functional specialists inside and outside the organization to ensure that they are working together to deliver the desired message to the customer.

One company that has experimented with this marcom manager system is AT&T. As already mentioned, AT&T, like its telecommunications rivals, makes heavy use of both direct-marketing programs and mass media advertising to reach out and touch its customers. George Burnett, the marcom manager for AT&T, explains the value of integrating direct mail and advertising this way: "Honestly, I think it is simplicity and clarity . . . That is one of the goals of integrated communications, because in this complicated world, adding complication on top of the competitiveness is really not in our customers' interest."[62]

Burnett adds emphasis to a theme we have developed throughout this book. Perhaps the major challenge in the world of advertising today is to find ways to break through the clutter of competitors' ads—and really all advertising in general—to get customers' attention and make a point with them. If the various media and programs an organization employs are sending different messages or mixed signals, the organization is only hurting itself. To achieve the synergy that will allow it to overcome the clutter of today's marketplace, an organization has no choice but to pursue integrated marketing communications.

58.   Kate Fitzgerald, "Beyond Advertising," *Advertising Age*, August 3, 1998, 1, 14.
59.   Jim Osterman, "This Changes Everything," *Adweek,* May 15, 1995, 44–45.
60.   Sally Goll Beatty, "Interpublic Group Considers Move into Hot Field of Direct Marketing," *Wall Street Journal*, April 19, 1996, B3.
61.   Don E. Schultz, Stanley I. Tannenbaum, and Robert F. Lauterborn, *Integrated Marketing Communications* (Lincolnwood, Ill.: NTC Business Books, 1993).
62.   Levin, "AT&T Exec," op. cit.

SUMMARY

◀▶ Identify the three primary purposes served by and explain the growing popularity of direct marketing.

Many types of organizations are increasing their expenditures on direct marketing. These expenditures serve three primary purposes: direct marketing offers potent tools for closing sales with customers, for identifying prospects for future contacts, and for offering information and incentives that help foster brand loyalty. The growing popularity of direct marketing can be attributed to several factors. Direct marketers make consumption convenient: credit cards, 800 numbers, and now the Internet take the hassle out of shopping. Additionally, today's computing power, which allows marketers to build and mine large customer information files, has enhanced direct marketing's impact. The emphasis on producing and tracking measurable outcomes is also well received by marketers in an era when everyone is trying to do more with less.

◀▶ Distinguish a mailing list from a marketing database and review the many applications of each.

A mailing list is a file of names and addresses of current or potential customers, such as those lists that might be generated by a credit card company or a catalog retailer. Internal lists are valuable for creating relationships with current customers, and external lists are useful in generating new customers. A marketing database is a natural extension of the internal list but includes information about individual customers and their specific preferences and purchasing patterns. A marketing database allows organizations to identify and focus their efforts on their best customers. Recognizing and reinforcing preferred customers can be a potent strategy for building loyalty. Cross-selling opportunities also emerge once a database is in place. In addition, as one gains keener information about the motivations of current best customers, insights usually emerge about how to attract new customers.

◀▶ Describe the prominent media used by direct marketers in delivering their messages to the customer.

Direct-marketing programs emanate from mailing lists and databases, but there is still a need to deliver a message to the customer. Direct mail and telemarketing are the most common means used in executing direct-marketing programs. Infomercials are another prominent tool. Because the advertising done as part of direct-marketing programs typically requests an immediate response from the customer, it is known as direct response advertising. Conventional media such as television, newspapers, magazines, and radio can also be used to request a direct response by offering an 800 number or a Web address to facilitate customer contact.

◀▶ Articulate the added challenge created by direct marketing for achieving integrated marketing communication.

Developing a marketing database, selecting a direct mail format, or producing an infomercial are some of the new tasks attributable to direct marketing. These and other related tasks require more functional specialists, who further complicate the challenge of presenting a coordinated face to the customer. Some organizations are now experimenting with marcom managers, who are assigned the task of coordinating the efforts of various functional specialists working on different aspects of a marketing communications program. To achieve an integrated presence that will break through in a cluttered marketplace, this coordination is essential.

KEY TERMS

direct marketing (595)
cost per inquiry (CPI) (602)
cost per order (CPO) (602)
mailing list (603)
internal lists (603)
external lists (603)
marketing database (604)

RFM analysis (605)
frequency-marketing programs (606)
direct response advertising (608)
direct mail (608)
telemarketing (608)
infomercial (612)
marcom manager (614)

QUESTIONS FOR REVIEW AND CRITICAL THINKING

1.   Direct marketing is defined as an interactive system of marketing. Explain the meaning of the phrase *interactive system*. Give an example of a noninteractive system. How would an interactive system be helpful in the cultivation of brand loyalty?

2.   Start a collection of the direct mail pieces you receive at your home or apartment. After you have accumulated at least ten pieces, review the three main purposes for direct marketing discussed in this chapter. For each piece in your collection, what would you surmise is the direct marketer's purpose?

3.   Review the major forces that have promoted the growth in popularity of direct marketing. Can you come up with any reasons why its popularity might be peaking? What are the threats to its continuing popularity as a marketing tool?

4.   Describe the various categories of information that a credit card company might use to enhance its internal mailing list. For each category, comment on the possible value of the information for improving the company's market segmentation strategy.

5.   What is RFM analysis, and what is it generally used for? How would RFM analysis allow an organization to get more impact from a limited marketing budget? (Keep in mind that every organization views its marketing budget as too small to accomplish all that needs to be done.)

6.   Compare and contrast frequency-marketing programs with those tools described in Chapter 18 under the heading "Sales Promotion Directed at Consumers." What common motivators do these two types of activities rely on? How are their purposes similar or different? What goal is a frequency-marketing program trying to achieve that would not be a prime concern with a sales promotion?

7.   There's a paradox here, right? On the one hand, it is common to talk about building relationships and loyalty with the tools of direct marketing. On the other hand, it is also true that direct-marketing tools such as junk E-mail and telephone interruptions at home during dinner are constant irritants. How does one build relationships with irritants? In your opinion, when is it realistic to think that the tools of direct marketing could be used to build long-term relationships with customers?

8.   What is it about direct marketing that makes its growing popularity a threat to the traditional advertising agency?

EXPERIENTIAL EXERCISES

1.   Spend an hour watching television, with the goal of viewing an advertisement by a direct marketer. What product was offered? Was the offer unique? Can the product be found in stores in your area? Describe what immediate action the advertiser wants you to take.

2.   Describe one direct-marketing promotion you have responded to, print or broadcast. What made you respond to the offer? Were you satisfied with the product after receiving it? Have you made additional purchases from the same direct marketer? Explain why or why not.

USING THE INTERNET

Several merchandisers have established Web sites that serve as direct-marketing vehicles. Visit the following sites:

Sharper Image: www.sharperimage.com

Fingerhut: www.fingerhut.com

Lands' End: www.landsend.com

Spiegel: www.spiegel.com

Virtual Vineyard: www.virtualvin.com

For each site, answer the following questions:

1. How attractive is the online catalog? Is it easy or difficult to navigate within the site and place an order? Make some suggestions on how the online version can be improved.

2. How does the shopping experience compare to more traditional ways of shopping? How does this site make it easier or less expensive for the company to sell and distribute its products?

3. Are any specials offered? Do you think the specials are effective tools for getting people to purchase products on this site?

4. Does the site adequately address the issue of security for those providing credit card numbers when placing orders?

In the "brick and mortar" world, information can be captured on consumers only sporadically. One can match customers with purchases, if they use a credit card, or a preferred customer discount card, but surveilling the customers, to know what they look at, is all but impossible. On the Internet, however, all those bits and bytes can be captured, by the site being visited, or by the consumer's Internet provider.

A controversial venture is ZapMe!, which offers schools free PCs and network connections, in return for the right to both collect information on the students who use them, and to tailor advertising for them.

Visit the ZapMe! site at www.zapme.com

1. What sort of offer does ZapMe! make to schools? Why might schools find it compelling?

2. What sort of downside consequences can you imagine if a school decides to take up the offer?

3. What role should commercial companies be allowed to take in the K–12 educational process?

Another company that surveills consumers is Customer Insites, which captures consumer behavior (with their permission) to assess the effectiveness of commercial Web sites. Visit Customer Insites at www.customerinsites.com.

What techniques does Customer Insites use to evaluate a client's Web offering?

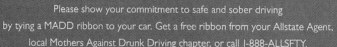

CHAPTER 20

After reading and thinking about this chapter, you will be able to do the following:

- Explain the role of public relations as part of an organization's overall IMC strategy and detail the objectives and tools of public relations.

- Describe two basic strategies for motivating an organization's public relations activities.

- Discuss the applications and objectives of corporate advertising.

In 1995, Microsoft Corporation rolled out its Windows 95 operating system with tremendous fanfare and flair. A tightly coordinated global launch included a guest spot on the Jay Leno show, a celebration for 3,500 people, a Ferris wheel, hot-air balloons, free copies of the software for dignitaries around the world, and a huge payment for the rights to use the Rolling Stones song "Start Me Up" as the product launch theme song. During the 12 months after the launch, Microsoft spent $200 million on advertising to support the introduction.

In 1998, Windows 98 was introduced with a low-key, waterfront, corporate affair in San Francisco attended by about 300 representatives from the press—no hot-air balloons, no Ferris wheel, no dignitaries, no Rolling Stones. Why the difference in intensity? As one journalist put it: "Windows 95—Jay Leno. Windows 98—Janet Reno?"[1] The reference, of course, is to the highly publicized investigation of the U.S. Justice Department into Microsoft's marketing and business practices regarding Windows software and the bundling of services within the basic operating system—specifically its Internet Explorer program.

The Justice Department investigation has presented Microsoft with a public relations challenge of huge proportions. Literally every major business publication (*Wall Street Journal, Business Week, Forbes, Fortune, Advertising Age*) has carried multiple stories about Microsoft's antitrust problems. Popular press vehicles from *USA Today* to *People* to the local newspaper have followed the story. And, of course, the Internet has been buzzing with each new development. Coverage of the situation has often portrayed Microsoft as "predatory" and "anti-competitive," borrowing language that often appeared in Justice Department reports.

The low point in the negative publicity onslaught came in late 1997, when attorneys for Microsoft submitted a court filing in which they described Justice Department attorneys as "poorly informed lawyers [who] have no vocation for software design."[2] Microsoft executives regretted the statement and said the company should have been more respectful of the court. The official public reaction came from Microsoft's chief operating officer and executive vice president, Robert J. Herbold, who met with the press and offered the public relations understatement of the year, "We need to do a better job of toning down the rhetoric."[3]

Microsoft was clearly struggling. It had never faced a negative publicity challenge like this before and it needed to respond to this challenge more effectively than it had been responding. Being a creative and astute organization, Microsoft crafted an interesting public relations and advertising response. First, the organization recognized that its efforts to date were inadequate. A good public relations and corporate image campaign begins with full understanding and appreciation of the situation.[4] Microsoft's own focus group research revealed that "bashing" Microsoft had become fashionable among information technology managers. Often, the first thing out of their mouths during a focus group session was "It's a monopoly."[5]

Once the firm had established an understanding of the situation, the next step was to evaluate the public persona it was presenting. The conclusion here was that Microsoft was, indeed, seen as a predatory giant seeking monopoly power. The solution was to recast the organization with a "kinder, gentler face" in its advertising campaigns. The firm set about doing this by carefully evaluating all advertising materials and recasting the organization in a more benign way. The main advertising campaign for Windows 98 concentrated exclusively on consumer magazines such as *Bon Appétit, The New Yorker,* and *Time* (see Exhibit 20.1). The ads highlighted features and used

1.   Catalina Oritz, "Fed Lawsuit Offers Best PR for Microsoft's Windows 98," *Associated Press,* June 25, 1998.
2.   Associated Press, January 9, 1998.
3.   Ibid.
4.   Geri Mazur, "Good PR Starts with Good Research," *Marketing News,* September 15, 1997, 16.
5.   Bradley Johnson, "Microsoft Aims 3 Ad Drives at Small-Business Users," *Advertising Age,* February 16, 1998, 43.

**WINDOWS HELPS
PEOPLE AND
MACHINES UNDERSTAND
EACH OTHER.**

Where do you want to go today?® www.microsoft.com/windows/   **Microsoft**®

©1998 Microsoft Corporation. All rights reserved. Microsoft, Where do you want to go today? the Windows logo and the Windows Start logo are either registered trademarks or trademarks of Microsoft Corporation in the United States and/or other countries. Windows is a registered trademark of Microsoft Corporation for its Windows brand operating systems.

EXHIBIT 20.1

In the midst of serious public relations problems, Microsoft developed "kinder and gentler" advertising.

such "friendly" headlines as "Shouldn't Your Computer be Smarter Than Your Dog?"[6] Another more friendly campaign was developed for the Microsoft-bashing information technology managers. In these ads, Microsoft offers such self-effacing revelations in the ad copy as "Apparently, there are those who do not subscribe to an all-Microsoft approach."[7]

But perhaps the most interesting, though not official, advertising response to the publicity-hostile environment was Bill Gates's decision to do an ad for Callaway Golf in which "Bill" reveals that he is a fairly poor golfer who is really trying hard to get better. Talk about your "kinder, gentler" faces. Here is Bill Gates (net worth about $43 billion with a reputation as a ruthless competitor) sheepishly admitting that he, "golly gee," can't play golf very well. This is certainly a much more humanized version of Bill Gates than the Justice Department hearings ever showed.

Microsoft used the tools of both public relations and corporate advertising as a way to deal with negative publicity that was outside the firm's control. This chapter will consider in detail the role of two separate and important areas that must be part of a firm's overall integrated marketing communications effort: public relations and corporate advertising. Each of these areas has the potential to make a distinct and important contribution to the single and unified message and image of an organization, which is the ultimate goal of IMC. Each has the potential for effective and supportive communication, but they achieve this in different ways.

Public Relations.

Public relations is a marketing and management function that deals with the public issues encountered by firms across a wide range of constituents. An important component of public relations is publicity—news media coverage of events related to a firm's products or activities. Publicity presents both challenges (as Microsoft learned) and opportunities. News reports about problems, such as those Microsoft had to deal with, represent challenges. Large investment projects in facilities or new product discoveries represent opportunities for positive publicity.

Public relations problems can arise from either a firm's own activities or from external forces completely outside a firm's control. Let's consider two highly visible companies—Intel and Pepsi—and their public relations problems. In one case, the firm caused its own problems; in the other, an external, uncontrollable force created problems for the firm.

Intel is one of the great success stories of American industry. Intel has risen from relative techno-obscurity as an innovative computer technology company to number 38 on the Fortune 500 list. Sales have grown from $1.3 billion to more than $25 billion in just 15 years.[8] But all this success did not prepare Intel for the public relations

6.   Bradley Johnson, "Microsoft's Win 98 Pitch Touts Product Advantages," *Advertising Age,* June 22, 1998, 4.
7.   Ibid.
8.   "The Fortune 500," *Fortune,* April 29, 1998, S1.

challenge it faced in late 1994. In early 1994, Intel introduced its new-generation chip, the Pentium, as the successor to the widely used line of X86 chips. The Pentium processor was another leap forward in computing speed and power. But in November 1994, Pentium users were discovering a flaw in the chip. During certain floating-point operations, some Pentium chips were actually producing erroneous calculations—albeit the error showed up in only the fifth or sixth decimal place. While this might not affect the average consumer who's trying to balance a checkbook, power users in scientific laboratories require absolute precision and accuracy in their calculations.

Having a defect in a high-performance technology product such as the Pentium chip was one thing; how Intel handled the problem was another. Intel's initial "official" response was that the flaw in the chip was so insignificant that it would produce an error in calculations only once in 27,000 years. But then, IBM, which had shipped thousands of PCs with Pentium chips, challenged the assertion that the flaw was insignificant, claiming that processing errors could occur as often as every 24 days. IBM announced that it would stop shipment of all Pentium-based PCs immediately.[9]

From this point on, the Pentium situation became a runaway public relations disaster. Every major newspaper, network newscast, and magazine carried the story of the flawed Pentium chip. Even the cartoon series *Dilbert* got in on the act, running a whole series of cartoon strips that spoofed the Intel controversy. One of these *Dilbert* cartoons can be seen in Exhibit 20.2. One observer characterized it this way: "From a public relations standpoint, the train has left the station and is barreling out of Intel's control."[10] For weeks Intel publicly argued that the flaw would not affect the vast majority of users, and the firm did nothing.

Ultimately, public pressure and user demands forced Intel to change its position. Consumers were outraged at Intel's initial policy of refusing to replace Pentium chips unless Intel thought the user needed one. Finally, in early 1995, Intel decided to provide a free replacement chip to any user who believed he or she was at risk. Andy Grove, Intel's highly accomplished CEO, in announcing the $475 million program to replace customers' chips, admitted publicly that "the Pentium processor divide problem has been a learning experience for Intel."[11]

Source: *Dilbert* reprinted by permission of United Features Syndicate, Inc.

EXHIBIT 20.2

The importance of public relations to a company is underscored in this exhibit. A cartoon character can make fun of your company's problems and there isn't much you can do about it. In checking out the Dilbert Web site, you can see that the "everyman" of corporate America has grown into quite a commercial enterprise. www.dilbert.com/

9.   Barbara Grady, "Chastened Intel Steps Carefully with Introduction of New Chip," *Computerlink,* February 14, 1995, 11.

10.   James G. Kimball, "Can Intel Repair the Pentium PR?" *Advertising Age,* December 19, 1994, 35.

11.   Grady, "Chastened Intel Steps Carefully with Introduction of New Chip," op. cit.

Syringes Found in Two Cans Of Cola in Washington State

SEATTLE, June 13 (Reuters) — Hypodermic needles were found in two cans of Diet Pepsi in Washington State this week, prompting a Federal investigation and a warning from a bottling company that Pepsi drinkers should rattle their cans before taking a sip.

Preliminary Food and Drug Administration tests of the two cans revealed no contamination, the regional Pepsi bottler Alpac Corporation said. Alpac has not issued a recall.

The first syringe was found in a Diet Pepsi by an elderly couple in Tacoma. Earl and Mary Tripplett discovered the syringe and bent needle Wednesday rattling around in an empty can of Diet Pepsi which they had opened and drunk. They reported no illness.

Alpac said the second can was found by a resident of Federal Way, about 18 miles south of Seattle. It was collected Friday and turned over to the F.D.A.

In a television interview on Saturday, the president of the bottler, Karl Behnke, urged consumers to "rattle the cans a little bit" before drinking. Alpac supplies Pepsi to Washington, Alaska, Oregon, Hawaii and Guam.

Source: *New York Times*, June 14, 1993, A-11.

EXHIBIT 20.3

Pepsi faced a potential public relations nightmare in 1993.
www.pepsi.com/

Intel's public relations and publicity problems were of its own doing. But in many cases, firms are faced with public relations crises that are totally beyond their control. One of these cases, which goes down in history as a classic, happened to Pepsi. In 1993, Pepsi had a public relations nightmare on its hands. Complaints were coming in from all over the United States that cans of Pepsi, Diet Pepsi, and Caffeine Free Diet Pepsi had syringes inside them (see Exhibit 20.3). Other callers claimed their cans of Pepsi contained such things as a screw, a crack vial, a sewing needle, and brown goo in the bottom. Unlike Intel, Pepsi assembled a management team that was mobilized to handle the crisis. The team immediately considered a national recall of all Pepsi products—no matter what the cost. The Food and Drug Administration (FDA) told Pepsi there was no need for such action since no one had been injured and there was no health risk. The Pepsi team was sure that this was not a case of tampering in the production facility. A can of Pepsi is filled with cola and then sealed in nine-tenths of a second—making it virtually impossible for anyone to get anything into a can during production.

The president of Pepsi went on national television to explain the situation and defend his firm and its products. Pepsi enlisted the aid of a powerful and influential constituent at this point—the Food and Drug Administration. The commissioner of the FDA, David Kessler, said publicly that many of the tampering claims could not be substantiated or verified. A video camera in Aurora, Colorado, caught a woman trying to insert a syringe into a Pepsi can. Pepsi was exonerated in the press, but the huge public relations problem had significantly challenged the firm to retain the stature and credibility of a truly global brand.

What happened to Intel and Pepsi highlights why public relations is such a difficult form of communication to manage. In many cases, a firm's public relations program is called into action for damage control, as the Pepsi ad in Exhibit 20.4 illustrates. Intel and Pepsi had to be totally reactive to the situation rather than strategically controlling it, as with the other tools in the integrated communications process. But while many episodes of public relations must be reactive, a firm can be prepared with public relations materials to conduct an orderly and positive goodwill and image-building campaign among its many constituents. To fully appreciate the role and potential of public relations in the broad communications efforts of a firm, we will consider the objectives of public relations, the tools of public relations, and basic public relations strategies.

Objectives of Public Relations. The public relations function in a firm, usually handled by an outside agency, is prepared to engage in positive public relations efforts and to deal with any negative events related to a firm's activities. Within the broad guidelines of image building and establishing relationships with constituents, it is possible to identify six primary objectives for public relations:

- *Promoting goodwill.* This is an image-building function of public relations. Industry events or community activities that reflect favorably on a firm are highlighted.

EXHIBIT 20.4

Pepsi (www.pepsi.com) moves to head off trouble—in this case, all of the facts are on its side, as it quashes an apparent hoax. Some firms have found the Internet a challenge, as it gives a voice—and sometimes, unwarranted credibility—to virtually anyone who can slap up a Web page or broadcast E-mail. Some of the hoaxes, myths, and urban legends coloring the Internet have been documented on one of the Mining Company's many expert sites (urbanlegends.miningco.com).

WEB SIGHTING

Pepsi is pleased to announce...
...nothing.

As America now knows, those stories about Diet Pepsi were a hoax. Plain and simple, not true. Hundreds of investigators have found no evidence to support a single claim.

As for the many, many thousands of people who work at Pepsi-Cola, we feel great that it's over. And we're ready to get on with making and bringing you what we believe is the best-tasting diet cola in America.

There's not much more we can say. Except that most importantly, we won't let this hoax change our exciting plans for this summer.

We've set up special offers so you can enjoy our great quality products at prices that will save you money all summer long. It all starts on July 4th weekend and we hope you'll stock up with a little extra, just to make up for what you might have missed last week.

That's it. Just one last word of thanks to the millions of you who have stood with us.

Drink All The Diet Pepsi You Want.
Uh Huh®.

DIET PEPSI and UH HUH are registered trademarks of PepsiCo Inc.

When employees of General Electric participate in the Habitat for Humanity program, this event is newsworthy in a public relations sense.

- *Promoting a product or service.* Press releases or events that increase public awareness of a firm's brands can be pursued through public relations. Large pharmaceutical firms such as Merck and Glaxo Wellcome issue press releases when new drugs are discovered or FDA approval is achieved.

- *Preparing internal communications.* Disseminating information and correcting misinformation within a firm can reduce the impact of rumors and increase employee support. For events such as reductions in the labor force or mergers of firms, internal communications can do much to dispel rumors circulating among employees and in the local community.

- *Counteracting negative publicity.* This is the damage control function of public relations. The attempt here is not to cover up negative events, but rather prevent the negative publicity from damaging the image of a firm and its brands. When a lawsuit was filed against NEC alleging that one of its cellular phones had caused cancer, McCaw Cellular Communications used public relations activities to inform the public and especially cellular phone users of scientific knowledge that argued against the claims in the lawsuit.[12]

12. John J. Keller, "McCaw to Study Cellular Phones as Safety Questions Affect Sales," *Wall Street Journal,* January 29, 1993, B3.

- *Lobbying.* The public relations function can assist a firm in dealing with government officials and pending legislation. Industries maintain active and aggressive lobbying efforts at both the state and federal levels. As an example, the beer and wine industry has lobbyists monitoring legislation that could restrict beer and wine advertising.
- *Giving advice and counsel.* Assisting management in determining what (if any) position to take on public issues, preparing employees for public appearances, and helping management anticipate public reactions are all part of the advice and counsel function of public relations.

Tools of Public Relations. There are several vehicles through which a firm can make positive use of public relations and pursue the objectives just cited. The goal is to gain as much control over the process as possible. By using the methods discussed in the following sections, a firm can integrate its public relations effort with other marketing communications.

Press Releases. Having a file of information that makes for good news stories puts the firm in a position to take advantage of free press coverage. Press releases allow a firm to pursue positive publicity from the news media. Items that make for good public relations include the following:

- new products
- new scientific discoveries
- new personnel
- new corporate facilities
- innovative corporate practices, such as energy-saving programs or employee benefit programs
- annual shareholder meetings
- charitable and community service activities

The only drawback to press releases is that a firm often doesn't know if or when the item will appear in the media. Also, the news media are free to edit or interpret a news release, which may alter its meaning. To help reduce these liabilities, consultants recommend carefully developing relationships with editors from publications the organization deems critical to its press release program.[13]

Feature Stories. While a firm cannot write a feature story for a newspaper or televise a story over the local television networks, it can invite journalists to do an exclusive story on the firm when there is a particularly noteworthy event. A feature story is different from a press release in that it is more controllable. A feature story, as opposed to a news release, offers a single journalist the opportunity to do a fairly lengthy piece with exclusive rights to the information.

Company Newsletters. In-house publications such as newsletters can disseminate positive information about a firm through its employees. As members of the community, employees are proud of achievements by their firm. Newsletters can also be distributed to important constituents in the community, such as government officials, the chamber of commerce, or the tourism bureau. Suppliers often enjoy reading about an important customer, so newsletters can be mailed to this group as well.[14] Exhibit 20.5 is an example of a company newsletter.

Interviews and Press Conferences. As in the Pepsi tampering crisis, interviews and press conferences can be a highly effective public relations tool. Often, interviews and press conferences are warranted in a crisis management situation. But firms have

13. Adriana Cento, "7 Habits for Highly Effective Public Relations," *Marketing News,* March 16, 1998, 8.
14. Joanne Cleaver, "Newsletters Prove to be Both Effective and Cost-Effective," *Marketing News,* January 4, 1999, 6.

Inside ILLINOIS

Volume 15   March 7, 1996
Number 15

For Faculty and Staff, University of Illinois at Urbana-Champaign

Faulkner's first two years as provost provide challenges

By Nancy Koeneman

Budget reform. Competitive salary structures. Preservation and enhancement of quality in the UI's programs. Technology. These and other issues have been on the agenda of Larry Faulkner since he became provost and vice chancellor for academic affairs Jan. 1, 1994.

He's shepherded these issues to various levels of discussion, inquiry and resolution through task forces and work groups. Some topics were being examined as he took his office; others became a focal point due to his efforts over the past two years. Recently Faulkner shared his thoughts on the progress made during his tenure as provost and of the challenges that lie ahead.

Budget Reform

"I think there is a certain amount of apprehension about what might take place, but the main thing is that we are proceeding in a careful way through the Budget Strategies Committee to address a budget-making strategy that can meet the real needs of the campus in the years ahead," Faulkner said.

"In the past, habits have built up in an environment where the mechanisms for state funding were very different from the way they are now and [in that time] the university has become larger and more complex," he said.

The current budget system makes it difficult for the deans to understand "the larger implications" of how they allocate their money. Complicating the situation, he said, is the fact that "the system forces too many decisions at too high a level." What the UI needs and what Faulkner wants to see is a "system that allows genuine empowerment of colleges and departments to direct programs," he said.

Subcommittees of the Budget Strategies Committee have been working on these issues, and members were expected to report back this month. The report will be made available to the campus, Faulkner said. Once the report is in hand, he and others on the committee will meet with the major decision-making groups on campus – including the Senate and its principal committees and the representatives of every college – to answer questions and "look at ways to refine this proposal," he said.

"This is a major initiative and it has involved a lot of people," Faulkner said. "I hope to move forward with some early elements [of the reform] in fiscal year 1996-97."

Undergraduate Education

A major theme in the orchestrated efforts to improve the UI is enhanced undergraduate education.

"We have, under the chancellor's leadership, put a strong focus on improving the students' first year here," Faulkner said. "The Discovery Program has received a great deal of attention. We have been working with colleges to provide a stable appropriations base and to increase capacity so that students who desire a course of this kind can get one."

Also, David Liu was appointed associate provost to focus on undergraduate education. "He's a leading faculty member and he will provide strong and more focused leadership in this area," Faulkner said.

Liu is involved in creating a Teaching Advancement Board, one of the recommendations in the Framework for the Future, and in a number of other undergraduate projects.

Salaries and Compensation

Faulkner said with the many topics under consideration, one that remains at the top of his list is improving the salaries for faculty and staff members and graduate assistants. "We're maintaining focus on this with hopes of making progress on an annual basis," he said.

A related issue – tuition and fee waivers for graduate students – has received a lot of attention lately.

"[The proposal] was developed to allow colleges to make their own decisions about support structures suited to their own programs," Faulkner said. "Proposals have been [made] to do that, within a framework governed with fairness by the Graduate College. Some colleges feel they don't have a support program that serves their needs within the competitive context that they face nationally." (For more information about tuition and fee

Enhanced undergraduate education, improving salaries and budget reform are among the items on provost Larry Faulkner's agenda.

waivers, see the Office of the Provost Web page, which is accessible under Administrative and Support Services on the UI's Web page.)

(See Faulkner, page 16)

Fans to honor Henson in post-game tribute

By Nancy Koeneman

Lou Henson's retirement announcement last month set off fireworks in the college sports media, but the real fireworks will be in his honor Saturday at Assembly Hall during post-game ceremonies on Lou Henson Fan Appreciation Day.

Saturday's program concludes with indoor fireworks; the event will sparkle with luminaries from the UI and the sports world as well.

Chancellor Michael Aiken, UI President James Stukel and Ron Guenther, UI's athletic director, are all expected to attend and comment at the post-game bash. Big 10 Commissioner Jim Delany also is expected to attend.

Several former Illini who are now playing in the NBA are sending videotaped tributes for the occasion.

Henson will be featured on the game program cover, commemorative T-shirts will be sold at the game and in the community (with proceeds going to the Fighting Illini Scholarship Fund), and a four-page pamphlet describing Henson's accomplishments in his 21-year history at the UI will be distributed to fans attending the March 9 game.

The last home game of the season, this is the fans' chance to give Henson a warm send-off, said Tom Porter, associate director of athletics in the UI's division of intercollegiate athletics.

"There are very few major NCAA basketball coaches who have an opportunity to retire," Porter said. "With the number of years he's coached and his success, I feel it's fitting to pay him a special tribute."

Guenther added, "We're pleased to honor Lou Henson following the Minnesota game. Henson has done a terrific job representing not only Fighting Illini basketball, but the UI through the last two decades. He is a true gentleman and has been a wonderful role model for our young men on and off the court. We're extremely proud of his accomplishments and delighted we have the opportunity to present him with a big send-off."

An eight-minute video highlighting Henson's UI career will be shown, along with the interviews with former UI athletes now in the NBA. The Rebounders, a basketball booster club, and the Alumni Association will make presentations to Henson, in addition to those by the chancellor, the UI president and the athletic director. Henson also will comment.

Former letterwinners from Henson's teams over the past two decades have been invited, Porter said, and many are expected to attend.

Since Henson's announcement, the game has sold out, Porter said. But those who want to see the celebration can hear it on WDWS-AM (1400) or watch it on WCIA Channel 3. ▼

Head basketball coach Lou Henson retires after this season, his 21st at the UI.

Inside ▼

2   Plans are under way for Cyberfest '97, a celebration of the birth of HAL from "2001: A Space Odyssey."

6   Recipients of the Chancellor's Academic Professional Excellence awards are announced.

also successfully called press conferences to announce important scientific breakthroughs or explain the details of a corporate expansion. The press conference has an air of importance and credibility because it uses a news format to present important corporate information.

Sponsored Events. Sponsored events were discussed as a form of emerging support media in Chapter 16. Sponsoring events can also serve as an important public relations tool. Sponsorships run the gamut from supporting local community events to sponsoring global events such as the World Cup soccer competitions. At the local level, prominent display of the corporate name and logo offers local residents the chance to see that

EXHIBIT 20.6

Oscar Mayer participates in community events to generate favorable public relations. www.oscar-mayer.com/

an organization is dedicated to the community. Exhibit 20.6 shows one of the ways Oscar Mayer participates in local community events.

Another form of sponsorship is fund-raisers. Fund-raisers of all sorts for nonprofit organizations give positive visibility to corporations. For many years, Chevrolet has sponsored college scholarships through the NCAA by choosing the offensive and defensive player of a game. The scholarships are announced weekly at the conclusion of televised games. This sort of notoriety for Chevrolet creates a favorable image for viewers.

One of the most difficult aspects of investing in sponsorships is determining the positive payoff the organization can expect from such an investment. Analysts are recommending that corporations (a) establish an evaluation procedure that tracks awareness generated from sponsorships, (b) establish an event tracking model that can identify target audience attitudes and purchase behavior, and (c) identify the components of the sponsorship that were most effective in achieving awareness and attitude goals.[15] In addition, the IMC box on page 628 offers suggestions on how to judge whether a sponsorship fits well within an organization's overall communications program.

Publicity. **Publicity** is unpaid-for media exposure about a firm's activities or its products and services. Publicity is dealt with by the public relations function but cannot, with the exception of press releases, be strategically controlled like other public relations efforts. This lack of control was demonstrated earlier in the chapter with respect to the situations faced by Microsoft, Intel, and Pepsi. In addition, publicity can turn into a global problem for a firm, as did the controversy created by Benetton's advertising explained in the Global Issues box on page 629. Public relations professionals can react swiftly to publicity, as the team from Pepsi did, but they cannot control the

15. Susan Sloves, "Do Sponsorships Provide a Gold Mine or a Black Hole?" *Marketing News,* February 2, 1998, 9.

EVENT SPONSORSHIP ACID TEST

Many successful, well-respected organizations are besieged with requests to act as an official sponsor of an event. Most managers, sensing an opportunity for good exposure for their firms, are at a loss as to when and whether to sponsor events and how to integrate the event into the firm's broader communications plan. The event promoters make it sound like a good idea, but how can a manager evaluate whether the sponsorship opportunity will fit the firm's overall IMC effort? The International Events Group, publisher of the IEG Sponsorship Report, offers these ten factors to use as criteria to evaluate sponsorship opportunities:

- *Audience composition.* First and foremost, does the audience for the event represent an audience with whom the firm wants to communicate and is reached by other IMC efforts the firm has underway?
- *Image compatibility.* Is the stature of the event consistent with the stature of the firm? This is particularly important for firms that want to develop or protect an upscale image.
- *Exclusivity.* Can the event promoters offer exclusivity of sponsorship in the product category, or will competitors also be sponsoring the event? Being the "official airline" or "official beverage" of an event creates a positive impression.
- *Media coverage.* Will the event be covered by television? Will the firm's brand be prominently displayed in the coverage area?
- *Administrative ease.* Will the sponsor handle all administrative details, or will the organization have to allocate staff to the event?
- *Leverageability.* Is the event sponsorship easily promotable in other ways, helping create a synergy in the IMC effort? For example, Powerfoods's print ads feature the PowerBar Women's International Challenge cycling race.
- *Measurability.* Who measures the attendance and media coverage of the event? If the sponsor doesn't, the firm will incur costs.
- *Continuity.* Is this a one-time sponsorship, or is the event annual? Long-term association with an event can create relationships with target markets and foster the overall IMC program.
- *Efficiency.* Are the terms of the sponsorship offering everything, or only what the firm needs? If the conditions include an official event auto or sponsor's tent and the firm will not use them, the costs are superfluous.
- *Trade and employee tie-ins.* Will the event excite trade partners and employees? Exciting events are all the more potent for an organization.

Source: Adapted from "Ten Steps to Evaluating an Event," *PROMO Magazine,* November 1995, 61.

flow of information. Despite the lack of control, publicity can build an image and heighten consumer awareness of brands and organizations. An organization needs to be prepared to take advantage of events that make for good publicity and to counter events that are potentially damaging to a firm's reputation.

One major advantage of publicity—when the information is positive—is that it tends to carry heightened credibility. Publicity that appears in news stories on television and radio and in newspapers and magazines assumes an air of believability because of the credibility of the media context. Not-for-profit organizations often use publicity in the form of news stories and public interest stories as ways to gain widespread visibility at little or no cost.

Basic Public Relations Strategies.
Given the breadth of possibilities for using public relations as part of a firm's overall integrated marketing communications effort, it is worth identifying basic public relations strategies. Public relations strategies can be categorized as either proactive or reactive. **Proactive public relations strategy** is guided by marketing objectives, seeks to publicize a company and its brands, and takes an offensive rather than defensive posture in the public relations process. **Reactive public relations strategy** is dictated by influences outside the control of a company, focuses on problems to be solved rather than opportunities, and requires a company to take defensive measures.[16] These two strategies involve different orientations to public relations.

Proactive Public Relations
Strategy. In developing a proactive public relations strategy, a firm acknowledges opportunities for it to use public relations efforts to accomplish something positive. In

16.   These definitions were developed from discussions offered by Jordan Goldman, *Public Relations in the Marketing Mix* (Lincolnwood, Ill.: NTC Business Books, 1992), xi–xii.

GLOBAL ISSUES

BENETTON FOULS OUT

The Italian sportswear retailer Benetton is no stranger to controversy. Throughout its history, the firm's leaders have thrived on developing an avant-garde image for the firm with off-beat advertising. Typically, Benetton's ads generate attention and controversy, and cofounder Luciano Benetton likes to get into the act himself—like the time he posed nude for a charity ad campaign for the homeless.

But the most recent publicity generated by Benetton ads caught the retailer off guard. While Benetton ads have been criticized by the conservative press for years, this time it was Benetton's own retailers who cried foul—and they did more than cry: They created a global publicity problem for the firm.

The controversy centers on two ads released by Benetton as part of its ongoing "United Colors of Benetton" campaign. The first depicted a white child wearing angel's wings alongside a black child sporting devil's horns. The second, meant to be a statement on the Bosnian war, showed a soldier's torn and blood-soaked uniform. The problem with these ads spreads beyond the financial discontent of the retailers, though. Trade and industry associations are criticizing the ads on an ethical basis. A spokesperson for the German ad agency association said that "Benetton's ad strategy is morally condemnable, legally untenable and economically extremely damaging." A German trade association spokesperson said, "They [Benetton] have ruined their own brand with the tasteless ads."

The situation was so unusual that press throughout the world carried the story of how Benetton managed to so offend its own partners in retailing that they pulled products from their shelves. The damage from this negative publicity remains to be seen, although the firm has moved to a much more limited advertising and promotional budget and put more effort (interestingly) into retailer promotions.

Sources: Dagmar Mussey, "Benetton, German Retailers Squabble," *Advertising Age*, February 6, 1995, 46; John Rossant, "The Faded Colors of Benetton," *Business Week*, April 10, 1995, 87, 90; Jennifer DeCoursey, "Benetton Illustrates New Battles on Ads," *Advertising Age*, July 24, 1995, 26.

many firms, the positive aspects of employee achievements, corporate contributions to the community, or the organization's social and environmental programs go unnoticed by important constituents. To implement a proactive public relations strategy, a firm needs to develop a comprehensive public relations program. The key components of a such a program are as follows:

1. *A public relations audit.* A **public relations audit** identifies the characteristics of a firm or the aspects of the firm's activities that are positive and newsworthy. Information is gathered in much the same way as information related to advertising strategy is gathered. Corporate personnel and customers are questioned to provide information. The type of information gathered in an audit includes descriptions of company products and services, market performance of brands, profitability, goals for products, market trends, new product introductions, important suppliers, important customers, employee programs and facilities, community programs, charitable activities, and the like.

2. *A public relations plan.* Once the firm is armed with information from a public relations audit, the next step is a structured public relations plan. A **public relations plan** identifies the objectives and activities related to the public relations communications issued by a firm. The components of a public relations plan include the following:

- *Current situation analysis.* This section summarizes the information obtained from the public relations audit. Information contained here is often broken down by category, such as product performance or community activity.
- *Program objectives.* Objectives for a proactive public relations program stem from the current situation. Objectives should be set for both short-term and long-term opportunities. Public relations objectives can be as diverse and complex as advertising objectives. And, as with advertising, the focal point is not sales or profits. Rather, factors such as the credibility of product performance (that is, placing products in verified, independent tests) or the stature of the firm's research and development efforts (highlighted in a prestigious trade publication article) are legitimate statements of objective.
- *Program rationale.* In this section, it is critical to identify the role the public relations program will play relative to all the other communication efforts—

particularly advertising—being undertaken by a firm. This is the area where an integrated marketing communications perspective is clearly articulated for the public relations effort.

- *Communications vehicles.* This section of the plan specifies precisely what means will be used to implement the public relations plan. The public relations tools discussed earlier in the chapter—press releases, interviews, newsletters—constitute the communications vehicles through which program objectives can be implemented. There will likely be discussion of precisely how press releases, interviews, and company newsletters can be used.[17]

- *Message content.* Analysts are now suggesting that public relations messages be researched and developed in much the same way that advertising messages are researched and developed.[18] Focus groups and in-depth interviews are being used to fine-tune PR communications. For example, a pharmaceutical firm learned that calling obesity a "disease" rather than a "condition" increased the overweight population's receptivity to the firm's press release messages regarding a new anti-obesity drug.[19]

A proactive public relations strategy has the potential for making an important supportive contribution to a firm's IMC effort. Carefully placing positive information targeted to important and potentially influential constituents—such as members of the community or stockholders—supports the overall goal of enhancing the image, reputation, and perception of a firm and its brands. Recently, firms are finding that event sponsorships offer an opportunity to add yet another instrument to the overall communications orchestra. The IMC box on page 628 explains that carefully integrating sponsorships with other communications will pay off for firms.

Reactive Public Relations Strategy. A reactive strategy seems a contradiction in terms. As stated earlier, firms must implement a reactive public relations strategy when events outside the control of the firm create negative publicity or circumstances. For firms such as Johnson & Johnson, swift and effective public relations can save an important brand from disaster. The makers of Tylenol had to rely on reactive public relations heavily in the infamous 1982 product-tampering case. Extra-Strength Tylenol had been tampered with and caused the deaths of several people. Within a week after the incident, Tylenol's market share had dropped from 35 percent to about 6 percent of the market. Public relations people handled literally hundreds of inquiries from the public, distributors, the press, and police. The firm then quickly and carefully issued coordinated statements to the general public, the press, and government authorities to provide clarification wherever possible. The result was that through conscientious and competent public relations activities, the firm came through the disaster viewed as a credible and trustworthy organization, and the brand regained nearly all of its original market share within a year.

It is much more difficult to organize for and provide structure around reactive public relations. Since the events that trigger the public relations effort here are unpredictable as well as uncontrollable, a firm must simply be prepared to react quickly and effectively. Two steps help firms implement a reactive public relations strategy:

1. *The public relations audit.* The public relations audit that was prepared for the proactive strategy helps a firm also prepare its reactive strategy. The information provided by the audit gives a firm what it needs to issue public statements based on current and accurate data. For the Tylenol case and for Pepsi in the syringe scare, a current list of distributors, suppliers, and manufacturing sites allowed the firms to quickly determine that the problems were not related to the production process.

2. *The identification of vulnerabilities.* In addition to preparing current information, the other key step in a reactive public relations strategy is to recognize areas where the

---

17. Ibid., 4–14.
18. Mazur, "Good PR Starts with Good Research," op. cit.
19. Ibid.

firm has weaknesses in its operations or products that can negatively affect its relationships with important constituents. These weakness are called *vulnerabilities* from a public relations standpoint. If aspects of a firm's operations are vulnerable to criticism, such as environmental issues related to manufacturing processes, then the public relations function should be prepared to discuss the issues in a broad range of forums with many different constituents.

Public relations is an prime example of how a firm can identify and then manage all aspects of communication in an integrated and synergistic manner. Without recognizing public relations activities as a component of the firm's overall communication effort, misinformation or disinformation could compromise more mainstream communications such as advertising. The coordination of public relations into an integrated program is a matter of recognizing and identifying the process as an information source in the overall IMC effort.

Corporate Advertising.

As we learned in Chapter 1, **corporate advertising** is not designed to promote a specific brand but rather is intended to establish a favorable attitude toward a company as a whole. A variety of highly regarded and highly successful firms use corporate advertising to enhance the image of the firm and affect consumers' attitudes. Toyota, Hewlett-Packard, Rockwell, and Coopers & Lybrand have recently invested in corporate advertising campaigns. A Coopers & Lybrand corporate campaign was conceived to show how the firm helps manage change in a dynamic, global environment. The goal was to establish the image of Coopers & Lybrand as a contemporary and visionary organization.[20] One of the ads from the Coopers & Lybrand campaign is shown in Exhibit 20.7.

Risks can be managed

with foresight.

Damage can be controlled

with hindsight.

Your choice.

Coopers & Lybrand L.L.P.

Not Just Knowledge. Know How.℠

Our profession-leading standards for assessing, measuring and controlling risks protect billions of dollars in reputational value for our clients. This proactive, preventive approach to risk is at the heart of our audit and assurance services. Which lets your senior management spend more time building your business and less time putting out fires. It's your call. 1-800-340-5524.

Coopers &Lybrand | Coopers & Lybrand L.L.P. a professional services firm

EXHIBIT 20.7

In what ways is corporate advertising similar to public relations? How are they different? In this corporate ad for Coopers & Lybrand, how does the image of the company as a whole come across? www.pwcglobal.com/

The Scope and Objectives of Corporate Advertising.

Corporate advertising is a significant force in the overall advertising carried out by organizations in the United States. The best estimates are that about 65 percent of all service companies, 61 percent of business goods manufacturers, and 41 percent of consumer goods manufacturers employ some form of corporate advertising as part of their overall marketing communications.[21] Billions of dollars are invested annually in media for corporate advertising campaigns. Interestingly, the vast majority of corporate campaigns run by consumer goods manufacturers are undertaken by firms in the shopping goods category, such as appliance and auto marketers. Studies have also found that larger firms (in terms of gross sales) are much more prevalent users of corporate advertising than are smaller firms. Presumably, these firms have broader communications programs and more money to invest in advertising, which allows the use of corporate campaigns. An

20. Kevin Goldman, "Coopers & Lybrand TV Ads Paint Inspirational Image for Accounting," *Wall Street Journal,* January 3, 1994, 12.

21. David W. Schumann, Jan M. Hathcote, and Susan West, "Corporates Advertising in America: A Review of Published Studies on Use, Measurement and Effectiveness," *Journal of Advertising,* vol. 20, no. 3 (September 1991), 38.

example of a company using just such a campaign is shown in Exhibit 20.8. Here DuPont touts its image with a very stylish ad and makes only an oblique reference to a specific product in the DuPont line.

In terms of media use, firms have found both the magazine and television media to be well suited to corporate advertising efforts.[22] Corporate advertising appearing in magazines has the advantage of being able to target particular constituent groups with image- or issue-related messages. Magazines also provide the space for lengthy copy, which is often needed to achieve corporate advertising objectives. Television is a popular choice for corporate campaigns, especially image-oriented campaigns, because the creative opportunities provided by television can deliver a powerful, emotional message.

The objectives for corporate advertising are well focused. In fact, corporate advertising shares similar purposes with proactive public relations when it comes to what firms hope to accomplish with the effort. While corporate managers can be somewhat vague about the purposes for corporate ads, the following objectives are generally agreed upon:

- to build the image of the firm among customers, shareholders, the financial community, and the general public
- to boost employee morale or attract new employees
- to communicate an organization's views on social, political, or environmental issues
- to better position the firm's products against competition, particularly foreign competition, which is often perceived to be of higher quality
- to play a role in the overall integrated marketing communications of an organization as support for main product or service advertising

EXHIBIT 20.8

DuPont is using this ad to enhance its corporate image more than it is trying to promote the specific features of the Tyvek HomeWrap insulation system. www.dupont.com/

The human body can detect a change as tiny as .2 degrees. DuPont Tyvek· HomeWrap· keeps out chilly drafts.

DUPONT

www.dupont.com   Better things for better living

Types of Corporate Advertising.

Three basic types of corporate advertising dominate the campaigns run by organizations: image advertising, advocacy advertising, and cause-related advertising. Each is discussed in the following sections.

Corporate Image Advertising. The majority of corporate advertising efforts focus on enhancing the overall image of a firm among important constituents—typically customers, employees, and the general public. When IBM promotes itself as the firm providing "Solutions for a small planet" or when Toyota uses the slogan "Investing in the things we all care about" to promote its five U.S. manufacturing plants, the goal is to enhance the broad image of the firm. Bolstering a firm's image may not result in immediate effects on sales, but as we saw in Chapter 5, attitude can play an important directive force in consumer decision making. When a firm can enhance its overall image, it may well affect consumer predisposition in brand choice.[23] Exhibit 20.9 is an example of an image-oriented corporate ad. Here, Huntsman Chemical Corporation is using a quality theme to create a broad image for the firm, based on both the quality of its business practices and the philanthropy of the company founder.

22. Ibid., 40.

23. For a recent, exhaustive assessment of the benefits of corporate advertising, see David M. Bender, Peter H. Farquhar, and Sanford C. Schulert, "Growing from the Top," *Marketing Management,* vol. 4, no. 4 (Winter/Spring 1996), 10–19.

A distinguishing feature of corporate image advertising is that it is not designed to directly or immediately influence consumer brand choice. In the case of Bayer Corporation, its corporate advertising campaign launched in 1995 had two specific goals: first, to announce its name change from Miles Inc. to Bayer Corporation; second, to change the perception of the company from that of an aspirin-product firm to that of a diverse, research-based international company with businesses in health care, chemicals, and imaging technologies. The ads show a wide range of nonaspirin and often nonconsumer products to demonstrate how Bayer regularly touches people's lives in meaningful ways. The target audience is business decision makers and opinion leaders. The media schedule reflects this nonconsumer target: the *Wall Street Journal* and *Business Week* in print and *Face the Nation* and *Meet the Press* in television. Exhibit 20.10 shows a print ad from this campaign.

While most image advertising intends to communicate a general, favorable image, several corporate image advertising campaigns have been quite specific. When PPG Industries undertook a corporate image campaign to promote its public identity, the firm found that over a five-year period the number of consumers who claimed to have heard of PPG increased from 39.1 percent to 79.5 percent. The perception of the firm's product quality, leadership in new products, and attention to environmental problems were all greatly enhanced over the same period.[24] Another organization that has decided that image advertising is worthwhile is the national newspaper *USA Today*.[25]

Quality People. Quality Products. Quality of Life.

Every day, more than 10,000 skilled and dedicated Huntsman employees and contractors work together to produce the petrochemical industry's highest-quality products...and to help find a cure for cancer.

Chairman and CEO, Jon M. Huntsman, donated $100 million to establish the Huntsman Cancer Institute at the University of Utah. His goal: Assemble the world's finest research scientists and clinicians to work together to help conquer cancer. And he has made the relief of human suffering, including helping to find a cancer cure, a Corporate spending priority.

A partnership of some of the world's best and brightest...petrochemical producers, research scientists, medical professionals...working to improve the quality of life for people everywhere.

HUNTSMAN

Corporate Headquarters • 500 Huntsman Way • Salt Lake City, Utah 84108 • (801)532-5200
www.huntsman.com

EXHIBIT 20.9

This corporate image ad for Huntsman Chemical Corporation uses a quality theme to tout the company's business practices and the philanthropy of the firm's founder. www.huntsman.com/

EXHIBIT 20.10

Bayer changes names and repositions the company in this corporate image ad. www.bayer.com/

24. Schumann, Hathcote, and West, "Corporate Advertising in America," 43, 49.
25. Keith J. Kelly, "*USA Today* Unveils Image Ads," *Advertising Age,* February 6, 1996, 8.

NEW MEDIA

TURNING GREEN AT THE CYBERMALL

For marketers who have environmental causes as part of their corporate advertising agenda, the World Wide Web offers another opportunity to get their green message to consumers. A large percentage of Web users earn a median income of $50,000 to $60,000 and are highly educated. These demographics match the profile of environmentally aware consumers. Many of these consumers got started on the Web by looking for global environmental information. Now they are surfing the Net for green products and business opportunities.

Two well-known green advertisers who turned to the Web early on are Ben & Jerry's (www.benjerry.com/) and Annie's Home-grown (www.annies.com/). Both firms maintain Web sites that offer up-to-date environmental and social information, green games and activities, and ordering information.

In addition to setting up and maintaining a Web site, one of the best ways for an organization to establish a green presence on the Web is to join an online green cybermall. For as little as $500, green mall operators will create and maintain a Web listing for a company and its products. The listing is positioned with other green advertisers and is accompanied by tips on green living, discussion of green issues, and listings of green organizations. Three green mall operators who offer such services are Eco Expo (www.ecoexpo.com/), Envirolink (www.envirolink.com/), and GreenMarket (www.greenmarketplace.com/).

For now, green advertisers are not expecting much in the way of sales from their Web presence. Rather, they feel that creating awareness at minimal cost, reinforcing a green image, and offering potential customers details about the green features of the organization and its products are reasonable objectives. As the vice president of marketing for Safecoat paints put it, "It's another way for us to communicate with people and to get our message out there. It lets our competitors know we're the first and helps us promote an image of cutting edge."

Source: Jacquelyn Ottman, *Marketing News*, February 26, 1996, 7.

The newspaper has spent $1 million on print and outdoor ads that highlight the four color-coded sections of the newspaper: National, Money, Sports, and Lifestyle.

Advocacy Advertising. Advocacy advertising attempts to establish an organization's position on important social, political, or environmental issues. **Advocacy advertising** is defined as "advertising that addresses and attempts to influence public opinion on issues of concern to the sponsor."[26] Exhibit 20.11 is an example of an advocacy corporate advertisement. Here, Chevron is touting its commitment to a clean environment. Typically, the issue is directly relevant to the business operations of the organization. Another company, W. R. Grace, which is a conglomerate in a variety of businesses, used to run advocacy ads warning the public about the disastrous effects of an ongoing federal government budget deficit. After one such campaign, the firm received 50,000 requests for its booklet on the issue.[27]

Cause-Related Advertising. **Cause-related advertising** features a firm's affiliation with an important social cause—reducing poverty, increasing literacy, and curbing drug abuse are examples—and takes place as part of the cause-related marketing efforts undertaken by a firm. The idea behind cause-related marketing and advertising is that a firm donates money to a nonprofit organization in exchange for using the company name in connection with a promotional campaign. The purpose of cause-related advertising is that a firm's association with a worthy cause enhances the image of the firm in the minds of consumers. The Allstate ad in Exhibit 20.12 fits this definition perfectly. The firm is promoting responsible drinking and driving in partnership with MADD—Mothers Against Drunk Driving. The social cause of drinking and driving, however, also affects the company's business activities.

Cause-related advertising is thus advertising that identifies corporate sponsorship of philanthropic activities. Each year, *PROMO Magazine* provides an extensive list of charitable, philanthropic, and environmental organizations that have formal programs for

---

26. Adapted from a definition offered by Karen Fox, "The Measurement of Issue/Advocacy Advertising Effects," *Current Issues and Research in Advertising,* vol. 9, no. 1 (1986), 62.
27. Bob Dietrich, "Mr. Nice Guy," *Madison Avenue,* vol. 26 (September 1984), 82.

EXHIBIT 20.11

Petroleum companies have applied considerable technological research to making fuels burn cleaner. Whether or not you prefer to bike, the companies can make this sort of claim, and do, in ads such as this one for Chevron (www.chevron.com). The American Petroleum Institute (www.api.org), the industry's trade association, dedicates much of its public relations effort to explaining the petroleum industry's contribution to the economy and representing corporate achievements in the aggregate.

EXHIBIT 20.12

Insurance company Allstate (www.allstate.com) and advocacy organization Mothers Against Drunk Driving (www.madd.org) team up for cause-related advertising. Clearly it's in Allstate's interests to see fewer alcohol-related accidents, and less alcohol consumption wouldn't hurt. Would MADD be as likely to share ad space with breweries like Budweiser (www.budweiser.com) or Heineken (www.heineken.com), which also request that their patrons drink responsibly?

corporations to participate in.[28] Most of the programs suggest a minimum donation for corporate sponsorship and specify how the organization's resources will be mobilized in conjunction with the sponsor's other resources.

Some high-profile firms have participated in cause-related marketing programs and have made extensive use of cause-related advertising. American Express first sponsored a major campaign as part of the restoration of the Statue of Liberty.[29] Next, it was the sole sponsor of a program in which the firm donated to a fight against hunger each time an American Express card was used for a purchase during the Christmas holidays. Another cause-related advertiser is Avon, the cosmetics firm, which has distributed more than 15 million brochures on breast cancer and underwritten a PBS special on the topic—all designed to encourage early detection of the disease.[30] Firms are also finding that new

28. For example, see the 1996 listing: "Causes That Move Cases," *PROMO Magazine,* February 1996, 34–38.
29. Bill Kelley, "Cause-Related Marketing: Doing Well While Doing Good," *Sales & Marketing Management,* March 1991, 60.
30. Sue Hwang, "Linking Products to Breast Cancer Fight Helps Firms Bond with Their Customers," *Wall Street Journal,* September 21, 1993, B1.

media outlets such as the World Wide Web offer opportunities to publicize their cause-related activities. The New Media box on page 634 gives information on these activities.

While much good can come from cause-related marketing, there is some question as to whether consumers see this in a positive light. In a study by Roper Starch Worldwide, 58 percent of consumers surveyed believed that the only reason a firm was supporting a cause was to enhance the company's image.[31] The image of a firm as self-serving was much greater than the image of a firm as a philanthropic partner.

The belief among consumers that firms are involved with causes only for revenue benefits is truly unfortunate. Firms involved in causes do, indeed, give or raise millions of dollars for worthy causes. Consumers shopping at Eddie Bauer outlets or ordering from catalogs are encouraged by salespeople to "Add a dollar, plant a tree." With this program, the clothing retailer is helping to raise money for American Forests Global ReLeaf Tree Project. So far, the program has raised more than $300,000, and Eddie Bauer has contributed another $75,000.[32]

Corporate advertising will never replace brand-specific advertising as the main thrust of corporate communication. But it can serve an important supportive role for brand advertising, and it can offer more depth and breadth to an integrated marketing communications program. One fundamental criticism corporate managers have with corporate advertising is the measurement of its specific effects on sales. If the sales effects of brand-specific advertising are difficult to measure, those for corporate advertising campaigns may be close to impossible to gauge.

31. Geoffrey Smith and Ron Stodghill, "Are Good Causes Good Marketing?" *Business Week,* March 21, 1994, 64–65.
32. Daniel Shannon, "Doing Well by Doing Good," *PROMO Magazine,* February 1996, 29–33.

SUMMARY

◀▶ Explain the role of public relations as part of an organization's overall IMC strategy and detail the objectives and tools of public relations.

Public relations represents another aspect of an organization's IMC programming that can play a key role in determining how the organization's many constituents view the organization and its products. An active public relations effort can serve many objectives, such as building goodwill and counteracting negative publicity. Public relations activities may also be orchestrated to support the launch of new products or communicate with employees on matters of interest to them. The public relations function may also be instrumental to the firm's lobbying efforts and in preparing executives to meet with the press. The primary tools of public relations experts are press releases, feature stories, corporate newsletters, interviews, press conferences, and participation in the firm's event sponsorship decisions and programs.

◀▶ Describe two basic strategies for motivating an organization's public relations activities.

When companies perceive public relations as a source of opportunity for shaping public opinion, they are likely to pursue a proactive public relations strategy. With a proactive strategy, a firm strives to build goodwill with key constituents via aggressive programs. The foundation for these proactive programs is a rigorous public relations audit and a comprehensive public relations plan. The plan should

include an explicit statement of objectives to guide the overall effort. In many instances, however, public relations activities take the form of damage control, and in these instances the firm is obviously in a reactive mode. While a reactive strategy may seem a contradiction in terms, it certainly is the case that organizations can be prepared to react to bad news. Organizations that understand their inherent vulnerabilities in the eyes of important constituents will be able to react quickly and effectively in the face of hostile publicity.

◀▶ Discuss the applications and objectives of corporate advertising.

Corporate advertising is not undertaken to support an organization's specific brands, but rather to build the general reputation of the organization in the eyes of key constituents. This form of advertising uses various media—but primarily magazine and television ads—and serves goals such as image enhancement and building fundamental credibility for a firm's line of products. Corporate advertising may also serve diverse objectives, such as improving employee morale, building shareholder confidence, or denouncing foreign competitors. Corporate ad campaigns generally fall into one of three categories: image advertising, advocacy advertising, or cause-related advertising. Corporate advertising may also be orchestrated in such a way to be very newsworthy, and thus it needs to be carefully coordinated with the organization's ongoing public relations programs.

KEY TERMS

public relations (621)
publicity (627)
proactive public relations strategy (628)
reactive public relations strategy (628)

public relations audit (629)
public relations plan (629)
advocacy advertising (634)
cause-related advertising (634)

QUESTIONS FOR REVIEW AND CRITICAL THINKING

1. Describe the two basic strategies a firm can select in determining its approach to the public relations function. Which of these two strategies do you believe Microsoft operated under in the Pentium example discussed at the beginning of this chapter? (Be careful! This is a trick question.)

2. Review the criteria presented in this chapter and in Chapter 16 regarding the selection of events to sponsor. Obviously, some events will have more potential for generating favorable publicity than others. What particular criteria should be emphasized in event selection when a firm has the goal of gaining publicity that will build goodwill via event sponsorship?

3. Would it be appropriate to conclude that the entire point of public relations activity is to generate favorable publicity and stifle unfavorable publicity? What is it about publicity that makes it such an opportunity *and* a threat?

4. There is an old saying to the effect that "there is no such thing as bad publicity." Can you think of a situation in which bad publicity would actually be good publicity?

5. Most organizations have vulnerabilities they should be aware of to help them anticipate and prepare for unfavor-able publicity. What vulnerabilities would you associate with each of the following companies:

R. J. Reynolds—makers of Camel cigarettes

Procter & Gamble—makers of Pampers disposable diapers

Kellogg's—makers of Kellogg's Frosted Flakes

Exxon—worldwide oil and gasoline company

McDonald's—worldwide restaurateur

6. Review the three basic types of corporate advertising and discuss how useful each would be as a device for generating publicity. What other forms of advertising or advertising tactics can be counted on to bring about publicity for its sponsor?

This exercise involves an examination and assessment of corporate advertising. You will need recent issues of popular business magazines. Find and copy three examples of corporate image ads. Which ad do you think does the best job of building a positive corporate image? Explain why. Find and copy one example of advocacy advertising. Describe the controversial issue and why you think the firm is taking a particular stance. Finally, find and copy a cause-related advertisement, and discuss how the firm can be certain it is sponsoring a good cause.

EXPERIENTIAL EXERCISES

1. Whatever happened to Microsoft and its antitrust case with the Justice Department? Track down the news reports about the case in the *Wall Street Journal*.

2. Obtain recent copies of popular business magazines like *Fortune, Forbes,* and *Business Week*. Look for "advocacy" and "cause-related" corporate ads. Do the positions and causes "fit" the corporations' main business areas? Explain.

USING THE INTERNET

Often, the goal of public relations is to support a company's corporate image in the minds of consumers. Public relations departments need to keep abreast of what people are thinking and saying about the company and its products to take any necessary actions to maintain the intended corporate image. The Internet is a worldwide public forum in which people discuss their experiences and evaluations of products. Visit the following sites:

www.markwatch.com

www.ewatch.com

1.   What type of information is available to a corporate public relations department through subscribing to each site? Of what value is this information?

2.   How does the information available through each site compare to other information a public relations department can obtain, such as in news reports?

3.   Make an argument for why a public relations department should subscribe to these sites. Are there specific types of industries that should subscribe to these sites?

The Internet is an ideal medium for the dissemination of corporate public relations documents, and several companies have been formed to serve as channels. Visit these sites:

Business Wire: www.businesswire.com

PR Newswire: www.prnewswire.com

A number of Web-based news services further "distribute" these releases through links on their own sites, e.g., on the Yahoo! stock exchange quotes site (quote.yahoo.com).

1.   What percentage of these press releases are business-oriented, as opposed to cause-related news releases?

2.   What sorts of biases does this news reflect?

The Center for Media & Democracy (www.prwatch.org) is an organization that challenges public relations "spinmeisters" on their facts (or, perhaps, "facts"):

3.   In what ways does the Center take advantage of the Internet in its work?

The Internet is also a cheap medium for companies' opponents, e.g., to disseminate rumors, or even outright hoaxes, or to set up protest Web sites. McSpotlight (www.mcspotlight.org) is a site dedicated to opposition to one corporate target: fast-food giant McDonalds.

4.   How large an audience do you think this site has? How well is it reaching its target audience?

FROM PRINCIPLES to Practice:

A COMPREHENSIVE IMC CASE

PART IV

Executing and Evaluating the IMC Launch Campaign for
Cincinnati Bell Wireless

As noted in Part II of this case history, one of the most laudable aspects of the IMC campaign designed and executed by Northlich Stolley LaWarre was the skillful mix of persuasion tools deployed on behalf of Cincinnati Bell Wireless in the spring of 1998. As you will see, it is reasonable to conclude that these tools worked in harmony from both the standpoint of communicating a multifaceted value proposition and the standpoint of creating awareness, credibility, and excitement for the CBW brand, which together culminated in a desire to purchase this service.

From Part II you should also recall the launch strategy that guided the preparation of the campaign: MOPEs (managers, owners, professionals, entrepreneurs) using other wireless services were targeted for conversion to PCS digital from Cincinnati Bell. The value proposition communicated through a diversified IMC campaign advanced this package of benefits:

- *Simple Pricing, Better Value.* Subscribers sign no contracts; they choose a simple pricing plan, such as 500 minutes for $49.95/month or 1600 minutes for $99.95/month.
- *The Coolest Phone on the Planet.* CBW launched its service with the feature-laden Nokia 6160 phone.
- *Member of the AT&T Wireless Network.* As a member of AT&T's network, CBW offered customers wireless access in over 400 cities at one "hometown rate."
- *Worry-Free Security.* Digital PCS allows secure business transactions that may be compromised over analog cellular.

As you will see in the sample communication materials that follow, the critical points advanced throughout the launch campaign were superiority over cellular, simplification, and hey, it's a cool phone! Various ads played different parts to yield precisely the kind of beautiful music that Jack Cassidy and others at CBW were waiting to hear: These ads made the cash register sing!

An Overview of the CBW Launch Campaign.
Here we will describe and provide examples of many of the different persuasion tools deployed in this multi-million-dollar launch. You will see that this was a multilayered campaign with different elements called on to contribute the best of what each has to offer, as represented in Chapters 15 through 20. We will discuss TV, print, radio, and outdoor ads, special events and promotions, direct mail, and point-of-purchase advertising. Each built on the other to advance the CBW brand. But we begin at the beginning, with public relations.

Public Relations.
As you learned in Chapter 20, there can be at least six different objectives for public-relation activities. Two of these six were very clearly being pursued by public relations staff on behalf of CBW. These included the use of press releases and staged events to

develop awareness for CBW, and active development and direct dissemination of information to employees of Cincinnati Bell to turn them into knowledgeable spokespeople for the company's newest offering. Pubic relations efforts often are initiated in advance of more conventional advertising. In this case, press releases were created and circulated as early as February of 1998 to announce newsworthy developments such as the signing of the partnership agreement between Cincinnati Bell and AT&T, which established the infrastructure to support CBW. One could think of this activity as preparatory awareness building.

Another excellent example of the PR function at work is illustrated through Exhibit IMC 4.1. This "Launch Highlights" document was part of a corporate newsletter distributed to Bell employees to advise them of the forthcoming launch. It provides a wonderful synopsis of the complete launch campaign in an effort to create interest and enthusiasm for the new service from within the company. Other internal, corporate communications included a special invitation to attend an employees-only sneak preview for Wireless on May 5, 1998. Hundreds of Bell employees turned out to watch the official countdown and blastoff for the new service. But guess who else got a special invitation to this "employees-only" event? That's right, the press! All the Cincinnati media were in attendance to make sure the whole scene was reported that evening on the local news and in the next day's newspapers. So here again, we see the two PR objectives of awareness building and internal selling working for CBW.

Television. May 11, 1998 was the official start of the advertising support for CBW. Three television advertisements were at the center of the advertising barrage. One of these, *Classroom*, was described briefly in Part III (see Exhibit IMC 3.1). The other two were titled *The Big Easy* (see the storyboard in Exhibit IMC 4.2) and *X-ray: Cool Phone*. These two ads advanced different aspects of the CBW value proposition. Many of the programs where these ads were initially aired are listed in Exhibit IMC 4.1.

Throughout this text we have emphasized that good advertising must be based on an understanding of the customer's concerns. NSL lives by this principle, and we see it brought to life very vividly in the two spots *Classroom* and *The Big Easy*. NSL's consumer research repeatedly identified that consumers were frustrated by the complexity of the wireless category. Their complaints were that the deals were confusing; they got locked in by a contract; and it was hard, even after the fact, to understand the pricing plan that applied to them. CBW's service tackled these concerns with its simple pricing plan and no contracts offer. *The Big Easy* presents CBW as a breakthrough service that eliminates all the hassles people associate with cellular. What's more, this is a service from "people you know you can rely on." *The Big Easy* ad set the stage for all that would follow.

Print, Radio, and Outdoor. As noted in Chapter 15, television is the ultimate medium for achieving broad reach for an appeal almost instantly. However, when repetition of the basic message is called for, the high absolute cost of this medium makes it an expensive option to exclusively rely on. It is common to use other more economical media

EXHIBIT IMC 4.1

CBW internal newsletter: launch preview.

EXHIBIT IMC 4.2

Cincinnati Bell Wireless storyboard: The Big Easy.

as a complement to television to achieve frequency or repetition of the basic message(s). For the CBW launch, NSL made heavy use of both print and radio ads to complement the messages being advanced in the television campaign. Actual spending levels for TV, radio, print, and outdoor are detailed in Exhibit IMC 4.3.

As reflected in Exhibit IMC 4.3, there was a consistent commitment to print ads as a means to keep the CBW offer on the table on almost a daily basis. Print ads like the one in Exhibit IMC 4.4 hammered away at the point that CBW is simply a better deal than cellular and that the world's most advanced digital phone is part of the package. Additionally, the actor shown in Exhibit IMC 4.4 is the same one featured in all CBW TV ads, which again reinforces the integrated look of the campaign. Per Exhibit IMC 4.1, print ads ran in both local newspapers and regional editions of several major magazines.

In many respects, radio parallels print. According to Chapter 15, radio is a very cost-effective medium for executing high levels of message repetition in a targeted geography. NSL deployed radio ads to achieve frequency of exposure of the campaign's basic themes. Using several different executions, the radio ads reinforced the claims that with CBW you get the best coverage, a great phone, no contracts, and much better prices than cellular. One sample of the radio ad copy is featured in Exhibit IMC 4.5. This particular ad emphasizes the point that, with CBW, you can roam far and wide and still stay in touch. The main actor in the radio ad is the same actor who appeared in the TV and print ads. Are you starting to get the picture that the folks at NSL took this "one look," "one voice," "integration thing" pretty seriously?

EXHIBIT IMC 4.3

CBW launch: media billing summary for the first half of 1998.

Description	January	February	March	April	May	June	July
TV					$142,982	$95,887	$0
Radio					49,904	22,844	27,536
Print					153,977	65,265	63,374
Outdoor					8,339	8,339	6,589
Production Totals	$19,179	$50,053	$281,165	$344,835	246,118	202,306	169,507
Media Totals	0	0	0	0	355,202	192,335	97,499
Total Spending	19,179	50,053	281,165	344,835	601,320	394,641	267,006

From the spending levels in Exhibit IMC 4.3, it should be clear that outdoor advertising was not a major emphasis but instead served its traditional role as a support medium. Billboard and transit ads bolstered the basic proposition that CBW is clearer, smarter, and better than cellular. As we pointed out in Part III of this case, the billboards definitely contributed to the uniform look of the campaign.

Promotions and Events. NSL and CBW also made adept use of promotions and special events for a variety of purposes. The schedule of launch events and promotions for May and June of 1998 is listed in Exhibit IMC 4.6. Several points are evident here. First, there was participation in city-wide spring outdoor events, such as Taste of Cincinnati, Day in Eden (Park), and Kid Fest, that provided exposure and lead generation for CBW at virtually no cost. Note as well that with an event like Kid Fest, CBW was also probing customers who were not part of the primary launch target. This gave CBW an opportunity to gauge the appeal of their service with a broader base of potential users, without diluting the focus of their primary advertising campaign.

Second, from Exhibit IMC 4.6 we see that CBW offered price promotions around traditional gift-giving occasions such as Mother's Day, Father's Day, and graduation. These promotions were supported by special radio and print ads and direct mail. One advantage CBW has over any local competitor is that its parent company, Cincinnati Bell Telephone, makes regular mailings to nearly every household in the city in the form of monthly phone bills. For CBW, the bill insert is a very cost-effective way to announce promotions.

Finally, Exhibit IMC 4.6 also notes CBW's participation as a sponsor of professional baseball and the women's professional golf tour. Through their "businessmen's special" promotions at Cincinnati Reds' games, CBW was afforded an awareness-building opportunity with its primary target segment—MOPEs. An affiliation with the Ladies' Professional Golf Association facilitated outreach to the primary target segment and beyond.

EXHIBIT IMC 4.4

Sample print ad from the CBW launch.

EXHIBIT IMC 4.5

Radio copy: Roadside America *(:60).*

(Sound effects: outdoor, nature sounds.)

Scott: This truly is a modern way to travel, Roy.

Roy: Yeah, the largest mobile home ever made. Theater-style seating. Sleeps 52. So big, it beeps when I back up . . . and when I'm going forward.

Scott: Wow! Now where have you been, what have you seen?

Roy: The world's largest talking cow in Georgia. A bicycle-eating tree in Washington. And pretty much everything in between.

Scott: Oh, that's great . . . now, you know, if you had a Cincinnati Bell Wireless phone, you could talk to virtually anyone, anywhere you went.

Roy: Oh yeah, is that right, even at the sand sculpture of the last supper?

Scott: Oh, the sand sculpture of the last supper . . .

Roy: All right, how about the lickable house of salt?

Scott: Oh . . . yeah, wherever that is. You know . . . plus home-rate roaming in AT&T cities across the U.S.

Roy: Well, what are we waiting for?!

(Sound effects: engine starts, then the familiar beeping sound a truck makes when it's backing up, continues under Scott.)

Scott: Get the nationwide coverage and simple more affordable rates than cellular: 100 minutes for 25 bucks or 500 minutes for $50. Stop by the Store@Cincinnati Bell or call 565-1CBW for details.

NOTE: This ad was voted *Best of Show* by the 1998–99 Addy Awards, Cincinnati Advertising Club.

Direct Marketing.

The set of communication tools described above—from PR, to various forms of mass-media advertising, to event participation—set the stage for the success of CBW by building awareness, excitement, and credibility for the brand. At this point, a MOPE may have been convinced to walk into a Store@Cincinnati Bell to purchase their cool phone and activate this new service; however, NSL was clearly leaving no stone unturned. To build on the broad base of awareness created by the communication tools described thus far, the direct marketing specialists on the NSL account team prepared a coordinated and extensive direct mail campaign.

The goal for this campaign was to prompt action in one of several ways. Recipients of the direct mail brochure were invited to either sign up immediately for wireless service by calling an 800 number or get more details at the CBW Web site. Or, as the brochure explained, they could sign up by visiting any Store@Cincinnati Bell or another CBW-authorized dealer. As part of this mailing, MOPEs also received a letter from Mike Vanderwoude, CBW's marketing director, detailing the benefits of CBW for the sophisticated business user. Attached to Mike's letter was a $10 coupon redeemable on any CBW purchase. Again, the goal of this direct marketing effort was to sway hesitant MOPEs to close the deal.

With the help of a list broker that specialized in geodemographic segmentation (remember Chapter 6?), NSL identified nearly 100,000 households in greater Cincinnati that contained a MOPE. Simultaneously, they were planning a campaign that included a built-in experiment. As we noted in Chapter 19, the mindset of the direct marketing specialist always includes experimentation to benefit future programs. For the CBW launch, four groups were created to facilitate this research:

1. 46,000 MOPE households were designated to receive the complete mailing package plus outbound telemarketing follow-up *and* extra offer of a free leather case for their Nokia 6160 phone.
2. 46,000 MOPE households were designated to receive the complete mailing package plus outbound telemarketing follow-up, but *no* offer for the free leather case.

645

EXHIBIT IMC 4.6

CBW launch: promotions and events schedule.

May	June
Taste of Cincinnati	**Day in Eden**
Target: Adults 25–54	Target: Adults 25–54
Objective: Introduce CBW and build awareness; generate leads (database)	Objective: Introduce CBW and build awareness; generate leads (database)
Vehicles: Event only	Vehicles: Event only
Promo: Booth at event; free trial (phone calls); contest entry	Promo: Booth at event; free trial (phone calls); contest entry
Mother's Day	**Kid Fest**
Target: Users and nonusers	Target: Users and nonusers
Objective: Drive response; store traffic	Objective: build awareness; drive response
Message: Safety; multiple phones per household	Message: Safety
Vehicles: Radio and print; bill inserts	Vehicles: Event only
Promo: Special price package; radio contest (best mother; mother in most need of wireless)	Promo: Booth at event giving away safety-related item (windshield distress sign; emergency flag) logo'd CBW; special offer to sign up for service and receive family pass to local amusements
Graduate Program (high school and college)	**Father's Day**
Target: Nonusers (soon to be young professionals); users (families)	Target: Users and nonusers
Objectives: Drive response	Objective: Drive response; traffic in stores
Message: Safety and productivity benefits	Message: Productivity benefits
Vehicles: Radio and print; bill inserts	Vehicles: Radio and print; bill inserts
Promo: Special price package	Promo: Special price package; radio contest (best father; father in most need of wireless)
Baseball	**LPGA**
Target: Businessmen (Businessmen's Special)	Target: Nonusers and Users
Objective: Build awareness; drive response	Objective: Drive response
Message: Productivity benefits	Message: Safety and convenience
Vehicles: Event only	Vehicles: Event only
Promo: Coupon on back of ticket for discount; raffle free phone/service	Promo: Coupon on back of ticket for discount; raffle free phone/service

3. 5,000 MOPE households were designated to receive the complete mailing package with follow-up by a second direct mail contact in place of telemarketing.
4. 1,500 MOPE households were designated to receive outbound telemarketing only.

It should be apparent that NSL's direct marketing department expected direct mail followed by outbound telemarketing to be the best combination to drive response. The overwhelming majority of the targeted MOPEs received this combination. Groups 3 and 4 were used to assess the relative effectiveness of other combinations for future campaigns. In addition, the comparison of responses from group 1 versus group 2 showed NSL the value of the leather case offer, again, for future reference. As it turned out, the incremental responses generated by the leather case offer were not enough to justify the extra costs associated with that offer. Looking to the future, there would be no more leather freebies, and direct mail followed by outbound telemarketing was established as the most effective tactical combination.

P-O-P Advertising, Collateral, and Sales Support. The final layer that must be addressed as part of any multilayered IMC campaign is point-of-purchase. At P-O-P, everything the customer hears, sees, touches, tastes, and smells must support the expectations that were made by other communication tools. While there isn't much tasting or smelling to worry about in activating a new mobile phone, there are plenty of other details.

At P-O-P, and particularly in the Stores@Cincinnati Bell, the prospective customer was reminded of the larger IMC campaign in many ways. As you saw in Part III of this case history (see especially Exhibit IMC 3.3), the numerous informational brochures developed by NSL shared many design features with other materials from the campaign, as did the interior design of the Stores@Cincinnati Bell. NSL used the same design features in the package sleeve that slid over the protective packaging of the Nokia 6160 phone.

In-store salespeople were also well versed in the messages and details of the larger IMC campaign. As already mentioned, the details of the campaign were communicated to all employees throughout the CBW system by newsletter announcements (see Exhibit IMC 4.1). Additionally, the multiple benefits that comprised CBW's value proposition were recast as a list of the top ten reasons why one should become a CBW subscriber (for example, reason number 1 was "No contracts to sign!"). This top ten list was featured on in-store placards and window posters to reinforce the benefit promises that customers may have heard in other campaign executions.

As you learned back in Part II, an IMC plan is characterized by anticipation of brand contacts. Brand contacts are all the ways in which prospective customers come in contact with the organization—through packaging, employee contacts, in-store displays, and sales literature, as well as media or event exposure. Each contact must be evaluated for consistency with the overall IMC program. We see this drive for consistency at every level of the CBW launch campaign.

Gauging the Impact of the CBW Launch Campaign. Hopefully, this overview has given you an appreciation for the breadth of the IMC campaign that NSL orchestrated on behalf of its client and partner, Cincinnati Bell Wireless. But were the campaign's objectives achieved? Did the client consider the campaign a success? Looking back now, we are able to accurately assess the outcomes from this launch campaign, and this assessment must start with the issue of objectives. You may recall from Part II that the client's primary objective targeted new subscribers. Success for CBW begins with service activations. The campaign's goal was 16,868 new subscribers by the end of the calendar year, a conservative and attainable goal that both the client and agency hoped to surpass. But no one really anticipated how much was possible.

It didn't take long for all parties to realize that they needed to think bigger. After just one week into the launch campaign, they had 10,500 activations. While this pace could not continue, the new subscriber goal for the campaign was easily surpassed in the first 90 days. By the end of 1998, CBW had over 60,000 subscribers, over three and a half times the original goal. And the profile of these subscribers was truly remarkable. Almost exactly half of these activations came from MOPEs who were converting to CBW from another mobile phone service. As you know by now, these MOPEs were the primary target segment. The other 30,000 activations came from young professionals who hadn't previously subscribed to a mobile phone service. To explain the outcome, Jack Cassidy, president of CBW, surmised that NSL's IMC campaign had been exceptionally effective in communicating the *no hassles*, *great pricing*, and *cool phone* elements of the CBW value proposition. Users and nonusers alike were persuaded that CBW was different and better than anything available previously. Users switched carri-

ers and nonusers signed on in about equal numbers. As you might expect, Jack Cassidy was very pleased with his advertising agency.

There are other concrete indicators of the campaign's success. One has to do with CBW's realized churn rate. Churn rates are expressed as a percentage and indicate the percent of current customers that a company is losing each month. Average monthly churn in the wireless business is about 4 percent. If a company is losing 4 percent of its customers every month, then after just a year, it will have lost nearly half its customers. Obviously, high churn rates are an indication of customer dissatisfaction. In 1998, CBW's churn rate was less than 1.5 percent per month, indicating that CBW customers were considerably more satisfied than the industry average. It also indicates that there was a good balance between the benefits promised in CBW advertising and the actual benefits realized in the use of the service. Striking this balance is one mark of great advertising.

You probably also will recall that the primary reason MOPEs were targeted had to do with their usage potential. The thinking was that MOPEs (that is, business users) make heavier use of their mobile phones each month than do household users. Thus, if NSL targeted their advertising efforts properly, they would attract heavy (more profitable) users. Here again, NSL delivered the goods. Industry averages provide the critical point of reference: average revenue per customer per month for analog cellular companies is $29, and for other PCS digital companies it is $45. In 1998, CBW 's average revenue per customer per month was just over $60, which means that NSL's communication tools were delivering the high-value mobile phone customers to Jack Cassidy's door, again making him very happy.

Finally, in the spring of 1998, CBW had intended to spend about $3 million on its IMC campaign. But astute marketers monitor their own successes carefully and make budget adjustments to support programs that clearly are working. Strong programs get budget increases and weak programs get budget cuts. Given that this IMC campaign clearly was working, which became obvious to all just one week into the campaign, what do you suppose Jack Cassidy did with his IMC budget? Well, he effectively doubled it. By the end of 1998, CBW had spent $6 million to support its aggressive launch. This spending is yet another indicator of the campaign's unprecedented success. As 1998 came to a close, investment analysts, AT&T executives, business journalists, and Jack Cassidy were all drawing the same conclusion about the CBW campaign: By any measure, this was the most successful PCS digital launch ever in North America.

IMC EXERCISES

1. Compare this CBW launch campaign with the iMac campaign described at the beginning of Chapter 8. How are they similar? How are they different? What aspects of the iMac campaign would have made it a more complex undertaking than the CBW launch?

2. In this CBW example we see that direct marketing people are most prone to learning through trial and error. Why is this type of learning so important to direct marketers? What is it about direct marketing that makes learning in this way more feasible? What did the direct marketers on NSL's account team learn in the CBW launch?

3. Make a list of at least five different communication tools that were used as part of the IMC campaign for CBW. Now critique each tool with respect to how well it supported or reinforced key aspects of the CBW value proposition.

4. Visit the CBW Web site at www.cbwireless.com. Obviously, the launch campaign described above was just the beginning for CBW. From the Web site now, can you infer any changes in marketing strategy? Has the value proposition changed? What about the primary target segment? Given the effectiveness of their launch campaign, how could CBW justify any changes in their marketing strategy, on the Web or elsewhere?

Appendix: Web Site Addresses

3com
www.3com.com/

ABC
www.abc.com

Absolut
www.absolutvodka.com/

Acura
www.acura.com/

Adobe
www.adobe.com/

Advertising Age
www.adage.com

Airbus
www.airbus.com/

Allstate
www.allstate.com/

Alpo
www.nestle.com/brands/html/b9-3.html

AltaVista
www.altavista.digital.com/

Altoids
www.altoids.com/

Amazon.com
www.amazon.com/

America Online
www.aol.com/

American Express
www.americanexpress.com/

American Honda
www.honda.com/

American Petroleum Institute
www.api.org

American International
www.aig.com/

American Association of Advertising Agencies
www.aaaa.org/

Anheuser-Busch
www.budweiser.com/

Annie's Homegrown
www.annies.com/

Apartments.com
www.apartments.com

Apple Computer
www.apple.com/

Arthur Andersen
www.arthurandersen.com/

Asian Pacific AIDS Intervention Team
www.youthhiv.org/apait/

Ask Jeeves
www.ask.com/

Association for Interactive Media
www.interactivehq.org/

AT&T WorldNet Service
www.att.net/wns/maxim/

Avis Rent A Car
www.avis.com/

Bargain Finder
www.bargainfinder.com/

Barnes & Noble
www.barnesandnoble.com/

Bass Ale
www.bassale.com/

Bauer Skating
www.bauer.com/skating.html

Bayer
www.bayer.com/

Bell Atlantic BigYellow
www.bigyellow.com/

Ben & Jerry's
www.benjerry.com/

Binney & Smith
www.crayola.com/

Bluefly
www.bluefly.com/

BMW
www.bmwusa.com/

Bobby
www.cast.org/bobby/

Body Shop
www.the-body-shop.com/

Boston Globe
www.boston.com

British Army
www.army.mod.uk/army/

broadcast.com
www.broadcast.com/

Builders Square
www.builderssquare.com/

Business Wire
www.businesswire.com

Campbell's
www.campbellsoups.com/

Carnival Cruise Lines
www.carnival.com/

cars.com
www.cars.com/

Cartoon Network
www.cartoonnetwork.com/

Casio
www.casio-usa.com/

Catalog City
www.catalogcity.com/

CBS
www.cbs.com

CD Now
www.cdnow.com/

Center for Media Education
www.cme.org

Centers for Disease Control and Prevention
www.cdc.gov

Charles Schwab
www.schwab.com/

Chevrolet
www.chevrolet.com/

Chevron
www.chevron.com/

Chiat/Day
www.chiatday.com

Chivas Regal
www.chivas.com/

Christie's
www.christies.com/

Chrysler
www2.chryslercorp.com/

Cincinnati Bell
www.cincinnatibell.com/

Cincinnati Bell Wireless
www.cbwireless.com/

Citibank
www.citibank.com/

City of Detroit
www.detroit.com/

City of Beverly Hills
www.ci.beverly-hills.ca.us/

Clamato
www.clamato.com/

Claritin
www.claritin.com

Classified Ventures
www.classifiedventures.com

Classified Warehouse
www.classifiedwarehouse.com

Clorox
www.clorox.com/

CNET
www.cnet.com

CNN
www.cnn.com/

Coalition Against Unsolicited Commercial Email
www.cauce.org/

Coca-Cola
www.cocacola.com/

Comedy Central
www.comedycentral.com/

CommerceNet
www.commercenet.com/

Commission-Based Advertising
www.markwelch.com/bannerad/baf_
commission.htm

CompareNet
www.compare.com/

Consolidated Cigars (H. Upmann)
www.hupmann.com/

Converse
www.converse.com/

Coopers & Lybrand
www.pwcglobal.com/

Coupons Online
www.couponpages.com/

Court TV
www.courttv.com/

Crackerjack
www.crackerjack.com

Cybercalifragilistic
www.cybercal.com/

CyberShop
www.cybershop.com/

Danskin
www.danskin.com/

Dassault
www.dassault-aviation.com

Data on Demand
www.ira-ondemand.com/

Defense Department
www.pentagon.mi/

Democratic National Party
www.democrats.org/

Diamond Center
www.adiamondisforever.com/

Dilbert
www.dilbert.com/

Diners Club
www.dinersclub.com/

Direct Marketing Association
www.the-dma.org/

Discover Brokerage
www.discoverbrokerage.com/

Disney
www.disney.com/

DM Group
www.dm1.com/

Dodge Neon
www.4adodge.com/neon/

Dogpile
www.dogpile.com/

Dove
www.dovespa.com/

Dr. Marten's
www.drmartens.com/

Dun & Bradstreet
www.dnb.com/

Dunkin' Donuts
www.dunkindonuts.com

DuPont
www.dupont.com/

E★Trade
www.etrade.com/index.html

Ebel
www.ebel.com/

Eco Expo
www.ecoexpo.com/

Edmund's Automobile Buyer's Guides
www.edmund.com/

Elle
www.ellemag.com

Envirolink
www.envirolink.com/

Excite
www.excite.com/

Exxon
www.exxon.com

FannieMae
www.fanniemae.com/

Fat Possum Records
www.fatpossum.com/

Federal Trade Commission
www.ftc.gov/

FedEx
www.fedex.com

Foote, Cone & Belding
www.fcbsf.com

Fox
www.fox.com

Fox Kids
www.foxkids.com/

Franco-American
www.francoamerican.com/

Frederick's of Hollywood
www.fredericks.com

FTD
www.ftd.com

Gap
www.gap.com/

Gatorade
www.gatorade.com

General Motors
www.gm.com/

General Electric
www.ge.com

GeoCities
www.geocities.com

Gillette
www.gillette.com/

Gitam International
www.gitam.co.za

Global Casino
www.gamblenet.com

Global Reach
www.euromktg.com/

GoldMine
www.formulanet.com/

Goodyear
www.goodyear.com/

Green Giant
www.greengiant.com/

Green Marketplace
www.greenmarketplace.com/

Grey Interactive Worldwide
www.grey.net/website/interactive/index
.html

Guess
www.guess.com

Guinot
www.lotions.com/guinot.html

Hallmark
www.hallmark.com/

Hard Candy Cosmetics
www.hardcandy.com/

Harley-Davidson
www.harley-davidson.com/

Heineken
www.heineken.com

Hemlock Society
www2.privatel.com/hemlock/

Hewlett-Packard
www.hp.com/

Holiday Inn
www.holiday_inn.com

Holland Festival
www.hollandfestival.nl

Hollywood Stock Exchange
www.hsx.com

Home Page
propaganda/fear.htm

Honda
www.honda.com/

Horst Salons
www.horst-salons.com/

Hot Sails Maui
www.hotsailsmaui.com/

Hot Wired
www.hotwired.com/

HotBot
www.hotbot.com/

HotMail
www.hotmail.com

Huntsman
www.huntsman.com/

I/PRO
www.ipro.com/

IAMS
www.iamsco.com/

ibid
www.ibidphoto.com

IBM
www.ibm.com/

Iconocast
www.iconocast.com/

Infiniti
www.infinitimotors.com/

InFocus
www.infocus.com/

INSYNC Marketing Concepts
www.fotoball.com/

Intel
www.intel.com/

interMute
www.intermute.com

International Social Survey Programme
www.zuma-mannheim.de/boege/issp

Internet Link Exchange
www.link-exchange.com

Iomega
www.iomega.com/

iQVC
www.iqvc.com/

Iridium
www.iridium.com/

Isuzu
www.isuzu.com/

iVillage.com
www.ivillage.com/

J. Walter Thompson
www.jwtworld.com/

Jack Daniel's
www.jackdaniels.com/

Jeep
www.jeepunpaved.com

Jell-O
www.jell-o.com/

Joe Boxer
www.joeboxer.com/

Johnson & Johnson
www.jnj.com/

Johnston & Murphy
www.johnstonmurphy.com/

Jolt
www.joltcola.com

Kenwood
www.kenwood.com/

Kibbles 'n Bits
www.kibbles-n-bits.com/

Kohler
www.kohlerco.com/

KPMG
www.kpmg.com/

Kraft
www.kraftfoods.com/

L. L. Bean
www.llbean.com/

Lancôme
www.lancome.com

Lazy Squirrel
www.middletown.com/lazysquirrel/

Lee Casuals
www.leecasuals.com/

Leggs
www.leggs.com

Levi Strauss
www.levi.com/menu/

Libertel
www.libertel.com/

Lucky Brand
www.juckybrandfootwear.com/

Lycos
www.lycos.com/

M & M Mars
www.m-ms.com/

MADD
www.madd.org

Magellan
mckinley.netcom.com/

Mall Internet
mall-internet.com/

Marriott
www.marriott.com/

Mass Mutual
www.massmutual.com/

MasterCard
www.mastercard.com/

Match.com
www.match.com

McDonald's
www.mcdonalds.com/

MCI
www.mci.com/

McSpotlight
www.mcspotlight.org

Mediamark Research
www.mediamark.com/

Mercedes-Benz
www.mercedes-benz.com/

Microsoft Sidewalk
national.sidewalk.msn.com/

Miller Brewing
www.millerlite.com/

Mining Company
urbanlegends.miningco.com

Mitsubishi
www.mitsubishi.com/

Mobil Oil
www.mobil.com/

Modern Technologies Corporation
www.markwatch.com

Multi-State Lottery Association
www.powerball.com

Nabisco
www.nabisco.com/

Nascar
www.nascar.com/

National Archives Online
www.nara.gov/

National Dairy Council (UK)
www.milk.co.uk/

National Geographic
www.nationalgeographic.com/

National Enquirer
www.nationalenquirer.com/

NBA
www.nba.com

NBC
www.nbc.com

NEC
www.nec.com/

New Jersey Devils
www.newjerseydevils.com/

New York Times
www.nytimes.com/

New York Lottery
www.nylottery.org

Nicorette
www.nicorette.com/

Nielsen Retail Index
www.nielsenmedia.com/

Nike
www.nike.com/

Nissan
www.nissan.com/

Northlich Stolley LaWarre
www.northlich.com/

Northwest Airlines
www.nwa.com/

Norwegian Cruise Lines
www.ncl.com/

Oldsmobile
www.oldsmobile.com/

Olivia Cruises and Resorts
www.olivia.com

Oneida
www.oneida.com/

Oscar Mayer
www.oscar-mayer.com/

O'Neill
www.oneilleurope.com/

P-O-P Advertising Institute
www.popai.com/

Partnership for a Drug-Free America
www.drugfreeamerica.org/

Pathfinder
www.pathfinder.com

Pax Network
www.pax.net/

PBS
www.pbs.org

Pepsi
www.pepsi.com/

Pharmacia & Upjohn
www.rogaine.com/

Pillsbury
www.pillsbury.com/

Pizza Hut
www.pizzahut.com/

Playboy
www.playboy.com

PocketMail
www.pocketmail.com/

Polaroid
www.polaroid.com/

Pontiac
www.pontiac.com/index.html

PowerQuest
www.powerquest.com/

PR Newswire
www.prnewswire.com

Procter & Gamble
www.pg.com/

PromoMart
www.promomart.com/

Propaganda Analysis
carmen.artsci.washington.edu/

Prudential
www.prudential.com/

Publisher's Clearing House
www.pch.com

Quaker Oats
www.quakeroats.com/

Qualcomm
www.eudora.com

Quicken InsureMarket
www.insuremarket.com/

Ray-Ban
www.ray-ban.com/

Red Spider
www.redspider.co.uk/

Red Dog
www.reddog.com/

Reddi–Wip
www.reddi-wip.com/

Reebok
www.reebok.com/

Republican National Convention
www.rnc.org/

Ringling Brothers
ringling.com/

Rolling Stones
www.stones.com/

Royal Viking Line
www.royalviking.com/

Rykä
www.ryka.com

Saab
www.saabusa.com/

Saturn
www.saturncars.com/index.htm

Schwinn
www.schwinn.com/

Scope
www.scope-mouthwash.com/

Screenvision Cinema Network
www.screenvis.com/

Sears
www.sears.com/

shabang!
www.shabang.net/

Singapore Tourism Board
www.newasia-singapore.com/

SkyMall
www.skymall.com

SKYY Vodka
www.skyyvodka.com

Smucker's
www.smucker.com

Snapple
www.snapple.com

Sony
www.sony.com/

Southwest Airlines
www.iflyswa.com

Sporting News Online
www.sportingnews.com/

SportsLine USA
www.sportsline.com/

Sprint
www.sprint.com/

SRI International
www.sri.com/

State of Idaho
www.idoc.state.id.us/

State Farm
www.statefarm.com/

Stoli
www.stoli.com

Sunbeam
www.sunbeam.com/

SuperPages
www.superpages.com/

Suretrade.com
www.suretrade.com/

Svetlana
www.svetlana.com/

Switchboard.com
www.switchboard.com

Tampax
www.tampax.com/

Television Bureau of Advertising
www.tvb.com/

The White House
www.whitehouse.gov

The X-Files
www.thex-files.com

theglobe.com
www.theglobe.com/

Thermador
www.thermador.com/

Ticketmaster
www.ticketmaster.com

Time
www.time.com/

Timex
www.timex.com/

Toshiba
www.toshiba.com/

TotalNEWS
www.totalnews.com

Toyota
www.toyota.com/

Travel City
www.travelcity.com/

Travelocity
www.travelocity.com/

Trojan
www.linkmag.com/trojan/

TRUSTe
www.truste.org

Tupperware
www.tupperware.com

Tylenol
www.tylenol.com/

**University of Illinois,
Urbana–Champaign**
www.uiuc.edu/

United Airlines
www.ual.com/

Urban Decay
www.urbandecay.com

U.S. Postal Service
www.usps.gov/

U.S. Army
www.army.mil/

U.S. Marine Corps
www.usmc.mil/

U.S. Navy
www.navy.mi/

U.S. News & World Report
www.usnews.com

U.S. Savings Bonds Online
www.publicdebt.treas.gov/sav/sav.htm

Versace
viabazaar.com/versace/versace_home.html

Vidal Sassoon
www.vidalsassoon.com

Virginia Power
www.vapower.com/

Virtual Mall
www.virtmall.com/

Visa
www.visa.com/

Volkswagen
www.vw.com/

Volvo
www.volvo.com/

WavePhore, Inc. (eWatch)
www.ewatch.com

Weather Channel
www.weather.com/

WebStep
www.mmgco/webstep.html

Wendy's
www.wendys.com/

Wilkinson
www.wilkinson-sword.com

Wilson
www.wilsonsports.com/

Wired
www.wired.com

Working Computer
www.clientsandprofits.com

Worldata
www.worldata.com/

Yahoo!
www.yahoo.com/

Yellow Pages Publishers Association
www.yppa.org/

Yokohama
www.yokohamatire.com

GLOSSARY

A

account planner A relatively recent addition to many advertising agencies; it is this person's job to synthesize all relevant consumer research and use it to design a coherent advertising strategy.

account planning A system by which, in contrast to traditional advertising research methods, an agency assigns a co-equal account planner to work alongside the account executive and analyze research data. This method requires the account planner to stay with the same projects on a continuous basis.

Action for Children's Television (ACT) A group formed during the 1970s to lobby the government to limit the amount and content of advertising directed at children.

adaptors In reference to the *adaptation/innovation theory* generated by a study of creativity in employees, adaptors are the ones who, when faced with creative tasks, tend to work within the existing paradigm.

advertisement A specific message that an organization has placed to persuade an audience.

advertising A paid, mass-mediated attempt to persuade.

advertising agency An organization of professionals who provide creative and business services to clients related to planning, preparing, and placing advertisements.

advertising campaign A series of coordinated advertisements and other promotional efforts that communicate a single theme or idea.

advertising clutter An obstacle to advertising resulting from the large volume of similar ads for most products and services.

advertising plan A plan that specifies the thinking and tasks needed to conceive and implement an effective advertising effort.

advertising research A specialized form of marketing research that focuses on the planning, preparation, and placement of advertising; more simply stated, advertising research is any research conducted by an advertising agency.

advertising response function A mathematical relationship based on marginal analysis that associates dollars spent on advertising and sales generated; sometimes used to help establish an advertising budget.

advertising substantiation program An FTC program initiated in 1971 to ensure that advertisers make available to consumers supporting evidence for claims made in ads.

advertorial A special advertising section designed to look like the print publication in which it appears.

advocacy advertising Advertising that attempts to influence public opinion on important social, political, or environmental issues of concern to the sponsoring organization.

aerial advertising Advertising that involves airplanes (pulling signs or banners), skywriting, or blimps.

affirmative disclosure An FTC action requiring that important material determined to be absent from prior ads must be included in subsequent advertisements.

agency of record The advertising agency chosen by the advertiser to purchase media time and space.

aided recall A method of testing research subjects in which an interviewer asks questions that use product-category cues in questions designed to assess what the subject remembers.

alternative press newspapers Newspapers geared toward a young, entertainment-oriented audience.

animation The use of drawn figures and scenes (like cartoons) to produce a television commercial.

aspirational groups Groups made up of people an individual admires or uses as role models but is unlikely to ever interact with in any meaningful way.

association tests A type of projective technique that asks consumers to express their feelings or thoughts after hearing a brand name or seeing a logo.

assorted media mix A media mix option that employs multiple media alternatives to reach target audiences.

attitude An overall evaluation of any object, person, or issue that varies along a continuum, such as favorable to unfavorable or positive to negative.

attitude-change study A type of advertising research that uses a before-and-after ad exposure design.

audience A group of individuals who may receive and interpret messages sent from advertisers through mass media.

average quarter-hour persons The average number of listeners tuned to a radio station during a specified 15-minute segment of a daypart.

average quarter-hour rating The radio audience during a quarter-hour daypart expressed as a percentage of the population of the measurement area.

average quarter-hour share The percentage of the total radio audience that was listening to a radio station during a specified quarter-hour daypart.

axis A line, real or imagined, that runs through an advertisement and from which the elements in the ad flare out.

B

balance An orderliness and compatibility of presentation in an advertisement.

bandwidth A measure of the computer resources used by a Web site on the Internet.

banner ads Advertisements placed on World Wide Web sites that contain editorial material.

barter syndication A form of television syndication that takes both off-network and first-run syndication shows and offers them free or at a reduced rate to local television stations, with some national advertising presold within the programs.

beliefs The knowledge and feelings a person has accumulated about an object or issue.

benefit positioning A positioning option that features a distinctive customer benefit.

benefit segmentation A type of market segmenting in which target segments are delineated by the various benefit packages that different consumers want from the same product category.

between-vehicle duplication Exposure to the same advertisement in different media.

blackletter A style patterned after monastic hand-drawn letters characterized by the ornate design of the letters. Also called gothic.

bleed page A magazine page on which the background color of an ad runs to the edge of the page, replacing the standard white border.

border The space surrounding an advertisement; it keeps the ad elements from spilling over into other ads or into the printed matter next to the ad.

brand attitudes Summary evaluations that reflect preferences for various products and brands.

brand communities Groups of consumers who feel a commonality and a shared purpose grounded or attached to a consumer good or service.

branding The strategy of developing brand names so that manufacturers can focus consumer attention on a clearly identified item.

brand-loyal users A market segment made up of consumers who repeatedly buy the same brand of a product.

brand loyalty A decision-making mode in which consumers repeatedly buy the same brand of a product as their choice to fulfill a specific need.

brand placement The sales promotion technique of getting a marketer's brand featured in movies and television shows.

brand switching An advertising objective in which a campaign is designed to encourage customers to switch from their established brand.

build-up analysis A method of building up the expenditure levels of various tasks to help establish an advertising budget.

business markets The institutional buyers who purchase items to be used in other products and services or to be resold to other businesses or households.

business newspapers Newspapers like the *Financial Times,* which serve a specialized business audience.

C

cable television A type of television that transmits a wide range of programming to subscribers through wires rather than over airwaves.

caching The use of a kind of active memory to conserve computer system resources.

cause-related advertising Advertising that identifies corporate sponsorship of philanthropic activities.

cease-and-desist order An FTC action requiring an advertiser to stop running an ad within 30 days so a hearing can be held to determine whether the advertising in question is deceptive or unfair.

celebrity endorsements Advertisements that use an expert or celebrity as a spokesperson to endorse the use of a product or service.

channel grazing Using a television remote control to monitor programming on other channels while an advertisement is being broadcast.

circulation The number of newspapers distributed each day (for daily newspapers) or each week (for weekly publications).

classified advertising Newspaper advertising that appears as all-copy messages under categories such as sporting goods, employment, and automobiles.

click-throughs When Web users click on advertisements that take them to the homepages of those advertisers.

client The company or organization that pays for advertising. Also called the *sponsor*.

closing date The date when production-ready advertising materials must be delivered to a publisher for an ad to make a newspaper or magazine issue.

cognitive consistency The maintenance of a system of beliefs and attitudes over time; consumers' desire for cognitive consistency is an obstacle to advertising.

cognitive dissonance The anxiety or regret that lingers after a difficult decision.

cognitive responses The thoughts that occur to individuals at that exact moment in time when their beliefs and attitudes are being challenged by some form of persuasive communication.

column inch A unit of advertising space in a newspaper, equal to one inch deep by one column wide.

commission system A method of agency compensation based on the amount of money the advertiser spends on the media.

communications test A type of pretest message research that simply seeks to see if a message is communicating something close to what is desired.

community A group of people loosely joined by some common characteristic or interest.

comp A polished version of an ad.

comparison advertisements Advertisements in which an advertiser makes a comparison between the firm's brand and competitors' brands.

competitive field The companies that compete for a segment's business.

competitive positioning A positioning option that uses an explicit reference to an existing competitor to help define precisely what the advertised brand can do.

competitor analysis In an advertising plan, the section that discusses who the competitors are, outlining their strengths, weaknesses, tendencies, and any threats they pose.

concentrated media mix A media mix option that focuses all the media placement dollars in one medium.

concept test A type of developmental research that seeks feedback designed to screen the quality of a new idea, using consumers as the final judge and jury.

consent order An FTC action asking an advertiser accused of running deceptive or unfair advertising to stop running the advertisement in question, without admitting guilt.

consideration set The subset of brands from a particular product category that becomes the focal point of a consumer's evaluation.

consumer behavior Those activities directly involved in obtaining, consuming, and disposing of products and services, including the decision processes that precede and follow these actions.

consumer culture A way of life centered around consumption.

consumerism The actions of individual consumers to exert power over the marketplace activities of organizations.

consumer markets The markets for products and services purchased by individuals or households to satisfy their specific needs.

consumer-market sales promotion A type of sales promotion designed to induce household consumers to purchase a firm's brand rather than a competitor's brand.

contest A sales promotion that has consumers compete for prizes based on skill or ability.

continuity The pattern of placement of advertisements in a media schedule.

continuous scheduling A pattern of placing ads at a steady rate over a period of time.

controlled circulation The number of copies of a newspaper that are given away free.

cookie A coded identifier that is downloaded to a Web site visitor's computer that allows an Internet server to keep track of, and collect data on, that visitor.

co-op advertising *See* **cooperative advertising**.

cooperative advertising The sharing of advertising expenses between national advertisers and local merchants. Also called *co-op advertising*.

copywriting The process of expressing the value and benefits a brand has to offer, via written or verbal descriptions.

corporate advertising Advertising intended to establish a favorable attitude toward a company as a whole, not just toward a specific brand.

corporate home page A site on the World Wide Web that focuses on a corporation and its products.

corrective advertising An FTC action requiring an advertiser to run additional advertisements to dispel false beliefs created by deceptive advertising.

cost per inquiry (CPI) The number of inquiries generated by a direct-marketing program divided by that program's cost.

cost per order (CPO) The number of orders generated by a direct-marketing program divided by that program's cost.

cost per rating point (CPRP) The cost of a spot on television divided by the program's rating; the resulting dollar figure can be used to compare the efficiency of advertising on various programs.

cost per thousand (CPM) The dollar cost of reaching 1,000 members of an audience using a particular medium.

cost per thousand–target market (CPM–TM) The cost per thousand for a particular segment of an audience.

coupon A type of sales promotion that entitles a buyer to a designated reduction in price for a product or service.

cover date The date of publication appearing on a magazine.

creative boutique An advertising agency that emphasizes copywriting and artistic services to its clients.

creative concept The unique creative thought behind an advertising campaign.

creative plan A guideline used during the copywriting process to specify the message elements that must be coordinated during the preparation of copy.

creative revolution A revolution in the advertising industry during the 1960s, characterized by the "creatives" (art directors and copywriters) having a bigger say in the management of their agencies.

creative team The copywriters and art directors responsible for coming up with the creative concept for an advertising campaign.

culture What a people do—the way they eat, groom themselves, celebrate, mark their space and social position, and so forth.

cume The cumulative radio audience, which is the total number of different people who listen to a station for at least five minutes in a quarter-hour period within a specified daypart.

customer satisfaction Good feelings that come from a favorable postpurchase experience.

D

dailies Newspapers published every weekday; also, in television ad production, the scenes shot during the previous day's production.

dayparts Segments of time during a television broadcast day.

deception Making false or misleading statements in an advertisement.

delayed response advertising Advertising that relies on imagery and message themes to emphasize the benefits and satisfying characteristics of a brand.

demographic segmentation Market segmenting based on basic descriptors like age, gender, race, marital status, income, education, and occupation.

design The structure (and the plan behind the structure) for the aesthetic and stylistic aspects of a print advertisement.

developmental copy research A type of copy research that helps copywriters at the early stages of copy development by providing audience interpretations

and reactions to the proposed copy.

dialogue Advertising copy that delivers the selling points of a message to the audience through a character or characters in the ad.

dialogue balloons A type of projective technique that offers consumers the chance to fill in the dialogue of cartoonlike stories, as a way of indirectly gathering brand information.

digital video (DV) A less expensive and less time-consuming alternative to film, it produces a better quality image than standard videotape.

direct broadcast by satellite (DBS) A program delivery system whereby television (and radio) programs are sent directly from a satellite to homes equipped with small receiving dishes.

direct mail A direct-marketing medium that involves using the postal service to deliver marketing materials.

direct marketing According to the Direct Marketing Association, "An interactive system of marketing which uses one or more advertising media to affect a measurable response and/or transaction at any location."

direct-marketing firms Firms that maintain large databases of mailing lists; some of these firms can also design direct-marketing campaigns either through the mail or by telemarketing.

direct response advertising Advertising that asks the receiver of the message to act immediately.

direct response copy Advertising copy that highlights the urgency of acting immediately.

display advertising A newspaper ad that includes the standard components of a print ad—headline, body copy, and often an illustration—to set it off from the news content of the paper.

display type Larger-size copy in the headline and subhead of an advertisement.

door-to-door sampling A type of sampling in which samples are brought directly to the homes of a target segment in a well-defined geographic area.

double-page spreads Advertisements that bridge two facing pages.

dummy advertising vehicles A type of pretest message research that consists of mock-ups of magazines that contain editorial content and advertisements; the mock-ups are given to a test audience, whose responses to the test ads are assessed.

E

economies of scale The ability of a firm to lower the cost of each item produced because of high-volume production.

editing In television ad production, piecing together various scenes or shots of scenes to bring about the desired visual effect.

effective frequency The number of times a target audience needs to be exposed to a message before the objectives of the advertiser are met.

effective reach The number or percentage of consumers in the target audience that are exposed to an ad some minimum number of times.

electronic, laser, and inkjet printing A printing process that uses computers, electronics, electrostatics, and special toners and inks to produce images.

electronic mail (E-mail) An Internet function that allows users to communicate much as they do using standard mail.

emergent consumers A market segment made up of the gradual but constant influx of first-time buyers.

emotional benefits Those benefits not typically found in some tangible feature or objective characteristic of a product or service.

environmental analysis A type of developmental advertising research that tries to assess the potential influence of social and cultural trends, economics, and politics on the consumer and the social environment into which the advertising will be injected.

ethics Moral standards and principles against which behavior is judged.

ethnic newspapers Newspapers that target a specific ethnic group.

ethnocentrism The tendency to view and value things from the perspective of one's own culture.

evaluative copy research A type of copy research used to judge an advertisement after the fact—the audience expresses its approval or disapproval of the copy used in the ad.

evaluative criteria The product attributes or performance characteristics on which consumers base their product evaluations.

event sponsorship Providing financial support to help fund an event, in return for the right to display a brand name, logo, or advertising message on-site at the event.

extended problem solving A decision-making mode in which consumers are inexperienced in a particular consumption setting but find the setting highly involving.

external facilitators Organizations or individuals that provide specialized services to advertisers and agencies.

external lists Mailing lists purchased from a list compiler or rented from a list broker and used to help an organization cultivate new business.

external position The competitive niche a brand pursues.

external search A search for product information that involves visiting retail stores to examine alternatives, seeking input from friends and relatives about their experiences with the products in question, or perusing professional product evaluations.

eye-tracking systems A type of physiological measure that monitors eye movements across print ads.

F

fact sheet radio ad A listing of important selling points that a radio announcer can use to ad-lib a radio spot.

Federal Trade Commission (FTC) The government regulatory agency that has the most power and is most directly involved in overseeing the advertising industry.

fee system A method of agency compensation whereby the advertiser and the agency agree on an hourly rate for different services provided.

film The most versatile and highest quality medium for television ad production.

first cover page The front cover of a magazine.

first-run syndication Television programs developed specifically for sale to individual stations.

flexography A printing technique similar to offset printing but that uses water-based ink, allowing printing to be done on any surface.

flighting A media-scheduling pattern of heavy advertising for a period of time, usually two weeks, followed by no advertising for a period, followed by another period of heavy advertising.

focus group A brainstorming session with a small group of target consumers and a professional moderator, used to gain new insights about consumer response to a brand.

formal balance A symmetrical presentation in an ad—every component on one side of an imaginary vertical line is repeated in approximate size and shape on the other side of the imaginary line.

fourth cover page The back cover of a magazine.

free premium A sales promotion that provides consumers with an item at no cost; the item is either included in the package of a purchased item or mailed to the consumer after proof of purchase is verified.

free-standing insert (FSI) A newspaper insert ad that contains cents-off coupons for a variety of products and is typically delivered with Sunday newspapers.

frequency The average number of times an individual or household within a target audience is exposed to a media vehicle in a given period of time.

frequency-marketing programs Direct-marketing programs that provide concrete rewards to frequent customers.

frequency programs A type of sales promotion that offers consumers discounts or free product rewards for repeat purchase or patronage of the same brand or company.

full position A basis of buying newspaper ad space, in which the ad is placed near the top of a page or in the middle of editorial material.

full-service agency An advertising agency that typically includes an array of advertising professionals to meet all the promotional needs of clients.

functional benefits Those benefits that come from the objective performance characteristics of a product or service.

G

gatefold ads Advertisements that fold out of a magazine to display an extra-wide ad.

gay and lesbian newspapers Newspapers targeting a gay and lesbian readership.

gender The social expression of sexual biology or choice.

general-population newspapers Newspapers that serve local communities and report news of interest to the local population.

geodemographic segmentation A form of market segmentation that identifies neighborhoods around the country that share common demographic characteristics.

geo-targeting The placement of ads in geographic regions where higher purchase tendencies for a brand are evident.

global advertising Developing and placing advertisements with a common theme and presentation in all markets around the world where the firm's brands are sold.

global agencies Advertising agencies with a worldwide presence.

globalized campaigns Advertising campaigns that use the same message and creative execution across all (or most) international markets.

government officials and employees One of the five types of audiences for advertising; includes employees of government organizations, such as schools and road maintenance operations, at the federal, state, and local levels.

gravure A print production method that uses a plate or mat; it is excellent for reproducing pictures.

gross domestic product (GDP) A measure of the total value of goods and services produced within an economic system.

gross impressions The sum of exposures to all the media placement in a media plan.

gross rating points (GRP) The product of reach times frequency.

guaranteed circulation A stated minimum number of copies of a particular issue of a magazine that will be delivered to readers.

H

habit A decision-making mode in which consumers buy a single brand repeatedly as a solution to a simple consumption problem.

headline The leading sentence or sentences, usually at the top or bottom of an ad, that attract attention, communicate a key selling point, or achieve brand identification.

heavy-up scheduling Placing advertising in media more heavily when consumers show buying tendencies.

heavy users Consumers who purchase a product or service much more frequently than others.

high-definition television (HDTV) Television that displays picture and produces sound from a satellite that sends a digital signal.

highly industrialized countries Countries with both a high GNP and a high standard of living.

hits The number of pages and graphical images requested from a Web site.

household consumers The most conspicuous of the five types of audiences for advertising; most mass media advertising is directed at them.

households using television (HUT) A measure of the number of households tuned to a television program during a particular time period.

I

illustration In the context of advertising, the drawing, painting, photography, or computer-generated art that forms the picture in an advertisement.

illustration format The way the product is displayed in a print advertisement.

impressions One way an advertiser can pay for space on a Web site page. In this case, a flat fee is charged for each time the advertisement is viewed.

Industrial Revolution A major change in Western society beginning in the mid-eighteenth century and marked by a rapid change from an agricultural to an industrial economy.

industry analysis In an advertising plan, the section that focuses on developments and trends within an industry and on any other factors that may make a difference in how an advertiser proceeds with an advertising plan.

inelasticity of demand Strong loyalty to a product, resulting in consumers being less sensitive to price increases.

infomercial A long advertisement that looks like a talk show or a half-hour product demonstration.

informal balance An asymmetrical presentation in an ad—nonsimilar sizes and shapes are optically weighed.

information intermediator An organization that collects customer purchase transaction histories, aggregates them across many firms that have sold merchandise to these customers, and then sells the customer names and addresses back to the firms that originally sold to these customers.

in-house agency The advertising department of a firm.

innovators In reference to the *adaptation/innovation theory* generated by a study of creativity in employees, innovators are the ones who, when faced with creative tasks, treat the existing paradigm as an obstacle.

inquiry/direct response measures A type of posttest message tracking in which a print or broadcast advertisement offers the audience the opportunity to place an inquiry or respond directly through a reply card or toll-free number.

in-store sampling A type of sampling that occurs at the point of purchase and is popular for food products and cosmetics.

integrated marketing communications (IMC) The process of using promotional tools in a unified way so that a synergistic communications effect is created.

integrated programming Programming produced through the combined efforts of advertisers, entertainment companies, and media operators.

interactive agencies Advertising agencies that help advertisers prepare communications for new media like the Internet, interactive kiosks, CD-ROMs, and interactive television.

interactive media Media that allow consumers to call up games, entertainment, shopping opportunities, and educational programs on a subscription or pay-per-view basis.

intergenerational effect When people choose products based on what was used in their childhood household.

internal lists An organization's records of its customers, subscribers, donors, and inquirers, used to develop better relationships with current customers.

internal position The niche a brand achieves with regard to the other similar brands a firm markets.

internal search A search for product information that draws on personal experience and prior knowledge.

international advertising The preparation and placement of advertising in different national and cultural markets.

international affiliates Foreign-market advertising agencies with which a local agency has established a relationship to handle clients' international advertising needs.

Internet A vast global network of scientific, military, and research computers that allows people inexpensive access to the largest storehouse of information in the world.

Internet relay chat (IRC) A component of the Internet that makes it possible for users to "talk" electronically with each other, despite their geographical separation.

involvement The degree of perceived relevance and personal importance accompanying the choice of a certain product or service within a particular context.

J, K, L

layout A drawing of a proposed print advertisement, showing where all the elements in the ad are positioned.

less-developed countries Countries whose economies lack almost all the resources necessary for development: capital, infrastructure, political stability, and trained workers.

letterpress The oldest and most versatile method of printing, in which text and images are printed from a plate or mat.

lifestyle segmentation A form of market segmenting that focuses on consumers' activities, interests, and opinions.

limited problem solving A decision-making mode in which consumers' experience and involvement are both low.

listservs Electronic mailing lists on the Internet.

live production The process of creating a live television commercial, which can result in realism and the capturing of spontaneous reactions and events but comes with a loss of control that can threaten the objectives of the commercial.

live script radio ad A detailed script read by an on-air radio personality.

local advertising Advertising directed at an audience in a single trading area, either a city or state.

local agency An advertising agency in a foreign market hired because of its knowledge of the culture and local market conditions.

localized campaigns Advertising campaigns that involve preparing different messages and creative executions for each foreign market a firm has entered.

local spot radio advertising Radio advertising placed directly with individual stations rather than with a network or syndicate.

local television Television programming other than the network broadcast that independent stations and network affiliates offer local audiences.

log analysis software Measurement software that allows a Web site to track hits, pages, visits, and users as well as audience traffic within the site.

M

mailing list A file of names and addresses that an organization might use for contacting prospective or prior customers.

mail sampling A type of sampling in which samples are delivered through the postal service.

make good A media buyer's promise to repeat ad placements, reduce the price on future ads, or offer a refund if the expected audience reach of an ad placement is not delivered.

marcom manager A marketing-communications manager who plans an organization's overall communications program and oversees the various functional specialists inside and outside the organization to ensure that they are working together to deliver the desired message to the customer.

market analysis In an advertising plan, the section that examines the factors that drive and determine the market for a firm's product or service.

marketing The process of conceiving, pricing, promoting, and distributing ideas, goods, and services to create exchanges that benefit consumers and organizations.

marketing database A mailing list that also includes information collected directly from individual customers.

marketing mix The blend of the four responsibilities of marketing—conception, pricing, promotion, and distribution—used for a particular idea, product, or service.

marketing research The systematic gathering, recording, and interpretation of information related to all marketing mix variables.

market niche A relatively small group of consumers who have a unique set of needs and who typically are willing to pay a premium price to a firm that specializes in meeting those needs.

market segmentation The breaking down of a large, heterogeneous market into submarkets or segments that are more homogeneous.

markup charge A method of agency compensation based on adding a percentage charge to a variety of services the agency purchases from outside suppliers.

meaningfulness In advertising research, a term used to describe the import of the information gathered.

measured media Media that are closely measured to determine advertising costs and effectiveness: television, radio, newspapers, magazines, and outdoor media.

mechanical A carefully prepared pasteup of the exact components of an advertisement, prepared specifically for the printer.

media buying Securing the electronic media time and print media space specified in a given account's schedule.

media-buying service An independent organization that specializes in buying media time and space, particularly on radio and television, as a service to advertising agencies and advertisers.

media class A broad category of media, such as television, radio, or newspapers.

media mix The blend of different media that will be used to effectively reach the target audience.

media objectives The specific goals for a media placement: Reach the target audience, determine the geographic scope of placement, and identify the message weight, which determines the overall audience size.

media plan A plan specifying the media in which advertising messages will be placed to reach the desired target audience.

media vehicle A particular option for placement within a media class (e.g., *Newsweek* is a media vehicle within the magazine media class).

medium The means by which an illustration in a print advertisement is rendered: either drawing, photography, or computer graphics.

membership groups Groups an individual interacts with in person on some regular basis.

members of business organizations One of the five types of audiences for advertising; the focus of advertising for firms that produce business and industrial goods and services.

members of a trade channel One of the five types of audiences for advertising; the retailers, wholesalers, and distributors targeted by producers of both household and business goods and services.

merchandise allowances A type of trade-market sales promotion in which free products are packed with regular shipments as payment to the trade for setting up and maintaining displays.

message strategy A component of an advertising strategy, it defines the goals of the advertiser and how those goals will be achieved.

message weight A sum of the total audience size of all the media specified in a media plan.

miscellaneous In regard to font styles, a category that includes display fonts which are used not for their legibility, but for their ability to attract attention. Fonts like garage and novelty display belong in this category.

mobile sampling A type of sampling carried out by logo-emblazoned vehicles that dispense samples, coupons, and premiums to consumers at malls, shopping centers, fairgrounds, and recreational areas.

monopoly power The ability of a firm to make it impossible for rival firms to compete with it, either through advertising or in some other way.

multi-attribute attitude models (MAAMs) A framework and set of procedures for collecting information from consumers to assess their salient beliefs and attitudes about competitive brands.

N

narrowcasting The development and delivery of specialized television programming to well-defined audiences.

narrative Advertising copy that simply displays a series of statements about a brand.

national advertising Advertising that reaches all geographic areas of one nation.

National Advertising Review Board A body formed by the advertising industry to oversee its practice.

national spot radio advertising Radio advertising placed in nationally syndicated radio programming.

need state A psychological state arising when one's desired state of affairs differs from one's actual state of affairs.

network radio advertising Radio advertising placed within national network programs.

network television A type of television that broadcasts programming over airwaves to affiliate stations across the United States under a contract agreement.

newly industrialized countries Countries where traditional ways of life that have endured for centuries change into modern consumer cultures in a few short years.

nonusers A market segment made up of consumers who do not use a particular product or service.

normative test scores Scores that are determined by testing an ad and then comparing the scores to those of previously-tested, average commercials of its type.

O

objective-and-task approach A method of advertising budgeting that focuses on the relationship between spending and advertising objectives by identifying the specific tasks necessary to achieve different aspects of the advertising objectives.

off-network syndication Television programs that were previously run in network prime time.

offset lithography A printing process in which a flat, chemically treated surface attracts ink to the areas to be printed and repels ink from other areas; the inked image is then transferred to a rubber blanket on a roller, and from the roller the impression is carried to paper.

online editing The transferring of the finalized rough cut of a television ad onto one-inch videotape, which is of on-air quality suitable for media transmission.

on-package sampling A type of sampling in which a sample item is attached to another product package.

on-sale date The date on which a magazine is issued to subscribers and for newsstand distribution.

out-of-home media The combination of transit and billboard advertising.

P

pages The particular pages sent from a Web site to a requesting site.

paid circulation The number of copies of a newspaper sold through subscriptions and newsstand distribution.

parallel layout structure A print ad design that employs art on the right-hand side of the page and repeats the art on the left-hand side.

participation A way of buying television advertising time in which several different advertisers buy commercial time during a specific television program.

pass-along readership An additional number of people, other than the original readers, who may see a magazine.

pay-for-results compensation plans When a client and its agency agree to a set of results criteria on which the agency's fee will be based.

pay-per-click The same as the terms under paying "impressions," the advertiser pays a certain fee each time the page is viewed.

percentage-of-sales approach An advertising budgeting approach that calculates the advertising budget based on a percentage of the prior year's sales or the projected year's sales.

peripheral cues The features of an ad other than the actual arguments about the brand's performance.

physiological measures A type of pretest message research that uses physiological measurement devices to detect how consumers react to messages, based on physical responses.

pica A measure of the width or depth of lines of type.

picturing Creating representations of things.

pilot testing A form of message evaluation consisting of experimentation in the marketplace.

point A measure of the size of type in height.

P-O-P advertising Advertising that appears at the point of purchase.

positioning The process of designing a product or service so that it can occupy a distinct and valued place in the target consumer's mind, and then communicating this distinctiveness through advertising.

positioning strategy The key themes or concepts an organization features for communicating the distinctiveness of its product or service to the target segment.

posttest message tracking Advertising research that assesses the performance of advertisements during or after the launch of an advertising campaign.

preferred position A basis of buying newspaper ad space, in which the ad is placed in a specific section of the paper.

premiums Items that feature the logo of a sponsor and that are offered free, or at a reduced price, with the purchase of another item.

preprinted insert An advertisement delivered to a newspaper fully printed and ready for insertion into the newspaper.

preproduction The stage in the television production process in which the advertiser and advertising agency (or in-house agency staff) carefully work out the precise details of how the creative planning behind an ad can best be brought to life with the opportunities offered by television.

price-off deal A type of sales promotion that offers a consumer cents or even dollars off merchandise at the point of purchase through specially marked packages.

primary demand stimulation Using advertising to create demand for a product category in general.

principle of limited liability An economic principle that allows an investor to risk only his or her shares of a corporation, rather than personal wealth, in business ventures.

principles of design General rules governing the elements within a print advertisement and the arrangement of and relationship between these elements.

private label brands Brands developed and marketed by members of a trade channel; they usually carry the retailer's name.

proactive public relations strategy A public relations strategy that is dictated by marketing objectives, seeks to publicize a company and its brands, and is offensive in spirit rather than defensive.

product differentiation The process of creating a perceived difference, in the mind of the consumer, between an organization's product or service and the competition's.

production stage The point at which the storyboard and script for a television ad come to life and are filmed. Also called the *shoot*.

production timetable A realistic schedule for all the preproduction, production, and postproduction activities involved with making a television commercial.

professionals One of the five types of audiences for advertising, defined as doctors, lawyers, accountants, teachers, or any other professionals who require special training or certification.

program rating The percentage of television households that are in a market and are tuned to a specific program during a specific time period.

projective techniques A type of developmental research designed to allow consumers to project thoughts and feelings (conscious or unconscious) in an indirect and unobtrusive way onto a theoretically neutral stimulus.

psychogalvanometer A type of physiological measure that detects galvanic skin response—minute changes in perspiration that suggest arousal related to some stimulus (such as an advertisement).

psychographics A form of market research that emphasizes the understanding of consumers' activities, interests, and opinions.

publicity Unpaid-for media exposure about a firm's activities or its products and services.

public relations A marketing and management function that focuses on communications that foster goodwill between a firm and its many constituent groups.

public relations audit An internal study that identifies the characteristics of a firm or the aspects of the firm's activities that are positive and newsworthy.

public relations firms Firms that handle the needs of organizations regarding relationships with the local community, competitors, industry associations, and government organizations.

public relations plan A plan that identifies the objectives and activities related to the public relations communications issued by a firm.

puffery The use of absolute superlatives like "Number One" and "Best in the World" in advertisements.

pulsing A media-scheduling strategy that combines elements from continuous and flighting techniques; advertisements are scheduled continuously in media over a period of time, but with periods of much heavier scheduling.

purchase intent A measure of whether or not a consumer intends to buy a product or service in the near future.

Pure Food and Drug Act A 1906 act of Congress requiring manufacturers to list the active ingredients of their products on their labels.

push strategy A sales promotion strategy in which marketers devise incentives to encourage purchases by members of the trade to help push a product into the distribution channel.

Q, R

radio networks A type of radio that delivers programming via satellite to affiliate stations across the United States.

radio syndication A type of radio that provides complete programs to stations on a contract basis.

rate card A form given to advertisers by a newspaper and containing information on costs, closing times, specifications for submitting an ad, and special pages or features available in the newspaper.

ratings point A measure indicating that 1 percent of all the television households in an area were tuned to the program measured.

reach The number of people or households in a target audience that will be exposed to a media vehicle or schedule at least one time during a given period of time. It is often expressed as a percentage.

reactive public relations strategy A public relations strategy that is dictated by influences outside the control of a company, focuses on problems to be solved rather than opportunities, and requires defensive rather than offensive measures.

readership A measure of a newspaper's circulation multiplied by the number of readers of a copy.

rebate A money-back offer requiring a buyer to mail in a form requesting the money back from the manufacturer.

reference group Any configuration of other persons that a particular individual uses as a point of reference in making his or her own consumption decisions.

regional advertising Advertising carried out by producers, wholesalers, distributors, and retailers that concentrate their efforts in a particular geographic region.

reliability In advertising research, a term used to describe research that generates generally consistent findings over time.

repeat purchase A second purchase of a new product after trying it for the first time.

repositioning Returning to the process of segmenting, targeting, and positioning a product or service to arrive at a revised positioning strategy.

resonance test A type of message assessment in which the goal is to determine to what extent the message resonates or rings true with target audience members.

RFM analysis An analysis of how recently and how frequently a customer is buying from an organization, and of how much that customer is spending per order and over time.

riding the boards Assessing possible locations for billboard advertising.

rituals Repeated behaviors that affirm, express, and maintain cultural values.

roman The most popular category of type because of its legibility.

rough cut An assembly of the best scenes from a television ad shoot edited together using digital technology.

rough layout The second stage of the ad layout process, in which the headline is lettered in and the elements of the ad are further refined

run-of-paper or **run-of-press (ROP)** A basis of buying newspaper or magazine ad space, in which an ad may appear anywhere, on any page in the paper or magazine.

S

sales promotion The use of incentive techniques that create a perception of greater brand value among consumers or distributors.

sales promotion specialists Persons who design and then operate contests, sweepstakes, special displays, or couponing campaigns for advertisers.

salient beliefs A small number of beliefs that are the critical determinants of an attitude.

sampling A sales promotion technique designed to provide a consumer with a trial opportunity.

sans serif A category of type that includes typefaces with no small lines crossing the ends the main strokes.

scratch track A rough approximation of the musical score of a television ad, using only a piano and vocalists.

screen printing A printing process that employs a stencil produced on a screen. Also called *silk screening*.

script The written version of an ad; it specifies the coordination of the copy elements with the video scenes.

script font A font that mimics cursive handwriting by connecting its letters.

search engine A software tool used to find Web sites on the Internet by searching for keywords typed in by the user.

secondary data Information obtained from existing sources.

second cover page The inside front cover of a magazine.

selective attention The processing of only a few advertisements among the many encountered.

selective demand stimulation Using advertising to stimulate demand for a specific brand within a product category.

self-expressive benefits What consumers gain by using products that they perceive will send a set of signals identifying them with their desired reference group.

self-liquidating premium A sales promotion that requires a consumer to pay most of the cost of the item received as a premium.

self-reference criterion (SRC) The unconscious reference to one's own cultural values, experiences, and knowledge as a basis for decisions.

self-regulation The advertising industry's attempt to police itself.

sentence and picture completion A type of projective technique in which a researcher presents consumers with part of a picture or a sentence with words deleted and then asks that the stimulus be completed; the picture or sentence relates to one or several brands.

serifs Refer to the small lines that cross the ends of the main strokes in type; also the name for the category of type that has this characteristic.

share of audience A measure of the proportion of households that are using television during a specific time period and are tuned to a particular program.

share of voice A calculation of any advertiser's brand expenditures relative to the overall spending in a category.

shoot *See* **production stage**.

single-source tracking measures A type of posttest message tracking that provides information about brand purchases, coupon use, and television advertising exposure by combining grocery store scanner data and devices that monitor household television-viewing behavior.

single-source tracking services Research services that offer information not just on demographics but also on brands, purchase size, prices paid, and media exposure.

situation analysis In an advertising plan, the section in which the advertiser lays out the most important factors that define the situation, and then explains the importance of each factor.

slogan A short phrase in part used to help establish an image, identity, or position for a brand or an organization, but mostly used to increase memorability.

slotting fees A type of trade-market sales promotion in which manufacturers make direct cash payments to retailers to ensure shelf space.

social class A person's standing in the hierarchy resulting from the systematic inequalities in the social system.

social meaning What a product or service means in a societal context.

society A group of people living in a particular area who share a common culture and consider themselves a distinct and unified entity.

space contract A contract that establishes a rate for all advertising placed in a magazine by an advertiser over a specified period.

space order A commitment by an advertiser to advertising space in a particular issue of a magazine. Also called an *insertion order*.

spam To post messages to many unrelated newsgroups on Usenet.

specialty-advertising items Items used for advertising purposes and that have three defining elements: (1) they contain the sponsor's logo and perhaps a related promotional message; (2) this logo and message appear on a useful or decorative item; and (3) the item is given freely, as a gift from the sponsor.

split-cable transmission A type of pilot testing in which two different versions of an advertisement are transmitted to two separate samples of similar households within a single, well-defined market area; the ads are then compared on measures of exposure, recall, and persuasion.

split-list experiment A type of pilot testing in which multiple versions of a direct mail piece are prepared and sent to various segments of a mailing list; the version that pulls the best is deemed superior.

split-run distribution A type of pilot testing in which two different versions of an advertisement are placed in every other issue of a magazine; the ads are then compared on the basis of direct response.

sponsor *See* **client**.

sponsorship A way of buying television advertising time in which an advertiser agrees to pay for the production of a television program and for most (and often all) of the advertising that appears in the program.

spot advertising A way of buying television advertising time in which airtime is purchased through local television stations.

standard advertising unit (SAU) One of 57 defined sizes of newspaper advertisements.

still production A technique of television ad production whereby a series of photographs or slides is filmed and edited so that the resulting ad appears to have movement and action.

storyboard A frame-by-frame sketch or photo sequence depicting, in sequence, the visual scenes and copy that will be used in an advertisement.

story construction A type of projective technique that asks consumers to tell a story about people depicted in a scene or picture, as a way of gathering information about a brand.

STP marketing (**S**egmenting, **T**argeting, **P**ositioning) A marketing strategy employed when advertisers focus their efforts on one subgroup of a product's total market.

straight-line copy Advertising copy that explains in straightforward terms why a reader will benefit from use of a product or service.

subhead In an advertisement, a few words or a short sentence that usually appears above or below the headline and includes important brand information not included in the headline.

subliminal advertising Advertising alleged to work on a subconscious level.

support media Media used to reinforce a message being delivered via some other media vehicle.

sweepstakes A sales promotion in which winners are determined purely by chance.

switchers A market segment made up of consumers who often buy what is on sale or choose brands that offer discount coupons or other price incentives. Also called *variety seekers.*

symbolic value What a product or service means to consumers in a nonliteral way.

T

target audience A particular group of consumers singled out for an advertisement or advertising campaign.

target segment The subgroup (of the larger market) chosen as the focal point for the marketing program and advertising campaign.

telemarketing A direct-marketing medium that involves using the telephone to deliver a spoken appeal.

television households An estimate of the number of households that are in a market and own a television.

testimonial An advertisement in which an advocacy position is taken by a spokesperson.

theater test A type of pretest message research in which advertisements are tested in small theaters; members of the theater audience have an electronic device through which they can express how much they like or dislike the advertisements shown.

third cover page The inside back cover of a magazine.

thought listing A type of pretest message research that tries to identify specific thoughts that may be generated by an advertisement.

three-point layout structure A print ad design that establishes three elements in an ad as dominant forces.

thumbnails, or **thumbnail sketches** The rough first drafts of an ad layout, about one-quarter the size of the finished ad.

top-of-the-mind awareness Keen consumer awareness of a certain brand, indicated by listing that brand first when asked to name a number of brands.

trade-market sales promotion A type of sales promotion designed to motivate distributors, wholesalers, and retailers to stock and feature a firm's brand in their merchandising programs.

trade shows Events where several related products from many manufacturers are displayed and demonstrated to members of the trade.

transit advertising Advertising that appears as both interior and exterior displays on mass transit vehicles and at terminal and station platforms.

trial offers A type of sales promotion in which expensive items are offered on a trial basis to induce consumer trial of a brand.

trial usage An advertising objective to get consumers to use a product new to them on a trial basis.

trustworthiness In advertising research, a term used to describe information that can be trusted.

type font A basic set of typeface letters.

U

unfair advertising Defined by Congress as "acts or practices that cause or are likely to cause substantial injury to consumers, which is not reasonably avoidable by consumers themselves and not outweighed by the countervailing benefits to consumers or competition."

unique selling proposition (USP) A promise contained in an advertisement in which the advertised brand offers a specific, unique, and relevant benefit to the consumer.

unit-of-sales approach An approach to advertising budgeting that allocates a specified dollar amount of advertising for each unit of a brand sold (or expected to be sold).

unmeasured media Media less-formally measured for advertising costs and effectiveness (as compared to the measured media): direct mail, catalogs, special events, and other ways to reach business and household consumers.

Usenet A collection of more than 13,000 discussion groups on the Internet.

user positioning A positioning option that focuses on a specific profile of the target user.

users The number of different people visiting X Web site during Y time.

V

validity In advertising research, a term used to describe information that is relevant to the research questions being investigated.

value A perception by consumers that a product or service provides satisfaction beyond the cost incurred to acquire the product or service.

value pricing The strategy of offering good-quality products at low prices to attract a high volume of customers.

value proposition A statement of the functional, emotional, and self-expressive benefits delivered by the brand, which provide value to customers in the target segment.

values The defining expressions of culture, demonstrating in words and deeds what is important to a culture.

variety seekers *See* **switchers**.

variety seeking A decision-making mode in which consumers switch their selection among various brands in a given category in a random pattern.

V-chip A device that can block television programming based on the recently developed program rating system.

vertical cooperative advertising An advertising technique whereby a manufacturer and dealer (either a wholesaler or retailer) share the expense of advertising.

videotape An option for television ad production that is less expensive than film but also of lower quality.

virtual mall A gateway to a group of Internet storefronts that provides access to mall sites by simply clicking on a storefront.

visits The number of occasions on which a user X looked up Y Web site during Z time.

vulnerabilities From a public relations standpoint, weaknesses in a firm's operations or products that can negatively affect its relationships with important constituents.

W

white space In a print advertisement, space not filled with a headline, subhead, body copy, or illustration.

within-vehicle duplication Exposure to the same advertisement in the same media at different times.

World Wide Web (WWW) A universal database of information available to Internet users; its graphical environment makes navigation simple and exciting.

X, Y, Z

zapping The process of eliminating advertisements altogether from videotaped programs.

zipping The process of fast-forwarding through advertisements contained in videotaped programs.

NAME/BRAND/COMPANY INDEX

SUBJECT  INDEX

Page references in **bold** print indicate ads or photos. Page references in *italics* indicate tables, charts, or graphs. Page references followed by "n" indicate footnotes.

A

Accountability, 126
Account executive
    for television advertising
        production, 408
Account planning, 211–212
    advertising planning strategy
        and, 259
    vs. research, 211–212
Account services, 49
Action for Children's Television
    (ACT), 85
Activities, interests, and opinions
    (AIOs), 189
Adaptors, 313–314
Ad blockers, 549
Administrative services, 51
Advertisements
    defined, 9
    length of, 450–451
    size of, 450–451
Advertisers, 42–45
    government and social organi-
        zations as, 44–45
    manufacturers as, 42–43
    resellers as, 44
    sensitivity shown by, 104
    service firms as, 42–43
Advertising. *See also* Evolution
    of advertising

annual expenditures on, 40–41,
    41, 42
as business process, 17–31
as communication process, 11–17
customer satisfaction and, 23
defined, 6–9
ethics of, 108–110
goals of, 24–27
    vs. sales, *570*
informative nature of, 99–100
marketing role of, 17–24
mass media effects of, 107–108
nature of, 4–5
noncommercial use of, 108
offensive nature of, 105–106
political, 9
profits generation, 23
programming effects of, 108
psychological process of,
    150–156
vs. publicity, 6, 9
public's attitude toward, 4–5
reinventing process, 90–91
revenue generation, 23
as social text, 172–175
society's social priorities and, 103
superficiality of, 100
truth in, 109
types of
    corporate, 26–27
    delayed response, 26
    direct response, 26
    primary demand stimulation,
        24–25
    selective demand stimulation,
        25–26

Advertising agencies, *43,* 45–48
    in advertising planning,
        260–261
    compensation plans
        commissions, 51–52
        fee system, 52
        markup charges, 52
        pay-for-results compensation
            plan, 52–53
    creative boutique, 46–47
    defined, 45
    full-service, 46
    global agencies, 282, 284
    income of, 45, *47*
        in-house, 48
    interactive agencies, 47–48
    international affiliate,
        284–285
    Internet specialist, 544
    local agencies, 285
    media-buying services, 47
    professionals of, 46
    redesign of, 53–56
    self-promotion, 53
    services of, *43,* 48–51
        account services, 49
        administrative services, 51
        buying services, 50–51
        creative services, 50
        marketing services, 49–50
        media-planning, 50–51
        production services, 50
Advertising campaign, 9
Advertising clutter, 154
Advertising industry
    scope of, 40–41

structure of
    advertisers, 42–45
    advertising agencies, 45–48
    agency compensation,
        promotion and redesign,
        43, 51–56
    agency services, 48–51
    external facilitators, *43,*
        56–58
    media organizations, *43,*
        58–60
transition of, 39–40
trends in, 40
Advertising plan
    advertising agency's role in,
        260–261
    for Apple Computers,
        240–244
    components of, *245*
        budgeting, 253–258
        evaluation, 260
        execution, 259–260
        introduction, 245
        objectives, 249–253
        situation analysis, 245–249
        strategy, 258–259
    defined, 245
Advertising research, 211. *See also*
    Research
Advertising research firms, 56
Advertising response function,
    255
Advertising substantiation
    program, 115–116
Advertorial, 349
Advocacy advertising, 634

CREDITS

For permission to reproduce the images on the pages indicated, acknowledgment is made to the following:

Chapter 1

2   Courtesy of Mercedes-Benz.

4   Courtesy of Mercedes-Benz.

5   Courtesy of Mercedes-Benz (both).

6   Courtesy of Volkswagen and Arnold Communications, Inc (left).

7   © 1995 The Coca-Cola Company. Reprinted by permission (left). Advertising Agency: Tanhouse Creative. Client: PowerQuest Corporation (right).

8   Reprinted with permission from Carter-Wallace, Inc. © Carter-Wallace, Inc. All rights reserved (top).

9   Courtesy of the Republican National Committee.

10   All photos © Geof Kern.

13   Courtesy of The Coca-Cola Company.

14   Compliments of InFocus, the world leader in data/ video projection systems.

15   Courtesy of TAP Pharmaceuticals (top). Courtesy of Rolex Watch U.S.A., Inc. (bottom left and right).

17   Courtesy of Daffy's.

18   Courtesy of Shapiro Luggage, Gifts, Leather.

21   Courtesy of Honda Motor Co., Inc. (top left). Courtesy of The Martin Agency (bottom).

22   BMW of North America, Inc. Photo by Michael Rausch (top left). Courtesy of Acura National Advertising (top right). Courtesy of Ben & Jerry's®. Photo Jeffrey Henson Scales (bottom left). © The Procter & Gamble Company. Reprinted by permission (bottom right).

24   Weider Nutrition International © 1995.

25   © 1996 National Fluid Milk Processor Promotion Board. Reprinted by permission of Bozell World-wide, Inc (left). Courtesy of State of Florida, Department of Citrus, 1994/95 (right).

26   Courtesy of Panasonic (top). Courtesy of Thermo-scan Inc. © 1992 Thermoscan Inc. (Bottom).

27   Courtesy of Foote, Cone & Belding (left). Courtesy of Toshiba America Consumer Products, Inc. (right).

28   Permission granted by The Franklin Mint and Sheffield Enterprises (left). © 1995 Lever Brothers Company "All" Laundry Detergent. Courtesy of Lever Brothers Company (right).

29   © 1993 American Plastics Council. Reprinted by permission.

31   Photo courtesy of Levi Strauss & Co. (top). Ray-Ban sunglasses by Baush & Lomb. © 1995 Bausch & Lomb Incorporated. Reprinted by permission (bottom).

32   Courtesy of United Airlines (left). © 1994 Waterford Wedgwood USA, Inc. Reprinted by permission (middle). Courtesy of Gucci (right).

Chapter 2

36   Ad provided by U.S. Navy.

38   © General Motors Corp.: used with permission.

39   Reproduced with permission from Red Spider. Portions Copyright Netscape Communications Corporation, 1999. All Rights Reserved. Netscape, Netscape Navigator and the Netscape N Logo, are registered trademarks of Netscape in the United States and other countries.

45   Ad provided by U.S. Navy.

46   Idaho Department of Commerce.

48   Portions © Netscape Communications Corporation, 1999.

50   Courtesy of the Pillsbury Company.

54   Courtesy of J. Walter Thompson Company (top). Courtesy of Arian, Lowe & Travis Advertising-Chicago (bottom).

56   Courtesy of O'Neill Inc., Santa Cruz, CA. Portions © Netscape Communications Corporation, 1999.

Chapter 3

66   Courtesy of Lever Brothers Company.

72   Courtesy of Lever Brothers Company.

76   Reproduced from the Collections of the Library of Congress.

78   Courtesy of The Coca-Cola Company.

79   © Archive Photos, Inc. (bottom).

80   Courtesy of H. Armstrong Roberts, Inc.

82   Courtesy of IBM Corporation (top right). Courtesy of Serta, Inc., Des Plaines, Illinois (bottom left).

83   ® Kellogg Company, © 1968 Kellogg Company; used with permission (top left).

84   Reproduced with permission of PepsiCo, Inc., 1995 Purchase, New York (left). Courtesy of Goodyear Tire & Rubber Company (right).

85   Photo courtesy of Polaroid Corporation; "Polaroid" and "One Step"®.

86   Courtesy of Nestle U.S.A., Inc. (left). Courtesy of Chrysler Corporation (right).

87   Courtesy of Kloster Cruise Line (left). Courtesy of the Republican National Committee (right).

88   Reproduced with permission of PepsiCo, Inc., 1995, Purchase, New York (left). © 1998 MTV Networks. All rights reserved. MTV, MUSIC TELEVISION and all related titles, characters and logos are trademarks owned by MTV Networks, a division of Viacom International Inc. (right).

89   Skechers In-House Advertising Department.

Chapter 4

96   Andy Warhol, "Three Coke Bottles," 1962. Synthetic polymer paint and silkscreen ink on canvas, 20 x 16 in. © 1999 Andy Warhol Foundation for the Visual Arts/ARS, New York.

99   © 1990 Anheuser-Busch, Inc., St. Louis, MO. Reprinted by permission (left). The Facing HIV and AIDS campaign is a collaborative effort by the Asian Pacific AIDS Intervention Team and Pacific Asian Language Services of Special Service for Groups and Healthier Solutions, Inc., under a CARE grant from the County of Los Angeles Department of Health Services, AIDS Programs office (right).

102 Courtesy of Good Humor–Breyers Ice Cream (left). Courtesy of Johnson & Johnson (right).

103 Courtesy of Lachman Imports.

104 Richard Avedon for Gianni Versace.

105 Courtesy of Unilever (left).

106 Courtesy of Procter & Gamble.

107 © Darlene Hammond/Archive Photos.

108 Courtesy of Partnership for a Drug-Free America.

111 Courtesy Federal Trade Commission. Portions © Netscape Communications Corporation, 1999.

Chapter 5

136 © The Procter & Gamble Company. Used by permission.

138 © The Procter & Gamble Company. Used by permission.

141 Courtesy Johnson & Johnson.

142 © General Motors Corp.: used with permission (top). Courtesy of Chrysler Corporation (bottom).

143 Courtesy of Acura Division, American Honda Motor Co., Inc. (top). Courtesy of Campbell Soup Company (bottom).

144 Courtesy of Northwest Airlines.

146 Courtesy of American Isuzu Motors Inc. (top). Courtesy of Casio, Inc. (bottom).

147 Courtesy of IAMS Food Company.

148 Courtesy of DeBeers Consolidated Mines, Ltd., and J. Walter Thompson (bottom).

149 Courtesy Wendy's International.

152 Courtesy of Sears, Roebuck and Co.

153 Thermador.

155 Singapore Tourism Board (right).

157 Photo by Thomas C. O'Guinn.

159 Dr. Marten's Airwair USA, LLC.

161 Courtesy of Kraft Foods, Inc.

163 Chivas Regal and the Chivas Regal Logo are trademarks of Chivas Brothers Limited (left). Courtesy Miller Brewing Company (right).

164 © Gonalco Productions, Inc./CBS.

166 Courtesy MasterCard International, Incorporated (left).

168 Used with permission of DFO, Inc. (left).

169 Ad concept by Mad Dogs & Englishmen. Illustration by Stuart Patterson (right).

171 Courtesy of Saturn Corporation (top). © Henry Diltz/Corbis (bottom).

173 Courtesy of Johnston & Murphy, Nashville, TN (bottom).

175 Courtesy of Joe Boxer (top). Courtesy of Harley-Davidson, Inc (bottom).

Chapter 6

178 Courtesy of Hard Candy.

181 Courtesy of Gillette (both).

183 Neither the United States Marine Corps nor any other component of the Department of Defense has approved, endorsed, or authorized this product. USMC advertising creative by J. Walter Thompson (left). Courtesy of Hard Candy (right).

187 © 1994 American Express Travel Related Services Company, Inc. Reprinted with permission.

190 Courtesy of Pillsbury Company; created by Foote, Cone & Belding (Chicago) (left). Courtesy of Pillsbury Company; created by Leo Burnett (Chicago) (right).

192 Ad for Mitsubishi Motor Sales of America, Inc., created by g2 Advertising. Photography by Vic Huber. Reprinted by permission (top left). Copyright, Nissan 1995. Reproduced by permission (top right). Courtesy of Volvo (bottom).

193 Courtesy of Arthur Andersen.

195 Reprinted by permission of Svetlana Electron Devices. Created in house by Svetlana Electron Devices. Creative Director: Terri Bates; Photographer: Jared Cassidy.

197 Courtesy of State Farm Insurance Companies.

199 Agency: DSW Partners. Photographer: Michael O'Brien.

200 Courtesy of Virginia Power/Richmond, Virginia (top). Courtesy of Saab Cars USA, Inc. (bottom left and middle). Courtesy of Rykä and Mullen Advertising. (Bottom right).

201 Courtesy of Norwegian Cruise Line (left). Property of Carnival Cruise Lines (right).

202 Courtesy of Saatchi & Saatchi.

203 Reproduced with permission of PepsiCo, Inc., 1995, Purchase, New York.

Chapter 7

208 © 1998 Pharmacia & Upjohn Consumer Healthcare. Agency: Jordan McGrath Case & Partners/Euro RSCG.

210 Courtesy of the Goodyear Tire & Rubber Company.

215 Courtesy of Harris Marketing Group.

217 JELL-O is a registered trademark of Kraft Foods, Inc.; used with permission.

219 © 1998 Pharmacia & Upjohn Consumer Healthcare. Agency: Jordan McGrath Case & Partners/Euro RSCG.

223 © 1994 B. Kramer/Custom Medical Stock Photo.

226 Courtesy of Leo Burnett.

228 Reprinted with permission of General Motors Corporation (left). Courtesy of Ford Motor Company (top right). Reprinted with permission of General Motors Corporation (bottom right). Courtesy of E★Trade Securities (bottom).

Chapter 8

238 Courtesy TBWA/Chiat/Day.

241 © Apple Computer, Inc. Used with permission. All rights reserved. Apple® and the Apple logo are registered trademarks of Apple Computer, Inc.

242 Courtesy of Apple Computer, Inc.

243 Courtesy of Apple Computer, Inc.

244 Courtesy of Apple Computer, Inc. Portions © Netscape Communications Corporation, 1999.

246 ©1996 American Express Travel Related Services Company, Inc. Reprinted with permission.

247 Sony Wireless Phones. Advertising Agency: Matthews/Mark (right).

248 Courtesy of the Pillsbury Company.

251 Dassault Falcon Jet Corp.

258 Danskin, Inc.

Chapter 9

264 Courtesy SkyPort TV, CS Service Center Corporation, Yokohama, Japan.

267 Courtesy of McDonald's Corporation (right).

268 Courtesy of PepsiCo.

272 Courtesy of Tropicana Dole Beverages North America.

275 Courtesy of Schieffelin & Somerset Co., 2 Park Avenue, New York, NY 10016 (left). Courtesy of International Business Machines Corporation (right).

277 Courtesy of Warner-Lambert Company. Lady Protector de Wilkinson is available in the French Market; it is a trademark of Wilkinson Sword GmbH (left).

278 Courtesy of Alan Powdirll, photographer, and Euro RSCG Wnek Gosper. Art director: Oliver Caporn (bottom left). © 1994 Oneida Ltd. (bottom right).

281 Courtesy SkyPort TV, CS Service Center Corporation, Yokohama, Japan (top).

286 Courtesy of Jack Daniel Distillery (both).

288 Courtesy of Yokohama Rubber Company, Tokyo, Japan; advertising agency IDUE.

Chapter 10
309 © Philadelphia Museum of Art.

312 © 1946 Time Inc. Reprinted by permission (top).

316 Garie Waltzer, photographer.

320 Courtesy Wesley H. Perrin, Chairman Emeritus, Borders Perrin & Norrander, Inc. Advertising Agency, Portland, Oregon.

Chapter 11
327 Art Directors: Mark Faulkner, Noel Haan; writer: Steffan Postaer; photographer: Tony D'Orio; clients: Callard & Bowser-Suchard; agency: Leo Burnett Company/Chicago.

331 Courtesy of Apple Computer, Inc.

333 © Heinz Pet Products.

334 Art Directors: Mark Faulkner, Noel Haan; writer: Steffan Postaer; photographer: Tony D'Orio; clients: Callard & Bowser-Suchard; agency: Leo Burnett Company/Chicago (left).

339 The John Hardy Collection (top).

341 © The Procter & Gamble Company. Reprinted with permission of P&G and Jack Perno, Photographer.

342 © The Procter & Gamble Company. Used with permission (left).

344 Advertising created for the New York Lottery by DDB Needham Worldwide.

345 Created by Publicis & Hal Riney (bottom).

346 Agency: Doyle, Inc. Art Directors: John Doyle, John Emmert. Copywriter: Kara Goodrich. Photographer: Geoff Stein. Client: Shreve, Crump & Low.

347 Courtesy of BMW.

350 Courtesy of FannieMae.

Chapter 12
357 Courtesy Richmond Technical Center (top).

359 Courtesy of Avis Rent A Car System, Inc. (left). Courtesy of C. F. Hathaway (right).

362 Courtesy Miller Brewing Company (left). Courtesy MCI (middle). Courtesy of the U.S. Army (right).

364 Courtesy of Goldsmith Jeffrey: Noam Murro, art director; Eddie Van Blaem, copy writer; Gary Goldsmith, creative director: Ilan Rubin, photographer.

367 Courtesy of The Clorox Company.

370 www3vw.com/index5.htm. (top left). Appears courtesy of Fat Possum Records (top right). Courtesy Cybercalifragilistic Gifts (bottom left). © Iomega Corporation (bottom right). Portions © Netscape Communications Corporation, 1999 (all).

376 Stephen Frisch/Stock Boston SUF3230R.

383 DILBERT reprinted by permission of United Feature Syndicate, Inc.

Chapter 13
393 Courtesy of Computer System Organization, Hewlett-Packard (top). Adobe and Photoshop are trademarks of Adobe Systems Incorporated. Portions © Netscape Communications Corporation, 1999 (bottom).

394 © 1997 by Kohler Co. All rights reserved.

396 © Apple Computer, Inc. Used with permission. All rights reserved. Apple® and the Apple logo are registered trademarks of Apple Computer, Inc. (top).

398 Courtesy of Volkswagen and Arnold Fortuna Lawner & Cabot Inc., Advertising (top).

400 Courtesy Arnold, Finnegan & Martin (all).

401 Courtesy Arnold, Finnegan & Martin.

405 TABASCO®, the TABASCO® diamond logo, and the TABASCO® bottle design are registered trademarks exclusively of McIlhenny Co., Avery Island, LA 70513 (top left). TVLand Online used by permission. Nick At Nite's TVLand (top right). Courtesy Orkin Pest Control (bottom left). Courtesy Jack Daniel's (bottom right). Portions © Netscape Communications Corporation, 1999 (all).

407 © Kobal Collection (left). © Paramount (Courtesy Kobal Collection) (right).

411 Courtesy of Portland General Electric (top).

413 Courtesy Miller Brewing Company (bottom).

414 Courtesy Miller Brewing Company.

415 © Apple Computer, Inc. Used with permission All rights reserved. Apple® and the Apple logo are registered trademarks of Apple Computer, Inc. (top

left). © Ladd Co. (Courtesy Kobal Collection) (top right). © Universal (Courtesy Kobal Collection) (bottom left). With permission of Nike, Inc., and 40 Acres and a Mule Filmworks (bottom right).

Chapter 14

439 Reproduced with permission of BAUER NIKE HOCKEY INC. © 1999. Portions © Netscape Communications Corporation, 1999 (left).

447 Courtesy of Toyota and Saatchi & Saatchi DFS; photos by Michael Raushe, David Lebon, and John Early.

451 Courtesy of The Quaker Oats Company (right).

459 © 1998 Turner Private Networks, Inc. All rights reserved. Used by permission of TPNI.

461 © copyrighted 1999 Chicago Tribune Company. All rights reserved. Used with permission.

463 © Christie's Inc., 1999. Portions © Netscape Communications Corporation, 1999 (left).

Chapter 15

468 Courtesy of Men's Journal Co., L.P. Photograph by James McLoughlin.

470 Trade Marketing Director, Michael Q. Griffin; Graphic Designer, Leslie Goodwin; Copywriter, Tom Wilson.

474 Copyright, Nissan 1994. Reproduced by permission. Infiniti is a registered trademark of Nissan (left).

475 Courtesy of The Peoria Journal Star.

477 Photography by Joe Higgins (top). Ebel USA, Inc. (bottom).

478 Photo Courtesy of Pizza Hut.

479 Courtesy of Leath Furniture Inc. Creative direction Sharron Hutto; art direction Sandia Chen.

480 Courtesy of Schwinn Corporation.

482 Courtesy of Challenge Publications, Inc., and Mountain Biking Magazine, Canoga Park, CA 91304 (left). Courtesy of Ogilvy & Mather, Chicago (right).

483 Courtesy of Clarins Corporation.

485 Courtesy of Men's Journal Co., L.P. Photograph by James McLoughlin.

486 Photography by Joe Higgins (bottom).

487 Company: Lenox Brands 1998. Agency: Grey Advertising, N.Y.

492 Courtesy of Fox Family Worldwide.

Chapter 16

508 Courtesy of The Bettmann Archive (both).

509 Courtesy of Horst Salons. Carol Henderson, art director; Luke Sullivan, writer: Fallon McElligot,

Minneapolis, agency (top). Courtesy of the Museum of Flight, Seattle, Washington (bottom).

510 Courtesy of David Auerbach Opticians.

512 Chris T. Allen, photographer (bottom).

513 © Bob Kramer/Stock Boston (top). Chris T. Allen, photographer (bottom).

517 Bell Atlantic Electronic Commerce Services, Inc. Portions © Netscape Communications Corporation, 1999.

520 Courtesy of State Farm Insurance Companies, Bloomington, Illinois (bottom).

524 © The Procter & Gamble Company. Used by permission.

Chapter 17

540 Excite is a trademark of Excite, Inc. and may be registered in various jurisdictions. Excite screen display copyright 1995–1999 Excite, Inc. (top left). © 1996–1999 Ask Jeeves, Inc. ASK JEEVES, ASK.COM and the JEEVES DESIGN are service marks of Ask Jeeves, Inc. All other brands are property of their respective owners. Patent pending (top right). Courtesy of Travelocity.com. (bottom). Portions © Netscape Communications Corporation, 1999 (all).

541 "America Online," "AOL" and the Logo design are all Registered Trademarks of America Online, Inc. Copyright 1999, America Online, Inc. All Rights Reserved (right).

544 Designed by mPhatic Ads & Design for middletown .com. Portions © Netscape Communications Corporation, 1999.

546 Courtesy Saturn Corporation. Portions © Netscape Communications Corporation, 1999 (bottom).

547 Courtesy women.com Networks. Portions © Netscape Communications Corporation, 1999 (bottom).

548 Reprinted by permission of National Enquirer, Inc. Portions © Netscape Communications Corporation, 1999 (top).

550 Web Premiere Toons, Pink Donkey and the Fly, characters, names, and all related indicia are trademarks of The Cartoon Network. © 1999. All Rights Reserved (left). Courtesy Meadowlanders, Inc. d/b/a the New Jersey Devils (right). Portions © Netscape Communications Corporation, 1999.

551 Copyright © 1994–99 Wired Digital, Inc. All Rights Reserved (left). Portions © Netscape Communications Corporation, 1999.